Cooper R.

Ashley R.

Charleston

JAMES I.

STO I.

O C E A N

N T I C

N
W E
S

A MAP OF
The Sea Islands
of
South Carolina

0   5   10   20

Scale of Miles

R.E. Falconer

A
Sea Island
Lady

Also by
FRANCIS GRISWOLD

THE TIDES OF MALVERN

A
SEA ISLAND
LADY

BY FRANCIS GRISWOLD

BEAUFORT BOOK CO.
Publisher
BEAUFORT, SOUTH CAROLINA

A Sea Island Lady

COPYRIGHT—1939
BY FRANCIS GRISWOLD

Beaufort Book Co.
Publisher 1971

910206

This edition published by Beaufort Book Co.
by arrangement with William Morrow and Co., Inc.
105 Madison Avenue
New York, N.Y. 10016

ISBN 0-685-06833-1

Published, October, 1939

PRINTED IN THE UNITED STATES OF AMERICA

To

THE LOWREYS

Miss Kate and Jake

Except for several historical figures appearing in the earlier pages, all the characters in
A Sea Island Lady
are imaginary and should not be identified
with any actual persons, living or dead. F.G.

Part One

I

THE MELLOW GLORY of Indian Summer had shone through the day, brightening from crimson to scarlet the woodland fires of sweetgum and maple, dogwood and sumac and sassafras. But now as the sun smoldered in the cold cloud bank of the horizon, a wind haunted with autumn stirred over the sea islands, fretting the quiet tidewaters and the sweeps of russet marshgrass. At old Beaufort, halfway between Charleston and Savannah, the trees along the sandy streets and within the white-fenced gardens sighed and writhed against the intruder, and blinds banged in sharp protest.

Horses champed and stamped and shook their harness as they waited with their carriages by the high brick wall that enclosed the graveyard of St. Helena's Parish Church. Within the yard, over the blackened marble slabs, long cobwebs of gray moss tossed and waved from branches of live-oak and sycamore. The fronds of the palmettoes were thrown into starched spasms, and even the resolute cedars bowed and shivered.

Only the church stood firm and calm, as it had stood through all weathers from its founding in 1724 to this fourth day of November, 1861. It acknowledged the presence of the wind, however, with a faint rattling of its windows and a moaning under its eaves. Gentlemen, with one hand holding their beavers, met a tussle at the double door, which had to be opened wide to admit ladies' hoopskirts into the vestibule. In the white interior of the church the candles at the scarlet-and-white altar, in the chandeliers, and on staffs fastened to the sides of the stalls along the center aisle, lurched as eyes and nods and whispers greeted each arrival.

To Alec, young slave boy of the Fenwicks of Marshlands on the Point, the chill wind was an added spur to unusual haste. Alec was

3

actually running: a flapping loose-jointed gait carried him away from the vestry door of St. Helena's, projected him through the side gate of the churchyard, and swung him eastward. His feet, cramped on this special occasion into a pair of his master's cast-off kid boots, flung themselves at the road regardless of the twisting pain of the treacherous heels. Leaves from the stricken trees twirled down around him, swirled into bands, and scurried crisply after him. There was something mighty scary about this movement in the ebbing light; and the mournful voices the wind made in the branches were scary too.

His boots slapped the hard surface of the Shell Road and he followed it southward toward the Bay. At Fenwick Street he turned eastward again, slackening his pace to a trot. He was pure out of breath, and the boots were killing him.

In front of the gate to the Rhett Langdon garden he sat down abruptly to tug off the cruel boots, talking to them as he struggled. He had suffered them since early morning, he could suffer them no longer. Too bad bare feet did not match the dark green footman's suit he was wearing, the strutting gold-braided and brass-buttoned uniform that his big brother Robert had worn when he had first served at the Fenwick table under Old Semp. This proud outfit that Alec was being allowed to wear today for the first time was still too large for him, as much too large as the kid boots were too small, yet it was the sign of approaching importance. He would have been willing to have had his feet shod with fire if the total effect had required it. But now he must give them one gasp of freedom.

He wiggled and rubbed his liberated toes, wondering how he had been able to stand the misery so long. His feet might be too broad for the master's narrow boots but they were not splayed like black nigger feet. He was no black nigger, thank God. He was light-colored, like his mother. No flat nose and thick lips. And brother Robert was light, and so was sister Phyllis. Because of that and because he belonged to the Fenwicks, Alec knew he could afford to hold his head mighty high. He knew the worth of himself and his family, white and colored.

His special importance at the moment flashed back, and he was up and off again, a boot in each hand. And now his free pace was in easy rhythm with the message that pounded in his throat and car-

4

ried him along on its rolling beat. Beyond the short causeway that bridged a marshy inlet, the street curved a little to the right. At the end of the street the tall gates of Marshlands were waiting for him. There was a light shining already in the lantern that was framed in the iron lacework over the gates.

"*Ki,* bubbuh!" Old Eva's voice cut across the wind from the yard of the Dedrick house. "De *Debble* mus' be 'pontop you' tail! You tek foot in han' fuh true."

"*Ki,* ol' tittie!" Alec tossed back at her. "You sho' is a po'-buckra black nigguh fool, fuh true!"

"Who you call black nigguh an' t'ing, you yalluh peanut! I gwine burn you' britches when I git muh han's on you!"

Her voice pursued him scorchingly. Alec drowned her wrath out of his ears with shrill derision and ran faster, glad that he was out of the reach of her stinging hand. He panted through the gateway and followed the shell drive as far as the turn-off to the back yard. The stables and quarter were deserted, but there was plenty doing in the kitchen-house—rumpus and singing and laughter. The good smells from there made his mouth water as he ran by. He caught a glimpse of his mother in her blue turban overseeing the cooking and wished for time to stop and steal a taste of something.

His bare feet took the steps to the back porch three at a time, and his shoulder and hip pushed open the heavy door, swung it closed in the face of the wind. In the dim space behind the base of the staircase he paused: the pantry door to the left was ajar, and he could see his big brother bossing in there where china and glass gleamed in the candlelight that was staggering from the wind's brief thrust. He stood in the path of light from the pantry long enough for Robert to see him in his importance; then with a bright grin and a tingle of pride he stepped from behind the staircase into the main hall.

The illumination against the white paneled walls made him blink. The Yankee War was making the mistress saving of candles, yet tonight they were all over the house: in the crystal chandeliers, in brackets, in candlesticks and candelabra on mantels and tables. Not all were lighted, but these in the hall were, shining bright and safe from drafts in their hurricane shades. An astral lamp glowed on the table near the tall hall clock, and in front of the clock in a halo from the lamp Alec discovered the awesome back of Maus' Joe Bramwell, from whom, rather than from the clock, seemed to come a slow and solemn *tock-tock*.

"*Reb'ren' say come suh!*"

Alec's knees went weak when he realized how loud his voice was. With the house family you could be free enough and never be noticed, but with this visiting brother of the mistress you had to mind yourself close.

Judge Joseph Legerton Bramwell, youngest jurist ever appointed to the Supreme Court of South Carolina, turned with a start from the clock, by which he was setting his watch for the third time within the last ten minutes.

"Less noise, boy!"

Alec whispered: "Reb'ren' say come please Maussa. She vaitin' on you at de westry in she robe an' t'ing."

"The Reverend Mr. Walker is not a *she*," Joseph Bramwell snorted. "How much longer are you going to jabber like a fieldhand? If you were mine, I'd put you on a rice gang! Where are your boots?"

Alec held them up, one in each shaky hand.

"Is that the proper place for them?"

Alec hung his head.

"Now clear out!"

Alec disappeared in a flash. Testily Joseph Bramwell finished setting his watch: that blasted boy had made the minute hand jump beyond the mark. If the young beggar were his, he'd discipline his *café-au-lait* hide in short order. Not that he'd have him as a gift. A few people—and his own brother-in-law, Major Michael Fenwick, was unfortunately among the number—held the perverse position that the lighter the color the better the servant; but it was Joseph Bramwell's conviction that in house as in field a negro's proper color was black.

The bulbous watch in his hand chimed six with faint but furious sweetness. His thoughts mounted to the dressing-chamber above, where his sister Susan, with the aid of the Fenwicks' young mulatto wench Phyllis, should certainly have completed by now his sister Isabel's toilette.

"Isabel! . . . Susan!" he called up the stair well.

Susan answered.

6

"We're hurrying fast as we can, brother dear!"

"The Rector has given the signal!"

Isabel's voice called: "They're fixing my veil, Joe dear!"

Joe's mouth softened. A slight mist came over his eyes as he studied the slim patent-leather boot that gleamed as it tapped the bottom step of the stairs. Isabel, the youngest of his three sisters, was far and away his favorite. He was fond of Susan, just as he was fond of Sophie, Mrs. Fenwick, who was ten years his senior; but they were both too competent to allow him to feel for them the protective love he felt for Isabel. Isabel was little more than a child. And he was about to give this child in marriage to a soldier bound for the front. It was some comfort that she was marrying an Allston, a Charleston cousin, and not someone beneath her.

Now if England would hasten intervention, the War would soon —but Joe had promised his harassed brain to forget the War for these few hours. His thumb rubbed slowly back and forth over the case of his watch. He returned it to his pocket and studied his nails. The inspection, casual at first, became interested: tapering fingers, well-kept nails,—an elegant hand, the hand of a gentleman. A wave of satisfaction, sponsored by two carefully measured brandies taken before the appearance of Alec, passed up his spine and spread to the roots of his cologne-scented mane.

Joseph Bramwell was not a tall man, but a certain burliness of chest, an erectness of carriage, and a superb head, gave the impression of commanding stature. It might have been supposed from his air of wisdom and dignity that he was the product of a long and fruitful life, when in fact he was not yet thirty. Even his dress contributed to the illusion of ripe nobility, for he invariably wore sober black broadcloth, shunning the passion of his contemporaries for checked trousers and fancy waistcoats. His high stock, almost hidden by a wide satin cravat, stopped just short of the point where compression of the larynx would have proved fatal.

Aside from his precocious elevation to the Supreme Court Bench, other factors contributed to his premature pomposity. While a law student at Harvard, where he was honor man of his class, he had suffered a loss that had saddled him with early responsibilities: his father, twice governor of the state, and his mother, on their way to England for a holiday, had been drowned in a memorable disaster of the sea. So he was now the guardian of the persons and estates of

7

his two younger sisters. And at Holly Hill, his Combahee River plantation, he was a conspicuously successful agriculturist. Moreover, despite these and a host of lesser obligations, he had taken it upon himself, in the half decade before Sumter, to play a leading part in championing Secession, smiting hip and thigh, in prose and verse, the Abolitionist Philistines. It was he who, in a paper for the *Southern Literary Messenger,* had compressed the soul of the South into a single rolling period.

"The South possesses the philosophic temper of Greece, the political vitality of Rome, and the beauty of Chivalry softened by the spiritual quality of Christianity."

In view of his imposing array of talents the majority of his neighbors in aristocratic Beaufort were inclined to be tolerant of his manner. It was understood that in a general way he stood for the proud little town, was certainly its spokesman and possibly its fittest representative.

The sound of steps in the hall above drew Joe's handsome eyes up the stairs, which reached with easy treads to a landing, lighted by a large palladian window, where it divided and reversed upward. Isabel came first; at the landing her crinolines were released to their full spread and she descended the broad lower flight with her flounced skirt filling the generous space from rail to rail. The candlelight caught the sheen of the silk beneath the lace of her pointed bodice and the luster of her dark hair, whose darkness, like the darkness of her eyes, was accentuated by the whiteness of her dress and skin. Points of light touched the pearls in her hair and at her slim throat and wrists. There were lace bows on her satin slippers, and each step down revealed a dainty ankle.

Joe stepped up to meet her. He took her hand and raised it to his lips with a feeling of intense agitation.

"Do I pass muster?" she asked breathlessly.

At the foot of the stairs she turned around before him, smiling over her shoulder, and Joe found it necessary to clear his throat before he answered.

"You are lovelier than a white japonica."

"Goodness, am I that pale?"

She touched a forefinger to her tongue and rubbed a circle on each cheek.

"Now!"

8

"Now," he smiled, "you are lovelier than a pink japonica."

She took his arm with a squeeze, and he escorted her down the hall past the dining-room door, where the servants had flocked from the pantry to gape and exclaim. Susan followed her brother and sister chattering superfluities to relieve her nerves, while Phyllis, white teeth shining, brought up the rear with the young ladies' wraps. At the front door Joe took Isabel's cape from Phyllis and placed it tenderly around his sister's shoulders; he performed the same service, with less ceremony, for Susan. Then, with a matter-of-fact snort to hide his feelings, he received from Robert his best English gloves and his new beaver, which he pushed well down on his head against the wind that rushed in with the opening of the front door.

When he had taken his sisters down the steps and handed them into the waiting barouche, he mounted the horse whose head Alec was holding: Bramwell men had never pampered themselves with coach-riding. After the ladies dresses had been carefully settled, the door safely closed, and Phyllis seated beside the coachman on the box, he gave the signal to start, leading the way as the barouche followed the curve of the drive with a fine jingle of harness.

There was a glimpse, between the silhouetted trees, of the calm rose glow above the dark cloud line in the west, and there was a reflection in tatters on the gusty river; but Joe, sitting very straight in his saddle, was no more aware of the twilight colors than he was of the stinging wind in his face or the sighing tempest in the branches. His thoughts were turned inward, lost in reverie, as he rode through the pool of light under the gateway arch and trotted along darkening Fenwick Street, where sound of hoof and wheel was muffled in ashy sand. . . . Joe's moments of introspection were normally of a self-congratulatory order. Yet there was one matter that sometimes popped up to give him pause, and in this hour of his sister's wedding it presented itself with peculiar force. Where was his bride? Or rather, where was his son, the Bramwell heir? Where was William Legerton Bramwell, great-grandson and name-sake-to-be of old "Yemassee Bill," early settler, Indian fighter, Revolutionary hero? But he soothed himself now as he had soothed himself before. He was a young man still, and being a Bramwell he could expect to be a potent man for many years to come. And, as Aristotle had said, no man was wise to marry before the age of thirty-six. Later, at the next convenient season, he would make a serious survey of belles at the Charleston balls and pick a young lady worthy of Bramwell attention. Later. . . .

At the inlet causeway he was drawn out of his reflections. Ahead to the left, rising from the edge of the brooding marsh, stood almost-finished Bramwell Hall, its Tudoresque battlements and chimneys sharply outlined against the dying afterglow. Here in good time some eligible lady, unknown now, would be honored as his bride. A band of wind-blown crows flapped away from the roof, cawing unpleasantly, and Joe was touched for a moment by a sense of vague sadness. But he dismissed the mood with ease. With a cheerful nod he returned the respectful wool-pull greeting of Mingo, the town lamplighter, who had dismounted from his tacky and was transferring a light from his lantern to the lamp at the street corner.

"What news, Mingo?" he checked his horse to ask.

"Maus' Joe, to tell de trut' suh,"—Mingo scratched his head apologetically—"I hear Mistuh Heyward an' dem gemmen whut been to Chaa'son say dey lookin' fuh dat big Yankee fleet mos' any day now suh."

"I know all about their Invincible Armada!" Joe snorted. "A dozen Yankee fleets couldn't take Charleston."

Mingo's worried brow relaxed and a grin spread his shiny black face.

"Now ain't dat de Gawd trut' suh! T'ank you suh! T'ank you, Maussa!"

Joe resumed his way ahead of the barouche, turning his head to watch the light from the lamp throw a turmoil of shadows over Bramwell Hall. Already those new walls were beginning to mellow. The War was responsible for the unfinished state of the interior, for those blind windows covered with crocus bagging, but when victory came the house would speedily be completed. For Susan's wedding and his own there would be no need to borrow his brother-in-law's house.

In a thoroughly comfortable frame of mind he convoyed the barouche along the several streets to the gate of St. Helena's. There he dismounted with a flourish, handed the ladies out, and with a reassuring pat gave a confident arm to Isabel. Susan took his other arm, leaving Phyllis to bring up the rear as they walked under the sighing branches of the majestic old trees, past the plot that held the brick-supported slabs of the Bramwell dead, toward the lights and the waiting door of the church.

Alec had jumped down from his secret perch on the back springs of the barouche and was trailing the little procession at a respectful distance. When they entered the vestibule, he slipped in behind and from a corner watched Phyllis's quick fingers arrange the veil on Miss 'Bel's head and freshen the lace flounces of the dress. Then someone opened a crack in the double door to the big room, and the organ began to play. With thumping heart he turned and scrambled up the steep steps to the gallery.

There he tried to squeeze into the packed front bench beside Maum Freeny Hazzard, who gave him a cuff for his no-manners. The rest of the benches were full too: all the quality color in town were here in their Sunday best, whispering and stretching their necks. He sat in the aisle on the bottom step. With elbows resting on the railing he could see the whole church and look down on the buckra. He spotted his own in one of the front stalls: his mistress, Stephen's cadet uniform, and little Miss Eugenia's curls sticking out from under her bonnet. Only Maus' Larry was missing, away in Virginia. Big Maussa, Major Fenwick with his sash and sword, was standing up by the altar with the man who was going to marry Miss 'Bel. The man was gray-looking as his uniform.

The organ music swelled up loud, and there was Miss 'Bel and Maus' Joe walking up the aisle slow as you please, with Miss Susan and Cap'n Pat Elliott following behind.

When the organ stopped, Reverend began to talk. Shivering from the cold of the church, Alec tried to hear and make some sense out of what Reverend was saying. But it was no use.

As the voice mumbled on, he smiled to himself, thinking of the fun ahead. He was lucky, in his fine boots and green coat with brass buttons and braid, luckier than Stephen in his old cadet uniform: he would have double fun, at the buckra party and then the kitchen party afterwards.

Presently he reached down to work off the miserable boots. Maum Freeny Hazzard had brought a hot brick to church like the buckra, and he moved his feet over close to it without her noticing.

Stephen Fenwick rode home with his mother and father and Eugenia. He had wanted to stay behind and find his cousin Rusty

Stewart in the church crowd, but the voice of authority had said to come along now, and he knew better than to argue with the Napoleon-the-Third imperial of the commander of the Beaufort Militia.

But riding beside him through the windy darkness and snatches of light, facing his mother and sister in the swaying carriage, there was nothing to keep him from arguing back inside. He resented his family. For some reason they always made him feel uncomfortable. He could feel more natural with neighbors or niggers or even strangers than he could with his own flesh and blood. Except Rusty Stewart.

Rusty was different. He was Larry's age, but he was more of a brother than Larry had ever been. Land's End, the plantation on St. Helena Island, was next to Cherokee, the Stewart plantation, and in the old days Stephen had always had Rusty to stick up for him, to thank for being allowed to tag around with the bigger boys, after the community school of knuckle-rapping Miss Libby Evans was out. It was Rusty who had taught him to swim and ride and hunt. Later, when Larry had gone off to college at the North and Rusty had gone abroad to Edinburgh to study medicine, Stephen had been sent to Porter Academy and the Citadel at Charleston, but he had never found any friend who could take Rusty's place.

Now the War had brought him back from Scotland to join the Medical Corps. Yesterday he had reached Beaufort with only forty-eight hours' leave before Virginia. The same Rusty—tall and lean, sandy-red cowlick hair, freckled face and hands, light blue eyes with a faraway look, the same easy-going voice, same old contagious smile—the same Rusty. Rusty had taken on over him before the whole family, saying how he had sprung up and filled out, thumping his chest and testing and praising his muscle. Nothing could be better than seeing Rusty again.

But so far it had been impossible to see much of him. Now riding home with the family Stephen ignored their talk about the wedding. He was living over his disappointment. Yesterday he had ridden out with most of the men left in town to Holly Hill for the last meeting of the Combahee Hunt Club, the old Free-and-Easy. No chance for a good talk with Rusty there. After supper the men had gathered round the fire to swap Gullah stories, forgetting the War for one night and monopolizing Rusty. And the hope of bunking down with Rusty had been broken by the sleeping arrangements that Uncle Joe had dictated. Stephen had found himself three in a bed with Peewee Hawley and Moultrie Pherson, who had snored like a trooper and taken over most of the covers.

Then cold dawn and the first stand, posted alone in the woods; only the dripping of frost melting in the first slanting sunrays, and now and then the fall of a crimson or yellow leaf breaking the chill silence. He remembered how he had pulled down moss to stand on. Up in Virginia perhaps his brother Larry's feet had been cold too, waiting for the Yanks. Soon Rusty would be there. Everybody would be there except himself. He was to stay home like a little boy.

It had been an endless wait before the dogs had jumped a deer and the driver's yell had echoed through the woods. Here in the carriage his ears were ringing as if he were back there on that stand again, straining to follow the swing of the chase. It was coming straight on now, headed straight for his stand, the dogs in full cry. His fingers stiff with cold were tightening convulsively on his gun. He was fighting off panic, praying to God he wouldn't miss, for Rusty's sake.

Without so much as the warning snap of a twig: the deer standing in the clearing across the road, motionless, listening, as if waiting for the trigger. Then a flashing glimpse of the phantom as it bounded to the left and vanished.

Stephen moved uneasily in the carriage, remembering the stinging words that had come when his father and Uncle Joe had galloped up to the stand to halt the dogs with cracking whips and curses.

"What was it?" Uncle Joe had snapped at him.

"Eight-point," his father had answered for him. "A beauty."

"Buck fever!" Uncle Joe had sneered. "We'll post him on the rump stand next drive."

After the dogs were curbed and quieted, his father had said: "You'll have to do better than that, son, if you ever hope to hunt Yankees."

But now as the carriage passed through the gateway of Marshlands and followed the drive to the front door, the smarting bitterness of the day dissolved in the thought that soon Rusty would be here.

He followed the family into the bright light of the hall, but let them go on up to the drawing-room without him. When they were safely out of the way, he went in the dining-room to the sideboard with its glistening decanters of sherry and port and brandy; but he had hardly taken the stopper out of the brandy decanter when he heard voices at the front door. There was just time to step behind the curtains at the nearest window alcove. He heard Uncle Joe, Aunt Isabel and her new husband, and Aunt Susan go through the hall and upstairs. When he came out from his hiding-place he found Phyllis in the room, smiling at him.

He turned to the sideboard and said to her over his shoulder, "Get me some cloves from the kitchen, and make haste."

He was able to swallow two drinks and pour a third before she came back with the cloves. He chewed some and put the rest in his pocket. His eyes were watering and he was gulping for breath, and she was grinning at his struggle to look natural.

"See you keep your mouth shut," he told her hoarsely. "And quit hanging around. Here, take my things."

When she had gone into the hall with his cape and shako, he coughed off his distress. Then he stood with his back to the crackling fire, chewing cloves as he waited for the first glow to come.

It was not long delayed. The fire felt good on his back after the cold church and the windy ride home. The crackling began to sound exciting, and there was excitement in the dining-room table with its damask and silver and in all the chairs lined up against the walls like a dress parade: he tugged down his tight-waisted cadet jacket, stretched his neck in the tight collar, and arranged his cuffs. . . . Everything was losing its commonplace expression and coming vividly to life. At any moment the guests would begin to arrive, Rusty among them. He thought he heard wheels on the drive right now.

He saw Alec scuffling down the hall to the front door and hurried out to intercept him.

"Hey! Where you think you're going in that rig?"

Alec stopped short with a look half sheepish, half determined. "To de do'."

"Remember to say *sir* to me, hear."

Alec blinked.

"Where's Robert?" Stephen frowned at him, then jeered: "You can't go to the door in that getup. You look too foolish. Look at yourself."

Alec looked at himself and made a sudden break for the door, and with a flush of rage Stephen went after him. For months he had been trying to teach Alec that he was a man now and master and no longer playmate. He grabbed his arm and shot at him in Gullah: "*Tek* you' han' fum dat do'—*yeddy!*" But Alec's lips pouted defiance, and he clung to the latchring with both hands when Stephen tried to pull him away. Then he started to sniffle, and with a sudden return of dignity Stephen let him go. "I'll tend to you later," he said ominously, smoothing his hair and straightening his uniform. All just in time, for there were voices and steps on the porch, then the tap of the knocker.

When Alec opened the door, no Rusty but only the Hamiltons and the Mowbrey cousins from Savannah. Stephen had to go up with them to the drawing-room, where the bride and groom and the family were waiting in an evergreen bower, opposite the big fireplace where the Stars-and-Bars hung. And then he had to act sociable with the cousins.

"Wasn't it just too adorable!" Cousin Betty beamed.

"Oh, I think it was just the most adorable wedding I almost ever saw!" gushed Cousin Corny.

They were always like that. Everything was *too* adorable, *too* cute, *too* something. They were so silly they made everything they talked about sound silly. They didn't seem to know there was a war, they didn't even know what they were saying, they just gabbed and giggled, giggled and gabbed. All he had to do was look polite, which wasn't hard with the brandy glow spreading all through him.

People were really beginning to arrive now, he saw, watching the door for Rusty. . . . The room was filling with faces and a confusion of greetings, laughter and talk and kissing the bride. People usually made him feel self-conscious, but not tonight. Tonight he felt strong and important, and when the currents of the room finally relieved him of the Mowbrey cousins, he circulated with ease from group to group. He kept away from corners and stayed in the main stream. He wanted to see everyone, to talk and laugh, though he instinctively lowered his voice when he was near his mother and father or Uncle Joe. He had quick replies now for any of the men who had been on the morning hunt and inquired solicitously about the eight-point buck and the tail of his shirt. With the ladies, old and young, he felt he was making a charming impression.

Faces and eyes. All, even the dullest, transfigured tonight. The room was getting more and more crowded, and it was getting more and more exciting to move about. The eddies of chatter and laughter made a pleasant giddiness. The warmth from the big fireplace made the flutter of fans more than an ornamental gesture; it was good to get a breath from them now and then. Things moved smoothly and easily, spontaneously, and he gave himself to the delicious movement. Rusty appeared for a moment and was drawn away, but it was impossible to feel depressed even about that. Somehow everything that was happening was right. It was all right, or at least it wasn't actively unpleasant, to have to take Cousin Corny down to supper, though Peewee Hawley had Nancy Malcolm, the best-looking girl in town.

Supper slowed things up a little. But after the calapee of turtle and the cold turkey and ham, champagne began to sparkle and bubble and the world was afloat again, flowing smooth and swift and serene. Syllabub and ices and more champagne accompanied the cutting of the tiered cake from Charleston.

He stood very steady during the toasts to the bride and groom. For them one day and a night together at Holly Hill; then separation. Virginia. . . .

His father was standing in the middle of the room with his glass held up, waiting for silence. Then his voice came, quiet and very sure.

"Ladies and gentlemen, I give you the President of the Confederate States of America."

Glasses and voices swung high. In the hall the orchestra struck up *Dixie*. Shivers of joy and pride ran up Stephen's spine as he joined in the chorus.

> *I wish I was in Dixie—Hooray! Hooray!*
> *In Dixie Land I'll take my stand,*
> *To live and die in Dixie;*
> *Away, away, away down South in Dixie;*
> *Away, away, away down South in Dixie.*

The room, the hall, and the room beyond were in an uproar. Everyone was going wild. Stephen felt that his chest was bursting with it. Then *Maryland* started. It started itself, and the orchestra had to catch up.

The despot's heel is on thy shore,
Maryland! My Maryland!
His torch is at thy temple door,
Maryland! My Maryland!

People in front of him and around him were crying, and he couldn't keep their tears from blinding his own eyes. He tried hard to wink them away, but everything stayed in a burning haze. When someone right next to him started *The Bonnie Blue Flag* he couldn't even see who it was. But he could still sing.

We are a band of brothers and native to the soil,
Fighting for our liberty with treasure, blood, and toil;
And when our rights were threatened, the cry rose near and far,
Hurrah for the Bonnie Blue Flag, that bears a single star!
Hurrah! Hurrah! For the Southern Rights, Hurrah!
Hurrah! for the Bonnie Blue Flag that bears a Single Star!

The room and all the people were hopelessly blurred now. . . .

People were moving out into the hall and up the stairs, taking the orchestra with them, and he was carried along with the tide. He was laughing now, hysterically, at nothing. But no-one noticed in the noisy press up to the drawing-room. . . .

The orchestra was opening the ball with a quadrille, Uncle Joe leading the cotillion march. Stephen wound up with Peewee Hawley's fat sister for a partner. But what difference did it make tonight. . . .

The next thing he knew everyone was trying to get down to the front door to see the bride and groom off. He swam against the tide this time and somehow glided out onto the promenade porch, where he found a few other smart ones. But the view was blocked by curtains of plantation cloth lashed from pillar to pillar to keep the wind out, and nobody seemed to know what to do about it. Well, he did. He ripped loose a whole section of the cloth. Laughter applauded him and heads and arms joined him at the opening. Below was the carriage: Isabel and her husband were just getting in through flurries of rice. People were crowding down the steps after them, pelting rice at the carriage, waving and laughing and shouting. . . . A regular hail storm of rice now. . . . Rebel yells. . . . Farewells. . . .

17

The carriage was gone.

. . . He was helping himself to rum punch, impartially from first one and then the other of the two bowls on a table in the upper hall. He was eating mints from the cutglass dishes of the silver tree-of-life, the White Elephant as it was called in the family, which stood tonight between the punch bowls. . . . He was dancing a schottish or polka, he wasn't sure which, with someone he didn't know and grace he didn't suspect he had in him. . . . He was waltzing with Nancy Malcolm, dizzily, having mysteriously stolen her from Peewee Hawley. Ordinarily Nancy treated him like a boy, but tonight she was treating him the way he felt. When they went out on the upper porch, he took her hand and kissed it, recovering his balance with ease. He was smitten with a desire to tell her how beautiful she was and how he was going to the War: he *was* going to the War. But his tongue was clumsy and thick when he tried to talk or even whisper, so it was easier to just laugh about it and go back inside to dance some more. . . .

Rusty had touched his arm and was taking him aside. "Been looking for you, Steve." Arm in arm they were leaving the drawing-room, weaving down through the couples sitting on the stairs. They were in the lower hall, at the front door, on the porch. At the foot of the steps there was a carriage with luggage waiting for them.

"Let's go, Rusty. Come on!"

Rusty steadied him as they went down the steps.

"Take it easy, old boy. I'm the one that's going."

The sharp air cleared his head a little then.

"I'm due in Charleston by morning," Rusty was saying, "so I've got to push off now. If I can trust you to take a little air. You're beginning to stand out a little, even in this crowd. How about it?"

Stephen nodded sensibly, steadying himself on Rusty's arm. Then suddenly he understood the whole thing.

"I'm going with you, Rusty. By God, I'm not going to stay behind!"

"Whoa boy, hold your horses," Rusty was smiling. Then he stopped smiling. "Somebody's got to look after things at home, Steve."

"Rusty, I got to go with you. I'm obliged to go. I can't stay behind."

Rusty's hands gripped his shoulders.

18

"I know how you feel, man. But don't be in too big a rush. Your chance will come before you know it. Now give me your paw. And take my advice and turn in, while the turning's good. At least let the party catch up with you, before your father or Uncle Joe does. How are you, all right?"

"Sure I'm all right. Perfect."

He stood back then, on his own. And there was something in his throat that made it impossible to say anything more, even after Rusty was in the carriage. He just shook hands again, grateful for the shadows that kept Rusty from seeing his eyes.

When the carriage was gone, he stood in a choked spinning misery. Then the dizziness that the cold wind had driven away swept back: the lawn and the river and the marshes beyond, under a moon racing through tatters of cloud, all began to swing wildly around him. By a great effort he steadied things and turned to the house, where the branches flung crazy patterns between the lights of the windows. But when he tried to climb the steps, they swayed and fell away from him.

He was on the lawn, talking to himself as he headed for the dark gleaming river. . . .

He was lying on the edge of the lawn near the seawall, looking up at the fronds of a palmetto. The stiff rustling sounded like rain. The wind had blotted out the moon with solid cloud. It was dark and cold.

He sat up, and finally got to his feet. He felt wobbly and weak as water, and there was a humming fog in his head. The humming remained but the fog cleared a little when he got going across the lawn toward the house.

At the front steps he hesitated and decided to go around and in the back way. All he wanted now was to avoid people and get to bed, in his temporary quarters in the attic. In the yard he was surprised to find no signs of celebration; there were lights in the kitchen and the servant quarters but no sounds of merrymaking. Puzzled, he slipped in the back door. Maum Minda, Robert, and some of the others were cleaning up in the pantry, talking in low voices. He tiptoed into the empty main hall. There were a few voices in the living-room. He tiptoed on upstairs, guilty and anxious.

At the head of the stairs he stopped again. There were loud voices in his room, the men's coatroom tonight. He listened, trying to make sense out of the jumble. When one voice—Uncle Joe's—stood out alone, he began to understand.

"Why shouldn't it be Port Royal, gentlemen? Isn't it the finest harbor on the coast and key to Beaufort? And isn't Beaufort the heart of the sea islands, the richest plantation country in the Confederacy?"

A faltering voice interrupted: "But Charleston or Savannah or New Orleans would be more strategic points for them to attack."

"Nonsense, sir!" Uncle Joe's voice rapped back. "Here they have a fine harvest of long-staple cotton and also a back door to Charleston and Savannah. Don't deceive yourselves, gentlemen. This is no feint to divert troops from our sister towns. Read Governor Pickens's dispatch again, Michael."

After a rustling of papers Stephen recognized his father's voice. "I have just received information which I consider entirely reliable that the enemy's expedition is intended for Port Royal."

"You hear that, gentlemen?" Uncle Joe's voice resumed. "Make no mistake—the expedition is intended for Port Royal!"

After a muttering of oaths the room was still for a moment.

"Then what's to save us?" the faltering voice asked. "With our waterways so easy of access for Federal gunboats, what hope is there of making an effective resistance? Beauregard himself has said——"

"I'm not concerned, sir, with what anyone has said! If Charleston and Savannah think it's dangerous and futile to lend us any of their strength, we'll go it alone, sir. Does any man here doubt that we'll fight for our homes?"

There was a sharp silence. Then the voices mingled and came toward the door.

Stephen hurried across the hall to the attic door and stumbled up the steep dark stairs. In the dusty-smelling room he lighted a candle and undressed. When he crept in between the cold sheets, he lay with a pounding heart, trying to think through the fog that was closing down on him again.

II

THREE DAYS LATER Stephen Fenwick, sitting between his mother and sister in the family stall at St. Helena's, was ready to jump out of his skin. What was he doing here with the women and children and old men, listening to the voice in the pulpit droning through the Penitential Service, while his father and the others, including even Peewee Hawley, were out in the fort at Bay Point.

Every now and then the windows shook with heavy jarring rumbles, punctuating the Rector's drone and sending an audible shudder over the stalls. Out of the corner of his eye Stephen watched his mother and sister: Eugenia's eyelids were fluttering like she wanted to cry, the baby scare-cat, but his mother looked like she always did. She was looking at the pulpit calm and steady, as if this was just an ordinary service back in peace times. And suddenly it gave him a funny proud feeling. It made him feel proud to be her son.

He suppressed an unaccountable twitching that came up from the pit of his stomach. The world, the secure and steadfast world of home, was on fire. Maum Minda used to sing when she was rocking him to sleep long ago: *"O po' brud-duh—when de worl's on fi-yuh—don' you wan' Gawd's boo-sum—fuh be yo' pil-luh?"* God's bosom would be a mighty fine pillow if it was half as good as Maum Minda's. But this was no time for bosoms and pillows, church and prayers,—this was crisis time, time for men to be in action. . . . At least his father had promised to let him go if the War lasted into the second year. But the Yanks would be squealing for mercy by then.

He felt his mother's hand touch his knee. She and Eugenia were kneeling. He knelt with them and closed his eyes, trying to focus on the Rector's voice.

"O most merciful and just God, give ear unto Thy children in this hour of dire peril. Abide with us, abide with us, we most humbly beseech Thee. Sustain our arms against the enemy at our gates. . . ."

The prayer was attended by an increased booming of the guns in the Sound and by prolonged rattlings of the windows. Stephen stole a look at his mother. Her gloved hands hid her eyes, but now her lips were trembling. It gave him a terrible catch in the throat to see that. He closed his eyes and pressed his forehead against his knuckles till it hurt.

O God, he breathed, I've never asked many favors, and I'll never ask another if you'll grant this one. Don't let the War stop before I get in. Give me just one shot at the damn Yanks. For Christ's sake. Amen.

After the service, out in the clear bright sunlight, everything was easier. He saw his mother and sister off in the carriage and then raced to Bay Street and the boat landing.

The batteaux that served as ferries across the wide tidal river to the Ladies Island shore were all missing. To the South, beyond Ladies Island, lay great St. Helena Island with Land's End plantation at its southwest tip. His thoughts leaped to that familiar ground and crossed Station Creek to the wind-duned barrier islands and Bay Point beach, where he had so often swum and fished with Rusty. But it was no longer the peaceful place of sea birds and ocean surf: now it was the place where his father and the militia were defending a shallow sand fort against the Yankee armada in Port Royal Sound. The thundering clouds of smoke would be visible from here where he stood on the landing but for the bend the river made as it broadened into the Sound.

But from reports that had come in earlier he knew how the battle looked. At nine o'clock the Yankee fleet had crossed the bar off Bay Point and opened the attack. The Sound had been quiet as a lake on a sleepy summer day, not a ripple or a swell to disturb the accuracy of fire from the decks. Like doom the nineteen warships had moved in from the sea in close file. Sudden white plumes had stood in rows over the blue water and thunder had jarred the horizon. When the ships had fired at Fort Beauregard on Bay Point, they had swung round and fired at Fort Walker on Hilton Head, three miles across the mouth of the Sound. They were making this circuit again and again, pouring their broadsides into the pair of makeshift forts.

Old Mr. Jenkins was at the landing, with several women and kids and a sprinkling of servants sent for news. When Stephen approached him and asked if any fresh word had come in, Mr. Jenkins scanned his face with a fierce scowl. The stout cane was shifted from right hand to left, and Stephen felt on his shoulder the big loose hand that so loved to descend on young heads with what was intended for a gentle pat. The big hand had been respecting his head lately, sure proof he was grown-up now.

"Lad," the big voice boomed shakily, "your father and the rest of them are knocking the living tar out of the boogers, same as your grandfather and me did the British when we were lads no bigger than you."

Stephen winced at that.

"I'd be there too if they'd let me."

"So would I, lad," the big voice grumbled and quavered, "so would I. If I just had me a boat,—that's the hell of it."

Stephen stayed for a polite few minutes to listen to Mr. Jenkins and then turned home through the confusion of the town.

A dazed weariness took hold of his senses, his brain and body rebelling against the tension that had been with him so long. The preparations for flight along the way seemed to have no personal connection with him; he felt a remote annoyance, that was all. Some of the houses were already deserted, at others carriages and carts were being loaded, and he caught glimpses of flats on the river and many-oared plantation piraguas, piled high with everything under the sun. People would have a lot of unloading to do when the news came that the Yankee fleet had withdrawn. His father had said the forts would hold, so they would hold, and all this rushing around of women and servants was ridiculous. There was the booming of the guns out there in the Sound, but it was no longer impressive: it lacked conviction, it was becoming tiresome. Beaufort abandoned to the Yanks! That just couldn't happen.

Fenwick Street burst, came slowly together, and stood still, the bright air stunned by the heavy thudding clang of St. Helena's bell. Stephen opened his mouth for breath. The second stroke shattered the spell and went eddying down the street, spreading panic. He started to run with leaden feet as in a nightmare,—the bell, signal for evacuation, tolling in his head as he strained toward the gates of Marshlands.

He found his mother in the hall. Her eyes gave him quick reassurance, for there was no panic there.

"Dear," she said quietly, "the clothes you need are all laid out on the bed. Don't try to take anything else in your room, unless it's something you really want."

The afternoon was a turmoil in which the only point of stability was the form of his mother, frail but wonderfully undismayed. Most of the furnishings from the house at Land's End had passed Marshlands yesterday in a plantation boat on the way to the Combahee River and Uncle Joe's Holly Hill; but none of the furnishings of Marshlands had been sent away yet, and now came the frantic task of picking out the few things that could be saved. He and Alec helped Robert with the bigger things, while Maum Minda and Phyllis followed his mother through the house with pillowcases to catch the smaller things.

He ran endless errands upstairs and down, sustained by a burning fever of excitement and by the look in his mother's eyes whenever he came to her. He was in a chaos of familiar things become suddenly sharp and strange, of yard servants gone jibbering mad, of half-blind comings and goings between the disordered house and the littered front driveway, where old George was in charge of loading the two carriages and the plantation wagon and cart, and where the sun shone with mocking brightness.

Late in the afternoon he was aware that his father had come back from Bay Point. His face was haggard and black with grime, and his uniform was torn and stained, but he was safe. Stephen wanted to ask questions, but he didn't dare. He waited for his father to tell him what to do next.

Things moved now with more speed and order. But the tide of the sun was ebbing away from the river and the marshes before the little caravan drove out to join the long procession that was making inland over the old Shell Road, draining the life of the town.

Stephen carried along with him the picture of his mother and father standing together in the driveway for a last look at home.

He had heard his father say, "You must come now, dear." He himself had checked his horse outside the gates to look back. The high wall hid the grounds and the tabby arches of the house foundations. A soft golden light lingered over the chimneys and the broad roof and touched the tops of the live-oaks. This light, like a voice saying farewell, became a stinging haze in his eyes as he turned his horse away.

He rode beside the closed carriage which his father was driving and in which his mother and Eugenia were packed among bundles and baskets. Eugenia held her white kitten and a doll in her arms and on her knees two silver candlesticks and a jewel-case; in his mother's lap was the pair of vases from the drawing-room mantel, and in each hand a crystal decanter. Behind was the open phaeton filled to overflowing with Maum Minda and Phyllis and bundles and boxes. On mattresses in the big lumbering plantation wagon rode Robert and Alec and the other house servants, with the moss-packed portraits of Grandmother and Grandfather Fenwick. The cart brought up the rear, driven by old George perched on trunks and hampers.

Stephen's setters, the pair Rusty had given him, kept close at his heels. They were subdued and grave, not frisking and frolicking like some of the fool dogs up ahead, acting like this was some sort of picnic. To the west, over the dusky fields and woods, the sunset was turning from gold to rose and placid jade.

It was late night before they reached the mainland ferry. Here was a congestion of vehicles and a long wait in line for the rope-propelled transport. Fires and torch-flares made wavering caverns in the darkness.

While Maum Minda prepared supper from a hastily-stocked basket, Stephen went with Robert to one of the fires to heat water for tea. There was quite a lively group at the next fire, and around one of the torches some boys were playing tag among grotesque shadows. But here at this fire most of the people were silent, staring into the flames, or talking in low voices as they warmed themselves and waited. . . . Watching the first wisp of steam curl from the pot of water that Robert had set at the edge of the fire, Stephen thought of home sitting empty and forsaken on the Point, deserted, alone under the cold calm stars.

III

At noon on the second day after the battle of Port Royal, Beaufort was visited by a trio of Federal gunboats. The men, coming cautiously ashore, found the town deserted except for a cluster of stray blacks, who received assurances that they were now free with stupefied grins. Some of the soldiers shook hands with them and joked, calling them Uncle Tom and Sambo, Cuffee, Topsy.

They watched the soldiers spread with fixed bayonets through the silent streets. They heard the thump of rifle-butt and boot against sacred doors; the sudden crash and tinkle of glass. They saw soldiers appear at the upper windows of one house in Bay Street with bottles in their hands and shout down to other soldiers, who shouted back in harsh Yankee voices and rushed to join them. From an upper window of another house a snowstorm was being shaken out of a feather-bed. A china commode came hurtling through the falling fluff and smashed in the middle of the street, narrowly missing the head of a Yankee officer, who looked up and cursed. That broke the spell, and the gaping blacks broke into chuckles and guffaws. The officer turned and cursed them too. When he had moved on, they slapped knees, bent double, pushed one another in their glee.

They were losing their shyness and their bewilderment at the spectacle of their masters' homes being thus freely invaded; they were beginning to understand this Freedom thing. Presently some of the bolder ones left the group and began to trail the soldiers. Soon all but two or three old slaves had overcome timidity and mixed in.

The officers of the landing force established headquarters at the Heyward mansion on Bay Street, issued orders that there was to be no pillaging or burning, and made themselves comfortable with an abundance of confiscated delicacies and demijohns of old whiskey, preparatory to a careful inspection of the town. Several hours passed before they felt sufficiently fortified to sally forth. They then made two very satisfactory discoveries: that the little town contained an excellent library, whose volumes could later be boxed and shipped to Washington as a suitable memento of the occupation, and that the inhabitants had left behind a number of fine pianos, which could be disposed of, by private treaty, to some of the adventurous merchants who had followed the fleet to Port Royal. They also discovered that the men were not observing the pillaging clause of the day's orders. The men, in fact, were getting out of hand. Those officers who were still sober enough to sense the necessity for immediate return to discipline set themselves to the task of rounding up the rank and file.

This proved complicated. Lawless elements among the troops had created a carnival, which by contagion was growing from strength to strength. By late afternoon fraternizing bands of drunken soldiers and blacks had plundered house after house, scrambling for valuables, smashing windows, chandeliers, glassware, china, furniture, pictures,—and pianos. The functioning officers became less and less capable of dealing with the situation. When they were able to suppress for a moment the looting in one part of town, it broke out with fresh vigor somewhere else.

One carousing party, absorbing a patrol sent out to subdue them, tore the organ pipes out of St. Helena's Church and played them jubilantly up and down Bay Street. In other streets impromptu parades formed and re-formed behind cowbells and improvised drums and triangles, manipulated by blacks in a jungle rhythm that made perfect music for the fantastic scene. One parade, which held tenaciously together till sheer exhaustion disrupted it, was led by a wild-eyed black buck, naked to the waist, his powerful muscles glistening with sweat despite the chill air of the waning day, his big hands thumping a savage beat on the sides of a lady's valise suspended from his neck by a curtain cord. He was followed with mincing steps by a tall Yankee corporal in a fluffy hoopskirt and feather bonnet, arm-in-arm with a grinning black youth. Next came two soldiers in Revolutionary uniforms and half a dozen riotous black women in a variety of looted finery, prancing and jerking along in time with the leader's drum. A boyish lieutenant, hatless

27

and with his coat ripped and befouled, brought up the rear of the parade, swaying dangerously yet managing somehow to keep up.

Captain Brooks, of the New Hampshire Highlanders, finding himself ranking officer owing to the total eclipse of his superiors, made a rapid survey of conditions throughout the town, found that matters had come to the point where gangs of soldiers and Negroes were barricading themselves in houses with Negro women and assorted liquors, and wisely decided that nature must be allowed to take its course for the night. Morning would bring a state of mind more amenable to discipline. Accordingly, he posted sentries on the outskirts of town, sent scouts out the highway to scent any raid of the enemy, and appointed a police squad to do what they could to quiet the waterfront and watch for fires.

That evening Captain Brooks confined his own private celebration to a bottle of claret with his supper. After supper he set out to do a little fastidious souvenir collecting. And despite the shocking vandalism that met him at every turn, he was highly successful. The first house he entered (he commandeered an orderly and two Negro boys with a clothesbasket to accompany him) yielded a pair of Lowestoft vases, a charming Sully portrait, an interesting old sword, and four Fraser miniatures.

Especially enjoyable and worthwhile was his last visit, to the house of a Major Michael Fenwick. An inspection by candlelight revealed a completely devastated dining-room and living-room, but the library beyond the living-room was almost intact. Although some of the books had been swept off the shelves, thrown about the room or through the windows, many were undisturbed. The Captain made a leisurely selection. Sets of Montaigne, Shakespeare, and Madame de Sévigné, all bound in the finest morocco. Old calf volumes of Hesiod and Plutarch, Horace and Virgil, each with the signature of Stephen Fenwick, a Colonial governor of South Carolina. A copy of Scott's *Marmion* in the handsomest binding the Captain had ever seen. And finally a bulky volume of Von Humboldt's *Cosmos,* autographed to "My respected Confrere, William Elliott Fenwick."

In the upstairs drawing-room the Captain found remnants of evergreen decorations. At the windows massive gilded clasps held a few shreds of the heavy damask curtains that had been wrenched from them. Even in its completely ravaged state the room fascinated him. He left the orderly and the Negro boys in the hall, closed the door, and set the candle he was carrying on the mantel.

From a corner he salvaged a small curio case of old yellow lacquer with Chinese figures in color, which had miraculously escaped destruction. Presently his eye settled on an exquisite Wedgwood medallion set into the frieze of the mantel. It depicted in delicate relief a classical scene: four maidens beautifully draped, symbolic of the seasons. He took the candle in his hand to study the figures closely. Then he returned the candle to the mantel and carefully pried the medallion out of its setting with the point of his saber.

It was almost midnight when he returned to headquarters, fatigued but well-pleased with Beaufort and this war to free the slaves.

Part Two

CAPTAIN WILL HERKIMER closed the front door of Marshlands behind him and stood in the cold bare hall. A frame of light from the dining-room showed him a guard lounging by the door to the sitting-room. The man's drooping head snapped up to attention, but his body was slow to brace itself for a salute.

"The Chief in there?" Will asked the blood-shot eyes.

The weary figure shifted his cud.

"Yes sir, him and General Sager. He give orders he ain't to be disturbed without it's important."

That settled the chance of getting into Sherman's warm and comfortable lair, and Will turned to the dining-room. But there was no space for letter-writing there. The table and chairs and candles were monopolized by a group of staff officers playing pinochle with the usual grimy cards; and the special correspondents of the *Post, Herald,* and *Tribune* had taken over the fireside for the swapping of flasks and yarns.

He felt his way along the dim hall to the stair rail. In the upper hall he paused to get his bearings. From the orderlies' fire in the yard enough flickering light came up through the window at the landing to indicate where the doors were. The one he was facing led to the big room, which General and Mrs. Sager had offered the Chief and which the Chief had refused in favor of the cozy library off the sitting-room downstairs. So Mrs. Sager would be lying in state behind this door, and Will had a vision of that masculine presence waiting to question her husband, who was no more than a bearded child beside her. A weird union. But no stranger than the one behind the next door—the Reverend Aaron Moffet and his young bride. Mrs. General Sager and her husband were a mating essentially comic, but this other was painful to think about.

Will tiptoed to his own door and closed it quietly behind him. Three years of war, he realized with a certain satisfaction, had not made him altogether thoughtless of others. Major Atwood, snoring somewhere in the stale darkness, would have come banging into the room, tramping across the floor and probably humming a ballad. Atwood was typical of this army of yahoos. To them the war was just a grand spree.

It was clammy cold in the room. Will could see his breath like smoke when he lighted the shapeless candle on the mantel. The pale light resurrected the dirty plaster walls above the dirty wainscoting, the rickety chair, the table made from a box, and the scarred old-fashioned bedstead where Atwood lay buried under a mound of blankets and clothing. Will put his overcoat around his shoulders and moved the chair over to the box. With a dispatch pad for stationery he began to write, stopping occasionally to rub his hands and wriggle some life back into the toes in his mud-stiffened boots.

HEADQUARTERS ARMY OF TENN.

BEAUFORT, S. C.

Jan. 23, 1865.

Mother dear,

I have not yet recovered from the joy of finding nine letters from home waiting for me at Savannah. "General Sherman & Staff" left there early this morning. We reached Beaufort this afternoon and landed in a cold rain, which is tonight turning to ice. Looks like a tough march through Carolina—very different from the Georgia weather.

I have had little opportunity to note the peculiar features of this "Newport of the South". I can tell you this much, though: none of the houses are modern, and I have yet to see any sign of running water. I gather that the "missionaries" were sadly disappointed; I suppose they expected to find pillared palaces such as you read of in Southern Romances. Nevertheless they have been having a glorious time of it in this quondam resort of the Aristocracy. As you probably know, Beaufort is the spot where the "noble experiment" (as the politicians call it) was begun. It is a Mecca for male and female humanitarians with pet schemes for regenerating the poor darkies.

We are quartered in the former home of a Major-General

Fenwick, who was killed at Holly Hill, an engagement on the mainland near here a few weeks ago. It is now the hdqts. of General Sager, Commissioner of Freedmen—Moses to the negroes. His Aaron in the enterprise is a Rev. Aaron (!) Moffet, who has pious sideburns and fanatical eyes and hails from our own Connecticut, but not Hartford I'm glad to say. I heard Mrs. Sager tell Sherman that Moffet was her conception of the Perfect Man of God. He looks more like a plain opportunist to me.

After supper this evening, while Moffet was buttonholing Sherman about some scheme for helping the mobs of freedmen that flock after the armies, I talked with Mrs. Moffet. All the officers have fallen in love with her. She's very young and pretty. She and her husband came with us from Hilton Head this afternoon. He had returned North, I'm told, to appeal for funds and workers and had met this girl in Boston and persuaded her to come back with him. He must have mesmerized her. When Sherman was introduced to her on the boat, he misunderstood "Mrs." Moffet for "Miss", a natural mistake, and though he is not noted for gallant remarks said to Moffet:

"Your daughter will be an ornament to the post, sir."

"My *grand*-daughter, General," Moffet corrected with a dry smile.

The Chief looked at him as much as to say, You don't look your age. It's been "Miss" Moffet since, and no one on the Staff has had the courage to put the Chief straight.

Hope I haven't bored you with the missionaries, but they're a novel experience in this war. For the rest it's just the same old game—men, horses, and ruin.

As far as I can find out we'll leave here and move up to Pocotaligo (see Atlas) day after tomorrow. I don't think we'll have much trouble marching through Carolina. The Secesh are pretty thoroughly crippled now. If you could see the state of the country, you would have to feel sorry for the people.

I haven't seen or heard from Barnard since we parted at Atlanta. Love to Dad, Sister, Aunt Mary, and the rest of the family, including Bridget.

Always your aff't son,

WILL

When he had sealed the letter he rested it against his hat on the mantel, stretched stiffly, and began to undress. He was feeling more

35

self-respecting these days, now that it was possible to keep clean. Soon the new campaign would bring gradual incrustation again, and it was hard to feel like a conquering hero in a coat of grime. To hides like Atwood's dirt was no burden however long borne. He exhaled a concentrated aroma of the entire campaign, from Atlanta to the sea.

Will opened the window and stood in the frost breath of the night. The house seemed suspended over an abyss of silence. The sky, free now from clouds, rejoiced with a multitude of stars. They seemed brighter here in the South, somehow.

He thought: the window next to this is the Moffets' room. The Moffets,—it had a false ring, that implied conclusive blending. "Miss" Moffet. Mrs. Sager had called her Emily. Her hair was light brown and soft, and her eyes were dark blue. Appealing eyes, wide-spaced and frank. Her mouth was perfect, and there was magic in her voice. There was magic and beauty in everything about her: a simple natural magic, and the kind of beauty a man could worship from afar and then know intimately without any loss of faith. Here was the thing long sought, come with quick and intense surprise. And too late.

He turned from the window with a shiver. . . . Atwood was snoring as if everything in the world were quite as it should be. For the Atwoods of the world it always was.

He blew out the candle and got into bed, easing some of the covers over his way and spreading his overcoat on top. Achingly weary yet wide awake, he lay watching the faint play of ceiling light that came through the back window from the campfire in the yard. Beyond the wall at his head: Emily Moffet.

He closed his eyes and turned over with an emphatic twist, determined to forget her in sleep. Atwood had terminated his snoring with a final snort, and his back was warm. But for a long while the room was full of disturbing images that would not dissolve and let him rest.

II

WHEN WILL came downstairs the following morning, there was commotion in the hall. General Sherman was greeting General Howard, one-armed and heavy-bearded, and his staff. Their arrival was clashing with the exit of General Sager and the Reverend Mr. Moffet.

"They're going to St. Helena Island on an inspection tour," Mrs. Sager was announcing to General Howard. "An inspection of the new freedmen schools before Mr. Moffet's departure on the morrow with General Sherman."

It was amazing how this woman's voice and keen gray eyes dominated a hall full of generals.

"Mr. Moffet," she continued, "is to follow the march through Carolina to shepherd the helpless refugees. A splendid work."

Will watched Sherman's strained face with amusement, knowing how he hated this business of rounding up the stray children of Ham. Then his eyes found Emily with a start. She stood behind Mrs. Sager, close to the wall, in a dress of dark red merino that made her hair look golden. Mrs. Sager turned and put her arm and part of her purple shawl around Emily's shoulders. They went out with Moffet and Sager to the porch steps, where an orderly was waiting with a carriage. The forms were fringed in the early morning dazzlement of the river beyond the frosted lawn.

He joined the group that was filing into the dining-room and took a place at the long table. The Chief presided with his back to a roaring fire; the fragrance of coffee and sausage mingled with the brisk crackle of the flames and the talk and laughter. Rubbing his cold hands together Will told himself he had a fine appetite, but his attention kept wavering away from the table to the hall. Finally

37

he caught a glimpse of her as she came back into the house with Mrs. Sager. He found himself trying to disentangle the sound of her tread on the stairs from the jangle of the table. That was too much, and he felt for something distracting to say to the fat pop-eyed correspondent of the *Tribune* at his right.

"If we make the junction with Grant in North Carolina, the War's over. That prospect must make your customers pretty happy."

The pop eyes regarded him sardonically.

"The small fry, sure. But not the big bugs. They don't care if you never meet Grant. The longer you birds go on sweating and bleeding for Home and Country, the better they like it. Why the easy pickings behind the lines are making a new batch of millionaires every day."

"They ought to stop all that."

"How are *they* going to stop it? They, the gang in power, the money gang, they don't want to stop it. Why should they? I know damn well I wouldn't if I was in their shoes."

The *Tribune* man finished his hot-cakes in one enormous mouthful.

"No, Captain," he went on thickly, "the profiteering gang think this war is a sweet act of God. You and I and the rest of us are the suckers. You kill or get killed and I write red-white-and-blue pap to make it sound glorious to the homefolks."

"It's all wrong," Will said.

"Sure it is," the *Tribune* man agreed, wiping his moustaches with the back of his fat hand. "And so is human nature."

"I wouldn't go that far," Will contradicted perfunctorily, to keep the conversation going.

"No?" The correspondent regarded him with raised eyebrows as he picked his teeth. "Well, I must say it does me good to find someone who's come through this bloody mess with his faith in man intact. I couldn't keep mine even back in peace times. You must be one of these incurable idealists. Or maybe it's just because you're young, or in love or something."

The correspondent of the *Tribune* was smiling good-naturedly, innocently, and Will was able to swallow his shock without batting an eye. It was just a chance remark, of course, asinine but harmless, without intentional meaning.

"That must be it," he smiled back, forcing an easy smile.

38

He finished his coffee in silence, trying to keep his thoughts in the room. But presently he heard steps on the stairs, coming down, and he caught another glimpse of Emily in the hall. Now she and Mrs. Sager had their jackets on. Where were they going? The front door answered with an enigmatic slam.

Breakfast dragged on. Cigars were lighted, chairs pushed back, and legs crossed. Impatiently he watched Sherman's face for some sign of relief, a dispatch, a telegram. The Chief, his elbow resting on the arm of his chair while his hand rubbed his close-grizzled beard, listened with an expression of dyspeptic alertness to Howard, who talked on and on. The staff officers were melting away from the table on a variety of duties, Will's envy following each one through the door. Howard continued to talk, his spade beard wagging. Sherman made brief replies, nodded or shook his head. . . . At last Howard pushed back his chair. Gratefully Will watched him leave the room. Sherman was writing an order.

A few minutes later, standing in the drive waiting for an orderly to bring his horse, Will frowned at the sparkling sapphire of the river between the tawny arms of the marsh. The world had changed overnight from somber cold grays, fit background for war, to a vast radiance of blue and gold: a world in which uniforms and salutes and all the monotonous paraphernalia of destruction became completely lunatic. But it was also lunatic to be pondering how to find out where Emily had gone with her amazon companion. A soft humming disturbed his thoughts, and when he looked around and up he saw a mulatto girl spreading bedding over the rail of the upper porch. She smiled down at him brazenly.

"Where have the two ladies gone, do you know?" he asked in a voice that made her forget her coquetry.

"I spec' to de chu'ch."

"What church?"

The girl thought it was the Tabernacle Church, but she wasn't sure. And her directions on how to get there were involved. When the orderly brought the horse, Will rode to the striped sentry-box just outside the gates for further information. The sentry, an Irishman with a musical brogue, located the Tabernacle in simpler terms. They did be using the church, he said, as a horsepital for some of them sick Georgia niggers, and it was only a minute back that he had saluted the ladies going out and headed that way. The young lady had had a good-morning smile for him, and faith it *was* a good morning, Captain. When would the fun be starting in Carolina, sir? From the house a high laugh broadened the sentry's grin of anticipation. The girl on the upper porch was exchanging pleasantries with the orderly below.

Will galloped his horse to Bay Street and traveled its length at a fast trot, despite the treacherous pot-holes and mud and the congestion of army traffic, soldiers and niggers, horses and mules and wagons under the bare winter trees along the mushroom growth of store-fronts. When he had delivered Sherman's order at the encampment to the west of town, he turned back and searched out the Tabernacle Church.

The outside of the place was alive with niggers. Will left his horse in the care of a black sentry and shouldered and picked his way into the whitewashed barn-like building. More niggers: men, women, children: some lying on hard benches, some sitting, most standing for want of any place to lie or sit. Their eyes stared vacantly at him, like the eyes of animals herded in a pen. The dress of these contrabands from Georgia made a pathetic masquerade; among the general plantation rags and near-nakedness of the children were feather bonnets and stovepipe hats, ponchos made of turkey carpet, capes of crazy quilt, lace shawls, ball gowns, and odds-and-ends of salvaged uniforms, Rebel and Yankee mixed. The air was heavy with the heat of a glowing stove, acrid with the stench of black bodies, and vibrant with coughing and suffering.

He stood just inside the door, eyes hunting Emily. He found her at the far end of the big room and followed her as she moved with Mrs. Sager from group to group. It was a blessing to be able to see her at all, but it was horrible to see her in this foul reeking place. He must get her out of here somehow. But then he came to his senses and looked at himself standing helpless and foolish in the shadows near the door. And turning on his heel he stepped out into the crowded sunlight.

He rode back to headquarters with his lips and thoughts set in a firm line. A bugle was calling somewhere behind him; it was excellent distraction to follow the thin silver thread of its promise of more campaigning. Several blocks away, in Bay Street, a band was brightly blaring *Tramp, Tramp, Tramp, The Boys Are Marching*. Looking to the right at cross-streets he could see the columns of men and covered wagons, the last of the division landing from Savannah. Tomorrow the moving-up would begin.

The band fell to the drub of drums, and he had to focus his attention sharply to keep from being swept back to the Tabernacle. That was a broken picket fence, a house with a belvedere like one at home, a bunch of gray moss lying on the sidewalk. Mistletoe hung like nests in the bare upper branches of a sycamore. A few snowdrops were blooming in a trampled rubbish-strewn garden. In the twilight of Northern winter nothing was even thinking of stirring in the frozen ground. Still, spring had by no means come to Beaufort yet: the air was warm in the sun, but in the shadows it was chill, and there were crystals of ice in the ditches. . . .

At headquarters he found Sherman waiting for him with enough desk work to keep him in a welcome oblivion the rest of the morning. He worked with a fierce concentration that carried him safely to the dinner-bell. But when he laid down his pen, buttoned his collar, and went to take his place at the dining-room table, he saw that she was there and resolution fell away from him like smoke in the wind.

She was up toward the head of the table, on the Chief's right, with stout and puffy General Blane on her right. Down here at Mrs. Sager's end of the table it was necessary to make some show of conversation. Only for a minute or two, however, for Mrs. Sager's voice soon suppressed all competition. Her theme was Charleston's imminent fate.

"When Secretary Stanton visited Beaufort last week on his way to Savannah, he showed me a communication from the offices of the General-in-Chief at Willard's Hotel, Washington." Frowns from the head of the table were lost on Mrs. Sager. " 'Nothing', the communication said, 'would suit the people so entirely now as to hear that Charleston, that hot-bed of rebellion, had been burned to the *ground* and the *ashes* sown with *salt.*' And *I* say," Mrs. Sager added in a tone calculated to reach Sherman's ears without fail, "that *nothing* would so certainly *immortalize* a general."

There was no doubt, Will judged from the sour look on the Chief's face, about his having heard distinctly. And satisfied that her words had registered, Mrs. Sager then launched into her own personal destruction of Charleston and its people. Through the smoking ruins he watched in vain for a glance from Emily, not sure what he would do with it if it came. If it were only possible to believe that she was deliberately avoiding his eyes, because she knew. Or if he could only stop this hopeless folly. That was the only rational thing to do; and with the assurance that he had enough reason left to do it, he forced himself for the rest of the meal to hang on every word of Mrs. Sager's Charleston jeremiad.

It was an immense relief when immediately after dinner he found he had to go with the Chief to Howard's headquarters. Riding through the clear sunny streets he took himself to task, finally and completely. He would stop tormenting himself with this madness. He would stop it now, at once, and keep it from coming back.

At Howard's headquarters the Chief, withdrawing for a long conference, told him to take the rest of the afternoon for himself. Will rode back to Bay Street with a gauntleted fist pressed firmly against his thigh, arm akimbo, and with his hat cocked resolutely on the side of his head. Emily—Mrs. Moffet—was probably at the Tabernacle again by this time, but that was no concern or interest of his now. Soon, within a few hours, he would be gone, and this absurd fever for another man's wife would vanish as quickly as it had come; for the remaining brief time he would avoid her, in person and thought. He would look around Bay Street, make a few purchases of things needed on the march, and return to the house at the Point, where he would write letters and sew on some buttons.

Bay Street was full of soldiers of Howard's division. There were black soldiers too. Colonel Higginson, white commander of the black regiment, was standing with a group of his men in front of the combination bookstore and post-office. Will studied him with curiosity, wondering what sort of man he was inside. Pluck he had certainly, because black troops were shoved into the front lines to keep them from running away and the man who led them must know his life wasn't worth a shuck if he fell into Confederate hands. He was welcome to his job, Higginson.

Will left his horse at a hitching-rail and went into the post-office. Here was a jam of lounging, drawling, spitting soldiery, black and white, and it was hard to get back to the book department. He scanned the long list of publications that had come in on the last steamer, then picked items from the shelves at random. *Shoulder Straps, A Romance of the War:* sentimental tripe. Hawthorne's new book, *Our Old Home,* about England: dull stuff. A scientific treatise called *Origin of Species,* which he couldn't make heads or tails of.

But it passed time just to turn pages. . . . He bought, finally, a copy of Halleck's *Standard Military Art and Science,* one book that really made sense.

From the bookstore post-office he walked along the muddy sidewalk past a barber shop, where Atwood, among others too lazy to shave themselves, was getting what would undoubtedly be his last shave in Carolina. Possibly his last shave anywhere. But no, Atwoods were never the ones to die; and anyway it would be a shame to lose that hearty laugh on the march, that rousing snore in the tent. . . . Next door was a pharmacy with a wooden awning over the street and a bright new mortar-and-pestle sign. Then a stationer's with a big pen for a sign over the window. In the window there was an untidy display of slates, copybooks, and illustrated papers, in the midst of which a large soiled cat was taking a nap, unmindful of the noisy crowded street. At Wilkes & Thompson, Printers, a notice said: "*THE FREE SOUTH*—To our Soldier Friends 50¢ for 3 months—Your paper will follow your regiment by mail—Send home, almost as good as *weekly letter.*"

He went in to get a copy, and walked on reading it. The headline was the fall of Fort Fisher. Sherman and Blane had been talking about that at dinner, across Emily. He turned hastily to the editorial page, *With Grant in Virginia.* But no need to go into that now, he was perfectly all right, everything was all right, sharp and interesting around him, and he would read the paper when he got back to the house. A sign stopped him at a shanty next to the Adams Express office.

MR. SAMUEL COOLEY, Esq.

Sun Pictures
At his Gallery.

| LARGE PORTRAITS | SMALL BUSTS | AMBROTYPES |
| CARTE DEVISETTES | | MELLAINOTYPES |

Pictures neatly inserted in Lockets, Pins, and Seals. All
pictures finished in the Highest Style known to the Art.

He decided to go in for a small bust to send the family: after all he had been putting it off for three years. There was a long wait in line before his turn came to enter a fenced-in yard, the Gallery. Mr. Samuel Cooley, Esq., was a bird. Wild hair proclaimed him an

43

artist and his breath was drenched with inspiration. It was all he could do to contain it, it was almost too much for him, in fact it was almost throwing him. He complained the sun was getting too low, he was ferocious with the head-clasp and erratic with his exposures. And after prolonged smotherings under his black cloth he finally staggered out with a flat refusal to even consider a small bust, or any kind of bust, it was all or nothing, take it or leave it; only a full-length portrait right down to the spurs would satisfy him and do the subject justice. So the subject was lined up with a marble column in front of a punctured backdrop showing the bombardment of Port Royal. And somehow, in the end, Mr. Cooley produced from this heroic scene a startling likeness, "clear as a bell and clean as a whistle". He personally guaranteed that it would leave for the North on the next packet boat.

Out in the pleasant turmoil of the street again, Will weighed the distractive powers of a game of billiards in the room over the Adams Express. No: he didn't feel sociable, and the place was jammed, they were hanging out of the windows. He went instead into Van Wie's General Store for needles and thread and some buttons. It took a long time to get a clerk to wait on him. Prices were sky high as usual. In the back room of the store, beyond a swinging door, were loud voices and laughter, a banjo and fiddle and singing. Time could be made to pass quickly enough in there; but no necessity for falling back on that method, he was succeeding very well as it was. He left the store and went back to the post-office hitching-rail for his horse, pleased with the way he had taken himself in hand.

When he reached Marshlands, he found the house almost empty. The only officer not out on some errand or other was Happy Stickney, who was sitting at the dining-room table over a map, nursing a head cold with a cup of hot toddy and obligingly instructing through his nose the fat correspondent of the *Tribune*. But there was one other person in the house, he discovered as he entered the sitting-room. She was in Mrs. Sager's armless rocker at the fireside, sorting over a basket of cloth remnants. She looked up with a quick smile.

"Good-afternoon, Captain Herkimer."

"Good-afternoon," he bowed, feeling his cheeks burning like a schoolboy's as he moved toward her. He was pleased that she remembered his name. But then in a flash displeased that she used it. It meant that she thought of him formally, impersonally, as just one of the staff officers. It was as bad as if he had said, Good-afternoon, Mrs. Moffet.

"Making bandages?" he managed to say. It was obvious that she was.

"Bandage rolls and strips for mustard plasters," she nodded. Her eyes were intent on her work again, so he could look at her without the obscuring confusion that came over him whenever she looked at him. "We're so short of everything," she was saying. "Mrs. Sager left me home this afternoon to see what bits I could salvage out of this rag basket. I really should be helping her at the Tabernacle."

She had been here, then, all afternoon, while he had been killing time in Bay Street.

"You shouldn't be risking your life at that place," he found himself saying. When she looked up at him, he added: "I thought you came here to teach."

"I did. But we've all had to help out with the sick refugees. And it's terrible how little we can do for them."

He wondered what to say to that. The War had showed him sickness and dying in so many terrible patterns that it was hard to feel much for the plight of a horde of misguided niggers, survivors of the mass flight from Egypt Georgia to the Promised Land of Freedom. But her caring about them finally made their fate important.

"Poor wretches," he said, envying them. And watching the hands that cared for them, the quick fingers tearing and rolling bandage from the remains of a sheet, the terrible thought kept cutting through him: She has been sitting here, alone, while I was wasting time in Bay Street.

"Any news in your paper?" she asked.

He snatched at this excuse to stay with her.

"Wouldn't you like me to read to you while you work?"

"I'd love it."

He moved Sherman's camp-chair near her by the fire and opened *The Free South* on his knee. He began with the Virginia dispatches, trying to concentrate on the meaning of the words. But it was just a jumble of letters, behind which his thoughts struggled to make the most of being with her. To forget the sudden pressure of time, and that his hands were tied and that it was all hopeless, futile and worse than futile, this torment in his chest, this tongue-tied gagged feeling in his throat. How strained his voice sounded, reading. And how easy and natural she seemed, listening. Naturally. He was just one of the army crowd to her. If he were someone else, anyone else, there would be no difference in her manner.

". . . On the Northern trip the *Fulton* captured another valuable prize, the celebrated blockade-runner, *Banshee,* a splendid steamer, built in Liverpool, 1862. . . ."

He read through the entire paper, grimly, down to the last item. When it was over, he groped helplessly for conversation and discovered that the log on the fire needed turning, which he managed with amazing awkwardness.

"I hope this clear weather keeps up," he said finally, to the last rays of the sun touching the mantel.

"I do hope so," her voice answered. "You leave in the morning, don't you?"

He met her eyes for an instant as he nodded.

Her hands were idle in her lap now; she had finished with the basket. He fumbled with his sword sash. Did she have no inkling whatever of his misery? It seemed as if he had dreamed of her all his life, known and loved her always, and now he could do nothing to show it, nothing to make her acknowledge it. He could only make small talk around the miracle of finding her, and even that was failing. So definitely that it was almost a relief when the front door opened and steps sounded in the hall.

It was Mrs. General Sager.

"Well," she declared ambiguously in her booming tone, taking the room in. "Turning much colder for your march, Captain," she nodded to him as she strode to the fire, pulling off her mittens. "Emily, I don't recommend your sitting in this drafty room entertaining people without a shawl. I must say you did very well with the bandages. Eleven refugees died today. And they've dumped a whole new batch on us. The army, Captain, is responsible for this deplorable situation. No judgment shown, I regret to say, and very little interest. Have our husbands returned yet, Emily? No, I didn't suppose they had. Come and help me make some tea, my dear. Captain, I won't ask you to join us,—it's entirely too scarce a commodity to be prodigal with. Come, Emily."

Will bowed and watched them go out.

Alone, he studied the fire glumly for a spell. Then he went to the

46

hall and out the front door, down the steps, across the cold lawn to the seawall.

The sun was gone and the western sky was aflame, and there was flame on the river and on the marsh pools. Along the far shore veils of mist hung like smoke after a battle. A wedge of wings sped high over the water, accenting the stillness with shrill cries. He stood working bits of oyster shell out of the seawall with the toe of his boot, while the flame in the west burned down to ash, the marshes and the land sinking below the incoming tide of dusk.

He had no idea how long he had been standing there when he turned and saw Atwood, Happy Stickney, and the correspondent for the *Tribune* coming across the lawn. When they were within a few yards of him, Atwood struck a pose, pushed up his sleeves and held his arms out to one side, exposing the palms of his hands and then the backs. "Nothing there, and nothing there—("And nothing there," the pop-eyed *Tribune* interrupted, tapping the magician's head)—*but* the hand is still quicker than the eye, how'zat, gents?" And Atwood tugged a bottle out of his hip pocket. "Have a swig, Herk."

"Not tonight, At."

"What the hell, man?" Happy snuffled. "I just cured a cold with it."

"I'll take another small one," the *Tribune* offered.

"In a pig's whistle," Atwood told him. "You newspaper leeches can buy your own booze. You got a snootful already anyways." And he took a long swallow, spat, and passed the bottle over to Happy.

"The more some people drink," the *Tribune* said to Will, "the worse they get. I just get better. In weeno weritas."

Atwood was saying: "Herk, did I ever tell you the one about the Frenchman and the lady elephant?"

"They brought that one over in the ark," the *Tribune* muttered.

Happy Stickney began to laugh and cough. Will turned his back on the stillness of the river and faced Atwood and the story with a set grin. Out of the corner of his eye he saw the unmistakable form of the Chief ride in the gateway.

". . . So the Frenchman takes off his hat and says, Pardon me, Madame. . . ."

The front door of the house was open, and for a moment the Chief

47

was silhouetted against the glow of the hall. Then the door closed with a report, and the glow returned to the fanlight. In a minute the supper bell would ring. . . . To Atwood and the rest he wanted to say, You poor miserable fools, get away from me with your noise, for I have found the most wonderful thing in the world.

General Sherman took Emily in to supper. The headquarters family was small tonight: there were no visitors, General Sager and Aaron Moffet had not returned from St. Helena Island, and Atwood with Happy Stickney and the *Tribune* correspondent had decided at the last to go to Bay Street where joy was less confined.

Will found himself sitting next to Emily. But though so intimately close she seemed more remote than ever tonight. Beyond the barest table civilities she had nothing to do with him. She talked with the Chief, leaving him to shift for himself. Once as she felt for a spoon her fingers touched his with an electric shock, but it seemed to him that not only her hand but her whole body shrank from the contact, as if she knew his feelings and rejected them completely.

After supper the men lingered over coffee and cigars. In a few minutes Howard arrived and the inevitable maps were spread out on the table. This final conference, Will thought with bitter satisfaction, would drag on till midnight; then a few hours' rest and departure at dawn. The door to the hall was closed and he had seen the last of her. Already she was lost, as if he had never found her. No, not quite that easy. The War had caught up with him at last, at this peaceful Beaufort bivouac. But at least the infliction part was ended. Now for the healing process of destruction, more raiding and foraging and pillaging, with some point to it now. Maps and routes were excellent things, like cool compresses on a feverish wound.

Sometime later there was a knock at the door, and being nearest he got up to see who it was. It was Mrs. Sager, inquiring with heavy facetiousness if any of the warriors needed to be darned. Emily was with her. The Chief took off his coat and exposed a loose lining. Other warriors found they were not intact.

"Are you all right?"

It took a moment to realize she was speaking to him. He started to say, All right thank you, but caught himself in time.

"I've got some overcoat buttons off. Can you do anything about that?"

"I think so."

"It's upstairs. I'll get it."

Upstairs in his room, breathless, he lighted a candle with shaky fingers and found the buttons of his overcoat perfectly secure. He worked two of them loose and pulled two off altogether. Then as he was turning to the door, a sudden idea stopped him.

He tore a sheet from his dispatch pad and wrote: *I cannot leave without telling you—*

He tore up the sheet and started again.

May a soldier beg for some token to carry through the coming campaign.

He corrected it in his mind, weighed it, then tore it up and wrote once more.

Forgive me, but may I ask for some small good-luck token to carry through the coming campaign?

That would have to do. But how was he to give it to her? Puzzling frantically he slipped the note into a side pocket of the coat, blew out the candle, and started downstairs. He must say something to be sure she read the thing. But with Mrs. Sager in the way how would that be possible?

At the foot of the stairs he saw thankfully that she was waiting at the sitting-room door. When he reached her, he saw that Mrs. Sager was already seated with her work-basket before the fire.

"There seem to be several loose buttons," he said in a flushed undertone as he gave her the coat, "and the ones that came off are in the pocket."

"You're very smart to have hung on to them," she smiled, in his own tone but quite impersonally.

"Yes,—well, you see, there's a little note in there too, if you'd please read it privately."

He turned away abruptly and went back to the dining-room, closing the door behind him with the same sense of deliverance that he used to feel as a boy after a journey through the dark. For many minutes after he had taken his place again at the table, a deep pounding and roaring filled his ears. There were blinding flashes in the room, like the bursting of shrapnel. He was afraid to think. When anyone spoke to him he tried not to look the way he felt. He forced himself to look at the maps and listen to the demented clash of voices around him.

49

Later, there was a knock at the door and Mrs. Sager handed in the mended coats. His was not among them. Evidently it was not finished yet. All those buttons took time. He hadn't meant to pull two off. One would have been enough. . . .

Minutes dragged by. He began to feel a cold sweat coming out on his forehead and hands, and his mouth was dry as ashes. The ashes of the sitting-room fire, where he hoped his note was reposing. That was all he asked now. That it be politely ignored, dismissed, forgotten. *Forgive me, but may I ask*—only to take it back, and to escape, be free again, on the march. . . .

The tension stretched into an hour, two hours, without bringing any release. It was after eleven when the door opened and General Sager and Moffet appeared, back from their day's trip to the out-islands. The round-table map conference broke up then into groups of talk. When the first chance came, he left the room and crossed the hall to the sitting-room.

The lamp was turned low, and there was no-one there. His overcoat lay neatly folded over the back of a chair. He looked at it, hardly daring to pick it up. The two buttons were sewed on and the others tightened. When he felt in the pocket, his hand touched something unfamiliar, which he drew out and held in the light. It was a small prayer-book with black binding and gilt edges. On the fly-leaf was written: *Emily Curtis Easton.*

He stood staring at it for a minute; then returned it to the pocket and put the overcoat on. In the hall on the way to the front door he met Moffet and Sager on their way to the stairs.

The General's stubby form stopped with braced shoulders to ask, in the voice that was always striving to outboom his wife's: "Not turning in yet?"

Suddenly and acutely aware of Moffet's tall frame, Will tried to concentrate on the General's bearded baby face.

"No, sir, not yet. Thought I'd get a little air."

"Look like you need it, kind of peaked," the General observed helpfully. "Well, good luck on the march, my boy, good-bye and good luck. Wish I was going."

Will shook the chubby little hand, and then saw that Moffet's hand was held out. A long strong hand but dead as mackerel. And the eyes that met his were smiling but cold as ice underneath.

"Good luck, Captain," the words slipped out smoothly, evenly. "I shan't say good-bye, because we shall no doubt meet again, on the march. I shall be rounding up the freedmen as fast as you release them. Good-night."

Will nodded good-night and went on to the front door, with his fist in his pocket, tight around the prayer-book.

III

After the tumult of the dawn departure, the house and the town seemed to sink into a cold gray torpor. Emily went with Mrs. Sager to the Tabernacle hospital and worked there through the day in a benumbed state, hardly knowing what she was doing.

This numbness lifted a little in the evening, after supper as she sat in the warm parlor making copies of Mrs. Sager's appeal to Northern ladies' aid societies for gifts of clothing, books, money. The wording was becoming so familiar that she could follow her own thoughts as she wrote. But then Mrs. Sager returned from her usual inspection of the kitchen and took her seat by the fire with a sociable sigh. It was plain from her expression and the way she took up her knitting-bag that she was well content to have the house free of men, Sherman on the march, her husband and his aide out for the evening on freedmen business. She was settling herself for a good gossip, and her voice was far too insistent to permit Emily to only pretend to be listening.

To begin with, Mrs. Sager had plenty to say about Sherman, mostly unfavorable. The march through Georgia was a glorious exploit, granted; but why had he spared Augusta? Rumor said he had avoided the town because of the memory of a sweetheart he had courted when posted at the arsenal there in antebellum days. Romancing stuff and nonsense. If he had actually allowed sentiment to deter him from the path of duty, he was at least a fool, and Mrs. Sager's only regret now was that she hadn't told him so to his face. Which she didn't like anyway. It was too squinched up, not enough nose. "Give me a man with plenty of nose and a good generous mouth, like your husband, Emily,—it's a sure sign of character."

"What's more," Mrs. Sager continued, "I don't like Sherman's attitude toward the freedmen. He lacks enthusiasm. To him they are merely so many freed slaves, nothing more. I cannot rank him with the splendid men and women working for racial equality."

Having disposed of Sherman, Mrs. Sager proceeded to the whole body of the army: it was impossible to approve the military without reservations, important reservations. Far too heavy consumption of spirits, for one thing, and this evil was by no means confined to the rank and file. It was not idle talk that sprawled a high general, a very high general, drunk on the floor of his tent during a certain disastrous battle in Virginia. Temperance was simply missing from the army manuals. Nobody would ever suspect from their appearance and conduct that these wild Indians were pilgrims on a crusade.

"Those rum-soaked soldiers we passed on the way to the Tabernacle yesterday were as insulting as street-corner toughs. No respect for women, let alone Abolitionists. And some of us are actually made apologetic by this sneering."

Moreover, the army was appallingly lacking in another important respect: virtue. To be frank, there was no doubt but that the men were using Negro women for lustful purposes on a large scale. Mrs. Sager said she spoke of the matter with reluctance, but she had heard of many instances from the refugees themselves. This bestial fornication put Northern men on a plane with Southerners. Did Emily realize that under the old regime every planter had one or more concubines in the yard? And now our men were tarring themselves with the same brush.

"No cause to blush, child," Mrs. Sager snapped. "It's best to face the truth, however unpalatable." Her knitting-needles made savage thrusts. "And while we're on the topic, I might add that the only salvation I can see for the rundown white stock of the South is to mix freely with the Negroes. If some of the washed-out belles of Charleston and Richmond and New Orleans——"

"Please, Mrs. Sager," Emily put down her pen to protest. "How would you like it if someone suggested that for the North."

"The North," Mrs. Sager answered with an emphatic jerk of her head, "is not in need of regeneration. Here in the South the whites will be forced to amalgamate, or the Negroes with their new freedom and their natural adaptability to the climate and the soil will take the country away from them. Mark my words. But whether the whites accept their fate openly or not, amalgamation will progress."

Mrs. Sager got up to thump another log on the fire, and Emily took the opportunity to put her work aside.

"I'm afraid I'll have to stop work for tonight," she said. "I'm so sleepy I can hardly keep my eyes open."

"Poor child," Mrs. Sager agreed, "I know you're tired, better go on up."

But she had had three cups of tea with her supper and was enjoying herself too much to be so abruptly separated from her audience. She accompanied Emily upstairs and stayed with her while she undressed, insisting on helping with hooks and stays and then watching the rest of the process with embarrassing interest.

"Frankly, my dear," she said as Emily hurried to get into her flannel nightgown, "I was very much concerned about what kind of person Aaron was bringing back with him. I was worried some fly-by-night might have taken his fancy. Men are so easily taken in. But I should have known better, of course,—Aaron Moffet is such an exceptional man. And you, my dear, are an exceptional young woman, a very attractive young woman but with Christian character and sense beyond your years, not flighty and vain. I know you will be worthy of him and make him a dutiful loving wife, a real helpmate."

Shivering under the covers, Emily thanked Mrs. Sager and tried to change the subject to tomorrow's work at the Tabernacle and the need for an early start. But Mrs. Sager ignored the hint and lingered on the edge of the bed, where she got back on the South, concluding her arraignment with a description of what Lincoln should do after the surrender.

"But you can't depend on him, that's the trouble. He'll shillyshally around, parading that wishywashy tolerance of his and letting the South get back on its feet, instead of exterminating the whole rotten system once and for all, root and branch. He'll rest on his oars with the race half won, canceling victory by not following it up. Why, he had to be pushed into the Emancipation Proclamation. His heart was never in it. As Aaron says, he never was a real Abolitionist, only a sham one, for political purposes."

"I'm afraid," Emily found herself saying in final exasperation, "I'm not a very good Abolitionist either. I don't seem to feel as strongly as you do."

Mrs. Sager stiffened visibly in the lamplight. But she quickly relaxed and patted Emily's hand, regarding her with indulgence from under heavy lids. "That's hardly to be expected, my dear. It takes time to make a true Abolitionist. You're too young and innocent to sense the full degradation of the South. But it will grow on you as you pursue your work among the freedmen. Have no fear."

Mrs. Sager wrapped her shawl more tightly about her; the cold of the room was getting the better of the tea. At last she leaned over and kissed Emily good-night.

"My little missionary sister," she said benevolently, "you are fretful tonight. And how well I understand. I know what a hardship it is to be separated from your husband so soon. Indeed I do. When I came here with the first party of teachers and married General Sager, I was inconsolable when he was called away for a single night. But duty comes before all else, and strength for duty comes with prayer. Shall I pray with you tonight for Aaron's safety? Shall we kneel together for a moment?"

"If you don't mind, I think I'll say my prayers in bed tonight."

"I understand, my dear," Mrs. Sager sighed resignedly. "I'm sure your prayers will be heard as well from there. I'll open the window for you. And if you're lonely in the night, or if there's anything you need, just rap on the wall and I'll hear you."

She went to open the window. And then the tall form moved to the door with the lamp, trailing shadows. But she stopped and turned to the bed for a moment before leaving the room, her voice recovering its precision.

"I shall call you early in the morning."

The door closed, and the room bumped into darkness, whirling flashing darkness at first. Then blank staring darkness; and finally, slowly, steady settled darkness, with dim windows of starlight and fresh clear air, salt-smelling from the low-tide marshes. As if really awake for the first time today, she lay with senses keenly alive to the night, free at last to think her own thoughts in peace and quiet.

But hardly in quiet. For the moment she began to live the day over, the room was full of confusion and the voices of dawn, the departure that already had happened so long ago. And hardly in peace. For it was frightening what she saw: not Aaron waving as he drove away from the front steps. Even as she recalled that picture it faded, and she was seeing a young officer of Sherman's staff, almost without a name, turning to look back as he rode toward the gates; and this refused to fade. Even when she tried to turn back to Aaron, here beside her one night ago, her body lay warm and cold torn between them, her husband and the man who had never come up to his room all night, herself listening, feeling him somewhere in the darkness outside, looking up at the house and these windows.

It was a blessing he was gone. A greater blessing if he had never come. She hated him, really. For in his brief passing he had brought great harm to her, wrought fearful secret changes, changes whose exact nature she could not fathom and whose effect she could not foresee, but profound changes, deeply hurtful, disruptive, confusing, altering the accepted course, the whole look and feel of things.

Prayer was the answer. Prayer for strength. Strength for duty and forgetfulness.

�   ✓   ✓

In the days that followed it was not hard to forget, because there was so little time for anything else. The sufferings and needs of others, the multiple pressure that surrounded her all day long at the Tabernacle hospital, left no room for absorption in her own trouble. And by night she was wrung too dry for thought or feeling.

From the stories she heard at the Tabernacle she was able to piece together the full tragedy of the freedmen's march to the sea. They were following the army out of bondage, their chains had been stricken off and they were marching to milk and honey. But even the religious frenzy of the exodus was not enough to sustain them against the privations of the army-ravaged country, the long cold and exposure, the terrible hunger and thirst. There were no masters now to order them about, no masters and no friends. Many of the children and old people were left behind to die in the wilderness, alone or in huddled groups in the winter fields and pine barrens, under the patient eyes of buzzards. One powerful mother had brought her entire brood through by tying the older ones to cords fastened to her waist, carrying the younger ones in rotation; but few families were so fortunate. Where thousands had set out for Freedom, mere hundreds had reached the refugee camps at Savannah and Beaufort, and of these hundreds only about a half were surviving the epidemics of dysentery and pneumonia.

Once every week Emily went with a group of "cures" from the Tabernacle in a government steamer to St. Helena Island, where

56

they were billeted around on Land's End and Cherokee and other big plantations. The stronger men were picked out for army fatigue, and the stronger women for field work; the rest were not welcomed by the government agents and private speculators who were trying to make the plantations show a profit with free labor. With the help of a young Philadelphia woman, Harriet Sheppard, who had a school at Cherokee, Emily settled the submissive and pitiably stoical refugees as acceptably as possible, but it was a complicated business. Yet despite the difficulties of these billeting trips she was always glad to escape from the hospital and go to this place where land and sea and sky met in crisp sunshine. When she mentioned how much she liked the island, particularly Land's End, Harriet Sheppard said:

"When you're through nursing and ready to teach, why not come out here? You'll find plenty to do."

Emily answered that she expected to start her teaching in one of the Beaufort schools under Mrs. Sager's supervision. But the thought of a school at Land's End stayed in her mind.

Getting acquainted with this sea-island world was in itself a means of forgetting. There was so much here that was different from the North. A new world, at once challenging and comforting. In faraway Boston weather was an abstraction; here it was intimate, immediate, exciting, like weather in the country, at the farm near Salem where she had spent so many happy holidays before her mother had died and her father married again. Here the sky was no longer a glimpse of remote blue or gray above rows of rooftops, but a vast and significant presence. And here the rhythms of winter fell into the most surprising patterns.

The last day of January, one of a sequence of cold gray days, had brought flurries of snow. Then there had been three days of serene sunshine, followed by a day like Northern June, half sun, half drifting shadows. Orange butterflies from nowhere fluttered over the dead grass of the lawn. On top of that an even milder day—till noon, when the sky went wild with wind-harried clouds of every shape and texture, and thunder announced a true summer shower. But by six the sky was free enough to make a purple and gold sunset over a bank of soggy clouds. Next a spell of bleak November days. Then the warm sun again, flooding the land and sparkling on a river of deepest blue: the song of the mocking-bird flung out in sweet and whimsical snatches, the bright whistle of redbirds, the coarse cries of jackdaws and bullying jays. The simple white beauty of wild plum trees in the yard, and the surpassing beauty of a crimson-budding maple against the white side of the house. Sea-island winter was a fantastic blending of all the seasons, autumn and spring, winter and summer.

At first this Carolina Low Country had seemed oppressively flat. In place of the close hills of New England there were sweeping horizons, disquieting reaches, as if the world had no end anywhere. But after her eyes had become accustomed to the openness, there was abundant compensation in being able to stretch sight as far as it would go, over golden marshes and broad waterways, now placid blue, now sea-green and whitecapped, changing tone ceaselessly in tune with the sky. And there was no monotony in the swing of the tides, brimming up the seawall at flood, draining away to marsh mud at ebb, rising and falling in an ever-changing flow, an infinite range of light and color. And so, as the weeks passed and her interest and delight in this island world increased with her knowledge of it, her heart and mind felt restored to order in its variety of moods, its lavish enchantments.

Besides the charm of Beaufort country there was an even more important counterbalance to her nursing work at the Tabernacle. Marshlands on the Point, this old house where she was staying with the Sagers, was home to her from the beginning; and she responded to its friendliness by noting its every feature, from the delicately-carved frame of the front door to the hand-hewn rafters in the attic, and from the brick kitchen-house and slave quarters and stables in the yard to the arched foundation masonry of oyster-shell "tabby" and the tabby seawall that curved with the river, bounding the lawn and the two side gardens that flanked the house. In the open east garden were rose bushes and hedges of boxwood, and an old marble sundial where the paths met in the center. The other garden, to the west of the house, was shut in by walls of evergreen shrubs, and its paths and octagonal latticed summer-house were almost lost in a tangle of vines; but even in its neglected state it was a charming place. And because no-one else ever went near it, she could feel that it was her own, a private hidden place that she had found and that now belonged to her. In the late afternoons, back from the hospital with a few free minutes to spare before supper, she did what she could to clear the paths to the summer-house, thinking of another garden she had known and loved: the garden of the house in Boston. It was just a pathetic little space, that lost garden, a cramped space between the basement and woodshed and the drab yard walls, but her mother had made things grow there, lilies-of-the-valley and bleeding-hearts. After her mother had died, the "new mother" had said it was a waste of time trying to have a garden in the city. One morning, before her father had left for the school where he was teaching Greek and Latin then, he had told the cook to dump ashes over the narrow beds. . . . But she felt that her mother must be here with her now, delivered as she had prayed to be from that changed and bitter world of home, here with her now, knowing this Southern world, this new home, this garden.

Some of the trees of Marshlands had been ruthlessly cut down for firewood since the Occupation, but many marvels remained. Particularly the old moss-draped live-oaks with their wide spreading branches, and the great magnolias solid from top to ground with big glossy leaves. It took time to learn the smaller trees and shrubs. Among the evergreens were the loquats and Carolina cherries. Among the bare trees were the crepe-myrtles, with limbs like hard and sinewy arms, and in the back yard the fig trees and the china-berries with their clusters of little golden balls. Some of the shrubs and exotics in the closed garden were still without names. The only trees that she had recognized on sight were the cedars and dog-woods and the silver sycamores. And the palmettoes along the sea-wall, which had not seemed absolute strangers because of Palm Sunday back North.

"Dem t'ing what stick like pin is call Sponish bay'net," Phyllis had told her.

Phyllis and "Maum" Minda, her mother, were very patient about answering questions. Often, while Emily was getting used to their Gullah dialect, the answers had to be repeated over and over. In exchange for this service they examined her about things Yankee, Phyllis usually being the spokesman.

"Mis' Moffit, to de Nort' de street is pave wid pure gold, enty?"

"Mis' Moffit, dey ain' make we color fuh work to de Nort', ain' dat so, ma'm?"

"Mis' Moffit, is Mistuh Linkum color man fuh true?"

Maum Minda was a handsome quadroon woman, proud and

taciturn. Phyllis's skin was even lighter than her mother's, but she had not inherited the patrician cast of features and she lacked the fine carriage and dignity. She was pretty, certainly, but she was slovenly in her dress and ways and her manner was too free and knowing. She was lazy, too, letting her mother do most of the housework as well as the cooking.

Mrs. Sager frequently complained of coming upon the spoiled girl leaning on her broom or the back of a chair and smiling into space. Mrs. Sager was not inclined to apply her principles of Negro philanthropy to a servant in the house who was being paid good hard cash for loafing, but she was prevented from giving Phyllis even the mildest rebukes for fear of offending and losing Maum Minda. And besides Maum Minda's general indispensability there was the difficulty of getting any Free Negroes to work. So the tongue-lashings intended for Phyllis were taken out on Emily. Once in a moment of extreme vexation Mrs. Sager actually said:

"There are times when I can almost understand the feelings of Southern housewives. What that insolent sulky do-as-you-please girl really needs is a good whipping!"

But Phyllis had two redeeming qualities for Mrs. Sager. There was her bright skin, testament of Southern sin. And there was her gift for reciting, with gestures, lurid tales of slavery-time beatings and lashings. Mrs. Sager would jot down details for her letters North, rewarding Phyllis with some trifle that had been broadly hinted for.

Emily learned Maum Minda's and Phyllis's story from Phyllis, with corrections by Maum Minda. They had belonged to the Fenwicks, former owners of Marshlands, and had been taken away by the family when Beaufort was abandoned. Mrs. Fenwick and a young daughter Eugenia had refugeed first at Augusta and then with relatives at Summerville near Charleston, where Robert, Maum Minda's son and the Fenwick butler, had been put to work with the harbor authorities. He had become assistant pilot on the *Indigo,* a little Rebel sidewheeler that had been giving the blockading fleet much trouble. One night he had smuggled his mother and sister and young brother Alec aboard the *Indigo* and had sneaked the boat out of the harbor to the Union fleet.

"Fuh dat," Phyllis explained, "de Gow'ment make'um Cap'm of de *Indigo,* an' he bring we back hyuh an' buy buckra house to de tak sale. But Maa ain' sotisfy fuh sit roun' like missie lady—he ain' sotisfy till he home hyuh to Maa'shlan'."

Neither Maum Minda nor Phyllis recognized any sex but the masculine: they always referred to each other as "he". Robert's speech was less picturesque. Maum Minda had proudly brought him into the sitting-room one evening for General and Mrs. Sager and Emily to see. He was a fine-looking man, quiet and self-respecting, and he spoke with little trace of the Gullah that made most sea-island people, even house servants like Maum Minda and Phyllis, so hard to understand. He was neat and clean, Cap'm Robert Fenwick, unlike the majority of uniformed freedmen, who swaggered about dirty and careless with forage caps perched at an angle.

Alec, the other member of Maum Minda's family, was a lanky boy, all arms and legs and neck, and no more responsible than his sister Phyllis. He was supposed to work regularly at Marshlands, waiting on the table and carrying wood and water, but he was always shirking and sometimes he disappeared for days at a stretch. Maum Minda and Phyllis went home after supper to sleep at their own house, but except when the *Indigo* and Robert were in port Alec stayed out all night. He had bought himself a flashy turnout at the new clothing store on Bay Street and his companions were the young colored sports. He came to work only when he was hungry and needed money.

"Son," Emily heard Maum Minda say to him once, "Satan find plenty trouble fuh idle han's. You' po' head gittin' turn so fas' he gwine pure twis'off one dese days, same like chicken fuh pot. Ain' nutt'n else gwine cure'um."

She no longer made any serious attempt to control him; the forces pulling him away from her were too strong. And she had her hands full keeping Phyllis straight, keeping her away from all the wild bucks that Freedom had turned loose.

Emily wrote of all this in her letters to Aaron. And letters came regularly from him as he moved from point to point up through Carolina, working to help the bewildered freedmen.

"Since Sherman's misguided feint on Charleston," he wrote from the town of Barnwell, "we have been heading with more consistency and success for Columbia, and there I hope to establish some sort of base of operations for ministering to these poor distracted creatures whom I have been called to save. You may tell General Sager that I am meeting with the usual treatment from the army, the callousness and indifference I have learned to expect; I shall report to him more fully on this at a later date. I pray God that I shall be able to terminate this arduous task by the middle of March and return to you, my beloved, and the pressing duties of the Beaufort district."

She could see now how mistaken she had been to fear her feeling for him had changed in any respect. She told herself how completely she had forgotten that sudden fear, and with it a fringe of lesser misgivings, left over from the girlhood she had so abruptly changed for womanhood when she had come South as his wife. These weeks of his absence, these days of work at the Tabernacle and these nights of exhausted sleep, were giving her time to catch up with the hurried courtship and wedding that had released her from Boston, the honeymoon voyage to Beaufort, and then the confusing cross-currents of the first days at Marshlands. That weakness, she saw now, was only a final phase of her adjustment to him, her acceptance of him as her husband. It was gone now, that shock of homesickness and fear, that brief interlude of uncertainty, leaving her strong in the assurance of how thankfully she would welcome his return, to show him how much she loved him, to make amends to him with a whole lifetime of devotion.

There was only the missing prayer-book. Mrs. Sager had noticed and admired it the first day at Marshlands in the unpacking, and later she had had to be told it was missing. "Try to think, child, where you had it last, it will come to you." Maum Minda and Phyllis solemnly denied having seen it, it couldn't have walked off by itself, and certainly it wasn't the kind of thing any of Sherman's staff would have walked off with. "We'll all keep looking," Mrs. Sager said, "it's bound to turn up in some unexpected place." She kept bringing it up. It was gone but she would not let it be forgotten. And later Aaron would have to be told. Then, at last, it would be possible to forget it forever, to say to herself as she must say to him that it was lost, that she had put it down somewhere, not remembering where.

♪   ♪   ♪

The weather was growing steadily warmer. The twin camellias flanking the front steps of Marshlands were covered with waxen pink blossoms, the big buds of the Japanese magnolia near the gates were almost open, and delicate little red blossoms had appeared miraculously from the black bark of the flowering quince in the closed garden. Some distance along Fenwick Street from Marshlands, at the house that looked like a Tudor castle and was used for an army hospital, narcissus were shining at random in the garden. Emily would have liked to stop and admire them, but the stares of the men sunning themselves on the lawn always made her hurry on by.

Late one afternoon in mid-February as she was coming home alone from the Tabernacle, Mrs. Sager being detained as usual by her instructions to the volunteer night nurses, she was hailed from the garden gate of the army hospital by its head, genial Dr. Ellis, who sometimes came over to help with the sick refugees.

"First day of spring, Mrs. Moffet," he squinted pleasantly. "It's in the air."

He chatted briskly for a minute before he came to the point.

"Mrs. Moffet, I realize you and Mrs. Sager have your hands full, but I'm going to make an appeal to you just the same. We're swamped here. We haven't the doctors, the nurses, or the beds for the wagon trains of wounded they're sending back to us. It's an emergency. We're distributing the new cases wherever we can find places for them, and I'm going to ask you to take care of some of the overflow at Marshlands. In fact, I've already sent one case over to you. Sorry."

"But there's no-one there," Emily remembered. "The servants left early today, and General Sager and his aide have gone to Savannah."

"My stretcher-men said they left him in care of the sentry," the Doctor informed her cheerfully. "I'll be around to see him after supper. Just let him rest till then."

And with thanks and apologies the Doctor excused himself and hustled back into the hospital.

Emily hurried on up dusky Fenwick Street, turning his words over in her tired brain. The sentry was absent from his post at the gates of Marshlands: it took a moment to recall why. In the house there was no light downstairs. She had to feel her way along the dim hall.

Upstairs a lamp was burning in the spare room next to hers, and when she went in she found the sentry sitting at the side of the bed. A man was lying there.

63

"They just brought him here and dumped him, ma'm," the sentry whispered to her as he got to his feet. "Said they was full up at the hospital."

She nodded that she understood, but he went right on explaining.

"I told them I didn't know nothing about it, but he kept moaning to them to leave him here and they left him and beat it. I didn't know what to do, so I just been sitting here with him waiting for you to show up, ma'm."

When she went closer to the bed, she saw that the wounded man was sleeping. His uniform was torn and caked with mud. The face was so grimy that it was seconds before she recognized him.

IV

THE HOUSE and the room hung in a heavy dead stillness, except for the quick beat of her heart. The sentry had gone back to his post and she was alone, waiting in the chair by the bed. The head on the pillow was turned toward her, the face clear in the lamplight. A stubble of many days' growth covered the hollow cheeks, the closed eyes were sunken in their sockets and dark-rimmed, the nose was pinched and gray. Long deep breathings passed between the parted gray lips.

Helplessly she sat waiting, listening for the opening of the front door. She felt that she was slowly suffocating and that only the tight clasp of her hands was keeping the room from reeling blackness.

After an endless time she heard the front door open and close, steps in the lower hall, and then on the stairs. But it was not the doctor. It was Mrs. Sager.

"What's the meaning of this?" her eyes flashed in the lamplight.

Emily started across the room to explain and caution her to be quiet, but Mrs. Sager brushed that aside with "I know all about it," advancing to the bed with a solid tread. There she folded her hands at her waist and frowned at the head on the pillow in silence for a moment.

"Well," she said coldly, without lowering her voice, "I didn't know it was this one. Our former guest returns to pay his respects. Where are you wounded, Captain Herkimer?"

When the question was repeated in a louder tone, the eyes dragged themselves open. They were bloodshot and dull, without recognition. Mrs. Sager repeated her question again: "Where are you wounded, Captain?" Finally his left hand moved feebly, touched his right side, and fell limply back. Emily saw clearly for the first

65

time that the right arm was not in its coat sleeve and that there was a bulge of bandage at the shoulder.

His eyes were closed again.

"When did the Doctor say he'd come?" Mrs. Sager demanded.

"After supper," Emily whispered.

Mrs. Sager sniffed. "That means any time. Well, we can't leave him sprawled here like this. See if you can get his boots off."

With a sigh Mrs. Sager took off her shawl and bonnet, laid them on the chair, and set to work to unbutton the coat. Emily tugged gently at one of the mud-caked boots. "You'll never get it off that way," Mrs. Sager told her. But it came off at last, and then she worked on the other till it too was off. Mrs. Sager had expertly removed the coat: underneath was a large bandage stained with blood.

"Get some hot water," Mrs. Sager directed. "We have to heat some for tea anyway, so we may as well wash his face and hands."

Downstairs Emily was able to breathe easier, but she was still in a helpless daze. It seemed a great accomplishment to even know how to get water heated, to make her thickened fingers strike a match and light the fire Maum Minda had laid in the woodstove, and to put the kettle on. Maum Minda had left cold supper under napkins on the table, but the very thought of food was distasteful. She sat by the stove and stared at the kettle till it gave in and began to simmer foolishly.

When she brought the kettle up to the room, Captain Herkimer was under the covers, and Mrs. Sager had the windows closed and the fire lighted.

Emily poured some water from the kettle into the basin on the washstand and carried the basin and a washcloth and towel to the chair by the bed, but then Mrs. Sager took charge. "Close your eyes," she said as she wet the cloth and wrung it out, and when the eyes were closed in their pathetic hollows she went efficiently to work. When she was through with the cloth she passed it on to Emily and picked up the towel. Taking the left hand first, Emily tried to make her hands work as matter-of-factly as Mrs. Sager's, but they were so clumsy and the grime stuck so hard that it took a long time. And when she came to the right hand she was so afraid of hurting him that she could make no headway at all. Her breath kept catching in her throat, and finally she had to turn to Mrs. Sager, who was watching her impatiently.

66

"I think—I think we better let this hand go," she said weakly and uncertainly.

"Good land, child, haven't you hadn't enough nurse practice yet,—give me that cloth." And Mrs. Sager took it and cleaned the hand in no time.

"There," she sighed when she had finished the drying, "now let's get some supper. I'm starved. And we have letters to write this evening."

"But don't you think one of us better stay here till the doctor comes?"

"I do not. And no need to whisper. The man's not dying."

"But I don't think we should leave him alone. I don't mind staying with him. I've had some supper."

Mrs. Sager shrugged her broad shoulders. "Very silly," she said, "but suit yourself." And picking up her bonnet and shawl and the kettle she stalked out of the room.

Sometime later, sitting on the edge of her chair at the bedside, Emily heard Mrs. Sager's voice in sharp debate with someone in the lower hall: Dr. Ellis. Finally she heard his creaking tread on the stairs, and then as she went to meet him he appeared at the door, his close little eyes twinkling between his bushy hair and beard. He was armed with the steaming kettle as well as his medicine-case.

"Well," he nodded approval, allowing her to relieve him of the kettle, "you seem to have made the patient very comfortable."

He bustled to work at once, opening his case on the chair, taking off his coat and rolling up his sleeves, and directing her to rinse out the basin and fill it. From the case he produced a pair of scissors and cut away the unstained portions of the bandaging. Then mumbling in his beard he dabbed the clotted remnants with hot water from the basin, which she held, and began to work them loose.

The Captain's hands were clenched, his knees were twitching under the covers, and tears forced their way out between the tight-shut eyelids and ran down his cheeks. She had seen much suffering in the past weeks, but this was different. She could feel it in the pit of her stomach, the room was swinging sickly, and her hands holding the basin were melting.

At last it was over. The Doctor was studying two bare wounds. One was in the shoulder, round and small: the other, like a rip, was in the upper arm near the shoulder.

"Now if you'll empty that," the Doctor's voice came through some muffling thickness.

She emptied the basin into the jar by the washstand, and burned the bandage pieces in the fireplace. Then she stood at the foot of the bed while the Doctor finished dressing the wounds.

"I guess that will hold him," he twinkled cheerfully. "We'll have him up and at them again in short order. But I'm afraid it will all be over by then."

Chuckling over that he held two fingers to the Captain's wrist and took the pulse with the aid of a dented watch. After that he selected some medicine from his case and left it on the bureau. She helped him on with his coat and went with him to the door. He beckoned her into the hall.

"If he works up a fever during the night, give him a teaspoonful or two of that medicine with a little water. Tomorrow he'll be ready for some nourishment, broth or gruel."

"Is he really going to be all right?" she asked him.

"Heavens yes. It's not bad. No bones splintered, grazed perhaps, but no swelling to speak of. They did a pretty fair job at the field hospital, but of course the ride here didn't do him any good. He's still suffering from shock and he's lost plenty of blood, but he'll pull through in fine style with a little good nursing."

He patted her arm. "You look a little pale yourself, young lady. Well, we're all doing too much these days. But how can we do less?" And he wagged his beard at her with a bright good-night.

But then suddenly he remembered something and bobbed back into the room, returning with the kettle.

"I had strict orders from below to bring this down with me," he chuckled as he passed her, "so I better. I'm in hot water enough as it is."

She watched him disappear down the dim stairway. Then she heard Mrs. Sager come out of the sitting-room to confront him in the lower hall.

"It's a perfect outrage and imposition," she heard Mrs. Sager say. "You may be sure the General will hear of this the minute he returns."

Dr. Ellis's voice protested mildly: "My dear Mrs. Sager, I'm very sorry but I've explained that this is an emergency. And you who devote yourself so generously to the refugees at the Tabernacle, don't you feel you owe a little something to your own color?"

"Well really, Doctor, I hardly expected to have insult added to injury. But remember one thing, I want that man out of here as soon as he can be moved. And don't try to palm any more of your cases off on us."

The Doctor went on to the front door. When he was gone, with a bang, Mrs. Sager came to the foot of the stairs to call up.

"Emily, coming down now? Don't forget we have letters to write."

Emily hurried down to the landing so her voice could be lowered.

"I can't leave him alone," she answered over the railing. "I don't dare, he might want something."

"Fiddlesticks," Mrs. Sager called back. "I suppose you're going to leave the letters to me."

"I'm sorry," Emily told her, starting back up the stairs.

"Yes, I know how sorry you are to get out of it." Mrs. Sager tramped back to the sitting-room.

In the upper hall Emily stopped at the door, in a sudden panic at the thought of going back into the room. When she had stood at the foot of the bed while his wounds were being dressed, she had seen the first sure sign of recognition in his eyes, and she was not ready to face that alone. Time to think was what she needed now, time to collect herself so she would not be carried along in stunned helplessness like this. Her hope was that he would be oblivious of everything again, lost in his dark maze of exhaustion, resting deeply, eyes closed.

They were closed when she went into the room, but they opened as she tiptoed to the bed. They looked at her listless and dull at first, and then with a light of recognition again. A wan smile came to his lips, but his brows contracted with pain when he tried to speak.

"Don't try to talk," she told him through a constriction of her own.

But he persisted, and she leaned down to catch his words as he brought them out in a broken husky whisper.

"I got them—to bring me here—to you. . . . Sorry. . . . Emily— Curtis—Easton. . . ."

Her heart tightened so that she could hardly speak herself.

"Don't try to talk now. Try to sleep."

69

His eyes closed then and his head rested easy on the pillow.

She sat in the chair by the bed for a time, without stirring, watching him, listening intently to his breathing. When she was sure he was sleeping, she moved the chair to the fireside and sat staring at the flames, trying to separate herself from him long enough to regain some measure of self-possession, to reach a point where she could think again. But she was hopelessly tied to the bed, and could think and feel nothing beyond its range. After a while, aware that his breathing was becoming labored, she gave him some of the medicine and water, holding up his head so that he could drink. When he was resting quietly again, she went back to her chair by the fire.

Later, when she heard Mrs. Sager coming upstairs, she tiptoed to the hall.

"Please don't make any noise," she whispered. "He's sleeping."

"And it's time you were sleeping too," Mrs. Sager condescended to half-whisper. "Here, I've brought you some cambric tea and a biscuit with butter and honey. I don't believe you touched a bite of supper. You're still much too easily upset, my dear. Now take this and come to bed."

Emily took the tray, but she told Mrs. Sager that she was not going to bed yet.

"Dr. Ellis says he's going to have a bad night."

Mrs. Sager clicked her tongue in disgust. "Well, suppose he does,—is that any reason for us to sit up all night? I'll leave my door open in case he wants anything."

"But I'm not sleepy anyway, really I'm not. I may just as well stay up a while longer."

"Perfect nonsense. You look tired to death. Now go to bed, child, go to bed."

"But we can't leave him alone tonight. And I'm not going to. I know he'll need medicine and water."

Mrs. Sager sniffed, shook her head and sighed, ending with a yawn. "Well, I certainly can't force you to be sensible. I promised your husband to look after you, but after all you're a free agent. I'm going to bed. Somebody's got to be on the job at the Tabernacle tomorrow."

And Mrs. Sager turned to her room, closing the door with emphasis to stress her disapproval.

70

A few minutes later, however, she appeared in the spare room in her wrapper, carrying a shawl.

"Put this around you, child," she whispered crossly, "and don't be an absolute fool."

After she was gone, the house and the room settled down to a final stillness. A slow heavy breathing, an expansion and contraction of rest, in which reason could function at last. But when the mind tried to think clearly, some obstruction intervened, some obstacle of will, blocking thought, rejecting it. Her brain felt drugged, in the grip of an overwhelming weariness, as if in the past few hours she had lived through whole days and nights of strain. And in this spell of exhaustion she lost all consciousness of time, so that she had no idea whether it was before midnight or after, and all track of place, where she was in relation to familiar things, people and events, whether she was here in the South or back North or somewhere strange and unknown. Only the bed remained sure. Even when little waves of drowsiness washed over her from the warmth of the fire, she was still able to hang on to that core of reality, the nearness of that deep breathing, that dark head on the pillow.

At intervals she left her chair to reassure herself that he was sleeping. When he tossed and moaned feverishly, she gave him more of the medicine with sips of water. Once she stole out of the room to get wood from the fireplace in her own room, and came back to find him murmuring her name. And once she was roused with a start from some moment of fitful easement by that same summons, her name murmured over and over. He clung to her hand for a long time before the fingers went slack, and then she smoothed back his matted hair and rubbed his brow till his head was quiet on the pillow. She waited till she was sure he was sleeping again before she went back to the chair by the fire.

It was cold and dim in the room. The fireplace had turned to empty blackness, and the lamp had burned itself out. A vague and obscure light was invading the room, inventing the shapes of bed, bureau, and washstand.

In time it got around to inventing her, too, so that she could rouse herself from this dream of sitting bound in ashen twilight and frozen gloom. With a shiver she drew the shawl tight around her shoulders, got up stiffly, and went over to the bed. Hardly breathing, she stood there looking at the shadowy head on the pillow till the features were clear beyond doubt, beyond hope or fear.

When she turned away and moved softly to the window, the garden lay still dusky with night. But already the branches of the trees were sharp against a rose tint in the sky. The birds were stirring to life, preparing to greet the dawn. Like musicians, she felt, before the footlights and curtain. And even as she watched the curtain seemed to be lifting. Slowly, imperceptibly, an unearthly ecstacy was beginning to pervade everything, mounting and spreading with the rising tide of light.

V

WILL HERKIMER opened his eyes with a start. For a moment he was lost, unable to get his bearings. Then the room began to make sense.

He pulled himself up a little in the bed, not minding the wince of pain that any movement involving the shoulder still gave him. Pain was the twist of fate that had brought him back to this house: it was no more than a reminder now of the joy of these days. The War, men and marches, bivouacs and bugle-calls, even the shout and shock of that last skirmish and the long dazed agony of the wagon ride back to Beaufort, all were dissolved now like the images of a bad dream, leaving a vast contentment, delight in the smallest details of living, the very act of breathing.

The morning air that stirred in from the open window was heady with spring. From where he lay he could see only branches, beginning to show a yellow-green mist of new leaves; the closed garden, Emily's garden, below across the driveway, was invisible. But he could see it in his mind as he had seen it so often from the window. The gay daffodils that she had set in a vase on the bureau had come from there. And today, at last, he would be out there with her, walking the secluded paths, sitting with her in the latticed summer-house.

His eyes began to travel along the cornice of the room, stopping as usual to calculate the number of dentils missing at the place over the closet door. Seven. The seven wonders of the world, the seven wise men of Greece, the seven deadly sins. Emily had thought of the seven hills of Rome, the seven sleepers, and the seven against Thebes. Also, seven was lucky. . . . Maum Minda was a great one for rattling pots and pans, but it was always a welcome sound, this early-morning clatter from the kitchen yard. It heralded a new day, bringing Emily to him again. Her eyes and her voice and her self. In those first days when he had been coming back from the turmoil of pain and fever, her hand had sometimes rested in his when she talked to him or read a little. The contact had seemed natural enough then. Now her hand was withdrawn, and it gave him an empty feeling to realize that as his wound healed she was being drawn away from him, back little by little to the point where they had met as strangers. It made him want to tear off the itching bandages and wrench his shoulder back to the first stage, the worst and best stage. But today, this afternoon in her garden, he would take her hand without benefit of pain. He would speak out at last, before it was too late, and trust to lucky seven to keep it from being a fatal mistake.

The back door slammed, and a voice was singing in the yard. Phyllis! He had been listening for some sound from Emily's room, beyond the fireplace. He could hear the mumble of voices in the big bedroom, where General Sager and the Amazon slept. Finally a door opened, but he couldn't be sure whether it was their door or Emily's. Steps were going downstairs.

Later a knock at the door made his heart jump.

"Come in."

But it was only the Amazon.

"Well, Captain, how did you rest?"

"Very well, thank you, Mrs. Sager."

She advanced to the foot of the bed and folded her hands at her waist, eying him with the patient heavy-lidded watchfulness of a campaign buzzard.

"Anything you need?"

"Nothing, thank you. Except breakfast."

Mrs. Sager sniffed at that. "So glad your appetite improves with your color."

The hell you are, Will thought. He said: "I feel better every day. The doctor says I can go out for a while today."

"Yes," Mrs. Sager nodded, "I was talking to Dr. Ellis yesterday. He says you'll be leaving us in another week."

Her eyes made a rapid inspection of the room and returned to the bed like a blight.

"We'll miss you, Captain. It's been very agreeable having you as our guest, with the Government paying expenses. The money has come in very handy at the Tabernacle, Too bad you're leaving us so soon."

And with a parting jerk of her head Mrs. Sager turned and left the room, closing the door with authority.

For a moment Will lay smiling to himself at the Amazon. But then, abruptly, he stopped smiling. Too bad you're leaving us so soon. . . .

He tossed restlessly in the bed. Somewhere below a door closed with a faint jar. He listened and listened till his ears hummed, till there was nothing to do but give up hope with a sigh. This morning, for the first time, she had left for the Tabernacle without stopping in to see him. For some reason, some good reason. Perhaps she had been late; or perhaps she had started very early and had not wanted to wake him. One or the other, of course. Anyway, it was nothing to get fretted about: she would explain when she got back. And now the afternoon could not come fast enough.

When Phyllis eventually appeared with breakfast, he ate ravenously, thinking how thoroughly he was exploding the old saw about food and the lovesick. No-one would suspect a man with an appetite like this. It was enough to keep even the Amazon off the scent.

While he ate, Phyllis leaned on the footboard of the bed, bubbling over with talk. Any original shyness she may have shown had long since passed. Her Gullah chatter amused him, but she needed watching: her slim fingers were light as a professional pickpocket's. His watch had been the first thing to vanish. Maum Minda had returned it with solemn apologies.

"Cap'm Hakmuh suh, da' gal ain' t'ink fuh do bad."

After the watch episode he had kept a close eye on her and had made a game of catching her in the act. Any brief remorse she suffered seemed to come from being caught rather than from being guilty,—she was shameless as a child. Now lying back on his pillow after breakfast, he wondered what her incurable fingers would fasten on this morning. Feigning sleep he watched her movements through his eyelashes. When she had put his tray out in the hall, she brought in her broom and dustcloth and began a casual cleaning, lightening her labor with one of her half-hummed half-sung spirituals. He had worked out the words of this one.

> *Oh Ma'y, don' you veep don' you moan,*
> *Oh Ma'y, don' you veep don' you moan,*
> *Fairy aa'my got drowndid,*
> *Oh Ma'y, don' you moan.*

He saw her glance slyly in his direction when her sweeping brought her to the open door of the closet. She seemed to be satisfied that he was asleep, for her hand reached in and searched the pockets of his uniform.

"Phyllis!"

She looked round with an expression of surprised innocence.

"Yassuh?"

"Come here."

She came reluctantly, with her hands behind her back.

"What you got this time?"

She lowered her eyes and swung her hips. "Nutt'n."

"Let me see your hands."

She brought her chin up defiantly and held out her right fist, clutching three greenbacks. He took them from her and looked at her sternly.

"How long is this going to keep up? How would you like me to call the sentry at the gate and have him arrest you?"

She smiled saucily at that.

"He ain' gwine res' me. I too quaint wid da' man."

"Then perhaps you'd like me to tell Maum Minda or Mrs. Sager."

Phyllis shook her head and her lips pouted.

"You ain' like me?"

"I like you well enough to see you keep out of trouble."

Her face brightened and she moved close to the bed. "You like me fuh gal, enty?"

"I'd like you to finish your work and clear out."

The smile died on her lips and she moved away from the bed, eyes flashing at him.

"Spec' I ain' good enough fuh you."

He didn't bother to answer that, and after a moment she backed away to the door.

"I know howcome you ain' hab eye fuh me," she said from there. "You hab eye fuh Mis' Moffit!"

The door banged and she was gone.

Will threw back the covers with an oath and yanked himself out of bed. He worked into his clothes in a blind rage, heedless of the stabbing pain in his shoulder. Blood was pounding in his ears and his knees felt wobbly, and he decided he better sit down for a minute in the chair by the window.

A few minutes later, while he was still sitting there trying to get the dizziness out of his head, the door opened to a cautious crack and Phyllis looked in. Her eyes were wide and her face long.

"Please Cap'm Hakmuh suh, mus' make up de bed."

Will pointed his forefinger at her.

"You get out of here and stay out!"

"Please suh, I ain' mean what I say, suh. I too shame."

When he started threateningly for the door, it closed in a hurry.

He went back to the chair and sat frowning out at the garden. It was a shock to discover there was someone his carefulness was not fooling. But what did Phyllis matter. Not at all, except that she forced him to think when he wanted only to feel and dream.

It was bad to think. For what if this Emily dream came true, as it must. This soft-scented sunshine, this gentle beckoning of spring branches, the summer-house in her closed garden, what if all this hope and promise came to life, as it would. What if he succeeded in making her acknowledge and accept his love, as she must and would. . . . If he only had the strength to keep silent, to make no attempt to possess her but simply to keep the dream, leaving her as he had left her before, as something hopelessly remote and unattainable, as if he had fallen in love with the picture of someone belonging to another age. For if he succeeded in getting her to break marriage vows, to disown all conventions and scruples, releasing her youth and trust from this Aaron, what could he offer her in return but scandal and disgrace, an outcast existence. Why did she, of all the girls he had known, have to be the wife of another man. He could see that face so clearly: the fishy eyes and mouth, the long hands, the whole hated body. He could even hear the voice again, with its smooth and smug inflections, its sneer-like smile of confidence, like a taunt and challenge. "Good luck, Captain,—I shan't say good-bye because no doubt we shall meet again."

But having reached that point, his thoughts slipped back to normal. No need to make a monster of her husband; the man **was** probably human, and must have some good traits or he would never have won her. Let it go at that. Dismiss him. Look at the garden, waiting. Forget everything else. No use going over and over the same ground: it was a circle that always ended where it started: it would all come out right somehow, because it had to, because it was impossible to believe anything else. The twist of fate had not brought him back here to cap a climax of torment. He knew better than that, as she must. And beyond that central assurance he refused to think. No use even trying to rehearse what he would say to her this afternoon, there in the garden. Fate would take care of that too.

He turned then to the batch of Hartford papers that had come with the box of delicacies from home. The family: he had overlooked that angle. Their expectations and hopes of him, his career in the firm when this war business was over. Well, that was easy: if they didn't care to receive Emily, that was their loss. Plenty of room in the world. But they would love her, of course. How could they help themselves. And so with mind drifting free again, he glanced idly over the papers, just killing time and not trying to concentrate, for nothing happening in the outside world really mattered anymore. It had ceased to exist, that world, or at least it had shrunken away to unimportance, leaving only this vital world of meaning, this house and room, the garden and the sparkling curve of river beyond the trees, a stream of spring morning and love on whose surface he could float toward afternoon, safe above the dark undercurrents of anxiety and fear, dreaming of her and trusting his dreams.

In the course of the morning there was one intrusion from the outside world, but he welcomed it because it helped time pass. He had forgotten about Mr. Monroe, the barber of Bay Street. He enjoyed the visits of this drawling philosopher from Portland, Maine, but he didn't remember the man was coming till he saw him ambling in the gateway, exchanging quips with the sentry.

Phyllis brought him up to the room with the usual pot of hot water. Brazenly, as if nothing had happened, she set to making the bed, while Mr. Monroe opened his satchel and laid out his tools.

"It's goin' to be a lot easier gettin' at you now," his shock of iron-gray hair nodded. "Guess you'll be skedaddlin' out of here shortly, but you'll have to go some to catch **up** with Sherman."

Will moved the chair away from the window and sat down, facing the light. "I can't even catch up with the news. What's the latest?"

Before answering, Mr. Monroe spread and pinned his cloth, being elaborately careful of the bad shoulder.

"Well, Captain, I don't set up to be no cornersewer of military affairs, but with Charleston in our hands now and Sherman pushin' up into North Carolina after burnin' Columbia, accidently on purpose, it looks to me like it's all over but the shoutin'."

"What makes you think he burned Columbia on purpose?" Will asked through the first slap of lather.

"Well, I'll tell you. It's been my experience in life to find rumors turn out to be true in most cases. Where there's smoke there's fire, as the feller says. In my opinion a man's guilty till he's proved innocent, and nine times out of ten I'm dead right in suspectin' the worst."

Mr. Monroe fell to stropping his razor, waiting for Phyllis to leave the room. When she was gone, he continued:

"Now you take what happened to me. I had the whole thing brung home three years ago when I caught my wife co-inhabitin' with another gentleman. Seems everybody else in town knew about it but me. There was plenty of rumors floatin' around, but you see I was one of these trustin' fellers then, the kind that thinks lightnin' can strike any house but his'n. Now I make a practice of believin' every rumor I hear. Believe the worst and you won't be far wrong—that's my motter now."

He indulged himself with a short croaking laugh.

Mr. Monroe was being a little too entertaining this morning. Will decided not to ask him what had become of the wife and the other gentleman.

"Go easy on that shoulder," he said between lathered lips.

"Pretty sensitive, hey?"

"A little. Any Beaufort news today?"

The razor hung poised in the air a moment while Mr. Monroe considered. "Let me see now." The razor descended for a clean smooth stroke. "They shot another deserter this morning."

Will relaxed with a mumble.

"Yes," Mr. Monroe sighed, "a young German boy. One of that outfit they got quartered in St. Helena Church. I used to cut his hair. Always talkin' about his home in Wisconsin. Got homesick, I guess. I get that way myself sometimes. Too bad he couldn't have hung on a spell longer and he wouldn't have had to desert."

"Mmm."

"Guess you heard about the riot between the soldiers and nigs last night."

"Uh-uh."

"Well, sir, they had theirselves a time. Them soldiers vamoosed out of Bay Street double-quick when the nigs started pullin' razors on them. Felt like pitchin' in myself with a few good licks at the nigs. I can't stand nigs. Can't stand the smell of them and the airs, and can't stand havin' them set in my chair givin' orders same as a white man. If I didn't have to make a livin' I couldn't hardly stand touchin' them. But I sure would enjoy slicin' a few of their throats."

Mr. Monroe's razor scraped smoothly up Will's neck as he gave a fuller account of the riot. Wine and women were at the bottom of it, of course, but it went deeper than that. White and black were like oil and water. They never would mix together equal, one was always going to be floating on top, no matter how hard the Abolitionists strained themselves and everybody else trying to change the laws of nature. . . . Will's eyes closed with an inner sigh. The soft fragrant air drifting in from the garden and the tide, cooling the lather on his cheeks, was too much for Mr. Monroe's riot philosophy. Only the drawl of that down-east voice survived, and finally even that lapsed into a sort of lullaby. To avoid being carried away by this seductive droning, he had to keep prodding himself back to consciousness of the razor.

Mr. Monroe took his calling seriously; each stroke was executed with deliberation and finesse. A good half hour had passed before he delivered the final pat of cologne and removed the cloth. Another quarter-hour was consumed in packing up. And then, with a little encouragement, he lingered on to tell a story or two.

After he left, Will found there was still too much morning left for comfort. There was still an hour before the midday meal, and there was no getting back to the earlier mood of passive waiting and dreaming: he was at complete loose ends now. But pacing the floor brought back dizziness, and sitting by the window only made him jumpy. He tried to look over the papers again, to think about the War; but all he could think of was four o'clock, the hour that usually brought her back from the Tabernacle. He remembered the way he used to feel at school as the hour of public speaking approached, only this was any number of times worse. In the end he stretched out on the bed and let himself fret in peace. It was easier than trying to fight it.

When Phyllis appeared at last with a well-filled tray, he found he had no appetite whatever. That was the last straw. While he picked at the food, making some pretense of eating, he allowed her to stay and talk. She seemed to consider their clash a thing of the distant past, forgiven and forgotten all around: she was full now of a Charleston jamboree she was going on soon. In a couple of weeks, first week in April, the Yankees were having a big celebration there. Celebrating, he finally gathered, the anniversary of the surrender of Fort Sumter, with a whole crowd of people from the North. Her brother Robert, who was downstairs right now, was going to take a boatload of people from Beaufort on the *Indigo*. He let her ramble on about it, disgusted with himself that he was grateful for the distraction of her company.

A few minutes after she left with the tray, General Sager came in with his cribbage board. At first it was a pleasure to see him, and for a while he was excellent distraction; his stubby self-importance and his excited interest in the game were really diverting. But today he stayed and stayed. The patch of sunlight in the room had moved from beneath the window and was creeping up the washstand toward the basin and pitcher, it was actually getting on toward four, and still the General was playing just one more game. At last Will's patience frayed out.

"No official cares today, General?"

"Not one, my boy, not one," in the voice that was so much too big for him. "Reports went off this morning. Glad to say. So my time is my own, my boy. And yours, all yours."

Will fidgeted through another game. But after that he called a final halt.

"I just remember, General,—Doc Ellis has given me permission to go out for a while today. I've been sort of saving it for afternoon."

"Why splendid. I'll keep you company. We can play a little croquet if you feel up to it. I'll give you a fair handicap for your bad arm."

"Very sporting, sir. But you see, as a matter of fact, Mrs. Moffet has promised to do a little letter-writing for me."

"Oh yes, I see. Very interesting. Well, how about some more cribbage this evening, if you can take another beating?"

"Very good, sir."

The General then bustled out with his cribbage board, and Will heaved a sigh of relief.

He sat by the window looking out at the driveway and the gates, holding himself in check, till his watch said four o'clock. Then he started downstairs.

It felt funny to be out of the room. He held on to the railing with his left hand: his pins were not to be trusted yet, bed had sapped the strength out of them. And each step down gave the shoulder a good jab.

Out on the front porch was a rocking-chair, and he sat there to wait, watching the gateway. The slanting sunshine made him squint, but it felt fine on his face and hands. Beyond the lawn and seawall the river was at flood tide, like a lake of placid blue. All the beauty and happiness in the world was locked in this afternoon serenity, if he could only find the word to release it. But it was all he could do to sit still and try to collect himself, keep from jumping out of his skin, stop shaking like a miserable schoolboy.

And when at last he saw her coming up the driveway, he could hardly get to his feet to start down the steps. His head was whirling perilously as her smile came toward him.

"Well! How does it feel?"

"Great," he smiled back.

But then he realized that her words meant nothing. They were automatic, perfunctory. Her eyes and smile were here, but she herself was standing far off, aloof and reserved, untroubled, unreachable. He saw now that his leaving the room had opened the breach between them, the breach that had been growing more and more threatening as his strength returned. She was hopelessly secure against him now, and with this realization his hopes stood confused for an instant, then tottered and plunged down.

Her voice came to him thinly. "How long have you been out here?"

It took all his strength to answer. "Only a minute or two."

Things seemed to hover at random then. Her face seemed to recede and blur, and extraneous things came forward, strangely sharp: the white dogwoods by the closed garden, the bright song of a mocking-bird. He felt a sudden need to laugh, and then unexpectedly her face came back clear, eyes unsmiling now, voice warm and close.

"Sure you feel all right?"

"What?—why yes," he heard someone say. "Sure, I'm all right."

Her lips said, "You mustn't overdo, this first day."

He took a deep breath. "I feel all right."

Her eyes were still solicitous.

"I feel fine," he told them.

They stayed with his for a moment, then looked away at the river, apparently satisfied.

"You know," he said as steadily as possible, "you promised to write a letter for me this afternoon. And show me your garden."

Her eyes came back to him with a smile and nod.

"So I did. I'll get my writing things. Is it to your best girl? Because if it is, I'll borrow some of Mrs. Sager's best notepaper."

"No thanks," he managed to grin. "Anything will do. It's just the family."

He waited for her at the foot of the steps in a blank misery, staring at the croquet wicket on the lawn beyond the flagpole. My best girl, he thought wryly. He could hear her voice inside, speaking pleasantly to the General in the parlor.

When she came out with her writing-case, they walked across the side lawn to the dogwood trees and the closed garden. There she showed him where her daffodils were growing, and the mockingbird's nest in the privet shrubbery, empty now but long and ably defended against Maum Minda's marauding cat. Around the summerhouse banks of azalea bushes were in full bud, almost ready to open, and the roof was decked with grape-like clusters of wistaria buds intertwined with sprays of banksia rose. In a few more days the roof would be a mass of purple and gold: he tried to show some appreciation of her interest in all this.

At last he was alone with her in this secret place of spring, just as he had been dreaming. And now he could only wonder, as he took his long-appointed place beside her on the bench of the summer-house, how even with the wildest conceit and presumption he had ever built the dream up to this ultimate madness. But it was still not too late to spare her the embarrassment and pain of his folly. For her sake he would have the final decency to keep silent. . . . Yes, he thought as he watched her open the writing-case on her knee, the onrushing tide would soon engulf this roof with purple and gold, but by then he would have stepped decently aside. Not to return home with the victorious army to a cramped office and desk, but to move on to the new western territories, where he could forget in open action, in style even, in some new dream perhaps.

That picture sustained him for a brief moment. Then he lost track of it in her hand waiting with the pen. The late sunlight, sending long shadows across the garden, made a wavering tracery of leaves on the paper. He watched the flickering pattern with a sort of doomed fascination, for its silent turmoil was suddenly his own and could no longer be controlled. He saw there was no escape now. He was acting under some fatal compulsion, as if the dream was not his but an independent will, taking charge of him, refusing to recognize the hopelessness of it, forcing him to go through with it regardless.

"That looks like pretty fancy paper," he found himself nodding at it. "Maybe we better make this to my best girl after all. If it won't embarrass you too much."

She looked up with her quick smile. "No,—I don't mind, if you don't. I should think she'd be anxious to hear from you by this time."

He shook his head.

"I'm afraid not. You see she's married."

"Oh."

"Pretty hopeless, isn't it. But is it wrong to love her?"

Her eyes were on the paper again, and her voice was a long time coming.

"I should think it would be wrong to tell her, certainly. Hadn't you better forget her?"

"I've done my best to. But it just gets worse all the time. And now I've got to tell her."

"I'm sorry, Captain, but this is a little embarrassing. I'm afraid you better wait and write that letter yourself."

"I'm sorry. I didn't mean to—well, thanks anyway. . . . I'll make it to Mother. Is that better?"

"Much better."

She gave him a flushed smile and then her hand waited with the pen. But it took him a good while to get started.

"Dear Mother," he began finally. But then the first scratch of the pen stopped him dead. He held his breath for a moment, grinding his hands together as he groped for words. "Please just say I'm about well now, and will be leaving Beaufort shortly. I expect to be ordered back to headquarters then, but I'll try to get a week's leave to come home first."

"Wait," she smiled intently at the paper, "let me get that down. A little slower, please."

84

He was able to slow down. But no stopping now, no turning back. He couldn't see her eyes, but he saw the words ahead clearly now, on her cheek and touching the delectable little ear, the long soft lashes, the tip of her nose and her parted lips, her hands giving his strained voice magic form and flow.

"I owe my recovery . . . and this letter . . . to a young lady here . . . who nursed me like an angel."

He paused there to ask, mouth dry as dust, "Too fast?"

She seemed to be trying to smile, but her cheek was deeply flushed now and her voice disconcerted, suddenly as strange as his own, its naturalness and impersonal friendliness gone. "Thank you for saying that. Of course you don't want me to write it."

"I want to say," he stumbled on, in a blind rush to get it out, "I have never known anyone like her. She's the most wonderful girl in the world, the finest and most beautiful. You will fall in love with her, as I did, the moment you see her."

Her pen had stopped somewhere far back, but the words wrote themselves now. "That first day, coming up to Beaufort on the boat from Hilton Head, I saw her standing by the rail, I saw her eyes and then her smile. And in that moment I saw all it means to be alive. Then I lost her and died. But finally a miracle brought me back to find her again."

And then at last words came with a wild burning exhilaration, headlong release.

"Emily, forgive me, but you must listen. You can't mean that it's wrong to tell you this. I've got to. I can't keep it in any longer. It's no use fighting it. Can't you see it's no use."

It was over. Said and done beyond any hope of recall. And now he had only to take his medicine, the last bitter drops from her hand. Anything she said would be fair and just. He could never lose her again and live, but already he could hear her kindest possible words: Please go now, I can never see you again, Captain Herkimer, no, no, it's impossible, this is good-bye, yes, I do, I do mean it. He could not even hope for forgiveness now. He only asked in this final torn moment that she would not find him merely ridiculous, and yet even her derision had been earned.

But her head remained bowed, as if she were carefully weighing her answer. And then, with utter amazement, he saw that tears were dropping on the paper where her pen had stopped.

VI

In the midst of an afternoon's work at the Tabernacle Hospital for Freedmen, Mrs. Sager was visited by an intuition. It came to her as she was passing from the sun-flooded yard, where the patients were being sunned and aired, into the sun-striped interior, where a crew of advanced convalescents were cleaning house. She stood looking sightlessly at the chattering workers for several minutes before she called to one of them.

"Sister Eva."

Sister Eva Toombs put down her mop and came across the room. Sister Eva, long since restored to bulging health from her exodus out of Washington, Georgia, was allowed to stay on at the hospital because of her ability and willingness.

"Yas, Mis' Saguh?" she beamed.

Mrs. Sager made a gesture of protest.

"I have asked you not to address me in formal terms. I am your sister."

"Yas'm, Tittuh."

"That's better. Now. Can I depend on you to take charge here till the night helper from the Teachers' Home arrives?"

"Yas ma'm, you sho can, Mis' Saguh!"

Mrs. Sager closed her eyes with a sigh. "Can't you understand we are sisters now—equals?"

Sister Eva grinned apologetically. "Yas, Tittuh, I understands all right, only I fuhgits."

"Well, you mustn't forget. Give the patients an hour more sun before you bring them in."

"Jes' leave 'um to me, Mis'—Tittuh."

86

Mrs. Sager gave final instructions to the cleaning crew and went out.

Emily had left more than an hour ago, she had been leaving early every afternoon since the hospital work had been growing lighter: Mrs. Sager's mouth was set in a tight line as she hurried through the streets toward Marshlands. March had shaded into April and full spring was coming on,—the hard bare trees were putting out fresh and tender green, masses of wistaria hung over fences and yellow jasmine torrented from branches, perfuming the air where birds sang joyously,—but Mrs. Sager was not impressed. Her attention was firmly fixed on her revelation.

Why hadn't she sensed the situation before? Very stupid, she was compelled to admit, but no use to go into that now. Now everything was transparent as glass. How easy it was now to interpret Emily's recent moods, not to mention the Captain's: how blind she had been! Their eyes, their glances, the very tone of their voices betrayed them. Her thoughts were unable to keep up with the pictures that now rushed to the support of intuition. And all this had been going on right under her nose, while Aaron Moffet was straining every nerve to help the freedmen in the wake of Sherman's army.

In a way, Mrs. Sager decided with a sniff, it served him right for supposing he could go off and leave a young bride. It certainly served him right for having ever married the girl in the beginning. Mrs. Sager gave her head a savage jerk: she would have made him a proper wife, a real mate and partner in his labors. She had set her cap for him the moment they had met on the steamer bringing the first delegation of missionaries to Port Royal in '62, but he had remained cold in the face of her warmest encouragement, had finally told her he was dedicated to his work, and in the end she had thrown herself away on the General. Then he had gone North to raise funds for the Cause and had brought back an unformed snip of a girl as his wife. After that, this was no more than he deserved.

At the gates of Marshlands Mrs. Sager gave the sentry a stiff nod for his salute.

"Have the General and his aide returned yet?" she asked him.

"Not yet, ma'm."

"Maum Minda and Phyllis have left?"

"Yes, ma'm."

"Tell the General I wish to see him the moment he returns."

Instead of approaching the house by the front driveway, Mrs. Sager turned off and followed Maum Minda's and Phyllis's path to the back yard.

She opened the back door quietly and tiptoed into the hall. There she paused to listen; then started cautiously upstairs, easing her weight slowly on each treacherous tread. At the landing she held her breath to listen again; and once again in the upper hall, damning the worn floor boards and a faint squeak in her shoe. The doors were all open except the one to the right, the Captain's room. She moved softly to it and held her ear close. Not a sound. Her hand felt for the knob: was it locked? With a sudden convulsive twist she swung the door open.

The room was empty.

With a twitch of chagrin she shut the door, crossed the hall to her room, and went out on the upper porch. From here she commanded a good view of the grounds, but Emily and the Captain were not in sight. Then her eyes settled on the side garden: so closed in with new foliage that even from this high angle it was all hidden, except the summer-house roof and that was buried under a cloak of blossoms. She was about to descend for an inspection of the premises, when she happened to notice that the rowboat was missing from the landing that ran out on stilts from the seawall. Her spirits rose with a bound at this clue, and she stepped back into the bedroom to get the General's field-glasses.

The marshes across the river were cut by many tideways, and on these Mrs. Sager trained the glasses. Unfortunately the marsh-grass, already turning from russet to green, screened the canals from view. But she was not prevented from seeing with the eyes of imagination. She herself had been rowing with the General through those placid water lanes with their walls of reed and ceiling of sky. If Emily and the Captain were there, and there was no sign of them up or down the river, then they were alone together in a secret place, very thoroughly alone and together in a boat with plenty of cushions.

It was a long tense wait before Mrs. Sager was rewarded by the sight of a rowboat emerging from the far marshes. And then live-oak branches and the flagpole on the lawn kept getting in the way of her glasses. But by shifting around on the porch she was able at last to get a good clear focus: it was the guilty parties all right. Emily was rowing,—hurrying them back so they could be found playing an innocent game of croquet. The Captain was on the stern seat, his white sling showing up bright in the sunlight,—that arm was no longer a serious handicap. As the boat came out into open water she could see he was smiling and his lips were moving,—if glasses only had the power to bring sounds as well as sights close up! . . .

She became so absorbed in the approach of the boat that she failed to note the arrival of her husband and his aide. So when they came upstairs and stepped out on the porch from the bedroom behind her, she was taken by surprise.

"You wish to speak to me, my dear?" the General asked, looking surprised at the glasses.

"I do,—but is that any excuse for sneaking up behind a person and scaring them out of a year's growth! I wish to speak to you alone."

She gave the aide's thick-lensed bug-eyed glasses a look that made him beat a hasty retreat.

"What's up?" the General asked, peering at the river. "Porpoises again?"

"Something a lot fishier than that," she snapped, prodding him with the field-glasses. "Look at that rowboat."

He took the glasses in his stubby hands and fumbled for the focus.

"Emily and Will Herkimer," he discovered finally. "Have they been fishing? Have they caught something?"

"It's Captain Herkimer and *Mrs. Moffet,* and they've been over in the marshes half the afternoon. They've caught something all right, and so have I!"

The General looked confused. "I don't understand, Mattie."

"Oh, naturally. I wouldn't expect you to know a clandestine affair if it bit you. Horace, Captain Herkimer is to leave this house to-night."

"Now really, my dear, after all,—aren't you jumping at conclusions? Isn't this all rather—sudden?"

"Far from it. It's been going on too long. But I haven't time to go into that now. All I want now is to get that man out of this house."

"Now, Mattie, I think you're acting very hastily, very rashly."

"I'm not asking what you think. I'm telling you what to do. Get him off this place, at once, the moment they land. You tend to him, I'll tend to her."

"But now, Mattie, hadn't we better sleep on this? We may find it wiser to let the matter rest, or blow over. After all, he's leaving for the North in a few more days."

"With Aaron's wife, very probably. Would you have us conniving in that? As the young woman's chaperon I have some sense of responsibility, if you haven't. Now don't make me lose my temper, Horace. We must go about this thing in a calm and dignified manner."

"But what explanation shall I offer young Herkimer? And where is he going to stay?"

"We're not concerned with that. If there isn't room for him at the hospital, he can put up at the Sea Island Hotel. As for explanations, we don't owe him any. He should have left here days ago. And he was an uninvited guest in the first place."

"But, my dear."

"No buts about it. If you don't tell him, I will."

"Very well, my dear. Let's get it over with."

They went downstairs to the front porch, and were posted there when Emily and the Captain came across the lawn from the landing.

"General," Mrs. Sager announced to her husband as the pair came up the steps, "you have something to say to Captain Herkimer, I believe. Emily, may I speak to you inside."

She led the way into the sitting-room, where she closed the door and confronted Emily with hands clasped firmly at waist.

"I'll come straight to the point. We're asking Captain Herkimer to leave the house, and I shall ask you not to see him again."

The face before her was white as a sheet, the eyes staring back, blank with shock. She waited for them to catch up with her words, for the blanched lips to make some response. They did, finally.

"What do you mean?"

"Well really, young woman, I hardly expected quite such a display of innocence. I was hoping it wouldn't be necessary to explain. After all, you must know a decent married woman doesn't go off alone with a man."

Color flushed back into the pale cheeks at that.

"I'm afraid I can't see anything indecent about rowing with Captain Herkimer."

"Perhaps you can't, but others can. Please don't think you're deceiving anyone. Don't you suppose I know what's been going on behind your husband's back?"

"Your insinuations are quite clear, Mrs. Sager."

"For your husband's sake, Mrs. Moffet, shall we say simply that you have been guilty of extreme indiscretion? The matter can rest there, if you come to your senses. And you will, if you wish to stay in this house. That is all."

She marched to the door, but turned there to add:

"While Captain Herkimer remains in town, your work at the Tabernacle will be very confining. And in our spare time we'll have many letters to write, you and I. There are some on the desk there now, waiting to be answered. I'm sure you're as anxious as I am to protect Aaron from all this, but if you object to my help you can complain to him on his return, or by mail if you like."

✐   ✐   ✐

Before going to sleep that night, after nudging the General over to his own side of the bed, Mrs. Sager had a little talk with herself. Captain Herkimer was out of the house, and Emily had shut herself up in her room all evening without supper. But this was hardly a satisfactory denouement to the great day of intuition; Mrs. Sager was beginning to realize, now in the darkness, that in the excitement of the moment she had not played her cards well. Not at all well. And the more she thought about it, the more it irritated her. She had exposed her hand too soon: if she had waited a day or two, she might have had something more specific to disclose to Aaron Moffet. She had gone off half-cocked, caught Emily a little prematurely. . . . Still, given a little more rope Emily might very well hang herself yet. And with that comforting thought, Mrs. Sager finally resigned herself to sleep.

The next morning before leaving with Emily for the Tabernacle, Mrs. Sager interviewed her husband's bug-eyed nasal aide. She pointed out that it would be to his interest to perform a slight service for her. When the aide agreed, she explained that she wanted him to locate Captain Herkimer and observe his movements.

At the Tabernacle Mrs. Sager spent the morning watching Emily out of the corner of her eye. Toward noon the aide reported to her there. Captain Herkimer had left a note with the sentry at Marshlands: the sentry had passed it on to Phyllis. Mrs. Sager gave the aide a nod of approval, left Emily in charge of the Tabernacle, and

91

went back to the house, where she summoned Phyllis to the sitting-room and came to the point at once.

"You have a note for Mrs. Moffet. Let me have it."

"No ma'm, I ain' got no note."

"Liar, I happen to know you have. Now give it to me."

But Phyllis was not so easily cowed; she held out against the sharpest browbeating, stubbornly denying she had any such thing as a note. Finally Mrs. Sager was compelled to sweeten her tactics, which was directly against her principles. She offered Phyllis a silver dollar: the girl produced the note from her bosom without further delay. Mrs. Sager dismissed her with contempt and ripped open the envelope.

I must see you tonight in the garden. All my love. Will.

Mrs. Sager read the message over several times, with twitching lips and a twisted smile. She stared out the window into space. It was difficult to decide what to do next: here was an embarrassment of possibilities. They could be prevented from meeting, or they could be allowed to meet. If allowed to meet they could be overheard. She saw herself stealing through the closed garden toward the wistaria-clad summer-house. When overheard they could be surprised at their tryst—or allowed to carry their madness into further meetings.

She was strongly tempted to surprise them in the garden tonight. However, there was the matter of her own dignity to be considered. And it would be difficult to explain to Aaron if she allowed Emily to receive the note and keep the tryst. No, there was really only one course to take. She would send word to Aaron by government dispatch, urging him to return at once; and in the meanwhile she would keep a close watch on Emily. There would be considerable pleasure, after all, in preventing the guilty pair from seeing each other again.

Mrs. Sager went to her desk.

Dear Aaron, she began, *It pains me beyond measure to find it my duty to inform you——*

She slowed her pen, took her time, savoring each word.

VII

EMILY studied her face in the mirror of the bureau. There were dark shadows under the eyes and the skin was white and drawn. But the eyes were dry at last. There were no more tears left.

Since that afternoon when Will had left the house, now days and years ago, it had been impossible to eat or sleep or think. It was still possible to feel, in one direction, endlessly, through throbbing temples: she must see him tonight. That necessity had broken the long stunned lethargy when General Sager had taken his life in his hands to tell her, last evening when his wife was out of the room for a minute, that Captain Herkimer had been ordered back North and was leaving tomorrow on the *Indigo* for Charleston. She had avoided repaying the General's kindness by asking him to risk his life again as an errand boy; but this morning in final desperation she had found a weak link in the chain of Mrs. Sager's you-will-thank-me-for-this-later-on censorship. "Sister Eva" Toombs at the Tabernacle had smuggled out a message in the ample folds of her dress, and had brought back a frantic answer from Will: he would be waiting outside the gates after dark.

She would go to him tonight, if she had to run openly from Mrs. Sager. She would go to him to tell him what she must, that he must go without her, forget her, go on with his life as if they had never met. No, not to forget, but please to remember her always as she would him. . . . He would reject all that again and rush on with his plans for their future, but this time she would be strong. She would quiet his arguments and entreaties with her hand firm on his lips, quiet him as she had in his pain and fever, like a sick fretful little boy, his head resting in her arms. She would be strong for his sake. And she

93

knew this time that it was true when she looked at her eyes in the mirror.

She had only to make herself ready. When she had come upstairs from the ordeal of supper, she had thrown herself on the bed, and now her hair was undone. She forced her lifeless hands to do it up again carefully; then as one hand held it in place while the other opened the top drawer of the bureau and felt for the box of hairpins, her fingers touched one of the collars Aaron had left there. She closed the drawer quickly. But at least that was something to be grateful for: that it would be days yet, perhaps weeks more, before his return from Columbia, giving her time to recover a little, a little of the lost ground, enough to rest on, enough to stand on at least.

When her hair was arranged, there was nothing to do but wait for the darkness, trying to feel nothing but the minutes passing and the shadows gathering in the room. She sat on the edge of the bed for a time, listening to the low ringing that was always in her ears now, till presently an obsession developed that her earrings, Aaron's wedding present, were the cause of this constant remote thunder. There was no escape from the tight gold band on her finger, but she took the earrings off and went back to the bureau to put them away, getting out the old ones, her mother's, to take their place. But the dull thunder persisted. Not strongly enough, though, to shut out the rapturous vespers of birds in the garden. After a brief shower in the early afternoon, an unearthly radiance had flooded the world of new green, sharpening every tone of spring to a final intensity; and now after sundown, with the light dying away to a last glow in the west, the fall of evening shadows was only heightening the fullness of things. Even here in the room she felt she was slowly stifling in the spell, as if she were holding her breath against it or drowning in its fragrant depths.

She went to the front window to try to get some of the clear cool river air into her lungs. General Sager and his aide were playing a solemn game of croquet in the fading light of the lawn, and she stepped back a little for fear of attracting their attention. On the lower porch a rocking-chair was creaking busily: Mrs. Sager. . . . That meant the back door, that way to the gates. In a few more minutes she would go, in the friendly darkness after the first stars came out and before the moon came up over the island shore across

94

the river. When she came back through that moonlight, it wouldn't matter whether the doors were locked or not. The clash with Mrs. Sager was inevitable, but it would be easier then.

As she stood waiting near the window, she was aware of a grind of wheels on the shell of the drive, and she saw the General and his aide drop their mallets and start toward the house. Someone calling on the Sagers: here was a final unexpected obstacle. She turned away in panic to the bureau, but there she saw that it could only mean a delay, and it might prove an advantage, after they were settled on the porch or in the sitting-room.

As she stood waiting, she heard steps and voices in the lower hall, then in the sitting-room. And then as she stood listening to the mumble of voices below, all sense of time and purpose fell away from her. She stood motionless, hands frozen to the bureau top, eyes staring at the mirror. Even when she caught the sound of steps coming up the stairs, she was powerless to move or prepare herself in any way for the approaching shock. She stood paralyzed as in a nightmare, waiting for the steps to cross the hall and the door to open.

Then at last she was able to turn to meet him as he came into the room. In the half light only his form was clear at first, his face and eyes obscure, and yet in those first moments she seemed to read his expression plainly and was unable to keep back the gasp of fright waiting to escape her lips. So that when he came forward eagerly and threw his arms around her, crushing his mouth against hers, she was too stunned to yield defensively but stood rigid against the pressure of his embrace, his voice speaking her name.

Even when he released her at last and stood holding her hands, smiling down at her, she could not force herself to make a sign or sound of response.

"Still a little shy of your big clumsy husband?" his words echoed weirdly in the dimness. "I was hoping this separation would cure all that. My darling, if you only knew how I've been longing for you. I almost sent for you, but decided to surprise you instead. . . . But I'm afraid I've surprised you too much. Your hands, they're like ice. Mrs. Sager tells me you have not been well. You should have told me yourself. But I guessed from your last letters that something was wrong. You have been too brave, my dear, not wishing to worry me."

Still she was unable to utter a word or rally her shrinking senses. A violent trembling seized and held her, and when he let her hand

95

go her knees were so weak that she could hardly stand and had to feel for the edge of the bureau to steady herself. Somehow she managed to keep meeting his eyes, but only to watch them helplessly in the failing light. And now they seemed to narrow, their look changed, his whole bearing and manner altered, and he was standing back nodding at her through the vagueness with a strange precision.

"I'm thankful," his voice came, cold and deliberate, "you have not chosen to dissemble. That I could never have forgiven. Well, what have you to say for yourself? Anything?"

She managed to speak, finally, in a weak whisper.

"I didn't know you were coming back. So soon."

He smiled at that. "Thoughtless of me, wasn't it. How you must wish I'd never come back. . . . Emily, you're not very good as a cheat. You're too young and inexperienced, you need more practice. And your lover is a very bad coach."

She fought then for words to fight back with and for breath to carry them.

"Aaron, wait. It's not that. You must understand and believe me."

"I believe I understand. My wife is unfaithful to me. Do you deny it?"

She leaned against the bureau, still facing him but unable to answer.

"Can you deny it?"

He came close again and gripped her hand. "I want the truth, from your own lips. Tell me you love him. Say it."

She tried vainly to free her hand. Then liberation came in a choked sob.

"I do love him."

She tried to stop the sobs that were tearing her throat. Her head was spinning so wildly now that it took moments to realize he was kneeling before her, his breath hot against her hand.

"O God, let this cup pass from me."

He pressed her hand to his forehead. "Emily, pray with me for forgiveness. God is merciful. Christ forgave the woman taken in adultery. Pray with me."

He started to pull her down beside him, but with a sudden strength of revulsion she wrenched her hand out of his and stood free.

96

"I don't want your forgiveness. I'm going to him. You can't stop me."

She felt an hysterical desire to laugh as he got to his feet. Even in the dimness she could see how darkly flushed his face was, his eyes gleaming with rage, but she was not afraid of him now. Shaking with sobs she flung words at him.

"I'm not afraid of anything now. I'm going to him, I tell you. I was going to send him away without me, but now I'm going with him. Nothing you say can change that now. Nothing. Nothing."

Her words struck back at her from the shadowy walls, as if many voices were repeating them over and over. Then the room was ringing with silence, his eyes still staring glassily at her. When he spoke at last, his voice came low and deliberate again, slow, precise and even.

"So you were going to send him away. Renunciation. Very noble. But now you weaken, saving me the trouble of kicking you out. A separation without freedom, you understand. Divorce is a complex and disgusting business, my dear, and I don't believe in it. So you will be going with him as my wife. And then what?"

His eyes seemed disembodied now. She could see nothing but their gleaming. Even his words seemed to come from them now.

"When the first fine frenzy of romance wears off and he begins to hate you for ruining his life—what then? If he has any social position or sensibilities, or any hope of a career in the army or elsewhere, don't you suppose he'll tire of his burden, the curse of traveling around with another man's wife? Even if he feels bound to you by some sense of obligation, even if you don't lose him to some other woman who can give him children with a name, you'll have to free him in the end. Then what remains? Do you think you can come crawling back to me? . . . I see you're careless of your own fate, and mine, but hadn't you better consider his?'

The eyes studied her steadily, and she felt her own flinching at these words that she already knew by heart. She tried to escape by forcing herself to awareness again of his face, his frame in this twilight doom, his fingers straightening his cuffs. But her eyes had to come back to his for the words that kept lashing at her.

"I'm sure you love him too much to take this final irrevocable step. And in any case I could not permit it. I suppose it is weak of me not to be willing to expose you both to the laws of propriety and retribution, the workings of justice human and divine, an atonement that would fall hardest on you because you most deserve it. But I love you too much to see you sacrifice yourself. Yes, in spite of this my love remains steadfast, faithful to my vow to cherish you in sickness as in health. I am a man of love and faith, Emily, dedicated to the cure of souls. And you are sick, mortally sick with sin and deception. It is my duty to heal you, make you whole again, for His sake."

He braced his shoulders and cleared his throat.

"Don't think that I hold myself blameless. I reproach myself for having failed you as a husband. In my devotion to my work I have neglected my duty to my wife. I promise to correct that now. . . . You seem to be coming to your senses a little, so I shall leave you for a while to think things over."

He stood looking at her in silence for a moment, then turned to the door. From there his voice came to her with final inevitableness and decision.

"You have my calm guidance now, Emily. Of course, if you prefer, I shall settle the matter with Captain Herkimer directly, but I'm sure you wish to spare him that. Mrs. Sager informs me he leaves tomorrow for Charleston and the North,—shall we allow him to depart in peace, without any farewells from us? I think that's best, decidedly. And now if you will pray for strength and forgiveness, your prayers will be answered. Pray for His compassionate redemption and purification. In good time His peace will follow, flowing into your soul like a blessed sacrament. Amen."

The door closed remotely.

She stood listening numbly to his steps descending the stairs. Then a mumbling of voices came up faintly from the room below. She felt her way to the bed and lay down in its darkness.

Steps and voices in the hall brought her back to consciousness. She was lying in a pale misty light: a ghost of moon looking in the front window. She heard Mrs. Sager's voice and the General's saying goodnight to Aaron. When the door opened with a flash of lamplight, she managed to raise herself on an elbow, but sank back as he came toward her.

She was blinded at first. But then she saw he was carrying a cup and saucer, which he put down on the bedside table.

"Some chocolate Mrs. Sager was good enough to make for you."

She wanted to turn her face away from him, but his eyes and voice held her.

"We have Mrs. Sager to thank for my return in time. I hope you appreciate that."

As he stood looking down at her, his eyes seemed to relent in the softening glow of the lamp.

"I suffer with you, my child. And I have much counsel to give, but that can wait. I want you to rest now, alone."

He paused, lips parted, watching her as if he expected some response. Then his mouth firmed into words again.

"Before I leave you for the night, is there anything I can do for you? I can see prayer has helped you already, but tell me how you feel now."

Staring up at him, she wondered vaguely how she did feel now. The only feeling she could be sure of was a dull tingling and smarting of her skin under the tightness of her clothes.

"Can't you say anything? After all, I'm the injured party."

He waited, watching her.

"Well," he said finally, "I hope you recover your speech by morning. We have certain elementary decencies to uphold through this. I wish especially to spare the Sagers any further embarrassment. I expect your coöperation in preserving appearances. That is an important part of our understanding."

She could only continue to stare up at him.

"Oh yes," he nodded with a slight smile, "I have news for you. The Fort Sumter Celebration is being held at Charleston on Saturday, and we're all going from here on the *Indigo* tomorrow. Mrs. Sager agrees with me that the change will do you good."

After a minute of silent appraisal, his eyes left her to look around the room. Then at last he turned to the door, and said to her from there:

"I am staying in the spare room tonight, Emily. Your lover's room, I believe. I have my own penances to do. When we return from Charleston, you can count on me to take you rowing across the river to the marshes, and there will be long talks in the garden summerhouse. By then you will be thanking me for keeping you from destroying this great love of your life, Emily. You can keep it always now, my dear, and dream of it as you lie here with me. . . . No need

99

to lock this door, of course, from the inside or out. I shall leave mine open, in case you need me in the night. And I shall call you early in the morning."

The lamplight was gone. The door was closed. The ghost of the moon crept back into the room and lay still at her feet, watching her, listening with her to the wall of darkness at her head.

VIII

A BELL TINKLED somewhere below and the little sidewheeler began to churn at the wharf, sloshing swirls of spume against the palmetto piles. The wharf and its crowd began to draw away. Shouts and laughter and shrill screamed messages were lost in a single sustained uproar.

From where Emily sat at the rear of the upper deck, she could see only the forward portion of the lower deck. There, sitting in the prow, a freedmen band was blaring and blurring in hideous sharps and flats over a thumping bass-drum—*Downtown Gal Won't You Come Out Tonight And Dance By The Light Of The Moon,* a recent favorite of Phyllis's. Phyllis herself, in bright calico and feather bonnet, stood in front of the band with her brother Alec and two young bucks dressed to kill. She had one arm around Alec's waist, the other resting familiarly on the shoulder of one of the bucks. Maum Minda, in dignified black, appeared and separated the girl from her companions, bringing her up to the pilot-house, where her brother Robert took charge of her.

Bay Street was sliding away behind. Ahead at a bend in the river was Marshlands, half hidden in its trees. An air of unreality enveloped the lawn and garden, the seawall, the boat-house landing. This was not the place she had come to that January day already so long ago; then the marsh had been brown and many trees bare, but things had been alive in that winter and now in this spring they were dead, as ghostly as last night's moon. And these people sitting or moving so plausibly around her, government officials, school-teachers, Bay Street merchants and their wives, General Sager, Mrs. Sager, Aaron Moffet: all phantom shapes. Their words and gestures, so matter-of-fact and authentic, only intensified the unreality. Even Will, at the rail near the pilot-house, the most unreal of all.

When she had come on board and had seen him standing there alone, the pattern of their meeting repeated as if she were seeing him for the first time again, the last strength to endure this death by slow torture had failed her. In that moment the only consequence to be feared was the unbearable one of losing him. But then for his sake this protective numbness had set in, this spell of final despair that rendered all things harmless. She could see everything with sharpest clarity, as in a nightmare, but nothing could touch her now. And she felt that the spell would hold as long as she could keep her eyes from his.

The day was overcast with a high veil of clouds. The *Indigo*, churning and throbbing along the river, trailed a hissing flounce of foam. Fields bordered the way, sometimes reaching to far fringes of smoky green, sometimes broken by thickets and sentineled by plumed palmettos. Occasionally a glimpse of a plantation house in a grove. Now and then the course widened at the mouths of marshy inlets and tidal creeks, and once it narrowed between sandy bluffs crowned with pines whose clusters of dark green needles had a sheen like metal. Here the paddle-wheels threw out from their dripping boxes pulsing and swishing rumbles that multiplied and rioted to escape.

The phantom shapes of people spoke and were somehow answered. They moved back and forth, came and went. The walking-beam, at the foot of the tall stack that puffed black smoke, worked smoothly up and down, up and down, with tireless panting sighs. As the minutes flowed by, this walking-beam under its canopy of smoke became a vast obsession. For long stretches nothing else existed.

At one time she was aware that General Sager was leaning over her chair. She had no idea what he was saying. But because something in the pale little eyes above the bushy beard wanted to be kind, she made herself find meaning in his words.

"Coming into St. Helena Sound now. Point on the right known as Brickyard. Probably a brickyard once. On the left we have Coosaw River and the delta of the Combahee. Very interesting."

She nodded and smiled to him. . . .

On the swelling breast of St. Helena Sound the boat began to roll gently. There were smiles and significant glances. The General said something waggish, which was greeted with hysterical laughter from the trio of maidenly school-teachers next to Emily. Then conversation lagged. Even the lower deck was subdued.

In the middle of the Sound the rolling mysteriously ceased. The school-teachers resumed their chatter. Their backs were turned to her now; they had definitely given up their efforts to draw her into their circle. . . . The *Indigo* seemed to be floating in infinity. To the right was the open sea. To the left, sweeps of marsh, far wooded shorelines, points and islands, half lost in the haze of distance. . . . The General discovered a school of porpoises, and the school-teachers flocked to the rail, where he gallantly offered them his field-glasses. Gulls flapped and soared over the wake of the boat with plaintive cries. One swung down, picked up something from the foam, and started for shore, pursued by two others. . . . The shorelines were closing slowly in again. A winding waterway through marsh plains. The ebbing tide left oyster banks and black mud that had a strong salt smell. . . .

Mrs. Sager gave the signal for lunch. The Marshlands basket of fried chicken, sandwiches, and cake was opened, and cold tea was poured from bottles into tin cups. Emily was conscious of Mrs. Sager's eyes watching her; her pride rallied a little then, and she forced herself to eat something, to meet all their eyes, and even talk.

After lunch the unreality deepened. There were long merciful stretches of oblivion when all sensation was lost, even the intimate pant and sigh of the walking-beam. It and the boat itself, the phantom faces and voices around her, water, shore, sky, all lost their identities and were merged in one hypnotic throbbing.

At one point in the afternoon, where the winding tideway was so narrow that there was hardly room to pass, a gunboat came tooting toward the *Indigo* and puffed tightly by with close cap-wavings and shouts. It was soon lost in the forgotten spaces behind. But for some time after, gulls wheeled and pleaded insistently over the water, their dangling claws and alert eyes urgently distinct, like Aaron's fingers rubbing his chin thoughtfully as he talked with Mrs. Sager. And finally, abruptly, from a mud flat ahead, beyond Will's healed shoulder, a blue heron rose against the sky and flapped away, and for one sharp instant as Aaron pointed to it she and Will were together, watching that flight forever.

But then the sky sank heavily back to the empty path of water. The course widened and narrowed again, winding endlessly on.

103

Marsh and field and woodland dragged by in a slow gray maze of numbness.

Streaks of scarlet sunset had broken through the gray when the *Indigo* came out of the narrow tideway into the broad Ashley River. Ahead lay the spires of fabulous Charleston, floating between the tinted sky and water.

The walking-beam assumed a leisurely gait as the harbor drew nearer. The water lanes were crowded: progress was slow. General Sager strutted the deck like a chesty little admiral, reviewing the great fleet. Those were troop transports over there, half sail and half steam. This slim vessel on the leeside looked to him like a captured blockade-runner. And just off the Castle Pinckney lighthouse, already glowing against the gathering dusk, were two monitors.

"Cheeses on shingles," the General chuckled in his beard.

The three school-teachers, clinging to one another, were beside themselves with excitement when he pointed out the dark shape of Fort Sumter.

Faces were becoming indistinct now in the growing darkness, as the *Indigo* crept along through the tangle of black hulls and silhouetted funnels and rigging. Lights hung like stars all around and snakes of light writhed across the water. Ship bells tolled, and sometimes voices could be heard clearly. . . . A pilot boat came alongside, and words were shouted back and forth between the two pilot-houses. Emily was aware of confusion around her. Everyone was suddenly babbling at once about something, exchanging shrill handclasps, laughing, weeping, shouting around her in a kind of grotesque dance. She felt General Sager touch her arm.

"Didn't you hear it?—Lee has surrendered!"

Lee has surrendered, she repeated to herself, trying to grasp its meaning. . . . Aaron's voice was launching *Praise God From Whom All Blessings Flow*. After that the General started *Three Cheers For The Red, White, And Blue*, which was followed after a pause for breath by Mrs. Sager's *Columbia, The Gem Of The Ocean*. The upper deck songs were clashing with the lower deck's frenzied *John Brown's Body*. . . .

The noise and confusion lasted through the landing at a torch-lit wharf. She saw Will standing near the gangplank in the jostling throng. For a moment their eyes met at last; then people came between, and he was lost. After that things became hopelessly blurred. Faces and voices, carriages, moving lights and shadows. Crowded carnival streets and streets of dark echoing stillness, clopping cobblestone streets, and finally a house.

A house with servants assigned to "General Sager and Party" by the Authorities. Supper was waiting. Afterwards some of the party went out to see the torchlight procession and fireworks, but Mrs. Sager pronounced this folly. Early to bed, she told her three schoolteacher disciples, was the only sensible course with such an important day ahead. Emily sat with them in the parlor, where the General and Aaron discussed the probable effects of the Surrender on freedmen affairs. At eight o'clock, by Mrs. Sager's locket watch, all knelt by their chairs while Aaron offered a prayer of thanksgiving. Then Mrs Sager led the way up to the second-floor drawing-room, the ladies' dormitory, equipped with army cots.

While they were undressing, Mrs. Sager talked to the teachers. Under the covers she continued her monologue for a while. Finally her tongue was hushed, eventually the whisperings of the teachers died out, and Emily lay in a void watching the faint window flashes from the illumination in the harbor.

Later the ghost of the moon invaded the room. It had found her even here in this strange refuge, as it would find her everywhere and always. No use to close her eyes against its filtering rays. They penetrated to the core of pain, where his name was aching to cry out against this lingering death, this descending spiral of night and recurrent defeat, herself in ever-weakening flight to him blocked by the wall of Aaron.

✓   ✓   ✓

She was roused at sunrise by the specter of Mrs. Sager, shaking her arm. Mrs. Sager was already dressed, in her best purple silk. She made a crisp rustle as she moved around the room waking the others.

After breakfast, General Sager assembled his "family" on the front steps of the house, where an official photographer posed the group for an instantaneous picture. Then official conveyance arrived to carry them on a tour of the city: the ceremonies were not to commence till ten. But on inspecting these complimentary vehicles, two army wagons with improvised seats, most of the General's family decided to see the sights on foot. To avoid too sweeping a rebuff to the Authorities, Mrs. Sager installed the three teachers in one of the wagons with the General's melancholy aide for an escort.

Through a nightmare in bright sunlight Emily set out with Aaron and the Sagers for the harbor. The sky was immaculate blue this morning, and a fresh breeze was stirring the foliage in abandoned gardens: the perfection of the spring day was a Sign and a Symbol, Mrs. Sager said.

When they reached the Battery and climbed to its esplanade, there was a magnificent view of the harbor and all the vessels dressed for the great occasion with flags of every color. And here, separated from the waterfront by a strip of scarred trees and breastworks and dismounted guns, stood the finest residences in the city, all bearing wounds of the long siege. Some had holes clean through them. Others had their broad piazzas smashed down, garden walls toppled over, walks fractured and torn.

"Four years ago to the day," Mrs. Sager finally ejaculated, "those windows, balconies, and rooftops, were crowded with Aristocrats, cheering the bombardment of Fort Sumter."

When she had had her fill of the Battery, she led the party on up Meeting Street, once the proud main thoroughfare of Charleston. Now it was ploughed by shell, its houses gaping with holes, its sidewalks weed-grown and littered with glass and debris and blocked at points by piles of brick and timber. But despite the difficulty of passage the way was thronged with people, well-dressed Northern souvenir-hunters and freedmen of every shade and age clothed in everything from the gaudiest finery to the filthiest rags. Mrs. Sager was intoxicated with this holiday concourse; walking with Aaron, Emily and the General bringing up the rear, she had a nod of greeting for everybody she passed, white and black, high and low. She was sorry when, after too few blocks, Aaron reminded her it was time to turn back to the harbor.

For Emily the day was now forming a jerky pattern of confusion, scattered impressions striking through tardily to her senses, as if she were lagging behind time and catching up only at random intervals. In this drugged chaos she clung to one thought to keep herself going: Will was still here somewhere. His boat was not leaving till after the celebration, tomorrow. There was still time, still time. And some-how this thought sustained her through everything, as if some blind hope were still left in this nightmare of farewell, this shining turmoil of extinction through which she kept searching for some sight of him.

. . . The *Indigo* moving away from the dock toward Fort Sumter. The breeze fluttering flags and whipping the harbor with white. Mrs. Sager's voice nudging Aaron: "That's the *Blackstone,* the boat for New York." . . . The whistles and bells of other boats heading for Sumter. Bands blaring brokenly across the waves. Choruses of voices competing with the breeze, distorted, demented, fantastic in this almost exultant turbulence of sun and water. . . . Sumter coming nearer. And then the congestion of boats at the landing. General Sager offering her his hand and tripping over his sword on the gangway to the powdered brick entrance of the fort. Walls battered shapeless. Soldiers at present arms: white soldiers on the right, black on the left. Inside the fort a new flagstaff, flanked by decorative pyramids of cannon balls. A platform trimmed with red-white-and-blue bunting and a golden eagle. Rows of seats, many already occupied. People talking in groups, promenading, collecting relics to take home. Her eyes searching in vain. . . .

The General finally found reserved seats in the front row, and there she was placed between Mrs. Sager and Aaron, like blinders on both sides. The General pointed out the six big guns mounted on the parapet ahead for a grand salute. Beyond the guns were the flags and masts, walking-beams and smokestacks of the boats showing above the parapet. . . .

The speakers of the day were arriving on the platform now. Everyone was clapping. Cheering now, as the speakers were recognized.

After an opening prayer, there was the reading of selected psalms. Then: great applause when William Lloyd Garrison introduced Major—now General—Anderson, hero of Sumter and guest of honor. His hair was sprinkled with gray. He spoke in a hesitant voice that hardly carried beyond the front rows.

"I am here, my fellow citizens and fellow soldiers, to perform an act of duty. Had I observed the wishes of my heart, it would have been done in silence. . . ." The last words of his brief speech were almost inaudible. ". . . And on earth peace, good will towards men."

Mrs. Sager's black cotton gloves clapped without enthusiasm.

"Disappointing," she said across Emily to Aaron, who nodded agreement.

Her expression of disappointment survived through the raising of the tattered flag, raised by the hand that had lowered it four years before; survived even through the cheers that followed it to the top of the staff; but perished in *The Star Spangled Banner*. The guns on the parapet thundered in Emily's head. Answering thunder came from the fleet and the surrounding island forts. Earth and air shook. Smoke blotted out the sun.

A hush fell over the crowd when Henry Ward Beecher came to the front of the platform. Emily had made no attempt to protect her ears from the din: she had welcomed it without even blinking, without hearing it really but only feeling the tremendous repercussions, as if it were a soundless end of the world, some blessed cataclysm of release. Now she sat stunned with deafness, watching the speaker struggle with his manuscript against the stiff breeze. He took off his hat, but the breeze was too much for the dignity of his hair, and he put it back on again. His mouth worked, his arms waved, on and on. The only words she heard clearly were the closing ones, which the speaker delivered with a disastrous skyward gesture that loosed his manuscript to the breeze like a flock of seagulls.

"As long as the sun endures, or the stars, may this flag wave over a nation neither enslaved nor enslaving. Peace, Union, and Liberty, now and forevermore!"

Then at last the Benediction, releasing her from this cramped position which she had held for hours, it seemed, between Aaron and Mrs. Sager.

"Almighty God, our Heavenly Father, bless this grand ceremonial, which must ever live upon the annals of our country's history."

But the nightmare dragged on, prolonging itself into the afternoon with a resumption of sightseeing. The City Hall, the Court House, the Slave Mart and Auction Block, all were thoroughly investigated. And then Mrs. Sager led the way to Citadel Square, where a mass meeting of freedmen was being addressed by Senator Wilson, Theodore Tilton, and other distinguished speakers from the North.

Later they visited St. Philip's quiet churchyard to see the tomb of John C. Calhoun, the arch-traitor, prime instigator of Secession. It proved to be a plain marble slab bearing the single word *Calhoun*, in letters hardly big enough to spit upon, as Mrs. Sager said.

They walked on from there to St. Michael's Church. Mrs. Sager was well pleased with a shell hole adorning the tower; and another that let daylight into the sanctuary, revealing a demolished altar and fragments of the Ten Commandments. On closer inspection Mrs. Sager called attention to the fact that the shell had broken all the Commandments except Adultery, the very precept Charleston most needed.

From there they went on to see the Ration House, where army rations were being doled out to freedmen. Mrs. Sager pointed out in the waiting lines several white women, dressed in black.

"Widows of Charleston Fire-eaters," she supposed in final triumph. But she still had to see the ruins of Institute Hall, where the Ordinance of Secession had been passed. When it was finally located, she pronounced it a fitting climax to a perfect day, a day she would never forget as long as she lived.

It was almost dark by the time they got back to the house. A figure waiting at the front steps turned out to be Alec, with a message from his brother Robert for the General, that the *Indigo* would leave at seven in the morning to catch the tide. Then as the General and Aaron were following Mrs. Sager up the steps, Alec slipped a piece of paper into Emily's hand. As her hand closed on it her heart came back to life with a wild race. Before she could whisper or even nod thanks to him, he turned and dashed off down the dusky street. Resisting an insane impulse to break away and follow his freedom, she fumbled the paper into her sleeve and started up the steps after Aaron and the Sagers.

The rest of the house party had already returned from their various expeditions. They were assembled in the parlor, awaiting the hour of departure for the Public Banquet at the Charleston Hotel. And there was no privacy upstairs: Mrs. Sager accompanied her, and remained to ease her stays and rest with her shoes off for a few minutes. Emily lay down on her cot, trying to quiet the pounding of her heart as she waited for Mrs. Sager to leave. But when she did finally, Mrs. Rutherford and Mrs. Crounse appeared and lingered to tidy themselves a bit. Then at last they too were gone and she was alone, her fingers like sticks unfolding the paper and holding it to the candlelight at the dresser.

I am making a last attempt to reach you. You can't let me go like this without a word or a sign. I shall be waiting across the street again tonight, hoping for some chance to see you.

The words rushed together in one thrust of pain. Her stricken eyes stared helpless at the wavering flame of the candle. And then she had to wait through a cycle of breathless sightless contraction before she could free herself and cross the room to one of the front windows.

There were no street lamps, and the moon—now suddenly an old friend longed for—had not yet risen. But patches of light from the windows below reached the cobblestones and were reflected dimly by the blank face of the deserted house across the way. In the shadows there she made out the form of a man.

Like a stab from somewhere behind her she heard her name called. It was not repeated, but steps were coming up the stairs. She barely had time to force her paralyzed body away from the window when Aaron stood at the open door.

"You're keeping us waiting."

"I can't go," she managed to tell him weakly. "I can't go another step."

He stood looking at her from the doorway, his features sharp and set in the candlelight.

"I think you better make the effort," he said after a moment. "You've done very well so far. I wouldn't spoil it now."

Her knees were trembling so that she could hardly stand, but she met his eyes steadily.

"Please don't ask me to go. I can't stand any more."

He came into the room then and closed the door.

"You do me final injury," he said in an altered tone, "by taking the attitude that this is a form of punishment. It isn't, in any sense. You're simply being given a chance to humble your spirit and test your strength for redemption."

Her eyes must have revealed all her hate and contempt at that, for his face hardened abruptly.

"Aren't you overlooking something? After all, you might have a farewell glimpse of him tonight, after watching in vain for him all day. Doesn't that possibility revive you?"

He waited, watching her eyes for an answer.

"Well," he sighed finally, "you must be pretty far gone if even that doesn't interest you. . . . Very well, Emily, I'll leave you in peace.

I haven't time to coax you. My only suggestion is that you lie down and try to rest quietly till we get back."

He was gone, leaving the door open. And for a moment the realization was staggering, as if her body had been braced against his presence and was now unbalanced by this sudden release. She held her breath, listening to his steps going down the stairs. Then there was a mingling of voices in the lower hall: the front door opened and closed. The voices were in the street now. They moved away, faded out. The street, the house, and the room vibrated in one stillness.

At first nothing could break this stupefying spell. If I go to him, she thought, I have no will left to let him go without me. But when she felt the paper crumpled in her hand, some deep reserve of strength was released within her: not to let him go like this without a word or sign. Weakness and indecision were swept away and she was sure of herself at last.

But when she hurried out of the room and down the stairs, in the hall an apparition appeared from the parlor, blocking the way to the door. It was Mrs. Sager, looking astonished.

"May I ask the meaning of this? I thought Aaron said you had a sick headache."

Steadying herself from the shock, Emily countered lamely, "I thought you'd gone with the others."

"No indeed. I have a headache myself. I was just going up to lie down, and see if you wanted anything. I must say you look as if you'd been buried and dug up. Do you want me to go out with you for a breath of air?"

"Oh no, thank you, I'm all right now. I decided to go on to the banquet."

"You certainly don't intend to go through the streets alone."

"I can catch up with them."

"Nonsense. If you insist on going, I suppose I'll have to get my bonnet."

"No—please—you mustn't come. I'll be all right."

She started on to the door, but Mrs. Sager was before her, hand on the knob. Panic desperation flashed up then and she struck the hand away with swift force. She swung the door open and slammed it closed behind her.

The night air, cool and calm, touched her feverish cheeks as she ran down the steps and crossed the street. She stopped for breath there. Down the street a short way an unmistakable figure was emerging from the darkness and silence. She was straining toward him, and with a cry she was in his arms, locked in his arms, hearing her name over and over from his lips.

She was holding his hand and they were hurrying away from the house and the street. When they had turned a corner, they slackened their pace. There was only an occasional trace of light through broken shutters in the houses along the way, but several blocks ahead was a street of torches and shouting and band noise, and they turned again to avoid that direction. They crossed to the other side of the street whenever voices came toward them in the darkness, gangs of freedmen laughing and singing, and once they drew back into the recess of a doorway to let a carousing militia patrol with lanterns pass. But as they went on, the streets became empty and quiet, with only the sound of their own voices and steps. And the deeper they went into this sheltering maze of night, the less it mattered to her whether they ever found their way back.

They came finally to a burned district, blocks of ruin where the first pale glow of moonrise showed only chimneys left standing, hearths of lost homes hanging among the stars. Beyond this area was a lane of deserted shell-torn houses, and at one of these they stopped. An iron gate still barred its garden, but there was a breach in the wall and they climbed over a mound of brick and mortar to the weed-grown paths. The breach seemed to heal behind them then. They were sealed in this strange sanctuary, as if they had found some forgotten corner of space where time was suspended, where only spring night and soft shadows existed, themselves and the rising moon.

The moon was low in the west, a ghost again and now forever, watching her as she climbed the steps of the house.

The door was locked. She tried it again to be sure. She was wondering what to do next with this wraith of herself, when a bolt was drawn and the door opened. She saw Aaron's form framed in a light from the hall, Mrs. Sager beyond. When he made a motion for her to come in, she obeyed mechanically.

In the parlor she sat down limply on the sofa. Her eyes looked vacantly up at him standing there with Mrs. Sager. His face was terrible to see, but she felt no terror. Only this limpness and with it a curious sense of detachment, as if she were watching a scene between them and some third party, herself a spectator, not directly involved.

It was Mrs. Sager who spoke first, her face livid with suppressed violence. "Well, young woman, you certainly are fortunate to have such a Christian for a husband. That's all I have to say. Any other man would turn you out in the street, where you belong. I know I would."

Aaron's voice intervened huskily: "I suggest we keep our voices down, Mattie."

"As if everyone didn't know about it now," she sniffed, her face working to control itself. "She's the only one that doesn't seem to realize what she's done. How can she dare face you like this."

"If you please, Mrs. Sager," he said to her, "I prefer to handle this in my own way. . . . Emily, how did you happen to come back at all?"

She had no will to resist his question. She answered as mechanically as she had obeyed his summons at the door.

"I had to see him, one last time. To make him understand. For his own good."

"And didn't he care what became of you afterward?"

"I told him not to worry. Just to forget me, and never try to see me again, or write. I made him promise so many things. Everything."

After a moment's silence Mrs. Sager disregarded Aaron's warning and lunged in again. "And now you expect your husband to take you back, as if nothing had happened."

"I don't expect anything. It doesn't matter what happens to me now."

"Then why didn't you stay on the street? What are you doing here?"

"I don't know."

She continued to stare back at them, blankly, without fear or feeling.

Finally Aaron spoke to Mrs. Sager.

"There's nothing more to be said for the present. Will you take her up with you? I am staying down here."

Mrs. Sager nodded. Mouth set in a hard righteous line, she waited with averted eyes for Emily to join her. She held her skirts back to keep them from touching Emily's, and then turned to the hall and led the way to the stairs.

✓   ✓   ✓

The April morning dawned without a cloud.

And because it was the Lord's Day as well as the end of the celebration, the Doxology was sung in farewell to the city as the *Indigo* left her dock. Shunned by even General Sager now, Emily sat with the wife of a Beaufort storekeeper, stout and comfortable Mrs. Van Wie, the only member of the party who didn't seem to feel contaminated by her company.

As the *Indigo* rounded the Battery and headed up the Ashley for the tidewater creek, Will's ship the *Blackstone* was just weighing anchor. Then the harbor and Charleston were lost behind. Only a vast blue and green emptiness around her now, vast peace of sky and marsh and shorelines drifting by, peace like death at last.

At eleven o'clock Aaron stood up before the company, near the forward rail for the benefit of the freedmen on the lower deck, who were requested to join in the Sabbath services. After hymns he gave out that he would take his text from Psalms 32 and 33: "And be sure your sin will find you out." He pointed out that this applied to individuals as it applied to communities of souls, like Charleston. But God's justice was tempered with mercy. God was merciful to them that repented and sought His forgiveness. . . .

The day turned slowly through noon. After lunch two of the school-teachers, unable to hold their heads up any longer against the sunshine and the languid motion of the boat, lay down along the railing seat with their heads on their arms. Everyone looked drowsy. Mrs. Van Wie dozed comfortably in her chair. Even Mrs. Sager nodded. The lower deck was subdued too, many of the people stretched out asleep. Phyllis was sleeping like a child with her head in Maum Minda's lap, Alec nearby, a handkerchief over his face. In the pilot-house, Robert seemed to slumber at his wheel, motionless, inanimate. Only the walking-beam remained actively alive, rising and falling with its rhythmic pant and sigh.

When the sun finally burned down to the west, a great yellow radiance spread over the marshes, reviving the decks. Later, at St.

114

Helena Sound, the whole world was transfigured in flaming glory. Mrs. Sager declared she had never in all her born days seen such a sunset. It was a fitting close to this journey of double celebration: the Redemption of Sumter and the Surrender of Lee. She discovered the shapes of angels and archangels in the fiery heart of the glory.

It was dark by the time the *Indigo* skirted the shadowy point of Marshlands. Then the lights of Beaufort winked among the trees and sent wriggling lines over the tide. The freedmen band was blaring full blast when the little sidewheeler churned up to the landing, but it was a strangely silent crowd that was waiting in the light of waterfront torches.

The noise of the lower deck had suddenly stopped. Mrs. Sager, face contorted in the flaring light, was passing some word along to Mrs. Van Wie. Mrs. Van Wie's placid eyes were wide as she turned to Emily.

"The President has been assassinated!"

After that it took a long time to get off the boat through the crowd. General Sager and Aaron were besieged with frantic questions.

"Uncle Sam dead, Gen'l?"

"De Gow'ment done dead, enty?"

"What gwine come of we now?"

Finally Aaron sent Emily on to the house with Mrs. Sager, while he and the General stayed to calm the bewildered people.

Alone in her room, Emily lay down on the bed. Sometime later she heard Mrs. Sager and the General come upstairs and go into their room; the mumble of their voices came through the wall. Later still she heard Aaron come up and go into the spare room.

She tried then to get up to undress, but her body refused to move. The bed was a black void where she lay lifeless, without hope or feeling. There was only a dim necessity, a faint knowledge formed on the boat, that tomorrow at daybreak she would leave here and go to St. Helena Island, to Harriet Sheppard and the Land's End school. Where she could bury herself decently, away from hostile faces and voices.

Part Three

MRS. GENERAL SAGER's robust limbs were making haste under the chaste dignity of her hoopskirt. She had come to Bay Street in her best black silk at this late afternoon hour to do some last-minute marketing at Van Wie's for the important guests who were expected for supper, and now she was hurrying home, followed by the grocer's handyboy with a basket. She was conscious of his bare feet padding along behind her.

She was conscious of the heat. All day the May sun had been blinding the streets, and although the shadows of the trees were now lengthening toward five o'clock the air was still sweltering. Her purple parasol could not protect her from the heat that still quivered up from the sandy sidewalk along the store fronts. She thought with vexation of the futility of the sponge-bath she had taken, and wondered if damp patches were showing through on the back of her dress.

Yet there was something in her mind beside discomfort. There was pleasure: pleasure because she had jewed down Van Wie, the robber, on the price of his preserved fruits; pleasure because these were such triumphant days,—now it was Chief Justice Salmon P. Chase who was coming to Beaufort. And it was rumored that General Grant himself was coming through soon on a tour of inspection. Exciting times indeed. Not that Mrs. Sager had any intention of showing it; she gave the people she passed purposely acid glances or greetings to prove that she was not one to wear her excitement on her sleeve. Her thoughts turned away to the Shell Road, where she saw the General and Aaron Moffet riding in the surrey to meet the Chief Justice and his party on the way from Charleston.

She drew her handkerchief from the pocket of her rustling skirt and wiped her moist forehead. It served Aaron right, she told the bottles of colored water in the drugstore window, all the trouble he was having with Emily. Pretty kettle of fish, she living over there on St. Helena Island teaching for the Philadelphia Freedmen's Aid Society, making a fool of her husband. He was altogether too patient, too ready to forgive, in Mrs. Sager's opinion. Absurd! What the young woman needed was a little physical discipline to bring her to her senses.

Mrs. Sager's gray eyes had every appearance of being focused on the barber pole that she was approaching, but as a matter of fact they were seeing Aaron Moffet disciplining Emily. It was really a calamity, she recognized for the hundredth time, that she herself had failed to get Aaron. He was a man. The General was hardly that. Still, she confided to the barber pole as she passed, any husband was better than no husband. Mrs. Sager sighed. In a way life was very unsatisfactorily arranged. If one didn't know that it was merely a way God had of testing souls for salvation, of separating sheep from goat, one might suppose that some imp of the perverse was playing a vicious game with people. Only in thought could reality be shaped to the heart's desire. In thought one could have things one's own way. One could substitute Aaron for the General in thought——

Mrs. Sager brought herself up with a snap. Often, far too often, she was shocked at this trick her mind had of straying off into forbidden pastures. Sometimes she wondered if there was any other Christian woman in the world so sorely tried in this respect. Certainly it was fortunate that one's mind-wanderings were not visible to anyone save God.

In the very midst of taking a new grip on herself, Mrs. Sager became aware of a stalwart blackman in uniform coming down the street toward her. She recognized with a tremor Sergeant Pritchard. Before he had been drafted into the First Carolina Volunteers, she had taught him in her school at the Tabernacle. She had been helplessly afraid of him then and ever since. Her fear had always been that she would meet him like this on a dark night in some back street, that she would be seized and dragged into deep shadows, a powerful hand over her mouth. No saving herself, for fright would have deprived her of all power of resistance. Swaggering toward her now he appeared to be leering lustfully.

It took Mrs. Sager several seconds to realize that Sergeant Pritch-ard had reached the whitewashed board gate that led through an alleyway to the government wharf and was turning in with a respectful grin and tip of his cap. Her fancies were further shattered by two Negro women who brushed by her just as she herself reached the alleyway. Looking after them she saw that there was some com-motion on the wharf. There was a crowd there, a noisy crowd. Turbulent heads and arms stood out against the white deck of the *Indigo* and the blue river and green marshes beyond.

With a sharp injunction to the grocer's boy to keep his hands out of the basket, Mrs. Sager dispatched him on to Marshlands and hurried through the alleyway to the fringe of the crowd. At first she tried to see what was going on by standing on her toes, but there was too much movement. Next she tried to clear a way for herself by the authority of her voice, but even that trusty instrument was of no avail in this tumult. Firmly she placed the weight of her substantial shoe on the nearest black foot; and this tactic, supple-mented with the point of her parasol, opened a passage for her to the front row of the crowd, where she found a handful of whites.

At the steamer end of the gangplank Mrs. Sager saw an emaciated young man in the uniform of a Confederate officer. The long dark hair that came from under his slouch hat and his dark mustache emphasized the pallor of his face. Behind him stood a shabbily-dressed woman of proud bearing, and with her was a frightened-looking girl. At their feet were several boxes and parcels.

"What seems to be the trouble?" Mrs. Sager asked her neighbor in the crowd, Mrs. Crounse, wife of the druggist.

"Why it's the first of those old Beaufort people coming back," Mrs. Crounse answered with feeling, "and the freedmen are worried. I don't blame them. Mrs. Elliott here says they'll never let them land."

Mrs. Crounse indicated a large coal-colored Negress nearby, who vehemently agreed.

"Dat ain' no mo'n de trut'! Dem Rebel buckra gwine study fuh pit we back in slabery quick as dey lan'."

"Quite right, Sister," Mrs. Sager nodded.

She saw with gratification that the crowd needed no stimulation from the outside. Black mouths and hands were growing more and more threatening, whipping up a great roar against the three frail figures across the gangplank. Mrs. Sager squeezed her hands together in self-congratulation,—she wouldn't have missed this for the world. The crowd was going wild. The voices of the men were punctuated with the shrill invective of the women. There was no tempering of abuse and threat: the mass formation made even the most timid brave. Although much of the crowd was plainly recruited from the ex-field-hand idlers of the hovels at the edge of the town, Mrs. Sager was able to translate their thickest gabbled Gullah. What a nice predicament these ex-aristocrats found themselves in! Further working out of Justice, thought Mrs. Sager.

A missile thrown from the rear of the crowd narrowly missed the head of the Confederate officer and crashed against the smokestack behind him. Laughter went up from the dock. It seemed to release the young man from his indecision. He started down the gangplank, and as he advanced those nearest on the wharf pressed back, leaving an open space. A hush fell on the crowd as he stood facing them From where Mrs. Sager stood she had a perfect view of the scene.

"Don' le'm lan'!" a voice yelled from the rear.

"T'row'um in de ribbuh!"

Others took up the refrain at once; even those in front joined in, avoiding the white man's eyes. He glared around, fixed on someone.

"Alec!" His voice commanded silence again.

Mrs. Sager saw with surprise that Alec and Phyllis, who were supposed to be at Marshlands with Maum Minda preparing for the special supper tonight, were standing there near the front of the crowd.

The white man's voice snapped out: "Come here! You too, Phyllis. Help us with our things."

In the silence Mrs. Sager saw Phyllis step out of the crowd. She stood with her shoulder and hip toward the white man and looked him over with a mocking smile. Her voice came bold and shrill:

"I *free*, hear! I ain' slabe no mo'. I free till I *fool!*"

The crowd took up her words. Mrs. Sager forgave Phyllis for leaving the house to meet the boat. There was a press forward; but the white man held his ground, and those in front, including Phyllis, pressed back to keep from touching him. Mrs. Sager watched him turn abruptly on his heel and stride back up the gangplank. The crowd pressed forward again, jabbering threats and curses. But when he brought the woman and the girl down the gangplank, a lane opened for them. Mrs. Sager frowned as she moved forward with the people around her. The frown vanished when she saw that the lane was blocked by the strapping frame of Sergeant Pritchard.

"Stand out the way!" the white man ordered.

Without moving the black grinned.

"You ain' yeddy de law 'bout Secesh button, lootenan'? You ain' know you ain' allow fuh wear'um?"

Black fingers closed over a button of the white man's coat and ripped it loose. Mrs. Sager saw a white fist strike out at the black jaw, which did not appear to be even jarred by the blow. When a black fist shot out with a thud, the white man fell back against the crowd and slumped to the ground, where he lay still. Sergeant Pritchard brushed his hands together, spat juicily, and grinned around at the gaping faces. Then the faces pressed in around the fallen man and the woman and the girl, and Mrs. Sager was unable to see what was going on.

Someone was forcing an opening in the crowd. Robert Fenwick, Mrs. Sager recognized. He was pushing the crowd back from the woman and the girl and the fallen man, over whom Sergeant Pritchard was leaning to pull off more buttons. Robert Fenwick brought the Sergeant to his feet with a blow on the shoulder. The two men stood facing each other, while the crowd stared open-mouthed.

"Dese people is my white folk, Saa'jint."

The grin had disappeared from Pritchard's face. For several moments he eyed Robert Fenwick threateningly. In the end he showed his teeth in a conciliatory grin.

"Jes' you say, Cap'm. Jes' you say."

Mrs. Sager suffered a sharp disappointment as she watched Robert Fenwick help the Rebel officer to his feet and lead him and the woman and the girl out through the crowd to the alleyway and from there to the street. The crowd yielded a quick path for the Captain of the *Indigo,* and the clamor fell.

Mrs. Sager was unable to make her way to the street in time to see the close of the incident; she was informed that Robert Fenwick had taken his white folks off in a carriage. She looked around for Alec and Phyllis, but they were nowhere in sight.

They, with a band of children and dogs, were following the carriage that Robert had commandeered. He was driving fast, so fast that by the time the carriage passed the brick wall of St. Helena's churchyard Phyllis had to hold up her skirt and run like a boy. She was even with Alec and only a little behind the carriage when it reached their house. There she watched Robert scatter the children and dogs, but when he took the buckra into the house and upstairs, she hung back and stayed with Alec listening in the lower hall. The excitement that had keyed her up to facing Stephen Fenwick on the wharf had subsided.

In the room upstairs Stephen treated his cut and swollen lip at the washstand. He heard Robert say to his mother:

"Anyt'ing you wish, Miss Sophie?"

"No, Robert. Thank you."

"T'ank you, my missie. I bring up some suppuh direc'ly, ma'm."

It was a conversation out of the dead past. When the door closed, Stephen turned and went to the window, holding his ragged handkerchief to his lip and avoiding his mother's eyes. Outside, across the street, stood a group of niggers staring at the house and talking. When one of the group discovered him and pointed, he drew back out of sight.

Eugenia wanted to see his lip.

"It's all right, Sis," he said, pushing her away.

"Stephen," his mother's voice came, "what is Robert doing here in the Prestons' house?"

"He says he owns it."

When he looked at her, her face made him wince. Absorbed in his own misery he had not looked behind the calmness with which she had met him two days before in Charleston and which she had preserved up to this moment. Her nerve had not failed when she had embraced him, nor when they had spoken of the death of his father and brother. Not even the reception at the wharf had seemed to shake her. But now at last control was breaking down in her voice and her stricken eyes, and he had to look away.

"Stephen, is there nothing we can do about Marshlands?"

He shook his head.

"What is there to do? We're no worse off than the rest. Every house in town is in the hands of carpetbaggers or niggers. We're lucky to have a place to lay our heads."

Her voice came quick and tense:

"We can't stay here."

His nerves frayed to exasperation answered: "Where can we go—

St. Helena's graveyard?" But when he met her eyes his throat tightened, and he said gently, "Mother, we'll have to stay here tonight. Tomorrow I'll see what we're going to do next."

He persuaded her to lie down on the bed. She lay with open eyes following his restless movements around the room. He avoided looking at her, fearing the sinking feeling that took hold of him when he saw that face unveiled now in all its wretchedness.

He let Eugenia cover the buttons left on his coat with pieces of stocking. Later Robert brought up a candle and generous helpings of cold meat and cheese, bread and butter, milk and jam, more food than was left in the world. Stephen could have eaten ten times his share: but not even the food he begged or borrowed in his dreams could ever fill the void, the gnawing emptiness he had carried through the last months of the War.

After supper Eugenia lay down beside her mother, and Stephen spread his army blanket on the floor and lay down too. But it was still light, and anyway his nerves were on fire, sleep was hopelessly out of reach. Finally he got up and went to the window: the street was empty now. When he was sure his mother and sister were resting, he put on his hat and went downstairs. In the hall he met Robert. Their eyes exchanged an old understanding, and Stephen held out his hand. Then he turned quickly to the door.

"I'm going out for a while," he said over his shoulder.

As he closed the door he heard Robert say: "Bettuh keep shy of Bay Street, Maus' Steve."

He walked to St. Helena's first, through the gathering dusk. It was hard to believe, standing here by the gates to the quiet old church, that so much had disappeared and was gone forever. Once he had been baptized here, held in his mother's arms. As a boy he had known this place through a chain of Sundays that had seemed then unbreakable. It was only yesterday that Aunt Isabel had been married here. Then the Bombardment and the last services, himself praying to get into the War before it was all over. If these things were true, could it also be true that he was standing here now like this?

He turned away and followed the dark side street that led to the Bay. The big rambling Heyward mansion at the corner was brightly lighted. There was a sign over the familiar iron-lace gate: *Sea Island Hotel*. Stephen stared at the sign and then at the house. There were voices and the forms of people on the wide double piazzas, the piazzas where he had played so often with the Heyward boys, whose bodies were rotting now in the Wilderness. Obeying a sudden blind impulse, he stepped in the gateway and walked through the garden. He avoided the long flight of steps to the second-story piazza, and went in the door to the ground floor. It was a big billiard room now with a bar at one end. There were plenty of Yankees, but the lamps had green shades that confined the light to the tables and he could keep his uniform from being noticed by staying in the shadows.

He moved over to a chair by a table in a dark corner near the bar. The next table was vacant, but there was a circle of men sitting and standing around the table beyond. He listened through a haze of exhaustion to the Yankee voices in the cigar smoke.

"I tell you," one voice was saying to the accompaniment of a fist banging on the arm of a chair, "Port Royal is the greatest harbor on the coast! You can't beat it. What it needs is Northern capital and push to make it the biggest proposition this side of New York. Why it'll be a gold mine to the fellers that get in on the ground floor."

He listened, feeling somehow detached from his body and wondering what it was doing here: it didn't even have the price of a drink. He gripped the arms of his chair to steady himself. Two men came over and sat down at the vacant table. He was about to get up and move away toward the door when he heard the word "Marshlands".

"Chase is staying there," one of the men said. "Know him? Great man. Hey, Mack!"

A man in an apron was coming around from behind the bar. Stephen sat rigid with his chin sunk in his coat collar. When the waiter had taken the order from the next table, he came over.

"What'll you have, sport?"

"Nothing just yet," Stephen mumbled without looking up.

The waiter sucked a tooth and slapped the table with his napkin.

"These tables is reserved for customers, mister."

The waiter went over to the next table. Stephen could hear his whisper to the men. He could feel their eyes on him now. He dragged himself to his feet and walked along the wall to the door, voices and laughter pursuing him. Outside in the darkness of the lawn he got his breath back and hurried to the gate.

Marshlands, he kept saying over and over to himself. He took back streets to avoid the lights and crowd of Bay Street. There were stars, and a cool breeze coming in from the sea. In the dim light all the change in the places along the way was softened. He could almost feel that he was going home after supper at the Heywards', back in the old days.

As he approached the gates to Marshlands he made out the shape of a sentry-box. He stopped short, then walked on slowly; there was no-one in sight. He stole through the old gateway and skirted the lawn, keeping close to the shrubbery of the side garden. There were lights in the windows of the house. A party seemed to be going on. In the middle of the front lawn where the flower-bed used to be was a flagpole, and he went over and stood by it, looking at the house. He could see people moving around inside and hear their voices. Two figures, a man and a woman, stood at one of the windows long enough for him to see that the woman was white and the man a nigger.

He turned away from the house and walked in a daze to the sea-wall. The tide was high, lapping along the wall. The wind made the same old rustling in the palmettoes. This was the sound he had dreamed of at endless homesick camp-fires. It seemed the same, yet it was heart-sickeningly changed, this rustling. It was mockery. It was whispering Yankee voices and derision. It was defeat and despair.

He went out on the plankway over the marsh to the boat landing. He stretched out on the flooring, and peered down over the edge at the tide, sliding by with streaked reflections of stars.

His jaw ached dully. That was final ignominy. . . . He remembered the first nigger he had seen in a Yankee uniform. That had symbolized the end of the world into which he had been born. What was left? Not even despair, really. Only the necessity to go on living, to keep on breathing and moving in a world of dishonor.

He became conscious again of the tide sliding under him and of the tranquil song of tree-frogs and crickets on shore. Gradually he recalled where he was and got wearily to his feet. He balanced his way back over the narrow planks to the seawall and the lawn. Voices from the porch startled him, and he made for the dense shadows of the garden. Stumbling along the dark paths past the old summer-house with its heavy canopy of wistaria leaves, he came out near the gates and hurried into Fenwick Street.

Early the next morning he made a bundle of the remains of his army kit and set out for Land's End. Part of the kit he bartered at the ferry steps for a batteau across to the Ladies Island shore, and the rest went in exchange for the use of a tacky mare to some niggers who were occupying the old Whitehall place near the landing. The little horse was half starved and her gait was miserably uneven, so he made no attempt to hurry her up.

His eyes, half shut against the glare of the sandy road, were alert to everything along the way. Some of the great fields were green with young cotton plants, but many were broken up into random patches of corn and peas and yams, and not a few were brown with the stalks of last year's cotton or abandoned to broomstraw. Evidently the Yankee speculators were finding it difficult to cope with free nigger labor. No signs of the old system: only a scattering of listless workers, mostly women, who stopped to lean on their hoes and gaze at him. The gang and the task and the driver were gone, and the golden age with them.

But the world of nature was still left, to put some heart into a man. Still the sun and the blue sky, so surprisingly blue and peaceful, and the good soil, and the woods already fragrant with bay blossoms and heavy with the foliage of summer. Here was soft air breathing from the sea. Pines and palmettoes again, the old oaks, roadside thickets of cassena and myrtle tangled with smilax and honeysuckle. The brave whistle of a cardinal, the lilting extravaganza of a mocking-bird, the lusty bullyings of jays and the rapid tappings of woodpeckers,—these were more than welcome homes: they were challenges to courage. Take heart, take heart. Even the buzzards circling high above the trees were reassuring, heartening, because they were part of home now and not the scavengers of defeat.

When he reached the causeway that crossed the marsh between Ladies Island and St. Helena, he had lost himself in the sights and sounds and smells that went back to earliest memories. Sometimes the family had gone from Beaufort to the plantation by water, but more often the trip had been made by land because of his mother's preference. This passage over the causeway had always been a leading event of the journey, for here was the place to spot a white heron, which counted ten points in the bird game Rusty had invented. Everyone had joined in that game, even Father.

Now the marsh plains to the right and left were empty. Only the maniacal mirth of willets and the screams of laughing gulls. The game was ended. Father at least would never play it again. Nor Larry. Nor all the others who were gone. Not even Rusty, who must be gone too, since there was no word of him.

At Frogmore Crossroads, beyond the causeway, there was a sharp reminder of changed times: ox-carts, mules, and tackies in the yard of a big cheap-looking new store, niggers chattering and sunning themselves out front. A continuous movement in and out of the doorway; from the crowded interior loud voices and a strong odor of rum. He gave the place as wide a berth as possible, keeping his little mare on the far side of the road, but his uniform attracted quick attention. A shout went up from the doorway, and those inside came crowding out to see. He was aware of a white man with a cigar in his mouth and a straw hat on the back of his head standing among the blacks. That voice stood out from the general laughter.

"Hey, General Lee, where you goin'? Desertin'? Or only jest retreatin'?"

The white voice was swallowed up in a hubbub of black laughter.

He rode on, eyes stinging, blood pounding at his temples and neck. Sweat came out on his brow, and his hand shook so he could hardly hold the rope reins. Beyond the store he turned the tacky off on the road to the right. The voices and laughter fell away behind then. When he was out of sight, his head drooped and his body slumped in the saddle.

He looked down at the dirty worn edge of his left cuff where the still livid scars of the stump of his wrist showed. He was back in the earthworks at Petersburg looking at his left hand and the bits of shrapnel imbedded all through the quivering flesh. "It ain't bad," he was saying to someone. The hardest part was trying not to faint. Then the stinking hospital tent and seeing his hand thrown into a bucket, like some loathsome piece of refuse.

"Still got your shaking and drinking hand, Fenwick," the hard-worked surgeon had grinned for him.

He looked at his right hand with the reins between the lean fingers. One of the fingers was loosely encircled by the great-grand-father seal ring, all that was left of the missing hand. All that was left, in fact, of that earlier Stephen Fenwick's great domain.

To forget himself he held his attention on his ancestor, whom he always visualized as a portrait, static like a stuffed bird. The old bird had been very much alive in his day, no doubt. It was he who had laid out this very road, before the British had come to ravage the Sea Islands in the Revolution. But that other Rebellion and those Rebels, all that seemed remote and unreal, like history; only the road survived, and the love of nature that had made these numerous twistings and turnings to spare fine specimens of trees. Some of them, youths in those days, were gnarled old giants now. Others had vanished, leaving deviations that seemed without logic.

From time to time he passed small groups of island people on foot or in ox-carts, all going his way. These were civil: they drew aside promptly to give him a free road. He was puzzled where they were headed till he reached the clearing in the woods where the little white chapel stood. Here a large crowd was gathering. He braced himself for another ordeal, but he was allowed to pass in silence. He only felt hundreds of eyes, staring at him from the space under the trees where his family had met other planter families for worship.

He rode on grimly, pondering what the mass-meeting was for. The people he passed now were all coming his way. A few wore the remnants of their last allotment of denim, but the majority were gotten up in the tawdry finery of Freedom. He found mirthless amusement in some of the more outlandish costumes. Sometimes he recognized a face from one of the neighborhood plantations. Sometimes, though seldom, a woman stopped to curtsy and mutter respects or a man removed his hat to pull wool.

Opposite the gateway to the Habersham place he met Isaac, the driver at Land's End, with his wife Leola and an assortment of children. Four years had made no visible change in this powerful gingerbread nigger who had held such a high place in plantation affairs. Then he had been a figure to be propitiated for purposes of adventure: he had held the key to many important locks beside the storehouse, symbol of his position. Now he was a staring stranger, and perhaps another enemy. Yet there was no passing him by without a word.

"How are you, Isaac."

The man's stare gave way to astonishment.

"Who dat? Great King!" A broad grin showed strong white teeth and Isaac snatched off his hat. "Maus' Steve, I sway to Gawd

I ain' replace my young maussa! Leola, ain' you know Maus' Steve when you shum? You blin', 'oman?—make you' mannuh! An' you chillun—pull you' foot!"

There was a great bowing and scraping from Leola and her offspring. The woman had acquired a resplendent dress and turban made from material that bore a striking resemblance to the curtains at Land's End; but she had lost some of the fat that had made her pregnancies such marvels of inflation, when she had worked as assistant cook in the plantation kitchen.

"How are you, Leola?" Stephen said to her.

"T'ank Gawd fuh life suh," she simpered. Her teeth were showing but her eyes were sullen.

Isaac left his family at the side of the road and came close.

"Maus' Steve, I too glad fuh see you come home suh! When fus' I look 'pon you, I ain' replace my young maussa, he done got so man-size fuh true. But when I look two-time, my haa't jumpup in my t'roat say, Bless Gawd!—he sho is change, but t'ank Gawd he ain' dead!"

"Everything's changed now, Isaac."

"Ain' I know, suh. When I t'ink how t'ing stan', I too shame. Free nigguh ain' fuh *lick*—free nigguh ain' fuh *dribe*—free nigguh ain' fuh *nutt'n!* Nigguh same like 'oman an' dawg ain' *wut* widout lick. Ain' you know dat, suh?"

"You're almost as out of place in this new freedom as I am, Isaac. Where all you people heading for?"

"Well suh, dey habin' a meetin' fuh yeddy de Chief Jestish of de U. S."

"On a junket to tell you poor niggers you can do as you please, I suppose."

Isaac grinned. "Maus' Steve suh, to tell de trut' dem Yankee people ain' onuhstan' we nigguh nohow. T'ings is goin' pure bad to Lan's En'."

"Yankees there?"

"Yas *suh*. Yankee been comin' an' goin' sense de gunshoot to Bay P'int. Dey done take ebery Gawdbless house 'pontop de oilan', 'scusin' Cherokee. Nigguh got dat. When Maus' Rusty come bock las' week——"

"Rusty! Is he—back?"

131

"Yas *suh!*"

He forgot all the questions he had to ask Isaac. He took hasty leave, prodding the tacky into a trot and finally a gallop.

But it seemed to take ages to reach the old tabby gateposts of Cherokee. And in the cool shady avenue the tacky fell into a stubborn walk, from which there was no rousing her. He stared in amazement at the approaching house. It didn't look like Cherokee: the white paint had completely worn off the wings so they were as gray as the tabby walls of the older middle section. All the blinds were gone, and paper and rags and moss were stuffed in the windows where panes were missing. Most of the trees around the house had disappeared for firewood, and the garden was completely obliterated with weeds. When he came up to the steps of the house and dismounted, he found the front door open. The frame was smudged and filthy. No need to step into the hall to know that proud old Cherokee had become nigger quarters.

There were ugly flashes in the sunshine when he turned away from the door. The engulfment of last night at Marshlands swept back over him, and he felt again the desire to vomit. He sat down on the steps till the sickness passed. . . . When he felt better, he stood up and cupped his hands to give the deer yell that Rusty and he had always used. He listened, then yelled again. His heart thumped when an answer came back, from somewhere off in the direction of the slave quarters. He swung into the saddle and turned the tacky's head that way.

Beyond the deserted street of the Quarter with its rows of tabby cabins, he came to a freshly plowed field, where Rusty's voice became Rusty himself. He was cutting across the new furrows, and Stephen swung out of the saddle and went stumbling to meet him, keeping the stump wrist out of sight. But when Rusty finished shouting Steve at him, pumping his good hand and thumping his shoulders, and got to looking him over to see if he was really all here, it was quickly discovered. He winced then, and felt like letting himself go; but the joy of seeing Rusty again held him in a vise, and all he could do was laugh and jabber.

Finally they went back for the tacky, and sat down in the shade of a chinaberry tree at the edge of the field. The ground around them was strewn with the tiny lavender blossoms of old times, but it was a long hard task getting back there, filling in the gaps that the War had made. Questions were few. Each let the other tell what he could as best he could, till it was all over and done with.

"Let me introduce you to Nellie," Rusty concluded, pointing to a mule in the shade across the field. "I bought her in North Carolina with my last hard cash. She's not much on looks, but she's good company and she carried me home. Well, we sort of carried each other on the home stretch. And now you find us engaged in a little late planting. Very fine for the nerves, and we hope the belly."

He took a cob pipe out of the pocket of his army shirt and regarded the empty bowl regretfully.

"No way of getting the nigs out of the house?" Stephen asked him.

He shook his head. "Not unless you want to touch a match to Government property, by tax default. Fortunately there's the Quarter. You couldn't hire a nig to stay there now. So I've got shelter till I can build myself a lean-to. How about bringing your mother and sister out here?"

"To live in the Quarter?"

Rusty's hand gripped his knee.

"Steve, we're back in the days of the early settlers. With nothing but our wits between us and extinction. We've got to start all over again, from scratch."

"It's hopeless."

"Not by a long shot. Man, I'll have us a crop of corn and cowpeas here before you know it. Meanwhile we'll live like royalty on the fish you catch, with oysters and shrimp on the side. And incidentally, I happen to know a hen that's fixing to lay an egg."

Stephen grinned and listened, taking comfort from Rusty's voice if not from his words. In his clear blue eyes and slow smile was the old contagious spirit that cast out fear. It was useless to be hopeless with Rusty.

When they had talked things out, Rusty unharnessed Nellie from the homemade plow. The mule and the tacky paced along bonily side by side to the Quarter, where he exhibited the one-room cabin he had cleaned up, the pine chair and table and bed he had made, the moss mattress, and the shelf of books he had salvaged from the Big House in return for his medical services after a Sunday night brawl.

"Before long, Steve, we'll have a regular cottage colony here. Like Virginia Springs or Flat Rock."

133

They rode to the avenue by a side path, avoiding the way past the Big House. At the gates they turned to the right and trotted on toward Land's End, making plans.

The neighborhood road came to an abrupt end at a rickety paintless gate, which Stephen was hardly able to recognize as the remains of the trim white gate that used to swing open at the touch of a hand. Now the thing had to be dragged open. A sign on it said: *Private Property—E. S. Philpott.*

"Who in hell is he?" Stephen said.

"A carpetbagger. Isaac tells me he's gone now, busted like the rest by free nigger labor. Seems a treasury agent has sold the whole place to The Philadelphia Freedmen's Aid Society, God bless them. Two Yankee school-marms in the house at present. I don't think they'll object to our looking around, briefly. They're probably at the meeting anyhow."

They rode on in silence between abandoned fields till they came to the house, on a low bluff facing the sparkling waters of Port Royal Sound, where Yankee men-of-war and merchant ships were anchored. The house was in bad shape. Boxes of rose geraniums on the edge of the piazza only added to the general forlornness.

"Would you believe this was home once?" Stephen said bitterly.

Rusty shook his head and puffed at his empty pipe.

As they stood in the front yard studying the house, a wiry young nigger girl came to the door with a broom and big eyes.

"Anybody home?" Rusty asked her.

"Nawsuh."

"You don't need to be scared. We just came to look at the old place."

"Yassuh."

Stephen said: "You're not a Fenwick nigger, are you?"

"Nawsuh. I was b'long to de Fulluhs to Brick House."

"What's your name?" Rusty said.

"Lucy."

"Well, Lucy, how does it feel to be free?"

The big eyes resented that.

"Nawsuh, I ain' no free nigguh. I b'long to Miss Em'ly an' Miss Hayut now. . . . If you leabe you' name, I tell'um you call."

Rusty shook his head. "I'm afraid they wouldn't appreciate the honor."

"All right," Stephen broke in, "let's go. I've had enough."

When they trotted back to the avenue, Rusty had to laugh over Lucy's rejection of freedom, though it only made Stephen curse louder and harder. Then in a patch of woodland before they reached the gate, they turned off into the ditch to let a buggy pass. Rusty tipped his hat.

"Who's that?" Stephen asked him when they were back on the road.

"Lucy's Miss Em'ly and Miss Hayut, I suppose. The Yankee school-marms."

"Yankee bitches. Do you have to tip your hat to them?"

Rusty flicked an overhanging branch with his hand.

"I suppose they mean well," he said. "Notice the younger one? Right pretty."

"They're nigger lovers, aren't they? And living at Land's End Isn't that about enough to notice?"

Rusty sighed and let it go at that.

II

EVERY MORNING at Land's End Emily woke to the frenzied chatter of the sparrows that slept in the magnolia outside the room. Their clamor carried her back to childhood: the chestnut tree in front of the house in Boston had always been alive with their chirpings. It was strange to find them here where so much was still unfamiliar.

She lay listening to them till the first red rays of the sun came spilling over the sill of the east window, burning a pattern on the upper wall. That was the signal for stepping out on the bare floor, making a hasty toilet before the crazy mirror of the washstand, and hurrying into clothes. Before she left the room she always had to go back to the bed to give Harriet the long shaking that was necessary to waken her. Harriet looked more helpless than ever in the early morning light: pale eyes blinked up from sleep with childlike bewilderment. It was hard to realize that this woman had been teaching among the freedmen for three years. Harriet Sheppard had left a home of luxury in Philadelphia to embark on this pioneer work. How she had been able to stick it out was a mystery.

In the wide upper hall there was a door that opened on the upper piazza and Emily liked to stop there on the way downstairs. This house had a much finer view than Marshlands, there was more than river and marsh to see from the double piazzas that extended around three sides. To the west lay the broad Sound with the far shore almost lost in the haze of distance. To the east were marshes and small islands of scrub growth and a stretch of tidewater called Station Creek, with long barrier islands beyond. But to the south lay the great sight: the high ground of the house sloped out to a marsh flat and the mouth of Station Creek, and beyond that was the silver tip of Bay Point, the white foam of breakers, and the blue ocean. Sometimes when the wind was right it brought the faint boom of surf on the beach. Opposite Bay Point, across the mouth of the Sound, was the Government supply base of Hilton Head with its ships riding at anchor. So the house stood facing the sea and flanked by the Sound and the Station Creek inlet, with its back to the wide fields and woodlands of the plantation. This was Land's End, and its beauty increased with each day that she knew it.

The house itself, as well as the site, was different from Marshlands. It was apparently older than the Beaufort house and simpler in design and finish: four rooms upstairs and four down, all square and plain of trim. If it had ever had a garden and lawns, no trace of them remained. But at the edges of the yard were tall oleanders with pink blossoms that swayed enchantingly in the sea wind, and dour Spanish bayonets that held surprising blooms, big white flower clusters that stood out against the horizon. Behind the house orange and lemon trees, pear and fig, made a little orchard. For the rest, only the bare ground under the veteran live-oaks and magnolias and cedars, ground swept clean of old leaves and tatters of moss by Lucy's industrious switch-broom.

Lucy was the third member of the household. She was a scrawny girl, pure black like most of the islanders, but her features were good and she was exceptionally willing and bright. She had appeared at Land's End several weeks after Emily had come from Beaufort. The moment had happened to be crucial: the Philpotts, with whom Harriet had been living since her arrival on the island, were leaving the plantation in disgust. After a three-year struggle to show a profit with the labor of freedmen who worked when they felt like it, and never worked when they had any money, Philpott had been forced to admit failure to the Northern syndicate employing him. The syndicate had directed him to sell the land to the people; but the people, waiting for their forty-acres-and-a-mule, had refused to buy at any price. In the end the syndicate had considered itself lucky to dispose of the property at a nominal sum to Miss Sheppard and the Philadelphia Aid Society. On the eve of the Philpotts' departure, Emily had agreed with Harriet that it was a good time to get a new cook: Leola, Isaac's wife, was a terror. Then Lucy had appeared, applying for work. Harriet had shrunk from the task of dismissing Leola, so it had devolved on Emily. Leola had quit, but not without spoils and a promise to cut Lucy's throat for her. The next day Isaac had come to register a polite protest, but Emily had held firm. Lucy was installed.

She spoke the modified Gullah of a sea-island house servant: Emily had heard her whole story the day of her arrival. She had refugeed with her buckra, a St. Helena family, in Camden. When Sherman had come through, she had followed the army for a while; when she had finally turned back, her buckra had disappeared off the face of the earth. Like a stray dog she had somehow made her way back to the place of her birth. But the plantation was in the hands of Yankee men and she was afraid to go near the Big House. Exhausted and half starved she had presented herself at Land's End.

Emily had had to nurse her back to health before she could be much help around the house. She was still very thin, but her strength had returned. She had little to say, expressing her gratitude by energetic work, and by attaching herself to Emily, even insisting on sleeping in the same room. In her old home, she explained, she had always slept in her young mistress's room: she felt "curious" sleeping in a room by herself. So every night she spread her pallet, an old tick stuffed with moss, at the foot of the bed in which Emily slept with Harriet, who also disliked the idea of sleeping alone.

Lucy had breakfast well started by the time Emily came down. The Philpotts had discarded the kitchen-house in the yard and converted one of the back rooms into a kitchen. While Lucy was busy over the stove, Emily set the table in the dining-room. Harriet never appeared till everything was ready. Then she would come tripping down, fresh and dainty in starched white piqué.

Since the departure of the Philpotts it was Emily's first duty each day to drive Harriet in the buggy to her school at Cherokee plantation. Harriet was deathly afraid of horses, so Emily had taken lessons from Isaac in managing Garibaldi, an old army steed, world-weary but capricious.

Sometimes at Cherokee they saw "Maus' Rusty" Stewart, who Isaac said was a doctor, and the Fenwicks, who had come to live with him in the slave cabins. According to Isaac the Fenwicks were former owners of both Marshlands and Land's End, so their hostility was easy to understand. Stephen Fenwick, a tall lean young man, darkly handsome, always had a fine long glare for the passing buggy, while his mother and sister merely turned their backs. For some reason lanky Dr. Stewart, a homely but nice-looking man, always tipped his hat and spoke.

"Why do you notice him," Harriet had once said. "Just look straight ahead, the way I do. He's only being sarcastic. They all hate us like poison."

"I don't blame them," Emily had answered.

"Don't blame them?"

"Of course not. Do you?"

"I despise them. All Southerners."

But then one day something had happened to modify her despising, in his case at least. Garibaldi had shied at some washing hung on the branches of a tree near the cabins, and Dr. Stewart, who was hoeing a patch of young corn nearby, had come running to their assistance. Under his hand the horse had steadied at once. Harriet had been compelled to admit there was nothing sarcastic about that friendly act, and from then on she had acknowledged his salute with a gracious nod.

Each morning when Emily got back to Land's End after taking Harriet to Cherokee, she unharnessed the horse at the stable and walked the half-mile along a woodland lane to the clearing where her own little school stood. Harriet's school, a remodeled cotton barn, was the largest of the five on the island. Emily's was the decrepit plantation praise-house.

The children were always there waiting, but she kept them outside till she had opened the blinds, aired the strong little room, and dusted the benches and the pine pulpit that was her desk. Then with the bell the children came tumbling in like monkeys. The first day there had been an inrush of dogs, too, and several of the older girls had brought their infant charges. The dogs had been banned on the second day when she had felt a little more confidence, and the babies and pot-bellied pickaninnies had been left outside in the shade of a mulberry tree in the care of alternate nurses.

With the final bell the class came to some semblance of order. Then the day's struggle began with the inevitable confusion of the roll-call. Some few of these Land's End children had been to school at Cherokee, but to most of them school was a new and dazzling experience. Many of them never seemed to be sure of their names in the excitement; many changed names from day to day. And all the black faces and appealing eyes had looked so much alike at first that she had despaired of ever learning to tell them apart.

The presence of some of the mothers on the opening day had helped her to make a beginning.

"What's your name?" she had smiled at the first child.

A finger in mouth and a wide stare had been the only answer. But a voice from one of the elders standing at the back of the room had come to the rescue.

"You yeddy what de lady ax, enty? You ain' know you'-own title, tittie? Shuh! He name Annie K, ma'm. Pull you' foot, chile, an' show you' mannuh!"

With infinite pains the names had been drawn from the benches. Very few were as simple as Annie K. There were Limus and Clinch, Hacklus and Gib, Weenia, Cully, Mona; there was a Hamlet, a Pontius Pilate, and a Cleo. Emily had finally got them all down. But the next day, with the parents absent, the roll-call had fallen into chaos. Now, at last after weeks, the thing had taken on some stability, yet it was still far from foolproof: there were always hesitations and lapses of memory. After the trials of the roll-call came the exultant singing of the ABC's, a happy and easy interlude in the drudgery of the morning. Then the complicated agonies of Gullah reading, writing, and arithmetic.

But the greatest trials came with the afternoon school. Then the grown-ups of the plantation assembled at the praise-house to "catch a lesson", and many of the children came back too: every bench was jammed, all standing-room taken, and some of the pupils were compelled to take their lessons through the windows. The roll-call of this afternoon class almost drove her to distraction. In the beginning all the grown-ups had given their names as Mr. or Mrs. Fenwick; in Freedom they had appropriated the name of their former owner and were loth to return to plain Dolly and Sam or even to such proud titles as Shadrach and Josephine, London and Venus.

Most of the class had not known at first what a book was or how to hold it. They were pathetic in their eagerness and in the faith they had in the miracle of book-learning, which they seemed to believe would put them in the position of their former masters. Often stalwart man and wife stood together, staring intently at the First Reader held in their clumsy hands. They scratched their heads if they were unable to get a word, but if successful they laughed and nudged each other. Most of the elders were harder to teach than their children, who mocked their efforts.

"Shut you' mout', boy, 'fo' I shut'um fuh you! 'Scuse me, Miss Em'ly, but da' boy bex me tummuch."

Something was always happening in this afternoon class. Once it was a mysterious peeping sound that sent the whole room, young and old, into suppressed giggles, till Emily located a brood of chicks concealed in one woman's ample bosom.

"Warmint an' t'ing gwine t'ief'um ef I lef'um home, Miss Em'ly ma'm."

But even without dramatic happenings, it was almost impossible to keep order. The most effective method was to set the whole class to writing, for which it was necessary to kneel before the benches and use the seats for desks. In this position and absorbed in making letters on their slates the class was reasonably quiet.

On the way South she had pictured herself gently instructing a class of neat black cherubs. But she was grateful to the Land's End people as they were, grateful for their infectious laughter and the trouble they gave her, the way they used her up and left no time or will for thoughts of herself. This island world of peace and hard work stood like a bulwark between her and that other treacherous world.

When she had first come to Land's End she had felt nothing. Then she had wakened to a period of pain so sharp that she had thought she was going mad. But finally the pain had burned down to a flat nervelessness, a ceaseless dull ache, to which there was no answer beyond movement, doing the next thing. The part of her that was not dead, the part that mattered least, was moving without purpose or hope, moving mechanically through this routine. This getting up with the sun and driving Harriet to Cherokee, going through the duties of school and fetching Harriet in the late afternoon, eating, sleeping, and getting up again.

❧   ❧   ❧

So these days of June moved by. The first memorable blooms of the magnolias had opened back in May and now some of the cupped petals were falling into slippery brown decay on the ground, to be swept away by Lucy's yard-broom. The pomegranate bushes at the side of the house had lost their orange-red flowers. But the blossoms on the graceful stems of the oleanders were endless. And now a delicate pink mist enveloped the hard sinewy limbs of the crepe-myrtles by the stable. The lane to school was fragrant with honey-suckle and gay with trumpet-vine, and the little porch of the praise-house was covered with morning-glory. Blackberries and sparkle-berries had been ripe for weeks, and on the last day of the month Lucy brought in the first figs for breakfast.

At the supper hour that day Isaac's boy Tunis, returning from the island post-office in the store at Frogmore Crossroads, brought a letter from Aaron, the first word she had had from him since she had left Marshlands.

"I have kept my promise," it said in his fine strokes, "to leave you to yourself for a time. And I should have continued to hold my silence a while longer, waiting some communication from you, were it not for a circumstance that has arisen. Secretary-of-War Stanton is here with us and wishes to visit a representative school on St. Helena. I am sure Miss Sheppard will be pleased to hear that we have decided on her school for this honor. Kindly inform her that she may expect us about ten o'clock tomorrow morning. If convenient we should like to go on to Land's End for the midday meal, stopping on the way to see your school. We shall return to Beaufort in the early afternoon.

"I hope there will be an opportunity for private conversation with you. It is my prayer that I shall find you improved and in a receptive frame of mind. Obviously we can't go on like this.

"Your husband, Aaron."

Next morning she went to the praise-house school with nerves sharpened to panic by a sleepless night.

It was almost noon before she caught a glimpse from her desk of General Sager's surrey arriving. The figures coming through the sunshine toward the open door made her knees weak when she got up to walk down the aisle between the rows of benches.

Mrs. Sager came in first. She gave Emily a quick peck on the cheek and went rustling up the aisle, hands folded at waist, eyes ranging the benches. General Sager, perspiring freely and more nervous than usual, shook hands, mumbled a greeting in his beard, and followed his wife. Harriet came next, wearing her sweetest expression. Then Emily met Aaron's eyes.

"Secretary Stanton," he was saying, "this is my wife."

Stanton was distinguished and lively. "Mrs. Moffet," he smiled and bowed, "this is a pleasure indeed." Walking up the aisle he said to her: "Your husband tells me you are so engrossed in your work that you quite neglect him!" He laughed pleasantly. "Well, it's a splendid work. Splendid. How many pupils have we here?"

She found it a great relief to say something. "Thirty-five. In the afternoon class about seventy-five."

"You don't say so! Splendid."

When she reached her desk, she gave the staring class the signal to rise. The National Anthem was disposed of with small success: she had to carry most of it alone. Nevertheless, Stanton pronounced it very good. He understood, he said, that the children were naturally a little timid before visitors.

"Now, Mrs. Moffet, may I put one or two questions to your class? How far advanced are they in arithmetic?"

"Not one can count beyond ten. I haven't even been able to teach them their left hand from their right yet."

Mrs. Sager exchanged a glance with Aaron. General Sager blinked. Stanton's eyebrows lifted.

Harriet rushed into the breach. "Mrs. Moffet," she explained, "has had the school only a very short time."

"I see. Of course. Well, let me put some questions to test their general knowledge. Children, who wrote the Constitution of our re-United States?" After beaming at the class for an expectant minute, he repeated the question. "Can any child tell me who wrote the Constitution?"

"Perhaps," he appealed to Mrs. Sager, "the question is a little advanced here on the island."

"It shouldn't be," she flashed. "If they don't know the answer to that, it's high time something was done about it." She pointed at a boy in the front row: "Young man, who wrote the Constitution that guarantees our freedom? . . . Come, come, speak up."

The only answer was a frozen stare. Mrs. Sager picked out an older boy.

143

"Moses," he gasped at her finger.

"Sit down! Next."

"Uncle Abe Linkum!"

"Next!"

"Gen'l Saguh suh."

The General blinked solemnly at the offender. "Know what the Constitution is, my boy?"

"Yas ma'm,—nawsuh!"

"Perhaps," the General whispered to his wife, "you better make it the Declaration of Independence."

"Not at all," she snapped back. "Next!"

But there were no more answers of any description. Mrs. Sager was very provoked now. "For important elementary questions like this," she told Emily, "you should have the answers on a blackboard or on cards on the wall, the way we do in the Beaufort schools. Can your pupils read anything for Secretary Stanton?"

The class came through the reading of *Little Red Riding Hood* with surprising success. Harriet looked relieved, Mrs. Sager and the General nodded approval, and Stanton smiled benevolently. He gave the children a little talk on growing up to be splendid useful men and women, good citizens, worthy of freedom. When the class was dismissed, he went to the door to shake the hand and pat the head of each child. Mrs. Sager stood beside him and distributed little Star-Spangled-Banners that she had brought with her. Outside, where some of the parents had gathered to see the visitors, the children forgot their shyness completely in the fun of waving the flags and shouting.

Harriet and Mrs. Sager, Stanton and the General rode on to the house in the surrey, while Aaron stayed to help her close the school for the day. When they left and were walking side by side through the sun-patched shadows of the lane, her cheeks were burning and her ears ringing as she waited for him to speak.

"Emily," he began finally, "I want you to come back to me."

The gentleness of his voice, so different from the abrupt cold tone of his note, took her by surprise and for a moment robbed her of the reply that came to her mind.

"Sager," he went on to say, "has been appointed district director of the new Freedmen's Bureau, with headquarters in Charleston. I am to remain here as his assistant. Marshlands will be ours in a few days—I have arranged to take it over. It will be our home, Emily, when you come back."

She took a quick breath to answer him. "I can't. I'm sorry, but it's impossible."

"But we can't go on like this, living apart."

The possible truth of that only made her voice more tense.

"Why can't we? I have my work here and my salary. I don't ask anything from you but just to be let alone."

He sighed deeply.

"You may still feel that way, Emily, but it won't last forever. The only way we can hope to be made whole again is by mutual forgiveness, by ending this separation and working things out together. There must be a final humbling of pride for both of us. It may seem like bitterest expiation at first, but in time I know we shall find ourselves closer than we could ever have been without this ordeal. . . . Yes, God has chastened us to strengthen our lives for His work. He joined us together to live for Him till death. It was His will, Emily, and our promise."

She was shaking so now that she could hardly keep up with him.

"I'm sorry, Aaron," she told him, trying to keep her voice steady. "It's no use. I'm not going back. It wouldn't help either of us."

It was long moments before he spoke again. They were in sight of the house when he finally said:

"Emily, don't ask me to go on living like this without you. It doesn't matter what you've done, I can never stop loving you, never. All I ask now is that you forgive me, for anything I said or did to add to your suffering. There must be something besides bitterness left in your heart. You must give us another chance."

There was such appeal in his voice and words that she was compelled to glance his way for the first time.

"Why do you want me back," she said, feeling his strength against her will. "I should think you'd be glad to be rid of me."

"It will never be that," he sighed, smiling faintly. "But I'd be glad to be rid of this terrible loneliness for you. I don't love the suffering you give me, young Emily. It's you I love, now more than ever."

She stopped then for a moment to meet his eyes directly.

"Aaron. I don't deserve your love or forgiveness. I know that. And I'd do anything I could to make up for the injury I've done. But that's all I can say now. I've got to work things out here alone. There's no other way."

"If that's what you wish," he nodded slowly, in a low voice: "I'm at your mercy, Emily. I certainly can't force you to come back, and I see it's no use telling you how badly I need you, begging you to come back. I'll just have to live on hope, and prayer."

They walked on to the house in silence.

III

WITH THE closing of the island schools the heat began to deepen in earnest. And this was not the heat of Northern summer. It was a vast stunning heat, burning away all energy. It brought clinging dampness to any activity. The house could be kept bearable with closed blinds, though even then heat seeped through the shutters. Outdoors was like the breath of a furnace.

Some nights were made sleepless by swarms of sandflies, tiny but fearful gnats whose acquaintance she had made one sultry afternoon in May. The mosquito-net over the bed was no bar to these pests; they fell like hot sparks on the arms and face, and it was futile to try to keep them off and ridiculous to waste energy killing them. She tried Harriet's scheme of wearing a piece of muslin over her head, but she had to leave an opening for breathing and the sparks invaded her nostrils. Back in May Isaac had said: "San'fly come wid de drumfish. When san'fly gone, skeetuh take chaa'ge." But the sandflies had not gone when the mosquitoes had taken charge; they could be depended on to appear whenever a land breeze was blowing. As for the mosquitoes, no matter how carefully the inside of the netting was inspected before bed, the singing of at least one would come to the ear.

There was some relief in the breeze that came in from the sea at the turn of the tide. With it the leaves and branches of the trees stirred to a semblance of life, and the pines in the grove beyond the stable whispered mockingly of the great winter winds that now seemed so desirable. Sometimes in the afternoon majestic thunderheads towered up from the south, bringing the brief refreshment of a shower. Thunder and lightning were terrifyingly close here: the tremendous flashes and crashes were just outside the house. When the rain was over, Land's End was cool and green for a few hours. Then the feverish monotone of the locusts, spirit of heat, came stinging back and the sky was again the ceiling of inferno.

"If I'd only gone North as I intended," Harriet kept sighing. "No Northerner should stay in this climate the year round. That's what ruined the Southerners, who came from just as good stock as we did in the beginning."

One day Emily's overwrought nerves asked: "Well, why didn't you go North, Harriet?"

"Oh, I couldn't leave you here alone. But I'll never stay another summer. And you mustn't either, you must come home with me. . . . Oh dear, I keep forgetting about your husband. I don't know what I'd ever do without you now, but we mustn't plan ahead, must we. You may be leaving me as suddenly as you came."

If it were only possible to see anything but memory ahead, Emily thought. If these flames of heat would consume the past and leave the future free. If she could only forget, even for an hour, her husband Aaron, wronged and forgiving, patient, waiting.

Letters came from him regularly now. They were invariably gentle and understanding in tone, healing without straining to be; and presently she began to realize they were undermining her position, weakening her resistance little by little. Slowly, subtly, they were replacing the Aaron of nightmare with the man she had first known.

The earliest of these letters told of trips through the state for the Freedmen Bureau and gave an account of the conditions he found. "Many whites," he wrote, "do not know that they are beaten, and many slaves that they are free. Our work, I fear, has scarcely begun. The movement to uplift the freedmen that we initiated in the Sea Islands is spreading throughout the entire South, but we must fight harder than ever now or the fruits of victory, so dearly bought, will be lost and the sacrifice all for naught."

In August he was canvassing Beaufort County for election to the Constitutional Convention. And finally, in September, he was in Columbia, as delegate for the only Republican county in the state: his letters contained a full report of the proceedings, with descriptions of the Democratic leaders. An attempt had been made to discredit his credentials and disbar him from the Convention hall; but it had failed and he had held his chair, a voiceless observer of the restoration of South Carolina to the Union. The War had broken the strength of Charleston and the Low Country, and now the more liberal and sane Up Country was in control. But for all their repudiation of the old fire-eating elements and their resolutions of loyalty to the Government, they were not to be trusted, they were already scheming to return the freedmen to virtual slavery.

In none of his letters of the summer was there any mention of the situation between them, any pressure or urging, and he never came to Land's End. But he often asked if there was anything she needed or wanted, and though she protested there was not, in her strained little answering notes, presents came just the same: packages of fine tea, material for dresses, a subscription to the Beaufort paper. And finally he sent out by the pilot boat a new style of oil lamp—"To Miss Sheppard with the compliments of an admirer"—which drew from Harriet expressions of frankness as well as delight.

"How thoughtful of him! . . . Really, Emily, I don't see how you resist him. I'm your friend and on your side always, and now that I've found you I only wish we could be together till we're old old ladies, but I must say he does seem a very fine gentleman, and a very exceptional considerate husband. I've only seen him once, of course, but I was very favorably impressed even then. And now what you read me of his letters convinces me all the more that he's a remarkably gifted man, devoted to a wonderful Christian work. . . . You're a very young woman, Emily,—perhaps it takes someone a little nearer his own age to appreciate a man of such unselfish nature. Oh, I know you don't like to talk about it, and I won't say another word. But if I were in your shoes it wouldn't take me long to forget this trouble and make up with him."

It was all true and fair; and she was only proving herself further wrong and prolonging the injury to him by this inability to yield. But that admission didn't help her to unbend in her answers to his letters. She could offer no words of interest in his work that didn't sound stilted and forced: there was a final sense of unworthiness, of failing him completely, in this hopelessness of ever recapturing the feeling of zeal and dedication she had once shared with him. For the rest her notes to him were just scraps of island news, labored little recitals of the incidents that marked the slow passing of the days.

Evenings when the heat was not too prostrating she sat with Harriet in the sitting-room to write him by the light of the lamp he had sent, or to read from the back numbers of *Harper's Monthly* that came in the Aid Society "missionary boxes". Harriet wrote endless letters, but she confined her reading to a well-thumbed copy of *Daily Strength For Daily Living,* from which she liked to read favorite paragraphs aloud. There was small comfort in listening to these readings. The abject resignation of the book and the didactic tone of Harriet's voice combined to create rebellion rather than a state of acquiescence.

But there was comfort in the prayers that she had said since childhood, and comfort in her contacts with the Land's End people. The contacts were much reduced since the closing of school, but the arrival of an Aid Society box always brought the whole plantation flocking, and between times people came to the house singly and in groups to "make manners" and ask favors. Sunday afternoon was the most popular time: it never failed to produce a good-sized delegation, mostly women. Many of them wanted letters written, in the great struggle to locate relatives and friends lost in the mix-up of war times.

Harriet felt that her nerves were not equal to any part of this correspondence work in the enervating heat, so it was all up to Emily. Sometimes, sitting at the dining-room table with the people packed around her, she wrote as many as twenty letters at a stretch, each presenting a highly individual problem. The addresses were often a matter of the wildest guesswork, but even when she knew it was hopeless she wrote the letter anyway and stacked it with the others, knowing what relief it was giving the sender.

"Please, Miss Em'ly, ma'm, tell Cun Millie to Sawannah howdy. Jes' say we is all well t'ank Gawd. An' tell'um don' fuhgit he praise." This from an old man.

Another. A strapping big woman.

"Dis gwine to Quash Stoo't what been in Waltuhbuh las' I hear. Ax'um don' he know de Wo' obuh, an' tell'um come on home."

"Is he your husband?"

"Well, no'm—ain' zac'ly hosban'. I ain' got no tiffity yet. So you mus' talk stiff to'um an' easy, all-two."

Emily wrote to meet these requirements as best she could. When she read the letter over, it received the endorsement of the room. But the big woman was not quite satisfied, and after some hesitation she asked Emily to put in a postscript asking Quash Stewart to excuse the poor writing.

Another letter that Emily remembered well was dictated by a dried-up little woman. She spoke with flashing eyes and gestures as if she were talking directly to the addressee, and her sisters, roused by her fire, spurred her on. The room was like a praise-meeting for a minute or two.

"Mistuh Hacklus Sams to Sams P'int, right-cheer on de oilan'. Do you t'ink I is a peach layin' vaitin' fuh you 'pontop de *groun'*? I is a peach may be, but I sittin' 'pon*top* de tree! Yas Lawd. I ain' fuh drop in you' mout', man, an' you cyan' reach me wid you' han'. If you wan' me you gots to *jumpup!* Tell'um dat straight, ma'm."

But there was one letter that Emily knew she would never forget. It was written for a girl named Mary, a young girl but long gone with child. She refused to say anything with the others in the room, and Emily had to move them out to the piazza. Then Mary began in a slow soft voice.

"Dis fuh Jim Fenwick wid de color regiment to Chaa'son. Please ma'm, talk to'um jes' like you talkin' to you' own man an' you lookin' f'um to come bock an' git marry."

"Well, if you'll just say what comes to you, Mary, I'll write it down."

Mary stared at the paper. Her fingers pulled at her dress.

"Jes' tell'um I cyan' fuhgit'um. Tell'um I stan' jes' like he lef' me, vaitin' f'um. An' if he don' nebbuh come, I be vaitin' f'um still."

Lucy always expressed relief when the Sunday delegation was gone. She carried their presents of an egg or a pat of butter to the kitchen with a scornful expression. One day Emily asked her if she wanted any letters written.

"Who me? No ma'm!" She was giving the room a savage sweeping after the callers. "My fambly all dead an' gone, an' I sho ain' studyin' bout no man like dem crazy 'oman. Uh-uh!"

"Don't you want to try to locate your people, the Fullers?"

"Miss Em'ly, you ain' ought talk so to me. You know good enough I gwine stay right wid you. You my white folks now."

Lucy was the greatest comfort of all through this long summer of heat and depression.

The torpid weeks of August had sulked into the oppressive hazes of September. But at last September too was gone, and with the first cool fresh days of October the schools were reopened. She was driving Harriet to Cherokee again, along the road that still belonged to summer but without the heat and flies and dust. The praise-house school, with its classes for children and grown-ups, was the center of life again. There were new textbooks from the Aid Society, and a large blackboard from Aaron.

After the first frosts the woods began to turn. The color was not so vivid as at the North, there were more evergreen trees and shrubs here, and yet this sea-island autumn seemed more beautiful than any she had known. For her it was a season of returning life rather than an ebbing-away of the year. Pain had burned itself out at last, like a lingering fever finally extinguished, leaving her with an intense eagerness of life, a strong new will to live.

She could not do enough with this revived energy. School no longer exhausted her, and she took a more active interest in the Land's End people. They were in a state of fluster over events whose excitement they caught but whose meaning eluded them. And in trying to answer their questions and explain things to them, she found herself examining critically, for the first time, the rapidly changing conditions that the freedmen were facing. Demoralized by their sudden emancipation, by the cash-money that had poured into hands for their war-time labor and produce, and by their hopes of a fabulous future, it was scarcely surprising that they had lost their bearings and found it hard to adjust themselves to this sober world of peace. Now it seemed the clear responsibility of every white person to help them settle down, but it was becoming clear now that most civilian Northerners were in the South only to stir up and exploit them.

And the army of occupation had very strange tactics for restoring order. All autumn long they kept the island in an uproar. The Georgia freedmen, who had been placed on the various plantations by the Government, were being rounded up like cattle for transportation back to their native state. There were a score of these refugees settled at Land's End, people whom she had helped nurse at the Tabernacle hospital, and they were thrown into a panic when the soldiers searched the plantation. Some came to the house for protection, others hid out in the woods and marsh islands, in a frenzy of fear that they were being taken back to slavery.

Another source of trouble was the St. Helena Protective Union Store, a coöperative enterprise which a group of freedmen had established near the White Church and to which most of the people were contributing their savings. Like the forty-acres-and-a-mule that they were expecting to receive any day now, the store immediately became an excuse for doing no work. Isaac explained about it.

"He operate like dish, Miss Em'ly. You see de Yankee people to Frogmo' sto' an' Beaufort, dey do chaa'ge we tummuch fuh grit an' t'ing. Bellden, we all put in a little money fuh sto' of we-own, an' den we git ration an' t'ing too cheap."

Theoretically the idea seemed sound, but she was beginning to know black nature well enough to foresee disaster. And within two weeks after the opening of the store its shelves had been stripped by rioting shareholders, each of whom felt entitled to unlimited credit. A week later, the treasurer having absconded with surplus funds, the very building itself was divided.

But the greatest source of disturbance was the collapse of the free-land dream. One November day word spread over the island, by the mysterious grapevine telegraph, that General Howard, Head of the Freedmen Bureau, had spoken to a mass-meeting of people on Edisto Island and had advised them to go back to hard work, because the Government was not going to give forty-acres-and-a-mule after all. A cloud fell over the people at Land's End. They stayed away from school, but at night used the praise-house for a "moan" that lasted till morning.

For two days a strange silence hung over the plantation. But on the third day—Thanksgiving—the pall was lifted when word came that General Sager had ordered all the Government land on the island sold to the freedmen for five dollars an acre. Cherokee was included. The Land's End people joined the rush to get choice holdings, and school was forgotten for a week. The store at Frogmore sold hundreds of red-white-and-blue stakes at a dollar apiece, telling the people that they must have them to stake out claims.

In December Aaron's letters began to hint that Christmas at Marshlands would be miserably lonely. Would the ladies at Land's

End have pity and either join him or invite him there? After a con- ference with Harriet, Emily wrote him to come, on Christmas Eve if he wanted to.

He came by boat the afternoon before Christmas. At first she felt an acute restraint with him, but this gradually relaxed under the quiet naturalness of his manner. And it helped her to adjust herself to his presence that he addressed himself largely to Harriet, who was breathlessly sweet for the occasion.

In the late afternoon she went with him to the woods to cut a tree and some evergreen boughs. She set out with misgivings, with a sick fear that he was going to say something that would break the truce between them. But as they walked in the crisp golden sunlight that slanted through the winter woods, he spoke of happy remote things, of Christmases he remembered as a boy on his father's farm in the Connecticut hills: of bringing in the tree with his brothers through snow drifted breast high, boots crunching on the porch, the frosted panes of a sitting-room bright with candles and fire- light. Life had been hard then but good. He talked well of those vanished days, and she found herself sharing his reminiscent smiles.

They came back through the sunset woods loaded with spoils. He dragged the tree, a young slash pine, and a bundle of boughs. Her arms were full of cassena branches, with red berries like holly, and branches of wild olive and bay. When they reached the front yard, the sun, a great ball of fire, was just at the horizon. They left their burdens on the piazza and went to the edge of the bluff: a highway of fire crossed the opalescent waters from the landing at their feet to the far islands where the sun was sinking. When it was gone, they stood watching the afterglow mount up the sky.

When they went into the house, he set up the tree opposite the crackling fire in the sitting-room. After supper he took charge of the decorating, balancing on a chair to reach the upper branches. When the last of Harriet's ornaments had been placed and the tip of the tree crowned with a silver star of Bethlehem, Harriet and Lucy went to bed, while she stayed to talk with him before the fire.

At first a silence stood between them, but when this was once broken they talked freely and without strain. She told him of the troubles of the island people; it pleased her that he listened with close attention, examined her about conditions here, and asked her opinion on the Government's action in the land question. He gave

154

her details of his work in the Beaufort district to protect the rights of the freedmen.

As he talked on about freedmen welfare, she studied his strong earnest profile in the firelight. This was almost the original Aaron. It was late when they banked the fire and said good-night.

In the morning, after breakfast, Aaron handed out the presents that had been placed under the tree. Harriet was all aflutter over a dozen lace handkerchiefs, and all apologies for her poor little present, a pair of common cotton handkerchiefs from the Frogmore store. Lucy was overcome by an envelope containing a shiny five-dollar goldpiece from Santa Claus. Emily watched him with flushed cheeks when he opened her present, a scarf crocheted so badly that she had had to sew up the holes. When she opened the tiny box he put into her hand, she discovered a brooch of carved ivory set in gold. Harriet and Lucy, pressing to see, covered her confusion for a moment with their exclamations, but then she had to face Aaron's smile.

"Don't you like it?" he asked her. "It should be a string of pearls. But try it on anyway."

With awkward fingers she pinned the brooch at her throat, wondering what to say or do beyond blushing thanks with Harriet and Lucy looking on. But later when they went to the kitchen for a minute, she found her voice.

"It's lovely, Aaron, but really I can't accept it."

"Hasn't a man the right to give his wife a small present for his own pleasure? It's not a bribe, Emily."

His eyes were searching hers so deeply now that she was forced to look down. At the sound of steps coming back from the kitchen, he quickly took her hand and led her through the hall to the piazza. There he sat her down on the top step and stood below her, so that their eyes were on the same level.

"Isn't it time yet?" he said gravely. "Marshlands is crying for its mistress to start presiding. And I'm slowly starving to death for you."

She raised her hand in a gesture of appeal. "Please, Aaron. You promised to let me decide."

"I'm sorry," he sighed. "I didn't mean to take advantage of your Christmas hospitality. But the sight of you is too much for me, young Emily."

After a painful moment she said to him:

"Aaron, if we can only get to be sure friends again. That's still all I can tell you."

"Well," he nodded sadly, "that's better than nothing. But it seems I have a special argument for you today. The Freedmen's Bureau is building a fine new school in Beaufort, and I want you to come and teach there. It's a splendid opportunity."

"But I couldn't leave my school here," she said lamely.

"Oh, surely Miss Sheppard could get someone to take your place. Let me speak to her about it."

"No, no, Aaron. She depends on me to stay with her, at least till she goes North."

"But I can easily get a teacher to substitute for you here. Emily, haven't we both suffered enough? Isn't it time to pick up the pieces and start over? I don't ask you to come back to Marshlands as my wife. I'll gladly agree to any conditions you name, if you'll only come back."

She managed to say to him, finally, "I want to try to start over too, Aaron."

The sound of her voice saying that released an urge to say all that was in her mind.

"I didn't till lately. I didn't care. I didn't care what happened."

She stopped abruptly there, her hands clasping her knees tightly. To get the sudden blur out of her eyes she looked beyond him at the waters of the Sound, sparkling serenely in the winter sunlight.

"I understand," he nodded.

Her eyes came back to him then.

"I must be sure of myself for you, Aaron. It mustn't be just because you've been so forgiving and patient, or because you need me or I feel I should, but because I want to. It wouldn't be fair to you any other way, no matter what you say."

He shook his head.

"I want you back on any terms, Emily."

She turned her head with a start to find Isaac and Leola coming across the side yard with their family of ten, all polished, all wreathed in smiles. On the strength of this interruption and as she got up to greet them, she gave Aaron's hand a hasty clasp.

"If you really want me back," she hurried to finish saying to him, "trust me a little longer."

Isaac, hat in hand, was bowing and scraping.

"Chrismus gif', Miss Em'ly," he grinned broadly.

"Chrismus gif'!" piped a shrill chorus of children.

Isaac and family had arrived early, but soon there was a little crowd at the front steps. When most of Land's End was assembled in the yard, the sitting-room blinds were closed and the candles on the tree lighted. While Lucy stood by with enough water in buckets and pitchers to extinguish a conflagration, the people were steered into the house and out again in batches, laden with cornucopias of candy and an assortment of presents from the Aid Society's Christmas box.

After it was over and they were all assembled again at the foot of the steps, Harriet gave them a little talk on the birthday of the Christ child and Aaron said a brief prayer. Then the people showed their appreciation with an old-time spiritual, the grown-ups starting it, the children quickly joining in.

I gwine set at de welcome ta-ble,
I gwine set-at-de-welcome-table-one-dese-days—Halleelooyah!
I gwine set at de welcome ta-ble,
Gwine set at de welcome table one dese days. . . .

Presently Harriet decided that the freedmen's singing was in danger of breaking down into a slavery-time shuffle and "shout", which would never do. She clapped her hands till the other clapping ceased, and then announced sweetly but firmly that the celebration was over.

Her conversational flutterings held Aaron's attention up to and through dinner, and soon after that his boat came for him: he had an afternoon meeting of freedmen to address at the Tabernacle.

When he was gone, and Harriet had finished singing his praises and had gone upstairs to rest, Emily went out for a long walk to try to think.

IV

As THE FIRST WEEKS of the new year firmed toward a month, she knew the time had come. She was whole again, she told herself, and ready to go back to Aaron. But more weeks slipped by, January and February had passed and March was here, and still she hesitated.

In the advancing spring there was a last obstacle to overcome. The swamp maples in the woods along the lane to school were flames of crimson bud: dogwood blossoms were beginning to shine among the dark trunks of trees whose branches were dissolving in mists of green. Saffron tendrils of jasmine were climbing the edges of the woods where judas trees glowed, and the fields were bordered with thickets of wild plum like drifts of snow. At Marshlands, she thought, the camellias by the front steps would be carrying waxen flowers among their glossy leaves. And soon in the closed garden,— azaleas opening in tinted masses, and over the summer-house the mantle of wistaria and banksia rose, fragrant lavender clusters woven with sprays of gold. Every shape and color of this sea-island world, even the air itself, was in conspiracy against her, torturing her with the past. That other spring, so safely far away at Christmas, was striking back full force. . . . Would his eyes linger and his voice echo through all the springs of her life? Was there never to be any final escape?

She saw that she must throw all her will against this tide of memory that was seeking to engulf her, deepening its force with each day. And it was this fear of being carried back to confusion and despair, all the hard-won ground lost again, that roused her to act at last.

The first move was to tell Harriet, and she picked the morning drive to Cherokee as the best time for that. Harriet was immediately tearful. But she was not going to be selfish, she said, and stand in the way by causing any delay. Now that Emily had finally made up her mind, there was to be no waiting for summer and the close of school. No, Harriet insisted she would close the schools and go North now, leaving Emily free to return to her husband at once.

But it was not accomplished quite that easily and swiftly. It took a nerve-racking stretch of days to get things settled. A date was finally set for Harriet's departure—the second of April—and Emily wrote Aaron, but then Harriet decided she would never be able to get off before the fifth. And the date was shifted once again, to the seventh, before everything was actually arranged. Aaron planned the journey for her and got the tickets: she was to go on the *Indigo* to Charleston and take the train from there. She had come from Philadelphia by water, but she would never attempt another ocean voyage no matter how bad the rail connections were. She was in such a fluster that even her packing had to be done for her. All the responsibilities of closing the house were left to Emily.

It was a long day, that last one at Land's End. The worst part was saying good-bye to the people, trying to make them understand that she was only going to Beaufort and would be back often to see them, and that Harriet would be back with another teacher at the end of summer. Taking leave of these island friends, these children and grown-ups who had helped her so, was like casting off moorings for exile, and yet it was an enormous relief when this parting demonstration was over with: almost as great a relief as it would be tomorrow when her return to Aaron was over with. Thoroughly exhausted, she went to bed right after supper, but it was long after the midnight crowing of cocks off at Isaac's cabin before she was able to get to sleep.

It was Isaac's knocking at the kitchen door before dawn that woke her to the fateful day. She had sent word to Aaron that Isaac would bring them to Beaufort in his sailboat. A pale light had begun to steal over the world by the time they had had breakfast and were standing on the piazza, waiting for Isaac to close the last blinds and shut and lock the front door. He handed the key ceremoniously to Harriet, who handed it back to him with reiterated instructions and cautions.

"Yas'm, sho will, Miss Hayut," he grinned. "Don' fret you'self ma'm—I been bo'n an' raise right-cheer in dis yaa'd, an' my maussa always lef' me in chaa'ge, like he paa done wid my paa an' he gran'paa wid my gran'paa. My fambly been 'sponsible pusson too long, ma'm."

He shouldered Harriet's trunk and carried it across the yard and down the flight of steps to the landing, where his sailboat, the *Rebecca,* was tied. His oldest son and constant companion Tunis, a slim but strong boy with a ready smile, picked up Emily's little trunk and started after his father. Lucy took charge of the hand-luggage; her own possessions were slung in a modest bundle over her shoulder, with the exception of two blue calico dresses worn one over the other and on top of several petticoats, which gave her a voluptuous carriage out of all proportion with her wiry young frame,—a spotless white apron and headcloth completed her costume. Harriet had offered to take her North, but Lucy had declared her intention of going to Marshlands. When Emily had written Aaron about her, he had answered that she would be welcome, for Maum Minda and Phyllis had left and his only servant was a slow and stupid woman from the mainland.

It took many minutes to get the luggage and passengers settled, the tide had not been flowing long and the boat stood all of Isaac's six feet below the level of the landing. Harriet was terrified of the ladder and had to be coaxed down step by step. But finally the time came for Tunis to cast off: he swung nimbly down onto the prow by way of the mast, Miss Hayut giving a little scream that made him grin as he hoisted the sail. As the boat moved away from the landing with the tide and the light breeze and headed north for the mouth of Beaufort River, Emily turned with Harriet to wave to the little group of plantation people who had gathered in the yard. Beyond their silhouetted forms and the silhouettes of the trees a rosy glow was inciting the morning star to a last bright twinkling and sparkle. But a quality of dusk still brooded over the Sound and deep shadows haunted the shorelines. And in the shrouded western sky the moon was no specter yet but still a living presence, lustrous and undimmed.

The air was shivering cold, and yet it felt good on her cheeks. They were burning, but inside she felt surprisingly calm. She listened attentively to Isaac's talk as with the eloquent hand free of the tiller he pointed out places of interest along the way. The only place she knew was the first one, the old house at Cherokee, with its cabins where Dr. Stewart and the Fenwicks had been living. She had wondered why she had seen none of them recently, and now Isaac explained that: Maus' Steve was keeping books for Van Wie's General Store and had taken Miss Sophie and young Miss Geenie to town to live, and Maus' Rusty had built himself a little cottage over at Pine Point on Station Creek facing the barrier islands. . . . When the boat was gliding up Beaufort River, Isaac pointed out the remains of a rice mill at abandoned Port Royal. And further on was old Spanish Fort, a tabby ruin half-sunken in the marshy shore. Presently the river narrowed, and now the boat was skirting a bluff where the outlying houses stood. Ahead at Government wharf lay the *Indigo*, resplendent in the first rays of the sun.

As Tunis let down the sail and the little *Rebecca* drifted up to the looming steamboat, she saw Aaron standing with Robert Fenwick by a gate in the rail. When the time came to take his hand for the step up from the prow of the sailboat, she thought he could hardly fail to see how flushed her smile was for all its ready sureness.

She sat on the upper deck for a last chat with her friend Harriet, while Aaron saw to the transferring of luggage and then sent the sailboat on to Marshlands with Lucy. She had held her breath for a moment when she had found herself back on this memorable deck. But the walking-beam was at rest now, and all the phantoms of that nightmare journey had fled: even the phantom of Will, standing so still at the rail near the pilot-house, even he was safely lost in this morning of new spring. Here now were only Harriet and herself, talking in the early sunshine, and a few people moving on the wharf, where a carriage was waiting.

The *Indigo* was gone and Harriet with it, and she was riding at Aaron's side through Beaufort. He talked with an ease and fluency that left no gaps for embarrassing silence, but she realized she must share the responsibility and groped for something to say.

"Wasn't that Phyllis and Alec on the wharf? They're both so elegant I hardly recognized them."

He smiled and folded his arms.

"Phyllis is quite the young lady of leisure now. She got so lazy at the house I thought I'd have to tell her to leave, but fortunately she and Maum Minda left of their own accord. I say fortunately because I'm glad I didn't have to offend Robert Fenwick. He's becoming quite a figure in our Republican circle here. I've had some interesting talks with him lately—very intelligent man. Comes as a guest now to the house where he once served as a slave."

He crossed his legs in the carriage. "By the way, this house on the corner has been bought back by the original owner." He was pointing to the "Castle" that last spring had been the Government hospital of Dr. Ellis. "A rebel by the name of Joseph Bramwell. He's set himself up as Democratic leader here, in opposition to the policies of the Freedmen's Bureau—not impressive opposition."

She felt his hand close over hers.

"Emily, this district is the opening wedge in the drive to uphold freedmen rights. And they're going to be upheld, even if it means Negro supremacy, the bottom rail on top. In the struggle ahead I thank God I shall have you at my side. . . . It's been a long hard courtship, Emily. A little more and you would have been a widow. Have I made up a little for rushing you into an elopement in the beginning? I guess that first courtship was too much of a whirlwind affair."

She tried to control her hand, to keep it from twitching for release, and to return his smile with some show of life.

"Now," he added with a sigh of satisfaction, "I can work with a whole heart. I don't want you to do any more teaching. Just let your youth and beauty shine at Marshlands. You'll have your hands full presiding there."

Her hand was still in his when the carriage rolled through the gateway where the striped sentry box used to be, when they went up the steps to the front door where Lucy was waiting for them, and when he then led her upstairs to the big room that had been the Sagers'. Cheerful flames were crackling in the fireplace and she was thankful for that, for she was cold to the marrow of her bones. As they stood before the fire, he raised her hand to his lips.

"Emily, I can't tell you what your homecoming means to me. There aren't words for it. I'll just say that my prayers have been answered."

She tried to meet his eyes, but it was too hard and she could only stare at the flames. If he failed to realize that she must adjust herself to this house of memories, she wondered if she could master a revulsion that would shatter everything. Her will was firmed to yield and yet her body shrank instinctively from any contact with his. Somehow this shrinking must be controlled till it was subdued. She waited, feeling his eyes on her. It was an immeasurable relief when he released her hand at last and left her free.

"I know," he said slowly, "you don't love me as I love you. You never could, and I never expected it. All I ask now is all I ever asked, that you let me do what I can to make you happy. You must let me know your every wish. If you say so, I'll leave you this room to yourself."

It took an effort to summon the voice to answer him.

"I came back to live as your wife, Aaron."

She turned then to face him with an uncertain little smile. "And now may I have a minute to unpack?"

"Bless your heart!" he laughed. "And that reminds me, I have something to attend to myself this morning, to keep me out of the way." He took out his watch and studied it. "Freedmen Bureau business—labor contracts. Look here, suppose I go on now, so that I can get back comfortably for dinner."

He was already at the door. Gratefully she called after him. "But what do you want for dinner?"

"Your duties don't commence till tomorrow, child. But if you want to have a conference with Rose, you'll find her in the kitchen, cross and rheumatic but a great exponent of the beaten biscuit."

He was gone. . . . She stood motionless in the middle of the room for several minutes before she could concentrate on unpacking. Her little trunk was placed at the foot of the big bed that stood waiting opposite the fireplace, the bed the Sagers had used, its massive head in shadow between pools of sunlight from the two front windows. The room felt suddenly close and tight, stifling, and she went to open the window at the right of the bed. The upper porch and its railing cut off the view immediately below, but she could see the lawn from the flagstaff to the seawall: the sun and the flames on the water hurt her eyes and it was only by peering through her lashes that she could make out the marshes beyond. Then her eyes searched for Isaac's boat in the blinding light that enveloped the landing. It was gone, of course: time was confused this morning. But a moment later she did discover a sail that looked like the *Rebecca,* tacking far down the river toward the Sound and Land's End.

She turned back to the trunk finally and began to unpack. There were two bureaus in the room. One was Aaron's. The other was empty except for one drawer that held the odds-and-ends she had

163

left behind when she had gone to Land's End a year ago. When she came to hang her dresses in the closet with Aaron's suits, this intimate mingling again of their clothes wakened her at last to the full meaning of her surrender.

She was thankful when Lucy's appearance interrupted her thoughts. The girl had shed her surplus clothing and returned to her normal shape. Under her arm she was carrying a suspiciously familiar bundle, which she prepared to stow away out of sight under the bed.

"Lucy, what are you doing?"

"Jes' settin' my pallet out de way. I mus' get me some mo' bettuh moss fuh stuff'um good, but he do fuh tonight."

It hurt to laugh, but it was a relief too.

"Lucy, I'm afraid you'll have to have a room of your own now. Mr. Moffet has put a cot in the attic for you."

With a long face Lucy removed the pallet and carried it off downstairs, returning with her things. Emily went up with her to the attic to see that she would be comfortable there. But she took no interest in this room of her own and made no comment on the view from the dormer windows. Her face remained pensive and sad as they went downstairs together and out to the kitchen-house.

Rose, cook and housekeeper, proved to be a formidable creature indeed. She was very large and moved with a slow heavy sway. It was easy to understand now why the house needed a thorough cleaning: it was hard to see how this unwieldy woman even managed to get food hot into the house. She showed at once that she resented any inspection of her kitchen. Her answers were short and sullen, and she had to be questioned at length to determine the state of the larder. It developed that dinner was planned but supper was not.

"Ain' my style fuh study 'bout nex' meal till I'm got dish one out de way."

The prospect of keeping house with such a helper was not exactly promising. Emily made a mental list of some of the supplies most sorely needed and went back into the house with Lucy. There Lucy could no longer keep her contempt to herself.

"Miss Em'ly, dat 'oman talk big 'bout bein' quality nigguh, but he ain' nutt'n but po'-buckra grease nigguh an' you cyan' eat he bittle nohow ma'm."

"We'll see if we can't arrange for her to have the afternoon off,

Lucy. You and I can get supper. I think you better keep away from the kitchen till then."

"Don' fret, ma'm, I ain' goin' near dat ogly 'oman."

A few minutes later when Emily prepared to go to Bay Street, an expression of shocked disapproval came into Lucy's face.

"Miss Em'ly, you ain' goin' to *maa'ket?*"

"Why not?"

"You cyan' do dat, ma'm. Ain' you know white lady cyan' go to maa'ket?"

Trying to make her face as serious as Lucy's, she said, "I'm afraid you'll have to let me go this one time."

Smiling to herself she went upstairs for her hat. But when she looked in the mirror of her bureau, the smile faded. When she came out into the hall she stood there for an uncertain moment. The doors to the other rooms were closed, but she felt drawn to what lay behind them. When she opened the door of the room that had been hers, there was nothing there, no furniture, nothing but blankness: a silence of walls so hollow that she could catch the sound of her own breathing. And it was the same with the spare room: it was bare and empty, without recognition or memory. Of the past, she saw now surely as she turned to the stairs, there was only Aaron and herself left, in a house of forgetfulness and future appeasement. If time would only hurry this day away.

In the lower hall she found Lucy sweeping savagely, with unrelenting disapproval of the trip to market. It was difficult to live up to Lucy's code of what a lady could and could not do: living up to it strictly would have eliminated most activity. At Land's End she had tried to avoid getting caught in the act of making a bed or dusting a room, or any of the many other known breaches of etiquette that gave Lucy "too shame" pain. But unexpected breaches were always being blundered into through sheer ignorance, like this present one of going to market.

"Lucy," she said impulsively, "do you know what a comfort it is to have you with me? What would I ever do without you now? Even when you scold me."

Evidently this was not etiquette either, for Lucy only swept harder, mumbling to her broom. But in a moment the sweeping slowed and she glanced up. A smile was struggling with the pout of her lips.

Bay Street was not the thoroughfare of war times. There were comparatively few white faces, and the only uniforms were worn by colored militiamen. Yet it seemed more crowded than ever: ox and mule carts, wagons and carriages, and throngs of strolling loud-talking freedmen. The only thing that made the narrow sidewalks passable was that all the freedmen were trying to exercise their new right to walk on the "inside", formerly the white man's special privilege.

Van Wie's General Store stood in the heart of Bay Street, its imposing false front facing the entrance to the steamboat landing and flanked by a crowded saloon and a handsome old house, now the home of the Freedmen's Saving Bank & Trust Co. The broad steps to the door of the store served as a lounging place for the overflow from the saloon. A barroom in the rear of the store, beyond a swinging door, increased the congestion of people between the long counters. Emily stood back as far out of the way as possible to wait till florid perspiring Mr. Van Wie or one of his clerks was free. When she looked around she found she was standing near the cashier's desk and that Stephen Fenwick was there: she remembered Isaac had said he was working here now. He was scratching down in a ledger the list of purchases a clerk was rattling off to him. She had always liked his looks in spite of the look of hate he had always given her whenever their paths had crossed at Cherokee.

"Two-forty-nine," she heard him say.

As he dipped his pen and prepared to scratch again, his dark eyes took hers by surprise. She looked away quickly, and kept her eyes away, watching the stream of people passing in and out the wide doorway.

Almost all were freedmen. The costumes were dazzling and the faces gay. In watching the noisy faces move by she noticed how many were not black or even brown. Of the trio in the doorway now: the taller of the two young men was black but the other was light-colored and the young woman between them was lighter still. Phyllis, she recognized with a start. Not the girl of a year ago, slouching through her work at Marshlands, but the Phyllis fleetingly glimpsed at the wharf this morning. Her dress was bright red silk, and her hair was drawn back into a tight chignon around which curled the feather of her scarlet hat. There was no longer any trace of Maum Minda's sobering influence. Her companions were her brother Alec, in a dapper checked suit, and a swaggering militiaman with a gold-braided zouave cap cocked over one eye. She came into the store with a high self-conscious laugh and flash of teeth, and when people turned to stare at her she stopped to look around with a smile and a tilt of her head. The militiaman left her side and strutted over to the desk, where he held out his hand with a grin.

"Howdy, Steve," Emily heard him say to the white man. "I hear you was come back. Sho glad to see you. How is you' fambly?"

She heard Stephen Fenwick answer in a low measured voice: "Who are you?"

The black man's grin broke down. "You ain' know me? Dublin—what used to b'long to de Heywards."

Stephen Fenwick put down his pen.

"Now that you have made yourself known, my name is Mr. Fen. wick. If you wish to speak to me, address me so or hold your tongue."

The man's jaw dropped. He pulled off his cap and whispered: "Scuse me suh. Scuse me, Mistuh Fen'ick." He fumbled with his cap. "You see, Maus' Steve, dem Yankee people teach me dat free talk."

He fell back stammering apologies, but Phyllis took his place.

"Howdy, *Mistuh* Fen'ick! Spec' you ain' know me too. Spec' you done pure fuhgit me an' you was raise togedduh. You ain' membuh Phyllis what use to play wid you an' t'ing?"

Her shrill voice had attracted the attention of the entire store now. Emily tried to move away, but the press of people trying to see what was going on held her where she was. Mr. Van Wie came shouldering his way to the desk.

"What's going on here?"

Stephen Fenwick said to him: "Get that wench away from me."

Phyllis answered that with a blast of Gullah abuse.

"Now wait a minute here!" Mr. Van Wie barked. "No call for that, young lady. We don't want any trouble here,—you folks better move on."

With a final shrill sneer Phyllis moved on with Alec and the black militiaman, in the direction of the swinging door to the back room. Mr. Van Wie began to gently herd his customers away from the desk. Emily heard him say to Stephen Fenwick: "I give you a place here to show I ain't a man to hold no grudge against Southerners,

167

but if you can't keep out of trouble with the customers I'll have to get somebody that can." He saw her then, looked hard at her for a moment over his glasses before recognition came into his face. "Well, Mrs. Moffet! I declare. Why I ain't seen you since the Sumter celebration year ago. You been teaching on St. Helena Island, they tell me. My wife and I was talking about you only the other night."

"I've come back to Marshlands to live," she explained, flushing at the loudness of his voice and the nearness of the desk.

"Well now, that's just fine and dandy. Bessie will be pleased to hear that. She always had a good word for you. That is, she always liked you, what little she saw of you." Mr. Van Wie laughed nervously and pulled out a blue bandanna to mop his face. He suddenly remembered his storeful of customers. "Well, what can I do you for, as the feller says?" Yes, he had nice apples, several barrels left in the cellar from the shipment that had come down from his own farm in Essex County, New York. "I'm afraid I have quite a list here," she told him. Well, beamed Mr. Van Wie, if she'd just give the order to the young gent at the desk, the things would get sent right over.

She went to the desk and gave her list to Stephen Fenwick. His hand shook whenever he dipped the pen. When the list was finished, he asked without looking up:

"Name please."

When she said "Moffet", his mouth twisted.

"That's Marshlands, isn't it. Thank you, Mrs. Moffet."

On the way back to Marshlands, her thoughts gradually returned to herself and Aaron. Bay Street and the incident at the store had given her a brief respite, but by the time she reached the house all that was forgotten in the fatal drift of this day. The sun had risen and was now moving toward noon; afternoon would come, and then at last, night. It was a matter of will, she assured herself, a matter of control.

As a final test of herself she went out to the closed garden to cut some flowers for the table. When she had taken sprays of banksia rose and clusters of wistaria from the ladened summer-house, she sat there for a while. When the garden seemed to blur and streak before her eyes, she pressed her hands tightly together till it stopped and she was alone again.

To make her share of conversation at dinner, after Aaron had finished telling of his morning difficulties with freedmen labor contracts, she mentioned the incident at the store. Aaron frowned.

"Yes, I know Stephen Fenwick. He was born in this house, you know. I advised Van Wie not to employ him. Of course Phyllis has a violent high-yellow temper, so I can imagine it was quite a scene. . . . I've tried to keep a fatherly eye on the girl, for Maum Minda's sake, and because I can't help feeling personally responsible for the conduct of every freed soul. The worse freedom goes to the head of an ex-slave, the greater responsibility I feel, naturally,—the blacker the sheep, the dearer to the shepherd." He cleared his throat with a shrug and sigh. "But I'm afraid I'll have to give up Phyllis and Alec as hopeless cases. Even their brother Robert can't do anything with them now. . . . As for the militia boy's clash with Fenwick, that's typical of the trouble we're having with the returned native whites. There's a perversity about the Southern mind that's past my comprehension. It's not thought wrong for a white child to be suckled by its black nurse. White children have Negro children for playmates. Negro servants use the same dishes as whites. Yet despite these familiarities, and others, the Negro forms a caste of untouchables who cannot be granted even the little human dignity that goes with the title 'Mr.'."

"But in the North people don't make social equals of their servants. They don't 'Mr.' them."

He shook his head and smiled indulgently.

"My dear child, there is no real analogy between the two situations. If these Southern whites aren't made to acknowledge the social equality of the Negro, they will try to deprive him of all equality. I trust you're not defending the Southern attitude."

"I must say I felt sorry for Stephen Fenwick this morning."

"You mustn't allow your sympathies to be enlisted because an ex-slave-owner finds himself in a humiliating position. These people have much humbling of the spirit to go through before they're chastened, Emily. They can't keep their old prejudices and live in this new age. They've got to accept the new conditions or go under."

She nodded, refraining from saying anything more on the subject.

After dinner they walked across the lawn and sat on the seawall, watching the ebbing tide as they talked of housekeeping matters. Aaron promising to give Rose the rest of the day off and let Lucy take charge of supper. Some men were coming to the house this afternoon to discuss freedmen affairs—"I can't keep even this day of days inviolate"—: he said she looked tired and suggested a rest while he disposed of this duty business, and after a talk with Lucy she went obediently up to the room. At first she sat in a chair by the window, staring out at the river. She was miserably tired, but she had no idea that she could rest. Yet when she finally went to lie down, rest came almost at once, as if she had long since completed her submission to this bed.

It was late afternoon when she opened her eyes. She had an illusion of being back at Land's End and it took a minute to dispel that sense of deliverance and realize where she was. When she got up and went to the washstand, the water felt cool and good to her hands and face. Now that the day was drawing to a close the currents of spring air stirring through the room seemed freshened and quickened, but it made breathing no easier. She straightened her hair with nerveless fingers and went downstairs.

There were voices of men talking with Aaron in the living-room. She walked softly to the back door and went out to the kitchen-house, where she found Lucy had supper almost prepared. The potatoes were already baking, the lemon pie was cooling, and the fish loaf was waiting to go into the oven. The table was set too, Lucy said, so there was nothing left to do except cut slices of cheese and open one of the jars of pickles that had been brought from Land's End, watermelon pickles that Lucy had had the energy to put up in the heat of last summer. But she stayed on with Lucy till she saw through the little window that Aaron's visitors were leaving. Two of them, white men, were in an open carriage, and a black militia officer was on horseback; the others, several freedmen in frock coats and stovepipe hats, were on foot. She watched the last of them down the drive and out the gateway into sunset Fenwick Street before she went back into the house.

At the door she met Aaron coming to find her.

After supper—"We'll dispose of Rose in the morning," said Aaron, praising Lucy—he closed the windows in the living-room and lighted the fire, for the night air was still chilly. They sat on the sofa watching the flames that paled the glow of the lamp on the table behind them. Her thoughts were in commotion to find things to say to bolster up the conversation that he seemed willing to let languish now. It was difficult to talk with animation, but silence was more difficult. Most of the time she hardly knew what she was saying, but it was helping the evening to wear away little by little.

After Lucy stopped to say good-night on the way up to her attic room, she made no further attempt to keep talk going. I am waiting, she told herself, ready and willing. And at last it was sheer relief to know that the long ordeal of suspense was nearly ended. The sooner it's over now, she kept repeating to herself. Yet when he released her hand and got up, stood with his back to the fire smiling down at her, her mind began to grope in a sudden uncontrollable panic for some excuse to delay, to ward off this hour to which she had committed herself so many weeks ago, this inevitable moment for which she had so carefully schooled herself.

"This," he was saying with a deep sigh, "is certainly the happiest day of my life. Honestly, I can't believe you're here."

Her hands were pressed so tightly together in her lap that they were white and tingling. It was all she could do to make her eyes meet his with a smile. Then she looked down at her hands, trying to relax them. She could feel the strength of his eyes on her for an endless time before his voice came again.

"You're not sorry you came back, young Emily?"

She looked up at him with a quick catch of breath.

"I wanted to," she told him. "I'm thankful, Aaron. Grateful and glad."

She had to look down again then. But a moment later her eyes returned to his with surprise. He looked toward the hall.

"Hear a knock?" he asked her.

She nodded.

The knock came again, unmistakable this time, from the direction of the front door. He frowned. "I don't know who it would be at this hour. Some freedman in trouble, I suppose. You'll have to expect this occasionally, dear, like being a doctor's wife."

She watched him go into the hall, wondering what effect this interruption would have on her taut nerves. When the bolt clicked and the front door opened, she listened to the voices. But she could make no sense out of what was being said: there were gullah voices, confusing Aaron's words. And then startlingly, without warning, there were sounds of a scuffle. The front door slammed and quick steps came toward this door.

Phyllis was standing in the room. For an instant of shock everything stopped dead: then came to life again with the remote immediacy of a dream. The figure of Phyllis, hatless and with rumpled hair, stood facing her. And now the figure of Aaron was there too. He took hold of Phyllis's arm, but she jerked it free.

"Keep you' han' off me!" She thrust clawing fingers at his face. "I gwine gouge you' eye out if you lay you' han' 'pon me!"

She stood glaring at him for a moment, panting, and then swung around. As Emily got to her feet she saw flashing bloodshot eyes, distended nostrils, and teeth set in a vicious grin. Minced sneering words came in breaths of rum. ·

"Scuse de 'trusion, Mis' Moffit. Me an' Alic jes' stop in fuh pay we respec'—on'y Mistuh Moffit ain' got no mo' mannuh dan t'row Alic out." She flung a guttural chuckle at Aaron. When her eyes came back they were narrowed to slits. She sucked her teeth. "You been gone long time, Mis' Moffit. T'ink you' hosban' been twillin' he t'umb all dis while?"

Aaron tried to seize her arm again, but she was ready for him, with such a savage scratch at his face that he stepped back.

"If you like you' looks, man, keep way fum me!" her tongue lashed at him shrilly. "Tellin' me I ain' fuh come to dis house! I ain' fuh come. You cyan' hide me out noplace. You ain' nebbuh gwine lose me—I ain' makin' way fuh no gal, black or white." She swung back to Emily. "I been waitin' fuh you to come crawlin' back to de bed I done warm! He gwine put me in secon' place fuh a piece like you, what ain' got no mo' bosom dan Alic!"

She spat.

As Emily turned to the door, she saw Aaron move out of her way. Then everything was whirling darkness as she felt her way up the stairs.

In the upper hall she turned first to the attic door to call Lucy, who came stumbling down the steep steps with a candle, eyes and mouth wide with alarm. "Get your things, Lucy," she heard herself say in an absurdly steady voice, "and hurry." Then she crossed the hall to the room. There was enough light from the moon so that she could see to get her bag and hatbox out of the closet and start packing. She was shaking now with hysterical release, at this repeated pattern of escape, fantastic second escape from the rooms of this house. But she steadied again when Lucy came down with her bundle and the candle. "Just get the things out of the bureau, Lucy, never mind the rest. . . ."

When they left the room and started down the stairs, Aaron was coming up, his head and shoulders outlined against the moonlight at the landing window.

"Listen to me, Emily," he stopped her. "You can't go like this. I forbid it this time."

"Please let me pass."

"No. . . . I can explain this to your entire satisfaction, and you'll do well to listen. You saw the girl was drunk. Her crazy brother put her up to this. It's a trick to blackmail me. That's how I'm repaid for my kindness in befriending them. And your leaving will make matters worse, if they try to 'expose' me to the Freedmen's Bureau. I advise you to accept my explanation and ignore the whole incident. I promise you it won't happen again."

"Isn't this enough without explanations."

"You have the gall to take that attitude, after all I've put up with from you?"

"It's funny, really. We're more than even now, Aaron."

"Oh no we're not. . . . If you think you can use this as grounds for divorce, you're badly mistaken. There's no such thing as divorce in this state, and you'll never get rid of me anywhere else without my consent. You're not through with me, Emily. You never will be. I warn you, you better stay."

"Let me go."

He stood aside then and let her pass. But as she hurried on down the stairs with Lucy, she heard him call after her:

"You'll regret this."

Things moved in violent streaks, with blank spaces between. She knew only that somehow she and Lucy were in a room at the Sea Island Hotel, and that she was saying finally in a voice calm with daze: "In the morning, Lucy, we'll get a boat to take us back to Land's End."

173

V

Emily had written Harriet from the Sea Island Hotel the morning of the return to Land's End. It was ten long days before an answer came.

"Emily *darling,*" it said with heavy underscorings. "I'm *dreadfully* sorry to hear that you have found a reconciliation with your husband *impossible.* I was always *very dubious* about your going back to him, though naturally I did not try to *influence* you. I am sure it will all be *for the best.* I have always said that everything works out for the best. I know you have been through bitter trial and tribulation, but remember we suffer for some *divine purpose* and must not *question* the why or wherefore but do God's will as it is revealed to us *day by day.*"

Harriet went on to say that she couldn't help feeling overjoyed that Emily would be with her at Land's End. "My *permanent colleague,* I hope." Harriet had always thought of marriage as a leap in the dark and was certainly thankful that *she* had escaped. After all, the only *real* satisfaction in life was in *service to others.* The educational work among the freedmen gave a perfect opportunity for that. She concluded by insisting that Emily come to Philadelphia for the summer.

When Emily sent a letter of warm thanks, she declined the invitation to go North: the summer months here would not be so bad now that she had been initiated; she could have a morning class for the children, and by autumn they would be that much ahead; there were rumors of smallpox at the other end of the island and the people might need her. She added as many other reasons as she could think of, but she knew the underlying reason was that she could not bring herself to accept,—the thought of going to a strange place and facing strangers was intolerable. Better to hide away here where there were only Lucy and the island people, with whom it was possible to feel as much at ease as with trees and fields and sky. For the one need now was peace; the one desire, to be lost, forgotten, buried alive in this isolated spot where land came to an end in sea.

The day after she received Harriet's letter, Emily harnessed Garibaldi and rode in the buggy over the sand and shell roads to the groups of cabins scattered around the plantation. On the morning of her return the people had come flocking to the house to welcome her back, informed of the event by their grapevine telegraph. Now they were all "too glad" to hear she was going to reopen school.

The letter that came from Harriet a week after the reopening of school was full of disappointment. She hoped that Emily would reconsider her decision about coming North for the summer and she was confident that Emily would when hot weather set in. She said she had submitted the smallpox matter to the Society and they were sending instructions.

The instructions came a few days later. ". . . We are sending you the serum via Charleston," flowed the secretary's copybook hand. "You will employ a doctor to administer it at once to every child who attends your school. The Board is of the opinion that the fee should be ten cents a child or less. . . ."

First it was necessary to find the doctor. There was a Freedmen's Bureau doctor in Beaufort, but the island people that Harriet had sent to him for treatment had reported that he was one half drunk and the other half mean. It was not very pleasant to think of assisting this man through a day of vaccinating children at ten cents or less a head. Then she remembered Dr. Stewart.

Isaac said that "Mistuh Rusty" was at Pine Point, but his directions on how to get there were so full of turns and forks that she took Tunis with her in the buggy to show the way.

The road wound through strips of wood thick with the fresh green of May and past old fields of which only small patches were under cultivation now. The homes of freedom, ramshackle cabins with mud-and-stick chimneys, were usually huddled together into communities of four or five, but sometimes they stood alone, set at random in a field or nestling in some woodland cove. Most of them had but a single room that had to serve as kitchen, dining-room, bedroom, and parlor for an entire family. Whitewash or a fenced-in yard, like Isaac's neat place near the Big House, was a rare sight.

She had to halt Garibaldi frequently to receive greetings and pass the time of day.

"Howdo, Miss Em'ly! Well, I'm makin' out po'ly t'ank Gawd, jes' po'ly. Got de misery in muh back—da's howcome you ain' see me an' Milly to school fuh t'ree day."

"Miss Em'ly, you ain' fuhgit 'bout dem stockin' you done primus me out de nex' mission box, is you ma'm?"

"No'm, Laa'ceeny ain' zac'ly sick, Miss Em'ly. To tell de Gawd trut' I too shame 'bout dat gal. He ain' know heself who done it. Look like dat good-fuh-nutt'n Change to me an' I been to he paa 'bout'um—he say Change gone to Sawannah. Bellden, I gwine fine a hosban' fuh Laa'ceeny if I got to lick'um. I sho ain' gwine allow no gal of mine fuh hab sin."

"If my boy Shad do bex you to school I hope you lick'um good, ma'm, but please don' hu't he feelin'."

"You ain' hear 'bout Auntie Cuba, Miss Em'ly? He hab *fit*. Yas'm. You know he ain' got Gawd toot' to he head—well ma'm yistiddy to meetin' de preachuh been preachin' 'bout dey shall be vailin' an' gnashin' of teet', an' he p'int to Auntie Cuba, say, Sustuh you gwine haffuh gum'it. Well ma'm Auntie let out holluh like debble got'um, an' de people done cyarry'um home stiff like bo'd. . . . Yath'm, he awright now."

Today there was a special cause for several of the halts. A few days ago a strapping black woman by the name of Lily had come to the house to ask if her newborn babe could be christened "Em'ly". She had rashly given Lily material for a dress for the baby and a small present of money. Almost immediately an epidemic of "Em'ly" christenings had broken out. The plantation birthrate was high, but she soon had reason to suspect that the majority of her namesakes were being reborn and rebaptized for the occasion. Today one destitute mother, with a naked infant astride her hip, stopped the buggy to introduce still another "Em'ly".

"But it's a boy," she protested.

"Miss Em'ly," the mother answered with dignity, "seem like I cyan' birt' nutt'n but boy-chile noway ma'm. Plenty 'oman be too glad fuh dat but not me—I too stribin' fuh birt' gal-chile fuh he'p me roun' de yaa'd. I blame muh hosban' fuh pullin' gains' me 'bout dat—he got no use fuh gal-chile. So now I gwine bactize dish boy Em'ly fuh spite'um, if I can git de chris'nin' dress an' t'ing, please ma'm."

It was a long time before the last interview was over and the end of the road in sight. Winding through a final strip of woods, the buggy came abruptly to a great field.

"Big fiel'," Tunis volunteered, forgetting for a moment his chronic shyness. "When Paa been dribuh fuh Ol' Maussa, dishuh fiel' make fo' hondred task!"

Big Field was a sea of weeds now, dotted with thicket islands. The road, almost obliterated by the rank growth that came up to Garibaldi's flanks, led straight across it to a pine grove. As the buggy slowly approached this grove, she could see the flashing waters of Station Creek beyond the columns of the pines. Before the road entered the grove there was a little log bridge over a marsh brook, bordered with feathery tamarisks. Then the deep dragging sand became a firm matting of pine-needles, and the sea air was scented with the aromatic breath of the trees. On either hand the trunks soared, with here and there at their feet a scrub palmetto or dwarf cedar, or a clump of cassena and myrtle; the carpet of pine-needles was littered in places with the cast-off fronds of the larger palmettoes. There was a soft music in the treetops. It was an enchanting spot, and she was glad to let Garibaldi settle down to his most languid walk.

They came out on a grassy open space, not immediately on the broad inlet as she had expected but on a little tidal stream that made an S through the marsh before it reached the main water. To the left at the edge of the grove was the pine-log cottage that Isaac had described. It stood well above the ground on palmetto posts, its roof, for which Isaac had hewn the shingles, extending to cover a front porch. As she gave the reins to Tunis and stepped out of the buggy, a brown setter came bounding down the steps of the porch barking ferociously: but when he reached her he thrust his nose into her hands, wagging his tail. When she looked up from patting his silky head, she saw Dr. Stewart coming toward her. At the sight of his master the dog resumed his barking, but perfunctorily now and with an accompaniment of apologetic whining.

"He's beautiful," she said with a flushed smile as Dr. Stewart came up to her. "What's his name?"

"Jeb. Excuse his manners—he's been living a pretty lonely life."

"But he has lovely manners."

"They do seem improved, all of a sudden."

There was a quiet assurance in his voice that made her feel at ease with him at once, as he stood smiling down at her. Other times that she had seen him had been from the buggy and she had not realized how tall he was: she hardly came up to his shoulder. She was struck again by his eyes of clearest blue and his sandy-red hair.

"What a wonderful place to live."

"Like it?" He was emptying the bowl of his pipe against the palm of his hand. "Fortunately no-one else does. Its only appeal is the view, luckily for us."

They talked about the view for a minute while she got up courage to explain her call. Hesitatingly she told him about the vaccination instruction and asked him if he would be willing to do the work.

"Gladly. My clients pay only in kind and in their own good time, so cash trade is very welcome."

She noticed his crudely patched gray army shirt and trousers and his worn shoes.

"But do you think ten cents a child is enough?"

"I think it's more than enough."

"I'll let you know then as soon as the serum comes."

They walked over to the buggy, and there she gave Jeb a parting pat before she took the hand Dr. Stewart held out to help her up the high step between the wheels. When she took leave of him and headed Garibaldi back to the road through the grove, she felt a pang of regret that the visit was ended. Those brief minutes had given her a strange sense of refreshment and comfort that remained with her as Garibaldi settled into his homeward-bound trot. Her thoughts kept turning back to Pine Point gratefully.

At Dr. Stewart's suggestion she made a tour of the plantation, several days in advance of the general vaccination, to enlist the coöperation of the parents. They were far from enthusiastic, but they promised to have every child on hand. As for the children themselves, she took great pains to explain to them in class that vaccination was only a pin prick followed by a bag of colored candy.

When the solemn morning arrived and all the children and many of the mothers were assembled at the praise-house school, she was prepared for a certain amount of trouble. It was too much to hope that these dozens of children could be herded into the room and up to the doctor without some difficult moments, despite the bags of candy piled on the desk. But she was not prepared for what actually happened when the first child felt the bone needle scratch her arm. Her piercing shriek froze every waiting face. There was a wild stampede. In a minute the yard was cleared of all except the mothers and the few children in their immediate charge. Some of the fugitives had scrambled under the building, but the majority had taken to the woods.

The rest of the day was full of commotion. But by late afternoon the last of the children had been rounded up, their arms scratched, smeared, and bound up, and their mouths stuffed with candy. As special compensation a three-day holiday was declared.

She was exhausted but happy when the long excitement was over. Dr. Stewart walked home with her and she persuaded him to stay for supper; they sat on the piazza steps and laughed over the adventures of the mad day, while Lucy amplified the sketchy evening meal. When she called them in, it was to sit down to a supper to match their appetites. They had interrupted the day's work only long enough for a hasty lunch of cornbread and sassafras tea at one of the island homes.

After supper they went back to the steps, with Jeb stretched on the ground at their feet. Emily felt peace in the company of this Dr. Stewart: with him her nerves were relaxed and easy. The quiet strength in his voice made her own voice seem quiet and strong. Under this spell she lost all sense of time. The red sun set behind the far islands across the Sound, and a soft wind swayed the tall blossom-ladened stems of the oleanders and rippled the leaves of the trees. Dusk was gathering about the house. And as they talked, the light in the west faded into darkness and the stars came out.

When he discovered that it was late and got up, knocking the ashes out of his pipe and apologizing for staying so long, she could honestly protest that it had been no time at all. She was worried about the walk he had before him till he told her of the short-cut he knew. She could see his smile and his eyes in the starlight as she gave him her hand to thank him again and say good-night.

After he had vanished with Jeb in the deep shadows of the yard, she sat on the steps with her elbows on her knees, listening to the throbbing song of peepers and crickets and watching the stars and the faint gleam they made on the darkness of water. She sat there so long that Lucy, impatient to lock up for the night, came to the front door with reproach in her voice.

"Miss Em'ly you ain' nebbuh comin' to bed? T'ain' good to set out in de night hair ma'm."

VI

THAT DAY of the "woccination", as the Land's End people called it, marked the beginning of a friendship that ripened quickly and surely. Almost before she realized it, Dr. Stewart had become by spontaneous transition Rusty.

More and more frequently, in the evenings, he walked over from Pine Point by his short-cut; and those evenings when Jeb failed to come panting up the steps to announce his approach, she felt keen disappointment. She who had determined to school herself in resignation to loneliness, who had thought there was nothing left for her but withdrawal as into a shell, was finding her confidence being subtly restored by the companionship of this man in whom her trust deepened with each time she saw him. She felt a new desire to meet adversity with courage, as he was doing. The whole structure of his life had been destroyed, but the foundation had stood firm and he was building again, without fear or bitterness. She hoped that she could somehow make his strength her own.

For the last weeks of school, at his suggestion, she moved her classes from the praise-house to the cool west piazza of the Big House. And he taught her the wisdom of taking an afternoon siesta, and showed her how to abate the fly and mosquito nuisance by tacking bobbinet across the windows; it was remarkable how these two simple expedients lessened the distress of hot weather. In the late afternoon she drove for visits to the plantation people, and often these drives included a stop at Pine Point. So it was seldom that a day passed without a sight of him, either afternoon or evening. On Sundays he usually went to Beaufort to see the Fenwicks or Stephen Fenwick came out to see him, but on Saturdays she had his company for the entire day. She tried on that day at least to get him to come to Land's End for dinner, when she could fill him with Lucy's good cooking; but he got so reluctant about it that finally she had to resort to taking Lucy and a basket to Pine Point and preparing a meal there, around his fish broiled over an open fire. This proved such a success that it became a weekly institution. After it they went for a walk along one of the plantation trails or sat for a talk on the bench he had built between two palmettoes looking out over marsh to the open water of the Inlet, while Lucy swept and dusted the cottage, a practice she refused to abandon despite Rusty's regular protests.

"Lucy!"

"Suh?"

"What are you doing in there?"

"I ain' doin' nutt'n suh."

"Are you housecleaning again after what I told you last time?"

"Now Mistuh Rusty please don' hinduh me suh. You know good enough a gemman what been bo'n an' raise quality wid a crowd of people at you' beck an' call cyan' make out by you'self like a common pusson nohow—somebody 'blige fuh look affuh you suh."

She had explained to Emily: "He need we bad, Miss Em'ly, me fuh clean an' t'ing an' you fuh talk t'um, 'cause when a man try fuh make out alone 'tis pure deestruction."

The cottage fairly shone after Lucy's ministrations. It was a happy little place. The sitting-room had a fireplace of brick salvaged from the ruins of the Cherokee smoke-house and was incongruously furnished with a homemade pine table and chairs, a dignified old sofa, and two fine paintings by a Low Country artist named Washington Allston, some kin of Rusty's. The paintings and the sofa had been returned, he had explained, by conscience-smitten Cherokee people who had been "gyaa'din'" them since "de gun-shoot to Bay P'int", that cataclysmic hour from which all island time was now reckoned. One of the two small side rooms was the bedroom, as barely furnished as a cell; but the other was filled to overflowing with a great assortment of things, most prominently a library of books that had been exposed to the weather and a number of Audubon colored prints of birds.

Emily had soon found that the study of birds was a major interest of Rusty's. He had said to her one day early in the growth of their friendship:

"How do you like *Curlew House* for the name of the shack?"

"I like it. But what does it mean?"

He had shaken his head at her. "Emily, is it possible you don't know what a curlew is?"

"It sounds like a wave or a feather or something."

"That isn't such a bad guess."

He had pointed to wings speeding over the marsh. Listening she had heard weird sad cries. She had thought they must be lost souls, but later when he had shown her a group of these migrating shore birds at close range, resting on a low-tide mud flat, they had looked cheerful enough. They were mottled brown and had slender legs and a long curved bill with which they expertly dug up fiddler crabs. She was delighted with them.

That was her introduction to an enchanted kingdom, peopled with marvels to whose existence she had been blind and deaf. The marshes and fields and woods were alive now with winged spirits and their voices. It was the end of the spring migrations and many of the discoveries—such special favorites as the curlew, the blue heron, and the painted bunting—disappeared soon after her first sight of them. But Rusty promised that she would see them again in the autumn, together with many another she had missed. Not till next winter, he told her, would she see the myrtle warbler and Carolina wren, the mass flight of ducks at sunset, the marsh-hawk hunting alone, and the great bald eagle circling high in the sun. Some fine day she might even see that rarest of all coast-country birds, the black-necked stilt, as elusive as ultimate wisdom.

"Have you ever seen one?" she had asked him.

"Not yet," he had smiled wistfully.

Of the land birds whose acquaintance she made as the summer deepened, the white-throated sparrow took her particular fancy. Its sweet tremulous little song sounded so pathetic beside the rowdy screechings of bluejays, the brilliant confidence of a mocking-bird, or the blithe whistle of a cardinal, that she wished she could do something to comfort the poor thing. But most of the new acquaintances were lusty sea birds. There were the willets, large gray-and-white birds whose crazy mirth was the characteristic note of the marshes now that the mournful curlews were gone; the wood ibis that looked like a stork; the laughing gulls, white with black heads, whirling and screaming over the water; the night herons that made a *qwok-qwok* over the marshes after dark. And one Saturday when Isaac took her with Rusty out to Bay Point in his sailboat, she saw her first sanderlings and an unbelievable pelican, flapping heavily along out beyond the surf line.

He always carried in his shirt pocket a notebook into which went the name of every variety of bird seen each day, a list that was transferred at night to the pages of a ledger. She tried hard whenever she was with him to be the first to spot a bird that was not on his list for the day. She ventured finally to keep a notebook of her own, but for some time her lists came out hopelessly shorter than his.

"Promise you didn't invent that ibis today, Rusty?"

Little by little her eyes grew sharper and her lists longer, till at last, at the end of a Saturday they had spent together, she found that her list was identical with his. His praise made her joyful. After that she got to the proud point of being able to see a bird the moment he did. It was an amazingly satisfying interest, this game that had quickened the first steps of their friendship. The only difficulty was the long scientific names that he wanted her to learn.

"They may be necessary for classification," she mocked, "but aren't you glad *Curlew House* doesn't have to be called *Domus Numenius Longirostris!*"

Nevertheless she revived her Latin and learned the awkward names. She would have cheerfully returned to the agony of Greek if it would have pleased him.

Through his companionship the sea-island world was unfolding in all its magic. It was as if her senses had been drugged before and were only now waking to appreciation of the sights and sounds around her. But he was bringing to intense life for her more than the present sea-island world, the foreground of marsh sweep and dreaming tidewater, of fields under burning sun and cooling shower, of woods fragrant and mysterious in their deep summer foliage, of color and light nuances that were like exquisite music. There was a hidden world that he was revealing to her, the buried past of the Sea Islands; and little by little she was piecing together from her talks with him a picture of times gone that gave another dimension to her surroundings.

A Spaniard was the first white man to see this part of the New World. Exploring the coast early in the sixteenth century, he paused long enough to give St. Helena Island its name and to carry off as samples of the fauna some of the natives who had welcomed him to their Hesperides. In the middle of the century a Jean Ribaut, follower of Admiral de Coligny, founded the first Protestant settlement in North America, on Parris Island, which jutted out into the Sound like an arrow head, its marshy tip opposite Land's End.

"Stand on your west porch," Rusty said, "and look hard at Parris Island till the open fields there have grown up into forest wilderness again and you see the frail smoke of the Huguenot fires."

But the Spaniards, raiding up from Florida, wiped out the settlement and erected a fort of their own, around which grew up a mission colony of some sixty houses. Franciscans attempted to instruct the barbarous natives in the arts of civilization, and were massacred for their pains. After that a three-cornered contest lasting a century was waged among the Spaniards, the English, and the Indians for possession of the coast. In the end the English triumphed and Beaufort, their little outpost in the heart of the sea-island country, took firm root.

Rusty's ancestor, a Scottish trader and frontiersman, was the first colonist to take up a grant of land on St. Helena. He turned his attention to naval stores in the beginning: the great live-oaks were cut into ship beams, from the pines came pitch and turpentine. At that time his laborers were indentured whites, indigent persons who sold themselves into seven years of slavery for the opportunity of getting to the New World; but when indigo culture was introduced from the West Indies, the first Negroes were brought to the island. There was a government bounty on the dye, and St. Helena indigo commanded the top price in the London market. The Stewart plantation flourished.

But with the outbreak of the Revolution, the bounty and the market vanished. St. Helena Parish was desolated by the British; the war dragged on year after year. When peace came at last, the Stewarts, the Fenwicks, and the Bramwells, the Combahee River rice-planting branch of the family, were ruined along with their neighbors. As they were struggling to build again, sea-island cotton came like a miracle to lift their fortunes on a great wave, a wave that rolled high and far before it struck the gray walls of Sumter.

"Now that the old plantation life is gone," Rusty said, "its faults are easily seen. Slavery was a fatal mistake, but it wasn't the cruel institution that fanatics conceived. At least I wonder that it never occurred to your Abolitionists that there were forms of slavery **at** their own doorstep,—wage slavery in sweat-shop and mill, child labor, slavery to poverty and ignorance and disease."

Preconceptions of the South and Southerners, the plantation and the Negro that Emily had brought with her from the North were dissolving. Whenever she saw Rusty with the Cherokee people, she realized with increasing force that such mutual understanding and good-will could not have grown out of a system of cruelty and misery. She began to see that the old way of life here on the Sea Islands had possessed a simple beauty transcending the shadow of slavery. Her own work among the freedmen was teaching her what a burden of responsibility must have been borne by the plantation master and mistress; it was really they, she thought, who had been liberated. As for the Negro, he was no longer a romantic figure, a sort of white man in blackface. He was a very human being. And a stubborn enigma. She had the feeling that while she was striving without much success to fathom the Land's End people, they had fathomed her instinctively and at once.

"It doesn't take them long to learn your moods and tenses," Rusty had told her.

But at least she was slowly learning what to expect of them, and what not to expect. Mr. Philpotts, the Northerner who had been supervising the plantation when she had first come to live here, had said to her on the eve of his disgruntled departure: "Profit by my sad experience and forget the sentimental twaddle you were taught about these people—they are utterly lacking in character, conscience, and initiative, and they will lie, cheat, and steal as naturally as they breathe." It was clear to her now that this was all true, though only part of the whole truth. Certainly lying and stealing were common enough among them, and getting something for nothing from white people was one of their greatest accomplishments; they were completely innocent of morals; and they seemed quite content to pursue a calm unhurried destiny, untroubled by the spur of ambition. Moreover, they were enormously superstitious, every act of their lives was sponsored by some magic formula: midwives put a hoe, plowpoint, or axe under the bed of childbirth to cut the pain, and death was accompanied by the covering of mirrors and stopping of clocks: they moved in an atmosphere of spells and exorcisms and cunjuh

Yet, strangely, as her illusions about them faded, she found her affection for them increasing.

This happy summer was giving her a better understanding of many things. In the hours she spent with Rusty, reading to him and talking as he worked on the sailboat he was building with Isaac's periodic help, she felt that she was learning to see clearer and straighter and farther than she ever had before. His simple direct way of looking at things was contagious. This new insight that was coming to her, this power to think about things and not just accept them at their face value, was showing her a little how things worked. If this fresh scrutiny was hard on old prejudices, it was also an amazing instrument for lighting dark bafflements, for making some order in the confusion of the world.

She thought she could see this change in the mirror when she studied her face, which was losing its delicate tint for a bronze tone of sun and wind. Her eyes looked steady and unafraid. I've grown, she thought; I'm really a woman now. Yet with him she felt like a child, sitting at his feet. She did not fully realize how dependent she had become on his companionship till late in the summer when he made a journey to Georgetown, beyond Charleston, and was gone four long days. She took some little comfort in his absence by making curtains of checked gingham for his cottage and by darning and patching the scanty washing that Lucy smuggled out. But, alone, she was still not strong enough to master the nightmare of the past and the fearful shadow it cast over the future. He had left Jeb in her keeping, and when at last the dog announced his return and she hurried to the door to find him coming up the steps, she could hardly conceal her relief and pleasure.

He brought back with him, in addition to a supply of medicines, a pair of old field-glasses: now they could study the wariest of the island birds at close range. And when the little sailboat was finished in September and christened the *Dolphin* after a lengthy debate, the whole sea-island world was open to them. Under his hand she learned the knack of tiller and sail. On week-day afternoons, whenever the wind and tide were right, he came to the landing for her and they went out on the Sound and were lost in a vast blue enchantment of sky and water. It was hard to say which days she liked best: the days when the wind was strong, making joyous thunder in her ears and dashing shining spray over the nose of the *Dolphin* to shock and cool her arms and face, or those days when the wind was lazy and they fished at one of the drops in Station Creek. Saturdays were for long explorations among the islands, to Coosaw and Pinckney Neck, Callawassie, and Hunting Island, where an old lighthouse rose high above bleak dunes. . . . The most memorable sails were those to the barrier islands. They had been wooded strips along the horizon before, floating in haze beyond the waters of the Inlet. Now they were intimately known: places of weird beauty, half jungle and half beach, far-flung battle lines between the land and the sea. At the edge of the dunes palmetto sentinels with blasted crests gazed gauntly out over the waste; behind them, at the edge of the jungle, fantastically twisted live-oaks and cedars, tortured myrtle and cassena bushes held the field against onslaughts of wind and sand. In the surf stood bleached skeletons of trees caught in the remorseless advance of the sea.

But all the days of this summer were in some degree memorable. A sustained happiness ran through them all, a happiness that was like a protecting wall around her, shutting out torment and fear. A sanctuary where she could rest while her wounds slowly closed and healed.

One day early in October a letter came from Harriet saying that she was leaving for Land's End in a fortnight. Would Emily have the Cherokee school opened and aired and scoured?

The praise-house school had already been reopened, so her time with Rusty was sharply reduced. And now every moment with him was doubly precious, for soon their companionship must be further curtailed and adjusted to make room for Harriet. . . . Her letter said: "I know what a lonely summer it has been for you." In answering, Emily resisted saying: I have never been less lonely. She had avoided any mention of Rusty in her previous letters, knowing Harriet's fixed distaste for all Southerners, but now she spoke of him briefly. "Dr. Stewart has made a most agreeable neighbor. When you get to know him I'm sure you will like him as much as I do."

VII

AFTER HARRIET's return Rusty continued to come over to the house several times a week, but her presence so muddied the clear waters of companionship that these evenings soon became more strain than pleasure. Her affected sweetness, painful politeness, and precise gaiety were poor masks for hostility. It was a relief when Rusty stopped coming, with the explanation that he was working on some medical papers.

That left the sails in the *Dolphin* for Harriet to spoil, which she did very thoroughly. In the deepening friendship with Rusty silence had become a means of communication sometimes more explicit and satisfactory than speech, but for Harriet an occasional quiet spell was an acute nervous strain and challenge. Finally, after one particularly unpleasant sail, it was easy to agree with Rusty that no sails at all would be better than including Harriet; so it was discovered that the little boat had sprung a leak, several leaks in fact, and would have to be laid up, scraped, and repainted.

They saw each other now only on those days when she finished early with the afternoon class of grown-ups and could stop at Pine Point for a little while on her way to get Harriet at Cherokee. Sometimes there was the special blessing of a Sunday morning together, when the weather was fair and Isaac took Harriet to St. Helena's in Beaufort. Emily excused herself from accompanying Harriet on the grounds that she did not like to go to Beaufort even for church. But there was another reason that she did not mention. It was vague yet profoundly disturbing, this other reason. For a time she struggled with it alone, but that seemed only to increase its strength. At last when it had become unbearable, she took it to Rusty, as she had learned to do with so many lesser problems.

Driving to Pine Point after school that late November day, she forgot the turmoil of her thoughts in the autumn glory around her. Scarlet flames of oak and blackgum, golden flames of hickory and poplar burned among the evergreens of the woods. The days were growing short again and the sun was low in the west, but the air was still mild. In the grove at the Point the cassenas were already covered with red berries for Christmas, but it was hard to believe that Thanksgiving was here and the year drawing to a close.

When she got out of the buggy, Jeb came bounding to her and she gave him the pan of scraps that Lucy always saved for him. The ebbing tide had left the *Dolphin* high and dry on the bank of the marsh creek: Rusty was sitting crosslegged on the seat of the boat, mending a crab net. He brought it with him when he came to meet her, and when they went to the bench between the twin palmettoes he continued his mending while she related the day's little happenings. She was feeling her way to the trouble that lay like a stone on her mind, but it was some time before she found a path that would lead there.

"Harriet saw you with the Fenwicks at church Sunday, Rusty. I didn't know you went to church on your trips to Beaufort."

"I don't, ordinarily. But sometimes the bells get the better of me."

She watched his long sensitive fingers tie expert little knots in the net on his knees.

"You don't feel the need of church?"

He shook his head. "You're looking at a heathen, Emily."

"But you couldn't be."

He glanced at her with a smile. "Why is a heathen such a baleful thing to be? By definition a heathen is a dweller on the heath. One living under the sun by day and the stars by night, remote from the crowded highways of orthodoxy." He laid the net aside and got out his corncob pipe and worn leather pouch. "But you haven't been to church for a long time, Emily. You haven't turned heathen, have you?"

She stared at the marsh where the late rays of the sun rested and at the barrier islands beyond the open water of the Inlet.

"I don't know what I am anymore," she said slowly. "I don't know what I believe." Her hands made a troubled gesture. "It used to be so easy. Have faith and question not. But the questions won't stay down any longer, and I don't know what's become of my faith."

When she looked at him, his eyes were smiling at her as he lighted his pipe.

"I'm pretty upset," she told him.

He crossed his legs and put an arm over the back of the bench, puffing thoughtfully.

"Well, it's a pretty old upset, if that's any comfort. Has it occurred to you that you might be having growing pains?"

"Growing pains?"

He nodded. "The picture getting a little too large for the original frame. . . . You've been thinking about things. A very serious malady."

He studied her solemnly.

"Well," she frowned at him, "I must have caught it from you. I certainly never had it till this summer. What can I do about it? What's the cure?"

"There's no cure that I know of. It'll be more or less chronic from now on. What stage are you in? How far along have you gotten?"

She thought a moment before answering.

"Well, far enough to know I can't believe in heaven and hell any more."

"That's quite a way," he nodded.

"And"—she took a quick breath—"I'm not sure I even believe in religion."

She expected to see the horror of her words reflected in his face. But his face and voice remained calm.

"If by religion you mean the separate cults and churches that do more to divide men than unite them, I don't wonder. . . . You seem to have discarded a good deal. What's left? What do you still believe?"

"That's just the trouble. The more I think about things, the more confused I get. I don't know what to believe. And I've got to believe something."

He shook his head at her and sighed. "Emily, Emily. Why couldn't you have kept that old-time religion? It was good enough for Paul and Silas, why isn't it good enough for you?"

"I don't know," she said weakly.

"Well, you're going to have a lot of trouble finding a satisfactory substitute." He examined the bowl of his pipe critically. "You'll have to go some to beat that old-time religion. Remember the words of the hymn?—'It satisfies my longings as nothing else can do.' "

"And if you've somehow lost it, what do you do?"

"Find a new one."

"You make it sound so simple."

"Not at all. It may take you the rest of your life."

Jeb had finished his pan of scraps and came over now with a panting smile to thrust his muzzle into their hands and get some attention. When he had received sufficient reassurances, he stretched out at their feet with a groan of contentment that made them both laugh.

"There's a boy with faith for you," Rusty nodded. "That good old-time animal faith. Takes life as the cook serves it."

He sat back and gazed over the marshes, puffing at his pipe, which as usual had gone out.

"Emily," he said after a moment, "anything I can do to help?"

"Of course. I don't even know where to begin."

He looked at her with an expression of gentle amusement. "Even Genesis is in doubt? You're back in primal chaos?"

"I'm afraid so. . . . Tell me what you believe, Rusty. Whatever it is, I know I can believe it too."

He wrinkled up his nose and rubbed the back of his neck.

"Now, Emily,—you can't do it that way. You've got to work it out for yourself. Besides, I'm in about the same boat as you, adrift on a sea of doubt."

"You don't look it. You look as if you had something better than old-time religion."

"I look that smug?"

"Not smug. Just sure."

"Well, I'm sorry I've deceived you. I haven't anything like a positive creed. Only a few tentative thoughts, which I'm sure you'd find disappointing."

"No I wouldn't. Please, Rusty."

"All right," he sighed. "I warn you I've never tried this before, but I'm willing to make a stab at it for you."

He recrossed his long legs and frowned at the barrier islands, where purple haze was deepening as the golden sunrays withdrew. Over the marsh curlews sped and dipped, accenting the silence with their haunting cries. She watched his face, waiting for him to speak.

"Well," he began with a slow meditative smile, "suppose I start by telling you what I don't believe. I don't believe man has solved the riddle of the universe yet. And I think it would be remarkable if he had, considering the short time he's been in a speculative frame of mind. Man is still in his childhood, the age of myths and fairy tales. . . . Some of these myths that we've invented to shield our nakedness, our helplessness against the winds of fate, are very beautiful and comforting. But if the dead rise not? What if the answer to this final question is like all the rest, simply a wish?"

His eyes returned to hers for a moment. She nodded quickly, intent on his words.

"There seems to be some vast and intricate order in the universe," he went on, "some evolving design, some dream working itself out. And perhaps in time man will solve the ultimate mystery that lies behind everything, from the falling of a leaf to the birth of a star. But meanwhile the mystery remains. Why has creation put forth man? What is it trying to get at through us in the midst of all these myriad changing shapes of the world, these marvelous shifting patterns of life and death and rebirth that by turns delight and torture us? I'm sure I don't know."

He took up his crab-net again, but his hands were idle as he gazed off into space. When he continued to stare out over the marsh in silence, she finally prompted him to go on.

"Isn't that what's called agnosticism?"

"With a dash of stoicism," he nodded. "But I'm prepared to go a little beyond that negative point, now that you've got me started and I'm in such good hands. In fact you're such a sympathetic listener, I'm ready to cut loose and go my limit. How about it?"

"Fine!"

"All right then, just stop me when you've had enough and no hard feelings. . . . Well, come to think of it, I guess I have a positive faith after all. I seem to believe in man. In spite of wars and all the rest of our cussedness and folly. In man as member of a great race of strivers and seekers. I believe in his lonely adventure, his groping toward the light, his persistent searching for a truth to reconcile good and evil, the things of Christ and Caesar. I believe in his suffering and wounds, his slow and painful growth. I admire his courage, his will to hope when all hope is gone. I like his spirit, the supreme spirit of life. . . .

"I'm willing to bet the time will come when man will find the answer to all his questions within himself, his own heart and mind, understanding at last that the only meanings life can have are those he gives it. As the spearhead of nature's growing soul he will learn to accept the challenge of his destiny without hope of supernatural reward or fear of supernatural punishment. And I can't believe that even God will begrudge him this new religion, because I have a sneaking suspicion God is patiently waiting to become a reality from man's dream of Him, just as man has become a reality from some dream of time. . . .

"I believe man will develop a sort of *esprit de corps* about himself and his fellow men. Yes, the brotherhood of man, old and new hope of the world. Faith in the forces that unite and strengthen against the forces that divide and destroy. Then will the day break and the shadows flee away. Man will at last find himself at home in the world, and seek to make his home a place worthy of his heritage and dreams. Then no longer will those about us be strangers to be feared or exploited, but sharers in the communion of a universal church and faith, comrades in the immortal adventure of our race."

His voice stopped abruptly, and his eyes returned to hers from their distant visions. His smile came back too. "Still with me?" he asked. She nodded and smiled vigorous encouragement, but something in her throat prevented her answering him. He looked away again, and presently his voice resumed its course.

"But what about you and me and the rest of us who are doomed to die in the wilderness and never reach the promised land. We must live our lives in a sort of twilight zone between dark and dawn, scarcely able to see our fellows in the mists of fear and blind selfishness that surround us. We live in an age whose policy is still every man for himself. . . . But even in a golden age of faith, man must still stand alone. As at last all of us must always in any age. For what millennium can protect us from the changes that time brings, the end of our dreams, the loss of those we love."

He was silent again, his eyes on the barrier isles and the sky above them, where the flames of sunset were reflected in a soft rose glow. After a moment he roused himself and turned to her.

"That would be a pretty sad and ungrateful note to end on, wouldn't it. No, that won't do. The last word, the final answer to life, had better be a thanksgiving. For all the splendor and wonder of the world. For friendship. And love.

"And that," he smiled, "is as far as I've gotten."

As he searched her eyes, a look of dismay came into his face.

"Have I hurt you by anything I said?"

The flames of the sunset were streaked and blurred, but it was easy to give him a reassuring smile.

"I'm afraid you don't know me very well yet, Rusty. I'm just thankful for your friendship, and this is the way it affects me. I don't know why."

She joined his laugh of relief and took his hand.

"Rusty," she said to him after a moment, "do you mind if I believe what you do?"

"But it isn't even finished yet."

"It's finished enough for me."

"But at least give me a little more time to tinker with it."

"No, I want it just as it stands. It's perfect."

"Thanks, but I'm suspicious of sudden conversions."

"You don't need to be of this one. I know it's right. I can feel it."

"Now listen, Emily. I trotted it out for your inspection, but I don't claim it's any good. It just happens to be my way of seeing things, and I may be suffering from acute astigmatism. No, you'll have to fit your own glasses, and keep correcting them as you go along."

"All right," she finally conceded. "But I'm going to start by testing yours. I know they fit me, and I know I won't ever have to change again."

"We'll see about that," he smiled.

As they sat watching the sunset sky, she felt a sudden shiver of cold, and with a start remembered Harriet, waiting at Cherokee.

When the buggy reached the main road and she turned Garibaldi's stubborn homeward-bound head in the direction of Cherokee, she saw Harriet coming toward her. Even at a distance and in failing light it was plain to be seen that Harriet was indignant; and as the distance grew less, the indignation of her walk seemed to increase. Her mouth was set and her face flushed when Emily reached her and backed the buggy around.

"Sorry you had to walk part way, Harriet. I didn't mean to be late."

Harriet got in without a word. And she remained tight-lipped and flushed all the way to Land's End. Unprepared for such rigid censure, Emily could find nothing to say. She felt her own lips becoming tight and her cheeks flushing. . . . At the stable Harriet got out and went straight to the house. Tunis came running from the kitchen to unharness Garibaldi, but Emily stayed to help him, dreading the scene that Harriet was working herself up to.

When she finally went in to find her, Harriet was stationed before the sitting-room fire looking very tense and inflexible.

"I'm really terribly sorry I kept you waiting, Harriet. I don't blame you for being provoked."

Harriet's voice came with a startling rush.

"It isn't just your being late to get me. It's where you were. You were at Dr. Stewart's and I happen to know you stop to see him most every afternoon. I don't say you're in love with him, but he's certainly in love with you. . . . Can't you keep away from the man? Haven't you had enough trouble with men? And you seem to forget you're still married. If I were in your position I'd confine my interest to teaching and leave the opposite sex alone."

And with that she hurried out of the room and upstairs, leaving Emily staring at the fire.

Later Tunis brought in an armful of wood, and she roused herself to answer his good-night. When he had gone, she sat down limply. The last light drained slowly from the room, till only the flickering of the fire was left. When Lucy came in with the lamp, she kept her face turned away.

"Suppuh on de table, Miss Em'ly."

"Thank you, Lucy. Call Miss Harriet, will you, she's upstairs."

Lucy's house slippers shuffled back to the hall, went softly upstairs, and after a minute came clopping down and faded away to the kitchen. Emily heard Harriet's footsteps in the bedroom overhead, then on the stairs. When she looked up, Harriet was standing in the doorway. Her eyes were red.

"I'm afraid I said too much," she faltered.

Emily got up and stood with her cold hands to the fire.

"No, I'm glad you were frank. I needed to be reminded of my position."

"I only want to save you from any more trouble."

"Harriet, you're a wonderful friend, but I can't offer any apologies for my friendship with Dr. Stewart."

"I can't see why I'm not friend enough for you. It's a woman's pure friendship you need. How can a woman be friendly with a man without the carnal element creeping in, in thought at least? . . . No, Emily, I can't approve of your seeing Dr. Stewart alone. But I will try to ignore it and not mention it again, if you'll promise to be careful and not let it come between us."

She came over to the fireside, eyes mournfully large, lips trembling.

"I can't stand to dispute with you, Emily, I just have to give in, it takes so much out of me. I only want us to be close, like sisters. You don't seem to have learned a single lesson about men from what you've been through, you're still just a headstrong young girl, impulsive and rash and terribly impressionable, badly in need of an older sister to look after you. But I didn't mean to say anything to hurt you. Will you forgive me?"

Emily put her arm around Harriet's shoulders.

"If you'll forgive me for being late," she said with a pang of wry amusement. "I promise it won't happen again."

✓   ✓   ✓

During the summer and autumn, the months since last spring when Rusty's friendship had come like providence to meet her need, she had remembered Aaron only in those moments of anguish when she had forced herself to speak of him, to tell Rusty what had happened; the rest of the time her mind had been closed like a door against all thought of him. Now Harriet's words, reminding her of her "position", had broken the door open and it could not be closed again. But she could face him now and every stinging memory that came back with him, for she felt strong in the armor that Rusty's friendship had given her. She could do more, in fact, than just face these Aaron memories: she could live with them without flinching, scrutinize them, come to dispassionate conclusions about them.

One thought that kept repeating itself in her mind was the strangeness of what had happened to her. Only yesterday she had been a daydreaming girl in pigtails, visiting Grandma Curtis at Salem and complaining that nothing ever happened. Vividly that animated old face returned, and the petulant dear voice with it.

"Nothing ever happens! Didn't you tell me you found a turtle in the brook today? Didn't the mailman let you ride to the Post

Road with him? Didn't you have strawberry shortcake for dinner? What more do you want, child, a witch on a broomstick or just an Indian massacre?"

"I mean nothing big ever happens, Granny."

"Nothing big! I like that. Someday, my fine fidgety young lady, you'll learn to appreciate the blessed small things of life. You'll have plenty of rough weather, if that's what you're after. Let me see that hand again. Mercy!—no-one in the family ever had a fate line like that, except your ne'er-do-well Uncle Ned that sailed the seven seas. A little patience, child, and you'll have no cause to complain about nothing ever happening!"

But she had continued to worry that life would never begin. And then with what sickening speed it had finally lifted her out of day-dreams into a bewilderment of nightmare happenings, to drop her here at Land's End as suddenly as it had snatched her up. . . . Time was not Granny, reading your palm or telling your fortune in a teacup, but a demented wind playing with lives like autumn leaves: you were lucky to be out of the whirl-dance, lodged in this nook where only echoes of the wind came, to make you tremble in retrospect. Your only wish and hope now was that the wind would pass you by, forget you, leave you here in peace. But always now there was the shadow of Aaron.

It was the persistence of the shadow that was most troubling. There was no driving it away. As the slow quiet months moved by, it neither advanced nor receded. It just stood there watching her, from beyond the woods and fields to the north where Beaufort lay hidden.

Even if by some force of will she could have broken this constant awareness of the shadow, there was the sequence of outside events to keep reminding her. After the Fourteenth Amendment was passed early in the spring of '67, the Union League sprang into existence to organize the freedmen vote. The excitement among the island people was enormous: the mystic initiation and rites of the League intoxicated them and they enrolled in droves. Spring planting and school were alike forgotten in the frenzy over "de boilit", which had now taken the place of land-owning and book-learning in their fancy as the miracle that would make them the white man's equal. Frogmore Store was headquarters of the League's activities on the island, but there were many branch meeting places. The Land's End people celebrated their mass membership with an almost nightly shout at the praise-house. Attendance at the afternoon class for grown-ups fell away to nothing, to the tune of long rigmaroles of excuse. She saw the futility of remonstrating with the tide and concentrated on holding the children's class together.

It was some time before she discovered that the leader of the League in the Beaufort district, the "Paa'son" whose name was on the tip of every gullah tongue, was Aaron. The people seemed to regard him as personally responsible for getting them the vote. She had known of former visits he had made to the neighboring plantations as agent of the Freedmen's Bureau, but those visits had been comparatively rare. Now he came regularly to the island. Twice Harriet reported his appearance at Cherokee to speak to the people, and one day he made a tour of Land's End. But she did not see him even then; she stayed in the house till Tunis came to say he was gone. He remained a shadow, invisible, suspended in silence, and for that very reason all the more sinister and threatening, impossible to disown or escape from. You'll never be through with me, she remembered his last words: We'll meet again, you and I, we'll come together, it's the only salvation for either of us, you'll find, the only solution. . . .

So the spring went by, and another summer came; and at the end of the summer the great Registration Day in Beaufort. Rusty brought back an account of the astonishing carnival. Twenty-five hundred blacks had registered, and fifty whites.

"Some of the out-island people," he told her, "having no idea what a ballot is, brought baskets to take it home in."

As the movement to turn the South over to the freedmen advanced, a hot shame for the North grew in Emily. When Harriet came back from Philadelphia glowing with praise for the work of Thaddeus Stevens, whom she had had the privilege of meeting just before she left, Emily listened till she could contain herself no longer.

"But Harriet, if the Republicans win the election, it will mean black rule—black over white."

"Well, why not?" Harriet flustered. "The Southerners don't seem to learn anything more from experience than some other people I know. They had a chance to show their good intentions toward their new fellow citizens right after the War, and what did they do?

Tried to return them to virtual bondage by disqualifications and restrictions of the most vicious nature. They must be made to accept the Negro as their equal. If that means the Negro in power, they have only themselves to blame. . . . I'm afraid you've been listening to your Dr. Stewart."

Emily gripped herself to keep from answering. She hated this blind hatred of the South, this vindictiveness that was only too willing to exalt the black man if it promised the debasement of the Southern white, but she realized she must keep her feelings to herself if she wished to avoid a serious quarrel with Harriet. As it was, Harriet had worked herself into a righteous indignation that lasted several days.

Early in the new year came the grotesque Constitutional Convention of Black Republicans in Charleston. The election in April was a sweeping victory for the Radical party. Harriet was delighted and postponed her departure for the North till July so that she could attend the inauguration of Governor Scott. The state was in the hands of a motley crew of blacks and tans, scalawags, and carpetbaggers.

"I'm tired of being a Northerner," she finally told Rusty.

"You're turning into sort of a Yankee Rebel," he said. "If you don't watch out you'll wind up as a sure-enough one, a regular sea-island lady."

VIII

IN THE OUTSIDE WORLD of the state and nation strange dark events were unfolding, but it was only their faint echoes that reached Land's End. Here time moved quietly, smoothly, like the ebb and flow of the little creek that passed Rusty's cottage on its curving way out through marsh to the broad Inlet. Island spring and summer, autumn and winter were like four walls of shelter, slowly revolving and changing yet always steadfast around her. She knew the island's moods by heart now, and each season had its special charm; but summer, which had been so unbearable the first year, had become her favorite, for then there was a rest from teaching—and Harriet went North.

Remembering the debt she owed Harriet, she was mortified with herself for feeling relieved when the separation of vacation started. But there was no denying the sense of ease that came when Harriet was gone. And this raising of spirits seemed to be shared by Lucy.

"Miss Em'ly, Miss Hayut sho do put we t'rough. Hope he don' come bock too soon dish time."

"Miss Harriet's been wonderful to us both, don't ever forget that," Emily had said, more as a rebuke to herself than to Lucy.

"No'm, I ain't fuhgit. But I ain' fuhgit he don' like Mistuh Rusty neiduh. He always lookin' fuh chonce fuh fuss wid you 'bout dat an' pick on we. I too glod fuh summuh, I know dat fuh true."

It was true: summer was the best time. But all times were soothing and healing here at Land's End, even those long days when Rusty was only near, when she missed seeing him out of deference to Harriet's nerves. Because of him Land's End, the house and the place and its people, was a blessing in all seasons, helping her to gather strength and confidence for some solution to free herself from the shadow of Aaron.

The spreading plague of Reconstruction, now fixedly associated with him in her mind, had not yet seriously affected the life of the island. The people had sobered from the intoxication of the ballot. They had seen what cunjuh their votes could make, it had placed members of their race in highest state offices and converted every county court-house into a Negro club, but here on St. Helena at least a plain man must still work or starve. Government rations were no longer available, and the paternalism of the Freedmen's Bureau and Union League greased no hungry mouths. The people had come face to face at last with the full implications of freedom, the drab responsibility of looking after themselves.

In the spring of '70 cotton was planted abundantly the island over. Rusty said it looked like old times. The routine of island living was set again to the rhythm of long-staple. Planting began in February with listing of the soil that had been fertilized with "saltmaa'sh", reed straw and rich mud hauled by batteau. In late March the seed was drilled into ridges. Hoeing ceased in July, when more saltmarsh was piled in heaps to rot for next year. In September began the harvesting. To see the white fluff opening on withered stalks was no longer for Emily the novel sight it had been her first year on the island, but it was surprising and exciting now to see so many fields of snow. It was November before the stiff brown bolls had surrendered the last tatters of fleece, and sluggish ox-carts began to carry the bags that had accumulated in yard and shed to Frogmore Store, where cotton became credit in a ledger. Some of the more independent carts dragged on to the Ladies Island ferry to see if they could get better terms from Mr. Rutherford, the Yankee who had put up a warehouse and gin on a wharf at Beaufort. A few of the people who owned flats took their cotton to town by water.

The women did the greater part of the work, including the heavy hoeing and the break-back picking. They seemed to accept their burdens as a matter of course. In slavery times, Rusty said, they had been the responsible heads of families: the cabins had been theirs, the children had been listed in plantation records as belonging to them, and any money made from the sale to the Big House of chickens and eggs and yard truck raised in the hours after the day's task had been theirs to spend. Since freedom the men had grown jealous of their rights, they wanted to be boss in the home, to fish and loaf as much as they liked and spend some of the family income to pleasure themselves; but they were willing to leave to the women the privilege of doing most of the field work, as well as buying rations, cooking, washing, ironing, mending, and raising the children "deestint". Yet the only complaint Emily heard the women make was about the little they got for their money at the store. As one Land's End woman put it:

"I is a flat-foot blue-gum pusson an' ain' know much, but I ain' sotisfy de way dem white people to Frogmo' do me, Mish Am'ly. I done make good crap but what I got fuh muh labuh? Dey say muh money in de book mos' gone already—dear Jedus, dat s'pose to las' out de year, fuh muh hosban' and seben hongry chillun what stan' pratchly start-naked dish berry day. You bettuh don' fuhgit we, please ma'm, when de nex' mission box come fum de Nort'."

The revival of cotton planting ended for good and all the afternoon class for grown-ups. But there seemed to be more children than ever for the morning class. Perhaps because the new crop of heads were a harder lot, definitely stupider, noisier, and more unruly than the older ones, many of whom had graduated to the field and home, the fishing fleet, or the Beaufort militia, a passion with the boys.

Her greatest loss among the charter members who were gone was Tunis. She saw him now only when he came to the house to do chores: a long-legged lad who had lost all resemblance to the bashful little fellow she had first known, though he still preserved his good manners, an ingratiating smile, and the liking for elegant speech inherited from his father. But his loss and the loss of his sister Weenia were compensated for, numerically at least, by the addition to the class of two more of Isaac's and Leola's endless offspring. The names, most surprising of the series, were Hard-Times and Breakfast. Leola had always scorned school for herself, though Isaac had attended for a while, but she was an unfailing source of pupils. Lucy, who came over for an hour in the morning to "catch" a reading lesson with the children, sucked her teeth over Leola's latest contributions.

"Miss Em'ly, dat 'oman cyan' read an' he cyan' write but he sho can multiply."

The number of new faces and the loss of old ones wakened her to the fact that she had been teaching here at Land's End for almost five years of being separated from Aaron without being free from him.

And added now to this realization were grave doubts about any permanent value in her teaching. There was so little to show for all the struggle with gullah spelling and grammar, reading, writing, and arithmetic, and above all gullah Latin, which Harriet insisted upon for all the older children. When they outgrew school most of them promptly shed any vestiges of schooling that had happened to cling to them.

"It's like pouring water through a sieve," she said to Rusty in a moment of blank discouragement.

"That's about it," he agreed. "They can't absorb most of it because it's not related to anything they need. How about concentrating on their everyday lives? They could use a good influence there."

She resolved to take teaching less seriously and find some way to enlarge the meager contact that school gave her with the younger generation of Land's End. In spite of the long hours of class she was really more out of touch with the young people than with their parents, who were continually bringing their troubles to the house. Finally she hit on the idea of a sewing class for the girls, on afternoons when they were not needed at home, as a means of getting better acquainted. When many of the boys clamored to join the sewing circle at the Big House, feeling they were being slighted, she organized a basket-making class for them. Harriet said she was afraid these "extra-curriculum experiments" would only relax school discipline, but when sample embroidery work and baskets sent North met with the approval of the Society, she withdrew her opposition. Emily was delighted with the success of the plan: it put her in close friendly touch with the boys and girls, helped school, and made up for lost illusions about the value of the formal lessons she had to continue to give them.

But of greatest satisfaction to her was her work with Rusty at his Saturday clinics. The growing fame of the "clink" brought people from every corner of the island to the little cottage at Pine Point. It was hard work, more difficult and complicated than even her first day with him, the memorable "woccination", but it was work she could believe in with all her heart.

As a preliminary task it was necessary to separate, at the porch steps, those who really needed attention from those who had come with ailments created or enlarged by curiosity. Then began the long day of examining and treating a variety of miseries, she and Lucy acting as nurses. Here all the physical ills of the islanders came to light; in spite of her experiences at Tabernacle hospital she had been too shaky at first to be much use as an assistant, but gradually she had learned to be steady and efficient. These clinics were revelations of the stoicism of the people under pain become chronic through neglect and witch-doctoring, of Rusty's unfailing skill and self-command, and finally of her own ability to stand at his side without flinching even when he was operating, even the time he had to remove the infected eye of a boy from Sams Point. When that was over he gave her a look and nod of approval that meant more to her than anything he might have said.

Harriet made it amply clear that she did not approve of this participation in the clinic. But Emily had become inured to Harriet's standing disapproval, expressed now always in tones of patient sweet reasonableness.

⚹   ⚹   ⚹

When Rusty first spoke of going to Charleston, telling her of the post he had been offered in the general hospital there, it was such a stunning blow to her that she was able to think only of herself, of herself alone. She knew at once that he should go, but the thought of losing him, continuing her life here without him, was so devastating that she accepted without question his flimsy reasons for rejecting the offer. Now at last she realized fully what his friendship meant to her, how dependent she was on him, how completely her own feeling of strength came from his strength, which had picked her up in the beginning and was still supporting the confidence it had given her: he was the prop she leaned on, the heart of this island life, the force that held everything together and kept the shadow of Aaron at bay.

But when she had had a little time to rally from the shock and overcome her selfishness and fear, she set to work to persuade him to take the post, urging him with every argument she could think of. He must go, he was wasting his life here, he should have gone to a city like Charleston long ago. He was needed there and he needed the equipment he would have there, the scope of practice, contact with other doctors. To say nothing of the salary, money for new instruments and medical books and the experiments he was always talking about.

"You can have a decent office and a real laboratory. And some clothes. New suits and shirts and shoes."

"And a hat, I suppose. A tall beaver hat with a frock coat, like an undertaker. And my name on a door with office hours."

"Oh please, Rusty. It's the only thing to do. You've got to go."

"So you want to get rid of me."

The hardest part was trying to give her voice spirit and at the same time keep back the pain.

"How would you feel if you were begging the best friend you or anybody else ever had to leave you?"

"You'd miss me then. Well, that's the first sound argument I've heard."

"Do you really want me to try to tell you how much?"

"No. Because I'm not going. Inertia has me."

But at least she was able to persuade him to ask the hospital for further time to consider. And finally, months after the offer, he gave in to her and agreed to accept—on one condition.

"That you come too. Being missed by you would be all I'd ask of life, but the catch is it would take a little too much missing in return. How do you expect me to get along without my partner? We'll fix you up with a nursing diploma or something."

"No, Rusty, I'd just be under foot there, in your way."

"All right, young lady, we'll stay here then."

"Rusty, if you'll only go I'll promise to come later. If you still want me, and I can wait that long. I want to do whatever you want me to."

"And what I want, first and last, is your happiness. Not to complicate your young life further. But I haven't accomplished much as a friend, have I. Even with the legal talents of my cousin Joseph Bramwell I haven't worked out any way to pry you loose from that husband of yours—short of murder, which would certainly be a pleasure. . . . All right, Emily, I'll go ahead and break the Charleston ice, if that's the way you want it. Then we'll see what happens next."

This day when it was settled that he was going to join the hospital staff was in the spring of '72, the third year of renewed cotton planting on the island. But there were more months of grace, a whole final summer with him, because he insisted on postponing his move to Charleston till Harriet returned from her vacation in the North. It was autumn and the third crop of cotton was harvested before he actually prepared to leave.

And then, with the separation finally at hand, panic took hold of her.

"You're sure you'll come back pretty often?"

He put his reassuring hands on her shoulders.

"If I can't arrange to get off every week-end or so for our clinic, the hospital post will be open again. And I'll be back in between times every chance I get. Don't worry, I'll be keeping close enough tabs on you. It's me you'll never be rid of, not Mr. Moffet."

She clung to that comfort to carry her through the preparations for his departure. It carried her safely through even the hour of leave-taking, when she took him in the *Dolphin* one November morning to get the train at Port Royal, the little settlement that had sprung up to the west of Beaufort at the terminus of the new branch line from Yemassee. But on the long sail back to Land's End, she had to surrender to the tears that were blinding her. Now there was only Jeb to see.

"He's coming back to us," she told the sad brown eyes, "he'll always come back to us."

As soon as she got back to the house, she had to drive Harriet to Cherokee. Harriet concealed her satisfaction poorly. From that day on she was very generally amiable, except for her pretense of being in deathly fear of Jeb.

The first days of separation from Rusty brought a loneliness so intense that she could hardly eat or sleep. But when a letter came from him, she discovered the solace of writing. To attempt to communicate with him by means of scratchings on a piece of cold blank paper seemed in the beginning a hopeless substitute for speech, speech that included seeing his eyes and hearing his voice in answer. But in her eagerness to reach him, she soon learned to forget the wretched medium of pen and paper and speak to him as if he were here with her, to talk to him as naturally as if they were still together.

Because she wanted to avoid intruding herself too much on his time and attention, she sent him a letter only once or twice a week. But she could not let a day pass without easing her loneliness for him by writing; it was a sort of diary she kept and mailed to him at intervals. Usually she wrote to him in the evening after supper, but sometimes when she visited the cottage at Pine Point with Jeb to satisfy herself that everything was all right there, she took a pad and pencil with her and wrote to him from the bench between the palmettoes, or if the day was cold from an armchair before a fire in his little sitting-room. So by this strange but precious makeshift, this pitiful substitute for the old companionship, she was able somehow to deny his absence, to break the silence of separation.

The actual time she had with him on those scattered week-ends when he came home was strictly limited. In theory the trains from Savannah, Augusta, and Charleston met at Yemassee at noon, and Rusty reached Port Royal about one o'clock; but the schedule was capricious, and it was seldom that she had more than a fragment of Saturday afternoon with him. When the weather prevented her from meeting him in the sailboat, he had to go to Beaufort and she drove Garibaldi to the Ladies Island ferry to meet him there, which meant the loss of much time. And Sunday morning and part of the afternoon had to be given to the clinic. Then before she could fully realize that he was with her, he was back in the city clothes he hated and gone.

The long days between his returns she kept herself as busy as possible with her work. She read a great deal now too, making astonishing voyages of discovery in the books borrowed from his little library. She read slowly, thinking of the bearing of what she read on her own life and the lives she knew, remembering whatever puzzled or particularly pleased her to take up with Rusty. He smiled at the resolution with which she was consuming the whole range of his shelves, from Aeschylus and Plato, Shakespeare and Montaigne, to *Pilgrim's Progress* and *Don Quixote, Tom Jones* and *Religio Medici*. Once when he came back from an absence of two weeks and she proudly reported that she had disposed of *Faust, Tristram Shandy,* and *Walden,* he offered to mix her a dose of paregoric.

"Let me see your tongue," he said.

She showed it to him. He took her pulse then, frowning heavily at his watch. In the end he had to admit that her digestion was remarkable.

"That's because I ruminate," she told him.

Harriet, whose reading was ostentatiously restricted to her missionary papers and a nightcap from *Daily Strength,* viewed all of

Emily's reading with raised eyebrows and some of it with a frightened expression. One evening after supper when she found Molière's plays resting on her *Missionary World,* she removed the offending volume with a shudder, using two fingers for tongs.

"It won't bite you," Emily couldn't resist saying.

That gave Harriet an opportunity to deliver one of her patient-voiced rebukes.

"Emily dear, I'd rather not discuss these books of Dr. Stewart's. His influence over you is so strong that I realize nothing I say could have any effect, except to cause ill feeling between us. I dread to think what all this is doing to your character, but I've given up trying to reason with you about anything. No, please don't say anything more. You know I can't stand arguments."

These periodic tiffs with Harriet were convincing Emily of the hopelessness of ever being able to revive their fading friendship. But in spite of Harriet, and in spite of the irremovable shadow of Aaron, her life and work at Land's End continued as an essentially grateful state. For from necessity she had learned to feel that even in his absence Rusty was not really away, but always here near her, watching over her as the months tightened quietly into another year of this strange island freedom in bondage.

IX

IN THE COUNTRY beyond the island the march of events grew more and more amazing, but remained remote. It was difficult to get a true conception of what was going on out there: the picture had to be pieced together from conflicting sources. The *Beaufort Republican,* to which Harriet subscribed, was a pro-Reconstruction paper, while the *News & Courier* that Rusty sent from Charleston was anti-Reconstruction. In the latter all the news was white; in the former, black. Her sympathies were now so definitely with the South that to keep from accepting every Southern attitude, at once and at face value, she had to remind herself of Rusty's warning: "Reconstruction is creating such a blindly solid South that everything Southern is right because it's Southern."

As for world events, her main source of information and understanding were the back numbers of magazines, *Harper's* and *Scribner's,* that came in the Aid Society boxes. In their illustrated articles she had followed, somewhat tardily, the course of the Franco-Prussian War through the siege of Paris to the birth of the German Empire, in the Hall of Mirrors at Versailles. While Chicago had been swept by fire, feudalism had been abolished in backward Japan. And while the East was waking from its age-old sleep to trade with the golden new West, Rome had become the capital of a united Italy. . . .

In the *Harper's* for July, 1873, she found a pair of ghosts from the past. They were in the first installment of General Sherman's triumphant tour through Europe. The last she had heard of General and Mrs. Sager was their transference from Charleston to Washington the second year after the War, but here they were again with Sherman. The party landed at Naples. They climbed Vesuvius. A

Pompeii, "assembled in the Public Baths", they were "moved by the beauty of the ruins to sing *Marching Through Georgia*"; however, "articles were so carefully watched by the police that it was impossible to take away souvenirs." "That evening the party dined *en famille* with the Grand Duchess Olga of Russia, who was visiting Sorrento for her health." For some reason the Sagers disappeared from the party after that, and with them went a large portion of Emily's interest in the remaining installments of the grand tour.

The magazines that came in the Society's Christmas box told in detail of the great panic that had struck the country in September. Payment of the French indemnity had loosed a speculative mania in Germany and Austria; when the bubble had burst it had hit the United States, where a boom headed by the railroads was in full swing. New York had been swamped with unmarketable securities, many banks and commercial houses had failed, three million men had been thrown out of work: everywhere glut, shrinkage of values, stagnation.

"Did you know we were having a panic?" she asked Rusty the next time he came back from Charleston.

"I don't know about the rest of the country," he said with a grim smile, "but how can we have a panic?"

But despite the affliction of Reconstruction there seemed to be first stirrings of better times in some parts of the South. At least so she gathered from a *Harper's* article, "The New South". South Carolina was in the depths of despair under the Carpetbagger-Negro machine of Governor Moses, but several of the states, including neighboring Georgia, had escaped the worst phases of Reconstruction and appeared to be on the road to recovery. In the Georgia section of the article the statements of two political leaders made a particular impression on her. The reactionary counsel of Robert Toombs, who opposed "Yankee innovations", emphasized by contrast the constructive plea of Benjamin Hill, who was urging the people of his state to make cotton their surplus crop, raise their own provisions, and so free themselves from bondage to brokers and merchants.

She wished she could pass that advice on to the Land's End people. Like the rest of the islanders they had become virtual slaves to Frogmore Store. Already many of them had lost their land and were hopelessly in debt.

They were such easy prey for every variety of folly. Even if they had been able to resist the white dominance of the Frogmore organization and the sophistries of the League and the Bureau, there were enough influences coming from their own color to turn their heads completely. Islanders who had gone as far as Charleston and Savannah and Columbia in search of work or adventure, youths who had joined the militia, those who had scraped and saved for the supreme pleasure of an excursion by steamboat or train, all brought back the same story: the country "b'long to we now", the bottom rail was on top with a vengeance. The accounts of Columbia were especially glamorous. There black folk dressed to kill, filled the State House and the adjoining saloons, governing the white folk and spending the tax money with a free hand. They lived in the best houses and rode in fine carriages. They smoked Havana cigars and drank French champagne.

Those stay-at-homes who were inclined to be skeptical of all this could see the new order of things for themselves by just going to Beaufort, and there were few who did not get there eventually for an Emancipation Day or Fourth-of-July jubilee. They could see members of their race walking the streets proud as any white man, talking loud and free, hobnobbing with the people from the North. They could see their own kind in the Court House, running the county. They could see Major Pritchard, swaggering black commander of the militia. And if they were lucky they might even catch a glimpse of Senator Robert Fenwick, with his silk hat and cane.

♪   ♪   ♪

Money, more than they had seen since the easy money of war times, was beginning to come into the hands of the island people through the new industry of phosphate mining. A plant had been established on Coosaw River near Port Royal to dredge up the fertilizer rock; the company was paying high prices for hand-picked rock, and every able-bodied man on St. Helena who could get hold of a batteau was diving for the stuff. The work was cruel, but it meant fat pay envelopes for gambling and drink at Frogmore Store. Rusty said that in slavery the only drinking was at the Christmas festival. But now a drunken negro was a common sight.

Manners were becoming absurd, revolting. She hardly knew whether to laugh or cry at some of the changes that were taking place around her. The Land's End women whose men worked at the Coosaw mines were beginning to go in for pin-backs, bustles, and button shoes, and were giving themselves all kinds of grotesque airs and graces. Frogmore was doing a rushing business in lotions for hair-straightening and skin-bleaching. One afternoon she met Isaac's wife Leola coming back from the store with a face that looked as if it had been whitewashed.

"Mercy, Leola, what on earth's happened to you?"

"Ain' nutt'n mattuh wid me," Leola blinked indignantly.

The ghastly complexion remained a mystery till later that afternoon when she saw Jessie Fenwick, leader of the plantation's burial club, "Ladies and Gentlemen of Charity of Thankful Baptist Church", and the social club, "Bon Ton League of Free Ladies". Jessie's complexion was even ghastlier than Leola's, but she was not in the least sensitive about it and readily explained that she was using Gardner's Alabaster Blanch, night and morning.

"I ain' shame of muh culluh, Miss Em'ly, but I jes' druthuh be white."

Lucy seemed to be the only person on the plantation who remained untouched by the times. She was openly scornful of "nigguh stribin' fuh be buckra".

"Dem people mus' be gone crazy. Nigguh cyan' be white no mo' dan mule can be haws."

She was especially hard on Tunis when he came back to Land's End full of brag after a semester at the University of South Carolina in Columbia.

"Boy," Emily overheard her say to him in the kitchen the day of his return, "don' come roun' me wid no hairs. I got no time fuh listen to you big-talk."

Tunis ignored the rebuke and continued. "Miss Lucy, you ain' know what Greek is, ma'm?"

"Who you callin' Miss an' ma'm? Don' you sassy me, I ain' no freedom nigguh!"

"Greek," Tunis said meekly, "is de talk of dead people."

He went on to tell her he was also studying literature, "de writin' of dead people", and history, "de life of dead people".

Lucy sucked her teeth. "What dat gwine git you, studyin' 'bout *dead* people? Shuh! Git out in de yaa'd an' break up some kindlin'. Make you'self useful nigguh, an' don' be pure fool."

Tunis's young brother Hard Times came to the house to do the chores now, but he could not be trusted to drive for the mail: Garibaldi's crotchets, increasing with age, were too much for him. So Emily had to drive to Frogmore. When Tunis had been going for the mail, she had rarely gone beyond the boundaries of Land's End and Cherokee; now every day was a forceful reminder of Reconstruction. It seemed to have become the chief ambition of the island people to spend as much time as possible at the crossroads store. The place was always crowded. Those who had no money for drinks and gambling in the noisy back room lounged around the porch and yard.

In the summer of '74, after Harriet had gone North, Emily avoided Frogmore except on Saturday mornings, when a message might come from Rusty if hospital work threatened to keep him in Charleston over the week-end. One Saturday she found the crowd at the store amusing itself with three youths who had made an early start on this favorite day of revelry. She saw that the youngest, who was too drunk to stand, was a boy from Land's End, one of the boys she had taught in the first year of her school. Recently he had been working at Coosaw, and throwing his money away as fast as he made it.

When she went into the store and faced Mr. Walters across the counter, she could no longer control her disgust.

"Mr. Walters, you're a Northerner, aren't you?"

He plugged a potato over the spout of the kerosene can he had finished filling, pushed his straw hat to the back of his head, and removed a mangled cigar from his mouth to give her a yellow-toothed grin.

"A Yankee, ma'm. And proud of it."

"Are you proud of your business here?"

Mr. Walters slipped his thumbs behind his suspenders and chewed his cigar good-naturedly.

"Coming from anybody but you, Mrs. Moffet, I'd be inclined to resent that question. But I know you don't mean nothing personal by it."

"Can't you see the harm your place is doing these island people?

As a Northerner don't you feel any responsibility toward them, to help them in their new freedom?"

He picked up the palmetto fan that lay on the counter and whisked the flies away before he answered.

"Mrs. Moffet, I'm just a plain human being. I ain't no nigra philanthropist. I come to these parts because I knew somebody was going to do the natives and I figgered it might as well be me as the next feller. I keep my nose out of other folks' business and I'll be obliged if they'll keep their nose out of mine. If you got any complaints to make about this place, better take them to your husband. He's boss here, I'm only his agent."

She looked at him in bewilderment.

"You mean he owns this store?"

Mr. Walters smoothed his stained moustaches with the back of his hand.

"That's right, you're kinda out of touch with your husband, ain't you. Well, let me tell you there ain't many pies the Parson ain't got a finger into. He's got a whole fist into this one."

Mr. Walters rested a confidential elbow on the counter.

"I got the greatest admiration for your husband, Mrs. Moffet. There's a man that knows how to make philanthropy pay. He don't miss a trick."

"Please give me the mail," she said weakly.

He reached into one of the pigeonholes of the post-office compartment and brought out two letters, examining the postmark of each before he handed them to her.

"Philadelphia and Charleston. That one from Miss Sheppard been here since Wednesday. Doc Stewart's come in this morning. Anything else I can do for you today, Mrs. Moffet?"

With numbed senses she left the store and went through the fringes of the crowd out front to the hitching-rail, where Garibaldi and the buggy were waiting between an ox-cart and a rickety sulky. All the drive home her eyes, half shut against the quivering sunshine, were seeing the shadow of Aaron.

The fragments of information about Aaron that had come to her from time to time had failed to make any connected picture of his life and activities, till this astonishing knowledge of his interest in

215

Frogmore fused them into an explicit whole. And now that she knew it was he who was robbing and ruling the island people through the manifold operations of the store, she wondered why she had not suspected it before. Ever since she had come to realize the malignant influence of Frogmore, she had felt behind it a force more sinister and resourceful than any of the visible members of its clique, Mr. Walters and the white and colored agents of the Freedmen's Bureau and Union League. But in spite of her awareness of his dominant position in the affairs of Beaufort and the islands, some lingering respect for his integrity, his steadfast devotion to a cause that she herself had once believed in, had prevented her from supposing that his activities went beyond the politics of Reconstruction. Now the last vestige of leniency was lost in the knowledge that his mind was behind this well-organized machine for exploiting the people; taking their hard-earned money in exchange for trinkets and bad whiskey and exorbitantly priced staples, stealing their land by "tax loans" and mortgage chicanery (there was a branch of the Freedman's Savings Bank & Trust Co. at the store), manipulating their votes and leading them deeper and deeper into the fool's paradise of Reconstruction.

What role he was playing in the affairs of the state was still partly obscure. She knew only that he had been elected Commissioner of Education on the Moses ticket of '72, and that he was running again on the Chamberlain "Reform" ticket in the approaching autumn elections. But from the beginning Marshlands had been headquarters for the Republican leaders of the coast-country Black Belt. And now she learned from Lucy that Tunis had brought back from Columbia reports of a house he had there, where he and Phyllis entertained the Governor and members of the black-and-tan legislature.

Lucy said: "He ain' deserbe to be white man, Miss Em'ly."

She had no conception of the extent of his power in the state till one day late in the summer when further revealing information came from Rusty. Rusty's cousin, Stephen Fenwick, had just been sentenced to three months' imprisonment in the penitentiary at Columbia for "night-riding". Major Pritchard, commander of the Beaufort militia and plague of the helpless little group of whites who had returned to the town since the War, had climaxed a series of frolics by leading a company of his men into Sunday evening service at St. Helena's Church. The whites had left to the accompaniment of black gibes and jeers. Several nights later Pritchard had been beaten by masked men. He had named Stephen Fenwick as their leader.

"The trial was a farce," Rusty said. "They had a nigger judge and a hand-picked jury of niggers and carpetbaggers. And Pritchard is Moffet's bodyguard and particular pet. It's a wonder the Moffet Ring didn't lynch Steve."

"The Moffet Ring—what's that?" Emily asked him.

"Well, strictly speaking the Ring is made up of Moffet and his Republican cronies here. But actually it includes the whole Republican organization of the state, from Governor Moses down. It runs the state, and Moffet runs it."

He stopped there and was reluctant to go on. "I didn't mean to bring him into the story. I know you don't want to hear about him."

But she urged him to tell her all he knew. "I want to see him as clearly as I can now."

"Well, I don't really know much about him. There are plenty of stories floating around about his private life, but you wouldn't like to hear them, take my word for it. But I can tell you this much, he's undoubtedly the brains of his party, the power behind the throne. He's the boss of this state."

"But how did he ever get such power?"

"By carefully building up influence. By fraternizing with the nigger leaders."

She was silent, trying to comprehend the full implication of his words.

"Few people," he went on, "have any idea of his real power. That Commissioner of Education business is just a screen. Politically he keeps well in the background and uses men like Moses for his puppets. We can't do much at the next election because even our own people are taken in by the reform promises of this new puppet of his, Chamberlain, who passes for a gentleman and scholar. They're attempting to whitewash Reconstruction now, but we're in for two more years of black corruption and plunder,—if the patient can survive that long."

He was right. At the autumn election Chamberlain was voted into office by an overwhelming majority. Then the "reform" platform was quickly scrapped, and the fate of the state sealed for another two years.

But now she was in a state of active rebellion against her own fate, her private Reconstruction. The cloud, so long safely distant and stationary, had suddenly moved nearer, looming up like a thunderhead on the island horizon. Her thoughts were never free now from this towering apparition of Aaron, and slowly out of the turmoil of revulsion a decision took shape.

It was hard to break the habit of resignation to her anomalous position, this strange chronic state of being neither married nor single. Since there had seemed to be no escape, she had long ago adjusted her mind to the hidden shackles, thinking of herself as a cripple who was living to overcome and even forget an incurable handicap. But the past months had changed all that, carrying her back to fearful consciousness of her position, its unfairness and absurdity, and giving her a desperate desire to escape. She had not, she now discovered, accepted her fate at all: she had simply been marking time, grateful to be physically free, to be let alone. Lulled into contentment by her life and work at this providential Land's End, through the sense of security that Rusty's friendship gave her, she had been afraid to consider any move that might disrupt the fine adjustment of this life. But though her mind had been avoiding the whole question of Aaron, as if she expected to be bound to him like this, invisibly, for the rest of her life, still some part of her will had been secretly protesting, always hoping for a way of escape, waiting from month to month and year to year for some move that would complete her release from this everlasting predicament. And now at last her whole being was aroused to effect some final break and deliverance.

A suggestion for action came, with the unexpectedness of fate, from the *Beaufort Republican*. One day, in a news dispatch from Columbia, it gave a list of the latest bills passed by the Chamberlain legislature, and among them were two startling items: one, legalizing miscegenation; the other, divorce.

"The first day of January, 1875," the editorial page declared, "will go down in history as the date when these two reform measures became law. At last marriage between white persons and persons of color, the only solution of the race problem, is to be recognized, giving the offspring of such unions full rights of legitimacy. And also for the first time in the history of this state, divorce will be obtainable, on any criminal grounds or by mutual consent of the parties concerned. In the mind of every progressive citizen these two liberal measures alone will insure the fame of our new administration, and allay all fear of any backing down or compromising with the reactionary elements. It is clear now that we can trust Governor Chamberlain to complete the great humanitarian objectives of the Reconstruction program, implanting them so firmly in the state that they will never be uprooted. Until then we must keep the opposition prostrate, and not heed the too soft-hearted sentiments of our good Commissioner of Education, Rev. Aaron Moffet, who feels it is time for a policy of appeasement. His 'era of good feeling' will have to wait until the business of the day is done."

That evening, after Lucy had cleared the dining-room table, Emily took her writing things there. It took a last tussle with her pride before she could put pen to paper. And then she wrote slowly and with agony, testing every word, trying to see her opponent and what his reaction would be to each phrase and sentence.

The address on the envelope was incredible. *Mr. Aaron Moffet, Marshlands, Beaufort, S. C. . . .*

It was a week before an answer came.

"I coulda told you your husband's in Columbia," Mr. Walters grinned through cigar smoke as he handed her the letter.

On the way back to Land's End, she fastened the reins around the whip in its socket and left Garibaldi to follow the road at his own somnolent gait while she tore open the envelope. She sat back in the seat to hold the shaky letter in the shade of the buggy top, out of the glare of the sun. The pounding of blood in her ears made her feel dazed as she began to read the fine handwriting.

My dear Emily,

Need I tell you with what delight I received your favor after so prolonged a silence—and with what dismay I read your proposal, or should I say disposal. I had been supposing, all this long time since our unfortunate separation, that you were quite content to remain my wife, in spirit at least, and now I find that you have been waiting for me to act!

You are quite mistaken in presuming I must want 'freedom'. I have freedom, all I can use. As for you, since your marriage vows have not interfered in the past with your freedom of action, I can only marvel that you have bethought yourself of divorce at this late date,—unless you are contemplating a second excursion into matrimony, which, if my information is reliable, seems quite probable.

Has it never occurred to you that had I wished to divorce you I would have done so ages ago in the neighboring state of Georgia, on the twin counts of infidelity and desertion? But as you know the whole idea of divorce is abhorrent to me. Particularly divorce from you. Times change and we with them, but not my tender devotion to you, which seems to have survived everything. And quite aside from that, I confess there is a selfish reason for my refusal. Now that the lawmakers of our adopted state have gotten a little out of hand and legalized both divorce and mixed marriage, I find it increasingly convenient, surrounded as I am by influential and maritally inclined ladies of color, not to be a technically free man.

No, Emily, you fail to make me see any advantage in coöperating with you to sever our connections. To be brief, you ask of me the one impossible thing. I shall be honored, of course, to be of service to you in any other matter. I am really embarrassed that you have never called upon me for financial assistance. Perhaps you will compromise to that extent.

Let me close with the hope that you will not be so rash as to sue me for divorce under our new law. One never knows where legal proceedings may lead before they are finished, and I am confident you do not wish to involve a certain Doctor of Medicine, as well as yourself, in a business so unsavory and futile.

With regrets that I cannot be of service to you in this matter, but always prayerful that some miracle will eventually bring you to see the light and rejoin me,

I remain, my dear Emily, as ever,

Your Devoted

HUSBAND.

P. S. Have I by any chance misinterpreted your letter? Was your appeal merely an example of woman's subtle strategy of indirection? Perhaps you are ready at last to come to some understanding, but your pride forces you to say exactly the opposite of what you mean. If this is the case, and nothing would make me happier, forgive me for being so dense.

I have often considered inviting you to preside over my prospering establishment, but I have always been deterred by the fear that life in Columbia would not be entirely to your taste. Now, however, we are about to clean house, tone things down and tidy up generally in preparation for the '76 elections: frankly you could be a great help here, not only to yourself and to me, but also to the Southern cause, which I hear you have espoused. I also hear that you have blossomed into loveliest womanhood at Land's End, which makes it all the greater pity that you have chosen to waste your fragrance there. Here you can have anything you want, on your own terms, of course. And I am sure you would find life here more interesting and worthwhile than teaching there forever, burying yourself alive in that barren retreat of yours, that hopeless cul-de-sac. All this requires of you is a little imagination, and the charity to forgive my transgression as I once forgave yours.

Let us meet and talk the whole thing over sensibly, Emily, like the civilized people we have both had time and experience enough to become.

AARON.

She made herself read the letter again. Then her numb fingers tore the paper into small pieces and let them fall at intervals along the roadside.

X

The spring of 1876 was delayed by a long and unusually bitter winter. But when at last the cold relaxed its grip and ardent sunshine flooded the Sea Islands, all the buds of woods and field and roadside burst open in one sensuous breath. Emily could remember no spring so lovely. Yet behind this extravagant manifestation of life lay memories of death, a swift crescendo of death that had come to shock and unnerve her.

Isaac was associated with each of these somber memories that lingered on to blight the season of rebirth. It was he who had shown her the stricken orange trees in the orchard near the stable.

"When I been boy," he had said with many shakings of his head, "wintuh ain' t'ink fuh be cole like dis. Dese time is pure crazy. Miss Em'ly, my maussa set dem tree out heself when dey ain' been nutt'n but seedlin', an' we done raise'um by han'."

And it was he who had brought first word of Garibaldi's passing. The veteran horse had been retired from active service the autumn before; Harriet had decided it would be cheaper not to replace him and had made arrangements with Isaac to drive her to Cherokee. Every morning Emily went to the stable pasture to comfort her melancholy old friend with a handful of brown sugar, returning at dark to see that he was safe in his stall. One morning Isaac came to the school to tell her he had found Garibaldi lying in the pasture at the foot of the big cedar, cold dead.

Then, Jeb. One day in Christmas week Isaac took him to the barrier islands: Rusty had given him permission to take the dog along when he went hunting. Emily expected them back by sundown, but she sat up till late that night waiting for them in vain. The next morning Isaac appeared at the house with tears running down his black cheeks. "Miss Em'ly, Mistuh Rusty ain' nebbuh gwine fuhgib me!" It was some time before she could get out of him what had happened. Jeb, following him through the underbrush, had suddenly sprung forward; only then had Isaac seen the rattler in his path; before Jeb's teeth had closed on its neck, the snake had struck the dog between the eyes.

"I done bring'um home, Miss Em'ly, an' I done lay'um to res' 'longside Gaa'baldi in de pasture. But I ain' hab haa't fuh tell you las' night. An' I ain' nebbuh gwine hab haa't fuh tell Mistuh Rusty."

And then, while she was still trying to realize that Garibaldi and Jeb were gone forever, death struck in a more terrible form, using Isaac once again as messenger. He had been to see Auntie Cuba on her sick-bed and she had sent him to the Big House. When Emily reached the little cabin in answer to the summons, the withered cataract-blinded old woman roused herself to clear the gathering of neighbors out of the room with hoarse abuse.

"Git out! I done help mos you git in dis worl'—Lawd hab mercy! —but I ain' need you fuh help me git out. Go on, eb'ry las' sinnuh of you, an' take you' moanin' wid you! Isaac?—wuh you at? Stan' to de do', son, an' keep out dat rabble."

Emily sat at the bedside and tried to comfort and reassure her. But Auntie Cuba, lying back exhausted now, only murmured: "T'ain' no use. I know when muh time come fuh true. When de tide out yonduh tu'n, he gwine cyarry me home."

Later she mumbled:

"Don' fret fuh me, chile. I ain' sad to be leabin' dis worl'. I too t'ankful I gwine home to muh Jedus."

It seemed to Emily that hours passed as she held the bony hand from which she could feel the last life ebbing away. From time to time she held a cup of water to the parched shriveled lips. Outside, voices moaned in the gathering dusk. Isaac's tall form stood motionless in the doorway, against the dying sky.

Afterwards, walking back to the house with Lucy who had come to meet her, she could hardly control the weakness in her knees. Harriet was waiting for her at the door with an injured expression.

"Why did you have to go? It was quite unnecessary."

She was too shaken to answer. She let Lucy make her a cup of tea, and then took her writing things to the dining-room table for a letter to Rusty, to ease the weight on her heart.

223

It would have eased the weight on her mind to have talked to Rusty about Harriet. Regularly he asked: "When are you coming to Charleston?" But she kept putting him off, unwilling to pass her troubles on to him till the last gasp. The Harriet problem, like the problem of Aaron, was a contest to be fought out single-handed now, a test of the strength that came from knowing Rusty, a final test of her ability to stand on her own feet, not an excuse for involving him. She would stick it out here with Harriet as long as possible before she turned to him for help. She would go on with her work and try to meet things calmly as they came, the way he always did.

Still, apprehension of some imminent crisis kept forcing its way through the defenses of her mind. She dreamed of herself being carried like a piece of driftwood by dark currents toward a hidden abyss. Was this a wish, she wondered, pressing forward from the back of her thoughts, a wish that something—anything—would come to break the curse that held her in this everlasting suspension. Or had some inner ear of awareness caught the actual approach of release. But what release could there be. If she were compelled to leave Land's End, if she left of her own will, there was no escape anywhere from this endless legal bondage to Aaron.

I've got to stop worrying, she told herself. It doesn't do any good. . . . It was all very well to tell herself that, but the presentiment of a crisis was too real to be dismissed. The trouble with Harriet was growing more acute with every day of the advancing spring. And after smoldering so long, it finally broke out in an open quarrel, when Harriet called her views on Reconstruction "shocking and disgraceful".

"Why? Haven't I a right to my own opinions?"

"Not if they're pro-Southern and you're working for a Northern organization. Unless you want to lose your position."

"I'm ready to give up my place here."

Harriet looked horrified at that. "Why, where on earth would you go? You told me your father disowned you when you ran away from Boston with Aaron Moffet,—would you go back there? Where else respectable could you go?"

"I don't know. Somewhere. Charleston, perhaps."

"Now, Emily, if you're going to make threats, I'm going to bed. From now on you may think, say, and do what you please, without any notice from me."

Harriet kept her word. The rest of the spring was one long reticence between them, gradually tightening till there was room left for only the barest civilities. Emily knew the deadlock could be broken with a few humble words: she would be sweetly forgiven. But then a new deadlock would build up, carrying their relationship one step nearer the inevitable conclusion. And she felt, at last, no desire to be forgiven. Some denouement was taking shape and she was braced to meet it, whatever it was, whatever the outcome.

One evening after supper she found herself disparaging Harriet's Philadelphia Centennial Exposition, celebrating a century of national progress. "When you think of conditions, a celebration does seem a little absurd, in spite of the marvel of the telephone invention and electric lights."

Harriet bridled at once.

"I suppose you got that from your friend Dr. Stewart."

Emily flushed. It was a foolish thing to have said, and she made an attempt to modify it. But Harriet was up in arms.

"You're always looking for a chance to belittle the North. I can't understand you at all anymore. You're perfectly hopeless!"

She checked herself there for an instant, but then the momentum of her anger swept her on. "I don't see who you are to criticize anything. If I'd made the mess of my life that you have of yours, I'd keep—I'd keep my thoughts to myself. I was going to ask you to come to Philadelphia for the Exposition, I was going to make a last attempt to get you away from the influences here that have warped your character. But now I give up. For good. Our relationship from now on will be purely professional."

When Harriet left for the North several days later, her good-bye was formal. This is the end, Emily thought. Still, it was not yet complete and final: the initiative for severing the long bonds with Land's End remained with her. And her will had not built up sufficient strength for action. It's the end, she kept telling herself, and now I must plan what I'm going to do. But the very thought of leaving this place that had become home numbed her mind. Pride could goad her, but it could not help her to come to any decision.

Through the deep languid days of early summer she continued her morning class for the children. Their faces and the faces of all the plantation people were sharpened in her eyes by the realization that soon she must be leaving them. When this thought hurt too much, something in the back of her mind whispered: Perhaps somehow the crisis will pass and you will stay on here, anyway you can postpone a decision till Harriet comes back in the autumn. But it was folly to listen to this voice. It was weakness, this reluctance to face the uprooting and make plans for the future now.

The June days moved by; and her thoughts, groping for direction, traveled in a blind circle. Then, abruptly, a sequence of surprising events came to take command of her.

Later in her life when she recalled the events of that summer, it was always Stephen Fenwick that she saw as the dominant figure. He was involved in the sequence from its beginning. It was his appearance on the scene, in fact, that marked the beginning, and that first day and its circumstances were unforgettably associated with him in her memory.

It was the first Saturday in July and Rusty was coming from Charleston. She had left for Port Royal in the sailboat earlier than usual: the wind was light, and she needed time to get provisions before his train came in. The little store stood with its back to the waterfront between a saloon and a real-estate office, which with some frame buildings in process of construction made up the main street of the infant town. Across the road from the false front of the real-estate office stood the sooty yellow station, its roof supporting a sign that said in dingy gilt letters: *PORT ROYAL—The NEW YORK Of The SOUTH ATLANTIC SEABOARD.* Midday heat quivered up from the burning sand and pressed down from above like a weight. Her eyes were half shut against the glare as she walked past the saloon, where somnolent forms of men and dogs roused themselves to stare at her from the torpid shade of the wooden awning. At the door of the store lanky Seth Robinson, the owner, met her with an expression of eagerness in his lean honest face. His voice, usually slow and drawling, was excited today.

"Been watchin' your sail clear from Land's End, ma'm."

Seth Robinson and his wife might be crackers, Rusty had said in telling her about them, but they were a long way from being poor white trash. The Robinson family had supplied old Beaufort with generations of harness-makers and artisans. After the War, Seth had married and for several years had struggled at tenant farming inland. When Port Royal had come into existence as terminus of the spur line from Yemassee, he had moved here to work at carpentering; and when this work had petered out, he had taken his little savings to open a store. Business was poor, Emily knew, but she hoped he would be able to hang on, for she liked this couple who were almost the only white people she had any contact with. She had soon learned the sorrow of their lives: in their farming days they had lost all three of their children from "fever". Swamp fever, Rusty had guessed.

Seth Robinson was saying: "Been hopin' you'd come today, ma'm."

"How is Mrs. Robinson getting on?" she asked him.

"Well, ma'm, that's just what I been frettin' about. You lookin' for Dr. Stewart on the train?"

When she nodded, he looked relieved.

"You see, ma'm, the niggers had their Fourth-of-July jamboree to Beaufort day before yesterday—salutes and brass band and speeches and all—and the girl we got to help out ain't showed up since, and I ain't been able to get nobody else. And now it looks like Marty's time ain't far off."

"May I see her?"

"Now I sure wish you would."

She let him take the market-basket from her arm and went with him through the store to a doorway hung with a jingling portiere of beads. They went on through the combination sitting and dining room and the kitchen shed to the yard on the waterfront, and picked their way around boxes and barrels to the outside stairway that led to an upstairs bedroom. It was a cramped sweltering little room; Seth had recently pieced it together out of odds-and-ends of lumber. Here his wife Martha was lying, and it was plain at once that her labor was far advanced. Emily had always thought of her as a good-looking woman: she had the same clean-cut features as Seth with high cheekbones and a strong chin, and fine eyes; but her face now was hardly recognizable: the skin was bloodless and drawn, the mouth distorted, the eyes glazed with sickness and pain.

After Emily had gotten Seth out of the way by sending him down to watch for the train, she set herself to the preparations she had learned from observation of the Land's End midwives, and from one memorable experience with Rusty in the delivery of the child of an unmarried plantation girl, a pitiably young girl. That had been three or four years ago, but every detail of the little drama, acted out in the lurching shadows of a cabin fire, was sharp and fresh in her mind. And now as she moved about this room she talked to comfort the woman on the bed, remembering Auntie Cuba's rhythmic phrases of encouragement. If Auntie Cuba were here, she would be chanting: "Bear down, chile, bear down. T'ain' no good to call 'pon Jedus—de Lawd gwine help dem what help deyself. Da's right, honey, help'um 'long, you comin' good now, comin' good."

Later, she went downstairs to put a pan of water on the little cook-stove in the shed and to bring up a basin of cool water to bathe the fevered face. As she sat at the bedside, stirring the suffocating air with the palmetto fan that Seth had given her, she listened for the first distant whistle of the train. But the only sound was Martha's breathing, and at intervals a fantastic note of men's blurred voices from the saloon next door. Even during the seizures of pain, no cry escaped the clenched teeth, though the head turned from side to side in torment and tears forced themselves between the quivering closed eyelids. If she would only cry out, curse and pray like the plantation women. . . .

As the minutes dragged by, Emily acknowledged to herself that Rusty was going to be too late, for the merciful spaces between the convulsions of pain were growing shorter and shorter, till there was no relief at all. Her heart began to pound and she was trembling inside with a curious mixture of fear and nervous laughter. And now, as if it had been carefully timed to increase her confusion, she heard the first faint sound of the train.

After that she lost all consciousness of everything except the suffering woman on the bed. Somehow she managed to keep her head clear; and when the final panic moments of birth came, she worked coolly, feeling Rusty's guidance and strength in her hands. But she was hardly prepared for the crisis that followed. For a few seconds her heart stopped dead as she struggled with frantic fingers to release the slippery cord knotted around the babe's neck. When a thin constricted little cry cut through the moaning of the mother, her heart began to beat again, but it took the room a long time to recover from whirling blackness.

Little by little, as she stood there steadying herself with a hand on the post of the bed, the train came back into her consciousness. No longer a faint promise, but a close reality now: she listened to its tired panting at the station. Yet it seemed an endless wait, as the clanging of the bell died down to a low hissing of steam, before she heard voices in the store. Then quick steps came up the stairs, the door opened, and Rusty was with her.

As he pulled off his coat, rolled up his sleeves, and snapped open the kit he always brought with him for the island clinic, his voice came to her in sustaining snatches. "Couldn't wait for me, eh? . . . Lord, it's hot in here! . . . You seem to have managed very well—have any trouble?"

"There was a knot," she told him weakly, "around the neck."

He glanced at her with approval. "Well. Had to work fast, didn't you. Better get a little air now."

"I'm all right," she assured him.

But she was glad to escape from the stifling room long enough to go down to the kitchen shed for the pan of hot water. Seth was standing at the end of the yard with some man, to whom he was talking earnestly. When he heard her step on the stairs, he looked around and hurried to meet her.

"It's a fine girl," she told his anxious eyes. He stared at her blankly, and she repeated, "A girl." When he continued to stare, she couldn't help smiling. "Wasn't that what you wanted?"

He came to life then and grinned. "Oh yes ma'm!—that's all right." He added quickly: "A girl's a mighty fine thing to have—mighty fine—and less trouble to raise, Marty always said."

He seemed completely bewildered and to help him she asked, "What are you going to name her?"

He had an immediate answer for that. "Dallas if it's a boy, Linda if it's a girl,—so it's Linda, ma'm."

"That's a fine name. . . . Can you get someone to stay with them tonight?"

"Well," he puzzled, "reckon I can get the station-master's sister. Least I can go see if she'll come. She's uppety like most all the niggers round here, but she owes us money."

He wanted to carry the pan of water upstairs for her, but she urged him on his errand.

As she went back up to the room she repeated the name Linda to herself with pleasure. When Rusty had poured some of the hot water into the washstand basin for his own use, she took the pan away from him. "Look here," he whispered, "you've done your share."

But over his amused protests and with as professional an air as she could summon, she set the pan on one of the two pine chairs in the room and drew up the other to face it, poured cool water from the washstand pitcher to bring the water in the pan to the right temperature, testing it with her elbow as she had seen Auntie Cuba do, and sat down with a towel spread over her knees. "Now I'm ready," she told him confidently. But when he brought her the helpless squirming little being that was Linda, her confidence forsook her. She was glad that he turned back to the bed, but she was aware that he was watching her out of the corner of his eye. In the next few minutes she could have used his help a dozen times, but she struggled on, clumsily and with flushed cheeks, refusing to appeal to him, wishing she had some of Auntie Cuba's reckless dexterity in handling newborn babes. Presently, however, she forgot him and herself in the ticklish business: always to support the little head, never to get a drop of soapy water in the wailing mouth and squeezed-shut eyes.

When it was over and Linda was safely dried and pinned into her first garment, Emily drew a deep breath of relief and held her up for Rusty to see.

"That settles it," he nodded. "There isn't anything you can't do. When are you coming to Charleston to help me?"

"Soon," she told him with a quick smile.

But he was looking at her with a not-to-be-put-off expression. "You've been saying that for a long time. I'm serious."

"So am I," she said, meeting his eyes.

"Young lady," he said to Linda as he took the bundle in his arms, "do you realize you owe your life, as well as your first bath, to your godmother here? See that you don't forget that." And he carried her to the bed to lie beside her mother.

He motioned Emily to the door. "Now go downstairs and take it easy, please. I'll be through in a minute or two. Look here, did you see Steve?" When she looked at him uncomprehendingly, he said: "Stephen Fenwick. He came out with me—forgot to tell you in the excitement. Didn't you see him when you went down?"

She shook her head.

"Well, he's down there somewhere." He opened the door and went out on the landing of the stairs. When he called, "Steve!", the man standing at the end of the yard turned and looked up. Rusty drew her out on the landing and performed a hasty introduction:

the man raised his hat and bowed stiffly. "Now go down and talk to him till I finish," Rusty said to her as he turned back to the room. "But Rusty," she whispered after him in a panic, "he doesn't want to talk to me. Let me stay and help you." "No, no, don't need any help, —I want you two to get acquainted."

Obediently she started down the stairs, but her mind was in a turmoil of rebellion and embarrassment. Three Stephen Fenwicks converged with a rush in her consciousness: the Stephen Fenwick of her own distant memory, the Steve of Rusty, and the man who was coming across the yard to meet her with obvious diffidence. The Stephen Fenwick of memory: the young man living with his mother and sister in the slave-quarters at Cherokee after the War, and then a little later working in Van Wie's store that nightmare day of her return to Aaron. And then the Steve of Rusty: the cousin that she had been hearing of as long as she had known Rusty: the Steve who had served a sentence in the state penitentiary for night-riding, and was now free-lance reporting for the Charleston *News & Courier,* while his mother and sister were living as "poor relations" with the Bramwells in the house that had once served as a Yankee hospital:—a figure of ever-increasing interest, this Steve, because of the life that Rusty breathed into him whenever he spoke of him. But this man coming towards her with lowered head: a disappointment, for his presence was an intrusion on her brief time with Rusty, and a problem, for she sensed at once what his attitude toward her would be.

When she reached the foot of the stairs, her eyes were disconcerted by the surprise of seeing not the young man of her early memory, or the young man that she had continued to visualize whenever Rusty spoke of Steve. Here before her was almost a stranger: he was taller and handsomer than she remembered, but he was no longer youthful. A heavy furrow in each cheek and twin lines between the brows had changed the expression of the face, given it more character and strength. It was a face that attracted her immediately, but the dark eyes that met hers were hostile.

For her first words to him she could find only: "I feel I know you already, Dr. Stewart speaks of you so often."

It seemed to her that he purposely allowed this banality to hang in the air for a moment before he answered.

"I feel the same way, Mrs. Moffet, for the same reason."

She thought she detected an inflection of contempt in his voice when he said "Mrs. Moffet", and surely identifying her at once as the wife of Aaron Moffet was a gesture of unfriendliness. But she promised herself in a flash to get along with him somehow on Rusty's account. During the exchange of further polite banalities she began to realize that he was trying to be civil, on Rusty's account of course, and she thought: It's harder for him, because he despises me.

Before the fragile conversation reached an impasse, she invented an excuse to go into the kitchen shed. Through the little window that looked out on the yard she watched him pace back to the water's edge. It was breathlessly hot in the shed, but she stayed there, making a little order in the confusion of Seth's bachelor housekeeping, till Rusty came down from the room and Seth came back with word that the station-master's sister had agreed to help out.

On the lazy sail to Land's End the afternoon became a strain in earnest, a mounting strain centering in Stephen Fenwick. She knew she was neither acting nor speaking naturally; she felt his eyes watching her, though she never found them looking at her when she turned to him with some word for Rusty's benefit. It was this that aggravated the strain, this necessity of showing Rusty that all was well, that his cousin and she were "getting acquainted" as he wished.

When they reached Land's End, one special worry that had been fretting her all the way from Port Royal, the embarrassment of asking this man into the house that had once been his home, solved itself. Lucy had already placed two chairs from the piazza in the cool shade of the east yard, and Emily sent her to bring a third. That still left the problem of supper. She must ask them to stay, but because of the vista of discomfort it opened, she would have postponed the invitation if Lucy had not brought the matter to a quick head by mumbling audibly, "Miss Em'ly, de udduh gemman gwine stay fuh suppuh 'long wid Mistuh Rusty, enty?" So there was nothing to do but ask them at once. It was an enormous relief when Rusty answered: "We better not. I know Steve wants to get into camp rig."

Rusty was in an excellent humor and seemed quite unconscious of the strain. Or did he think, she wondered, that he was helping things along that way? His banter with her, anything he said to her in fact, grated very obviously on Stephen Fenwick, who was making no attempt now to hold up his corner of the conversation. Whenever she tried to include him, the conversation entered a polite blind-alley from which she had to withdraw without betraying her discomfort to Rusty. She thought behind her words: I hope you don't think I'm doing this on your account, Mr. Fenwick,—if you only knew it, I resent you as much as you do me. But that, she realized, wasn't fair: his resentment was natural. To him she was nothing but a Yankee, schoolmarming niggers, living on the plantation and in the house that were rightfully his.

Somehow she managed to remain outwardly at ease, till the conversation turned to the field of politics and the approaching election. She had helped to steer it there in an effort to find some subject that would draw him out, and at first it had promised success, for at last he was talking with some show of animation. But when in an impulsive moment of relief she spoke of her interest in his *News & Courier* articles, the hostile expression flashed back into his eyes. Although he thanked her courteously, she saw what a mistake she had made: he was interpreting her remark as an attempt to ingratiate herself. Her cheeks began to sting, but she kept her eyes steady and undisturbed. Still, she was not prepared for the elaborate rebuff that followed.

"By the way," he said to Rusty, "have I told you about the latest bunko game of the Ring?"

Rusty shook his head and frowned, but Stephen Fenwick paid no heed.

"It's just come to light and I want to work it up for the paper sometime next week. It seems that when the United States Government discovered they were going to have trouble finding enough authentic remains of Union soldiers for their National Cemetery on the outskirts of poor old Rebel Beaufort,—well, the Ring came to the rescue by organizing a grave-finding syndicate."

There was real animation in his voice now. "Any nigger who can produce enough cow or mule bones to rattle in a box gets one dollar from the syndicate, which turns around and sells the box to the Government for ten dollars. How is that for a neat little sideline for the Ring and Aaron Moffet? Of course I can't name your husband in the article, Mrs. Moffet, but the syndicate operates through the Freedmen's Bank and everybody knows the Parson's behind the bank."

After that it was no longer possible to hide her distress from Rusty. When they got up to leave an awkward minute later, he sent Stephen Fenwick on ahead and turned to her with the darkest look she had ever seen in his eyes.

"Forgive me for bringing him here, will you?"

She put a reassuring hand on his arm, and felt a relaxing of tension in him.

"Please, Rusty. I don't blame him. Now see here, you wanted us to meet and be friends,—well, we've met, so that part's over with, and if the other part's something you want, that's all I need to know. It will take a lot more than this little snub to put me in my place. We're going to be friends if it kills us."

As he stood looking down at her, his face began to soften in response to her smile.

That night she went to bed soon after supper, the supper that was to have been shared with Rusty. She was worn out, but sleep was slow in coming and then brought disturbing dreams in which were crazily mingled Stephen Fenwick and Aaron, Seth Robinson and Martha and the newborn Linda, Rusty and herself and the Port Royal train. It took the golden morning light to dissolve the last of these phantoms. And after that a very real worry harassed her as she dressed and went down to a nervous hurried breakfast: Rusty would talk to Stephen Fenwick about her and that would make matters worse, he would resent her more than ever. And this worry would materialize at any minute, for they were coming over from Pine Point early, Rusty to take her back with him for the clinic, Stephen Fenwick to go on to Beaufort in the sailboat to spend the day with his mother and sister at the home of his uncle, Joseph Bramwell.

But when she finally caught the sound of their voices and went with heavy misgivings to the piazza to meet them, it was a new Stephen Fenwick that confronted her. He looked rested and cheerful, and whatever Rusty had said to him had made a remarkable change in his manner. He seemed sincerely anxious to be friendly now, and above all his eyes were no longer hostile.

He left so soon for Beaufort that the completeness of the change in him did not become apparent till his return later in the day. Meanwhile there were happy hours with Rusty to restore her spirits. On the walk to Pine Point he talked to her about his cousin, making her see the man once and for all through his eyes. And when the long clinic at the cottage was over and they were able to talk freely again on the walk back to Land's End, he told her why Stephen had come. "Along with his newspaper work he's sort of a traveling agent for the Red Shirts." The Red Shirts, he explained, were rifle clubs organized throughout the state to put a little authority behind the campaign for Wade Hampton's election. "We don't know how much we can accomplish here. There's only a handful of us to convert thousands of Black Republicans, so you can judge for yourself what our chances are. But we're not going to surrender this section without a struggle." After he had gone over the plans they had made for campaigning the Beaufort district, he said: "You see how I trust you." "I'm proud," she told him. "But why can't I do something to help? I'm afraid I wouldn't be much good at intimidating carpetbaggers and scalawags, but I ought to be able to convert a few of the plantation people." "Sure you could," he smiled. "I'll bring you a red shirt next time I come out."

When they got back to the house they sat talking on the piazza till Stephen came back from Beaufort with the late-afternoon ebb tide. He managed the sailboat clumsily and made the mooring with difficulty even under Rusty's guidance. Watching from the head of the steps that led down to the landing from the edge of the yard, she realized for the first time and with a shock of pity that his left hand was missing. In the stress of her contest with him yesterday she had only sensed there was something the matter with one hand, vaguely noticing he always held it behind him or thrust into his pocket.

They had supper with her before Isaac took them back to Port Royal to catch the evening train. Rusty did most of the talking, for Stephen had little to say despite his new attitude of friendliness. He'll always be on the defensive with me, she thought: we can never really be friends. But she was grateful for the change in his manner, and she was happy because Rusty was so well pleased.

✓   ✓   ✓

For the rest of the summer she saw Stephen Fenwick only the few times he came from Charleston with Rusty, but he was interwoven with the passing days through his articles and dispatches in the *News & Courier,* and he was often in her thoughts. This she explained to herself on the grounds of the distress her initial experience with him had cost her and the fear that at their next meeting he might revert to his original attitude. But when she saw him again, she was convinced he had definitely accepted her. Still, she could never feel really at ease with him even though Rusty was there to lean on; and she thought that if she ever had to talk with him alone they would be swept back to the impasse of their first meeting. Yet underneath she was developing a curious feeling of kinship with him, and she wondered if he too recognized it in some degree: that Aaron was their common enemy. He was being very careful, she knew, to avoid mentioning that name in her presence again.

It was from his reporting in the *News & Courier* rather than from the headlines and editorials that she caught the crescendo of events leading up to the crucial election. His work, written with a fire that burned through the cold cramped print and made the neighboring columns sound peculiarly stilted and lifeless, was of three kinds: exposures of the endless corruption at Columbia, accounts of the race riots that were breaking out all over the state, and reports of the more important rallies of both political parties. The exposures were put together with some regard for "literary style", but that did not shake the accuracy of their aim or soften the impact of their fury. A few were summaries of the careers of Republican leaders, damning as simple catalogs of fact; most were direct attacks on the Parson and the Ring.

"They're really on his trail now," Rusty said. "They may be laying some crimes at his door that he's not responsible for, but the important thing is that they're finally smoking him out of his hole, forcing him out in the open."

The accounts of the riots of that summer, the bloody clashes between whites and blacks, carried Stephen from one end of the state to the other. His dispatches from Hamburg, a little town on the border near Augusta, were written the day after his first visit to the island; that morning at Port Royal he had heard rumors of trouble at the other end of the railroad and had taken the train on through instead of changing at Yemassee with Rusty, and so he had been an eye-witness of the closing scenes of the tragedy that had flared up from a few words between a white man and the captain of the local

Negro militia. His description of those hours of stark daylight horror had brought home to Emily the desperation of the times, the savage chaos that lay just below the tense surface of things. Even Rusty's cool head had turned hot then. He had written her: "The blood is on the hands of every Northerner who has supported Reconstruction in any way, whether from ignorance or vindictiveness or greed. They have sown the wind of hate, and the South—black and white alike —must reap the whirlwind. . . . Governor Chamberlain has telegraphed to President Grant for more Federal bayonets 'to restore order'. That will have the effect of bringing every last sane white man into the Hampton camp." But the Hamburg riot was only a beginning. During August and September outbreaks increased in number and violence, as the election drew nearer and the campaigning reached a turbulent pitch of excitement.

Stephen made lively pictures of the big political rallies: sardonic pictures of the Chamberlain rallies, jubilant pictures of the Hampton rallies. But Emily's imagination was stirred more deeply by the firsthand descriptions he gave her, one of the times he came from Charleston with Rusty, of the village and crossroad rallies. It was these pictures, of little bands of Red Shirts riding into Republican meetings to demand a hearing with the speakers of the day, that stayed in her memory.

Unaware how crucially her own fate was involved in this tide of events sweeping towards the election, she would have felt herself a mere onlooker but for the way Rusty and Stephen took her into their confidence. Listening to their talk and discussion when they came to the island, corresponding with Rusty between times, and following Stephen's articles in the *News & Courier* made it impossible for her to view the rising turmoil with any detachment; through them she was directly involved. And there were her own small efforts at proselyting to sharpen her sense of participation. In her contacts with the people she took every opportunity during the weeks before the election to solicit Hampton votes, using the line of persuasion that she had learned from Rusty, that he applied with his medical aid whenever he was on the island for a Sunday clinic. She worked on the families of voters as well as on the men themselves, taking a cue from the local preachers who were exhorting the she-lambs of their flocks, in praise-meeting and out, to see that no ram-lamb strayed from the fold,—"De 'oman-folk mus' hope de man-folk fuh do dey duty fuh de Lawd an' de 'Publican Paa'ty fum who-um all blessin' flow." Yet despite their potent influence and the influence of Frogmore Store, which was distributing hand-bills announcing that *Valuable Prizes will be Presented immediately after Election to each and every Lady whose Husband voted the Republican Ticket,* Emily was elated by the number of converts she was making. There was hardly a man she talked to at Land's End and Cherokee who did not respond with nods and expressions of agreement: "I b'liebe da' so, Miss Em'ly"—"Yas'm, 'tis de pure trut' us cyan' make-out widout buckra fuh frien' "—"Da's right, ma'm, da's right"—and a promise to vote for Hampton. But one day late in October she had a talk with Isaac that caused her spirits to drop with a thud. "Miss Em'ly," he said, shaking his head, "dem nigguh ain' gwine vote no Dimmycrack ticket—I ain' mine how polish dey talk to you' face, ma'm." And in the end she had to admit to Rusty that the only vote she felt sure of was Isaac's.

In these last weeks of the campaign Rusty and Stephen were concentrating on a reorganization of the Beaufort Volunteer Artillery, with Joseph Bramwell and other men whose names had become familiar to her. Stephen was elected Captain, and led his little company to meet General Hampton when he came to town for the Democratic Rally on the twenty-fifth of October. Emily wanted to go, but the old fear of encountering Aaron, the dread that had prevented her from ever going to Beaufort, kept her away now. Rusty did not get to the island that trip, either before or after the rally, so her first description of it came from Seth Robinson when she went to Port Royal in the *Dolphin* the following day. It had been a disastrous affair. The nigger militia had wrecked the speakers' stand the night before and Hampton had had to make his address from the porch of a house on Bay Street. There were only a few white people present, but the street was jammed with niggers. They heard Hampton out in silence; the heckling began with the next speaker. The meeting broke up in roars of black laughter.

But the chagrin of that day was wiped out by Stephen's report in the *News & Courier* of the great Charleston rally, when General Hampton and General Gordon led a parade of ten thousand Red Shirts down Meeting Street to the Battery. And three days before the election there was another great demonstration, at Columbia. After that the long strife of the campaign came to a sudden end. The world stood tense and still, waiting, listening.

That enigmatic Seventh of November the plantation was deserted; even the women and children had gone to the polls at Frogmore. The following morning Isaac went to Port Royal, but he brought back no news. The next day Emily went herself. Seth Robinson met her at the waterfront with a perplexed face. There was no definite word yet: the station-master was getting all kinds of conflicting reports on the telegraph, but nothing definite. She sat with Martha and the baby in the back room of the store till late in the afternoon, while Seth made frequent trips to the station. But she had to start back to Land's End without an answer.

The next day solved the mystery at last. The result of the election was in doubt: both parties claimed the victory, each accusing the other of wholesale fraud. So the *News & Courier* said, and a brief letter from Rusty added: "I don't know how they'll ever settle the thing. Every man in the state must have voted two or three times, and whites and blacks came over the Georgia line in droves. It stands a tie now, but it can't stay there—the national election is at stake and the S. C. vote in the electoral college will decide whether Tilden or Hayes is to be president. Meanwhile we have the nice little problem of a dual government at Columbia, and the plot thickens. . . ."

XI

After the election and its strange outcome, there was a pause, a lull in things. Emily felt this in herself, in the plantation and the people, in the world beyond the island. Suspense instead of breaking had been sustained and increased, but the feverish excitement had gone and a repressed hushed excitement had taken its place. Everything was at a standstill, suspended in an expectant void. Even nature seemed involved in this universal uncertainty: summer had passed, but autumn had not yet revealed itself; day after day a hazy noncommittal sunlight watched over land and sea, and there was no breath of wind to rouse the brooding waters or stir the still-green leaves of the trees.

As Emily waited and listened, her eyes began to turn back to herself and her own unsolved problem. But she felt no nearer a solution, though now the time had almost come when a solution could no longer be postponed. For Harriet must soon be returning, was already overdue. Yet each day failed to bring the letter she had always sent to give the date of her arrival. Perhaps she had decided not even that was necessary in the new "purely professional" relationship. But there was something mysterious about this continued silence. The only communications from the Society were the yellow envelopes that arrived punctually on the third day of every month containing the invariable notice in the secretary's prim hand: "I am herewith enclosing a draft on the Society for the sum of Thirty Dollars in payment of your services for the month of so-and-so, as assistant to Miss Sheppard at Land's End, St. Helena Island, S. C."

These checks had taken on a significance they had never had before. Out of the long line of them that stretched back to the unforgettable satisfaction of the first one, her first earned money, she had never been able to save much; after her share of the living expenses had been paid, there were always needy cases among the plantation people. Still, during the period of her work for the Society a few hundred dollars had accumulated bit by bit in the Charleston bank that Rusty had recommended for her. It stood there now, that frail sum, a bulwark against the uncertainty of the future.

But twist and turn as she might through these fretted days and nights, there was no answer to the main problem of the future, no escape from this endless squirrel-cage of indecision and worry. I've got to stay here, she told herself, till Harriet comes back, till she can find someone to fill my place. Of course. But after that? . . . It was getting impossible to breathe in this atmosphere of unbreakable suspense. You've got to decide and plan, she demanded of herself. You can't sit here helpless till you're forced to act.

The familiar routine of teaching would have given her some outlet for this constant anxiety, but she kept putting off the opening of school, waiting for word and instructions from Harriet. And then at last, suddenly one day at noon, she was standing on the piazza with the letter in her hand, brought from Frogmore by Isaac, and everything was turning sharp with premonition in the clear November sunlight. She went down to the landing and sat on the bench there at the water's edge for a steadying minute before she tore open the envelope.

In the first hurried reading only the high points registered on her mind. Behind the tight little writing that followed so evenly the lines of the paper, with its faint scent of violet sachet, Harriet's sweet fragile voice was saying: "I have delayed this until I could give you positive information. I am not returning to St. Helena. The terrible political situation in South Carolina has decided the Society to abandon its work there and turn its efforts to more promising fields. . . . The plantation has been put up for sale through the Beaufort bank. I see no necessity for you to leave there, however, until you receive notice. They have instructions about the furniture, etc., including my things. . . . A dear friend and I are going into welfare work in the slums of this city. I have been deeply concerned about what you are going to do, but I am at a loss what to suggest for you. Our lives and characters are so absolutely opposed. . . . Your salary will be paid to the first of the year. If there is anything I can do, please feel free to call upon me. . . ."

After the signature Emily's eyes went back and fastened on the line, "The plantation has been put up for sale through the Beaufort bank." The soft lapping of water along the side of the *Dolphin* and the fishy salt smell of low tide came back into her consciousness then. Her eyes lifted from the letter and looked up the Sound toward Port Royal. And in the brief space of that look all the long suspense and indecision came to an end.

The strength of this abrupt liberation carried her through the afternoon without a falter. She knew exactly what to do now, felt and acted resolute, confident. She went to Port Royal in the sailboat and at the station wrote out on a soot-smudged telegram blank the message to Rusty that had framed itself on the way: *Tell Stephen Land's End for sale Beaufort bank*. After that she went over to the Robinsons' store to see Linda and talk with Seth and Martha. It was after five when she went back to the station to see if any answer had come. The mulatto agent with the sullen eyes pushed a telegram under the bars of the ticket window. Out of his scrawlings she pieced together Rusty's message: *Just heard about sale but too late arrive Saturday expect you return with me Charleston*.

The sun was setting when she left the Port Royal dock. It was a long journey home: hardly a breath stirred over the Sound and the ebb tide was slackening. The fire in the west was almost out and dusk shrouded the shoreline before the sailboat drifted into the slender path of light that came to meet her, with Lucy's anxious voice, from the lantern glow on the landing.

"Miss Em'ly, you got me worry to deat'! I sho goin' wid you nex' time."

When she handed up the basket of provisions, she said as calmly as if it were the most natural news in the world: "There isn't going to be any next time, Lucy. We're going to Charleston to live."

And that night, for the first time in months, she slept like a child, like Linda in her cradle.

But it was three long days to Saturday.

Wednesday passed with some ease, thanks to the packing and housecleaning and a visit to Isaac's cabin with odds-and-ends of presents. After that time began to tighten and grow tense. Thursday was Thanksgiving; she had expected to pay a farewell visit to the plantation settlements, but the morning brought muggy rain, breaking the stretch of fair days. She moved aimlessly through the house, pausing at the kitchen door to talk with Lucy or at the front windows to stare at the curtained Sound. Now that Land's End was lost, it was agony lingering on here. And under this strain of delay, this marking time and waiting, her mind was prey to an insistent clamor of speculations.

She wondered now what exactly she had hoped Stephen Fenwick would be able to do about Land's End. He had no money, but Rusty would have found some way to help him. What were the details behind Rusty's telegram? How had he heard about the sale? From Joseph Bramwell in Beaufort, perhaps. What did the "too late" mean? The Freedmen's Bank must have made a quick disposal of the property. Of course they were not interested in seeing it return to the original owner: rather than have that happen they would probably have given the place away. In the end it would doubtless be broken up and parceled out to the people, like Cherokee and the rest of the island plantations. . . . But it was idle to speculate about things: Rusty would explain everything. Would it stop raining by Saturday so she could go for him?—it was impossible to keep her mind from repeating that question over and over inanely. And all the time she recognized that secretly she was listening for something, she had no idea what. Perhaps for the "notice", she thought finally, remembering Harriet's words, "I see no necessity for you to leave there until you receive notice." It might arrive before Saturday. Today. At any moment. . . . At last in desperation she took her writing things to the dining-room table and settled down to the task of a last letter to Harriet.

She had no appetite for the Thanksgiving dinner of wild turkey, a present from Isaac. Faced with a fretful afternoon in the house she made up her mind to walk to Pine Point, in spite of the rain; she put on rubbers and went down with an umbrella to the landing to get Rusty's hooded poncho out of the locker of the sailboat. She had to put down the umbrella to free both hands for the feat of tossing the weight of the grappling line over the anchor line, to draw the boat in from the mooring, and by the time she had dragged the poncho out of its lair she was drenched. But she had no intention of changing her clothes: the discomfort suited her mood. She struggled into the great loose folds of the poncho and turned back to the house, intending to stop only long enough to leave the umbrella on the piazza. But there was no escaping Lucy's watchful eyes.

"Miss Em'ly, wuh you fixin' fuh go?"

"Just over to Mr. Rusty's. And I want to stop to see Isaac a minute."

"When you comin' back?"

"Long before dark, don't worry."

The moment she got away from the house, her spirits began to rise. And as she followed Rusty's shortcut, through dripping woods and along the edges of fields where cotton stalks and scarecrow ranks of corn survived the harvest, motion released her mind from its trammels to explore the new life that was about to open for her. Outwardly her senses were entranced by the circle of rain that accompanied her: it had the same intimate yet vast sound as the sea wind in the crests of the pines at the Point. When she reached the grove and its thick carpet of needles, she stopped to pick up some of the cones in her path. On the porch of the cottage she shed the poncho, got the key out of the pocket of her skirt, and unlocked the door with a shiver of pleasure.

She felt his presence at once, his eyes and smile and easy-going voice, waiting to welcome her. And when she had built a fire to dry her clothes and combat the low hypnotic roar of rain on the roof, she felt that he drew the other armchair up beside hers and was sitting there puffing his pipe, hands behind his head, long legs crossed, comfortably ready for talk. As she tossed the wet cones one at a time into the fire, where they smoked and sputtered angrily before they burst into purple flame, she shared her thoughts with him as they came to her.

Looking ahead, it was still impossible to see any Charleston but the city of the past, the Charleston of the Fort Sumter celebration, a place of ghosts and nightmare memories. But with Rusty there she would soon be able to forget: it would be a new city, wiped clean like a slate at school. And what would her life be there? Not like anything she might expect or plan or imagine. It never was. . . . She remembered a day of revelation years ago, in the orchard of the Salem farm, when she had suddenly wakened to full awareness of herself and the world, and had foreseen in a vision of ecstacy the whole course of her life. That poor benighted girl had fancied that

244

by this time she would be thoroughly married to her first beau—where on earth was John Grenville now?—her hands very full indeed with a house in Boston, a little place in the country, and the orderly bringing-up of five children, three boys and two girls. . . . As she sat gazing wistfully into these flames where the future lay hidden, she decided it was just as well that the future was inscrutable: it left you room for hope, however vague now, and some illusion of shaping your own destiny. A necessary illusion, that, but an illusion nonetheless. For through the inevitable working out of cause and effect it was clear that your fate and the fate of the world were already as fixed as the present and the past. The future was not unformed but simply invisible, waiting in time and space for the miracle of consciousness to bring it to light for an instant, before it became the past by the miracle of memory. You had the illusion of continually making decisions, of your own free will, but it was only your past and the pressure of circumstances making decisions for you. You were merely one of a countless multitude of actors, playing an infinitesimal part in the great drama. Yet despite the magnitude of the setting and the plot, you clung to the quaint notion that your part was somehow desperately, splendidly, infinitely important.

Well, as Rusty said, it certainly was—to you. She smiled at the memory of a quizzing he had given her when she had announced her conclusions about fate and free will. He had said: "You worked that out all by yourself? And now what are you going to do with it? If I were you, I'd wrap it up and put it away. We may not have free will, but it's a sure thing we have to act as if we have. We may be puppets of fate, but we also have to keep moving." . . . If those early dreams of mine had come true, she thought, I'd be worrying about domestic matters, not vain abstractions. Yet fate could scarcely be dismissed as abstraction: already it had altered the pattern of her life beyond recognition, by the sheerest chances. They were myriad, these tiny accidents that produced such enormous consequences, but two loomed at once in her mind as prime examples. In Boston she had happened to go to a meeting of the Freedmen's Aid Society when Aaron Moffet was the speaker. A few months later in a skirmish on a plantation road somewhere in South Carolina, a bullet had struck Will Herkimer's shoulder. . . . Harriet would have said: "It is all part of the Divine Plan, and we must question not, but do God's will as it is revealed to us day by day." Fate—Divine Plan—

God's will: only names for the ultimate mystery of things. The mystery remained. Meanwhile you had to keep moving, making the best you could of things as they came. Thankful for the good things. Thankful, above all, that you had a friend, that you were not alone.

Meditations always came to rest like this on Rusty. But today there was a tendency to go a little beyond him. She resented this intrusion of Stephen Fenwick. He too would be in the new Charleston life, but she thought: I don't know how I feel about that. He was still such an unknown quantity, and she wondered if it would ever be possible to get to know him. He promised to be only a disturbing figure in the future and she was sure she wished he were not going to be there. But because he was part of Rusty she must try to make the best of him. And with that she abruptly reminded herself of her promise to Lucy to be home early.

On the way back to Land's End some remnant of agitation hovered at the edge of her mind. Perhaps it was the thought that Land's End was no longer home, that she was leaving the house and the island; but it was less than that and more, for it was no distinct thought at all. Whatever it was, it slowly dissolved in the trance of rain, leaving only the restored sense that the visit to the cottage had given her.

Before she reached the house she turned off the shortcut into the lane to Isaac's cabin. In answer to her hail from the gate of his neat little yard, he came out on the porch with several of the younger children at his heels. When she asked him what the weather was going to do, he scratched his head: it was hard to say exactly, but far as he could see it looked like more rain, then a wind from the north and pure cold. If the weather was still too bad on Saturday for sailing to Port Royal, he promised to hitch his mule to Garibaldi's buggy and drive to the Beaufort ferry to meet Rusty.

When she got to the house, she went down to the landing to be sure the sailboat was properly moored for the night. Not far out from the landing, half obscured by the mist of rain, a sloop lay anchored. It was no unusual sight to see any kind of craft from a fishing smack to a three-mast schooner becalmed in the Sound, unable to make port till the turn of the tide, but her sympathy was particularly aroused for this unlucky crew: they were having as cheerless a Thanksgiving as she was. She could make out the forms of the men moving about the deck in oilskins, but the sounds that would have carried to her easily if the weather had been clear were lost in the hissing of rain on the gray water.

When she went up to the house, Lucy met her in the hall with popping eyes and a stuttering jumble of gullah. There was no understanding Lucy when she was really excited about something. She had to be made to repeat her story slowly before any connected sense could be made of it. A soldier on horseback, a militia officer black as crow, had ridden into the yard. He had gone down to the landing first, then come back and pounded on the front door. He had prowled all through the house, and even looked into the stable and old bake-house before leaving.

"But what did he want, Lucy?"

"He ain' say. But he done quizzit me plenty. 'Who you?—What you' name?—Wuh de white lady?' I talk back to'um, till he grab muh aa'm an' staa't fuh hu't me. Den I jes' study'um close-mout' an' ain' crack me teet' fuh nutt'n. Miss Em'ly, I scare of dat nigguh. He ac' like he own dis place."

She managed to say calmly: "Maybe he does, Lucy, but there isn't anything to be scared about. If he comes back before we leave, we'll simply go over to Isaac's, or the cottage."

But that night, after a wretched evening of pretending to Lucy and herself that she was reading, sleep stayed beyond her reach for hours. The rain had subsided to a drizzle, but there was an endless dripping from the eaves and the trees. Whenever she shifted her position in an effort to escape the apparition of the afternoon visitor, she heard Lucy move on her pallet beyond the foot of the bed.

She opened her eyes the next morning to find the house enveloped in a dense fog. It breathed in the open windows like smoke, and when she went to close them she could see clearly no farther than the railing of the piazza. The trees nearest the house were ghosts; beyond them the world was lost in dank muffling grayness.

The day had a smothered quality. It would have been hard enough if the sun had been shining, but this submerged mood of nature was worse than rain and drove her back on her last reserves of endurance. There was nothing left to do in the house to relieve the impatience of waiting, and it was impossible to go groping through this fog to the settlements to take leave of the people: she would have to leave her good-byes with Isaac and ask him to explain that she would come back often with Rusty for the clinics. She thought that the day would never wear away to night. And then, when night came, that it would never end.

The first murky light of Saturday revealed a world still buried in fog. But today it did not press in on her senses with quite the suffocation of yesterday: she could keep reminding herself that now only a few hours stood between her and Rusty's arrival. And during the morning the soggy wall of gray thinned away a little, not enough to permit any hope of meeting him at Port Royal but enough so that she could see most of the yard again, though the upper branches of the trees remained shrouded in mist. When she looked out the dining-room window to see if the sailboat was visible, she could make out a mast, but it was too tall to be the *Dolphin's;* it took a minute to recognize the sloop that had lain off shore in the rain of Thanksgiving afternoon, and apparently in the solid fog of yesterday. As surprise passed she began to resent this trespass: if they were too timid to feel their way on to Port Royal or Beaufort with the tide, they might at least have asked permission to tie up at the landing. But that, she realized, was an absurd attitude to take, for she herself was only a trespasser here now.

At noon Isaac stopped at the house on his way to meet Rusty at the ferry. And after that she forgot the ghostly presence of the sloop, forgot everything except the clock on the living-room mantel. She sat by the fire there, pretending to read but secretly timing Isaac's journey.

But something was wrong. Even with the generous allowances she forced herself to make for delays all along the line, Isaac failed to return with Rusty. . . . As the afternoon dragged by, the fog closed in on the house again. She had some tea with Lucy in the kitchen and then went back to watch the clock. When it began to get dark in the room, she lighted the lamp and put more wood on the fire. It was after five before she caught at last the sound of Isaac's return.

She was standing on the kitchen porch staring down at him. He was saying apologetically: "So'm, when I see de ain' no use fuh wait no mo', I jes' come on back home."

She found the voice to say: "Something must have kept him in Charleston at the last minute. I'm terribly sorry you had the trip for nothing."

"Naw'm," he blinked up at her in the light from the doorway, "I too glad fuh do anyt'ing fuh you, Miss Em'ly. Anyt'ing mo' you wan' me fuh do, ma'm?"

"Oh no, Isaac,—nothing, thank you."

But when he turned away into the gloom, it was all she could do to keep from calling after him.

When she went back into the kitchen, she said quietly to Lucy: "Isaac will take us to the ferry in the morning. We can meet Mr. Rusty in Beaufort if he comes tomorrow. If he doesn't come, we'll go on to Charleston anyway."

This quick decision and the steadiness of her voice checked the panic that had taken hold of her the moment she had seen that Rusty was not with Isaac. But when she faced the clock in the living-room, she realized that for the first time in the years she had lived in this house she was afraid. A nameless terror was closing in on her. It was stealing up through the darkness from the landing, coiling around the house, peering furtively in at the windows. It seeped through the walls, and lurked in the shadows at the corners of the room and in the hall.

She went to the kitchen to be near Lucy. And after supper Lucy came in to the living-room to sit with her by the fire. The blinds were closed and fastened, and the shades pulled down.

She looked up with a start from the fire to the mantel. The fact of five-minutes-past-eight somehow confirmed the reality of that first undefined sound from the back yard. In Lucy's eyes she found further verification, and as the clock ticked off the next enormous seconds she realized with an uprush of deliverance that Rusty had come.

On the way to the kitchen the whole burden of tension and ridiculous fear left her, left her smiling with shame. She saw in a flash what had happened: the fog had made his train hours late and then missing Isaac he had had trouble finding someone to bring him out: she must not betray to him how upset she had been. But when she unbolted and swung open the door and stepped out on the porch, she could hardly keep from shouting her relief to him.

The glow from the kitchen lamp made a golden cloud of the pall beyond the steps: she could only hear. And in that moment of listening all greeting died on her lips, for the sounds that came to her were suddenly confusing. There were unknown voices talking, the sound of carriage wheels not yet at rest, and the champing of horses.

From the obscurity before her emerged the figure of a man, a strapping negro in the uniform of a militia officer. The shock was so great that only a surface impression of what followed reached her. She saw him come up the steps toward her, tip his cap and bow, a grin on his shiny black face as he stood in the light from the doorway. She was aware that he was speaking to her and that she was answering him, that he then went into the kitchen, said something to Lucy, and went on into the dining-room. After an indeterminate time, during which she was powerless to move or think, he came back and vanished into the mystery of the yard. After a minute of low voices he reappeared, followed by a colored woman and a white man. As they came up the steps, she recognized the woman at once. When she finally recognized the man, things began to move in a jerky blur.

She was facing them in the living-room, and now full consciousness was returning. But a sense of unreality, a conviction that this could only be a bad dream, protected her from the impact of their presence: she was acutely aware of what was happening, yet some part of her was able to stand aloof and skeptical, sustaining the rest of her. Although she saw with entire clarity these figures before her, —Aaron, so changed and coarsened that he was almost a stranger, slouched in the easy-chair at the fireside across the hearthrug from where she stood with Lucy, his overcoat thrown open and his beaver hat pushed back off his forehead—Phyllis, still pretty, seated on the arm of the chair with her gloved hands on her hips and a smile on her painted lips—the big buck officer standing in the doorway,—for all their cruel vividness they remained phantoms in a nightmare, terrifying but incredible. Even Aaron's words, perfectly understood now, though they came to her with a hollow reverberation as if they were spoken into a shell, could not break this protective sense of unreality.

He was saying in a tired drawl: "Didn't expect to have this pleasure, my dear. Mrs. Moffet, this gentleman is my loyal friend, Major Pritchard. He reported you were still on the place the other day, but I was afraid you'd be gone by now."

He nudged Phyllis off the arm of his chair and said over his shoulder, "Major, will you be good enough to relieve me of this leech for a few minutes?"

For a moment Phyllis stood looking down at him with narrowed eyes. But then the contagion of an oily chuckle from the man in the doorway was too much for her. She broke into a sneering laugh.

"You sho got me by de right title! You bes' quit studyin' 'bout losin' *me.*"

"Get out," he told her in the same listless tone and without looking up.

"Wellden, gib me dat whiskey you got wid you."

She made a reach for the smaller of the two handbags at his feet, but he kicked her hand away and sat up with sudden force in his eyes and voice.

"I told you to keep your dirty hands off those."

She glared at him, nursing her hand. "You don' trus' me no mo'?"

"You think I ever did?" he asked as he pushed the larger bag under his chair and opened the other. "I may have my weaknesses, but trusting women isn't one of them." He pulled a bottle out of the bag and snapped it shut, turned and held the bottle out to the man in the doorway. "You better take charge of this, Major." To Phyllis he said with a jerk of his head, "Now get out."

Her eyes were sullen, but her teeth flashed in an easy smile. "Good t'ing I don' nebbuh fuhgit I'm a lady." She glanced at Emily and her lips curled. With a shrug she turned to the door. "Come on, bubbuh," she grinned at the black man as she took his arm, "we leabe de white folk fuh stew in dey own culluh."

The man in the chair called after them: "Check up on your sloop, Major. And tell your fishermen to report here to me."

As the door closed and the phantom of Aaron turned his eyes back to her, her protective illusion snapped and she was defenseless against the reality of his presence. A shuddering sickness took hold of her, and her knees went so weak that she could hardly stand. But somehow she was able to meet his gaze without flinching, even to see him distinctly, the lines in his face, the heavy pockets under the eyes, the sag and bloat and grayness of the skin. Only his eyes seemed alive, burningly alive in a repulsive mask.

"Like seeing a ghost, isn't it," he said.

His mirthless laugh ended abruptly in a cough, and he leaned forward to spit into the fire. When he sat back, he glanced at Lucy as if he were seeing her for the first time. "Mrs. Moffet," he said as his eyes came back to her, "I have a desire to be quite alone with you."

She saw the hopelessness of any immediate escape, but it took all her will to summon the voice to say to Lucy, "Wait for me in the hall." Her eyes did not move from his and she could only sense the reluctance of Lucy's withdrawal. When the door closed and she was alone with him, she drew a quick breath of resistance. He smiled faintly at that and rested his elbows on the arms of the chair, locking his hands in a way that was instantly familiar to her. In defiance of her will her thoughts flew off at a wild tangent: Here is the church and here is the steeple. . . . The steeple of his forefingers tapped his chin as he studied her. She felt she had been standing before him for hours when he said at last with a nod toward the sofa:

"Why not sit down?"

His eyes were beginning to have a hypnotic sway over her, and she had to fight off an impulse to yield to his voice.

"I'm not detaining you, surely. You weren't going anywhere on a night like this, were you?"

When she made no response, he raised his eyebrows and crossed his legs with a sigh. "You know, this touches me deeply. I can't guess how you feel about it, but to me it seems an absurdly happy accident. I can hardly believe it's true. It's like something in a play. But then our life was always like that, wasn't it. Melodramatic."

She thought: This has all happened before. A strange sense of recognition hovered over her mind, and she felt that if she could concentrate intently enough she could know what they both were going to say and do next. But when she tried to grasp the idea firmly, her thoughts were thrown into confusion, and she was left with only a baffling impression that his words were familiar the instant they were spoken. He was saying in a slow reflective voice:

"Honestly, I can't tell you what it means to me to see you standing there. I've dreamed it so often. And coming now just at this time of stress, it seems doubly impressive. But I won't bore you with myself. It's too much to expect others, even one's wife, to appreciate the exquisite little ironies of life. Let's talk about you. Standing there in the flesh. No longer a dream."

He paused for a moment, inspecting her with a sardonic smile.

"But in my dreams you were never this inflexible. You were proud.

252

yes, but yielding, or at least ready to yield. It was always as if you wanted to tell me something, and couldn't quite. I felt you wanted to tell me—I blush for the fatuousness of the male—that there had never really been any other man in your life. That after all there could be only one man for you. The man you promised to love and honor and obey till death."

He shook his head with a gesture of dismissal. "But all that bitterness is gone, my dear. I remember you only with gratitude. Why when I married you I was helplessly idealistic, an almost perfect fool. It pains me to recall what a sentimentalist I was then. I used to believe life was a morality play. I believed particularly in the goodness of woman, and hence in the goodness of life. Now, to pursue the confession to its conclusion, I believe in nothing. Except myself, at intervals. . . . For a long time I've wanted to thank you for my education. And then too I've been wanting to see what time has done to you. Very pleasant things, evidently. You've improved immensely. Of course to me you were always beautiful beyond compare. In the past, though, it was a beauty a little too dependent on the virginal for its appeal. But then you were very young and unformed. Now you are a woman indeed."

She had been trying desperately, all the time he had been talking, to find words of escape and the voice to utter them. Now as he paused again, she was able to say in a shaky whisper:

"Will you let me go now."

He affected surprise. "But why hurry? I can't have bored you this quickly. I should think you'd find it rather interesting to see your husband again after so long a separation." He raised his hands to rub his forehead, smiling wryly. "Yes, I know. Looking a little the worse for wear, I'm afraid. Ah well, success must be paid for. . . . My dear, you left me too soon. Where have you gotten, here in this hole? Wasted years, wasted charms. I could have given you anything you wanted. I can now. Though just at the moment things have become a little complicated."

His hands fell and hung limp at the sides of the chair. As he sat looking at her, his eyes seemed to turn blind and all animation drained out of his face. When he spoke again, his voice was lifeless.

"I won't detain you any longer. This meeting has great possibilities, but I can't play up to them. I'm mortally tired."

For a minute he seemed to be listening, slumped in the chair, his head half turned to the door. With a visible effort he straightened up and sat forward. Then his eyes searched hers through so long a silence that she felt they had both been changed to stone and were doomed to hold their positions forever.

"Emily," he said at last, "I'd give anything on earth to have you with me again."

Against all her reason his words, the change in his voice, his use of her name, touched chords of memory and pity that made her throat close tight. A sudden haze came over her eyes, so that his face was a blur before her. Then as she was wondering helplessly how far this absurd weakening would carry her, the sound of voices in the hall came to check it. Stability returned in a flash when someone knocked at the door.

When he got to his feet and went to open it, she caught a glimpse of Major Pritchard and two white men in the hall. He went out to see them, closing the door behind him. It was several minutes before he came back into the room: by that time she had recovered some control over herself. And now as he stood facing her his eyes were intensely alive again, and his voice had regained its hard suavity.

"At this point, my dear, I'm afraid I must ask your plans, if I'm to arrange for your comfort. As fellows in this house we must talk with some frankness. To begin with, will you have the good grace to be seated."

She went to the sofa, and he returned to his chair.

"That's better. . . . Our paths have crossed at a remarkable moment, Emily, but I'm just superstitious enough to believe it wasn't entirely haphazard. I think you'll find it was providential for both of us. Where are you planning to go now—Charleston?" He searched her eyes and nodded. "I see. Your friend the doctor has kept you waiting. Well, I think I can account for that. Today every Red Shirt in the state is in Columbia, or headed there."

He smiled as her lips parted.

"I'll explain. Recently I allowed myself to be persuaded that the only way to break the political deadlock was to—break it. Smash it, clean out the Hampton crowd, thus settling both the state and national election at one fell swoop. Now in Charleston there happens to be a social organization known as the Hunkidory Club, a beautiful collection of nigger cutthroats, and last night a trainload of them packed off to Columbia to see the sights. As good citizens what could be more natural than that they should take it into their heads to visit the capital of their state? Well, unfortunately there was a leak somewhere. By daylight Red Shirts were pouring into town to welcome the excursionists. So I decided to leave. . . . I've had my eye on this place for some time, my dear. Not only because you were here but because the seclusion and quiet of it always charmed me. I've often thought what a splendid health resort Land's End would make. And then at a most convenient moment your Philadelphia Aid Society abandoned it. So I shall rest here till the storm blows over. If it doesn't blow over, I have a boat handy. To cruise up or down the coast, according to the political wind. In a few hours I expect a weather report."

He sighed wearily and the tired look came back into his eyes. And with it some trace of the old intimate appeal returned to his voice. "I guess the Carolina days are about ended. The vein's played out. Time to strike out for new fields. A new life. Well, I'm ready for a change—spiritually and financially. With the exception of this place and Marshlands, all my assets are liquid. I want to go back and start all over again, with you."

He leaned forward. "You can help me, Emily. I need you, I want you with me, and I'm prepared to pay any price for your company. Just name your own terms."

She felt she was using the last of her strength as she got to her feet. "Won't you let me leave?"

His brows contracted. "You mean leave the house?"

She nodded weakly.

He shook his head. "No, Emily. Couldn't think of turning you out into the night. And then too you must realize I'm not anxious to have my whereabouts advertised. I've been to some pains to get here with only the Major, and Phyllis. You'd be surprised how many people would give their eyeteeth to know where I am at this moment. Sorry, but the most I can do is let you go to your room. And that under protest. . . . Emily, can't you be a little less tense about this? After all I'm only a harassed human being, like yourself. I have no designs on you. I just want your company. You see, there's something in you I still cling to. Nothing's been able to kill that. You remember I used to call you my guiding star. You used to tell me you liked it."

He laughed dryly and moistened his lips. "Not interested, are you.

Well, I'm beginning to lose interest myself. It's rather tiresome being stared at as if I were some sort of monster. I'm disappointed to see you haven't learned to understand life and relish its contrasts. You miss the whole point and all the fun by being so rigid. . . . Go upstairs and do try to relax, you're quite safe under your husband's roof. Besides, I have certain matters that require my undivided attention. I'll see you later, after you've had time to consider my offer. I want to rehitch my wagon to your star, on any terms you name. I'm sure we can make some sort of bargain. Think it over. I think you'll find this chance meeting was a genuine inspiration, just what we needed to bring us together again."

On her way to the door, past his chair, she felt that she was dragging weights of lead. In the hall things lost their sharp outline, began to jerk and blur again. There was a whirling impression of Phyllis and men in the dining-room. Then Lucy was with her on the dim zigzagging stairs.

Golden rays penetrated her half-shut eyes as she lay on the bed, but it took many seconds to realize that Lucy had lighted the lamp on the bureau. And a little later, when the soft glow was cut by crackling flashes, it took time to grasp the simple fact that Lucy had lighted the fire. Gradually the excitement of the flames stirred her out of this stupor and her mind began to beat again. But her thoughts could only revolve in a tight little circle whose center was the utter insanity of what had happened. When she closed her eyes, faintness returned with a rush, blackness bombarding her senses; and when she opened them, there was the grotesque play of light and shadow over the walls and ceiling. Despite the spreading warmth of the fire, cold crept up her spine and held her in a shivering grip. Even after Lucy had spread a blanket over her, the chills kept coming back to shake her till her teeth chattered. When they stopped at last, she lay in a void of exhaustion, thinking and feeling nothing.

Sometime later she became aware again of the room, of herself lying on the bed and Lucy standing near. In Lucy's eyes she saw her own helpless bewilderment reflected, and that finally roused her mind to action. She threw off the blanket and got up.

She had to steady herself before she could go to the door. There she listened for a moment, hand on the knob: the only sound was a mumble of voices from the room below. But when she drew the bolt and opened the door softly, she saw the form of a man sitting on the top step of the stairs. He turned a leathery face to the light and looked at her with curiosity, rolling a wad of tobacco in his cheek. She shut and bolted the door with numb hands.

Before terror could close in on her she turned quickly to the windows. But when she raised the shade of one and peered out, she saw another man posted on the piazza. He was sitting propped against the railing, his head bowed forward as if overcome by the smoky wisps that curled in from the fog mass at his back. Though the shock of his presence, barring this last wild hope of escape, held her powerless to move, yet she found herself observing with irrelevant intentness his appearance,—the oilskin suit and hat, the old army coat over his shoulders, and when he blinked up at the window, the youthfulness of his face. It was only when he got up and came to stare at her through the damp panes, shook his head at her several times with an almost frightened expression, that she was able to gather enough strength to lower the shade.

She stood by the fire then for a time, mechanically warming her hands and trying to calm herself by talking in calm whispers to Lucy. But behind her words her mind searched in a frenzy for some means of escape. Even after she went back to the bed and lay down, determined to force herself into a state of acceptance that would permit her a little respite, some part of her mind continued to grope frantically for release, picturing fantastic ways of escape from the room and the house, and repeating them endlessly.

With the fading out of a final picture of herself and Lucy running and stumbling through foggy darkness toward Isaac's cabin, she began to wonder what time it was. Out of entire vagueness she developed little by little a sense of midnight, which became finally so strong that it was as if all the clocks she had ever known were chiming the eerie hour here in this room. But when this appalling illusion ran down, she again lost all sense or thought of time and lay in a stupor between the dying firelight and the wakeful lamp.

At intervals she was dully aware of sounds beyond the bounds of the room. Frequently it was a mumble of voices broken by muffled laughter, from the room below. Sometimes it was the tread of the youth on the piazza, trying to keep warm, she imagined slowly. And once she was roused to full consciousness by the banging of the front door, followed by loud voices in the lower hall. But now even this disturbance was unable to create any answering turmoil in her senses: she listened and heard and that was all. And when it was over and silence returned to the house, she was without memory of it. For it seemed not to concern her, even remotely, here in this long void where she lay.

Lucy was shaking her arm. Lucy in lamplight, eyes wide with alarm, was whispering something to her. She was aware too of the knocking at the door, grown loud and insistent now from that first remote tapping. But for many moments she could make no response to either summons.

When she roused herself at last, motioned Lucy to go to the door and raised herself from the bed, she felt drugged and nerveless. Even when she saw Aaron come into the room, she felt no fear, no emotion whatever. It was as if she had already lived through this second encounter, drained it of all feeling, so that her only reaction to his presence was simple perception.

She watched him go to the window and raise the shade. As gray daylight smote the glow of the lamp, as he opened the window and cold dampness flowed into the room, she saw that the fog had receded. The branches of the trees in the yard, beyond the outline of his head and shoulders, were free.

She heard him say to the form on the piazza: "Get some coffee in the kitchen and go to the boat."

When he turned back to her, she realized that he was drunk. It did not show in his movements, but his eyes were glazed and staring and his breathing was labored.

"Well," he said thickly, "I've come for your answer. I've had a little message that spells the end of my Carolina days. The end of Reconstruction too, I imagine. I'm clearing out. And I want you with me."

He stood looking at her, breathing heavily.

"I haven't much time," he said after a moment. "No time for coaxing. I laid my cards on the table last night. I told you you could have things your own way. I may have forgotten to mention that Phyllis is being left behind. Though she doesn't know it yet."

He seemed amused at that thought, but his dead white face sobered quickly. "Another thing. I don't want you to feel coerced in any way. You can have this place, and Marshlands too. I've got no further use

258

for them anyway, and they're already in your name, for good and sufficient reasons. I want you to make a free choice between staying here and going with me. I'm pretty played out, Emily. I need someone I can trust, for a while at least. What do you say?"

She made no answer, and he came a step nearer. When she moved back, he put out his hand in a gesture of conciliation.

"Don't worry, I'm not going to drag you away with me. . . . Can't you say anything?"

When she still made no answer, he sighed heavily and shrugged his shoulders.

"I'm afraid I haven't any more time. . . . Well, good-bye, Emily. Till we meet again. We always do, you know."

The door was closed and he was gone, faded like an apparition from the room. But his voice and his words remained, reverberating in the gray hush of the room. Even when voices came up from the hall and the rooms below, his words continued to echo around her, more real than any sound.

As the minutes passed and she stood numbly rubbing the hand he had touched and staring at the door, many sounds came to her. Voices, groups of voices, and the tread of feet; voices on the lower piazza and in the yard; a shout from the landing. But his voice lingered on in the room, surviving every other sound. Even a final tumult in the room below, a sudden scream, the overturning of a chair, and the slam of a door, could not dissipate the mocking persistence of his last words to her. *Till we meet again, Emily. We always do, you know.* . . . It was only when a profound stillness settled over the house that his voice began to recede beyond her hearing.

Little by little, as she listened and waited, the meaning of that final tumult invaded her consciousness. They were leaving Phyllis behind, bound and gagged in the room below. She thought she could detect sounds to verify this: a muffled groaning, a faint struggling against tight bonds.

She went to join Lucy at the window. It was open as Aaron had left it, and by leaning out she could see over the edge of the piazza to the landing. The sloop was gone. The fog, thinned now to a diaphanous haze through which the sun seemed to be trying to shine, had lifted enough so that she could see gray water for some distance. But though she could catch stray fragments of voices on the still air, the sloop was already far out from shore and invisible.

"We can go now, Lucy."

That realization and the sound of her own voice released her will at last from its weight of limpness.

"We'll have to leave our things here. No, don't try to take anything now. Isaac can come for them."

The pounding of awakened life at her temples and in her ears seemed to make resounding detonations in the stillness as she led the way down the stairs. In the lower hall the hanging lamp was gasping for oil, its fluttering flame blackening the chimney: she resisted an absurd impulse to stop to draw the thing down on its pulley chain and put it out of its misery. From the slams she had heard she expected to find one or more of the doors closed, but they all stood open. At the dining-room door she saw that the table was littered with the remains of a meal. As she turned to the living-room, her heart stopped dead.

From behind her Lucy's *Jesus* and *O Gawd* racked up from the pit of her stomach as though they were her own response to the horror before her. He lay on the floor, his head and shoulders slumped against a leg of the overturned armchair, his eyes staring at her drowsily. His coat was cut to ribbons, the shirt soaked with blood. There were open gashes on the neck and cheek, and the hands and wrists were slashed. Around him were strewn the contents of a shaving kit, mirror, brush and soap, and an ivory-handled razor smeared with blood.

She spoke through frozen nausea. "Get Isaac."

And when Lucy hesitated, she gasped sharply: "Go for Isaac—quick."

Alone in the clammy shuddering stillness, she began to repeat to herself, over and over: Do something, do something. But she could no more move toward him than she could turn away from him or look away. He held her there as powerless to move as himself.

As horror seeped into the deepest recesses of her spine, the ghastly gray and crimson mask before her seemed to smile and the glassy staring eyes to wink slyly. *Good-bye, Emily. Till we meet again. We always do, you know. . . .*

His eyes, his face and body, the furniture of the room and the room itself melted into a fuzzy whirling sickness. When she put out her hand to grip the frame of the doorway, the room expanded dizzily, contracted, expanded again. A voice within her, the voice of a frightened child in the dark, began calling to Rusty, crying for him to come to her.

*   *   *

But it was Stephen Fenwick, not Rusty, who came at last, found her at Isaac's cabin, where she was trying to collect herself.

He was not much help at first. He seemed to mistake her stunnedness for steady calmness, capable of understanding him at once. And after he had explained something about Rusty being tied up in Columbia and sending him instead, his one thought seemed to be to get her story straight for the *News & Courier.* Somehow, with Lucy's promptings, she managed to answer his rapid-fire questions and tell him what had happened.

"I'll leave you out of this of course, Emily," he assured her, his dark eyes flashing with excitement, "——I just want the Aaron Moffet part. This sure was a lucky break for me. I had a hunch he might come here. When I came through Beaufort, a posse of Red Shirts were turning Marshlands and the town upside down looking for him. How long ago did that Pritchard gang get away?"

She had no idea of time.

"Well," he shook his head, frowning, "it doesn't matter. It's too late now to get them. They'll never get them,—like looking for a needle in a haystack, trying to locate that sloop in the islands, north or south. . . . I got to get this to the paper right away. I can telegraph the high spots from Port Royal and write the rest on the train. I see they scuttled Rusty's sailboat,—lucky I was able to get a boat to bring me out. And I better get you away from here in a hurry, before that posse arrives. They'll just ask a lot of fool questions. We'll save all that for the coroner's inquest."

Then, finally, he did seem to realize her dazed state.

"Say," he stared at her with suddenly solicitous eyes, "I've been asking quite a few questions myself. I'm sorry, Emily, I forgot what you've been through."

He held out his hand, clumsily, to support her arm. "Afraid I'm a pretty poor substitute for Rusty. Won't he give me the devil for not taking better care of you. Think you can get to the boat?—shall *I* carry you?"

"I'm all right, Steve," she tried to smile.

"Sure? Feel faint?"

"Not very. I think I can wait till we get to Charleston."

She held on to his arm as they left the cabin with Lucy and started back to the house and the landing, where the boat of flight and escape was waiting.

Part Four

I

MRS. FENWICK was returning with Eugenia from a morning call on the Broughtons, one of the few old families that had returned to Beaufort. The town, half-buried in the rich foliage of early summer, was drowsing under a spell deeply scented and languid; resting in exhaustion, it seemed to Mrs. Fenwick, after the desperate struggle that had established the Hampton government and ended the long agony of Reconstruction. To be sure, here on the Sea Islands, in the very heart of the Black Belt, the Republicans by weight of overwhelming numbers had been able to hold most of the local offices,— the Chief of Police was still black, the Clerk of Court, the Probate Judge, the Town Treasurer, and the Coroner. But the turn of the tide throughout the majority of the districts of the State had broken the confidence of the Negroes and reduced their objectionableness amazingly. It was almost possible to believe that Beaufort had returned to its golden age.

Almost, but not quite. There were certain painful facts to quench the illusion. For one thing, Mrs. Fenwick was conscious of the darns and patches in her black muslin dress, in Eugenia's white muslin dress, in their cotton gloves and stockings, the faded cotton parasol over their heads. Not all of these endless mendings showed, only one or two were conspicuous, but they were there and Mrs. Fenwick could not forget them: each was like a wound in her flesh. For another thing, she and Eugenia were not in a carriage and were not returning home. Home no longer existed. Marshlands still stood on the Point, of course, but in hands other than Fenwick it had become merely a bitter reminder of incredible changes. They were returning, she and Eugenia, to Joseph Bramwell's home, not theirs. Far from it. Their purgatory. Some blessed day Stephen, earning

265

barely enough on the *News & Courier* to keep himself alive in Charleston, would come to the rescue. Some blessed day. But how much longer could they hold out? Sometimes it seemed impossible to Mrs. Fenwick that she could stand charity from her brother for another instant.

And there were the hostile eyes that she knew were watching her and Eugenia from behind shutters closed against the mounting heat and glare. The eyes of Carpetbaggers and Negroes who occupied the old houses along the way. In Fenwick Street! No, Miss Sophie, you are not back in the lost days. You hold up your head and look alive because you are the daughter of a Bramwell and the widow of a Fenwick; but you know that actually you are a ghost wandering aimlessly in a dead world.

Eugenia, following her mother through the gateway and garden of Bramwell Hall, was not conscious of being a ghost. She was daydreaming as usual. With her mother to worry about the problems of the external world, she could spend her time in the satisfactory world of her fancy, except at those intervals when she was interrupted by summons—

"I asked you," her mother repeated, "who that is on the porch with your Uncle Joe. I'm lost without my glasses."

Eugenia's pensive eyes brightened.

"It's Cousin Rusty," she whispered, "back from Charleston."

"Oh——. I suppose he has a message from Stephen."

Eugenia was blushing. She stood behind her mother when they reached the brick-paved porch and gave Rusty a quick shy smile of greeting. As a matter of course she followed her mother's example in ignoring Aunt Susan and Aunt Isabel, who were engaged in an unnecessarily animated conversation with Uncle Joe. That was part of the technique of the Feud, which had been in progress for so many months now that its gestures were as formalized as a Javanese dance. Eugenia heard Cousin Rusty say he had something to tell Mother. Mother asked him to come upstairs. Eugenia followed them into the house with a little smile, after a sufficiently casual glance had revealed to her the suppressed curiosity in the faces of the Aunts.

Their animated conversation died the moment Eugenia disappeared. Ex-Judge Joseph Legerton Bramwell, sitting in his easy-chair between Susan's straight-back and Isabel's armless rocker, re-crossed his legs and pinched his nose, waiting for the remarks that would come when the steps had climbed the stairs. Susan, sitting on the edge of her chair, opened in her sharp rapid voice:

"What on earth has Cousin to tell Sophie that he has to be so mysterious about?"

"If he doesn't care to enlighten us," Joe answered testily, being piqued by curiosity himself, "that's his privilege, isn't it?"

"I can't see why he should be so evasive about it."

"And I can't see," Joe snapped, "why you should be so everlastingly inquisitive."

Susan settled against the stiff back of her chair and resumed her sewing without resentment. Poor Joe's temper had naturally grown shorter and shorter with the years of frustration and idleness since the War. She accepted his outbursts of irascibility: they served as a cathartic for the bad humors that accumulated around his enforced inactivity.

Isabel's slow chronically-tired voice wondered if that Moffet woman had anything to do with it.

Susan and Joe looked at each other. Isabel's impassive remarks might at first seem random and obscure, but it was seldom that they were not found to contain surprising penetration. It was understood between her brother and sister that the stunning blow she had received when her young husband had been killed at Sharpsburg— a blow from which she had never quite recovered—had somehow endowed her with sixth sense, a heightened perception. She was the family oracle. The Judge and Susan encouraged this occult power as they encouraged her semi-invalidism, the continued wearing of black, the attitude that her loss at Sharpsburg was irreparable. Her loss had, in fact, become one of the family's most cherished possessions.

"What," Joe asked gently, "has the Moffet woman to do with it?"

Isabel smiled vaguely from her low rocker, which was in mild motion as usual. "I heard Rusty say he brought her from Land's End to Marshlands in his sailboat this morning. That makes the third time she's come to Marshlands this month."

Susan, again on the edge of her chair, made an effort to anticipate her sister. "So maybe she's going to live at Marshlands instead of Land's End. But I don't see what that has to do with Sophie." She frowned at the garden, and added absently: "I don't see how Cousin Rusty can associate with that woman."

267

"Now my dear," Joe put in, "Rusty has assured you several times that Mrs. Moffet is not the creature you imagine."

"Wasn't her husband the vilest Carpetbagger that ever set foot in the State?"

"But they were completely estranged, and surely she is not responsible for his crimes."

"In any event she's a Yankee. Can that be denied? Well then! I don't know what more needs to be said. I simply don't understand how Cousin can allow himself to be so intimate with her. How *can* he do it?"

"Perhaps he likes her," Isabel rocked.

"Likes her?" Susan flared. "Likes a *Yankee?* Isabel! . . . What's probably happened is she's played on his chivalry and sympathy."

"And do you realize," she added irrelevantly with a little jerk of her head, "she's never been seen in church? Not even the Baptist Church." She pronounced the words *Baptist Church* with a suitably scornful inflection; no right-thinking Beaufort Episcopalian would ever forget or forgive the schismatic bastard birth of that church out of the side of St. Helena, after the visit of a great English revivalist in 1840.

"Maybe," Isabel suggested, "she don't belong to either church."

"Maybe," Susan sniffed, "she's one of those Boston Unitarians, which is certainly next door to nothing. But that don't excuse her. After all, the Lord's House is the Lord's House and any denomination is better than none. The fact remains she never goes to church— unless she attends services at the praise-house at Land's End, which wouldn't surprise me."

Isabel joined her sister in a brief little whoop of laughter. "Well," she sighed a moment later, "Rusty don't go to church either—except once in a blue moon, like Easter."

"It's different for a man," Susan contested. "You don't necessarily expect a man to attend services regularly. Look at Grandpaa Mowbrey—he didn't go to church in Savannah from one year's end to the next, and did anyone ever call him a freethinker? But if a woman don't go to church, you can make up your mind there's something radically wrong with her."

"One minute, Susan!" Joe said crossly. "All that is entirely beside the point. Bel, I fail to see what this Mrs. Moffet has to do with Rusty's present interview with Sophie."

Isabel smiled enigmatically and pressed her black-bordered handkerchief out on her knee. Susan restrained a sudden surmise, waiting to see if the oracle would commit herself. When it was apparent that the oracle intended to remain silent, she explained to her brother in a tense voice:

"I believe Bel is hinting that Cousin Rusty came to tell Sophie he's thinking of *marrying* that Moffet woman!"

Isabel rocked a little faster, and Susan was emboldened to elaborate her startling interpretation.

"That's just it! She's snared him—why, she's had every conceivable opportunity to play on his sympathies over a long period of time. And now he's come to tell Sophie. It's all plain as day. He hopes to win Sophie over—she's always been clay in his hands. He knows better than to come to you, Joe. He knows well enough what *our* stand would be. A Stewart married to a Yankee, the widow of Aaron Moffet!"

Joe snorted.

"Do you think that's what Rusty came to see Sophie about?" he asked Isabel.

"I can tell," she answered, giving her handkerchief a particularly emphatic pressing, "something's going to happen."

Joe examined this abstract prophecy. Abruptly he became aware that he had exposed his curiosity; clearing his throat, he shot out and adjusted the immaculate cuffs whose laundering Susan personally supervised. "I haven't time or inclination," he told his sisters, "for idle speculation. I have work to do."

When Joe announced he had work to do, it was understood that the matter under discussion was closed. "Work to do" meant his imminent retirement to the "office"; the library-study had been converted into a chamber of law, but clients were so rare that the Judge's time was quite free for reading, meditation, and rest. His sisters entered into the conspiracy, Susan actively, Isabel passively. When the Judge was in his office, the house was hushed to the silence of the grave.

"Remember the heat," Susan counseled. "Don't overdo."

Joe might have suspected his sister of sarcasm if he had not known she was incapable of it, with him at least. He got up, braced his shoulders, and went into the house.

"I put a bowl of figs on your desk," she called after him.

269

Joe went through the hall and the darkened parlor, into his office. He left the door open so that he could hear Rusty come downstairs from the third story, the living-quarters of his sister Sophie and his niece Eugenia since the beginning of the Feud. He stood before the gilt-framed pier glass and made a little ceremony of the removal of his black frock coat and white linen waistcoat, his black-and-white cravat and standing collar. An elegant figure of a man, he admitted; and essentially youthful still, despite a distinct thinning away of the hair at either temple and a slight thickening of the waist-line. . . . Stimulated by his own image and the curiosity aroused by Rusty's mysterious call on Sophie, Joe's thoughts were active, but not altogether serene.

He could never get used to the appalling disaster that had smashed the pattern of his life. As a matter of fact, he had not suffered so cruelly from the War and Reconstruction as most of his neighbors. After two years service under Memminger in the Treasury Department at Richmond, he had been sent during the last year of the War to Nassau, the little capital of the Bahama Islands and halcyon center of blockade-running, to look after Government interests there. In this tropical paradise he had been able to spare his sisters and himself the hardships of the War's final phases. At the collapse of the Confederacy he had taken his sisters to England, where he had for some time been accumulating bonds. He had been well received in London, but he had suffered there the humiliation of not being able to trace the gentleman, representative of a Liverpool cotton firm, who in Nassau had asked Susan's hand in marriage. Susan had speedily recovered from the jilt; she had acquiesced in the courtship to please her brother, who had behaved as if he had been the jilted party.

When President Johnson had promised amnesty to Confederate officers and officials, Joe had prepared to return to South Carolina and face the future with his own people. In Beaufort he had learned that Sherman had burned Holly Hill on the Combahee, but he had been able to buy back Bramwell Hall from the United States Government. The house had been thoroughly scoured and fumigated after its contamination as a Yankee hospital, the unfinished rooms finished, common wooden mantels put in where imported marble ones had been intended, and a little furniture bought: the interior was a travesty of Joe's original plans for it. There had been enough money left for a modest income, which Susan managed admirably.

Immediately upon his return he had felt it his duty to campaign for the reorganized legislature. Snowed under at the election by the Republican candidate he had withdrawn into his castle, and for the duration of Reconstruction he had seldom set foot out of his yard. One of his rare appearances had taken him to the court house, where he had defended his nephew, Stephen Fenwick, against a charge of night-riding; he had not only lost the case but had also suffered the ignominy of being fined for contempt by the presiding mulatto judge. He had taken in Sophie and Eugenia as a matter of course when Stephen had been sentenced to three months in the penitentiary. When the Feud had developed out of nothing, he had been inclined to the side of his younger sisters: he had always entertained a high respect for his oldest sister, but his affection was limited to Susan and Isabel, who looked up to him. This hidden partiality had prevented his effecting, in the role of mediator, a graceful truce. Sophie had finally severed all relations with Susan and Isabel and retired with Eugenia to the attic floor, where their meals were brought to them on a tray. . . .

He turned away from the mirror and stood undecided in the middle of the room. His eyes ran absently over the shelves of law books kept carefully dusted by Susan, avoided the desk, debated the relative attractions of the armchair and the lounge, whose springs sagged. He chose the lounge and stretched out with a heavy sigh. With one ear he listened for Rusty's step on the stairs; with the other, he listened to himself. If Rusty was actually contemplating matrimony with the relict of Aaron Moffet,—but Rusty was too reliable for that.

Joe fanned a fly from his forehead and closed his eyes the better to visualize Mrs. Moffet. He had seen her for the first time only a day or two ago when he had taken a morning constitutional to the gates of Marshlands. Curiosity had led him well within the grounds before he had discovered her presence there, working in the garden, which had fallen into sad neglect during the Moffet regime. He had apologized stiffly and departed with as much dignity as the situation allowed, taking with him the picture of a slender disturbingly lovely woman. For good and sufficient reasons he had not mentioned the incident to his sisters, but he had reviewed it many times in his thoughts. It was not to be wondered at if Rusty had lost his head.

Joe sighed. How miserably different these years since the War had been from what he had planned for them, the achievements, advancements, honors. The future would have to be very splendid to make up for this appalling vacuum. Thank God, there was the future. An appointment from the Hampton government to begin with. If he could only get it. Everyone was clamoring for an appointment at Columbia. . . . The utter defeat of the War had offered certain compensation. A man had been able to think of himself, through the hopeless Reconstruction period, as a classic figure crushed by inexorable fate. There had been tragic dignity, even grandeur in ruin so complete and unjust. But now it was possible, and therefore necessary, to enter the arena again,—in a minor role. He was not sure he could marshal enough influence for an appointment of any kind, with the loss of prestige the Low Country had suffered. . . . Well, an appointment would come. It would come. Great God, the Old State couldn't do without Joseph Bramwell: the dominant Up-Country faction wouldn't pass his talents by. It was necessary to wait. A little more patience. It would come. . . . What was Rusty telling Sophie? It was necessary to wait. Patience, always patience. . . . In the garden beyond the partly drawn blinds, a locust's stinging monotone accented the heat. . . .

He sat up with a start. He had been betrayed into that abominable laxity, a forenoon nap. He listened, wondering if Rusty had gone while he had been sleeping. Now beyond the blinds the turn-of-tide breeze was stirring softly in the trees: evidently he had been dozing many minutes. Well, he could interview Sophie after dinner and find out what Rusty had come for. It was his usual habit to pay a visit upstairs after supper, but he would change the schedule today.

He got up, put on his coat before the mirror, and went out to the porch. Isabel was alone, rocking and waving a palmetto fan.

"Where is Sue?" he asked her.

"Seeing to dinner. We're going to have the first corn fritters today."

That would have been very beguiling news ordinarily, but Joe did not allow his thoughts to be diverted from the matter in hand.

"Has Rusty gone yet?"

"Left while you were working. Sue couldn't get anything out of him."

He gave a little snort and sat down. He picked up the fan he had left at the side of his chair and began to fan himself briskly.

"I hope she didn't forget to ask him to stay to dinner," he said after a moment.

"She didn't forget. But he said he had a patient to see. Didn't say who it was."

Joe discarded his fan, realizing that it was only a nervous gesture, for the sea breeze was refreshingly strong now. A few minutes later Susan appeared on the porch with a flushed face from supervising the fritters.

"He's gone," she told her brother. "Too provoking—not a word out of him. Joe, I was wondering if, after dinner, you wouldn't go up and—perhaps—Sophie will say something about it."

Joe looked annoyed. "My dear Susan. To begin with you know I never go upstairs till after supper."

"I thought," Susan said meekly, "you might make an exception of today."

"An exception to satisfy feminine curiosity! I consider it presumptuous of you to suggest such a thing, Susan. Do you think I have any intention of cross-examining Sophie?"

"I didn't mean that."

"Then it's a mystery to me what you do mean. We'll say no more about it."

Susan went to the porch rail and trained a wandering vine tendril to hide her chagrin.

"I wonder," Isabel said innocently, "if the Moffet woman will sell Marshlands if she goes to Charleston to live."

Joe's elegant fingers beat a petulant tattoo on the arm of his chair.

"Come Joe dear," Susan sang, "dinner's ready and we're going to have okra soup, shrimp pie, and corn fritters!"

Susan and Isabel usually took a rest after dinner in the summertime, but today they sat in the cool dark parlor waiting for their brother to come downstairs. He had gone up after all, as they had guessed he would, though he had explained elaborately that it was merely to find out how the Broughtons were.

When he came down, much sooner than they expected, he made

straight for his den without a word. Susan was able to control herself till he got as far as the door. Then she broke down.

"How did she say the Broughtons were, Joe?"

He turned in the doorway. "Very well," he said shortly.

"Did she say anything about Rusty?"

"No! She volunteered nothing. And naturally I didn't question her."

"What did you talk about?" Isabel asked.

"Nothing of any interest that I recall. I saw they were busy, so I didn't stay but a minute."

Susan's ears pricked up. "Busy? Doing what?"

"Sophie was in the midst of a letter to Stephen, and Eugenia was making calling-cards out of pasteboard."

"What!" Susan gasped from the edge of her chair.

Joe went into his sanctuary and closed the door. He sat down in the armchair with the *News & Courier,* which had come in the morning mail. Presently he moved to the lounge and surrendered to after-dinner torpor. He knew he could trust his sisters to watch for any developments, while he gave his undivided attention to mastering a meal that had included four helpings of fritters.

Susan and Isabel sat with their eyes glued on the hall. At four o'clock their vigilance was rewarded by the descent of Sophie and Eugenia. Susan at the moment was talking so earnestly to Isabel that she appeared wholly oblivious to the passage of her sister and niece through the hall to the front door. But the instant they were out of the house, she scurried to the window and Isabel followed. Peering between the shutters they could see Sophie and Eugenia turn up Fenwick Street. They then hurried upstairs to the north bedroom, in time to see Sophie and Eugenia cross the little causeway and proceed under a single parasol toward the Point. After that trees cut off the view. Breathless, Susan flew downstairs to send the yard boy to trail the parasol. It was not the first time he had been dispatched on the same errand.

The sisters waited on the porch, Isabel quietly rocking, Susan twitching on the edge of her chair. When the boy came back at last, he looked surprised at what he had to tell.

"Miss Soozie, Miss Sophie and Miss Geenie done gone to Maa'shlan'!"

When Susan had collected her convulsed wits, she went straight

274

into the house and to the office. It was the first time she had ever approached the closed door without hesitation. She knocked boldly.

It was five-thirty before Joe, Susan, and Isabel in their respective chairs on the porch caught sight of the returning parasol. It came through the gateway and up the path, was lowered at the steps.

"Quite warm for a walk, isn't it, Sophie?" Joe asked as he got to his feet.

"Joseph," she said, ignoring his question, "I have some news I think will be as welcome to you as it was to me. Cousin Rusty brought a message this morning that Mrs. Moffet wished to return the Fenwick properties."

She paused to observe the effect of her words and to steady the agitation of triumph in her voice. "Of course, I was not able to accept the offer as it stood. But I have arranged to rent Marshlands. And Stephen has been offered a position with the English phosphate company that's begun mining off Land's End—they've leased part of the plantation for their operations. If you will come upstairs a little later, I shall give you some details. Come, Eugenia."

When they were gone, Joe cleared his throat heavily. Susan and Isabel were speechless.

"Well," he said finally.

Susan found her voice.

"*Oh!* Why! I never heard of such a thing! It's too horrible! Accepting favors from a Yankee! Accepting favors from that Moffet woman!"

"Now my dear," Joe said half-heartedly, "calm yourself."

But Susan was not to be calmed. She began to laugh hysterically. Then suddenly she burst into tears and rushed into the house.

Isabel smiled vaguely and continued to rock.

"I knew something was going to happen today," she told her brother complacently.

STEPHEN FENWICK stood in the wide doorway of the commissary of the Land's End Mining Company, watching the closing scene of the week's work: the excitement that followed the Saturday noon whistle from the steam-engine in the crusher building.

Autumn was come, yet the midday sun was hot as summer. It was hot even here in the shade of the porch. In the sandy road in front of the store the crowd of women, who had come to waylay the men on pay day, gossiped and laughed and quarreled. Beyond them the dump-car railway ran past the washing and drying sheds and the crusher building to the long wharf that reached out into the shining waters of the Inlet. Beyond the Inlet lay the long narrow chain of the barrier islands, and beyond them the ocean. Under the tides of the Inlet lay the gold of phosphate, covered with a deep layer of rich black pluff-mud. During his father's time, Stephen mused, and his grandfather's the mud had been hauled to the fields for fertilizer; the value of the phosphate rock beneath had not been dreamed of then. Now these rich deposits of the bones of prehistoric creatures had come miraculously to light when they were most needed.

The men were swarming onto the wharf from the dredges and barges and small boats. Swarthy stalwart bodies, still wet from the water, glistened in the sunlight; these were the "hand-pickers", prime bucks who dove for the pure "phoskit". Pneumonia would get them in a season or two, Rusty said, but they made high wages while they lasted. Those sleek strong bodies had no sense of doom: he could catch their laughter from where he stood. Within the hour most of them would be incased in flashy store-clothes and headed for Bay Street in Beaufort, where rotgut and dice and women were waiting for them. The beefy form of Peter Bethel, British manager of the company, dominated the crowd on the wharf. His booming voice was delivering a profane harangue. The women in the road whispered and snickered.

Stephen watched Bethel coming toward the store over the palmetto ties of the railway, followed by the men. Peter had the frame of John Bull, the nose and chin of Mr. Punch, a bushy moustache, eyes of concentrated fierceness, and a blasting tongue; it had been surprising to find a soft heart behind this formidable façade. Little by little, from bits of information casually dropped, Stephen had pieced together the man's history. As a youth he had studied for the church in accordance with the desires of his family; he could quote pages of Latin from the church fathers. Attacked by skepticism he had run away to sea. Eventually he had enlisted in Her Majesty's Army, where he had reached the rank of Major in active service. His army adventures had marked him from the top of his bald head, which carried a livid scar from the Sudan, to the soles of his feet, which bore marks of torture fire in India. During the Franco-Prussian War he had joined the French Army and had come out with a slight limp and a profound contempt for both the winners and the losers. After two obscure episodes in Ireland and Corsica he had come to America as manager of the phosphate company because at the moment nothing more exciting presented itself. A breathing spell, he called it.

When Stephen had come to work at the plant, he had moved into Rusty's cottage at Pine Point; and one Saturday soon after, when Rusty had come from Charleston, Stephen had brought Bethel home with him for a supper of deviled crabs baked by the house "boy", Washington. Rusty had readily fallen in with Stephen's suggestion that his boss would be more comfortable at the cottage than in his present dark quarters over the commissary. His battered camp cot had been set up in the side room where Stephen slept, and the chest that contained the cherished relics of his campaigns and travels had been placed against the wall of the sitting-room opposite Rusty's cot, where it served as a seat.

Bethel had left the railway and was coming toward the porch, blasting his way through the group of women and the hubbub of their greetings, questions, and appeals. Stephen turned away from the bright sunlight and stepped into the cashier's cage just inside the doorway. When Bethel came in he took a firm post in front of the cage, where he could check and control the press of men and women, children and dogs. He admitted one worker at a time, and as he called out the name, Stephen selected an envelope from the basketful that had come out from Beaufort that morning on the *Pilot Boy*. Stephen counted the money out, slid it back in, handed the envelope to Bethel, who handed it to its owner with a word of personal advice.

"Give your woman some of that to put away in her sock and put the rest in groceries, not rotgut and general Goddamn foolishness."

"Jerry, don't forget what I told you about sharing your pay with your old mother. Stay home one Sunday in your life and keep away from those twitching yellow wenches in town."

"Sample, you grinning ape, pay your debts or by God I'll collect them out of your black hide. I'll take what you owe Dr. Stewart now."

Stephen smiled as he picked out the envelopes. No-one was spared. They took their medicine with good-nature.

"Yas *suh*, Mistuh Bet'l, I sho gwine do like you tell me."

"Cap'm, I ain' been to Beaufort fuh t'ree week suh. I too t'rough wid dat place."

"Da's right, boss man, burn me up--I ain' wut! But I gwine do mo' bettuh direc'ly suh."

The big dim store was gradually filling with gullah gabble and oily laughter. When all the envelopes were distributed, Stephen went with Peter behind the long counters to help Seth Robinson and his wife distribute groceries, drygoods, and hardware. The Robinsons were tending store for the company and living overhead: Emily had arranged that. It was half an hour before the crowd was reduced to a number the Robinsons could handle. Then Stephen went out with Bethel and around to the shady side of the building, where there were boxes that served for chairs and tables. Bethel put down the things he had brought out with him for lunch, crackers and cheese and a tin of beef. He had forgotten beer and sent a boy to fetch bottles and glasses.

When they had finished eating, they walked the half mile of sandy road to the Big House. Emily was waiting for them in the *Dolphin* at the landing, ready to sail to Port Royal for Rusty. While Bethel exchanged his usual pleasantries with her, Stephen untied the painter and hoisted the sail. The boat dipped a little as the light west wind carried her away from the wharf. Bethel had seated himself at Emily's left on the curving seat and his weight made good ballast against the dip; he sat solid and at ease with his arms stretched along the rim of the cockpit. Stephen begrudged him the place: it meant that he had to sit with his missing left hand next to her. He balanced his way to the place at her right, where he sat stiff and glum and jealous.

Bethel carried the burden of the conversation,—no hardship for him, Stephen thought. He was a poor listener but he certainly could talk; the only pauses were for the elision of expletives. Stephen remembered the first time he and Rusty had taken Peter to see Emily. They had carefully coached him beforehand. "It's no bloody use," he had insisted, "I'm no blinking good in polite society. I'm not respectable, my lads. I can only disgrace you." In the end he had agreed to go and hold himself in check. "I shan't open my blank trap," he had whispered at the door. But early in the call he had suddenly joined the talk, and had come through without a break. "It was worth the struggle," he had admitted afterwards as he mopped the sweat from his face. "That's the first damn respectable woman I ever liked, except my mother, God bless her."

Stephen wished he had the man's spontaneity and assurance. But there was compensation in taking a minor part in the talk: he could secretly watch Emily. That had become an increasingly absorbing occupation. It seemed impossible now that once he could have hated her so bitterly. Yet when he was near her like this, he felt he still hated her, hated her for the calmness with which she seemed to accept the distance that still separated them and that he felt powerless to reduce.

When they had met Rusty at the train and were sailing back to Land's End, he felt better. He always felt better when Rusty was around. At the landing he did not join Rusty and Bethel in begging Emily to go on to Pine Point for supper; for a special reason he was pleased that she refused. "I'm not going to spoil a perfectly good bachelor party," she told them. "It's enough to let me go fishing with you in the morning." He had gone forward to lower the sail and ease the landing, and when he helped her out she spoke to him directly for the first time today.

"Are you going to see your family tomorrow, Steve?"

He nodded. "I'm going soon as we get back from Bay Point."

"Will you take a note to your mother? She sent me some delicious preserves by the *Pilot Boy* this morning."

"I'll be glad to."

A minute later, as he was about to push off, he remembered the Marshlands rent money in an envelope in his pocket. He jumped to the landing and overtook her.

"I forgot this," he explained.

He saw a flush come into her cheeks as she took the envelope and thanked him. "Thank you," he smiled awkwardly. As usual he avoided trying to say more; that would only increase the embarrassment. He stood irresolute before he found the voice to say:

"Are you going to be busy this evening? I'd like to talk to you about Marshlands."

"Of course. What time will you come?"

"About dark?"

"All right, Steve."

On the sail around the tip of Land's End, past the "mines", and up the marsh creek to the cottage, his thoughts were in confusion. Fortunately Bethel and Rusty were lost in one of their prolonged rambling dialogues, which they transferred from the boat to the bench beneath the rustling fronds of the twin palmettoes. He left them there and took the crab-net to the bank of the creek, where he could carry on a secret dialogue with himself while he went through the routine of baiting the net, sinking it, raising it, disentangling the crabs, and dropping them into the bucket that Washington had brought from the kitchen. The bucket was overflowing within an hour, but he kept on, allowing the surplus catch to scuttle back into the water.

When Washington came for the bucket, Stephen wandered aimlessly over to the bench and stretched out on a patch of grass nearby. He closed his eyes and tried to close his ears, but bunches of Bethel's words were continually breaking through. ". . . You had one man who could outfight every Yankee strategist God ever made—Stonewall Jackson, the greatest soldier that ever lived. . . . War is hell, obviously. But if you ask me, the chief curse of man is thought. It gets us neatly out of the frying pan—into the blinking fire. . . . I've never been able to see what blanking difference it can make to me or any other individual whether the human race goes forward, sidewise, or backsidewise. After life's fitful bloody fever, we'll all sleep well. We'll be bloody well out of it, in my humble opinion. It's a bit thick, as a matter of fact, to have to pay the piper for a few moments of jig-time one's parents enjoyed. I can't recall having asked to come here, and I don't expect to get out of the bloody place alive, so what in the name of God do I owe Society? . . ." Rusty's quiet amused voice came through only at intervals. Generally Stephen relished the Englishman's talk, but today it was pure irritation. He sighed inwardly with relief when Bethel finally slapped his beefy thighs and said he must go in to see if that nigger had remembered to put plenty of curry in the chowder.

"Steve, my lad, you seem uncommon aloof and superior today. What you need is a good shot of old Irish. And the Doctor says he'll take a wee drap with us being he's Scotch and it's Saturday."

Stephen raised himself on an elbow and started to shake his head, but thought better of it and got up to go with Bethel to the house. There Peter brought out a bottle of whiskey and bellowed to Washington for glasses and water.

When he went into the kitchen to season the chowder, the cockney he always used on Washington mingling crazily with the nigger's hilarious gullah, Stephen poured most of the stiff drink he had given himself back into the bottle and carried Rusty's glass and his own out to the bench.

It was the hour of sunset and a great peace hung over land and water, but it only increased the agitation in him. Rusty smoked his pipe in silence, watching the flight of curlews over the marsh. Stephen dug his heels into the sandy ground in front of the bench.

"Rusty," he blurted out at last, "I'm——." He stopped short. When Rusty's eyes turned to meet his, he finished it: "I'm in love."

When Rusty continued to look at him without speaking, he repeated, "I'm in love, man."

Rusty nodded slowly. "And have been for some time."

Stephen's frown deepened. "How did you know?"

"Well, it hasn't been so hard to see."

They sat looking at each other. Stephen leaned forward and rested his elbows on his knees with a sigh.

"I suppose it started back yonder, summer before last. When you introduced us, in the back yard of Seth Robinson's store at Port Royal."

"You picked a peculiar way of showing it. Remember how you treated her?"

"Yes. I got off on the wrong foot all right. . . . You know, it really goes back farther than that. Way back. When we were camping at Cherokee after the War while she was living at Land's End with that other Yankee schoolmarm—remember?"

"Vaguely."

"Lord, how I hated her then. But it was just love upside down. I was in love for the first time in my life and didn't even know it. It's sure taken me a long time to find out. . . . I hate the thought of her having been married to Aaron Moffet. And the Yank officer that was in love with her,—what was his name?"

"Herkimer. Will Herkimer."

"What's the difference. It's all past now. Why, I was even jealous of you, till I realized you and she were just friends. . . . Think she knows I'm in love with her?"

Rusty emptied his pipe against the palm of his hand and studied the caked bowl with a faint smile.

"I wouldn't be surprised."

Stephen frowned at the wooded shore of the barrier islands, dissolving now in purple haze. He let his thoughts stumble out as they came to him. "I can't tell how she feels about me. Sometimes I could swear her eyes were trying to tell me something, or trying not to. But it's come to the point where I've got to tell her how I feel."

He got up and paced to the edge of the creek. When he came back to the bench, he said: "If she won't have me, I don't know what I'll do. I need her, Rusty. I'm not like you, I can't go things alone."

He dropped down on the bench, and his right hand closed over the stump of his wrist. "I don't know whether she even likes me. She's always so damn friendly and natural, the way she is with everybody, I can't tell whether she feels anything else. Maybe she just pities me. Maybe I'm repulsive to her." He held up the stump of his wrist. "Is that pretty?"

He felt Rusty's arm on his shoulder.

"Forget that pity idea, Steve."

The sun had dipped down into the far horizon beyond Land's End, and swirls of cloud there were beginning to take fire. It was fire without warmth: the air was turning chill. Stephen moved uneasily on the bench.

"What would you say my chances are, Rusty?"

A shout from the porch broke in on them. Bethel, glass in hand, was calling to them to fall in for mess.

"Well," Rusty said as they got up, "there's only one way to find out."

After supper they sat around the fire, Bethel with his banjo on his knee. Ordinarily this was a mellow hour, but tonight Peter's repertoire—the *Rebel Song* Stephen had taught him, his English music-hall and army ballads, the gullah songs and spirituals he had picked up from the phosphate gang—all sounded flat and stale. Stephen kept listening for the last words and the final twanging chord. He was anxious for Peter to get started on his regular Saturday night jaunt: he was in no mood for an exchange of banter if he had to leave first. But Peter was loath to lay his banjo down. It was a quarter to eight and Stephen's nerves had reached the snapping point when Peter finally announced he was shoving off.

At the door, with a bottle tucked under his arm, he made his usual speech.

"Gentlemen, I have a little residuary business to transact. I regret that you will not join me, but I respect your prejudices against working after hours. It is a matter of some wonder to me that you feel no need to change your luck, but I shall let that pass."

As soon as his lusty whistle had faded away outside, Stephen grabbed hat and coat and swung open the door.

"See you later, Rusty," he said with a nervous grin.

Rusty followed him out on the porch.

"Good luck, Steve."

He watched Stephen's form disappear into the blackness of the grove. Then he went slowly down the steps and across to the bank of the creek. He stood there under the stars for a long time, watching the dark tide flow smoothly silently along the flank of the *Dolphin*. The cold breath of the sea made a rustling in the palmetto fronds and the faintest of music in the pines behind the house. From the Big Field came the last thin choruses of crickets, ghostly echoings of the summer that was gone: all the summers that were gone. A dog barked at the nearest settlement beyond the field. To the west, just above Land's End, hung the slender crescent of the new moon.

It had dipped down out of sight when he turned back to the

house, chilled to the bone. He livened the fire with some kindling, as much to break the stillness as for warmth. When the cheerful crackling flames had taken some of the numbness out of him, he filled and lighted his pipe and drew a chair up to the table. When he opened the package of medical papers he had brought with him from Charleston and spread them out in the lamplight, he could force his eyes to follow the lines of print but he was powerless to hold his thoughts there.

It seemed hours before he heard quick steps on the porch. As he looked up, the door opened and Stephen came in, his dark eyes flashing with excitement.

"Well, I did it!"

He flung his hat and coat on the chest and came over to the table.

"My God, man, I did it!"

He paced around the room, blowing for breath. And he kept in restless motion as he told the story of the evening in disjointed snatches. Rusty listened and watched him with affectionate amusement: accustomed as he was to Stephen's confidence, it had been a long time since he had seen such a complete breakdown of reserve in Stephen's eyes and voice, in his whole manner. He was like a kid again.

"I couldn't get my nerve up," he was confessing sheepishly, "till the last minute. She sure looked surprised!" But she hadn't said No. And she had promised to give him an answer in a day or two, maybe tomorrow. "She didn't turn me down, man!" And she had admitted she loved him. "Can you beat that, Rusty?"

His face clouded. "If she means to turn me down, wouldn't she have said so tonight? It's just that she wants a little time to think it over, eh?"

Rusty got up to stir the fire.

"Sounds like you have a pretty good chance, Steve."

"That's the way to talk! You're with me?"

Rusty put his hands on Stephen's shoulders and searched his eyes without speaking. When he relaxed the grip, he said quietly: "With you all the way, Steve. Providing you never forget, if she takes you, how lucky you are."

They stood looking at each other for a long moment. Stephen nodded.

They settled down in the armchairs before the fire to talk. It was after midnight when Rusty suggested a little sleep might not be a bad idea. "Sleep?" Stephen protested, "—how do you expect me to sleep tonight!" But a few minutes later he agreed to go to bed. "I suppose I better try to get some sleep," he admitted as they undressed before the fire. "Better calm down,—after all, she hasn't said Yes yet. She may be days thinking it over. But maybe she'll tell me in the morning. Say, when we get to Bay Point, keep Bethel occupied, will you?"

When he had finally gone into the side room, Rusty blew out the lamp and lay down on his cot. His eyes stared up at the last flickering shadows from the firelight playing over the rafters, as he listened to Stephen's voice that kept coming to him intermittently from the other room.

"Rusty, I honestly believe she's going to say Yes."

"I think there's a good chance, Steve."

". . . What do you suppose she wants to think over?"

"It's natural to want a little time, isn't it?"

"I suppose so. . . ."

Later.

"What do you think Mother will say?"

"She's bound to like it."

Still later.

"You know, after the War I was all tied up in knots. I didn't think I'd ever get straightened out, to say nothing of finding happiness like this. . . . You asleep, Rusty?"

"Not quite."

"Well, you don't know what this means to me, man. . . . Say, how come you never fell in love with her? You may be ten years older than us and a natural independent bachelor, but how could you help falling for her?"

". . . Well, Steve, now that you ask, it's sort of a relief to tell someone. I fell in love with her all right, who wouldn't? But I had to keep it to myself. Her life was complicated enough then. . . . And by the time she was free, we were just old friends. And she was in love with you."

"You don't mean you're in love with her now? You didn't step aside for me?"

"No. I'm afraid not, Steve, not even for you. No, I'd cut your throat as quick as anyone else's, if it would help. But she wanted me for a friend. And that's what she's got."

"Good God, Rusty. I never realized, you're so damn—quiet. God, I'm sorry."

"Sorry? You mean lucky. . . . No, I'm satisfied. There never was anyone in the world like her, and there never will be. It's more than enough to be her friend."

". . . But I can't understand why she passed you up, for me."

"It's the way your eyebrows grow, man, or the way you laugh. That's what does the trick. . . . No, Steve, there was just some vital spark missing with us. The spark that makes things inevitable for you two. . . . And now how about a little sleep. You'll be needing it."

Light was beginning to frame the windows when Bethel came in. "All hands on deck! What you doing awake, Rusty? Steve!"

A sleepy groan came from the side room. Bethel went to the door to bellow: "On deck, my hearty! The tide waits for neither man nor beast, and we said we'd be at Land's End by sunrise."

When he came back to the table to light the lamp, his face, coming to life out of the dimness, looked none the worse for wear. Rusty sat up.

"Peter, how do you manage to look fresh as a daisy without sleep?"

"What in hell do you think I've been doing, man?"

He picked up the lamp and went chuckling into the kitchen. From there came the sounds of a fire being built in the woodstove to the tune of a sea chanty and a clanking coffee-pot. Rusty got up and began to dress. Stephen's voice yawned from the other room: "What time is it?"

"Time to get up."

Rusty went out to wash his face at the pump by the back porch. When he came back through the house to get his rod and tackle and surf boots to take to the boat, Stephen was shivering into his clothes before the cold hearth.

"How goes it, Steve?"

"Not a word," he chattered with a frozen grin. "I feel like a m-murderer waiting for the j-jury to come in."

286

A great orange-red glow was spreading from the barrier islands when they were ready to leave. The air was still frosty as night, but the sun would soon be up to make a warm shining day. Oar and ebbing tide carried the little sailboat out of the winding creek to the open water of the Inlet, where the reflected glory of the sky was hardly disturbed by the light land breeze. Then the sail flapped up the mast to the creaking refrain of the pulley. It was slow going past the Company wharf to the mouth of the Inlet and around the marshy tip of Land's End. And it took a long tack into the Sound and back to reach the landing, where Emily was waiting for them.

She sat next to Rusty on the sail out to Bay Point. The sun was well up by the time they landed. As she took his hand to balance herself in the step from the prow of the boat to the wet sand, she said to him privately, "I want to talk to you about something—can't we be looking for curlew nests."

He gave her hand a reassuring squeeze, and a few minutes later when Stephen and Bethel were committed to their boots, he walked up the beach with her. His field-glasses hung by their worn strap from his shoulder: they were not raised to bring near any of the hosts of migrant birds that moved away in short flights ahead of them. When they had gone far enough, they turned away from the sea and left the hard beach for the deep sand of the dunes. In a sheltered hollow they stopped and sat down. The roll of the surf was muffled here to an undertone, against which the cries of the birds and the crisp rustling of sea-oats stood out sharply. As he waited for her to speak, his long fingers traced designs in the powdery sand.

"Rusty," she began, "I need your advice."

He looked up at her, but her eyes were so deeply troubled that he had to look down again.

"You know Steve has asked me to marry him, don't you."

He nodded, sifting sand between his fingers.

She seemed unable to go on, and to help her he asked, "What have you decided?"

"Nothing yet."

"You love him?"

"I guess I've loved him since the beginning, without quite knowing it."

Her face was turned away from him now. And as he studied that beloved head, so great a tenderness took hold of him that he could not trust himself to speak for a minute.

Finally he asked: "Well, what advice do you want?"

"I want to know," she said, her eyes coming back to his, "what you think about it."

He shook his head, smiling as he lowered his eyes to watch the streams of sand pouring between his fingers. "Emily, I'm a bad person to ask that. Steve is like a younger brother to me, but no man on earth is good enough for you."

She put a protesting hand on his arm. "No, Rusty,—I mean I'm afraid it might change us. Are you sure I won't lose you?"

"Hardly. Unless you want to."

"That's the one thing I couldn't stand, ever."

"Well, if that's all you're worrying about. . . ."

After a pause, he added with an involuntary sigh.

"It's all in the family. If you're happy, I'm satisfied."

When he looked up, it was difficult to tell for a moment whether this strange mist was in his own eyes or in hers, or in both.

III

THE NEWS of Stephen's approaching marriage struck his Aunts Susan and Isabel with the force of a thunderbolt. Word had not come from a member of the immediate family but from one of the Broughtons, a scandal to begin with.

Joseph Bramwell's reaction was confined to head shakings and snorts because of his preoccupation with Public Life, to which he had at last returned as a circuit judge; but his sisters, left to themselves for days at a time while he held pompous court at crossroad villages, were exposed to the full impact of the news. At first they were simply speechless. They could do no more than exchange shrill little noises. When cups of strong tea had revived their shocked senses, they were able to examine the hideous thing that "Cousin" Sally Broughton had dropped in their laps. But the more they turned it over, Susan sitting on the very tip of her chair, Isabel rocking perilously, the more utterly incredible it became.

"The son of a Bramwell and Fenwick wedded to a Yankee!"

"The widow of that Aaron Moffet creature!"

When they had sobered down to cold analysis, Susan declared: "You can't tell me our dear sister Sophie didn't have a hand in this. Instead of discouraging the thing, she's been fostering it by having the woman to Marshlands and going out with Eugenia to Land's End to call on her."

"The marriage," Isabel discovered, "would bring the property back to them."

"That's it exactly! And Sophie would stop at nothing to effect that. Not even at seeing her son, the last of his name, mated to a Yankee."

"What if they have children?" Isabel's morbid imagination suggested.

"Do, Bel!"

"They'd be Fenwicks," Isabel pursued ruthlessly.

"Not Bramwells, I'm thankful to say."

"They'd have Bramwell blood in their veins."

"Oh! Horrible little Yankee Southerners—half-breeds!"

When the cards came, delivered by hand from Marshlands, announcing that the wedding would take place at St. Helena's the Thursday before Christmas, the Aunts were spurred to drastic action. They dispatched a tea invitation to the Rector.

"Is it possible," Susan flashed at him from the edge of her chair, "you intend to perform this ceremony?"

"Is there any irregularity?" the Rector asked, stirring his tea in mild surprise.

"Irregularity? Are you aware the bride-to-be is a Yankee, widow of Aaron Moffet?"

"I'm afraid I don't quite follow you, Miss Susan."

Susan's eyes snapped.

"Would you bless the union of our nephew to a Yankee woman in a church where his forefathers were baptized, married, and buried? The whole connection would turn in their graves!"

"On both sides," Isabel put in with startling vehemence.

The Rector said he was sorry and quite understood their feelings in the matter, but he didn't quite see what he could do.

"Have you forgotten," Susan asked him shrilly, "who desecrated our altars, ravaged our country, and killed our loved ones? And then set up our slaves to rule over what was left of us!"

"But, Miss Susan, your nephew Stephen——"

Susan raised her hand. "Please don't speak his name to us. His father and brother were murdered by the Yankees, as was Isabel's husband. Yet he is willing to make this woman his wife."

"His mother," the Rector said timidly, "has raised no objections."

"May we ask what that has to do with it? It seems to us your duty should be clear without reference to the weakness of others."

"But hasn't the time come for us to forgive those who have trespassed——"

Susan stood up.

"There are some of us, I am thankful to say, who will remember to our last hour the people of the North. We see that you are not one of us. We must beg to be excused."

The Rector did not stay to finish his tea.

The next day, as the only retaliation they could devise at the moment, Susan and Isabel Bramwell withdrew their subscriptions to the Foreign Missions.

When the day of the wedding came, they were able to draw a certain grim satisfaction from its very inauspicious nature: it was cold and gray. The next morning they received a report of the proceedings from Sally Broughton, who gave them a full description of how everyone looked and behaved. The honeymoon, she had heard, would be spent at Land's End, because Stephen could not leave his work just now.

When Sally had gone, Susan moved that the case be closed. Isabel was agreeable. Stephen's name, and Sophie's, would never pass their lips again. So far as they were concerned the Fenwick branch of the family was completely dead and lopped off.

IV

THE MAIN WING of the upper piazza at Land's End, facing south, was warm with sun almost every day in these winter months, so that Emily could sit out to sew or read and dream when there was a pause in the work of the house.

Two worlds met her here: the visible world of home—Stephen's work-place at the "mines" and Rusty's cottage at Pine Point to the east, Bay Point and the ocean to the south, the Sound and the sunset isles to the west—and the great invisible world beyond the horizon, whence came the ships of the English line that carried away the phosphate rock that rumbled into their holds. Stirring sights, those ships, with Stephen's future entangled in their sails and the black smoke that trailed from their stacks; but they were powerless to beguile her with any interest in their world. No doubt there was plenty of happiness out there, mixed in with all the misery and splendor and common monotony of living, but it was impossible to believe that any happiness anywhere could be greater than her own, here at Land's End.

Or any peace more sure and deep. For it was possible now to think of the past as a necessary voyage to these untroubled waters. As Stephen put it in cherished words: "Maybe if we hadn't had plenty of trouble getting here we couldn't appreciate it so much. It's like coming into port after a storm. Or having somebody hand you a Thanksgiving dinner when you're about to starve to death."

"As if anybody," he had gone on to say with a sigh and grin, "could describe what it's like having you. All I know is it's like being born all over again. I can't even remember what it was like before."

Yes, the past was safely extinguished now. Even the nightmare of

Aaron's death, that climax hour of horror and deliverance, had become so unbelievable in the light of these days that it was without power to harm her. After the final ordeal of the inquest when she had come back to Land's End with Lucy, Rusty along to see them settled in the house, there had only been quiet sunlight touching familiar objects. Actually, she had feared she could never convince herself of this. But in the end horror and its sleepless aftermath had dissolved in the slow mercy that made unreality of unbearable memories.

So the long troubled chapter of the past was closed and sealed, and a new chapter of the greatest joy and promise was opening before her. "I don't know how you feel," Stephen insisted, turning a deaf ear to her protesting lips, harping on his own happiness, "but for me this is the beginning of everything. I'm just starting to live, and I want to shout about it, not whisper. I don't know how it happened and I can't believe it, I thought you had to die to get to heaven, but here I am and I can sure use it. And don't ask me what happened back in those lonely no-account days, because I wasn't even born then."

Every day in this new chapter of life brought problems, but how small they seemed and how easy they were to meet now. Even the difficulty of establishing comfortable relations with his mother and sister was being resolved without much agitation.

It was comparatively simple to make an adjustment to Mrs. Fenwick. Prolonged adversity had worn her nerves thin, and her sensitive pride, inflexibility of opinion, and unpredictable temper made vigilance necessary to keep from treading on her toes. But beneath the formidable exterior lay rare charms. She was excellent company with her fund of family reminiscences, household lore, and practical philosophy. Emily had liked "Miss Sophie" from the first, and she was learning to enjoy even the skittish moments now that she knew how to deal with them.

Stephen's delicate and pretty sister Eugenia was a different story. It was easy to say: I hate her, she's hopelessly spoiled and self-centered. But since it was necessary to be friendly she tried to see her sympathetically as an unhappy young woman who had inherited all her mother's pride and none of the graces, and to concentrate on the only satisfactory contact that could be made with her: dressmaking. Eugenia was indulging a starved passion for clothes, and

Emily was thinking about styles for the first time since the welcome revolution, several years ago, when following Harriet Sheppard's lead she had abandoned hoopskirts and the head weight of the chignon. Now it took an effort to bring herself back to preoccupation with tucks and bows and flounces, but Stephen wanted her to be in the fashion and it gave her one interest in common with his sister, so she studied the magazine patterns in earnest. However, she modified for herself the more exaggerated forms of draped overskirt and bustle and fussy hairdressing that Eugenia went in for.

She saw Miss Sophie and Eugenia almost every week: Stephen seldom failed to bring them out in the Company steam launch, the *Pilot Boy,* when he went to Beaufort Saturday morning for the payroll. Sometimes they stayed over Sunday, but more often she and Stephen went with them in the launch to church at St. Helena's and dinner at Marshlands, coming home in the late afternoon. . . . Once or twice during the week Peter Bethel came to supper and enlivened the meal with his yarns; she urged him to come more often, but she was secretly grateful that he insisted he was not going to make a nuisance of himself. Rusty's increasing practice kept him in Charleston for weeks at a stretch. But when he did appear, the circle of her happiness was complete.

It was when she was sitting here alone on the upper piazza, overlooking her little world, that she could feel its goodness most intensely. At these pauses in the routine of housekeeping, these quiet intervals of self-communion, she could marvel over her blessings.

If life, she thought, will only stay like this always.

When she had said that to Stephen, the night of their first full moon together, he had sighed and nodded.

"Yes, let's stop the clock right here."

But he had quickly thought better of it. "No, I'll take that back. With you life can only get better. The moon bigger. Spring forever, honey. . . . God, when I think of all the moons and springs we've missed. All that time lost, wasted."

"Aren't we doing pretty well at catching up?"

"No, we'll never catch up. We haven't a chance. It's nice trying, though. . . . We should have grown up together."

"Would we be here now if we had?"

"Sure. You don't think they could have kept us apart, do you? You don't seem to realize we're what people mean when they say, Now there's one couple who were made for each other. At least you were made to order for me. I couldn't have done better if I'd raised you myself. Only I'd have taught you how to take on over me and love me the way I do you."

"You really think you love harder just because you can squeeze a little harder?"

"Sure I do. Nobody has ever loved anybody, or ever will, the way I love you."

And he had lifted her off her feet, up toward the moon, and held her there with his arms around her waist till she had agreed.

"But I should have had you from the cradle on up," he had sighed. "I can see you then. And in pigtails too. It was a dirty trick I didn't know you when you were a kid."

"It was probably just as well you didn't."

"It's nothing to smile about. When I think I might never have found you at all—well, it was a close shave all right. I don't like to think about that. No, I'm not making any complaints."

But then he had held her at frowning arm's length. "Except about one small item—small till it starts getting in the way. Speaking of cradles in the midst of love, now I ask you isn't this a fine time to start having a baby. We haven't even had a honeymoon yet. A fine state of affairs. Pretty soon I suppose I'll have to start handling you with gloves, go back to holding your hand and just looking at you." And drawing her close he had planted a chaste kiss on her brow.

"You don't want a son?" she had smiled up at him.

"Oh, someday maybe. Say in about fifty years. When we get back from our golden wedding journey."

"Too bad. I'm afraid you're changing your mind a little late."

"Well, if you can't postpone my rival, I'm afraid I'll just have to make the best of it. But let's get one thing straight right now. One is the absolute limit. Is that perfectly clear?"

"Perfectly, dear."

✔   ✔   ✔

Winter had passed and spring was stirring over the island. The air was vibrant with warm sunshine and alive again with the ecstacy of birds.

In the late afternoons she walked to the mines and came back with him along the narrow sand road between walls of new green. After supper they went to watch the sunset from the bench on the landing, or took a little sail on the flaming waters of the Sound in the old *Dolphin*. He liked her to take the tiller so that he could stretch out on the side seat with his head on her knee. When bad weather forced them to spend the hour before dark indoors, her lap was his pillow on the living-room sofa and she was inclosed with him in an enchanted citadel. He was her little boy then: the assertive manhood of morning, so independent and important, had faded by the end of the day when he came home to her for comfort and renewal.

It seemed impossible that the happiness of that spring could be surpassed; yet when the soft accents of April and May deepened into the full pitch of summer, happiness continued to rise in a steady crescendo. This was the season of "marooning" parties, as the family called the trips to Bay Point, the sails among the islands, and the fishing expeditions that Stephen and Peter Bethel relished. Rusty came more often from Charleston and special good times were planned for him. All things seemed united in one conspiracy of happiness.

But with the final breathless heat of late summer, the smooth surface of things was disturbed. Miss Sophie and Eugenia came out to stay at the house, "to save Emily". She protested to Stephen that she didn't need saving, that she could manage perfectly well with Lucy, that she really wanted to be alone.

"Nonsense, darling," he laughed at her. "Mother's going to take all responsibilities off your hands. This is no time to tax yourself, you've got to take it easy. And it's no burden for her—she wants to do it, expects to. Her feelings will be hurt if we don't let her."

So Miss Sophie took over the housekeeping. And, as she had feared, it was a nerve-racking business from the start. Miss Sophie ran under a tension far too strenuous and sustained for the simple easy-going routine that Lucy was accustomed to. Lucy's poise was upset, and within a few days the entire household was on edge. Three high-strung Fenwicks under one roof created an atmosphere of nervous pressure that was like the closeness before a summer storm. She felt that her own nerves were beginning to snap: control was withering in the tremendous heat. As the time of her confinement approached, she had to fight to keep from showing her particular resentment at Eugenia's presence in the house. Miss Sophie's over-solicitude was endurable, but Eugenia's furtive virginal glances, in which seemed to be mingled curiosity and disgust, were almost unbearable.

The first week of October brought a heavy storm of wind and rain that swept away the pall of heat and left the earth fresh and green. The atmosphere of the house cleared as if by magic, and her spirits were restored.

That week-end she had an opportunity for a talk with Rusty, and his reassurances checked any tendency toward panic. Her own observations, too, were reassuring: of the plantation women, the majority of whom were narrow-hipped, two types suffered the most, the sickly and the very strong, and she was neither. Some few, like Isaac's wife Leola, big loose machines for procreation, bore their young without any fuss. Leola had had her last child, the fourteenth, in the neighborhood of the praise-house, where she had been overtaken during a shout. And in contrast Emily remembered the fate of the girl Ruth, who had been straight and strong-muscled as a man, and had died with her child after three days of agony.

"Rusty," she said to him that day of their talk, "it's got to be a boy. You realize that, don't you?"

"I do," he told her. "And all you have to do is just hold the thought." And he had added with magnificent gravity: "Someday you'll be surprised at what medical science will do in that direction."

"Sorry but I can't wait that long. And it's simply got to be a boy."

"We'll see what we can do," he promised.

She could joke with him about it, but underneath she was saying to herself with desperate seriousness: It has got to be a boy, a son for Steve,—I can't disappoint him. . . .

In these last days she forgot any impatience she had felt with his mother in the preceding weeks. She saw little of Eugenia, who confined herself to her room with her poems and water-colors and sewing, but Miss Sophie was constantly on hand. The elaborate information and advice of the earlier phase of her visit had been largely exhausted: now her company was restful and a great comfort. Emily's eyes felt too heavy for reading, so Miss Sophie read aloud, from *Henry Esmond* and *The Virginians*, *Vanity Fair* and *The Four Georges*. Miss Sophie had settled on Thackeray as her favorite author—hadn't that English gentleman said all that needed to be said about life, superbly and for all time? And how vividly she recalled his brief stay at her father's plantation on the Combahee, in the spring of '53, when he had planted a live-oak tree that had been destroyed when Sherman had burned the house on his raid to Columbia. With Miss Sophie one reminiscence led to another; her stories were filling in the distances beyond her shoulders like landscape in a portrait. Behind the expectant grandmother-to-be Emily caught glimpses of the girl, the bride, the wife and mother, the widow, all moving in the vistas of a background whose bright colors memory made brighter and whose somber colors had become merely enriching shadows. So many people, Emily thought, went to make up a single life, all strung together on the mysterious thread of personality. She was growing very fond of the accumulation of people that was Miss Sophie.

So the days moved toward the crisis. In the mirror she saw a woman whose eyes were veiled and languid, whose skin had lost its healthy tone of sun and wind. A morning brought the first vague pains. It's not going to be very bad, she thought.

And then, abruptly, she was lying in bed, her teeth gritted against pain that was no longer vague, pain that clutched her with claws of fire and loosed its grip to clutch again. Cold sweat came out on her forehead as the cruel rhythm advanced.

It was late afternoon, she understood dimly. Miss Sophie was moving about in the room. Once she recognized Eugenia standing white-faced in the doorway. At sunset Lucy came in with the lamp and a basin of water. Then she felt the grateful coolness of a washcloth bathing her face. She held Lucy's hand.

"Stay with me, Lucy," she whispered.

Between the pains she could talk to Miss Sophie, but she was not sure what she was saying or what Miss Sophie was saying to her. Everything had taken on a submerged quality. In one feverish breathing-space she remembered Stephen.

"Where is he?" she heard herself ask.

"Downstairs, dear," Miss Sophie's lips moved. "Do you want him?"

"No. Just—give him my love, please. Tell him I'm all right."

Sometime later she realized that Rusty was there, from Charleston.

"I'm sorry," she smiled weakly. "I'm sorry. . . ."

His words came to her through a blanket of pain. She had no clear understanding of their meaning, but his voice was a blessing. Still: she was alone, beyond his reach, and sinking deeper and deeper into the wrenching suffocating darkness. Don't, don't let me cry out, she implored her inmost self; and she remembered Martha Robinson that day of Linda's birth. I didn't realize then, she thought, how brave. . . .

Great waves of pain were crashing through her. In the flashes of consciousness between, she could breathe and see familiar faces as she clung to Lucy's arms. . . . That was her own voice, screaming. But it didn't matter now. Nothing mattered now. She was alone in a writhing hell of pain. Pain that was shattering the world beyond any hope of recovery.

This, then, was death. There could be no return from this ever.

Downstairs in the living-room Stephen was trying to sit still for a few minutes. He threw the cigar he had just lighted into the fireplace: his tongue was burned and his mouth tasted bad. His resentment focused again on the form of Bethel, snoring comfortably on the sofa with his hairy hands folded complacently over his belly. All the excited good-feeling of the early evening, when they had taken several fortifying drinks together, had burned out. Nobody but an unfeeling ass could sleep at a time like this. Stephen moved his chair noisily.

Bethel's snoring terminated on a high note and he sat up with a start.

"What news from the front?" he blinked in the lamplight.

Stephen grunted.

Bethel rubbed his bald head and yawned. "What the hell bloody time is it, my lad?"

Stephen indicated the clock on the mantel with an impatient jerk of his head.

Bethel peered intently at the shadowy dial.

"Well, four-twenty. *Hmm.*"

He stood up and stretched. He rolled down his shirt-sleeves and slapped Stephen's thigh.

"Wager you ten pounds it's a blooming ten-pound—girl."

Stephen groaned.

Bethel chuckled. "Come along, man, you're in need of a drink. And I'm ready for coffee, and a few ham-and-eggs."

Stephen shook his head. "Help yourself."

When Bethel had gone to the kitchen, Stephen got up and went into the hall. It had been quiet upstairs for many minutes now. Why didn't someone come to tell him how things were going?

He climbed the stairs softly and stood outside the door. He could distinguish Rusty's voice and his mother's, speaking low. The door across the hall showed a crack of lamplight and when he looked around he saw his sister. He tiptoed to her. As they whispered, he hoped his face wasn't as pale as hers. For the first time in ages he felt close to her: they were both outsiders.

When she closed her door, he went back to the other door and waited there in a sweat of suspense. Light was beginning to frame the narrow windows that flanked the door to the upper porch, at the end of the hall. His heart jumped when the door in front of him opened and Rusty came out, closing the door behind him.

Rusty was smiling and nodding.

"He'll be out to have a look at you in a minute."

Stephen caught a glimpse of Emily when Rusty went back into the room. Her face was turned away from the light, and he could see only the frail line of her neck and the light brown mass of her hair on the pillow.

A few moments later Lucy appeared with a white bundle in her arms. In the circle of light from the hanging lamp, Stephen stared. He reached out clumsy fingers to take hold of the tiny hand.

"Michael Fenwick," he said in a husky whisper. "A pleasure to know you, sir."

When Lucy went back into the room, Rusty came out again. He put his hand on Stephen's shoulder and they went downstairs together. In the lower hall Stephen remembered Bethel and went to the kitchen to tell him.

Rusty went on out to the piazza and sat down on the steps. He got out his pipe and filled it absently, his eyes on the east where the trees of the barrier isles stood out in black filigree against the saffron of the dawning sky. The waters of the Inlet carried the reflection without a tremor. The air was fresh and clear, and glorious with the rejoicing of birds.

V

THE DAYS flowed over Land's End like waves advancing endlessly from the sea. The surface of life was infinitely varied, like the surface of the Sound. Now the waters were calm dreaming sapphire with highlights of turquoise and patches of amethyst cast by leisurely sailing clouds. Now they lay a mirror for the chromatic fires of sunrise and sunset: scarlet and gold, mauve with pools of cool jade. Sometimes they danced and sparkled under a radiant sky, or glistened softly in moonlight. There were terms of vast sea-green white-capped animation; and moods of turgid brooding and dark turmoil, of savage wind and hissing rain. But always beneath the shifting surface, the deep tides, serene and strong.

The months and the slowly revolving seasons brought changes, astonishing changes, changes of the greatest magnitude; but time was so stealthy that they were not revealed till they had matured. Then they sprang up in sudden confounding moments of realization. That Michael could be six years old was incredible, yet it was impossible to doubt because there had been a cake with six candles and one to grow on and she had fought with Stephen and Rusty to prevent them from keeping the boy all day long in the saddle of the pony they had given him.

"No Fenwick," Stephen had insisted, "ever got beyond the age of six without learning to ride, and you may be sure my son isn't going to be an exception."

Emily had been compelled to surrender. But she had held her ground on the subject of a small rifle that Stephen wanted to get him.

"No Easton," she had insisted, "ever learned to shoot before the age of sixteen, and you may be sure my son isn't going to be an exception."

Stephen and even Miss Sophie had been so dismayed by this that Emily had compromised on fourteen. That would be tomorrow, she sighed to herself, for it was only yesterday that the boy had been a babe-in-arms. Margaret, born a year ago, was now the babe-in-arms; but Emily had a feeling that if she looked away for a minute or two, tricky time would transform the babe into a little girl with a seven-candle cake and a will of her own as strong as Michael's.

"Is it a family custom," she asked Stephen, "to boost little girls into a saddle?"

"Sure."

"Do Fenwick girls have to learn to shoot?"

He shook his head. "The men of the family will do all the shooting."

"I'm relieved to know that," she told him.

Stephen was a crack shot and he rode superbly. When Peter Bethel's wanderlust had at last drawn him back to England and fresh adventure, Stephen had celebrated his promotion to manager with the purchase of a saddle horse, christened Pete.

"We'll have to go halves on him," he had said. "We can't afford two just yet."

She had been glad to have him teach her to ride. At first it had been decidedly more of an ordeal than a pleasure, but she had stuck to it because it meant being able to keep track of Michael on his pony. But more satisfactory even than to ride with the boy herself was to see him and Stephen start out together for a late-afternoon canter.

"Hold him in, sir!" Stephen would shout as the pony prepared to make short work of the long avenue. "Grip those knees! And keep your hindquarters where they belong!"

Stephen carefully concealed his tenderness behind a mask of discipline; only his eyes gave him away. But Miss Sophie made no attempt to conceal her pride and satisfaction.

"He's well-named Michael Fenwick," she loved to repeat to Emily, "for he's the very image of his grandfather. Of course, dear, he has some of your expression, and no doubt the Bramwell in him will crop out somewhere, but his dark eyes and hair and his features are pure Fenwick—the Huguenot strain. The resemblance to his

302

grandfather Fenwick is really remarkable. Oh, if they could only have known each other."

Emily was reminded of another grandfather the boy would never know. At the time of her marriage she had written her father, and she had written again after Michael's birth. Both letters had been returned unopened. She had thought: It doesn't matter. But when, a month before Margaret's birth, a message had come from a lawyer telling of his death, her heart had turned sick with grief for him, remembered now only as the father of her young girlhood. She had been tortured with bitter speculations: perhaps he had never received the letters, perhaps she should have addressed them to the Academy instead of the house where the stepmother was, perhaps if she had made a journey to Boston to see him. . . .

"What was the color of his eyes?" Miss Sophie had asked when she had studied the picture of him that Emily had shown her.

"Blue, like Mother's."

"Well, you see Margaret favors you Eastons. But Michael——."
And she was off again on her pet subject.

Emily had no other feeling than amusement at Miss Sophie's insistence on the Fenwickness of Michael. What did it matter whom he resembled so long as he was her son. Her son and Stephen's: herself and Stephen blended in a living symbol of their love. That was miracle enough. . . . It could hardly have made any difference if he had resembled the most ill-favored of all his ancestors since the beginning of time, but it was good to see what a fine-looking well-made little fellow he was. Someday, by a series of changes that would take her as much by surprise as this one of his sixth birthday, he would grow to manhood, strong and true. Nothing in her life now was so important as that. There were no bounds to her dreams for him.

But those changes belonged to tomorrow. Today her thoughts and heart were busy making adjustments to this first great transformation,—her baby of yesterday astride a pony! And there were all the other realizations that this one evoked.

No change was more amazing than the change that had come over Stephen. Success had made him over. The drawn worried look was gone from his face, and his tall lean frame had filled out, his ribs and his nerves were well covered. The new gloved hand that Rusty had ordered and fitted for him had cured his excessive consciousness of disfigurement, though sometimes that left hand still hid itself behind him instinctively. He had developed a magnificent vanity in his personal appearance; his friend, courtly Captain Todd of the phosphate fleet, who was always entertained at the house when he was in port, brought in fine English cloths, which Stephen had made up in the latest Bond Street cut by a Charleston tailor. Clothes for the rest of the family as well as himself must be of the best. That and the occasional wines and food delicacies imported through the Captain were his only extravagances. Each month the surplus from his salary went into shares of the Company. And each month his confidence in himself and the future expanded.

"We're going to be rich some day, sweetheart," he told her one night when they were talking over expenses. "I mean sure-enough rich. And the first thing we're going to do is take a vacation and catch up with that honeymoon we missed."

One Sunday when they were at Marshlands, she heard him say to Miss Sophie: "Mamma, one of these mornings bright and fair you're going to put on wings and cleave the air! You're going to have a fine carriage and a whole flock of servants. It's going to be like old times again. Only we'll have more money than Pappa and Grand-pappa put together!"

He laughed when she hastened to knock wood and solemnly chided him for saying such rash things.

Miss Sophie showed scarcely any change. Her hair had turned a little grayer; that was all. According to Stephen she was well over sixty, yet she was the same energetic and erect woman that Emily had first known. Her birthday came two weeks after Michael's, but her eyes snapped at the mere mention of a celebration.

"None of that, if you please. Why, I'm just beginning to get my second wind. Haven't I got to raise Michael? Time enough to think about birthdays and chimney corners when that's done."

"Nobody said a word about chimney corners," Stephen smiled.

"Never mind—I know what you're thinking."

For Michael's sake she had evidently made up her mind to remain vaguely middle-aged as long as necessary.

It was Eugenia who showed that six years could bring unpleasant changes. As the lives and fortunes of the family expanded around her, she seemed to contract. Her chief characteristics were sharpening to the point of eccentricity; she was thinner and paler, her dark eyes were more introspective and her voice more petulant than ever. The last bloom of youth had left her when Sally Broughton's brother Bob had gone to Savannah to work; she had rejected disdainfully and as a matter-of-course the embryonic attentions of Donald Van Wie, son of the carpetbagging storekeeper. Her only companion now was Sally, whose cheerful disposition accented Eugenia's unhappy qualities without having any tonic effect on them.

"Nobody can do anything for her," Stephen sighed. "To begin with, you can't get at her. You know that yourself—certainly nobody's tried harder than you have. She makes me mad, and Mother can only scold or pet her. She's going to dry up into an old maid like Aunt Susan and Isabel, only worse."

"Oh, Stephen, don't take that attitude."

"Well, isn't it the truth? The South is full of single women and not half enough men to go round—why should any man pick her? Bob Broughton was the nearest thing to a beau she ever had, and he always kept at a safe distance. Can't blame him. I don't mean to be hard on her—she's my sister and I'd do anything I could for her. But she's got herself all tied up in knots and I defy anybody to get her untied."

"If she had some kind of work to do. . . ."

"Work in a hardware store like Sally? No thank you, not while I have my health. She couldn't do it anyway. She might help Mary Hamilton with her school, but she hates children."

"If she had some interest to take her out of herself. . . ."

"Interest? What about her water-colors? Doesn't she write poems? Have you forgotten *The Heiress of Holly Hall?*"

Emily had not forgotten *The Heiress of Holly Hall.* It was a long narrative poem recounting the abduction of a Southern maiden by Indians and her eventual rescue by her lover. Like other shorter poems Eugenia had sent it to *Scribner's Magazine* and, like them, it had been returned with polite regrets. The manuscript was dedicated to: *My Uncle, Judge Joseph Legerton Bramwell, whose ante-bellum verse has been my inspiration.* Her uncle had returned the compliment by having a limited edition of two hundred copies of *The Heiress* privately printed in Charleston; twenty-two autographed copies were disposed of through the Broad Street Bookstore, fifty or sixty were distributed as gifts, and the rest were deposited in a neat bundle on the top shelf of the closet of Eugenia's room at Marshlands. Having launched his niece as a poetess the Judge had tactfully suggested that she try her hand at some other branch of literature,—something in the historical or genealogical line, perhaps. She was now engaged in collecting notes for a Life of her maternal grandfather, Governor Bramwell of South Carolina.

The Judge called at Marshlands every Sunday afternoon he was in Beaufort and Emily often saw him there. She understood that in the past certain differences had existed between him and Miss Sophie, but these had apparently been removed. Their relationship, however, remained peculiar: they seemed to come together largely for the purpose of contradicting each other. Miss Sophie took sober delight in puncturing her brother's flights of eloquence with little needles of irony; he returned the attack with elaborately polished sarcasm, couched in legal parlance and directed at her by way of someone else in the room, usually Emily. Sometimes in the midst of a discussion they both appealed to her for support. She managed to stay on neutral ground, but secretly her sympathies were with the Judge, who was certainly the underdog; ordinarily he was attacked without provocation or warning, and his lines were taken by quick assault before he had time to bring up his heavy artillery.

But it was not always warfare between them. There were truces, notably at Thanksgiving and Christmas, when perfect harmony prevailed and they encouraged each other to dizzy heights of storytelling and reminiscing. Emily had to go back to her earliest memories of family gatherings at Salem to match such times.

When she had first met the Judge, he had addressed her as if she were a courtroom of people and given her a condescending account of his university days at Harvard. She had thought then that he was the most pompous self-satisfied bore she had ever known, but her feelings toward him had soon changed. She was not sure how the change had come about; perhaps it had started the day Stephen had brought him out to Land's End and he had made such pathetically awkward efforts to get acquainted with his grand-nephew Michael. At all events she was positively fond of him now. She took him at his own valuation, and he rewarded her by being always his most magnificent self. It gave her amusement and pleasure to play audience to his sense of personal grandeur, his elegant manners, and his sweeping pronouncements.

"Look here," Stephen said to her, "what are you doing to my Uncle Joe? You've got him eating out of your hand. And you're spoiling him worse than the Aunts do."

There was no change whatever in the Aunts. They remained as damningly invisible as ever, two witch-like creatures of her imagination mingling in a kind of fantastic dance with the ghosts of genial Dr. Ellis and his soldier patients. But Bramwell Hall, the hospital of her first memories, within whose mysterious depths the Judge's younger sisters lurked, had undergone a remarkable change. Its tabby walls, its battlements and molded chimney-pots had taken on a mellow age that made it look older than the old places along the river. At dusk, when its surroundings were shrouded in shadows and the last brooding reflections were ebbing away from the marsh pools under its east windows, it was definitely a Tudor castle, standing bleak and lonely and proud against the dying sky. It made a haunting picture when the family was returning in the launch from a Sunday with Gran'ma. Michael stared at it with awe.

"Mamma."

"Yes, dear?"

"Uncle Joe comes to see us—why doesn't he ever ask us to come and see him?"

"He's a very busy man, dear, and he's away a great deal, like Uncle Rusty. I'm sure he'll ask us some day."

Michael pondered that. His enthusiasm for the adventure seemed to wane at even so remote a prospect of its fulfilment.

"Lucy says Uncle Joe keeps two female wildcats."

Emily glanced at Lucy, but Lucy was absorbed in bundling up the baby against the night air. Stephen, no help at such a time, was smiling foolishly.

"Lucy must be mistaken, dear," she told Michael.

His wide eyes continued to stare at the Castle till the lights of the Bay Street waterfront captured his attention.

These years since Michael's birth had not neglected Beaufort. The whole atmosphere of the little town had changed. It seemed to have recovered some of the dignity and serenity of the old days that Miss Sophie and the Judge loved to tell about. There was plenty of activity, stimulated by the rapid growth of phosphate-mining and by the increased trade that came from neighboring Port Royal, where the railroad from Augusta met the ships of the Mallory Line; but it was a healthy controlled activity, not the feverish inflation of war times or the fetid blatant disorder of Reconstruction. Bay Street had a new bank, several new stores, and a new cotton warehouse; and a new Court House was being built to replace the one that had burned—*been* burned, the Judge always insisted, to destroy records of Reconstruction chicanery.

The Negro population had quieted down. They were objectionably in evidence only on Saturdays and on their days of celebration, when augmented by a great influx from the islands they took over the town. Their leaders had disappeared one by one since the Hampton election; Robert Fenwick, the last to desert, had gone to found a "free community" in California. The people were beginning to lose interest in elections, and the Judge was growing more and more hopeful of making them politically impotent. He was campaigning to oust the remaining Negro office-holders at the next election, to restore the Black Belt to complete white rule. He had State and even Federal ambitions for himself, and he urged on Stephen the duty of making himself a candidate for at least a County office.

But Stephen had other ambitions, which were drawing him into the business life of the community. It was a great satisfaction to Emily that he invariably made a point of talking things over with her. In the evenings when she came downstairs from getting Michael settled for the night and from taking a peek at the baby, Stephen put aside his *News & Courier* and came to the sofa to stretch out. After the kinks of the day had been ironed out, he came to the matter that was continually in his thoughts now.

"You see, what I want is a little of everything in this section,—the railroad, the bank, Bay Street and Port Royal real estate. Old Beaufort, the Beaufort you hear Mother and Uncle Joe tell about, is dead and gone, and it's too bad but it can't be helped. The only thing to do is make the most of the hustling new Beaufort that's coming sure as judgment. And take my word for it, we're going to be in on the ground floor."

Phosphate, of course, was the main thing; it wasn't going to be long before they'd have to make him a partner in the Company.

But meanwhile he was getting a foothold in Beaufort and Port Royal. There was one big obstacle: most of the business men were Yankees. The worst of the Carpetbagging element had cleared out since Reconstruction, but there were some fine specimens left. He would have no dealings with them. For one thing, he would never accept a directorship in the bank as long as a skunk like Sam Koenig was on the board.

Emily knew there were several Yankees whom Stephen respected and with whom he was beginning to make business contacts. Rutherford, president of the Port Royal Railroad; Van Wie of the General Store; and the Turner Brothers, who had come from the North recently to open a hardware store. But Stephen never invited them into his home and never went into their homes; Emily had only a bowing acquaintance with them and their families on Sunday at St. Helena's. For the Fenwicks, as for the Bramwells, society was confined to the handful of Old Guard families that had drifted back to the town,—the Rhetts and Elliotts, the Broughtons, the Hamiltons, and a few others.

This jealous remnant of Old Beaufort was thrown into a spasm on "Decoration Day", when ex-President Grant came to dedicate the National Cemetery to the north of town. A few weeks before, Stephen had been made a director of the railroad and now was expected to serve on the committee of welcome. After several painful family conferences it was decided that he must go through with it. Emily went with him to the reception at the Sea Island Hotel with bitter resentment in her heart against this figure that had presided over the South's darkest hours; and it gave her a flash of delight, when the procession of carriages passed Bramwell "Castle" on the way to the cemetery, to see that the Judge's sisters had taken advantage of his absence to shroud the gateposts with crepe and hang Confederate flags out the windows. But when she sat behind the guest of honor, her bitterness melted into pity. Could this mussy broken old man, addressing in a faltering voice the Negro crowd and the aisles of immaculate new headstones, could this be the Grant of Appomattox and Reconstruction? Here was not even a tragic figure, of nemesis and retribution; here stood only a little old man, peevish, sick, pathetic.

Somehow the sight of him that day brought Emily her fullest

realization of change: of how relentless it could be, had been to her in the past, and of how kind a face it was turning to her now. The years that had crushed this man had performed miracles for her. Time had become her patron, her friend and ally.

✓   ✓   ✓

There was a special place where time conveniently crystallized its changes for her. On the two lower shelves of the living-room bookcase were accumulating the paper backs of *Harper's Monthly*. By some magic they had become a record of memories, of significant moments and moods of the past.

Stephen never went near the bookcase: his reading was confined to the newspapers. And she herself had no leisure now for the little library that regarded her reproachfully from the upper shelves. With the world so full of Michael and the baby and Stephen and home, what time or inclination was there for looking into books. She was grateful to them for former companionship, but they were become as irrelevant as friends who have ceased to play any part in one's life, and she was impatient of their silent importunities.

But with *Harper's* it was different. The magazine had subtly grown into her life, it was a habit of long standing now, it was not to be denied or neglected. When a new number came in, it was often several days before she could find time to look into it, and it might be many days before she was able to get through it; but in the end it was read from cover to cover and installed with its fellows on the slowly filling bottom shelves of the bookcase. In the intervals between the finishing of one number and the appearance of another, she went back to keep in touch with the older ones, which she felt she knew almost by heart.

Her attachment to the periodical had little to do with its intrinsic worth. It simply happened to be the core around which her memories had collected. There they were, from the first year at Land's End to the recent miracles of Michael's sixth birthday and Margaret's weaning. . . .

With the next money that could be spared she would have all these loose copies bound, and someday she would buy the numbers that were missing, the first number that marked the month of her own first birthday and the others that held her childhood and girlhood in the North. Then there would be thirty-four trim volumes, resting here like the years of her life under the seal of time. But those missing numbers at the end, those volumes of the months and years ahead that would slowly and surely fill the space left: what would they hold? She kept this sacred gap clear of the things that everyone loved to tuck here,—Stephen his papers, Michael his knick-knacks, Miss Sophie her crochet-bag when she came on a visit,—for here the mysterious future would reveal itself, little by little. With some number the world would end for her, somewhere here time would stop forever like the flame of a candle snuffed out, but for the children life would reach far beyond, shining and happy. . . . No, *Harper's* was not to be neglected even in the fullness of these days, and its shelf was a place not only of memory but also of propitiation and prayer.

Usually she did her reading in snatches while keeping an eye on the children's play, indoors or out depending on the weather. The cove, a tiny crescent beach lying below the tip of the front yard, was the favorite spot for sunshiny days in autumn, winter, and early spring. In late spring and summer the sun was too hot there, and play had to be transferred to the shade of the trees at the side of the house, or to the cool and generous spaces under the tabby arches supporting the piazzas. The cove had no fine white sand and no shells like Bay Point, and there was marsh grass growing where the surf line should have been, but it had one attraction that compensated the children for its shortcomings,—the little bluff, six feet of sandy soil rising from the beach to the coarse Bermuda grass of the front yard. This was the background for most of their games. Today it was a cliff with ledges and recesses for mud huts, an idea Michael had derived from the illustrations of an article on Cliff Dwellers. Tomorrow it might be anything from a fortress to an avalanche.

Michael's playmates were Linda and Dallas Robinson. Every morning as Stephen was leaving for the mines they appeared hand-in-hand on the front piazza, spic and span from their mother and prepared to spend the day. Linda, age eight, was a fine handsome child, with golden hair and light blue eyes and a bright cheerful expression; she was more than a match for Michael when he got too obstreperous, but most of the time she was content to follow wherever his fancy led. Dallas, two years younger than Michael, was as different from his sister as night from day: brown-thatched and somber-eyed, he was dull and incurably shy,—Emily would gain his confidence one minute to lose it completely the next. He was always being hustled and ordered about for the purposes of the latest game Michael had invented; he was the rank-and-file, the rabble, the drone, indispensable yet scorned. The only times that he could be himself and enjoy himself were during intermissions in Michael's and Linda's exploits, when his services were not required and he was allowed to go his own way. Then he could turn with a timid smile to the pen where the baby staggered and played havoc with her blocks and a rag doll named Juba. Margaret never failed to greet him with a tipsy grin and the immediate offer of whatever she happened to have in her hand at the moment. He was at ease with her. She understood him.

Seated in a camp-chair near the pen Emily had to go back over every page of her reading several times to get the meaning. Even when the children and the baby were not actively demanding her attention, she couldn't help watching them out of the corner of her eye. And their voices kept breaking through the print, the baby's babbling and humming, the children's sea-island dialect. It was a dialect, no doubt about that, and when they got excited it was close to pure gullah. Stephen only laughed at her alarm about it. She needn't be surprised, he told her, if someday Margaret repeated the words of the island belle attending her first ball in Charleston: the young lady's patience was sorely tried before one of the town gallants asked her if she cared to dance, and she replied with spirit, "Sho I dance. I come fuh dance! What you t'ink I come fuh—to tack root?"

Stephen was no help whatever. "I'd rather have my children talk gullah than Yankee any day. You don't know how much your own speech has improved with a little softening and slurring."

"But Steve dear, we can't have them saying *kee-uk* for cake, and *vell* for well, and *pilluh* for pillow. And I *yeddy* for I hear, and I *shum* for I see—or saw—him or her or it or them!"

He was only amused. And there was no combatting the combined influence of Lucy and Tunis, who was now general handyman in the house and yard. The most she could do was concentrate her attack on a few special gullahisms, during the morning reading lessons she gave Michael and Linda. But even in this limited field, she foresaw with a despairing smile, defeat was inevitable.

At the close of each long day, as the afternoon sun was sinking toward the horizon islands across the Sound, Lucy took charge of the baby. Then Tunis took Michael to meet Stephen, and Linda and Dallas home. When she had seen them off,—Michael on the pony, Dallas clinging to Linda on big Pete, Tunis on his marsh tacky,— she went into the house for the few minutes that were her own. She valued this quiet solitary time of the day not as an escape from the family: things seldom got to that harassed point. Its value lay in the breathing-space it gave her to appreciate the blissful flow of life.

The piano stood between the corner windows in the living-room. And it always seemed to be waiting expectantly for this hour, shafts of late sunlight illumining the keyboard and the portfolios on the rack, Mozart and Bach, Chopin and Brahms. She would never forget the hesitations and misgivings with which she had approached the old Steinway after its arrival from the North. When the lawyer's letter had come, asking what disposal she wished to make of this single bequest to her in her father's will, she had decided with Stephen to have it shipped. When the crate had finally appeared from Port Royal on the *Pilot Boy* and been grunted up from the landing by a good-natured quartette of Stephen's huskiest mine hands, and when Seth Robinson had carefully unpacked the familiar square shape, a host of memories had been released with it, aching homesick memories of her mother and her childhood at the house in Chestnut Street. After it had been placed in the living-room, there had still remained the problem of tuning, but Stephen had solved that by having a man come out from Charleston, a painstaking old German whom Joe Bramwell had located. Then at last everything had been ready and waiting.

"It looks simply elegant in the room," Stephen had smiled, "but can't you do anything but poke at it with one finger after all this trouble? Why even I can play chopsticks. If your mother was a teacher at the Boston Conservatory of Music she must have raised you better than that. Didn't you say you were an infant prodigy once, or at least good at it? Haven't you been telling me for years that the only thing you missed in the South was a piano? Well, here it is. Do something."

But she had found some urgent house matter as an excuse for begging off, and another day had passed before she had summoned the courage to replace her mother's image at the keys. It was this same late-afternoon hour that she had picked for the test. Then: the triumphant thrill of discovering that her fingers had not stiffened beyond recovery, had not lost their feel and response to the notes that her eyes were able to read with little faltering.

That night she had found confidence to play a Chopin *Nocturne* for Stephen. He had listened with more affection than attention. And after other experiences with him as an audience she had begun to realize he was not listening at all but merely watching her, indulgently. Once when she had played a Bach *Fugue* that she had practiced for him with great pains, she had turned to find him absorbed in his *News & Courier.*

"You don't like that?" she had asked him lightly, hiding her disappointment.

He had put down the paper with a guilty smile. "Oh, sweetheart, I'm sorry,—please don't stop. I love to hear you, but—well, I'm afraid I haven't much of an ear for music."

"But if you'd really listen, you'd learn to enjoy it."

"Oh, I like the old-time songs you play all right. But complicated pieces, I just don't understand what they're all about."

"They're about life, just like the songs."

"I still don't get the connection. That heavy stuff's too much for me, that's all I know about life."

He had come from his chair then to give her an apologetic hug. "Don't mind me, honey, I'm hopeless. Play for Mother—she'll appreciate it. Now come and talk. I'm not getting any attention since that piano appeared."

After that she had stopped playing any "complicated pieces" or "heavy stuff" in the evenings. One Sunday she had played for his mother, but Miss Sophie had very soon announced she had "short patience with classical compositions". She was partial to "simple melodies", which she executed with expression and a system of pedaling all her own. *The Last Link Is Broken, Long Long Ago,* and *Stabat Mater* were her favorites. And for contrast she had a thundering "descriptive selection", *The Battle of Prague,* which enthralled Michael with its elaborate cannonading and realistic cavalry charge.

But when Rusty had come from Charleston, his enthusiasm had more than repaid her for the apathy of the rest of the family.

And now as she sat here alone, with the shadows gathering softly around her and the last shafts of the sun glowing across the pages of Brahms, she was secretly playing for them all, all her loved ones

This hour was the transfiguration of her happiness, as sunset was the transfiguration of the glory of earth. Here in this magic flow of sound the day was washed clean of fatigue and fret, all things fell into a pattern of seemliness and order, life was exalted. Under this spell of music time and its laws were suspended: the past and the future were blended in the light of an eternal present whose master she was, memories and dreams were secure here against the endless shiftings of change.

VI

John Easton Fenwick was born on the third day of April, 1885.
The Easton was Miss Sophie's generous suggestion. Having secured
Bramwell for both Michael's and Margaret's middle name, she was
prepared to make this concession to the Yankee side of the family.

Emily's strength was slow in returning. Finally one morning
she made herself get up, but she felt so shaky that she had to go back
to bed after barely an hour downstairs. She fretted through this
delay, worrying about the children and Stephen and the house despite
Lucy's reassurances; waiting impatiently for Rusty's next visit, yet
steadfastly refusing to send for him. "I'll be all right in a day or
two," she kept telling Stephen. But the wretched weakness persisted, and when Rusty came at last he shook his head over her.

"What's the matter with me?" she pleaded.

"Nothing serious. Just played out. You need a little vacation."

That evening after supper when Lucy had taken the baby and his
crib into the children's room, Rusty and Stephen came up to announce a plan they had worked out. "You're going to the mountains," Stephen told her, "with Mother and Eugenia."

She stared at him blankly. "And what about the children?"

"Oh, Lucy and I'll take care of them. Rusty says you've got to
have a complete rest."

She looked at Rusty and then back at Stephen. "Are you both
mad?" she asked them with a panic-stricken little laugh. "Do you
suppose I'd have a moment's peace away from you all?"

When she realized that they were serious, that they expected her
to abandon even the baby, she rallied all her forces to demolish the
plan. She met argument with counter-argument and appeals to her
reason with appeals to theirs. "Well," Stephen concluded hotly,

"you've simply got to go without the children,—you've got it to do, that's all." "I won't," she told him. "You gentlemen may just as well trot downstairs and have another conference. And if you want me to listen to you, you better come back with at least a compromise." But they made no move to leave the room, and in the end she wore them down to conceding every point.

When Rusty went back to Charleston he made arrangements for Stephen to rent the summer place of the Pinckneys at Flat Rock in the North Carolina mountains. The price sounded enormous, but Stephen insisted. Miss Sophie and Eugenia set out ahead with Ella, their Marshlands servant, to open the house; Emily was to follow several days later with Margaret and the baby and Lucy, leaving Michael to come up with his father after the Boat Club races. But on the eve of this first separation from Michael, courage failed her.

"Stephen," she said hesitatingly, "I really don't think I ought to leave just yet."

It was after supper, the children had been packed off to bed, and Stephen was comfortably settled with a cigar and the *News & Courier,*—as good a time as any for arbitration. "What's the matter, dear?" he asked with indulgent half-attention. "Don't feel quite up to snuff yet?"

"Oh no, I'm all right. It isn't that."

"What is it then? Worried about the baby on the train? That was your idea, you know."

"No,—I talked that all over with Rusty."

He glanced at her facetiously. "Perhaps you can't tear yourself away from the piano. Or don't want to miss the boat races."

She encouraged his good-nature by being amused at that.

"Well," he sighed, "if you're still worrying about us, you're wasting your energy. We're going to make out like white mice,—Michael goes to the mines with me and starts learning the business, Tunis keeps house. So what's there to worry about?" He rustled and scanned his paper, signal that the subject had been covered and closed. "Here's another chess problem for you and Rusty. Better take it along and work it out with Mother when the pair of you get fretting about us." A minute later he chuckled: "How you must hate to be told the men of the family can get along without you for a few days."

"Of course," she smiled. "But that still isn't quite it."

317

He lowered the paper and studied her with a frown, all attention now. A surmise came into his eyes.

"Is it Michael?"

She nodded.

He crumpled the paper to the floor and got up with a groan. "I was afraid of that!" He thrust his hands into the tight pockets of his trousers and pulled them out again. "Why didn't you say so in the first place? Why in the devil can't women be direct about a thing? Why not come right out and admit you want to keep him tied to your apron-strings?"

"But Steve darling. He isn't seven yet. It's too soon——."

"Too soon to start making a man of him? Not on your life! If you had your way, you'd keep him at your skirts till he was seven-teen. Or twenty-seven."

"Oh now please, Stephen. You understand—he's so very young. I'll promise not to protest later on."

He threw up his hands. "Have it your way!"

"But you do understand, dear."

"I understand you're making a big mistake, yes. It's too bad you can't see the sooner apron-strings are cut the better it'll be for both of you." He picked up the paper and resumed his reading with an expression of disgust. "But we're not going to have any mother's boy in this family. Make no mistake about that."

So it was settled that her departure be postponed till the day after the boat races and that Michael would leave with her then. So the first separation was staved off, deferred.

And that Saturday she had the joy of seeing Stephen and Michael win the races with the trim new *Gleeful*. Rusty had come out from Charleston to enter the old *Dolphin*, overhauled for the occasion. It was a glorious day of sun and flying shadows, a day made everlast-ingly memorable by the ecstasy of returning strength, which gave significance to even the slightest things—the rustling of palmetto fronds in the yard as she went down to the landing with Margaret, the scudding patches of wind on the water, the arcs and hoverings of gulls. When the sails appeared at last in the Sound from the mouth of Beaufort River, it was a struggle to hang on to Margaret with one hand and focus Rusty's binoculars with the other. And when she had disentangled her two particular sails from the rest in the sparkle and glare, the problem was to keep them separated in the confusions that developed with all the tacking and cross-tacking.

For the first half of the race her heart was in her throat most of the time, as treacherous puffs dipped the sails perilously. At the height of the excitement Lucy left the baby in his crib on the piazza and came to the edge of the yard to relieve her feelings with jabber and prayer and frenzied wavings of her apron. But after the boats rounded the buoy off the tip of Parris Island, the danger of cap-sizings was past. From then on it was clear running before the wind, and the *Gleeful* stepped briskly away from her chief rivals, the Rutherfords' *Spray* and Sam Koenig's *Captain Jinx* and *Jessie B.* By skillful handling Rusty brought the old *Dolphin* to the buoy on the heels of the leaders, but on the home stretch he was left far behind.

Beating Rusty seemed to give Michael much more pleasure than winning the "Port Royal Cup". In the late afternoon when they came back with the trophy,—on the launch with the sailboats in tow, for the wind had fallen and the tide was against them,—the first thing Michael shouted across the water was "Mamma! we gave Uncle Rusty an awful beating!" And on the landing he was convulsed with joy telling her about it. "Monkey," said Rusty, "if I'd had your swelled head along for ballast, it would have been a very different story." When the victor grew too objectionable, Rusty scooped him up by the seat of his sailor pants and suspended him over the side of the landing till he squealed for mercy.

It was a formidable matter getting him settled for bed that night: the day's excitement and anticipation of tomorrow's departure for the mountains were too much for him. For once he was beyond Lucy's control, and Emily had to go up to the nursery to quiet him and get Margaret and the baby to sleep again. She had hardly come back to the living-room and announced success with a smile of relief when there was a scamper of bare feet on the stairs and Michael appeared at the door—wearing only a flushed and uncertain grin. In a crisis of this kind Stephen and Rusty were worse than no help, and their breakdown demoralized her completely. By the time her eyes and voice had recovered some authority, Michael was sure enough of himself to be gigglingly defiant. And when she had finally sobered him, he wrinkled up his nose and tried being pathetic.

"But it's so hot, Mamma. I just can't get to sleep. If you'll let me stay just two minutes, I know I'll be all right."

As a last resort he made a dash for Rusty's chair. This strategy won him the two-minute respite, for it took that long to maul him into submission. Then Rusty carried him upstairs piggyback, which of course roused the nursery again, and once again Emily had to go up to restore order. This time she gave Michael a serious talking-to, keeping herself very firm against his blandishments and suppressed glee; and she stayed till she was satisfied he was really settled for the night.

It was a good half-hour later, and well after ten o'clock, when a desolate stage whisper came from the head of the stairs.

"Mamma."

She gave Stephen a weary look of appeal and he straightened his face and went into the hall. Her eyes met Rusty's for support as they listened.

"Now, son, we've had enough of this."

"I want to tell Mamma something."

"Did you hear what I said, young man?"

"I just want to say good-night to Uncle Rusty."

"Michael!"

"But, Pappa, I can't get to sleep at all. I've tried and tried."

"If I come up there, sir, you'll get to sleep in short order. Now don't let me hear another sound out of you—understand?"

"Yes, sir."

Silence. And then a whimper.

"I got the stomach-ache bad."

So in the end it developed that something besides excitement and heat was causing the feverish unrest. It developed, in fact, that Michael had consumed three lemonades, a bottle of ginger-pop, and two slabs of Lady Baltimore cake at the Boat Club buffet.

"Just a sample," she told Stephen, "of freedom from apron-strings. I see how well the men of the family get along on their own."

But next morning at the Port Royal station she was overcome with qualms. In the excitement of avoiding a first separation from Michael she had lost sight of the fact that this was to be a first separation from Stephen. And she was leaving him with nothing but work and heat for company.

"I think I'll stay with you," she said to him privately out the window of the train.

"Now that's more like it," he smiled up, reaching for her. "Come on, jump,—you're only young once. Think of the honeymoon we could have with nobody around, not even Lucy." But then he shook his head and sighed. "No. Rusty says we can't even hold hands all summer. Doctor's orders."

"You don't think we're smart enough to fool the doctor?"

"Not me. The only person I'm smart enough to fool is myself,—I cut my own throat by having three children. Listen to them clamoring for you. Even begrudge me a private good-bye. . . . But I'm getting used to it now. Only it's going to be pretty tough this trip. I won't even have you to look at this time."

"Darling, I'm sorry."

He grinned up at her. "Oh I'll take it out in work. And love letters. Say, that's something else we've missed, along with a honeymoon. You'll turn red as a beet when you read them. You'll have to burn them on the spot. Look at you, blushing already!"

"Please, Mr. Fenwick. At my age?"

"You never blushed better in your life."

"It's a little public here, after all."

"Well, that's easily remedied." And he pulled her hand down for a kiss. "That better?"

"You don't seem very depressed. Sure I can trust you alone?"

"Why, are there any other women in the world? I haven't noticed for years. Sorry, honey, I'm afraid I'm not the exciting type of husband. Should I try to improve?"

"Please don't, even in fun. . . . Steve, you will take care of yourself and remember everything I told you?"

"Now don't try to change the subject. They say ladies thrive on excitement. Or have you had enough?"

"I'm having enough, thank you."

"You will if I ever get you alone again, before we're old and gray. Maybe you'll appreciate me again someday. Maybe someday we can have that honeymoon instead of a separation. . . . Well, there's Conductor Gilroy's signal. You're as good as gone, honey. Let me say good riddance to that gang of yours."

But before she left the window to make way for them, her anxiety rushed out in a last jumbled appeal.

"Yes, yes," he nodded with smiling impatience, "I'll toe the mark, don't worry. No, I won't work too hard. No, I won't forget to have Joe out for company." But then he sobered suddenly. "And don't you forget to go easy. I'm letting you get away with murder taking that gang with you, but I expect to see a new woman by the end of summer. Now no nonsense. I'll be up to check on you as soon as I can get away. Just keep one thing firmly in mind,—this is to be a nice quiet vacation adventure for you."

After the confusion of good-byes in the clanging start of the train, after the last wave to his diminishing form at the station, it took her a long time to settle down to any sense of adventure. It was shocking, this separation, this leaving him alone. But finally she was able to quiet herself with the repeated thought: He needs a rest from all of us—it will do him good to have no family for a while—he'll be pretty glad to see us when it's over. . . .

She was sitting with Rusty facing Michael and Margaret. Lucy and the baby in his basket had the seat across the aisle. He was behaving beautifully, cooing and gurgling against the train noises as if he too were aware of high adventure. Lucy was stolid with dignity, but her eyes gave her away: they had a wild almost frightened look. Margaret, shy and bewildered, hugged her old friend Juba in a strangling embrace and took all her cues from Michael; she was learning to talk, but all this was too much for her, and not even Rusty could get more than a slumping little smile from her.

Michael was beside himself with excitement and popping with questions. This was not his first journey: the summer before he had been taken to Charleston for the "Centennial of Incorporation". But that had been by boat, the stimulations had not been so violent, and he had had the freedom of the whole upper deck. Here he was confined beyond endurance, and to keep him from making expeditions up and down the aisle Rusty resurrected a game that the grandfathers of the family had used to ease the tedium of travel: the one who could spot the greatest number of "living creatures" was the winner. And except for the change at Yemassee Junction and later the opening of the lunch hamper, the game was pursued without interruption to the outskirts of Charleston, when it was lost in the slow clanging approach to the station through blocks with too many living creatures to count.

Rusty went with them in the omnibus of the old "Charleston

House" and saw them settled in a spacious suite; then he had to hurry off to his hospital. He had wanted them to stay at his little house in Legare Street, but the size of the party made that impossible this time.

Toward evening it turned a little cooler out in the street, but the rooms stayed hot and close. After supper she took Michael for a walk: he was far too restless for bed. He strained at her side, trying to look in every direction at once and full of questions. When they had walked as far as St. Michael's (he took a proprietary interest in the old church), a horse-car came along and to his intense delight they rode the rest of the way down Meeting Street to the Battery. They stayed till dusk settled over the water and the stars came out, till the outline of Sumter was lost in the darkness and there was nothing left of the harbor but twinkling lights and the toll of a ship's bell. Even then he was reluctant to leave, for though vision was thwarted there were still the voices of the city people passing and the shouts of invisible boys at play in the park to keep him excited. He was still hopelessly wakeful.

To insure his sleeping she decided to take him back to the hotel by a roundabout way. The route was clear in her mind: King Street, Legare, side streets to Broad, and then Meeting again and the hotel. King Street was familiar to her; and to Michael too, for here last summer he had seen the city's first arc lamps and they had made a greater impression on him than even the Centennial fireworks. And Legare Street, where Rusty's little house stood back in a tangled garden and bird sanctuary, was familiar ground. But when they turned off Legare, the streets were nameless and confusing and it was difficult to keep a sense of direction.

Michael wasn't worried about direction: his only concern was to get to the next street intersection,—the whole city was lighted by arc lamps now. At each corner he would stop to squint up at the dazzling bluish light with as much fascination as if it were the first he had seen. He was distressed about the swarms of bugs hurling themselves against the faintly spluttering globes. From the gutter under one light he salvaged the fragile body of a lunar moth, and he discarded the fragments of carbon sticks he had been collecting so that he could devote an entire hand to preserving it intact for Margaret and the baby and Lucy to see.

It was the mid spaces of the blocks, beyond the reach of the lights, that attracted her. It took a shroud of darkness to complete the haunting magic of the city. Stirring of shadowy palm plumes over an old wall, languid voices from a window above the street, the melody of laughter from a vine-hidden piazza: sounds that came to break the surface of the night were like pebbles cast into a still pool, spreading gently conflicting circles of memory and reflection. And a breath of fragrance from a sleeping garden was enough to revive a whole era of the past. . . . Night revealed beauty and sadness that day only obscured. You could see better at night; the blinding glare was gone, the glittering curtain of commonsense vision lifted, and you were free to see the realities that lay behind the superficial everyday aspect of people and things. At night the wonder of the world came to light, and the lives and homes of strangers in strange streets lost their remoteness and became intimately yours. You felt the kinship of yourself to other selves. Understanding and sympathy took the place of hostility and indifference. . . . The direct pain of her early memories of the city had long since vanished. Only the memory of memory remained. Yet this lingering essence was intense enough to heighten her consciousness like music and to give her a sense of approaching some profound secret. It seemed as if the very meaning of existence lay hidden somewhere in this mood that was Charleston at night, and as if, as a kind of reward for her faraway suffering here, an answer to the mystery of things might be revealed to her at any moment, in any doorway or around the corner of any street.

That, she recognized abruptly, was a fantastic conception. The reward and answer to everything was here with her now, his hand in hers. And she observed that his steps were at last beginning to lag. He blinked up at each arc lamp now without pausing and with obviously waning interest, and when they came into Broad Street there was the open confession of a yawn. The sudden chimes of St. Michael's clock startled him into dropping his lunar moth; but after that had been retrieved, nothing, not even the glitter of the hotel lobby, could rouse him from his sleep-walking.

Then, when he was finally in bed and Margaret and the baby had been inspected on whispering tiptoe with Lucy, she was free at last as she undressed to forget them and Charleston and the journey and turn back to Land's End and Stephen, alone for the first time since their marriage, alone at home as she was here in this strange room of separation.

Next morning Rusty came to have breakfast with them, take them to the station and see them off. Leaving him behind made a bad gap in the party, and all sense of adventure wilted on this second leg of the journey.

Michael was soon at loose ends in the crowded stuffy car. The monotony of pine barrens and desolate farms offered no distraction, and being read to only aggravated his fidgets; he was in a continual chafe for the forbidden freedom of the aisle. Margaret, clutching Juba, remained fortunately in a state of docile bewilderment. But the baby grew more and more fretful as the heat increased with each rackety mile. By midday all nerves were thoroughly frayed, even Lucy's stoical mask showing signs of stress through its luster of sweat. By the time the train had dragged itself out of flat country into the sand hills and jarred to a halt at Columbia, the family was reduced to a pulp.

Changing cars at the broiling station brought a few minutes of welcome distraction; but after this brief relief the journey relapsed into a torpid fever. The baby finally cried himself into a nap in Lucy's arms. Margaret, still clutching Juba, was laid out on the seat. Michael, his eyes red from staring out through cinders and puffs of acrid smoke, refused to give in till his head dropped of its own weight and slipped from Emily's shoulder to her lap.

He was the first to revive when the mountains came in sight, beyond Spartanburg. But there was a long hour of approach before the train began to chug up slow grades between timbered slopes and to rouse the echoes of a thousand panting engines through rocky gorges where cool torrents rushed and tumbled. By that time the whole family had returned to life, and the sense of adventure was resumed.

Now that the journey was ending, the people in the car became interesting. They seemed to have new faces. And the voice of the brakeman was exciting when he appeared to sing out the names of the final "station-stops": Campobello, Landrum, Tryon, and at last—Flat Rock!

And there waiting for them at a funny station that looked like a miniature Swiss chalet were Grandmother and Eugenia with a carriage and a luggage cart. For that tumultuous moment of greetings and hugs and kisses Michael seemed glad to see even Aunt Genia. Afterwards he wanted to make a bee line for the little horse, no bigger than his own pony, harnessed to the cart. But there was no squirming away from Grandma till he had blown the soot of the journey into her black-bordered lavender-scented handkerchief.

✻ ✻ ✻

The Pinckney place, Oakmont, like the other little estates of Flat Rock, lay in the foothills of the mountains; the mountains themselves made the rim of a vast bowl whose center was the town of Asheville, invisible some miles off to the west. The country of the bowl reminded Emily of New England, and she felt immediately at ease among the tilted meadows and woodlands, the fields of hay and grain, the winding roads and snug homesteads. There were brooks and ponds, orchards of apple and pear, even stone walls to accent the resemblance. And all the Northern trees were here, from elm and maple to willow and birch. But it was the pines that gave the prime note to the landscape: white pine and yellow pine, spruce and hemlock and balsam, their comely dark green shapes were everywhere. It was a land of pines. The woods were carpeted with their needles, and day and night you breathed the aroma of their boughs. . . . A smiling pastoral country, marked in its contrast to the brooding moss-draped coast. The days were hot, but it was not the steaming enervating heat of the Low Country. Even at midday the air remained clear and fine, and the nights were cool enough for blankets.

From the stone entrance gate of Oakmont you followed a woodland road banked with rhododendron and laurel till you came to a gravel drive that wound through a park of old oaks. A pair of deodars flanked the house, which resembled Land's End with its double piazzas and wide halls, but there were no trees on the back lawn to break the view over a great valley to hazy blue mountains, where the sun set long before dark. At the end of the lawn an evergreen hedge bounded the flower and vegetable garden. Beyond that were the stables and the caretaker's cottage, and an apple orchard sloping down to pasture land and a red barn. Horses and cows, sheep and chickens shared the pasture. Off to the right, half hidden by a grove of "Christmas trees" as Michael called all pines, was a little rock-bound lake fed by a forest stream.

Miss Sophie performed the introductions to Flat Rock. Emily was allowed only one day of grace to rest from the train trip and get her bearings at Oakmont. Then, still a little muddled by the change of altitude, she was taken out sightseeing in the Pinckney carriage, an obsolete affair that had evidently been retired to the mountains for a rustic old age after a gilded youth in Charleston. On this first drive Miss Sophie was content merely to point out the places of chief interest. Like Low Country plantations they all had names,—Boxwood, Kenmore, Argyll, Dawn Hill, Runnymede,—and like Oakmont they were well hidden from the highway. It was not till the following day that the houses and their occupants, each fully described in advance by Miss Sophie, came to light.

There was no denying the charm of these Flat Rock people. They were "real" gentlefolk. And in appearance at least they were as pronounced individualists as Miss Sophie. But, perhaps because of the uniformity of Charleston accent and manner, they all seemed cut out of the same cloth: they seemed to share the same belligerent prejudices, to have identical reactions on every subject. This solidarity of viewpoint, this language of an old and tenacious society that they all spoke, was not calculated to make it easy for a stranger in their midst.

"Don't be put out for a moment," Miss Sophie had warned, "by their Charleston smugness,—they're smug as bugs in a rug. They even make me feel like a foreigner sometimes. Simply because I wasn't born in the shadow of St. Michael's spire and don't pay dues to the St. Cecilia Society."

They seemed to consider themselves tolerant and almost recklessly broad in their outlook; but they were, Emily decided, if anything more provincial and suspicious than a group of Boston Brahmins. But her judgment of them, she had to admit, was largely splenetic. She resented the fact that, despite their friendly gestures and alert kindness, despite even their apparent liking for her, she must stand an alien among them, a Northerner; shrived a little by her marriage and long residence in the Low Country, but still and essentially a damned Yankee.

And, she feared they must think, a damned unsociable one. For after the initial interest of meeting them it was impossible to sustain any enthusiasm for their endless gossiping and whist parties. The truth of the matter, she realized, is that I'm the smuggest bug of all. It's my outlook that's really restricted. I'm getting to be the worst sort of provincial: I can't see or think or feel anything beyond home any more. . . . Fortunately, a new baby and two young children and uncertain health made reasonably good excuses for keeping social activity down to a minimum.

So after that first inescapable flurry of calls life settled back into the tight happy pattern of the family. Diplomatic relations with the members of the colony fell upon Miss Sophie's shoulders, where they were no burden at all. Her social talents, so long parched and withered in the desert air of post-war Beaufort, burst into giddy bloom here in the company of her peers; and even Eugenia came a little way out of her shell. But for Emily sometimes a week would pass without sight of any of her neighbors,—except on Sundays, when she always ran into all of them in a swarm after church at mellow old "St. John's-in-the-Wilderness". Then there was more than enough hubbub of sociability to last her for the next six days.

It was hard to tell where they went to, these Flat Rock days. They came stealing through the cool dawn mists of the front park, consumed the last breath of her energy, and vanished into the sleepy afterglow and haze of the great valley to the west. Vaguely she begrudged the fall of each day's curtain; yet it was good to be used up utterly, to be living to the very full, to have nothing of herself left at bedtime but dreamless ashes. For the first week or two she had followed Rusty's instructions conscientiously, allowed Miss Sophie to manage the house, swallowed a wineglass of bitter tonic after every meal, and rested for an hour morning and afternoon; but after that she had rebelled, quietly taken over the housekeeping, reduced the tonic dose to a teaspoon, and telescoped the rest periods into a single brief siesta. Even then it seemed precious time wasted.

Housekeeping at Oakmont presented certain difficulties in the beginning. Lucy had learned a great many recipes out of the *Boston Cook Book* to lend variety to her "Southern style", but Lucy's time was largely taken up now with the baby and the upstairs work, so the kitchen was in Ella's hands. Ella was what Miss Sophie called a good plain cook, and she certainly knew how to beat biscuits, make light corn breads, and steam rice to perfection. But she also knew—

only too well—how to fry. Since chicken was the chief meat of the country, fried chicken ruled as the specialty of the house till Emily was able to persuade Ella that chicken could be baked and even fricasseed occasionally. And that vegetables could be cooked without pork fat. From then on the family digestion was distinctly easier; and though Miss Sophie protested that the vegetable dishes had lost all taste, it was remarkable how much longer a tin of baking soda lasted.

The supply of vegetables from the garden was supplemented by purchases from the ladened wagon of Mr. Lockhart. And sometimes Mr. Lockhart carried cuts of lamb or a mess of fresh-water fish in a tarpaulin-covered icebox at the back of his wagon. His appearance every Wednesday and Saturday morning was a great event for Michael and Margaret. At first they had been attracted by the more obviously picturesque aspects of his visits: his Santa Claus beard and strange mountaineer speech; his white poodle, who could walk on her hind legs, say her prayers against her master's knee, and chase her tail in the dizziest of circles; the big patched and faded umbrella that shaded the high seat; and last, but by no means least, the straw bonnet that the horse wore;—all this was as good as a circus in the beginning. But in the end it was the personality of Mr. Lockhart himself that held the children's fancy. He was a spellbinder; and, listening with gaping and wide-eyed attention, they made an audience worthy of his best efforts. Sometimes, when they were able to elude Grandma, they went to ambush him as he turned in the gate from the highway and he would lift them up to ride back to the house beside him. But even when Grandma was on guard and their freedom was restricted, they were always aware of his approach and ready for him long before he arrived, for the harness of his horse was studded with an assortment of sleigh-bells.

"Ah! there's my fine lad and wee lassie," he would beam down at them. And before he had left his high seat, he would have begun one of his wild tales. "And did I ever tell you about the mad mare of Pompey's Knob? . . ."

A dozen times during the course of his tale he would interrupt the work of sorting out vegetables for Ella's basket or cleaning fish for her waiting pan to illustrate his words with dramatic gestures. And usually the proper conclusion of his tale would necessitate his lingering at the kitchen steps, which upset Miss Sophie, who seemed to feel that he was not only neglecting his business and keeping the neighbors waiting, but demoralizing the children and Ella as well. Miss Sophie's aversion to mountaineers extended even to the benign figure of Mr. Lockhart.

"Brigands and moonshiners," she called them. Renegade stock, trash, worse than crackers. And Republicans and scalawags during the War, every last one of them! "If I were you, Emily, I wouldn't allow that dirty old peddler to come near the children. Heaven knows what diseases they might catch from him."

What worried Miss Sophie even more than Mr. Lockhart's entertaining of the children was his custom of bringing them a "pretty". He passed through the village of Hendersonville on the way from his little farm in a "cove" up the "pike" a "piece", and he never failed to stop at the Hendersonville General Store for a "poke" of rock candy or licorice or gumdrops. Miss Sophie was put to it to see that his presents were not consumed on the spot, and she had to keep a supply of peppermint sticks and homemade popcorn to exchange with Michael and Margaret for the outlaw sweets, which were turned over to the children of Mr. Pittman, the combination caretaker, gardener, farmhand, and coachman at Oakmont.

Waits-on-the-Lord Pittman, Waits for short, had a child to commemorate each year of his married life, and he had been married eleven years. The precincts of the house would have been overrun with young Pittmans if Miss Sophie had not taken an early and firm stand. Her stand had been a little too firm for the Pittman pride: the entire clan had sulked in their cottage. A conciliatory call had been necessary, and Miss Sophie had to face the fact that, whatever her private opinion of mountaineers might be, their opinion of themselves was very good and they must be treated accordingly.

Emily was thankful for the existence of the Pittman children. Flat Rock was largely a colony of grown-ups; most Charleston children were taken to the beach colony on Sullivan's Island, referred to frequently and simply by the ladies of Flat Rock as "The Oiland". Of children near Michael's and Margaret's ages there were only the little Ravenel girls and the Lowndes boy, and they were almost useless as playmates: Christopher Lowndes was a frail child with bad eyes and weak lungs, and the Ravenel girls were so bound round with rules and regulations and starched dresses and sashes and bows that to fetch them, preserve them through a harum-scarum afternoon, and deliver them home in something like their pristine state was a responsibility that Emily was unwilling to assume very often. So the Pittman children, immediately accessible and practically damage-proof, came in handy indeed. Like Linda and Dallas Robinson and the youngest of Isaac's black brood at Land's End, they made an excellent check-and-balance for Michael's growing will. With them he was not able to have his own way by any means. From grown-ups he got altogether too much attention, and Emily herself had to be constantly on guard to keep from spoiling him in one way or another. She realized how fortunate it was that he was not an only child. With Margaret and the baby to divide her attention, he was safe from the dangers of being the center of things.

But of one universe Michael was obviously, openly, frankly the center. Miss Sophie was devoted to Margaret and the baby, but Michael was far and away her favorite: he was the apple of her eye, and she made no bones about it. But like most highly-prized objects he was extremely elusive. "Where is Michael?" she was continually demanding of some member of the household, as if he were being concealed from her. The only time he was completely hers was Sunday at church; then she had him securely under her wing, and there were no bounds to the pride with which she displayed her grandson to the colony assembled for worship. The rest of the week he was hers only by dint of pursuit, bribery, and cunning. But he was adept at keeping out of her way, and it would have been an endless game of hide-and-seek between them but for the lure of the lake and the quiescent evening hour before bed.

The lake was the center of attraction for the children. Not so much the lake itself, for its inviting waters were hedged about with Don'ts. The shingle boats with paper sails that Waits Pittman made could be navigated back and forth across it; but neither the flat-bottom skiff nor the graceful cedar-wood rowboat, with its brass rowlocks and leather-trimmed oars with curved copper-tipped blades, could be loosed from their mooring rings on the boat-house landing, unless Mother was on hand. And swimming was waiting for Father's appearance. And the whole lower end of the lake, where the greatest attractions were,—the dam and the waterfall and the old tumble-down mill with its wheel overgrown with ferns,—was strictly for-bidden ground. But despite these tantalizing restrictions the lake offered plenty of excitement. There were the log boat-house and the landing out over the water; the little pebble beach near the spring-house; and, above all, the stream that slid down rock terraces to feed the lake, a series of pools and cascades that inspired a variety of pastimes besides plain splashing and wading. And all games seemed more enjoyable when played at the cool shady borders of the lake. The crags and boulders and mossy glades were made for hide-and-seek, and certainly there was no place like the little glen behind the boat-house for ambushing and scalping stray Pittmans.

Michael was not permitted to go near the lake without one of the grown-ups; and since Mother and Lucy were usually too busy to go, and Eugenia too afraid of snakes to venture beyond the boundaries of the lawn, Grandma was in frequent demand. Several times a day he would beg her to take him with Margaret and some of the wild little Pittman goats to the lake; and though she was opposed to the place on a number of counts, she never refused. For all the needles-and-pins she suffered here, for all the perils she felt to be lurking round about the dark waters, it was better to have Michael where she could keep some kind of an eye on him than to have him roam-ing the fields and woods at large, jumping from high beams in the hayloft of the barn, or playing in the rowdy yard of the Pittman cottage. Here at the lake Michael could be relied on to stay within bounds, and while the black mop of his head was not always in sight from her post at the boat-house, he could always be summoned to her side by a little ringing of the dinner-bell she brought from the house with her. It was understood that if he failed to answer the summons, he would find her unavailable the next time he wanted to come to the lake.

But it was evening that she chiefly depended upon to bring them together. With her power of hastening or delaying the signal for bed, he was wax in her hands. Over a game of jack-straws or parchesi she could feast her eyes on him to her heart's content; and, more impor-tant than that, she could talk to him and know he was listening. She was always talking to him, but it was only in the evening hour when bed was hanging over his head that she felt sure he was paying attention to what she was saying. He would even encourage her to talk then, leading her on with questions, and becoming very attentive indeed whenever a lull in her story permitted an intrusion of the fatal *tock-tock* of the Pinckney grandfather clock in the hall. It was a game that Emily watched from her sewing with secret amusement.

". . . How old were you, Gran'maa, when General Lafayette came to Beaufort?"

"Not a day older than your little sister."

He looked at her with wonder, trying to imagine a time when Grandma was not a day older than Margaret, who only a short while ago at supper had drowsed over her milk and had had to be carried up to bed by Lucy.

"The tiniest tots," Grandma continued, "were allowed to stay up that night, you may be sure. It was after dark when he arrived from Charleston, on his farewell tour of the States. We were stationed, a band of little girls, at the steps of the Rhett house. It's been called the Lafayette house ever since, an honor that used to turn the Rhetts' heads—before the War came and Sam Koenig got it."

"He's a Carpetbagger, isn't he?" Michael assisted.

"Of the worst possible stripe. Well, in any event, there we were at the steps, our curls bound up with *Lafayette* fillets, wearing *Welcome to Our Hero* sashes, and with tricolor rosettes pinned on our tight little bodices. I have all those souvenirs in a chest in the attic,—remind me to show them to you when we get home. And I still have the candle I had clutched that night in what must have been a very sleepy little hand."

Miss Sophie paused for a crooked smile and a reminiscent sigh. And Michael, fearful that the tale might end on that note, rushed in to fill the breach.

"They didn't have lamps when you were a little girl, did they, Gran'maa?"

Miss Sophie shook her head without suspicion, too lost in reverie to notice the barefaced artifice of the question. "No indeed, child. The town was ablaze with candles. None of your smelly oil lamps in those days." She warmed anew to her theme. "As he alighted from the coach, he patted each of us on the head. And when my father said to him, 'General, this is my little girl sir,' up he lifted me in his arms and kissed me before all the people!"

Michael was delighted with that. "Lafayette kissed you!"

Miss Sophie was quite flushed. "Kissed me on the forehead and both cheeks!"

When Emily looked up from her sewing to join the laughter, Miss Sophie chuckled to her in an aside: "Poor dear weary old gentleman, I realized later in life what a hideous old thing he was, but that

333

night he looked to me like a saint in shining armor. It's my first vivid memory, and I suppose it will be my last,—they say we all go back like that at the end." Her eyes, mirthful and a little moist, came back to Michael. "There was so much excitement that night that it must have been midnight before we youngsters were properly in bed."

"Midnight!" Michael echoed enviously.

He tried to cover his blunder with an extravagant smile of innocence. But at that moment the clock in the hall gave him away.

"Gracious!" Miss Sophie gasped, "can that be half past eight? Why, I didn't know it was eight yet. Didn't hear it strike, did you, Emily? To bed, to bed, sleepy head, fast as your legs can carry you!"

"Oh, Gran'maa, please tell me some more! Tell me"—he made a desperate lunge at one of her known weak spots—"about Refugee Days. Tell me about the time Sherman came through Camden and dug up the yard with bayonets!"

"Not another word, sir. You've taken quite enough advantage of me for one evening."

"Well, one more game of jack-straws then."

"No more of that fidgety business, thank you. March!"

"Just one short game of hearts or snatch-the-bundle?"

"There's no such thing as a short game of hearts or snatch-the-bundle. They both go on forever. To bed, Michael."

As a last resort he turned to Mother.

"Do I have to go to bed, Mamma? I'm not the least bit sleepy."

She smiled at the tired dark eyes, always so reluctant to yield.

"I'm afraid there's no escape, dear. . . ."

This summer, for the first time, it became clear that Miss Sophie's conversations with Michael were not so random as they seemed. They had direction: there was purpose, intense and increasing purpose, behind all her talk about the past. And as she became more and more absorbed in this story-telling business, she seemed to feel more and more pressed for time.

"Your old grandmother has a great deal to tell you, young man," Emily once heard her inform him, "and she's not going to be with you forever, so you'll do well to listen. It isn't every boy that has your proud heritage to carry on. Yours is an honorable and distinguished name as far back as the records go. Your mother will have to tell you about your New England forebears,—I have no doubt

334

they were excellent people. I can only tell you about the Bramwell and Fenwick branches of your family tree."

The Southern branches were of such luxuriant foliage that the Northern branches were left sadly in the shade. Emily felt there must have been Indian Fighters among the New England roots of Michael's tree, and she knew positively there had been several officers in the Continental Army. But what hopeless wraiths they seemed beside such figures, vividly conjured up by Miss Sophie, as "Yemassee Bill" Bramwell and Colonel John Fenwick, "the Scourge of Tarleton". And when it came to the more recent ancestors, how could a drab collection of merchants and professors, plus one whaling captain, compete in Michael's imagination with a perfect procession of dashing, hard-riding, duelling, deer-hunting planters and statesmen. In her family Emily could recall no particular belles, whereas the Bramwell and Fenwick women seemed never to have been anything else. If only Grandmother Curtis were here to uphold the Yankee strain and balance things up a little, but even that sharp warm personality must remain the wannest of ghosts for Michael beside the electric presence of "Gran'maa".

And Miss Sophie had aid this summer in her mission of steeping her grandson in the Bramwell-Fenwick tradition. In mid August, before Stephen was able to get away from work, Joseph Bramwell came up on a visit, and for a solid week Michael was the center of an orgy of ancestor worship, family lore, and Beaufort legends. The Judge was a specialist in the histories of the entire "connection". He knew the earliest settlers by their first names and could even hark back to roots in England, Scotland, and France.

As the means of introducing Michael to his ancestors Uncle Joe employed the dramatic anecdote. But the effectiveness of this method of resurrecting the family dead was badly impaired by his passion for digression: in the rich and varied country of the past the temptation to wander afield was too strong for him, and by the time he was ready to return to the highway of his narrative with a "Let-me-see-where-was-I" the interest was usually lost beyond recall. This tendency to digress, which Miss Sophie found so charming in her Thackeray, was maddening in her brother. "Stick to your story, Joe," she was continually warning him. And equally maddening to her was his interrupting, when she was telling a tale, to put her straight

335

on some point that she felt to be completely trivial. She was not concerned with exact details, she was working for a general effect, she was out to make her story interesting to Michael at any sacrifice of accuracy; and she usually succeeded, while her brother often failed. His pedantic love of facts led to so many squabbles between them that it began to look as if this controversial double tutelage would produce in Michael only a profound distaste for ancestors.

Fond as Emily had become of Joe, and glad as she had been to receive his assurances that Stephen was working hard but bearing up well in his bachelor state, it was a relief when the visit was ended. Joe was not an easy guest, and by the time he left everyone was saturated with genealogy. Even after he was gone, there were echoes that had to be stilled before peace and quiet was restored.

It was apparent that something was preying on Michael's mind, but it was several days before it came out. One evening at bedtime he asked with a deep frown: "Mamma, can you get the answer to this riddle? If one Confederate can lick ten Yankees, how many Confeds will it take to lick a hundred Yanks?"

She might have guessed, she realized then, that Rebel yells would not be omitted from Joe's fosterings. While she was trying to collect her wits to meet the emergency, Michael answered the riddle himself.

"Ten!"

"I wouldn't be too sure of that," she managed to tell him. "What other riddles did Uncle Joe tell you?"

"He didn't know any more."

He sighed and counted the row of buttons on her dress front, up and then down. When he looked up at her, his eyes were very troubled.

"Mamma, I'm not a Yankee, am I?"

"Why—no, dear."

"Well, what am I?"

She put her arms around him with a little ache of laughter. "You're a mighty sleepy boy."

But he was not to be put off with that. "I'm a Confederate, ain't I? Uncle Joe said I was."

"Well, Uncle Joe is a very wise man. What else did he tell you?"

He put his arms around her neck and hid his face from her.

"He said you were a Yankee once, but grew out of it. He said you turned into a Confederate when you married Pappa. I'm terrible

336

sorry you had to be a Yankee once, Mamma. I'm too glad you got over it, in time for me to be a Confederate."

"Oh, darling, darling," she hugged him tight, "of course you're a Confederate! A Confederate and an angel and a monkey and every-thing else in the world."

"And you're a Confederate now," he insisted, bringing his face out of hiding.

"Yes, yes, darling. And Pappa and Grandma and Aunt Gene. And Uncle Joe and Uncle Rusty."

"And Margaret and the baby?"

"And Margaret and the baby."

He gave her a one-tooth-missing grin. "And Lucy?"

"Oh, most emphatically Lucy."

"And Mr. Lockhart?"

"And Mr. Lockhart. And Waits and Mrs. Waits and all the little Waitses."

"And Linda and Dallas? And the pony!"

"Yes indeed. Every last one of us."

He was smiling all over now and getting very wide-awake. But finally she sobered him down.

"I wish Pappa would hurry up and come," he sighed, his head at rest on the pillow.

"He will, dear. Just as soon as he can get away. . . . Now let me ask you a riddle, and then we're going to sleep. If one good boy can lick ten bad boys, how many good boys would it take to lick a hun-dred bad boys?"

He pondered that with a grave yawn.

"Ten?"

"Correct. And now let me tell you something Uncle Joe over-looked. I think he must have forgotten to mention that it doesn't really matter whether you're a Confederate or a Yankee, Abe Lin-coln or Robert E. Lee, an Eskimo or a Hottentot, as long as your heart is pure. If your heart is fine and strong and kind, then your strength will be as the strength of ten. Think you can remember that?"

He thought he could. But what was a Hottentot and an Eskimo?

When she had explained the difference, she stayed with him till his eyes were closed and his breathing satisfied her he was really settled for the night. Then, after a peep at Margaret and the baby, she went back downstairs to finish a letter to Stephen. Thinking, with a smile to herself: The strength of our Yankee Rebels will be as the strength of ten.

At last, early in September, Stephen arrived, bringing Rusty with him for a week's escape from work and heat.

"Darling, I'd just about given up hope," she sighed with joy when they were finally alone in the bedroom, his arms around her. "I guess the separation didn't bother you so much after all."

"Now isn't that appreciation for you! Even the love of my life doesn't know the trouble I've seen. Can't you see I'm a wreck? . . . And I don't like the way you thrive on separation. All those letters about how you were pining away in the pines! Why you look like a blooming rose."

"If I do, it's for you."

"Now don't try to pretend you really missed me," he laughed, squeezing the breath out of her. "You've got too many babies for that. I should be getting resigned, but all the time I get jealouser and jealouser."

"I'm the one that's jealous. Of your work."

"Well, if I didn't attend to business, how would we ever get ahead?"

"I don't know. All I know is I've got you and I'm not going to let you go."

"Suits me," he said with a grin that was only a shade older than Michael's. "Let's just curl up here till you're ready to come home."

But a few moments after that, Michael and Margaret were clamoring for them out in the hall.

She went to the door to tell the children that Mother was talking to Father about something important, and would they please go down and entertain Uncle Rusty, show him the lake and the hayloft.

"How was that?" she asked when the door was closed again.

"I didn't think you had it in you," he laughed. "You're too sporting, honey, it takes the wind right out of my sails. I'll spare you till things quiet down around here. Come on, let's go out and get some of your pine air. It's really a great climate."

But by evening the climate was getting on his nerves.

"It makes you feel logy. I'll take island heat."

"You get over it in a day or two."

"I suppose so. Just when it's time to leave."

And when he opened his eyes the next morning, after a restless night, he answered her smile with a preoccupied frown and an announcement that he felt worse, much worse.

After breakfast he took her aside.

"Honey, I've simply got to get back. No, it isn't the mountain air. It's the two ships that came in just as I was leaving. You see, the hands have to be kept on the jump to load them on schedule. I should have stayed over, I had no right to a vacation now. I hate like hell to leave, but you understand. The main thing was to be sure you and the kids were doing all right. Well, I'm satisfied about that, so I better get back on the job. I'll leave Rusty with you. And you'll all be coming home soon."

She made no serious attempt to dissuade him. He looked dragged out, but if he was going to fret, it was better for him to go.

"But I'm going with you," she decided.

"Oh no you're not. No thanks, honey, I'm not crazy enough to kidnap you. You wouldn't be worth shooting, worrying all the time."

While she was repacking his bag, he had a hurried few minutes' romp with the children. Then there was a wild dash for the morning train, and he was gone.

But Rusty's staying on was some compensation for this bitter disappointment. If he felt his hospital work and practice were suffering at the hands of a substitute in his absence, he never showed it. He gave himself with abandon to the children. Michael and Margaret clung to him all day long, climbed over him, ate him up. And he was not content, as Joe Bramwell had been, to chuckle self-consciously over the baby's crib; to relieve his feelings he had to pick him up and parade him around, to the consternation of Miss Sophie, who seemed to feel that his time with the children should be devoted to a series of medical tests.

And he taught Michael to swim. In the past two summers Michael had done some spectacular splashing at Bay Point with one foot touching bottom, but this was the real thing. First with and then without Rusty's hand under his chin he learned to swim dog-fashion all the way across the lake, Margaret paddling at his heels on her water-wings, her curls tied up on top of her head; while Miss Sophie, looking remarkably like a hen whose chicks had turned into ducklings before her eyes, supervised the proceedings from the boat-house landing, frequently interrupting to see if lips had turned blue yet or fingers shriveled at the tips.

Up to the time of Rusty's visit there had been no long walks. Often in the afternoons, while Miss Sophie went calling in the carriage and Eugenia daydreamed in her tasseled hammock, Emily had taken Michael and Margaret with her to the Flat Rock post-office, but that was only a little way from the house. Now she found herself able to go on real hikes without getting tired. "You're made over," Rusty told her. And it felt true, for even the picnic climbs to High Falls and Creation Knob were not too much for her.

This week she had more of him than she had had for ages. It was a rare opportunity to catch up on "back talk", as he called it.

"Well, life seems to be agreeing with you all right," he said the last evening of his visit, as they were following the path down to the lake under the stars.

"Rusty, I'm so happy it hurts," she told him soberly, reaching out to rap the trunk of a tree in passing. "It doesn't seem right to be so well-off. It makes you feel guilty somehow."

That amused him. "You sound like a rich man with a tender conscience."

"I feel more like a thief with a bagful of loot."

"But you've earned it."

"Wouldn't it be nice to think so. Too bad there's been a little too much luck mixed up in it for that. Maybe that's why I get suspicious sometimes."

"You suspicious? That's a new one."

"And scared, too. Scared stiff that it's all too good to be true, to last. If things are as good as they are, how can they possibly get any better?"

"Well, at least they can stand pat."

"Or slip. But they can't do either. They've got to get even better, for the children. And Steve's business. Don't you see?"

"Sure I see. But I've never seen you scared before."

"Oh, I'm everything now, since we've begun to really tempt fate. I don't dare leave any stone unturned. I go to church every Sunday and pray every day. And I'm getting so superstitious I go around with my fingers crossed, knocking wood. And you should see some of the slick cunjuh tricks, black-magic spells and things, I've picked up from Lucy. Any objections?"

"None whatever, if it helps. But what does Steve say about all this?"

"Oh, he's too busy with business to even notice my propitiation leanings."

"Well, I must say you're doing a thorough leaning job all right. You seem to have tried everything but the kitchen stove, and me."

She took his arm as they went down the boat-house steps.

"I'm saving you. I'll fall back on you when I'm really scared."

"That's better," he sighed. "I was beginning to get a little jealous."

When they were settled in the rustic chairs on the landing, with the shadowy mirror of the lake before them, she gave him time to light his pipe before she turned to him with an abrupt question.

"Rusty, how do you bring up children?"

She could see his smile in the starlight.

"Why ask me? You ought to know."

"But that's just it, I don't. I used to think I did, before they started arriving and complicating things. Now all I can do is feel my way blindly, without any system."

"Maybe that's the perfect system, in your case at least."

"Just blundering along by instinct?"

"Just being yourself. With that example they ought to turn out to be pretty all-around decent."

"Very handsomely put. But I'm afraid it isn't quite enough. Rusty, do you realize these children have got to be something special? You may as well start facing it."

"I'm facing it," he nodded. "Seems to me if they're all-around decent they'll be very special."

"Rusty, really they have got to be special. The boys must have careers, creative work of some kind, a calling like yours, not just a business like Steve's. And Margaret must help some man with a calling. Do I sound like any doting parent?"

"No,—like a very special doting parent. And I'm glad to hear it. Only I wouldn't advise holding me up as an example of anything special, unless it's a horrible example. You don't know how many failures I have on my professional conscience."

"I don't believe it. And I've got to have your help."

"Well, it's yours, such as it is. What do I do?"

"Just be yourself, as you say. And let the children see as much as possible of you, Michael to start with. That's all."

341

"If that's what you want, that settles it."

"There. Now I feel fine. . . . Now how about you doing a little leaning for a change. Don't you ever have any problems?"

He shook his head, the bowl of his pipe glowing in the dusk.

"Not anymore. Oh, I have a few small ones, but they don't count since the big one got solved."

"What big one?"

"You."

And he added with a comfortable stretch in his chair: "So you see life is agreeing with me too."

After Rusty's visit there were still three more weeks of the mountains. Outwardly they were glorious weeks, but her enjoyment of them was qualified by her anxiety to get home to Stephen.

Autumn was early this year, and Waits Pittman, bringing in great armfuls of wood for the fires, told how all signs pointed to a hard winter. But winter and bleak trees and snowdrifts were a long way off yet: now there were only exhilarating rumors of ice-bound days and nights. Heavy rains in August had made the leaves tenacious, and when frost came to nip them they turned to brilliant flames that no gusts of wind could extinguish. Every hillside and mountain slope was a resplendent tapestry, a pageant of gay colors as far as the eye could see. Along the roadsides clusters of goldenrod and wild aster still shone bravely; in the garden the marigolds and zinnias, the showy dahlias and the last frail nasturtiums defied the frost together; even the chorusings of crickets and katydids were not yet silenced. But Halloween was already in the air, which sparkled with a light as rich and mellow as the harvest fields where pumpkins smiled among stacked cornstalks.

This was a season of early-morning mists yielding to crisp sunshine, of apples and cider, roasted chestnuts and roaring fires. The days were cold enough for jerseys under jackets, and the nights called for plenty of covers well tucked in. By the first of October the entire household, including Lucy and Ella, were in flannels; the baby's crib was lined with coverlets, the children and Eugenia were sleeping between blankets, and Miss Sophie was resorting to a steaming hot toddy before bed. But never had the family been in better health and spirits, and the only flaw and regret was that Stephen and

Rusty could not be here for this crowning final phase of the mountain summer.

When it was over at last and she was looking back on it from the train, she could begin to appreciate in retrospect its full value. And it had been a time singularly free from worries. There had been the trouble between Lucy and Ella, brought on by some slighting remark Lucy had made about Tunis while deciphering for Ella a letter from him, but the strained relations had been healed by keeping Lucy out of the kitchen. The only other happenings worthy to be called trouble had been Michael's poison ivy and his rumpus with Eugenia. The itchy rash on his wrists, diagnosed by Miss Sophie as chickenpox or hives caught from the Pittman children or something worse caught from that horrid Lockhart peddler, had been checked and dried up before it could spread by old Dr. King, Flat Rock physician recommended by Rusty. But the rumpus with Eugenia had been more serious. Michael had used a nasty word and been generally rude and impertinent. It had been impossible to learn from either party what the nasty word had been, but Michael had admitted the charge in general, so there had been nothing for Mother to do but punish him. In the absence of Father she had prepared to administer her first spanking with the only implement at hand, an ivory-handle hairbrush. At the quivering initial blow the handle had miraculously snapped, and the awful suspense following had been broken by their both breaking into a fit of tears and laughter. . . .

As the train chugged and rattled on toward home, she knew that this summer, already receding like a dream into the misty distances behind her, would stand always among her most cherished memories. If Stephen had only been able to share it with her, if they could only have had it to remember together. That was the only drawback: this straining forward to end the separation, to close this first—and last—breach in their union.

✓   ✓   ✓

And that seemed to be his one idea too, for the first words were: "Never again. You've had your first and last vacation. The next separation will be over my dead body."

"Was it really that bad, darling?"

"It was so bad I don't even want to talk about it."

"But you've been working so hard, how did you find time and energy to miss us?"

"Listen, don't judge me by yourself. The kids may use you up, but work is not my consuming passion. Sure I've been busy, up to my neck, but I couldn't concentrate. Now will you all please settle down and stay put, home where you belong, so I can catch up. I'm way behind, and I've got to make up for lost time, all along the line."

But for the first few days even the joy of being with him again was not strong enough to lift the sense of depression that went with return to the Low Country. Here were the dregs of a long parched summer; and the flatness of the sea-island world, the brooding quality of the marshes, the drabness of the picked cotton fields, the desiccated green of the woods, the somber cobwebs of moss, the change of air,—everything combined to emphasize the loss of the mountains and produce a terrible feeling of letdown. It even interfered with proper appreciation of the great surprise he had prepared for the return: a bathroom at Marshlands, the first in Beaufort, and one at Land's End. Bathrooms!—yet her reaction to them in the beginning was negative. The Marshlands bathroom cramped the upper hall. The Land's End one shut off light from the back window of the upper hall. Besides, it was unnatural and unpleasant to see a windmill showing above the trees beyond the stable. And the scaffolding that supported the windmill and the reservoir tank offered a pluperfect hazard for Michael's simian moods.

But then the first autumn winds came to freshen the jaded air, dispelling the fag-end remains of summer and bringing back the winged music of migrating hosts. It was not the flamboyant autumn of the mountain country, but surely its magic was greater than any in the world. She was home. It was good to stretch the eyes across shining waters and smell the salt tides; good to see again the faces of the island people and the smoke of their cabins, receive their greetings and hear the ups and downs of their summer. It was good to leave home for a time, but it was better to return. And she was viewing Land's End with new eyes and finding beauties that had somehow been hidden from her before. Absence had increased the enchantment of this place that was now so deeply her own.

When she told Stephen that, one afternoon when he came home from work to find her at the piano, he said with an indulgent pat: "You see, that's the difference between you and me. When you get to be as old and wise as I am, you won't need a separation to sharpen your appreciation of things. Or a piano to thump it up on. . . . Say, how do you happen to be childless for a moment? No, don't let me interrupt you, go right ahead and enjoy your fleeting freedom in peace. I've got a batch of reports to make out and I better get started on them before supper."

"More night work?"

"Now don't mind me, honey. I'm only slaving so we can take it easy later on. We've got to get ahead before we can relax and enjoy life."

"Getting ahead is getting to be quite a rival."

He grinned at that. "Better than a flesh-and-blood rival, isn't it?"

"I'm afraid so. But hadn't we better enjoy life as we go along?"

"Well, aren't we? And haven't I got three growing rivals to your one? Where are they, by the way?"

She could afford to smile with him as she left the piano and set out to find them. For in spite of his increasing preoccupation with reports the cup of her happiness was full to the brim. Full to the brim and running over.

VII

On the *Harper's* shelves at Land's End the volume for '85 was bound and settled in its appointed place, and five numbers of '86 had collected in their brown paper covers, when a momentous family decision was made: to move headquarters to Marshlands.

Stephen's business affairs were thriving, slowly but surely his dreams of prosperity were coming true. Already the shares of Company stock that he had accumulated were worth ten times what he had paid for them, and his other interests—the Beaufort bank, the Port Royal railroad, and real-estate holdings in both places—were steadily building up his capital and income. And with the expansion of his interests, the center of gravity had gradually shifted to town. For some time he had been hinting that Marshlands would be a more logical base of operations than the island.

And there was Michael's schooling to be considered. He must start in September; the time had come to surrender him to Miss Hamilton. Despite the strides he was making in his lessons at home, Emily could no longer feel justified in keeping him from the competitions and adjustments of school with a group of children. Still, she might have held out for one more year's delay if Stephen had not taken such an emphatic stand against it.

"He's going to school this autumn, and that's that."

"But there's no desperate hurry, dear. We want him to learn to think for himself before he's exposed to cut-and-dried instruction. We don't want him poured into a mold and turned out like every boy in Beaufort."

"I see. We want our boy to think for himself,—I suppose that means thinking like you and Rusty. Strange that both of you were exposed to a cut-and-dried system without damage to your mental independence. Why even I have an occasional thought of my own, a glimmer of intelligence now and then, in spite of the old Beaufort Grammar School."

She had surrendered with a laugh, but he was not through with her.

"Now let's get this thing straight for once and for all. I'd rather have a plain ordinary manly boy in the family than a prodigy or a freak or a mamma's darling. Anyway, I'm not worried about his being poured into a mold. He's going to have to live his life among molds, isn't he? Well, the moldier he gets, the easier time he's going to have. And while we're on the subject, I'm getting sick of this music business. I can't see my son doing trills and frills on a piano. That's a game for girls. And you know he hates it."

No denying the truth of that.

"He can stop if he likes," she had conceded, "when he starts school in September."

The move to town was a major upheaval, a violent wrenching of ties, a staggering change. But she forgot the greater part of her own distress in Michael's. To visit at Grandma's was one thing; to transfer home there was quite another matter. He was heartbroken at leaving Linda and Dallas, the cove, the mines, all the associations of the island place. Margaret and her dolls—including the perennially revived Juba, battered but indestructible—were at ease at Marshlands within an hour after their arrival. And to little Jack, who was beginning to get his sea legs, one place was as good as another in this bright and exciting world, as long as the joggling-board and the sand-box and his chair swing went with him. But for Michael it seemed impossible to make any adjustment whatever to Marshlands as home.

To beguile him till he got accustomed to living "at Grandma's", Stephen bought him the bicycle intended for a birthday present in October. Emily's heart skipped many a beat as she watched from the house while he wrestled with the strange new steed hour after hour in the drive.

"Don't worry about him," Stephen said. "Leave him alone with the thing."

But Grandma was unwilling to hold aloof, and as soon as Stephen was out of the way she supervised Michael and the bicycle from her chair on the porch, summoning Tunis when he was available to support the course of the wobbly wheels. Even at that there were skinned hands and knees, and once a bumped head from a collision with the inevitable tree. But in the end balance and steering were mastered, and by that time Michael was at home at Marshlands.

Emily was not sure that she would ever be able to feel at home here. The painful memories of this house, like the chimeras of Land's End, had long since been lived down, buried under the years of happiness and fulfilment. Now it was certain comparatively superficial aspects of Marshlands that made adjustment to it so difficult.

To begin with, there was the matter of "crowding". At Land's End there had been two extra rooms: a guest room, and a spare room that had served as a combination store-room, sewing-room, and indoor playground. At Marshlands there was no extra space at all. The big bedroom, the former upstairs drawing-room of the house, was the nursery; she and Stephen had the small room next to that; Miss Sophie and Eugenia occupied the two back bedrooms; Lucy, who refused to stay in the yard quarters with Tunis and Ella, slept in the attic; and Michael's setter, Trig, a Christmas present from Rusty, took over the upper hall, where she could set up a howl when anyone groping through darkness for the bathroom door tripped over her. The only way a spare bed could be contrived, in case one of the children was sick or Stephen had an out-of-town business guest, was by asking Miss Sophie and Eugenia to double up, which always upset Eugenia.

It was clear from the beginning that this intimate mingling of personalities, this arrangement of a family living within a family, this attempt to blend the two parts of the family into a harmonious whole, had enough potential dynamite in it to blow Marshlands to bits. Emily soon realized that it was her job to prevent petty frictions from leading like sputtering fuses to a general explosion; Stephen, out of the house most of the time and preoccupied with his own affairs, seemed unaware that there were any problems involved in the situation. Fortunately, Miss Sophie remained the paradox of an almost perfect mother-in-law even under the strains of continuous contact. But with Eugenia it was a different story, and it was she who presented the central problem of the united family. Nothing ever quite suited her, she was forever getting her feelings hurt about something, and she could sulk for days without weakening. When Miss Sophie was nettled about anything, there was a magnificent outburst and that was the end of it, it was over as quickly and thoroughly as a thunder-shower. But the weather of Eugenia's moods never cleared to sunlight: she brooded endlessly under sultry clouds that no lightning could release.

"If she'd only get mad," Emily said to Stephen during one of Eugenia's spells of injured retirement from the family circle. "If she'd only get mad and get whatever it is out of her system, it would be so much easier all around."

"Oh, don't pay any attention to her," he smiled absently. "She'll get over it."

And of course she always did get over it, in her own good time. But with one or more of the children usually involved, it was impossible to pay no attention to the spells. However, for this problem which promised to be chronic there was apparently no solution but chronic patience. For the sake of peace in the family there was nothing to do but try to sympathize with Eugenia's moods, even when they seemed more childish than any moods of the children's.

Another aspect of Marshlands that made adjustment difficult was the strangeness of the furnishings. Land's End was assorted but simple and livable, while Marshlands was fitted out in garish style, pretentious and ugly. Stephen had disposed of the house's tainted Reconstruction trappings and had refurnished with pieces even more out of keeping with the dignity of the rooms. Every table and chair and bed was at least slightly startling in design, and none was free from some sort of excrescent ornamentation. Most of the upholstery was plush. Even the album on the weird center table of the living-room was plush-bound.

The living-room was particularly cluttered up. There were tortured whatnots, crowded with knickknacks, in all four corners; and a gallery of drab steel engravings in elaborate frames marred the white paneled walls. The arms and backs of the fussy chairs and sofa were dotted with Miss Sophie's antimacassars, which were always slipping out of place despite pins. A set of water-color "studies" and a pair of mantel candles hand-painted with forget-me-nots were Eugenia's contribution to the room. But it was the center table, sacred to the family album and Bible, that supported the

349

crowning glory of the room and the house,—an amazing lamp of brass with a shade studded with glass gems, rubies, diamonds, topazes, and one large emerald.

And of course no changes could be made or suggested without treading on someone's toes. But finally Stephen himself suggested that the honest old-fashioned magnolia-wood furniture of the Land's End bedroom be moved over to replace the funereal walnut suite of Marshlands. She breathed easier after that, resting relaxed and comfortable again back in the bed where Michael and Margaret and Jack had all been born. And when the piano was settled in a corner of the living-room, and Rusty's old binoculars and the "Toby Fill-pot" that he used for tobacco placed on the library mantel, then at last Marshlands began to look and feel a little like home.

By the middle of summer even the knotty problem of keeping house with Miss Sophie had been straightened out. That was a complicated business, though. She once remarked: "Those carpetbagging Rutherfords have changed cooks again, Ella tells me. That makes the third since Memorial Day. I have yet to see a Yankee that knew how to get along with colored people, except you, Emily. You're neither too hard nor too soft. I admit I'm too easy on them, like most Southern women." So she imagined, but actually she was the terror of the kitchen. She left Lucy, who was not afraid of her, scrupulously alone, but she kept Ella and Tunis and the poor inoffensive yard-boy in a constant stew, using them as a sort of vent for her high-strung nerves and the vapors and vexations of living. Hardly a day passed that she did not threaten to run one or more of them off the place. As a result there was always a pout to be soothed. Sometimes Emily felt that her chief part in the housekeeping was nursing hurt sensibilities. But somehow the house was kept running, satisfactorily if not smoothly.

In the end there was only one situation arising from the moving of home to Marshlands that seemed impossible of adjustment. At Land's End Stephen's evenings had been hers. Even those evenings when scarcely a word had passed between them, when he had worked on his reports or read his *News & Courier* while she sewed and darned, even those evenings of silence had been a source of comfort and enjoyment to her. But in Beaufort he soon formed the habit of dropping in at the Commercial Club after supper. It became a rarity for him to spend an evening at home. And then the old sense of intimacy was broken by the necessity of sharing him with Miss Sophie and the taciturn presence of Eugenia.

The sudden loss of those cherished evenings meant a terrible curtailment of her time with him. But because the Commercial Club seemed an important new interest in his life, because she understood that it was to his advantage as well as pleasure to mix with the leading citizens of Beaufort, she was determined to conquer her own feelings in the matter. I'm not going to feel like a martyr, she told herself. I'm going to be sensible about it. . . . But inside something continued to hurt.

And then, just as she was getting accustomed to Marshlands as home, along came an abrupt and amazing event to jostle her out of it.

It was the last day of July, and Stephen was back from Bay Street earlier than usual.

"Pack up your duds," he told her with a broad grin. "Here it is. This is it."

"What?"

"The honeymoon, of course. We're leaving for Washington and Virginia Springs on the morning train. Had a meeting at the Commercial Club about the proposed Navy Yard,—we're going to fight Charleston and Savannah and New Orleans for the honor. We've got the logical harbor and a delegation to sell it to the Government. Port Royal's going to be the biggest thing south of Newport News! And while we're at it, you and I are going to run over to White Sulphur and catch up with that honeymoon we missed."

Laughing at her blank astonishment, he took her into the library and closed the door. There he sat down and pulled her down on his knee.

"Now, here we are away from everything. It'll be just like this, just the two of us, alone at last,—no family butting in, no worries, nothing but love. Well, how does it hit you?"

It was impossible at the moment to say anything except "Oh, Steve darling, it's wonderful!" And in the panic of discovering she had nothing to wear and packing that and his things as well, with the disorganizing assistance of Miss Sophie, and in all the rush and confusion of leaving the children and the house and attending to a congestion of last-minute details, it was not till the train was actually pulling out of the station that she was able to realize what had happened. Then a flood of conflicting emotions swept over her: delight in the journey and pride in Stephen's mission, dismay over suddenly remembered things she had forgotten to tell Lucy, agony over the thought of being separated from the children for a solid month,— separation from Michael, the First at last.

She finally had to turn for relief to Stephen's profile, slightly unreal through the network of her veil.

"You really think everything will be all right?"

He glanced at her with a frown and shook his head. "No indeed. I look for an orgy of calamities in our absence. Fire, burglary, murder, earthquakes, hurricanes, tidal waves,—to say nothing of mumps and measles."

"Hush! dear."

"Now, honey, you're not going to work up a lot of silly worries to spoil the trip, I hope." He chuckled and gave her hand a reassuring pat. "Of course, we could have carted the children along, but wouldn't that be a little embarrassing for a honeymoon couple?"

After he had shown his pass to Conductor Gilroy, a big man with a mild affable manner, Stephen excused himself to go forward to the smoking-car, to join the other members of the delegation.

"You don't mind, dear,—I see you've got your magazine. And we've got to map out our campaign."

"Of course, dear." She mastered a flash of disappointment to return his smile.

After all, she thought as she watched his tall handsome stride up the aisle, I'll have him all to myself after this Washington business, all to myself for the first time in ages. . . .

It was disturbing how quickly the excitement of that burned itself out. Instead of leaping ahead as it should, her mind kept turning perversely back to Marshlands. She had to remind herself forcefully how really wonderful it was of Stephen to have thought of this honeymoon.

She raised her veil finally and settled herself to take up the August *Harper's* that had come just in time to travel with her. This number could be read straight through from cover to cover, from Pear's Soap to Baker's Chocolate in fact: no interruptions to see what Jack was screaming about or if Ella had remembered to make the pudding sauce. But when she turned to the frontispiece, a portrait of Nathaniel Hawthorne, the distinguished melancholy white head blurred and grew to enormous blank proportions. And with a sudden stab of sight and pain she found herself back at Marshlands, the children rushing shouting to meet her at the door, Michael in the lead, the first to reach her aching arms.

✓   ✓   ✓

On the morning of August 31st, Eugenia's first thought when she opened her eyes was of her friend Sally Broughton. She smiled up at the ceiling, where the reflection from the river made a pattern of soft shimmering loveliness. But it was going to be another sweltering day; already the new waves of heat were pressing into the pool of night air that lay in the room. And the morning sounds of the house —Ella's activities in the kitchen, the noise of the children between the nursery and the bathroom, her mother calling something to Lucy—added to the sense of torpid fretfulness. Peculiarly irritating were the sounds that came through the windows: Tunis jabbering with the yard boy, the whirr and clatter of the lawn-mower, the rake-raking of the shell drive. Preparations for the return of the Master and Mistress. The Honeymooners!

Eugenia sighed in disgust. She only hoped this heat spell would hold out to welcome Emily and Stephen after their month at White Sulphur. There was some satisfaction in knowing that the Beaufort delegation had failed at Washington and lost the navy yard to Charleston; that must have cast a pall over the "honeymoon". But the pictures remained, the pictures that Emily's letters had brought: the frivolous routine of a great resort, morning Germans, champagne lunches, afternoon bridle paths and carriage drives and woodland trails, evening balls. Those pictures flashing through the shimmer of the ceiling were so painful that she soon turned them off. But after a moment she revived the background of White Sulphur to see herself moving there. Beautiful clothes, envious eyes of women, admiring eyes of men. . . .

"Eugenia!"

She answered the summons with a tired sigh. "Yes, Mother."

"Are you awake, child?"

When you were beginning to wonder what had become of your youth, it was comforting to be called child. But that hardly neutral-ized the irritation of the question.

"Of course not. I'm having a beauty sleep in this peaceful house."

353

Her mother continued to rap on the door, and knowing there was only one way to end that Eugenia got up, slipped on her kimono, and went to unlock it. "Well," her mother greeted her from the hall, with the genial little smile that was so vexing at this hour of the morning, or any hour for that matter. Keen eyes peered into the room, suspiciously, Eugenia thought, as if they hoped to find something out of order. "Just wanted to be sure you were up,—the children's party today, you know, and the servants must get breakfast and the house out of the way. If you'd leave your door open at night like the rest of us, you'd sleep much cooler." She went on to the stairs, and Eugenia closed the door emphatically in protest.

She was barely back between the sheets when the door burst open and in came the children with a rush: Michael ahead, Margaret scrambling to keep up, and little Jack reeling and chortling after them. Michael and Margaret could be controlled to a certain extent, but Jack not at all. And when Michael boosted him onto the bed, she was overwhelmed with smacking wet kisses.

"Oh, Jack!—stop it! Please, children! . . . Now just look at this bed. Lucy!"

Lucy was watching from the hall.

"Lucy, do take them down to breakfast, hear. And Jack shouldn't be allowed to run with them, he's too little."

"Ain' nobody gwine control dat case, Miss Gene. Come 'long, you chillun, you' Gran'maa vaitin' on you."

The everlasting impertinence of that Lucy!

When they were gone, leaving the door wide open of course, and had taken their noise and confusion downstairs to the dining-room, Eugenia got up to close the door. Back in bed again she relaxed with a long sigh. They were always such a strain, the children. She felt she had had all the strain of each of them since the days they were born, and none of the joy that the rest of the household seemed to get out of them. They belonged to the others. She was jealous of them, with Emily and their grandmother, with Stephen and Rusty, with the servants even; yet when they were hers for a moment, she could only submit to them, never respond. To show affection for them, she felt, would be like *touching* Emily. They were all part of Emily, extensions of Emily: Margaret's blue eyes, Jack's blue eyes, even Michael's dark brown Fenwick eyes were all somehow Emily's eyes. Besides, she knew they didn't really love her. This demonstration was just part of the excitement of getting up, more excited than usual this morning because of the party today and the homecoming of their mother and father tomorrow. No, they were nothing to her but strain, one of the chief vexations in this endless circle of vexations that encompassed her life. Sometimes she felt that if she didn't get away from them all soon, escape from the prison of this house, she would simply go crazy.

At this point thoughts of Sally Broughton came to her rescue, as they always did when Eugenia was at the end of her rope. Someday when she had saved enough, month by month and year by year, from the allowance that Stephen was giving her, she would propose to Sally that they go away somewhere together. Already the fund had reached an appreciable figure, deposited in a Charleston bank through Uncle Joe Bramwell, who had been sworn to secrecy on the plea that she wanted to surprise Stephen with her thrift. Of course the plan required the elimination of Sally's mother, whom she supported by her clerking at Turner Brothers hardware store; but Eugenia had arranged all that in her mind,—Mrs. Broughton was old and ailing and she would certainly have the good grace to die before the hour of emancipation struck. . . . Meanwhile, Sally remained Eugenia's sole defense against the loneliness that was forever driving her back upon herself. Sally understood her. Sally was the only human being she loved.

And Sally had promised to spend the night with her, the last night before the return of the "honeymooners". It was this thought alone that gave her courage to get up to face the inevitable trials of the day.

The first trial was—as usual—the bathroom. She had, in a fastidious way, enjoyed the bathroom, till Emily and Stephen and the children had moved from Land's End. Then the wholesale latching and unlatching of the door had begun; it had become an obsession with her, that sound; it had almost driven her to revert to washstand and commode. Her towels and toilette articles she kept in her own room, but that was no protection from the litter of the children's things. Of course the most offensive aspect of the bathroom was the family intimacy involved. It was an ordeal she hurried through with every sense contracted.

Back in her room, a little out of breath, she took her time about dressing. She liked to get downstairs after the children had finished and taken their insistent voices and persons outdoors. And she liked to linger over every phase of this transformation of her slim unashamed self into a figure of stylish respectability; this sheathing of her private self—"all eagerness and grace"—against a world careless of the waste. Before her in the bureau mirror stood a prim-and-proper person in draped polonaise, tight bodice and sleeves, high-buttoned neck with a bow in back for chic. She leaned forward. If the skin of her face could only have kept the smooth soft whiteness of the rest of her. But nothing now could rouse those cheeks from their sallow deadness, and the wrinkles at the corners of the dark eyes had come to stay. Somewhere she had read: *The beauty of Southern women blooms like the rose, and as soon fades.* But as she brushed the bang of dark hair down on her forehead, she searched for reassuring things to say to herself, and found them. By the time she was ready to turn her back on the mirror, her confidence was restored.

When she went down to the dining-room, the children were gone but her mother was still there. Eugenia always started the day with a determination to allow nothing to disturb her serenity. The determination seldom carried her far, and this morning it was defeated more quickly than usual. No sooner had she slipped into her chair and opened her napkin than resentment began to stir within her against the cheerful debonair old figure across the table. Since the advent of prosperity her mother had evolved into a living symbol of the new order; she radiated well-being. And in her recent amazing acceptance of age, she had almost in a day shed the last troubled vestiges of middle life and proudly donned the very livery of grand-motherhood, an elegant costume of her own designing,—loose black taffeta dress gathered at the waist, immaculate lace cap, lace collar, lace cuffs, lace handkerchief. There was something positively treacherous about all this, Eugenia couldn't help feeling: it somehow advanced her own age, robbed her of years, left her exposed to middle-age. She felt the treachery of it more keenly than ever this morning.

She waited till her mother had poured and passed the coffee and tinkled the silver bell for Tunis. Then, in the faintly petulant voice that was her defense against all members of the family, she said: "I thought you were going to stay in bed this morning."

"Gracious no. I have the children's party to attend to."

Eugenia watched her take another helping of fig preserve.

"That's about your fifth helping, isn't it?"

"And what if it is, my dear?"

"Oh nothing, of course. Yesterday you had one of your worst attacks of dyspepsia, but don't let that give you any pause."

"That was yesterday. And it was not dyspepsia. It was the heat."

"I'm glad you can jest about it. If I'd fainted dead away, I'd be a little concerned about myself."

"And well you might, at your age. But at my time of life I hope I've earned the right to a touch of vertigo, if I please."

Eugenia sighed. Nothing was more provoking than her mother's facetiousness.

"Well," she said with an air of resignation, "I only hope Cousin Rusty comes with the Honeymooners from Charleston tomorrow, so he can give you some medicine."

"Hmm! I'm always glad to see Rusty, but I'll take none of his medicine,—unless he prescribes a little bourbon for a tonic. No need to look so puritanical, child. You'd do well to take a toddy yourself now and then."

"That's a nice remark."

"Merely a little friendly advice, my dear. There's nothing like good food and good bourbon for what ails you, as your Grandfather Bramwell used to say, and the older I grow the more wisdom I see in it. Put that in your little portrait of his life."

Eugenia thought she detected a note of disparagement in this reference to her latest literary interest. It spurred her to find a suitable retort.

"My advice to you is to let Cousin Rusty give you a thorough examination. After yesterday I'm afraid there's something *organically* wrong with you."

For a moment Eugenia thought she had at last touched a vital spot. But her mother's reply was flatly disappointing.

"Eat your breakfast, child, before it gets cold."

"Mother!" Eugenia discovered in a shocked voice, "isn't that your third cup of coffee?"

"It is. Those carpetbagging Van Wies have one redeeming trait, they do carry good coffee. Ready for another? Plenty more here.

. . . By the way, do you want the carriage for the Malevolent Society meeting? Because if you do, I must send Tunis to Bay Street in time to get back by eleven."

"I suppose it's witty to call the Benevolent Society by that name. You seem to forget that Grandma Fenwick started it."

"My dear Eugenia, I wasn't born yesterday. I know quite well what women's clubs are for, and with all due respect to the memory of Grandma Fenwick she was undoubtedly the greatest gossip in the parish,—she herself, being an honest woman, would have been the first to admit it. Now when *I* feel like gossiping about my neighbors, I don't purpose to do it under the guise of distributing Christmas baskets to the poor." She gave her lace cap a little pat and added, before Eugenia could get her breath, "But I suppose you want to see your dear aunts."

"You know I don't even look at Aunt Susan and Isabel," Eugenia found the voice to protest. "I go because Sally does."

"Well, it's not a bad idea to have one member of the family present, for protection's sake. They won't slander you to your face."

Eugenia began to realize she was no match for her mother this morning. She finished her breakfast in injured silence, while her mother summoned Tunis and Ella to give them instructions for the day.

When she went out to find Lucy and the children, she had to call repeatedly before an answer came from the summer-house in the side garden. She hunted them down there, her vexation with her mother carrying over to them. "Didn't you hear me calling?" she demanded of Lucy. "And why do I have to come to get you children? If Aunt Eugenia is willing to give her time, I should think you'd at least have the courtesy——!" They stood frozen, staring at her with round eyes. Even little Jack was stiff with awe at the tenseness of her voice, though he knew he was not involved in his brother's and sister's predicament. When her indignation focused on Michael, he looked down and wriggled his toes in misery; but a moment later his dark eyes flashed up with an inspiration.

"Ladies first," he grinned, coaxing Margaret to the front with his hand on the back of her pinafore.

"Now, Michael, none of that, if you please."

"Oh please take Margaret first this time, Aunt Gene.'"

Eugenia's temper was not improved by Lucy's amusement.

"Michael!"

His reluctant bare feet followed her out of the garden, across the fragrant new-cut grass of the lawn, over the sharp shell of the drive, up the hot porch steps, and into the hall with its cool smooth relief of matting. In the living-room the piano was waiting for him with the slightly malicious expression it always wore except when Mother was playing. Its mahogany squatness stood out against the white paneling of the walls and the white slip-covers of the chairs. The room was darkish: the blinds had already been closed against the mounting heat and glare. He went to open the shutters of the window nearest the piano before he sat down, limply. Suddenly remembering his bare feet and his hands smudged from the summer-house railing, he pounced on the keyboard to distract Aunt Eugenia's attention. It was too late.

"Your shoes, Michael."

He turned the stool with a protesting squeak. "Aunt Gene, please don't make me put them on. It's so hot. And the pedals feel so nice and cool."

"I'm not interested in how the pedals feel. Let me see your hands."

When he held them out for inspection, she made such a face that he took them upstairs without argument. "You may bring down my writing portfolio," she called after him.

In the bathroom he lingered soapily over the offending hands. After he had stopped in Aunt Eugenia's room to get the mysterious portfolio, he peeked into his grandmother's room in the hopes of a "Well, what are you up to, my darling?" and a little chat; but she wasn't there. Her absence reminded him of the party, and then the banister rail couldn't take him downstairs fast enough. He sobered as he went into the living-room and put the portfolio in Aunt Eugenia's lap, but when he adjusted the stool he couldn't help snickering at the squeaks it made.

"That will do, Michael. Didn't I hear you sliding down the banister?"

"Yes, Aunt Gene."

"Haven't you been told repeatedly not to do that?"

"I forgot."

"That's the worst possible excuse. I shall have to tell your father, the moment he comes home. Now get on with your practicing."

With a sigh he settled down to the torture of scales.

Eugenia opened the portfolio to the familiar first page with its carefully printed letters: *Life of Governor John DeSaussure Bramwell, by His Grand-daughter, Eugenia Bramwell Fenwick*. After that the manuscript was an elaborate jumble of notes. And there would be additions if Uncle Joe came over this evening. She hoped he would; and, because Sally was coming, she hoped he wouldn't. Her thoughts struggled against the stumbling repetitions of the scales, the clatter of the lawn-mower, and the stinging song of a locust.

"You're not counting, Michael," she discovered crossly.

"Yes I am—under my breath."

"Well, I want to hear it."

He began wearily to count aloud, nodding the dark mop of his hair in time, and she made another effort to concentrate on the sheaf of papers in her lap. Here were slowly accumulating the remains of her grandfather. But sometimes she wondered if a likeness of the old gentleman could ever be assembled from these ashes, these dusty facts of his life. And sometimes, in moments of extreme stress, she wondered if it mattered very much. There were even occasional moments, of pure vagary, when she wondered what chronicle of emotions lay behind the chronicle of events she was preparing to record, what his inside life had been, the part that didn't show. In her own life, she knew, all the really important events were submerged below the surface of decorum and respectability, as her person was hidden under clothes. But, after all, appearances were what counted. And I am, she thought, what I appear to be: a still young, attractive, well-dressed lady author, poet, and artist. . . . She would have dwelt on that pleasant thought, but Michael's scales kept intruding. And presently she gave her undivided attention to his torment, enjoying the fretting of his hands, the agonizing of his toes on and off the pedals, the whole increasing exhaustion of his slender body as the ormolu clock on the mantel ticked off the seconds. When a half-hour was up, he turned on the stool to plead with her. "Don't make me do any more today. My back aches. Really it does."

"Do you suppose this is any pleasure for me? Stop frowning and finish."

"I'm not frowning," he frowned.

"We won't have any impertinence, if you please."

She held him to the last fretful minute of the forty-five. When the signal for his release could no longer be put off, he started out of the room with a whoop.

"Michael!"

"Yes, Aunt Gene?"

"Go out properly. And tell Margaret to come in."

He went out very properly, as far as the front door, where he broke loose again.

Margaret behaved much too well to furnish any enjoyment; it was Eugenia who did all the squirming in this case. As the minutes dragged by to the nerve-racking tune of scales and locusts' hot dry raspings, she began to worry seriously that Tunis would not get back from Bay Street in time. But at ten minutes to eleven, she heard the carriage on the drive.

She hurried upstairs to wash her hands, on general principles, and to look at herself and her hat in the mirror. When she came down and went out to the carriage, she raised her parasol against the blazing sunlight with a feeling of really blissful anticipation.

But the meeting of the Malevolent Society was unsatisfactory in every respect. Only five members responded to the roll-call: Mildred Rhett, Mrs. Nat Elliott, Aunts Susan and Isabel, and herself. It took her some time to admit that Sally was not coming.

After the official business was disposed of, a lively discussion developed as to when rain would come to break the heat wave. She sat tense in her chair with an air of detachment, to conceal the discomfort of being in the oblivious presence of the Aunts. Release came when Aunt Susan broke up the meeting by contradicting Mildred Rhett and Mrs. Elliott into an offended silence about the duration of the '82 drought.

When she was back in the carriage she told Tunis to stop at Turner Brothers, and then the post-office.

It was no pleasure to drive through town. She knew what a charming picture she made in the carriage with the delicate shadow of the parasol over her face and shoulders, but there were only unappreciative, hostile, common eyes to see. And at the green facing the Grammar School, once the proud Library that her grandfather had given to Beaufort, a special ordeal was waiting for her today in the shape of the town sports playing a languid game of ball. Donald Van Wie and Allen Rutherford, whom she had somehow come to think of as rejected suitors, were among the group and tipped their caps politely; but some of the others made insulting bows and noises at the carriage.

For the rest of the way to Bay Street she held herself very rigid. It was a curse to be sensitively attuned in a world composed so largely of callous and vulgar people, and provoking and painful circumstances. Still, without sensitiveness how could you feel the subtle beauties and nuances of life? How could you be Eugenia Fenwick?

The thought was still echoing in her mind when she stepped out of the carriage several minutes later to pass under the sign of "Turner Brothers Hardware & Furniture Emporium". Ordinarily she avoided Bay Street and its stores: they were all run by carpetbaggers, or sons of carpetbaggers, or crackers. But in an emergency of this kind she had to swallow her distaste.

It was Hal Turner who came forward to meet her.

"I wish to speak to Miss Broughton, if you please."

"Why certainly, Miss Fenwick."

She stared coldly after him as he went toward the door of the office at the back of the store. The Turner Brothers were handsome men and courteous enough, but that didn't remove the stigma of their Yankeehood. And it was this Hal who had had the gall to propose marriage to Sally. In confessing it Sally had seemed only amused, but Eugenia had been hotly indignant.

When Sally came smiling toward her, the many-sided tension of the morning relaxed.

"Well, Gene! Where did you drop from?"

Eugenia always regretted that Sally wasn't a little more dainty in manner and looks. Everything about Sally was so big and hearty,— her person, her voice, her smile, and her laugh. Particularly her laugh. Eugenia had never learned to resign herself to the sheer good spirits of it, any more than she had learned to resign herself to Sally's habitual carelessness of dress and untidiness of hair, and the paper cuffs she wore in the store.

Eugenia's reserved little smile of greeting faded quickly into a frown of reproach.

"Why weren't you at the meeting? Wouldn't he let you off?"

"Inventory. Can't even get off for dinner. And we all have to work tonight."

"But you promised."

"Well, won't tomorrow night do just as well? My, you look cool and fresh and sweet!"

"I told you the Honeymooners were coming back tomorrow."

In the midst of her panic disappointment Eugenia suddenly remembered Uncle Joe. She hated to use him for a decoy, but this was an extremity.

"And Joe's back from circuit court, and he's coming over. I thought we could all have such a nice evening together."

This was a naked lie, she knew well enough: Uncle Joe was back in town, but there was no reason to suppose he was coming to the house this evening. However, the ruse worked like a charm. Sally colored and looked confused.

"Well. . . . I might possibly be able to get off early. I'll try to jog things up here. But don't count on me for supper. I'll try to get there by eight."

Not a very satisfactory victory. But Eugenia left the store with composure.

It did not stay with her long. At the post-office she had to go in for the mail herself: Tunis couldn't leave the horses. She loathed the post-office. She loathed the people moving in and out, and she particularly loathed the impossible little turned-up nose of May Lou Mason, who always presided at the window. May Lou Mason was not only the wife of the carpetbagging post-master, but she was also a cracker. It stuck out all over her. Eugenia shared with her Uncle Joe the conviction that it was better to be nigger than cracker, and her manner showed it. She never spoke to the woman: she merely presented herself at the window. May Lou Mason retaliated by pretending not to recognize her at once. This morning she went so far as to ask, "Name please?"

Without looking at the creature Eugenia answered, "The Fenwick mail."

When the mail was slapped down before her, she found there were only letters from White Sulphur, business letters for Stephen, and another rejected poem from *Scribner's,* which was supposed to be so partial to Southern material.

Back at the house, she walked out of the living-room when her mother began to read aloud from the White Sulphur letters. Her own letter from Emily she left unopened on the table. She went up to her room and stayed there till dinner time. And after dinner she withdrew immediately, for her siesta.

She undressed and lay down without putting on her nightgown. It was hotter than ever now, and for a long while she made no attempt to sleep. Although the blinds were closed, enough light burned through the shutters to make Tennyson's *Idylls of the King,* her bedside favorite, easy reading. She dreamed over the pages, till the children came up to dress; after that, her fancies were jostled into confusion. . . . Michael was humming in the bathroom. It wasn't just the party, she knew, that was making him so happy: he had been getting happier day by day as his mother's homecoming drew nearer. He was no longer a little boy, he was beginning to stretch and grow up, but the first nights after his mother had left he had behaved like a child. What he had needed then, and what she had recommended for him, was a good licking. . . . She thought: If I could only get him punished for something: if I could only fix it so Stephen would have to lick him, first thing, what a nice homecoming that would make for Emily. *Michael has been too impudent and horrid.* Or better: *Michael used some nasty words to me,—much too nasty to repeat, and much too nasty for mouth-soap-washing. . . .*

She recalled the entirely unsatisfactory Flat Rock spanking. And that somehow reminded her of the Rose episode.

She put the *Idylls* aside and began to reconstruct that memorable affair. Mulatto Rose had been the cook before Ella. She had a coal-black son about Michael's age; her husband had disappeared. One Saturday night in spring Eugenia had gone out for a walk in the garden before bed. It was an enchanting night, moonlit and scented. But her poetic reflections were disturbed by sounds from the servants' quarters in the yard. They were such strange and provocative sounds that she felt drawn toward them as by invisible and irresistible hands. She moved softly, keeping in the shadows. The windows and blinds of the quarters were closed, but she crept around to the back and found a broken shutter through which she could see into the dimly lighted bedroom. Her heart leaped up to a furious beat at what she saw and heard. Armed with a strap Rose was licking her naked screaming son around the room, which was in the wildest disorder. For a cycle of minutes, the most exciting in her life, Eugenia watched the monstrous scene. She was able to turn away from her peep-hole only when the boy lay moaning in a corner and Rose knelt by him, panting, the strap fallen from her hand.

Living over that night, Eugenia remembered she had not closed her eyes a wink. The next day she had said nothing to anyone about the whipping.

Her memory veered erratically: to Bob Broughton, Sally's brother, and the single kiss he had once given her. That too had happened in the rose garden, and in moonlight. The poison of it was still working in her blood. She turned over on the bed, turned her face into the pillow, away from his. To escape him completely her thoughts returned with a staccato rush to Michael. She saw him stripped and lashed, herself lashing him around this room. After that, a deep languor and stillness possessed her. She lay on her back again, hardly breathing, her thoughts moving in a gently meditative rhythm. The children's voices were gone downstairs. With a little sigh she took up the *Idylls,* but the words and lines refused to form even the vaguest images. Everything around and within her was becoming pleasantly blurred. Outside in the tremendous sunlight a locust's rising and falling monotone was like a sorcery, sorcery of Merlin, sorcery of Merlin the Magician, stealing through her most secret senses. Slowly with Sally she felt herself sinking under its stinging swelling spell. . . .

Voices, children's voices, the voices of the children were weaving in and out of her dreams, and she realized dimly that the party was in progress.

Fortunately the joggling-board, the rank-a-tank, and the swing were on the other, the shady side of the house; and after their charms had been exhausted, the rout moved to the side garden, which was far enough away from the house to keep the noises remote. But presently a game of tag destroyed the unity of the group, and shrill shouts and laughter were scattered in every direction like leaves in the wind. Sometimes she would be brought to the surface of consciousness with a start as a whoop or a wild laugh broke loose under her very window. She could make out individual voices: Linda and Dallas Robinson, brought from Land's End for the occasion by their father; Allen Rutherford's boys; the Van Wie grandchildren; Betty and Nancy Elliott. All trash, except the Elliott children, and they were impossible little things. . . . By the time the game shifted from the tumult of tag to the giggling suppressions of hide-and-seek, Eugenia was too wide-awake to profit by the change.

Eventually the scattered elements of the party were collected and herded into the house. But this only made matters worse. Treble voices and laughter came up through the floor in a muffled nerve-racking bedlam. Chairs were being moved. They were being brought into the living-room from the hall, from the dining-room, from the library. Tunis even came upstairs to get some from the bedrooms. Eugenia knew what that foreboded, and she called to him angrily as he passed her door.

"Tell them not to dare use my gilt chair or the bamboo rocker!"

A few moments later her fears were suddenly confirmed when the piano began to thump in march time. Feet tramped. The piano stopped abruptly. There was a wild screaming and scrambling for chairs. After a minute the piano and the tramping started again. The piano stopped; started; stopped again. She could hear her mother's gleeful commands above the din. Where did they all get the energy for such a roughhouse in this terrible heat? Desperately she tried to turn her thoughts away from the endless Journey to Jerusalem.

. . . *Jerusalem the Golden, with milk and honey blest. Beneath thy contemplation sink heart and voice oppressed.* Heart oppressed. Certainly the heart was oppressed. Why not? What a mess things made! A wretched Journey to Jerusalem, a stupid marching in a circle, a mad scramble for chairs that soon left you standing in a corner, watching others scramble for a place, till the music stopped for good. A child's game, a no-sense jumble. Vexation of the spirit. Frustration. . . . This house, would she never escape from it? She had been born in this very room: was she doomed to die here too? Her eyes rested on the gap in the cornice where several dentils were missing,—one of the numerous scars that the house bore, one of the souvenirs of its raping by Yankees and niggers. This house was poisoned. Everything was poisoned. . . . She remembered having once read that someone died somewhere every second. Every breath that she drew marked the end of some life. On Greenland's icy mountains, it might be, or India's coral strands. More likely India's coral strands. People died like flies in India, a human life meant nothing. If you could escape to India, with a little money, you could live like a princess, with dozens of servants to do your bidding. Slaves, practically. The slavery of the old South would be as nothing beside this voluptuous oriental slavery. . . . But she would never escape to any such earthly paradise. The most she could hope for was escape with Sally to some respectable place miles away from Marshlands and Beaufort.

But when would that be? Never, perhaps. And with that thought her mind swung back to the thought of someone-dying-somewhere-every-second. Well, sometimes she felt that her own particular second would be welcome. After all, why wouldn't it be a plain relief to be through with frustration? The heart oppressed would stop beating, stop like a clock run down, come at last to rest. A final tick, setting her free.

She began to feel that already she was free. Free from the time-bound ticking of her heart, free from a world of millions upon millions of ticking hearts. Detached from her body, she felt that she was floating away into space, toward God. . . . *My poor child, it's been lonely and hard for you.* Yes, Father. Lonely and hard. . . .

When she opened her eyes, streaks of blood-red light from the blinds stained her arms and breasts and the pages of the *Idylls* at her side. Slowly she became aware that the party had dissolved and the house was at peace; that the locusts had ceased and the bird vespers were beginning; that the sun was almost set, but that it was hotter, more sultry than ever. Not even a stir of the usual sea breeze to cool things off a little.

It was only the thought of Sally that gave her the heart to raise herself from the heavy languor· of the bed. The prolonged siesta seemed not to have rested her at all. She felt more tired than when she had lain down.

When she had opened the blinds and dressed with care, she waited till the children came up with Lucy for early bed before she left the room. Downstairs she found her mother in the dining-room, enjoying a cup of tea and a piece of angel-food cake while she perused the *News & Courier,* in the failing light. She looked as cool and collected as she had at the beginning of the day, in spite of the party.

"Well, my dear, I thought you were going to sleep forever. You missed a treat. The party was a great success."

"It certainly sounded like it. I never heard such disgustingly noisy children."

"You may be sure, child, that you and Stephen and Larry made quite as much noise when you were young."

"I don't believe it. Have you left anything for me?"

"You'll find plenty of sandwiches and sherbet in the pantry. Paper says more hot weather. If this keeps up, the lawn will be burned to a crisp."

"I hope it will be," Eugenia tossed over her shoulder on the way to the pantry. "And I hope it's hotter than ever tomorrow."

At exactly eight o'clock Eugenia left the house to meet Sally. She hoped they would meet at the gateway, but when she reached it there were only the shadows of the hot dusk to greet her. Strolling on along Fenwick Street, her thrill of anticipation was dampened by remembrance of the lie she had told Sally. To answer that first lie she would have to tell a second. She would say: Uncle Joe sent word he couldn't come this evening after all.

And then she saw coming toward her not one figure, but two figures. And her wits, as the distance between her and the figures closed, would do nothing whatever to help her. She could only repeat to herself: It's Sally and Uncle Joe, Uncle Joe and Sally. At the Rutherfords' driveway she paused to delay the meeting and rally her forces. But she was still hopelessly confused when they reached her.

Sally's laugh came to the rescue. "I bearded the lion in his den and brought him along!"

It was not too dark to see that Sally was very flushed indeed. And even Uncle Joe seemed a little thrown off base for a moment.

"Well, Gene," he said with a rather stiff bow, "and how are you, my dear?"

"Oh, Uncle Joe," she stammered through her disappointment, "I'm too glad to see you."

Her disappointment, during the course of that evening, blossomed into a perfect blight. Uncle Joe proved to be in fine fettle despite the heat, which forced him into an unprecedented breach of his dignity,—with many apologies to the ladies he shed his coat and gave them stories from his last session of court in his linen waistcoat and shirt-sleeves. Eugenia grew more and more glum as her mother's and Sally's enjoyment increased. She made several half-hearted attempts to divert the conversation into the channel of Grandfather Bramwell, but Uncle Joe held the floor and quickly steered back to his own interests. When he got on the subject of politics, the threat of "Pitchfork Ben" Tillman and the rising cracker movement, Eugenia gave up completely and resigned herself to waiting.

Once, when he seemed on the point of leaving, juleps were introduced to prolong the agony. Miss Sophie was responsible for that.

"Joe," she urged perversely, "I'm sure that you and Sally will take some refreshment. The ice boat came in this morning, just in time for the children's sherbet, and there's plenty left over. The bourbon's in the sideboard. Call Tunis to get you some mint."

Uncle Joe smacked his lips in approval.

"You'll have one with us, Sophie?"

"Don't be a fool, Joe, how could I refuse on a night like this."

With a little snort of amusement he turned to Eugenia.

"And you, Gene?"

"Oh no, thank you. It's much too hot to drink anything."

The rebuke was lost on him, lost on them all. For that matter her very existence seemed to be lost on them. For the rest of the evening Sally hardly took her eyes off Uncle Joe. And she laughed a great deal too heartily at his jokes, much more heartily than they or her julep warranted.

Finally Eugenia could stand it no longer. She felt that she was going to explode, scream something at them. How startled they would be, not suspecting the storm that was building up within her. The fools! I hate you all, she told them; you most of all, Sally.

Suddenly she was standing up,—just in time, she felt, to avert the explosion, the scream.

"I'm going up. I've got a headache."

Her voice sounded calm enough. But evidently it had a tenseness she could not detect from the inside, for they all stopped fanning abruptly and looked around at her sharply as if she had actually screamed at them. Sally was immediately solicitous, but Eugenia cut her off curtly: "Aren't you about ready?—it's almost ten."

Sally's face fell, but Miss Sophie came to her rescue.

"Leave Sally here, Eugenia. It's much too early and hot for bed."

"I'm not trying to take her away. I simply thought she might be tired."

Sally brightened. "Oh, I'm all right! You go ahead, Gene,—I'll stay and chat a few minutes longer with Miss Sophie and Cousin. I'll be right up. Don't mind, do you?"

"Why certainly not. Come up when you're ready."

Upstairs in her room, Eugenia faced this final humiliation and vexation in the mirror of her bureau. . . . In the pool of lamplight on the marble top of the bureau an assortment of scorched bugs were writhing. It was a mystery how they got into the room with even the fireplace chimney stuffed up with bagging. One by one she put them out of their misery with the tip of her palmetto fan. . . . But this day, she thought as she began to undress, for all its disappointments and frustrations was not lost yet. It could only be a matter of minutes now before Uncle Joe left, his boots grinding the shell of the drive; Aunt Susan and Aunt Isabel would be sitting up for him. And then Sally would come up and a long spell of loneliness and oppression would be washed away in a flow of close intimate whispered talk with her bosom friend.

When she had undressed she put on her best lace-trimmed night-gown. Though there was nothing dainty about Sally, she did appreciate dainty things. Poor Sally perspired so, but what could she do about it? It was certainly a blessing not to perspire at all. Cousin Rusty said it was bad not to have open pores, but it was a great comfort just the same. . . . Cousin Rusty would be coming with the Honeymooners from Charleston tomorrow to stay over the week-end, but that meant nothing to her. They were in Charleston from Washington by now. . . . Through her thoughts she was lis-tening to the voices and laughter downstairs. Every second that passed now, killing someone somewhere in the world, seemed a precious length of time stolen from her night with Sally. Sally was such a perfect fool where Uncle Joe was concerned: she acted like a love-sick schoolgirl. But she was wasting her time. There was no threat there, and no cause for jealousy; Sally would never get so much and so little as a passing kiss in the garden from Uncle Joe,— his sisters made him perfectly comfortable, and the Law was his passion.

Eugenia smiled faintly as she groped under her pillow for the chain of her locket watch. When she pulled it out and turned the face to the light, it looked like ten past ten. But she couldn't be sure: the watch seemed to be vibrating in her hand. As the thought flashed through her mind how curious that was, she realized that not only her hand was trembling but her whole body as well and the bed and the room. As her heart pounded to a dead stop there was a rumbling of thunder as if a storm were coming to break the pall of heat. And then, after an instant of weird silence, everything went suddenly and violently insane. All the furniture in the house was being moved wildly about. The walls creaked and shivered: the pictures danced before her eyes: patches of plaster fell from the ceiling and spattered on the floor. The lamp jiggled on the rattling bureau, toppled, crashed,—a blue flame shot up and went out. Through the panic din and darkness came crazy snatches of bells ringing and voices shouting near and far.

A scream—the scream that had been stuck in her throat for so many moons, years, ages—burst free as she strained convulsively from the bed. She could hardly stand: the floor shook, seemed to buckle, to rise and fall under her as if it were breathing. Somehow she reached the door, but it was stuck fast and there was no strength in her paralyzed hands to budge it. Then abruptly, whimsically, it gave way and swung open of itself. She was in the hall.

As she gripped the quivering banister rail she saw, in the hall below under the swaying light of the hanging lamp, Sally in Joe's arms. She stood transfixed, only dimly aware of her mother coming up toward her. Her mother's passing voice smote her, but though the words were distinctly heard they were void of meaning. It was not till moments later, when her mother came back past her carrying little Jack and with Margaret at her skirts, that Eugenia came to life. She felt Michael's hands grip her arm, and with him she hurried down the treacherous stairs.

They were all somehow assembled on the front lawn,—her own arms were tight around Michael, Margaret and Jack were with her mother and Lucy, Sally was still clinging to Joe. Tunis and Ella and the yard boy were there too, wailing and moaning.

Jedgmen' come fuh true! Jedus hab mercy! End of de worl'!

A mist of dust hung between them and the house. The tremors of the earth were dying, but the rumbling continued.

"Stop that racket!" Uncle Joe snorted at Tunis. "Hush up, you damned niggers!"

But they kept up their wailing.

"The worst's over," Eugenia heard him tell her mother. "I'll take

Sally home and stop at the house. Stay right where you are till I get back."

As they passed her, Eugenia closed her eyes against Sally. But she watched the pair of dim forms skirting the lawn till they were lost completely in the blackness toward the gates. Simply and without emotion she thought: Things will never again be the same with us, Sally.

Her arms tightened around Michael and she spoke to him softly. "Everything's all right now, dear."

She pressed his head tight against her breast. And when she felt his arms respond and tighten around her waist, so great an ecstacy gripped her throat that she could scarcely breathe. In her whole life she had never known anything like this rapture of joy and release. In the midst of dark turmoil she stood steadfast and unafraid, utterly sure of herself and serene. Judgment? The End of the World? Rather it was as if the world were just beginning, as if she had only at this moment come to life.

✧ ✧ ✧

For Emily the day after the earthquake was more terrible than the earthquake itself.

Those frenzied hours of darkness in Charleston had carried their own anesthetic. Rusty had met her and Stephen at the station; they had been on their way to his house when the first shock struck. After the miracle of escape from toppling chimneys and crumbling walls, she had worked with Rusty till dawn at the dressing-station he had set up under a torch flare in the little park across from St. Michael's. Every detail of that lurid night was impressed on her memory; but there had been no time to think, only an oblivion of feverish activity.

But when the last of the injured had been treated and daylight came to reveal the full extent of the havoc, one consuming thought took possession of her. . . . For hours Stephen had been working frantically and impotently to get some communication from Beaufort: the office of the *News & Courier* and the telegraph office at the station could give him no information whatever. Home might as well have been in China, or on another planet. By seven o'clock he had been able to learn only that the rails out of Charleston were so badly twisted that no trains would be running for days. It was

372

impossible to get a carriage through the narrow debris-strewn old streets and clear of the town; even then it would take a day and a night to reach Beaufort by way of Green Pond and Gardner's Corners. The only hope was the water route. But it was mid-morning before he was able to charter a pilot boat, at a price that took her breath away.

As the little boat rounded the Battery and headed across the Ashley into Wappoo Creek, the slumbering blue of the water, the dreaming expanses of marsh, the serene blue of the sky only increased the turmoil in her heart. Stephen kept trying to reassure her: "Now, honey, the center of the thing was Summerville, so Beaufort couldn't have been hard hit,—why they'll be laughing at our fears, just rocked a little in their sleep, that's all. . . ." But he was obviously talking to reassure himself as well; and he could no more sit still, in the chairs the captain had set forward for them, than she could.

Through noon into afternoon, hour after hour the boat followed the winding course, dragging a leisurely wake that lapped the edges of the marsh. For long periods it seemed hardly to move at all. It seemed suspended in an unearthly mystery of marsh and shining water and sky over far-flung sea islands. And finally in the interminable repetitions of its puffing sunlit path there was a mesmerism that blunted the sharp fear of disaster and the unknown.

With sunset and the opening of the narrow course into the broad waters of St. Helena Sound, the unreality of the journey deepened. The only continuous reality now was the stinging of her cheeks from the day of sun and breeze; everything else was frayed into fantasy by exhaustion and the constant straining forward. Weaving in and out of her troubled numbness was a persistent illusion that all this had happened to her before. And then delayed recognition of something familiar in this journey came at last to mingle its memories of another sunset long ago with the images of this dreaming. . . . She was torn between her present self and that former Emily, that stricken girl who knew the world had come to an end and there was nothing left for her, sitting alone among strangers on the deck of the *Indigo* after the Fort Sumter Celebration, a shadow among nightmare shadows. She was aware again of the intimate presence of the walking-beam, its rhythmic rise and fall, pant and sigh; and Mrs. Sager was reviewing hosts of angels and archangels in the flaming glory of this sunset: Lee had surrendered, the War was won.

As memory led to memory in this fevered reverie, whole zones of the past melted and flowed together into a present where the most incongruous elements mixed with grotesque ease: the children and Harriet Sheppard, Sherman and Miss Sophie, Rusty with Phyllis, Stephen and Will Herkimer with Aaron. Finally she lost all sense of time and place, drifting in helpless confusion.

But in the last hour of the journey, after the boat had left the luminous waters of the Sound and entered the darkening coils of Beaufort River, she came back to life. Because it took her a few paces nearer home, she went to the bow of the boat. Stephen brought her a wrap from the luggage and stood with her there, in the cool air above the swishing cleavage of the tide, the prow feeling cautiously for the channel.

Finally, abruptly, a bend in the endless tortured winding brought gleams of light converging from the waterfront. She could see Fenwick Point brooding in the dusk, the landing and the curve of the seawall. And there at last, nestling among the trees, its chimneys dimly silhouetted against the starry sky, stood home, safe and sound, its fanlight smiling the most radiant of welcomes.

Nothing could match the relief and joy of that hour of homecoming.

And after the tumult had subsided and Stephen had satisfied himself that the only damage to the house was cracked plaster, there was the excitement of the presents. Miss Sophie and Eugenia, Lucy, Tunis and Ella were willing to wait till tomorrow for their presents, but the children had to have theirs on the spot. More cars and track for Michael's railway, and another company of lead soldiers. For Margaret, Japanese flowers that opened in water and sheets of cut-out dolls. Picture books and a new kind of building blocks for little Jack. Then there was an aftermath of excitement that made it look for a while as if they would never get settled for the night. And when they were finally, Michael in his private corner of the big room and Margaret and Jack separated by a bolster in the double bed, she could hardly bear to surrender them to sleep, starved as she was for them, their clinging arms and the sweetness of their bodies.

After she had given them a positively final good-night and taken away the lamp, Jack tried clamoring for his father, and to quiet him

Stephen had to go in and lie down beside him. A few minutes later when she was picking up in the bathroom, Stephen came back on tiptoe with eyes twinkling.

"Dead to the world, I hope," he whispered.

They smiled over his escape.

He put his arms around her. "Had about enough yourself, honey?" She acknowledged it with a relaxed sigh, and after a comforting moment of intimacy he patted her back as he released her. "You see, I told you not to worry."

His brows contracted then and he consulted his watch. "I'm going over to the club a minute, honey, to get the news. I'll be back in no time, but don't wait up for me. Better turn in right away."

She nodded and lifted her face cheerfully for his hasty kiss. But when he was gone, she stood motionless, trying to clear the sudden mist in her eyes. She was unprepared for this abrupt relapse into separate existences: the happy month with him had lifted her up to forgetfulness of the dead taken-for-granted level to which love and companionship had sunk, somehow, by inexorable degrees. Now it was ended, their little journey into the past together, their "delayed honeymoon" with its recaptured sense of oneness. They had returned, she to the children and home, he to business and the don't-wait-up-for-me Commercial Club evenings. . . . An anguish of rebellion flared up in her. As if she could ever do more than twist and turn till he came in at night! Back to that. Back to the status of housewife.

But then she thrust bitterness away. There were altogether too many blessings in her life to leave room for any repining because every detail was not working out in accordance with the pattern of earlier dreams. It was childish to cry for a moon of everlasting romance; ecstacy, like beauty, was the rare and unpredictable wine of life, not the bread-and-butter. It was folly to expect marriage to be a prolonged intoxication. You were lucky if you were able to salvage in the end a friendship of understanding and mutual respect.

Taut nerves and strain, she told herself, had opened this seam in the armor of her peace. Sleep would close it again.

On the way to her room she stopped in to see Miss Sophie, who was already in bed but sitting propped up, looking expectant.

"Well, my dear! And how does it feel to be home, now that things have quieted down a bit? Come and sit down a minute, and let me take your hand. Your eyes are tired, child, and no wonder. I won't press you for a report tonight. I already know from your letters what a grand time you had."

"Oh, darling, we did have the most wonderful time. But I am a little tired. Won't things keep till tomorrow?"

"Of course. When you're my age you'll be surprised to find how well things keep—till your tongue begins to wag, and then it's hard to stop. Poor child, your eyes are in the back of your head,—get to bed before I get chatting about the quake. An earthquake in Carolina! Thank God we're all safe, but who ever heard of such a thing? —I thought they only had them in strange places like South America. It just goes to show we never can tell what's going to happen next in this life. Did I hear that wretched son of mine go out?"

"He wanted to get the latest news."

"I could have given him all the news there is. But he never stopped in here to even say boo. He might have stayed home the first night, at least. Truth of the matter is that Commercial Club means more to him than his own family."

"But, dear, his club contacts are important to him, for business reasons. And you can't blame him for wanting to see his friends after a month away and an earthquake."

"Friends! A pack of carpetbaggers and crackers, not fit for a gentleman to associate with. Stuff and nonsense, child. We're his friends. But he don't mind neglecting us. . . . No use trying to defend him. I hate to admit it, but Stephen is a selfish man. Perhaps it's enough to say he's a man. Men—sons, husbands, fathers—they're all alike, all incurably self-centered. And the older they grow, the worse they get. God made them so to teach us patience and forbearance, I suppose. But don't let me get started on that subject. Or any other. Good-night, good-night, my dear,—we'll dispose of Stephen and many another matter in the morning."

In her own room Emily undressed wearily. By the time she came to platting her hair, her fingers were almost too limp for twining the long strands into braids. She wondered if ever in her life she had felt this tired: it was as if she had been on her feet for days and weeks. But it was a tense kind of exhaustion: beneath fatigue lay quivering agitation. Even when she was stretched out in bed at last, it was impossible to relax this miserable tenseness.

And resentment returned to plague her. There was no dismissing it this time; her mind was caught in a squirrel-cage of exasperated speculation, memory and discouragement. She had fought so hard to preserve their love against change. . . . If she could only eliminate these futile hours of bitterness and learn acceptance for once and for all, resignation complete and final. What other solution was there. No amount of wishing and prayer, no fretting and certainly no re- criminations could ever change Stephen back to the original lover and keep him there; she might as well try to spare herself further worry and regret. But trying was not going to help her tonight. She must lie on this rack waiting for him to come in, very steady on his legs but breathing heavily, and then she must pretend to be asleep.

At some point in the dreary circling of her thoughts she was vaguely aware of sounds from the children's room. But they were too faint and undefined to attract her direct attention. When a moment later a hand touched her arm, she started violently.

It was Michael. Not since his little-boy days had he come to her like this in his sleep. There was not a drop of will in her to give her the resolution to take him back to his bed: she took him into her arms with a joy and relief beyond her control. But he did not wake in her embrace, his body yielded to hers with a sigh of content. And now in a flash all tenseness and distress were gone from her and her whole being was at rest. My darling, my darling, her heart whispered to him over and over, the first separation ended. How could she have lost sight of that, forgotten him, in her barren and exaggerated fret- ting about Stephen.

It was hard to believe that he was here with her again, close to her breast, living and breathing in her arms. If she could only hold him here like this forever, her little boy. So soon she must begin relin- quishing him for his growth into manhood: like the ties of birth these later ties must be severed for his independence. But gently, Time, gently,—I can surrender him to you only at the dearest cost and slowly. . . . If that ultimate and invincible force could be bent to human will by offerings and sacrifice, how gladly she would ex- change her lifeblood for its favors. But the face of time was as in- scrutable as the face of a clock, as inscrutable and as impassive. There was no wrath there and no malice, but no mercy either and no pity: only a ceaseless becoming, eternal flux, the ebb and flow of everlast- ing tides. The world and home were being swept along on a dark stream. Swifter and swifter the current moved, bearing them helplessly onward, shifting, changing, altering, but never pausing, never returning.

Cold fear gripped her throat as she stared up into the darkness. But his life stirred in the shelter of her arms, releasing her again in an instant. She was not alone but home with faith, and her son— the still unborn and the babe, the child and boy, youth and man—lay sleeping at her side, close as breath. Even the earthquake seemed now as remote and fantastic as a nightmare, an absurd *fee-fi-fo-fum* of fate. And time was standing still.

And now so deep a peace suffused her heart that, despite her will, despite the needles-and-pins in her arm under his head, and the necessity of taking him back to his bed before Stephen came in, she was powerless to hold herself above the eddying waves of sleep.

VIII

THE YEARS OF MICHAEL's growing out of boyhood presented Emily with plenty of agitations, a long succession of problems. They were not, she recognized, in any sense unique or even unusual; they were the worries that all mothers of sons had to face, though that knowledge hardly lessened their special importance to her or made them any easier to bear. The fact that they grew more complicated in form, more difficult to get at as Michael grew older did not dismay her too much. She had confidence that each problem would work itself out in the end as the earlier ones had, those stubborn problems of the past,—bed-wetting, refusing to drink milk, "forgetting" to brush teeth, sucking thumb, biting nails, teasing sister, reading with eyes to the light and book in shadow, and so on.

But there was one problem that never dissolved; it was with her always, chronic, persistent. It was the central problem, she felt, for upon it depended the right solution of everything now. It was the problem of bringing Michael and Stephen together as much as possible, to give the boy every opportunity to be under the influence of the man.

But now, when he was most needed as father, Stephen was simply not there. He had almost no time anymore for his family: every month that passed seemed to carry him a little farther away from them all, to sink him a little more deeply in his eternal business affairs. Days when he was not at the offices of Fenwick and Company on Bay Street, he was at Land's End or the Coosaw River plant, or in Charleston or Savannah or Augusta; his grips were forever being packed and unpacked.

For her own part, she felt resigned to the situation. The change had been gradual, there had been plenty of time to adjust herself by degrees to living largely without him. Once it would have been impossible to believe that she could be content with so little of him in her life, but that was before the children had begun to use her up in earnest; when they were through with her for the day, there was as little left of her as there was of Stephen after business. And it helped to reconcile her to her loss of him to see that his energies spent away from home were steadily strengthening the security of home and the future of the children. It was not cotton padding she wanted for them, but a good start; already the time was approaching to begin to plan about college for Michael.

Even the cold fact that Stephen no longer took her into his confidence, asked her advice as of old, was endurable when it was becoming increasingly clear that he knew exactly what he was about. She had felt in the beginning that he was deliberately sacrificing, burying, the more sensitive parts of his nature for the sake of success, prosperity at any cost: poverty and defeat had always held so mortal a terror for him. But she wondered now if she had not been mistaken there, he had developed talents for business with such ease. In any case, there was no doubt about his success: in his business world he was greatly respected and trusted, and—what was evidently more important in some quarters—feared. But the only comments he made to her about all this were when they went over the bills together at the end of the month and he smiled at her carefulness, her little economies.

"Honey, when are you going to wake up to the fact that we're rich? No need for all this cramping. I want you to stop counting pennies, like a New England shopkeeper. I want you to splurge a little. I want to see a dressmaker around here working on you. Have some new clothes made. I'll get the material next time I go to Charleston."

Once when she had asked him some question about a piece of Port Royal waterfront she knew he had bought (she had promised herself immediately afterwards never to repeat that mistake), he had answered shortly: "Now don't you fret about my business, dear. Home's your sphere,—God knows you have your hands full. You tend to your business, I'll tend to mine. Perfect combination—partners. Neither any good without the other, but each operating in his own sphere. Isn't that reasonable?"

Reasonable enough, she had had to admit. And as each year went by and she became more accustomed to the arrangement, the more reasonable it seemed. And it would have been quite acceptable, but for one thing: the children.

What's become, she wondered with an ache, of the Steve who used to walk the floor in the middle of the night with "Michaelovitch Bawlski"? If he gave any time to the children now, it was certain to be Margaret or Jack. They were children still and could he handled as such, while Michael was fast becoming something else, a person of rapidly shifting moods and baffling tenses, an individual requiring more than superficial attention. And the longer his arms and legs stretched, the more awkward his hands and feet became, particularly the more his eyes revealed the turmoil of deepening awareness of himself and the world about him, the more Stephen seemed inclined to avoid any intimate contact with him.

"That son of yours," he told her, "is just one too many for me."

"But, dear, you don't try to understand him. You've forgotten what you went through at that age."

"You're quite mistaken. I remember very well indeed what it was like to be all arms and legs. But there was none of this supersensitive business with me. He reads too much, for one thing,—ten times as much as I read at his age. You let him pore over that set of Dickens till his eyes are popping out of his head. I suppose he'll be going into the Shakespeare set next. And Mother feeds him Thackeray. Is it any wonder he's got a morbid imagination?"

There was no longer any use trying to thresh a point out with Stephen. His patience was too short to brook any contradiction.

But Michael was not always "your son". There were times when he was spoken of as heir to the business, and then he was "our son" or "my son". She knew that Stephen expected him to step into Fenwick & Co., when it would become Fenwick & Son, and later—when Jack joined—Fenwick & Sons; that was already understood, taken for granted, all settled. And perhaps, she thought, he'll want to. But she was bent on seeing that he had as free a chance as possible to decide that for himself. In her own heart other plans for him were forming, vague as yet, but certainly opposed to Stephen's. There must be something better for him than the second-hand routine of a business that his father had built. He must create something for himself: he must have a profession of his own, some work that would bring out the best in him, engage his deepest interest, develop to the full the potentialities of his mind and spirit. . . . But as yet there was no need to worry much about Fenwick & Son. Stephen was evidently going to wait till Michael was well out of the "too-much-for-me" stage before he began any actual grooming of him for the firm.

Meanwhile his neglect was causing her to turn more and more to Rusty for help. Michael must have a man to look up to, someone he could feel close to, imitate and pattern himself after, someone who would influence and guide him: that much was clear and certain. That the man could not be his own father was a great misfortune, but not a complete misfortune, since the substitute was a man for whom her admiration had deepened to bedrock with the increasing years of their friendship. As time went by and the favorable aspect of the situation grew in her consciousness, regrets faded. And finally any remnant sense of disloyalty to Stephen that she still felt was dispelled in an instant by Stephen himself on Michael's thirteenth birthday.

He had stayed home from the Commercial Club that evening to help chaperone the party. It was afterwards, when they were undressing for bed and she had one of her rare opportunities to talk with him when he was not sodden from an evening of highballs and cards, that she brought up a subject that had been on her mind for a long while and had come to the front with particular force today. She began hesitantly, for it was difficult enough to discuss the simplest matters with him these days, and there was nothing simple about this matter; every word, she felt, had to be carefully chosen.

"Steve, have you ever talked to Michael, about himself?"

He looked up at her blankly from unlacing his shoes.

"What do you mean?"

"About himself. About his—oh, you must know what I mean!"

"I'm sorry, but I haven't the ghost of an idea what you mean."

She floundered helplessly. "Things he ought to know about himself. Haven't you told him anything?"

Understanding and amusement came into his eyes. "I see! You want to know if I've called his attention to the fact that he's changing from a boy into a man, is that it?"

She nodded her relief.

He shook his head. "No, dear."

"Well, don't you think you ought to talk to him?"

"Why?"

"Why, for every reason. Isn't it better to have his knowledge come from us, from you, than from outside sources, the village boys, or— just anyone?"

"Now isn't that just like a mother. I'm afraid, dear, I'd be a little late. I guess there aren't many facts of life he hasn't picked up by this time."

He smiled at her while she pondered that in obvious dismay.

"Now, darling, put your mind at rest. A boy comes by his knowledge in his own way, like a puppy. He doesn't require any information or stimulation from his parents."

"But I really think you ought to say something to him."

His smile frayed into impatience then.

"What is this, another of your schoolmarm theories? It's a wonder you didn't tell the parents of your pupils back in your nigger-teaching days that they should instruct their children in sex! Now, look here, who would naturally know best about male problems, you or I? I don't know anything about Yankee practices, but I know my own father never told me anything and I can't see I'm any the worse for it. I picked up my knowledge from other boys and the servants in the house, if you want to know the truth. And I'm sure that's a damn sight more natural method than the shock and embarrassment of a fatherly sermon on keeping your mind pure and your privates clean, and steering clear of girls with loose ways and diseases."

"Sermons," he added more gently, "don't do any good. You've just got to trust to luck, and pray a little if you like. Of course we'll try to keep him away from the wrong kind of girls, at least till he's old enough to sow his wild oats with some discretion, but that's all we can do."

But she continued to protest. "Steve, you've got to say something to him. It's a mistake for us to avoid the whole subject with him, as if it were something shameful and evil and nasty. It's a mistake to leave him to find out things for himself, furtively, on the sly, in dark corners, away from us."

"You've got a hopelessly exaggerated and silly slant on the thing. Can't you see that?"

"No, I can't," she answered weakly. "I think you have the wrong slant."

"Well, that's where we disagree,—that's all. But if you think telling him things will do any good, go ahead. You have my permission and best wishes. You can give him little talks on the holy temple of his body, and tell him about the mating of the birds and flowers."

"If that's the way you feel about it, I'll ask Rusty to talk to him."

"Fine! Say, why didn't you have sense enough to marry Rusty in the first place?—he'd have made a perfect father for you. But it's not too late even now. Call in the Doc by all means. He can show Mike a chart of his anatomy and give him lectures on personal hygiene. Whoop the thing up, the pair of you, you're always in cahoots,—get the boy hipped on the subject. Only get one thing straight. I didn't start this argument, but I'm going to finish it. You can get as hysterical as you like about this thing, but count me out. I don't want any part of it."

After that conversation she felt no further reluctance in turning to Rusty for help in every problem of Michael's coming of age.

Whenever Rusty was able to get away from Charleston and his work at the hospital, she packed him and Michael off in the launch or sailboat for a day at Land's End or Bay Point, where they could surf-fish, watch the sea birds, or just loaf and talk. But such opportunities were rare: Rusty could seldom come to Beaufort now for a week-end. So she was reduced finally to letting Michael spend part of his school holidays in Charleston. And during the summer vacations she let him spend several weeks there. On these visits Rusty took Michael "calling" with him, and to his office at the hospital when there was not too much going on there; and sometimes they were able to take the ferry across the harbor for a few vagrant hours on Sullivan's Island and Isle of Palms. The rest of the time Michael filled in with some boys of the Legare Street neighborhood whose parents Miss Sophie knew and pronounced safe wardens for her grandson.

But even the longest visits to Charleston came to be considered mere makeshifts by Emily. In the end she found herself actually looking forward to the time of dread separation when Michael would be going off to the Citadel School there. Then he could stay with Rusty and be constantly under Rusty's eye and influence.

What college he was going to afterwards could still be considered an entirely undecided problem, though there had already been some stiff tilting about it between Miss Sophie and Stephen. Miss Sophie, who had made up her mind that Michael was going into Public

Life ("a statesman, Emily,—not a politician"), was in agreement with her brother Joe in favoring Harvard Law; Harvard might be a Yankee institution, but it belonged to the family tradition, having been purified for all time of any sectional taint by the attendance of three generations of Bramwells: Joe, his father, and his grandfather. This was in direct opposition to Stephen's stated intention of sending Michael to the University of Virginia.

"I seem to have made out fairly well without benefit of college. But if he's got to waste several years, he can do it just as well—better —at a Southern college. Virginia was good enough for his Grand-father Fenwick and his Uncle Larry. I guess it's good enough for him."

Emily kept out of these discussions. It was her secret hope that when the time came Michael himself would decide in favor of Charleston Medical College, where Rusty was a trustee and lecturer in surgery. But it was too soon to expose her hope, except to Rusty. He was her fellow conspirator.

Before Michael had begun to grow up in earnest, Rusty had once remarked to her: "I'd never want a son of mine to go in for general practice or surgery."

"Not medicine at all?" she had asked in alarm, for the hope of Rusty's profession for Michael had already taken root.

"Medicine, yes. But let him go in for the science of medicine, pathology, laboratory work. Research is the thing."

"Have you ever wanted to do research work?" she had asked him.

"More than anything. But I haven't the background. And when you're in practice, it's hard to stop for study. You feel you're needed where you are. And then of course there's the old element of iner-tia,—you decide research had better be left to gifted youngsters."

And he had added: "It takes special gifts to get anywhere in a laboratory. As well as luck and the most dogged kind of perseverance and faith."

"Do you think," she had asked him, "Michael could ever become a great scientist in medicine?"

"Would you like that for him?" he had smiled at her.

"More than anything."

"Well, it might be arranged. At least we can try to steer him in that direction."

That had been the beginning of the conspiracy. From that time on there had never been any question about what she hoped for Michael's future. And though they seldom spoke of it even obliquely, she knew that Rusty was with her, seconding her hope and furthering it by every means in his power.

But it was still almost three years to the Citadel, and beyond that three more years to Medical College. It was very strange to be trying to speed time. But that was what she found herself doing: counting the months, trying to hasten Michael's separation from her and from home, straining for the autumn when he would leave for Charleston and Rusty's wing.

"What are you smiling about so smugly?"

It was Christmas Eve of '91, and she was enjoying one of her few chances to have Rusty to herself. They were sitting before the living-room fire, waiting for Stephen to come back from the Commercial Club to hang up the stockings and put the presents out under the tree, whose tinsel ornaments and colored balls glistened expectantly in the lamplight near the piano. The children were long since in bed, Michael worn out from an all-day expedition with Rusty to Hilton Head,—a not entirely bootless excursion, Miss Sophie had admitted, for they had brought back holly, a bucket of oysters for the turkey dressing, and some sea trout for Christmas breakfast. Eugenia had retired early, as usual; and Miss Sophie had left in disgust after three successive checkmates at Rusty's hands, vowing to confound him in the morning with a new opening from the "Chess Chronicle" of the paper. Emily had played a pair of games with him, but then they had put the board aside for talk.

"It isn't a smug smile," he told her.

"Indeed it is. It couldn't possibly be any smugger,—you just can't see from the inside how smug it is. I'd be ashamed to get any satisfaction out of that last easy mate."

"Still a little piqued?"

"Naturally. I wasn't watching when you took my queen, and after that you couldn't have lost if you'd tried. Now tell me I shouldn't have opened with my king's-bishop pawn or been so bold with my knights or castled when I did."

He got up with a chuckle and went into the library to fill his pipe from the belly of Toby Fillpot on the mantel.

"It wouldn't do any good," he said to her from there. "Your mind would still wander off to the bigger game."

When he came back into the room and took up the tongs to turn the fire log, she asked him mockingly: "How can you tell when my mind's wandering?"

"Well, I'd hate to think what my chess would be like if I had three growing youngsters. And one of them almost as tall as his father."

"I suppose you think I don't think about anything but the children."

For answer he held up his pipe. "Look at that,—fresh tobacco. Trouble with you is you think about everybody but yourself."

She reached out for his hand. "Oh, I do think about you occasionally. But not nearly as much as I should. Now come and sit down and let me catch up with you. What about that new ophthalmic ward you're working for at the hospital?"

He shook his head. "No, we're going to talk about Michael, Margaret, and Jack."

"No we're not," she protested firmly. "Do please, Rusty, help me to get away from them all for a few minutes. Tell me what's going on in the world."

"As far as I know, the same old things."

"But I'm serious. I need some fresh air. Why, I don't think of anything anymore beyond the family and this house."

"Isn't that enough? What more do you want?"

"I want to think about things in general. And read some good books again, and talk about them the way we used to. That's going to be my New Year's resolution. Oh, you can smile, but it's not funny never being able to concentrate on anything but home and the children. And the situation's getting worse all the time."

"Can't you save chess and books and abstract thought for a little later, when the children are grown?"

"Oh, I'll be hopelessly ingrown by then."

"You happen to be the most outgrowing person I know. Emily, I'm afraid you're indulging in a little exaggeration."

But she was afraid not. It was true that scarcely anything beyond the circle of home existed for her now; everything that happened be- yond the high gates of Marshlands seemed so remote and irrelevant. The only newspaper that would have had real meaning for her would have been a sort of home journal. Its headlines would have gripped and held her.

MICHAEL SLAYS FIRST DEER

BRINGS DOWN EIGHT-POINT BUCK
WITH PARKER SHOTGUN
ONE BARREL AT TWENTY YARDS

MOTHER BOWS TO TRADITION
BUT BARELY SURVIVES ORDEAL

Following in the footsteps of his ancestors the fourteen-year-old son of Mr. & Mrs. Stephen Fenwick attended the Christmas hunt on the Combahee River plantation of his great-uncle, Judge Joseph Bramwell, and brought down a splendid buck. He was credited with having conducted himself like a true sportsman when bloodied by his father, but there was much chaffing later when he carved his first saddle of venison and refused to touch his own plate. . . .

CLOSE CALL FOR MARGARET AND JACK

CHILDREN HAVE NARROW ESCAPE
AT BAY POINT

On an outing at the beach yesterday Margaret and Jack Fenwick had a bad scare when a man-eating shark grazed so close to them that they could feel the swish of the tail fin. They had gone with their grandmother and Lucy for a day of crabbing and hunting conch shells and king's crowns. There was no surf to speak of, and after lunch Grandma had allowed them to go wading. It was Lucy who saw the fin cutting toward them like a little sail and gave the alarm just in time. . . .

MICHAEL LAUNCHES RAFT

BEAUFORT RIVER SEES STRANGE CRAFT

Inspired by Huckleberry Finn *and with the aid of several schoolmates Michael last Saturday launched a log raft, which filled Mother with graver misgivings than had any of his reading-inspired exploits since the* Swiss Family Robinson *tree house. Her fears were duly confirmed this morning, when the raft attempted a maiden voyage across the "Mississippi" to the Ladies Island shore, with Jack aboard against orders. The ebb-tide current carried the unmanageable craft down-stream and stranded it on the marsh flats below town. A rescue was effected by Tunis and the yard boy in a batteau. . . .*

FENWICK & CO. PLAN PORT ROYAL DEVELOPMENT
FORESEE GREAT PORT AT TERMINAL

Last night Stephen Fenwick announced that he has com-pleted the purchase and leasing of key properties on the Port Royal waterfront for the construction of docks, warehouses, and a grain elevator. Work will start as soon as contracts can be let. . . .

A ROOM OF HIS OWN AT LAST
LIBRARY CONVERTED INTO BEDROOM
FOR MICHAEL

On his fifteenth birthday and soon after the opening of his final year at grammar school, Michael was moved out of his corner of the "children's room" and installed, with his books and bird pictures and an accumulation of very personal be-longings, in a room of his own downstairs. At the same time it was decided that in a year or so a wing with another bath would have to be added to the house, for him and Margaret and Jack. The library would then be redeemed, and Mother and Father would move into the big room from their present quarters, which would become the guest room. . . .

If Michael featured in most of these mental headlines, it was not because of any lack of Margaret and Jack news. There was plenty of both. Margaret was what Miss Sophie called a "naturally good child, as lovely and gentle as her looks"; and certainly she was easier to manage than the boys. But she was a delicate girl,—growing too fast, Miss Sophie thought; she was the member of the family most susceptible to anything contagious in the air, and she was always getting hurt in the games of the boys who came to the house: her mishaps alone would have been enough to keep her on the front page of the home journal. Jack, on the other hand, kept in the lime-light by continually getting into hot water; he was forever embroiled in some sort of trouble; he loved action and hilarious excitement, and when they did not exist in his surroundings he created them.

389

Miss Sophie, who was the first to damn him when he trod on her toes, was the first to take his side when anyone else took him to task. "He can't help it," she would condone; "he's a direct throwback to Yemassee Jack Bramwell. And besides, it's a healthy sign,—a young colt should be frisky. I'm always suspicious of a boy that behaves too well. Deliver me from that kind of a grandson." She was thoroughly delivered, as Jack frisked from one healthy sign to another.

But Michael held first place in the family news. In these momentous years of his growing toward manhood the things that were happening to him were of more importance than any other developments within the gates of Marshlands. All the biggest headlines were his, reaching at last that supremely important culmination point:

MICHAEL TO ENTER CITADEL NEXT AUTUMN!

✓   ✓   ✓

The imminence of the Citadel separation was not the only factor, or even the chief factor, in Emily's final realization that her son was no longer a boy. There were several striking circumstances, belonging to the spring of '93, any one of which would have been enough to jar her into full awareness of the change that had taken place so slowly under her eyes.

His voice could now command, when he was talking with his father or Rusty or Uncle Joe, really dramatic depths, though in unguarded moments with her and Grandma and Lucy it was still apt to go treble. And he was training his hair as well as his voice: hours were given to the fretful mirror struggle to make that stubborn black mop lie back flat. And there was the first long trousers, a pair of Stephen's altered remarkably little, in which he appeared at St. Helena's on Easter. The following Sunday, experimenting with his father's razor, he cut himself so badly that he had to stay home from church.

But it was something else that most poignantly completed her realization.

After Michael had outgrown the period of contemptuous indifference toward girls, there had been a series of yearnings. Suddenly girl-conscious, he had gone rapidly through all the pretty girls at school, exchanging heaven alone knew what inner pangs and jealousies for their unabashed coquetries, skillful note-passings, and capable maneuverings. During this feverish phase Linda Robinson had been the only girl, except Margaret, with whom he could be natural: his relationship with her remained as spontaneous and companionable as with boys. But now, this spring, it was evident that a great change had come over their friendship.

The summer before, when the family had again rented Oakmont at Flat Rock, Michael had formed an attachment that had cost Emily some real worry. Waits Pittman's oldest girl was plain but lusty, and—in Miss Sophie's phrase—"a little too knowing". The situation might have been worked out calmly if Miss Sophie had not felt it necessary to take extreme measures. She had begun by removing the girl from all work in the house; but not satisfied with that, because she was less able than ever to keep track of Michael, she had paid a peremptory call at the Pittman cottage and demanded of Mrs. Pittman that the girl be confined to her home. This had been too much for the mountain blood of the Pittmans: relations between house and cottage had been strained beyond mending. And the reaction on Michael had been toxic: his interest in Millie Pittman had become a lingering sickness, which he had carried back with him to the Low Country.

For this reason particularly Emily had been relieved and pleased when he had begun to forget Millie in Linda. But his new interest would have been pleasing to her in any case: if the choice had been her own, she couldn't have picked a more satisfactory object for his youthful dreams and affections. As Miss Sophie said, "There must have been good blood from somewhere in the Robinsons to produce such a girl." It showed in her frank eyes, her slender hands, the bone structure of her tanned face, the even whiteness of her teeth, the natural grace of her strong lithe body. And she was as fine as she looked: she rang true all the way through.

She had already passed the awkward stage and gained the first poise of her womanhood, while Michael was still trying to shed the last vestiges of boyhood, trying to appear at ease on the threshold of manhood. What misery to be in love with so many handicaps,—self-conscious eyes, treacherous voice, unmanageable hair, halting tongue, gawky arms and legs. And his agony could not have been much assuaged by the daze his changed relations with Linda produced in him. He seemed himself to be puzzled, in the beginning, by his desire to go to Land's End at every opportunity.

It pleased Stephen, who decided his son was finally taking an interest in the phosphate branch of the business. If he noticed that Michael spent most of his time at the mines hanging around the commissary, where Linda helped her father, he certainly saw no particular significance in it or he would have spoken of it. And at first Emily attached no great importance to the new love; her only feeling was that Linda was the best possible solution of the problem at this period. She could be sure that Linda, in contrast to other girls, was not disturbing him selfishly. Ample proof that he was in good hands came with the approach of the grammar school examinations: when he showed an inclination to shirk his studies for too-frequent visits to Land's End, Linda used her influence to keep him at his books.

It was not till late in the spring that the depths of his devotion became apparent. One evening at supper Stephen announced to the family a golden journey, and when the table had been cleared, he spread out a map to illustrate the route: first, New York and Newport, where Miss Sophie had summered with her parents before the War; then on to the Chicago Exposition in the cool of September, by way of Lake George and Saratoga Springs, where Grandfather Fenwick had once kept a racing stable. The family was wildly excited about the plan, with the exception of Michael. Emily saw his frown grow darker as the journey was discussed from every angle; and when just before his bedtime he used her presence as a shield to talk to his father, she guessed what was coming. He wanted to stay at Land's End for the summer, work at the commissary, while the family was away. When he had gone upstairs, Stephen shook his head.

"Can you beat that? I tell you, that boy has me stumped. Here I've been hoping he'd show some interest in things, and now—just at the wrong time—he suddenly develops a little initiative. But I can't let him miss this trip. He's got to go. And I don't want any nonsense from him about it."

He was spared any nonsense about it. The next day she talked to Michael, and in the end he accepted the prospect of traveling far away from Linda. As for enthusiasm all Emily could do was trust that it would replace acceptance when the journey actually began.

It came out now that Stephen's original plans for the summer had been expansive indeed: a trip abroad. But business was in the doldrums; a "cyclical readjustment", he called it. Nothing to be alarmed about, but under the circumstances he felt it would be wiser to tackle a less ambitious plan, one that would take him not too far from his base. Europe could wait till Fenwick & Co. was better able to get along without him, and the children grown to more appreciative ages.

May was a month of furious preparations. Dressmaking was the chief activity; everyone had to have new clothes, from Miss Sophie to Lucy. Eugenia went into such an orgy of puffed sleeves and flounced skirts and giddy hats that Stephen wanted to know if she thought she was going on a wedding journey. "With that trousseau," he told her, "you won't look decent without a man." And because she was well pleased with the additions to her wardrobe, for which he had given her a special check, she received his chaffing about making Newport and Saratoga sit up and take notice in amazingly good part. Emily had never seen her in such high spirits. But then the whole family was elated as never before. Even Michael began to show a little excitement toward the end of the month.

By the first day of June everything was in readiness. Memorial Day was past, Michael was safely graduated, the summer matting was down, the slip-covers were on the furniture, the silver trunk had been taken to the bank. And then, on the very eve of departure, there was a sudden delay.

Miss Sophie was the unhappy cause. She had finished her preparations a full week in advance of the great date: every article in her room had been carefully covered or put away, even the pictures on the walls had been taken down and stored in bureau drawers, and in her impatience she had gone so far with her traveling-cases that she had continually been forced to unpack this or that to "make out". On the last day, in getting down a bandbox from the shelf of her closet for something or other that she had forgotten—she had pieces of reminding string tied round most of her fingers—she lost her balance on the chair and fell. "Don't know how on earth it happened, I just suddenly got light-headed and everything went black as night." Although badly bruised and shaken, she insisted it was nothing. But when Rusty came from Charleston to see her, he found a sprained wrist and shoulder and said they must be allowed to heal before she could travel. At that she might have overruled him, if her nose had not been quite so prominently skinned.

As bags were unpacked and the silver brought back from the bank, there was an acute prostration of spirits. Only Michael seemed pleased at the delay: he went to Land's End every morning on the Company launch. Everyone else was at the worst of loose ends. Miss Sophie was in what she herself admitted was a "terrible pet". Eugenia relapsed into melancholy. Ella and Tunis were irritable because their vacation was being postponed, and Lucy suffered by contagion. And Margaret and Jack were able to concentrate on no games. The magic-lantern Rusty had given them, which had not yet lost its Christmas novelty, was of some help, and in this emergency they were permitted to seal all light from the living-room two or even three times a day. But soon the last glamour faded from the grotesque slides on the hot sheet, and there was nothing left for the children to do but fret till Grandma's wrist and shoulder and nose healed.

And when they were healed, a second obstacle checked departure. While the family—except Michael—stewed in disappointment, Stephen wrestled with some last-minute problems of the Port Royal project. He expected to be able to leave from day to day, but there was a hitch in one of the contracts and the delay extended into weeks.

So June passed, Miss Sophie was able to enjoy the new fig crop after all, and Emily was able to do some preserving. But those were the only compensations for the increasing fret and fume to get off. "When I'm all set to go somewhere," Miss Sophie declared, "I want to *go!*" On the first of July Stephen decided they would have to leave without him. He was sorry, but there was no other way out: the Port Royal complications might hold him up for a week or two longer, and there was too much at stake for him to leave things in the hands of subordinates. He would join them in Newport as soon as possible.

The tension was released just in time to save the family from exploding of internal combustion. But Emily was distressed that he was not leaving with them. He was frayed out with the Port Royal business and sorely in need of a change and rest.

The morning of the departure Emily awoke at daybreak, but lay quiet to let Stephen get as much sleep as he could. But Miss Sophie was already astir in her room. First, a chair was dragged across the floor and back, over Michael's head; then, the window shades were released with sharp reports; and finally, there was a great shooing of blue-jays off the beds of the rose garden, followed by an extended argument with Tunis in the back yard. Unconsciously, perhaps, Miss Sophie was doing her best to rouse the house, and she presently succeeded. Michael came up to the bathroom, Lucy came down from the attic, and Margaret and Jack capered in the hall in a sleepy frenzy. There was not much point in lying quiet any longer for Stephen's sake. The journey had begun.

. . . A few last hurried words with Stephen at the station, Jack's shrieks of good-bye, Miss Sophie's final admonitions out the window to Tunis by the carriage. Then Conductor Gilroy's beaming face when he came to honor the passes with an elegant tip of his cap. He had a word for each member of the party, the back of his big hand smoothing the generous moustache that went so well with his big smile and the big watch-chain that crossed his bulging vest. Not Flat Rock this time? The North?—Well! The World's Fair?—Ah! And what a treat that would be, particularly the Midway for the children! But plenty to make grown-ups open their eyes: he'd read where there were exhibits from every corner of the globe, the latest contraptions of science, wonderful new-style buildings, the whole march of progress passing in review as you might say. Ah, but the Midway!—that was the thing, hey Jackie my boy? He shook all over when he chuckled.

"Can't hardly keep track of these young-ones, ma'm, they're shooting up so fast. Reckon they're all going to take after their father and run tall."

When he was gone, a smile lingered on her lips as she watched them with eyes sharpened by his words and the general excitement of the departure. In the seat across the aisle Jack sat next to the window, hemmed in by the only person who could control his nine-year-old fidgets: Lucy, proud in her new black dress, a black sailor hat over her white headcloth and single gold earring. Ahead of them Eugenia sat by herself, having resisted Margaret's overtures to keep her spreading finery company. Margaret sat here with Mother, her dreamy eleven-year-old eyes admiring her aunt, and yearning no doubt for the day when prim pigtails could be frizzed up with a bang; a really lovely child,—it was quite proper to admit that in secret. In the seat ahead Michael sat stiff and erect with his grandmother. Her alert and vehement little bonnet, trimmed with lace and tied with ribbons in a bow under her chin, was turned to him most of the time; she glanced out of the window only occasionally, and then absently. The bonnet nodded as she talked, and her ivory-headed cane tapped the floor for emphasis. He was plainly suffering from the fact that she seemed to feel no necessity for lowering her voice from the people in the car. His own voice came seldom and then very deep, as befitting the man of the party, while she rattled on, gaining momentum with the train.

"Southerners made Newport, of course," she was telling him. "Even before the Revolution packets ran there regularly from Charleston. The Fenwicks never went there, to the best of my knowledge,—they preferred Virginia Springs. But it was a favorite place of sojourn with your Great-Grandfather Bramwell, and in his day many of the most representative low-country families still frequented the place. I was first taken there as a young girl, a mere child, but I well remember what a gay colony it was then. . . ."

. . . Charleston, with Rusty as the only point of stability in the agitated wait between trains. In this brief hour the family was recklessly scattered: Emily stayed with Rusty and Eugenia and the luggage in the waiting-room, Lucy took Jack and Margaret to stretch their legs in the neighboring streets, and Miss Sophie rushed Michael off in a hack to the City Hall to see the Trumbull portrait of Washington. It was an expedition she had planned weeks ago, when she had learned that there would be an hour's wait at Charleston. The portrait had been painted, she explained, just before Washington's stay at the Bramwell plantation on the Combahee, so Michael simply must see it.

They got back with only a minute to spare. Emily had been too anxious about them to breathe freely with Rusty; the precious moment with him had been distracted by frantic pictures of departing trains and missed connections. And she had hoped Michael would have a little time with him. But Miss Sophie had to blast even the minute of good-bye with her disappointment in the portrait: It might be good as a *painting* but it was *wretched* in every other respect, or at least it certainly wasn't flattering with its sickly pale forehead and sunburned nose and false teeth out, and what on earth was the point in a portrait so unseemly?—why, she infinitely preferred the portrait of Beauregard hanging in the same chamber. By the time she was through there was barely time for scrambled good-byes with

Rusty. Never mind, Emily thought, he'll have Michael under his wing from next autumn on. But as the train began to move and she exchanged hurried last words with him, a sudden pang of distress flashed into her voice. "If you were only going with us! Couldn't you come with Steve? But please don't work too hard.—Go to Land's End as often as you can.—Promise me, Rusty. . . ." And the pang stayed with her, together with her final glimpse of him on the platform and his farewell words—*I'll be with you in spirit*—and the last wave of his hand, long after the train had clanged out of town and was rushing and crying through the pinelands. I'll write you, she told him: I'll write you the kind of letters I used to when you first went to Charleston, before so many things came to divide us. . . .

And then the utter confusion of New York, a night and a day of complete stupefaction. Stephen had insisted they stay at the fabulous new Waldorf-Astoria instead of the old Fifth Avenue Hotel, though any quiet place would have been preferable to this mad "Rendezvous of the Elite", where spectacular figures of Society and Fashion rubbed shoulders with Barons of Wall Street and Rough Diamonds from the West. But Miss Sophie was not daunted for an instant by "Peacock Alley"; almost belligerently arrayed in her best,—dress of black moiré, black point-lace cap, white point-lace collar and cuffs, black kid shoes, black chantilly shawl, fine gold chain from neck to watch pocket at belt, *and* the remarkable brooch with its miniature of herself in youth,—she paraded her family through the lobby. They all seemed delighted with the great city. But when it was over and the party was settled again in a pullman, Emily could recall only a dire bewilderment of tall buildings and crowded streets, show-windows and getting in and out of cabs, stamp and book stores and the bird wing of the Natural History Museum for Michael, and faces—haunting faces, hungry faces, hurrying scurrying faces. . . .

And then finally, the moment of arrival. The jolt of the train stopping before daylight at Wickford Junction, the jarring switch-off of the car onto a siding, the clanging and panting of the engine and its fading away at last into distance, leaving a prostration of silence that accented the breathing and drowsy whisperings from the berths of intimate strangers. Margaret waking up in her arms and peeking under the shade for a first dim glimpse of the new world. Then the difficulties of dressing, the sleepy exit from the

cramped stuffy car, the chilly half-awake ride to the ferry. . . .
Trim white-and-green farm houses, neat stone walls and orderly
fields and pastures revealed themselves in the mystic dawning light,
bringing back nostalgic memories of girlhood days at Salem. This
she had been expecting, but she was unprepared for a resurgence of
such force. And she had forgotten how great was the contrast between this country of her birth and the country of her adoption,
the brooding languid old sea-island world.

On the ferry even Michael's eyes shone as he forgot his man-of-
the-family dignity in the excitement of approaching Newport. Jack,
who was celebrating his final release from trains, could hardly be
confined with Margaret to the newspapers Miss Sophie had spread
for them on the mist-wet seat: he leaned so far over the briny cold
rail that she had to hang on to him with one hand while she pointed
her cane with the other. This was Beaver Tail Light they were rounding, on the tip of Canonicut Island. Now Jamestown was on the left,
Aquidneck Island on the right, Newport ahead,—that was Trinity's
white steeple rising above the trees. . . . Emily's impressions and
enjoyment came to her by way of the children, intensified and
heightened. She saw through their eyes the silvery loveliness of the
harbor, the sailboats and yachts floating like magic in the diaphanous
light, the calm reaches of water and land and sky blended in a single
dream-like entrancement. It was as if all the beauty of the world
were focused here to welcome them. And she thought, If Stephen and
Rusty were only with us, this moment would stand matchless. . . .

After the turbulence of the docking, there was the confusion of
getting the family and the luggage into the hotel omnibus. Then a
jouncy climb up steep cobblestoned streets, past Touro Square, across
Bellevue Avenue, and under a gateway arch onto a smooth shady
drive. And there before them at last loomed the great Ocean House,
its long façade and tiers of verandahs resplendent in the first golden
shafts of the sun.

And at first glimpse it seemed that the reality was more magnificent than the "views" that had answered Stephen's inquiries. But only
at first glimpse. Where were the galleries hanging over a tumble of
surf on a rugged coast, with a sea of limitless blue stretching away
to the ends of the world? The Ocean House was lost in a park of
majestic elms. And the only sight of the sea was in the picture at the
top of the breakfast bill-of-fare.

IX

For the first two or three days the charms of Aquidneck, "Isle of Peace", were obscured by the confusion of getting settled. But when the adjustment period was over and a routine had been worked out for the children, the beauty of the place began to assert itself.

In the mornings, while Miss Sophie and Eugenia went window-shopping along old Thames Street in the town or stayed to chat on the verandahs of the hotel, Emily took the children with Lucy to the beach. A rather pathetic little affair of coarse sand and pebbles in a rock-bound cove, it suffered particularly in the inevitable comparisons with the fine wide beaches of the Sea Islands. Miss Sophie, who was finding nothing but change and decay in even the natural aspects of Newport, paid it one visit and pronounced it impossible. "Not a shell, but plenty of seaweed and trash. And undertow. And freezing cold water for cramps. Yankee beach, Emily." She didn't see how she could have enjoyed it as a child. Michael shared her disapproval; most of the morning he spent on the rocks watching the sea birds and sunning himself and dreaming, or reading in the shade of the bath-house. But Margaret's and Jack's critical sense was not yet developed to the point of destructive contrasts: to them a beach was a beach, and one was as good as another. And Emily had no fault to find with any frame of land and water and sky that held her three. Besides, for Margaret and Jack at least, there were playmates; among the ladies and gentlemen of Newport bathing was evidently not fashionable, but there were plenty of children on the beach.

In the afternoons Miss Sophie liked to take the entire family out for the air in two carriages, along shady and assured Bellevue Avenue, with its elaborate "cottages", and on out Ocean Drive to bare open country, where ambitious newcomers were building Italian villas and gardens in honest hard-bitten old stonewalled Yankee sea fields. The journey was a congestion of very dressy people in flashy turnouts: victorias, coaches, phaetons; swank traps and swankier dog-carts; elegant tandems and more elegant four-in-hands; high-stepping horses, ramrod footmen, glistening and clanking harness. Vulgar display, Miss Sophie called it.

"In the old days," she said with feeling, "nice people from the South and the North came here and lived simply, pleasuring themselves naturally and with dignity. Not a trace of this artificiality and idiotic parading. There were no upstart rich then, and no 'show-places'. And who on earth are they, these people? Where did they come from? What are their antecedents? It's plain to be seen they're bloated with money, but what about taste and intelligence? Our best people indeed! The truth of the matter is that real society has been dead as mutton since the War, except for a few isolated communities like Charleston. You may be sure money alone never made a society and never will."

She never failed to complain of the circus-like traffic that cluttered up the highway and made quiet enjoyment of the scenery impossible. But she never missed her afternoon drive.

Her grandchildren soon lost interest in the spectacular social aspects of Newport, and finally Grandma was unable even to bribe them into taking the air with her and Aunt Eugenia. They preferred to go on foot with Mother and Lucy to one or another of the picnic spots, or to Cliff Walk skirting the high sea lawns of the Bellevue Avenue estates, from which you could look down at clear green water sliding in over rock ledges and splashing up into brilliant spray. Even Michael was soberly finding Newport full of delights. It was only Miss Sophie who continued to find nothing but faults and disappointments in the place. However, she derived inverted but intense pleasure from a relentless indictment of the people.

Her fun began each morning at breakfast. Holding her gold-rimmed glasses to her eyes, for she never allowed them to pinch her delicate nose, she read with satirical inflections items from the society column of the *Newport Daily News*. ". . . And you will be interested to learn, Emily, that Mr. and Mrs. Ogden Goelet are entertaining the Grand Duke Alexander of Russia. . . . The Duke of York, Prince George of Wales, and Princess Victoria of Pless will attend the Grand Ball to be given tomorrow evening by Mrs. August

Belmont. . . ." Usually she was satisfied to read without comment, trusting the tones of her voice and the items themselves to convey withering enough implications. But sometimes a paragraph called for more explicit attention. "Mrs. Julia Ward Howe (*Aha!* the *Battle Hymn of the Republic* lady again—Mine eyes have seen the glory of the coming of the Lord—the Abolitionists' Lord of course)— Mrs. Julia Ward Howe will read a paper on *Optimism and Pessimism as Social Forces* (social fiddlesticks!), at the first meeting of the Town and Country Club at the home of Mrs. William B. Rogers (whoever she is) on Tuesday next. If there's anything I despise it's an intellectual woman, or a butterfly posing as a bluestocking. . . . And here's a notice that a golf links is being laid out in a cow pasture north of town. A pretty picture, effete millionaires, grown men, tagging around a field after balls no bigger than turtle eggs! Deliver me from these cracked people. If this is our new aristocracy, God help the country,—that's all I have to say. . . ."

But of course it wasn't: not by any means. She never seemed to tire of the sport of breaking these frail butterflies on her heavy wheel. And in exploring the foibles of the "self-styled elect" she took particular pleasure in the company of Colonel and Mrs. Williams, a handsome white-headed couple from Richmond, who were not only congenial Southerners and her own kind but also very competent guides. Through many vicissitudes and changing years the Williamses had managed to cling to the little summer cottage they had bought on their honeymoon before the War; and while they were, like Miss Sophie, mere onlookers of the gaudy present-day pageant of Newport, they were able to give her a comprehensive collection of anecdotes and family histories and could rattle at least one skeleton in the closet of every great house on the Avenue. They accompanied Miss Sophie and Eugenia on the afternoon drive and identified the Mighty of the colony, the Has-been's and Would-be's, the rout of Strivers and Hangers-on. After a lesson or two their apt pupil could spot for herself such conspicuous figures as James Gordon Bennett, Ward McAllister, and Harry Lehr; and soon she was on intimate terms with the Vanderbilts and the Astors, the Whitney Warrens and the Stuyvesant Fishes. In the end she had mastered even the least of the lesser lights. It whetted her appetite for the slaughter enormously.

To prolong the day's entertainment Miss Sophie often invited the Williamses to dinner at the hotel. Emily would leave them to go for an evening stroll with Michael, leave them chatting busily on the verandah or in a corner of the lobby, and return an hour or so later to find them still huddled amiably over the corpses of the Herman Oelrichses or the Pierre Lorillards. They were as merry and unmerciful as a trio of coachmen exchanging backstairs gossip.

In her first letter to Stephen, she attempted nothing more than family news and a few surface impressions of Newport to supplement Miss Sophie's description of "life among the goldfish", for anything beyond that would simply have bored him. But when she wrote Rusty, she felt free to set down her thoughts.

". . . Miss Sophie is having a high old time at the expense of our best people,—that is, as much of them as she can see over the garden walls with a boost from the Williamses. Well, it does make an offensive spectacle, all this extravagant mummery. If this is the best these people can do with their wealth and power, I'm agin 'em, charity or no charity. After all, it's a pretty sad show for the price. It isn't easy to forget the wholesale poverty and misery behind the scenes, the miles of city slums we crawled through on our way here.

"The complacent palace and the festering gutter, you can't have one without the other. But why have either? If asked, I'd say eliminate both extremes, if only on the humane grounds of releasing the idle rich from their weary traces and paces. They might not like it in the beginning, but it would be a sight healthier for them in the end. And while it would destroy many high and low lights dear to the student of pure art and abstract beauty, it would certainly make a cleaner and sweeter picture for everyone else.

"I recognize the hazards of disturbing the tooth-and-claw balances of nature, and I haven't forgotten the cautioning you once gave me about remembering that questions like coins have two faces, and that contrasts are what make values and meanings in the scheme of things—that bitter ultimate paradox. But don't you agree we'll have a much more valuable and satisfactory arrangement when we get around to ironing out our violent social contrasts? Some sort of great Republic is coming, you assure me, and I believe you, but what a pity we can't get together and speed up the process. Increasing knowledge and machinery, but no common will and purpose.

Meanwhile the best our leisure class can do is invent games to while away the time.

"But who am I to cast stones at these glass houses? Don't I live in a little glass house of my own? Aren't we Fenwicks parasites too, on a small but vicious enough scale? The average phosphate diver, the Land's End Mining Company reckons, is good for a year or so and a couple of hundred tons of fertilizer rock before his sinuses rot or his eardrums pop. He's lucky if he's maimed and laid off before pneumonia gets him.

"If I wrote my Steve in this vein, I'd be promptly shied into his wastebasket. He has no patience with me as a moralist, or as a mental free agent of any sort for that matter. Woman's sphere is still the home, the old plane of instinct, and anything else is out of bounds, so I have to unburden on you. I used to bother him about conditions and how the plant was gradually devouring the manhood of the island—the pick of the young men, of course, for in phosphate mining as in war it's the cream of the crop that's wanted. Why, I once asked him before I knew my place, couldn't there at least be a rule that no man be employed long enough to be injured? I was properly rebuffed. Didn't I realize that any men the Company laid off in sound health would simply go to one of the competing mines? If the business was going to be conducted on a philanthropic basis, the Company might as well balance its books and shut up shop. Business was a man's game and no place for feminine sentimentality. So I tried to mind my own home business and forget the boys I used to teach in the praise-house school. It was an enormous relief when we moved to Marshlands and I could avoid close contact with the mines. Since then I've grown a protective hide, and yet I still wince a little when I spend a day at Land's End.

"What a miserable coward I am. I talk these unpleasant matters out of my mind and return with a sigh of composure to the children.

"But it's not all composure even here. There's a sea serpent in this Eden, here at the beach where I'm writing you, and a very sly old fellow he is too. Can you believe that dark and rather aloof young man is the Michael you taught to swim? And this tallish and blossoming girl at my side, waiting impatiently to add her messages, is this the Margaret we brought into the world only a summer or two ago? As for that rowdy boy playing duck-on-the-rock over there with his new chums, if that's Jack then where is the infant of just a few minutes back, worrying even Lucy because he was learning to walk too soon and might get bow-legs? Possibly you can keep up with them, but the pace is too much for me. In my more rational moments I see the necessity of their growing up, even the desirability of it occasionally, but why can't they take their time about it? Soon I'll be left trailing superfluously in the dust, no longer needed or heeded,—that pathetic object, an outgrown mother.

"So you see there's some soul-searching and stock-taking going on up here in the bracing Yankee air. I begin to realize I must pay more attention to you and Steve before I lose both of you through long and gross neglect. I must mend my ways before it's too late and I have no-one to fall back on.

"I really am going to reform. It's time Steve got some undivided attention: I'll prepare for his arrival by weaning the children one and all. As for you, I need a return to closer communion. Certain questions have appeared on the horizon, and while they're still no bigger than a man's hand they trouble me by their stubborn refusal to disperse. Please help me nip them in the bud when we get home.

"If you were only coming with Steve! That's Michael's idea too. He's writing you a long letter in installments, but he wants me to enclose this list of birds he's seen so far. I haven't seen one of them yet. Which proves how much worthier he is of you. He won't ever fall down on you, my friend. . . ."

By the time Stephen arrived, the second week in August, the children were well weaned. It had not required much effort. They had practically weaned themselves.

Michael had made the acquaintance of two pretty girls from Hartford,—or rather, they had made his acquaintance by a series of after-dinner maneuverings in the lobby. The fact that they were sisters by no means softened their rivalry for his attention; and though he was scornful enough of their wiles, he allowed them to fight over him when he had nothing better to do. But usually his resourcefulness provided him with something more interesting. It was most likely to be a lonely expedition to Agassiz Point or 'The Reefs, with a box of lunch, a book, and Rusty's old field-glasses for the sea birds. But when the wind was right he often went for a sail around the island or to Narragansett Pier, with a retired lighthouse-keeper whose acquaintance he had made while exploring the water-front. When the weather was bad, he browsed in the Redwood Library; or paid a surreptitious visit to the Music Hall, where from a gloomy back seat he could watch a rehearsal of the "Vanguard Repertory Company". Every evening before bed his head was bowed over a long letter to Linda. And so, with one thing and another, his hands were quite full.

As for Margaret and Jack, they were now in league with all the younger elements at the hotel, so they could be depended upon to scare up almost too much amusement for themselves: the ever-vigilant Lucy was put to it to keep them within any bounds. On the Avenue they had discovered Huyler's, where you could get a big ice-cream soda for a ten-cent check. And on Thames Street, the roller-skating rink. This wildly exciting attraction,—with its blaring merry-go-round music and dizzy roar of wheels, its glaring artificial lights, stale air, and motley crowd,—held such fascination for them, and for the nursemaids of their young companions, that all their time would have been spent there if it had been allowed. But after an inspection of the place Mother had decided that despite the flushed and delighted faces with which they circled round and round, despite the triumphant grace with which they recovered from the most shocking spills, this form of entertainment would have to be restricted to rainy days. Then, when even the generous lobby and verandahs of the Ocean House were too confining for the explosive energies of Jack, the rink was distinctly the lesser of two evils.

With the children off her hands well in advance of Stephen's appearance, she had been free to make thorough plans: selecting the spots on the island most likely to please him, deciding which should be visited first, dreaming how this or that mood of her native North-ern land and sea would affect her Southerner. In the beginning, of course, he must sleep late in the mornings, for he would certainly arrive worn to nothing. But even if he stayed in bed till eleven, that was not too late to start out with lunch for a leisurely ride through the farm country north of town, where crickets sang reminiscently in sunny clover fields and apple orchards. Bicycles were the craze now and quite fashionable here; as a novelty he might submit to them once or twice,—after that he would probably want to hire saddle horses or an expensive trap. Whatever the conveyance, they need not return from their rides till the last golden light had withdrawn from the field tops and scented mists were rising in the hollows, till dusk was stealing along the old stone walls and the roadside thrilling with insect choirs.

And in the evenings, they would drive to Agassiz Point and spread a robe in some nook of the rocks, where only the faint tolling of a buoy and the muted music of the sea could reach them. Across the dark waters of the bay the lights of Narragansett would twinkle like stars, and overhead the vast real stars would shine, undimmed by moonlight. But there would be the slim burnished crescent of a new moon, and close by the evening star, the same mystic sign that had watched over their wedding night at Land's End, far away and long ago.

It was absurd to be so excited: a young girl waiting for her sweetheart could be no more tremulous. But it was absurd and spiritless to have been so discouraged about Stephen. This reunion would carry them back to the old vital intimacy, and this time she would see that it was not lost. After all, much of the fault for the waning of their marriage had been hers, and she was going to repair the damage—before, as she had written Rusty, it was too late. Yes, she was freeing herself from her intense and everlasting preoccupation with the children; and she was going to hold herself free. An opportune time: soon now Michael, her first thought for so long, would be at school in Charleston under Rusty's wing. Already she was free to meet Stephen, a Stephen free from business. And he too would be eager. Together they would recapture the lost ground. They would turn back together to the enchantment of those blessed early days at Land's End. . . .

And there were three marvelous days together. But after that things fell so quickly into a different pattern that she could only wonder if she hadn't been hypnotized by her hopes into dreaming the three days.

Across Bellevue Avenue from the Redwood Library stood the Reading Club. "Our sporting club," Colonel Williams had explained, in pointing it out as one of the sights. "They have a rack of newspapers, but that's about as far as the reading end of it goes." And on the morning of his fourth day in Newport Stephen announced that he was taking a membership. They had a stock ticker and bond and cotton quotations, and it was necessary just now to keep in close touch with the markets. Besides, it was an unusual opportunity to make important contacts, to meet some of the really big fellows and hear what they had to say about the financial situation; for whatever else Yankees were, there was no denying they were born business men, and a Southerner could well afford to take a lesson or two from them in this age of expanding trade and industrial vision. And soon he was spending all his mornings, most of his afternoons, and many of his evenings at the Reading Club. The shining sea and sparkling air, the singing fields and starlit nights of Aquidneck were speedily forgotten in telegraph clickings and market gossipings, in the chink of poker chips and the convivial tinkle of ice in tall glasses, against a background of cigar smoke and sporting prints and portraits of financial giants.

Her first rather dazed concern was to keep her distress to herself; keep it not only from him but from Miss Sophie as well, and from Eugenia, and the Williamses. She hastened to make excuses for him when Miss Sophie began to notice that he was spending "too much time at that club place".

"Why don't he take up bachelor quarters there?—it would save him the walk. You tell me he sleeps here, Emily, and occasionally I see someone that looks like him at meals. But that's about all."

"Now, dear, it's not quite that bad. And after all, isn't this his vacation? He needs to get away from his family as well as his work, once in a while."

"Nonsense, my dear,—hasn't he just had a vacation from us? It's plain selfishness. Do you realize he's been with the children only twice since he's been here? And he's taken me driving exactly once!"

"I'm sorry about that."

"Don't apologize to me, child, for the shortcomings of my own son. A wise mother learns to make no demands and to expect nothing. But there's no excuse for a man neglecting his wife."

"Goodness! dear, do I look like a neglected wife? I'd be upset if he didn't neglect me for business. And for the rest,—well, I want him to do just what he likes up here."

"Well, I don't! No man on earth was ever safe when left to his own devices. You're entirely too easy on him, Emily."

"No, seriously, I'm glad he's getting his mind off his worries. We both know he's had plenty of them lately."

"That's all very fine, my dear. But you know as well as I do that what he needs is to get out in the open air with you and the children."

To pacify Miss Sophie, she found herself pretending to meet him every afternoon at driving time, though actually he seldom left the Club till the afternoon was over. It called for some sharp practices to support this deception, but she felt they were justified, for somehow at this moment nothing seemed so important as peace in the family.

But she was not so successful in meeting the problem from another angle.

"Emily," Miss Sophie said one day when Stephen had come in very late for lunch, "I see no objection to an older man indulging himself as he pleases. The old should be allowed to get what comfort they can. But intemperance in a younger man is unreasonable. It's not good for his nerves, and I don't like to see it. His father never took spirits in any form till the day's work was done, and then never to excess. The fact that he conducts himself like a gentleman don't disguise the fact that he's had too much,—you can always tell by his eyes. I really don't know what's come over him in the past year. Something should be said about it. You've noticed it of course?"

She had been "noticing" it for a good deal longer than Miss Sophie's "past year". Ages had passed since she had sipped a tranquil glass of sherry with him. But she had always been careful not to show any serious disapproval of his drinking, his just-one-more-before-dinner visits to the sideboard. It would only have aggravated the trouble, and it would have cost the last saving dignity between them. There was that to be supremely thankful for, she had never nagged him about things. Even the mildest nagging was worse than futile, it was a perilous confession of weakness and disunion. And it quickly became a disease. No, she had safely avoided that pitfall and she was not going to fall into it now, or at any time. The solutions of problems must come from within Stephen himself, they couldn't be forced or prompted from the outside. She would certainly rather have her tongue cut out than speak to him about his drinking.

But just two days after Miss Sophie's comments, something happened at last to snap that confident resolution.

He had offered to take her for an afternoon stroll: she was to be at the entrance of the Casino at four, on the dot of course. As usual he was late, and finally she started down the Avenue to meet him. It was the driving hour, and she paused at the shop windows along the way to watch the reflected images of the equipages that passed with such an elegant clopping of hoofs and clanking of harness chains, amused at herself for being too proud to stare at them directly like any other rubberneck tourist. At the window of Worth's it was her own reflection that she studied, contrasting her homemade white muslin dress and cotton parasol with the superb patterned silks (parasols to match) beyond the glass. The striped green, labeled *"Très Recherchée"*, was still there. In the flush of excitement before Stephen's arrival she had seriously considered getting it, despite the breath-taking price; but then Eugenia had taken a mordant I-saw-it-first fancy to it, along with the ones labeled *"Distinguée" and "Dégagée"*; and by the time she had changed her mind—"I've discovered the English dresses at Redfern's are the thing, Emily"—and relinquished Worth's, Stephen had arrived and the excitement had faded. And now she knew she would not recapture the recklessness necessary to put that much money into any dress however *recherchée,* despite the piping prosperity of these days, and despite the urge to look her best for him and with him.

At least, she thought with affectionate bitterness, he was still the perfect escort. No woman had a handsomer man: admiring and envious eyes had been telling her that always, and there was much reassurance in that single knowledge. His tall frame was as straight in its finely-tailored clothes as it had been twenty years ago; and would still be, no doubt, twenty years from now. The recent graying of his dark hair at the temples only enhanced his good looks. . . . What was that saying of Miss Sophie's?—A woman bows to time while a man is in his prime. I wonder, she thought as she searched the street ahead for him, I wonder how long I'll be presentable enough to walk with you? But the reflection in the window of Worth's had not been altogether disconcerting. That still-slender person with the bright eyes was not yet ready for any bowing to time.

And so presently her musing and her anticipation brought her to the gate of the Redwood Library, opposite the Reading Club. And here she innocently lowered her parasol to wait in the shade of the trees.

It was not till several minutes later, when she saw him come out on the verandah of the Club with two other men, that it occurred to her he might not like to find her waiting to meet him almost on the doorstep of his haunt. She hastened to open her parasol to start back toward the Casino. But it was too late: as she turned away she glimpsed him taking leave of his companions. And then as she walked slowly on, nervously waiting for him to cross the street and overtake her, she could feel his displeasure approaching with the sharp click of his heels. But she was hardly expecting the intense resentment in his eyes when she turned to greet him. He raised his hat curtly.

"I thought we agreed to meet at the Casino. Was it necessary to trail me here?"

"I'm sorry," she managed to smile. "It never occurred to me there'd be any objection."

"I think you might have waited for me there, as I asked you to."

"And I think you might have been there to meet me, as you said you would."

"I had some important business to attend to, after the close of the market. When you saw I was detained, why didn't you wait in the Casino?—plenty of comfortable chairs there. You didn't see any other wives mounting guard at the Club, did you?"

Now, suddenly, she had her own temper as well as his to deal with.

"Well really, you're beginning to make me feel I've done something pretty terrible. Think of it, when my husband was an hour late I calmly walked up the street to meet him. That must have shamed you before all the members."

"If you can't see what a damned undignified position it puts me in, to find my wife posted outside my club, you must be losing your grip."

"I don't suppose there's anything undignified about reprimanding your wife for nothing, and on the street. Couldn't you control your indignation till we get back to the hotel, or at least till these people pass?"

She realized her words and the even tone of her voice were calculated to infuriate him. But some demon of accumulated bitterness was driving her now; and when the trio of young women had passed, she was unable to resist a final thrust.

"While we're on the subject of dignity, is there any particular dignity in drinking so much that you forget yourself as well as me?"

Of course, an instant later she would have given anything to have

410

been able to recall that little speech. His glance told her how deep the thrust had gone.

"If you're going to get nasty," he smiled wryly, "perhaps we had better postpone this. Before I do forget myself as well as you. May I have the pleasure of your company as far as the hotel?—I think we better head straight there, don't you?"

She nodded. "And be sure I shan't embarrass you again, Stephen."

"Suits me. You know, on top of the day's worries, this kind of conjugal bliss doesn't sit so well. I'll take a whiskey sour and male consolation any time."

They walked on to the hotel in a flushed silence. Miserably she wondered what had happened to break down her control so disastrously, and what she was going to do to repair the damage. He was whistling softly, one hand lightly swinging his stick, the other jingling the change in his pocket: he was going to pass the scene off with an air of jaunty indifference, leaving any conciliatory moves to her. The palms of her hands grew moist within their gloves, but it was not till she had closed her parasol under the elms of the hotel gateway that she could summon the resolution to touch his arm.

"Stephen, I'm sorry I spoke that way."

She was grateful for his quick smile and pat. "Oh hell, honey, let's forget it. I'm sorry for being late, and abusive. Call it the heat."

After that fiasco, she was relieved that he suggested no more afternoon strolls. She told herself she was quite content to see the last Newport days go by without further struggle. Perhaps when he got away from this club, perhaps at Saratoga and the Fair, things would improve. But no, she wasn't going to build any more vain hopes and illusions.

And she wasn't going to scuttle back to the children for solace. The time had come to start standing on her own feet again, to test and prepare herself for a hard new phase of life. And she felt that for the first time in years she really wanted to be alone, to think and collect herself, to get a fresh grip on things.

She first tried solitary walks in the country and along the shore. Yet, strangely, this natural method of escape and restoration only aggravated her smarting nerves. She turned then to the Redwood Library, which seemed to promise certain sanctuary,—using the side entrance to avoid the precincts of Stephen's club. But the quiet of the place oppressed rather than comforted her. It was a dusty quiet, static and tomb-like, and her thoughts fell appalled before all the accumulated experience and wisdom of the ages looking down on her from the towering shelves. In her contracted state of mind even the lowest of the shelves were beyond her reach.

The town suited her mood better. Especially the old quarter, the neighborhood of Trinity Church and the Commons, where the old markets and the State House stood. She liked Thames Street too, with its throngs of plain people and unpretentious little shops, so different from the grand promenade of Bellevue Avenue. She felt at home in this New England crowd, these faces that approached, passed, and were lost forever with their secret joys and woes. They somehow did not seem the faces of strangers: there was an old kinship and understanding in their eyes. The shops seemed friendly, too. And in the window of a musty secondhand-store she discovered a pair of fine naval glasses with Zeiss lenses, for Michael to send to Rusty.

But the place that best suited her mood was the Casino. It was here, listening to the afternoon concerts of Mullaly's orchestra, that she came to a final understanding with herself about Stephen.

The Casino presented to Bellevue Avenue a long brown-shingled front, with a string of expensive shops on the ground floor. Redfern and Tiffany flanked the entrance. When you turned your back on the driving-hour parade, you passed through a foyer, where you bought your ticket, and came out on the "ombre", where you were met by a battery of stares. Before you lay an oval of fine lawn, flanked by wings of the main building containing extensions of the ombre and, above, an elaborate system of shingled balconies and hooded turrets pleasantly overgrown with ivy. At the end of the lawn stood the orchestra stand, and beyond this were the lawn tennis courts and a big brown building containing the community ballroom, theater, and bowling alleys. In the central tower of the main building a large clock, with a black face and gilt hands and numerals, presided over the scene.

The lawn was set with tables and chairs, but she was always careful to pick a place well back in the shade of the ombre, or at least far enough removed from groups of chatterers so that she could enjoy the music. The great vogue of the Casino had evidently waned, for it was rarely that one of the ranking butterflies appeared here, and then only for a fluttering moment and as if by mistake. But there were plenty of unidentified personages who carried themselves with an air of social importance. And there was plenty of high fashion, incredibly slender waists swelling upward to astonishing puffed sleeves, striking little hats and parasols of distinction, novel veils and modish fans.

And the gilded youth of America were well represented. With contemptuous indifference to the concert scene, they passed through the ombre to and from the tennis courts: young ladies in light blue blouses, dark blue serge skirts, and Eton jackets embroidered with rackets; young men in Eton jackets and knee-breeches. They all drawled with what seemed to be a British accent of some sort, and their faces wore the most bored expressions. It was quite apparent that they had already found life out very thoroughly, that the last word had been said on everything, and that nothing except tennis was worth any effort.

But when the orchestra appeared, she quickly forgot the denizens of the Casino. Here certainly was a fine body of men, a valiant little brotherhood who seemed not at all disconcerted because even their highest efforts were received merely as a pleasant accompaniment for conversation, like tea and cinnamon toast. Instinctively she admired them all, from shaggy-haired Professor Mullaly through to the disembodied Bass Horn at the rear. Her chief interest at first was the pianist, whose performance she could follow with a critical eye and ear, but later her attention wandered to the trombonist and the French-horn player. They were Germans, she discovered one afternoon when she sat quite near the stand; between numbers they conversed earnestly in their native tongue over the sheets on their racks, or exchanged a few words with their neighbors in broken and apologetic English. One was a youth who looked only a year or so older than Michael; the other, she decided, was his father. Their faces touched her, and she wondered what their lives were, what town or village of their country they came from, whether the rest of their family was with them or had been left at home across the sea.

The programs were made up of good, bad, and indifferent pieces, but she was too starved for music to resent even the trashiest overtures and the most insipid medleys. When something good came along, one of the Tschaikowsky symphonies or the C-Minor of

Brahms or Schubert's Unfinished, she longed for Michael to be hearing it with her. He was still deaf to everything but the simplest melodies, but someday, finally at some moment, the spell of great music would enter his soul in answer to her prayers. . . . You may not leap out of your chair, she told him, as you did that day at Land's End when you suddenly got the swing of reading (*Once upon a time,* you panted, *there was a Fisherman and his Wife!*). But you will waken to it someday, waken to the greatest of the arts. . . . And to explain to herself and him what she meant by that, she wore her card-case pencil down to the quick one concert afternoon trying to consolidate her feelings about music on the margins of her program. *When you have learned to listen, my son, music will lift your spirit above the dust and confusion of the world. It will keep the springs of your being from drying up, keep them from choking up with the sediments of everyday thinking and living. It will release you from your busy ordinary self, and permit your deeper wiser self a moment of freedom to remember the wonder of the world. To remember the sorrow of the world, too, but sorrow transmuted by beauty, transcended by faith and hope and love. And you will see more clearly through the eyes of music the comradeship of men, the place of your own life in the life stream of the race, see greater visions in your medicine, find greater joy and purpose in your work. And perhaps in the end you will see, through the beauty of music, Beauty itself, —the essence of all things, the unity at the heart of multitude, the harmony and order in the turmoil of reality. . . .*

The hopeless inadequacy of that, she thought as she reread the cramped lines. Where words ended, music began. And then, quite irrationally, she made a fresh attempt on another program the next afternoon. But in the end she was back where she started, reduced to a bare and simple prayer: that music might come to enrich his life. And somehow that prayer must be answered, along with all her other prayers for him and for Margaret and Jack. For there could be no compromises ever with her dreams for them.

I accept my compromises with you, Stephen, she told him finally out of her musings. And she saw, as one looking back from a hilltop at a long-traveled road, saw for the first time how far back their ways had parted. I've been walking alone, she realized now, talking to myself all this time; telling myself you were still at my side, and somehow never quite doubting it. . . . Well, she would continue to talk to empty air, pretending he was still there, for the sake of the children and Miss Sophie, and Eugenia and General Appearances and her own peace of mind; for the sake of everyone, in fact, except Lucy, who couldn't be fooled and had probably known the truth for ages anyway. The truth that Stephen was lost and gone forever. Yes, that was it. Not strayed or stolen, but lost—irretrievably, completely, finally.

Not strayed or stolen? she wondered, pausing. A woman was supposed to know intuitively if there was another woman, or other women. She wondered. And then, beginning to resent the abrupt intrusion of this question, she answered curtly that he was absorbed in his business to the exclusion of everything; and that even if it were possible and true, she didn't care really, as long as he was discreet about it. Because, she added bitterly, he's lost to me forever. And looking back over the country of her past, from the hilltop of these lonely Newport afternoons, she saw him standing dead at a far fork in the road. Stark dead he stood there in the sunlight of their early marriage; just this side of Jack's birthday, she thought, or at least near that first summer at Flat Rock; his head silhouetted against the nightmare valley of Aaron and her teaching years at Land's End. The head and shoulders of his deadness loomed up, so that the sun, dipping imperceptibly down from high noon, had sent his shadow pacing after her, deceiving her into believing him still with her. Now, she knew, it was only the shadow of him that kept her company; while a stranger, a ghostly Stephen, moved forward on a road of his own parallel to hers, too intent on his own affairs even to pass the time of day with her.

She reproached herself for feeling no great pain. There was only a dull remote sadness, as if all the deadly little compromises she had had to make with her marriage dream had secretly drained away all but the dregs of feeling, so that now she could make no deep response to this full realization of her loss. It was a fact, a truth to be faced, like the end of a beautiful summer, or the falling of leaves in autumn, or the discovery that one was middle-aged. She thought: It's ended, I admit it and I'm sorry, and now what is there left to do but continue to darn his socks and find things he's misplaced and pack and unpack his bags? . . . And she demanded of herself: Of all the countless millions that have lived and died and will live and die in this old slaughter-house careening through space—how astonishingly calm and collected everything looked here in this secure enclosure of lawn, how matter-of-fact and substantial—why should you be immune, why should your little dreams be spared? For whatever else could be said about human life, one simple fact was clear enough: for everyone, everywhere and always, it was a struggle to cling to cherished possessions, your home and loved ones and dreams, as you were swept along in the turbulent stream of time down to the great sea of death. The inevitable engulfment, where all dreams became one and none. . . . And were they then, these lost dreams, lifted up by the sun to drift again in cloud shapes over the land where you had lived and to fall as tender rain among those you had loved or could have loved? Or was there actually some sort of Heaven, where lost dreams were found in truth and all men equally blessed (the gentleman with the Ascot tie, Professor Mullaly, and the waiter in the background furtively cleaning his nails with the corner of a wine-card), and you sat passing the time of infinity over a cup of celestial tea, absolutely at peace, utterly at rest, all rapture through and through, congratulating yourself and your neighbors at having made the steep grade, nodding familiarly to the Lord as you waited, with just a trace of earthly apprehension perhaps, for those loved ones left behind to catch up with your translation? Or did you wake at last to find yourself merely in a place where no wind stirred and no tides ebbed and flowed?

But then she rebuked her thoughts for their extreme waywardness, when she had asked them only to help her prepare for the next phase. They fell back, leaving her to comfort herself against the three tomorrows (one so near, none far) when she would lose her three and stand again childless as well as husbandless. And to promise herself she would escape the fate of so many outgrown mothers and lonely wives: she would never become like an abandoned house, doors swinging aimlessly open and shut on puzzled querulous hinges, blinds rattling and banging about nothing in the winds of other lives, bleak empty windows staring vacantly at spring morning and autumn dusk.

And now, she assured herself confidently, she was ready for the years ahead: restored, composed, and ready. All lay in order before her: the loss of Stephen accepted (she would darn his socks as carefully as ever), the growing up and away of her three prepared for (but no compromising ever with her dreams for them), and the increasing spare time of the future to be given to the Land's End people and music and books and gardening. To crown and insure the whole: Rusty, the one constant in a world of change. There!—it was settled. And abruptly she became very impatient with Professor Mullaly and the Casino, for she wanted no more music or musing, for the present at least, but only to return to her life now that she had freed herself to return. And now she could enjoy the last days at Newport, and look forward to Saratoga and Lake George and Chicago, and face with resolution what lay in wait for her beyond the glittering excitement of the World's Fair: Michael's empty bed, almost immediately, and then other and other encroachments that she would defeat by continually reconsolidating her position, within a contracting circle but always presenting a solid front to the enemy.

But first she was to have him to herself for a day or two, when she took him alone to Boston while the rest of the family went on to Lake George. A weird idea, Stephen called this side journey, declaring himself unable to understand how anyone would wilfully return to the home of the cod and the bean having once successfully escaped. But how could he understand what a sad and happy pilgrimage it was to be for her.

She saw herself with Michael driving up Beacon Street in a hack from the station. And here at once she became confused, for how much of the city would be as she had left it that winter day with Aaron, on the way to New York and the steamer for Port Royal? Wouldn't it be as much of a stranger to her now as she would be to it? Wouldn't she find everything changed beyond recognition? And as she wondered, confusion became worse confounded: she was overwhelmed by such a horde of memories, her girlhood in Boston mixed crazily with the fantastic outcome of the Beaufort dream, that she finally had to discard all of the city but the house itself, her birthplace on Chestnut Street. They would leave the hack at the corner and proceed on foot, counting the numbers to *108*. But once again she had to pause, for she was visualizing a street of snow: the old chestnut tree, outside the bay window, robed in snow. And when she had swept that cold whiteness away, she had to eliminate the vivid image of a spring tree, fragrant with blossom clusters set like candles on its branches; and then the image of a gusty autumn tree, shedding brown leaves and dropping on the mocking soil of the pavement the sleek mahogany nuts for which the boys of the block scrambled. But at last she reduced the tree and the street to the leafy slumber proper to a late-summer day. And with Michael's hand in hers she stood again in that grateful shade, looking up with him at the bay window. . . .

She relinquished his hand, remembering that he was a man now, and wondering if any sadness could match this: that the hand of her son was no longer hers to seek and that she could never again expect it to seek her hand.

But the concert for this afternoon was over: Professor Mullaly was collecting the sheets of music from the racks, and his men were packing their instruments to return to whatever their private lives were. And she was returning, she reminded herself briskly as she renounced her lonely Casino chair, to her life. Returning, she twitted the presiding clock (for she was through with meditations, restored and whole again, and only annoyed now that it had taken so long), returning to her family and to blessings greater than any dream of perfection.

✓   ✓   ✓

The last Sunday at Newport she was favored with more of Stephen's company than she had had since the day of his arrival.

He had promised to take Margaret and Jack for a stroll before church. But Saturday night at the Reading Club had been too much for him, and he got up only in time to shave and dress for Old Trinity. There she had him on her right and Michael on her left; Miss Sophie and Eugenia were several pews ahead, with Jack and Margaret. In other times that had always been the benison of church, kneeling with her husband and her son, communing with them through the service. But then she had felt they were all three mysteriously one. Now she could only wonder what was going on in the dark head on her right (business, last week's quotations, next week's aces) and the dark head on her left (another expedition to Agassiz Point perhaps, and tomorrow's sailboat races, and certainly Linda). And now, she wondered, did they think of her (if they thought of her at all) as anything but a comfortable buffer between their very separate egos?

But during the Offertory, *There Is a Green Hill Far Away,* she had the surprise and pleasure of a sign from Michael at least. He nudged her arm and shared a secret smile with her: Grandma's

418

bonnet was nodding in solemn time with the hymn while an invisible hand was keeping Jack in order. The pleasure of that little moment remained with her through the day.

In the afternoon Stephen offered to take her for a drive. It was hot, and he wanted to escape the Williamses, whom Miss Sophie was entertaining at the hotel. Most of the drive he spent damning the Williamses. The Colonel tried to be a good fellow, but the struggle only made him a worse stiff-neck and prig than if he'd left bad enough alone. Virginia men were all alike, conceited asses. And she was a tiresome frump. . . .

He yawned through an evening in the lobby. It was a decided relief when he suggested early bed.

On Monday she saw him only at breakfast. And then it was the usual thing: to avoid conversation he read snatches from the *Newport Daily News*. "Well, President Cleveland has issued a proclamation calling Congress to a special session for financial relief. That's news, all right. . . . Here's something to read the children about the Fair,—Streets of Cairo, Samoan village, models of St. Peter's and the Eiffel Tower, the great Ferris wheel, lagoons with fountains of flame, gondolas and electric launches. You can skip the item about Little Egypt, the Hootchy-Cootchy artiste. . . . Listen to this from the editorial page: 'The stock market has taken another slump. The depression now extends throughout the civilized world. So true is it that when one of the great family of nations suffers, all suffer with it. But don't be alarmed; this great country, with its boundless resources, will survive. The times are out of joint, but reconstruction will come. The pendulum will swing back; old time prosperity will return and before we know it. It always has. So stop croaking.' Well, I'm not croaking. This is the time to snap up a few bargains. . . . How'd you like to hear yesterday's results at the Saratoga races? . . ." He expected her to acknowledge each item with a nod. But he was not interested in hearing any comments. And if she asked questions, he rustled the paper impatiently.

On Tuesday morning, she left the table before he opened his paper; there were still two days before her departure with Michael for Boston, but she wanted to get the packing started. When he came up to the room, he slapped the paper down on the bureau.

"Can you beat that? Read that despatch from Columbia, S. C. Last night at midnight your adopted state went into the saloon business! Every bar in the state closed. Dispensary system. Another damn Tillman play to the Baptist and Methodist galleries! God knows where we'll wind up now that the Crackers are in the saddle."

A few minutes later, as he was preparing to leave for the Club, he interrupted her packing.

"I won't forget the reservations today. If you still want them. I think it's foolishness myself, separating the party."

She looked at him with a faint smile. "But you really understand, don't you?"

"I suppose so," he said indulgently.

When she turned back to her packing, he took her arm and led her to the window. He left her there for a moment while he went to close the door to the children's room, where Jack was having some argument with Lucy. When he came back to the window, he put his arms around her.

"Honey," he said with his old intimate smile, "I've been neglecting you pretty shamefully, haven't I?"

Flushed and confused she had to look out of the window for an answer. The fog that before breakfast had been pressing thick and gray against the panes was luminous now. It was a dazzling mist now, veiling the trees and the lawn in shining white magic. She nodded. And then as pride rushed back to stiffen her against his embrace, she told his eyes lightly, "But it's quite all right. I understand. I'm not bitter about it, you know."

"No?" he said with an air of surprise. "Resigned?"

"Not even conscious of it anymore."

"That's bad!" he laughed, and held her tighter. And now, abruptly, all resistance was gone and she yielded to him completely. When he bent his head to kiss her, her lips met his as eagerly and naturally as if time had swept them dizzily back to the beginning.

He whispered, "I'd like to go into this a little more thoroughly. What are you doing this evening?"

"I have an engagement," she told him soberly, "with a tall dark gentleman with nice teeth and an old-fashioned smile."

He shook his head over that. "I better be around with a shotgun. What are you doing this afternoon?"

"Nothing." She straightened his tie. "You see, my husband's a confirmed clubman, and my children have become free agents. With us it's every man for himself now."

420

"Well then, why not meet me at the Casino? If you're not feeling too self-sufficient."

"Would you actually be there?"

"Four sharp."

"I'll look for you about five."

When he released her, they stood smiling at each other for a moment in silence.

"Are you serious by any chance?" she asked him.

"Yes sir! You and I are going on an old-fashioned bender, starting at the Casino and lasting well into the night. Dinner at Keeler's—lobster and champagne, or filet mignon and burgundy. Then the Casino theatre and the ball. And then,—well, how does the program hit you so far?"

She touched his forehead. "You're feeling all right, dear? No fever?"

He kissed her hand gaily and turned with a chuckle to the bureau mirror. But as he put on his straw hat and used the finger tips of his good hand to brush back the graying hair at either temple, the smile faded. "Just because I don't unburden on you," he frowned at the mirror, "don't think I haven't had plenty of worries to keep me from relaxing."

"But why don't you unburden?" she asked quickly. "Can't we have a little old-fashioned unburdening on this bender?"

His face brightened again. "Sure we can! And we're going to start taking things easier from here on. We're turning over a new leaf. Less strain, more home life. This slump may be hell for a lot of people, but it's going to put the finishing touches on our fortress. Which reminds me of another little item I meant to show you."

He picked up the paper. "Listen to this: 'General Wade Hampton, U. S. Railroad Commissioner, has returned to Washington after his long tour of inspection on Pacific railroads.' Doesn't that somehow bring the whole amazing business home to you? Look where we are and think where we were! You see, darling, you can't keep good Southerners down."

He tapped the paper with the stiff fingers of his gloved hand and slapped it down on the bureau again with a satisfied jerk of his head. "It's a crazy world," he told the mirror as he gave his moustache a final twist, "—very pleasantly crazy. And I hope to die if I haven't had more than my share of luck. Take you, for instance." He turned back to her, put his arms around her waist and lifted her off her feet.

"Please, dear!" she begged, "you'll hurt yourself."

"Oh!" he panted, "so you think your old shipmate is too brittle for this kind of thing. Well, I'll show you." And with a gasping laugh he set her up on the chair by the window. *"Phew!*—there now, I guess that'll teach you to respect me." He pressed his face against her breast, and his hat slid to the back of his head and fell before she could catch it. "Let'er rip," he said with a muffled sigh of content; and shaking with a stifling laughter that came up from the pit of her stomach she tightened her arms around his neck.

"Well, honey," he mumbled solemnly, "it isn't such a bad game after all, is it? But where would I be without you? You're my luck. Still love me?"

Holding his head tight was not stopping the absurd constricted laughter that kept racking up through her, and she could only nod in answer. "Much?" he demanded; and she wanted to say, More than ever, but she could only nod again. He tried then to look up at her, but she held him where he was, afraid to let him go. "More than anyone?" he persisted, "and for ever and ever amen?" And she kept nodding and clinging to him, till at last he had to pull away to look up at her.

"What in the name of God," he smiled, "are you sniffling about?"

She caught her breath finally. "Nothing. And I'm not sniffling. I'm laughing."

He was delighted with that. "Darling, you're a terrible fool."

"I know it," she sighed. "Let me down now,—I've got to finish packing and you've got to run."

"Well, that's nice,—chasing me off just as I was about to make a proposal. But perhaps discretion is better, what with the family on the right and left of us and the maid about to knock at any moment. Ah, honey, it's good to see you blush."

"Haven't you any shame?" she asked him as he lifted her down.

"Sure," he said blandly, "but I'm saving it for our wheel-chair days."

A glance at his watch sobered him. "By George, it is late!" And he hastened to retrieve his hat and make a final appraisal of himself in the mirror.

At the door to the hall he paused to tip his hat jauntily.

"Oh, by the way. I'm buying you and Mother a fistful of Union

Pacific today,—got a hunch the market's ripe for picking. So you see our little bender is by way of being a celebration, among other things. How do you like the idea anyway—you and I on a complete bender?"

"I can't tell you how I like it. Particularly if it's real."

"It's real, all right,—real enough to make your head spin. All you have to do is meet me at the Casino about four-thirty."

When he was gone, she stood at the window in a long trance of bewilderment and bliss. Try not to be a fool, she asked of herself. Yet beyond doubt everything had changed: the room, everything about her was magically altered, looked gay and bright and new. And there was no denying or resisting the rhapsody in her heart. Now you'll have to unpack your best evening dress, she thought with cheerful annoyance. But when she went to kneel before the trunk, her hands rested at the rim while her thoughts went off on a joyous rampage.

She was still kneeling there when Jack came bursting into the room.

"Where's Pappa?"

She mimicked his wild-eyed breathlessness. "Have you looked under the bed?"

He glanced at the bed and looked back at her blankly. Then he grinned. "He's gone! Ain't he?"

"*Hasn't* he," she corrected automatically. "Yes, I'm afraid so."

He put a fretful hand on her shoulder. "Mamma, have you got just a dime in pennies? I wish Pappa would give me an allowance like Michael, so I wouldn't have to ask him every time."

"You know what happened to your bank," she reminded him.

"I couldn't help it if I dropped it, could I?"

"And you still don't think it's strange it happened to get dropped from the attic window?" She tried to make a little order in his stubborn brown hair, smiling into the blue eyes that were her own, thinking how different even the shape of his head was from Stephen's and Michael's. "When you grow up to be a young man like your brother, then you'll know how to take care of money."

"Not if I don't get any practice. He ain't a man anyway. I'll soon be up to him." All his grievances settled on the trunk. "Why do you have to pack now? Why can't you go to the beach with us?"

"But you have Grandma and Lucy, and Margaret and the Alanson children. And Aunt Gene's going to sketch. You don't need me."

"Sure we do! It's no fun without you,—they won't let me do anything. Oh please come, Mamma, it's almost the last day!"

"Well, dear, if that's the way you feel about it, I'll go."

He beamed at her. "And will you go with us this afternoon to pick blueberries? Gran'maa's going to pay us five cents a handful."

She shook her head. "I'm sorry, but this afternoon I have a very important engagement."

"Where you going?"

"Can you keep a secret?"

"Sure. I keep them for Gran'maa all the time. I'm keeping one for her right now."

"Well, if Grandma can trust you I guess I can. Your father and I are going on an old-fashioned bender."

He gave her a puzzled grin. "What's that?"

"Well, it's a very special sort of party."

"Can I go too?" he immediately wanted to know.

"Darling," she said to him very seriously, "can you keep another secret? I love you so much I could eat you up."

He received that with a perfect grin, and she drew him into her arms for a hug so big that they were both left breathless and dazed beside the astonished trunk.

That afternoon, of course, everyone would decide to go to the Casino, everyone except Margaret and Jack, who had gone berrying with Lucy, and Michael, who was off on a last all-day sail with his friend the retired lighthouse-keeper. The luminous fog had dissolved by noon into burning sunshine, and Miss Sophie had declared at lunch that it was too hot and glary for anything but a late drive: after a siesta she and Eugenia would pick up the Williamses and carry them to the concert for a while,—five o'clock would be early enough to have the carriage come back to take them driving.

So now, at four, Emily found herself seated with them all at a table on the Casino lawn, tasting a fruit sherbet and trying to concentrate on what Colonel Williams was saying against the opening bars of Elgar's *Pomp and Circumstance*. Across the table Mrs. Williams and Miss Sophie were in a huddle over their sherbets; at intervals Miss Sophie fumbled for her glasses at the end of their gold chain and held them to her eyes to examine new arrivals, nodding as

Mrs. Williams made covert comment: it was a crowded afternoon at the Casino and there was much to see. Eugenia was simply not amused, not even by her sherbet, which was languishing into pink soup.

"Your husband was telling me," the Colonel was saying as he pulled at one end of his stained white mustache, "that the best phosphate deposits are in the waters around Beaufort and Port Royal. He described how the rock is washed, ground, and treated with sulphuric acid, to free the phosphoric acid from the lime. . . ."

She had expected to spend this hour in serene anticipation of Stephen. And in her handbag was a letter from Rusty that she had planned to reread here at her leisure. But now she was lost in a confusion of tongues. Crisscrossing her surface attention to the Colonel's voice were snatches of chatter from the neighboring tables and strains of pomp and circumstance from the orchestra. Lingering memories of the morning jostled one another for her inner attention: the strangely disturbing gray fog at the windows before breakfast, the shock and ecstasy of the moments with Stephen, the spell of the beach and the glassy sea under slowly lifting veils of translucence, with Margaret and Jack. And there was the dark red rose at her waist. Perhaps it was Eugenia's presence that kept her cheeks faintly flushed about that: she had offered Eugenia one from the armful that a florist's boy had embarrassingly appeared with just at lunch time,—They don't go with my dress, Eugenia had said, and besides I never cared for crimson roses. . . . Above confusion hovered a persistent prayer that the presiding clock would be kind enough to delay Stephen after all, delay him till five, till the party had departed for their drive. And through everything the last lines of Rusty's letter kept repeating themselves. *At your insistence I am going to the island next week to loaf* (he was there now, she rejoiced). *With Land's End empty and deserted I shall miss you worse than ever.* Then some lines about the clinic. That would be his idea of a loaf, doctoring the plantation people when he should be sailing and fishing and smoking his pipe in peace. If she were only there to make sure he got a real rest. . . . *And I have a hunch that with these marvelous new eyes Michael has sent me I shall spot at last a black-necked stilt. You remember how we used to refer to that elusive bird as ultimate wisdom? . . .*

"You don't care for sherbet?" the Colonel was asking Eugenia, in a benevolent effort to draw her out. "I find it so much more refreshing than hot tea on an afternoon like this. Of course these Newporters would observe the rite of hot tea in Hades, in order to appear English."

"I perceive you're no Anglomaniac," she smiled at the Colonel when he turned back to her, from Eugenia's lukewarm reception, for appreciation of his hot-tea-in-Hades whimsy.

"I admire the English—within reason," he said expansively. "But I have no use whatever for Americans who ape English manners." He finished his sherbet and gave his mustache a careful wiping. "A great people, the English, as a matter of fact." And he added with becoming modesty, "Natural I should feel so, I suppose, being a tidewater Virginian of Cavalier stock. And I suppose," he nodded at Eugenia, "you feel very much the same way about it, being a tidewater Carolinian." He was rewarded for that with a decidedly tepid smile; but he continued undaunted, dividing his attention impartially now between the two parts of his audience. "You know, I have observed that the English take to Southerners—Southerners of breeding, that is. We seem to be spiritually akin. Of course, the English failed us in the War. But that was not the fault of the upper classes—from the Queen down, they were with us heart and soul. It was the masses that opposed us. Your sentimental middle-class Englishman, intoxicated by abolition and reform doctrines, and your radical lower-class workers of Liverpool and Manchester,—which was strange when you stop to consider that cotton was their bread and butter. . . ."

So it went on, through *Invitation to the Dance* and *Liebesträum* and Selections from *Faust.* . . .

Now the clock said it was almost a quarter to five. The intermission had arrived, and it was possible to hope that Stephen would not appear till the others had left. He would be annoyed to find her not alone, particularly with the Williamses. Taut, she secretly watched the clock and the entrance through the lingering confusion of table talk. . . . A breeze had sprung up. It came in hot little gusts that flapped the skirts of the tablecloths and stirred into sudden brief frenzies the leaves of the trees beyond the orchestra stand. But it failed to dislodge her party and shoo them away on their drive.

By intense concentration she finally forced the clock to concede five explicit chimes. The intermission was over: the orchestra had worked their way back to their chairs among the congestion of racks and were tuning up. And the Williamses were waiting expectantly for the signal to rise and depart. But Miss Sophie was in no hurry.

"Shall we stay for one more number?" she asked, glancing around the table for objections.

There were none, so they stayed for Tschaikowsky's *1812*. Through Professor Mullaly's inspired conducting with gusts of the increasingly playful wind in his hair, through the spasmodic tempests in the trees and the hazy agitated stirrings of sunlight and shadows over the lawn and the tables, she tried to resign herself to meeting Stephen in this congested company and to feel only anticipation of the bender with him, renewal of this morning's miracle, the return to intimacy, the recapture of all lost ground. But when the barbaric splendor of the *1812* ended in a hymn of victory and a triumphant jangling of bells, with Colonel Williams bristling martially and almost shouting at her ear "Napoleon's retreat from Moscow, you know", she felt defeated herself, as completely wilted as if she had been through the entire campaign.

"Have you read *War and Peace?*" the Colonel asked the table in general, when the battle was over. "Tolstoy, you know. It's at the library."

"I never could finish it," his wife told Miss Sophie. "I did read *Anna Karenina,* though. That's not so long drawn out, and it's more human. A chronicle of emotions, not just events."

"I hear it's shocking," said Miss Sophie absently, as she gathered herself together for a faultless exit. "All about a woman who deserted her husband and child to go traipsing off with a lover. Not exactly edifying."

"She was punished in the end," Mrs. Williams countered.

"Give me Thackeray, my dear," sighed Miss Sophie, taking a firm grip on the ivory handle of her cane. And as she rose she added, more to the surrounding tables than to Mrs. Williams: "He said the final word on everything,—men and women, love and marriage, death and taxes. Emily, tell Stephen we're sorry we missed him, child."

And then, at last, they were gone. And she was sitting alone at the table, with the sherbet glasses and Stephen's lateness.

. . . This capricious wind that had sprung to life from dead sultry sunshine had furnished an excellent atmospheric accompaniment for the blusterings of the *1812*. But for the tenderness and anguish of *Romeo and Juliet* it was as demoralizing as a pack of mischievous

427

boys of Jack's age. Professor Mullaly's conducting was erratic and irritable: he had evidently determined that the somber mood of this number called for a brooding head, pensive and sad, but the prankish imps of the wind were too much for him,—his left hand was hopelessly divided between assisting his baton hand and keeping his hair from standing on end. And each member of the orchestra faced a problem of his own, the necessity of turning his notes and clipping the sheets down again before a boisterous gust could snatch them away. It was a tussle between lawless nature and the will of man. And somehow the music won out, transcending the demons of discord to soar on wings of dark beauty. As the spell heightened, her amusement and even her impatience for Stephen vanished in a spine-tingling response to the tragic rhapsody.

Just at the finale a vengeful gust of wind rumpled Professor Mullaly's hair down over his eyes and frisked whole sheaves of music off the racks, scattering them like autumn leaves over the lawn. But it came just one moment too late to disconcert the orchestra: with a magnificent blind upthrust the Professor sustained his men through the last swelling chord. For several seconds his disheveled head was bowed in utter prostration; then suddenly he jerked it up, clearing his eyes of hair, and turned briskly to receive the patter of applause.

The spell was broken. Waiters were gathering up the stray sheets of music among the tables. And Stephen was coming down the steps from the ombre.

Out of the corner of her eye she had discovered him a minute before, first searching for her and then waiting for the music to end. But an absurd flash of shyness had prevented her from nodding to him. And even now, as he came toward the table, she was intent on her program and only sensed his approach. It was not till he reached the table and stood before her that she glanced up at him with a flushed greeting.

"Well, dear, it's good to see you again, after all these years."

"Well, honey," he grinned, "I see you had company. I don't feel so bad about being a little late."

At first she was simply unable to believe in the thickness of his voice. "Mother and Gene," she said numbly. "And the Williamses."

"Always those damn spongers."

He sat down with a chuckle, moved Eugenia's pink soup out of the way and rested his arms on the table. Avoiding his eyes she saw with sharp irrelevance, her stunned wits clutching at anything to escape the realization that for all his steadiness he was quite drunk, she saw on her program that tomorrow's concert included Bizet's *L'Arlesienne Suite,* Gilbert & Sullivan's *Mikado,* and César Franck's Symphony in D-Minor. "I simply couldn't get away any earlier, honey," he was explaining. "It was some day! You and Mother are now the proud owners of the Union Pacific Railroad—or at least a nice little block of it. And ten years from now the children will be blessing their old man for the shares he picked up for them at today's bargain counter. I invested for Lucy, too. I loaded us all up with every share we could carry. Now what do you think of that?"

"Wonderful," she smiled weakly.

"Calls for a celebration, all right."

The orchestra was swinging into the relaxed rhythm of the concluding number, *The Blue Danube Waltz.* He gave them his attention for a moment, looked over the tables, and then sat back in his chair and crossed his legs. "Well," he said with a smile of satisfaction, "it was the chance of a lifetime. I had it all planned out weeks ago, but I just sat tight, watching our two big rail bugs at the Club buying on a steadily falling market, ten, twenty, thirty points above what I finally paid for it. But today things looked good and I dove in. Slid off a point or two at the close, but I'm not worried. The tide has turned."

He took a cigar out of his case and clipped the end with the silver cutter on his watch-chain, lighting it carefully and evenly. "You know," he exhaled with a sigh of ease, "you can't expect to get the absolute bottom on a stock. But I'm satisfied. . . . Say, what about our little bender? All set?"

She nodded, her eyes still on the program.

"You don't look very enthusiastic," he told her. "Mad because I was late?"

She looked up with a forced smile. "Of course not."

"That's better. What you need is a drop of sherry, for a starter. Then let's get out of this place,—we can take a drive before we go back to the hotel to dress."

He blew a heavy ring of smoke that would have delighted Jack and Margaret, and for an instant she could hardly resist an impulse to poke her finger through it. Quivering inside with insane laughter she watched it enlarge, waver, and wisp swiftly away in a breath of wind.

He signaled to the waiter who was clearing up a vacant table nearby.

The music had stopped, she realized, and Professor Mullaly was taking a final bow. She kept her dazed eyes on him while she spoke to Stephen. "Would you mind terribly if we went back to the hotel now?"

He concentrated a puzzled frown on her.

"What's wrong?"

"The sherbet I guess. I feel a little sick."

"Well, that's tough. But a little drive ought to set you up."

She managed an apologetic smile. "I'm afraid not."

"But I've got a surprise,—a dress at Redfern's I want you to see."

The waiter made a merciful interruption.

"Let me have the bill for these poisonous concoctions," Stephen said to him.

She kept a tight grip on herself while he paid for the sherbets and added his usual extravagant tip. When the waiter was gone, she said quickly, "I'm terribly sorry. I hate to fall down on the celebration."

"Oh hell, honey," he told her with an amiable shrug, "don't let that worry you. I'm only sorry you feel bad." He knocked the ashes off his cigar. "After all, the celebration will keep till tomorrow. Or we can make a reunion of it at Saratoga. . . . Well, are you ready?"

A hot breath of the wind sent a shiver through her as she got to her feet. And then an infinite expanse of lawn separated her from the steps to the ombre.

After dinner he went back to the Club.

She sat for a while with Miss Sophie in the lobby. When she went up to say good-night to Margaret and Jack, a few minutes after Lucy had finally corralled them for bed, she stayed in her room to answer Rusty's letter.

If he were only here with her, or she there with him, his healing smile and voice and eyes. But there was only the art calendar over the desk and the mocking vase of crimson roses on the bureau, and at the dark windows hissing little gusts of rain. And there would be no release from this turmoil till she was with him again: no answer of his would reach her on the rambling journey home. Still, she could get some relief by writing him, frankly and without reserve as of old.

But when the letter was finished, she found she had given him no hint of her depression and bewilderment. Only family news, closing on a note of absurd composure. She wanted to tear it up. But she felt too washed out for another attempt, so she compromised on a postscript. "The truth of the matter is that while you're looking for a black-neck stilt I'm seeing ghosts. I don't think I'm exactly scared of them yet, but they humbug me, as Auntie Cuba used to say about her plat-eye hants. I'm not having much luck shrugging them away, so please don't be surprised if they come trailing home with me for your inspection. After you've told me what the elusive bird of ultimate wisdom looks like face to face, I'll show you my hants and you can amputate them in that blessed dressing-station of yours, cure of all ills."

At least that would indicate her troubled state of mind to him, if only by contrast with the complacent body of the letter. Explanations would simply have to wait.

She wrote at the end: "In a shifty world you alone remain unchanged." . . . Her pen stopped there. But from that he would understand all she wanted to say. How further would she ever be able to satisfy the longing to express what he meant to her? She folded the sheets quickly.

The envelope she addressed to Legare Street, Charleston. And as she sealed it, she saw it drop through the letter-slot to the floor of the hall, where he would find it on his return from the island at the end of the week. But she had to revise that picture: Santee, his house-boy, would have it waiting on the desk in the office whose windows opened on the wild and fragrant garden, his bird sanctuary in the heart of the city,—where Michael would be with him often, after the beginning of school, at this time next month. . . .

She felt a little better after that. But when she went down to the lobby, and the letter disappeared from her hand into the mail-box, a miserable loneliness closed around her again.

In a cozy corner of the lobby Miss Sophie was engaged in animated conversation with some of her hotel acquaintances. In another corner Eugenia was reading with her back to the world. And in the writing-room Michael's head was bowed over a letter to Linda.

To avoid a signal from Miss Sophie she made a detour to the front door.

She stood suddenly in the midst of confusion made manifest, a mood that perfectly matched her own. Fine driving rain stung and cooled her cheeks. The line of tall-backed rockers along the glistening deserted verandah stirred with phantom life. On the lawn a string of colored lights swung wild shadows among the swishing branches of the trees.

On the south wing of the verandah she found a sheltered nook and a dry chair.

After a time she closed her eyes against the swaying blackness beyond the railing. The sound of the wind and rain then became a sighing languor, at once close and remote, intimate and vast. Slowly it filled every particle of her being, blotting out all thought and feeling. It took nothing from her and gave her nothing. It was neither sleeping nor waking nor dreaming, but a sense of perfect equilibrium, like death.

The last day at Newport. Outdoors, a bedlam of writhing branches: spasms of rain blinding the windows, seething torrents of rain sweeping over the lawn and pounding up wavering mists from the driveway. Indoors, a bedlam of bags and trunks and littered beds and chairs and bureaus. Margaret and Jack rampant from confinement and excitement, Miss Sophie in a fluster of eve-of-departure generalship, and Eugenia making attempt after attempt to cram her Newport purchases into a trunk already bulging full.

Through the morning and most of the afternoon three principal refrains bobbed in and out of her dazed consciousness: Miss Sophie's certainty that if the storm got any worse every craft in the harbor would be wrecked, railroads washed out, all communications cut off; Eugenia's continual appeals, "Couldn't you tuck this dress in somewhere in your luggage or the children's?"; and her own inner chidings, Brace up now, can't you?—after all you're packing for home, where things will straighten out, and tomorrow you're going to Boston with Michael. . . .

By late afternoon Miss Sophie's dire prophecies were partly confirmed. When Michael came back from the waterfront, where he had gone to say good-bye to his friend and witness the storm at close range, he brought with him a soggy 5:30 extra of the *Newport Daily*

News. When Grandma had ordered him to change his clothes, for he was soaked to the skin despite his raincoat, she read the extra's chief items in a voice of triumph. " 'Mr. John Jacob Astor's handsome steam yacht *Nourmahal* is hard on the Blue Rocks!' " And: " 'On account of the storm today we have received no telegraphic news.' You see, Emily, this is just what I feared!" But by the time Stephen came back from the Club in a closed carriage for supper, the worst of the storm was over. "Just a gale," he said, "to cool things off for traveling." So Miss Sophie's refrain was silenced. And with a sigh of relief, for what she had feared was not wreckage but a delay, she proceeded to tell the children about a real storm remembered from her own childhood.

But the stubborn sense of depression and turmoil remained. Perverse and unreasonable in the light of all her blessings, it spread a deepening pall over everything. It was silly and weak to be its victim, yet she was powerless to break its tightening suffocating grip. It was like a bed of quicksand: the harder she struggled to free herself, the deeper she sank.

The next morning before breakfast she took a carriage with Miss Sophie and Margaret and Jack, the other early risers of the family, to drive out to see Spouting Rock after the storm.

An aftermath of wind was still blowing and the cold gray sky was wild and ragged. Bellevue Avenue was strewn with fresh green leaves and branches. Awnings were torn and sagging, and there were glimpses of bedraggled shrubs and beaten-down flowers in the gardens along the way.

There were groups of people on the rocks watching the heavy churning sea. . . . The billows were dark green till they reached the base of the rocks; there they swelled up with a hollow thud; then up through the crevice leapt a great fountain of spray, a hiss and splatter trailing off into mist to Margaret's and Jack's delight. "Keep back!" Grandma kept warning them. The waves struck the headlands to the north, one after another, rising over each in towering white fury. The Coney Island boardwalk of the pavilion at Easton's Beach, where Newport servants and excursionists bathed, was awash with the high surf.

When they got back to the hotel, Stephen was waiting in the lobby; and while the others went on into the dining-room, he drew her aside

433

and showed her the morning paper. "Great Storm," she read aloud. "Sweeps Atlantic Coast." She took the paper from his hand to steady the smaller print: *New England felt only the tail of a great West Indies hurricane that struck Savannah and Charleston.* Her eyes met his in a sagging swirl of recognition.

"It's too late to get the train," he said very distinctly and from a fabulous distance, "but the Fall River boat will get me to New York by morning. I'm afraid the rest of the trip's off. You'll all have to stay on here till you hear from me."

When she continued to stare at him, he nodded, "It looks bad." Had she spoken? But then she clearly heard herself say: "I'm going with you."

He shook his head. "I'll have enough trouble getting through myself."

"Steve, you've got to let me go with you."

At the moment that was the most amazing thing: the calmness of her voice, the steadiness of her hand on his sleeve.

"All right," he said finally.

. . . The red carpet of the cabinway muffled her steps after she left Stephen talking with some men in the main salon, but that only increased the ringing in her ears. And she found the cramped cabin unbearable.

She changed it for the forward upper deck. Here, with her cloak wrapped tight around her, the thunder of the wind and the slapping of the flagstaff cord drowned out the ringing: and the moving beam of the searchlight fascinated her eyes as it cut through the darkness. But she became aware at last of the resentment of a honeymooning couple enfolded in a steamer-rug, and she went to the after deck. Here were a number of people, but the space was more generous and she found a chair.

Some of the stars were out. The Big Dipper was complete, but the North Star was missing. Beyond the hissing spectral wake lay an expanse of dread black water, between her and the frail lights of Newport. And there was the bright intermittent star of the Beaver Tail revolving light. From time to time a sable cloud of smoke blotted out everything in the past but the wake.

From somewhere below the songs of a negro quartette reached her in tatters. She pieced together *Juba,* and *That Old Time Religion,*

434

and *Roll, Jordan, Roll.* The voices of the people around her sounded quite real. They spoke and laughed so naturally that it was impossible to doubt their sincerity. They must believe the world a sane enough place, she thought. Life as usual,—sometimes hot and sometimes cold, but always sane. At intervals their arguments almost convinced her, she could almost believe with them. They reduced the terrible magnitude of the night to human dimensions, at comforting intervals.

At some point she left the chair and went in to the quivering glare of the staircase, along the red-carpet corridor to the door of the cabin. Stephen was not there. She took off her cloak and hat and turned down the smoky lamp.

At intervals now muffled treads passed the door, strange snatches of talk came to her, and the clatter of keys in locks. A man and a woman entered the next cabin, just beyond the wall of her berth. There was an extended conversation, dying out in intimate laughter and whisperings.

At last there was nothing but the trembling and squeaking of the walls. A central throbbing. The swish of water outside the latticed window. The incessant rattle of a glass over the wash-basin.

It was an almost timeless journey. Everything that came within range of her senses smote her with painful sharpness, acute and exhausting meaninglessness; yet a great stupefaction blanketed her mind, so that she was conscious of only a few major impressions, a slow and inevitable crescendo of realization.

In New York a newspaper told her frankly and impersonally that the Carolina and Georgia coasts were devastated, and that Port Royal Sound had borne the brunt of the storm.

A Washington paper added that Beaufort Township was reported to be the scene of indescribable havoc.

At Richmond Stephen got off the train to get a paper. "The worst storm since 1804," he read to her. "St. Helena Island swept by tidal wave. Hundreds drowned. Starvation threatens survivors."

But it was not till Charleston, on Sunday morning, that details began to break through her protective numbness.

At the station, she sat with the luggage in the waiting-room while Stephen went to find out what connections he could make for Beau-

435

fort. When he came back he said: "They're making up a train now. I can get as far as Yemassee,—they can't tell me what happens from there on. The Coosaw River trestle's gone. . . . You'll simply have to stay here, dear, I'm not going to take you into that mess. You can go to Rusty's. And stay there till you hear from me."

. . . He kept out one bag and put the rest of the things into the carriage with her. He tossed a *News & Courier* onto the seat beside her. "Don't move till you hear from me. . . ."

The town was steeped in sunshine: her eyes winced from the brightness. Except for an occasional pile of debris in the gutter—leaves, branches, chimney brick—it seemed to her, as the carriage joggled along the quiet old cobblestoned streets, that this might be any summer Sunday morning in Charleston. And the illusion deepened as she rode down Meeting toward Broad and the chimes of St. Michael's came nearer. . . . Then there was an incredible sense of repetition in everything. She had experienced it before in her life, this sickening shock of recognition, this sense of familiarity and foreknowledge, as though long ago she had known all about what was happening now. And because anything would be less painful than this, she took up the paper.

It was littered with dispatches from the Sea Islands. Against the motion of the carriage she struggled to fix Beaufort items, deciphering the jerky print in fragments. Phosphate works between here and Savannah are reported to be in bad shape—Land's End, Coosaw, and Broad River plants wrecked—Tugs and dredges sunk or flung up high and dry. St. Helena Island was completely washed over by the tidal wave—It is reckoned that upward of fifteen hundred persons were drowned on that island alone—Crops ruined everywhere. . . . It was a sad trip this correspondent made to Port Royal and back to Yemassee from which this dispatch is being sent—The country is utterly devastated—Whites and blacks are working together in teams —Dead being buried in trenches as bodies are found. . . . The Beaufort waterfront has been almost obliterated—Wharves gone— Bay Street looks like a shipyard. Chancel of St. Helena's Church blown out—roofs ripped off many houses exposing rafters—windows smashed—fences crumpled—yards and lawns deep with marshgrass and mud. Every tree left standing is bare of leaves. . . .

Next to advertisements for Bon Ami and Hires Root Beer she found and read: Little hope is held out for the life of Dr. James

Stewart, well-beloved surgeon of this city. Dr. Stewart is known to have been on St. Helena Island at the time——

With suffocating precision the Bon Ami and Hires Root Beer closed over the exquisite pain. . . . But I knew, she pleaded with all that was before her eyes,—I did know, so perhaps you can change it.

And with astounding clarity she saw herself enter Rusty's house in Legare Street, while she was still seated in the joggling carriage, still passing under the echoing chimes of St. Michael's; heard herself answer the house-boy's welcome. She saw herself standing in the office, among his things, his sunlit wind-torn garden beyond the windows.

As she stood staring out, a curtain stirred toward her and touched her bare hand. Mechanically then she took off the other glove and pressed them together into a tight white ball, and turned away from the window to his desk.

On the blotter lay her last letter to him, unopened, waiting.

In a shifty world, she remembered she had written at the end, *you alone remain unchanged.* . . . And here, she thought in a last position of defense, was the final fatal evil at the heart of life. For this, as he himself had said, would be the same always and everywhere, in any world, at any time.

Part Five

I

In the hostile parlor of the Castle, Eugenia confronted her Aunts Susan and Isabel Bramwell with dramatic eyes.

"I'm leaving Beaufort forever!"

The sound of her own voice, the release into spoken words, permitted her to taste at last the full flavor of her decision. It was no longer merely a decision: it was a sensation. For one heady moment she shivered in an ecstasy of satisfaction. All that was lacking now, —gasps of shock and protest from the Aunts.

Suspended in mid-air Eugenia stared at them in bewilderment. Was it possible that they could be receiving the tidings without so much as a flicker of surprise? Susan's face, always so alert and expressive, seemed this morning a perverse mask, faintly quizzical and ironic; Isabel's face showed something less than its habitual vagueness, was a blank pit into which Eugenia felt herself and her precious announcement toppling with no prospect of a break to the sickening fall. She suddenly hated herself for having come. In the flush of intoxication that had followed her decision, she had turned to the Aunts as the only audience of importance at hand, for Uncle Joe was holding court at Walterboro. It had happened simply before she knew what she was doing: the jangling of the Castle doorbell had wakened first misgivings as to the wisdom of the call, but it had been too late then to consider turning back. She had forgotten her pride to bring them news the nature of which she had supposed would insure her at least an interested reception. Yet here they were regarding her as impassively and ambiguously as a pair of cooters on a log. It took all the wind out of her sails.

"I'm leaving Marshlands for good," she tried again, in a pathetically reduced voice.

Susan's short nod was as explicit as though she had said in so many words: Well, we're not surprised to hear that.

As a matter of fact, the impact of recent events had quite numbed the Aunts against surprise. Although six months had passed since the great storm, they were only beginning to recover from that night of stark terror, when they had huddled in their bedroom while the wind roared at the windows like a furnace and downstairs in the hall the dark water rose inch by inch; while out on St. Helena their cousin Rusty was sharing the fate of hundreds of the island people, —Susan and Isabel had never forgiven him for siding with the Fenwick faction, the Enemy, but they would hardly have wished him punished so conclusively. . . . And on the very heels of the storm Clara Barton, Yankee queen of the Red Cross, had descended with her retinue upon desolated Beaufort. A second wave of Carpetbaggers. They had passed over Joe and other leading white citizens and consulted nigger politicians, hobnobbed with them, so demoralized the black people with charity that they would not work to clean up the wreckage and rebuild. Another Reconstruction Era.

And then the Aunts had watched Stephen's struggle to save something from the ruins of his world, his desperate squirmings to extricate himself. Finally, only two weeks ago, had come the death of Sophie. How they had begrudged her even her last gesture! Stricken with heart failure on the stairs at Marshlands, she had clutched as she fell at the pictures on the wall, pulling them down with her in a great clatter and to-do: a giddy end, theatrical and absurd. But by dying their sister had obviously capitulated, so they had been able to attend the burial services at St. Helena's,—without of course recognizing Stephen or his wife. Amnesty had then and there been granted Eugenia, because she was judged neither responsible for the Feud nor worthy of its continuation. And they had foreseen that their niece's departure from under the roof of Marshlands would be only a matter of time now that Sophie was gone.

"Where you going?" Susan asked curtly.

Eugenia failed to realize that the tone of the question was caused by the simple fact that she was occupying Aunt Susan's special parlor chair instead of the chair reserved for visitors, thereby seriously disturbing the fitness of things. She interpreted the tone as a sneering reflection on her capacity to go anywhere. But the question gave her an opening: she brightened perceptibly and answered boldly.

"Charleston. I can stay with the Hazzards."

"Don't see how you could stand that," Susan said with a twist of her head. "They're uncommon tiresome, particularly Cousin Charlie."

"Always bragging," Isabel put in, "on their wonderful cistern water. You don't hear them bragging on their roaches, though. Susie, where'd we read about roaches would inherit the earth someday?"

"Do, Bel. Can't you find a place to board in Beaufort?" she asked Eugenia. "What about the Broughtons? There's only Sally and her invalid mother in that house."

Eugenia shook her head emphatically. "No I thank you. I've been off speaking terms with Sally for ages. And I can't abide invalids. Anyway, I've had enough of Beaufort,—it isn't really Beaufort anymore."

"No?" Susan bridled. "Strange we haven't observed that. Your Uncle Joe and we have been under the impression that Beaufort was still enough Beaufort to be worthy of our continued allegiance."

"I mean," Eugenia retreated, "everything's so changed. And there's nothing to hold me here now."

She drew a handkerchief from her belt, and to forestall any demonstration of that kind Susan promptly turned helpful.

"Of course," she conceded, "there would be plenty of contacts for you in Charleston."

Eugenia nodded appreciatively. "And I can get loads of material for my book on Wade Hampton. And Uncle Joe will be there on and off."

"I thought Joe was helping you with a biography or something of Grandpaa Bramwell?"

"He was. But I feel I've grown stale on that, so I've put it aside for the present. I'm terribly interested in General Hampton. He's such a great man, such an inspiring figure, a hero in every sense of the word."

"I won't dispute that point with you. But so was Grandpaa, though not so conspicuous."

"Must have been in the paper," Isabel interrupted, still pursuing the roach question.

"Well," Susan shrugged, "suit yourself about Charleston, Eugenia. But I should think you'd find the Mowbreys and the Savannah connection a sight pleasanter company than the Hazzards."

"I could never forget," Isabel smiled, "that Savannah's in Georgia."

"Mamma did come from Savannah," said Susan, "but of course she was descended from a staff-officer of Oglethorpe, so she wasn't a Georgian in the ordinary sense."

"Mamma was a great belle," Isabel sighed, and began to rock gently.

Susan pressed her lips together and closed her eyes to accent her nod of agreement.

"The greatest belle of them all," Isabel chanted, "the greatest belle of the ball."

Susan opened her eyes. "And a very great wit as well, Bel. Mamma's beauty was not of the shallow and frivolous sort. She had beauty of both heart and intellect. Why, any one of her *bon mots* would have made the reputation of another woman. Her remark to the Minister from Poland is history."

Eugenia felt that the conversation was being diverted into wholly irrelevant byways.

"So I'm going to Charleston," she insisted. "I'd have left long ago if it hadn't been for Mamma."

Susan regarded the floor severely.

"I suppose," she said presently, "you've saved some of the allowance you've been getting. And Joe says Sophie—Joe says you were left some bonds."

"She didn't leave us a hairpin," Isabel mused.

Eugenia's lips began to tremble. "Stephen's been trying to make me give up what little I have. He'd make a pauper of me too. He's taken all the money Emily had, and the funds they were building up for the children, and everything Cousin Rusty left in his will except the medical books for Michael,—he's even used Lucy's little savings. He's borrowed everywhere he could, and Marshlands and Land's End are both mortgaged up to the hilt. And it's all just been thrown away."

"Joe lent him money," Isabel told the black-bordered handkerchief she was pressing out on her knee, "but he says he won't let him have a penny more."

"How can he?" Susan flashed. "He has his own obligations to consider. It was folly trying to revive phosphate with the new Florida deposits and the Tillman tax. Joe said all along it was folly. . . . Well, what are they going to do now? We hear they're letting Marshlands and moving to the island."

"I'm sure I don't know what they're going to do. All I know is I'm leaving in the morning."

"Rats leave the sinking ship," Isabel rocked.

Eugenia gasped. "Why, Aunt Bel!—what a perfectly horrid thing to say!"

"Eugenia!" Susan snapped from the edge of her chair, "you're not to speak to your Aunt Bel in any such tone of voice."

"But I'm not a rat! I've been planning this for months and years, to get away from that house. And now I don't dare stay under the same roof with Stephen for another day. I'm afraid of him. He threatens me. He's drinking terribly now. He's——"

"Sally Broughton," Isabel interrupted placidly, "saw him being taken home from Bay Street in a carriage Saturday evening."

"He's——," Eugenia tried to continue.

"*And,*" Isabel smiled, giving a final pat to her handkerchief, "that wasn't all."

In exasperation, Eugenia raised her voice. "He's gone all to pieces! I tell you he's gone mad!"

Susan was not impressed. "Goody gracious, you don't have to shout. We're neither of us deaf, thank heaven."

Eugenia played her last card in a whisper.

"I'd just like you to know some of the scenes I've been through in that house lately."

For a moment Aunt Susan was obviously on the verge of betraying her curiosity: she hesitated on the edge of her chair like a fish inspecting a morsel of choice bait. But for the sake of other and greater satisfactions she resisted the temptation, and rose with a fine toss of her head.

"Eugenia, we're not interested in anything that concerns your brother. We're neither glad nor sorry that God has seen fit to punish him. For us he ceased to exist when he mingled his blood—our blood —with the blood of that woman. As for her, it will be entertaining to see how a Yankee meets disaster."

Since the beginning of the interview Susan had suspected Eugenia of having come to make overtures about living at the Castle, and to blast any such proposition she added quietly: "If you had had the delicacy to avoid the subject of the Fenwicks, your Aunt Isabel and I would have been only too glad to hear your plans and help you in any way possible. As it is, we must ask you to excuse us."

After that there was really nothing for Eugenia to do but gather up the shreds of her dignity and leave.

And the following morning she actually left Marshlands and took the train for Charleston.

II

THE LAST DAYS of February were languid with spring, but March brought to Land's End savage west winds that kept the Sound in an uproar of whitecaps and lashed to pulp the opening buds and flowers lured out too soon. Tender shoots, withered by freezing nights, drooped in the sun that was without power to revive them; and the new leaves that had begun bravely to hide the scars of the great storm hung now like sodden paper, limp and dead in the wind.

Just before the coming of the wind, Emily had wakened—her first morning on the island after the move from rented Marshlands—to find the world muffled under a light blanket of snow. For the Sea Islands this was extraordinary. During her years in the South it had happened only once before: on a January Sunday, when Michael was thirteen. White magic had enveloped Marshlands, the house and the lawn and the trees; the palmettoes at the seawall and the lone sago palm near the gates, the last damasks of the rose garden and the shrubbery of the closed garden; the roofs of the summer-house and boat-house, the fringes of the marsh, the Ladies Island shore across the gray river. Everything had stood transfigured in unforgettable beauty, the somber enchantment of New England winter in the air, the heart aching with memories.

. . . Rusty had come "home" from Charleston and Joe Bramwell had dropped in for dinner, so there had been plenty of recruits for the snowball battle that afternoon. The children had been beside themselves, and in the excitement even Joe had taken leave of his dignity and joined in the fray, scooping up snow with both hands and hurling it loosely in any direction. Weakly defending herself against Jack's giggling raids, she had laughed at Joe till her sides hurt. The very abandon of his attack had soon cleared the field; but his triumph had cost him his breath and had left him in a state of flushed impotence, so when the children had combined forces against him (a strategy prompted by Miss Sophie from the front steps), he had been put to ignominious flight. After that they had turned on Rusty and driven him into the closed garden. There for a while he had repulsed every assault and even made several spectacular sallies, but in the end a flanking movement had forced his retirement to the summer-house, where he had been o'erwhelmed. Then Lucy had rounded up and subdued the giddy victors, herding them into the house for a change of clothes. And that evening when the family had been gathered in drowsy peace before the living-room fire, she had read them *Snowbound* as a fitting close for a memorable day.

> *The sun that brief December day*
> *Rose cheerless over hills of gray*
> *And darkly-circled gave at noon*
> *A sadder light than waning moon. . . .*

Now at this second time of snow, here at Land's End, she wondered if the children had opened their eyes yet to the miracle. What a blessing to know they were safe, out of range of disaster: Michael in Charleston, thanks to Joe's help in getting him a scholarship at the Citadel, and Margaret and Jack boarding in Beaufort with their teacher, Miss Hamilton. They were taken care of, for the time being at least, and that was the important thing. As she crept out of bed and dressed before the dead hearth, quietly to keep from disturbing Stephen, she repeated this comfort to herself over and over to fill the awful emptiness.

It was that afternoon, when the snow had melted from everywhere except the places of deepest shadow, that the west wind began to blow. For four days it roamed the island like a wild beast, resting at night to permit visitations of black frost. At each noon the sun was able to thaw out a little of the ice sheet that clung to the north slope of the roof, releasing a mournful tattoo on the tin roof of the back porch, but beyond that the sun was helpless against the relentless cold of the wind. Once she had loved wind; now even its gentlest stirrings would be an echoing of the storm, a whispering of anguish and death. And when it blew like this from the west, bitter and malevolent, mocking the feeble sunlight through which it swept,

448

jarring the windows and shuddering down the chimneys to convulse the fires, it was the voice of doom.

Lucy, who went about her work swathed in layers of clothing, was always on the lookout for something comforting to say.

"Miss Em'ly, dey's one good t'ing 'bout dis bad spell. 'Tis sho gwine do 'way wid dat crap of las'-season skeetuh what de wintuh been too mile fuh kill."

Emily felt solicitous eyes watching her.

"Now jes' set in dat big cheer to de fiuh an' *res'*. Le'me git you a book an' a cup of good hot tea."

That faithful heart. What would she ever have done without Lucy. It was to Lucy's arms that she had turned when the first protecting shock had passed. It was Lucy who had stood by her through the period of Stephen's disintegration, when each day had brought fresh misery and disaster. And it was Lucy who had come to share with her this last stand against chaos.

"Miss Em'ly," Lucy had replied when she had been told she must find other work, "you know good enough I ain' gwine do no sech t'ing."

"But you must, Lucy."

The eyes had filled with tears.

"I too shame fuh hab you talk so to me ma'm. What I keer what Tunis an' dem no-'count nigguh do? I ain' gwine lef' you nohow. I ain' nebbuh gwine lef' you."

All her will had been powerless to break that stubborn loyalty. And now, as she watched and nursed Stephen, so Lucy was watching and nursing her. Every morning when she came downstairs she was taken in hand.

"Miss Em'ly, when you done hab you' breakfas', do go set to de fiuh an' res' till Mistuh Steben wake-up."

Rest! There was no longer any such thing as rest: it had ceased to exist, it had vanished out of the world together with all peace, leaving only exhaustion and an endless futile harassment of body and mind. To sit down for so much as a minute was to be engulfed. She must keep moving, moving from room to room, doing anything that involved movement.

It was noon before Stephen rapped on the floor above, signaling that he was finally awake. When she went up with his tray, opened the door and met his sunken eyes, her nerves began to quiver. She was still fighting to forget those last days in Beaufort, to drive out of her mind the picture of that Stephen—besotted, brutish, and frantic as an animal at bay; to see only this sick man, this broken Stephen. It was his defeat that she found most difficult to meet. If he had been able to stand up against the collapse of their world, she could have faced catastrophe with courage. But his failure had left her miserably shaken and afraid.

After she had fed him like a child, she sat at the bedside through the long afternoon, moving only to put wood on the fire. He seldom spoke, but he seemed to need the sound of her voice and she read to him as long at a stretch as her eyes and lips could follow the print. When he drowsed, she kept on to drive back the bleak turmoil of the wind in the trees. When she had to stop, a stinging faintness was waiting for her, a smothered agitation that was the nearest thing to rest she knew during these first days at Land's End.

At night he slept like a dead man. Lying tense beside him in the ringing darkness, she was exposed to the full fury of the torment that daylight and daylight activities partly blunted. If she lost direct consciousness for a time, it was only to enter a place of desolation where strange elements from the past mingled in a phantasmagoria of pain and despair. But consciousness seldom released her; she was caught in a net of mental twistings and turnings, vain reflections and speculations. And now one thought repeated itself with more cruel persistence than any other: how had she failed to take matters into her own hands till so late? If she had had the wits to step in sooner, perhaps the final and worst phases of disaster could have been averted.

I was dazed, she told herself. . . .

But there was the one great blessing to cling to,—the children had been protected from the worst. And for the present they were safe. Someday, somehow, the family world would be rebuilt for them, must be rebuilt, made whole again from these shattered fragments. Somehow, despite the pitiless heartsickening wind.

So, somehow, these nights were lived through.

✓   ✓   ✓

The wind had spent itself at last. A friendly day dawned, and she put on old clothes and walking shoes for a journey over the plantation.

When she was free of the house and Lucy's protests, a little of the dead weight on her spirit began to lift. In the avenue the great interlocking arms of the live-oaks, sturdy survivors of the storm, made a vaulted ceiling over her head: through the tattered cobwebs of moss that still clung to the branches were glimpses of the sky, serene and spotless blue. The shafts and pools of early sunlight that fell across her path held warmth and life. Birds sang, and the earth seemed already to have forgotten the recent treacheries of cold and wind. It was possible to believe that the soft bright air was whispering promises, indefinite but sincere.

But when she reached the end of the avenue and followed the main road as far as the right-hand turn to Pine Point, she realized that the mood of the avenue was isolated and deceptive. The maimed woods and barren littered fields along the way had not forgotten either the storm or the false spring. They had the appearance of shrinking from the renewed ardor of the sun; they held themselves aloof, as if unwilling to risk another betrayal. And their mournful distrust was contagious. Heaviness closed down again, leaving only mechanical movement, mechanical perceptions.

Apathy hung over the settlements along the route. The wind and tide of the hurricane had left a great blight of hopelessness on the lives and homes that had not been swept away. From cabins supported at crazy angles by pole props the survivors came to the roadside to greet her sadly and tell their stories in listless voices. It was appalling the number of faces that were missing. Few family groups had been spared intact, most had suffered cruel losses, some had vanished completely. The morning developed into a long repetition of sorrows. And nobody seemed to be doing anything about the present or to have any plans for the future, though the period of hibernation on Red Cross rations was ended and the planting season had come.

It was noon before she reached Jessie's house. A two-story affair, substantial and well anchored, it was the only home in its neighborhood that had escaped serious damage. Jessie herself sat on the porch with an assortment of people around her. When she recognized who it was, she came to the road with a warm greeting. But this was not the old Jessie, light-hearted leader of plantation society: she was shabby and dejected, and after the greeting all vivacity faded and her voice went flat as she gave her version of the storm. Her husband

and two of her sons had been drowned when the phosphate dredge had foundered; only Duke was left to her, the most no-account and ill-favored of the lot. That made the third husband she had lost. She had been able to give the other two decent burial; her main regret about the last one seemed to be that a watery grave had claimed him, —"De spirit cyan' nebbuh fine no res' in dat element, Miss Em'ly." And then a plague of relatives and orphans had descended upon her, some come from as far as Sams Point at the other end of the island. She hadn't the heart to run any of them off, though they were crowding her out of house and home and she had nothing to feed them but hoecakes and sassafras tea. Her voice trailed off. Everything was ruination these days, and all signs were failing. She pointed to the drooping branches of her pet camphor tree, killed by the frost. If she could make up her mind to cut it back, it might come up from the roots. . . .

Emily looked past Jessie at the little band that had straggled after her from the porch and stood now in a half-circle behind her, the children in front, the grown-ups hanging back. Beyond them lay a big pine that had fallen across the yard: they had all had to climb over it on their way to the gate. Although there were several able-bodied men among Jessie's pensioners, nothing apparently was ever going to be done about the obstacle. It lay there a symbol of the lethargy and defeat that gripped the whole plantation.

"What are you all going to do, Jessie?"

"I ain' know, Miss Em'ly. Seem like nobody ain' got no haa't fuh nutt'n no mo'."

"But you've got to do something. We've all got to do something. Can't these people help you plant?"

"Who?—dem nigguh?" Jessie sucked her teeth. "Miss Em'ly, dey done git too lazy fuh raise han' fuh scratch wool! All dey studyin' 'bout is eatin' an' sleepin' an' might-be fishin'. De debble heself cyan' dribe'um."

But Emily was unwilling to let the matter rest on that fatalistic note. She was waking from her own lethargy as she talked, and before she was through she had succeeded in waking in Jessie a determination to take the situation in hand. Once definitely aroused Jessie became something of her old forceful self.

"All I been need, Miss Em'ly, is somebody fuh straight-talk me like dat fuh gib me backbone fuh cuss dem nigguh out good."

And she turned on them with flashing eyes. "Listen-yuh, you nigguh! I gwine chase eb'ry Gawdbless las' one of you out dis yaa'd!" Their gaping mouths and pop eyes inspired her to a shouting rage. "I mus' be pure lose my mine, lettin' y'all fasten 'pon me same like tick 'pon cow! But I *t'rough,* hear. Now mine what I say. I gwine plant peas an' collard. Maybe cotton an' co'n. An' dem willin' fuh wuk can stay. But dem what ain' fuh wuk can *git out!"*

She singled out one man in the group for special attention. "Max, t'ain' gwine do you no good smilin' so foolish. Jes' 'cause I ain' got no hosban' no mo', don' t'ink you' sweet-talk an' t'ing done turn my head,—you gwine wuk same de res' ef you wan' my roof obuh you' triflin' caa'cuss. Gawd'a'mighty, I hope I ain' so haa'd-up till I'm got to keep no blue-gum ape!" She swung back to the group as a whole. "When de white lady gone, I gwine bless y'all out *plenty.* I ain' staa't yit."

And when Emily left after a few final words with Jessie, the harangue was resumed. When she was far down the road she could still catch its blistering exclamation points.

There were two more stops, and then the road brought her at last to the Big Field.

For a long time she stood motionless in the warm sunlight, looking out over the wild expanse of dead weeds and vine-tangled scrub thickets. Above her tired body her thoughts were feverishly active, but they were unable to take any direction. Talking with the people, listening to their troubles and trying to offer some comfort had shaken her out of absorption in her own troubles, but there was no vaguest solution for the problem of the future. It remained a blank wall, casting a numbing shadow over her, and she was powerless to find any passage through it, any opening and escape to what lay beyond. In these dazed months since the storm life had come to a full stop, and the word, the sign to set it in motion again was still lacking; though today the world around her, the great field and the blue sky, the very road under her feet seemed suspended in hushed expectancy, waiting and listening with her for an answer.

Straight ahead, at the end of the road, was the grove of pines that marked the Point. Between their shafts came flashes of light from the shining waters of the Inlet. As she stood gazing she was swept back to the moment when she had first seen the grove, that faraway day when she had driven over—in the old buggy behind Garibaldi with the boy Tunis seated shyly beside her—to see Rusty about the vaccination. That day and this one, it was hard to believe they were equally true; yet here they both were, existing together for her by the time-obliterating magic of memory. With an effort she drew her stinging eyes away from the grove; but she could not hold them away; they kept turning back. And presently she found herself walking towards it, moving as in a dream towards the end of the road, against her will, against the realization that she must avoid this place, that she was not yet ready to face this final confirmation of her loss.

When she reached the marsh brook, she saw that the little bridge of logs was gone and the tamarisks stripped of their feathery plumes. To cross the brook she had to walk along the bank till she came to a spot where a shoal of oyster shells gave her firm footing. On the opposite bank there was no trace of road: all the space under the trees where the thick brown carpet of pine-needles had been was a gray waste now of sand and dried mud. The dwarf cedars and fragrant myrtle bushes and the cassenas and hollies, on whose red berries flocks of robins used to feast, had been whipped to shreds like the tamarisks. Only two of the great pines had fallen, but the proud crests of all had lost branches and the bark for several feet from the ground was crusted with mud that no winter rains had been able to wash off.

When she came out on the far side of the grove, the sparkle of the water beyond the marsh blinded her for a moment. Then her stricken eyes began to take in the desolation around her. There was scarcely anything recognizable to cling to. The cottage had vanished; tilted foundation posts were all that was left to mark the site. Of the palmettoes only two or three remained, and they were half-uprooted and dying, a last mournful rustling in the bleached tatters of their fronds. For the rest: swirls of mud-caked debris stranded at the edge of the marsh.

As she moved to the bank of the creek, scores of fiddler crabs sunning themselves on the ebb-tide flats vanished so quickly that it was difficult to believe they had been there an instant ago. And for an instant the image of the *Dolphin* stood before her on the gliding water. Then it too vanished, leaving her at the mercy of a vast and impersonal silence. In the past this same silence had been an intimate

454

medium of communion with him who was gone. Now it was a terrible vacuum, draining away the remnants of her being.

Where are you? her heart pleaded.

But there was only the enormous solitude, magnified by the remote cries of sea birds and the ticking sound of the tiny crab holes in the pluff mud at her feet. An emptiness as of death shuddered through her, and instinctively she turned to flee, stumbling blindly over the ridges of sand toward the shelter of the grove.

Her hands gripped the rough bark of the first trunk she came to, and for a few moments the strength of the great tree steadied her. But there was no shutting out of her ears the muted plaint of birds over the marsh and the murmuring lament in the branches high above her head. The breath of the sea was a whispering of horror, a rising moan of grief and despair. It mounted swiftly in her senses, a crescendo of savage wind and rain. It was become tumultuous, frenzied. She could no longer stand against it. A tremendous black tide was crashing, thundering over her. In her throat she could feel her drowning voice cry out to him. . . .

She lay still, hardly breathing. The storm was past, she knew dimly: the wind gone, the dark waters subsided. Beyond that for a long time she could think or feel nothing.

By sluggish degrees her mind regained consciousness of the sunlight, the sand, the base of the tree near which she lay. But even then she was unable to say where she was. Around this core of uncertainty a sense of extinction formed, and she thought: I am dead with him, this is my body lying here beside his. . . . Slowly her open eyes recognized the absurdity of that. And then she explained to herself rationally: I've tried to do too much today—I was weak and faint— I should never have come here at all. . . .

But when she closed her eyes against the thought of him, grief rushed back with such force that she cried out his name. And now because full realization of her loss had at last overtaken her, she fought for strength to destroy that stifling knowledge, for faith to deny it, faith to redeem him from the dead, call him back to her.

"It's not true that you're gone."

She threw her whole heart against the terrible solitude that was pressing in on her. "You're here with me now. And you always will be. You promised me. And I believe. I believe. . . ."

Out of the numbing silence a pulsing as of many wings quickened the air around her. She felt strong arms lifting her. And despite the stinging haze that obscured marsh and inlet and even the trunk of the tree near her hand, she saw in a surge of revelation his face, his eyes and his smile clearly before her.

After that first piercing ecstasy had passed, she clung to him like a child, fearful that he would be torn from her again by the doubts and impacts of the visible world. But far from fading in the blind white light of reality and reason, the conviction of his living presence grew in strength with every moment. He was hers, completely and finally, beyond the reach of any power of darkness and time.

When she left the grove and recrossed the marsh brook, she took the old shortcut that skirted the Big Field and wound toward Land's End through woods and clearings. The path had been erased at many points by the storm tide, but knowing so well its vagrant course she was able to retrace every twist and turn even when it became at times a trackless waste of sand and silt. And through her thoughts she was aware of him striding ahead of her: she was following him as she had in the long-ago days of their first friendship, as he had always insisted she should for fear of meeting a rattler or moccasin. But there was no more fear in her heart now than there had been then. And though so persistent a mist blurred her eyes that she had to keep brushing them to see the way, there was no longer even memory of loss. Her mind, freed at last from its dark stupor, was hastening to make up for lost time, seeking his guidance, turning over with him the problem of the future.

When she reached a cross-path to the mines, she turned off to the left and followed the trail worn by the feet of the workers from the plantation settlements. Like the shortcut it was erased at many points, and not being familiar with its windings she lost her way several times before she came out abruptly on the Company property.

She was unprepared for a scene of such complete desolation. From his visits here since the storm Stephen had brought back descriptions of the havoc, but she had been too stunned to take in much of what he had told her. Even now the picture before her eyes could not at once dislodge the pictures of the past, the sights and sounds of the place as she had known it for so many years:—the bustle of activity around the buildings, rumble of grinding mill, smoke and steam of engine house, sweating forms of men, snatches of song, masts of schooners at the wharf, the dredge and its barges on the Inlet. Now all that was gone, leaving an incredible wilderness littered with drifts of mud-caked debris, against a background of shining blue water and dreaming barrier isles under a sky serene and innocent.

Her eyes came to rest on a little white house that stood like a miracle in this wasteland, near the spot where the road from the mines to Land's End led away through a strip of woods. The last time Seth Robinson and Linda had come to Marshlands they had told of this new home they were building with lumber salvaged from the wreckage of the commissary and the drying-sheds. In the neatly fenced yard the figure of a young woman was taking down washing from a line.

To be sure of herself Emily waited a little time before she started toward the house. When she was in hailing distance she raised her hand and called out. The figure in the yard shielded her eyes, hesitated a moment, then waved and called back and came running to meet her.

After a warm embrace Emily held her at arm's length in happy appraisal, smiling helplessly before the joy of her greeting and the breathless rush of questions. And as she searched Linda's eyes, level now with her own, the poignant surprise was renewed. It seemed so short a time ago, that day in the sweltering little room over the Robinsons' store at Port Royal: she could still feel the weight of the newborn babe in her arms. And only yesterday Linda and Michael had still been children. Today they were grown, but by what alchemy remained a mystery, though she had been so intimate a witness of every phase of the transformation.

As they walked arm-in-arm to the house, she felt behind their talk the sense of refreshment that Linda's company always gave her. Linda was one of the truly good things in the world. "She's as reassuring," Rusty had once said, "as sun-up and a bird on the wing." To be with her was inevitably to be reminded of your own age,—yourself deep in the forties while she was not even eighteen yet, standing where you had stood when you had first come to these islands,—but it was also to be made to feel young again by contagion and sympathy. And Linda had the perception to see in this older you a contemporary as well as a middle-aged friend.

At the house Seth met them. He still limped from the injury to his back, and his face was longer and sadder than ever. But his welcome was heartwarming.

After she had answered his close inquiries about Stephen and Michael, Margaret and Jack, he showed her through the little house. It was neat as a pin, but scantily furnished.

"We're fillin' in piece by piece, ma'm," he explained, "fast as I can turn 'em out. Which ain't none too fast 'cause I got no proper tools. Now take them makeshift beds,—had to just throw 'em together best I could. But soon as I get me a lathe, I aim to turn out some pretty beds, like them old-type magnolia ones I made for the big house. Right now I'm workin' on a table to replace this here jackleg critter. Like to see it?"

She went with him out to the side yard, where an "old-type" wing table stood in a nest of shavings. It was cleverly pieced together from scraps of salvage, recognizable remains of the well-seasoned pine counter of the commissary; proudly he displayed his only implements, a penknife and chisel dug out of the debris of the Company tool shed. "When I get it sanded down and oiled," he said, stroking the top affectionately, "you won't never know the mournful patchwork that's in it."

When she had finished admiring the table and his resourceful craftsmanship, they went to sit on the porch. Linda left them to talk while she made tea.

As Seth told what they were planning to do with this plot of land that Stephen had sold them out of the Company property, Emily marveled how little time had changed him from the man she had first known at Port Royal. He had seemed oldish to her then; now he really looked no older. Perhaps it was because his spare frame had so little to lose. He was like some gaunt tree on the edge of the barrier-island dunes: weathered to bleakness, almost bare of leaves, twisted and gnarled and dried by the winds, but also toughened to a kind of ageless durability. Only his eyes were a little more sunken, and his voice a little more drawling and slow.

"Yes ma'm," he was saying, "I reckon we'll all make out somehow, sorta piecin' things together again from wrack and ruin, like I'm tryin' to do with that table there.

"Now I got me a patch of peas and corn in, over yonder where you see the scarecrow standin'. And I'm fixin' to put in some sure-enough crops quick as the people come alive and I can get help.

Linda's been after me to get her some settin' hens from the main-land, where every last fowl on the island was blowed clear to in the storm. And she's got her heart set on a cow and I don't know what all."

He smiled at that, but his eyes saddened again.

"Young wounds is soon healed, and that's as it should be. But when you're old, it takes a right smart of time to get over the hurt of things. Seems like I can't never get used to havin' Martha and Dallas gone. . . .

"When the roof of the engine-house come crashin' into us that night and our walls begun to buckle and give, I didn't have time to reach out my hand before they was gone, her and Dallas, in the howlin' flood of wind and rain that come lashin' in on us. Swallered up without a sign or a sound, they was, in that churnin' black tide. How me and Linda ever fetched up safe in the woods I can't rightly say.

"I never was real pious and sure of salvation like Martha, and I ain't never been much of a hand for church-goin',—never felt worthy someway. But we always had home prayers of a Sunday and readin' from the Scriptures, and we still do, Linda and me. And I'm full of praise to the Lord for sparin' her, but I'm still wonderin' why he couldn't have took me in place of Martha and the boy. I'm still ques-tionin' the wisdom and mercy of that."

His tanned fists relaxed. "But it ain't meet for a man to be a-questionin' the will of God. He spared Linda, and I reckon that's sufficient answer for me.

"Bein' young she's hopeful-like, and that puts heart into me,—a body can't stay downcast with her around. She keeps pert and cheer-ful, but I know she gets mighty lonesome with nobody but me to talk to. It's sure fine, ma'm, you took a notion to come back here to live. Things'll seem a heap more natural now, like they used to. We was fixin' to pay our respects to you and Mister Fenwick, directly we heard you was in the big house. But—well, we thought we better not put our oar in—in a manner of speakin'—better wait till you got settled and not push ourself forward, knowin' how sick he was and all."

She reassured him gratefully. "He'll be up soon, and it will be a great help if you'll come to see him."

"Well now, I sure want to. You see, ma'm, you and Mister Fenwick was ever powerful good to me and mine. And I thought maybe——. Well, for one thing, I better take a look at them repairs I made to the roof and chimneys right after the storm, see how they're holdin' up. And—I been meanin' to speak for a little more land, if he was willin' to parcel me off a few more acres. And then there's the old Company launch a-settin' back up yonder in the woods nigh to the head of Station Creek,—I was aimin' to haul her out on rollers, and patch her up some, and tinker with the engine. And I been a-thinkin'— maybe——." His voice trailed off to a hoarse whisper. "I been a-tellin' Linda. . . ."

He seemed unable to go on. His eyes blinked under the strain, and a vein stood out on his forehead. But when at last he found his voice again, words came with a rush. "Mis' Fenwick ma'm, you been a-lookin' out for us since way back when the mines was first opened, and now I'm takin' the liberty to ask permission to do a little some-thin' in return like, till Mister Fenwick gets his health back. I got bank savin's over to town I never would had if it hadn't been for you-all. It ain't no big sum, but we ain't goin' to be a-needin' more'n a mite of it, me and Linda, to make out till we get our little farm here a-runnin'."

She was staring miserably off into space, unable to control her eyes and voice to thank him.

"I hope I ain't give no offense, ma'm," he faltered. "It's just that we been a-hearin' things has been a-goin' powerful bad with Mister Fenwick—since the Company failed. And I been a-tellin' Linda I was just goin' to ask—well, if they wasn't *somethin'* we could do, ma'm."

Under the necessity of making some immediate response she man-aged to force out a few words of thanks; wretchedly inadequate words, but they were received with a deep breath of relief. And then, abruptly, an idea came to her aid.

"Seth, you can help us. In another way."

He nodded and blinked expectantly.

"You see, the doctor in Beaufort says it will be a long time before Stephen can get his health back. And—meanwhile—the plantation is the only hope we have left. It's got to be made to help us. I don't know how, but somehow it's got to be made to work for us."

He nodded again, with dawning comprehension. And she groped on, feeling her way as the idea expanded. "If we could plant—on a small scale, of course. And rent some of the land to the people on shares. Don't you think we could make the place pay us something?"

"Yes ma'm, I do. Leastways, I don't know why not. It's the same land that yielded a fortune to Mister Fenwick's grandfather, and his father before him. Only o'course that was in slavery times, and things is changed now. But I'm certain sure somethin' can be done."

"Isaac was always urging Stephen to plant. He said the land was well rested and it was a pity not to work it."

"It's a-lyin' good and faller, the land, and ripe for mighty nigh any crop you had a mind to put in. Won't take no fertilizin' to speak of neither, though it will take a heap of clearin'. Yes ma'm, I remember how Isaac used to go on to the boss. This place was his heart. He could call the name of every field on the plantation—and Cherokee too—like they was his own young-ones, and he sure hated to see the place runnin' to sedge and brush. He never took to phosphate,—it was only the high wages and that Leola of his that drove him to it."

He shook his head. "Sea-island cotton was his line. They ain't nobody left that knows long-staple like he did. But most of the people has it in their blood, as you might say, so you could make out with them. And I done enough dirt farmin' in my time to be some help, I reckon. Was it cotton you had in mind, ma'm? That's about the onliest money crop they is."

"I suppose so." She had to smile at the vagueness of that. "You see, I need your advice,—it's just a hazy idea in my mind."

But by the time Linda called them in to tea, the idea had begun to take distinct shape. And by the time she left to hurry back to Stephen, the idea had become a definite plan.

To begin with, the Big Field was to be cleared for planting. And Barty and Ned would do the plowing. Barty and Ned were twin deaf-mutes, but they were powerful men and hard workers; and they had saved their yoke of oxen from the storm by driving them—against all protests—into Thankful Church, which stood on high ground and so had served as a sanctuary against the storm's great tide. Today, Seth said, the Twins had borrowed the batteau he had patched up for fishing, but when they got back he would tell them to report to the big house first thing in the morning.

There the plan began.

Linda walked part of the way home with her. Quivering inside

461

with excitement, and a little stunned too by the scope and daring of the plan, she was content to let Linda do most of the talking. And it was easy to listen: flushed but frank, the girl wasted no time getting to the subject of Michael.

After she had made Linda turn back, she slackened her pace. Cold shadows were closing in on the lonely road, but she simply could not hurry, even though it was late and Stephen and Lucy would be fretting. She was conscious now of heavy fatigue, increasing with each plodding step; and the nearer she came to the cluster of trees that hid all but the chimneys of Land's End, the harder it was to sustain the new confidence this day had given her. Little by little, as she approached the house and its mood of defeat, her spirits drooped under a weight of questions and dreary uncertainties. So that by the time she reached the stable and the yard she found herself back in the grip of emptiness and fear.

Lucy met her at the kitchen door with a solicitous scolding. That was balm. And waiting for her in the house to revive her spirits with a bound were two letters from Michael, with the mail and groceries that Mr. Van Wie had sent out by boat as he had promised. But when she went up to Stephen, she was lost again.

When she had succeeded in quieting his fretfulness, she gave him a censored account of her day, telling him only about her visit to the settlements and the Robinsons' new home. Then she opened the precious letters from Michael. They were not the long homesick affairs of his first weeks at the Citadel: they were short and hasty now, and she had to read them slowly to make them sound like anything. And at the end of both she had to invent messages for Stephen. It was her fault, of course, that they were missing; in keeping her letters scrupulously free of worry or any reminders of family disaster—what he knew and what he had seen at the Christmas holidays was terrible enough—she had made no mention of Stephen's breakdown.

Later when she went downstairs, after she had fed him the bowl of bread and broth that was still the only food he could keep in his stomach, and had finally settled him for the first phase of the night, she read the letters to Lucy. And after supper she read them again, to the living-room fire, lingering over each abrupt sentence till it yielded its last possible significance. She found courage then to look over the rest of the mail. It was mostly bills, as she had feared, and

News & Couriers. There was one bright spot, though: a check from the Fowlers for the Marshlands rent.

While she was looking wearily through the bundle of papers, trying to make sense of the news of the day as her mind skirmished feebly with the multiple worries ahead, she heard Stephen's rap on the floor above. When she got him settled again, she stole back downstairs. She was suffused with tiredness, her very bones ached with accumulated fatigue, but the thought of staying upstairs, of lying tense and motionless in the darkness beside him, was unbearable.

When she had persuaded Lucy to go to bed, she took the lamp and her writing things to the dining-room. But when she sat down at the table she could find nothing to say to her son that was not related to disaster. . . . To protect him from useless worry, to permit him to forget disaster or to think of it as past, that was what had to be kept rigidly in mind through every letter to him. They were not ears, these letters, for the unburdening of her troubles. They were reassurances that home was functioning again, on a reduced scale of course, but confidently: that all was well, secure again, or at least improving, so that he could meet his life with a whole heart and will. And at last, by a weary process of elimination, she managed to piece together a letter that sounded plausibly cheerful. Mostly it was about the final emergence of spring on the plantation and today's visit with the Robinsons, with natural emphasis on Linda. Of the nebulous plans for the future she made no mention. She hesitated to speak of them even to herself tonight.

But after she had sealed and addressed the envelope, her mind began to move tentatively and fearfully back over the day. Slowly, before her stinging eyes, the glow of the lamp splintered into lances of flame and the dead silence of the house became an eddying roar. She seemed then for a time to lose all consciousness of herself and the room: she was many places, and nowhere: with many people, and alone. And when the roaring turned back into the whisperings of the fire and the splinters of flame melted into the faintly humming glow of the lamp, she returned to a room she was not sure of. She was not sure which of its selves it was, or which self she was; till looking at the old writing portfolio and seeing herself seated at a table without faces, she thought clearly: Rusty was gone. And then: He's gone away, he's with Michael in Charleston, leaving me here alone, but I can write him. . . .

A shivering sense of flight passed and left her still. She wrote down the date and his name.

She thought: First I must tell him of this day, the day as I lived it. And then he will want to hear everything that's happened since he left. . . . It was no illusion, no dream of exhaustion and despair. She could tell him. And he would hear. And answer. . . . And as she began to write, all weariness and uncertainty left her. Her pen moved easily and quickly across the paper, setting down her hopes and fears, her love for him, her trust and faith.

The paper was so blurred now that she could no longer see what she was writing. But it was true. She was neither afraid nor alone. He was here with her, beyond any power of darkness and time.

III

THE NEXT MORNING she was dressed and downstairs by daybreak. And she had finished breakfast and was ready for the arrival of Barty and Ned, the deaf-mute twins, by the time the first shafts of the sun came streaming across the yard.

When they appeared at last, there was the problem of communicating with them. As boys at her school they had learned with great difficulty a little reading and writing, but evidently they had forgotten it long since; despite their polite smiles and nods and gurgles, in response to the message she spelled out with a stick in the sand at the foot of the steps, she soon realized she was not reaching them at all. She resorted then to pantomime, repeating her gestures over and over, quivering inside with pained amusement at her own antics but persisting till she was sure the meaning was clear. In reply Barty, as spokesman, conveyed to her in an elaborate language of signs that he understood they must come to help burn over the Big Field: tomorrow morning—when the sun had set and risen again.

Then she left Stephen in Lucy's care again and traveled the plantation roads, visiting the settlements to talk with the people about renting and share-cropping and work in the Big Field.

During the years of prosperity Stephen had been heedless of all plantation affairs: the plantation had become merely a source of labor for the mines. "I have no time," she remembered his saying, "to play landlord,—dunning a pack of niggers for back rent is just too much more trouble than it's worth." But now even a minimum rent on the cabin acres was a matter of vital importance. Taxes to be paid, mortgage notes to be met, family survival till Stephen could get back on his feet: these were in the forefront of her mind. But she was thinking too of the people, how a reorganization of plantation life would benefit them, deliver them from their fatal do-nothing, start them on a road less seductive than the paths to the mines but kinder and better. And it helped her determination to feel that she was working for their interests as well as her own. She held this double purpose over herself like a whip, to make her voice and eyes firm as she talked with them. Those that wanted to stay on the place must pay a small rent for their land, or crop on shares, or work in the Big Field.

On her way home, late in the day, she had a sense of tangible success to lift her out of weariness. She had taken with her a notebook to jot down the names of the people and the agreements made with each; and of the heads of families she had seen, many had grumbled but only one had threatened to move away. She realized her troubles had only begun, for it would take endless perseverance to hold them to their agreements: a harassing vision opened before her, her own* uncertain will opposing a regiment of stubborn black wills. But there was no room left for failure.

The next day was a peculiarly memorable one. It was a day made for the memory to hold not only because of its dramatic events but also because of the aura, the special atmosphere that enveloped it. It had the spell-bound quality of one of those strangely momentous days on the beach at Bay Point when the children were younger. Then, the elements of magic were the long hypnotic roll of the surf, the lambent dance of the waves, the soaring arc of the sky; the sea's breath, the swaying incantation of the sea-oats on the dunes, and the children's endless delight. Today, the magic came from very different elements,—the crackle and roar of a blazing jungle of weeds and brush, the shouting of excited gullah voices, the billow and drift of smoke against the frail pinkish new green of the woods. But the effect was the same: a dream-like spell, a sustained entrancement.

She had opened her eyes at daybreak with the fear that there might be a wind or a threat of rain. When that fear dissolved in the peaceful early sunlight, another took its place: perhaps the people would fail her after all. But when she reached the Big Field by way of the short-cut, with Seth Robinson and Linda, there was the little band of picked workers waiting. Barty and Ned; strapping Lily, her husky son Shad, and her latest husband Rod; One-Eye Richard and James

Washington, two of the phosphate hands that had survived the storm. And Tad, Lily's youngest boy, to fetch water.

Seth directed the undertaking. At first she had some misgivings about his ability to direct, having known him only in the passive role of storekeeper. But the misgivings left her when she saw the quiet authority with which he took charge. He divided the party into teams and set them to work with brush-hooks and hoes clearing a safety zone along the edge of the woods. The field was to be burned from the woods toward the marsh: the teams were to patrol the safety zone, beating out any trails of fire that might creep back to threaten the woods. This clearing process took several long hours. And after that Seth made a deliberate inspection of the zone. But at last all was ready, and there was a breathless pause of expectancy. Then the first tentative blue smoke coiled upwards into the bright still air; sudden flames began to lick at the tinder-dry tangle of weeds and brush.

That was the beginning, and there was no rest till late that afternoon. Even when Lucy arrived with lunch, a basket on each arm and a jug of coffee wonderfully balanced on her headcloth, there was no time out. Food and drink had to be taken on the run.

Armed with an old broom Emily was stationed, in the early afternoon, with Linda and Barty and Ned behind the middle advance of the flames. The heat, even well back from the fire line, was terrific; and she had to cover a wide area of smoking hot ground, to beat out treacherous "stragglers". But with the Twins bearing the brunt of the battle in this sector, she could lean on her broom now and then for a breathing spell or exchange a few words with Linda to relieve the throbbing excitement. At such moments she could grasp the tremendous drama of the scene, the savage and unforgettable beauty of the flames advancing eastward toward the marsh and the great pines of Rusty's grove, protected by the little tidal creek. She could see the field already swept clean, cleared, redeemed; the rich dark soil ploughed and harrowed and listed; the seed planted, sprouting; the cotton growing in myriad rows,—thriving, ripening, opening bolls of snow to the harvest sun. And, unhappily, she could also see one immediate cost of that vision: a trio of hawks, keen-eyed and pitiless, circled silently above the crackling tide of fire, watching for prey, hovering down to close range whenever a thicket blazed up. . . .

Later in the afternoon Barty and Ned were transferred to the north boundary of the field, where Lily and her family were hard-pressed keeping the fire from crossing the safety zone to a strip of pine woods; and after that there was no time for breathing spells. Although most of the mid field was burned over by now, constant vigilance was still necessary, for little trails of flame were continually threatening to sneak back toward the deep leaf carpet of the plantation forest. With the buffer of Barty and Ned removed, she and Linda had to patrol the blackened acres alone, hurrying back and forth without pause. The soles of her shoes were like hot coals. The broom in her grimy aching hands grew heavier and heavier, though there was now only a charred stump left at the end of it. Faintness came and went in waves through a daze of smoke no longer stimulating but acrid and stifling. At times it seemed impossible to think she could raise her arms again or force her legs to carry her another step; but then, just at the instant when she felt she must give in, stop or drop, from somewhere a renewal of strength would come to her support and take her one measure nearer the fulfilment of the day.

Many moments of fag, many tense moments of threat, but only a single moment of real fear. It came toward the close of the afternoon, when the fiery conquest was almost complete, when the field was safely burned over from the west to the east and north and the last blazes were devouring the thick stubborn brush along the south border. It came with a sudden far-off hallooing and arm-waving from Seth at that end of the field. Panic tightened her throat as she started to run with Linda. They were so hobbled by their skirts that Barty and Ned and then Lily (whose skirt was sensibly tucked up to free her strong legs) and Rod and Shad overtook and passed them on the way. But they reached the scene in time to play some part in this frantic climax to the day. Sobbing for breath, her arms constricted almost to helplessness by the terror of the crackling patches of fire spreading through the grasses on the very edge of the woods, she smote at the creeping fringe with her absurd broom-stump weapon, between Richard's cursing tearing hoe and James Washington's whacking spade. They were foes now, these sly eager little tongues eating their way toward the leaves and undergrowth where they could leap up into wild flourishings of flame, rampant and invincible: they had turned against her, this multitude of demons loosed from one spark; menacing the finest stand of timber on the plantation,

468

they menaced the settlements and the big-house as well,—they even seemed to menace, in that enormous moment of desperation, the whole island, the very world.

And then, as suddenly as it had come, the crisis was passed. Choking and trembling she saw Seth stamp out the last truant flame. She felt then that she must collapse, like Tad the water-boy, whose spindly legs had simply given way under him, leaving him stretched flat and panting on his back; or that at least she must sit down with Linda and the others for a little rest. Yet several minutes later she was still on her feet, talking with Seth as they watched Barty and Ned beat out with myrtle boughs the final patch of fire in the corner of the field.

The sun was almost gone now, and the woods, veiled in quiet lilac mists of smoke, reached far cool shadows across the charred sea of the field and the smoldering islands where thickets had been. The day, she realized slowly through a haze of exhaustion, was won. And hardly less amazing, her legs were still supporting her.

They were even able to carry her home, after Seth had assured her the fire was safely out and she had thanked the people. But when Lucy met her at the kitchen door, she gave up with a limp sigh.

"Great Gawd! Ain' I know you was gwine git in trouble widout me? Mm-*mm*, look at you! Face an' han's all black-up, clothes all tore-up an' smooty!—dat skirt too swinge 'long de bottom fuh t'ink mend, I could tell you right now. Miss Em'ly, you le' dem people see you like dis? I too *shame*."

It was not till Lucy's displeasure had spent itself that she ventured to ask, meekly, about Stephen.

Lucy's voice was still cross. "He ain' gib hese'f no res' an' he hab me runnin' up and down all day. But I studyin' 'bout you now,—I got a pot of tea waitin' fuh yuh an' planty hot water fuh bat'."

"Did he ask where I was?"

"Yas'm, an' I tell'um you is gone fuh see sick people. I see he bex, but he ain' say nutt'n."

"You understand we can't let him know about things yet, Lucy. It would just upset him."

Lucy nodded. "I know *dat* fuh true. He ain' gwine like no paa't of what you doin'. He gwine be pure *hot*."

Her mouth remained disapproving, but her eyes gleamed with the excitement of the conspiracy.

469

IV

THE FOLLOWING WEEK she was able to give most of her time to nursing Stephen, while Barty and Ned were guiding their oxen and plows endlessly back and forth over the Big Field. On Monday morning she went to see the first furrows turned, but after that she left the Twins to oversee themselves. She could trust them to finish their heavy task as soon as possible.

Late each afternoon, however, after the Twins had left the field, she traveled the short-cut to see how the work was progressing, to count the furrows, and relieve a little the strain of her own inaction. But in spite of the reassurances that each day brought, another good strip of the field converted from charred stubble to fresh rich earth, she could not shake off a sense of time lost that was almost intolerable to her new energies. Lily's boy Tad was cleaning up the house grounds and making real headway; but his activities, just outside the open window of the bedroom prison where she sat by the hour with Stephen, only increased her restlessness.

They fretted Stephen in another way.

"Can't you keep that damn nigger quiet?" he groaned whenever Tad broke into song to lighten his labor.

Even the cheerful whistle of a cardinal or the rapture of a mockingbird in the branches beyond the piazza railing was too much for him.

"I'm afraid I can't do anything about that," she told him.

But when drowsiness came over him, she went down to the yard to be sure Tad sang no songs. And then she could do a little work herself and release some of the pent-up energy.

And twice during the week she stole off to the settlements to try to locate and talk with the people she had missed before. But neither of these journeys was particularly successful. And the second

470

aroused Stephen's curiosity, for the first time. Sitting up in bed now part of the day he was beginning to take some notice of things.

"Where have you been?"

"Trying to help the people get straightened out. They're still in a daze."

"Don't you think you better get me straightened out first?"

Out of that long week Saturday was the only satisfactory day, the only day that gave her a sense of real accomplishment. In fact there was almost too much crowded into that day.

On Friday afternoon Seth had proudly appeared off what was left of the landing—seven forlorn palmetto posts—in the puffing launch with a battered dory in tow. The salvaged *Pilot Boy* was sorely in need of paint, even her name was weathered out, but aside from that she looked none the worse for her drydocking in the woods. When Seth came ashore in the dory to take her out for an inspection, he announced simply, "Well, ma'm, she's a-runnin', and she ain't a-leakin' to speak of"; and then, as if he had said too much for modesty, he added quickly: "I'm sorry I ain't got her lookin' more presentable for you. But I need paint for that, and to close her seams up good. If you'll let me carry you to town for supplies tomorrow, I'll get paint then. And on high tide Sunday I'll take and beach her in the cove, where I can get at her."

"Seth," she said with enormous relief that the isolation anxiety was ended, "you're really wonderful. Is there anything you can't do?"

"Well now," he blinked in embarrassment, "Martha always said I had a little of everythin' and not much of anythin', and I reckon that's about got it. 'Bout how long will you want to be in town, ma'm?"

"I have quite a few errands, if you have time to spare."

"Well, that's just fine, ma'm, 'cause I'm aimin' to locate a cow somewheres and settin' hens for Linda."

So the next morning they went to Beaufort. It was another fine day: a little rough on the Sound, but the *Pilot Boy* puffed bravely along, as if everything were quite as it had always been. The familiar shorelines, bewitching in their shining and delicate new foliage, had a deceptive air of old times and a world unchanged. It would have been an enchanted journey, if her mind had not been so full of the cares that lay ahead. And in spite of herself she could not help remembering, with recurrent apprehension, Stephen's parting shot:

"He'll blow you right out of the water in that resurrected tub."

But with puffs of perfect self-possession the *Pilot Boy* entered Beaufort River; passed the bluff, where the three-mast schooner *Liverpool* lay stranded high and dry, with the same astonished expression of seven months ago; and came to rest, with only a minor jar, at the rebuilt Rutherford wharf.

To get the unpleasant business of the day out of the way she went first to the bank, to cash the Marshlands rent check, and then to Turner Brothers' and Van Wie's. Facing people was even more of an ordeal than she had anticipated: it was impossible not to sense a mixture of pity and delight behind their solicitous inquiries. You've got to stop being on the defensive, she told her pride. But she could feel her cheeks flush at each encounter, though somehow she managed to keep her eyes and voice natural.

Sally Broughton was the easiest encounter. When she came forward in Turner Brothers', she didn't assume a long face to ask about Stephen and the children and how things were going on the island and so on. She said, simply and cheerfully, that she was "glad to see you", and really looked it. And after a perfectly spontaneous little chat about the weather, she took the order for three bushels of long-staple cotton seed without a flicker of surprise and without comment.

The encounter with Van Wie was the most difficult. The fact that his solicitude rang true didn't make matters any easier. He insisted on waiting on her himself, which made the necessity now of pricing everything more embarrassing than it would have been with one of his clerks, particularly since she suspected he was quoting her a special price on every article. And when she had finished her list, and made arrangements to have the boxes of groceries delivered to the wharf later, she had to go through a painful controversy about paying for them in cash.

"With me," he beamed, "the Fenwick credit is always good. It goes on the bill, as usual."

"But you see," she told him again, trying to keep her nerves steady, "we don't want to run the bill any higher than it is. We'll pay as we go from now on, and pay up the back bill as soon as we can."

He looked at her over his glasses with an injured expression. "Did I ever press you for money, ma'm? Can you imagine me taking cash from the best credit customer I ever had? I ain't scared just because

Mister Fenwick's got a little hard times. You can pay my bill any time you like,—ten years from now."

In the end he yielded to her insistence with a sorry shake of his head.

With the smarting business of the day behind her, she turned with a sigh of relief to the post-office to mail her letters to Michael. And there was a letter from him waiting for her, along with an accumulation of *News & Couriers* and bills and stale business mail for Stephen. As soon as she was out in the sunlight again she tore open Michael's letter; and though it was little more than a page and there was the necessity of making it last for days, she was unable to return it to the envelope till she reached Miss Mary Hamilton's gate.

Margaret was in the garden with Miss Hamilton and came flying to meet her. But Jack was off somewhere with schoolmates and had to be sent for. And when at last he appeared, hot and disheveled and wild-eyed as usual, there was the problem of crowding into a half-hour whole weeks of loneliness for them, and then the problem of leaving them again.

Jack was no trouble at the parting. After the excitement of seeing Mother had worn off, he strained to get back to his mates; all he wanted was a final smacking kiss and some pocket money, which she made herself deny him so that Stephen would have it to give him next week-end. But Margaret grew tearful and clung to her, and in the face of that it was all she could do to carry her cheerful pose through to the end.

"Next Saturday's only a few days off, darling. And before you know it Easter will be here, and then you'll have a whole week's vacation and Michael will be home,—all of us together again."

She could hardly tear herself away from the comfort of these slender arms around her waist and this young breast pressed tight against her. And to fill the emptiness in her own breast, on the way back to Bay Street, she had to keep reminding herself how well both children looked and how good it was that they could be in Miss Hamilton's care. And soon, she repeated over and over to the spring sunshine, Easter will bring them all back to me and we shall be one again.

When she came to the Castle, she thought of turning up Fenwick Street to the Point for one homesick look through the gateway of Marshlands. But she resisted the impulse by telling herself firmly that there was no time for sentimental digressions today; and eased her disappointment a little by remembering that no purple-and-gold mantle of wistaria and banksia rose would be flung over the summer-house. All the gardens along her way were bankrupt this flowerless spring.

On Bay Street she stopped first at Fortner's Pharmacy and climbed the rickety outside stairs to Dr. Wright's grubby little office, marveling how either the stairs or the shaky flooring were able to support his ponderous tread. When she had received his asthmatic assurances that he would meet her on the wharf in half an hour, she went on to the "Lafayette" house, where Joseph Bramwell had opened law offices after his recent retirement from the bench.

"I am returning to private practice," he had told her the last time she had seen him, several days before she had taken Stephen to Land's End. "And I shall remain in private practice as long as the State remains in the strangling toils of Tillman and his cracker rabble."

His new offices occupied the entire second story of this place of business that had once been a proud residence, Beaufort's reception-place for Lafayette on his farewell journey; and as she climbed the generous staircase, she remembered Miss Sophie's story of the great night when the tired old hero with rouged cheeks took up in his arms a little girl clutching a welcome candle. In the upper hall she was confronted by four open doorways and sounds of much activity: Joe was evidently not yet installed. She hesitated for the guidance of his resonant voice. Since it was not forthcoming, she decided on the first doorway to the left as the best bet.

She paused on the threshold, reluctant to intrude, for two women were standing before the fireplace intent on the hanging of a large picture, which a colored boy was supporting against the over-mantel for their inspection. But when they stepped back to get a better effect, she ventured to interrupt them.

"Will you tell me where I can find Judge Bramwell?"

It was only then when they turned with a start that she recognized them. They fixed her with eyes of frozen horror; and unable to move she could only return their stare with a sort of numb merriment at her predicament and theirs. Even the boy holding up the portrait of General Robert E. Lee behind them looked frozen by contagion. And it was beginning to seem that they might all very well remain standing here till Judgment, when Joe appeared at the door of the adjoining room and broke the spell with a dynamic greeting.

"Come in, come in, my dear Emily! Well, you honor us." He cleared his throat deeply: *"Mmm,* Mistress Fenwick, I don't believe you know my sisters, Susan and Isabel. . . ."

Among the fragments of the shattered tableau she was conscious of Susan and Isabel Bramwell's bustling exit, the drawing aside of their skirts as they passed her. Their precipitate descent of the stairs echoed in the room. Joe's face was crimson, from the immaculate white of his high standing collar to the receding gray of his mane.

"I must apologize," he said grimly, "for my sisters' shocking conduct."

"I'm afraid," she told him with a tentative smile, "I must have given them quite a start."

"I'm grateful," he bowed, "for your lenient attitude, Emily. My sisters are kind women at heart, I may even say saintly women, but as I once told you they suffer from certain extreme prejudices. If you will accept my apologies for their indefensible rudeness by your leave we'll say no more about it. Come into my private chambers."

"Aren't you too busy for me today?" she asked him.

He dismissed the objection with an elegant gesture: "For you? Never!"

As he was ushering her into the next room, she remembered the poor boy still supporting the heavy picture.

"Doesn't he deserve a little recess now?" she asked gravely.

Joe directed him to put the picture down. "Careful there! Do you realize whose portrait that is?"

"Yath'm," the boy grinned.

"Well?"

"I dunno 'zac'ly."

"Well, do you know approximately?"

"Yath'm."

"Tut-tut!—no nonsense, boy. That great man, upon whose noble countenance you have the honor of gazing, is the man who would have *saved you from yourself,* but for the damnable insubordination of—of a trusted general at Gettysburg!"

With that cryptic information Joe sent him to sweep out the fireplaces of the rooms across the hall, and ushered her on into the private chambers.

The pictures here were already hung. From the panel frame over the old fireplace Wade Hampton dominated the room. The portrait on the side wall, above a new roller-top desk, had to be identified for her,— Judah P. Benjamin, Confederate Secretary of State. In the cramped space between the windows opposite, overlooking the tar-papered roof of Van Wie's store, the *Banshee* was making her Last Run from Nassau through the Blockading Fleet into Charleston Harbor, 1864; while between the front windows, overlooking Bay Street, the *Alabama* was sinking the *Hatteras*. There were fresh white curtains at the windows, a worn leather couch in a corner of the room, bookcases flanking the fireplace, a comfortable armchair there, and a new swivel-chair facing the desk.

With apologies he handed her over stacks of law books to the armchair and lowered himself cautiously into the swivel-chair. When he relaxed, it responded with a derisive squeak, and he sighed heavily.

"Emily, this confounded contraption masquerading as a chair is easily the most flagrant fraud, the most barefaced swindle, in the entire range of my legal experience. In a weak moment I accepted this junk"—he pulled the top of the desk down with a testy clatter—"in lieu of a fee. Modern equipment!"

He shot out his cuffs and washed his hands of the offensive furniture. "And now tell me how you are. And how is Stephen? You see, I have kept my promise to wait for you to come to me."

When he had adjusted his cuffs and put on his pince-nez, he pursed his lips, and with the tips of his fingers touching judicially prepared to take her testimony. As she told him about Stephen and briefly described conditions on the island, avoiding any mention of her activities and plans, he followed her with nods and grumbles of understanding. She bore his cross-examination as patiently as possible.

"And now," she said when he was satisfied, "let me hear about Charleston."

He allowed his glasses to topple dramatically from his nose, depending on their heavy black ribbon to check their fall at the bottom button of his waistcoat. "Well, except for the meeting of the St. Andrew's Society and a chat with Eugenia, I spent my entire time with Michael. And I am happy to report that I found him in excellent health, and keeping well up to scholarship standards both in his studies and the military end of it. I made a point of seeing each of his masters. And this time I made a thorough survey of the school, attended classes, inspected the dormitory, barracks, kitchen, wash-room,—in short, every aspect of the place. I lunched in the buttery, mess-hall I believe it's called now, with Michael and his roommate from Camden,—fine boy, discovered his mother was a Cantey, Sea-Island stock originally, good family,—and in the afternoon I witnessed a guidon drill of the battalion on the parade grounds."

Hanging gratefully on every word, she was nevertheless not un-mindful of what Michael's feelings must have been during this exhaustive inspection.

"Needless to say," Joe continued, "I found the Academy much altered from what it was when I was a lad. Not physically, of course, for I felt perfectly at home seated again at one of those scarred old desks in the study-hall. But a spiritual change, a change shall we say in the mental atmosphere, there certainly has been since my time. A radical new tendency to shift curricular emphasis away from the humanities to the sciences. I regret that Michael elected to take up chemistry instead of going on with his Greek."

"But don't you think he's wise to choose the subjects most closely related to his life and work?"

Joe pinched his nose to moderate a snort of dissent. "My dear Emily, could any subject, with the exception of the New Testament, be more relevant to any life in any age than the language of Socrates and Plato, Homer and Sophocles? They speak with the tongues of men and angels, for all times in all climes."

"But he really hates Greek, and I'm afraid any more of it would give him a distaste for the classics that might last the rest of his life. Why can't he read them in good translations, when he's ready for them and they'll be a great experience—not a grind?"

"Nonsense, my dear. The classics must be read in the original for their full beauty and meaning; and if he doesn't 'grind' over them now, he'll probably never be 'ready' for them. The old rule still holds: good things come hard, or not at all."

"But aren't the sciences good? And more in line with his plans to study medicine? Rusty had years of Greek, but he wanted Michael to concentrate on chemistry and physics, and physiology and bi-ology."

Joe shook his head sadly. "I keep forgetting the boy's contemplating a medical career. I'm not condemning it,—though naturally if he were my son, and I like to feel that in a way he is, I'd infinitely prefer to see him trained for the Law. The state and the nation are sorely in need of leaders, men of caliber and integrity. However, my feelings don't enter into the case."

Since there seemed no sense in trying to force her point through this impasse, she retreated to Charleston and the St. Cecilia Ball.

"Ah yes," he brightened, thrusting his thumbs into the armholes of his waistcoat and leaning back with a comfortable squeak in the despised chair. "Well, he was an unqualified success at the ball. Carried himself like a man. Turned the heads of all the young ladies without losing his own!" He permitted himself a restrospective chuckle. "You may be sure I kept him in constant circulation, and I saw that he met his peers of all ages. He wrote you all about it, I presume?"

"Yes indeed." And he had, in one short sentence: *Uncle Joe sure put me through.* "You were a saint to let him tag along."

"It was a pleasure and an honor to introduce my grandnephew to his spiritual kinsfolk. Of course on this first occasion it must have been a somewhat confusing experience for him, getting the names and faces straight. But he'll have many invitations between now and the end of the semester, and by next season he'll be thoroughly at home in Charleston society. And at some future ball he'll find, I expect, some young lady of more than passing interest."

With a reminiscent smile he speculated further. "Possibly he's already met his bride-to-be without recognizing her. Possibly he's already in love without our knowing it. Has he written you of any girl in particular?"

"Not yet," she smiled back.

"Well," he frowned, discarding romance, "so much the better. A young man should get his bearings, complete his education, hang up his shingle,—in short, establish himself on a firm foundation, before he contemplates marriage. Then he's much more likely to make a wise choice. . . . Michael is a lad of great promise, and I'm confident he'll conduct himself with prudence and propriety. And he's in good hands. There has been a serious weakening of the moral fibre of the nation since the War, but so far as I have been able to judge, the younger generation in Charleston at least are still well under the control and discipline of their elders, notwithstanding certain laxities in manners and chaperonage that would never have been tolerated in my day. Since you're unfamiliar with Charleston quiddities, I better take a minute to run over the names of some of the people I was particularly pleased to have Michael meet at the St. Cecilia."

Since running over the names meant lingering over the genealogy of each, the minute easily stretched to a quarter of an hour before she could find any kind of opening.

"Stephen must hear all this," she told him gently as she moved to get up. "I want you to save it for him, when you come out to see us. But I have one more question for you before I leave," she answered his protests as he struggled out of his treacherous chair. "Is he still homesick?"

He gave the question heavy consideration, pondering it through half-closed eyelids as he ran the clasp of his pince-nez ribbon up and down, up and down.

"Yes and no," he announced finally. "He's a boy of uncommon, and very commendable, reserve; so his real feelings can only be conjectured. But I would say that his somberness comes now less from homesickness than from a thoroughly awakened appreciation of his loss, his double loss,—Rusty and his grandmother."

He frowned at the window curtains fluttering in the spring air. A faraway look came into his eyes, and he stared out over the roofs to the spire of St. Helena's.

"How true it is," he sighed, "that we must lose those we love before we can really possess them. It's only when they're gone from us beyond recall that we can forget their little foibles and certain quite superficial differences of opinion. It's true of my cousin, whom I alternately damned and admired; and it's particularly true of my sister, who never missed an opportunity to rub me the wrong way, as you well know."

He shook his head. "Sophie was undoubtedly the most exasperating of women,—contentious, sarcastic, short of patience and quick of temper, contrary-minded to the last degree. But I wonder if it would be possible to feel the absence of anyone more acutely. From childhood we fought like cats and dogs, but what about I have no more recollection now than she has."

He whisked a handkerchief out of his pocket, made a pretense of polishing his glasses, and then blew his nose hard.

When he turned away from the window, his glasses were back on his nose and he was quite himself again. "Time is still our master, Emily. And if you'll accept my translation of a great line from Sophocles, 'Only to the gods in heaven comes no old age nor death of anything.'" He braced his shoulders and inhaled deeply. "Ah, to live nobly we must breathe the classic air! Greek philosophy, Roman law. And Christian charity. Here, in a blessed trinity of truth and beauty, is all we know and all we need to know. And by however much we of the modern age turn our backs on the great tradition, by just so much do we retrogress to Babel and primordial chaos. . . . But I shan't afflict you with my crying in the wilderness. And I'll let you go, when you tell me how I can be of service to you."

"Haven't you done more than enough already?"

"On the contrary, I don't feel that you've allowed me to do anything yet. Have you been troubled with any more bills and legal communications?"

She got them out of her handbag.

"It's just as well," he said as he thumbed them over, "that Marshlands and Land's End are in your name. The Fenwick Company bankruptcy will take care of these, of course. Now may I ask what you propose to do about current expenses? Will you do me the honor of turning over all bills to me, for the present at least?"

She shook her head gratefully but firmly.

"You're prepared then to let me open that checking account at the bank?"

She shook her head again. "No, we're going to try to piece out expenses for the next few months with a little cash and some credit. And we have a plan that we hope will put our heads above water by the end of the summer."

He raised his eyebrows inquisitively. "A plan?"

"But I'm not going to tell you about it till later. Because I'm afraid it won't stand close inspection yet. You see, it's still in the pure faith stage."

"I see. Something Stephen's trying to hatch out of that hopeless china egg of phosphate?"

"Now never you mind. As a matter of fact, he doesn't know about it yet either. I'm keeping it from rational male scrutiny as long as possible."

"*Dux femina facti.* But don't you think you better take me into your confidence?"

"Very soon," she promised.

"There's nothing I can do at the moment, then? You're sure, my dear?"

"You can take the children promenading to Port Royal again, if you will. They're still talking about last Sunday."

"I've already planned to do that. And now can I depend on you to call on me for anything you need?"

"You can, positively."

She refused to hear of his escorting her to the wharf, but he had to see her down to the door. On the stairs she asked him: "How would you like to be our factor someday, Joe?"

"Factor?"

"Can't a lawyer be a factor too?"

"Why, I suppose so. That is, in the past it was frequently the case that a man's factor was also his solicitor, and vice versa."

"I'll remind you of that later. I really wanted to know."

"But what do you want with a factor?"

At the door she said, "I'll try to be less mysterious next time." And then, in the midst of her shame for baffling him so, she remembered Eugenia.

"Oh, she seems well enough," he told her. "Left the Hazzards, of course. I helped her find comfortable quarters in Tradd Street, and I mean to drop in to see her whenever I'm in Charleston."

"I hate to think of her living alone."

"She can't get along with anyone else."

"But you'll let us know, won't you, if you find she ever wants to come back to us."

When she had taken final leave of him, she hurried down Bay Street to the Rutherford warehouse and through the alleyway to the wharf, where she found tobacco-chewing Dr. Wright impatiently waiting with Seth. The box of groceries was there too, along with a crate of hens and a rooster that Seth had bought for Linda.

"And I got the promise of a likely heifer," he told her proudly, as he helped her onto the roof deck of the *Pilot Boy* (for the tide was out and the main deck stood too far below the level of the wharf), "and then we'll have plenty of milk and butter too." And her delight with that swelled to sudden ecstacy as she passed through the hot acrid breath of the smokestack and climbed down the steep forward steps to the prow, and so past the engine boiler with its familiar smell of steam and oil to the horseshoe seat of the open cabin. For the cares of the day were successfully behind her, and she could yield herself now to the rapture of this boat so ladened with memories of the happy years: as ferry between Land's End and Marshlands, as picnic carry-all to Bay Point and excursion cruiser among the islands, this old "Company tub" had accumulated such a cargo of family memories that it was a wonder it could stay afloat. But it did, valiantly, joyously; and the lilt of hope and renewal in the air, the thought of Easter and the children and the whole family (visible and invisible) together again, melted all weight out of the memories and gave them wings. So that as she glanced out over the river there was a flash of sheer delight, the purest bliss, when for a single instant of lapping water and gull wings and sparkling rippling tide she was lifted out of herself on an upsurge like music, her essential being fusing with the essences around her.

And then, a moment later, the spell was gone and she was sinking back into her reasonable self again, moving over on the seat to make room for Dr. Wright's ponderous stern.

He spent the trip to Land's End spitting in the general direction of the *Pilot Boy's* wake and complaining of the scurvy treatment he had received at the hands of the specialists that Miss Barton had brought down from the North with her Red Cross circus. The community was well rid of them, he wheezed. They gave themselves great airs and called themselves sanitary experts, but they were nothing but a pack of kid-glove grafters and know-it-all theorists, leaving him to do most of the dirty work. And patronizing him because he was a plain country doctor with a Southern degree and not up on the latest Yankee medical fads and newfangled notions! And as she struggled to subdue her dislike of the man, she began to develop serious misgivings. Perhaps, she thought now, she should have spoken to Stephen about it. But then he would have flatly refused to hear of it. No, she was doing what had to be done the only way it could be done.

But the misgivings had become a panic by the time the *Pilot Boy* was anchored off the forlorn remains of the landing. And when Seth had taken them ashore, one at a time in the little dory, she left the doctor to wait on the piazza while she went very uncertainly upstairs to prepare Stephen.

In the room, confronted again by his sickness and defeat, the cheerful account of the day that she had planned to give him deserted her along with every lightness of feeling and thought, and she could summon to her aid not even an artificial animation. Soberly she reported her visit with Margaret and Jack, and mentioned seeing Joe Bramwell.

"But I'll tell you all about that later," she said, trying to keep any expectation of trouble out of her voice. "Because Dr. Wright's downstairs,—he came back with us to see you."

With more life than he had shown for weeks, he roused himself, hitched himself up in the bed. "Oh he did, did he? Damn considerate of him. Well, you can tell him when I want to see him I'll send for him! You can tell him what you like, but I'll be damned if I'll see him!"

His protest was no more violent than she had expected: he had said, in fact, almost exactly what she had guessed he would say. But because tears were so treacherously near the surface these days, she was afraid for a moment that she was going to cry, simply and thoroughly. She was surprised when she heard herself say quite calmly:

"I'm sorry, dear, but you've really got to be gone over. You've been very sick, and I can't keep proper track of you with just a thermometer and counting your pulse."

"Well, if you think I'm going to have that Goddamn cracker horse-doctor fooling around me, you're cracked—that's all! Hell, I'm getting along all right. All I need is a little more time to get myself together here." He flopped back on the pillow and closed his eyes with a sigh. "God knows all I ask is to be let alone."

Sitting on the side of the bed watching his drawn face, a nerve in his neck quivering, she sighed too, in spite of herself.

"If you won't see him," she told his closed sunken eyes as she got up, "then you'll have to let me get someone from Charleston."

He opened his eyes and looked up at her wearily. And whether it was her eyes or the lack of any further strength to resist, he suddenly yielded. "You win. If it can't be Rusty, it might as well be this leech as any other. Show him up."

During the interview she waited downstairs, helping Lucy stack the groceries on the shelves of the kitchen safe and listening impatiently. When she heard the doctor's heavy grunting tread on the stairs, she went to meet him.

"Your husband's a downright cussed patient," he told her with nasal spleen as she walked with him to the landing steps, "and to be plain with you, I hope I don't have to treat him again." Nothing more he could do anyways, he said. The heart seemed strong enough, but the nerves was all shot to pieces and only time could remedy that, months of rest. Had the cascading stopped? Well then, the stomach was healing up, which was something. "I reckon I don't need to tell you he can't touch no licker—kill him dead as a poisoned dog." When he could keep it down, he could be given a little solid food, without seasoning. "I'll send him back a bottle of tonic. And I'll be obliged if you'll pay me now."

"Of course," she flushed. "How much will it be?"

Well, he'd have to charge her double for coming out here. That would be four dollars. And one dollar for the prescription made five.

She went back to the house and got five precious bills out of her purse. After she had paid him and thanked him, and seen him and Seth off in the *Pilot Boy*, she turned again to Stephen.

"Satisfied?" he asked her as she came into the room. Trembling and feverish, he was supporting himself on a shaky elbow. "Well, get this straight. If anybody thinks I'm going to lie here and rot they got another guess coming! I'm getting up. Tomorrow."

✓   ✓   ✓

But it was days before he could actually drag himself up, over her beseechings.

It was only then, as she helped him to dress, that she realized fully in how terrible a condition his sickness had left him. Instead of restoring him to any health the weeks of bed seemed to have sapped the last of his vitality: he was emaciated to skin and bones and weak as a kitten. When he peered into the mirror, steadying himself against the bureau, rubbed his unsteady fingers over the growth of grayish beard, and then turned to her incredulous, she had to busy herself with the bedclothes to escape his eyes.

She supported him down the stairs with an arm around his thin waist, his weight resting on her. When she settled him in an armchair on the piazza with a blanket over his knees, the living spring sunlight accented the deathly pallor of his face and hands, the black circles under his eyes, the whole pitiable contraction of his being. There was no response in him to the sunlight. He sat inert, staring listlessly at the dancing waters of the Sound.

She hated to leave him alone today, but she had to be at the Big Field. Seth Robinson was going with her to inspect the Twins' finished work: the plowing and listing were over, the last preparations for planting complete.

She got back to him as soon as she could, and found him sitting just as she had left him. He had not moved, she felt, had not raised his hand or turned his head while she was gone. He was not even fretful today about her absence, and did not press her with any questions. When she asked if Lucy had given him his bread and broth and if he had enjoyed it, he nodded. Had any boats passed on the Sound? He hadn't noticed. Had he slept? He wasn't sure. . . . Sitting on the steps at his feet she tried to distract him with a description of the Robinsons' increasing menagerie. There were pigs now and more chickens and a fine cow; she had brought back a pail of milk and a pat of sweet butter that Linda had sent him; he could have egg-and-milk drinks now to build up his strength. And Seth was coming over to see him soon, and bringing a hen and a setting of eggs for Lucy. Seth had brought the cow from the mainland in style on the *Pilot Boy!* But he wasn't amused at anything she told him, till she remembered Linda's first venture at milking. That made him smile a little. But his smile hurt her more than his unresponsiveness. It was empty as his eyes.

After early supper, the air was still mild enough so that they could sit outdoors, and she read to him while the light lasted. He insisted on her opening all the *News & Couriers* that had come in the mail, but he accepted her rigid censorship, her selection of only the items that had no reference to business. In spite of her care she sometimes stumbled upon something she feared might disturb him, but glancing at him she knew that he was paying less and less attention, that finally her reading was a meaningless chant through which he could stare at his own dark reflections in the golden afterglow of the Sound. As usual, he was somewhere else, far away from her. And when the light failed and she could stop reading, something about diamonds and Boers in South Africa, nothing she could find to say seemed to reach him. Even disaster, she thought bitterly, can't bring

485

us together. . . . But then, when a few moments later she got up to take him in, his hand—as if to confound her thoughts—touched hers with a tenderness that made her shiver.

"Emily."

"Yes?" her breath caught as she answered him. "Yes, dear?"

"Don't fret about me, honey. Everything's coming out all right."

She nodded, unable to speak for a moment. And then steadying her lips and squeezing his hand she nodded again and smiled with him.

V

FROM THAT DAY his strength began slowly to return. Little by little the deadly inertia was leaving him; his appetite improved, and he recovered enough flesh to hide his skeleton. He shaved, dressed with care, and began to look a little like himself again.

His coming back to life raised her spirits mightily, but it also presented her with acute problems. First, there was the difficulty of keeping her plantation activities secret from him. He could no longer be put off with evasions or general statements about helping the people adjust themselves: he wanted to know what the devil was going on, what was she up to anyway? And when she had to tell him about the rent and share-cropping system, she had his scorn and sarcasm to deal with just as she had feared.

"But it's working," she protested. "It's going to take time to get everything regulated, of course, and it's going to be hard keeping them all up to their end of the bargain. But we're making a good start, and I'm not worried."

"I see. You put up the stake, the land and the seed and a hoe to this nigger and a sack of meal to that one, and they do the rest. Why should you worry? All you have to do is try to collect at the end of the summer. It's easy as rolling off a log."

"I never supposed it would be easy, dear. But it's certainly worth a fair trial, isn't it? The only risk is a little cash, and some credit perhaps, and a lot of faith."

"Faith! Aren't you cured of your optimism yet? And you're willing to stake any little cash you may have and part of the Marshlands rent on a collection of free niggers? Well, it's going to make a pretty picture all right, my wife dunning a pack of nigger tenants."

"That simply isn't the way to look at it, dear."

He had to laugh at that. "That's right, you tell me how to look at it! Leave you to yourself and you revert to type in a jiffy—right back to Yankee tricks. All a nigger needs to make a white man of him is forty-acres-and-a-mule. Well, go right ahead with your foolishness, if it amuses you, but don't expect any help from me, or any sympathy later."

And when Seth Robinson, in his first visit with Stephen, innocently exposed the Big Field conspiracy, she had to face something more serious than sarcasm and scorn. He was furious with her. He would listen to no explanations, he only wanted to condemn the whole idea.

"I can't understand why you didn't tell me about it! What damn folly made you rush into these crazy schemes while I was flat on my back? You didn't have to put on the pants of the family,—you knew I'd be back in the game in a month or two. Christ! . . . Well, you can get yourself out of this mess. Just count me out,—I don't want anything to do with it and I don't want to hear about it. I've got something better to think about. It's going to take something better than insanity to pull us out of this hole!"

Her confidence was firmly enough rooted not to be shaken by that, but it hurt badly. And while it was a relief to be done with evasions, it was an affliction to be working under his silent but burning disapproval. And having taken that stand his stubborn pride, she knew, would never permit her to enlist his interest and help.

And now she worried more and more about what was going on in his mind, what he was thinking and plotting. Quivering inside and suffering with him, she watched his terrible and increasing restlessness; watched helplessly, for there was nothing she could do to ease his torment. There was no real force behind this feverish new stage of his sickness, he was merely being driven by the laceration of his nerves. Aimlessly he wandered through the house or paced the yard. He could stand before the bureau mirror long enough to brush his hair, train his mustache, and adjust his tie, but if he sat down for a moment, his feet and hands began to tick, and the tension grew till he had to jerk himself up and start moving again. His brows were set in a chronic frown of concentration, yet he was able to concentrate on nothing, not even the *News & Couriers* that Seth brought twice a week when he went to town for mail and supplies. But worst of all was his insomnia. He would stay awake at night for hours, tossing and threshing in bed, or pacing the floor till sheer exhaustion gave him a little respite from himself.

He took no interest in anything going on around him. He noticed Tad working in the yard only when the boy disturbed his brooding with a lapse into song. When a spring thunder-storm set all the up-stairs ceilings to dripping and every receptacle in the house had to be rushed up to the attic, he stayed down in the living-room as if it were no concern of his whether the plaster held or fell. When Seth appeared immediately after the rain to locate and seal the leaks in the roof, he looked on for a few minutes with indifference and then turned away. And when Seth spent several days repairing the boat landing, he avoided the front yard altogether.

The only subject in which he showed interest was cigars. He was accustomed to a special panatello from the Commercial Club; when they had moved to the island she had packed three boxes, but these were soon empty. He then seated himself at the living-room desk, one morning after breakfast, long enough to write an order to the steward of the Club—"Courtesy of Mr. Seth Robinson"—for three more boxes. When she tried to spare him a humiliation, he told her curtly: "My business credit may be nil, but I think my personal credit is still good,—no thanks, I won't deprive you of any of your nigger money." And when she got back from the Big Field that afternoon, she found him fuming over a box of cheap cigars that Seth had brought back from Van Wie's.

"They were out of my brand at the Club," he told her with a flush. "And I don't suppose it'll be worth their while stocking them anymore, now that I'm not buying them wholesale for the office. That bunch of pikers hanging out there now aren't going to buy specials for themselves, to say nothing of handing them out, the way I used to."

But he simply could not smoke these damn Van Wie cigars, he told her the following day: they hurt his throat, they made him cough. And on the eve of Seth's next trip to town he sullenly offered to borrow from her.

"I can't smoke rope. Better lend me a ten spot,—Seth ought to be able to get me a couple of boxes of some half-way decent brand at the Sea Island Hotel."

She gave him the money from the little store in the bottom of her jewel-case.

"Wouldn't this be a good time, dear, to cut down on your smoking?"

"Thanks for suggesting I give up the one comfort I have left. If that's the way you feel about it, you can keep your money. And throw it away staking niggers and raising weeds."

And then she had to pacify and conciliate him, resolving that she would be doubly careful not to provoke him in the future. For she saw clearly now how important it was that she should never forget for an instant, in the months that lay ahead, his sickness and touchiness, the rawness of his nerves, the prostration of his spirit. Her contribution to his recovery must be unshakable patience, constant vigilance over herself, constant regard for his pride, to protect it and bolster it up. Certainly she would make no more suggestions about his cutting down on smoking. In her worried budgeting she would have to allow for a regular cigar item.

Not that cigars were helping his nerves any. Like everything else they simply made him more irritable. The only times he seemed to have any peace were at the weekends, when Seth fetched Margaret and Jack from town in the *Pilot Boy,* and on those evenings when Seth and Linda came calling. For the children he somehow managed to forget himself and expand; they knew he had been very ill and that the Storm had altered the family's mode of living, but they were unconscious of anything wrong beyond that; they continued to look up to him, without questions or doubts or reproaches in their eyes, and he responded by being their usual father, a little sick-looking but otherwise unchanged. And it was the same with Seth and Linda: they treated him as if he were still master of himself and his world and of them in a way, and he braced himself for them too. She had to bear the brunt of his relapses afterwards, but she was glad he had these opportunities to raise his head and rally his self-esteem.

She was not so pleased with his man-to-man talks with Seth. Listening with one ear as she chatted with Linda, she gathered that he was attributing all his troubles to bad luck. Understanding his desperate need of martyrdom, she could not firmly begrudge him these cigar-smoke rationalizations of his defeat: perhaps for the present it was better for him to be allowed to deny all mistakes and admit no personal failure, make himself a victim of circumstances purely, exonerate himself on any basis he chose. But when one evening she heard him telling Seth that things would be "picking up directly", that he was "going back into the game", that he was going to Charleston in a week or two to look over the business field there, she took alarm. And when Seth and Linda had left, she found the courage to speak to him of a plan that had been on her mind for days.

"Dear, don't you think we better start a vegetable garden? This summer we're going to have three ravenous young people on our hands, and a garden will help a lot."

He was irritated at once. "Well? What do you want me to do, go out and make one? With this?" He held up his gloved hand: the first time she had ever known him to refer to it pathetically.

"Of course not. I just want you to direct. Tad will do the work, and Lucy wants to help."

"Say, what are you trying to do—make a po'-buckra farmer out of me? Thanks, but I'll leave all that kind of nonsense to you and Seth. By this summer I'll be back in business, where I belong."

"But, darling, you've got to get some real strength back first. Of course you're going back into business later on, but please don't even think about it yet. Try this garden scheme. It will help us and help you."

"Now isn't that sweet? Got everything all worked out for me, haven't you? Too bad it doesn't happen to coincide with my plans. Do you honestly expect me to hang around here and rot this summer?"

His nerves were on fire now.

"While we're on the subject, *darling,* I'll be obliged to you for a little less Yankee-schoolmarming. I don't need any more nursing, and I haven't asked for any suggestions about what I'm to do. I'll continue to wear the pants in this family, if you don't mind."

"Of course, dear."

"I'm letting you go on with your damn foolishness because it seems to amuse you, and because it takes your mind off me. I'll leave you alone just as long as you leave me alone. Is that understood?"

She nodded.

"And one other thing, while we're on the subject. Did you bring any liquor out here?"

Her throat tightened as she shook her head. He avoided her eyes then, busying himself emptying the ash-tray onto the embers of the fire.

"Well, what became of the bottles in the sideboard?"

She sat down weakly on the sofa. "I left them there." And she added irrelevantly, in a feeble attempt to distract him: "I had all the best furniture, except the piano, stored in the attic, when the Fowlers moved in. I want to bring the piano out as soon as possible. I'd like to have it here for Margaret by Easter vacation. Seth thinks he can handle it on the *Pilot Boy*, with Barty and Ned's help."

"You haven't anything hidden?" he asked over his shoulder.

Sudden tears blurred his image before her, so that she was unable to see whether or not his eyes were still avoiding hers, now as he stood with his back to the fire. She shook her head again.

"Well, there ought to be something in the house. It's ridiculous not to have anything to offer people. Asking Seth if he'll have a glass of water! And I'll tell you frankly, I can't down another one of those milk-and-egg drinks unless there's something besides nutmeg in it. A fine state of affairs when there isn't even a drop of cooking sherry in the house. We'll simply have to get some rye out here, that's all."

Don't let him think I'm resorting to tears, she prayed. But there was no checking them now, they were rolling down her cheeks for him to see. And her voice was choked with them.

"Stephen, you promised me. And you can't break that promise. I know how terrible it is for you, but I couldn't stand it."

He stood looking at her for a moment in stony silence.

"All right, all right," he said finally. "No need to work yourself into a lather. It's a mistake to make promises of any kind, and I must have been out of my mind. But if I gave you my word, you can count on me to keep it. Have I ever failed you in that respect?"

His exasperation had burned itself out. He came and slumped down beside her, rested his head back and closed his eyes with a sigh of exhaustion. Presently his lean nerveless hand sought hers, and then clumsily he put his arm around her.

In a day Barty and Ned plowed and harrowed enough of the rich pasture behind the stable for generous patches of corn and potatoes, beans and greens. Stephen took an active hand in laying out the paths and beds and rows with string lines; in his good clothes, of course, for he insisted he had no others,—and anyway, if he was going to be a farmer he was at least going to be a gentleman farmer. But after that preliminary activity, he directed the proceedings from a chair in the shade of the stable, strolling out into the sun only when Tad and an assistant needed something more stimulating than a long-distance harangue.

"Why didn't you give me men?" he complained cheerfully, for he was enjoying himself and already he was sleeping better and his nerves were steadying. "How do you expect me to get anywhere with a couple of no-account boys? Tad Lincoln's got hookworm and that other black son-of-an-ape's got the thinnest wobbliest shanks on the plantation. Now if I had some of my stout old phosphate hands, we'd make things hum here."

And another time: "I hope my sires aren't looking down on me driving a pair of free-nigger dragtails. Why, Lucy comes out here and does more work in ten minutes than I can get out of them in a day. I could take a hoe myself and beat them with one hand."

But she was satisfied that he was occupied and interested. She could go to her own duties at the Big Field with a lightened heart. And she needed to be free to devote all her attention to the work there. Things were moving fast. The seed had come and the planting had started.

She discouraged Seth's help now: he had his own planting to attend to. And she was learning to oversee the work herself. On the technical side this was not difficult; it was only necessary to follow a routine outlined by Barty and Ned, amended at one or two points by plantation veterans who had worked in the field in slavery-times, and approved by Seth. The hard part was controlling the human elements. Each day presented her with a fresh set of problems: disputes to be settled, excuses and "miseries" to be accepted or rejected, truancies to be dealt with. About a fifth of the plantation people had agreed to work out their rent for the year by giving her sixty days' labor in the field; even on a generously staggered schedule, to give each hand time off for his own pursuits, this arrangement theoretically provided her with an adequate gang for the planting and all later operations. But most of the people, after several days' consecutive work, seemed to feel they were entitled to several days' leave-of-absence, schedule or no schedule, and without notice. This general delinquency threatened such complete demoralization that she was compelled to institute a bonus system, a small cash wage to be paid at the end of the planting period to each hand who had appeared according to the schedule. There was no further trouble about labor: everyone immediately wanted to work in the Big Field. Even when, at Seth's wise suggestion, she gave notice that only part of the bonus would be paid after the field had been planted, the remainder to be paid at the end of the season, even then there was no falling-off of enthusiasm. The problem now was to still the clamorings of those who had decided at first to plant for themselves but were now suddenly eager to join the Big Field gang.

Almost overnight the grumbling and discontent became so serious that she saw she must act at once. It was hopeless to try to talk to the people separately. She must try to rally them as a group. She had thought of this in the beginning, but she had lacked the courage for it then. Now she felt surer of herself, and necessity was driving her.

But when she actually stood facing them, all resolution deserted her. She had first considered assembling them at Thankful Church, which had sheltered most of them through the storm; but remembering this had again become the praise-house of a jealous minority, she decided to speak to them in the open air and on common ground, under the old live-oak that stood where the road from the settlements came into the Big Field. This was her field headquarters; and here one noon, standing on the bench Seth had made for her, she confronted a pack of expectant black faces.

Looking back on that hour after it was over, she wondered how her knees had supported her through it. It was one thing to talk to the people as individuals, but to address scores of them collectively, stand up before them all and try to put into plain words what she wanted to tell them, was a very different matter. The necessity of speaking with authority, the struggle to recall the opening sentences she had rehearsed so carefully, the taunting felicity of a mockingbird's song, everything was in conspiracy to paralyze her tongue. And when at last she forced herself to begin, began haltingly to tell them that she had asked them to come together because she could not talk with each separately, she saw before her Stephen's derision. But then, an instant later as she caught the echoes of her own voice, his face vanished and she saw the wide field already half planted, the bags of seed waiting at intervals in the road that cut across the field to Pine Point and Rusty's grove. In a flash she was no longer alone, and confidence flowed back into her breast.

"But it's better," she heard herself saying, "that we talk like this, together. We belong together. We must think and act together." She gripped her hands behind her to stop their trembling, and her voice steadied as she went on. This plantation was their home and hers, and they must work together to preserve it. But a ship must have a captain. They must trust her to do the steering. No-one was asked to do more than a fair share of the work, but everyone would have to do his share without fail, or the ship would never make port. Those who lived up to their agreements, whether they were working in the Big Field or planting for themselves, would be rewarded. Those who shirked would be cast off. There was no other course.

"But I promise you this: if everyone does his part faithfully, we can't fail. We're going to make life over on this plantation, we're going to rebuild our world here, together and better than it ever was before. And no man needs to be jealous of his neighbor. Because every man that hoes out his own row will share in the harvest."

She was no longer conscious of herself addressing them. She had forgotten herself in her appeal: she was speaking to each of them directly. And seeing and feeling their response spurred her on.

". . . It's best we forget the Reconstruction years. The phosphate years, too. They were both false times, there was no true blessing in them, and they're gone for good. And now the storm has left us only the land and our bare hands. We must start all over again, but this time our house will not be built on shifting sands.

"And now I'm asking you to return to your tasks and follow me. I ask you to do your part without shirking or grumbling. If anyone has a complaint or a question, something you don't like or don't understand, come to me at once with it. . . ."

And at the end she had assurance enough to smile. "It's going to be a hard road, but it's not going to be a lonely road. We're all working together,—remember that one thing. And we're all going to sit at the welcome table. By next winter there'll be chickens and pigs and a cow in the yard of every home on the plantation."

The success of the meeting was so evident that, even as the people crowded around her to promise their faithful support, she warned herself against too great elation. They were so quick to respond, and they could forget so easily; she knew them well enough to know that only constant patient effort would keep them in line. But at least the meeting had some effect toward quieting discontents and fostering a sense of coöperation. And it produced Biggie.

He came up to her after the crowd had thinned away. Looking up from her lunch-box on the bench she beheld a dark bronze giant of a man, his great hands fumbling a battered felt hat, his teeth set in a broad grin. He wore the remnant of a jacket many sizes too small for him and held together by a strained safety pin, his tight trousers were shredded almost to leglessness, his feet were innocent of shoes. The swelling muscles of his arms and chest and thighs were so thoroughly exposed that it was impossible not to realize at once that here, suddenly and for no apparent reason, was the finest physical specimen she had ever seen or imagined. While she had been speaking to the people she had been vaguely aware of him at the edge of the crowd, an unknown standing head and shoulders above the tallest man near him. And now as he stood before her, she still failed to recognize him, though it was plain he expected her to know his name.

"You want to see me?" she asked him.

He answered in a voice as rich and smooth as molasses, "You ain't know me, ma'm?"

Studying his face, recognition came to her slowly. Soon after she had first come to Land's End she had helped old Auntie Cuba with Laura, one of the plantation's Freedom crop of young unmarried mothers, "social delinquents" as Harriet Sheppard called them, simple cases of "hab sin" to Auntie. Laura's sin had not only found her out but had also killed her. But Auntie had slapped life into the fruit of the sin and had christened him, with realistic fitness, Biggie. At the praise-house school he had been easily the most difficult boy in the class. When the mines had opened, he had quit school and gone to work sculling a batteau for his uncle, one of the Company's best divers. Soon he had learned to dive himself and in a few months he had outstripped the best of the grown men. Then one day, his jeans full of hard-earned silver dollars, he had skipped the island and disappeared off the face of the earth. Now in this dusky Hercules before her it was only the disarming and infectious grin that permitted her to recognize young Biggie.

"Of course I know you! How could I forget you after all the trouble you used to give me? Biggie, where have you been?"

His muscles relaxed and his grin exploded into an oily chuckle. "Aw'm, my missie, I been too all-about! I cyan' call de name of all de places I been at, ma'm."

"You look as if you'd done some hard traveling. Why did you run away?"

"My missie, de ole people hab sayin', Ef crob no walk he no see nutt'n."

"And they have another saying to go with it,—If crab no walk he no see pot. Well, have you seen enough of the world?"

"Yaz'm, I spec' I is. Mostes' place whuh I been at I done mek good money, but trouble is he go out mo' fas' dan he come in. An' time come vhen I git full-up wid dat humbug. I say to muhse'f, Biggie, you ain' gittin' nowhuh,—go home, boy, whuh you b'long an' whuh you' white-folks is."

She shook her head at him. "Biggie, I'm afraid you've fallen among thieves."

"Aw naw'm!—I ain' t'ief nutt'n, naw me! I gwine tell you de trut', Miss Em'ly. Some of dem policemens done pit me in de jail-house fuh fightin' an' t'ing maybe two t'ree time, but I ain' been in no udduh trouble,—scusin' one mean ugly 'oman."

"You ought to be satisfied to settle down for a while now, Biggie."

"My missie, I too sotisfy. I ain' nebbuh gwine roam no mo', fuh true. I come bock fuh wuk fuh you an' Maus' Steve."

The whites of his eyes, she noticed, were blood-shot and yellow. "You've been sick, haven't you?"

"Vell ma'm, I ain' been feelin' too good sence 'long 'bout Chris'-mus-time. But I sho feels mo' bettuh now."

She considered him in silence for a minute.

"Biggie," she said finally, "I'm glad you've come back, and I'm sure we can find a place for you. But you'll have to understand one thing clearly at the very beginning. Everything's changed here from what it was when you left. This is a plantation again. If you start a task you've got to finish it,—no picking up and leaving. And no fighting. You'll have to be sober and peaceable. You'll get rations of cornmeal and brown sugar and bacon, but there'll be very little cash pay and you won't get that till later on. You'll have to fish and make out as best you can, like the rest of the people. Next year things will be easier, but this year's going to be hard. Now, do you still want to join us?"

He nodded vigorously.

"All right, Biggie, you can start in the morning. You have a place to sleep?"

"Vell, naw'm, not e'zac'ly. Seem like muh skinfolks is all done daid in de flood."

"I can put a cot in the stable for you. And I think I can find some clothes that will fit you a little better than those. Hungry?"

He admitted it with an apologetic grin.

She gave him the rest of her lunch. And while he moved away to a respectful distance to wolf it, she tore a leaf out of her notebook and scratched a message to Lucy.

"You remember Lucy?" she asked him when he was through. "Well, take this to her at the house. She'll look after you."

So Biggie came home to Land's End like a shorn lamb to the fold. And though later he was to prove himself a prime asset, at the beginning he was only another problem, and a tough one.

Trouble started with his appearance in the field. The men resented him at once and instinctively; not, as it developed, because of any overt offensiveness,—his manner was friendly towards all,—but on the simple grounds of his physical superiority and the self-assurance that went with it. Apparently even his good-natured grin seemed a condescension and a challenge to the plantation bucks.

James Washington was the first to take umbrage.

"Why, what's the trouble?" she asked him when he came scowling and grumbling from the field.

"Miss Em'ly, I cyan' wuk wid dat mon nohow! He too big-mout' an' proudsome!"

"Well, I wouldn't let that upset you, James. He probably likes to boast about his travels. Just don't pay any attention to him."

"I ain' pay no 'tention to'um, but he try fuh mek me bex!"

"What did he do?"

"He ain' *do* nutt'n 'zac'ly, ma'm."

"Well,—what did he say then?"

"T'ain' what he *say,* ma'm. But he *look* at me too meanly an' uppety, like he is some big somebody an' I is nobody. He same as suck he teet' fuh onsult me, ma'm, an' I ain' tek dat fum no nigguh!"

She saw that the situation called for gravity.

"Very well, James. Your sensitiveness seems a little extreme, but if you can't work with Biggie you'll have to work by yourself,—which I'm sure you won't like." And she sent him to a lonely part of the field.

Before the day was over One-Eye Richard had also suffered some obscure slight at Biggie's hands, and had to be sent to keep James company.

The next morning, distracted by other worries, she made the mistake of hastily deciding that this excessive touchiness of the male element could be cured by the simple expedient of removing the cause of irritation from their midst, by segregating Biggie with the women workers; it would be bad, she felt, to isolate him completely, for working alone he would remain an outsider indefinitely, he would never be assimilated. And the mistake did not make itself evident that day: everything seemed to go very well indeed, and noting how well the women worked with Biggie she congratulated herself on having found so easy a solution.

The following day, however, it developed that the solution had only aggravated the situation. Neither Richard nor James appeared for work, and Biggie bore the marks of a brawl.

"You've been fighting, Biggie."

"My missie," he explained shamefacedly, "I too sorry 'bout dat. But I ain' staa't nutt'n. Seem like some of dese mens is too ogly an' squalsome an' too sp'ilin' fuh trouble. Las' night, ma'm, dey try fuh gang me, but I ain' allow dat."

She hated the thought of losing Biggie: he was worth ten ordinary hands, and already she had begun to see in him a possible successor to Isaac, a plantation overseer, a leader of the people.

"Biggie, this is very serious. I told you I would not tolerate any fighting. But I'm going to give you one more chance."

Later she presented this ultimatum to Richard and James, and exacted promises of good behavior and mutual forbearance from all parties to the encounter. And to insure peace, in the field at least, she put Biggie with the Twins, Barty and Ned, the only men who had shown no resentment toward him.

He was a marvelous worker. Tireless and cheerful, he moved with an ease and grace pleasant to see. He seemed to revel in work, and soon he was enough at home in the field to lift his voice in song. And his singing and hustling infected the others, so that the planting progressed with a new rhythm and energy.

From her post under the old live-oak, or from one of the seed-bag stations along the road that crossed the field, she watched intently every step of the routine. The rows, running north and south the full length of the field, were about five feet apart. The countless holes for the seed were cut by hoe along the crests, about one foot apart. The sowers moved up and down the long aisles with pouches slung from their shoulders, dropping several seeds into each hole, which must be neither too deep nor too shallow. The women workers followed the sowers, covering the seed carefully with their hoes, and patting the soil down lightly with the blades. A kind of monotonous process, Seth called it, but to her its repetitions seemed infinitely varied and engrossing.

All the years she had been at Land's End she had seen cotton planted, but she had never observed the routine closely. It had been taken for granted as part of the island scene, accepted without scrutiny, like the unfolding of the seasons or the swing of the tides. Now, suddenly, it had become vital and immediate. So vital that she could hardly stand her passive role. She longed to join the women workers in the great bright field.

VI

On the second day of April the planting was finished. The pause that followed might have been one of fretful dimensions but for the many other issues that absorbed her time and kept her from watching too intently for the field's first sprouts.

Stephen came first. His vegetable garden was made, and the interest and occupation it had given him were past; he was at complete loose ends again. And though there were a dozen matters in connection with the house and grounds clamoring for attention, particularly the state of the trees and shrubs at the edge of the yard where the storm tide had washed most of the soil away from the roots, he refused to show any concern.

"Let them die," he said of the trees, "or slide down on the beach. What difference does it make? It would take a carload of dirt to save them anyway. Besides, they always blocked the view from the lower piazza,—you used to say so yourself. With all that's happened you ask me to worry about the fate of a few trees and a mess of Spanish bayonets! No thanks." And he took the same attitude about everything.

If she thought her spare time now could be used to comfort him, she quickly saw her mistake. Talking to him was like walking a tight-rope; whenever she found a topic that she felt sure would make safe conversation, he managed to twist it around to the old theme of disaster. And her very company seemed to irritate him. He seemed to enjoy interpreting her every offer of tenderness and understanding as a gesture of superiority, of insufferable tact and pity, to be met with sullenness and sarcasm. It's the only outlet he has, she reminded herself when he hurt her or wore her patience dangerously thin. But she began to realize that his unconscious purpose was to break her down to his own level of despair and negation; that alone would satisfy him. And from that she must certainly protect herself, and him.

Yet it was impossible to avoid him, leave him to the mercy of his nerves. If she could do nothing for him herself at this phase, then something must be found to engage his interest, something to take the place of the vegetable garden, which had worked sufficiently well as a distraction. But the merest hint that anything else around the place needed attention was enough to send him into a sulk. Puzzling desperately for a solution, she thought finally of the boat-building that was in progress on the bluff where the Company's drying-sheds had stood. There, under Seth's supervision, several men from the settlements with carpentering experience were knocking together, from salvage and a little new lumber, a plantation fishing fleet of batteaux and skiffs. Wouldn't that interest him?

"It would not," he replied to her mention of it. "Suggesting I take up shipbuilding as a livelihood? Or just lining me up for a little fish-peddling? I had about enough of that, you know, back after the War when we were living in the slave-quarters at Cherokee, Mother and Eugenia and Rusty and I, while you and Miss Sheppard were occupying the house here. And has it occurred to you I might not have much appetite for fooling around the Company ruins?"

But after he had gotten that bitter rejection off his chest, she was able to persuade him to pay a visit to the scene and give the amateur boatwrights some advice. He ended by staying all day; and when she saw him at supper-time, there was a new light in his eyes. He made a fine show of indifference, however, keeping any trace of enthusiasm out of his voice.

"It's just as well I decided to drop over there," he frowned. "They were all working at cross-purposes, of course, and Seth is no good at bossing a job. It takes something more than hammers and nails and boards to make a shipyard,—someone with initiative and authority has got to oversee the thing. So I suppose I'm the goat. We'll have to lay down keels for two or three sailboats, if we want any Spanish mackerel steaks this summer. You can't get out to the big drops in a batteau."

So, her mind at ease again, she was free to devote herself to other concerns, chief of which was inspecting the people's cotton and vegetable patches. It was a wearisome business, visiting every family in the settlements, commending the industrious and prodding the laggards, listening to complaints and troubles and excuses. The planting of the cotton, the cash-money crop, was going well enough, had almost kept pace with the Big Field, but the vegetable patches needed vigorous encouragement. In fact, there was still such general procrastination about getting in the seed she had distributed that she felt compelled to make a drastic threat: any family that failed to plant its quota of corn and turnips and yams, without further delay and excuses, would be issued no more rations of fat-back and meal, salt and sugar. This broke up the passive resistance so completely that by the end of the week she was able to make a trip to town with the comforting knowledge that another problem had been solved.

After she had finished with the bank and Van Wie's, she went on to Marshlands. It was no pleasure to see this half of home in the hands of strangers, with no redemption in sight; and it was no pleasure to call on the Fowlers, particularly Mrs. Fowler. Captain Fowler, who controlled the piloting business of Port Royal Sound and had made money in the phosphate years, was agreeable enough, but his wife was distinctly offensive.

At the front porch she found old Mr. Fowler, the Captain's father, basking in the sun. He greeted her with his frightened look and shuffled into the house, and presently Mrs. Fowler appeared, tidying herself in a fluster.

"Well, if it isn't Mrs. Fenwick!" she nodded with a smirk. "Didn't Father Fowler ask you to come in? He's getting so absent-minded. But maybe you rather sit out here—it's chilly inside. Well, how are you folks? How is Mr. Fenwick doing?"

"He's much better, thank you."

"Oh, that's good,—we heard he'd never be a well man again, but I always say doctors don't know everything. Come to look at the garden?"

"Not today. I came to see about getting the piano."

Mrs. Fowler stiffened. "Well, that's going to make a bad hole in the sitting-room, I must say. They don't none of us use it, but it's ornamental-looking. Hope you're not afraid we might hurt it,—they's only George and me and Father Fowler and Cousin Meta—no children or pets to scratch it up. And we always keep a shawl over it."

"I'm sorry, Mrs. Fowler, but if you remember we had an understanding about the piano."

"Well, I don't remember. Nothing about it in the lease, neither. If you want the piano, you can just take and knock a couple of dollars a month off the rent. Everybody says we got stung anyways."

"Why, we'll gladly cancel the lease if you wish it, Mrs. Fowler."

"No thank you, Mrs. Fenwick, we don't ask favors. When we make a bargain, no matter how bad it is, we stick to it. Only we don't allow ourself to be took advantage of."

"I think I understand. Now will Monday be convenient for moving the piano?"

"No, it won't. The Ladies Circle of the Baptist Church is going to meet here Monday. You can come Tuesday. And I'll ask you to let us know ahead when you want to do any work in the garden,—we might have folks calling that day."

A charming interview. Shaken and disgusted she wondered afterwards if it would ever be possible to meet an experience of that sort with tolerance; or if tolerance was beyond reach, then with amusement or plain phlegm. It called, surely, for a reaction more satisfactory than mere self-control, the stifling of an impulse to box Mrs. Fowler's Baptist ears, to drive her out the gates of Marshlands or across the lawn and into the river.

But at any rate she had the piano. Seth reckoned that with Biggie and Barty and Ned to do the handling it could be transported in the *Pilot Boy*. This proved to be a miscalculation: in the end it had to be ferried across the river on a flatboat and hauled out to the plantation in the Twins' ox-cart, well cushioned with bags of moss. But when it stood again in its place in the island living-room, gently illumined in the glow of sunset from over the lulled waters of the Sound, she realized how light a ransom she had paid for it.

That first evening her fingers touched the keys with misgivings. In her enthusiasm she had not stopped to consider what effect it would have on Stephen. But his only protest was against her playing so softly.

"Come on out with it," he told her over his *News & Courier,* "I'm glad to hear some sounds of life around here. I only wish you'd had it before,—might have kept you out of all this plantation foolishness."

Every day now, morning or afternoon, she went to the Big Field, sure each time that she would find it sprouting. Yet when the miracle came at last, after a day and night of gentle showers, it took her breath away with surprise and unbelief.

It was several days before Palm Sunday and she was on her way with Biggie and Tad to spend an afternoon cleaning up the worst of the debris at Pine Point. When work was resumed in the field, there would be no time for this long-planned expedition. And there was a special reason for delaying it no further: Miss Sophie's cherished custom of palm crosses for the heads of the children's beds must not be broken, and the crosses (Michael's small enough to fit into an envelope) must be made from the palmetto shoots that were springing up at the feet of the stalwart old monarchs of Rusty's grove, among the reviving cedars and cassenas and myrtles. Her mind was so taken up with thoughts spreading from the grove that she came out of the shortcut, the woods still damply fragrant from the night's rain, and into the sunshine of the Big Field without any thrill of expectation. So that it was a long minute before she could grasp the miracle.

Even then she had to turn to Biggie for confirmation.

"Can you believe it, Biggie!"

"Naw'm, I sho cyan'," he grinned, "if I ain' shum wid my yown yeye."

There it was, actual and indubitable, a marvelous expanse of tiny sprouts. Not in orderly ranks, as she had dreamed, for only a small percentage of the sprouts was cotton: the rest was weeds. But in the excitement of the moment that seemed a matter of slight importance.

Her first impulse was to tell Stephen. But her pride decided against it; she would wait for him to ask how she was making out. And if he stubbornly refrained from asking? Well, that was all right: soon Michael would be home for the Easter holidays to share her triumph. Meanwhile she would look to Seth for appreciation. And she sent Tad to find him, while she and Biggie went on to the Point.

When he appeared, his appraisal of the field was sobering.

"A powerful perty sight," he admitted. "But it'll be a sight pertier when it's clear of weeds. That's goin' to be the rub from now on, to keep them weeds from chokin' you out. And it's goin' to be a fair tussle, ma'm."

Going home, by way of the settlements to tell the people of the field gang that they must be on hand without fail in the morning, her enthusiasm was able to discount the weight of Seth's words. It might be a little early for self-congratulations, but after all a mess of baby weeds was nothing to be afraid of.

But before the next day was over, she understood what Seth meant by "a fair tussle". And by the time she reached the brief respite of Palm Sunday, she was ready to acknowledge a solemn respect for weeds.

For this was a hand-to-hand struggle. It made the work of preparing and planting the field seem like child's play. More showers over the week-end helped the cotton sprouts but positively pampered the weeds; the cotton grew fast but the weeds grew faster: they flourished almost perceptibly in the muggy sunshine, the beds were ragged with them, and they flooded the aisles, their teeming myriads were spreading a coverlet over the uncleared part of the field. And at the end of Monday's work the unredeemed territory was still greater than the redeemed. The acreage cleared each day was always so much less than she had reasonably expected; and though she made allowances for the tediousness of "haulin' "—drawing up earth to the fragile little plants after the weeds had been hoed out—she felt there was a conspiracy among the hands to avoid any danger of overworking themselves.

Auntie Adelaide offered a plan to break this up. After Auntie Cuba's death, "Yan' Yaddy" had taken her place as the plantation's senior midwife. Stephen had pensioned the "gabby old crone" before the storm, but now in this plantation emergency she was unwilling to sit back and do nothing for her rations: when work had begun in the Big Field she had appeared to offer her services as a mauma. She was knobbly with rheumatism but far from incapacitated, and nursing was a business she understood well. In her reminiscing, under the live-oak where she minded the babies of the women hands, she told of the times just before the Gun Shoot at Bay Point when she had had as many as "t'irty head" to look after. "An', my chile, I haffuh cyarry each an' ebery one of dem out to dey mudduh in de fiel' fuh suck duh." She was now minding the "grands" of some of those same infants, but she had nothing good to say for any generation since slavery times.

"Befo' my maussa done tek me fum fiel', I been a willin' han'. Ole Maa'cus—dat been Isaac paa—he ain' haffuh dribe me! I done my task an' den I gone home fuh ten' me-own li'l yaa'd. But dese people ain' no-'count. De mans got Dispens'y likkuh an' 'oman on de brain tummuch, an' de 'omans cyan' t'ink 'bout nutt'n but silk dress an' plague de mans fuh cyarry'um to town."

Her advice was to put the field on a task basis. "Biggie an' some udduhs is doin' all de wuk, an' dem striflin' gals, like Alish an' Wishy, dem ain' do eben one task 'tween'um de day t'rough. Tell'um dem cyan' do you dat way, honey. Tell'um dem cyan' git credick an' leabe de fiel' till dem done full task fuh yuh."

That sounded fair enough; fairer, in fact, and more practical than the present system. So on Tuesday morning of that strenuous Holy Week the remainder of the field was paced off into quarter-acre tasks, and she explained to the hands that they would be credited for the amount of ground covered. There was considerable grumbling at the change, but when work was once resumed it proceeded at a much better pace. The only hitch was that some of the people were satisfied when they had finished one task. At least half a dozen of them were prepared to leave the field by noon, and had to be coaxed into starting another task.

Despite the extra progress made that day, so much of the field still remained unweeded that she began to worry about finishing in the two more days before Good Friday. Nobody would report for work on Saturday: that was clean-up day for Easter. And Monday everybody would be too dead to work. So unless the field could be cleared by Thursday evening, a heavy handicap would have to be carried over the three-day festival.

When she talked to Biggie at the close of Tuesday's work, he scratched an idea out of his kinky head.

"Missie, if you could full-up de fiel' wid mo' han', could clean-up in mos' no time. An' den dat gib we good staa't fuh nex' veek, an' den us could mek-out too yeasy wid dishyuh smalls gang, less'n duh come tummuch day rain."

Following his suggestion she sent out a general call for hands to work Wednesday and Thursday in the wage field. Because preparations for Easter had already begun at the settlements, there were many excuses; but the response was satisfactory enough. On Wednesday morning there were nearly fifty hands in the field, to the prime delight of Auntie Adelaide, who was inspired to a rhapsody of reminiscing at the sight.

It was too thrilling a sight just to watch. By mid-morning it was no longer possible to resist the urge to play a more active part in the proceedings. Leaving the shade of the live-oak to Auntie Adelaide and her nursery, she armed herself with a spare hoe and joined a little group of women hands in a corner of the field. At first she worked awkwardly, embarrassed by the weight of the hoe and the surprised glances of the people. And except for her hat, an old straw from the attic, she was hardly dressed for the part: she could only envy Wishy and Alice and Gertie, her neighbors in the field, the stout cords they wore bound tightly around their hips to hold their skirts up and "gib strain't". But what did it matter if she tore and soiled the hem of her skirt a little, providing she could get into the house without Lucy detecting her state. As she saw the people's surprise subsiding into tolerant acceptance, and as she began to get the swing of the hoe, her spirits climbed. It was ticklish business rooting out the weeds along the crest of the bed, and often she had to pluck them out by hand for fear of cutting the delicate cotton plants; but now she was not just eating and sleeping weeds and fighting them through mercenaries: she was fighting them herself now, she was at actual grips with the enemy. These rampant hordes were personal antagonists, her foes as surely as the cotton plants were her allies. And in fighting and conquering them she soon became oblivious of the field and the people and herself, of everything but the good sound and feel of her hoe chopping fervently along the row.

By noon the hoe had grown heavy as lead, and she had to rest after her lunch. But later in the afternoon she went back into the field. And the following morning, after she had finished her time-book, she joined Wishy and Alice and Gertie again. Her arms and back were so stiff and sore that at first she could hardly wield the hoe at all and thought she would have to stop; but she was determined to stick it out, and it was not long before she began to limber up.

It was an aid to rhythm to listen to the talk of the women across the aisles. Yesterday they had had little to say among themselves, in deference to her presence; but today they were unable to sustain this unnatural muteness and soon their tongues were wagging freely, normally. As oldest member of the trio Gertie held the floor most of the time. She was delivering to tittering Alice and Wishy a forceful sermon, this shining spring morning, on the wisdom of feminine cynicism.

"Don' laugh, tittuh," she was telling them, "befo' you fine you'self cryin'. Dey ain' no man wut no 'oman. You cyan' trus'um, you cyan' mek'um sansible, you cyan' do nutt'n wid'um. Vhen dey haa'd dey sof', an' vhen dey sof' dey haa'd. Dey gwine lie to you, dey gwine t'ief you' money vhen bock tu'n, dey gwine two-time all time. Don' fool wid'um no mo' dan snake in grass. Dey cyan' brung you nutt'n but trouble."

She seemed to see in Biggie, lightening his labor with song not many aisles away, a special snake in the grass.

"Don' t'ink I ain' see you gal cut you' eye at'um! An' I yeddy you miratin' 'pon'um, how sweet he stan' an' all. But ef you got one good green of sanse, bes' keep you' eye pure cyas' down vhen you pass'um in fiel' an' road. He ain' got no time fuh de like of you, less'n be de time snake got fuh cunjuh young bird fuh *yam*. He mek one po' mout'ful of you an' den he *gone!*"

"You is speak wid sech high feelin'," Alice countered, "mus' be you is studyin' 'bout Biggie you'self."

"Who—me?" Gertie sucked her teeth in scorn. "Jedus, chile, I hope my Sabeyuh is gib me mo' bettuh sanse dan foolish wirgin by dis time!"

"Who you call name?" Alice demanded.

"Ax paa'don, tittie. I ain' mean fuh onsult you,—Gawd know you an' Wishy ain' no wirgin. But you is sho foolish enough to mek-up fuh dat. An' you is pure co'tin' trouble vhen you looks 'pon dat big nigguh. Mens is a pain, an' de mo' bigguh dey come, de mo' haa'duh dey is fuh han'le."

"Fox call grape sour," Wishy put in, "vhen he cyan' reach'um."

And so it went on through the morning, making a welcome distraction from the increasing weight of the hoe.

It was not till the noon hour that she realized the work was almost finished. The beds stood free of weeds the length and breadth of the field except for two small patches at the south boundary, and these could surely be cleared by the end of the day. And now at last her pride was overwhelmed, and she sent Tad off with a note for Stephen, begging him to come and share her triumph.

She was back in the field when he finally appeared, late in the afternoon. She had begun to fear that her note had been too flip, that she should have worded it more carefully and soberly, for it would be no easy matter for him to surrender his position, his stubborn and studied indifference; so her heart pounded up with relief when she caught sight of him coming out of the shortcut. As he came along the edge of the field she saw that he was dressed as smartly as though he were on his way to the office: the only concession he had made to the dusty tramp from the house was the turning-up of his trouser cuffs. Quickly she wiped her face and hands with her handkerchief and tidied her clothes before she started to meet him. He stopped in the shade of the trees at the end of the aisle and stood waiting for her. It was not till she reached him with a breathless greeting on her lips that she recognized, through a flushed haze of pleasure, the horrified expression on his face.

"For God sake," he glared down at her, "have you completely lost your mind?"

Even when she realized his anger, she couldn't believe in it.

"Well, that's nice! You don't like my surprise?"

"Did you expect me to like the spectacle of my wife working with a gang of nigs?"

She let go of his arm then.

"Oh, that." She tried to dismiss it lightly. "I just wanted to see what it felt like to do a task."

"I see. Just wanted the experience."

"Well, I suppose I was a little carried away by enthusiasm, and a desire to get this first weeding done before Michael gets home. I'm sorry if it upset you. I had no idea I was committing a serious breach of etiquette."

"No, you wouldn't. How could you be expected to."

That wrenched from her a sudden gag of laughter. "Is it really as bad as that?"

"It couldn't be worse. I'd rather see you dead."

For a moment she regarded him with a twisted smile, and then she had to look away to the field.

"If I'd had any idea," she heard him say, "that anything of this kind was going on. Haven't you any judgment at all? Why, a white *man* couldn't afford to do what you've done."

He raised his voice to shout at the nearest hands: "You niggers get on with your work there!"

When he spoke to her again, his tone was less harsh. "I suppose you didn't know what you were doing. But I should think your common sense would have told you you can't mix in with niggers and expect them to respect you. If you're bent on continuing this heroic act of yours, please at least try to keep your head a little better. Nobody can help being a Yankee, but you might remember you're supposed to be a lady and my wife. Please don't make a worse fool of yourself, and me, than you can help."

She turned back to him with eyes steadied from the shock of his words by the sight of the field.

"Very good, sir. I'm thoroughly ashamed and sorry for this lapse. And in the future I'll do my best not to forget my position, and your dignity. And now will you please admire our field a little? You've been so busy lecturing me, you haven't even so much as glanced at it yet."

"No thanks. I've seen quite enough."

And he was gone.

But when she got home, he was waiting to renew the discussion.

"I didn't make much of an impression on you this afternoon, did I? Guess I didn't make it strong enough, you took it so lightly. Well, I want to tell you something. I'm sick and tired of this whole damn planting nonsense. Suppose you do succeed with it, what does it amount to anyway? But if you're set on it, you've got to remember that I have some pride left, if you haven't."

"All right, Stephen," she sighed. "I understand how you feel."

Her weary acquiescence only infuriated him.

"But do you?—that's the question. I doubt if you have any conception of the imbecility of your actions. To have you bossing a gang of niggers is bad enough, God knows, but to find you working in with them,—well, that's the limit!"

"Stephen, I said I was sorry. And I've promised it won't happen again. What more can I say?"

"You might admit you've been a fool."

"All right, I will, if that gives you any satisfaction. It was a piece of disgusting imbecility. Is that enough?"

"You see, you refuse to admit the seriousness of it. In your eyes it was just an innocent, harmless gesture."

"No, it was a mistake. If only because it's gotten you so wrought up. But I can't honestly say I think it was very serious. And now I'd rather not talk about it any more, if you don't mind."

And through supper and the evening she was too depressed to attempt to break the grim silence that stood between them.

But when she opened her eyes to the first light of morning, her hurt and disappointment had vanished as surely as the darkness. She hated, then, to leave the house without saying a word to him. When she went back upstairs after she had had her early breakfast, she hoped to find him stirring; but he was still sound asleep, and her movements in getting the wage money out of her handkerchief-bag in the bureau failed to wake him. So she had to resign herself to a deferred making-up with him.

It took a provokingly long time to settle with the people. When she reached the field she found them all assembled and waiting under the live-oak, but many "respectful" objections were raised to her sums in the time-book and it was a complicated process satisfying and silencing each individual objector, for everyone was in a talkative holiday mood and in no hurry whatever. And of course, despite the general spirit of festivity, there was an inevitable amount of grumbling at having a part of the wages withheld: a severe test of her patience, because she herself had an aversion to this precautionary measure, though she recognized the necessity of it. But finally the last hand was paid off, and she was free to make a brief appraisal of the field and start home.

And now, with the responsibilities of the plantation behind her for a few days, her mind was free to stretch out of its cramped concentration on weeds. She stopped at the Robinsons' for a minute,—Seth had already left for town in the *Pilot Boy* to fetch supplies and Margaret and Jack, but Linda was there, to rejoice with her over Michael's homecoming on the afternoon train tomorrow,—and then she hurried on, her own excitement heightened by Linda's, her senses reveling in the glory around her. Till this hour her obsession with the work and worry of the field had blinded her to the coming of full spring. But now she was intensely aware of the change.

Like the shadow of a cloud the old dark thought crossed her enchantment: of how quickly this flood-tide of spring must perish. Soon this crest of beauty must break and ebb away into the cauldron of summer. Too soon the great white chalices of the magnolias at Land's End and Marshlands would open and fall, and swarms of sand-flies would come to make still hours miserable; then the clustered bloom of the Spanish bayonet would flame up and burn down to a clump of ugly pods, while mosquitoes laid siege to the house after thunder-storms; and finally the delicate blossoms of the crepe-myrtles would come and go under a sky no longer vivid happy blue, as now, but pale and hazy from the tremendous heat. And soon this supreme season of music would pass: the migrant wings and voices would be gone, the faithful mocker and cardinal would stand aside for gangs of grackles, and at last song would be all but lost in the stridor of the insects. . . .

But it was summer, she reminded herself, that would ripen the cotton, bring the children home to her for whole months, carry disaster farther and farther away. And it was pure folly to allow anything, past or future, to mar the perfection of this morning. The future could take care of itself; and the past,—well, in an astonishing world nothing was more astonishing than the way memory made order out of chaos, casting out or transmuting evil, treasuring and magnifying good. The scars of the past, far and near, were as surely healed as the island's storm scars were healed now in this final triumph of spring.

And in the light of this serenity within and without she could only wonder how she could have allowed her chagrin to stand against Stephen yesterday. She saw so clearly now what she should have said and done. What difference did it make what he said? The vitally important thing was never to forget the sickness of his nerves, never to lose patience with him. That was the test of her strength. There was no place for pride in this matter: she must make whatever amends were necessary for yesterday, and then firmly promise herself not to fail again.

By the time she reached the pasture and the stable, she had prepared what she was going to say and she was in haste to get it over with. But in the yard an interruption was waiting for her. Lucy, feeding the hen and chicks that Seth had given her, was in a pout about something.

"Why, Lucy, they look fine! I believe they've grown since yesterday."

But Lucy's response was mumbled and she continued to scowl darkly at the clucking hen and peeping chicks at her feet. This was a formidable pout: something must have gone very wrong. Perhaps Stephen had spoken crossly to her. But there was no hope of getting to the bottom of it in a minute and she was in a hurry to see Stephen now, she would have to investigate later. It was better, anyway, to give Lucy time to cool off a little. And there was always the chance that a pout of Lucy's would cure itself, vanish without treatment and as suddenly as it had appeared.

"You gave Mr. Robinson the list, Lucy?"

For a reply she got a morose nod. A really serious pout this time, she thought as she hurried up the porch steps and into the kitchen.

His breakfast, hardly touched except for the coffee, was still on the dining-room table. He was not in the living-room, and when she called upstairs silence rang back. She went out on the piazza: he was nowhere in sight, and the only answer to her calls were the scoldings of a bluejay, the cry of gulls from beyond the landing, and the roll of the tide coming in over the flats. Puzzled, she went back into the hall and upstairs. Where on earth had he gone? But she quickly found an explanation to check her rising alarm: he had had a tiff with Lucy and had left the house to cool off. Perhaps he had gone to the field to meet her, and she had missed him when she had turned off the shortcut to stop at the Robinsons'.

Before going downstairs she went to the bureau to put back into her handkerchief-bag the change left over from the payroll. When she opened the bag, she saw that most of the money was gone. She saw that it was gone, but she had to count what was left several times before she could believe her eyes. This morning after she had taken out the wage money there had still been over three hundred dollars left in the bag, in bills, silver, and the ten-dollar goldpieces that Stephen used to give her "for luck" after directors' meetings of the bank and the Port Royal Railroad. Now there was exactly sixty-two dollars and ten cents.

As soon as she could rally her wits, she hurried down to the kitchen porch. But she was careful to keep any panic out of her voice.

"Lucy, do you know where Mr. Stephen's gone?"

Lucy shook some crumbs out of her apron and came reluctantly toward the porch. By the time she reached the steps she was sniffling.

"I done my bes' to sway'um fum goin'."

"Going where?"

"Miss Em'ly, I been dat worry I ain' pit one drap of food to my mout' dis mo'nin'. I tell'um you gwine be bad bex wid'um if he gone to town wid Mistuh Rob'son."

Her heart stopped there. But she had to say something, and say it calmly.

"Oh,—well, I suppose he wanted to see Mr. Joe. And come back with the children."

"He say, 'Tell'um I gots business fuh ten' to.' Da's all he say."

"And is that all you've been fretted about? Why didn't you tell me what it was as soon as I got here?"

"Miss Em'ly, I been too shame."

"Well, I think we better forget that now and attend to our own business. We've got a thousand things to do today."

She managed to make her share of the housework tide her over the rest of the morning. Making up the beds, cleaning the silver and trimming the lamps, dusting and doing the last-minute odds-and-ends that Lucy always considered superfluous, she worked frantically to keep from thinking. These preparations that would normally have given the finishing touch to her anticipation were become a desperate anodyne against panic. Even her bath and the special grooming she had promised herself had to be rushed through at a frenzied rate.

But when the dinner hour came and went without any sign of the *Pilot Boy* returning, she could no longer evade her thoughts. Trips to the landing only increased the suspense: the ebb-tide Sound was a mirror of staring presentiments, at once full and empty. She went up to the attic then, hoping to lose her fears in rummaging through the old cedar-chest for the children's bathing-suits. Margaret and Jack, at least, would not find the water too cold for swimming; and though she had intended to leave the chest to them, for they liked to be the first to open and explore it, they would have to forgive her for stealing a march on them in this emergency. But when she lifted the lid and began her ransacking, the scent of the chest, the sight and feel of half-forgotten garments—things of the children's and Stephen's and her own, a jacket of Miss Sophie's, a bathing-suit of Rusty's—released such a flood of memories that she had to give up the search and retreat downstairs, to the kitchen and the unfailing reality of Lucy.

But even Lucy was no comfort now.

"For goodness sake, Lucy, stop looking so solemn."

"Pusson cyan' help lookin' like he feel, Miss Em'ly."

To escape the house and Lucy's black mood she went out in the yard. And then, to give herself an active distraction, she took several oat sacks from the stable out to the avenue to fill with moss. It was too soon to stuff up the chimneys against early mosquitoes and moths, for there might be one more spell cool enough for fires before summer set in, but gathering up the moss litter would improve the

515

appearance of the avenue for Easter. Biggie and Tad had already dragged aside the great branches that the storm had snapped off, but the roadway was still strewn with bunches of the fallen moss, and it was a good time to remedy that.

The cathedral-like avenue, with its soft lights and shadows, was a charmed spot. And the venerable trees, with their long gray beards swaying meditatively in the sea air, were old friends, full of immemorial years and wisdom. But today they stood as remote as ancient prophets. Their endurance was a mockery and their wisdom was as far beyond her reach as their arching branches and the sky. But by steadfastly denying to them that she was either alone or afraid, and by diligently gathering up the moss at their feet, she was able to breathe freely as she listened for the signals of release: the toot of the *Pilot Boy's* whistle, and then the bang of the kitchen screen door as Margaret and Jack came dashing through the house and out to find her.

She saw herself meeting them at the end of the avenue, and then going on to meet Stephen. That picture was a blank, its elements unknown, but it was not going to be bad; she was confident of that, despite the quivering of her nerves. He couldn't allow it to be bad: there was too much at stake. It was just a threat, this trip to town and the taking of the money,—he was scaring her, teaching her a lesson, punishing her for yesterday. He wouldn't let himself carry out the threat. He would come back with the children, his torment relieved by the escapade. And when he was safely home, how readily she would accept any explanation he had to offer! After all, she was to blame for his going, her poor handling of yesterday's encounter had precipitated this.

. . . Actually, she was standing on the piazza and it was late afternoon when the *Pilot Boy* came puffing in sight at last. And when, a few minutes later on the landing, the children scrambled out into her arms, she had to face the fact that Stephen was not with them.

"He had important business in town," she found herself explaining to them in a plausible voice, "and I'm afraid he won't get home till long after you're both in bed."

And she sent them on to the house with their arms full of groceries before she turned to Seth.

"We waited on him till after five, ma'm," he reported glumly as he handed out the rest of the things, "but he never did show up at the dock. So I figgered he must not have finished his business and we better get along before dark, for fear we might fetch up on a shoal. And I figgered you and Linda might be gettin' a little fidgety. This evenin' she can stay with you and I'll catch the tide back and try to locate him."

"Oh no, Seth. He can easily get a boat to bring him out."

"Well, just whatever you say. Let me tote this sack of ice up to the house,—I left gettin' that till last, so it ain't melted none."

"Please don't, Seth, Lucy and I can manage it easily. Now you must hurry home to Linda. And I know you're starving."

It so embarrassed him to be thanked for anything that she made no attempt to say more than that.

"Well, I'll stop by tomorrow, ma'm," he told her as he went forward to push off, "on my way to get Mr. Michael."

She nodded back. And then for the next few minutes, as she watched the *Pilot Boy* swing away from the landing and head for the mouth of the Inlet, she stood transfixed in slowly tightening coils of consternation. It was not till Lucy came down from the house that she was able to break the spell of shock and suffocation.

When they had carried the sack to the back porch and buried the ice in the sawdust box, she forced herself to eat some supper with the children. After that she took them out to the edge of the pasture woods to get sprays of jasmine and branches of bay for the house. And with senses stricken mercifully numb between their bright chatter and the turmoil of her brain, she kept them out as long as possible, fearing the gathering shadows of dusk less than the living-room and its circle of lamplight.

She knew what was ahead of her. A night of waiting and listening, listening and waiting,—against the frail idiotic repetitions of spring peepers, the endless gyrations of her thoughts, the ironic serenity of a world steeped in moonlight,—waiting and listening for the sounds of a boat and voices at the landing. A night of dread and of grotesque shapes and astounding parallels risen from the dead strange places of the past. A night of nightmares, new and old.

She had depended on daybreak to scatter the phantoms of the

517

night and coördinate her faculties. But a dark residue of horror carried over to stain the sunlight and paralyze her will. Her mind was drugged, and for a long while after breakfast she was powerless to frame any course of deliverance.

Even when finally she was able to decide what to do, her will remained too numb to translate the decision into action. Perhaps, after all, it was better just to wait: perhaps he would appear of his own accord. And there were convenient delays to lean on. A delegation of women from the settlements presented themselves at the kitchen steps to beg newspapers "fuh dress-up we house fuh Yeastuh"; gratefully she left the urgent haunted daylight to rummage in the dusk of the attic for an armful of *News & Couriers*. But when they had gone, the situation had to be faced again and finally.

"I'm going to take Margaret and Jack to the Robinsons'," she told Lucy. "They can stay with Linda while Seth and I go to town."

And having put her determination into words, action suddenly became easy.

Margaret and Jack were glad to go for a tramp and see Linda. But when it came to being left with her and missing a ride in the *Pilot Boy* there were protests, loud ones from Jack.

"If you're getting Easter surprises, Mamma, you don't have to be scared of us. We won't even get out of the boat. And we won't peek or ask questions or anything."

It was hard to find a reasonable excuse to offer them, and for a moment she wondered if it wouldn't be wiser to take them and leave them with Miss Hamilton till this trouble was over. But when she thought of the explanations that would involve, she quickly abandoned the idea and concentrated on reconciling them to staying with Linda.

The moment she and Seth were safely off in the *Pilot Boy*, doubts began to assail her again. Perhaps she should have taken the children back to Miss Hamilton's after all. Perhaps she should have let Seth go alone. Perhaps it was a mistake to have done anything at all but wait. And then the full shock of the situation struck with a sickening force.

Yet despite the dazed ringing in her ears she managed to talk rationally and calmly to Seth. There was no sense in trying to keep up any pretense with him, and she questioned him frankly and received a frank answer.

"Where do you think Mr. Fenwick went yesterday, Seth?"

"Well, ma'm, I reckon he was headin' for that Commercial Club when he left me."

And when they reached the Beaufort waterfront and tied up at the new public wharf, she found she could move and think with astonishing ease.

Bay Street was crowded with Easter Saturday shoppers, mostly window-shopping colored folk with no money to spend this poverty-stricken year; yet most of the faces, the eyes and mouths and voices eddying around her were startlingly gay, as if trouble was only a sick state of mind unworthy of the season. . . . While Seth went on to the Commercial Club, she stopped in at Fortner's Pharmacy for candy and egg-dye, quite as if this was any year of the past and the children were still children. But they would expect rabbit nests and an egg hunt tomorrow morning, if only as a joke, just as they had expected Christmas with all the trimmings a few months ago in the midst of falling skies. They were the cruelest of tyrants, she thought with a terrible tightness in her throat at that moment of shrill Mrs. Fortner and the correct change: "Don't let me cheat you now. And how you all making out on the island? Well, that's nice, but I know it must get mighty lonesome sometimes with the children at school and all. Michael coming home? Well, that's nice. Come see us again soon, Mis' Fenwick, we sure miss seeing you so seldom now. Oh, Mis' Fenwick, is it all right for Jack to charge up candy? Well, it's perfectly all right with us, but I told Fred I didn't know how you'd feel about it. I got a list right here,—it comes to a dollar ten." . . .

She was able to get back to the boat without having to more than nod to anyone else.

After an interminable time Seth came back.

"Didn't have much of no success," he reported glumly, taking off his hat to scratch his head. "But I got what you might call a clue. The boy cleanin' out the place there says he got a carriage for him long about daylight, and heard him tell the driver to carry him to Port Royal. Heard him say somethin' about catchin' a train."

"Well," she told him after a moment, "I suppose that means he's gone to Charleston. I'm afraid there's nothing more we can do, Seth."

"Well, ma'm, appears to me like it might be a good idea to stop by Port Royal. Appears to me like they's a chance he missed the train."

519

When she saw his meaning, she acknowledged it with a feeble smile.

"All right, Seth, if you're willing."

On the way back down the river to the Sound and around the marshy point of Old Fort Plantation, Charleston loomed before her eyes. The picture was so strong and convincing and certain that it took time for the reality of Port Royal to break through. And then there was a flash of an old and appalling illusion, that strange crisis sense of not being sure just where in her life she was standing. Perhaps, she thought as it passed, because here was the Port Royal she had first known. Unlike Beaufort this waterfront still lay as the storm had left it, and the storm had reduced it to the well-remembered essentials of Reconstruction. Here was the station, grimy and sleepy again, and across the dusty street the same vacant-looking row of brick and frame buildings where Seth and Martha had had their little store where Linda had been born. There were even the same lounging forms, white men and black and nondescript dogs, to complete the relapse. All that was left of the newer buildings, the offices and warehouses of Stephen's dreaming, was a little wreckage, barely enough to mark their sites; nothing was left of the long wharf but a section of rails that hung out over the water like a pair of drooping fish-poles. Of "Port Royal—the Royal Port of the South" only the giant grain elevator survived. But its gray bulk, roofless and torn, seemed a survival without substance, without existence in the present: it had no traffic with the moment but stood aloof, a phantom of aspiration and memory.

The tide was high enough, so they could tie up at a remnant of the seawall. She left Seth there and went across the dusty "square", where the bird-stained granite pedestal stood patiently waiting for the Jean Ribaut statue that Stephen had planned, past a trio of tobacco-spitters on the station platform and through the smudged penknife-carved doorway. The face that appeared at the window of the ticket office was unknown to her, but she thought he must know Stephen.

"Has Mr. Fenwick been here this morning, can you tell me?"

The face regarded her blankly. "Mr. Who?"

"Mr. Stephen Fenwick. I want to find out if he took the morning train."

"Don't know nobody by that name. Live here?"

"No, but I thought you might know him. He used to come here a good deal."

"Must have been before my time, lady. I reckon I have heard the name, but I wouldn't know him by sight." He looked beyond her at the trio of loungers, who had moved silently in from the platform. "Any you boys seen a gen'leman by the name of Fenwick?"

None of them had. "I know who she's speakin' of all right," one of them volunteered with a tug at his hat, "but he's been makin' hisself mighty scarce round here since last winter,—owin' folks money, maybe."

"What's he look like, lady?" the face at the window asked.

At that moment it was almost impossible to think what he looked like.

"Why, he's tall and dark. With a mustache. And he was wearing a gray suit and hat."

"Well, wasn't nobody answerin' to that description got on. Only a couple of nigs, far as I know."

She thanked him and hurried out.

A voice called after her: "If you're lookin' for your husband, reckon you might find him sleepin' it off over to Pete's place."

At the end of the platform she met Seth.

"I located him, ma'm. And I told him you was lookin' for him, but he ain't exactly hisself, ma'm."

A flash of darkness like night sped past her, but in an instant the spring sunlight was clear again.

"Can you possibly get him to the boat, Seth?"

"Yes, ma'm, if you say so."

"If you can, Seth. And I'll be there in a moment."

Back in the station, her fingers seemed to take hours to print out a telegram to Michael. And then it had to be spelled over twice before the face at the window finally got it straight.

But for the ringing numbness that stood between her and the impact of things, the rest of the morning would have been unendurable. And when it was over, and she was able to leave the room and the house and go down to the landing for a breath of air, it was impossible to see how she had held up even with that protection.

It was gone now, and her whole being smarted as though she had been thrashed. But the flooded Sound, gleaming blue under the midday sun and pure sky, was tranquil and soothing. Just off the landing a school of dolphins broke the surface, singly and in pairs, with slow fins and sleek arched backs; a few stray clouds trailed patches of shadow over the water. The song of a mocking-bird from the yard behind her exalted the peaceful pattern into splendor. Little by little the smarting faded and the feeling of nausea passed.

But it was many minutes before she could muster the courage to go back to the house and up to the room. And then, when she stood again at the bedside listening to his heavy breathing, sickness came back with such force that she had to turn away. She picked up his coat and collar and tie, and put his shoes together under the chair by the dresser. After that she had just enough strength left to lower the shades and get out of the room. In the hall she sat on the top step of the stairs till she felt better. Then she carried the coffee tray down to the kitchen, where Lucy was making oatmeal gruel, stirring briskly to relieve her agitation.

"Dis is de bes' t'ing fuh settle stomach," she said without raising her eyes from the stove, "an fix'um up good. I knowed dat coffee wasn' gwine stay wid'um no time."

"Lucy, will you take some blankets and things to the Robinsons' and ask them to keep the children overnight. Just say Mr. Stephen is very sick."

"Yes ma'm. An' now you bes' res' you'self whiles he sleepin'."

She left Lucy muttering to herself and went to the living-room to lie down on the sofa. She had left the door of his room ajar so that she could hear any sounds of his stirring. She lay waiting and listening through a pounding headache.

It was late afternoon when she opened her eyes and came to with stunned bewilderment out of a leaden doze. After recognition of the living-room her first consciousness was of being miserably cold, despite the shawl that Lucy had spread over her. Then, sluggishly, she became aware of sounds in the room above, but for many seconds she was unable to get up.

In the hall she met Lucy with a bowl of the gruel.

"Has he been awake long?" she asked as she took the tray.

"I ain' hear'um til jes' now."

"You better start for the Robinsons' before it gets dark."

"Miss Em'ly, I ain' gwine leabe you alone in dis house wid him."

"Please don't argue, Lucy. Everything's going to be all right now."

But it took all the firmness she could command to get Lucy started on her journey.

When she went upstairs with the tray she found Stephen sitting on the edge of the bed, his head in his hands. He looked up as she came into the room, and when their eyes met her body began to smart again and quiver. Shakily she put the tray down on the dresser.

"How do you feel?"

He hid his face in his hands again. "Whatever you got there" he said thickly, "take it away."

"It will do you good, dear."

He waved it away. "Get it out of here. Take it away."

She stood helpless, unable to think what to say or do next.

After a moment his head jerked up. "Go ahead,—get it off your chest. Say it! But let me tell you one thing. I did it because I couldn't stand any more of this damn game of yours. I tried to start a comeback, and I lost. And what's the odds? What's the difference between my dropping it in a poker game and your throwing it away on the Big Field and the niggers? What's the difference between gambling with cards and chips and gambling with cotton and weather? We're all gamblers. And eventual losers. So what the hell. Only trouble with me, my luck played out too soon. Take it or leave it."

"You lost all the money?"

His head wobbled slightly and he smiled. "I was seven hundred dollars ahead about midnight. And I had that bunch of pikers sewed up,—but you wouldn't be interested. No woman can understand a man's game, or what it means to be a sport. Let it go. . . . As it happens, I got enough left for another crack at that outfit tonight. Saturday's the big night. Sam Koenig will be on deck."

"Please take a little of this broth, while it's hot."

"Don't bring that stuff over here! Say, I had a bottle with me, where is it?"

"Oh, Stephen, please try to pull yourself together."

He gave her a long steady look. "You know, you're an awful fool. If you had any sense or were any kind of a good sport you'd act human. Pull myself together! That shows how well you understand what I've been through. Just pull myself together,—I believe you really think that's all there is to it. Well, thanks for the suggestion. Where'd you hide that bottle?"

"I haven't seen it."

"Now don't get the idea you can palm off anything like that on me. I had a bottle with me. Now where is it?"

"I tell you I don't know. Stephen, I can't stand any more of this."

"Oh, *you* can't stand any more. I see. Well, get this straight. I've taken all I'm going to from you. And if you're wise you'll keep out of my way."

He lurched to his feet and came toward the dresser, shoving her aside with his arm. He stood swaying before the mirror and began to put on his collar and tie.

"Feel pretty sorry for yourself don't you?" he grimaced at the mirror. "Well, I got to admit you've had hard luck with husbands. First a son-of-a-bitch Yankee and now a no-good Southerner. Better try a Westerner next time and change your luck. . . . Where in hell are my shoes?"

She moved away from the chair. 'Steve, what are you going to do?"

"Three guesses."

"You can't ask Seth to take you back to town."

"Watch me."

"But the children are there. If your own pride won't stop you, think of them."

"Now don't try to hand me any of that guff. And don't try to tell me what to do! I may not be the boss of this family any longer, but I'm still my own boss."

He finished lacing his shoes, and then swung his coat on. She was shaking uncontrollably now, but she faced him squarely, blocking his way to the door.

"Steve, you can't go. I beg you not to."

"For Christ's sake get out of my way, before I hand you one! Yes, look as horrified as you Goddamn please, but keep out of my way!"

He jostled past her. But at the door he turned to say: "I advise you not to have any sermons cooked up for me when I get back. If you're wise you'll take a tip and keep your mouth shut from now on, whatever I see fit to do."

"If you go back to town," she told him in a low voice, "I'll leave you. I'll take the children away."

In a seething silence she saw fury explode in his eyes, but his words came with slow precision.

"There won't be any need for that. I'll arrange to have Seth bring my things to the Sea Island Hotel tomorrow. I realize you've stuck by me this long only on the children's account. Well your martyrdom's ended. And so is mine. It wasn't so bad while you were still functioning as a woman. But after the glory of motherhood set in,—and now you're mistress of the plantation and I might as well be married to a four-poster. Well, there happen to be other women in the world. . . . Hold up your head, you got one more home truth coming to you before we part. What do you think I married Aaron Moffet's widow for? I married you to get back what belonged to me. So you see I lost out all along the line. And now Land's End and Marshlands are yours for keeps, if you can hang on to them. I wish you luck."

The door closed with a slam that shook the walls of the room. Through thundering pulses she heard him stumbling heavily down the stairs.

Instinctively she moved to the window; and as she was trying to breathe, she saw his form in the side yard. He was walking at a quick and steady gait, but under the old magnolia he stopped. He stood for a moment with his hand on the tree and then went on.

She stared out at the empty yard. The trunk of the magnolia stood up very straight among the crooked arms of the live-oaks, its big sleek leaves and brown-furred buds as scornful as ever of the moss-trimmed bouquets of little leaves that were proffered from all sides. This familiar pantomime seemed new for an instant, as new, she felt dimly, as when she had first perceived it long ago. The thunder in her ears thinned away to stinging specks of silence, a nest of tiny abstract repercussions. These swelled in time to incredible proportions: as in a moment of ecstasy, the world and her life were suddenly one. But now it was a fusion of supreme bitterness, and an insane echoing, through which came at intervals the early vespers, astounding clear and true, of birds in the shadowy recesses of the ilex thicket at the edge of the yard.

Some time later she found herself in the yard. And then she was hurrying as fast as her shaky legs would carry her across the pasture to the mine road. Oh help me, Rusty, help me. . . .

She had gone only a little way when she saw him lying face down at the side of the road: intent on the road far ahead she had almost passed him. She knelt and lifted his head, and breathed again when he opened his eyes and closed them with a sigh. She moved him and tried to get him to his feet, but he was like a dead man. Crying to herself she loosened his collar and vest and rubbed his hands. She sat helpless then with his head in her lap, the dusk from the woods closing in around her.

It was almost dark when she made out a figure coming down the road toward her. When she called, the figure stopped and then came running. When she was sure it was Lucy, her senses began to steady. He made convulsive resistance to the first efforts to rouse him. But when they finally got him on his feet, he yielded to guidance and walked supported between them, his eyes shut, his head lolling. And so they brought him back to the dark house.

In the room, she sent Lucy down to heat the gruel and some milk, while she undressed him and got him into bed. She put blankets over him, for his teeth were chattering and his lips were blue with cold.

The next morning she let Lucy take up his breakfast, while she busied herself with nothing and tried to keep Easter hymns from running idiotically through her brain. *Sun of My Soul,* Miss Sophie's hymn for all occasions, was the most persistent obsession. It took possession of her.

Lucy brought down a message from him but she ignored it. It was not till later in the morning, after he had rapped for her several times, that she went up to the room. And then she stopped on the threshold and stood with her hand on the doorknob, regarding him impassively.

"Well," he sighed, "I guess you have every right to look grim."

"How do you feel?" she asked him calmly.

He rubbed the back of his neck. "Pretty low."

"Anything we can do for you?"

"Yes," he nodded. "Forgive me."

She drew a secret tremulous breath. "Let's not talk about things till you feel better."

He propped himself up on an elbow. "No, I've got to tell you now. Emily, I was out of my mind,—I didn't know what I was saying or doing. Some devil made me want to hurt you and I said anything that came into my head, but you know I didn't mean any of it, you know I couldn't have meant it. You should have laughed at me."

"Yes, I suppose so. I seem to have fallen down on you rather badly. But I'm afraid I'm not much of a hand for laughing at the right time."

"Emily, you've got to understand. I simply didn't know what I was saying. You've got to believe that because it's true."

"Were you also out of your mind when you went to town without giving me any warning?"

"Yes," he frowned, "I must have been. Oh Emily, have a heart!— I've been punished enough. I'm disgusted with myself and sorry as hell about everything, and I'll do anything in the world to make up for it if you'll only forgive me." He held out his hand. "Please come over here. You're so damn far away."

"I don't think you understand," she told him without moving, "that I've had a slight shock this time. I think we better postpone this till we've both had a little more time to think."

He sank back on the pillow with a groan and closed his eyes.

"Well," he sighed after a moment, "I guess I'll have to take my medicine. I've got it coming to me. But it's sure going to be tough to take from you, of all people. Things were bad enough when I had you on my side."

He turned his face away from her.

"I can't see," she said with a coldness she had to force, "how I've been any help to you. I seem to have only made things worse by trying to help."

He turned on his side and his hand jerked up to his face. "You're the only thing," he said in a voice so low that she could hardly hear him, "that's held the pieces together at all. The only thing that's been sure."

He turned back to her. But now she found his sick eyes too disconcerting to meet, and her own fell.

"Where are the children?" he asked after a pause she was powerless to break.

"Margaret and Jack are spending Easter with Seth and Linda. I telegraphed Michael you were very sick and he better not come home just yet."

After a long moment he said: "I didn't realize what I was doing. . . . What's left of the money is in my wallet. I can sell my English guns to make up the rest. I wanted the boys to have them, but Sam Koenig will give me a fair price. . . ."

She looked at him with unveiled misery as he stared up at the ceiling but she kept her voice inflexible. "I think Sam Koenig would rather have some of the family heirlooms and jewelry. That's the customary final gesture, isn't it?"

He held out his hand again. "Emily, come here a second, will you."

Against her will she went to the bed. And before she could recover herself he had taken her hand, and suddenly all her resolution broke down. A terrible sobbing, soundless and without tears, shook him and tore through her own breast. She made one last effort to hold out against him, and then burning tears blinded her eyes as she yielded to his arms.

". . . It's all right, darling," she comforted him. "Don't think I don't know what you've been going through. But why take it out on me and the children."

"Oh, darling, I've been a rotten husband to you. God, the one human being I care a damn about. The one real thing in the world. I deserve to lose you, but I can't go it without you."

"You're not going to have to. As far as I'm concerned we're together forever, for better or worse."

"There's going to be no more worse."

She wiped her eyes and managed a smile. "You know, that would be a help. You had me in a tight spot this time."

"Honey, you've taken it right and left, above and below the belt, but you're not going to have to take any more from me. I'm cured."

"You really think you got the poison out of your system?"

"I know it. And you honestly forgive me?"

"Better than that, we're going to forget the whole thing. We've got to, quickly. There! And now we're going to make a fresh start."

"And we're going to fight it out on this line if it takes all summer, in the words of another invincible Yankee."

"And it did take all summer. But he got to Richmond in the end."

"And saved the Union—for Reconstruction, Republicans, and panics. But no more Civil War. Is that the program?"

"Well, don't you think we have our hands pretty full without fighting each other?"

"It's a bargain. The Union forever, one and indivisible. . . . God, how I love you, Emily."

VII

When that summer was at last over, she felt as shaken as a sleep-walker waking to the achievement of an incredible balancing feat. And catching her first deep breath as she looked back at those hazardous months, boundlessly thankful that they were ended though it meant losing the children to school again, she realized that only blind faith had held the summer together and carried her through the prolonged strain, the complication of strains.

Reliving the summer through days of sudden leisure, after Michael had left for the Citadel and Margaret and Jack were back at Miss Hamilton's and the cotton crop was safely harvested, she saw that the worst strain had not come from the plantation problems. The people had been kept in line only by constant vigilance, and the Big Field had grown into a far more desperate struggle than she had dreamed of in any early moment of doubt: the unceasing weed warfare of June and July had been followed by the long unbroken heat of a dry August, fine for ripening the bolls and keeping down the caterpillar peril but dangerous as a builder of storm pressure, and September had brought day-to-day suspense, when the fate of everything had hung in the burning haze of the sky. But, terrible as those plantation strains had been, they had not given her the most serious trouble. Nor had it come from the frantic planning, week after week, to make the little store of cash and rent money, with a minimum of credit at Van Wie's, stretch to meet all needs. The worst stress had come fatally from within, from the family, the moods and tenses of home, where she was most vulnerable.

Caught between Stephen and Michael from the very beginning of the summer, she could side with neither.

Trouble appeared the day Michael came home from Charleston.

As soon as an exchange of stiff greetings was over, he began to avoid his father. It was as if, having spoken, he felt there was nothing more to say. And it was not long before Stephen showed his irritation, to her at first.

"Maybe you can tell me what's the matter with him, I can't figure him out. What's he got to pull a long face about? He's like a clam. Can't talk, can't smile, can't even look at you. I don't know what kind of discipline they have at the Citadel nowadays, but they certainly haven't improved his manners any. He may be good at his studies, but he's damn backward in respect for his elders. What he needs is a good dressing-down, and he's going to get it if he don't snap out of this directly!"

That outburst could hardly be laid to the state of his nerves. As a matter of fact, his nerves had been steadily improving, were better now than they had been for months; he seemed to have resigned himself to his Easter promises and to have adjusted himself, definitely and finally, to an idle recuperative summer. Margaret and Jack played a great part in this phase of his recovery, they continued to look up to him as though nothing had happened for which he was responsible. The storm had made drastic changes in the family's way of living, which they accepted, and their father had fallen sick,— that was everything. They were still too young to sense any undercurrents. And knowing they were innocently his, he made every effort to live up to their unshaken faith in him. He had had hard luck, his manner was calculated to assure them, but the reverses were of an entirely temporary nature, and he was not too sick to laugh with them and take them fishing and swimming at Bay Point. And how could they think of bad luck and ill health as calamities when now he had more time to give them than ever before?

But with Michael it was a different story. And though his moroseness might be provoking, she felt he was even less to blame than Stephen.

In her excitement at his homecoming she had made him stand back-to-back with his father, not thinking how that would make them both squirm: he had grown a good two inches taller than Stephen. And his voice had settled at last into a stable bass. Outwardly he was now fully developed, but the secret ferments of adolescence had not yet worked themselves out. This inner turmoil betrayed itself most immediately in the somber sensitiveness of his eyes, and it was scarcely concealed by the restraint of his voice and words. She saw how cruelly disaster had struck through his uncertain defenses. Old enough to feel the full impact of what had happened, he had yet had no armor of self-possession to reduce the force of the blow, the double blow of Rusty's death and his father's defeat. Of the family it was he, she realized now, who had suffered the darkest and most helpless anguish.

And now, watching him hungrily through these first of his days home, she had to keep reminding herself that she did not love him more than Margaret and Jack but only differently. Yet there was no use denying that he stood at the very center of the world, and that her devotion had grown with every amazing phase of his growth. It was not, she thought, that her love had actually grown in size: she had loved him always to the limits of her heart. But with each year of accumulating memories and dreams her love for him was taking on deeper significance and meaning, increasing intensity. Since the pains of his first teeth her capacity to suffer with him had expanded enormously, so that everything that touched him touched her to the quick. And as the workings of his heart and mind had become more and more involved and clouded, her perceptions had sharpened to keep pace with the changes in him, to divine even the least obvious troubles of his spirit.

But understanding was hardly enough. The problem was to reach him, and that remained a problem. For after the excitement of getting home had worn off, he seemed to want to avoid even her, as if his hurt extended to her, as if she too was somehow a part of disaster. With apparent relief he accepted her assurances that there was nothing he could do to help with the plantation, her insistence that she wished him to have a free summer and that he could best help her in that way. Much of his time he spent with Linda, and the rest was given to his books and lonely walks and fishing. He condescended to swim with Margaret and Jack off the landing, but except for that he was intolerant alike of his sister's gentle overtures and Jack's boisterousness. In the house only Lucy enjoyed his confidence and light moments.

Perhaps it was best, she thought in her quandary, just to let him alone, leave him to work out his torment in his own way. But that was impossible, the situation was getting steadily worse. And when she tried to relax the tension through Stephen, explaining to him as tactfully as she could Michael's state of mind as she understood it, he lost all patience.

"What do you expect me to do, lie down and let him walk over me? No thanks! He's a man now, let him behave like one and cut out this childish sulking."

He had such a knack for making matters worse, with his policy of "drawing the clam out of his shell", that she wondered in moments of extreme stress if he wasn't enjoying the situation, finding in it an outlet and release for his own torment.

"Well," he told her one day when she came back from the Big Field, "I had a little talk with your son this morning. Decided to give him a few pointers, about steering clear of diseases and keeping himself clean and so forth. And do you know the thanks I got? Flushed silence."

She looked at him with misery.

"I also told him," he added, "I didn't want him to see so much of Linda. I don't want him fooling around her. I haven't anything against Linda personally, always liked her, but I don't intend to have a son of mine getting mixed up with any cracker girl."

When the shock had passed she said to him with forced calmness:

"Stephen, will you trust my judgment in this one instance? Please just leave him alone, dear. I believe things will work out better that way. At least let's try it, please."

He agreed finally. But the only result was an increase of friction. Helplessly she watched the tension growing toward a crisis.

Meals were the most difficult times, particularly supper, climaxing the day's heat and fatigue. She tried to make the atmosphere of the table endurable, but with Michael and Stephen not speaking to each other and Michael seldom raising his eyes from his plate it was a sorry struggle, even with Margaret's and Jack's help. And in the end, at supper one humid evening late in June, the tension snapped suddenly and violently.

She saw Stephen, his face crimson, glaring at Michael, but it was too late to check him.

"What do you mean by speaking to your mother like that?"

Michael's face turned pale, but his eyes challenged his father's. "What do you mean, sir? I simply told Mother I didn't want any more salad."

She tried then to intervene, but her heart was pounding her throat closed and her body was rigid with panic.

Stephen's hands slapped the arms of his chair. "I'll show you what I mean, sir!" He sprang up and stepped to Michael's chair across the table from Margaret's and Jack's wide eyes, grabbed him by the arm and yanked him to his feet. "We'll see who's master here!"

They were out of the room and in the hall before she could move or think or breathe. But the slam of the living-room door restored her faculties.

As she crossed the hall, she heard Stephen's voice hoarse with rage. "If you ever speak like that to your mother or me again, I'll whip you within an inch of your life! I've taken all the nonsense I'm going to from you!"

After a moment's hesitation she opened the door. Stephen's furious eyes turned from Michael to her.

"Please keep out of here,—I can handle this without any assistance."

"Let me speak to Michael for a moment, please, dear."

"I'll be glad to, when he's offered you an apology."

"Leave that to us, won't you?"

Facing his shaking anger she thought he was going to lash out at her. Instead he satisfied himself with a long look of damnation while he got his breath.

"Very well," he nodded, "go ahead and baby him. But just remember one thing both of you. I've taken the last nonsense I'm going to from him, and I mean it!"

When he was gone, banging the door after him, she was left facing Michael's bowed head. And at first, miserably at a loss where to begin, she could only think what a blessing it would be if she could baby him as Stephen had said, take him in her arms, comfort that proud head against her breast.

"Come here, dear," she said finally, turning to the sofa.

He came to the sofa, but he was unwilling to sit down. He stood tall and dark, alone and unyielding, reluctant for her to see the humiliation of his eyes.

"I'm afraid," she began, trying to keep her tremulousness confined to her tightly clasped hands, "this was my fault. I should have talked to you when you first came home. I kept hoping you'd see and understand things for yourself, but I should have known there was so much you couldn't be expected to see or understand."

His fine long fingers chafed the arm of the sofa. "I think I understand all right," he said grimly.

"No, dear, you couldn't. You don't know what he's gone through. Just as he doesn't know how tormented you've been."

His eyes met hers at last, with flashing bitterness. "I hate him! It's all his fault, the whole business. And now he—he just sits back and let's you worry about everything."

"That's not fair," she said quickly, following up the advantage of seeing his eyes. "When things went wrong after the storm, he did everything possible to save us. It was too much for him, that's all. And now it's up to us to help him till he gets his strength back."

"I can't see that he's so sick. He's stronger than you, I know that. Why can't he do something?"

"He will, just as soon as he's able."

"But why can't he at least help you with the place?"

"Because I've asked him to leave what little worry there is to me. The important thing is for him to have a summer of rest, so he'll be ready to go back into business next winter."

"But why can't I do something?"

"Because I want you to have a vacation. You've earned it. You've worked hard and done well."

He sighed heavily.

"Oh, you don't understand,—how can I have any peace when you're doing everything? It makes me feel rotten. It makes everything terrible."

"But can't you see, dear, that the little worry I have isn't anything compared to the strain of having you unhappy, and on the outs with your father? If you want to help me, try not to be so unhappy about things, won't you?"

"Sure I'll try. But can't he leave me alone? I don't bother him."

"Dear, it isn't just a question of you two leaving each other alone. You've got to try to understand each other's troubles and make allowances. Remember your father's had a hard time, later you'll realize how bad it's been for him, and forget the rest. I'm not asking you to look cheerful, I'm asking you to feel cheerful. After all, the worst's over. We're on our way out of the woods. So brace up. Won't you?"

"Suppose he starts picking on me some more about Linda?"

"Leave that to me. I want you to concentrate your thoughts on making this a good summer to take back to school with you."

And in the end she had his promise. She resisted a longing to take his hand, knowing how he would hate that; she kept her hands locked, contenting herself with his smile and nod.

Later she had a talk with Stephen on the delicate subject of Linda. And, finally, the general tension was so relaxed that when Joe Bramwell came out for a visit, he quite lost track of his umbrage with her, for wrestling with the plantation without his guidance and backing, in his pleasure at being the center of the united family's attentions.

"Not being an old bachelor uncle," he assured her in a jocular parting at the landing, "you'll never know what an unfailing delight this family has been to me."

"Not being an old mother," she told him, "you'll never know what you've been spared. Or what it means to a family to have a faithful friend."

But, despite the harmony of that day and other days, the basic discord remained. And though there were no more scenes or serious tensions, the rest of the summer was a prolonged struggle to keep the family from splitting too obviously into camps: Stephen and Margaret and Jack on one side, Michael on the other, and herself caught miserably somewhere between them.

Yet there were many recompenses for the strain of that summer. Happy hours with Margaret and harum-scarum Jack, even much peace with Stephen. And, above all, certain moments with Michael.

After her talk with him his tendency to avoid her disappeared and he began to seek her company, with painful self-consciousness at first. He came to the Big Field more and more often; and finally, though she refused to turn over her notebook with its complex accounts in smudged and erratic shorthand, she yielded to his desire to do something to help and gave him the time-book to keep. Getting him straightened out was decidedly more trouble than continuing the timekeeping herself would have been, but it was worth the trouble. For it both eased his mind and gave him a close and healthy contact with the plantation people, whom he had been inclined to shun. Soon he knew every name; and as he came to see that they liked and respected him, his diffidence vanished and he felt confident not only to joke with them but also to inquire into and treat their

535

aches and pains, real and imaginary. That permitted her to recognize the deadly fear she had been hiding from herself, the fear that with Rusty gone his interest in medicine might wane or be diverted into some lesser aim. Here was the answer to that fear. And listening to him as he talked to one of the people about some ailment, she would see so much of Rusty in the expression of his voice and eyes and hands that she would have to find some pretext to turn away. The actual knowledge he had picked up from Rusty was rudimentary, but his manner was already sure; and within the limits of his knowledge and the family medicine-chest he was soon doctoring the plantation.

When he skillfully treated a sprained leg for Jack, who had made up for being forbidden to climb the water-tower ladder by falling through the floor of the tree-house, even Stephen was impressed.

"But how did you know what to do, son?"

"Rusty showed me once," he frowned. It was the first time he had spoken the name, and he added quickly, "Anyway, it wasn't anything."

"Well, I don't know about that. I hear you're treating all kinds of complaints with success."

"One or two. Anyway, it's better than herb-doctoring and cunjuh-healing, and patent medicine. And later on, when I have a clinic here, maybe I can patch up any damage I do now."

That was quite a speech for him. Often, when he went with her to the field in the morning with his time-book, he brought one of Rusty's medical books along to pore over under the oak, and sometimes he read his findings aloud to her; but he always shied away from talk, particularly about himself. In the beginning he had submitted to an examination about school life, and had even volunteered some intimate reflections on the theme; but afterwards there had been such a glum reaction,—as if by giving her confidences he had somehow given himself away, exposed himself unduly,—that she had resolved to curb her eagerness and refrain from pressing him or questioning him at all. Mentally he was still avoiding her. And she couldn't help jealously wondering if he was quite so reserved with Linda.

But however much she longed for his confidences she knew she must content herself with the crumbs that fell her way, piecing together by intuition his deeper thoughts and feelings. After all, she told herself, the really important thing was to have him near her, and certainly she was not stinted in his companionship. For he was hers not only through the days but also most evenings. Those evenings when he wandered off to Linda's after supper he was always back in time for a game of chess or a little book-browsing before bed; so that, between moves on the chessboard or over her sewing while he read, she could secretly study him to her heart's content and treasure up the sight and feel of his presence against the barren season of his next absence.

And there were deeply stirring moments of communion with him through the old Steinway. They were not so frequent as she wished, because she seldom had time to sit down at the piano when he was on hand except in the evening; and then it was no pleasure to try to play for him, even very softly and casually, against Stephen's irritable throat-clearings and newspaper-rustlings and Margaret's and Jack's interminable game of snatch-the-bundle. But though she was rarely able to have him alone, and in a mood to listen, she made the most of her opportunities when they came along. And by the end of the summer she was satisfied that his ear was developing sound discrimination. Except for one waltz he was still uncomfortable with Brahms, but he had learned to like many good things. And for two things at least he had formed a positive attachment, always asking her to play them again and never seeming to get his fill of them. They were the "Moonlight" Sonata of Beethoven and the enchanting middle passage—the one part, fortunately, that she could play without stumbling—of Chopin's A-Flat Major Polonaise.

Here at last was the real beginning of music-loving for him. And for her that was the high point of the summer, except for one heart-to-heart talk she had with him just before he left for school.

It came at the moment of her greatest anxiety about the plantation, when the fate of the venture hung finally and precariously balanced between success and failure in the scales of the enigmatic September skies. The heat of the days had built up terrific potential storm pressure, and at night there were tremendous displays of heat lightning over the mainland, silent demoniacal menacings. Late in May, before Michael's homecoming, a southwest gale had struck the Sound at flood tide, carrying away part of the new landing and badly washing the bank, blasting the shore trees with brine, and littering the yard and island roads again with branches and moss and leaves; but the young cotton had not been hurt, and Seth had said then, and still insisted now, that the gale was as good as insurance against a late summer storm. But with the Big Field a snowy expanse of fine fully-opened—and fully-exposed—bolls, with the picking barely started and no hope of augmenting the field gang with recruits from the busy cabin patches, it was impossible not to feel that these were the most fearfully vulnerable days and nights of her life.

And in this hour of feverish activity and apprehension, and congested last-minute preparations for school, she lost track of her disappointment in Michael's continued reticence. So that it came as a distinct surprise when she realized, one evening when she went down with him to the landing to get a clear view of the eerie inland lightning, that he wanted to communicate with her. But he seemed unable to speak out then; and later, when they reported the sight and were alone again while the others went to see, he again failed and retreated frowning into his book, leaving her to puzzle about him over her darning. But the next day, his last day home, he came at noon to have lunch with her in the grove at Pine Point, and then at last he was able to talk: hesitantly at first, but with increasing freedom as he went on. It was as if now, with the end of vacation staring him in the face, he had suddenly wakened to the need of unburdening himself for the return to school, of relieving his spirit of a confused accumulation of thoughts and feelings. Words released words, and he poured out his confidences with such a lavish hand and skipped so eagerly from one thing to another that it was hard to follow him at times. . . . She was careful to suppress her own eagerness for fear he might shy. Listening with rising delight and excitement, she spoke only when it was necessary and then briefly and quietly to keep from breaking the spell, to avoid disclosing to him the importance of the moment to her, to make it seem a perfectly normal conversation.

"I'm sure glad," he was saying, "I don't have to be a business man. If you're successful there may be a lot of money in it and all that, but think of the price you have to pay. Lord, think of spending your one and only life buying and selling, scrambling for pennies and trying to do your neighbor. I'm glad I can leave that to people that like it, or at least don't mind it."

"We all can't have professions, son."

"Well, then I'd rather be a planter, like you. Or a farmer like Seth. Or a carpenter or something. Or even a cropper, like the island people,—honest I would. That's doing something, making something. I mean that's producing things,—not just turning things over, handling them for a pinch of profit."

She smiled in her heart at the contrast between his man's voice and his boy's frownings.

"But things have to be distributed, dear."

He sighed over that and shook his dark head at the ground.

"Oh, I don't know," he said after a moment, looking up and brushing a tuft of unruly hair back from his forehead. "The harder I think about things, the more mixed-up I get. Do you ever get like that?"

"At least once a day. In fact, whenever I try to think."

He glanced at her with a mixture of surprise and doubt, but then quickly joined her smile.

"What do you do for it?"

"I'm afraid," she told him with a sudden sharp pang, "I haven't found anything specific to do for it. Except to keep on trying. There seems to be a sort of cure in trying to find a cure."

He gave that his solemn consideration.

"Well," he said finally, "I'm sure of one thing. There's something wrong with the way things are."

"What would you do if you were in charge of things?"

He stretched out with a profound sigh and made his elbow comfortable in a patch of pine-needles, propping his head up with his hand.

"I don't know," he pondered deeply. "Sometimes I think I do, but then I get mixed-up again. But I do know there's more trouble and ugliness and meanness than there's any excuse for. I mean people could be so much better and happier and—well, sort of beautiful."

"Pretty hard for most people to be happy and beautiful, son, when they've got to keep their noses to the grindstones of the world to exist at all."

"That's just it. People ought to get together and help each other, instead of everybody grubbing for themselves."

"Isn't that what Christianity's been preaching for ages? But how are you going to bridge the gap between preaching and practice? How are you going to get people to forget their selfishness and fear?"

He selected a pine-needle from the nest at his elbow and chewed it meditatively.

"There's got to be an awakening," he decided at last. "People have got to stop being so blind and stupid and start being more intelligent and kind."

"Don't you think we've made a pretty good start already? Seems to me we've climbed quite a long way."

"I'm not so sure of that. People prey on other people just the same as ever, only it's worse now because they do it under the cloak of Christian Civilization."

A flash of self-consciousness came into his eyes and he turned on his back and squinted up at the crests of the pines. It made her aware of the sharp scales of the tree-trunk at her back, but she sat dead still, afraid to stir. For a moment she watched his face and then risked an inducement for him to go on.

"Well, son, I'm afraid you'll have to accept the fact that progress is a slow process."

"I don't see why it has to be," he frowned at the sky.

"Because human nature is still its two-faced self, I suppose. Vision pulling against blind fear and greed, enlightenment against old night. We're in the distinguished but uncomfortable position of being a battleground for the forces of light and darkness. And it seems to take everlasting time and patience to arrive at even a little better living climate."

He was silent for so long after that, she began to fear her declamation had smothered him out. But finally his voice returned, and with intensified ardor.

"Well, I believe it's time people stopped thinking so much about heaven and all that and started putting more faith in themselves and what they can do together on earth. Look what's being done in medicine and all the sciences—all the wonderful inventions and all. And yet most people go grubbing along alone, dreaming and shouting about heaven and praying for salvation and jostling their neighbors out of the way, when they have the tools right in their hands for making a better world, if they weren't so darn blind and self-seeking."

He sat up with a shamefaced grin. "I guess that must sound pretty crazy."

She shook her head as emphatically as she dared. "Not half as crazy as accepting the situation. I don't think any man's worth his salt who doesn't feel that way about things. And I'm glad you're going to have a chance to do something about it, make some contribution to your better world through medicine."

"I'm afraid," he flushed, "it'll be a darn small contribution."

"Well, that will certainly be better than none, won't it?"

He dug a heel into the ground. "Yes, but I want to do something big with my life. I want to find a cure for some big disease. That's what Rusty was after."

He stopped there; and after waiting a moment she said: "I know you're going to do something very fine."

"Don't say that," he took her up quickly. "It makes me feel sort of superstitious."

"Well then," she smiled, "I'll silently pray for you. Will that be all right?"

He gave her a flushed grin and nod, and then fell to frowning. After a moment he lay back with a sigh and put his arms under his head and squinted up at the crests of the pines again. He stirred restlessly several times before he spoke. "I don't want to give you a jolt, Mamma," he said finally, "but there's something I think I ought to tell you. . . . I don't want to get confirmed. And I'm glad you haven't been after me about it, like Gran'ma was." He hesitated. "You see, I'm afraid I don't believe in church much. Rusty didn't either, except Easter music."

A sudden lump in her throat prevented her from answering him at once. But when he glanced at her apprehensively, she swallowed hard and forced words out, managing somehow to keep her voice steady.

"Son, I've always wanted you to work things out for yourself, as much as possible. I wanted you to see things clearly and make your own beliefs. But I hope you're not going to be anti-church, or anti-anything. Rusty's religion wasn't founded on negation of other people's creeds. He had a positive faith, which included understanding other faiths, and the comfort and freedom they give."

He put a hand over his eyes to shield them from the sun. And he lay perfectly still in that position for so long that the cries of terns over the marsh began to break through her thoughts, and she became painfully aware of sounds in the field and the end of the noon hour. From moment to moment she feared that here too was the end of their talk. But he continued his deep meditation; and presently he said slowly: "Rusty and I worked out a lot of things together. But there's one thing we never got to, and it's the thing that bothers me more than anything now. . . . I can't help feeling he's still alive. I don't mean up there in the sky somewhere,—I don't believe in that idea anymore. I mean alive right here. . . . I know that must sound pretty crazy, but I really feel that way about it. I mean I feel he's sort of living in me, so he can go on with the work he didn't finish. I don't mean I could ever be like him. But I know what he wanted to do, and I can try. . . . And maybe someday a son of mine will feel the same way about me, and want to carry on my work where I have to leave off. . . ."

He turned his head to look at her, and she nodded but made no attempt to speak. It was a sharp relief when, a moment later, he discovered a flock of birds in a cedar at the edge of the grove and got up to investigate. That gave her a chance to conquer the mist that was threatening to blind her; and by the time he came back to help her clean up the lunch things, she was ready to meet his eyes with a smile.

"Bunch of martins," he told her, "so that's the end of summer. And I see noon hour's up."

He gave her an awkward grin as they started back to the field. "I'm sorry I made you late talking. But I sure feel better. It's hard trying to figure things out by yourself. What do you think?"

"Darling," she smiled, "I think you're a really great person and I want you to know it. And I think you're headed in the right direction and doing fine. Will you let me know once in a while how things are working out with you?"

"Sure I will," he grinned.

✓   ✓   ✓

When he was gone back to the Citadel, and Margaret and Jack to Miss Hamilton's and the Beaufort school, she gave herself to the plantation with a whole heart. She felt strong and sure and keenly alive; more alive, certainly, than she had ever been in the prosperous years. If this eager and vigorous and sun-tanned new being that she recognized in herself had any affinity with the past, it was with the determined young woman who had taught a praise-house school full of monkeys in the years after the War.

542

For the last few days of the picking she recruited some of the older children to help in the Big Field. And by driving force and prayer she was able to get the cotton all picked, bagged, and flatted to town before the rains came at last. So that when the first heavy drops caught her on the settlement road and drove up into her nostrils the acrid odor of dust, it was like perfume. . . . For days the house was enveloped in a smoke of seething rain and wind. But she made happy use of the time catching up with long-neglected duties and checking over the accounts of the summer; and in installments she wrote Michael a bulky letter, in answer to his sketchy "Sunday Eve" note, which had somehow become sadly crumpled and soiled from its journeys to the field and frequent rereadings, despite the care she had tried to take of it to preserve it for the silver-chest, where his older letters lay with other precious fragments of the past.

And when the rains and her cheerful confinement were over, came the first splendor of autumn. In the past she had never been able to decide which was the more beautiful, April or October; but this year there was no doubt in her mind. After the prolonged heat and strain of the summer the songs of the mocking-bird and cardinal, roused from the half-sleep of the torpid months, sounded more brilliant and more welcome than at that other shining season: they were the spirit of the harvest air made audible and visible, after an age of prostration and obscurity in the steaming earth processes. It was still hot at noon and the stinging note of the locusts was not yet subdued, but the chill mists of early morning and dusk were turning the roadside dewberries and creepers crimson, and already a few yellow leaves were straying crisply from the trees. And the first fires and the first nights under blankets seemed blessings greater than anything spring had to offer. There was nothing sad, this year at least, in the coming of autumn: it was like clear cool water after a burning thirst. Even the beginning of the bird migrations and the thought of winter could not disturb the perfection of these sparkling days and her sense of strength and fulfillment.

And the results of her business visit to the office of Joseph Bramwell, to whom she had intrusted the sale of the cotton, made her head spin. The price of long-staple was still low, ridiculously low in contrast to the high prices of the phosphate years when the plantation had lain idle and unconsidered except as a source of labor for the mines, but even after the credit account at Van Wie's had been settled and the field-hands' back wages paid off, there was left the clear and fabulous sum of almost two thousand dollars. It was incredible for days.

The share-croppers, whose cotton Joe had sold with hers, were jubilant. But after the shares and rents had been deducted she surrendered the people their money in portions, knowing that without guardianship most of them would rush to town or the Frogmore store to spend the hard-earned dollars on nonessentials and then look to her to see them through the winter. Firmly she saw to it that they used their first portion to buy blankets and other necessities before she gave them the balance. There were few protests about this rationing out of the money; and when all accounts were settled, only one family wanted to leave the plantation, and their cabin was quickly taken over by a family from Cherokee.

Even Stephen had to concede the success of the venture.

"Well, you certainly fooled me, Emily,—I admit I thought it was a hopeless undertaking. I have to take off my hat to you."

In the excitement of praise from him she was rash enough to say: "I really believe we can do better next year. We'll have more confidence and experience, and we can get an earlier start. And Joe says prices are going up."

"Joe's as congenital an optimist as you are. Now don't get cocksure and let this business go to your head. Just remember you had beginner's luck with the weather and all. If you're wise, you won't risk another spin. Besides, I'll be back in the game directly, and there won't be any call for you to perform any more handsprings."

It was his urgent suggestion, advanced politely at first and then impatiently, that the thing to do with the profits of the summer was to invest them in "a couple of good sound securities". "It isn't too late to get aboard, but you'll have to get a move on! If you'll let me handle this thing for you tomorrow morning, I'm positive you'll double your money by spring." But she had foreseen the inevitableness of this and was prepared to meet it, gently but firmly. Throwing away "the chance of a lifetime", she applied a little of the money to the Land's End mortgage, set aside a sum for fertilizer, and deposited the rest in the bank.

Later in the autumn, after careful consideration, she allowed herself several purchases. The first was a cow, selected for her from a mainland dairy by Seth, who volunteered to teach Lucy to milk. Seth also did the trading for a horse, a sturdy little tacky; the old buck-board was resurrected from the stable and harness pieced together from remnants. And for cutting up the fallen live-oaks in the avenue, she bought Biggie a crosscut saw. And finally, with a feeling of guilt, she allowed herself one luxury purchase: a tuning for the piano.

When she wrote to the Charleston Music Store, asking them to send her old friend Mr. Hans Christian Kopp, she received word that they regretted to inform her that the infirmities of age had caused Mr. Kopp's retirement but they were sending the best man in their establishment. The best man, when he finally appeared, proved to be a dyspeptic youth with wild manners. He had no information to give her about Kopp; and after complaining of the hardships of the journey and the condition of the piano, he announced that his tuning-fork didn't vibrate right with people in the room asking questions and staring. Left to himself he went at the trembling instrument with hammer and tongs, received his lunch resentfully while Stephen fumed upstairs, and at five o'clock was still plugging away at the dismembered keyboard. But half an hour later, when the boat that was to take him back to Port Royal arrived, he had somehow brought order out of the chaos of strings and was prepared to submit his craftsmanship to her testing. After listening with an air of condescension to her playing, he sat down to demonstrate his own talents with a series of solf-pedaled scales and a sudden savage crescendo that carried him dramatically from deepest bass to highest treble, leaving her flushed and giddy with suppressed merriment.

Hours after his departure the house was still vibrating from that final flourish. But the old Steinway was in fine voice again, and ready to accompany her thoughts through winter twilights.

VIII

'95—'96—'97: these years stood bracketed in her memory as the term of Stephen's recovery. Remembered in two main phases, which had been the harder she could no more tell than how she had weathered them at all.

The first phase marked his final relinquishment of drink as a means of escape from defeat. Soon after the children had gone back to school, the struggle was renewed; alone with him that winter at Land's End she had to use all her will to keep him away from town. In this grim and largely subterranean warfare there were truces when Michael came home for the holidays and Margaret and Jack for weekends. And Linda's frequent calls eased the tension of the house, for despite Stephen's criticism of her as company for his son he never failed to respond to her cheerful presence. Then too, outside matters claimed attention and gave breathing-spells from the house: after the autumn plowing and the hauling of "maa'sh" to bed down the Big Field there was a long lull in the plantation routine, but the various needs of the people persisted and required many visits to the settlements. And there was Penn School.

Penn School, near Frogmore Crossroads, was all that remained of the ambitious educational system that the Freedmen Aid Societies had tried to establish on the Sea Islands. That it had survived at all, after most of its Northern support had been withdrawn, was a tribute to the heroic perseverance of the two women who had dedicated their lives to it, and a touching proof of the islanders' unshaken faith in book-learning as the key to success. But the very doggedness that had sustained the school through every test since its founding during the War seemed to have frozen its curriculum against any growth. It was certainly marvelous that the "grands" of field-hand slaves could be taught to recite the names of the English kings backwards; but having long since demonstrated that freedmen could learn by rote geography, Latin, and even algebra, wasn't it about time to move on to a course of training less extraneous to the lives of the people? The chief purpose of Penn School was to train teachers for the county schools and prepare "scholars" for the county examinations; but couldn't this purpose be transformed from a plastering-on of trumpery academic education into a training of the young for better lives on the island farms? At Land's End she was trying to get the people to work together in matters beyond the praise-house and the burial society. Why couldn't Penn School, at the heart of the island, become a center of community life, a training place for old as well as young in the things that really touched their lives,—better farming methods, better homes, better sanitation and health?

With such ideas whirling in her head she visited the school, marveling at her own temerity, for she had never had more than a bowing acquaintance with Miss Towne and Miss Murray, who seemed to view her as a sort of deserter, a Northern woman and onetime teacher fallen from grace, the wife of a hostile Southerner. But during the years of prosperity she had contributed to the support of the school, and she was relying on that to protect her from being considered a mere intruder and busybody. And though she paid regular visits to the school that winter and itched from the first to make suggestions, —why, for example, couldn't the arithmetic class be taken out in the yard and shown in practice how to measure a cord of wood or an acre of ground?—she kept her thoughts to herself, allowing them to accumulate toward a concrete plan, while she was getting better acquainted with Miss Towne and Miss Murray.

So that winter Penn School gave her an absorbing new interest. But in spite of that and her other concerns and releases, she was shut in with Stephen's festering idleness much of the time.

If she could only escape from the deadly position of keeper into which he had forced her. How gladly she would let him go back into business, in any capacity, if she could only trust him. But she couldn't trust him; as a final humiliation she had to keep the house money hidden, giving him only enough change to jingle in his pocket. Even that didn't stop him: by Christmas he had twice broken his "final" promise, with money borrowed from Lucy and then Seth. Both times he was violently sick and remorseful afterwards, and she was too sick and disgusted herself to lecture him.

After Christmas he began a campaign to wear her down to approving a trip to Charleston.

"Beaufort's finished," he told her, "but the fertilizer manufacturing business is picking up in North Charleston. And I've got the best of connections in Broad Street."

"Wait till you're feeling a little better, dear," she begged. "There's no rush. Give yourself a little more time."

"For what? I'm well now. But I'll lose my mind if I have to stick around here any longer. I tell you I can't stand any more of it!"

And he added a well calculated note of appeal. "If Michael's going to medical school, I've got to get back into the game on some basis without any further delay. I have to hand it to you for what you've done with the plantation this year, but it's a gamble at best and you can't expect your luck to hold out another season. If you can't see the necessity for this trip to Charleston, I'll have to borrow the money, that's all."

But despite that threat she continued to oppose him, sparring for time, hoping that when the planting season came she could interest him in the vegetable garden at least. Perhaps somehow she could hold him on the island through another summer. And perhaps then some real improvement, some basic change would restore her confidence in him.

But when spring came with its renewed activities for her, he refused to show the slightest interest in anything concerning the plantation. And seeing that now all the stir of life around him only aggravated his trouble, deepening his moodiness, heightening his petulance and sharpening his sarcasm, she realized that she was beaten, that she must let him go. The Charleston trip was inevitable: she could only pray that it would not bring fresh disaster.

"Now don't fret yourself," he insisted. "I'll be back by day after tomorrow, at the latest. And with good news."

And for the first two days of his absence she was able to quiet her fears with the thought that possibly she had been mistaken in not trusting him. But when a third day passed and then a fourth, she grew sick with fear.

When he finally appeared, she wondered how he had ever found his way home at all. And this time he very nearly died.

His first account of the trip was brief. "Charleston's doomed. Everything's at a standstill. No place for me."

But later, when he was able to sit up in bed, he expanded that a little. "If there's one thing I want my sons to learn while they're young, it's never to expect anything of a friend. Don't depend on *anyone*. God, I'd rather count on a nigger than a man I'd given a helping hand to. . . . I'll have to make one exception to that. You remember Jeff Farnsworth who used to work at the yards at Port Royal? Well, I staked that bird to a start in the coal-and-wood business in Charleston, and now he thinks he may be able to offer me a bookkeeper's desk at twelve dollars a week, when things begin to pick up again!"

That was his only explanation of what had happened to him. But she could fill out the rest.

When she had nursed him back to life, as soon as he was able to get out of bed, he wrote a number of letters to men and firms in Savannah: there were at least a dozen of them that he gave Seth to mail. Two or three answers came back, which he promptly tore up. He went back to bed then, voluntarily. And though she failed to recognize it at the time, that was the end of the first phase.

✦   ✦   ✦

When she finally realized that at last all desire for drink had been burned out of him, she also realized what the cure had cost. He was gutted. There was nothing left of him but the shell.

In the long fight toward his cure she had never considered the price of victory, had never foreseen for a moment this appalling change. Where before the struggle had been to curb his desire for town, now it was to revive in him some signs of life and ambition, to waken him from his deadness, to rouse some spirit in his eyes. But now there were not even negative expressions of vitality to work on: petulance, sarcasm, bitterness were all gone from his voice and words, leaving only a terrifying emptiness, a profound hollowness that she was powerless to reach or touch. He seldom had anything to say, and when he did speak she shrank from words that seemed to repeat a single refrain: Everything's futile, so why struggle or worry?

At first, after his recovery from the Charleston trip, she had interpreted his slump as resignation to a few more months on the island, peaceful resignation at last; and she had even had the optimism to hope that now, finally, she could enlist his interest in the plantation. But it soon proved that he was quite willing to let her worry along alone.

"No, I'm not going to interfere," he told her. "Play your hand your own way. I admit I couldn't do half as well, and I might break your streak of luck."

And impassively he watched her struggle with the land and the people, the rents and taxes, through a second and a third summer of planting. He was content to do a little fishing, in the Inlet or in the surf at Bay Point, and a little net-casting for shrimp in the tidal creeks; and occasionally he took the dogs for a day's hunting on the barrier islands. The rest of the time he wanted to be let alone in his easy-chair with his *News & Courier,* from which in the evenings he sometimes read items to support his contention.

"Country's going to the dogs all right. Look at these strikes and receiverships and bond defaults,—the whole nation's rotten to the core. We're in a fatal jam this trip. Cleveland's a good man, but what's a good man worth when the odds are all against him. There's no way out."

Before the revolutionary changes in her private world she had had little inclination to try to understand public affairs. In Reconstruction times, when she had lived politics, she had at least understood their importance; and ever since she had known Stephen and Joseph Bramwell and Miss Sophie, she had heard politics discussed heatedly and at length. But then her tendency had been to shut her ears against everything but the children's voices and the pertinent sounds of home; and even the times when Rusty had talked to her about questions of the hour in terms that struck below the surface, she had listened with her heart rather than her head, taking what he said as her own without troubling to make it her own, satisfied that a very general appraisal of the affairs of the outside world was sufficient unto the day. But now she was aware of a necessity and a keen desire really to understand: she was wakening to a practical interest in the mysterious forces, the social and economic pressures at work behind government and taxes, cotton prices and living expenses, and finding them not so hopelessly incomprehensible as she had supposed. And in the first flush of thinking things out for herself and arriving at a few seemingly reasonable conclusions, she wanted to air them, try them out on Stephen. Here, she thought confidently, was one subject of conversation that would be of mutual interest. A little companionable debating would test her theories and be stimulating and good for him, for surely he must get tired of holding the floor without any opposition. So one evening, when he had finished reading aloud an anti-Cleveland speech of "Pitchfork" Tillman's and was settling down to a routine damnation of up-state politics and the Farm Movement in general, she ventured to challenge him.

"But if the farmers can't make money, how can they buy manufactured goods? And if they can't buy, how can industry sell? Business comes to a standstill because a vital part of the population is denied fair prices for its goods. I don't see how you can blame them for putting up a fight."

He looked surprised, and then mildly amused.

"I'm not blaming them. I'm merely pointing out the futility of the thing. Where on earth is squawking for free silver going to get the honest farmer? Exactly nowhere. Just where strikes get labor,—a Federal injunction slapped on them and the militia. Better commodity prices, higher prices for manufactured goods. Higher wages for labor, higher cost of living. It's all grist to the mills of the Yankee bankers in the end." And he lighted the stump of his cigar and settled back in his chair with a sigh of finality.

"Well," she puzzled out, "things ought to be managed better, made fairer for the little fellow. The government ought to take a hand and regulate things."

"I see. Currency inflation, I suppose, and confiscation of wealth by income taxes. And government ownership of railroads and public utilities. Say, when did you join the People's Party?"

"Do you have to join a party to think, dear?"

"What are you trying to do,—start an argument?"

"Yes. A nice friendly one. I have some ideas, and I want you to tell me what's wrong with them."

He gave his paper a stiff shaking.

"I can tell you before you start. They're going to be idealistic, and idealism has about as much to do with politics as it has with making a living, or with any of the other hard facts of life."

"I still have some ideas."

He put down his paper and raised his eyes to the ceiling with a resigned sigh. "All right, let's have them. Coming from a long line of slave-traders and transcendentalists, you ought to have some pretty sound ideas for freeing the farmers and wage slaves. What reforms would you suggest, doctor, for restoring the health of the nation?"

"Well, to begin with, I think agriculture and labor should organize for an effective voice in the government."

"Ah! A mob of hicks and ditch-diggers in the saddle. That'll be nice. Radical rule."

"But surely farmers and laborers aren't radicals. They're just plain people trying to live."

His tolerance was beginning to break down. "I see. Now you're going to tell me what a radical is. Well, suppose I give you my definition. A radical is a nobody that's got nothing and so naturally envies the somebodies that have something. But don't think the some-bodies are going to allow their cloaks to be confiscated and divided among the poor." And he picked up his paper with an air of dismissal.

"You know," she said after a moment, "Jesus of Nazareth was pretty radical, wasn't he. Could anything be more radical than the Sermon on the Mount?"

He gave her a glance of irritation. "I suppose that's intended to be funny. If you're going to drag religion into this, I guess we better call it off. We all know the devil can cite Scripture for his purpose. . . . Why is it a woman's mind can't work logically? We started out discussing local politics and now look where you've got us switched to, religion! Do you wonder I don't like to discuss things with you? And now you seem to be drifting into the William Jennings Bryan class. Well, let your poor radicals eat cake. I'm on the conservative side of the fence. I'll take the frying-pan in preference to the fire any day."

"Yes, and you may have a revolution on your hands someday."

He had to smile at that. "A sort of French Revolution, I suppose. Well, you know how that finally wound up. And anyhow, you've got a fat chance of starting anything of that kind in this country. Revolutions don't breed in a lottery system where any clod can hope to draw a winning ticket and rise from rags to riches overnight."

"We had a revolution once," she countered, trying to think against the assurance of his voice.

"You don't call that a revolution, do you? That was just a change of dealers, a new shuffle among the upper-crust players. The rabble didn't have a look in."

"Well, this is supposed to be a democracy, and I can't see why——"

"*Supposed* to be is right. And maybe it actually was—on paper, in Jefferson's day. But the boys on top saw to it that the dear old Constitution safeguarded their inalienable rights, don't make any mistake about that. The boys on the bottom were able to rear their ugly heads for a few minutes under Andy Jackson, and I think we both have vague recollections of the times when black and tan niggers romped on our necks, with the aid of a Connecticut Yankee named Aaron Moffet. But those happy days are gone now and we're living in a full-fledged plutocracy."

He slapped his paper down and turned in his chair to face her. "You know, if you'd get a few elementary facts straight, you might be able to look at things from a realistic standpoint. Now if there's one thing I understand it's politics. And I can assure you that the nearest we ever came to having a literal democracy was in the beginning, when we made a nice theoretical frame. After that we went about our business, and since the War we've embarked on a Roman holiday,—and the portrait in the frame has been finished in oils and gold, wheat and tobacco and steel. It's the same old story, only on an elaborate modern scale. It's still every man for himself and devil take the hindmost. As it was in the beginning and will be to the bitter end,—or at least as long as human nature remains human. And I say Amen." And once again he resumed his paper with an air of finality.

But she was too wrought up now to be cut off here. "And you don't object to seeing the majority of people ground down by poverty while a few men grab and control the wealth of the country through monopoly and special privilege and every kind of sordid means?"

"I not only don't object," he tossed over his shoulder, "—I envy them. I hoped to be one of them myself, once. As usual the smart boys go to the head of the class. The rest stay where they belong. . . . And a damn good system. The only system that's ever worked or ever will. It may be rough-and-tumble, sordid as you say, but it's life and the natural order of things. And God deliver us from the static paradise of the socialists, where all men are free and equal brothers and everybody's nobody,—all of us reduced to the dead level of the lowest common denominator. You'd love that, if you were ever unlucky enough to get it."

"But why can't it be a leveling up process?"

"And why can't silk purses be made out of sow ears? Why can't pigs be taught to fly?"

"But almost all your big men were nobodies once. If the masses had decent wages, a fairer share in the profits of their own labor, and better living conditions, they wouldn't stay miserable and ignorant nobodies. I don't see why we can't make a better social order, a better world for everybody. Why can't we be a really great and happy people? Think what a fine and exciting thing it would be if we all dedicated ourselves to making this a true democracy."

He put down his paper for the last time and shook his head at her with a weary sigh. "Sure. You and me and Abraham Lincoln and Lucy and Mr. Rockefeller and Sam Koenig and the Tillmanites. . . . Emily, seriously, why don't you get yourself a fine and exciting soap-box? You know, it's always been a marvel to me the way your mind works, but I'm afraid time is going to your head instead of sobering you down. Haven't you learned enough geography yet to know that Utopia is in the State of Nowhere? Does the joker in the beautiful horizon still elude you? When are you going to stop chasing will-o'-the-wisps and accept things as they are? . . . Now suppose you listen patiently to me for just a minute. You said you wanted to know why we can't make a so-called better world,—all right, I'm going to give you a brief summary of the world we live in."

He paused to light the stub of his cigar.

"The country," he puffed as he shook out the match and tossed it onto the hearth, "is run by the government, and the government is run by politics. And politics, in turn, is run by politicians. And politicians are run by power. And power is money. Money! And money is in the pockets of the big boys. Now where are you going to get a wedge into that combination?"

When he stared at her for an answer, she said uncertainly: "Elect honest politicians."

"Greatest fallacy in the world! Joe's delusion. You can't get them. And if you could, they'd soon have to compromise with realities. And who's going to elect them in the first place? Most people in this land of the free and home of the brave have some small stake in what Joe calls the *status quo,* if it's only a sentimental stake, and they're not going to vote for a candidate with radical leanings, from a natural fear that he might tip over the whole cart and spill their precious little apples. . . .

"All right now, let's get on with the story. This is a plutocracy and the big boys run us. But there's one catch, if you reformers were bright enough to make use of it. Money attracts money, and periodically the good old ship of credit gets a trifle too topheavy with success and keels over. That's what's happening right now. Heretofore the boys on the upper deck have managed to get out from under, but I don't know about this trip. But even if the crew and the stokers and the steerage mob were able to stage a successful mutiny in the midst of panic and disaster, where would it get them? As soon as the ship was righted and patched up, there'd be a new crop of officers and salon passengers. It's just the nature of the beast. The same old game goes on and on, and if you're wise you'll like whatever berth you happen to fall into."

He tossed the stub of the cigar away, brushed his hands together, and took up his paper. "In other words, in such times as these the goose that lays the golden eggs is too busy being strangled to take advantage of the situation and turn itself into a truly democratic eagle. . . . Let me give you one word of advice, dear. Stick to your class and the interests of your class, and let the farmers and laborers worry about their own troubles. And please spare me the next time you feel another dizzy spell coming on."

She had succeeded, certainly, in reviving signs of life in him. But the reaction, tacit and expressed, was painful. And she decided she would attempt no more debates with him. It was better to let him alone and keep her speculations to herself.

He was still able to be something of his old self when Jack brought a pack of schoolmates out from town for a Saturday of scrimmaging, or when Margaret had one of her friends over the week-end. But as the months went by he made less and less effort to keep up appearances even for them; and as they grew in inches and awareness, they began to see him with critical eyes, which caused him to withdraw still further within himself. Not that they were in the least reproachful in their new understanding: on the contrary, Jack's reaction was simply a light-hearted assumption of increasing freedom as his father's authority diminished; and Margaret seemed to find in his self-imposed isolation only a challenge to her expansive nature, and in his weakness an object for the protective tenderness and sympathy of her firming womanhood. Certainly neither of them was made miserable, like Michael.

His despondency became so heavy in the second summer at Land's End that she resolved he would never, at whatever cost to herself, spend any time longer than a holiday at home till the situation cleared. So it was with the greatest relief that she received a piece of news in one of his letters from school the following spring, just as she was giving up hope of anything better than the place Joseph Bramwell wanted to make for him in the law office. His roommate's father, he wrote, was organizing a company to mine kaolin and feldspar and mica near Asheville and had offered him a job for the summer on the prospecting and surveying party, but he wasn't considering it because he was going to help her with the plantation. She rushed a letter back to him, urging him to jump at the chance and assuring him he could best help her that way. And finally, after another exchange of letters, he wrote that he had "jumped".

Any painful regrets that he and Linda had about not seeing each other except for a few days at the beginning and end of the summer, they kept well hidden. As for her own loneliness for him, she kept reminding herself what a fine healthful summer he was having, with mountain air in his lungs, with the heat and strain of home far away. Reminding herself, too, that by the time he returned she would have all but the harvest of another planting season behind her. And Stephen mended.

And when he came home at last, beaming proud of his first earned money and his tanned muscles,—though he was still too lean to suit Lucy, who made a heroic attempt to fatten him up for his junior year at the Citadel,—there was a first-rate crop of cotton to show him, and good harvest weather and prices in prospect. But with Stephen she had made no progress whatever. With him she remained defeated.

Up to this point she had tried only mild and indirect tactics. There had been the restraining fear that if she did succeed in rousing him the pendulum of his failure might swing back to the other extreme, and she doubted her strength to see him through that again. His evasion of all responsibility, this flight into hopelessness and apathy might be an ignominious retreat, but at least it was not so devastating as that other form of escape. Perhaps, after all, it was better not to try to force him, better to let bad enough alone. Then too some remnants of an old pride had stood in the way of any downright and drastic attempt to stir him. And, finally, there had always been the hope that he would rouse himself.

But now the more satisfied she became that his craving for drink was gone, the more clearly she saw how helpless that tattered victory had left him. And he was not only powerless to rouse himself, gradually she realized that he was content to be powerless; he was not only rotting before her eyes, but he was willing to rot. He was making it plainer every day that he didn't care what happened. He had even reached what was in him a supreme symptom of indifference: he no longer considered his dress, the appearance of his clothes, and he went for days without shaving. He was letting himself go so completely that now it was becoming a mortal struggle for her to keep impatience from submerging all other feelings. She couldn't hang on much longer to any shreds of sympathy. Despite every allowance she could find to make for him she knew this supine disintegration was killing the last of her respect by slow and fatal attrition.

It was this final deadly fear that drove her to speak her mind at last. And because the impulse had been so long restrained, her words came out in a rush of emotion that she could not stem or control.

"Stephen, you've got to do something. You can't sit and stew like this. It's killing you. You've got to take some interest in life, for your own sake."

"Go ahead," he told her impassively. "Take a good crack at me,— I'm down. Tell me what a failure I am. I won't argue with you."

"But you're not a failure, and there's no excuse for acting like one. I don't blame you for anything but that. Certainly no man who was really a failure could have done what you've done."

"I suppose you refer to drinking. Well now, that's certainly generous of you, but let's keep the records straight. Don't give me any credit. It wasn't will power. If you want the truth, it was simply that things don't make enough difference to me any more, one way or another, to take the trouble to get drunk."

That made her wince.

"You can't mean that. Oh, Steve, can't you see everything's coming out all right now if you'll just show a little gumption."

"Gumption, eh. Sure you don't mean guts? Why not come right out and say what you mean,—I'm yellow, I'm a quitter."

"You know I don't believe that."

"Well, why not? I am."

"But you're not. You never have been. It's just that—you've been through so much you've gotten a wrong slant on things. You've got to get back your old attitude and grip."

"I see. I don't suppose it's ever occurred to you that my present attitude might make more fundamental sense, to me at least, than yours does. It just happens that you're an incurable optimist unfortunate enough to be teamed up with an incurable pessimist. You may just as well resign yourself to that, and save your breath."

"You certainly didn't used to be a pessimist, or anything resembling one."

"That shows how little you ever really knew me. I've always been a pessimist underneath. I used to have a motto that it was better never to expect things to come out right and then you'd never be disappointed. And you might be pleasantly surprised, occasionally."

"You must have forgotten your motto when you had so many pleasant surprises for so many years in a row."

"I did. But you see, I've had considerable time to think lately. And I don't believe the game's worth the struggle. That's all."

"But you don't object to someone else struggling."

"That's their look-out. I'm not asking anyone to do any struggling on my account, God knows. And I don't believe anyone is, on *my* account. I believe someone's trying to hold the family together, and I have no objection to that whatever. And that someone's doing too well to get any sympathy from me. Far as I'm concerned anyone can struggle as much as they like, providing they don't try to drag me into it."

"Steve, that just doesn't make sense."

"I think it makes all kinds of sense. Why struggle? Everybody gets it in the neck sooner or later, no matter what kind of a fight they've put up. The higher they go, the harder they fall. Well, I've had my fall, I'm out of the running. I'm on the sidelines now, and able to see what a crooked damn race it is. But I don't expect you to share any such lily-livered views as that."

"No, I'm afraid I can't."

"Well, being a thoroughbred, you naturally couldn't. You see, I'm just a broken-winded sea-island tacky."

"Steve, this just isn't you talking. I can understand your feeling bitter as gall about things, but I can't understand being willing to give up and lie down."

"You'll learn. I admit you're a stubborn one, but you'll learn in time. . . . Oh, what's the use. Go right on dreaming your beautiful dreams about life being a noble adventure, a challenge to courage, and all that rot. Despite hell and high-water you're going to be a romantic till the bloody end. But kindly count me out. I've done my share of struggling. And so have you. Why not let the children carry the family bag for a while? Pass the torch on to them. Drop this heartbreaking backbreaking ambition of yours to give Michael a medical training, and give him a chance to show a little unselfishness and take a permanent job with that mining outfit. It would be a better healthier life for him, and he could grow up in a business with a great future. The medical profession isn't going to collapse without him, you know, and it's the hardest life in the world,—it was killing Rusty. And Jack's old enough now to get out and dig up a job for himself, and be a lot better off than marking time in school. Or let him help you around the place here."

By that time she was too shaky and afraid of tears to continue the discussion. But at least she had smoked him out of his hiding-place and forced the fight out into the open. And besides permitting him to get some of the toxins out of his system, it produced one happy effect: he announced, grudgingly, that he was going to "show Jack" what could be done with a vegetable garden. And that winter he pored over seed catalogues, made a long order list, and laid out on paper an elaborate plan for a garden of several acres.

But when it came to staking out the actual acres that spring, the plan began to break up. He began to complain of headaches and backaches. But lost again in her plantation cares,—and they seemed greater than ever, for this year at Seth's advice she was planting the Big Field in corn and shifting the cotton to three separate smaller fields on the Sound,—it was not till one afternoon late in March, when she came home to find him in bed with a hot-water bottle at the small of his back, that she realized he was through with gardening. For the rest of the spring damp weather kept him invalided with an unbroken series of backaches and cricks, colds and congestions; and the garden was left to Lucy and Tad Lincoln to do what they could with.

And that summer marked the beginning of his neuritis.

At first she was all sympathy. It was obvious that he was suffering acutely: sometimes a spell lasted two or three days, with no let-up of the quivering pains in his arms and shoulders. Yet it was impossible not to observe, as the summer months passed, that the pains had a way of magically disappearing whenever wind and tide were right for a fishing trip.

Once when he was leaving with Jack to stand casting for hours in the surf at Bay Point, she ventured to wonder if it wouldn't be bad for him.

"Sorry to see me well enough to have a little sport? I'll bet you'll be glad enough to have some bass for supper."

"Not at the expense of another siege."

"Oh, I'll be having one anyway. Might as well get a little pleasure while I can."

"Dear, I wish you'd see a doctor."

"I knew that was coming. Veterinary Wright, I suppose."

"A Charleston doctor."

"Not on your life. Anyway, how can we afford a doctor? We got to save our pennies to turn our perfectly good mining-engineer son into one."

"But I'm serious."

"So am I. No thanks, I'll wait till Michael gets back from the mountains and let him do a little amateur prescribing."

"I'm sure he could make some sensible suggestions, about what not to do at least."

"I'm positive he could. Well, let me tell you something, this game happens to be bad enough without having to listen to suggestions along with it. If you think it's a joke, try it yourself sometime."

"But I know it's terrible."

"Oh no you don't. You think it's one part pain, two parts bad habits, three parts failure to take suggestions,—and the rest put on."

So she made no more suggestions. There was simply nothing to

do but nurse him, and watch his sickness grow into a cherished fast-
ness, a combination of asylum and citadel and cloister where he
could rest in peace from all proddings.

And so he hibernated through another winter, coming to life only
when he and Jack were planning a hunting trip, and then he could
work over the guns several days in advance without incapacitating
himself for the week-end. And when spring began to lengthen and
warm the days and he saw the vegetable garden was safely started,
he began to show marked signs of improvement; he was able to
work over his fishing tackle—oiling the reels and tinkering with the
rods, sorting hooks and testing lines—for hours at a stretch without
any ill effects. But as the end of Michael's senior year approached, he
weakened again. And by graduation time he was having the worst
attack yet. It was impossible to think of his going.

"It's just as well," he told her. "You and Joe will be quite enough
of the family on his hands when he's parading for the girls. I'd send
him a note if my hand wasn't so bad."

"Let me write it for you," she volunteered quickly.

"All right. Just tell him I'd be there if I could but anyhow I'm
wishing him all kinds of luck. Tell him we're proud of him, and
expect to be even prouder in the future. I guess I can manage the
'Affectionately, Dad' part. And tell him I've got one or two things
of his grandfather's I want him to have."

"He's going to be badly disappointed you're not there."

"Yes, I can imagine. That shows how well you understand fathers
and sons,—you don't know what a relief it will be. And I'm damn
glad I don't have to go through any song-and-dance with old classmates. I'm not exactly in shape for a reunion."

So he was left home with Margaret to nurse him while she went on
with Joe Bramwell to the graduation. And at least that gave her a
good opportunity to talk with Joe about him. But Joe had something
else on his mind.

"Emily," he began as soon as they were settled in the train, "for
many months I have been considering a proposition which I now
wish to lay before you." He cleared his throat and proceeded with a
flushed face. "As you know, Michael has always seemed like a son
to me. I have watched his development with an interest that I think
I may say has been second only to his mother's and father's. And
having had no son of my own, in a literal sense, I had at one time

hoped, as you also know, that he would decide to study law and read in my office.

"The Law," he continued in a voice that made no concessions to the other passengers in the car, "has had the allegiance of four generations of Bramwells, and they have served her with devotion and honor through crucial periods of the Nation's history. But at no time in the past has there been a greater need for men of integrity and sanity in public life than there is today. However, I believe you are familiar with my views on the subject. Suffice it to say, it was a keen disappointment to me when Michael elected to dedicate his life to medicine. But there is one aspect of the case to which I have not been able to resign myself,—to wit, that anything less than the best in training is good enough for him. In short, I am proposing that if it is not to be Harvard Law School then it must be Harvard Medical School."

He extracted a catalogue from his pocket, opened it on his knee, and adjusted his pince-nez. He glanced at her over the top of them. "I trust you don't find my suggestion presumptuous, Emily?"

"Why, Joe, it's marvelous. But you'll have to give me a moment to get my breath."

"I've had it up my cuff for months," he beamed at her, "but I've been making inquiries and conducting a little investigation, so that I'd have all the data to give you when I broached the subject."

"But I'm afraid," she told him as the first thrill of the idea faded in misgivings and Boston shifted swiftly from a nostalgic inspiration to merely a place very far away, "—I'm afraid Charleston Medical School is going to be as much as we can swing."

"It's a good school," he conceded, "but not good enough. If Rusty were there, it would be a different story of course. But as it is, the facilities and the faculty and prestige of Harvard far exceed anything he could get—I'm reluctant to admit—in the South."

"But the tuition rates and living expenses would be so much more. Suppose our plantation luck gave out, or cotton prices fell, what then?"

"I'm coming to that." He took off his pince-nez and tapped the catalogue. "This came only yesterday so I haven't had time to make a study of it, but from a cursory examination I judge that the differences in expense will not be great. And then there seem to be a number of scholarships for which a student of Michael's ability would be eligible. But that's all beside the point in any case, for what I'm after is the privilege of sponsoring Michael through Harvard."

She shook her head slowly.

"But if we call it a loan, Emily."

She smiled at him and touched his sleeve, and shook her head again.

"Emily," he said dejectedly, "you haven't the heart to cut me out entirely. You don't recognize what this means to me."

"Joe, you don't seem to have learned what a hard-hearted person I can be. But would you mind continuing in an emergency capacity? You have no idea what an important position that is."

He gave her a brief smile and pulled his nose. "I feel like a suitor," he grumbled, "tactfully rejected for the nth time. But," he quickly added with a flush, "an emergency position is better than none. I mean to say, let's confine our attention for the present to my first proposition." And he resumed his pince-nez with a snort and began to thumb the pages of the catalogue.

And every spare moment of the graduation journey was devoted to Harvard Medical School. Little by little she found her doubts crumbling before Joe's arguments and persuasion; and when Michael showed enthusiasm, she yielded her last uncertainties. By the time they got back to Beaufort, the matter was settled.

But the problem of Stephen had not been solved. And that summer of '97 was too full of plantation activities and worries, and excitement over Michael's future, to leave any room for wrestling with him. She was satisfied to leave him to his own devices for those crowded months; and it was not till Michael came home from his job in the mountains and was packed off for Boston and entrance examinations that her mind was free to turn back to Stephen. But she was unable to organize her thoughts till word came that Michael was safely entered. And even then she waited till the tension of harvest was past before she made any move.

Then one day in the second week of October, when the last of the cotton had been shipped to town for ginning and it was time for her annual business visit to Joe's office, she prepared herself to attack the problem of Stephen from a new angle. It was a day made for venturesome tactics: the shores and marshes were still summer green, but the air was golden brisk with autumn. And the astonishing yet strangely familiar sight of a warship anchored in the Sound was quixotically converted by her determination into a personal champion. From the moment that morning when Stephen had spelled out the name *Maine* through field-glasses from the upper piazza, she had felt that the government had sent this "floating fortress" here for her private benefit, rather than as a firm and final reminder to the Spanish that it was time to put their Cuban house in order. This man-of-war had come to blast Stephen into animation. And already it had had the effect of galvanizing him into a greater interest in life than he had shown for ages,—a good base for her plan, by a happy chance.

At Joe's office, when the business of the day was out of the way and she had read him Michael's first letters from the North, it was not easy to introduce the subject of Stephen. Joe was in the most expansive of moods and not readily to be diverted from his own topics. Watching for an opening as he promenaded between his desk and the window, with a profusion of flourishes and a good deal of cuff-shooting and nose-pinching, she was struck with particular force today by his energy and verve. The graying of mane and the increasing stoutness that were so perfectly rounding out his dignity only accented his essential youthfulness. At sixty he was at the height of his powers; and though he was ten years older, he looked younger than Stephen.

"No," he was saying pensively, "I'm afraid there are no signs of an emergency. Your crop was smaller, but prices are higher. Now see here, Emily, when Rutherford's check comes in you'll have enough money in the bank to see Michael through,—why don't you take the advice of an old friend and give the fields and yourself a rest?"

She shook her head. "Not with the Marshlands mortgage still hanging over our heads."

He paused in his promenading long enough to give her a look of fierce indulgence. "By George, I can't tell you how I admire you for what you've done!"

"But why?"

"Because it's been magnificent."

"Now Joe, we both know better than that. It may have been a little risky the first year, but it's more or less taken care of itself since then. I've just been very lucky, as Stephen likes to remind me. And you don't know what support I've had. If I'd been some miserable person without friends or backing, I might think I deserved some applause."

"Your modesty is as becoming as your hat, Emily."

"Well, I don't know quite how to take that! Do you know how old this hat is? If you were a woman you'd be laughing at it."

"To that," he said, resuming his promenade with a flush, "I can only reply that any hat you wear is inevitably becoming and stylish. And I repeat my advice to you to take a rest."

"I can't keep up with you," she laughed. "Do I look frayed at the edges?"

"Frankly," he told her gravely from the window, "you look tired. Your eyes, particularly. I'm worried about you, as a matter of fact."

"As a matter of fact," she said soberly, "I feel fine. But I am going to take things easy for a while."

"I wish I could trust you to," he frowned down at the street, "but I know you too well. You'll spend the winter doing for the plantation people and worrying about this, that, and the other. Anything, in fact, to keep from letting up on yourself."

"No, you're wrong this time. I'm going to take a deep breath and relapse into my natural lazy self. I think I'd sleep straight through to Christmas, if it wasn't for Stephen. With the exception of him everything seems pretty shipshape. At the moment he's my one worry."

He turned away from the window with a snort. "It's outrageous! I can't tell you how his behavior has affected me. But I want you to understand, Emily, that his is an exhibition unique in the annals of our family. The only excuse I can find for him is that he was insufficiently grounded in the old order before the War. He's a member of a lost generation of South Carolinians, but that's no excuse for him. I can hold no brief for him whatever. If he had an ounce of manhood,—but I better not start on that."

Purple and out of breath he allowed himself a moment's respite in his swivel-chair. But before she could say anything, he was up again with a whole series of snorts. "Up to this point I have respected your wishes and refrained from any act of remonstrance. But by now, Emily, you must be willing to concede the futility of a passive policy. This is a matter between men, and I ask that you now allow me to assume my responsibility as his only kinsman."

"Joe," she said when his snorting had subsided, "I don't blame

Stephen for anything. I know what he's been through,—things were just too much for him, that's all. And he can't be lectured or nagged back to life. I've made that mistake. He's got to have something to do—almost anything, but it can't be forced on him. It's got to come from him."

"It seems to me," he exploded at that, "Stephen's had considerably more than enough time to act on his own initiative, if he ever intends to."

"Well, I have a plan I want to talk over with you. Why can't something be suggested to him in such a way that he'll think it's his own idea?"

He examined that solemnly and then broke into a deep chuckle.

"May I ask how you propose to insinuate an idea into a man's head in such a way that he'll accept it as his own, without suspicion? And what precisely are we going to suggest?"

She sighed frankly. "I don't know."

He stood regarding her absently.

"I don't suppose," he said to the portrait of Wade Hampton behind her, "he would be any more receptive now to my offer of a position here than he was in the beginning."

"No, I'm afraid not. I'm afraid that and the plantation will have to be counted out."

"He informed me that what I needed was an office-boy. Of course Stephen has always been extremely difficult,—couldn't have been anything else with Sophie for a mother. But I'm confounded if I can see how he can afford to be arrogant any longer."

"Perhaps," she suggested, "he feels he can't afford to be anything else now."

He greeted that with a vague "Mmm", and turned again to the window. There he thrust his hands into his pockets and gave himself to intense concentration, silent except for an occasional faint snort. After several long minutes of this, he turned back to her with an abrupt discovery.

"Insurance! Fire and life. Storm and theft. Fellow from the Mutual Life in here only the other day,—had quite a talk with him. What those Charleston agencies need is a good representative in this territory. Sam Koenig's in the field, but primarily to cut his own premiums,—no aggressive competition there. I have social and legal contacts with the heads of several of the larger agencies in Charleston, and we can make excellent connections and handle the business right here in this office. By George, Emily, it's an inspiration, if I may say so!"

"You certainly may! I knew you'd have an idea. And it's in Stephen's line, too."

"Exactly. Why haven't we thought of it before? Insurance and real estate were a sideline with Fenwick and Company, but—yes, and I see no reason why he can't handle rentals and sales as well as policies. He can have the room across the hall for an office."

"Joe, you're not only a saint but a genius."

But then they both sobered.

"And now," he frowned, "how are we to transfer our inspiration to Stephen? You don't think we can broach it directly?"

"I know *I* can't. One word from me would be enough to give him a fatal prejudice, and that would be the end of it. But coming from you, subtly, at least it will get a hearing."

"I fear I'm not much of a hand at subtlety, Emily. But I'll make the attempt. And now how and when am I going to see him?"

"Well, I can try to get him to town. But I don't know how I can do it without making him suspicious."

"And I suppose he'll be on his guard if I descend upon him at Land's End."

"I'm afraid so. But what about neutral ground? Can't you go fishing or hunting or something together?"

"Possibly. Yes, that's it! As a matter of fact, I've been promising myself a trip to Holly Hill. I'll ask him to go with me for a hunt. That ought to get him,—he stopped his first deer at the old plantation. Lost his shirt-tail there, too."

He rubbed his hands briskly and with satisfaction. "Fine! And now you can't refuse to do me the honor of drinking a short toast to our conspiracy. I have here some very commendable port."

"You don't think it will interfere with my marketing?"

"On the contrary, I can particularly recommend it for marketing."

He produced his key-ring with a flourish, unlocked the closet, and brought out a bottle and glasses. He filled the glasses with ceremony.

When she was preparing to leave, after they had rehearsed his role with Stephen, he insisted on making a package of the bottle. "Take a little every day after dinner," he prescribed, "there's no better tonic than port." And she had to carry it off with her.

Back at Land's End, she wasted no time before giving Stephen the message from Joe. But she was careful to seem preoccupied with other matters and to make her voice casual.

"And he says he'll meet you," she concluded, "at his office tomorrow afternoon at five."

"Well, it's about time he came across with a hunt. He's got the best deer drives in the country at Holly. And the best duck-shooting, with those old Combahee ricefields. What's he want me to bring?"

"Nothing but one extra gun."

"He's probably got that fine English piece I gave him rusted up already. He never knew how to treat a gun. How do we go?"

"Drive, I suppose."

"I thought so. Too damn tight to loosen up for a boat. Well, I can see myself driving all the way out there behind one of those carriage nags of his. I knew there was some catch. Nothing doing."

In sudden desperation she suggested, very casually, the *Pilot Boy*. "Linda can stay here overnight, and Seth would be tickled to go."

"Can you imagine Seth on a deer hunt? We're not after rabbits, you know. Anyhow, I'm sick of asking favors of the Robinsons."

"Well, I'm going to drive to Frogmore tomorrow after dinner, and I can easily take you on to the ferry."

"And how do I get back?"

"I'll meet you. Or send Tad."

"No thanks, I wouldn't ask him to wait around till maybe midnight, with only a lantern to warm his hands. No, it's too damn complicated."

She was afraid to make any further suggestions. But as a last resort she tried reverse tactics.

"Well, dear, I'm sorry you have to miss a good hunt, but it's probably just as well. I shouldn't think a cold damp stand at dawn would be the best thing in the world for that bad shoulder of yours."

He made no answer to that and with an air of dismissal began opening the papers she had brought in the mail. She had Michael's regular Sunday letter to reread, and for a while she was able to drown her disappointment in that. But then her mind began to grope for some way to reopen the subject. It had to be reopened: she couldn't be balked like this at the first step. As usual when she had some worry that made the house seem cramped and oppressive, she went out for a walk with the dogs along the old praise-house lane; but she came back hopelessly stumped.

After supper Stephen himself broke the impasse. He slapped his paper down and demanded if she had any soft scraps in her rag-bag for wiping down the guns. "I've got to go, I suppose. He'll have everything set, and I'm not going to let him down."

She kept her eyes on her knitting to hide the relief. And to clinch his decision she risked a mild remonstrance. "You better think that over, dear. Remember your shoulder."

"That's just what I want to forget. And please quit trying to make an invalid of me. . . . If you'll drive me to the ferry, I'll manage to get back somehow."

And the next day, after dinner, she drove him to the ferry in his hunting togs.

On the way back she stopped at Penn School and stayed for supper and an evening of talk with Miss Towne and Miss Murray, driving home by starlight so bright that there was no need to light the lantern. At the house all the downstairs lamps were burning and Lucy was waiting with a good scolding for her. It was late but she was still much too wide-awake for sleep; after she got Lucy to bed, she wrote Michael and then read till past midnight.

Suspense made the next day drag terribly. And by night she had a fully developed case of what Miss Sophie called "hunt funk". At nine o'clock the special okra soup that was to welcome him was moved to the back of the stove, but still feeling he might come she sat up till midnight again before she gave up hope. Even then she left the hall lamp burning low and lay awake listening for a long time despite herself.

The next day, Friday, he at last appeared, in the afternoon with Margaret and Jack—and a ten-point buck plus three wild turkeys. But there was too much excitement to give her a chance for anything more than snatches of talk with him. And after supper there was a long family evening, with Jack insisting on a detailed description of the hunt. Even when he and Margaret were out of the way, she feared that Stephen was going to yawn himself off to bed without giving her an inkling of anything important.

"You haven't said much about Joe," she told him in a voice of restrained desperation when he got up to wind the mantel clock.

"What do you want to know? He's as poor a shot as ever, and he has the worst driver and the sorriest little pack of rundown hounds I ever saw. And unless he can get a good tenant, the place is going to degenerate into a poachers' paradise."

"I mean didn't he have anything interesting to talk about? You haven't seen each other for so long."

"Oh, he's more tiresome than ever, if that's what you're after. He whips me down flat. Now he's got a whole nest of political bees in his bonnet. I honestly believe he's got his eagle eye on the Mayor's office. And then I had to listen to a lot of rot about going on with my Mason degrees, keeping the family's Grand Master tradition unbroken for Michael's sake and Jack's and their children's children. But don't ask me to go over all that. I'm ready for some sleep."

But in the hall he stopped to stretch and decide on a place to hang the new antlers,—she had managed to keep the walls of the living-room and dining-room clear of trophies but the hall bristled with them,—and while he was deliberating he said, absently: "By the way, I wish you'd have Lucy press a suit for me before Monday. I'm going in to town with the children."

"What for?"

"Business." And he flushed slightly as he studied the set of antlers over the dining-room door. "That's about the only spot for it, alongside that old-timer of Pete Bethel's. But I'm not going to crowd them. Say, what about placing this fellow over the dining-room mantel or the sideboard?"

"Why yes, of course," she agreed without thinking.

"Well! a change of heart! The bars are down at last. We'll be breaking into the living-room next. . . ."

"What business are you talking about?" she finally had to ask to make him go on.

"Oh, something I'm cooking up with Joe. An insurance agency, if you must know. I've been considering it for some time. Real estate on the side, maybe. I'm dickering with him for one of his rooms for an office. It's a good location."

"Why, dear, that's splendid! Why didn't you tell me about it?"

"Now don't get excited. That's just why I didn't want to mention it yet,—you always fly off the handle at the drop of a hat. There's nothing settled yet."

But there was enough settled to give her a good night's sleep.

She woke with the fear of a reaction, expressed in sick terms. But he showed no ill effects from his hunt and was able to go surf fishing with Jack. Sunday, however, found him bedridden with rheumatism in the knees. Unwilling to risk any delay at this crucial point she gave him drastic treatment: liniment and massage, hot-water bottles, and milk toast. And Monday morning she gave him a big breakfast and got him off bright and early with Margaret and Jack, in the *Pilot Boy*.

He was home at noon.

"Well," he told her as he came up the piazza steps, "it's all settled."

It was impossible, then, to keep back tears of joy. "Darling," she said with her arms around him, "I can't tell you how glad I am."

"You better save that," he frowned, "till we see how it works out."

He patted her arms and released himself to slump into his piazza armchair. She sat down on the steps at his feet.

"Oh, Steve, of course it's going to work out."

"Don't be too sure. I've got Sam Koenig to compete with, and he's a very slick article. And you realize what this will mean, don't you? We'll have to move back to Marshlands. And what I make, at the start at least, isn't going to make up for the rent we'll lose."

"But we'll have Margaret and Jack living home again!"

"What about this place?"

"Well, Biggie can direct the work. And Seth will keep an eye on things."

He was immediately skeptical of Biggie's reliability. But she was sure. He had long since established his leadership among the plantation people beyond any fear of dispute; and the past winter his marriage to Jessie had stabilized the domestic side of his life. He was now in every respect and just as she had hoped a worthy successor to Isaac. "And of course I can come over once or twice a week. Tad can meet me at the ferry with the buckboard."

"Well," he said finally, "there's no point in getting yourself keyed up yet, because we can't get the Fowlers out of Marshlands before Christmas. We got to give them at least a month's notice. And I'm certainly not going to try to commute till then."

Here was a serious last obstacle, threatening a fatal delay. And the next morning, on the plea of having some cotton business to wind up, she went to town to see Joe.

No dealings with Mrs. Fowler had ever been pleasant; and this interview, even under Joe's diplomatic auspices, was particularly disagreeable. But in the end, by offering to refund the rent for September and October, she was able to induce the Fowlers to give up their lease on the first of November.

The following morning she began preparations for leaving Land's End, over Stephen's protests.

"Why do you always have to rush into things like a madman," he complained. "I wish you'd let me regulate this business. It's my idea and I'd appreciate being allowed to handle it in my own way, and in my own good time."

"Of course, dear," she told him from the cedar closet, "but I know you won't want to be held up now that you've made your plans." And with burning excitement she hurried, that day and the next, to make the dismantling of the house conspicuous and decisive before she settled down to the packing.

But on the last day of the packing, despite her warnings, he stripped off his coat and pitched in with such sweating abandon that when the morning of moving arrived he was badly crippled with cricks and strains. When she tried to postpone the moving and keep him in bed, he insisted on "getting it over with",—with the result that for the first days at Marshlands she had a complete cripple on her hands. And when she nursed him out of that, he drifted into the familiar combination of invalid nerves and inertia, and lingered on in bed.

While this relapse lasted, she was powerless to do much of anything herself. And to make Marshlands home again there was so much to do, not only in the house, which the Fowlers had left in a wretched state, but also on the grounds: the lawns were grown rank and seedy, the closed garden was a tangle of shrub branches and wild vines, its beds and paths almost obliterated, and the rose garden had apparently been used for a chicken runway. Everything about the place was crying for attention and loving care again, yet she was inhibited from doing anything more than the immediately necessary unpacking by this last stubborn resistance of his, which kept her quarantined with him in a final miasma of fretful lassitude.

But then abruptly, one morning after a week that had strained her nerves to the breaking point, he gave in and got up. He was going, he announced crossly, to the office. And he would be home for dinner at two o'clock sharp.

. . . It was hard to believe her senses as she stood in the hall after breakfast, waiting for him to satisfy himself with his image in the hatrack mirror. In a daze of delight she went out with him to the porch and down the frosty tabby steps, so hard to get used to again after the wide piazzas and broad wooden steps of Land's End. In the leaf-strewn drive she detained him a moment while she hurried to the rose garden and found a dwarfed half-open bud, the last pale flower left in a world of deepening autumn colors. He fidgeted self-consciously when she slipped it into his buttonhole and gave his lapel a pat.

"You'd think I was going to a wedding, or on the stage," he said peevishly. "You know how I hate to have a fuss made over things."

The sunlight was softly radiant and still, more like expectant spring than Indian summer. She walked on with him to the gates, where he gave her a hasty kiss and a reluctant brief smile. She stood watching him as he walked very erect and business-like down Fenwick Street, her heart swelling to suffocation. So that when she turned back to the waiting house, it and the lawn and the old trees and the shining river all swam together in a blur of joy and thanksgiving.

IX

"I'M GOING TO GET you a real doctor from Charleston. No Doc Wright for you!"

Having for a nurse a fiercely solicitous Stephen was at least as strange as spending Christmas week in bed.

"But I don't need anyone," she protested meekly. "I'll take just a day or two more and then I'll be up in fine style."

"You'll do nothing of the kind. You'll stay there till I tell you you can get up. And that won't be for at least a week, till I'm satisfied you're really rested. Otherwise—Charleston doctor. So you better take it easy."

It was impossible to do anything else really, she thought as she submitted with a mildly rebellious smile and an inward sigh of relief, luxuriating in his despotic attentions. . . . It was strange and wonderful to be lying in bed with her hair in comfortable braids, every nerve quiet, her whole being relaxed, limp as a rag. This would have been inconceivable if Michael had come home for Christmas. Stephen's starting back to work had liberated in her a tide of energy that had carried her through everything with a rush; but after Marshlands had been restored to the state of home, there had been a series of wearing trips to Land's End to see the people and confer with Biggie about the winter plowing, the cutting and hauling of marsh for the compost piles, and a hundred lesser plantation concerns. So that she had found herself on the threshold of Christmas in a terrible fag. And when it had been decided at the last minute that Michael would not make the long expensive journey home for the holidays, she had suffered a sudden and complete collapse. At first she had struggled weakly to conquer this appalling breakdown of her forces, but she had soon found that her body and mind were decisively on strike: they had seemed to realize that at last they could afford to let go for a spell. And now there was only profound peace. The fire crackling and singing against the cold gray of the world beyond the windows. The Christmas tree shining in the corner to the right of the fireplace. And to the left, the door open to the upper hall so there would be no feeling of being shut off from the rest of home, and so she could see as soon as possible whose step it was on the stairs.

What Stephen called her "genius for worrying" remained shamelessly suspended, but she was beginning to be able to think again. The agitation of deep memories stirred up by the moving from Land's End had not yet subsided; and now this pause in her life, here in the room that she had first known as the bedchamber of General and Mrs. Sager, was giving the long past a chance to catch up with her in quiet earnest, wave upon wave. But she was not swamped in the eddying stream. Her thoughts were like reeds broken from the river marshes beyond the seawall: tossing at the will of random winds and tides, swinging back and forth in whimsical currents of time, yet ever floating light and unharmed. . . . Serene reveries in the end, for wasn't her house in order? Wasn't her whole world, present and future and past, in order? Even the hard sharp years since the storm were losing all their sting; the dark places of the near past were already fading into unreality, to match the dark places of the far past. Those troubles could be viewed with detachment now, and she felt the time had come when she could indulge in a little discreet happiness, savor with thankfulness the great mercy of her success with the plantation and the people and with Stephen.

He was saved. It was inescapable that something vital had died out of his eyes and was gone from him forever, but he was in sure possession of what was left, and that knowledge alone was enough to make the core of life sound and whole again. He was saved and the world was balanced again, centered, its integrity restored. And now from this vantage-ground of bed and suspended activity, rest and peace, she could range her world without fear.

But mostly her thoughts were of Michael, what he was doing and thinking and feeling. He would be sorry of course about Christmas, family Christmas broken for the first time, but he would certainly not be moping; in healthy enjoyment of being on his own in the

North he would be too busy for loneliness. Part of the holidays he was to spend with his roommate, at a place not far from Salem and the old Curtis farm where she had had the happiest times of her own youth. It was such a great comfort to see so clearly the background of his days: in that land of hills there would be snow now and ice, drifted roads and crunching footsteps and frozen breath, frosted window-panes, icicles hanging from eaves and bare branches and from evergreen boughs ladened down with snow. And her Southerner would be having his first chance at skating and toboganing, coasting and sleigh-riding. There would be frost-bitten toes and ears, too, and a cold if he didn't take all the precautions she had underlined in her last anxious letter. And what if he fell sick there among strangers, so far beyond her reach! But he would be careful. He had given her solemn reassurances in his Christmas letter.

He would be at no loss how to spend the Cambridge and Boston part of his vacation. He would browse in the University library. There was the theatre. He had promised to try a concert at Symphony Hall. And he would get acquainted with the great city, from Beacon Hill to the waterfront. . . . In the trance of accompanying him everywhere, she saw herself not as this limp self but as the eager young self that had last known Boston. She felt herself his contemporary there; in fact, he was several years her senior and she was Margaret's sixteen; and so it seemed natural for her to take his arm as they explored the old city together. And sometimes the associations of a particular scene carried her even farther back into the past, and she was a little girl clinging to his hand. . . . Palely she wondered if this vivid resurgence of early memories was an intimation of declining vitality. No, she told herself promptly: for fifty was still a year or two away, and in any case fifty was not old. A few wrinkles perhaps, but scarcely a trace yet of Stephen's "distinguished iron-gray". No, she was not in any sense old; not even weary and worn, really; she was only resting here for a moment to catch her breath and gather strength for the final effort that would carry the children safely over into maturity. When they were all three well established there, standing firmly on their own feet, with homes and families and lives of their own, that would be soon enough for reminiscences of youth and acceptance of time and age. Then she would be willing to let the tide ebb slowly and gently back to the beginning and end.

But not all the time of this pause for breath could be given to musing and reverie, for she was alone only at intervals through the day.

Because of the measles epidemic that had closed school for the first three weeks of December, vacation had been cut to the bone, the bare week-ends of Christmas and New Year's, and Margaret and Jack had to be launched off each morning in response to the doubly irksome warning of a holiday hurry-up bell. When they were out of the way, Lucy came up for the breakfast tray and a conference. And it pleased her to prolong her stay to spite Tunis, who was not allowed to enter till she was ready to leave. Soon after the move from Land's End, and after all the heavy work of getting settled at Marshlands was over, Tunis and Ella had appeared to apply for their old place; and when Stephen had satisfied himself that they were actually out of work and were not deserting another post, they had been taken back, to the great disgust of Lucy.

"But you won't have so much to do," Stephen had smiled at her black pout. "You ought to be glad. It's to your advantage."

"Maussa, t'ain' no 'wantage to hab dem striflin' people humbuggin' roun'. Dey ain' wut fuh tek back nohow. An' us cyan' 'ford'um no mo' suh."

"Suppose you leave that to *us* to decide. As a matter of fact, they've agreed to come back for very low wages."

"Maussa, you ain' know dem crofty nigguh gwine mek-up fuh dat by t'ief bittle suh? Dey gwine pure eat we out! Bad enough when dey was libbin' in yaa'd, but now dey got home of dey-own an' fibe hongry mout' fuh feed an' dey gwine be cyaa'tin' off sugar an' meal an' tea an' coffee an' eb'ry Gawd t'ing fum pantry eb'ry bless ebenin'. On'y dey ain', 'cause I ain' gwine let'um."

"That'll be enough, Lucy. We want you to be able to take things easier from now on,—you've certainly earned it. So they're coming back. And we don't want any fussing, understand?"

"No suh, I ain' gwine fuss wid nobody. I too look down 'pon'um. I know dat Tunis ain' gwine staa't no trouble wid me, less'n he git half hot on dat *Fuss-X* dispens'ry lickuh. An' as fuh dat freemale I jes' ain' gwine pay'um no mind, less'n he git uppety an' I got to tek'um down. Nawsuh, won' be no fussin'."

And there hadn't been. At least none that was audible above stairs. What went on in the kitchen could only be surmised. . . .

The only sign that there was never to be any final peace in this old warfare was the look of uncompromising contempt Lucy gave Tunis as she passed him in the hall, each of these Christmas-week mornings when she carried out the breakfast tray. The pantomime was plainly visible from the bed. Tunis came into the room grinning to show his indifference, bringing an armful of wood for the fire and the grocery order-book, for which the boy from Van Wie's was patiently waiting in the warmth of the kitchen.

By the time Tunis was disposed of, Stephen appeared. The initial drive that had started him to the office by nine, the first few weeks of his new business, had gradually declined and now he seldom got off before ten: a more sensible hour, he explained, because there wasn't enough business yet to justify clashing with Margaret and Jack at the bathroom door and the breakfast table. Fortified by a leisurely hot breakfast and two cups of coffee he was in fine form for delivering a lecture, as he stood at the side of the bed frowning down at her. She was starting the day all wrong: she couldn't be trusted, worrying with housekeeping when she had promised to do, think, and feel nothing: well, she was simply postponing indefinitely her getting-up. And when he had cross-examined and recautioned her, had his tie patted and given her a business-like kiss, he too was disposed of; and the house and the room sighed, and the fire settled down to a meditative companionable singing. . . . Her closed eyes followed him down Fenwick Street to his left-hand turn at the Castle; then the two short blocks to Bay Street, wondering if he was walking ahead of or behind the pace she was setting for him; and so to the Lafayette house and up the old steps to the proud sign at the entrance: *JOSEPH LEGERTON BRAMWELL, ATTORNEY-AT-LAW,* and *STEPHEN B. FENWICK, INSURANCE & REAL ESTATE.* Nothing could match the wonder and importance of the money he had been able to send Michael for Christmas,—the entire sum of his first little commissions, except for a few pieces of change kept to jingle with the key-ring in his pocket. And it was not till she had settled him comfortably in his chair at the office, and brought him in a client, that her thoughts began to waver away to Michael in Boston.

Her musings merged into a nap before the morning was over, but by the time they were all back for two-o'clock dinner she was awake again and expectant. Although Michael had been guarded from any suspicion of her collapse, there was always a chance that he might write something besides his regular Sunday evening letter: a postcard, of Bunker Hill perhaps, with just a word from him. But always she was disappointed, for he was taking literally her injunction that with so much else to do he was not to think of writing oftener than once a week. Yet when Stephen began to sense her disappointment and blamed him, she was quick to defend him and to blame herself for being disappointed.

After dinner Stephen took a little siesta over his *News & Courier* before he went back to the office. He left the paper for her, but she hardly glanced at it, for this was her time with Margaret. Jack made a brief appearance,—to cram his grin with stale popcorn from the festoons on the tree, like a small boy instead of an overgrown lad with a man's hands and jaw and voice, almost fourteen and only two years from the Citadel,—and then dashed off in some unknown direction, as if tarrying for a minute would make him miss something of vital importance; it was more difficult than ever to keep track of Jumping Jack, and it was only Stephen's sporadic discipline that had any curbing effect on him. But Margaret spent most of the afternoon with her. And Margaret was the greatest of comforts. Balanced in nature somewhere between Michael and Jack-in-the-box, good-looking and good-tempered, quick in perception and understanding, she was a most agreeable companion as well as a most satisfactory daughter.

And this helpful person, who had given her so little trouble in growing up, was beyond any question a young woman now with mature findings in her heart and head. During the past year she had become obsessed with the idea of teaching, a final result of her devotion to Miss Mary Hamilton. Summer visits to Penn School had given her a desire to start her teaching with the island children, but the mere mention of this enthusiasm had been enough to call forth a withering blast from Stephen. "Unfortunately I can't speak for your mother," he had told her, "but I can positively promise you that no daughter of mine will ever be caught schoolmarming niggers." However, the roots of the original urge had survived the blast; and now, at the mid-term of her last year at school, she was more anxious than ever to make definite plans. And the opportunity of these Christmas-week afternoons for uninterrupted talks brought the matter to a decision.

579

"I want to *do* something, Mother. I don't want to sit around and be a burden on you and Father, till somebody kindly asks me to marry him and takes me off your hands. Or till I'm an old maid."

"I'm afraid, dear, that isn't a very sound reason for going into teaching."

"Well, of course that isn't the main reason. I really want to teach. I want to do something useful with my life."

"You don't think marriage is very useful?"

"Of course I want to marry someday. But now seriously, don't you think teaching would be a fine thing to do first?"

"The finest kind of thing. And just about the hardest. You realize that, don't you? . . . Your Miss Hamilton has a gift for teaching boys and girls without blighting them or herself. If you've caught the secret from her, if you feel you can teach children without giving them an everlasting distaste for learning, by all means go ahead. I believe you can do it."

"Of course I'll have to go to a teachers' college. Miss Hamilton says Winthrop's the best place. And she says expenses there won't be much. But can we manage even that with all Michael's expenses?"

"I'm sure we can, dear."

"What about Father?"

"We'll manage him too."

"Oh Mamma, you're a darling! . . . I know I can't be like Miss Hamilton, but I can try. And I'll be earning my own living. And I'll be able to help Jack along at the Citadel,—you know *he's* never going to get a scholarship! . . . It is a selfish idea, though, isn't it? I could help you more by staying home, couldn't I?"

"You can help me most by doing what you most want to do."

So at this time it was settled that Margaret was going to Winthrop Normal College, at Rock Hill in the upper part of the state. And Stephen was brought around with much less trouble than had been anticipated. This supine state of bed made a strategic position for persuasion, and he was forced to moderate his objections.

"And you're quite sure," he insisted, "this is her own idea and not yours?"

"Hers entirely."

"It's a safe bet you encouraged it."

"I did."

"I thought so."

After a good deal of grumbling he said finally: "Well, all right, if she's really set on it. I suppose we can swing it somehow. Of course, it's beyond me why she wants to deliberately make an old-maid schoolmarm of herself. Why isn't she satisfied to stay home? Does she realize she's probably spoiling her chances to get married?"

There seemed small danger of that, for already, disturbing and conclusive proof that she was grown-up in earnest, she had two desperate beaux; not school boys but young men of affairs in Beaufort.

"Yes," Stephen scoffed, "and who are they? One's the grandson of a carpetbagger, and the other's a cracker! Fine company for my daughter. Why, they're not even good enough to look at her."

Only one thing upset him as much as these impertinent young men, and that was to find women callers in the house when he got back from the office.

"They wouldn't have had the nerve," he fumed, "to come traipsing here in the old days. Now, because we've been through hard times, they think they can patronize you."

"It isn't that, dear. They just want to be neighborly. We never gave them a chance before."

"And I can't see why you do now. I should think your pride would keep you from stooping to be pally with people you used to hardly speak to."

"I just didn't know them then, or care about knowing them. I had my hands full with you and the children and home. It's a little different now."

"I see. Well, if that's the way you feel, it won't be long before they make you president of the sewing-circle. It'll serve you right. . . . At least they might have the decency to leave you alone while you're in bed!"

Realizing that his irritation was caused, in part at least, by trespassings on his sacred hour-before-supper, she always tried to clear any lingering callers out of the way before he came in. Not that he had anything much to report to her, but he liked to be questioned about his day. It was like a return to the old days, his early business years, the first years of their marriage.

After supper Joe usually appeared to tell her how much better she looked. He always brought one or two of his elaborately droll yarns, with which it was always easy to be amused because his ponderous manner alone was enough to insure their success. But what gave her deep delight was Stephen's revived sense of amusement. Straight-faced and dry, it most often directed its barbs at the heavy underscorings and involved obviousness of Joe's humor. But she was not neglected, particularly in the matter of her old tendency to confuse names.

"We had a call this afternoon," he told Joe one evening, "from Mrs. Hotchkiss."

"Mrs. Hotchkiss?" Joe frowned. "Who is Mrs. Hotchkiss?"

"Well, she's probably still just plain Mabel Hitchcock to you. But we got tired of calling her that, so now she's Mabel Hotchkiss."

"I'm afraid I don't quite get the point."

"Then I'm afraid you're not going to get the point of calling Mrs. Fortner Mrs. Fowler, and Mrs. Fowler Mrs. Fortner, or Foster, or Peabody."

"Peabody? . . . Oh, I see!—of course. Yes, yes, that's a good one, —huh-huh! . . . Don't let him make game of you, Emily."

"Game of *her*? Don't let her make game of us, you mean. And what a game. . . . For example, if you were poor inoffensive Mr. Boutelle, pillar of the Baptist Church and somewhat belated admirer of our Emily,—that potted plant was delivered by the gentleman in person,—how would you like to be referred to as Mr. Belknap? And with no assurance that tomorrow you wouldn't be Mr. Knapsack."

There was no reason, she had to admit through aching laughter, why this should be particularly funny to Joe, or to anyone else; but to her it was something more than funny. It meant that the past was already so healed that merriment, even to the point of tears, was again a normal expression of home.

"Perfect nonsense," she assured Joe.

"And the weirdest part, Joe," Stephen went on, "is that she can call people these strange names to their faces and get away with it. They must like it, because they all come back for more."

When they were satisfied that she had had enough entertainment for an invalid, they turned their attention to the latest developments in the Cuban crisis. Joe was still insisting that intervention was preposterous, and Stephen that it was inevitable. And after the evening's debating started, drowsiness speedily overtook her, so that it was all she could do to keep her eyes open for the series of yawns that were always necessary to acquaint them with her sinking state.

"By George!" Joe would discover with a flush and the help of his fat watch, "I had no idea it was so late. Once again you must forgive me, my dear."

And, when she had assured him that it wasn't late and she wasn't at all sleepy and he mustn't go, he made his eloquent departure. And soon after that all good-nights had been said and she was alone again. With the decorations of the Christmas tree gleaming softly in the last glow from the hearth, with the windows open to dim starlight, with frosty air stealing in to chill the warmth of the room and crinkle the embers of the fire. . . .

But if Jack was still out, doing his homework at the house of one of his chums, she was never able to get to sleep till she heard his voice with Stephen's downstairs. No matter how great a weight of weariness was pressing down on her from the darkness, it was not till the whole house was still that she could surrender to the spell that was to restore a little more of her strength. And even then she was not able to quite let go till she had gathered in all the separate parts of her being, those divisions of her mind and heart waiting near and far in the darkness and quiet.

On New Year's afternoon the curtains of the room were drawn and the tree was lighted for the last time, for the entertainment (much to Lucy's disgust) of Tunis's and Ella's children. Five polished faces and shy grins and five pairs of wide eyes reflected the illumination; five pairs of black hands were quick to grasp the candy canes and cornucopias that Margaret had arranged; and five stricken tongues found speech only at the very end and after considerable prompting. Then there was a perfect shout of thanks.

The following morning the tree was dismantled and the ornaments packed away in the attic to wait for next year, when Michael would surely be home. She hated to see the tree carried off, to be thrown on the ash-heap behind the stable. Each year's tree seemed more beautiful and memorable than the last, and she had become especially attached to this one. The room seemed bare and empty after it was gone, and she told Stephen she was ready to get up. But he refused to even hear of that yet.

However, as a great concession, she was allowed to sit up in bed. So now propped up with pillows and wrapped snugly in Michael's

Christmas present, a knitted jacket of soft wool, she was at least able to catch up with some of her reading and writing.

On the bedside table was a formidable assortment of reading matter. The accumulation of magazines was easily disposed of, but the books were not so lightly dismissed. When Joe had gone to Charleston just before New Year's for meetings of the St. Andrew's, the Huguenot, and the Library Societies, in all of which he held proud life-memberships, he had offered to bring her some books from the Library to "soothe the savage convalescent breast". She had asked him to see if he could get any one of a list of French novels recommended by William Dean Howells, the new Editor of *Harper's*. It was Howells's own fine novel, *A Hazard of New Fortunes,* that she had recently finished reading in installments; and just before her sickness she had reread his *Rise of Silas Lapham* for its scenes of Boston. And it was Howells who had recommended the great Russian novels that she had read in lonely winter evenings at Land's End: thanks to his persuasion and Joe's Charleston Library, she had come to discover Turgenev, Dostoievski, and Tolstoi. . . . And now Joe had brought her not one but all three of the list she had given him: Stendhal's *The Red and the Black,* Flaubert's *Madame Bovary,* and Zola's *The Dram Shop.* To her dismay she learned that they must go back with him when he went on business at the end of the week. And to her further dismay she perceived that procuring them had caused him acute embarrassment.

"You're quite sure these are the titles you wanted?" he asked her with a flush. "They were not on the general circulation shelves at the Library, and since dipping into them on the train, I can understand why,—and why the ladies were taken aback by my request for them."

"Oh, I'm dreadfully sorry, Joe. Are they really that bad, these innocent-looking books?"

"My dear, I'm not addicted to the novel in any form, so possibly I'm not in a position to judge. But if compelled to render a verdict I would, even at a cursory glance, without hesitation and with considerable relish consign them to the flames."

"But you see how censorship works,—already you've whetted my appetite for them. What's actually wrong with them?"

"I struck no passage that I would brand overtly objectionable. It was the tone of each book, the point of view, the *raison-d'être,* that

I found in each instance so reprehensible. On the principle that no book can be better than the man behind it, and using as a standard some such sound example as—say—Edmund Burke and his works, I am forced to the conclusion that the several authors of these books were simply not gentlemen. And I can't see why anyone should elect to consort with them. . . . A case in point. You remember I brought you some Russian novels when you were staying on the island, and there was one entitled, I believe *The Brothers Karamam——*"

"Karamazov?"

"*The Brothers Karamazov*—precisely. Well, in glancing over that one I had a feeling that I was in a madhouse."

"I felt the same way about it."

"Exactly. And I forthwith concluded that the author was a madman, and that his testimony was therefore highly immaterial, impertinent, and irrelevant, to say the least. By a similar deduction I arrive at the conclusion that these French authors must be depraved men. And accordingly I want no traffic with them or their brainchildren. Isn't that logical?"

"Eminently so."

"However, now that we've got them, I hope you'll be able to derive some distraction from them."

"But I don't read for distraction. I'm distracted enough as it is. I read to see how the world looks through other and wiser eyes."

He granted her an indulgent chuckle for that. "My dear, in that case I fear you have three disappointments ahead of you. . . . Well, if no benefit I hope you get at least some sort of enjoyment out of these French concoctions."

And she did, intense and enormous enjoyment. Crowded enjoyment, too, for there were not only the usual interruptions of home but also long letters to be written to Michael. And she read slowly, stopping often to think about the actions and motives of the people and their relationship to her own life and the lives around her. And, greatest impediment of all, in the middle of the week the cold skies cleared and the sun came out warm and brilliant, casting on the pages a light inconsistent with somber scenes and dark events and emotions. So that it required a real effort to finish *The Dram Shop,* the last of the three, in time for Joe when he came for them Friday evening.

"And you actually waded through them?" he asked her with an incredulous smile.

"Actually. And practically word by word."

"And what was the net result?"

"A feeling of slight congestion. And a sense of having survived three devastating experiences. You find me older, sadder, and wiser, Joe."

"On the contrary, I find you younger, gayer, and—more beautiful."

After he had shot his cuffs and settled himself comfortably in his accustomed chair, he cleared his throat and pinched his glasses onto his nose, studying her over them.

"In Charleston, tomorrow," he told her precisely, "I'm going through the preliminaries necessary before introducing Margaret to the society of her peers by way of the St. Cecilia. I trust I have permission to act as your proxy and Stephen's."

"We're honored. And Margaret will be simply delighted."

"It's nothing," he said with a flush and a flourish. "That is, nothing more than her due. And the honor is mine. . . . Tillman's accursed dispensary system has made it necessary for us to accumulate the champagne bottle by bottle, shades of our ancestors! . . . By the way, may I get you *Quo Vadis* from the Library? It's highly recommended. A little on the *Ben Hur* order, I'm told, but more authentic."

"Thank you, sir, but I'm through with books and bed. I've won Stephen's permission to get up tomorrow, and I'm going downstairs Monday morning, at nine sharp."

Sitting up in a rocker before the fire Saturday and Sunday, she used part of her time alone to study the only reading matter she had patience for with release so near: the book of Brahms's last piano pieces that Margaret had given her for Christmas. She was prepared not to be allowed much freedom downstairs at first, and she had to admit to herself that even walking across this room was shaky enough business, but they couldn't deny her the piano.

The rest of her time alone she spent plotting how to outwit Stephen and Joe and their combined solicitude, so that her hands would be free to take a fresh grip on the plantation. For despite their insistence that she must "take things easy now", she felt that this year was the time for a supreme effort. With Michael actually in medical school, Margaret preparing for teachers' college, and Jack not far from the Citadel, it was hardly time yet for relaxing, despite the proud balance at the bank and Stephen's confidence that his business was bound to pick up soon. . . . No matter how much he and Joe objected, she was determined to make this a banner year on the plantation. And she was so sure of her will and strength that she planned to sandwich into her schedule for the spring a good deal of work in the neglected garden.

✓   ✓   ✓

But it turned out that she had underestimated her opponents' determination. Their interference cut her plantation schedule down to one trip a week, at the height of the January plowing and February listing. She made the most of each trip by spending the night at Land's End with Linda for company, and with Margaret and Jack and the dogs if the night was Friday, thus stretching out her time on the island. But even so she had to leave altogether too much to Biggie and ask of Seth, who had his own work to do, much more supervision than he had time for. Last autumn, when she had assured Stephen how easily the plantation could be managed from Marshlands, she had not foreseen all this shifting of responsibility. But now, before the preparations for planting had gone very far, she was forced to realize that her ambitious plans would have to be scaled down to the modest acreage of the smaller fields on the Sound.

So she found her renewed energies engaged this spring not with much planting and a little gardening on the side, but with much gardening and only a little planting.

Since a mere cleaning-up of the grounds was not enough to satisfy her thwarted energies, it was necessary to invent large-scale operations. For a long time she had had a theory in the back of her head that the grounds were too open to the Fenwick Street houses next door. There was the iron fence that Stephen had put up during the flush years to replace the old wooden wall that belonged to the Marshlands of his boyhood and of her early memories of the place; and there were a few deciduous shrubs set at random along the fence. But now, seeing Marshlands with fresh eyes after the years at Land's End, she decided that it was time to extend the evergreen

587

privacy of the summer-house closed garden to include the entire grounds.

Mention of the plan brought immediate protest from Stephen and Joe. It was viewed with alarm not only as too much of an undertaking for her at this time, but also as a sort of desecrating assault upon the natural order of things.

"It's not my affair, Emily," Joe told her, "but I must say it seems to me an ill-advised project."

Stephen was more explicit. "What's the idea of tearing the place up? What's the matter with things as they are? Can't you confine your fidgets to the house? Why can't you just plain take it easy for a while?"

To show them exactly what she had in mind, she spent days making a careful sketch of the grounds as they would look after the changes. She indicated where each wild-olive and Japanese plum and privet of the closed garden screen would go in the new background planting along the fence, leaving the summer-house to stand free in its mantle of wistaria and banksia rose and its skirts of massed azaleas. Then, because it stood a little too free and bare at the end of the west lawn, she sketched in a thin grove of dogwood that would veil the summer-house without hiding it. The dogwood would come from the plantation. And from Land's End would also come holly, and ilex from the dense thickets near the house, to fill out and vary the evergreen of the background. . . . Certain badly placed shrubs and small trees, such as the spindly mimosas on the shady side of the stable, and the stunted old tea-olive cramped against the tabby at the northeast corner of the house, would be moved out where they could have space and sun and air. . . . Paths, bordered with ribbon beds of jonquils and hyacinths, would wind across the lawn to the summer-house; and across the back lawn to and around Michael's cedar tree,—the once forlorn seedling that his childhood hands had proudly brought home to her, its roots wrapped in wet moss, one day long ago when he and Rusty had been on an expedition to the barrier islands. He had planted it for her in the middle of the back lawn, and there it had had to stay, protected with pickets against the yard-boy's careless mower. Twice in the course of its too-rapid growth it had been blown almost flat by storm and wind, but both times it had been successfully righted with stakes and wires. And now it was grown to a brave plume, secure of root and three times as tall as Michael: slender, symmetrical, and very handsome, it stood like an exclamation point among the softer contours. It would be a feature in this new garden that was to expand the walls of home to the fence lines.

"How does it happen," Stephen mocked at the finished sketch, "you're not shuffling any of the live-oaks and magnolias around? Here's a mistake,—surely you didn't mean to leave the twin camellias in their old place flanking the steps. And you're really not disturbing the seawall palmettoes? . . . Well, I can see one advantage in all this. It will shut out the neighbors in more ways than one. After this affront you'll never make the sewing-circle."

But because it was helping to resign her to his plantation restrictions, and because it was too late in the season to do any actual transplanting, he withdrew his opposition to her "fidgetings".

Although for the present all the transplanting had to be done on paper, she found plenty to do in checking over her sketch, revising and amplifying the original plan as enthusiasm and confidence increased, tagging each shrub that was to be moved and staking out its new position, first with the aid of her work-basket tape-measure and then realigning by eye from the focussing angle of the front steps. In laying out the winding paths she had Margaret's help, and was even able to enlist Jack for a few afternoons, on the plea that the complicated system of string-lines and stakes called for the masculine brain and sighting eye of the engineer he was, at this particular moment, planning to become. And when these preliminaries were finished, she plunged into as much of the actual work as could be done now. With the slow and clumsy proxy hands of the yard-boy she began the making of the paths and the narrow trenches for the flanking ribbon beds, and the digging of the scores of holes for the transplantings.

She was constantly seeing these beginnings of the new garden reflected in Michael's surprise and pleasure, when he came home at last: he would have only praise for her. . . . When she paused in her work to reread his latest letter, carried as always with her, she could feel his arm around her shoulder as she explained the rest of the plan to him. And sometimes, in some rare moment of entrancement that was reality in its truest essence, an inner ecstacy would swell to burst the bonds of time and permit her to feel in this garden the presence of his children, see their eyes and hear the magic of their laughter.

By the middle of February she had finished cutting and rolling the paths and digging the trench beds and holes, and had shifted operations to the east lawn and the rose garden. It was here that Stephen found her, directing the tearing up of the old uneven walks and relaying the bricks in sand over a well-tamped base of oyster shell, one day when he appeared early for dinner, with the air of intense casualness he affected when he was excited about something.

She let him take his own time about telling her. After he had thoroughly criticized the laying of the walk and started for the house with her, he waited till she had pulled off her gardening gloves and then handed her his *News & Courier*.

"Handle it gently," he cautioned, "and please keep it away from Jack and the servants. I want to salt it away in the silver-chest for my grandchildren."

When she had scanned the headline with shocked eyes, she turned to him in bewilderment.

"The *Maine?* But how did it happen? What does it mean?"

"How it happened," he smiled grimly, "seems to be a mystery. But there's no question about what it means. It's all that's needed to touch off the war."

And at dinner, after explaining the situation to Margaret and Jack, he told her continued bewilderment: "If you hadn't been too busy with the plantation and your garden to read the paper or listen to Joe and me, you'd have seen this thing coming long ago."

But at first she could think only of the *Maine,* which short months ago had lain peacefully at anchor on the Sound off Land's End, its launches puffing jauntily to Beaufort and back, its bells making a faint tinkle in the late autumn air, its lights at night sending shimmering trails across the water; and of the men, whom she had seen walking in Bay Street, talking and laughing; and of their families. And then—suddenly—of Michael, whose St. Valentine's card Stephen had brought in the mail.

"Are you going to help set Cuba free?" she heard Jack's thrilled voice ask.

"I'm afraid not, son," Stephen smiled. "They'll want new blood for this war. But they may let me do a little recruiting for the old Beaufort Volunteer Artillery."

"Think it'll last long enough for me to get in?"

Stephen shook his head with a chuckle. "Afraid not. When I was your age, I was worried about that too. But this one's bound to be short and sweet,—we're fighting Spaniards, not Yankees, this trip. It's going to be like taking candy from a baby. Or rather, a senile old man. . . . But your brother, well, I suspect he'll have to settle that with his mother."

. . . From that moment through the following weeks she watched the fatal drift toward war. But when it came at last, one day in the flood-tide of spring, she was as unprepared as if it had been totally unexpected.

Joe had brought back from a trip to Charleston a small Stars-and-Stripes on a stick,—in Beaufort there was none of any description to be had for love or money,—and with this miniature banner and Miss Sophie's large Stars-and-Bars he and Stephen and Jack staged a flag-pole ceremony on the front lawn, the day war was declared. She and Margaret and Lucy and Tunis and Ella and the yard-boy were all rallied round the pole to witness the strange flag-raising and Stephen's pistol salute, and to join in a ragged chorusing of the National Anthem and then *Dixie,* led by Joe's booming voice and erratic cane baton. For a finale there were three cheers and a pro-longed barking from all the dogs in the neighborhood.

"My dear," Joe said to her with unashamed mistiness afterwards, as he mopped his flushed face, "the importance of this hour can hardly be exaggerated. I believe this national crisis will do much toward healing, generally throughout the South, the wounds of the War."

"It will be all to the good," Stephen told him, "if they don't send any Yankee bands down here to play *Marching Through Georgia* for us."

She laughed with relief, but Joe was not to be lightly diverted.

"Only this morning," he said, "I was struck with the thought of how Michael stood as a symbol of it all. Just as in his veins flows the blood of North and South, so now the blood of the states is uniting again and blending in the veins of one nation under God." And he

591

added with deep feeling: "Today we all stand blessedly united under these two united flags, whose honor we will defend henceforth as one people."

Against her will her throat tightened instinctively at that, and she had to turn away from him.

"Have I said anything offensive?" he asked Stephen in alarm.

"Gracious no, Joe," she assured him quickly.

"You just picked an unfortunate symbol," Stephen told him with a dry smile. "We're raising our boy to be a doctor, not a soldier. We'll let somebody else's boy have the privilege and responsibility of defending the united nation's honor."

But then he saw her distress and said seriously to her: "Now don't get rattled, honey. I promise you this volunteering business is going to be left strictly to Michael and you."

"But," Joe protested, "I said nothing whatever about Michael's volunteering. On the contrary, I for one wouldn't hear of it. I mean to say, I consider it his duty to continue his professional studies."

"Why even discuss it," Stephen said with finality. "The whole show will be over before he even hears about it, up there in the cloisters of Fair Harvard."

. . . In his letters now there were plenty of indications that the war fever had invaded his cloisters. But though it was evident enough that he was a victim of the general contagion, he was carefully refraining from telling her, and in this one case she was only too willing to let him deny himself for her sake. And as the first phase of the war developed phantasmally out of fragmentary and often contradictory dispatches in the paper,—and as Stephen and Joe fought and reminisced at the office and at home, requisitioned Jack's geography for maps of Cuba and the Philippines, argued over the pronunciation of Spanish names, damned the Government, and prescribed tactics that would end the war in a month,—her tension relaxed, all her energies flowed confidently again, and she began to feel that it had been a little absurd to have feared that the strange and remote maneuvers of this military game constituted any actual threat to the peace of her life, the final hard-won order and surety of her world.

And in the last week of April, just as the first cotton sprouts were beginning to show in the Sound fields, a dazzling stroke of good fortune came to bring the strange game home like a benediction and to buttress the family and all plans against any further money worry.

Since the declaration of war Stephen and Joe had been discussing the prospect of Government activity on Parris Island. A drydock had been constructed there several years ago, but being of wood and faulty design it had promptly warped and rotted, and now the contract for a new concrete war-time drydock was going to the Charleston Navy Yard. But there still seemed to be a possibility of a Marine Corps encampment. So when one morning as he was leaving for the office Stephen told her, as casually as if they were back in the old days of frequent business guests, that he was bringing two men home for dinner, she thought at once of Parris Island and a real-estate commission.

"Now why," he demanded with a frown, "do you have to leap at such wild conclusions? And never mind the buttonhole bouquet, I'm in a hurry!"

"I want to know," she persisted, holding his lapel, "how good a dinner to have. If it's just insurance men from Charleston, I shan't be quite so particular."

"It may be nothing," he told her with a noncommittal shrug. "But you better have a good dinner because Joe's coming too." And he added: "Better make it late, we're stopping by his house on the way. . . . *No,* I'm not taking anything—as usual."

"I'm not worried," she said with a flushed smile. "And I promise you a good dinner, if you're not too late."

They were very late. But she had allowed for that, so the planked shad was not ruined when they finally appeared in a carriage hired for the occasion. But when she went to the door to meet them, to her acute confusion Stephen presented not insurance men from Charleston but Government officials from Washington.

"Dear, this is Captain Logan of the Engineer Corps. And Mr. Pendleton of the War Department. And they're both hungry as wolves."

They proved to be extremely amiable gentlemen, beamingly redolent of Joe's old bourbon; but her heart was pounding so hard that it was a struggle to keep her end of the first weather pleasantries from sounding as excited as a discussion of Spanish atrocities. And when she took her place at the table, with Captain Logan on her right and Joe on her left, she could only pretend to eat. But, mercifully, Stephen came to her rescue before she was reduced to jibbering idiocy.

"Gentlemen," his voice came at last from the other end of the table, "with your indulgence I think it's time we took Mrs. Fenwick into our confidence, she being the high contracting party of the first part. . . . Dear, the people of the United States, through these duly appointed agents, are offering you roughly eight thousand dollars for forty-odd strategic acres of Land's End. The parcel is bound by the praise-house woods to the south, by the Cherokee line to the north, by the main plantation road to the east, and by the Sound to the west. All you have to do is sign your name to the deed that Joe has drawn up for us."

In the shock of the moment she could only say: "But those are the very acres we've just planted. And the cotton's already up."

That made everyone laugh.

"Gentlemen," Stephen chuckled, "I'm afraid the deal is off!"

"As a matter of fact," Joe hastened to reassure her, "that item was generously allowed for in framing the transaction."

"Now," Stephen smiled, "is it a deal?"

"If you and Joe approve," she told him, rallying at last, "the deal is closed."

After that it was dizzily easy to talk to Captain Logan and Mr. Pendleton. And when it was all over, after the deed had been signed and Joe had left with the amiable gentlemen to conduct them back to their quarters at the Sea Island Hotel, she went with Stephen into Michael's den off the living-room and released her pent-up joy and tears in his arms.

"Why, darling, why didn't you give me some warning? The shock was terrific!"

"Better than a terrific disappointment, wasn't it?" he asked as he hugged her. "I couldn't tell you because it wasn't settled till this morning. Not such a bad surprise, was it, honey?"

"I'll be able to tell you about that when I recover, and can take it all in. Oh, darling, how did you ever do it?"

"Well, when you get down to cases, you did it. But we won't go into that big subject just yet. Joe did most of the talking. And the Captain and Mr. Pendleton did the rest. About all I did was worry. . . . And now there'll be no more worrying for you. And no more planting, thank God. Only cakes and ale from now on. . . . And it looks as if we might also collect commissions on some little Parris Island deals with the Government. Not such a bad war after all, is it? . . ."

The temptation to advise her to invest the money in war stocks was too strong for him; he seemed to try to resist it, but after a brief struggle he was telling her how easily—if she moved fast—the money could be doubled before summer, when he expected the war to be over. But he was a little sheepish about it, as if admitting he was acting under compulsion. And when she gently but firmly held her ground, that part of the great windfall should be used to finish paying off the Land's End mortgage and the rest should go soberly into the savings account, he gave in with a shrug and an expression of relief, though for the sake of his pride he still had to reproach her for passing up a practically sure thing.

"And," he concluded, "the fact that I once had a bad break of luck doesn't mean my judgment is worthless, you know."

"Of course not, dear. But don't you really think we better err on the side of caution?"

"Suit yourself. After all, it's your money."

"Oh no it isn't. It's ours."

"Well, I'm not willing to take the responsibility of arguing you into something you don't like the looks of. Even if it does mean passing up the chance of a lifetime."

With plantation work cut off completely now and gardening suspended till autumn, there was nothing to do but watch the sudden excitement and activity around her. The town looked almost like the bustling war-time Beaufort of her youth. The waterfront was lined with boats, the wharves loaded with supplies, and there were uniforms again and commissary wagons and drays in crowded Bay Street. The stores were doing a land-office business, and the Sea Island Hotel was packed with officials and strangers. A Marine Corps encampment had been established on Parris Island. And loads of materials and tons of stone had already been lightered to Land's End, where the Sound fields were becoming "Fort Fremont".

One day she went out to the island with Stephen and Joe to see the progress of the work. In the short weeks since the sale of the property a network of streets had been made across the trampled fields of young cotton. Captain Logan conducted them over the site, showing them the rows of barracks, the landing wharf, the observation tower, and the big masonry displacements where three ten-inch disappearing guns were to be mounted. It was all very impressive, but her eyes could not escape the mute rebuke of these ravaged fields which had served her so well and which she had rewarded by signing them away forever into this strange bondage: from now on they would bear not life-giving crops but a malignant growth, a plant of death and destruction. The sense of guilt and confusion became so intense that she had to keep reminding herself of the constructive uses to which the money would be put, for Michael's medical education and Margaret's teaching and Jack's engineering. And as an additional quietus there was the immediate good that was flowing to the island people from the sacrifice of the fields; scores of the needy were exchanging their labor for Government cash wages. Yet it was impossible to shake off a sense of depression and bitter irony about the sale, and a deep regret that the same results could not have come from her own continued planting efforts instead of from this evil chance advantage of war.

At first she kept these misgivings strictly to herself. But toward the end of May, when Michael's letters began suddenly to display warning signals that he was frantic to volunteer, it seemed a confirmation of her forebodings and she confessed to Stephen what had been on her mind since the visit to Fort Fremont.

"It's not at all like you to nurse superstitious feelings," he told her lightly. "Don't you realize the Government takes what it wants whether you feel like selling or not? If it actually bothers you to see your fields turned into a fort, ease your conscience by figuring that you saved somebody else's fields from such a fate—and such a nice tidy little profit. After all, you know, it's a fort for home defense. Or would you have us welcome the Spanish fleet in, if it comes knocking at our door? . . . I hate to admit it, honey, but I'm no nearer understanding how that head of yours works than I was twenty years ago. If you keep letting absurd and far-fetched qualms worry you in this hard life, you'll simply wind up in an asylum. All I know is that we were damn lucky to make the sale. Why can't you let it go at that and take it easy? . . As for Michael, leave him to me. Something tells me he's going to want to get back to that surveying job with the feldspar company the minute he gets out of college. But if he comes home with a Harvard accent, it'll be safer for him in Cuba with the Spaniards than in North Carolina with those mountaineers."

So she left Michael to him. And though she could only guess at what correspondence passed between them, the results were better than she had dared hope. In the last letters from the North there were no more names of classmates who had enlisted, no more hints that he was desperate to join them, no more mention of the war. And his final letter told that he had arranged to go back to his job of past summers.

Almost before she could breathe a sigh of thankfulness and relief, he was home. But she scarcely had time to look at him before he was gone again: he stayed only one night, just long enough to smile at his family's excitement, see Linda for a moment, and pack and repack; then he was off for the Asheville country, where, Stephen assured her, they didn't even know that Grant had taken Richmond. . . . It gave her heart a wrench, this glimpse of him after all the long months of waiting; but her joy at his being safely removed to the mountain country, far from war talk and enlistment fever, was enough to make up for everything else.

And he was out of the way just in time. For a day or two after he left, the town had a scare that started an epidemic of enlistments. While the *News & Courier* was still celebrating Dewey's great victory at remote Manila Bay, people suddenly began to wonder where Admiral Cervera was. It was known that the second Spanish fleet was lurking somewhere in the Atlantic, but now there were wild rumors that it was prowling along the Southern seaboard, preparing to strike Charleston, Port Royal, Savannah, Tampa, and New Orleans. Nervous shivers ran up and down the coast, and Beaufort was in an uproar. Was there to be another gun-shoot at Bay Point? Another invincible armada steaming into the Sound? Another sacking of the town? . . . Stephen was sardonically amused: What justice it would be to see the carpetbagging element fleeing and refugeeing! And he and Joe laughed at the panic at Jekyll Island, a sea island below Savannah which had lately become a winter resort and game preserve club for Yankee bankers; they were screaming through their Georgia congressman that the Atlantic squadron be recalled from Cuban waters and distributed up and down the coast. But neither he nor Joe were worried about Beaufort: Fort Fremont was not yet completed, but the three disappearing guns had been mounted and manned; and a naval tug had sown the harbor with mines, connected with a switchboard at the fort.

And all that came of the scare were several weeks of feverish suspense. And the accidental throwing of a ten-inch shell, during a morning of overzealous practice at Fort Fremont, across the Sound to Hilton Head, frightening the island people there out of their wits. And finally the news that Admiral Cervera was bottled up in Santiago Harbor.

And then, at the end of July as she and Lucy were finishing the fig-preserving, the war was suddenly all over.

"Just as you predicted," she reminded Stephen in the midst of the rejoicing.

"And if we'd taken a little flyer in cotton," he told her, "we'd have doubled our money, just as I said. And I'm afraid we've cheated Michael out of a pension. But we can't complain. The fort deal, my little Parris Island commissions, and Michael intact. What more could you ask of a war? . . . And Cuba free, and Porto Rico and the Philippines as good as in the bag. We're a spread-eagle for true now, a colonial empire, a world power. That ought to make some of those European birds sit up and take notice. And hardly a man lost on our side, in naval engagements at least. Of course there's a howl about the army's embalmed beef and yellow fever losses, but you can't expect a war to be a complete picnic. And anyway it's not the Fenwicks' fault, or loss."

It was true. Whatever the war had meant to others, to the Fenwicks it had been pure profit. When the Sound fields had been converted into Fort Fremont she had bemoaned the loss of her already sprouting cotton, yet even that loss was transformed into a gain. For a terrible "dry-drought" was parching all the sea-island fields and wasting the labor of the people. In June the cotton had nowhere grown beyond the sprout stage; on July 15th, St. Swithin's Day, there had been no signs of rain; and now, as August opened, the drought was breaking all records and still going strong. Last year at this time the cotton at Land's End had stood almost to her shoulders and touched across the aisles, but this year the cotton in the people's patches came barely to her knees, was hopelessly stunted and withered. And the provision crops were ruined, too. There were more than the usual number of fish peddlers on the streets of

Beaufort, singing the old songs of "swimp" and "sof'-crob" and "blockfish an' whitin'"; but this summer there were no "I gots gyaa'den on my haid" women, gracefully balancing baskets of vegetables and flowers.

"Now don't fret yourself about the people," Stephen said; "they don't need sympathy. You let them out of their rents, isn't that enough of a contribution from us? And plenty of them got good government wages out of the fort. They'll make out all right."

She awaited the end of Michael's summer work in the mountains without anticipation of anything more than another tantalizing glimpse of him. And when he came home, he had even less time than she had expected, only a few hours before his return to the North. And even this precious flash of him she had to share calmly with the rest of the family and Joe, and with Linda.

Joe's introduction of Margaret to Charleston society, by way of the St. Cecilia ball last spring, had produced invitations, several correspondences, and at least one serious beau,—Bill Beckwith, a determined young man bent on preventing Margaret from entering Winthrop Normal College, which he seemed to regard as a sort of convent. But Michael had proved a poor social disciple for Joe; the young ladies of Charleston had left him cold. He remained faithful to Linda. And now he was plainly frantic because he could have only a glimpse of her and then must leave her in the midst of the pack of Engineer Corps and Artillery officers posted at Fort Fremont, who spent most of their spare time hanging around the Robinson farm as if it were an army canteen. On his flying trip home in the early summer he had overlooked these rivals, but in the mountains he had had plenty of time to realize the situation, and he was worried. His last words at the station made that clear.

"Keep an eye on her for me, will you, Mother?" he asked with a forced lightness in the few moments she had alone with him before train time. "She's a steady one, but all those brass buttons might turn her head, even if there is supposed to be safety in numbers."

But then, just at the end, he spoke her thoughts. "We haven't had much of a chance to see each other, have we? But don't forget I'm positively coming home this Christmas, and then you and I are going off by ourselves. Yes sir, we'll make up for this at Christmas."

And from that moment she started to live for Christmas.

X

AFTER MICHAEL LEFT it was only a few days before Margaret too was gone, to Winthrop College; and she was left with a family reduced to Stephen and Jack, neither of whom needed her attention except for a few stray moments of each day.

But she had plenty to do to fill these autumn days to the brim. While she was waiting for a black frost to still the flow of sap in the garden for her transplanting, she gave the house some attention. At the beginning of their tenancy the Fowlers had demanded stoves for the living-room and dining-room, and the ugly objects continued to squat untidily on their squares of tin, reaching tin flues into fireplace shields of tin. She was bent now on getting rid of the unsightly stoves and unsealing the old fireplaces. But Stephen objected; open fires might have been all right in the old days but winters were colder than they used to be and blood was thinner and he liked the warmth of the stoves. Joe suggested cutting the generous fireplaces down to the dimensions of cozy coal grates, as he had done at the Castle. But she longed for the fireplaces as they had been, and to recover them she presented Stephen with an extravagant solution: the complementary heat of a small furnace. He made no objection to parting with the stoves on that basis and promptly consulted Turner Brothers, who recommended either a big steam furnace with radiators in every room or a hot-air furnace with registers cut through all the floors and ceilings. He seemed to think that either of these elaborate and expensive systems would be a good investment; but when it developed that neither the pipes of one nor the flues of the other could be hidden in the walls without taking the house apart, that all pipes or flues must be exposed, she was able to convince him that both heating systems would be far more disfiguring than the stoves. And in the end he agreed to her solution: a modest little hot-air furnace with one main register in the downstairs hall, which with the open fireplaces would heat the house well enough to warm thinner blood against colder winters.

So the stoves were removed and sold to help pay for the furnace. And after it was installed, she proposed to Stephen that the house shamefully needed painting. Although he admitted the place was in bad shape, he felt it could wait one more year; but when pressed he gave his consent to an estimate. And then, after the outside was finished in gleaming white, she was able to coax him into having the inside freshened up, the paneled rooms painted, the other walls and all the ceilings kalsomined. With the result that Marshlands looked like new, lovely and proud, to welcome Michael home at Christmas.

By the time the work on the house was done, November had come and it was safe to begin the transplantings she had planned in the spring. She imported Biggie and the Twins, Barty and Ned, from the island and put them up in the Quarter in the yard; they went back to the plantation on Saturdays and Sundays, but the rest of their time was hers for a solid month. And without the help of these three powerful and willing men she would have been lost, for this reshaping of the garden, which had seemed such a simple matter on paper, proved in fact to be a tremendous task.

From early morning till dusk each day she lived for weeks in a trance of driving purpose, leaving the garden only for a little while at noon, trusting Lucy to run the house, and resisting Stephen's every protest. Sun and wind and grime kept her face chapped and smarting, and despite work gloves her hands were painfully blistered and cracked. And at night, after she had written Michael or Margaret, she was almost too tired to get to bed. But through it all she was conscious of a pervading and sustaining serenity, a peace of spirit that she felt was deeper and surer than any she had ever known. And each day saw the work a little farther advanced, bringing Christmas and Michael that much nearer home.

By Thanksgiving she could stand at last at the front steps and survey the outlines of the plan achieved, the background screen an accomplished fact in spite of drastic prunings, the whole grounds a closed garden now, open only to the dreaming river and the marshes and the Ladies Island shore.

✓ ✓ ✓

One gray afternoon early in December she was in the stable sort-ing and counting bulbs collected from random corners of the garden and spread out on the floor, calculating how many dozens of new bulbs she would need to order from the seed catalogs for the beds bordering the lawn paths, when Joe appeared. He had just re-turned from a trip to Charleston, and it was obvious from his ex-pression and bearing that he was bringing her something besides an armful of yellow and white chrysanthemums, the last blooms from his garden. While in Charleston he had attended a special meeting of the St. Cecilia Society: the Boston Symphony Orchestra was planning a Southern tour during the holidays, and the Society was sponsoring a concert at the Academy of Music on the evening of the twenty-third of December. As a member of the Society he was privileged to make reservations in advance of the general public, and since there would undoubtedly be a stampede for tickets for such a major musical event, quick action was advisable.

The news went straight to her heart. Flushed with delight she promised Joe to let him know at the earliest moment how many tickets the Fenwicks would need, and after he had gone she went into the house to write Michael and Margaret at once. That evening she was unable to enlist the interest of either Stephen or Jack; they both flatly refused to be "dragged to a concert", so two members of the party had to be counted out at the beginning. And two days later came Margaret's answer, saying that she had already accepted an invitation to stay with her roommate at Columbia for a very important dance on that date. But a letter from Michael more than made up for these disappointments. By cutting a class or two, he wrote, he could get to Charleston on the afternoon of the twenty-third instead of the twenty-fourth. So in plenty of time to reserve good seats she was able to tell Joe that there would be only two in the Fenwick party.

However much she regretted that the rest of the family were going to miss this great event, it was impossible not to be overjoyed when she realized how perfectly chance had arranged things for her. Once home Michael would have to be shared with everyone, but for

602

those hours in Charleston he would be hers alone. And Stephen's understanding helped to relieve her feeling of selfishness, the element of distress in her delight.

"Now just curb yourself for once," he told her the day he came home from the office with the two tickets Joe had bought for her, "and don't spoil your pleasure by lamenting because your whole crew isn't in on this. It's worked out fine,—you'll have the concert and Michael all to yourself. And don't think I don't know what that means to you."

But there was still one catch: the difficulty of making time pass. Two solid weeks stood in the way, and with gardening finished it was a problem to find enough to do to divert her eagerness. Advance preparations for Christmas were too soon disposed of, and that left only her own personal preparations. For the past five years she had been living on the wardrobe of prosperous days, remodeling old dresses as she needed them; now, with Lucy's help, it took no time to make over her best winter dress. And the Persian-lamb jacket and toque that Stephen had given her, at the high tide of Fenwick & Co., would do as they were without altering: the cut of the coat was a little old-fashioned and the hat a little too trim for present styles, but Michael wouldn't mind that. Her face and hands needed careful attention, and she studied herself in the mirror more closely than she had for years, in her anxiety to look her best for him. Yet when she had done what she could with a weather-beaten and veteran complexion, had spruced herself up to an appearance as presentable as possible for his sake, and was ready, there was still a whole set of days left before the twenty-third.

But at last this fretsome time obstacle was disposed of and she was really living the scenes she had been enacting over and over in her thoughts and dreams. It was the day itself. She was dressing for the actual journey. Stephen had come back early from the office in a carriage and was taking her to the station for the noon train. Then she was in her seat, Stephen was waving from the platform, the train was moving. . . .

Her old friend Conductor Gilroy, big and hearty as ever, was acutely embarrassed at collecting a ticket fare from a Fenwick instead of honoring a pass with a tip of his hat. He lingered at her seat like a benevolent jumbo, the tight silver frame of his spectacles imbedded in his temples and the broad bridge of his nose like fence wire in a tree. He made elaborate inquiries about every member of the family, and in return gave her particulars about his children and grandchildren.

When he was gone, she tried to settle down and relax: excitement had allowed her hardly a wink of sleep the night before, and she hoped now to rest a little. But it was no use. The muffled roar of the train, the creaky sway of the car, the clacketing of the wheels and the jumble of voices refused to blend into a hypnotic spell or even a monotonous accompaniment for her thoughts: they remained immediate and insistent. And beyond the window the December fields and woods, gray with a warm mistiness that threatened more rain and a humid Christmas, only made her eyes more wakeful and alert. Finally she gave up trying to rest and surrendered to the mounting joy and agitation of seeing Michael, in his train, speeding to meet her.

At Charleston she found herself confronted by a final obstacle: his train was an hour late, and that meant a wait of almost two hours. Coming at the crest of her expectancy even so little an extra delay seemed an age.

For a time she tried to sit passively in the waiting-room, watching the life of the station, the faces, somber and bright, young and old, that moved past her under the phlegmatic eyes of the clock. And at first every face was sharp and interesting, touching her with old regret at the absurdity of barriers that kept the faces of even the most kindred-seeming fellow travelers the faces of strangers. But soon all faces began to blur against the newsstand and the ticket windows, the constantly opening and closing doors to the smoking-room, the restaurant, the gray street; till presently people and their luggage were like stray wisps of smoke caught in the eddies of some demented wind. A sense of discomfort beset her, a sense of confusion and loss, and a sudden rebellion against the hardness of the bench, the damp-smelling cindery air of the big room, and the cold imperturbable stare of the clock. She roused herself to take her bag across to the check-room counter; and when she had freed herself of its hampering company (not without a twinge of extravagance, for it was hard to remember that not every penny needed pinching now), she pushed open the heavy door to the street.

After she had passed through a cordon of cabmen and bootblacks and beggars, she found herself in a district of warehouses and work-shops, grubby little hotels and grocery stores. Beyond this dingy area lay the cobblestoned streets and faded mansions of "Mazÿck-borough", once one of the most elegant quarters of the city. It was a neighborhood with which she had long been familiar from train and cab glimpses, but now she was offered a chance to become better acquainted.

A chance to become intimately acquainted, she presently discov-ered, for the blocks of tenement mansions withheld few secrets from the passerby. Although it was late afternoon, the heavy gray air of this unseasonable day was still mild and most of the doors and win-dows were open, revealing murky hallways and the wretched fur-nishings of rooms that were homes for whole families. And their life, ragged and filthy and unashamed, harsh and clamorous against the impotent dignity of the scarred and dying old houses, overflowed into the squalid yards and refuse-littered streets. . . . When she had left the station for a quiet walk with her expectancy through this old quarter of the city, she had hardly bargained for this collision with slum humanity. In these forgotten back streets it was evident that there were no laws of segregation, no White and Colored signs. All vital barriers were down: packed together by dire poverty the races lived shoulder to shoulder, with no room left for pretensions or dis-tinctions. There were only human beings here, standing with their backs against a last wall, and it was a triumph merely to survive.

Yet it was the houses rather than the people that roused her com-passion as she walked on through the swarming streets. These pale relics of glory,—so far removed from their fellows in the lower city, those lucky other mansions that had been redeemed and were cher-ished now as of old, their gardens in bloom again,—these ghosts of the feudal South had never recovered from the cataclysm of Recon-struction, and they seemed to know they were never to be rescued from adversity and dishonor. They all wore the same expression of desolation and despair, as if they were mourning their lost youth and their vanished families, and shrinking in shame and disgust from the spawn of their present plight. Doomed to basest oblivion, they seemed to be striving to hasten extinction, to bury themselves in their own decay and corruption. Their faces and hollow eyes haunted her. . . . There were haunting human faces and eyes: faces twisted into grotesque masks by vice and disease, eyes dead with betrayal or sullenly alive with fear and hate: eyes and faces that revealed at a glance the depths of poisoned souls. But most of the faces she glimpsed in passing were in no sense haunting; they were arresting, but only because of a certain quality they all possessed, a quality of essential hardness and skeletal strength, a kind of lean and final endurance, as if every weakness and softness had been beaten out of them long ago. And this was particularly true of the young. Not surprisingly so in the boys, toughest of toughs, cursing the passage of every vehicle that interrupted their gutter ball. But shocking in the girls. They looked at you from their shrill-voiced sidewalk games with hard sharp challenging eyes that froze pity. Their insolent and penetrating glances proclaimed a knowledge and understanding of life that made them your masters. Even when she encountered a youthful face of beauty, shining like some flower in this rank growth of weeds, she was repulsed by this quality of hard vitality and wisdom. There was no call for pity here, she told herself: the pupils in this school of hard knocks and grim realities were being well trained to shift for themselves. Pity might better be reserved for their contemporaries growing up in the gentler traditions of the lower city, children playing now under the watchful eyes of nurses in Battery park and in cloistered gardens, those favored youngsters who would someday have to meet and compete, in an increasingly democratic South, with the resourceful graduates of "Mazÿck-borough".

That thought, she realized vaguely, was nothing more than petty defense against the impact of these cruel streets. She had come here to pass time, to walk and be alone with her secret joy, not to be shocked by a spectacle of human degradation, slum scenes worthy of Zola. She was unwilling to be disturbed, to feel any pang for lives less fortunate than her own. She felt she had earned the right to keep at least this high hour of life free from painful entanglements, disruptive and futile intrusions. . . . But then, walking safely with Michael through these noxious regions, she saw that she was the in-truder. Yet she stubbornly rejected the impulse to retreat. It would be no farther now, she told herself, to continue on a roundabout way back to the station.

She was still deep in the quarter when dusk overtook her. It was a dusk thick with mist, so that as the street-corner lamps came on, their beams were restricted to luminous little pools, while the rest of each block was submerged in heavy shadows. The district of generously-spaced old mansions was behind her now; she was in a neighborhood of small brick houses pressed tightly into solid rows along narrow sidewalks. And these streets were relievingly quiet after the racket she had passed through: there were no clamor and confusion of children's games, no shrill snatches of gabbling older tongues, no distracting jolt and rattle of wheels over cobblestones. Most of the houses were dark and hushed; and when at intervals a window or a doorway sent a frail glow of light and a muffled accompaniment of voices across her path, these subdued interruptions deepened the obscurity and silence ahead. Once a burst of laughter from a back yard broke the muted shadows around her, and in the next block, in a house displaying a *ROOMS* sign under a dim red light, a piano jangled mechanically; yet even these sounds seemed only to accent the stillness that enveloped this strange neighborhood like some nostalgic dream of city nightfall. With a dog's sleepy barking substituted for the persistent flat monotonings of the piano, she could easily have imagined herself walking home after dark in Beaufort, instead of pacing away the time to Michael in these mysterious back streets of Charleston.

It was only after she had passed a pair of startling figures standing together under a corner light,—one a haggish white woman with scarlet lips and cheeks, the other a young colored girl with a face painted to match her companion's,—that she awoke to the true nature of these byways. Mystery then speedily dissolved in the sinister cat-like shadows of doorways and alleys, and she quickened her pace. But the uneven and broken pavement made haste treacherous; and after she had bumped into a lurching apparition, a man with a cap pulled down over his eyes, she proceeded with caution, leaving the sidewalk for the street when she heard steps coming toward her through the misty mid-block gloom or saw forms ahead under the corner lights. In one block while she was making one of these fantastic detours out into the street, the clopping approach of a cab from behind sent her back to the sidewalk, and when the cab passed and drew up to the curb to discharge its passenger, she had to stop to avoid interrupting his hearty doorstep welcome by a beaming and unmistakable madam. When the door closed and the cab moved away, she hurried on, thinking of what Stephen would say and Michael's shock if they knew the dismally ridiculous predicament she had walked into, if they could see her—on this great eve of the Boston Symphony concert—attending the waking-up-for-the-night of Charleston's red-light district.

The sense of the ridiculousness of her predicament faded as the sense of its dismalness deepened. She was beginning to lose confidence in her sense of direction; and as the cab with its sound and solid clopping and its twin lamps, dim but reassuring lodestars in this murky maze, moved away from her, she resisted a panic impulse to call after the driver. She determined, instead, to keep the cab in sight: if it was not heading for the station at least it would lead her to some thoroughfare where she could get her bearings. At the end of the block she found the cab halted under the corner lamp, the driver counting his fare. He thrust the coins back into his pocket when she came into the light, and she could feel his suspicious scrutiny as she paused to glance to the right and left for the lights of the station plaza. Disappointed again, she resisted a second impulse to turn to the cab, assuring herself that she must be near the station now. But when she hurried tiredly on into the next block, she felt actual fear in the cold shadows lurking ahead and closing in behind her; and the thought that Michael's train might come in while she was still wandering in this back-street labyrinth unnerved her decisively. When the cab caught up with her, she hailed the driver. He peered down at her from his perch, hesitated, then tipped his hat and reached back to open the door. "Please take me to the station," she told him as she got in. The cab was upholstered with hard slippery grease-slick leather and smelled like a livery-stable, but she sank back in the seat as gratefully as if she were resting on down cushions.

To her chagrin the station proved to be a journey of only two blocks, a right turn and then a trolley-track street to the gloomy lights of the plaza, but she was glad to give her black rescuer a liberal tip and the promise of a fare to the Charleston House when the train from the North came in. There was still a half-hour's wait, she discovered in the station; but, spent and chastened, she was content now to mark time patiently in the staring brightness. When she had redeemed her bag from the check-room, she settled in a corner well back from the lane of traffic, wondering why she had felt any urge to escape the impassive face of the clock and the drifting people.

She had fully recovered her composure when the train at last came in. But when she hurried out to the platform, her heart began to beat wildly in the clanging panting glare of the engine. She started down the platform; but, fearful of losing him in the press of people, turned back, put down her bag near the station door, and took her stand there. The platform's string of dim globes and the succession of pale squares from the car windows were weakened to impotent haze by the fogginess, so the people were only obscure forms without distinguishing features. But straining her eyes against the dazzling glare of the headlight she caught a glimpse of one approaching form and singled him out at once by instinct. As her throat tightened with joy, he was lost to her for a breathless moment in a cloud of steam from the engine. When he emerged, his tall frame leaning with the weight of his suitcase, he made his way toward her through the crowd, though it seemed a full minute before actual recognition came into his face. And then, despite all her resolution, a sudden absurd mist blurred and haloed the lights as his grin came toward her.

That perverse mist, strange irrational expression of her happiness, was a recurrent problem from then on. It reappeared at the most disconcerting instants, when she was smiling with perfect assurance, when she was most confident that it had passed for good. She finally had to resign herself to its persistent returns and concentrate on suppressing it quickly, hiding its shining confusion as best she could.

It obscured her vision when they came out of the station and he asked, "How about this one, Mother?", as her puzzled cab-driver pressed forward to claim them. And again at the desk of the Charleston House, when he took charge of registering. When they were alone in the rooms, the secret pressure seemed reasonable, for she was sure these were the same connecting rooms that Rusty had reserved on the first trip to Flat Rock, one long-ago summer when Michael's head came only to her waist. But it was senseless that at dinner, in the very midst of realizing finally how complete his manhood was, how steady and assured and frankly adult his eyes and smile had become, how well he talked, without hesitation or strain, the last traces of self-consciousness gone, and how alert and vigorous he looked (though too lean and admittedly a little fagged from studies and the remnant of a cold), it was exasperating that she had to avoid his eyes so often.

But the real struggle to conceal this treacherous mist began at the concert.

They had planned to walk the few blocks from the hotel, but it was drizzling and they had to take a cab, driving in style over to glistening King Street, where many of the stores were still open for late Christmas shopping, show-windows gaily challenging the umbrellas and drab forms silhouetted against decorated brightness. After the chill silver wetness of the street the golden warmth of the Academy of Music seemed doubly cordial. They found themselves in good middle seats, and early enough to see most of the audience arrive. . . . It was a gala night for Charleston: everyone was here in finest feathers. Michael recognized some of them, people he had met in his Citadel schooldays. And when Joe appeared with his sisters, and had ushered them ceremoniously into front seats (where Miss Susan sat rigid while Miss Isabel stared round as she pleased), he came back to greet Michael and lingered to talk, at flushed and consequential random as he nodded to numerous acquaintances, near and far, and identified each in expansive whispers. So the concert approached in a slow rising tide of faces and voices. An erratic distracting crescendo that blunted her awareness, separated her from Michael, and seemed even to dissolve all sense of personal identity as it mounted at last to the stage, as the orchestra came on singly and in groups and joined the discord, mocking and multiplying the confusion of tongues with their tuning. While she was trying to make sense of her program, this primeval babble reached a culminating high; then subsided with anticipation. *Franz Kneisel, Conductor,* she was reading, when a break of applause swept the audience like a sudden invasion of rain, and she looked up to see a wiry little man stride onto the stage. On his podium he bowed brusquely, abruptly turned his back, and raised his arms for silence. When he was satisfied with the hush, his baton clicked, his arms lifted again.

And then in the twinkling of an eye, with the opening chords of Beethoven's Fifth Symphony, the world was transformed. For an instant she was thrown back upon herself by the impact of the music, every sense tingling with the strangeness and wonder of being at last actually here. But after that flash of solitary consummation she was lifted to full awareness of the miracle of Michael's presence, his nearness, his tangible closeness; and from there her awareness expanded with the music to embrace the people round her. Expressions of separateness began to dissolve in the great crucible of sound. Faces seemed to combine and flow together, fusing with the lights and contours of the hall, so that finally every listening entity was drawn into the music stream. And as the first magnificent movement came to an end, and the *andante* emerged and swept onward into the *scherzo,* the very walls were pushed back and the flood roamed a world confined only by the skies. Like the Sound at Land's End, the sea at Bay Point, the river at Marshlands, the music held all moods: sun and radiant warmth, gentle clouds and soft fragrant rain, moonlight and brooding waters, muffling dripping fog, cold and bleak stars; and dark troubled waters and blasting storm clouds, turmoil of writhing shadows, winds of despair and doom. But at last all weathers and all moods were gathered up in one mighty concord and harmony. Out of the long conflict of titanic forces an unconquerable will ascended to overwhelm and dominate the old dark chaos of the world, a deathless glory flamed up to light the way, and all hearts beat together, all minds aspired as one, all voices were united in a final triumphant hymn of courage and faith.

After the last heroic beats of this great music of darkness and light, conflict and triumph, it was a long moment before she came to herself. Then as the audience recovered its many identities in the disruptive downpour of applause, faces lapsing with a babble of relief into separateness and the releases of intermission, she realized that Michael had been having a struggle of his own to conquer a fit of coughing. He reassured her with a flushed grin.

"Train dust, I guess."

She blamed herself for not having sensed his discomfort. "It's all cleared up now," he smiled at her concern. But he agreed to go out for a drink of water.

While he was gone Joe came back to sit with her, but she knew he had Charleston acquaintances to greet and she insisted upon his going on out to the lobby. That gave her an opportunity to study her program notes and anticipate its two remaining marvels, the Prelude and *Liebestod* from Wagner's *Tristan and Isolde* and the Shepherds' Music from Bach's *Christmas Oratorio.* There was time, though, for only brief appreciation of the program; it seemed no more than a minute or two before the orchestra was back on the stage tuning up, and then she began to fret for Michael's return.

At the last moment he and Joe came down the aisle together. When he was settled in his seat he showed her a package of horehound drops in his pocket. "Taking no chances," he whispered, popping one into his cheek just as Conductor Franz Kneisel appeared from the wings, and joining the applause with an expression of small-boy innocence and a side smile that twisted her heart.

She refused to accept the Prelude to *Tristan and Isolde* till she was sure his remedy was effective. And even after she had satisfied herself that he was all right she determined to hold the music at a safe distance, for its subdued opening passage forecast a power not to be trusted. There was no promise here of light out of darkness, classic order and an all-embracing unity out of chaos, the triumph of heroic courage over the massive rhythms of disaster. Here was sorcery that spoke not to the whole soul, the heart and mind and will as one, but only to the heart, and fatally, stealing like a secret potion through the veins toward the center of feeling, shivering the spine and nerves, seeking to penetrate to the inmost core of emotion. In her overwrought state at Michael's homecoming this music was too moving, too intense and intimate: she must protect herself from its probings, resist its enthrallment, not allow it to take possession of her. But it was impossible to stand aside and watch its power grow, dispassionately following the tonal progression, listening only with her ears, rejecting its significance, its profound implications. It was no use trying to stifle her instinctive and full response; surrender was inevitable. And as the spell increased, as the music rose like flame to envelop and consume her defenses, she was soon involved to the loneliest recesses of her being in the terrible surge of the Prelude.

This was not the tragic song of Tristan and Isolde, but of all love and lovers. As the Beethoven symphony was a supreme expression of human victory over the forces of darkness, so this was an ultimate voicing of the victory of darkness over the forces of light and life. It stripped away every protective shield and exposed the heart naked to the fires of ecstasy and mortal anguish. It melted the firmest seals of the past, so that the highest joys and sorrows of living were released to meet in a doomed reverberant confusion of times and memories. No hope, no prayer, no rebellion could stem this fatal surge of life toward death. And as the throbbing tenderness and despair mounted to the last unbearable song of farewell, the fingers quivering her spine stole up to close her throat and blinded her eyes with tears. But in the final agony of the Love-Death, when it seemed that if she were ever to breathe again the mute sobbing of her heart must betray itself in answer to the stricken music, she felt Michael's hand seeking hers. In a flash of relief and joy she responded to the clasp of his hand, answering the music there with a swift exultant affirmation, and then relinquishing his hand without delay in quick instinctive fear of prolonging this touch of unbelievable intimacy and understanding an instant beyond his wish. But this brief contact was enough to redeem her heart and the whole world of memory and faith with a dizzying uprush from the fearful dissolution of the music. And at the end even the music was converted and made to turn upward on immortal wings from darkness to the light.

And then, before she could comprehend through the applause and pause this moment of supreme fulfillment, she was caught in the Shepherds' Music from the *Christmas Oratorio*. But this music of Bach was neither triumphantly nor tragically stirring. It was no heroic adventure of the will against fate, or transfiguration of love in death. It was music that blended the heights and depths of life in a sublime entrancement of balance and serenity. At once earthly and celestial it grew like a proud dream, its many voices weaving a pattern of transcendent beauty from the contrasting threads of reality. Its melodic thoughts budded and opened like flowers; its theme put out stems, branches, leaves to form a symmetry of loveliness and wisdom whose truth reached toward both the sun and the stars. Healing, blessing, it communicated simply yet with unimaginable glory a sense of health and sanity, rightness and goodness, wholeness and peace and strength. It spoke the language of the soul, translating infinite mysteries for the consolation and inspiration of mankind. Here was music of pure revelation, an incomparable expression of faith, a supreme illumination of the wonder and beauty of the world. It confirmed all the heart knew most deeply but could never utter. It was an ultimate psalm of thanksgiving. Like the Shepherd Lord of David it restored the soul.

And under its benign auspices she was able to recover her self-possession. So that when the applause ended and the orchestra and the audience began to break up, each individual intent on reasserting his identity and resuming his little destiny, she could face Michael and the people round her in the crowded aisle with steady eyes. But within she remained entranced, the rapture of the music still echoing, continuing as if it might last forever. And when holding Michael's arm she reached the lobby with its numbing congestion of voices and faces returning to normal, her intense reluctance to leave, to believe that this precious hour of life was over, delayed her acceptance of the matter-of-fact resumption of time and the reality of the street and departure. It was only when Michael left her to try to find a cab that she came out of her daze sufficiently to recognize that the earlier drizzling rain had become a downpour, a tumultuous drowning applause, and that it had turned so much colder that she could see her breath like smoke. Michael was gone a long while, but as she stood aside watching the slowly thinning crowd she was glad to be alone at this moment of readjustment.

Riding back to the hotel was a disappointment, for she had pictured a companionable walk after the concert. But when they were back in their rooms this omission was fully compensated for. Michael was burning to talk; and the small fact that the heat was off for the night and the radiators already cold, and his shoes soaking wet, seemed no reason for not settling down at once for a good chat. But she firmly refused to talk till he had taken off his things and was under covers. Then, sitting on the edge of the bed with her coat still on for warmth, she was ready to listen.

At first she was too intent on the sound of his voice to follow his words. The pleasure of hearing and seeing him, of observing every inflection of his voice, every shade of meaning in his eyes, every expression of his hands, the sheer joy of having him made words seem unimportant. But when he got round to telling how he really felt about the concert, she began to pay close attention to what he was saying.

He locked his hands behind his head finally and lay back, eyes on the ceiling, his voice measured and subdued, as if he distrusted his own enthusiasm. "It's sort of hard to talk about, isn't it," he smiled soberly. "Like religion, or love, or anything deep. It's hard to say what you feel without sounding cracked. Maybe it's best not to try to say anything, except to yourself."

"Or to your mother?" she asked him.

"Sure! But, you know, sometimes it's hardest of all to say things to you. Can you explain that?"

She shook her head.

"Well," he frowned, "maybe it's because things mean so much more when they're said to you. As if I was trying to tell you a lot of other things at the same time. That's the way it's always been." He was silent a moment, frowning. "But you've always understood everything without being told."

"Perhaps some things. But not how you feel about the concert. I'd like to hear some more about that."

"All right," he grinned, "if you can stand it." But back on that hard theme he was soon gravely perplexed again. "It was simply great," he kept repeating. "Simply and absolutely great. It just made me see stars, that's all."

He shared her amusement and then seemed to find it easier to go on. "Remember how I used to hate music lessons. And now music seems about the greatest thing there is. Poetry and art and all try to get at the essence of things, but it takes music to do the trick. It works like magic. It wakes you up, opens your eyes. Makes you see and understand things better."

He paused for confirmation and encouragement, and when she nodded went on eagerly. "It sort of tunes you up. Lifts you out of the everyday flatness of things. Don't you feel that?"

"Yes. And I think it does more than that. I think it lifts the everyday flatness along with you."

He considered that. "Guess you're right. It changes the looks of everything. It really makes everything seem important and wonderful somehow. . . . Of course, you can't hold the feeling. Like the plantation people you get the spirit but you can't keep it long. You have to come down to earth again, you can't stay tuned up or your strings would snap. But when you hear real music, you bring something back with you. As if you'd been up on some high place where you'd had a long view of the world. And seen things as they were, and are, and ought to be. And can be and will be."

He stopped there abruptly and looked at her with a half-apologetic smile. But after a moment of silent reassurances he continued in a tone of absorbed animation. "You know what I mean. Music makes you feel good about life, that it's a privilege to be alive. And it makes you realize you're not just yourself but also a member of the human race. It gives you a feeling of comradeship, not only with the living but with the dead, and the unborn. I don't know, but it seems to give you an increased sense of purpose and responsibility,

615

a sense of being part of the whole show, so that you want to make the very most possible of yourself and give something in return, some small contribution toward the—well, toward the inheritance of your race. . . . Right now I'd like to be able to compose great music better than anything. But I guess medicine isn't such a bad road. They both seem to lead in the same direction. If I could tell you all that's being done and planned in medical science, you'd feel the same way. It all fits in with the visions of music. . . . I guess maybe in a way that's my religion. Anyway, that's how I feel about music, near as I can express it. Now suppose you tell me a thing or two. You always let me do all the talking."

Having unburdened himself he was plainly anxious to shift to a lighter mood, but she had one thing she wanted to tell him in all seriousness. "The only thing I'd like to say is a short prayer, that you'll never lose the ideals you have now. That you'll never let anything change you. Not grind or disillusionments or even success."

He nodded with a solemn grin. "Not even success."

Then he wanted to talk about home, and was even willing to talk about college to escape going to bed. "Don't leave me yet," he begged; "I'm all steamed up and ready to talk all night." And though nothing would have pleased her more, though she hated to surrender him and end this day, she stood firm, knowing how much he needed rest. "All right," he gave in at last, settling down with a resigned sigh; "but I sure know someone who's in no danger of ever changing,— you're just as positive as ever about bed-time, no matter how much I have to get off my chest." He took her hand solicitously. "You're getting cold, and I know you must be dog tired, so I'll let you off till tomorrow. I've got plenty of things to tell you, but I guess they'll keep overnight."

She tucked him in like old times, as if he were still a little boy instead of a grown man, and made sure that his window was open enough but not too much with the cold and rain before she finally turned out the light and went to her room.

There, as she undressed, fatigue caught up with her at last and numbed her senses like a drug. But when she got into bed and pulled up the thin skimpy hotel blankets she lay hopelessly tense and wakeful. Even when the clammy sheets warmed up, and she began to relax a little in this strange bed and lose the contracted feeling of being one of a long line of transients, the ceiling patch of light from a street lamp just below the window and the unfamiliar noises of the city kept her eyes wide open. She was unable to resist the full impact of every clopping carriage that passed, the clang and rattling grind of each trolley bound for the intersection of Meeting and Broad, where a block or two away the chimes of St. Michael's sounded the quarter-hours. And even after the carriages had ceased and the last trolley had retired for the night, leaving only a spell of diminishing rain and at intervals the aloof punctuations of the chimes, even then sleep remained far beyond reach. Her mind refused to succumb to its weight of weariness and became instead increasingly alert and active. Her thoughts roamed the city, searching out points in the past, recalling the parts Charleston had played in her life and finding them all incredibly remote and unsubstantial in the light and living reality of this present, the joy of Michael's homecoming, the lingering rapture of the day. This was no night for sleeping: the satisfactions of lying awake, remembering and dreaming, were too great. For in whatever direction her thoughts moved they moved safely, and returned invariably to the central reality of a world at last in order, a world in which everything had come right in the end, astonishingly and wonderfully right. This was a time not for rest but for appraisal and appreciation and thanksgiving.

She thought of others who might be lying sleepless in this night, sharing with her each recurrent tone of the chimes. Pain and worry, beds of fire, would be keeping some poor tormented souls from rest; and others would be restless from some bright joy, some blessing recalled or anticipated. But of any souls who might be lying happily wakeful through these small hours, of all souls who in peace had ever listened or ever would listen to these rhythmic after-midnight pulsations of time, no-one surely for greater happiness than hers. . . . How, she wondered, could such happiness be accepted in the face of all the world's misery. But that qualm only made her clasp her happiness closer. She felt she had known enough trouble in her life to entitle her to take this final dispensation without apologies or reluctance or any sense of guilt. And so finally her thoughts gratefully encircled her little world, seeking Michael in the next room, Margaret in Columbia, Stephen and Jack at home, and gathering them all into the embrace of tomorrow, when the family would be one again on the eve of a truly joyful Christmas.

. . . She realized sometime later that it had turned much colder. And when she got up to take a blanket in to Michael, she saw at the window that the diminishing rain had become a light faintly-hissing sleet. Stealing into his room she managed to spread the blanket without rousing him. She laid his overcoat over the lower part of the bed, and then stood scarcely breathing for a minute watching his dark head outlined dimly against the pillow. It was so hard to believe he was really there.

Back in her room she converted her own coat into a cover before she got into bed. And as she lay curled up in a shivering knot she remembered freezing nights that last miserable winter at Land's End, when the family comforts and best blankets were divided between Michael at the Citadel and Margaret and Jack at Miss Hamilton's, the rest on Stephen's bed, while she and Lucy had slept in wrappers under heaps of anything that promised warmth. But how completely all bad memories had lost their sting. The most they could do now was sharpen appreciation of the present. At the moment, to be sure, it was cold; but what a different cold from the past, and how easily repulsed when the heart was glowing warm. . . . So in the end there was only an inexpressible peace. And the periodic confirmation of St. Michael's chimes, echoing in her breast like the Shepherds' Music of Bach, remote and serenely aloof as the stars, immense as the sky of night encompassing the earth, yet inherent and close as breathing.

Toward dawn she lost track of the chimes and slept a little, fitfully at first as if her thankfulness resented any intrusion of oblivion, even the briefest interruption. But finally she drifted off into a deep sleep. A sleep so deep that when she was wakened suddenly by a terrible banging noise, she sat bolt upright, heart pounding wildly, senses stunned for a long moment before she could realize that the cannonading in the room was just the heat coming on, steam exploding into the ornate gilt radiator by the window, where gray morning light was waiting.

There was no heat in the train going back to Beaufort. Something had happened to the pipe connections, Conductor Gilroy explained with deep chagrin. The air of the car was freezing.

Outside through frosted panes everything was transfigured by the cold. The night's rain had turned to ice, and on treacherous rails the train, its engine wheels spinning impotently for a time after each little station-stop, moved cautiously through a world of glacial wonders. Every tree, every shrub, even the humblest grasses of the field were arrayed in crystal splendor. Patches of broomstraw were transformed into cloth of silver and gold, and golden reaches of marshgrass were silvered as if with frosty sea spray. It was a miraculous world of silver and emerald and gold, a world of such enthralling loveliness that any fears she felt for the garden at home, for branches perhaps perilously weighted and tender shoots and buds ice-nipped, were dispelled by its magic beauty, a beauty that finally seemed to be the music of inmost joy frozen and fixed and immutable forever.

It was such a dream-like journey homeward that even the cold was forgotten. In this spell of enchantment her heart was immeasurably warm, and she was numb to all else except her awareness of Michael. Already she was beginning to lose him to the others: at her insistence he sat now across the aisle with Joe, who had deserted his sisters in the front of the car to come back for an energetic talk. Their words were broken into unintelligible fragments by the noises of the train and the jabber of the people in the seats ahead, so that only the sound of his voice was hers at intervals. But she was content with that. She was well content to sit alone, smiling to herself in this secret entrancement in which she possessed him completely. And by nightfall the family would be one again, reunited and whole.

✦   ✦   ✦

That afternoon, after he had been welcomed home by Stephen and by Jack, whose greeting was such a strange mixture of affection and defense, by Tunis and Ella, who were all blandishing grins, and by Lucy, who was ready at once and without any foolishness to start feeding him up against his return to the poor rations of the North, he left for Land's End to see Linda. Seth had come in from the island with a cargo of Christmas gifts for Marshlands, and Michael went back with him, along with Marshlands's presents for the Robinsons.

Stephen wanted her to lie down and take it easy for the rest of the afternoon. "You look as if you'd been on a three-day bender," he told her; "you won't be worth shooting for Christmas if you don't take a little time out." But he seemed more pleased than provoked when she insisted there was too much to do. He was not going back to the office, he was through for the day and at loose ends, and he needed to relieve some of the pressure of his restrained excitement at Michael's homecoming. Talking in interrupted snatches he followed her trail from the dining-room to the kitchen, from the cellar preserve shelves to the attic store-room, and finally out to the garden for an inspection tour. The sun was breaking through rifts in the heavy sky, but it was too late for any thawing; it only increased the splendor of the ice world, touching the crystal leaves and boughs with diamond fire. And by the time she had scrutinized every corner of the garden with Stephen at her heels and had satisfied herself that no serious damage had been done, the frail sunlight had faded back into grayness and freezing dusk was beginning to steal out from the garden shadows. Then as they returned to the house she felt such a cold tiredness come over her that she agreed to rest for a few minutes on the sofa by the living-room fire, while he left for the station to meet the five-o'clock train and Margaret.

She was so glad to have Margaret home that her disappointment was overridden when Michael failed to get back from the island in time for the traditional pick-up supper of Christmas Eve. And she knew how much it meant to him to see Linda again, appreciating how well he had concealed his eagerness—and his anxiety, for he had had to leave her exposed to the attentions of the garrison of young bachelors in uniform still stationed at the Fort Fremont barracks, next-door to Land's End. She was even able to share Stephen's amusement at the hopelessness of ever getting all hands together, of ever corralling the entire family without one member missing. But when the decorating of the tree started and still no Michael, she began to fret for his appearance.

"We can't expect to have him all to ourselves, you know," Stephen told her from the step-ladder, as he took the memory-encrusted ornaments she handed up to him from the old Christmas bandboxes. "I've got plenty of notes to compare with him, but you see I haven't forgotten what it was like to be young and in love. Give him a chance. And please don't give me any more of those cone candle-holders till I get all the balls on. Which reminds me we'll need to replenish our stock of balls before long, at least before our grand-children start arriving."

Everyone embarked on the decorating with a will, but soon the two most energetic workers fell by the wayside. Margaret was the first to desert; she wanted to do up her presents. Then Jack vanished mysteriously. He was discovered later in the back hall, polishing his rifle. . . . This was the first intimation that there was going to be a deer hunt. Stephen did the explaining, from his step-ladder: Joe had planned an old-fashioned Christmas morning hunt at Holly Hill in honor of Michael, nobody except Jack was particularly enthusiastic about it, but Joe couldn't very well be turned down flat. It was certainly nothing to get upset about, all hands would be back in time for three-o'clock dinner, positively. Christmas stockings would have to be omitted or postponed because the party was leaving shortly after midnight, but after all weren't stockings getting to be a little too much of a good thing?

"Why wasn't I told about it?" she asked him in exasperation at the whole idea.

"Well," he admitted blandly, busying himself with a glass icicle, "perhaps there was some hesitancy, some feeling you might object."

"I should think you'd all have realized that Michael needed rest, not a dawn deer hunt in freezing weather."

She was thoroughly provoked, but having expressed her disapproval there seemed to be nothing to do now but accept the situation. And when Joe stopped by briefly to hang his customary cornucopia on the tree, she had no heart to upbraid him. The hunt was on and she could only resign herself to it, feeling as powerless to stop it as if it were some force of nature rather than an idiotic inspiration of Joe's.

After Joe had gone, and after she had got Jack headed for bed and had sent Lucy up too, she stayed working with Stephen for a while longer. But now the tide of weariness was catching up with her in earnest, submerging her will in overlapping waves; and finally she had to give up, leaving him to finish the tree alone. Before she left, though, she helped him set the Star of Bethlehem, steadying the stepladder so that he wouldn't dive into the tree when he reached up to the tip. And she gave him three solemn injunctions about Michael: when he came in, he must not be kept up talking but allowed to get some rest before the hunt; he must be sure to wear his warmest things; and if he looked worn out he must be discouraged from going at all, Joe or no Joe. But Stephen was in high and heedless spirits, inattentive, already rehearsing for the Santa-in-plainclothes role which would climax with his special act for distributing the presents and leading the carols after Christmas dinner: he was not to be depended on in the way of solemn injunctions, and she thought it wise to write Michael a note. But even when she had pinned the note on his pillow and laid out his warmest underclothes on the bed of his room off the living-room, she was still not satisfied and lingered downstairs a few minutes longer hoping he would appear. At last she went out on the frosty porch to see if she could discover the light of Seth's boat on the river. Somewhere above the heavy blanket of darkness a full Christmas moon should be shining, but here below the night and the river were inscrutable.

When she came back shivering into the hall, she stopped a moment at the living-room door to unburden on Stephen her obscure but growing anxiety. "I don't think he should stay so late," she worried aloud. "It's almost ten, and the river's black as ink. It's pretty hard on Seth."

He answered her absently, without pausing in his task of stringing strands of silver and gold tinsel over the tree. "Nonsense. Seth doesn't mind doing a little night ferrying. The tide's right, and he knows the channel by heart."

"You don't suppose anything could have happened?"

"Oh yes, dear, of course! Certainly. I imagine they're stuck on a mudflat, or they've hit something and gone down with all hands. I imagine every conceivable calamity. . . . I thought you were headed for bed. If you're going to sit up imagining things, fretting about nothing because you're all in, you may as well untangle some of this tinsel for me. Why don't you call it a day. You've had about enough."

Upstairs she stopped in to talk with Margaret. And then she went to Jack's room, as much to delay herself as to make sure he had turned in and was not reading in bed. In her own room she continued to play for time, undressing as slowly as possible; and even when she was finally settled in bed, after a last window-peering at the river darkness, she fought off the weight and pressure of exhaustion, trying to stay awake till Michael came home. . . . To hold her wavering consciousness she kept repeating over and over the firm resolution that, as soon as this hunt and Christmas were out of the way, he was positively going to get the rest he needed. Rest and sleep, positively and in spite of any objections. And so she somehow managed to hold herself awake till she heard at last the faint chugging of Seth's boat coming up the river. A few minutes later there were voices at the seawall. Then, finally, the opening and closing of the front door. From the living-room the muffled tones of the two men of the family came up to her, and with a sigh of relief she let go then and sank down to them in deep sleep.

She woke with a start to find that it was shockingly late in the morning. By now the hunt was over, the hungry huntsmen already on their way home from Holly Hill, and there was so much to be done before they arrived; yet she could hardly drag herself out of bed, and the first minutes up were like sleep-walking. With mis-guided consideration Margaret and Lucy had allowed her to almost sleep the clock around. Even Fenwick Street firecrackers, which to her still made Christmas morning sound like Fourth-of-July, had failed to rouse her.

They were nearly ended now, these salutes to Christmas; only an occasional belated one stirred up the dogs of the neighborhood to a perfunctory and weary barking. But though the earlier din had failed to wake her it had invaded sleep, leaving a memory of fantastic hor-ror. There were elaborate details to be recalled, she felt, but when she tried to bring them into focus they faded completely; only the central picture remained, clear and distinct. It had developed out of a strange dream of Michael returning to her for primal shelter and protection, growing back to her from manhood to boyhood and from boyhood to infancy. She could remember no phases of transi-tion but out of that felicitous sleep reverie a monstrous vision had gradually taken shape. The scene was a wintry Northern woods, seemingly the cherished Salem woods of her girlhood, deep in snow. In a clearing stood Jack, waiting with his rifle, watching a snow-bound thicket. Before she could warn him, before she could move her leaden feet or utter a voiceless cry, he raised his rifle and fired. And when the smoke lifted, there in the blood-stained snow beyond the thicket lay Michael.

And this cheerful Christmas dream lingered in her mind all through her work with Margaret and Lucy to prepare for dinner and the return of the hunters. Neither shrugs nor the most deter-mined dismissals could rid her of its inexcusable and imbecile pantomime: it pursued her like a malicious shadow as she hurried from one errand to another. Far from losing its nightmare force in the daylight bustle of her tasks, it seemed to pick up strength as the hours passed, increasing in vividness and reality. Nothing she could say to herself could release her imagination from its baneful grip. It was casting an outrageous pall over Christmas, but the harder she tried to free herself the more obsessing it became.

When the last preparations were finished, the table set and trimmed with sprigs of holly and mistletoe and cassena-berry, smilax, moss, and cones from the old trees at Rusty's Pine Point, and everything else all ready, then she was confronted with a blank wait. The hall clock said two-thirty, and theoretically that left only a half-hour before the hunters' return; but practically she scarcely expected them to be on time, and Tunis and Ella had been warned to keep the dinner hour elastic. In an effort to keep herself busy she invented a few last-minute odds-and-ends to attend to, and in her extremity even ventured to fasten the candle-snuffer with rubber-bands to the tip of Miss Sophie's silver-headed cane, a rite that Stephen always reserved for himself. Then she tried talking with Margaret for a while. But when the hands of the clock passed three-thirty and began to creep toward four, she grew too fidgety for quiet sitting and talking or even for nervous wandering from room to room. And finally she put on a wrap and went out to the garden to ease her agitation.

The short afternoon was almost ended, but the sun, which since noon had been shining wanly through cirrus veils, had done its work: the air had turned mild, and all that remained of the crystal splendor of yesterday was a general droopy sogginess. For a while she wandered aimlessly through the garden, pretending to herself that she was concentrating on individual plants and shrubs and deciding just what damage had been done by the combination of ice and thaw. But it was useless to try to deflect her attention from the central concern, and in the end she gravitated to the gate, where she lingered watching and waiting. When she was unable by any legerdemain to make the hunters appear in Fenwick Street, she finally left her post and went to the back yard and the kitchen door to confer with Ella about the dinner emergency. Then she returned with her anxiety to the vicinity of the gate.

After a time she decided that it must now be five o'clock. The sun was gone, staining the cloud banks of the west dull crimson, and the garden was growing dark. Already the hunters were two hours overdue, and at this rate there was no telling when they would reach home. She should have expected them, she told herself, to be not late but scandalously late, disastrously late, ruining dinner and the whole day with their Christmas hunt. And she thought: it would only make matters worse to show them how furious she was and how worried. No, she would let the ruins of dinner shame them all and speak for her. . . . But no speculations, indulgent or impatient, could conceal the fact that her uneasiness was becoming genuine alarm.

So that when at last they actually arrived, intact and full of apologies and explanations and before dinner was hopelessly ruined, she was too relieved and delighted to berate them, and left all the scolding to Lucy. With her morbid fancies dispelled she was so elated that she could take even Jack's plight in good part: Michael was smilingly emptyhanded, and Stephen had only a wild turkey to show for his deer hunt, but Jack, who insisted he had spared three doe, had brought down a fine buck and had been "baptized" for it: proudly he displayed the dried gore in his hair, the traces left round his ears, the smears on his coat. And so with the excitement of their return it was not till they had cleaned up and were finally assembled at the candle-lighted table that she realized Michael had caught fresh cold. He was doing his best to disguise coughs and sniffles, but his bloodshot eyes and feverish face and hands gave him away. Yet the mere mention of putting him to bed produced such general consternation and protest that she had to take him into the hall to argue it out away from the others.

"Mother," he grinned down at her when they were alone, "do you honestly mean no turkey with oyster and sausage dressing, no Kentucky ham, no plum pudding with flaming sauce? Only castor-oil and hot-water bottles for Christmas?"

But she stood firm against him. It was a terribly hard thing to do, but she refused to let him stay up "just for dinner and the tree". It was impossible now to understand how she could have been so easy about the hunt. But she was not giving in this time. He was going straight to bed. And he was going to stay there till his cold was cleared up and he was thoroughly rested.

Colds were an old story in the family: every winter there were several. Usually they responded quickly to Rusty's old prescription,— bed, quinine, and hot lemonade. But this cold of Michael's was no common cold. It was a chest cold to start with. It had a past, a long head-start. And it hung on stubbornly, not yielding an inch even to Lucy's mustard poultices. Yet at first it was impossible to take it very seriously, perhaps because it was impossible to believe that it could be dangerous, perhaps because Michael himself took it so lightly. Despite his fever and heavy breathing and coughing his only serious discomfort seemed to be mental, that he was spoiling the holidays, wasting precious time in bed, wasting everyone's time nursing him. Each evening he confidently assured her he would throw the whole thing off that night and be up the following morning.

But after his third day of bed without any sign of improvement, she began to quiver inside with an uncontrollable fear. "Now just hold your horses," Stephen told her when she could no longer keep her alarm to herself. "I admit he's got a bad cold, and naturally he's running a little temperature, but there's certainly nothing to get wrought up about." He agreed, though, that it might be a good idea to move him upstairs: the weather was continuing rainy and bleak with only fitful spells of sunlight and the downstairs bedroom was damp and confined and cheerless. So he was moved up to the big room with its many windows and big fireplace, and Jack moved downstairs giving his room to her; and this new arrangement relieved her mind to some extent, for now only a thoroughfare closet separated her from Michael and by leaving the doors ajar she could keep close track of him through the night. And so for another two days she fretted on, trying to let Stephen's composure and Michael's own reassurances stifle the inner voice of dread. But when his fever, instead of breaking or even standing still, kept climbing higher and his breathing became increasingly heavy, she decided that he simply must have a doctor, whether he and Stephen thought so or not. Stephen refused to have "Doc" Wright in the house, but he finally agreed to "call in" the medical officer at Fort Fremont "for a consultation".

The medical officer proved to be an affable youngish man, not in the least military in spite of his tight uniform, and only too glad to oblige. She was grateful for his courtesy, but his bedside manner inspired no confidence whatever. After an examination that struck her as being perfunctory and entirely inadequate, he settled down

for a casual chat. He seemed to feel that Michael needed entertainment more than medical attention, and he and Stephen joked
at length with the "patient doctor" on the diverting theme of physi-
cians' singular inability to heal themselves. At last in exasperation
she made an excuse to leave the room and went down to wait in the
lower hall. When the consultation was finally ended and the affable
medical officer came downstairs with Stephen, he accepted her
thanks for his kindness and trouble and in return gave her a reassuring smile for her anxiety. It was only grippe. Yes, there was a
slight lung congestion, but he was leaving some pills to take care
of that. Tomorrow or the next day he would be making a trip in to
town from the island and he would be glad to stop by and see how
the patient was doing. By then he expected to find the fever broken
and the congestion cleared up.

"You see," Stephen shrugged at her after the man was gone.
"That ought to satisfy you. Now if you'll hold yourself together and
stop making mountains out of mole-hills, I'll go on to the office."

But she was by no means satisfied. She tried to show Michael a
calm and cheerful face, but underneath she was more worried than
ever; and by evening she had convinced herself that there was a
decided turn for the worse. Stephen did his best to quiet her fear, but
that night she was unable to close her eyes, and by morning she was
in a panic. When Joe dropped in after breakfast on his way to the
office, she confronted him and Stephen together with the necessity
of doing something, of getting a real doctor, a doctor from Charleston,—if possible Dr. Ravenel, old associate of Rusty's.

"Why you can't drag a man like that down here to treat a case of
grippe!" Stephen protested. "Michael wouldn't hear of it. If it was an
emergency it would be different. I'd telegraph Ravenel in a second."

But Joe, who in the last two days had worked up a flustered anxiety
of his own about Michael, took her side violently. An emergency did
exist and something must be done without delay: it was not enough
to telegraph Ravenel, he or some other good doctor must be
fetched, and Joe was going to do the fetching. Stephen then decided
that if anyone was going it was up to him, but Joe insisted he was
better acquainted with Ravenel and better equipped for persuading
and for getting quick action. So after a prolonged wrangle that drove
her almost to distraction it was finally Joe who rushed off just in

time to catch the morning train for Charleston. And, to Stephen's astonishment and her infinite relief, he came back on the afternoon train with Dr. Ravenel.

Dr. Ravenel was no amiable medical officer. A big gruff grumpy man, he was neither benevolent nor sociable, and he had no bedside manners at all. But she trusted him implicitly at once. . . . After he had made a preliminary examination, he interrupted his tapping of Michael's chest to ask her and Stephen and Joe to wait in the hall. That left the hall too congested for his liking, so he sent Joe and Margaret and Jack and Lucy on downstairs, allowing only Stephen and her to wait at the door. After minutes that seemed hours he appeared at the door and beckoned Stephen into the room. And then after more minutes that seemed years long, so long that she began to feel faint and had to sit down on the top step of the stairs, the door finally opened again and Stephen came out. As he closed the door behind him, as she got up to meet him, she saw all her worst fears confirmed in his face. He tried to evade her at first, but her eyes begged him to be direct and at last the truth flashed between them. It was pneumonia. Both lungs.

"But it's all right," he kept saying. "It's all right now. We've got a good man." And in idiotic fragments: "Says he'll pull through all right. Young heart. Looks for the crisis tonight. He knows his business, this man. Now don't worry. Everything's coming out all right."

Everything stood dead still around her. He held out steadying hands, as if he expected her to collapse. But after a moment of stunned sickness she found herself in possession of sudden strength and calmness.

And from that moment on this strange calm force persisted, sustaining and safely guiding her through the ensuing nightmare hours. Things and faces and voices, all expressions and aspects of normal life and reality, were at once very sharp and close and very remote and intangible. Meaning and significance were lost, she was scarcely aware of what she was doing, yet she was able to move and speak with perfect control. It was only her inner consciousness that remained stunned and benumbed. Her body and the working surfaces of her mind were alert, quick to respond, functioning with mechanical efficiency and precision like a clock.

At some vague point in time she realized that the crisis had not yet come though the night was gone. As she moved on through day toward another night, she began to lose all track of time, so that it was impossible to be sure whether it was night or day, early or late. Time was mercifully telescoped, there were no reflective spaces between the active moments, and she was able to keep going without faltering or any sense of fatigue. There were plenty of willing hands to take her place in the sickroom, Margaret and Lucy were anxiously waiting their turns, and Linda had come with Seth from Land's End: but Dr. Ravenel had picked her alone for his assistant, and he kept her on, and everyone else was barred from the room. . . . And so she lived through an eternity of moments, hardly daring to breathe for fear of taking precious air from Michael as he lay wavering between delirium and coma. Till at last only his dark head on the pillow remained clear and distinct. Dr. Ravenel was no more than her own will acting as a separate entity, and the faces she encountered when she left the room on some errand were like the blurred faces of strangers met in the mazes of a dream. Joe, Linda and Seth, and the others were become as shadowy as the neighbors who dropped in with solicitous phrases that had to be answered without being heard. They were all alike, unsubstantial figures existing on a different plane, once removed from essential reality. Everything outside the contracting lamp-light circle of Michael's bed was growing dimmer and dimmer. In the end nothing really existed beyond this circle, and she was alone with him in a world of tightening shadows.

Later, at a moment when she was standing across the bed from Dr. Ravenel, fighting a double obsession that the fire was stealing the last good air from the room, smothering Michael, and that despite their clasp of hands he was also slowly drowning in the pool of lamp-light, she became aware of the doctor's eyes studying her closely through his thick-lensed glasses. He seemed now for the first time directly aware of her existence. He left his chair and motioned her to the fireside.

There he said to her in a low voice: "He's sleeping now, and I think you better get a little rest."

She denied she needed any rest. "But you do. You must go and lie down for a while. I'll call you if there's any change."

He shook his head. "I'll rest here in my chair. But I want you to go to your room and try to sleep."

She assured him she was all right, but he was insistent, and finally she went obediently through the thoroughfare closet to her room and bed.

As she lay rigid listening to every faintest sound in the big room, she was certain it would be impossible to relax her clenched tenseness, close her eyes, rest. But though her eyes remained wide open against the very thought of sleep, some treacherous subtle oblivion stole over her senses from the darkness, and in time she lost track of even her own breathing. And then with a horrible start she found herself sitting bolt upright, her heart pounding wildly. As she struggled to collect her wits, she heard through a nauseous daze the sound of Stephen's voice in the big room.

He met her as she came into the room. But his expression and words failed to convey any meaning to her. She hurried past him to the bedside, where Dr. Ravenel stood in the circle of light wearily polishing his glasses with a crumpled clumsy handkerchief. Michael's labored breathing had stopped: his sunken eyes were closed and his head rested on the pillow in what seemed peaceful sleep: and for a moment she was able to cling to an illusion that the crisis was safely past. But then the lamp flashed like lightning and her heart was transfixed by recognition of the instant, by an old foreknowledge, a fatal sense of having lived through it before, of having known it was coming. Swiftly this was succeeded by a sense of disaster still impending, still escapable. Michael was in desperate peril, he was wounded, he lay dying. Quick—quick—not yet too late. But the figures of Dr. Ravenel and Stephen were deaf to her frantic appeals; like her they stood frozen in postures of eternal impotence. In helpless agony she prayed to Rusty, but he was bound and only his compassion and suffering reached her. Through a last moment of clarity she felt that Stephen was trying to reach and comfort her, but now she was hopelessly alone in a swirling emptiness. Somewhere in the room a voice not her own, a voice hardly human, was groaning in mortal anguish, as she slumped to her knees at the side of the bed, her heart sinking down into unfathomable darkness.

She knew she was lying in Jack's room, but beyond that nothing was definite. She had a sense of being detached from herself, of lying outside of herself, feeling nothing. After a time this outside self became aware of mumbled voices and faces in lamp-light: with great effort she was able to recognize Stephen and Dr. Ravenel near her. But after that impressions grew jerky, disconnected, and vague again. She wanted to be left alone, but it was impossible to make them understand. She could only turn her head away.

Sometime later she realized that Lucy was with her in the room. But even Lucy seemed now an alien presence to be rejected with the others. And now the defenses of numbness were deserting her, leaving her exposed to the furies of appalling torment. She was lying flayed on a bed of fire, and no position was sufferable. Mingled with this increasing fiery torture was a tightening sense of suffocation. And at last it seemed impossible to endure the bed any longer, impossible to breathe without escape from the room.

It was uncertain and obscure how she was finally able to dispose of Lucy. Perhaps Lucy was persuaded to go to her attic room to rest for a while, or sent on some errand; or perhaps she was watched and wished to sleep in her chair. But in the end she was somehow eluded and the room escaped from. For there was a sure sense of flight, of being in the hall, and then on the stairs. In the lower hall there were voices from the living-room, and she turned quickly to the back door. And then at last, out in the reviving air of the yard, she was able to breathe again.

It seemed near dawn but the sky was still dark. Just above the roof line of the quarter-house a burnished fragment of the lost full moon of Christmas was shining, without casting any glow to pale the brightness of stars. A wind of surprise intimations and promises cooled her face and filled her lungs so deeply that she felt her veins throb with a sudden hope, a strange wild buoyancy and elation. It was not too late: a mistake had been made, this time a mistake of measureless horror, but it could still be corrected: she would wake to find it all only a nightmare threat, a monstrous apparition of night and unreality. And as she hurried round the side of the house to the front lawn, the wind swaying the dark branches of the garden made the stars dart exultantly and the world seethe with a secret music of release. But at the seawall her heart contracted. The river had stopped. No tide or current flowed. It lay like a dim inscrutable mirror, a lake of ice bound by unbroken and unbreakable bands of black shadow, without egress, offering no reflection of life, no escape.

For an interminable time she seemed to stand there waiting for some sign of deliverance. In the end from the house, as from some far-off place, she felt a summons to return to the others, a necessity and a desire to comfort and be comforted. She turned back, and went in the front door. But in the hall she saw Michael's overcoat hanging on the rack. And then at last her whole being turned to cold stone, and she stood there motionless forever.

Part Six

I

ONE NIGHT in the autumn of 1907 Susan and Isabel Bramwell were roused from their slumbers by a great pounding at the front door of the "Castle". They had retired early, leaving their brother pulling his ear over some legal papers; but they had scarcely fallen asleep, back to back for warmth against the blustery night, when the pounding came to wake them with a violent start. And then, after a moment of excited voices from below, a confusion of alarms smote their stupefied senses: Joe stumbled upstairs to bang on their door— St. Helena's bell began to toll—the telephone in the lower hall jangled hysterically. A minute later Susan and Isabel were working frantically to free their heads of curl-papers, and Joe was rushing out of the house to join his volunteer fire brigade.

The exact cause of the fire remained a mystery, but there was no doubt about the effect. Sped by a brisk wind the flames raged through the heart of town, sparing a building here and there as if to accent the general devastation. Under the intrepid leadership of Joe Bramwell the volunteer brigade and shiny engine were nothing short of magnificent. But in the face of such a holocaust they were also completely impotent; despite the support of the ladies of St. Helena's auxiliary, who requisitioned and distributed gallons of hot toddy,—a remarkable exhibition of adaptability on the part of an organization whose chief charities began as far from home as possible, the maintenance of a *Fling-Out-The-Banner* Bed in Shanghai Missionary Hospital and a Bible Woman in Yokohama.

In the middle blocks of Bay Street only two old buildings survived: the Cowdrey house and the "Lafayette" house, both landmarks of antebellum days when Beaufort had no business section. The escape of the Lafayette house, a frame structure, seemed entirely fortuitous, though Joe's sisters felt that only a special dispensation of Providence could have saved their brother's office from the flames. They would have considered it even more of a dispensation if Stephen Fenwick's office could have been dissociated from their brother's for the occasion and separately consumed; but Stephen Fenwick's office, like Joe's, was only thoroughly smoked and watered. The Cowdrey house, home of the bank since the storm of '93, was protected by its tile roof and tabby walls. Not that tabby walls were positive insurance for a building: the big Talbert house in the center of town was gutted, and only their encircling graveyards saved St. Helena's and the Baptist Church.

And the Girls themselves had a great scare shortly after midnight. While in the neighborhood of the Baptist Church, which they were privately praying would somehow take fire from the showers of sparks pelting its roof, they were suddenly called out of their role of spectators and lady cup-bearers to take a hand in unloading their own home. The flames had veered in the direction of Fenwick Street, threatening the Castle. But after scorching a tree in the garden they veered away again, though not soon enough to spare the Girls the ordeal of seeing some of their most intimate possessions piled in the street like an eviction.

Yet that tribulation would have been nothing, even the loss of their home would have been almost bearable, if in return they could have been guaranteed the destruction of the rest of Fenwick Street. Since Hampton and the end of Reconstruction there were no colored families left in what had been the most fashionable quarter of Beaufort, but the leading carpetbagger families were still entrenched there. And on the Point, at the end of the once proud street, stood Marshlands, abode of the Girls' deepest abomination.

It took days for the ruins to smolder out and cool. Relief work was under the chairmanship of Joseph Bramwell, and normally his sisters would have joined with zeal in the work of succoring the stricken and homeless. But Joe, with his usual perversity where Emily Fenwick was concerned, had invited her on the committee, and that was more than the Girls could stand even in an emergency. They promptly resigned, on the plea that unless the smoked and watered law books in his office received immediate care they would be mildewed beyond hope of salvage; but they made the rebuke and their chagrin perfectly evident by forming a relief committee of their

636

own. Submissive to their brother's will in all other matters, the Girls hesitated at no insubordination when confronted with That Woman.

Months later, when the burned portions of the town had been rebuilt along modern lines, the Girls had less of their Beaufort than ever. They thought of it as a fine old shawl patched and darned with inferior goods till it was but a pathetic travesty of its former self.

Up to the time of the fire the Girls had clung to the notion that Beaufort was still somehow Beaufort, in appearance at least; but now it was not even superficially the place of their birth. When Ed Sands, Beaufort's enterprising contractor and cracker politician, was through with Bay Street, it might have been the main street of any small town. Country people came in from miles around to gape at the gingerbread store fronts and see the new-style "bungaloos" Ed Sands was building in a section of the burned area. The old houses that the fire had spared only emphasized the general change and decay.

By the spring of 1908 the Girls were ready to admit that Beaufort was no longer Beaufort but only common shoddy. If there was any health left in the place, if there was any of the old town left at all, it was confined, they felt, to the Castle, their brother, and themselves. They were the keepers of the last flickering light.

But the Fire had not been all loss. There had been certain gains, certain grim satisfactions that the Girls had been able to derive from the calamity. Retribution was slowly but neatly overtaking the last of the big carpetbaggers. To be sure, the sly and mysterious Sam Koenig, most objectionable of the lot in some respects, had not yet been anything like exterminated. He seemed to thrive on disaster. An uncanny talent for timely and heavy insurance had permitted him to more than weather the Great Storm; and now from the very ashes of his home and place of business this stumpy little fox, once an immigrant boy and least of the buzzards from the North, had risen on the phoenix wings of another whopping policy collection to compete with Ed Sands in gobbling up distressed properties at sheriff's sales. However, the Turners and the Van Wies, who had been badly shipwrecked in the Storm but had escaped by clinging to rafts of patient creditors, both were thoroughly sunk now. And the Rutherfords, who had somehow survived the buffetings of '93 despite their long cotton commitments, were swamped in the 1907 waves of flame. In fact, it was only through the legal intervention of Joe, who was not the man to kick a fallen foe, that they still had a roof over their heads.

And then, too, the Fire had given the Girls something almost as satisfying as the destruction of the Rutherfords and Van Wies and Turners, something they prized very highly: a story.

"It was shortly after midnight," Susan would invariably begin, "and we were hurrying back to the house, for the flames were veering that way. As we crossed Carteret Street at Coligny, we paused for a moment under the lamp."

"My stocking was coming down," Isabel usually explained at this point. But it might have been anything. And it was this unpredictable quality in Isabel as chorus that kept Susan on her mettle and gave an air of spontaneity and adventure to what might otherwise have been too tidy a recital.

"Not that there was any light from the lamp," Susan would continue. "It had been smashed and extinguished, like many another that night, by rowdies in the mob spirit that Joe says always manifests itself at a time of crisis."

"Just like Halloween," Isabel might contribute here.

"Precisely." Caught from her brother this was Susan's stock expression for weaving her sister's whimsies into the pattern of the tale. "And so we would have been enveloped in pitch black darkness but for the flames, which threw a lurid light over the street and the houses and yards. . . ."

"When suddenly——"

"Wait now, dear. When suddenly a figure emerged from the Koenig house on the corner. We drew quickly back into the shadows of the Tysons' yard, so that we were not seen, though we saw *him* clearly enough. And there was no mistaking who it was."

"Or *what* he was carrying!"

"One minute, Bel. It was Sam Koenig carrying——"

"Sally Broughton's *great-grandmother!*"

"Do, Bel! An oil portrait, in a big old gilt frame."

"When we told Sally about it, she almost died."

"Sam Koenig carrying that great Southern lady down the street in his arms! . . ."

638

"She was painted in England by some famous artist as a young girl,—who was it, Susie?"

"Can't call his name, off-hand. Joe will know. But anyway, that's where the missing portrait is, in the possession of a nasty little carpet-bagger. The Broughtons had to leave it behind when the Yankee fleet came, and when the town was looted I suppose some Yankee soldier or colored person stole it. And then Sam Koenig got it, and he's had it hidden in that robber's den of his ever since. And there it will remain, I expect,—nothing Sally can do about it now, Joe says."

"I'd steal it back."

"Pappa always said that Germaine Broughton was the greatest belle—next to Mamma—that ever married into Beaufort. She was a Levert, from Louisiana. What parish was it, Bel?"

"Joe'll know. Mamma always said she was too dark-complected."

"Do, Bel! Mamma only remembered her as a very old lady."

"Think of Sally's great-granny living with Sam all these years, and nobody the wiser till we saw it. I expect someday he'll be passing her off as one of his own ancestors."

"*Do* don't, Bel! . . ."

As the story aged in the Girls' cupboard (they always served it with their best blackberry cordial), Isabel found increasingly heady delights in it. But for Susan it was developing a dreggy taste: Isabel as chorus was getting entirely out of hand. And it was useless to try to fix her with an affectionate but firm eye. That seemed only to spur her on her wilful way.

Unfortunately her wilfulness was not confined to the Sam Koenig story. It extended now in practically every direction. When the Girls had been younger, Susan had felt she understood her sister as perfectly as it was intended for one human soul to understand another. Then Isabel's most whimsical vagaries had made sense, had seemed always charming and frequently inspired. But now there was something disturbing about everything she did and said. And there were moods that simply could not be fathomed at all.

This particularly applied to her moments of mirth. Formerly, Susan had enjoyed and shared her sister's smiles; even when she failed to grasp the point, even when she realized she was being gently mocked, she had never found Isabel's amusement anything but engaging. But lately a subtle change had come over Isabel's smiles: they were no longer engaging and intimate. Her mockery, too, had changed: it was not the mild and agreeable astringent of other years. And an alarming new note had crept into her laughter, a raucous note, perverse, irresponsible, destructive. Sometimes it was almost as if she were laughing to herself about things.

Not that Susan showed she detected any change. Never by the faintest innuendo or indirection did she attempt to convey her dismay to Joe, who seemed entirely unaware of any unpleasant metamorphosis in his pet sister. And she never betrayed to Isabel by so little as the bat of an eyelash that anything coming from her was seriously exceptional or startling: she continued to treat her sister as she always had, with affectionate indulgence. To acknowledge the change to herself was bad enough; and sometimes, when her sister was having a stretch of good behavior, she felt guilty about even that. But then Isabel would have a plangent relapse and try Susan to the very limit.

The Sam Koenig story was sure to bring on such a relapse. But the main trouble with this story, and with all the Girls' stories for that matter, remained the lack of an audience. And here perhaps was the central problem of their existence. Of course, there was Joe, and Sally Broughton, and Nancy Elliott and Henrietta Rhett. But once around that brief circle was barely enough to warm up a good tale.

❦ ❦ ❦

Since Reconstruction times, when their nephew had married the widow of Aaron Moffet and they had fastened on her the core of their rancor, Susan and Isabel Bramwell had lived on their hatred for Emily Fenwick. So during the period of her rising fortunes, Stephen's success, the birth and growth of the children, their life had been bitter indeed. In the long desert of Fenwick prosperity, up to the fatal last day of August 1893, there had been but one mirage to revive a little their drooping spirits. It had appeared toward the close of the period and by way of their cook, whose social traffic with the Marshlands cook, Tunis's wife Ella, they had fostered in every manner possible. It had come to them as no more than a hint, a mere morsel, but they had hungrily pounced on it. And when they had extracted the last drop of nourishment from the thing between themselves, they were not able to resist an urge to present it to their brother, whose dereliction, whose going-over to the camp of the enemy, had always been a matter of supreme chagrin to them.

It took courage. Because he was always more patient with Isabel, Susan allowed her sister to introduce the subject.

"Joe," Isabel began in a casual enough voice, "have you noticed anything wrong between Stephen and his wife?"

He put down his book. "Anything wrong? What do you mean by that?"

Susan blanched: Isabel was to have led up to the thing gradually, and she was never to refer to Stephen by his name. And as usual Joe was turning to her for an explanation.

"Isabel means," she said without looking up from her tatting, "we've been hearing things."

"What kind of things?"

"Ugly things."

Isabel put her handkerchief to her lips to hide a smile. "You may as well come out with it, Susie."

"Well, if you must know, we've been hearing that your nephew and his wife——"

"One minute! Who's your authority for whatever statement you're about to make?"

"It's common gossip."

"And what are my sisters doing soiling their skirts with common gossip?"

"Well, if that's the way you feel. We won't take any more of your time, Judge Bramwell."

"Very good!" he snorted, and snapped his glasses back on his nose.

Seething inwardly, Susan calmly resumed her tatting, waiting for her brother to put down his book again as she knew he inevitably would.

After a minute or two of twitchings and half-suppressed snorts, he put the book down with a bang that made her jump.

"Do, Joe!"

"Well, I better hear what you have to say."

She shook her head, her eyes on her work. "No I thank you, we're not going to have our heads snapped off, for merely wondering if some of the things we hear are true. It don't matter to us whether your Marshland friends are having trouble."

"What do you mean 'trouble'?"

"Just what I say. We've been hearing your nephew and his wife are at dagger points."

He relaxed into a chuckle. "Dagger points, eh? Strange it's completely escaped my notice, don't you think?"

"Very, considering the amount of time you spend there. But then a man can be curiously unobservant and dense about things. And a sense of loyalty makes him doubly blind sometimes."

"Now look here, Susie, I've had enough nonsense." He slapped the arm of his chair: "I insist on being told what you're driving at, without any further beating about the bush!"

"Has it escaped your notice that your nephew spends days at a time away from his home, at Charleston, Savannah, Coosaw and Land's End? Has it occurred to you that might mean something besides business?"

Joe's glasses dropped from his nose of their own accord. "What the devil are you insinuating?"

"We're not insinuating anything. We're trying to tell you what we've heard,—that Stephen—your nephew—has *affinities*."

"Concubines the Bible calls them," Isabel put in, and began to rock gently. "So I don't see why we should have to beat about the bush."

Joe was aghast. They had never seen him so fuming and so nearly inarticulate. He was flushed to the roots of his mane.

"Outrageous! . . . Absurd and ridiculous! . . . Good God!—I travel about too. Am I also under suspicion? Does anyone suspect me of—philanderings?"

"You're exceptional, Joe dear," Susan conceded without guile.

"Nothing of the sort! I think I can say without fear of contradiction that a man can have red blood in his veins and remain continent. Stephen is wedded to his business, as I am to the Law. I mean to say, the whole subject is too preposterous for discussion."

"We heard," Isabel sighed, fearing that the fireworks were over when she was just beginning to enjoy herself, "that they were not all white."

For the first time in his life Joe glared at his younger sister.

"That," he told her sharply, "will be enough."

"It's what we heard," she smiled at her folded hands.

642

"From whom? Where are your witnesses? What proof have you, and what evidence?"

"Softly, Joe dear," Susan interposed; "Bel's stomach's been upset. I think it's time we all went to bed."

He got up with a savage snort. "Let me out of this madhouse!"

That meant he was going to walk around the block, his way of letting off steam at times of intense stress. But Susan, who was already planning to have a basket of nuts and a plate of fruit-cake at his bedside against his return, ignored the violence of his wrath.

"Better wear your coat," she called after him as he went into the hall.

A moment later he appeared in the doorway with his hat jammed down to his ears, and pointed the raging forefinger of his cane hand at them.

"I'm ashamed of you! Heartily ashamed of both of you, upon my soul I am! And let me warn you for the last time. I will not tolerate the whispering tongue of scandal in this house! That's positive and final."

With the Great Storm the tide had turned in the Girls' favor. The lean years had come to an abrupt end. Life after that was fat with satisfactions for Susan and Isabel Bramwell.

But there was never any ultimate and complete satisfaction, for their mortal enemy refused to be downed by adversity. She had survived the loss of her friend Rusty, the decay of her husband, the death of her son. There was no final triumph to take the wind of hate out of the Girls' sails, and they watched Marshlands with increased alertness.

But now the interest was divided. Emily Fenwick remained the center of the circle of their hate, but there were two much more active points on the periphery that began to engage their serious attention for the first time.

Stephen was not one of them. He was too obviously licked. With eyes of mere contempt they watched him pass the Castle on his way to and from Bay Street, carrying himself as erect as ever but surely fooling no-one except perhaps himself with that pathetic shamming. For anyone could tell, a block away, that he was a man of straw. And who could look into his face without seeing at a glance failure and defeat. They had nothing to fear from him: he was out of the picture. And he might have dropped out of their thoughts altogether but for his passing the Castle, month in and month out, parading to his office to sit and talk through another day.

But Margaret and Jack were far from licked. They were up and coming. And though the Girls concentrated more and more of their attention on these youthful extensions of Emily Fenwick, it was a long time before they were rewarded with any results; so long a time, in fact, that they began to fear they had lost their knack for calling down wrath. And even then the results were meager and inconclusive. For bad marriages were not necessarily fatal.

There was no apparent reason why Margaret should have made a bad marriage. She was good-looking and she was said to have charm and brains of a sort. And she had plenty of admirers, not only local youths but also several quite respectable out-of-towners. If the information they pieced together from Sally Broughton was reliable, there were at least three serious suitors that summer of the elopement, any one of whom would have made a good match for the girl. One was a young professor of English at Winthrop College, an uncommonly handsome man in a common up-state way, who passed the Castle every day for two solid months in courting her from the Sea Island Hotel. And there was the minister of the Methodist Church at Rock Hill, with whom she was to do welfare work or some such rot in connection with her first year of teaching; he was an older man, and while loathing his denomination the Girls could see spiritual advantages at least in this match. And, finally, there was Bill Beckwith from Charleston, ugly as homemade sin but with money and good low-country blood on both sides. It was during her reported engagement to him, in fact it was just after her return from a stay with his family, that she had up and eloped with a traveling-man that nobody had ever heard of before.

"Wrong on both counts," Joe contradicted them across the dinner table, when they first referred to the event, between themselves to draw him out. "It was *not* an elopement, and he was *not* a traveling-man."

As their brother grew older, the Girls were becoming more and more daring. "What was it," Isabel asked her teacup, "a runaway?" And Susan put down her mincing fork to say directly: "Sally certainly told us she heard he was an itinerant salesman of some sort."

"Nothing of the sort! He was an insurance agent who had some business here. Came into the office several times to see Stephen, and put a little business his way if I'm not mistaken. One day Stephen took him home for dinner, and that's how he came to meet Margaret."

"And it was love at first sight, I suppose," Susan mocked.

"Exactly. And when his business called him back to North Carolina, she simply went with him, after a quiet marriage ceremony at Marshlands."

"What did he look like?" Isabel demanded. "I'll take another cup, Susie,—was he tall?"

"I didn't observe him closely. A man of good bearing, as I recall."

"Well," said Susan stiffly as she poured Isabel's tea, "what I don't understand is why it all had to be so quiet and hushed up, unless somebody was ashamed of something."

"Something funny about it, all right," Isabel agreed, smelling a rat in the sugar-bowl.

"I see no call for any such comment," he told them severely. "How they were wedded was, I take it, entirely their own affair."

"And you don't think it was over-hasty?" Susan pursued. "Why, Joe Bramwell, she hardly knew the man!"

"She knows him now, I'll wager," said Isabel, sipping her tea.

Up to this point their brother had not allowed the discussion to interfere with his enjoyment of the meal, pompano with plenty of butter sauce and hominy, but now he slapped down his napkin with a snort. "I repeat I don't consider it any of my concern, or yours, *how* they were wedded!" And he turned his chair away from the table, crossed his legs, and presented them with his profile to emphasize his disapproval.

Susan asked calmly: "How did her mother take it?"

"I am not at liberty," he answered punctiliously, "to divulge the confidences of a friend or a client, as you must know." They made no retort to that, and beguiled by his phrasing of the sentiment he added: "I can say she was not enthusiastic, but decided—wisely—that the girl was old enough to know her own mind and heart. After all, what more can a mother do in such a case?"

"Sounds to me like her speaking," Susan sniffed.

"It's *I* speaking!" he snapped over his shoulder. "Is that clear?"

Isabel snickered.

"Perfectly clear," said Susan. "And I suppose it's not a mother's duty to protect her daughter when a stranger comes along and turns her head. Let her fold her arms and trust to early training, I suppose, sink or swim." Warming suddenly to her theme, she slid forward to the very edge of her chair. "It was the same as a runaway marriage, Joe, and you know it as well as we do! Only you won't admit it. But you'll have to in time, for no good can ever come of it. Mark my words! . . . And her mother's obviously at fault. But what can you expect of that woman? Whatever happened to her daughter, *she'd* have no cause to complain, *she'd* be nobody to say anything."

"What do you mean?" he glared at her.

"I mean, for one thing, the girl never *was* properly brought up. Or properly chaperoned. She's been allowed to run loose with a perfect string of men! The only time she was ever decently chaperoned was when you squired her to the St. Cecilia. Well, too bad you couldn't have traipsed along when she used to go riding out to the woods with that army officer from Parris Island. Everybody knew what he was!"

"A perfect rake," Isabel put in.

"And," Susan went on, "in the second place, I mean what could you expect of *her* daughter? *She* had an army officer of her own once."

"Confound it!" he blasted them, swinging his chair back to the table with such force that the teacups slopped over, "—what the devil are you saying?"

In the face of this assault, Susan subsided: she hadn't meant to carry things quite so far. "Do, Joe," she protested mildly, rearranging the dishes with injured precision. "If you're going to get upset, I think we better drop the matter. Finish your supper before it gets cold."

But neither her brother nor her sister was willing to drop the matter there. "I demand an explanation!" he frothed. And Isabel chimed in with an hysterical little giggle: "The cat's out of the bag, Susie!"

"I'll tell it," she said, stiffening her back, "providing I'm accorded common courtesy. After all, it's not my story, and I disclaim any responsibility for it."

"It becomes your story," he warned her, "and your responsibility the moment you repeat it."

646

"In that case I have nothing to say. I'll thank you for the jam."

Isabel leaped into the breach. "I'll tell it, then."

"No, Bel!" Susan protested.

"Yes I will! We've known it for years, and it's time he heard it. She did have an army officer. When she first came to Beaufort as the bride of Aaron Moffet, she took a lover."

"Sally told us," Susan explained. "Old Mrs. Van Wie told Hal Turner, and he told Sally."

"It was an officer on Sherman's staff. His name was Herkimer."

"Old Mrs. Van Wie was here at the time and saw the whole scandalous affair."

"He was sent back here wounded and she nursed him at Marshlands. Her husband was away at the time."

"Part of the time he was here under this very roof when they were using it for a Yankee hospital!"

"Stop!" he shouted hoarsely. "I won't tolerate this!"

He pushed back his chair and stood up, livid with rage.

"If either of you scandalmongering women were a man, I'd take pleasure in horsewhipping you! If either of you were a brother instead of a sister, I'd horsewhip you out of this house!"

And after focusing all his rage into one terrible look at them, he stamped out into the hall.

For several minutes after the front door banged, they sat dead still, staring at each other through the stunning reverberations. Isabel was the first to break the silence.

"He'd horsewhip us," she sighed, hugging herself. "Wasn't that a nice thing to say. He was piping hot all right."

"Too hot," said Susan, removing the cozy to drain into her cup the last drops from the teapot. "You shouldn't have told him, Bel."

"You started it."

"But I had no intention of finishing it. We went too far this time. But he's too maddening about that woman! She plays on his fatal weakness for flattery, that's how she does it."

". . . Aaron Moffet had her, and then the soldier, and then Rusty, and then Stephen. Maybe Joe'll be next."

"Hush up, Bel! Now that's enough! We must put his plate in the oven and keep the biscuits hot."

"It was the same as a runaway marriage," Isabel said finally. "It was a disgrace, and no good can ever come of it."

So, for the time being, they disposed of Margaret. And when months later their brother announced to them, in a vindictive burst of confidence, that she was living very happily in Charlotte thank you and that there was a baby girl now, they were disgusted (the Bramwell blood gone further astray and under the trash name of Kennedy!) but they were not dismayed. A calculation of the time elapsed between the marriage and the birth netted them no scandal; but they remained satisfied that it was a bad marriage and must still end in disaster, that Emily Fenwick had been hurt by it and would be worse hurt before it was finished.

Their attention was now focused on Jack. Here was perfect material for breaking a mother's heart. . . . He had flunked out of the Citadel his first year, and that was the end of his schooling. Joe helped him to get a position in the bank, but he was tired of that within a month. He lasted a little longer as a hardware clerk at Turner Brothers', before he was discharged for chronic lateness. Why he left Van Wie's after only two days of clerking was obscure: general shiftlessness, they imagined. After that he made no further pretense at working. He loafed openly and without shame, tacking lazily up and down the river in his sailboat, disappearing for days on camping and fishing trips with one or two of his cronies, or just plain hanging around Bay Street corners. A likely youth, well able to begin a man's work in the world, yet already a perfect ne'er-do-well. Always in some scrape, but always getting out of it somehow.

But in the end he got caught, as they had foreseen, and in a grim trap. Sally Broughton brought the news. She had it from Hattie Fowler, prime gossip of the town, who had it straight from the County Clerk's office. "They took out the license here," Sally explained, "but they were married at Yemassee." The girl was from Port Royal, where she enjoyed an unsavory reputation; she was five or six years older than Jack; her father was an engineer on the railroad. "I understand he arranged the match," said Sally.

"A shotgun wedding," Isabel sighed. There was no question but that here was a crushing blow for Emily Fenwick. But they had hardly begun to relish the situation when their own brother stepped in to snatch the fat out of the fire.

"I'm arranging an annulment," he told them himself. "The boy was under age to begin with, and there's every evidence of gross fraud and collusion, to say nothing of coercion."

"A little late for an annulment, isn't it?" Susan asked him tartly. And Isabel was completely explicit: "Even an old law veteran like you can't annul a baby, can you, Joe?"

"I don't care to go into details," he said. "It's sufficient to say that if there are any damages involved, they were incurred before the boy was acquainted with the—defendant. I have already located several material witnesses, and no doubt there are others. As a matter of fact, the defendant herself has made several damaging admissions. In short, the case is as good as won, hands down and out of court. And I predict that the annulment proceedings will not be contested."

"A fine kettle of fish," Susan sniffed. "In all your years of practice, Joe, you've never stooped to anything like this."

"Poppycock! I'm not defending the boy. I acknowledge he's an irresponsible scapegrace. But——"

"He's the son of your good Yankee friend."

"That's entirely beside the point. In this case he was the victim of circumstances. I mean to say he was trapped by that little strumpet, and I consider it my duty to see common justice done."

And within a month after his marriage Jack Fenwick was free.

For a winter and a spring they saw nothing of him; he was working, they heard, at a lumber camp on the Combahee River near Holly Hill plantation. Then one fine June day he reappeared in town looking healthier and more irresponsible than ever, and again he was walking the streets or sailing his boat as bravely as if nothing whatever had happened. There was a rumor that he intended to enlist in the Marine Corps, but nothing came of it. He was fully developed now, a man physically, yet he continued to fritter away his time like a truant schoolboy. When he needed pocket money, he did odd jobs for his friend Ed Sands, the cracker contractor. The rest of the time he ate the bread of idleness at Marshlands and cheerfully loafed.

His favorite haunt now was the Sea Island Hotel. . . . After Reconstruction and carpetbagging days this hostelry, once the largest home in Beaufort, had fallen into disrepute and partial decay under a succession of shabby proprietors. But with the coming of the Spanish-American War, the construction of Fort Fremont, and the establishment of a Marine Corps base at Parris Island, the hotel had taken a new lease on life under the able proprietorship of a shrewd

649

and hearty woman by the name of O'Grady. It was flush times again: Bay Street was crowded with uniforms and the register of the Sea Island Hotel was fat with names. It was a short war, in Mrs. O'Grady's opinion, but she was not complaining. When the excitement was over, she and her husband found themselves well entrenched in the hotel business. And soon after the turn of the century a substantial peace-time revenue began to flow their way.

For many summers there had been a sprinkling of up-country visitors in Beaufort, but now they began to appear in numbers. Evidently, Susan and Isabel observed, there were Southerners of means again, and plenty of them: specimens of the New South who could afford to send their families to the coast to escape the inland heat. Each summer an increasing number descended upon the little tidewater town to regale themselves with sea breeze and sea food, bathing and boating. The Sea Island Hotel was fast becoming a resort. During July and August weekends they had to put cots in the attic to accommodate the overflow.

And the gaiety of the hotel gave a great fillip to the social life of the town. Everyone went to the Saturday night hops at the hotel. Formerly social festivities had been the prerogative of the Jean Ribaut Cotillion Club: the Girls remembered the days when the Ribaut Club had been an honorable and exclusive organization patterned after the St. Cecilia Society of Charleston; when it had been revived after the War and Reconstruction by their brother and a few survivors of the Beaufort Volunteer Artillery, they had rejoined as a matter of course; but later when the bars had been let down to admit the Rutherfords and other leading carpetbaggers, they had as a matter of course resigned. Now every Tom, Dick, and Harry belonged to the Club; and it was this assorted membership that flocked to the hotel hops, and in reciprocation issued wholesale invitations to the hotel guests for the Club's card-parties, barbecues, and fortnightly Germans.

The Girls were not too critical of their brother's continued allegiance to the Ribaut Club. They understood that he maintained his membership in that debased organization, allowed himself to be elected and re-elected its president, for good and sufficient reasons. After the Spanish-American War he had at last tossed his square derby into the arena of public life, to redeem his state—locally to begin with—from the yoke of the cracker machine. In his first bout with the machine he had felt it undignified and unnecessary to do much more than announce his candidacy, and as a result he had come off a very sad loser. But at the next election he had fought the devil with red fire; and with the help of the simple fact that the town was ripe for a change, his scorifying of the machine, his eloquent enunciation of his own platform ("Back to the eternal virtues and verities of Our Forefathers"), and his successful routing of all hecklers at a free-for-all fish-fry had swept him magnificently into office. And as Mayor, his sisters conceded, the Ribaut Club and his other diplomatic activities were justified means to worthy political ends.

But was it necessary, they questioned, for him to lead a German at the Sea Island Hotel with Mrs. O'Grady on his arm? She might be a good client and a figure of growing importance in town, but was it possible to draw the line nowhere between political and social life? There was a limit, and Joe had certainly overstepped it with this piece of buffoonery, which was more than they could stomach. More than he himself could, for that matter: as a result of the affair he was prostrate for three days with indigestion, which they might have thrown up to him as a lesson if they hadn't been so worried. They had no hesitancy, however, about expressing their disapproval to Sally Broughton, whom Joe had escorted to the hotel. When she appeared the morning after to visit the patient, they arraigned her on the carpet of the parlor.

"When you saw he was overdoing," Susan said severely, "we think you might have suggested leaving. Instead you kept him out till two A. M. and let him make himself deathly ill eating cake with green frosting and swilling green punch."

Because of her devotion to Joe, Sally always went out of her way to keep on amicable terms with his sisters. But she stood in no awe of them. "I'm not his guardian, Miss Susie," she replied with her generous laugh.

"And you don't have to nurse him," Susan said sharply.

"I'd be glad to, if I had a chance," Sally smiled,—and sobered, for that seemed to imply much more than she intended.

"Not while we're alive," Isabel told her with simple malice.

"We're none of us," Susan proceeded quickly, "as young as we used to be. Least of all Joe. He may have a Bramwell constitution, but the time's past when he could afford to stay up all night dancing jigs. And why should you want to attend a hotel ball, rubbing elbows with those people?"

"It was fun, Miss Susie."

Susan raised her eyebrows. "How could a dance presided over by that Mrs. O'Grady be fun for a lady?"

"She's really quite a character."

"Quite a bust," said Isabel, describing with her slender hands a gross arc out from her maidenly dress-front.

But beyond that there was really nothing the Girls could do about all this, except withdraw more deeply into their Castle shell. They would have shut out of their ken Mrs. O'Grady's Sea Island Hotel if it had not become Jack Fenwick's stamping ground. . . . He was now a fixture there. He made easy friends with the guests, young and old. He carried picnic parties to Bay Point in his sailboat for any recompense offered, arranged fishing trips and looked after the bait and tackle, taught the children to paddle like ducks in the swimming-crib under the bathhouse. He initiated after-supper games in the parlors, played poker with the men after the Saturday night hops, and could tell stories and hold his share of drinks like an old-timer. He met everybody with a smile, and people seemed to take to him instinctively.

"He's a scamp but you just can't help liking him," Sally was tactless enough to tell the Girls one time when she was giving them some particulars of him.

"We'll see what becomes of him," Susan said ominously.

One afternoon toward the end of June, two summers before the Fire of 1907, the Girls were taking their customary drive out the old Shell Road. Quite purple from holding their breath through "Sheba", a disreputable colored settlement on the fringe of town, they were breathing hard to catch up before closing their noses again to pass the Federal Cemetery, when they were confronted by a sniffling, snorting, rattlety-bang apparition. The horses shied, bolted, and swerved the carriage into the ditch, depositing the Girls with their coachman-butler in a heap at the very entrance to the Cemetery.

So the first automobile came to Beaufort, bearing the Riddocks of Atlanta, Georgia, for a vacation at the Sea Island Hotel. Frank Riddock, big and paunchy, of Riddock & Co., Cotton Brokers; Mrs.

Riddock, a queenly person with a heavy veil over her pansy-trimmed mushroom hat; and Nellie, their blonde peaches-and-cream daughter. And when Frank Riddock extricated himself from the wheel of the Stevens-Duryea, removed the cigar from his clenched teeth, and advanced in duster and goggles to the assistance of the ladies, he lifted his cap to receive an hysterical duet of abuse and a promise from the ladies that he would most certainly hear from their lawyer in the morning.

This promise the Girls were not, unfortunately, able to keep: their brother informed them that, outrageous as it seemed, the law provided no redress in their case. But at least they had the satisfaction of telephoning the hotel, each afternoon when they contemplated a drive, to caustically inquire if That Automobile was being taken out. If it was, they walked to St. Helena's Church and back, hoping to be passed on the way by the horrid honking contraption so that they could wither its occupants with contempt; which they were actually able to do on several occasions, though the Riddocks were not people who withered easily. . . . And despite the shock, bruises, and indignity they had suffered, the Girls were able in time to view the whole incident philosophically. For it had introduced them, most vividly and at the outset, to people who were to play a large part in Jack Fenwick's life.

That summer the Riddocks practically adopted Jack.

But the Girls were disappointed in their expectations that sensational developments would immediately arise from the combination. Without anything dramatic having happened between Fourth-of-July and Labor Day, Frank Riddock honked his family away from the Sea Island Hotel and Beaufort, his daughter apparently perfectly intact. Then there was a development of a singularly unsatisfactory nature. The following winter Jack Fenwick went to work for Riddock & Co. in Atlanta.

Confronted with a sudden blank where Jack had been for so long, the Girls were compelled to fall back on Emily and Stephen, living alone at Marshlands. But now there was practically no action at the center of the stage, and they were reduced to making the most of such paltry matters as Emily's "patronizing welfare work".

"I hear she's going in for poor white trash now," Susan told Isabel across the hearth-rug one evening that winter, for Joe's benefit. "Not satisfied uplifting the poor island darkies."

653

"She must think she's Lady Bountiful," said Isabel, watching her brother out of the corner of her eye.

It was not long before he was goaded into putting down his book.

"May I introduce the thought," he asked them ponderously as he took off his pince-nez, "that nothing you say can alter or obscure the fact that Emily Fenwick is a public-spirited woman. Without a trace of show she has quietly and generously given of her time, of herself, and of her very modest resources to people of this district, white and colored, who were friendless and in distress. I only wish I could say as much of my sisters."

"Well," Susan smiled grimly, "we only wish we had the arrogance, or whatever it takes, to think ourselves wise and superior enough to go around telling other people how to manage their lives. As for charity, we don't pretend to set ourselves up as an eleemosynary institute on your hard-earned money. There are organizations to take care of the needy, and we don't believe in it anyway."

"We believe," Isabel rocked, "in minding our own business."

For once in his life Joe refused to be drawn into debate. "I don't always," he continued, addressing the andirons with heavy complacency, "find myself in accord with Emily Fenwick's social theories."

"We're surprised to hear that," Susan sniffed.

"But," he went on, "I applaud her social practices. On democracy and progress, education for the masses and related subjects, we hold opposing views, but I respect her idealism for its sincerity and her good-will for its intelligence. She's a rare woman, and she's earned her popularity with all classes of people in this community."

"Stuff!" snapped Susan. "Not with *us*. She's earned our everlasting hate, and she'll be paid off some fine day!"

". . . Susan," he said to her deliberately, "you and I have been living together on this planet for some time, haven't we?"

She was too busy twitching with indignation on the edge of her chair to give the question any explicit acknowledgment.

"Haven't we?" he repeated.

"Do, Joe," she answered without looking at him.

"We've been living together," he pursued with a sigh, "since you were born and as long as I can remember. Not a very long time measured by eternity, but long enough to get fairly well acquainted, wouldn't you say?"

She was rigidly attentive now, but made no answer and continued to look at Isabel.

"Fairly well acquainted," he went on with relentless deliberation. "And yet do you know I'm compelled to make a very humiliating confession. I find after all these years I don't really know you at all."

"What are you talking about?" she asked him.

"Why, all these years I've been laboring under the delusion that because my sisters attended church with me and professed Christianity they were Christians. Have you ever in your life stopped to consider what that term means?"

"Do, Joe!" she flashed at him. "You can't be serious."

"Don't evade the question. When you take unto yourself the high title of Christian, follower of Christ, what obligations does that put upon you?"

"I've always supposed it put many 'obligations' upon us."

"Precisely. Many. But primarily what?"

"Faith. Faith in God, and Hope of salvation."

"Ah. And now abideth these *two*: Faith and Hope! And where, may I ask, is the rest of the Thirteenth Chapter of Corinthians? Is Charity no longer the supreme word? Don't all the law and the prophets still hang on this, that thou shalt love thy neighbor as thyself?"

Susan sat speechless, frozen at this unprecedented attack. But Isabel entered the fray with zest and abandon.

"Sam Koenig's your neighbor, ain't he? And Ed Sands? What about them—do you love them as thyself?"

"There's nothing in the commandment," he snorted, "about loving skunks, carpetbaggers, or crackers."

Susan recovered her breath to snap: "It only applies to a certain *lady* carpetbagging neighbor, Bel,—Aaron Moffet's widow, nigger-loving schoolmarm, freethinking Yankee hussy who married his nephew! Joe Bramwell, you can insult your sisters till you're blue in the face, but you can't make us believe that black is white or that we should tolerate your devotion to that Yankee woman! And if hating her makes us Pharisee Christians in your eyes, we're proud to be damned!"

"Your pride makes you blind," he shrugged wearily. "I feel sorry for you, that's all."

And he resumed his pince-nez and book with a serene finality that blocked any further discussion.

On several later occasions they found opportunities to sneer at the woman's "Good Samaritan exhibitions", but he continued to give an exhibition of extraordinary self-control at this period. He could be neither lured nor prodded into a decent argument, a real hot and heavy give-and-take.

↑   ↑   ↑

So the Girls had been almost at the end of their rope when the Fire of 1907 came to their rescue.

But after the excitements of the Fire had burned out, life began to pall again. By the following spring they were put to it to find any entertainment in the vapid happenings around them, and there were simply no Fenwick developments at all. Then suddenly, like an act of God, back on the scene came Margaret Fenwick.

Sally Broughton brought the news. . . . After the razing to the ground of Turner Brothers' store in the Fire, Joe had gallantly taken Sally into his office as secretary; and though she seemed definitely beyond the age of allurement, the Girls had not been able at first to view this abrupt propinquity with any detachment. As their brother's keeper they had even felt it their duty, in the first month of the arrangement, to make several surprise visits to the office. But finally, after time and complete lack of success had restored them to their senses sufficiently to abandon the sensational, and after milder and subtler tactics of argument seasoned with insinuation had failed to dislodge Sally, they had reviewed the whole case soberly and arrived at acceptance; grateful acceptance, when they had realized that Sally as secretary was really a blessing in disguise, for it might have been a younger woman, a very much younger woman, some unprincipled and dangerous young baggage in fact. And then, too, Sally was now situated to keep them well posted. But for her in her new and strategic position they might not have heard this momentous news of Margaret Fenwick's return till hours or even days later, for certainly Joe would never have mentioned it to them.

"What's wrong?" Susan asked from an immediate suspicion.

Why nothing, so far as Sally knew. Just a visit home.

"How does she look?" Isabel wanted to know.

Fine, Sally thought. And the little girl was with her, a really lovely child.

"Anything else?" Susan urged.

Well, Sally guessed through a slight flush, there was another baby on the way.

Isabel was inclined to look into that, but Susan cut her off.

"You might have spared us that detail, Sally. But you better keep your ears open at the office. Joe don't realize how shut in keeping house for him keeps us, and he forgets to tell us what's going on outside. I happen to think there's something more to this than a visit. . . . We want you to try a package of this special Ceylon tea from Charleston, dear."

But they didn't depend entirely on Sally's ears for developments. For all her good sense Sally remained, in their estimation, an essentially ingenuous person. It would be like her to overlook some highly significant clue.

Fortunately there was the telephone. . . .

In the years between the blowing-up of the *Maine* and the Great Fire there were several events of importance, in the Girls' lives, that did not issue from Marshlands and the Fenwicks. Foremost, of course, was their brother's election and reëlection to the office of Mayor. But other events jostled for second place in their favor. Certainly their initial traffic with an automobile, the Riddocks', was an event and a landmark. And there was the trip to Charleston with Joe to see their first motion picture, living shadows of the Russo-Japanese War. The experience left them blear-eyed and shrilly critical of the new medium: it was their first and last, as they told Sally. And within a few days their only clear recollections of the thing were a recurrent disappearing gun and the impression that the war had been waged in a heavy rain-storm. But there was no denying that it was an event, and they cherished it as such.

And then there was Theodore Roosevelt's appointment of Crum. That was really an epic. They had not attempted to follow their brother's elaborate demolition of the Rough-Rider President as a statesman; he was a Republican and a Yankee, and that was quite enough against him. Yet when—after volunteering an assurance, during a visit to Charleston, that the South had nothing to fear from him—he had turned around and appointed Dr. Crum, a man of color, Collector of the Port of Charleston, it had simply taken their breath away. And serving under Crum at the Custom House was Miss Mary Washington, a descendant of George Washington! It was no wonder they were not surprised when, later, Roosevelt entertained Booker T. Washington at the White House.

And there was the event of Owen Wister. A friend of Roosevelt's from Philadelphia, he had appeared in Beaufort and taken rooms for several weeks. It was quickly reported that the author of *The Virginian* was writing a novel about Beaufort, and immediately the whole town was aflutter. No-one more than the Girls, for the distinguished visitor frequently strolled by the Castle and paused to study it. But the upshot of their self-conscious suspense was a grating anticlimax. When the book materialized and they put aside their steady diet of *Confederate Veteran* and *Spirit of Missions* to plunge into it, *Lady Baltimore* proved to be only a cake after all, and a Charleston cake at that: an icing of patronizing familiarity spread over a flat batter of satire, melodrama, and romance.

When Frank Stockton, author of *The Lady or the Tiger?*, wandered into town some time later, he too was reported to be engaged on a story with a Beaufort setting and he too seemed singularly impressed by the Castle. But the Girls were not taken in a second time; they not only did not linger in the garden in lavender and lace, as they had done for the benefit of Mr. Wister, but they ostentatiously pulled down shades when Mr. Stockton paused at the gate. And, as they foresaw, nothing came of the visit,—except a vulgar pun attributed to him after his departure. He was said to have referred to the black waitresses at the Sea Island Hotel as the "Colognial Dames" of Beaufort.

A dire event was the erection of an oyster-canning factory on the Ladies Island shore across the river from the marsh inlet where the Castle brooded. To the Girls, who were so sensitive to sleep-disturbing noises that Joe often had to go out in his slippers with a lantern and a paddle to silence frogs in the garden pool, a steam whistle at dawn was the last straw.

"It's enough to wake the dead!" Susan told her brother.

"It keeps us awake all night, waiting for it," Isabel added.

"I find it rather melodious," he answered them. "Like a ship coming into port."

But they became so shrill about it that he was goaded at last into threatening the owners with a public-nuisance warrant. An unfortunate move, because it provided Ed Sands' cracker party with just the ammunition they needed for the next mayoralty campaign: Joseph Bramwell was a reactionary seeking to obstruct the industrial development of Beaufort. And when Joe, running for his third term, was defeated in the primaries, a sawmill and lumber yard were promptly located as near the Castle as possible; within a block, in fact, on a waterfront lot burned bare in the Fire. The Girls then found their view down the river shut off, to the accompaniment of a rasping saw, a chugging engine, and acrid smoke, a combination particularly effective when the wind was from the south, the prevailing wind in summer when the windows had to be left open. And Joe, who was finding that a slight tendency toward deafness had its advantages, told them they better start getting used to the situation because there was nothing he could do about it. And so, finally, there was no escape from the decay of the town, not even within the confines of the Castle.

These, then, were the outstanding other-than-Fenwick events of the Girls' lives in the decade after the *Maine*. These and one other, which turned out to be the most important of all. The installation of a party-line telephone.

Strangely enough, neither of them grasped its importance at first. Undoubtedly it was, as Joe said, "an invention second only to the electric light in its wonders and potentialities, an instrument for the gods"; and not the least of its wonders was the way it made itself so perfectly at home on the wall of the back hall. But its potentialities eluded them for weeks, while its presence overawed them. . . . They approached it more bravely than Jenny, their latest cook, who could hardly be driven to answer it when they shouted down the banisters. But Isabel answered with closed eyes and became mildly hysterical before she turned the receiver over to Susan, who did most of the talking, with wide eyes and in a very rapid voice.

Soon, however, they learned to spin the handle without flinching, to give the number distinctly, and to speak to Joe at the office in as normal a voice as if he were with them in the back hall; to hang up quickly if Stephen happened to answer instead of Joe or Sally; and not to jump when the bell jangled for them,—one, two, three, four, *five*. But it took some time for them to grasp the significance of the rings, to realize that all Fenwick Street was their oyster. The great illumination came one bright morning when Susan lifted the receiver to call the meat market and found herself connected with Hal Turner's wife gossiping with Mabel Hitchcock. That was almost three weeks after the installation. But now, in a single hour of investigation and deduction, they worked out the whole party system. Number one was the Van Wies; number two, the Turners; three, the Allens. The Rutherfords were number six. And number four was the Fenwicks.

In the rush to make up for lost time, and in the first blush of their inexperience, they received many cuts and bruises. And even after they learned that sneaking the receiver off the hook was only subjectively better than snatching it off, and that the best time to break in was just at the end of the ring, still there was Mrs. Fowler to contend with. Somehow Hattie Fowler, widow of the pilot captain, had mustered enough backing to secure for herself the position of night operator. The day operator, Louella Simpson, was a harmless young person with an almost deferential voice; and there was no danger of any rebuffs from the head of the exchange, Mr. Boutelle, whose pleasant voice, baritone of the Baptist Church choir, was on between the hours of twelve and two. But after seven, when Hattie Fowler came on, the telephone was charged with dynamite. She was the watchdog of the system and reserved to herself the right to listen in. In their first recklessness the Girls had tasted the evening hours and found them best of all, but after several direct encounters with Hattie Fowler they had restricted their attempts to the fateful moments when the bell jangled four for the Fenwicks. That was close enough to their own number, fortunately, to make an occasional mistake only natural.

"But you rang five," they countered when they were caught.

"I rang *four*, Miss Bramwell!" Hattie barked at them.

"Well, this bell certainly rang *five*."

And they hung up with a bang.

In time, when they had learned all the ropes, Susan came to feel the need of an etiquette to dignify their moments of success. "I picked up the receiver to ring Joe," (she simply ignored the fact that the ring preceded the receiver-lifting) "and I couldn't help hearing ——. . . ." And it pained her that Isabel refused to take the hint and made no bones whatever about her discoveries. "I just got in on

660

Stephen talking to *Her* from the office! . . ." And though they were both equally quick to detect any suspicious clicks while they were talking, Susan regretted her sister's failure to abide by an impersonal formula of rebuke. Susan always said: "I believe there's someone else on the line,—I wish people would have the courtesy to keep off when they know the line's in use"; and then, after a patient pause, "The line's in use, please." But Isabel said anything that popped into her head, and it seldom lacked sting. For example: "I hear you, and I know who you are too!—Why don't you mind your own business?" And once she went so far as to call the offender by name, with the result that Joe received a visit from Hal Turner on behalf of his insulted wife. After that, Isabel was compelled to soften her inflections and keep her conjectures anonymous.

And just as the Girls were perfecting their technique in this complicated game, everyone else on the party line perfected hers. It was becoming extremely difficult to score a point. But the Girls were not much chafed, for already the game was beginning to drag. They were getting a little tired of expending a ton of nervous energy to discover that the Rutherfords were having pork chops for dinner again; of eavesdropping on the Allen boy miserably stammering the same old mawkish maunderings to his girl; or of trying to make heads and tails out of the cunning code that Mrs. Allen and the Baptist preacher's wife had devised for the exchange of gossip. And though Emily and Stephen Fenwick, unsuspicious of or indifferent to the ears of their neighbors (the Girls could never decide which it was), continued to use the telephone without inhibition, even when Hattie Fowler could be avoided there was nothing of importance to be picked up. Only occasional clues that had to be painfully pieced together and then still made absolutely nothing.

After the Fire there was a sensational reshuffle and new deal on the Fenwick Street line, which revived the Girls' interest and sustained it through the following winter. But by spring the new deal had become old play, and the Girls' interest was flagging again. So they were in a highly receptive mood for Sally's tidings that Margaret Fenwick was in town, with her little girl—and another child coming.

And now they all but lived in the back hall, where the telephone returned their watchful gaze inscrutably from the dark wall. They even gave up their afternoon drives for fear of missing a clue. For their initial surmise that something was radically wrong was blossoming into conviction with the deepening of spring. It was all very well for Sally to maintain that there was nothing unusual about a daughter visiting her parents without her husband: since her marriage she had been home twice before. But why was she staying so long this time? Why did she look like a ghost when she passed the Castle with the little girl? Something very strange about the whole business. And though it was impossible to verify their conviction by any bits of Marshlands telephoning they were able to pick up, as spring passed into summer with still no sign of departure or the husband, they became surer and surer and more and more alert.

According to Sally's calculations Margaret's confinement was expected about the middle of September. But the summer passed and September came and went without any news, though Margaret and the little girl were no longer seen out walking. Two weeks of October faded away; the first tang of autumn was in the air; and still no news. . . .

One day toward the end of the month the Girls broke their own long confinement and went out for an afternoon drive. They were practically forced out by internal pressures. Over the Castle for days had hung the cloud of their brother's defeat, at the hands of Ed Sands and the cracker machine, in the mayoralty contest. And at noon of this day Judy Chizzum, their latest cook, had run amok in the kitchen,—presumably a church-supper hangover complicated by cooking sherry and a dram or two of Joe's old bourbon. Now they were quieting their shaken nerves with a drive into the country, to gather roadside golden-rod and a few last passion-flowers. . . . They returned to find Sally waiting to tell them that Emily Fenwick had taken Margaret to Charleston to the hospital on the afternoon train.

But two days later, on Halloween, they were able to beat Sally to the denouement.

Although this was the festival of devils and witches, black cats and bands of marauding boys, Joe had felt it was more important to go to sit with Stephen than to stay home to protect his sisters. Normally they would have retired the moment he was out of the house, but there was nothing normal about tonight; they were worn to exhaustion by a day of interviewing applicants for Judy's place and at the same time listening for the telephone, but they were determined to sit up till their brother got back. Last year, they had reminded him as he left, the town boys had torn pickets off the fence and carried the porch chairs off to St. Helena's graveyard: this year, Isabel had dreamed, they were going to cut down the great coral-vine that she and Susan had trained so faithfully for so many years,—so faithfully that it not only shrouded the porch with its leaves and grape-like clusters of autumnal bloom but also reached up to the very battlements, covering the whole face of the Castle so that openings had to be cut periodically to free the windows and blinds. . . . And at intervals during the evening they did leave their fireside chairs to peep out, at the edge of the shades, for dark forms in the garden. But these little tiptoed journeys were not allowed to interrupt the telephone listening.

By ten o'clock their nerves, still frayed from the Judy incident, were jumping at every little pop or crackle of the fire. But they stuck it out till eleven. Then, though Joe had not yet come in, they had to give up.

They had hardly bolted their bedroom door when the telephone jangled *four*. Quick as they could they rushed downstairs and grabbed the receiver.

Hattie Fowler's unmistakable voice was saying: "The telegraph office at the station was closed, so they had to telephone it from Charleston. Anything I can do, Mr. Fenwick?"

A tired voice answered: "No, thank you. . . . Wait a moment. Yes,—I want to get my son, in Atlanta."

"All right, Mr. Fenwick. Now if you'll hang up, I'll call you when I get the connection. . . ."

Susan hung up with a gasp. And for the next quarter of an hour she and Isabel waited in a state of suspense too acute for word or movement, almost for breath. At last the bell jangled and Susan snatched the receiver to her ear again.

"Hello?" Stephen's voice said. "Hello,—Jack?"

"Oh, Mr. Fenwick," Hattie Fowler's voice rasped, "they say your son's out and they don't seem to know where he is or when he'll be in. I could try Mr. Riddock's residence,—he might be there. Or would you want to leave a message with this party?"

"I'll leave a message, please."

There was a moment of confusion, a sudden tumult of buzzings and voices, through which Hattie Fowler called idiotically, "Atlanta?—Atlanta!—Atlanta?" Then abruptly the tumult subsided to

663

a dull and distant roaring, like the ocean on some far strand, and Hattie sang: "Go ahead now, Mr. Fenwick."

". . . Hello," Stephen said, "—will you take a message for Jack Fenwick?"

A remote voice squeaked something.

Hattie Fowler broke in: "Louder, Mr. Fenwick,—connection's bad."

Stephen Fenwick cleared his throat and spoke louder. "Hello! . . . I want to leave a message for Jack Fenwick. This is his father speaking. . . . A message!—I want to leave a *message* for him. . . . Please tell him his sister died tonight. . . . His *sister*. . . . *Died*. . . . That's right. . . . Yes. . . . Thank you. . . ."

So the next morning when Sally telephoned from the office, they were ready for her.

"I've just heard some bad news," Sally began excitedly. "Joe says he forgot to tell you."

"Yes," said Susan dryly, "he forgot. He always forgets. But fortunately we're not dependent on him or anyone else for news."

Sally's voice was incredulous. "You mean you've heard?"

"Yes, we've heard."

"About Margaret Fenwick?"

"Of course. We knew all about it last night."

But there was still the old problem: the lack of a fresh, virgin, and susceptible audience upon whom they could spring full-force their feelings about all this. And that at least had something to do with the fact that their first feeling was pleasure when, on the afternoon of the following day, their niece Eugenia Fenwick appeared from Charleston.

✓   ✓   ✓

Her appearance was not unexpected. They knew she had been on the verge of leaving Charleston since the beginning of cold weather, and now Margaret's death had precipitated the move; Joe had warned them that she was coming for the funeral, that he had telegraphed her to come from the train to the Castle and wait for him to stop by for her. So they could hardly feign surprise. But they could certainly conceal their pleasure, and they did, rigidly. Particularly when they saw that the hackman was unloading not only several traveling-cases but also a trunk.

When Eugenia had paid the man she came fluttering up the garden path like an autumn butterfly, between the beds of Joe's chrysanthemums, and up the porch steps. When with disconcerted fingers she succeeded in lifting her veil, her aunts submitted their cheeks to her pecks. Through a little tempest of greetings then they examined her candidly, observing with satisfaction what they had expected: that she was now completely faded and dried-up.

"You've come for the funeral, I suppose," said Susan without circumlocution, after the formalities were disposed of.

Eugenia was unable to keep astonishment out of her nod, for she on her side was observing that her aunts had changed not a hair since she had last seen them, ages ago in Charleston at the time of the concert. They were the same pair of alert gray creatures, a sort of cross between birds and mice. The only change, she realized, was in herself: she had somehow caught up with them. Yet they still had the power of making her feel like a child. And by the glint in their eyes she knew they were as ready as ever to pounce on her, and that she must be intently on her guard.

"Yes," she answered, mistily. "I—I couldn't stay away. Margaret was always my favorite."

"We didn't know you had any favorites there," Susan pursued, returning with Isabel to the work that Eugenia's arrival had interrupted,—the training, with bits of string, of stray tendrils of the coral-vine that shrouded the porch. "Didn't know you could abide any of them. To say nothing of attending a funeral of theirs."

Cornered, Eugenia's eyes shifted frantically from the porch to her luggage waiting at the gate like a supplicant dog, to the street for sight of Joe coming to rescue her, and then back in a panic to her aunts' busy fingers. Recognizing the futility of trying to escape, she said bravely: "After all, blood is thicker than water."

"Not when it's part carpetbagger Yankee," Susan snapped. "At least, not for us."

"Don't see," Isabel put in softly, "how she could have the face to go, after being on the outs with them all this time."

"Some of us have very convenient forgetories, Bel," Susan told her sister significantly.

"Oh, I didn't think she could hold the pose much longer. The strain was too much for her kind of backbone."

"Well," Susan conceded with hasty charity, "I suppose we must all follow the dictates of conscience, no matter where they lead."

Stifling her feelings, Eugenia defended herself in a mild and apologetic voice. "I've learned that time heals all wounds. We must forgive and forget, at a time like this at least. That is the light I have now."

Susan stopped her work and confronted Eugenia sharply.

"You're not really going to try to make up with them, are you? Is that what you mean?"

"Goodness, no. I hope I have some pride."

"I hope so too. But I doubt it. . . . Why did you bring all that hand-luggage and that trunk with you, then?"

"But surely you didn't think I was going back to Marshlands."

"We had no notion what you contemplated. You might have been entertaining some wild idea of staying here, for all we know."

It took Eugenia a moment to catch her breath after that rebuff. "I'm on my way," she finally rallied herself to say, "to Savannah."

Susan's eyes narrowed and she regarded Eugenia absently while she considered that.

"Savannah. . . . Well, while you're waiting for Joe you may as well come in and have tea."

Eugenia hesitated. "Is it safe to leave my things there?"

Susan cast a quick but disdainful glance at the forlorn luggage at the gate.

"Perfectly safe. Joe will be back in about half an hour. And he'll see that your things get to the hotel."

So burning with hate and injustice and suppressed tears Eugenia followed her aunts into the parlor, where a grate fire was simmering cozily. The atmosphere of the room was distinctly sedative; and by the time the tea-tray was brought in and the chairs settled, her nerves were measurably steadied. She was still quivering inside, but her confidence was sufficiently restored from the porch encounter to attempt a fresh approach, as if she had just this instant arrived.

"I must say," she ventured brightly as she peeled off her gloves, "you both do look wonderfully well."

"One or two lumps?" Susan asked her with peremptory suspiciousness. ". . . Wish we could say the same for you, Eugenia. You do

666

well to try Savannah,—it's evident Charleston hasn't agreed with you."

"It's a wonder we're alive," Isabel interposed. "Tell her about Judy the cook, Susie."

"Let's wait till we hear about Savannah, Bel. You may as well take off that hat, Eugenia, and be comfortable while you're waiting. It gives me a headache just to look at it. If women could see what they really look like in those ridiculous overstuffed headgears, they wouldn't make such fools of themselves."

"Why, I've been told it's very becoming," Eugenia protested with a forced little laugh. "And it's the very latest model."

"I can assure you it's very unbecoming."

Eugenia raised her eyebrows. But she pulled out the bachelor-button hatpins and removed the offensive member.

"Look!" Isabel popped, "—she's got rats in her hair, like Sally."

Instinctively Eugenia put her hands up to protect her hair. "Why, Aunt Bel," she gasped, "what's wrong with that? Everybody's doing their hair up like this now."

"Everybody isn't," Susan contradicted. "We're not. And we know other ladies whose heads aren't turned by every puff of the wind. The trend of all fashions has been getting worse for years, but we haven't been led astray or deceived for a moment. . . . Rats! Unsightly and unsanitary. Do you realize they're made from the hair of dead Chinamen?"

"And just look," Isabel pursued relentlessly, "—her hair was turning gray and now she's got it jet black! She's *dyed* it!"

"Oh!" Eugenia quivered. "Is there any harm in that?"

"Don't you snap at Bel," Susan flashed from the edge of her chair. "And don't be so pettish and touchy. I can't see myself why you should be ashamed of gray hair. It should be a badge of distinguished service and wisdom attained. And it certainly softens a woman's face."

"Shall we tell her about the Fire?" Isabel blandly asked her sister.

"One minute, dear, till we hear about Savannah. What are your plans, Eugenia? Your funds must be running low, to say the least."

"Well, I'm going to Savannah to live,—that's all. I'll stay with the Mowbreys, if it's congenial."

"I wouldn't count on that, if I were you. I suspect you'll find the Mowbreys very distant cousins if you try to get close to them."

"Oh, I'm not counting on them. Or anyone else, for that matter. I long ago learned not to look to other people for anything."

"Very philosophical," Susan sniffed. "And so much easier said than done. You've been looking to Joe for some time now, if we're not mistaken."

"Joe said," Isabel rocked, addressing Eugenia directly for the first time, "you didn't have a friend in Charleston. Said you'd worn out your welcome with everybody you knew."

"It's not true! And I don't believe he ever said it."

"Eugenia!" Susan warned. "Now we don't care for any more of that, if you please. If you can't tell your story without bad-tempered digressions and rudeness, we better leave you to wait for Joe by yourself."

Eugenia subsided in her chair with an inward sigh of impotence. When she had recovered a little, she went on with a sort of desperate patience. "I'm sick and tired of Charleston and Charleston people. They don't wear well. Savannah will be different. I know I'll be able to organize several classes for children there, in French and dancing and water-color painting. And I particularly want to collect material for a life of General Oglethorpe."

"General Oglethorpe? We thought you were interested in General Wade Hampton. What's become of him?"

"I've given that up. I don't think he was quite—the figure I thought he was."

"Just what do you mean by that?"

"Well, I don't like the way he served as United States Senator. And I don't like what he is reported to have said on his death-bed,—'God bless my children, white and black'."

"Poppycock," Susan jeered with a jerk of her head. "Don't be a fool, Eugenia. Wade Hampton redeemed the State from carpetbag and black rule, from Yankees and niggers,—isn't that enough? . . . As for your Oglethorpe," she added as an afterthought, "his claim to fame rests on the founding of a colony for the release and propagation of bondspeople and felons, criminals and fallen women, the riffraff of English prisons, the scum of the earth. Your Oglethorpe is responsible for the state of Georgia. A splendid theme."

Eugenia made no attempt to debate the point. Instead she made a gesture of acquiescence, which permitted her to shift her position so that she could steal a glance out the window at the gate and the street. But there was no sign of Joe coming to her rescue; there was nothing to do but face his sisters again.

"The future is all so nebulous," she said sadly to her teacup. "Only the past is clear. And I'm so out of touch with everything that's happened since I left here."

Susan sniffed at that. "We supposed," she said in her most matter-of-fact voice, "Joe had been keeping you well posted."

"I never asked him anything about Marshlands."

"Well, don't ask us. Joe never tells us anything,—what little we know we have to pick up by chance or from Sally. And besides you know well enough we're not interested in Marshlands and never discuss those people."

"How," Isabel suddenly shot at Eugenia, "did you know Margaret was dead?"

"Why, there was a notice in the paper. But I don't know yet what she died of."

"Blood poisoning," Isabel told her, rocking gently. "They took her to the Charleston Hospital in the baggage-car, and brought her back dead. But the child lived."

"It was a septicaemia operation, we hear," Susan nodded.

"What really killed her," Isabel rocked on, "was a broken heart. He deserted her in Charlotte, her husband did. That Kennedy creature. She crawled back home a sick woman, and when her time came she just had no strength left. She looked like a ghost. We told Joe in the beginning how that marriage would turn out. And it serves them all right, those damn Fenwicks!"

"Do, Bel," Susan remonstrated.

"Sally says she hears," Isabel rambled on, "she gave the child a name before she died. *Jane.* That may be a Fenwick name from way back, but it ain't Bramwell. It's most as bad as her other child's name, *Eleanor.* Rhymes with Kennedy and cracker and Yankee blood, don't it? But Joe told Sally he's going to make both children Fenwicks by law, in case the father ever turns up to claim them."

"Wait, Bel dear," Susan interrupted. "Now I think we've gone far enough. It's not dignified for us to discuss those people for Eugenia's edification. It's enough to say simply that they're gradually getting what they deserve. If she wants particulars, let her get the information herself first-hand from them, after the funeral."

Isabel smiled vaguely at her sister and without resentment fell silent. Eugenia decided there was no point in looking injured; with an expression of strict indifference she merely looked away, glancing again at the window to see if she could make Joe appear. Unsuccessful, she lowered her eyes to her teacup and waited, mute and tense. They were now going to give her a dose of silent treatment, she realized, and she promised herself that for once in her life she was not going to let them get the best of her. She had made the old mistake of approaching them with a flag of truce instead of with banners flying, and so in the opening encounters she had been as badly routed as usual; but now she was going to show them that she was more than a match for them now, if it was war they wanted: she could beat them at their own games, she would teach them what a real "stopper" was. Rather than break this uncomfortable silence she would sit here with them like a bump on a log till doomsday, or at least till Joe arrived.

Isabel was the first to crumple under the strain.

"Should we tell her," she asked with a sudden fidget, "about Jack?"

Susan shook her head.

"Well," Isabel mutinied, "there's certainly no harm in telling her about the Robinsons, about Linda and her child."

"I know all about that," Eugenia cut in coolly.

Susan stared at her. "You knew she had a child by one of those men stationed at Fort Fremont?"

"I heard," Eugenia wavered, feeling a sickening return of cowardice and self-pity as she faced Susan's steel, "that she married an Engineer Corps officer. He was ordered to the Philippines just after the marriage and was killed there, leaving her a widow with child."

"And did you know," Susan demanded from the very edge of her chair, "that there was some question about the paternity of the child? Did you know it was rumored her boy was born prematurely, too soon by weeks if not months? Or did Joe spare you the sordid details?"

"She was supposed," Isabel inserted sweetly, "to be soft on Michael. But it was only a few months after he died that she married the soldier."

As they closed in on her, all Eugenia's resolution weakened to water. But at that moment she caught sight of Joe's carriage at the gate at last, and the sight went to her head like some swift and violent stimulant. Her spine stiffened, and in a flash she had set down her teacup and grabbed up her hat. For a second she stood before the dim mantel mirror to guide her tingling fingers as they thrust in the hatpins. Then she turned on her ancient tormentors with eyes burning with ages of suppressed rage and hate.

"My light," she lashed at them in a voice that startled even herself, "is to resist not evil. But I've got to forget that long enough to tell you how I loathe you both. I came here peaceably inclined, as usual, —and as usual I've been browbeaten, abused, and insulted. But now I'm going to show you I have some pride. You'll never have another opportunity to insult me. I promise you that!"

They were both struck dumb for a breathless moment.

"Eugenia *Fenwick*," Susan finally found the voice to say, "you're an ass. You always were, and you always will be."

"And you're a pair of horrid old buzzards! I never want to see your faces again. I'll never speak to either of you again as long as I live. And I won't be among the mourners at *your* funeral!"

She turned her back on them and started for the front door.

"No," Isabel called after her, "because you won't get a chance!"

But that was not a sufficiently satisfactory last word, they realized as they watched her drive off with Joe. And after they had made fresh tea and exchanged hysterics over the afternoon's sensational fray, they were forced to acknowledge to each other that they had been badly worsted, and by Eugenia of all people.

This was humiliation and vexation of such caliber that even the funeral procession, which they watched from an upstairs window overlooking Fenwick Street, failed to restore their poise. When the slow file of carriages had passed, they put on their shawls and went out on the porch to work off their spleen on the old coral-vine while they waited for Joe's return home.

It was almost dark and they were on the point of going in when a carriage drove up to the gate. The driver got out and began to load in Eugenia's luggage.

"Who's that?" Susan called sharply, peering through the dusk.

"Hit's me, Miss Susie," Jackson, their coachman-butler, called back. "Maus' Joe sen' me fuh fetch Miss Eugenia t'ing."

"Where you carrying them to—the hotel?"

"Naw'm. To Maa'shlan's, de Fen'ick place out to de P'int."

Susan dropped her challenging like a red-hot plate and allowed Jackson to finish his loading and depart in peace. Flushed and wildly confused she and Isabel then went in to wait for Joe by the parlor fire.

It was long after supper-time when he finally appeared. Susan wasted no time and made no allowances for his depressed state.

"Why," she demanded at once, "did you have Eugenia's things carried to Marshlands? You told us she was spending the night at the Sea Island Hotel, and she said so herself. Said she was going on to Savannah in the morning."

"She's staying," he explained quietly and wearily, "at Marshlands."

"Over night?"

"Over many nights, I expect. In fact, I believe she'll stay on indefinitely. A happy solution."

It was only then that the Girls realized what a great and fatal mistake they had made that afternoon. By heedlessly and needlessly affronting Eugenia, by allowing themselves the easy sport of provoking her to the limit, by baiting her once too often, they had succeeded at last—and at just the wrong moment—in mortally alienating her. The worm had at last turned, turned and struck with the venom of a cotton-mouth moccasin. And they had lost an eavesdropper beyond price, an informant strategically and perfectly placed in the very citadel of the enemy.

DAYS SO EASILY became a month, months rounded so gently into another year that for long intervals it seemed to Emily that time had stopped and the world was standing still. To watch the sun was to detect no movement; only when you missed it for a while, when your thoughts were turned away and then brought back by some sharp reminder, could you see that it had moved; though now before your eyes it was standing innocently suspended again, as if it intended to hold forever this exact position in the fathomless sky. But it had moved, behind your back, subtly stealing another fragment from the arc that remained.

It was two years since Margaret's death. . . . Three years. . . . Four. . . . And Emily was scarcely aware of their passage till some special moment came to waken her from the hypnosis of everyday living, the routine of home, the endless repetitions, the little tensions and releases, the multitude of little events that made the flow of time so smooth and imperceptible, carrying pain farther and farther away.

Awareness might rise from some obvious source. A birthday, an anniversary, a New Year "art" calendar from Coleman's Model Meat Market. A spell of housecleaning: the first of May, when Tunis and the yard-boy grunted the rugs up the steep attic stairs and brought down the summer matting: the autumn day when the blankets were taken from the cedar-chest and hung out to air. The opening of buds, the migrations of the birds, the falling of frost-nipped leaves. Or it might be some unique and dramatic event that roused awareness: the substitution of a glaring electric light on a tall pole for the soft glow of the antique oil lamp on a post, just outside the gates of Marshlands; and the consequent loss of Old Clinch, the lamp-lighter, and his patient pony Brag; a change that brought home all the changes that had come over Beaufort since she had first known the place.

But realization could also spring from some fleeting suggestion to the senses. A flash of wings, or the rustling of a palmetto frond. A shifting pattern of sunlight and leaf shadow; a shiver of secret wind over the breast of the river. A scented breath from the garden or the sea. And often one of these slight brief signals could do more to waken perception than any of the manifest markers of tide and season, time and change.

Thus the most stirring force of revelation was a faint far sound, a small voice that spoke to her from inland at still hours. It was never expected, this faraway cry of a train, and it never failed to transfix her heart and mind; particularly when it came at night, a haunting call, remote yet intimate and close. It was like a phrase of great music muted by years and distance, a profound rejoicing and an eternal longing for the lost and the unattained: within a single prolonged note, at once major and minor, it somehow held all moods, all hope and sorrow, all dreams and all memories. But more surely than any music it had the power to heighten awareness in an instant, lifting her above the dust of the moment, swinging her up to a magic hilltop from which she could see and comprehend the transformations of her world. And long after it had died away, its echoings lingered, strengthening her will and her faith.

Under the date *April 1st, 1912* Emily wrote in her diary to those who were watching together from a place beyond change:

"Can you believe that Eleanor became eight today, and that Jane will be four next autumn? A fine piece of irony, Stephen says, in Eleanor's birthday being presided over by All Fools and Jane's almost by All Saints, for he's sure there never was a brighter child than Eleanor and he's afraid Jane bears no earthly resemblance to any saint except when she's asleep. Now Eleanor with her light hair and blue eyes is child of spring to Eugenia, and Jane with her brown hair and eyes, child of autumn. But for Lucy and me they're too assorted for any tags. Today we think we have them by heart, but what they'll say and do and be tomorrow there's simply no telling. The only thing we know is that they're growing like a pair of wild plantation sunflowers. . . ."

When everything had come to nothing at Michael's death, it had

674

taken her an eternity to drag herself back from the dead. But after Margaret's death there had been only a brief break in living and breathing. For there had been no time for mourning, or for fear, or for groping with cold hands for some remnant of faith and courage. There had been no time even for hesitation: the two children, these merciful responsibilities that Margaret had left her, had claimed her at once, demanding immediate and unfaltering attention. And then she had become conscious of a vital renewal of energy. Life was like an old slow-burning fire revived by an armful of kindlings.

"Can't you take things easier?" Stephen was continually complaining; "you're worse than Lucy." And she felt it was true that she was at least as bad as Lucy, who was thinner and more wiry and energetic than ever. But what else could he expect. Just when she had been learning to accept, with a little good grace and even a certain gratitude, the crossing of the years of her life over the sixty line; just when she had been learning to think of herself as a grandmother and a woman of age, adjusting herself to a circle that must inevitably contract from here on: suddenly and without warning the tide had turned, whirling her back to an age of high noon and expanding horizons. No chance to reason why or flinch at this trick of fate, this reversal of time that had swept her back to make a new start toward a goal that had already proved itself a mortal delusion. She had known only that she was a mother again, and that she must somehow begin again to live and plan with spirit for these two children who had become her own through a terrible mingling of death and birth.

And in a world of endless mutations what change could be more fearful than change in which there was so much of return and remembrance. Before Eleanor and Jane had come to her, she had already learned the essential trouble of age: the host of reminders with which the world was stocked, making you pray at times for deliverance, escape, flight to some country free from every trace of even the most blessed memories: the horde of big and little reminders lying in wait for you no matter where you turned, watching to pierce your poor defenses with recollections of the vanished years, with aching homesickness for the world of the past and all its blended good and ill. And now, by the miracle of this present that was giving her another chance at both the past and the future, the power and number of reminders were appallingly increased. Now through these late children of her life she was exposed to a resurgence of memories that would have been unbearable but for the children themselves. It seemed as if everything that was touched turned into something that was gone; but now the sting of things was healed in a flash by the very presence of these two young magicians, Eleanor and Jane.

Of the multitude of reminders a few stood out for their conglomerate associations. . . . The joggling-board, the old "rank-a-tank", triumphantly resurrected by Stephen from its grave of high weeds behind the stable, and given a springy new plank to replace the warped and weathered original. . . . Shoe-boxes of shells—sand dollars, kings' crowns, queens' beads—chosen with the same old care and wonder from the lavish surf-strewn treasures of the beach at Bay Point. And from the dunes, under the wings of curlews and willets and laughing-gulls, armfuls of golden sea-oats gathered again by child hands. . . . Old toys roused from their attic sleep to mingle on rainy days with strange new toys, on the floor of the room that had been a nursery before. . . .

There were new books that were fast becoming favorites: *The Wizard of Oz, The Counterpane Fairy, Davy and the Goblin.* But such battered veterans as Hans Andersen's *Tales* and *Alice in Wonderland* and *Black Beauty* had been called back to the colors for full service. The world was peopled again with figures of enchantment, but most of them were poignantly familiar figures; *The Night Before Christmas* had not displaced *Snowbound* at the season of deepest memories. . . .

And there were the river boats to be waved to again, the three old white sidewheelers of the line to Edisto and Charleston, with their gold-lettered names of the past: *Planter, Sea Island, Mary Draper.* When one of them passed the Point in the early morning or late afternoon, with a tinkling of the bell and a foamy churning to slow down for the Beaufort landing or to speed up after leaving the landing, Eleanor and Jane were on the lawn with Lucy and anyone else available. The captain was always kind enough to wave back from the pilot-house, and if he happened to be in a very good mood he would oblige with a toot of the whistle that set the children shouting and dancing with delight. For the bend at Cuthbert Point up the river the steamboats had a long full blast, a deep disturbing note that shocked the gulls and land birds and stirred echoes from the fartherest reaches of the islands, and made Eleanor frown and Jane shut her eyes and hold her ears. And sometimes, when the wind was from the sea, smoke from the twin stacks came trailing in over the lawn, acrid smoke that made them wrinkle up their noses; and then for a moment, though they continued to wave bravely, the gestures of the walking-beam and the muffled throbbing of the engine seemed to frighten them. But the rhythm of waves that spread from the wake soothed and reassured, rocking the moored Marshlands rowboat as gently as a cradle, swaying the marshgrass like the lightest of breezes, lapping at the seawall so softly that it was as if a dream had passed. . . .

And, above all, there was music. It was the old Steinway that held the greatest reminders of the past, the greatest store of memories; particularly in some of its simplest pieces that had been favorites long ago and were now again. Brahms's *Lullaby*. Wagner's *Dreams*. The *"Moonlight"* *Sonata* of Beethoven, and Michael. . . . For ages they had lain hidden, rigidly forgotten. And then, when she had brought them out for Eleanor and Jane, there was the fear that she lacked power to make of them anything but dirges. And now, still, it was only at surest moments that she dared play them.

Through Eleanor and Jane she was exposed again to the full force of time. But from these children of her child, these two beings who stood now at the heart of all change, came strength to face a present that held so much of the past. Memories had stopped ending in themselves, like roads leading nowhere in a world fatally seared and shriveled by disaster and defeat. Because of these two, memories now ended in hope reborn and faith renewed, journeying on into the future again.

*   *   *

She understood that there were others besides herself for whom Eleanor and Jane now stood at the heart of all change. Especially for Stephen they had become the center of everything, reviving his interest in life and restoring his energies to an amazing extent.

His business had taken on a new meaning. After Michael's death he had let his affairs slump badly, and it had been all she could do to prevent him from giving up completely again; it had been the very stress of that struggle to sustain him, to keep him from relapsing into his old hopelessness and sickness, that had helped her to keep going. Then the fire of 1907 had come to boost the insurance end of his business, and the situation had eased with little or no effort on his part. But since Margaret's death he had been working with increasing determination: for these two "pigtails" of his, who could barely be kept in shoes and stockings and would be demanding party dresses before he could finish paying for their middy-blouses and bloomers. Now he was getting most of the small amount of real-estate business in town, and that took genuine initiative and push. And soon after Eleanor's eighth birthday a notice appeared in the *News & Courier,* which he allowed to be discovered for itself. Since it happened to appear the same day the paper carried tragic world news in one of its rare spread headlines,—TITANIC SUNK BY ICEBERG 1500 LIVES LOST,—it was evening before the notice was finally discovered on the back page by Eugenia. *"The firm of Stickney & Co., Shippers and Factors,"* she read aloud, *"announce with pleasure that Stephen B. Fenwick, Esq., will act as their Beaufort agent from this date."*

Now there was so little time for talking politics at the office that he and Joe had to keep up with the presidential conventions at home, in the evenings after Eleanor and Jane were in bed. But for their hot debates she might easily have forgotten the issues and men of the coming election in reviewing home affairs over her work-basket; as it was, she listened as she sewed and darned, thinking how little time had altered the prejudices of these two old wranglers. Only in appearance were they changed since the years when she had had to warn them against too-loud voices, for fear of waking not these sleepers but those others. Stephen was quite gray now, and there were permanent dark circles round his eyes. And Joe was now pure white of mane above the noble brow, pontifically stout, and chronically flushed. But politically he was as unchanged as Stephen. He remained the incorruptible Tory, the unreconstructed Bourbon, the steadfast conservative and die-hard; while Stephen remained the bitter and scoffing cynic, blowing smoke-rings of futility from his skeptical cigar.

Through June evenings she listened in silence to their discussions of the tense Democratic Convention at Baltimore; accepted silently their criticism of the way the show was being run; and silently shared their excitement at the dramatic outcome, when Bryan on the forty-sixth ballot broke the deadlock and swung his

678

support to Woodrow Wilson. And through torrid August evenings she patiently and quietly followed their derision of the Republican Convention and their jubilation at its even more dramatic outcome: the sensational bolting of Roosevelt and the forming of a third party: the "Bull Moose" Convention in Chicago and the nomination of Roosevelt to head the Progressives, to the tune of the *Doxology* and *Onward Christian Soldiers*. But when they settled down to final dissections of the candidates and planks in the three-cornered contest, she joined the fray one evening.

Joe had been holding the floor for a solid stretch, summing up his feelings in a sort of soliloquy-peroration. ". . . In short, I find I prefer Taft to Roosevelt. There was more actual busting of trusts in Taft's single administration than in both of Roosevelt's, despite all his strenuous flourishing of the Big Stick. A Harvard man of sound heritage why he is not also a gentleman baffles me. But the fact remains that he had shown himself to be an opportunist, a careerist, an actor,—a political peacock. And, let me add, a political charlatan of the first water. For, despite all his histrionic championing of measures designed to stem radicalism on the one hand and exploitation on the other, he ended by conciliating the hierarchy of Northern industrialists and turning the helm back to them. The Rough Rider! The Big Game Hunter! The Third Termer when two were good enough for Washington!"

Flushed, he paused a moment for breath, and then panted on. "I'll pass over in charitable silence his entertaining of negroes at the White House. He's quite sufficiently damned without that. . . . As for Woodrow Wilson, well, after all he's a Virginian. We'll cast our ballots for him with the hope that he can carry us back to true democracy, the democracy of the Founders."

"Yes," said Stephen, "we'll cast our ballots for the Professor with the hope that he'll carry us back to Ole Virginny. And because we've got it to do."

It was here that she found herself stepping in with a sudden question.

"But why do you have to vote for him?"

They both looked at her with an expression of mild shock. Stephen was the first to relax into a smile.

"Well, dear, another county heard from. How would you vote, Yankee style?"

"If I had a vote," she said with an apologetic nod to Joe, a little surprised at herself for breaking into their sacred male stamping-ground, "I'd vote for Wilson. But not just because he's a Democrat and I'm a Southerner."

"Granted," Joe nodded back, with a ponderous fluster.

"Let me have this witness, Judge," Stephen told him, "she seems to be right up my alley. Now, dear, will you tell us why you prefer Woodrow to Teddy and Big Bill?"

"Because of his record as President of Princeton and Governor of New Jersey."

"You're pretty well posted, aren't you. You like his reform record, is that it?"

"I believe he's an honest liberal and progressive."

"I see. And has it occurred to you that honesty and good intentions might not pack much of a punch against resourceful giant trusts schooled in cunning and discretion by three administrations of muck-raking?"

"Have you ever heard," she asked him, "the story of David and Goliath?" And when Joe applauded that with a heavy chuckle, she added: "Or Jack the Giant-Killer?"

"Oh well, of course," he shrugged, "if you want to joke about it, that's different. And better. I thought you were serious."

"I am."

"Well, I wish I could be. Don't you good people ever get discouraged? Joe believes in getting back to the Golden Age, and you believe in getting ahead to it. And I believe in standing pat, because with the years I've grown a little suspicious of all compasses."

"That's beside the point," Joe decided.

"On that basis," she said to Stephen, "you never suffer any defeat. Nothing ventured, nothing lost."

"That's it. And someday I still believe you're going to wake up to that elementary truth yourself."

She shook her head. "I'm afraid not, dear."

"No," he sighed, "I'm afraid not too. I don't suppose it will ever occur to either of you extremists that the whole show, public and private, might be nothing more than a spectacular wild-goose-chase. A tale told by a driveling idiot, signifying exactly nothing."

"This is all," Joe decided again, "entirely beside the point."

"Jeffersonian Democracy!" Stephen shot at him. "New Era! New Nationalism! New Freedom! Same old game. And the new candidates? Tweedledee, Tweedledo, and Tweedledum,—and anyone who can tell them apart gets my vote."

"Rubbish, sir!" Joe snorted. "If those are your true sentiments, why do you trouble to vote at all?"

"Habit, sir. The same tune that makes me dance many another silly jig."

But, happily, his cynicism was limited now to such moments of talk. It only colored his words, occasionally; his thoughts and actions were too involved with the pigtails and welfare of his sprites to be anything but sanguine. These gestures of nihilism, she thought, were now no more than an old pose that he seemed to feel he had to strike at intervals, perhaps as a kind of superstitious deference to the furies of fate, who of late had become so benign. Yes, at intervals he still had to go through the rite of making a sacrificial bonfire of home and the world; but now it was no longer as a compensation for failure and defeat, but as an act of appeasement to the fortune that had given him his Eleanor and Jane.

If these two magicians of youth had wrought an amazing transformation in Stephen, it was even more amazing what they had done for Eugenia. Amazing and nearly incredible, for she had not only become an aunt again but such an aunt as she had never been to Michael and Margaret and Jack.

People never changed, Stephen liked to say; yet here before his eyes was a case of the most radical change, a complete conversion of attitude and disposition. "She's still the perfect spinster," he insisted, unwilling to acknowledge the transformation. But though he permitted her no other manner toward him than that of spinster sister, in every other direction she was able to demonstrate a spirit altered almost beyond recognition.

When she had come back to Marshlands from her long self-imposed exile, Stephen had been sure that she would be "worse than ever". Instead, he had had to admit that the years of loneliness in Charleston had not turned her fatally in upon herself; and soon it must have become clear even to him, though he had refused to admit it, that under the spell of Eleanor and Jane she was blossoming into a new person. Vestiges of her old vanity and primness remained, but her moods of melancholia, her unaccountable fits of depression and seclusion, her excessive touchiness were gone for good.

Her devotion to the girls was not only moving to watch but also disturbing. For Eleanor and Jane were the center of too many circles. Stephen, Eugenia, Joe, and even Lucy seemed bent on spoiling them.

"All right," Stephen would answer whenever she protested to him, "why don't you send them to school then? They certainly won't get pampered there."

But Miss Mary Hamilton was gone, and school without Miss Mary or anyone like her was a place to be avoided as long as possible.

"Naturally," said Stephen, "the sooner they start rubbing elbows with other children, the better off they'll be."

"But they get plenty of elbow-rubbing in their play with other children," she reminded him.

"All right. But I tell you you're all wrong again. You started out before with the idea of making extra special cases of your children, but fortunately you didn't have a free hand. And you're not going to have all the say this time either. The girls are going to grow up as normally as the neighbors' children. They're not going to be freaks of nature, if I can help it."

And he went about his spoiling more conscientiously than ever.

But she had one ally whose staunch support helped to sustain her against these odds.

At the time of Margaret's death there had been an interne named Hervey Caldwell at the Charleston Hospital, a young assistant to Dr. Ravenel who by his thoughtfulness had done much to ease the nightmare. Later she had written to thank him, and this had been the beginning of a correspondence that had ended in bringing him to Beaufort to start practice. His appearance had brought her great relief, for Dr. Wright had become totally unreliable. She had persuaded Joe to give him office space in the Lafayette house, and she had tried to make him feel at home at Marshlands, and to help him in every way possible to establish himself in Beaufort.

Stephen, jealous perhaps at the speed and thoroughness with which his Eleanor and Jane had taken to the stranger, had been inclined at first to resent him. "Why does he have to be urged to drop in here any hour of the day or night? It's all right to give him a helping hand, but do you have to adopt him? After all, what do we know about him, except that he's a doctor and comes from Anderson up-state? . . ." But after the children had been pulled through several spells of sickness by the young man from Anderson, Stephen had changed his tune. He and Joe had begun to back him to the limit, and their combined support had had a good deal to do with getting his practice well started.

At first glance he was unprepossessing as a man and unconvincing as a doctor. He lacked height and presence, and he had a definitely lean and hungry look. An unruly shock of sandy hair, a cowlick, and freckles gave him a boyish appearance that made people hesitate to commit themselves to his scrutiny and care. Even his smile and laugh were against him, for they were entirely too youthful to belong to a responsible and disciplined man of medicine. He undoubtedly suggested, as Stephen said, a schoolboy giving a bad imitation of a doctor. But his eyes were sure and his hands steady. And behind the too-youthful exterior were a set of finely coördinated nerves, a warm heart, and a good head.

"But you can't get to really know him," Stephen complained; "he won't talk about himself. I don't say that isn't a commendable trait, but he carries it too far. He ought to realize by this time that he's among friends. We've known him now for almost four years, but all I know about him for sure is that he had a barefoot boyhood, and that he isn't burning with any cracked notions about setting the medical world on fire."

That might be true, his lack of ambition beyond doctoring Beaufort, but she had found him the opposite of evasive. He had taken his time in telling her about himself, but as their friendship deepened he had pieced together the facts of his early life and the scraping of his way through state university and medical school, a story that reduced to absurdity the whole system of "advantages". As he had gradually become a member of the family, he had remained more or less tongue-tied with Stephen and Joe; but with her he was responsive and at ease, and eager to talk about anything and everything.

Stephen found it amusing the way their long after-supper talks grew out of a little music at the piano or a few moves on the old chess-board. Evenings when Joe dropped in, Stephen always greeted him with a warning stage whisper. "Quiet, man,—the sophomore class is in session again, clearing up one or two little problems of the universe left over from last night. And plotting how to keep us from spoiling the girls."

In the generally unpopular venture of making "special cases" of this "second batch of hopefuls",—"All I hope," said Stephen, "is that they don't expect too much of life, and the only talent I'd like to see developed in them is the knack of telling friend from foe, on sight or at the earliest possible moment."—in this struggle to keep the household from "just enjoying them" she had to continually renew her resolution to keep from weakening. It would have been so easy to have given in, or at least to have slacked off here and conceded a point there. But by turning to young Dr. Caldwell she could clarify her ideas and intentions, thrash answers out of tough questions, and return to the fray with fresh strength and determination.

He disagreed with her on only one main issue. He thought that Eleanor should start school by another year at the latest, and that Jane should follow suit as soon as she was old enough.

✓　　　✓　　　✓

If the Beaufort school had been run along the lines of Penn School on St. Helena Island, it would have been easy to agree with him. She would have rushed the girls to school, in fact, if its curriculum and system of training had been as well adapted to preparing white children for living as Penn School now was to preparing black children for coping with the actual conditions of island life.

What she had long ago dreamed of had come to pass. Two young college women from the North had taken over the school and begun the work of transforming it into an agricultural and health center, merging school and community in a common adventure toward better living standards. The school's old object, to drill pupils academically for county examinations and school-teaching, had been discarded for a sounder purpose. Now the fields and homes were the chief subjects of study, and the whole island was the classroom.

"Oblige me," Stephen asked her, "by keeping out of that mess." But it was impossible to lose interest in a movement so vital and full of promise. For Penn School with its all-year rounded training touched essentially the whole life of the people. There were still "blackboard classes" in the three R's, but the emphasis was now on learning by practice rather than by rote. The center of learning for the boys were the carpentry shop and the school farm, where rota-

684

tion of crops and modern methods of fertilizing and planting were demonstrated. For the girls there were sewing classes and a school kitchen, where they were taught good cooking and the value of a varied diet. And both boys and girls attended classes in "cow", "chicken", and "turkey". . . . And the good work was not restricted to the youngsters. Grown-ups of all ages came to school from all the old plantation districts of the island. For the men there was the "Farm Forum", and for the women the "Community", a combination home-improvement, quilt-making, and midwife association. . . . For both young and old there were the school sociables and suppers; the big Spring Bazaar, Autumn Fair, and Christmas; and the "Weeks"—Clean-up Week, Visiting Week, and Health Week.

It was a happy change that was coming over the island, but it was presenting her with a serious problem at Land's End. Most of the tenant people on the plantation were no longer willing to work on a share basis or even for cash-wages in the field. They wanted to buy land on terms and work for themselves. Already all the acres and cabins in the settlement neighborhood were in their possession.

The best of the men who had been keeping the planting going with Biggie were on their own now. But fortunately Biggie felt differently about working for himself. He didn't want to be burdened, he said, with property. His wife Jessie could have all the land she wanted in her own name, and it looked like she wanted the earth, but she'd have to look after it herself with the help of her trifling kinfolk. He wanted to feel free. The only land he had any eye for was the fields on the Sound, the "Reservation" as the people called the forlorn remains of Fort Fremont.

The place was a jungle of weeds and thickets. Even the paved streets were almost obliterated. The disappearing guns had disappeared for good and the emplacements were overgrown with vines. The barracks were in a state of rotten sag and collapse, and every pane of glass had long since been smashed out of the high room of the rusting tottering observation tower. The brick hospital was too badly damaged to serve any longer as a trysting-place for lovers brave enough to invade its haunted shadows, or even as a daylight encampment for the warring gangs of town white boys and island black boys who had once kept its plaster walls smudged with obscene challenges; the plaster had broken and crumbled away from the lathing like dead flesh from skeleton ribs, the doors and windows and blinds were gone, the roof and floors had caved in. But the land beneath this jungle and these ruins was the best on the island. And from the solid shell of the hospital Biggie saw how easily he could make a mansion for Jessie. But maybe it was just as well, he decided, that the Government never got around to putting the place up for sale on easy terms. Because he wanted no millstones round his neck. He wanted to feel pure free: free to be up and *gone* any time he took a notion.

As long as he felt pure free, she thought, there was little danger of his taking the fatal notion. Which was certainly a blessing, for Biggie was the force that kept the plantation going.

But even Biggie could hardly do the work alone, or with a few incompetent hands, the odds-and-ends of plantation labor. In recent years she had been satisfied to make taxes, but now she was beginning to wonder if the planting could be kept going at all. And when she consulted Stephen, he simply redoubled the pressure of his old insistence that the plantation be given up entirely.

"You get all the credit in the world for what you did with the place in the past, but isn't it just a nervous tick now? It's ridiculous keeping this game up year after year when there's no need for it. If you simply can't sit still, there's plenty for you to do right here at Marshlands."

"But we can't just let Land's End go to wrack and ruin."

"Of course not. Sell it. Sell what's left of the plantation in one parcel, instead of turning it over to the people bit by bit. It's served its purpose. From now on, with cotton prices drifting down all the time, it'll only be a growing liability."

"But, dear, you know we can't give up the house, and the house acres and the Big Field."

"Don't know why not. If I can stand the thought of parting with the place, I don't see why you can't. . . . If we had more money, it might be different. As it is, the only sensible course is to let somebody else hold the bag. But if you're not willing to sell, at least we ought to lease the place for a term of years. Say the word and I'll list it tomorrow."

But she was unwilling to abandon the Land's End part of home even on that temporary basis. His suggestion, though, gave her an idea for settling the situation in a way that would satisfy him without any relinquishment of the plantation.

For the two summers since the storm of 1911 Seth Robinson had been doing no planting. Without the help of prime hands the work of cotton was too heavy for him now; Linda had been keeping him from attempting anything more than a few acres of corn and a "table" garden. Jim, Linda's son, was big enough to wield a man's hoe and even to manage a horse and plow, but Linda was letting him help only with the lighter chores. So the Robinson farm was marking time. But Seth was by no means incapacitated for overseeing, and he quickly accepted her proposal of a three-cornered partnership to plant the Big Field. He was to supervise the work and keep the time-book and accounts, she was to put up the land and the seed, and Biggie was to captain the field gang. At planting time and harvest extra hands were to be imported from the mainland, where there was no shortage of labor.

It was an arrangement that worked well from the beginning. And it satisfied Stephen because it meant her practical retirement from the plantation scene. She still made trips to the island, but now it was primarily to give Eleanor and Jane a day of adventure there.

They were passionately attached to Land's End and to Seth and Linda and Jim. Jim was like a brother, in fact, and easily their principal hero. A well-developed lad, strong and good-looking and smart, with a steadiness beyond his years, he had inherited more of his grandfather's sad reticence than of his mother's open manner and shining spirits, and he was still inclined to be quiet with grown-ups; but with Eleanor and Jane he was able to expand to his full stature. A lonely boy he was always glad to see them, and they could tag after him all day if they liked. They seemed to feel that he knew everything and could do anything, but of all his accomplishments the one they most admired was his seamanship, for that took them to the wonders of the beach. Already he sailed a boat like an old hand: he knew the waters around Land's End as well as he knew every inch of the plantation, he was master of winds and tides, and Seth trusted him now to carry the party across the Inlet to Bay Point.

Just as Linda had always seemed like a daughter to her, so Jim was like a grandson; she had shared with Linda his growth from babyhood, just as Linda had shared with her the anxiety and pleasure of watching Eleanor and Jane grow. So, despite the separations of Land's End and Marshlands, the years had deepened and strengthened the old friendship between Fenwicks and Robinsons. And in the autumn of 1913, just after the planting partnership was formed, something happened to tighten the relationship of the two families. Not from choice but because of the lack of a white school on the island, Linda had been teaching Jim as best she could at home, but now she felt his need of regular schooling could no longer be denied. The faithful old *Pilot Boy* was at last definitely out of commission and at present a new launch was out of the question, and it was too much for Jim to ride all the way to the Beaufort ferry and back every day, so Linda and Seth decided he would have to board in town. It was a hard task to get them to let Jim stay at Marshlands, but she finally succeeded in persuading them, to the great delight of Eleanor and Jane. That left Stephen and Eugenia and Lucy to be reckoned with, but she was depending on Jim himself to do the persuading there. As she hoped, his quiet manners and consideration and his general unobtrusiveness soon won Eugenia and Lucy. And Stephen withdrew his objections when he discovered his lambs wanted to follow Jim to school.

"You sure missed your calling," he told her. "To be really happy what you need is a large boarding-house leaping with lodgers. With the girls, and Eugenia, and Joe and Hervey Caldwell dropping in for dinner or supper or breakfast, and three servants to feed, it would seem to me that we have about enough people on our hands without Jim. But I'll put up with one more addition to this the-more-the-merrier full-house game of yours, if you'll give in and start the girls to school."

So under this combination of pressures she finally gave in. And one week after Jim started school in the seventh grade, Eleanor was admitted to the fourth and Jane to the first. The first day Jane appeared home in the middle of the morning, but after this initial protest she suddenly took a fancy to school and began to share Eleanor's enthusiasm for the new adventure that Jim had inaugurated.

Their enthusiasm somewhat eased her sense of having made a fatal compromise, a concession that might be the opening seam for a whole flood of concessions. Also school was something of a relief, for home tutoring had been getting a little out of hand; she had been feeling for some time that instead of competently guiding the girls' development she was having all she could do to keep up with them. Now, with her mornings free for other concerns, she found that her time with them was sharpened to greater effectiveness. By contrast with school, home was taking on a new significance for them and a new importance.

❧ ❧ ❧

So life was still full of change, but change that thanks to Eleanor and Jane was forming a harmony of all elements. All mutations and memories, all plans and hopes were settling into a final pattern of peace and order; and she felt safe in believing that after a long day of wind-turmoiled sun and shadow, the sky had cleared at last for good, leaving of her life a gentle and unthreatened radiance as of some perfect autumn time. She must be on her guard always against abrupt treacheries of tide and sky, but in her heart she felt an unshakable conviction that it was to be clear sailing now.

And serenity was not limited to the air she breathed, to the world of home. It extended to the world at large, the places and peoples beyond the sea-island horizons. The whole world was at peace.

Stephen seemed to share her confidence that all was well at home, but he saw no health abroad. And when he read the news of Carnegie's World Peace Foundation at The Hague, he scoffed: "Pittsburgh steel shares into universal plow shares! And our hard-fisted battling Andrew calls the Kaiser 'a peace lord'. All the big chiefs are peace lords now. God, what a farce."

"But now," she protested, "the nations can settle all disputes by arbitration."

"Sure! When they have another Morocco incident, all the boys can meet in Andy's peace palace and cool off, with Bryan taking pulses and temperatures. Well, all I know about peace is what George Washington told me. It's a damn good time to prepare for war."

"But it's that attitude that breeds war."

"I see. Then we ought to do away with preparedness in civil life, I suppose,—police protection breeds crime. Well, when Woodrow gets you ladies the vote, you can change all that, and reform the world on the first ballot."

And before that, at the time of Wilson's inauguration, Stephen had mocked the promise of a new national order. The evening when

Joe had read the inaugural address aloud from the front page of the *News & Courier,* she had been stirred by the President's words. ". . . There has been something crude and heartless and unfeeling in our haste to succeed and be great. Our thought has been, 'Let every man look out for himself, let every generation look out for itself,' while we reared giant machinery which made it impossible that anyone but those who stood at the levers of control should have a chance to look out for themselves. . . . This is not a day of triumph; it is a day of dedication." And Joe had found one sentence that gave him such delight that he reread it three times with rising inflections: ". . . We have made up our minds to square every process of our national life again with the standard we so proudly set up at the beginning and have always carried in our hearts. . . ." But by way of rebuttal Stephen had felt that it was sufficient to pick up Jane's school reader and mimic Joe's declamatory style: "The north wind doth blow, and we shall have snow, and what will poor robin do then, poor thing."

But she was not disturbed by his pessimistic attitude toward the national and international scenes. Already the President's policies were shaping a better social order; and peace was in the air of the world. For the latter years of her life there was to be peace and order everywhere, at home and abroad, and she had firm faith in the progressive world that Eleanor and Jane were inheriting.

✦   ✦   ✦

But in this trend of the world and her life toward a final stability and harmony, there was one element of change that continued to trouble her deeply.

There were moments in her most secret thoughts when she found herself wishing that Jack had taken leave of her as Michael and Margaret had, swiftly and surely as nightmare flashes back in the dark forest of time. For as it was he was being taken from her by a living death, a slow disintegration of sympathy and understanding which seemed more terrible than any severing of earthly ties. This man in Atlanta, who had been her boy and was still her son, was very much alive; yet for all his prior claims on her devotion and interest he was coming to mean far less to her than Eleanor and Jane. She told herself that at heart her love for him was unchanged and unchangeable, but she knew it was the memory of him as a boy that she was clinging to, and despite all she could do to prevent it she was losing beyond recall even that Jack.

He had not failed her; she felt, rather, that she had failed him. She blamed herself for her neglect of him during the critical years at Land's End, when her thoughts and energies had been centered on Michael and Stephen and on the plantation and on holding the family together. She felt herself responsible for the scrapes he had gotten into, for the hurts he had given her, and for the development of his character along lines of least resistance. But that made it no easier to face his crystallization into a man responsible only to his own desires, a man of vain and ruthless selfishness, using his wits and engaging smile to promote himself on any basis.

When she had first come to recognize this crystallization, she had desperately denied to herself that it could be the finished mold of his manhood. He had always been a law unto himself, but she had always been able to think of his unruliness as a healthy sign of life and of spirits too high and independent to be easily brought under control. His earlier scrapes had alarmed her no more than they had Stephen, and even his later serious scrapes had seemed a final phase of youthful recklessness and blundering before the advent of maturity, a maturity that would be all the more disciplined and sure because of the trouble with which it had been won. But by the end of his first year in the cotton-brokerage business in Atlanta it was becoming clear that he was to bear no resemblance to the image she had made for him long ago. And each time thereafter when he came home on one of his whirlwind visits, he looked more prosperous, more dissipated, more self-centered and pleased with himself, and more disappointing to her. Till finally it was impossible to deny that this bundle of conceit was actually her son as a man.

"You don't seem very enthusiastic about his success," Stephen sharply observed after one of the flying visits. "Or is it just a mother's natural sadness and resentment because her boy doesn't need her anymore? After all now, you ought to be glad he's finally settling down and making something of himself."

He was certainly settling down, but not into anything resembling the fine strong manhood she had hoped for and once confidently expected; and he was certainly making something of himself, but something directly opposed to every wish and prayer she had made for him since the day of his birth. And since this warping of his character away from the true of her dreams could no longer be denied, since it was having a fatal effect on her feelings toward him, and since she was evidently beginning to show traces of her profound disappointment and chagrin to Stephen at least, she determined that she must reconcile herself to what he was. It was surely better to accept him on his own terms than to lose him on hers.

But it was no use. The harder she tried to hold him, the farther he slipped away from her. In spite of herself she kept seeing him as he might have been, as he could have been, as he should have been; kept contrasting him with the man Michael would now be, the man Rusty had been, the man Stephen was again. And when she tried to see him through Stephen's eyes—as a success, a good sport, and good company—she saw only a failure, a distorted figure, a half-man one side of whose nature had developed at the expense of the other: an egoist and opportunist whose one aim was to outsmart people and "get ahead" and have a good time; a charmer whose smile was as easy and shallow as his ideas and ideals, whose attractiveness was as superficial and transparent as a coat of shellac; a man for whom the things that seemed important and vital to her simply didn't exist.

"You're condemning him and torturing yourself," Stephen told her, "because he's turned out to be just a plain normal man, instead of some sort of dreamer with his head in the clouds." But if that was why she was condemning him and torturing herself, it would have to continue to the bitter end; for it was impossible to suspend or lower, even for her son, her own standards of what constituted normal manhood.

"You're not being fair with him or yourself," Stephen said to her on another occasion. "You've been watching him so closely for so many years you're full of near-sighted obsessions and prejudices on the subject. Loosen up and stand back and take a fresh look at him. . . . And remember to make allowances for the fact that he naturally isn't at his best with you. I mean to say, you know too much about him and he feels he can never shine here at home. I try to show him the past's all cleared up and forgotten and he and I are equals now, men together. But you somehow manage to make him feel uncomfortable. He senses that you're always applying invisible yardsticks to him and deciding he doesn't quite measure up. You don't mean to, of course, but you do. . . . Now why not give him another chance?

Take a new look at him. He isn't Michael, but he's all right in his own way."

While acknowledging the truth of most of that, she doubted the value of giving him "another chance". She was always giving him and herself another chance, trying desperately to adjust herself to him every time he came home. But perhaps the very desperation of her attempts was the force that was widening the breach between them. If she could take a good fresh "new look" at him, if she could free her eyes of emotion and see him dispassionately, meet him without a host of connotations and past references, perhaps she would come to share Stephen's confidence that he was "all right in his own way". So she determined to make a final attempt to see him with real detachment, to face him calmly and intrepidly as the stranger he was so rapidly becoming, to meet him as if she were meeting him for the first time.

His next visit was delayed till late in this autumn of 1913. Then he telegraphed Stephen that he was coming down for a week-end of fishing. He appeared in a flashy Benz roadster, and with the news that he had just been made a junior partner in the Riddock cotton firm. . . . "I've always told your mother," Stephen patted him proudly, "that you'd be the big money-maker of this family." . . . The excitement over the news and the automobile intensified the problem of seeing him with detachment. And she had little opportunity to see him at all: after he had taken time to give each member of the family a spin through the town, he and Stephen left on their overnight trip to the island, and almost as soon as they got home it was time for his start back to Atlanta. But in the snatches of time she had with him she tried resolutely to see him without fear or favor, in the direct light of the moment. And even that brief clear vision was enough to make her shrink hastily back to her old blind love for him, for as a stranger her son was a man whom she disliked at once.

And that winter something happened to bring her to final despair. She had come to pin her last hopes on his finding a good wife, a contemporary of intelligence and character, a woman of fine qualities who would help him to develop the dormant sides of his nature, who would succeed where his mother had failed. But Nellie Riddock was hardly the right woman. She was almost perfectly the wrong woman.

693

He brought her down from Atlanta in his roadster the Sunday before Christmas. The visit was announced by telegram well in advance, so she was able to make full preparations, send word to
Biggie that the Christmas turkey was needed a week early, see with
Lucy that the family's best china and glass and table linen were
ready, and make sure that Tunis had a spotless starched shirt to wear
with his long-tail coat. And the purpose of the visit, announced by
Jack the moment of their arrival,—"Mother, this is little Nell, and
I'm making an honest woman of her next June!",—came as no
surprise, for Stephen had guessed and prepared her for it. But
she was entirely unprepared for the shock of Nellie. At first it was
impossible to believe that this young woman with the pretty face
and baby stare and affected manners, this blonde doll in fluffy-
ruffle clothes that she was welcoming into the house and the family,
could be Jack's idea of a wife. Surely there must be some mistake,
she told herself through the exchange of greetings: if this was actually her son's fiancée, then she must be badly mistaken in her first
impressions; there must be hidden virtues, qualities of fineness behind this spoiled-child face and voice, and she must discover them
at once.

Dinner, with Nellie on Stephen's right, went well. But after dinner, when he and Jack lingered at the table to talk cotton and sports
through cigar smoke while Nellie and she withdrew with Eugenia
and the children to the living-room, conversation became strained
and ragged. And when later Eugenia, whose manner was a little
too formally gracious, excused herself with the children, leaving
her alone with Nellie, the following minutes were torture. For
Nellie let every offering fall at her feet with an apathy that said
plainly enough, It's up to you. And when at intervals she did make
some adequate response, it only strengthened first impressions and
made it increasingly difficult to go on with any show of sincerity.
So that by the time Stephen and Jack came to the rescue the conversation had reached an appalling impasse of politeness and inanity,
and her first impressions of Nellie Riddock had hardened into conviction.

Joe, in a most expansive mood, arrived just in time to see them off,
and his pleasantries eased the departure immeasurably. In the last-
minute chatter he made himself thoroughly charming to Nellie, and
she repaid him by dropping all pout from her smiles and popping

her eyes at him winsomely. After she was gone, he was the first to speak.

"Well, I'm delighted! Nice girl. Fine girl. Pretty, too. I'm satisfied Jack will settle down now! It's plain to be seen how deeply in love he is. Of course, I suppose we would have selected a sea-islander for him, but love doesn't follow family preferences, I've observed. In any case, under the circumstances, it seems to me an eminently happy solution. I mean to say, I don't see how he could have made a better choice."

"I wish I could agree with you," Eugenia dissented. "I didn't like her manner at all. And I didn't like the unnatural way she behaved with the children. It's a bad sign, I've always observed, when a person don't know how to act with dogs and children."

"I can remember the time," Stephen told her good-naturedly, "when you couldn't get along with dogs and children."

"I admit," she acknowledged stiffly, "that children and animals used to make me nervous. But you'll notice I grew out of it. *She* never will. She'll always be what she is now,—a spoiled Georgia peach with all the trimmings. I can tell. And there's plenty of temper and meanness behind that wishy-washy sweetness."

"She may not be long on brains," Stephen smiled, "but she's pretty enough for any man. And she's a Riddock."

"And who are the Riddocks?" Eugenia demanded.

"Very successful people. They may have no family portraits, but they've got plenty of cash, and that's what counts these days. . . . I gather Emily's not too well pleased. But what mother ever did think her daughter-in-law was good enough for her son? How about that, dear?"

She made no attempt to deny it. But she was careful to keep the depths of her dismay from him and the others. She had that out with herself in her room, later.

III

HOWEVER WELL she succeeded in hiding from Stephen and Eugenia and Joe her real distress about the marriage, she knew there was one person she was not fooling. It was perfectly clear that Lucy shared her feelings in this as in all things. There were no words of fellow-feeling, but there were signs more expressive than words. On that first day when Jack had brought Nellie Riddock to Marshlands, Lucy, in washing the dinner set of English china (a rite she never trusted anyone else to perform), had broken a dessert plate and the big platter. And since that spectacular protest there had been plenty of other signs of disapproval: prolonged frowns, poorly-suppressed mumblings, and a pronounced shortness of temper with Tunis and Ella, who were keeping close grinning track of the approach of the wedding on the kitchen calendar.

Not able to follow Lucy's example and give even indirect vent to her feelings, she tried to keep herself so busy with the affairs of home that there would be no time left for futile brooding. But with Jane in school and needing in the play hours little more watching than Eleanor now, and with Eugenia extremely sensitive about being relieved of any of the housekeeping duties she had assumed to balance her spasmodic water-colors and her researches into the Life and Times of General Oglethorpe, home was altogether too smooth-running for purposes of distraction and forgetfulness. And with Seth and Biggie in full charge of the plantation, and with Penn School taking under its island-wide community wing the last of the plantation families, she was not needed at Land's End. So she was reduced to the garden for most of her activity and escape.

In perusing the grounds for further developments, for revisings and improvisings, her eyes came to rest on the back yard; by elimination she arrived at this spot, the only part of the place that remained in its perennial state of rundown shabbiness and offered possibilities of extensive alteration. She had contemplated its shabbiness and its possibilities many times before, but now her eyes studied it with a glint of determination. . . . Stephen found the tumbledown kitchen-house "nice and old-timey"; but the perilous sag of its brick walls, the broken tile roof, the crumbling chimney, and the ease with which its musty interior accumulated litter and junk, made it look to her a plain eyesore. The longer she regarded the obstacle and considered how it cramped the life of its fragrant bay tree, and the more clearly she visualized a new and better order in the back yard, the higher her courage mounted for a drastic action. Finally one shining spring morning, a Saturday morning when Eleanor and Jane and Linda's Jim were out of school, she enlisted them and the yard-boy and Tunis for a sudden assault on the obstacle. And by the time Stephen came home from the office, the kitchen-house was reduced to a pile of brick and mortar and tile, and the green bay tree stood in astonished emancipation in a wide open courtyard.

"That's right—bust'em up," Stephen commented in disgust. "Can't you dislike Nellie Riddock without taking the place apart?"

Afternoons after school the following week Eleanor and Jane helped her to plan flower beds and vine and shrub plantings around the back porch, the stable, and the long two-story Quarter. Then she set the yard-boy and his moseying assistant to digging and preparing the beds. And though it was already late in the season by the time they were ready, she planted an ambitious experimental assortment of seeds: larkspur and phlox and snapdragon, calendulas and zinnias and nasturtiums, and Stephen's favorite, French marigolds.

The yard's transformation was now far enough along so that he had to concede he was beginning to see what she was driving at.

"But don't be surprised when the tradespeople start coming to the front door, and callers back here. You can't present two fronts to the world without confusing people,—everybody knows one of them must naturally be a behind. You better put up signs."

Eugenia was less grudging, and promised to paint a water-color of the new yard as soon as the flowers bloomed. And Joe and Hervey Caldwell and the grocery boy and all callers were so flattering, and Tunis and Ella and the yard-boy took such enthusiastic vows to mend their ways and respect the "court" and remember that the back yard was now behind the stable, that she wondered why she had hesitated so long to make the changes.

But, glad that she had waited because of the sorely-needed distraction the work gave her, she turned next to overseeing the yard-boy and his assistant while they laid the cleaned kitchen-house bricks along the edges of the lawn paths to the summer-house and to Michael's cedar tree. An exacting and extended task it was, painstakingly setting with slow clumsy proxy hands each individual brick in the winding rows that followed the path curves and the borders of the flanking ribbon beds of hyacinths and jonquils. It absorbed all her spare time, keeping her safely busy through the rest of spring and up to the very day when the Tiffany-engraved wedding invitation arrived from Atlanta.

After that a decision about the wedding present could no longer be postponed. At Stephen's suggestion, and with the reluctant concurrence of Eugenia and the manifest disapproval of Lucy, it was finally decided to send the old family tea-service of Georgian silver, relic of colonial Fenwicks and of Miss Sophie's and Eugenia's refugee days at Camden. And after the cherished set had been carefully polished and packed and expressed to Atlanta, there was the sudden problem of what to wear. "The latest thing" had not been an obsession with her since the years of youth, and she had long ago lost interest in the game of keeping pace with minor swings of the fashion pendulum; even in the prosperous years dressiness had seemed a nuisance, and she had usually failed to catch up with a new mode till it was quite old and already preparing to change; and now, just as she was still arranging her graying hair in the fashion of years ago, parted in the middle in front and drawn up from the sides and back into a tight flat coil, so too the cut and style of her clothes had changed little since the middle years of her life. But, she realized abruptly, she must have a new outfit for the wedding, and hastily she put herself in the hands of a seamstress and Eugenia, who was feeling too indisposed for the wedding but never for dressmaking.

After a struggle with the seamstress's hobble-skirt pattern and Eugenia's undiminished enthusiasm for the latest frills, she succeeded in coming out with a dress very much like her old Sunday best, even to the fullness of skirt and the collar of netting. She firmly resisted Eugenia's insistence on a fussy "picture" hat, idiotically puffed-up and ungainly, instead of a neat and sensible old one retrimmed.

Then, still avoiding consecutive thought and feeling about the real significance of these preliminaries, she was hugging Eleanor and Jane good-bye and leaving with Stephen for the station and the morning train for Atlanta.

✓   ✓   ✓

But on that long hot journey it was no longer possible to ward off her thoughts and feelings.

There were protective distractions at first. Mr. Gilroy, veteran conductor and friend of the family, stopped for a chat when he took up the tickets. But his company proved more depressing than comforting. He was a broken shuffling old man now, and his pathetic attempts to brace up and be his former hearty self for them hurt worse than his questions and his answers to questions. He was alone now, he told them finally; his wife was gone, and both his children were living away from Charleston. But, he was glad to say, he always had plenty of people to pass the time of day with, and next spring the Road would be retiring him on a pension and then he could visit back and forth between his children and get acquainted with his grandchildren. . . . He was mixed up about Margaret, he seemed to think Michael was still living—at the North, and he wanted to know all about "Harry's" wedding. But he remembered the Fenwick family's earlier trips with him well enough, too well. And his voice, his frayed uniform with the tarnished brass buttons, and the very click of his ticket-puncher resurrected such a host of confused and aching memories that she drew a breath of relief when he was gone.

"Poor old duffer," Stephen sighed with a frowning smile and a shake of his head. "If I was still a director of this damn jerkwater road, I'd have pensioned him off ten years ago. He must be far gone in his seventies by now. . . . Well, we'll all be up there before many more moons. But if I'm unlucky enough to live that long, please slip some knockout drops in my coffee at the first signs of dodderishness."

When she met his glance with perfectly solemn eyes, he added: "Don't worry, second childhood doesn't run in our family. We either die good and young or else go on forever with never a dodder. Look at Joe. He's well up in the seventies and still going strong as ever. He'll live to be a hundred, easy. . . . How about a little current news for a change?"

And he opened the paper he had brought with him.

". . . Well, here's something that ought to please you. A summary of what the President is up to,—single-handed, apparently, and without the aid of a net. To begin with, we're going to have a nice British-style income tax. Which certainly won't cost the Fenwicks much, with the exception of Jack. And the good old Sherman Anti-Trust Act is to be enforced at last. We're going to have child labor laws to protect our young, pure food laws to protect our health, and slum improvement to ease our conscience. The tariff is to be adjusted downward for the poor but honest farmer, and the financial system is to be jacked up with a Federal Reserve Act to prevent panics. Well, I've got to admit it begins to look as if your friend Wilson means business. At this rate you Suffragettes will get the vote all right. And he'll sure need you when the Republicans dust themselves off and start closing in on him.

". . . Don't suppose I can interest you in the White Socks and the Cubs. Or the possibility of a Jack Johnson-Jess Willard fight. . . . But how does this item hit you. *Wireless Communication Established Between Germany and U. S. Kaiser Wilhelm Sends Greetings to President.* Won't be long, honey, before you get your wish,—pretty soon we'll be in such close communication, all around, that the only logical conclusion will be a United States of the World. Then we'll be a happy family of nations, and all our wars will be strictly civil.

". . . Ah!—here's a bet we almost overlooked. *General Federation of Women's Clubs Decry Tango, Hesitation, and Suggestive Magazine Stories.* Now there's Progress for you with a capital P. Votes for Women!"

On the strength of that he decided he needed a cigar and a stretch. Besides, he wanted to peel off his coat and stuff a handkerchief under his collar to keep it from wilting to a pulp in the heat, and maybe he would take off his shoes like the cracker party across the aisle: none of which he could very well do while sitting with a lady, and such an elegant lady. So he excused himself and, looking very handsome and well-pressed, went forward to ease his discomfort and restlessness in the smoker.

Since there was no way of escape from her own restlessness, she took up the new *Harper's* she had brought with her, determined to make the pages of print stand between her and her thoughts. The stories were all insipid and dull this month,—certainly nothing here to rouse the General Federation of Women's Clubs. But the assorted articles were interesting. And the last of them, *American Contributions to Medical Science,* more than held her attention. It concerned chiefly the work of Dr. Alexis Carrel of Rockefeller Institute, but there was considerable mention of Harvard Medical School and a Professor Theobald Smith. This name was disturbingly familiar, yet she was unable to place it at first; she read quite a way before she realized in a flash of remembrance that Michael had often spoken of him with admiration.

When she finished her eyes were smarting so badly that she had to keep blinking to see the little that remained to be read in the magazine. Still she clung to the final pages, trying to make something better than nonsense out of the assortment of familiar advertisements. But recognition of two old trade-mark figures in fatal combination,—Baker's prim maid carrying her tray of Chocolate toward Hires' lusty infant flourishing his stein of Root Beer, the same dread idiotic tableau that had attended the first shock of Rusty's death,—made her relinquish *Harper's* abruptly.

She tried then to avoid her thoughts by way of her fellow passengers, watching and wondering, seeking to fathom the secrets of other lives, profiles and backs of heads, voices jumbled and broken by the train din. But that only brought her back to herself, to considering the strangeness of being her particular self, instead of some other self. . . . At a certain point of contemplation reality became fantastic. It was absurd to be imprisoned within one's own skin, enmeshed in a private set of nerves, limited to one's own special little universe: committed forever to the life and person of Emily Fenwick. There was a secret conviction at such an instant that the soul was more than the flame to the candle, lighted at birth, extinguished at death. A conviction that the sense of personal identity must be a separate living entity and hence detachable, a bird-like spirit confined in its particular cage so by chance and illusion that merely a wish would be enough to free it to take wing and fly away.

Unable to sustain this flight, she turned to the window to watch the country drifting past flatly in the blinding sunshine. This down-pouring June sun flooded the world with such dazzling light, soaking into the fields and invading the deepest shadows of the woods. But its brilliance only sharpened the mood of darkness within, the shadows of speculation and memory.

Against this cankerous dejection she was powerless. It spread like a slow poison, numbing and subtly converting to its own uses any defenses she could rally. The opposite of joy and confidence in life, this festering mood of doubt carried overwhelming conviction. What were hopes and dreams but illusions? What were beauty and happiness but signals of imminent change? Beyond the blessing of acceptance, stoical or humorous or orthodox, what possible faith? . . . And the incredible matter-of-factness of existence. The slack half-awake ordinariness of living. Perhaps in the end that was more baffling than the most violent or stealthy cruelties, the most fantastic contradictions, even the ultimate enigma. As the train panted and rattled hotly from one dingy little station to another on this interminable but frequently interrupted journey, the drab monotony of the breathless sun-baked country grew into a vast obsession. Here in this inland zone of pine barrens and cotton plains the very spirit of everyday monotony and drabness seemed to have settled permanently, a blighting pall too heavy for any wind to lift. Here life seemed to have gone stagnant as a miasmic swamp pool in a world of weary unrelieved horizons. The vacant faces at each dusty station-stop were like the faces of sleep-walkers; the eyes looked as blank as if they were closed, and the listless figures seemed drugged by an atmosphere of overpowering inertia and insensibility. . . . They were Tom, Dick, and Harriet of Crossroads, South Carolina, dead-level center of an earth still flat as a pancake, and they were making out on cotton, corn-pone and fat-back, pellagra and hookworm, and that good old-time religion.

She was able to call a halt there, realizing that she was trying to ease her burden by shifting it to the countryside and the people, by making her private tedium universal. And then, in a final attempt to escape, she tried to lift the world and herself to the better plane of tomorrow. . . . Change conditions, change men; improve conditions, improve men. In that dictum of the Enlightenment there was reason as well as rhyme, the only reason and sanity of society. Men would never be born equal, but they could all be given a fairer chance to become free. They could be born into a world less stupid and wasteful and cruel, a world of struggle not for personal gain and advancement but for human advancement, the welfare of all. A world of human solidarity, expanding horizons, transforming faith.

Impatiently she broke with her thoughts again, rejecting this last tangent of escape, this flight into the blue of futurity, this "straining for sublimity", as Stephen called it. For even in a shining new world, even in the best world that goodwill and reason could create, there would still be no cure for the basic ills of living. No miracles would ever heal the mortal lesions at the heart of life, or break the spell of time, or stay the fatal hand, or raise the dead. No dreams of heaven-on-earth could save the dreams of the individual: always the old bleak winds of autumn would roam the world, snuffing out the candles of spring, for each spring forever. Sooner or later you were left wandering in the dark of essential loneliness, lost in a helpless present to which the future was only a mirage of the past in the desert wastes of loss.

And now Jack was gone. . . . It was no use to pretend this need not be the end; underneath she knew it was the end. With his marriage the last ties would be cut and he would be lost to her beyond any hope of recall. And with final complete recognition of the bitter absurdity of this farewell journey, this festal journey to celebrate the wedding that was to seal her loss, her heart sank to the depths of dejection.

There was even a stricken sense of being confronted with the disposal of remnants of his life, a litter of things left in his bureau, an old pair of shoes, a coat hanging in his closet. But after touching this bottom her spirits tended to rise a little, as if full recognition of her loss lifted some part of the weight. Then, provoked and ashamed, she made an effort to throw off the whole burden of the journey, to turn her thoughts back to the harbor of Marshlands. And when she was safe again with Eleanor and Jane, her dark mood began to dissolve in the radiance of home as she took up her life where it had been interrupted. How good it would be when this journey was ended and she was free to return to them and resume the sure flow of days on toward their future. . . . But there abruptly she had to relinquish them. For fear of contaminating them and corrupting the years ahead with doubt and unfaith, she exiled herself again and returned to her captive journey.

In the end it was the journey itself that released her. The monotony and hot breath of the sun-sodden country sent her senses swimming, and at last the hypnotic roar and clacketing of the train lulled her into such a drowsy state that even the jerky braking and bell-clanging of station-stops failed to rouse her. And she could offer no resistance to this trend toward oblivion; her consciousness was like a straw in a stream, now drifting along on the surface, now submerged by the current, now caught in eddies of reverie and vague musing. Clear thoughts still came through at intervals, but they were meaningless, aimless, unconnected with any living issue and so without force to hold her. In time she became so lost in the squeaking rattling din of the car that it was impossible to say whether recurrent sharp sensations were pricks of distressful memories revived or only the sting of cinders in the puffy heat from the window. She no longer wondered when Stephen would come back from the smoker, or felt the stiff discomfort of the seat, or cared about the approach of Atlanta. At last everything was blended in a general blur of forgetfulness. Even the train's long harsh blasts at crossings were transformed into a kind of celestial music, like chords from beyond the sky, like faraway choirs in a dream.

Then suddenly she was wide awake, Stephen shaking her arm. The train was dragging into a city station: but it was only Augusta, where they were to change cars for Atlanta.

"You better start bucking up about here, honey," he prompted her with a pat as they got off the train. "This isn't a funeral we're heading for, you know."

✶   ✶   ✶

When it was all over and she was home again at last, only disjointed fragments remained, like the lingerings of a bad dream. . . . A general impression of the world Jack had attained: a high place of ornate houses and the Piedmont Driving Club, fine gardens steeped in the heavy fragrances of June: a world that seemed to have sucked up all riches, all substance and strength, leaving the nether world bloodless and drained. . . . After an embarrassing search with gushing Mrs. Riddock through mounds of presents, elaborate up-to-date silver pieces and objects-of-art, the plain old Fenwick tea-service located behind a door. . . . The Wedding March. . . . The champagne reception: a confusion of tongues and names and faces, the *Beautiful Lady* waltz, and something called *Too Much Mustard,* over and over. . . . The release of Mrs. Riddock's tearfully lyric contralto: "The lambs have flown! They've *slipped* away through the service entrance without a *soul* knowing!" . . .

And finally the night, what was left of it, in the Blue Room of the Riddock show-place. When she had succeeded in drifting off into a suspended state that was a far cry from sleep but better than nothing, Stephen had roused her with complaints of indigestion, not to be marveled at. Toward morning he had quieted down, and at daybreak a light rain had cooled the room a little, so that she had been able to imagine herself back at Marshlands with the breath of the sea stirring the curtains. . . .

Now, this morning after yesterday's return journey, Stephen had left for the office and she was in the garden with Eleanor and Jane. On the way home from Atlanta there had been a two-hour wait between trains at Augusta, and she had persuaded Stephen to take her to Berckmans' splendid old nurseries there, to pick out some new things for the garden. It would be months before they were shipped, but now she was impatient to plan where they would go.

Jane was her faithful assistant in placing and replacing the stakes that stood for pear trees and flowering peaches, banana shrubs and tea-olives, roses and camellias. Eleanor started out with enthusiasm, but when the stakes had been shifted and reshifted a few times she began to lose interest in the game, and presently she retired to her perch in the live-oak on the front lawn. A broad fork where the heavy horizontal branches of the big old oak met afforded her a generous lounging place and retreat, far from the madding crowd; she had first used it as a house for her dolls, but since her dolls had been turned over to Jane it had become a study, where she could read and meditate in peace. This vantage point commanded views in all directions, and now, though she had withdrawn from the tiresome staking experiments with an armful of books, she kept track of the world below, and was not above contributing suggestions to speed the garden proceedings into some other and more interesting channel.

From her crow's-nest she also kept a weather eye peeled for the approach of any possible excitement in Fenwick Street. And it was just as the last stakes were getting themselves settled that a sudden nautical whoop burst from the lookout:

"Carriage ahoy! Callers off the starboard bow! All hands on deck!"

She was unable to supply more specific information immediately, but after an expectant moment or two she came sliding down from her perch and made a dash for the driveway. "It's Pappa and Uncle Hervey!" she turned her head to shout. And Jane dropped the stake she was holding and rushed after her sister.

Watching them race down the drive toward the gates was perplexing. It was much too early for Stephen to be bringing Hervey Caldwell home for dinner. . . . When the carriage came through the gateway, she saw the girls stop dead, their joyous greetings abruptly stilled as the carriage passed them. Then her heart gave a panic thump. And as the carriage rolled sharply up the drive, with Eleanor and Jane in pursuit, she hurried across the lawn.

When she reached the carriage at the front steps, she saw Stephen slumped against Hervey Caldwell on the seat, his eyes closed, his face deathly white and drawn. After an instant of paralyzed shock her first response was to get Eleanor and whimpering Jane out of the way, send them to find Lucy. Then as she was trying to grasp what Hervey was telling her, Stephen's eyes opened and he straightened up with a weak smile.

"This young medico of yours," he told her in strained gasps, "is trying to make me believe—I've had a heart attack. Nothing but a dizzy spell—from indigestion. If he and Joe had given me a chance, I'd have pulled myself together—without all this damn foolishness."

Before she or Hervey could stop him, he tried to get up, but fell back on the seat, his face twisted with pain, sweat breaking out on his forehead. After that he waited limply; permitted them to help him out of the carriage, and up the steps into the house.

When he was stretched out on the living-room sofa and the pain had eased, he roused himself to glare up at Hervey Caldwell.

"I'll put up with this nonsense just long enough to get my stomach settled. I'll take soda, but don't leave any of your damn prescriptions around here. And tell Joe I'll be back at the office this afternoon."

And when he caught sight of Eugenia's white face in the doorway, he raised his voice to shout: "Keep out of here! Everybody clear out, except Emily. And stay out! What do you think this is, a sideshow? Can't a man have a few cramps in peace?"

But then he allowed himself to be quieted. He sank back and lay still, getting his breath, while she knelt by the sofa. After a moment his eyes opened with a sigh and looked into hers. He winked and touched her hand.

"Take it easy, honey. Sorry to spring this on you, but it's nothing. Nothing but a little too much wedding. I'll be all right in no time. Just take it easy a minute."

IV

FROM THAT DAY Stephen was a constant anxiety to her. On the second day after the attack he was defiantly back at the office; but from what Hervey Caldwell told her she understood how closely he must be watched and guarded. Far more than Eleanor and Jane, who were growing up so fast and learning to look after themselves so well, he needed her attention now.

But nothing could have been more difficult than trying to take care of him. He was worse than a child to look after, infinitely worse. It was impossible to protect him from himself and his three dangerous old cronies: coffee and cigars and late hours. By a valiant effort he succeeded in giving up his second cup of breakfast coffee and one of his morning cigars, but even these slight concessions were enough to shatter his nerves for the rest of the day. And any attempts to ease his insomnia seemed only to aggravate it. For the years since Michael's death he had been sleeping in the downstairs bedroom, and sitting up till midnight reading; but now he seldom got to bed before two or three o'clock. And sometimes when she came downstairs in the morning she found him asleep in his armchair in the living-room, his *News & Courier* draped over his head or crumpled at his feet, the table light still burning.

"It's no use, honey," he would answer her pleas. "Even you can't reform an old dog like me. You'll just have to take me as part of the way things happen, and make the best of it. . . . I'm getting along fine now. Let's let it go at that."

It was ironical that now she was engaged in the reverse of the long struggle she had once had to get him back to work and keep him at it; that now she was willing and anxious for him to give up his work; and that now he wouldn't hear of it. But though he paid

no heed to her pleadings and warnings and refused to consider retiring, she did succeed finally in getting him to give up the office in
the afternoons, leaving that much of his business in Sally Broughton's capable hands. He was won over to this not by direct appeal
or persuasion but by being made to feel that he was devoting too
little time to Eleanor and Jane.

So now he spent the summer afternoons with them. Usually they
went for a row, after his siesta and after the high heat of the day
was past: the yard-boy at the oars, Eleanor taking a pull at them
when the tide was not too strong, and Jane minding the trolling
line, while he dazzled their eyes with tall tales and reminiscences
of sea-island glory. If it was no day for the river, he took them for a
stroll, one on each proud arm. Or, if it was rainy and no weather
for either rowing or walking, he entertained them, and they him,
in the house. . . . If Sunday happened to be a bad day, he dutifully
escorted them with the family to church. But if Sunday was fair,
St. Helena's was left to Eugenia, and he took the rest of the family
by launch to Land's End. And that was best of all, for it gave
Eleanor and Jane not only joyful hours on the plantation but also
a trip to the beach at Bay Point, where he could watch his fairly
sober pigtails revert to frenzied sea-urchins in the wild spell of the
surf.

But before the end of summer this happy arrangement was disrupted by a sudden turn of events. In the first shock of war headlines Beaufort stood stunned in a staring and listening silence, while
the pulse of life stopped and business sagged; then Bay Street caught
its breath, and business bounded upward on a wave of long-staple
cotton buying orders:—and Stephen was quickly drawn back to the
office in the afternoons. "Everything's going up," he told her, "and
I've got to be on the job all the time." And she realized at once the
futility of trying to protect him from the office now, for even without prospects of better business he would have been drawn back
there by the urge to talk, by the necessity of discussing with Joe and
other men the astounding and incredible moves that were being
made on the map of Europe.

It was like that to her at first: moves on a map, echoes in the
paper, a fantastic game remote and beyond belief. A continuing
sense of shock prevented her from seeing it in terms of human
reality; she grasped only its spectacular outlines, its lurid and tumul-

tuous masses; and these only by reflection, as they affected Stephen. All the excitements of this great new interest were a menace to him, a very grave danger. And on that basis alone, in the beginning, she prayed for its speedy end.

For a time she was able to take comfort from his and Joe's insistence that it would all be over in a jiffy. He was confident that the magnificent German Army would break straight through to Paris again, and Joe was equally confident that the Vandals would be hurled back and cracked like a nut between Russia and the British Empire plus France; yet they agreed that it was too big to last more than a few months at most, so she waited in a daze for one side or the other to make the winning moves that would end the game and its thrills, and permit Stephen to quiet down. But with autumn the uncertainty and suspense increased, quickening her anxiety, for cold weather meant the lighting of the office stove. The office was bad enough for him in summer with all the windows open, but when the windows were closed and the stove lighted it meant his spending his days in a sealed stifling room, breathing stale air blue with cigar smoke. And that winter, as the war game settled into a deadlock, he had a series of severe colds, each of which frightened her badly. His own method with a cold was to treat it with contempt, to shake it off or wear it off, not to give in to it and not to let it get him down; with the invariable result that by the time he was willing to submit to her treatment, bed and hot drinks and hot-water bottles, the sore throat and stuffy head had become an alarming chest cold with high temperatures and a heavy cough. And the moment she succeeded in nursing him over the worst of it, and before he was half well, he was up and back at the office again.

He was always late for dinner now, and often for supper too. And as if the days were not long enough for talk, Joe dropped in almost every evening to resume discussion and debate, just as he had in Spanish War times. Her own faculties remained too stunned and confused for perception and analysis; she still saw only a spectacle, involving forces of tremendous magnitude yet remote and essentially implausible, like a summer night's thunder-and-lightning storm vaguely reverberant from far inland or from far out at sea. But from their evening talks it was becoming perfectly clear to her how Stephen and Joe felt.

It was Joe's rabid contention that the United States should rush to the aid of the Allies without further delay.

"How can you be willing," he hotly demanded of Stephen one evening, "to see us stand idly by while England struggles to save France from the fate of Belgium?"

"I tell you it's none of our business, man. We're neutral."

"None of our business? Neutral, when civilization is at stake? England and France represent civilization, sir, England being the masculine pole and France the feminine, so to speak,—and civilization hangs in the balance, sir!"

"That's one way of looking at it. As I happen to see it, we're all dogs the world over, and it's still dog eat dog. . . . Too bad Emily's Hague Tribunal for the Pacific Settlement of International Disputes couldn't do much with a plain old-fashioned dog-fight. What they needed was a Hague Dog-Catcher, armed to the teeth."

"Accepting for the moment your canine analogy," Joe growled, "I'll remind you that there are high and low breeds of dog. And I submit to you, simply and logically, that our lot should be cast in with our own kind. There's such a thing as blood allegiance, man."

Stephen smiled at that. "Nothing doing, Joe. If it was a question of strafing dogs of a different race and color,—well, that would be another story. As it is, we're well out of it. It's not our fight. We didn't start it, and our bones aren't involved. Not yet, at least. . . . Look here, you never used to be down on the German people."

"I never really trusted them," Joe flushed. "I always recognized that they were a people with chaos in their souls, a people of violent extremes and dual nature, capable of anything."

"I see. Like the little girl with the curl. When they were good they were very very good, but now that they're bad they're horrid."

"Precisely. They've shown themselves in their true colors. In the past you may have heard me praise them for certain virtues, but even then I never for a moment forgot that in their veins runs the blood of the Goths and the Visigoths who destroyed classical civilization."

"I'm no authority on antiquity, so I can't dispute you there. But I know something about hindsight and foresight."

"I have no idea what you mean to imply by that, but I find it impertinent and irrelevant on any count. The point I'm making is

711

that the Teutonic people are barbarians at heart, like their confederates the Turks."

"Barbarians hell. All they ask is a place in the sun, like all the rest of us. And I believe they're going to get it with the spring offensive. By summer at the latest. And as far as I'm concerned they're welcome to it."

"Ah! You don't object to atrocities, then?"

"One man's atrocities are another man's strategies. There's no such thing as civilized warfare, as our Yankee brothers taught us. If we didn't happen to remember British atrocities in Revolutionary times."

"Very well. But when the Hun hordes have ground civilization under the iron heels of their bloody boots and come to turn lustful eyes toward our shores, I'll warrant you'll change your tune!"

"Well, of course, that's a horse of another color. But suppose they do conquer the world, what of it? We might have peace then. If Alexander or Caesar or Napoleon had been able to establish a world empire, we wouldn't be a pack of brawling nations now."

"A *Pax Germanica,* I suppose!"

"Well, personally I'd prefer a *Pax Britannica* or a *Pax America* to goose-stepping Kultur. But I suppose any old *pax* is better than none."

"Rot, sir! I mean to say, you can't be serious. After all, we fought the North to prevent just such an enslavement."

"And lost, to our great advantage. Now we're one nation instead of two, and in union is strength. Live and learn."

"Am I to infer that if war came again you would fight for the Union against South Carolina?"

"What do you take me for, man, a damn fool? What's that got to do with this case anyhow?"

"I'll be frank with you, Stephen. I don't like this pro-German championing of yours."

"Who's pro-German? I'm pro-nothing! I'm neutral!"

By this time Joe was flushed purple, Stephen pale as ashes, and both were hoarse from shouting. They had reached their usual impasse and were waiting to be separated. Her intervention and quieting they were able to accept readily, for she had never taken sides, having still no clear thoughts to express.

But by the end of the winter, after listening to many evenings of

712

their war talk, at least her feelings were clarified. By a process of accumulation, of mounting protest against both their attitudes, she found herself in possession of a fully-developed sense of horror. Legions of youth were being herded to slaughter like cattle: youth against youth in mass butchery: shining countrysides become vast shambles for the bodies and souls of youth. Countless multitudes of men, with their dreams and the dreams of those who loved them, being sucked like gnats into a flaming death-trap of blood and fury. A man-made cataclysm so horrible and insane that the mind shrank from the sight of it, recoiling into disbelief to escape dissolving in the chaos and mockery to which it reduced all human values. Nothing—no banners, no cheers, no words—could cloak its ghastly futility; all its victories were defeats; its calm maps and carefully-planned drives and grand strategies only accented the stark madness, and the press bulletins and despatches and debates it inspired were like the trivial chatterings and flutterings of birds on the fringes of a seething forest fire. It was appalling horror and insanity, a mad carnival of death: this, in her understanding, was its essential reality.

Yet this prime element and aspect of horror seemed to elude Joe and Stephen completely. In their talks the War appeared as a reasonable conflict of national interests and honors, of raw materials and armies and leaders: a sort of glorified game of chess, tremendous and absorbing, with plenty of pawns. And when Jack drove down from Atlanta for a weekend visit after New Year's,—Nellie and Mrs. Riddock having gone to New York on a shopping trip,—it was the same with him: a great game, with French names thrown in as a joker. Tough on the boys that had to spend Christmas in the trenches with the cooties, but great for the cotton business. . . . Even Eugenia, so sensitive to a scratch or a pin-prick or a misplaced chair at home, seemed to see in all the carnage and devastation abroad only an elaborate kind of play, with Germany in the role of villain, Belgium and France as virtue in distress, and England as the hero-savior. And the talk of the town, comments heard in the stores and at the post-office and at social gatherings, seldom betrayed any feeling beyond excitement or indifference. Of all the people she knew only young Dr. Caldwell shared her awakened sense of overwhelming horror.

One evening late in January, when Stephen had torn himself

away from his after-supper easy-chair cigar and paper to give her his annual help with the garden seed list, she made an attempt to express her feelings to him. It was an unusual opportunity for talk with him alone: Joe was in Charleston, Jane had had her spelling heard and was safely in bed, and Eleanor was studying her lessons in the living-room under Eugenia's eye. And tonight she felt a great need for talk: the festive garden catalogs, whose arrival was always so sure a sign that spring was at hand, lay spread out with their expectant order-blanks on the dining-room table like gay invitations; yet somehow they were also rebukes, sharp reminders of the blighted gardens of the zones of horror. Even the gentle and contented glow of the fire seemed at moments a reflection of horror, of brutally dead hearths, of other homes consumed in blasts of blind and savage hate. And in her thoughts were lingering the disturbing echoes of an article she had read that afternoon, an account of the opening of the Panama Canal, which had stirred her deeply with its story of the years of struggle, the courage and ingenuity and labor that had gone into its making.

She waited till he had finished the order-blanks and was sitting back in his chair, well pleased with himself for the help he had given her. Then she mentioned the article and told him how it had affected her, how good it was to read of what men could accomplish by working together constructively, as opposed to the deadly alliances of war. She tried to speak with restraint, but her feelings once loosed were too strong for cool and measured words. And she found she had placed herself at an immediate disadvantage, for he was amused at her vehemence.

"Yes," he smiled tolerantly, "it's too bad we can't spend all our energies on noble achievements, great public works, inspiring engineering feats."

"But why can't we?"

"Are you asking me seriously? Because if you are, I'll have to refer you to God. Ask Him why He made men of us, instead of angels. Ask Him how He happened to give us a fighting instinct."

"But why can't we use our fighting instinct to destroy our old enemies—disease and stupidity and chaos—instead of one another?"

He sighed, pushed back his chair, and got up. After a stretch and yawn before the fire he locked his hands behind him and shook his head at her. "You know, it's really amazing the way you manage to bring any discussion around to that old refrain of yours, and Rusty's. Change human nature and transform the world! With never a thought of consequences, of what a transformed world would actually be like if carried to its logical conclusions, what a hell of uniformity and law and order and sweetness and light. You've never been able to see that your heaven-on-earth dream—no strife, no suffering, no tears—is nothing but death in disguise."

"You think doing away with unnecessary evil would make a hell of sweetness and light?"

"Oh, you perfectionists wouldn't be satisfied with anything less than perfection!—you're worse than the early Christians. That's why I don't trust you with even an inch of reform. A fanatic wouldn't be a fanatic if he knew when to stop. . . . Too bad you can't accept my humble slant on things. You could save yourself so much useless wear-and-tear if you'd only learn to take life as the cook serves it, with the sauce of humor if possible. It's a tough game all right, but you have a gambling chance, and in my poor opinion that's a damn sight better than living in a safe-and-sane Reformatory. In your world of no sickness and sin but only co-operative building, there'll be no gambling allowed. Even God has to have the devil, but in your fairyland of the future all the witches and hobgoblins, all the dragons and demons and werewolves will have been killed off, leaving only a collection of pixies and fauns and nice busy brownies. There won't be even a plat-eye left to haunt the colored fairies."

He gave her an indulgent chuckle. "I guess it's just as well you reformers can't change the rules of the game by wishing."

"That's all terribly smart," she assured him. "But it happens to be a fact that the rules have already been considerably changed. And I suspect they'll be changed beyond recognition as time goes on."

"Well, maybe you're right. But personally I'm content to bleed and perish on this side of Jordan. I wouldn't feel comfortable in the Promised Land. . . . And now let me put a question to you, for a change. Why is it you're always wandering off into abstractions? We started with realities, the Panama Canal and the War, —why can't we stick to that? How do you feel about the Central Powers and the Allies? Which side are you betting on? It's about time you declared yourself."

"I'm afraid I don't see it as a game, Steve. To me it's like some horrible world plague and madness. If there are any 'sides', it's death against life, barbarism against progress. No national rights and wrongs can justify the crime of it. It's just madness and horror. That's how I feel about your war."

He raised his brows sardonically, but carefully refrained from smiling.

"Well! You certainly have some decided feelings on the subject. And maybe you're right, maybe it doesn't make sense. But, honey, there'll always be war. It's the nature of the beast. We'll always find excuses to blow off steam, to get the strain of peace out of our system, the old heat out of our blood. Men must fight, and women weep."

She studied him for a moment in silence, and then began gathering up the seed catalogs.

"You honestly don't see the horror of it, do you?"

"Sure I do! Plenty of horror. But plenty of other things, too. Good and bad generalship, brilliance and fatal blundering in high places. In the ranks bravery and cowardice, strength and weakness, endurance and collapse. Good luck and bad luck. Glory and honor, amazing scientific cunning, suffering and agony and death. Yes, and humor, plenty of humor. And any other elements of life I've omitted. . . . That's what it is,—an intensified magnified game of life."

"You've quite forgotten the horror you once went through, haven't you?"

He paused over that, with a frown. But then he shrugged impatiently and turned his back on her, moving the fire-screen aside, and with tongs firmly gripped in his good hand began to settle the fire for the night.

"Time," he told her over his shoulder as he plied the tongs, "has a way of arranging things in their proper perspective. I don't recall much actual horror. Or much fighting for that matter. It was mostly marches and camps and talk, blisters and lice and bloody flux. . . . Of course, we didn't have barrages and machine-guns and barbed-wire and shell-shock in those days."

He straightened up and put the tongs away with a clatter. When he had moved the screen back in place, he turned to face her again, hands locked behind him. "If there was any madness and horror, my darling," he said sharply, "it came later. In peace times. In Reconstruction. . . . Get this sentimental notion of the horror of war out of your head! If war is horrible, then so is peace. When you get down to cases, do you honestly believe it's any worse for a man to die fighting for his country than it is for him to die of some peaceful disease—like Michael?"

"I do," she answered quickly and without flinching. "In war men are driven to kill men. That's the whole madness and horror of it."

He heaved an exasperated sigh. "That's simply not it at all! Can't you see that military warfare is no worse than civilian warfare, the struggle that goes on every day, all the time, in every peaceful corner of the world? They both come to the same thing in the end, war and peace. Only it seems to me that death in open battle is a damn sight cleaner and sweeter than all the miserable little lingering deaths of peace. . . . In peace even if you're lucky enough to beat your neighbor, you can't keep your winnings. Every success turns into failure in the end, and every gain becomes a loss. Slow or fast everything is stripped from you,—your dreams, your loved ones, your strength,—till at last the hour comes when you lie in peaceful state, and naked as the day you were born, on your undertaking neighbor's embalming-table."

He stopped for breath and then went hotly on. "No thanks, I'll take war any day. Give me death and destruction on a grand and glorious scale. You can have the creeping paralysis and all the slow rot and defeat of peace!"

His agitation began to alarm her, and she avoided any further dispute, allowing his fuming voice to subside.

"By this time," he told her finally, "I should know better than to get into an argument with a woman. You can't get anywhere. Particularly when she's an incurable idealist. . . . If you're not going to be able to discuss the War sensibly, I wish you'd just drop it. Just be thankful we're out of it. Cultivate your garden and enjoy your home and your grandchildren. Leave the War to Joe and me and God. We'll have it cleared up for you, one way or the other, in short order now."

. . . And that spring she did try to "drop it", to leave the War to them and lose herself in the blessings of home. She made a firm point of never being drawn into Stephen's evening debates with Joe, and when she could she avoided even listening to them. And though they failed to clear up the War in short order for her, though sometimes at the most shining moments the dark faith-destroying horror of it invaded the garden and spread through the radiant and fragrant air like some evil counter-charm, some noxious fume, laying a blight of doom over the blossoms, the new leaves, the laughter of the children, still she could always dispel the evil, drive it back across the river and the out-islands and the sea, by her own conviction that it could not last much longer. Soon, tomorrow perhaps, the world would return to humanity and hope, to building the future, to forward-looking peace, peace to match the peace of home.

↗   ↗   ↗

But before the War was a year old her conviction was worn thin, and even Stephen and Joe were beginning to lose confidence in their powers of prophecy. They continued to announce approximate dates for the end of hostilities, the breaking-through to Paris or the nut-cracking of Germany, but they made their predictions now with a waxing dogmatism that betrayed their waning assurance.

"At this rate," Stephen finally admitted, "they may string it out for another six months, or even a year."

And it was not proving so advantageous a game as he had expected. Cotton prices were climbing and business was better all along the line, but the cost of living was rising faster than profits. "H. C. of L." was coming to stand for something more serious than a household jest.

"If you had let me pick up a few shares of war brides and babies," he complained, "we wouldn't be worrying about high prices. We'd be sailing with the wind. As a matter of fact, it isn't too late to get aboard, if you could only get up your nerve. . . ."

"It's your damn British blockade," he told Joe, "that's causing all the trouble! What right has England to interfere with our neutral trade with Germany? And where does she get the gall to seize our cotton consigned to Holland and Denmark and Sweden? If that isn't flagrant violation of international law, what is it?"

"It's grim necessity," replied Joe blandly. "England is fighting for her life. The blockade is essential, and on that basis I find it eminently justified. *And,* in point of fact, it may well prove to be a positively humane action, by breaking the Western Front dead-lock."

"Don't talk through your hat, man! The Germans may be mis-guided fools, but their babies can starve as well as Belgium babies. If your blockade isn't the lowest kind of ruthlessness, I'll eat your hat! Why, damn it, it's the British navy that's starving Belgium! Open your eyes, man. Or are you too damn stubborn to see?"

Joe was stumped for an answer to that,—till Germany declared a blockade of the Allies and laid a submarine zone round the British Isles. Then he was able to demand: "The shoe's on the other foot, and now what have you to say to that?"

"I say it was provoked. Tit for tat. And you ought to applaud, —it will very positively and humanely break the Western Front deadlock."

But the words were scarcely out of his mouth when news came, with a shock that recalled the appalling *Titanic* headlines, of the sinking of the *Lusitania,* torpedoed off the Irish coast by a U-boat. Not since the *Maine* had there been such a furore of national ex-citement: the press burst into patriotic flames and the whole coun-try caught fire. This was not destruction of American trade. This was destruction of American citizens.

"What have you to say now, sir?" Joe snorted triumphantly. "Are you still neutral after this?"

"They were warned!" Stephen shouted back. And for a time he continued doggedly to defend Germany. When the *Deutschland* bobbed up mysteriously and ominously at Baltimore that summer, and when the *U-53* appeared at Newport after sinking nine mer-chantmen off Nantucket, he jeered at Joe's fits of indignation and alarm: "It's like you to mistake a sporting proposition for a threat." And later when Joe returned from a trip to Charleston with accounts of a lurid motion picture he had seen there, *The Bat-tle Cry of Peace,* whose theme, taken from Maxim's sensational book *Defenseless America,* was nothing less than the invasion of the United States by Germany,—"the heroine's part was played by a girl named Norma Talmadge, a face and form typical of our best young womanhood",—Stephen mocked him unmercifully. "You come back with your lungs full of poison gas, your heart riddled with machine-gun bullets and the charms of a picture-show actress, your womenfolk raped, your hearth and home desecrated, your country ravaged by an invasion far worse than anything Sherman ever dreamed of,—and you expect me to keep a straight face! Man, that settles it. You're plain crazy."

But that did not settle it. That only marked the end of one phase of his dangerous war fever, and the beginning of another phase. Already there were signs that his resistance was weakening, and soon it became evident that his opposition to Joe was gradually being converted into agreement. Little by little, as rapidly as his pride allowed, he was abandoning Germany and shifting his support to the Allies. By late summer, and the first anniversary of the outbreak of hostilities, he and Joe were in almost perfect accord. . . . But far from quieting his excitement, checking the over-stimulation of his heart and nerves, as she had hoped, this fireside *entente* only added fuel to the flames of their evening conferences. In accord, in damning together the "lady-like" foreign policy of Wilson and Bryan and praising the preparedness movement of fire-eating Teddy Roosevelt and General Wood, they were more violent than ever.

But toward the close of the year there was an astonishing interlude that relieved the heat and stress of their talk with long laughter. All through the Christmas holidays they made merry over the fiasco of the Ford Peace Ship, the *Oscar II*.

By the spring of 1916 Stephen's early neutrality was completely transformed. And after the sinking of the *Sussex,* torpedoed without warning despite Germany's pledges, he exploded into a more rampant jingo than Joe.

Everything was the War now: nothing could compete with it for his attention. He was becoming totally oblivious to the little problems and events of home, and even the little miracles failed to surprise him. Eleanor's high marks at school, Jane's talent for drawing, the love of music that both of them were learning from the old Steinway, these great developments received affectionate nods of commendation when they were brought to his notice, but he no more grasped their significance and promise than he recognized the presence of the lesser home developments, the hanging of new curtains, the reupholstering of a sagging armchair, or improvements in the garden. These vital home statistics were unable to reach his central consciousness; they were lost in his *News & Courier* headlines and columns, swamped in the endless flood of war news. He could give home only a vague and abstracted attention when he came back from the office like a man in a trance, his head in clouds of smoke and talk.

And that summer, as the presidential election loomed, his excitement rose to fever heat, mounting alarmingly as it became clear that the election was to be fought out not along regular party lines and on domestic issues, reform *vs.* the business boom, but solely on the administration's foreign policy,—"He Kept Us Out of War" *vs.* the Preparedness Group. The issue was War *vs.* Peace, and everyone was taking sides on that basis. And there was no way of checking or controlling the consuming passion this crisis produced in Stephen. . . . By autumn he and Joe had whipped themselves into such a state of patriotic frenzy that it seemed they might easily break all their most cherished precedents and carry out their threats to support Hughes with two solid Southern ballots. But in the end, at the last minute and almost on the threshold of the polls, they found a handy excuse for voting the straight ticket. They might as well stick to Wilson, they agreed, because the country was going to be forced into the War anyway and it better be under the Democratic banner.

But election day brought no release from this spell of tense and grinding strain. There were three extra days of supreme excitement, of nerve-shattering suspense and an orgy of coffee and cigars, while the result hung in doubt. It was certain that Wilson had carried the South and Hughes the East, and that the Midwest vote was about evenly divided, but what about the West? Stephen insisted on sitting up for three straight nights waiting for a telephone call from Jack in Atlanta or from Joe, who had rushed to Charleston as if to be that much nearer the electoral college and see personally that the Republicans didn't steal the election "as they did in the seventies".

When the final returns came in,—nine million votes for Wilson against eight-and-a-half million for Hughes,—Stephen was a wreck, his eyes bloodshot, his face ash-gray from strain and exhaustion. He tried to keep going, for of course the election had to be all refought at the office; but after a single day of that came the reaction she feared, and he had to give in. He refused to let Hervey Caldwell doctor him, but since there was no choice he grumblingly consented to a few days' rest in bed.

But he was up and back on the job, with renewed strength, in plenty of time to apply a critical eye and tongue to the first moves of Wilson's second term. And when just before Christmas the President sent out a world peace proposal, identical notes to all the belligerents, Stephen was feverishly involved again.

"A nice piece of sentimental tripe and feminine meddling! A perfect way to celebrate the anniversary of the *Oscar II*. A fine spectacle!—why these schoolmarm tactics are making us out a collection of damn fools and yellow-bellies! . . . Germany may accept because she's up against it, but the Allies aren't going to throw up their hands at this stage of the game."

And, as he predicted, the Allies declined the peace-conference invitations.

But before the end of the first month of the new year—1917— she had another thrill of hope when the President went before the Senate to propose a concert of nations, a league of peace.

"God Almighty," Stephen fumed, "the man's a maniac! He wasn't satisfied with being President of Princeton, where he belonged. He wasn't satisfied being reform Governor of New Jersey. He isn't even satisfied to be President of the United States. Oh no,—he wants to be President of the World!"

And it was impossible either to quiet him or keep out of his way.

"Come on, dear, give me some back-talk," he kept goading her. "Show some spunk,—pacifists should be game, like the early Christians. Still sticking up for your prophet? Still think he's sane?"

"Of course," she finally had to talk back. "Doesn't this war prove that the only hope is in some kind of league for international peace? Countries have got to learn to live together on the same basis of order and coöperation as states. You can make all the fun of it you like, but sooner or later there's got to be a United States of the World."

"I know! And sooner or later, because life is such an unsatisfactory arrangement, we've got to have a Brotherhood of Man. Well, I suppose you latest chosen people who have substituted utopia for heaven in the old game of consolations, I suppose you've got to

722

put us ordinary mortals through before you wake up and find it was just another dream. You just can't accept the hard fact that life is strife and can never be anything else. . . . Now can you seriously imagine a collection of nations joining hands in friendly intercourse. Only a Jew could concoct such a world. And only Jews could stand it. . . . No thanks. Fortunately there's still such a thing as healthy discrimination left in the world. And if actually faced with international peace and its inevitable amalgamations, I think most of us would prefer to join the German experiment and seek salvation breeding Supermen for the domination of the world."

"But don't all kinds of people live together in harmony in this country?"

"Sure, if you call our battle for existence harmony. But countries aren't people. They're mobs of people, a very different thing you'll discover when we get to race wars."

"Oh Steve, you're hopeless. Can't you see that world peace could give world civilization a chance? We've got to believe that and make it come true. Just as we've got to believe in human progress and the future."

"Oh, of course! Faith in a glorious future,—for our great-grandchildren, who won't even know our names! We've all got to rally round and believe the world's going to be as full of earnest loving kindness as you are,—or you won't be comfortable!"

"Well, I guess I've had enough, dear. You're beginning to shout, and we don't seem to be getting anywhere."

"Of course. You're getting the worst of it, so I'm beginning to shout, dear, and we're not getting anywhere! We better drop it and go peacefully to bed, I suppose. That's sporting, isn't it?"

"Well, all right. But what else is there to say? I'm pretty well demolished now."

"Oh no you're not! You never will be. It's congenital, this faith of yours. You'll always fall for messiahs and idealistic egomaniacs like Wilson. Hope for humanity is your special weakness."

"And perhaps my special strength."

"I don't doubt it. People have drawn strength from all kinds of strange delusions since time began."

She was able, at last, to let the discussion rest there. And vexed with herself for having allowed him to get so wrought up, she tried to placate him with a smiling surrender. Having exhausted himself he was willing to accept her submission, but not without a final word.

"All right, we'll drop it. But get one practical point straight in that flighty head of yours. The worst of Professor Wilson's more recent asininities is that now Germany thinks we'll stand for anything. Which is all to the good, as a matter of fact. We'll speedily have an overt act. You'll see."

And, sure enough, on the first day of February the *News & Courier* carried the staring headline: *Unrestricted Submarine Warfare.* Germany had sent a note of warning that all neutral vessels in the Mediterranean or waters adjacent to Great Britain would be sunk on sight. "That settles it," Stephen decided; and he and Joe jubilantly sent in a joint subscription to the *New York Times*. The paper would reach them a day or two late, but it would give them the complete and unabridged news.

Events moved so fast now that she could hardly keep up with them. The camellia bushes at the front steps had just opened their buds when the President went before Congress to urge the severing of diplomatic relations with Germany; and a few days later Ambassador Von Bernstorff was handed his passport, just as the snowdrops were beginning to blossom again along the fences of Beaufort. The old enchantment of swamp maple and jasmine, judas tree and wild plum, had barely touched the sea-island woods when the news broke of fantastic German intrigues: the British Intelligence Service made public an intercepted telegram, the "Zimmerman Note" to the German minister to Mexico, inviting that country to attack the United States and promising in return the states of Texas, New Mexico, and Arizona. . . . By the first of April,—as the deepening spring sunlight was bringing the whole magic of the garden to life, the gay daffodils along the paths, the dogwoods and the young flowering peaches against the walls of evergreen, the azaleas and the wistaria and banksia rose mantle of the summer-house,—the President was reading his War Message to Congress. And a few days later, on Good Friday and at the moment of the garden's full glory, came the Declaration of War.

"Well," Stephen told her soberly, "I didn't think your Professor had it in him. Don't care much for his flowery language, but his signature looks good. And with Russia in collapse they'll be needing us."

✦   ✦   ✦

At first she was helplessly confused by the President's sudden about-face. Stephen had his usual pat interpretation of the course of events: "We're pitching in because we've got to protect our loans to the Allies." And Joe had appropriated the thunder of Senator Lodge, leader of the war-whoopers of the East against La Follette and the laggards of the West and Midwest: "This war is a war, as I see it, against barbarism." But neither of these ideas satisfied her in the least, and she was lost till she found at last, among the stirring cadences of the President's War Message, a certain utterance of purpose and faith that restored her confidence in his leadership. ". . . We shall fight for a universal dominion of right by such a concert of free peoples as shall bring peace and safety to all nations and make the world itself at last free." That disarmed her resistance, and became and remained her reliance. It was clear now that from his high post Wilson had come to see that the madness and horror could be terminated only by force, that this nation must use its might to win peace and then its power and prestige to insure world peace. The end, he had decided, would justify the means; and she trusted him. Surely no nation had ever gone forth to war with such honor, not to win victory or spoils or glory but to save the world. This was to be, in truth, a crusade.

And there her thinking stopped. Reflection withered in the hot blasts of patriotism that swept the country, and misgivings were drowned in the released torrents of emotion, the frenzied chorusings of the newspapers, the clamor and surge of mass preparations. Beaufort was in an uproar: the little Marine Corps station on Parris Island was to be expanded into a great Base. Sam Koenig's dachshund was stoned in the street by a gang of town boys, and after that "The Hun" kept himself well barricaded in his house against the rising tide of hate. In front of the post-office appeared a large poster of Uncle Sam pointing an accusing finger: *I Want YOU for the U. S. Army!* . . . At the post-office, at street corners, in stores, in homes, at church nobody talked about anything but the War. It was in the air everywhere, like the lingering incense of

725

autumn bonfires. To try to think through it was like trying to think at the beach on a day of high wind and surf. All reasoning faculties were numbed and suspended, and you were carried along with your neighbors on an irresistible current of feeling and action.

Stephen was drawn at once into a whirlpool of activity. Immediately after the Declaration of War the inanimate village of Port Royal found itself suddenly resurrected as railroad terminal for Parris Island, and he plunged into the real-estate boom there. And as if that were not enough to tax his strength to the limit, he accepted a post on the local Draft Board.

"First," he explained to her, "we register every able-bodied male between the ages of twenty-one and thirty. Then they draw numbers out of a lottery hat in Washington, and the winners will be in uniform and camp before they know what struck them. They'll be heroes on a grand spree. And any possible squawks will be drowned out in a blare of congratulations and cheers, and bands playing *Tipperary* and *Dixie*."

He was on the go from early morning till late at night, he swilled coffee all day and chewed up uncounted cigars; but he was in heaven. She had to think far back to recall a time when he had been as happy as he was now. And she was disarmed by the way he seemed to thrive on this strenuous diet: he actually slept better and looked better. She had promised herself to keep a close watch on him and call a positive halt at the first signs of exhaustion, but as the summer advanced and the heat and pressure mounted, he appeared so well and vigorous that she felt she could afford to relax her vigilance and concentrate on her own activities.

And that summer she herself was busier than she had been for years. Home was not to blame for this, for these days home almost ran itself: Eleanor was ready for high-school in the fall and conscious of being a very grown-up and responsible person, competent to direct her own energies; and though Jane at times was still satisfied to be treated as a child and still clung to her dolls despite Eleanor's derision, she really knew how to look after herself now with few cautionings. It was outside activities, the duties of Beaufort-at-war, that so congested the days. Early in the summer she found herself chairman of the Ribaut Chapter of the Red Cross. And before this task of getting an emblem in the front window of every home was half finished, up popped an invitation to serve on the committee of the "Citizens' Community Hall League".

"Take it," Stephen urged her. "After all, you've brought these honors on yourself by being impartially nice to everybody. You're the only woman in town they'll all listen to and back, because they all know you don't run with any of their little packs. They'll tear you apart someday on general principles, but don't let that faze you now. Go ahead and accept. It's your duty. And maybe you can talk them out of building a Greek temple with Gothic trimmings."

When she accepted an invitation to serve on the board of the new Library Society, of which Joe Bramwell was elected first president, Stephen heartily approved of that too. "You and Joe," he smiled, "may be able to keep the board meetings from becoming a permanent arena for town spites. And now you're in no position to complain of my overdoing. You're the party that needs watching now. Red Cross, Community Hall, Library Board,—you're up to your ears."

And that was not all. There was the plantation, and the plantation had returned to prime importance. In April cotton had soared to 21¢ a pound; by June it was selling at 24¢; and farm truck was bringing unheard-of prices. But Seth was laid up with a combination of old rheumatic ills, and Land's End was paralyzed by labor shortage. The island people were in the demoralizing grip of flush times again: a ferment like Reconstruction was in the air, and few were immune from the general contagion. Penn School, despite new buildings and equipment donated by Northern benefactors, was losing its prestige and its ability to keep the island families in co-operative line. As prices had climbed since the beginning of the War, the people had grown restive under the communal authority of the school and had come to act with increasing independence. They wanted to be on their own again, to be free to do as they pleased, to loaf after a crop sale, to spend their cash without overseeing; to exchange their fresh butter and milk and eggs, and even the hens that laid the eggs, for goods from the shelves of Frogmore Store, canned salmon and sardines, sweet biscuits and soda-pop and showy shoddy clothes.

This relapse, most vividly signalized by the women's breaking-out in a rash of cheap finery and bad manners, had been serious enough, but now a fatal complication was developing. For years there had been a slow leak of migration from the island, a seepage of spirits restless for one reason or another and eager to try their luck in the city; after 1914 the annual population loss had trebled; and now, with the country at war, the migration fever was assuming epidemic proportions. Almost everyone, young and old, wanted to be on the move: the city with its bright lights and quick cash-money was pulling them like a magnet. It was useless to try to talk them out of it, the ones that seemed the most surely convinced it was best to stay settled were among the first to disappear. Already the pick of the island bucks, those who had escaped the draft or conscription for stevedore jobs at Parris Island and deck-hand jobs on the new mosquito fleet sub-chasers, were gone to Savannah or Charleston or the fabulous North. And the younger women were even wilder than the men to get away. One Land's End girl, recently a model student at Penn School but now in close communication with a sister in New York, was apparently speaking for most island maidens when she declared she knew she would rather be a "lam'-pos' in Haa'lem dan a whole plantation 'pontop St. Hel'na!" . . . The young people were leaving in batches, and the only thing that seemed to be preventing their elders from selling out and migrating in mass to Savannah or the North was the bewildering difficulty of clearing land titles; every family holding, however small, had several sets of scattered heirs all claiming a slice of the property.

Biggie shook his head over the situation. "Miss Em'ly, de 'omans is mos' fuh blame, 'cause he pit de mans up to goin', coaxin' an' sweet-talkin' an' plaguin' um till he got no good sense lef' an' don' know he own mine. An' seem-like de 'omans do pure t'ribe 'pon dat high city life, but de mans ain' wut in de city,—he do widduh-up same like cotton in haa'd dry-drought groun'. But mans an' 'omans, dey all-two come home fuh *bury,* I know dat! . . . My missie, I comin' frank wid you now. Vhen I been young I hod good privilege fuh run off an' all about, but time gone an' I ain' studyin' 'bout dat no mo', ma'm. I could be in Sawannah right now, an' I could be to de Nort', an' I could be *daid,*—do Gawd. Naw'm, I ain' studyin' 'bout leabin' de oilan' like dem po' peoples dat ain' nebbuh been no place an' seen nutt'n. I gots too much wuk fuh do, makin' de noo crap, fuh study 'bout fool. An' de mo' dem

728

crazy nigguh gone, de mo' my own two han' gots fuh t'ink 'bout, ma'm."

After this speech, with its personal reassurances, Biggie's desertion came as a double shock. Bright and early on Fourth-of-July morning, as the first salvos and salutes were waking Beaufort and accenting the already breathless sweltering heat of the sun, he appeared at the front steps of Marshlands like an apparition, abashed and resplendent in a new outfit of store-clothes,—green woolly suit, peg-top trousers and a box coat with the price-tag left on for elegance, orange button shoes with arched toes, and a red knitted tie. He was discovered by Eleanor and Jane; they stayed to entertain him while Lucy brought the news grumblingly upstairs. "Miss Em'ly," she announced through the bedroom door in a voice salted with old disdain, "dat Biggie is here an' say he mus' see you,—shall I tell'um no, ma'm?" Puzzled, she sent Lucy back with a message for him to wait and hurried to finish dressing. When she went down to the front porch she found Biggie presenting the girls with a pair of Roman candles, but she knew at once from his appearance and manner that this was no "gif'" call; and the moment he began to speak she guessed what was coming. He had been reading in the papers, he stammered with a huge frozen grin after an aimless preamble, that the Germans were sinking ships too fast and that the Government needed good hands bad in the shipyards. After this stumbling declaration, which had plainly been rehearsed with gestures, he became completely tongue-tied, his jaws were locked and beads of sweat ran down his tortured bronze face like tears. But by this time she had recovered sufficiently to help him. She said she thought he was making a serious mistake but that she was glad he had not run off without a word, like most of the people. She wished him good-luck, and hoped he would not feel he had to wait till he was dead and ready to be buried before coming home.

"You were wise," Stephen told her at breakfast, "not to try to talk him out of it. It's tough, but what did you expect? By this time you ought to know you can't count on any of them."

Biggie's desertion left Land's End squarely on the Robinsons' shoulders, and Seth being crippled with rheumatism that meant Linda's and Jim's shoulders; and to do what she could to help them she began now to visit the island regularly. There was not much she could do, except round up and try to animate and keep at work the few stray hands left on the plantation, people who lacked the initiative to either run off or crop for themselves. To young Jim fell the heavy task of leading this sad little crew in the field, while Linda took over his yard chores to add to a daily routine already congested with housekeeping, nursing Seth, and tending a substantial vegetable garden.

Fortunately, despite Stephen's spring predictions that cotton prices would soar and that it would surely pay to go the limit this year, only a modest acreage had been planted; so Jim and his make-shift little field-gang were not overwhelmed. Still, it was a close race. Jim at seventeen was already a man, full-grown and strong and in complete command of himself, but he had not yet learned to command others; he could do the tasks of three ordinary hands, chop weeds from early morning till dusk without tiring, but he was not so good at bossing a collection of shiftless helpers who were ready by noon to lay down their hoes and quit for the day. Like Seth's his voice was low and reluctant and rare as his smile; he had all his mother's energy, but her expansive qualities were subdued in him almost to stolidness. He was by nature self-contained, in-clined to think and act alone, to go quietly about his own business in his own way, without any talk and fuss and without much re-gard for what anyone else was doing; it was a real effort for him to show any authority, particularly when it meant calling one of the hands down, or shouting orders across the rows of the field that Biggie's great bellow had so easily spanned. Yet, though he could hardly fill Biggie's shoes, he was doing remarkably well as man of the plantation. . . . Every time she saw him that summer, realiza-tion of his new manhood made her throat tighten with memories of Michael at seventeen. They were so different in superficial ways, but so alike in the essentials of fine youth. And now she could only pray that Linda's dreams would not be outrun as hers had been. Jim was through with high-school and ready for Clemson Agricultural College in the fall, as soon as the cotton was safely harvested; perhaps Linda was fortunate in having her ambitions for her son limited by him to the soil of the island. Jim wanted to be a farmer, and with mercy fate would touch him genrly in that life close to the earth.

His inheritance of manhood was not the only transformation unmistakably revealed to her that summer on visits to the island. Eleanor and Jane usually accompanied her to the plantation, and here—where they were removed from Stephen and Eugenia and Lucy, from Marshlands-at-war and all the associations and background of their childhood, and stood in a setting of half-lost memories and the faded visions of another age—here they could be seen with a clarity impossible at home. It was fully apparent now that Eleanor was definitely in her teens and must soon be allowed to do up her hair. Although she was several years younger than Jim, she had the air of being his senior; and though she had once worshipped him as a combination of hero and older brother, she now seemed bent on balancing the score by behaving toward him like a captious older sister, a role she was forced to carry to excess because of his good-natured indifference to her rudeness and his stubborn refusal to take her seriously as a grown-up young lady. Jane was still willing to accept her standing as a mere fledgling, but already she was beginning to show signs of precocious maturing. Her own peculiar brand of madcap spirits was perceptibly shading and sobering, and she seemed to be subtly changing identities with Eleanor: she was becoming more reflective and governable, while Eleanor was growing steadily more mettlesome and impulsive.

They were changing places romantically, too. Eleanor always went out of her way to let Jim know she had come out to the island not by any chance to see him but to see his mother and grandfather, to talk with Linda and play checkers with Seth if his rheumatism was not too bad; to swim, exercise the plantation tackies, make a sketch, read a book, or take a daydreaming siesta in the shade of the Land's End veranda. But Jane was equally anxious to show Jim that she had come for the express purpose of seeing him, if it was only a glimpse of him in the field, or a spell of silent admiration while he munched his lunch at noon under an old live-oak. This was her first great love, and she surrendered to it with abandon, heedless alike of Eleanor's high scorn and Jim's inattention. During the past winter she had been through a series of school crushes, but with vacation these attachments, fitful at best, had quickly flickered out; and early in the summer Dr. Hervey

Caldwell, whom she had always adored, had deserted her, turned over his Draft Board work to the doctors at Parris Island and gone away to join the Army Medical Corps, leaving her free to devote all her attention to Jim. The fact that her devotion was going begging, unrequited and even unnoticed, seemed only to be deepening her concentration; and the fact that he persisted in treating her like a child, a frisky little girl in middy-blouse and bloomers, seemed only to be hastening the unfoldment of her nature. It was as if her whole slender being were straining to grow up to him, catch up with him in a single summer, standing on tiptoe to show him she was already tall enough for serious consideration.

So the trips to the island that summer proved to be more than errands of aid to Jim in his struggle to keep the plantation going with a shiftless remnant of hands: they were also little voyages of discovery and realization, revelations of the amazing and poignant changes that had come over Jim and Eleanor and Jane. These island pauses, these escapes from the confused comings-and-goings of home embattled, were like lulls in a tempest or the lifting of a mist: swift young changes that had been obscured or only dimly perceived were coming now vividly to light. It was like reliving the manifold past, awakening again to the old mysteries and miracles of youth as they had been known long ago. And because of this accompaniment of the past, this fourth dimension of memory, these changes were doubly moving.

Yes, the days at Land's End were like flashes of revealing lightning. They were moments of lucidity and comprehension in a fog of blind activities. She was aware, for the moment, that the girls were fast growing up; and that during these breath-restoring head-clearing island hours, the cannibalistic business-as-usual Western Front had devoured the regular daily quota of its own youth. . . . Glimpses of essential realities, before she was swept back and lost again in the hypnotic wartime bustle of patriotic Beaufort and Marshlands.

✓   ✓   ✓

The garden was sadly neglected this summer: the flower beds had to shift for themselves with only a little spasmodic weeding, and the roses would have been chewed to shreds if Jane had not taken pity on them and delegated herself to pass among them every morning with a cup of kerosene for the bugs. But the vegetable garden, in the lot behind the stable, was lavished with attention. Everyone in the family was willing and eager to help tend it.

There were two big new posters in front of the post-office. The first, a list of names of assorted nationalities under the emblem *AMERICANS ALL!*, was of doubtful appeal in Beaufort, where the only "foreigners" were Sam Koenig, Sam Levy of Levy's Drygoods Store, and the Brothers Nicopolis, proprietors of the Busy Bee Cafe and Shoe Hospital,—all more or less suspect as 100% Americans though they had been respected business citizens for years. But the other poster, Columbia flourishing a jar of preserves with the exhortation *Women of America Work for Victory!*, struck home like a bugle call. Every yard, large or small, was responding with a canning garden, miniatures of the great truck gardens that had sprung up in the broad fields beyond the bounds of town. . . . The Marshlands war garden had started out in the spring as a very modest affair, a patch small enough for the yard-boy to handle without complaining. But in June, with the appearance of the Columbia poster, it had been expanded with rows of late vegetables to the limits of the back lot. To make all the room possible the young pear trees had been transplanted to the fence line near the gnarled old fig trees; the chicken coops and runways had been removed to a cramped corner behind the Quarter-house; and patient Mrs. Moo, latest of the long line of Mrs. Moos, had had to give up her private pasture and submit to the public indignity of being led, like any common cow, through the streets every morn and eve to and from the Green, the grammar school park where most town cows were tethered to graze in a circle, browse moss from the liveoaks, and swish their tails in company. And to make this war garden a success every member of the household was doing his bit: Stephen and Eleanor and Jane, Tunis and Ella and Lucy, and even Eugenia, elaborately gloved, veiled, and bonneted.

By good fortune Tunis and his family were not taken with the traveling fever till autumn, till almost Thanksgiving. The surplus vegetables of the garden were safely harvested, put up in every available jar, and stored in the pantry and on the shelves under the furnace-room stairs when the blow fell. More wary than Biggie, Tunis avoided direct explanations. He deputized the pastor of his church to deliver a note, which stated with apologies that he and

Ella had decamped with their entire family for parts unnamed, where they would make more in a day than they could make in a week at Marshlands.

The worst immediate effect of this calamity was the effect it had on Stephen. The morning the note arrived he worked himself into a lather, and that evening when he came home from the office his face was still gray with fury. Like Lucy he would have been willing to have boiled Tunis and Ella in oil or skinned them alive. "If I could get my hands on that pair! . . . I warned you not to take them back after they'd quit us once when we were in a tight spot. But no, you wouldn't listen to me and Lucy! Well, it serves you right!"

Since Tunis's oldest boy was the yard-boy at Marshlands and his oldest girl the handy-maid, the departure of his entire family meant the loss at one fell swoop of the entire staff of home. And home, intent on the War and unprepared for this wholesale desertion, was thrown into confusion. But the forces were speedily rallied and the breaches closed. Eleanor and Jane took charge of Mrs. Moo, escorted her to the green on their way to school and brought her back in the afternoon; they took milking and churning lessons from Lucy; and they fed the chickens and collected the eggs. Eugenia helped with the bedmaking and the sweeping and dusting. Lucy took command of the kitchen and demonstrated that she had lost none of her cunning during Ella's long tenure. And while she was in charge of meals, Stephen was careful to be promptly on time for them: that was his contribution to the emergency regime. . . . Once intrenched in the kitchen Lucy was not easily dislodged. She insisted it was less trouble to do the work herself than to break in some trifling somebody these rotten-spoiled days, and it was hard to get her even to try out a new hand. Finally, grudgingly and as a great concession, three cooks of diverse ages and appearances were admitted one after another into the kitchen, put through a set of stiff tests, and within a day or two rejected and ejected before a fourth candidate named Pearl, an alert girl of good manners, was accepted as worthy clay. And then the same grim process of elimination had to be gone through before a yard-boy satisfactory to Lucy was found. It was nearly Christmas by the time the wounds of the Tunis clan desertion were healed and home was in good running order again.

In the turmoil of getting these household problems settled,—plus the Red Cross drive, long-winded sittings of the Community Hall Committee and the Library Board, Christmas shopping and wrapping, shipping a box of family presents to Hervey Caldwell at Base Hospital No. 1 in France, and knitting in every spare moment with Eugenia, who was clicking out yards of olive-drab socks and sleeveless sweaters,—in all this surface commotion an event of deep significance was almost overlooked. She had almost forgotten her fortieth wedding anniversary. And if she had failed to remember the date till this last minute, she was sure Stephen would never remember at all. In profound fear of that she tried to prepare herself by excusing him in advance, by telling herself that with all he had on his mind, his Draft Board work and insurance business and the booming market for real-estate, it would be anything but surprising if his end of the anniversary got lost in the shuffle: he could hardly be expected to remember. In her gathering anxiety as the day approached she even tried to pretend it was not vitally important anyway; but that was futile, for she knew too well she was praying he would remember.

Hope was shattered when he left for Charleston, "Government business, and I may have to stay overnight," the day before their anniversary. He allowed her to pack his bag, but he crossly refused help in his nervous search to find some official records in the silver-chest, where he kept important papers; she assured him all his papers were in the top tray, but he ransacked the entire chest before he was through. He was on a high and skittish horse about something, he didn't want to be bothered with questions, he was *not* going to wear or carry his rubbers, he would have no time to do any Christmas shopping for anyone, and in this disagreeable and uncompromising mood he hurried off to the station without a proper good-bye to even Eleanor and Jane.

Hope was dramatically revived when he came home on the night train. But the next morning, fortieth anniversary of their life together, her last hope faded when he left for the office without a word, with only the usual hasty peck. . . . All day she suffered a miserable loneliness, an irrational sense of isolation and affliction, a distress that was able to recall of the past only the unhappy times, the bitter disappointments, the disasters, the losses. And when Joe came by in the late afternoon with hearty felicitations and a present, a bottle of madeira that he had been saving for "this proud occasion," his remembering made Stephen's forgetting harder than ever to bear. She was careful not to betray Stephen's dereliction, and she tried to show her appreciation and look very happy and pleased about the proud occasion, but the strain of this double deception only drove the pangs deeper.

He had had no opportunity, Joe said, to congratulate the "cumulatively lucky party": his sister Isabel was indisposed and he had stayed the morning home to humor her; and when he had arrived at the office after dinner, Sally Broughton had informed him that Stephen had driven over to Burton to close a land deal and had left word that if he was not back before closing time she was to telephone Marshlands that he would not be home for supper. Joe was now delivering this message with his present and felicitations. No, he could not stay for supper this evening: he must hurry back to Isabel. "Nothing serious, just a touch of the vapors, but Susan is too excitable to be a good nurse." And he excused himself from even drinking a hasty health to the proud occasion.

"Every drop of this rare old wine," he told her with intimate eloquence, "is for you and Stephen alone, to share as you have shared the years."

That made her suddenly aware of age and the lateness of time, and for a moment she felt shrunken and frail and very old; as old as Joe, but without the stout perennial bloom that made him seem as eternal as a live-oak tree. But then, as a magnificently faraway look came into his eyes, she swung back to the feeling of suppressed youthfulness he habitually inspired in her, the sense of belonging more to Eleanor's and Jane's generation than to his, the giddy illusion of being not old or middle-aged or even grown-up at all. He seemed to be scanning her entire past, not only the parts he had known but also the hidden parts, her girlhood and childhood in the North; and his own entire past as well. And then, as if what he saw was too much for him, his eyes returned to her and the present, while his hand fumbled for the ribbon of his pince-nez. "My dear," he said, purpling with undisguised emotion, "you know how I feel." And saddling his glasses on his nose he picked up the bottle of madeira, glowered at it, and put it down with a snort of dismissal.

"Last year," he veered abruptly, clearing his throat, "the Cracker party voted the State dry, and we smuggled from Savannah. Now Georgia has gone dry, and we smuggle from Florida. Soon Florida and the whole country will be dry, and we'll be smuggling from the West Indies and Canada. When this singular procedure extends to the ends of the earth, we'll be compelled to smuggle from the moon,—or buy flyblown corn from the tin-can stills of our bootlegging Cracker prohibitionists!" He glared at the bottle, as if it were a gazing-crystal. "As the dregs rise and the upper classes are plowed under, we're doomed to see increasing experiments in social control as opposed to self-control. It is a source of supreme satisfaction to me that I shall not be on hand to witness the complete breakdown of civilization, the full consequences of the pandemonium the North let loose when they forced the Confederate War on us. Pandora's box is open, the lid is off, and all the demons of mischief are swarming over the land."

Grateful for this elaborate shift from the sore anniversary point, she ventured to encourage him by contradiction. "Didn't Pandora succeed in keeping Hope from escaping?" she asked him.

"Indeed she must have," he acknowledged with ponderous indulgence, "for surely there is no sign of hope in the contemporary scene. Nor in the future. The next pages of history will be a tragic record of the rise of the masses, the decline of all high and classic virtues, the leveling of the topless towers of Ilium, the spires of culture and law and reason. Like clouds of locusts the masses will rise, darkening the heavens, blotting out the sun and choking the air, strangling individual liberty and initiative, blighting the gardens of the world and the poetry of life. . . . In a few decades I'll warrant they'll be telling us what to eat, wear, and think. For the good of the Majority! They'll be telling us whom we may marry, whether we may beget children, and if so how many and of what sex, creed, and color. Only human nature will remain as ever free, to confound in the end all pseudo 'progress' and 'reform.' And there, my dear, lies the eventual hope."

Having unburdened himself of these sentiments he returned, with equanimity restored, to his felicitations. And then, suddenly remembering Isabel, made an abrupt departure.

Eleanor and Jane, rehearsing for a Christmas play, were late for supper, and she hoped the delay would give Stephen time to appear. But the girls had finished their studies and gone to bed, and

737

even Eugenia had put away her knitting and retired, before **he** finally came in. She had kept some supper hot for him and had set up a card table before the living-room fire so that he could warm himself as he ate: but he had already had some supper.

"I told Sally," he complained wearily, "to telephone you not to save anything, but nobody ever gets anything straight. I'll take some coffee and that's all."

He was still in the irritable mood of the last few days, he looked worried and frayed out, and she hesitated to ask any questions.

"Amuse yourself with this while I wash up," he said, tossing a clipping into her lap; "someone brought it into the office this morning,—it's months old but it's still good."

While he went up to the bathroom, she tried to concentrate on the clipping. It was from the *New York Tribune* of April 5th, the day before the Declaration of War, and seemed to suggest the discovery of an alleged plot to raise "a black rebellion throughout the South." American Negroes were to rise, it appeared, shake off white bondage, seize Texas and turn it into a Black Republic in which Mexicans and Japanese were to have equal rights with Negroes. . . . It was difficult to relate this stale news fantasy to the immediate reality, the complete failure of the day. For it was certain now that the day must end without a sign from him. There was no hope now of even the dregs of a celebration, a belated awakening to the passing of this milestone of memories, a last-minute recognition prompted by some reminder. Joe's present lay hidden away in the sideboard cabinet, and she knew her pride would never allow her to drop any gentle anniversary hint.

When he came downstairs he wanted to know what she thought of the clipping. "Isn't that a collector's item? You see, your Yankees were afraid we needed a shot in the arm to raise our war pulse, and they selected a brand of propaganda calculated to make the South see double red. Please salt that carefully away in the silver-chest when you go up. I want to preserve it for our great-grandchildren."

After he had swallowed a cup of coffee he prepared to stretch out on the sofa with the paper. "You better get to bed," he told her. "You look tired."

"I'm not. But you should be."

"I'll turn in directly," he frowned with an impatient ruffle of the paper. "Haven't had a chance to even glance at the news all day. And I want to take a look at the furnace. Just leave the coffee, I'll clear things up when I've finished."

"I think I'll sit up a little longer. I'm not sleepy. And I want to finish a letter to Hervey Caldwell."

He crumpled his paper with a sigh. But when he met her eyes, his frown relaxed. "You can do that in the morning, dear. Now run along and get some rest."

"But you haven't told me anything about your day."

"Oh, I finally got that Hotaling outfit to sign. Had to round up the whole damn clan. I'd rather do business with a nigger than poor-white-trash." He pulled a deed out of his pocket and gave it to her. "Here, put this precious document in the silver-chest, with the clipping. By the way, your chicken hatcheries" (two extravagant pairs of incubators and brooders she had saved all summer to order by mail, one pair for Marshlands, the other for the Robinsons on the plantation) "have arrived at the station. I told them to hold one set till the day before Christmas, and I fixed it up with old Abe to cart the other over here in the morning. He'll show up about six-thirty, so you better get your sleep."

She made no further protest, but lingered over her good-night, straightening the inevitable disorder of the center table, picking up a book Eleanor had left in a chair, and clinging finally to the silky brown ear of Cob, grandson of the setter Rusty had given Michael. He flopped his tail heavily on the rug and looked up at her with an apologetic smile for his drowsiness. But then his brown eyes seemed to turn misty, as if sharing her hurt; and her memories, too, for he was the reincarnation of all the family's dogs since the beginning. Reluctantly she relinquished his ear and withdrew her hand from his head, and resisting a last impulse to turn to Stephen—the many Stephens of past ages all converging in the news-engrossed form on the sofa—she turned to the hall and the lonely stairs.

In her room she had to fight to keep back the tears. It was weak and foolish, she admitted, to allow herself to be overwhelmed by the amassed strained sentiments of the long day; yet it was impossible to throw off this fearful sense of depression, this sense of standing utterly alone, cut off from all living ties and references. Everyone—Stephen reading downstairs, the girls sleeping, Eugenia, Lucy in her attic room—everyone seemed removed to an immeasurable distance like pale remote stars, leaving her alone in a house haunted by tense silence, a silence ready to spring. Because Stephen had failed her, this day, which might so easily have been transformed by a single word or sign into a serene music of remembrance, this day had become instead a nightmare, a sense of being lost in an enormous midnight forest, exposed to every crouching shadow and ghostly wind of the past, every rooted treachery of time.

She undressed in haste, as if that promised escape; brushed her hair strenuously, as if brushing torment away; and as her fingers hurriedly worked the graying mass of hair flowing over her shoulder, parting it into three strands and weaving them into a braid (the same pattern since youth, before she had known Stephen or this house or the sea-island world), she parried the sympathetic stare of her other self, her old intimate the mirror, and with firm eyes demanded the dismissal of this mood that was only a mixture of hurt pride and weak tired brooding. But the moment her back was turned, she was lost again. And when she returned to the bureau and stood there supplicant, shivering with cold despite the heavy wrapper over her nightgown, her will was powerless to rally her eyes. And now the image before her refused to stay fixed and steady: the face, incontestable sixty-odd written on the lined forehead and the thin cheeks, tended to blur and fade. Only the eyes remained clear, vital dark blue, intense and unfaded; yet they were confused, in suspense, unrelated to anything but themselves; so that it became impossible to say whose reflective eyes they were—her own or her own or her own—and what lay behind them forever and what lay ahead unknown. . . .

His deed and the clipping, by her brush on the bureau, claimed her at last. And here all the malaise of the day culminated in a flash of resentment. She might have been spared this final stress. The silver-chest, now waiting for her in the closet, was an ordeal on the best of days. Its assorted random mementoes, pathetic fragments of great vanished times, were sacred relics, precious talisman vestiges with the power of conjuring up at glance or touch whole eras of the past. . . . She went to the closet desolately and opened the door with a numb hand. When she lifted the lid of the chest and laid the deed and the clipping on the tray of papers, something caught her resistant attention with a shock. It was an old gold dragon pin of Miss Sophie's, risen to the surface of the chest as magically and mysteriously as Excalibur, for having lost its jade stone it had been lying for ages in the pasteboard box of lockets and bracelets, rings and earrings at the very bottom of the chest. When she picked it up, her heart skipped a beat. The hole in the center was no longer blank but set with a bright emerald.

She was so stunned at the sight that she could do nothing, think nothing, through the suffocating pounding of her heart. In that first moment her only response to the pin as she held it up to the light was the tingling of her fingers, as if an electric current were prickling them. Then she became aware of a card on the tray where the pin had rested. *For a few of the things,* it explained, *that can never be said.* But even then it took a full minute for realization, for the miracle to penetrate. And then she remained kneeling bewildered before the chest, unable to move, hardly able to breathe, overcome by this sudden salvation, this redemption of the day.

When she had recovered sufficiently to fasten the pin at the neck of her nightgown and come out of the closet to hurry downstairs, she found him in the room, beaming at her as he closed the door to the hall.

"I was afraid," he whispered as he tiptoed toward her, "you were going to overlook the entire bet."

With his arms around her, all strength dissolved: no longer standing alone she could no longer keep back the tears. "I was afraid you had——" but she couldn't say "forgotten," and finished with a choked sob, trying to return his smile.

"Not on your life," he laughed softly, holding her tight. "What do you take me for, a plain ordinary husband? Don't you think I know what's what, even if I don't show it all the time?"

He held her away for a moment, frowning down at her, and then took her back in his arms and held her close again. "Honey," he told her with a grave sigh, "there's something I better get off my chest this trip. The longer I put it off, the harder it gets. You may as well know you're the one thing that's been real and sure and right from start to finish. You make everything seem all to the good, and—well, I just can't figure out how I was lucky

741

enough to get you. There just isn't anybody in the world like you. I realize that more and more all the time. Nobody ever had such a wife."

She hugged him and kissed his cheek in thanks, and when she could trust her voice she assured him that nobody had ever had such a husband.

"I'm afraid that's too true," he nodded wryly. "If I could only have been the man you deserve. At least if I could have spared you the trouble that came through me."

"Hush, darling," she begged him. "I wouldn't have had anyone but you." A great tenderness for him swept her back to the very beginning of their life together. And in this moment she seemed to have in her embrace not only the gray man who was Stephen now but also the Stephens who were gone, the man of the tempestuous middle years and the young lover and even the Stephen of boyhood. So that she felt she understood and possessed him as never before, that she was closer to him than she had ever been, that she was knowing him fully for the first time. And from this autumn hilltop where she stood with him now all the deepening colors of the past were blended into a golden harmony; and looking back she was overwhelmed by the richness and wonder of their journey, by all they had seen together, by all they had been through.

"You know," he said in a tone of determined matter-of-factness, "an emerald wedding is no laughing matter. We're getting to be something to think about. We're getting together quite a tradition as a team, you realize that?"

She could only nod in answer, holding her head pressed against his.

He spoke with easy briskness now, shaking off all anniversary reflections. "Sorry for the delay, honey. It wasn't exactly fair to wait till the last minute, but I couldn't get the stone set in Charleston yesterday. Old Gilroy brought it on the evening train, just in the nick of time. And just about his last official act as friend of the family, now that they're actually getting around to pensioning him off the first of the year. . . ." He fingered the pin with a disparaging grin, giving her time to collect herself. "It's a pretty pathetic size all right. Should be big as your fist, but it was the only one they had in stock. But just wait till we get to our Golden

Wedding, and the Diamond Jubilee. We'll have you decked out like Queen Victoria in all her glory, or a Christmas tree in full bloom."

"It's beautiful," she smiled up at him with eyes at last clear and steady.

"I know," he nodded wisely, "what's going on in that head. You're wondering how much even a small emerald costs. You're thinking of the extravagance of it,—every penny should be salted away for the girls' advanced education. Well, they're advanced enough for me right now. But don't fret, at the rate we're going there'll be plenty of money in the bank for their hope chests. . . . Say, doesn't all this call for a little celebration? I know it's late, but come on down by the fire and let's talk over old times for a while."

She told him then of Joe's present, the bottle of madeira.

"Great. Come on." And he took her arm and started for the door.

In the hall she had to caution him against waking the house. "Oh, I'm tired of tiptoeing," he protested in a rebellious whisper "We don't have an emerald anniversary every day of the year,— let's wake them all up." But he quickly thought better of that. "No, we're lucky to have them out of the way. Not so easy to get you alone for a little privacy as it was forty years ago." And he was careful to be quiet till they reached the lower hall.

While he went down to settle the furnace, she got the madeira from the sideboard and glasses from the pantry and took them to the living-room, where the firelight was waiting with a blissful glow of expectancy and fulfillment.

When he came up from the furnace, he stood with his back to the fire smiling at her on the sofa. But then he turned frowning and picked up the poker to prod the embers, shaking his head with a deep sigh.

"Well, that was a sigh from way back," she laughed softly. "What's the matter?"

"Life. Just life."

"What's the matter with life?"

He came over and sat down beside her, taking her hand.

"Only one thing, really. They ought to give you another chance at it."

He was completely and thoroughly himself again in the morning. Assertively, even belligerently again his everyday self, preoccupied with business and the War, anxious to get back into harness after this emerald interlude, this anniversary interruption. Not that he failed to show how well pleased he was with the success of the celebration. While shaving he whistled snatches of *Listen to the Mocking-bird, There Was an Old Sailor,* and *Little Nell,* old expressions of satisfaction that no modern syncopated airs or even war tunes had been able to displace in his favor. And before leaving for the office he cheerfully volunteered to demonstrate just how the new incubator and brooder should be set up and operated in the stable; though in the end he lost patience and left her to puzzle out the leaflet of directions with the yard-boy.

But for her the anniversary was not so quickly forgotten. It was slow to fade, lingering to warm her heart like the glow of that night's firelight. And with Christmas, the flood time of memories, its spell was revived and sustained by confirmations that carried over into the turmoil of the new year.

V

Warm sunlight and the rejoicing of birds were stirring the garden back to life, and the russet winter reeds of the river marshes along the seawall were beginning to turn lithe and green again in the brimming spring tides. And when you paused for a moment to perceive these old wonders, it passed belief that the carnage beyond the sea could belong to the same world and time, that the horror could be searing its way into still another year and the grim parade of headlines still marching on and on.

When was it ever to end? What could stop it? For it was no stalemate, as Stephen and Joe called it, but a fixed vortex of flame sucking in an ever-increasing quantity of blood and iron: from the farthest corners of the earth it was draining the "raw materials" of life, and what could stop it but the exhaustion of the fuels on which it was feeding? A year ago, with America's entry into the War, Joe and Stephen had agreed that it would all be over by Christmas, at the latest and without the landing of a single Marine. "They don't need men. Arms and oil, money and morale will do the trick." But this was the spring of 1918, and there was still no end in sight, no dawn of peace but only deepening darkness.

And now malignant tentacles were reaching into the world of home in deadly earnest. The first intoxicated flush of excitement and enthusiasm was past, and Beaufort was settling down to stark realities. As the illusion of an easy quick victory faded, it was becoming apparent that the War involved elements more serious than catch-phrases and flag-wavings, booming sea-island cotton prices, Red Cross meetings and sock-knitting, and community singing of *There's a Long Long Trail, Pack Up Your Troubles,* and *Keep the Home Fires Burning.* Beaufort boys were actually leaving for France now. And now the town's adopted boys from crowded Parris Island were being shipped overseas in droves, loaded like cattle in camouflaged transports. The more and more frequent departures were festive occasions with plenty of cheering and bright band blarings of *Over There, Smiles,* and *Frenchy* in the spring sunshine; but for all the air of glorious adventure, for all the brave inscriptions of "Hock the Kaiser" and "Berlin Express" and "Paris Excursion" chalked on the sides of incoming and outgoing trains at the Port Royal terminal, it was no longer possible to ignore the ultimate destination of these shipments of jubilant youth, or to escape realization that for many it would be a one-way journey.

Already there were few Beaufort males of draft age who had not been called. "If it wasn't for the Parris Island boys," said Stephen reminiscently, "we'd soon be looking like Beaufort just before the Yanks came, when there were only women and children and old men left in town." With the exception of near-sighted Harold Van Wie, who seemed to consider himself a slacker and pariah because the Board had rejected him, all the young men of the Fenwick Street neighborhood were gone. Of Jack's particular boyhood pals three were in France or on their way. Jack himself was in uniform, but safely in an armchair post at Atlanta. . . . Of the town boys she had known best, boys she had watched grow up, most all were gone. While of those who were still the merest lads, who yesterday had been only a grade or two above Eleanor and Jane and who the day before yesterday had been babes in arms, many were already in camp or waiting anxiously for the next draft.

And there were lesser reminders that the War was striking home. The H. C. of L. was becoming a serious matter, even in this sea-island land of plenty. Herbert Hoover of Belgium Relief fame was the new Food Administrator, and the tightening restrictions of Conservation were beginning to pinch. The black Victory bread of wheatless Mondays and Wednesdays. Meatless Tuesdays and Thursdays. And sugar rationed out at the rate of a pound a month per person. To Eugenia, who was diligently compiling a list of persons she suspected of hoarding, this was nothing: didn't she remember refugee tea-times in Camden when one lump of sugar was passed around in an old silver bowl to be politely refused by all? And Stephen felt there was no excuse for even a peep of complaint: "Now if we were in France or England, we might be in a position to squawk." But Eugenia and Stephen didn't have to do any of the planning and fretting to make housekeeping ends meet and keep the family fed, and always have something on hand to offer ravenous young visitors from Parris Island.

The restrictions of the Fuel Administration made little impression. The experiment of Daylight Saving proved to be rather an agreeable change; and though lightless nights interfered with Stephen's newspaper-browsing and Eugenia's sock-knitting, noticeably straining their morale, Eleanor and Jane seemed to find it fun to do lessons by candlelight, and it was easier to get them early to bed. Even heatless nights, which must be producing acute distress at the North, were hardly felt here at home; there was no coal for the furnace, but there was wood enough for the fireplaces, and by banking rugs at the bottom of doors the main rooms were kept snug through the last cold snaps of spring. But the food shortage and the steadily rising cost of essentials were becoming a really serious problem. Every kind of sea-island commodity, from livestock to potatoes, was being shipped away. Butter was bringing 60¢ a pound, eggs 60¢ a dozen, and the price of meat and even fish was climbing skyward. At this critical point faithful Mrs. Moo was giving out, and there was no hope of replacing her. And the Marshlands chicken yard was emptying at an alarming rate. Linda sent a whole batch of setting eggs from the plantation for the new incubator, but through some tragic temperature slip of the yard-boy's the first experiment resulted in a hard-boiled catastrophe. Lucy took full personal charge of a second batch that she was able to scrape together with Linda's help, and this time a number of shrill peeping chicks emerged from the incubator and survived the brooder. It seemed as miraculous a spectacle as the gay opening of daffodils in the garden; but the daffodils took care of themselves, while this flock of helpless arrivals, clamorous as nestlings, had to be provided for somehow. There was plenty of oyster-shell grit to be picked up along the driveway, but skimmed milk was precious now and store feed at a premium and hard to get at all; Linda came to the rescue with as much corn and mash as she could spare, but for the rest these poor little orphans of war had to shift largely for themselves. And, as Lucy said, it took chicks long months to grow into laying hens, or even fryers.

The sky-high cost of living, the difficulty of balancing the family budget, of making income cover expenses, would have been no desperate problem if it had not been decided that Eleanor and Jane were going to a Northern college. But with that goal now definitely set, and with only two years left before Eleanor would be through high-school, money was again as vitally important as it had been in the plantation years at Land's End when Michael was preparing to study medicine. Stephen's business was flourishing, but expenses were eating up the commissions almost as fast as they came in and bank savings were practically at a standstill, while Eleanor and Jane were continuing to grow up at a great and alarming rate. So the cost of mere day-to-day living was a source of increasing worry, gravely threatening the whole planned course of the future and helping to bring the War home in earnest.

"There's not going to be any future," Stephen told her, "if we don't speed things up. People don't realize it's getting to be a damn serious game." And reversing his earlier stand he now declared: "It's man power that's needed. Supplies are all right as far as they go, but we've got to get the men there before it's too late. Don't get the impression we can't be licked."

Every day now seemed to bring some new development to intensify his excitement. He fumed over Wilson's snubbing of Roosevelt and Wood, who had fought such a hard and thankless fight for Plattsburg and Preparedness, and the appointment of Pershing, "who couldn't catch a few Mexican fleas with a whole army corps," to supreme command of the A. E. F. He ranted with Joe over a belated discovery by the *News & Courier* that toys plainly marked "Made in Germany" had somehow been sold in Charleston during the past Christmas holidays. He fretted and raged over the exposure of a major Administration scandal: last summer Congress had appropriated more than half a billion dollars for an air force, but to date not a single plane had been shipped to France.

And now he was up to his ears in work, the multiplying labors of the Draft Board and the booming business of real-estate. Truck farming was coming into its own and there was a wild demand

748

for land; Northern markets were clamoring for early Southern vegetables, and with fancy prices assured this season every available patch of land in the Beaufort district not already committed to cotton was being planted in potatoes and corn, peas and beans, lettuce and cucumbers and tomatoes. The favored fields were those just west of town, within easy hauling distance of the railroad: it was said that Ed Sands had sold 20 acres there for $27,000 and that the canny Hun Sam Koenig had refused an offer of $65,000 for his 40 acres near the station. But the fever had also spread to the out-islands, and at Land's End plantation Jim Robinson had decided to postpone Clemson College and stay home with Linda and Seth to raise corn and potatoes along with as much cotton as he could handle. According to Stephen every able-bodied citizen left in the county was borrowing from the bank to buy land and equipment, seed and fertilizer on the installment plan, confidently expecting to better the last-year record of the farsighted "profiteer" Sam Koenig, who had reaped 100 barrels of potatoes from each of his 40 acres, at $10 a barrel! There were disquieting rumors of a possible shortage of cars to move this year's harvest, but that failed to dampen enthusiasm and the lively bidding for land. And in the midst of this scramble stood Stephen, spotting prospects and skirmishing for commissions.

But he showed no signs of cracking under the strain and seemed only to thrive on this increasingly strenuous diet. He even had enough surplus energy to captain the local corps of "Four Minute Men"; and he and Ed Sands and Joe, a strangely assorted but impassioned trio, made trips to Savannah and Charleston to harangue torpid audiences between reels in the motion-picture theaters. And he somehow found time to take an active part in the local Liberty Loan drives. The community's generous oversubscription of each bond quota was, in fact, tending to become his and Joe's most urgent concern. The extent to which they were being carried away by the Over-the-Top spirit of the drives was apparent from the place of honor they gave to a picture clipped from the *New York Times*: stuck conspicuously in the frame of Stonewall Jackson's portrait over the mantel at the office, Mary Pickford, Douglas Fairbanks, and Charlie Chaplin were inspiring a vast crowd of hats and upturned faces in Fifth Avenue from a platform between the Public Library lions.

. . . It was Chaplin's *Shoulder Arms* that introduced her to the astonishing world of film and screen. "Movies" were an important item of entertainment at the Parris Island canteen, and the canteen was now her chief activity; as a member of the civilian committee chosen to help run this refreshment and recreation center, she was in charge of the big barnlike building four afternoons and two evenings each week. On the strength of *Shoulder Arms* she tried the next Special Attraction, which turned out to be a lurid drama of sin and retribution starring a strange heavy-eyed tight-lipped "vampire" named Theda Bara, erratically accompanied by the canteen phonograph. After that she decided to let the movies age a little longer in the wood before she sampled them again. Here was indeed "a great new popular medium," certainly one of the most amazing of all the magic inventions that had come in her lifetime, and perhaps an art that might someday swallow up every other art; but, for the present at least, she felt quite sure of her ground in not yielding to Eleanor's and Jane's clamorings to see even *The Birth of a Nation,* the "colossal spectacle" which at last under cover of the War had ventured to invade the South. Or even Mary Pickford of Sunnybrook Farm, or Doug Fairbanks as the spirit of gallant pep rampant and ever triumphant—the American Galahad of bravado and gusto with the smile that matched the curls of America's Sweetheart.

While the canteen movies were easy enough to avoid, the same could not be said for the canteen phonograph. It was continuously in use, insistently grinding out assorted selections in a tinny nasal screech. Already through Eleanor and Jane, by way of the succession of popular ballads they had picked up,—*Everybody's Doing It, Won't You Wait Till the Cows Come Home,* and *Darktown Strutters Ball,*—she had become inured to and even tolerant of ragtime. But such well-worn canteen favorites as *I'm Forever Blowing Bubbles, My Buddy, How You Gonna Keep 'Em Down on the Farm After They've Seen Paree?, K-K-K-Katy,* and *Sister Susie's Sewing Socks for Soldiers,* these were sore afflictions. And the best she could do in self-defense was to see that the needle was changed regularly. But except for the phonograph the canteen with its multiple contacts was a great experience. The work was taxing, but it gave her a surer sense of participation in the tide of vital events.

So without any pauses for breath the second spring of America at war swept on into a second summer, still with no victory in sight. Then in July came the last great German drive, and the desperate speeding-up of the war machine. Under the new Draft age limits young Jim Robinson was drawn in; Stephen assured Linda and Seth that exemption could be claimed in his case, but Jim went on to training camp at Spartanburg. Already a million men from the cities and farms of America were assembled in France, swarming like moths toward the flame: "But," as Stephen said grimly, "unless we can get another million there quick, they'll break through before the end of summer."

But somehow they, those other human pawns from the cities and farms of Germany, failed to break through. By some frail thin chance they were checked at the last minute on the pocked scarred face of Stephen's and Joe's pin-pricked map.

"It was a close shave all right," Stephen perspired with relief.

"It's the end," Joe contended. "We've come through our baptism of fire with flying colors, and now all we have to do is counterattack and mop them up."

"Sure," Stephen told him dryly. "Well, don't fool yourself. They may have played their last offensive cards, but don't overlook that ace in the hole, the little old Hindenburg Line. . . . Trouble with you is you never make any allowance for miscalculations. If I remember correctly, back in Confederate days you were so positive cotton was king that you knew England would have to come to our rescue and cinch the game right off the bat. You were afraid poison gas was going to end this war three years ago. And then two years ago you were betting tanks would do the trick. Maybe improved bombing planes and chemicals will make the next war short and sweet, but I wouldn't bank on it, and in this war spades are trumps. And you never can tell what Germany still has up her sleeve."

But Joe seemed to be right this time: at last the tide seemed to have turned decisively. With the Allies' counter drive in September all the ground that the wily Foch had yielded so strategically and the Boches had bought so dearly was being bought back mile by bloody mile, inch by inch on the map. Brilliant salients and glorious bulges, each representing only a few thousand lives, were appearing in the "Yankee" sectors (Stephen frothed, "The

Yanks are coming!—I never thought I'd see the day when good Southerners would fight under that name.") ; and the impregnable Hindenburg Line was beginning to waver and break. Yet for all the victorious advances there was still no final victory. Weeks drifted by, autumn colors glowed in the garden and the river marshes were turning russet again, and the War seemed to be dragging on into another winter.

Then suddenly, incredibly, it was all over.

First word of the Armistice flashed into Beaufort by long-distance from Charleston on the evening of November 7th, and Hattie Fowler on duty at the telephone exchange ran wild over her switchboard. Then the new fire siren whooped and screamed, church bells began to toll, shrill tootings and whistlings came from the waterfront, from the canning factory across the river, and from a locomotive at the station; guns boomed at Parris Island; and everyone in town turned out to join the joyous din.

Bay Street was like a carnival. Horns and pans, firecrackers and cowbells, anything and everything that would help swell the noise, accompanied the outburst of rejoicing, the shouting and singing and laughter. Impromptu parades formed and reformed, jostling and disrupting one another as they contended good-naturedly for the right of way; neighborhood feuds were forgotten in the excitement and old foes marched arm-in-arm up and down the crowded street. Toward midnight all the separate parading elements merged into a single jamboree, a torch-light procession featuring a carriage drawn by willing civilian hands and containing the crumpled remains of the evening's heroes, three Parris Island musketeers overcome by victory: two war-scarred young liaison training officers in full regalia, a French chasseur and a plaid-trousered Highlander, with a buck private of Marines. It was a memorable night in Beaufort, a night of crazy uproar and abandon, a fiesta and mardi-gras as incredible as the Armistice itself.

Although by morning the peace balloon lay punctured, false and flat, four days later it rose again and this time it was the real thing beyond any doubt. After the premature but fine frenzy of the first celebration this second seemed anticlimactic and tame, but what it lacked in spontaneity it made up for by being well organized.

A business and school holiday was declared, and Bay Street was properly decorated with flags and bunting. There was a morning parade led by a Marine band, followed in order by the Mayor mounted on a white mare, veterans of the Confederate and Spanish Wars riding the half-dozen blocks of Bay Street in the town's half-dozen automobiles, and on foot the Red Cross, Beaufort Chapters of the U. D. C. and Colonial Dames with a rout of school children at their heels, members of the Merchants Association, and bringing up the rear the shiny new fire engine and a float bearing pretty Miss Louella Simpson of the telephone exchange as Democracy Victorious, escorted by Boy Scouts. It was such a representative turnout, in fact, that only colored folk were left on the sidewalks to cheer. In the afternoon there was a mass-meeting at the Federal Cemetery on the outskirts of town, with flag services, speeches, and the *Doxology*. And in the evening a Victory Ball, attended by the Commandant of Parris Island, was held at Community Hall to conclude Beaufort's celebration of the Great World War's end.

❦   ❦   ❦

But actually it was not yet ended. Peace had returned, but peace haunted by an aftermath that was in a very real sense an extension of the War.

Soon after the Armistice celebration the casualty lists began to come in, and at last the price of victory could be realized. Among the assorted periodicals donated to the canteen library were copies of *The London Illustrated News,* and in each copy there were pages of Empire heroes killed in action; and in studying the faces of these distinguished dead she had always been reminded of those others who had also left their loved ones, the nameless lost host, the plain rank and file, the men and boys of all countries who were like Beaufort's own. Now that final full meaning of war was striking home. Beaufort's toll of dead and wounded might be light compared with other places; but the handful of missing boys, boys who had played in the garden and learned to swim off the seawall and been here in the sun only a moment ago, stood in her heart for all the rest the world over. And first on this representative home list of those who had exchanged life for gilt letters on

Rolls of Honor, listed there before the last of his letters had reached her from a field hospital in the Argonne, was the name of Dr. Hervey Caldwell.

Stephen and Joe were both shocked by that. "It's tough all right," Stephen frowned; "I know how you feel about it. And I feel sorrier about him than any of the others. But I suppose we ought to be glad we got off as easy as we did." And Joe nodded in vigorous endorsement: "Yes, they were cut off in the prime of life, young Caldwell and the others, but we must remember that they died with honor. And that our losses in the Confederate War were a hundred times worse. And then our homes were ravaged, our resources wiped out, our cause lost. While now, at a comparatively trifling cost, we have victory and the world at our feet."

Victory. Human sacrifice on ancient altars rechristened. And the *Doxology* again. . . . How, she began to wonder now that the smoke of battle was lifting, could any nation claim victory in a war that had cost the world millions of lives, untold suffering, and the destruction of enough materials and energies to have cleared the slums of the earth. Was it possible that the Great War had been nothing after all but a turning back of the clock to dark ages, a betrayal of the peoples of the earth by their leaders, a suicidal assault of man upon himself? Perhaps even America had been duped and misled. And to avoid such questions and doubts, to escape disillusion and a growing suspicion that the crusade had been no more glorious than holy wars of old, it was necessary to hold fast to the faith that peace and reconstruction would somehow make up for all the staggering losses.

As if America's losses had been too trifling and needed balancing up, the next phase of the War's aftermath came in the shape of a corrective plague. Under the mysterious name of Spanish influenza it swept the country, spreading like wildfire. Centers of population were hardest hit, and all through the winter Stephen's *New York Times* brought details of appalling conditions in the big cities of the North where there was a desperate shortage of doctors and nurses and hospital space; and the still-full training camps were focal points of infection. In the South it was not so bad, and little towns like Beaufort seemed almost immune; but crowded Parris Island, whose population was constantly being increased by transport loads of returning heroes, was transformed from a proud Marine base into a vast pesthouse.

Against Stephen's will she continued her work at the canteen, and to protect the family from contagion while the epidemic was at its height she stayed on the island, sleeping on an army cot in the canteen office and leaving the girls and Eugenia and Lucy to look after Stephen and home. These disastrous times carried her back to her first winter in Beaufort and to the "Tabernacle" hospital, where she had helped nurse the hundreds of stricken black refugees who had followed Sherman's march to the sea and Freedom. There was no nursing that she could do now, but there were moments when this canteen work seemed harder than anything in her life. For she found herself delegated to the task of meeting the mothers who came to Beaufort to be near their sons, and the canteen was as near as they were allowed to come to the sick wards of Parris Island. The battered canteen phonograph of *Till We Meet Again* was silent now, and each day was an ordeal of heartbreaking interviews, of futile attempts to give aid and comfort, of sharing and trying to ease the anxiety and the agonized waiting and the grief of women whose sons had escaped the War only to be caught in this death-trap of peace. And at the end of each day she had to go through the canteen files and remove scores of cards, the names of boys who had vanished like Michael into thin air.

"This is the absolute limit," Stephen fumed in his insistence that she give up the canteen without any further nonsense. "Of all the jobs you've ever wished on yourself, of all the trouble you've ever gone out of your way to find, this is the worst yet." But she managed to stick it out till the end. And the end came only when winter was gone, when crimson swamp-maples were beginning to glow in the woods again and pink flowering-almond blossoms opening in the garden, and in the Federal Cemetery rows of new white crosses sprouting under the moss-draped arms of the live-oaks.

But even that failed to mark the end of the war fever. After the flu epidemic had passed there was a final phase of aftermath, a plague of hate as virulent and contagious as any germ disease. As the tide of battle ebbed and demobilization proceeded,—bring-

755

ing Jim Robinson home from camp to Linda and Seth, safe and sound but hungry to get out of his uniform and into the spring fields and to resume his interrupted plans for Clemson Agricultural College,—as the Over-There spirit subsided and the amazing socialistic war organization of the nation began to fall back into the peace ways of individualistic competition, a residue of unexpended energy was left over, a store of pent-up emotion that the War had not lasted long enough to exhaust. The bands had stopped, but mass passions were still on the march, unable to halt so abruptly, and there had to be some outlet for this remaining patriotic pressure. Chief targets for majority wrath were any minorities that could be labeled radical; the great Russian Revolution, hailed at first, was not working out along good American lines, so any elements that could be suspected of menacing the existing order were branded Bolshevik and held up for persecution. And then there were Jews and Catholics and members of unfortunately colored races to be baited. It was hard for little Beaufort to see Red or Yellow, or find Catholics and Jews to harass, but it was always easy to see Black. Under Ed Sands' leadership a local K.K.K. chapter was established and night-riding revived. Joe and Stephen and one or two other surviving red-shirts repudiated and denounced the whole proceedings, but there was no abatement of the night-shirted Klan spirit till a negro youth, accused by a white woman, was mutilated and lynched near the village of Yemassee. Ku Kluxing was too good a sport to be dropped there, but the lynching served as a temporary appeasement of the lust for blood. And presently even cracker attention was attracted, along with the rest of the country and the world, by the spectacle of a President of the United States in Europe, endeavoring to impose a lasting peace on an assembly of diplomatic lions and tigers, buzzards and hyenas, in the Hall of Mirrors at Versailles.

✓   ✓   ✓

A bad heart attack had been the penalty of the Armistice celebration for Stephen. But after only a single day's rest in bed he had insisted on getting up, and a day or two after that he was back at the office again. She had confidently hoped that the end of the War would end the prolonged strain, that he would be willing finally to settle down and take better care of himself. And

756

for a time, though she had failed to keep him away from the office, his nervous tension had seemed definitely broken and he had seemed prepared to take things at a much slower and easier pace. But she had soon realized that secretly he was craving a resumption of violent stimulation and that his relaxing was only a superficial and temporary lull, a kind of involuntary quiescence like the dazed exhausted state of a man recovering from the effects of some powerful drug. And presently, by the time the Peace negotiations had begun, he had caught his breath and was ready to start off on this fresh new tangent of interest and excitement.

Although she was free now to concentrate on him, watch him closely and try to restrain him, there was little she could do to quiet his feverish excitability and unrest. Eleanor and Jane were more successful: using school problems and plain fun for bait, they were able to lure him into devoting some evenings to them and reposeful relaxation, instead of winding up an active day of business with a home session of hot debating with Joe. But even their soothing ministrations served only as brief interruptions to his compulsion to keep going at top speed, his obsession to keep pace with every twist and turn of events. He seemed bent on taxing his weary system to the limit, and driven by demons to expend his last reserves of nervous energy if not by actual movement then by keyed-up talk and discussion or by the tense inner activity of frowning over his newspaper. He was impatient of the slightest remedial suggestions and quick to detect and reject any schemes designed to protect him from himself; the most tactful hints only ruffled him, and he was particularly irritated by any attempts to wean him from his coffee and cigars and from his habit of swilling a mixture of baking soda and aspirin in as little water as possible, his pet nostrum for indigestion, headaches, and neuritis.

"Now if you'll just leave me alone, dear," he told her, "everything will be all right. Concentrate on the girls and stop worrying about me. I ought to know how I feel, and I feel fine."

It would have been a blessing if she could have followed Eugenia's example and advice to "simply keep out of his way." For all her restraining efforts seemed only to aggravate him without checking in the least his high-strung nervous animation. And as tension and strain increased with the progress of the peace negotiations, she had her hands full merely trying to escape being drawn into his fiery indictments of the proceedings. He was satisfied to allow Eugenia to keep out of his way, but he never missed a chance to provoke "our Wilson fan," and it was all she could do to avoid adding fuel to his flames by engaging in the kind of heated controversy he relished and was always seeking.

In his Armistice Day message Wilson had said: "Everything for which America fought has been accomplished; it will now be our fortunate duty to assist by example, by sober, friendly counsel, and by material aid in the establishment of just democracy throughout the world." But to Stephen and Joe that had not been high and inspiring idealism but only the tinhorn trumpeting of an egomaniac with messianic delusions. And when, before Christmas, Wilson had embarked for France to be present at the opening of the peace negotiations, they had washed their hands of him completely. His great reception abroad had only proved to them how easily people could be fooled. "The second coming of Christ," Stephen had nodded. It was all a grand farce, with the President of the United States as star clown.

When Wilson came home in the spring and then returned to Paris with his second wife and a corps of experts for final drafting of the peace treaty, Stephen and Joe worked themselves up to a frenzy of disgust and derision. And when the Versailles Treaty was signed at the end of June, they whipped each other into a lather. Even in that state Joe remained politely tolerant of her allegiance to Wilson, but Stephen kept after her, trying to drive her into a corner and make her fight back.

"Are you satisfied now?" he demanded. "Just look at the way they've got that map carved up!—it's a worse mess than ever. Can't you honestly see what a damnable carpetbaggers convention your League of Nations is? The whole layout is the damnedest stew ever concocted in the name of humanity, and your Wilson is responsible. No victors and no vanquished! . . . And you better take a good look at your Man of Destiny in his hour of triumph, before he starts fading into history. Because when they get through with him, he's going to look more like a plucked duck than a shepherd of the people. . . . And good-bye to reform. Big business is back in the saddle, with plenty of little fellers ready to fall in line and do their bit to bring down the champion of world democracy. The average citizen is sick and tired of the whole mess. He's had his bellyful of idealism and regulations and restrictions. He wants to be on the loose again and make some money, like the big boys. . . . The Professor's licked all along the line, only he doesn't know it yet."

And he was right again. The months of that summer and autumn brought the spectacle of the President touring the country in a desperate personal appeal to the nation. But the nation had suddenly gone deaf to the magic of his voice; or perhaps his voice was drowned in the tumult and shouting of peace and in the booming of million-share days on the stock exchange. And trailing him, yelping at his heels for the kill, was a pack of Republican isolationists led by Lodge, Borah, and Johnson. At Colorado Springs the pathetic tour came to an abrupt end. There he seemed to realize at last that he was crying in a wilderness, a prophet without honor; and from there he returned a sick and broken man to Washington and the White House, to remain in embittered seclusion for the rest of his term.

"The fate of a crackpot Icarus," Joe pronounced classically over the fallen figure. "The wild-eyed visionary lies shrouded in his crumpled wings. Our proud Achilles, having forgotten his vulnerable heel and the commonsense that still survives in the American people, now sits sulking in his tent."

"Haven't you forgotten your own heel," Stephen reminded him. "If I remember correctly, you once hailed him as a modern Jefferson, who was going to carry us back to good old Virginia."

As always in times of stress and bewilderment she found herself wondering what Rusty would make of all this, what he would think and say; and Stephen's and Joe's heel references recalled words of his that seemed to apply more justly to the fate of Wilson. One autumn night at Land's End long ago when she had been watching the stars with Rusty, he had traced out for her with his pipe-stem the great constellation of Orion. In Greek legend, she remembered he had said, Orion was a heroic adventurer who dared boast that he could rid the earth of all monsters and slay all beasts of prey; but as he set forth, at his own doorstep a scorpion stung him in his heel.

While Stephen and Joe had been following with relish every phase of Wilson's downfall, she had watched this sequel to war and treaties with a sinking heart. The repudiation and defeat of the President seemed to her in this moment a disaster worse than the

War, for it laid bare at last the full catastrophe of the War. Now every shred of possible justification was gone, every clinging remnant of hope and redeeming purpose was torn away, leaving only the War itself, stark catastrophe.

"Cheer up," Stephen advised her. "Your Wilson may be finished, but your League seems to be alive and kicking. They'll find it diplomatically useful and make a going concern of it over there, where it belongs. Unless it dies a natural death without us."

"If we joined in," she countered weakly, "it wouldn't die. And we would have joined, if the isolationists hadn't betrayed Wilson."

"Now don't blame them. They happen to be right. The League by itself might be harmless as The Hague, but it's all tied up with the Versailles Treaty, and we're not suckers enough to be willing to hold any part of that bag of European tricks. As Joe says, since the Founding Fathers we've always had sense enough to avoid foreign alliances and entanglements."

"Wasn't the War pretty much of a foreign entanglement?" she asked him.

"Now, dear, there's no point in talking through your hat. Be a little less bitter and a bit more graceful in defeat."

"Oh, Stephen, can't you honestly see that the League is the hope of the world? The treaties may be bad, but the League can work everything out if we help."

He shook his head over her. "Faithful unto death. Still hoping to see mountains move, and water flow uphill."

She nodded uncertainly. "Faith can do anything for us."

"I see," he smiled and sighed. "Well, please call my attention to it if you ever see old human nature flowing uphill. It never has and never will. And idealistic popguns have a way of backfiring. You all got what was coming to you. . . . I'll admit it's a rather sad sight, the finish of a public hero. They ought to invent some quick and painless method for putting ex-limelighters out of their misery. However, Wilson's getting what he deserves for revising Sherman and babbling about war to end war and make the world safe for Democracy."

"If the League fails," she said in final protest, "then victory and peace mean nothing. There's nothing left but the War and defeat, and all the horror and destruction have just been for nothing. All the life forces that went into it, enough strength and spirit to have rebuilt the world, were just wasted, thrown away. Everything lost, nothing gained."

"Oh, I wouldn't say that. We went in a second-rate debtor nation, and now look at us. The profiteers in particular. . . . I can imagine what jolts you've been getting, dear, but don't take it too hard. Maybe your next national dreamer will have better luck. And after all you're getting a vote out of this, to say nothing of Prohibition. And a liberal education. Isn't that enough?"

"You may be surprised at the results of women's voting."

"Yes, I know. The future is practically in your hands. . . . Dear, couldn't you possibly just take all this for what it's worth? A final lesson, a grand-scale demonstration of the futility of trying to square an incurable circle. You see where altruism gets you,—worse than nowhere. Can't you now make some final adjustment to reality, come to some sort of peaceful understanding with yourself about life, and stop worrying about the damned human race for once and for all?"

And she had to grant him the last word. "You've got a private utopia in a walled garden here at home. And two fine young disciples, almost grown-up now and ready to carry on the good fight of faith. You should be satisfied. So relax and enjoy life. Rest on your oars and laurels. Take it easy and let the world take care of itself."

He frowned down at her comfortingly, wisely, conclusively, and patted her arm with a dismissing paternal high hand.

But there was one sense in which the end of the Wilson epoch seemed a relief and positive good. She was confident that now Stephen would be content to relax and enjoy life in his walled garden. So at least a home victory and peace would be salvaged from the world ruins.

But she soon discovered that once again she was overlooking opponent factors. 1920 was something more than a promising new year, a gift of time that would bring great home developments, a sixteenth birthday for Eleanor, and for Jane more brave striding to catch up with her sister in age and height, in high-school, and in general deportment and assurance. 1920 was also a presidential election year. And Stephen, after a Christmas interim of comparative peace and quiet away from the office, was soon back on the job, following tensely like a veteran bird-dog every scent on the campaign wind, and pointing and flushing covey after covey of political quail.

She kept out of his way as long as possible, hating and fearing to provoke him and still hoping he would mend his ways of his own accord. But at last the strained pace at which he kept himself going, the constant whipped-up state of his nerves, so worried her that she could stand aside no longer. And finally at the end of an evening of listening to his and Joe's violent debating, after Joe had departed and the rest of the family had gone to bed and he was preparing to settle down with his papers to rehash the day's news far into the night, she took him seriously to task.

"Please don't sit up late, dear," she appealed to him to begin with.

"All right," he nodded absently. "Good-night."

"No," she told him firmly, "I'm not going till I've had a chance to talk with you, till you've promised."

"Promised what?" he frowned over his paper. "What's on your mind?"

"You. I'm worried about you. Dear, you must go slower. You keep yourself so keyed-up and on the go all the time. You don't give yourself any rest. You don't take any care of yourself at all."

He squirmed in his armchair and put his paper down with a sigh. "Now please don't start gnawing on that old bone again, particularly at this hour. This is the only peaceful moment I have all day."

"Is it nagging to ask you to take better care of yourself? You're always telling me to take it easy, but you don't like me to tell you."

"I don't like it," he nodded, "but I get it just the same. Don't fret, you always have your say. Seems to me I lead a fairly blameless existence in my old age, but that doesn't save me from getting lectured at regular intervals. Because I haven't yet lapsed far enough into second childhood to be able to sleep like a baby, and because I still derive a little toothless comfort from an occasional cup of coffee and a mild cigar! . . . Now I'm *all right*. Is that clear? Everything's all right. If you'll just let me alone." And he resumed his paper with a conclusive rustle.

"But, dear," she persisted, "can't you cut down on the everlasting strain just a little? You and Joe both need to quiet down. Can't the election take care of itself? And you say business is slowing down, why can't you? Can't you spend more time home with us now, and just sit back and enjoy life, and forget about everything but Eleanor and Jane?"

He put his paper down again, with emphatic exasperation this time. "That's just it! Your job of raising the girls may be about done, but my job of providing for them isn't, not by a long shot! That's why I've got to keep wide-awake and on the jump, while I'm still able. I can't afford to relax yet. The slower business gets, the harder I've got to plug at it."

He got up and went to stand with his back to the fire, his agitated fingers working his cigar-clipper abstractedly. "There's one thing you and I agree on absolutely," he frowned at her, "and that's that Eleanor and Jane are going away to college. You can be sure it isn't college itself I care about for them, but I am interested in getting them away from Beaufort. They're far too good for this deserted village."

He turned to the fire and picked up the poker to prod the embered logs savagely. "There's nothing for them in this dying place,—not even any good carpetbaggers left, only crackers and niggers. And they're not going to stagnate here, make no mistake about that! You can send them to college at the North or art school or a conservatory of music or anywhere you like, just so long as it's away from here. It's up to us to get them away while we're still on the job. And that's going to take money, as much change as we can lay our hands on."

"But, dear," she said to him gently, "we've saved enough to see them through college."

"Enough maybe," he grumbled, turning to face her again, straightening up with a twinge of some obscure pain that made her flinch with him. "But no surplus, no emergency fund. Now if you had been willing to let me pick up some stocks when they were dirt cheap five years ago, we'd have a surplus all right. But no, that would have been gambling,—as if everything wasn't gambling, refusing to ever gamble most of all. And we'd be sitting pretty if you had agreed to let us get in on that sure-thing Atlanta Coca-Cola stock that Jack recommended. It's been going up and paying dividends ever since he wrote me about it last year. But no, you couldn't take a tip even from your own son. So where do we stand, what have we got to show for your caution? Some cash sitting in the bank, a few Liberty Bonds, and a little insurance. Enough perhaps, but no margin of safety, no surplus. That's what worries me."

He went back to his chair and picked up his paper. "Of course in a pinch," he nodded with mock cheerfulness, "we can always mortgage the old homestead again, for something I suppose. But that thought doesn't comfort me much. In fact, I can't seem to settle down and relax. For some strange reason I still feel tense and strained."

She waited for him to calm down before she ventured to say anything further. And then she prepared to retreat in defeat, for she had to recognize that as usual she was simply provoking him and accomplishing nothing. "I suppose," she conceded finally, "it isn't much help to be nagged. I can't help feeling you can afford to go slower now,—you've done wonders and everything's going so well, you deserve a little rest. But I won't say anything more, and I'm sorry I upset you."

She started for the hall, but he was in no humor now to let her off that easily. "I'm not upset!" he called after her. "I'm just bored. And you're not sorry. Oh, I know you mean well, but you're damn right nagging isn't any help. But I suppose your nerves are a little strained too. Well, what of it? At our age we're entitled to a few nerves. Let it go at that."

"Dear," she told him from the safe distance of the hall, "I still think you should take better care of yourself."

"All right, all right," he sighed from his chair with weary patience. "You win. I'll try. I promise. Anything for a little peace and quiet."

And he did seem to try. He took the following Saturday off and gave Eleanor and Jane a full day's outing, a sailing and fishing trip to St. Helena Sound and up the Combahee to Joe's abandoned Holly Hill plantation. For several afternoons he stayed home from the office after dinner, to putter around the house and try to work up an interest in the early spring garden. And for a whole string of evenings he religiously refrained from engaging in any political debates when Joe dropped in.

But after that the excitement of the approaching election reasserted itself and his will to abstain began to break under the strain. It was too much for him; the remedy only aggravated the ailment; almost with relief she watched his surrender. And for the rest of spring and through the summer, except for brief respites contrived by Eleanor and Jane, he devoted himself with Joe to the election show, spending his inflamed nervous energy freely and without any pretense of restraint or any interference.

VI

ASIDE FROM its effects on Stephen the approaching election was of special and serious concern to her. Resolved to make the most of her first vote, she began to examine the party platforms and candidates conscientiously and well in advance. Through arrangements made by Joe with Charleston friends who ran a girls' camp in North Carolina, Eleanor had secured a post as assistant instructor in swimming and riding, music and drawing, and at the close of high-school Jane went along with her to the mountains for the summer; so time hung heavy at home and there were plenty of spare hours for acquir- ing political enlightenment.

Earnestly she perused Stephen's newspapers and studied articles in *Harper's* and Joe's *Atlantic* and in other magazines borrowed from the new Public Library. And in the evenings when Joe dropped in for a little debating with Stephen, she listened with one ear while she wrote letters to Eleanor and Jane or conversed in fragments over her work-basket with Eugenia, who still had a knitting hangover from the War but no interest whatever in post-war politics. Hope- fully she exposed herself to every oracle that might help to clarify election issues and cast some light on the dark tumult of national affairs. But at the end of summer, when the girls came home from their mountain camp brown and fit as Indians, she had nothing but confusion to show for all her determined concentration. And as the girls started back to high-school, senior and last year for Eleanor, and as October brought the first flaming colors of autumn and the final torchlight flares and blares of the campaign, her confusion mounted. By Halloween she was so hopelessly muddled, so perplexed and uncertain about how to vote, that at last on the very eve of elec- tion she had to confess her predicament to Stephen and Joe.

The girls were at the community hall this evening for the first rehearsal of a Thanksgiving play, so with no fear of disturbing studies the home debaters were making the most of their opportunity, wrangling at the top of their voices. Out of deference to the presence of Eugenia, who had taken the stand months ago that votes for women were silly and unladylike, she hesitated to join the fireside fray. But after vainly waiting for Eugenia to stop knitting and retire, she finally decided to declare herself anyway.

"It must be a great comfort," she said thoughtfully, taking advantage of a brief lull in the debating, "to know just where you stand."

Joe peered at her solemnly and respectfully over his puzzled pince-nez, but Stephen was immediately amused.

"Not stumped by any chance, are you?" he asked her with a dry smile. "Why I got the impression you had your vote all lined up. I thought of course you knew exactly where you stood."

"I know what I believe," she told him tentatively. "But I can't seem to make either candidate fit. And I can't get the platforms straight in my mind."

"If you weren't new at the game," he smiled, "you wouldn't let a little thing like that worry you."

"I can't really believe," she went on more positively, "in either Harding or Cox. They both seem like good respectable citizens, but that isn't enough. It seems to me a presidential candidate ought to be a great man, and at least as well trained for his job as—well, as a locomotive engineer is for his."

Stephen shook his head and sighed and continued to smile, but Joe nodded understandingly. "I agree with you, my dear. It was very different in the past, when we had men like Jefferson at the helm. But now, when we need expert guidance as never before, any old demagogue will do."

"Oh, I wouldn't call either candidate by that harsh name," Stephen dissented soberly, with his tongue prominently in his cheek. "They may not be great engineers, but they both seem to be sound conservative gentlemen with plenty of commonsense. Of course, the betting odds favor Mr. Harding. He's got a glad hand and a nice smile, he's better at kissing babies than Mr. Cox, and he'll look a sight handsomer at the throttle. The ladies will shower him with bright new ballots. They'll go for him like a flock of colored sisters getting religion with a strapping Baptist preacher"

Joe snorted: "That's a fine way to put it, I must say."

"Well, it's the truth, isn't it? You don't expect the average woman to vote as rationally as our Emily, do you? Most of the ladies will side with the heaviest artillery, naturally and regardless, now and forever."

"Did you say *ladies?*" Eugenia suddenly broke in from her knitting. "Ladies won't vote at all."

"Not many Southern ladies," Stephen conceded with a chuckle.

Joe turned in his chair to confront Eugenia, allowing his pince-nez to topple off his nose for emphasis. "You're quite mistaken," he contradicted her flatly. "Ladies will vote. Many ladies, in the South as well as at the North. For they will recognize that it's a responsibility, a duty, a trust."

"A sacred trust," Stephen suggested.

"Yes, a sacred trust," Joe turned back to nod vigorously. "A responsibility that no person of character can afford to shirk. Every qualified voter should exercise his or her rights at the polls as a matter of course. And better-class women, you may be sure, won't neglect their opportunity to counteract the rabble element and combat the subversive doctrines and tendencies of the times."

"Are your sisters going to vote?" Eugenia challenged him.

"No," he flushed. "But they should."

Eugenia sniffed. "They have more sense than I gave them credit for. It's undignified and silly, lowering yourself by tramping to the polls with a pack of cracker people. And what's the good of it anyway?—the South is going to be Democratic no matter how many or how few people vote. I still say no lady is going to vote. I'm not referring to you, Emily, or criticizing,—I'm speaking of ladies in general. Though I must say I don't see how you can do it."

"I don't either," she freely admitted. "It's certainly easier not to."

"That won't do," Stephen shook his head at her. "No backsliding now. We'll let Eugenia off because she's a conscientious objector, but that doesn't apply to you. After all the squawking about votes for women, it's up to you to declare yourself."

"But how can I," she asked him, "when I don't believe in either candidate? If they'd put up a man big enough for all the social problems that confront us, it would be a positive joy to vote. We need a man who understands that human welfare must be brought up to date with material progress, before it's too late."

"Pretty sassy," he smiled. "But just because you haven't any public-spirited giant to vote for, just because all the best brains are busy in industry these commercial days, that's no excuse for your trying to squirm out of voting. You asked for a vote and you've got it, and now it's up to you to show us how to use it. If the regular candidates don't suit your fastidious taste, why not write in an artist-scientist-saint ticket of your own? At least that will give the local supervisors a turn. And you'll be able to enjoy the memory of having registered a formal protest."

He flicked the ashes of his cigar in the direction of the hearth and settled back to puff out a series of smoke rings. "Whatever you do, don't revert to type and vote Yankee-style Republican," he told her pleasantly as he watched the rings expand and wobble toward the ceiling, "or they'll boil you in oil."

"Pay no attention to that kind of talk, Emily," Joe advised her. "Vote as you see fit."

"How," she asked innocently, "have you two finally decided to vote?"

Joe flushed and cleared his throat awkwardly, and Stephen rebuked her with a tolerant shake of his head. "That's not polished, dear. You're not supposed to ask, even in the bosom of the family. It's not according to Hoyle, but seeing you're a beginner we'll let you off this time. . . . I'm voting the straight Democratic ticket, from force of habit I suppose. But Joe here seems to be flirting with Harding, the dark horse from Ohio. He likes the swing of that campaign refrain: 'America's present need is not heroes but healing, not nostrums but normalcy, not revolution but restoration, not surgery but serenity.' It's got him. But I suspect, when it comes to a showdown, blood will tell. He'll wind up at the polls as a true son of the Old South."

"That remains to be seen," Joe snorted, darkly flustered.

Stephen enjoyed his discomfort for a moment, and then turned back to her. "To get down to cases, dear, I should think Cox would be your logical choice. He inherits what's left of Wilson's League-of-Nations toga, the tattered mantle of the prophet, and he may be able to pick up the reform movement where the War interrupted it. I don't think there's much danger, but there's no harm in casting a hopeful vote. And if you vote Republican, we'll only cancel each other, if that's any satisfaction to you."

He yawned and stretched in his chair. "Vote for Cox, but put your money on Harding. Nobody ever heard of him before, but millions of free and intelligent citizens of this great Democracy will surge forward to put their stamp of approval on him. He'll win, you can gamble on it. As a matter of fact, big business will win, no matter which nag comes in first. As usual the People won't place or show. They'll be lucky to even come in last in their own Democratic race."

"I'm opposed to big business and Wall Street finance," Joe declared with a snort, "but I certainly don't trust this demagogue Cox."

"Haven't we cleared that up yet?" Stephen sighed patiently. "I tell you you don't any more have to worry about Cox being a radical experimenter than you do about Harding entertaining darkies in the White House. The South is safe and sound no matter which man gets elected. As for big business and high finance, I'm afraid you're just going to have to accept them along with the other facts of life."

"I don't care for your cynicism," Joe retorted hotly.

"Maybe not. But it suits me a lot better than your futile harping on getting back to the Founding Fathers, and Emily's increasing progressive-mindedness. Why can't you face facts? Tne War to end war didn't make the world any safer for Democracy, but it sure gave the bankers a big boost. They're our lords and masters, more than ever the power behind the Democratic throne, and we may as well like it."

He got up and tossed the stub of his cigar into the fire, then turned to her. "Dear, let an old hand and an old friend give you one steer on the eve of your first vote. Don't strain yourself. Don't lie awake tonight puzzling. You can't win. Politics isn't an instrument for social reform,—it's a framed-up battle-royal, with the big boys always coming out on top. There's nothing in it for you, take my word for it. You might better stay home with Eugenia and knit."

And he told her with an air of finality: "You'll have a first-rate government when you have a majority of first-rate voters. And you can imagine when that will be. The Democratic whole is never going to be any greater than the sum of its parts. Get that straight in your mind, and if you feel you must vote, vote accordingly—with your eyes shut. You remember the children's old blindfold game of pinning a tail on a donkey? Well, voting is about as significant and satisfactory as that. Leave it to old fool addicts like Joe and me."

And that was as much aid and comfort as she could get from them.

Election day dawned cold and foggy, a perfect natural setting for her state of mind. The autumn colors of the garden were subdued by the sodden grayness, and the river looked leaden and dreary. It was almost noon before Stephen was ready to leave for the polls, and the long waiting aggravated her suspense and dejection. His excuse for delaying was that he wanted to get there after the early worms were out of the way, but actually he was preparing for his appearance with the care of an actor; and when they finally left the house for Bay Street, after Eleanor and Jane had delighted him by wrestling for the honor of putting one of the garden's last French marigolds in his buttonhole, he cut a handsome figure indeed, a positively dashing figure challenging the drabness of the day. She hadn't seen him so dressed-up and spruced-up for ages, and he started down the Fenwick Street roadway at such a striding pace that she had to take his arm to keep up.

"You seem to be in a great rush now," she told him breathlessly.

"And you're dragging," he laughed at her, "like a child being taken to school, or a reluctant bride. Looks as if I'd have to pick you up and tote you before we get there. After all the suffragetting! But I'm glad you have spunk enough to take your medicine."

At the Castle they stopped to pick up Joe. After Stephen had whistled for him several times from the garden gate, and she had had embarrassing glimpses of his sisters' startled faces at an upstairs window, Joe appeared dramatically at the front door. He was as resplendent as Stephen, but even before he joined them it was apparent that his mood fitted hers and the day's and was no match for Stephen's high spirits. He was plainly preoccupied, and as they walked on to Bay Street he seemed willing to let Stephen do most of the talking and all the jesting.

Bay Street was undergoing a deplorable change: in preparation for new concrete pavement and sidewalks all the old sugarberries and maples had been cut down, leaving the storefronts dismally bare. Work was suspended for the election holiday, and the walk to the polling-place at the Court House beyond the Sea Island Hotel was littered with branches all the way. It was a sorry sight, hardly calculated to improve the feel of the day, but at least it had the effect of rousing Joe out of his abstraction. He spent the detouring journey

770

denouncing the Mayor, the Town Council, and Contractor Ed Sands.

"Don't be a damn mossback obstructionist," Stephen told him. After all, the old trees only blossomed in spring, gave shade in summer, and pleased the eye in autumn; while the ornamental new electric lamp-posts would light the way of poolroom loiterers and the night rounds of the police force. "We can't have Progress without change, and we must have Progress at all costs. Can't you see this is a step toward Jerusalem the Golden, the far-off divine event toward which all creation is lumbering like a bloody juggernaut? Stand aside, man, before you get crushed by the steamroller of Progress."

Her nerves were thoroughly on edge by the time they arrived at the Court House. And here the strain of the day reached a climax. The steps and hall of the dingy building were crowded with men, and in making her way in she was unable to single out and speak to those she knew; it was just a congestion of staring faces, gaping and smirking at the spectacle of a woman come to vote. Then she found herself in a room full of tobacco smoke and more men. At a table surrounded by spittoons sat Ed Sands, the sheriff, and two other supervisors, looking to her like a kind of reign-of-terror tribunal. This was the audience before whom she was to stand proudly forth to assume the responsibility and privilege of enfranchisement, denied now only to minors, negroes, and the insane.

Ed Sands exchanged only formalities and the barest civilities with Stephen and Joe, but he was more than polite to her. He personally conducted her to the voting booth, which sat like a combination slot-machine and Punch-and-Judy-show in a corner of the room, and before leaving her he took courteous pains to explain just how the contraption worked. . . . Alone in the musty booth, with the curtain drawn behind her and the strange machinery of election confronting her, she had to suppress a panic of idiotic amusement and desperation. She felt paralyzed, unable to move or think, and a demented refrain kept running through her head: If Rusty were here, if I could vote for his wise men, the best brains of the nation, the League of Nations, all would be well, all well. It seemed scores of minutes before this spell of frantic impotence passed. Then at last, mindful of Stephen's coaching, she went through the motions of voting the straight Democratic ticket, with plenty of mental reservations and a distinct understanding that she was voting for only the lesser of two evils. And then, after she had satisfied herself that she had not slipped into the Republican fold by mistake, and after Ed Sands had obligingly extricated her from the booth, she saw her first vote safely deposited in the padlocked ballot-box that sat on the table in front of the grinning sheriff.

She was anxious to escape then, but she had to wait for Joe and Stephen to take their turns in the booth. To make conversation while waiting she asked Ed Sands if any other women had voted. "Yes, ma'm," he told her genially, "Hattie Fowler from the telephone exchange was here when we opened the doors, but you and her is the only ladies so far." He went on to ask about Jack. "He sure don't get home much these days, reckon they keep him mighty busy up to Atlanta. I never did get to know Michael, but I always liked Jack, and I always said he'd do well. I'd be obliged, ma'm, if you'd tell him Ed was asking for him next time you write, providing he ain't too proud to hear from old friends."

Joe was out of the booth by this time, but he failed to come to her aid and stood apart, flushed and belligerent, refusing to have any traffic with the elements whose latest atrocity was the desecration of Bay Street. So she was left at the mercy of Ed Sands's further probings into the old wound of Jack. And when Stephen joined her, it was only to prolong the agony. Demonstrating to Joe that he was not afraid to beard the cracker lions in their den, he gave Ed Sands details of Jack's progress in Atlanta, and then made a point of speaking affably to the sheriff and each of the other men at the table.

After that she was finally free to get out into the gray but fresh air, the ordeal of the day at last over.

On the way home there was a pause at the Castle, with disconcerting glimpses of Susan and Isabel at the window again, while Joe cut an armful of his white chrysanthemums and presented her with an "initiation bouquet" in honor of her first vote. Then as they left him and turned the corner into Fenwick Street, with the high gates of home ahead, she breathed an audible sigh of relief. Stephen glanced at her with a quizzical smile.

"Feeling better?"

"I'm glad it's over," she admitted.

His homeward pace was slowed-down and easy, and she took his arm not from necessity now but from a desire to be that much closer to him. She felt very small and old and futile, and needed the reassurance of contact with his tallness and confidence.

"That Joe bouquet," he chaffed her, "is the last straw. And the way you're carrying it gives just the right finishing touch. You look like some disgruntled public servant retiring from office with a parting nosegay from the force. . . . What are we having for dinner?"

It took a moment to collect herself and concentrate on home before she could answer that. "Eleanor and Jane are running the house this week," she told him finally. "I'm sure they'll have something special for you today."

"Ah," he nodded, "an election-day surprise." He sniffed the air expectantly. "Planked shad, I'll bet. And lemon pie for dessert."

In his exuberance he reached out to catch a large brown leaf that came drifting down from one of the old sycamores along the way. Smiling to himself he turned the crisp brittle parchment over, examining the veins closely as if he were reading the palm of a hand.

"You know," he said to her after a moment, "this election just about marks the end of an era. And it's been a pretty damn interesting one. I don't pretend to know what the future holds for Eleanor and Jane, but they'll have to go some to match our times. From Confederate days through the World War, that's quite a helping. . . . But I'm not thinking of it from the point of view of history and all that. I mean the things that have happened to us. We've had what I'd call a full life in any age or language. How about it?"

She met his eyes in agreement.

"A few years ago," he went on with a reminiscent smile, "a Yankee girl in hoopskirts came to the Sea Islands to help uplift the poor downtrodden negro, freed at last from his chains. At the same time a lanky youth was gunning for Yankees in Virginia, in defense of home and country. And now look at us. And tell me what you make of it."

A sudden lump in her throat made it impossible to answer and she could only press his arm in response.

"No," he amended with a chuckle, "I'll take that back. I know what you'd make of it. A tale with a moral, or some kind of social message." But he amended that too. "Maybe you'd be right at that. But all I can make of it is the story of a poor Rebel who got a stray Yankee angel by some fantastic good luck."

He looked to her for reassurance and appreciation, and when she returned his smile he became absorbed again in the brown leaf in his hand. After a moment his fingers ground the leaf into bits. When he had rubbed the bits into snuff-like powder, he let the particles fall and brushed his hand clean.

"Yes," he frowned cheerfully, "I'd say we'd had a full enough life for anybody. But you're still not satisfied. I suppose you'd like to have about nine lives, to hopefully watch the dog of Progress chasing his tail. Wouldn't you?"

She nodded to please him; absently, for they were almost at the gates and home thoughts were claiming her attention.

"I thought so," he sighed. "I honestly believe you'd be willing to live forever."

"Of course I would," she told him abstractedly, torn between his voice and the voices of home. "The longer we live, the more interesting life becomes. The world grows bigger, and we can see and hear better, and our appreciation of things is quickened and sharpened. It's like new doors opening all the time."

"Sounds mighty drafty," he grinned at her. "But I suppose if you can manage to keep feeling your way about life, you'll die young at a hundred. . . . As for me, I'm satisfied. I've had more than enough. And as for your opening doors, my idea of a perfect wind-up is to close all doors and stuff up the cracks, and dig in at the fireside in an easy-chair and carpet-slippers."

She looked at him with a quick smile of hope. "Dear, you're willing to give up the office now, aren't you? You will, won't you?"

"Oh no you don't!" he laughed. "Don't take me so damn literally. When I retire, it'll be to the cemetery,—not before."

And he was still laughing at her, at the quickness with which she had taken him up, as they went through the gateway into the garden.

Next day when he came home from the office for dinner, he brought the news that Harding had won the election, as he had predicted.

"Its just as well," he said with a shrug. "We can all use a little Republican normalcy for a change."

For her it seemed at the moment a final sealing of disillusionment. It meant complete surrender to the reactionary forces whose creed was business-as-usual and a national policy of *laissez-faire;* it meant return to the visionless system of muddling along lines of least resistance, abandonment of liberal ideals, and indefinite postponement of all progressive legislation. But in this dark denouement there was one bright ray of light. With election out of the way and the excitement ended, Stephen of his own accord turned over a new leaf. From now on, he announced to her surprise and delight, he was going to clean up his work at the office by two o'clock every day so that he wouldn't have to go back after dinner.

"Business is pretty dull right now," he told her. "You've got to expect a slump after a war, naturally. Things will pick up directly, but in the meantime I may as well mark time at home as at the office. I can get everything done in the mornings and take the afternoons off. And I'm knocking off for the whole day Saturdays."

When she tried to tell him how pleased and relieved she was, he cut her short. "Now don't get the idea I'm doing it to please anybody, or because I'm feeling tired or anything. It's simply because things are slow at present. . . . I'm going to spend my afternoons checking up on Eleanor and Jane. I know you think they're so well raised they don't need watching, but I'm keeping a close eye on the game till we get them safely off to college. I don't want any town boys hanging around them. They can spend their spare time entertaining me."

Because it annoyed him to have any fuss made over his new-leaf-turning, she did her best to refrain from any show of gladness. But within herself she sighed with deep content at this partial relinquishment of the office. It seemed like a special dispensation to compensate for the disheartening turn of affairs outside the world of home.

But her contentment was short-lived. Once again she had to face disappointment: after scarcely a week of living up to his resolution he was back on a full-time schedule at the office. Something had happened to stir him up and engage his whole attention again, he was on fire with some new enthusiasm, his nerves tied up in tight knots, but he offered no explanations and seemed determined to keep her in the dark. Finally, late one evening when they were alone in the living-room, she was driven to protest. And then at last he took the trouble to explain.

"You know I don't like to spring a thing till it's all set," he scolded as he paced the hearth-rug while she sat meekly attentive on the sofa. "I'm working on something big, and I hate to have to put my cards on the table before I've worked the hand out. But I don't suppose your curiosity can stand the strain of waiting."

"Now here's the situation," he paused in front of her to frown down. "Beaufort's share of the post-war slump is beginning to look mighty serious, if not permanent. This year the Texas boll-weevil raised hell with the crop, and next year you can just about kiss sea-island cotton good-bye. Stickney & Co. are no fools, those old Charleston birds know what they're doing, and they're getting out of their sea-island commitments as fast as they can. They're dropping their agency here, letting factor collections go by the board, and cutting out their steamer service to Beaufort and Edisto."

When he had given that time to sink in, he resumed his pacing. "And that's only one item. On top of that we've got a frozen real-estate game on our hands. The land boom's over. Truck farms you couldn't buy at any price two years ago they can't give away now. During the War we couldn't produce enough,—now it's a case of over-production, and Florida and California can beat us to what market there is. We're up against it for fair."

"But what are people going to do?" she asked him.

"Don't ask me. I'm no humanitarian. I've got enough to worry about looking out for our own end of it." He stopped his pacing again to confront her. "Now here's the idea, and please don't interrupt till I'm through. The boom in farm land's over, yes, but there's a new kind of special land boom coming. I've already gotten in touch with Dexter Giddings, head of a Charleston real-estate firm. We're going to be associates in selling old plantations to new-rich Yankees."

He enjoyed her astonishment for a moment and then hurried on. "The War made a whole new crop of Yankee millionaires and they're beginning to go in for plantation estates, for hunting and background and entertaining. Giddings is running Low-Country advertisements in all the sporty Yankee magazines. He's sold a dozen old places around Charleston already, and now he wants to line up places down this way. . . A man named Kress has bought the old Hugenin place near Yemassee. He's going to raise bulbs for his chain of ten-cent stores. And Hutton, a broker, is looking at five thousand acres on the Combahee, just across from Joe's Holly Hill. So you see the ball's started rolling our way."

"But, dear," she braced herself to protest, "you don't want to rush into a thing like this. You can't do it. It's too much of a strain."

He threw up his hands and heaved a pained sigh. "There you go again! Now isn't that a fine attitude. Instead of telling me what a smart idea it is, you have to throw cold water on it." He assumed an expression of extreme patience, as if instructing a backward child. "There's no strain involved. I don't have to go out and scare up customers. All I have to do is line up sea-island plantations with old houses, places like Land's End. Incidentally, if we can get an appropriation for a bridge to Ladies Island, we can bring all the St. Helena plantations into the market. But we'll have to start with mainland places." And he wound up on a briskly jocular note. "You ought to be delighted,—this game will keep me away from the office and out in the open air. . . . I'll need a car, of course. Eleanor can do the driving till she gets off to college, and then Jane can take the wheel. And when they're both gone, we can get a boy to drive, or you and I can pick it up. I wouldn't care about steering through city traffic, but we ought to be able to negotiate plantation roads. How does that hit you?"

But even this outing angle failed to reconcile her to the new real-estate scheme. "I'm sorry, dear," she told him firmly, "but I don't approve of it at all. I'm afraid. And I can't see any need for it. We have money enough saved. And even if your other business is gone, you still have your insurance agency."

"Insurance!" he sighed wearily. "Why that's only chicken feed. And at the present rate even that will be done for soon. How can you sell insurance to people who can't pay taxes? . . . Now try to understand this: we can use every cent we can get our hands on. We may have enough to see Eleanor and Jane through college at a pinch, but what then? Are we going to let them go to work to support us instead of getting married? Or are we going to turn to Jack and *Nellie* for help?"

She answered with a flush: "We'll manage somehow."

"The Lord," he nodded, "will provide. Yes, we'll manage all right —in the county poorhouse or the old folks home. The way things are going now, I have an idea not even your ingenuity could save us."

When he was satisfied that he had silenced her protest, he went on more calmly. "I don't like to use strong-arm tactics, but you've got to realize what we're up against here. This new game that you're so afraid of is just about our last chance to cinch our old-age independence. We've got to grab it. And it can easily be the biggest thing that's ever come our way. I hope to have the whole Beaufort territory to myself. It would be a great time to be a few years younger, but I can handle it, don't worry about that. And it'll only take two or three Yankee commissions to put us on easy street for the rest of our days."

And he concluded briskly: "If an altruistic angle will help reconcile you to the proceedings, just look at it as a form of social service or welfare work. If we can get a few rich Yankees settled in this district, it'll provide work for a lot of people and revive business. I'm not much on turning the land over to Yankees, but their money's as good as anybody's and it's better than letting the country go to seed. It's a bitter salvation, but it's better than none."

It was useless to try to argue him out of his scheme. He was off on a dangerous new tangent and nothing was going to stop him. He was bent on putting himself through an orgy of nervous strain, but there was no hope of heading him off, and she could only watch tensely and try to save him from the worst excesses of his enthusiasm.

Two days later, at noon, he telephoned from the office to say that he wouldn't be home for dinner, that Dexter Giddings was coming from Charleston on the afternoon train to stay overnight, and could she scare up a steak or a roast for supper?

"Tomorrow," his keyed-up voice told her, "I'm showing him some plantations, and I want to give him a taste of our sea-island hunting on the side. Ducks and boatmen are more plentiful at the Inlet at Land's End, but he wants to see places out Combahee way near the Hutton proposition. So I'm getting Joe's permission to scout around Holly Hill."

His voice rattled on with a chuckle: "Holly Hill's positively not on the market, Joe says. He doesn't approve of this business any more than you do. I told him it would take us back to the good old days of big baronies, but he says this new Yankee invasion is going to be worse than the carpetbagging years of the locust. But he's not too proud to have supper with us scalawags, so you better set a place for him. He'll probably monopolize Giddings all evening, talking Charleston."

On such short notice it was no simple matter to prepare for a guest. There was no good steak or roast to be had from the meat-market, and the substitute leg of lamb the boy finally brought was pathetic; it would shrink to one poor portion in the oven, Lucy pronounced in disgust as she sent it back and set out on a foraging expedition to round up roasting chickens to meet the emergency. Eleanor and Jane arrived home from high-school barely in time to tidy up their own rooms and too late to help Eugenia clean out the spare room, which had been converted into a sewing-room and had accumulated an amazing amount of litter. Then at the last minute, when everything seemed ready upstairs and down and the dining-room table was set, a stain was discovered on the cloth and another had to be put on and the table all reset. But somehow the house was in calm order, the fires lighted and crackling a cheerful welcome, when Stephen appeared at dark with Joe and Dexter Giddings, —a man of most charming manners, but to judge from his careless dress and air not one who would have minded or even noticed if the house had been upside down.

Mr. Giddings was a born talker, and in the living-room after supper even Joe was content to sit back and listen while he held the floor. It was hard to think of him as an inimical force, a promoter of mischief, seriously complicating her long struggle to get Stephen settled down to a pace of peace and quiet. And it was hard to get Eleanor and Jane and Eugenia started upstairs, so that the men could have the living-room to themselves. . . . When the girls went to their rooms to study, she talked with Eugenia till Lucy came up with the kitchen clock and stopped in to have the alarm set; Lucy resented the alarm and made a point of never understanding how to set it, always protesting her ability to wake up at any hour without being scared out of her senses by the clanging summons. After Lucy had gone grumbling on up to the attic and Eugenia had decided to retire, she prepared for bed herself. But she made no attempt to sleep till she heard Joe leave, and finally Stephen bring the guest up to the spare room and go back downstairs. Even after he had settled the furnace for the night, she lay wide awake in the stillness, wondering if he were straining his eyes over the paper instead of getting a few hours' rest.

She felt she had had only a minute or two of actual sleep when from Lucy's room overhead came the faint jangling of the alarm, set for three-thirty. When she got downstairs she found the lights on and Stephen already up and dressed in old clothes for the trip; whistling cheerfully to himself he was lugging gun cases and fishing tackle out of the closet of his bedroom off the living-room. "You and Lucy didn't need to get up," he told her over his shoulder by way of good-morning; and added, with a jerk of his head toward the windows glistening wet against the darkness: "A nice cold drizzle, but fine weather for ducks and fish, and it'll clear up later,—rain before seven clear by eleven." He glanced at her jauntily, with an air of having outwitted her and forestalled any use she might have made of the weather as grounds for an appeal. Despite all his chipperness, she observed with distress, the lines of strain in his face and the circles round his eyes were more marked than usual; she saw that his bed had not been disturbed and she doubted if he had even closed his eyes in his easy-chair; but it would do no more good to reproach him for not resting than it would to ask him to give up at least the hunting part of the trip. While he hastened upstairs to wake the guest, she went dejectedly to the kitchen to help Lucy with breakfast and the lunch hamper.

The car Stephen had hired for the trip appeared promptly at four, and a few minutes later she saw him and Mr. Giddings off into the rainy darkness. After that, at Lucy's behest, she went up to her room to lie down till the family breakfast hour. . . . Her eyes smarted with tiredness, but she was unable to close them and get back to sleep. And now she became conscious of an element in her thoughts more serious than disapproval and dejection. Starting in the back of her mind as a vague general apprehension, it presently came forward as a tangible fear: it took the shape of old dread revived, and she realized she was living over the time of the deer-hunt to Holly Hill the Christmas before Michael's death. Then and now, the former pattern of menace and this startling repetition, grew inextricably confused in her brain, forming a conviction that doom was again being sealed. Lying rigid in the combined grip of alarm and nightmare memory she tried to throw off this unreasoning fear, resorting finally to the desperate logic of chance, that disaster could never strike twice in the same way. But the harder she struggled to free herself the more deeply enmeshed she became. And in the end she had to get up and go downstairs to the kitchen, to be near Lucy till the girls and Eugenia came down to breakfast.

She spent a restless miserable day, unable to settle down to any task. Tension was relieved a little when the drizzling rain stopped before noon; but no sun came out and it continued cold damp, wretched and dangerous weather for Stephen to be out in. Her gloomy mood grew, feeding on itself. Even when Eleanor and Jane came home from school their presence could not break the spell of fear. And when dark came and supper-time passed without bringing any sign of him, her agitation kept her at the living-room windows watching the driveway and Fenwick Street for the lights of the car.

It was after eight when he appeared at last, apparently quite intact. He was late, he explained, because he had had to take Dexter Giddings to Yemassee to catch the evening train back to Charleston. His spry appearance failed to convince her at once: it was hard to believe that her forebodings had been entirely groundless, and she had to take careful stock of him before she was satisfied that he was perfectly safe and sound. Even then she felt it would be wise to steer him into a hot bath and immediate bed as a precautionary measure.

"Now wait a minute," he laughed at her concern, "if anybody needs nursing it's you. I suppose you've been fretting all day about me."

"I've been worried," she admitted.

He shook his head over her. "Well, if you will torment yourself, it can't be helped. Sorry to disappoint you, but there's nothing the matter with me, except I'm starved. Didn't even get my feet wet. And everything came out fine. Great day."

His trip seemed only to have braced him up, and she had to confess to herself that her anxiety had been overdone.

The next morning he was up bright and early, to escort the girls to high-school on his way to the office. But by noon he was home, complaining of an "upset stomach". The moment she saw him she knew what had happened. It was his heart again.

"I won't go back to the office," he said, allowing himself to be put to bed without protest. "I'm going to take it easy for a while."

He refused to consider having a doctor: he would doctor himself with the medicine Hervey Caldwell had once prescribed, which was certainly bitter enough stuff to clear up anything. And he stayed in bed only one day. But in that brief time an amazing change took place in him.

At first she found it impossible to believe in this change, fearing the usual disappointment. And even when she began to feel it was really to be permanent this time, a lasting reformation, she became afraid of the consequences. He was giving up not only the office but also his cigars and coffee, and losing interest in his newspapers and in evening debates with Joe, and surely these drastic renunciations would lead to a violent reaction sooner or later. Yet the days passed without any sign of relapse. The long tension seemed broken for good, like a fever, leaving him in a kind of comfortable daze.

Under this new dispensation his nights remained wakeful as ever, and the only sleep she could be sure he was getting came after dinner when he lay down till the girls appeared from school; yet now he seemed always rested. He seemed always relaxed and at ease: there was no indication of lacerated nerves, in fact he seemed to have no nerves at all. If his old neuritis was troubling him, he kept it to himself, along with heart pains and headaches or any other aches and pains he might be having. He received the family's anxious care and persistent attentions without protest or chafing, and he was patient and good-natured about everything, even the little things that used to provoke him so. The only sign he gave of strain and impatience was when the girls failed to get home on time. He looked for them by three-thirty at the latest, and when they were later than that he fretted about them.

That this transformation, this outcome of her long fear, was no weary slump of sickness and despair but the final release and peace she had prayed would come to him, seemed to her an ultimate miracle. But it was difficult to adjust herself to this strangely passive and receptive Stephen, whose voice even was calm and gentle. And one late-November afternoon, eve of the girls' Thanksgiving vacation, when she was walking with him through the garden on a roundabout journey to the gate to meet them, she took the opportunity to tell him how hard it was to get used to his new identity.

"You're so well behaved," she said, compressing all her pleasure and deliverance into the tone of banter he preferred for serious matters, "I don't know how to deal with you. You're so changed I don't recognize you."

"Well," he nodded with a slow smile, "I don't quite recognize myself. It's a strange feeling sometimes, like walking in sleep. If this is old age, it's not half as bad as it's cracked up to be. . . . No, I simply realized I couldn't argue with a skippy pump any longer, that's all. I'm not retiring, you understand,—I'm going to keep track of Dexter Giddings and the Yankee real-estate game by correspondence, with the help of Sally Broughton. But I'm through with the office, for good."

So at last came the belated blessing of his retirement, and the end of her long struggle and all the worry and strain that had started with his first attack, after the return from Jack's wedding in Atlanta before the War.

It made Thanksgiving a day of special significance.

✓   ✓   ✓

He seemed to be getting along so well now, he seemed so surely and comfortably settled in his transformed state, that she felt it was safe after Thanksgiving to consider a long-delayed trip to Land's End. Eleanor and Jane were eager for an island outing, and she was anxious to look the plantation over and see the Robinsons. With Jim away at Clemson College and Seth a bed-ridden invalid, Linda was having a hard and lonely time of it, and her letters kept hoping for a visit from Marshlands. But when Stephen was shown her latest appeal, a Thanksgiving note brought with the turkey by an island boatman and inviting the whole family for a week-end visit, he shook his head.

"You can't beat Linda," he smiled; "she takes after you. Now how in the name of commonsense could she put all of us up in that little farmhouse of hers? We'd have to pitch tents in the yard, or open the big house and camp out there, and I'm afraid Eugenia's camping days and mine are over. You and the girls go by all means, but count the rest of us out."

Since he felt an overnight stay on the island would be too strenuous, she suggested going just for the day. A day's trip would do him good without tiring him. But he still shook his head.

"No, we'd just pile up on Linda and give her a lot of trouble for nothing. She's looking for a real comfortable visit with you. You go and take the girls, that's what she wants. I'll mind the house and keep Eugenia and Lucy in order while you're gone."

He insisted on this arrangement and laughed at her hesitating to be away from him for a single night. "Don't fret, I'm not going to take advantage of your extended absence to have a relapse,—I promise to wait till you get back." When it was finally settled his way, when she had telephoned to Penn School and asked Miss Cooley to

783

relay a message to Linda by one of the pupils from Land's End, her reluctance redoubled, but in the end it was impossible not to be reassured by the fun he made of her frownings. "Anyone would think you all were going away for a year or so, a month at least. I admit it'll seem that long, but we'll manage to survive overnight somehow. Now do let this be one trip you don't spoil by worrying. I promise you we won't get into any mischief."

The next morning, the Saturday after Thanksgiving, after he had given Eleanor and Jane and her each an extravagant good-bye hug and kiss, he listened with solemn amusement to her last-minute cautionings and her conference with Eugenia and her instructions to Lucy; and when they were leaving, he called mocking injunctions after them about remembering to brush their teeth and not forgetting to write regularly. And a few minutes later, when they were crossing the river from town on the flatboat ferry to Ladies Island, they caught sight of him on the Point waving a handkerchief in elaborate farewell, as if they were embarked on an ocean voyage. Even when they had landed and found Linda waiting to meet them with the old plantation surrey, they could still see him on the seawall at Marshlands, waving mockingly as if they were setting out on a long long journey.

As they drove away from the landing and the river, she could see him in her mind's eye smiling to himself as he turned back to the house. And in the face of all his amusement at her agitation about the trip, and in the pleasure of seeing Linda, the last vestiges of doubt subsided into a simple regret that he was not along to share this day with them.

It was a glorious day. At first the morning sunlight came through a haze, a misty chillness that seemed translated from the rime that clung to fence-line grasses and the patches of fallen leaves under roadside trees whose shapes she knew by heart; but before they reached the old causeway across the pungent salt marshes between Ladies Island and St. Helena, the sunlight became clear golden. In the light of this Indian-summer glory the dreary rains and winds of November were all absolved. Colder winds and drearier rains and the bleak empty silences of winter would soon disrupt this radiant interlude of peace, but for the moment the world was suspended in a spell of profound clarity, a poise and balance, a harmony and wisdom that seemed inviolable.

Glad as she was to see Linda, she was content after the first exchange of news to let Eleanor and Jane do most of the chatting while she took in the richness of the day. . . . The brightest autumn colors were gone, most of the trees stood in blasted silhouette against the sky, only in the woods a few tenacious ones still clung to their glowing mantles; but these unextinguished flames, crimson of sweetgum and blackgum and smoldering gold of hickory, burned with a special splendor among the dark undying fires of the pines. Of all the roadside flowers only a few stray sprays of goldenrod survived, and in the resting fields the vibrant clamor of summer was hushed to a last scattered thin trilling of crickets; but these brave remnants of the year were enough to call up all years and all seasons of the island past. And there was one field where pumpkins lay mellowing among stacks of crisp cornstalks, as at Northern harvest and cider and frost time; and she saw robins from the North, come to feast on sea-island holly and cassena berries and the clustered golden balls of the chinaberry trees: and these were visions that extended the day's vista back to the earliest years and the country of her childhood. . . . There was a greatness about this day, a breadth and spaciousness that permitted it to transcend its explicit horizons. It had a quality of timelessness, a quality of all times, embracing all memories; not specific memories but memory as a whole, as a sense of times past, an essence of the world. It was a day of days, an epitome of time, a summing-up of life. And so along with its far-reaching greatness it held deep sadness: it was the prelude to the end of another precious year, a pause for appraisal between fulfillment and extinction: here the beauty of the world and the sadness were met on even terms for a moment before the scales tipped downward. Like the smoke that she was becoming aware of in the air, smoke that was both fragrant incense of autumn and disturbing proof of the island people's unregeneracy about burning over their fields and seedling woodlands, this day had a double meaning. And like the smoke it caught at last in her throat and made her eyes smart with its dark implications.

But she had only to turn back to Eleanor and Jane to clear the air, to dispel the day's somber aspects with a thoroughness that left only the pure radiance and goodness. For the girls stood for the season of resurrection waiting beyond autumn and winter: they were the spirit of hope and promise that converted the year's dying into a preparation for rebirth. They would be more than taken aback if they knew what she was thinking behind her little share in their gay chatter; they would certainly be convulsed if presented with a picture of themselves as springtime incarnate, yet that was what they certainly were. Eleanor most surely, perhaps, for there were no elements of uncertainty in her: she was fully-developed spring, her whole tall slender being was animated with the grace and force of April. Jane was grown almost up to Eleanor, but she was still awkward, her eyes and smile and her hands and voice lacked assurance, she flushed easily, and she was inclined to follow her sister's confident lead: she was like an early tentative expression of spring. But together these two perfectly reflected the season of unfolding beauty and purpose: they were good for old eyes to look at: they stood for all the redeeming faith-renewing signs of earth, all the divine and natural wonders of the world. And, though she was mindful of other earlier points at which she had wished she could stop time, she was sure now that this was the best moment of all, the point at which she would most like to hold them always, as once she had wished to hold Margaret and Linda. . . . Eleanor and Jane stood now where she herself had stood, between girlhood and womanhood, when she had first come to the sea islands. Yet they seemed different from that remembered self, different even from what Margaret and Linda had been in youth. It was hard to define this difference; perhaps it was best defined by the contrasts between the world then and now, the sharp differences in emphasis and pace. But she was satisfied that these modern young adventurers, setting out on the eternal quest, were equipped to cope with the accelerated and complicated world they were inheriting. And so their presence, along with the thought of Stephen's final reformation, confirmed and insured the serene splendor of this day.

And she needed these basic reassurances to keep the perfection of the day safe from something besides sadness, for there was active trouble as well as latent melancholy in the island air. She knew that times were bad again, but now she could see and hear for herself: by the time the wheels of the old surrey had followed the deep tracks of the sand road past Frogmore Store and then stopped under the live-oaks at Penn School, she began to make first-hand contact with island troubles. The indomitable ladies of Penn, Miss Cooley and Miss House, gave the visitors a warm welcome and displayed with pride the school's latest hard-won acquisitions: a new library, housed

786

in a bright little cottage and already well stocked with books, and a framed letter from Herbert Hoover, now Secretary of Commerce in the Harding cabinet, awarding to Penn School third prize in the "Better Homes in America" campaign. But after this good news Miss House and Miss Cooley disclosed their worries. The island people, barely recovered from wartime fever, were becoming demoralized again, stampeded this time by the boll-weevil calamity; the exodus to the city, checked at the War's end, was being resumed with a vengeance, particularly among the young and strong. School attendance and influence was falling off at an alarming rate; when the people most needed community solidarity and a guiding authority, they were turning their backs on the school, as if it were somehow responsible for their plight. Miss Cooley and Miss House seemed undaunted by the problems confronting them, but it was a gloomy picture they gave of island conditions and prospects.

And from Penn School on there was plenty to corroborate this picture of hard times and worse to come, plenty to bear witness with both mute and vociferous testimony to the devastating invasion of the boll-weevil army, which in the short time since the War had marched from the Rio Grande to the Potomac. It was apparent that the cotton fields along the road to Land's End had produced the very sickliest of harvests, and every person interviewed along the way was full of lamentations. Sea-island cotton was done for: by next season the pest would hold complete sway: there would be no crop at all, and no cash money. Storms could wipe out a man's planting overnight, and dry-droughts could bring his whole year's labor to nothing, but there was always another year and hope of better fortune; with the boll-weevil there was no hope, for no spray could protect the fine fleece of long-staple from this misery. Short-staple up-country poor-folks cotton might resist the blight better, but the Lord never meant short-staple to grow in low-country fields and it was not worth trying to raise a crop of that trifling stuff. Yes, years had been lean before and had come fat again in the Lord's good time, but now it looked like judgment for true.

Jessie, at the settlement at Land's End, summed up the situation. Since Biggie's desertion during the War, Jessie's proud homestead had run down noticeably, and Jessie herself looked seedy and careworn; the dejected air with which she came to the gate to greet her callers contrasted sadly with a gay crazy-quilt sunning on the fence and the gaudy Saturday wash distributed among the yuccas in the yard,—formerly Jessie's spirits would have been more than a match for the brightest colors on earth. But she was still social leader and spokesman of the plantation, and what she had to say was of special interest.

"Yas'm, Miss Em'ly, times is pure bad, an' cyan' see'um gittin' no bettuh no mo'. Ain' sayin' I ain' got li'l speck of money in de bank to Beaufort, an' maybe got speck bury right in dishyuh yaa'd, all-two, but I know dat ain' gwine he'p dem dat ain' got nutt'n fuh rainy day, like mos' folks ain'. An' hit sho gwine be rainy fum now on. I can feel'um in muh bones."

It was distressing to see Jessie so down in the mouth. She seemed to hold Biggie to blame for the state of affairs. "Ebbuh since de day Biggie walk out an' lef' me, eb'ry bless t'ing been goin' wrong. He ain' oughta done me de way he done, ma'm. I too good to dat man, but seem like he too ras'less and wag'rous fuh study 'bout dat. . . . Eb'ry day I look f'um to come back home smilin' big an' polishizin', but time gone an' I ain' shum. Dey mus' be got planty trouble to de city where he at, but hit ain' smoke'um out yet. But Biggie ain' sick, neiduh dead, I know dat, 'cause bad news trabel fas'. An' I know I gwine shum some day, eben if t'ain' till he come home fuh bury."

Having disposed of Biggie, Jessie went on to fasten blame on other heads. "Miss Em'ly, I been lookin' fuh somet'ing like dishyuh boll-evil. Gawd gwine plague evil wid evil. An' de people 'pon dis oilan' is too sinful." She lowered her voice to spare Eleanor and Jane in the back seat of the surrey. "Miss Em'ly, young gal gittin' in trouble too fas' dese day. Dey eye too open an' dey ain' t'ink fuh shut'um. Planty gal hab sin an' chile at breas' befo' milk dry 'pon dey own mout'. De boys is too big fuh britches, but I blame de gal 'cause dey make de plan an' don' check'um none. Yas'm, de young people is pure backslidin' bad as de grown people nowday. Dey 'bel agains' Gawd an' got no respec' fuh nutt'n an' nobody. You cyan' blame Gawd fuh lose patience wid'um."

Strange, this moral indignation from Jessie, who had been so lusty in her own youth. After enlarging on her theme of sin, she arrived finally at righteous resignation. "Gawd make all t'ing be like dey is. If we do de bes' we can, He will bless. We gotta come fuh res' 'pon Jedus bosom, I know dat, Miss Em'ly." She ended, however, on a note of blackest pessimism concerning the future.

It was a depressing interview. But when the surrey had left Jessie's place and the settlement and was back on the main plantation road, the golden spell of the day reasserted itself, like placid tidewater recovering its composure after the whirligig dip of an oar. In this enchanted air it was impossible to sustain any dark hopelessness. The sea islands had weathered times of stress and demoralization before; life here was as deeply rooted as the avenue of live-oaks leading to the big house, and those sturdy old trees had ridden out storms that had stripped off their leaves and torn away limbs and they had come through each ordeal stronger and sounder than ever. And, as Linda said, the island people were in a much better position than mainlanders to withstand hard times: Penn School had taught them to raise their own provisions, and they had good strains of livestock now, and always the sea to fall back on for food.

She expected to find Seth in bed, but when the surrey reached the tidy Robinson farm he was sitting on the porch with an army blanket of Jim's over his knees, waiting their arrival expectantly. After he had welcomed her and taken on over the girls, she stayed on the porch to talk with him while they went in to help Linda with dinner. He looked piteously feeble, and as he said himself he was no more than a pack of bones, but his eyes in their sunken sockets burned with a concentrated light, and though he spoke in a halting quavering voice his words were full of spirit. When he had inquired about Stephen and answered questions about his own health, he gave his views on the island situation.

Yes, times looked mighty bad in a way, but not half as bad as the plantation people were making out. The boll-weevil had left poor pickings of this year's crop and next year it was more than likely no cotton would be planted at all, but nobody was going to starve on account of that, unless they was too no-account and stubborn to lift a hand, just too plum lazy to live. "There's a powerful heap of wailin' bein' done, ma'm, but it looks to me like cryin' before gettin' hurt. When people is real hard hit, reckon they're mostly kind of quiet-like and don't raise much fuss." Now with cotton it was always a feast or a famine, up and down, up and down, till a man never knew where he was at; and as long as that went on, as long as people kept believing cotton was king for better or worse, what chance was there for plain honest farming? But with sea-island cotton sure-enough done for at last, maybe now shipshape farming, the good all-around brand that Penn School was backing, would come into its own. So maybe the boll-weevil plague was a blessing in disguise. And it might be a downright good thing for the whole South to be free of its tie to one-crop cotton. It would make for troublesome and unsettled times in the beginning, but in the end it would make the South true solid.

"Reckon sometimes we don't know what's best for us, ma'm. Seems like bad times if they ain't too bad is good for us, in a manner of speaking. It's a funny thing."

He was sorry in one way that Jim was getting started in hard times, but then again it would be good for him not to have things come easy. It would toughen him from the word go. And now, launched on the subject of Jim, he spoke with intensified feeling, and his gnarled brown old hands, which had been lying inert on the blanket over his knees, came actively to life.

"Jim's a good boy, Mis' Fenwick, and I ain't ashamed to take up for him even if he is my own grandson. Now you take most young fellers his age, they got an itch for the city, but Jim ain't like that. He never did show no inclination to run off, and he's got no taste for city ways. He's level-headed and he's lucky. He just naturally takes to this place where he was born and raised,—knows he belongs here by rights. There ain't a livin' thing on Land's End, from trees to critters, that he don't treat like they was folks. And as I tell Linda when she gets to frettin' sometimes about his bein' a farmer instead of somethin' else, he won't lose by it in the long run and he stands to win a sight more peace of mind. . . . You know at Clemson, ma'm, they're learnin' him what they call this-here scientific diversifyin', same as Penn School and same as old-type dirt farmin' only more advanced-like. But Jim ain't one to be satisfied with a self-supportin' farm and just makin' ends meet and a bare livin'. He's got ideas of his own for a cash crop to take the place of cotton. Cattle-raisin' in particular. Cattle don't need shelter here like up North, and fodder and pasturage works out a mighty lot cheaper. He's got it all figured out on paper, startin' in gradual and buildin' up to a regular herd, and he talks like he's got his eye on the Big Field, ma'm, for a pasture of carpet grass and lespedeza. Looks like he's aimin' to take over the whole plantation, if you and Mister Fenwick is willin' to rent, when he gets through with Clemson next spring."

790

An expression of pain came over his gaunt deeply-lined face then, and his hands fumbled impotently on his blanketed knees. "There's only one thing bad a-frettin' me, ma'm," he said in a voice sunken to a hollow whisper. "There was a time, back before the War, when I allowed Linda might take a notion to marry again—in particular that feller that was workin' for the government inspectin' the right-of-way of the inland water route. She never gave him no encouragement, but seemed like he was fair gone on her and he kept a-comin' back here to see her for a long spell after his work was done. And durin' the War I allowed she might take one them Parris Island fellers that was always hangin' around here a-pesterin' her like back in Fort Fremont times. But now I reckon she never will marry again, even without me to look after. I been a sore burden on her since my back give way and my joints got crippled up, but I been company too in a way, while Jim's been attendin' college. And I got to keep a-goin' till Jim takes hold. It ain't too far off now, but there's days, ma'm, when I just don't feel like I'm goin' to be able to make it."

She hastened to comfort him as best she could, assuring him and herself that he would most certainly be on hand not only to see Jim take hold of the plantation but also to welcome Jim's sons, Linda's grandsons, his own great-grandsons, into the world. He smiled sadly at that and shook his head, but he allowed her to lead him back to Jim's plans for cattle-raising, and on this subject he was firmly optimistic.

After dinner she talked with Linda and Seth on the porch, while Eleanor and Jane rode Jim's pair of tackies to the settlement for a visit with the people and a look at new babies, of which there were sure to be several. During the afternoon a number of the people appeared at the porch to pay respects and air their troubles, like old times. Their first concern seemed to be the serious island shortage of newspapers, which they used for so many purposes, practical and decorative; this simple need was easy to remedy, and she promised to send them batches of Stephen's *News & Courier* and *New York Times* from the Marshlands attic. As for their other and deeper problems, she felt she could best help by advising them one and all to stand together and hold fast to Penn School.

In the late afternoon, after the last of the people had left and

Linda had gone in to start supper, she was alone again with Seth for a time before the girls came back from the settlement.

As she listened absently to his voice roaming fondly over the past, she became aware at length of magic unfolding before her eyes. Out of the invisible sea beyond the barrier islands a golden full moon was rising, just as the glowing ball of the sun stood poised above the western horizon. They were like infinite reflections of each other, these twin spheres, and for moments the world seemed a mirror of remote unearthly splendors. As she watched in silent rapture this marvel of sorcery, fitting climax to the day of autumn glory, she realized that she was seeing it not for the first time. It was strangely and hauntingly familiar, like some nameless music heard again after many years, yet she was unable to place it. Had she seen it one time long ago with Rusty? Did it belong with Stephen? Or Michael? Or had she witnessed it not with anyone but alone? She could find no certain answer, and the wonder of the sight was pierced by the wretched inadequacy of memory.

Still puzzling futilely to place her former experiencing of this magic spectacle, she watched its dissolution. With majestic deliberation the sun withdrew its last crimson rays and smoldered into the earth, releasing with a tremendous mute detonation and repercussion a backrush of turmoiled memories, shattering the spell and leaving the moon to brood in pale introspective solitude at the margin of an unstable twilight. She clung then to the steadying reality and closeness of Seth's voice, and to the love of the sea-island world that reposed in his dim eyes and in his reluctance to heed Linda's warnings that it was time to come in by the fire. And against her susceptibility to this disruptive approach of dusk, that was seeking to break the golden harmony of the day before it could be transposed into a night of silvery peace, she opposed the cheerful crackling of the fire and the lamplight that reached out to the porch and Linda's soft humming in the kitchen and finally the agreeable sounds of the table being set. She was grateful for these good offices, yet as comforts they lacked some vital quality and in the end they failed to reassure her at all. It was absurd, this encroaching mood of sadness and oldness, but it was fast overcoming her defenses. She looked with tightening anxiety for the girls' return. And it was a profound relief when they appeared at last, flushed from their ride in the crisp air and full of news of their afternoon, and mortified to find they were too late to help Linda with supper. They were promised the dishes as a means of atonement. And now with their return the moon was safely risen and all sense of oppression lifted.

After supper and the dishes, she went with them for a walk to the big-house, while Linda was getting Seth to bed.

The old road was almost bright as day in the full moonlight, and the girls, relishing this evening adventure, kept up a lively exchange of chatter on the way. But when the road skirted the deserted pasture and the empty stables and led into the shadowy hushed back yard, the chatter stopped rather abruptly. They never had seen Land's End from this angle and they were distinctly impressed. On the way round the side of the silent house through heavy shadows, they stuck close to her: Jane hugged her arm and Eleanor admitted with a laugh that the place felt "creepy" tonight.

They both visibly relaxed when they came into the clear moonlight of the front yard, for there was obviously nothing spooky about the face of the house. It looked positively diffident basking in the soft light: even the shadows lurking in the recesses of the double verandahs seemed bland. She detected an expression of reproach about the door and the shuttered windows, and the moonlight enchantment could not gloss over an urgent need of paint. But this neglect was going to be corrected. Tomorrow, she promised, you shall have an airing, and a bright new coat of paint at the earliest opportunity. And having made her peace with the patient old house, she went with the girls to the edge of the yard, to the bench at the top of the landing steps for a look at the moonlit Sound.

The moon gleam swelling the flood-tide waters formed a brimming overflowing world and gave a sense of sitting on the brink of eternity. There were no snug limits to the Sound tonight, for the boundary islands were submerged, drowned. The string of lights along the Parris Island shore, the beacon on Hilton Head, the little cluster of sparks at Port Royal were low stars hovering just above engulfment; the upper constellations were lost in the gleaming vastness. Land's End always had a seaward temper, almost the feel of the beach at Bay Point, not the sheltered tone of Marshlands with only the tidal river gently lapping; but tonight Land's End seemed directly exposed to the sea. The Sound was the sea itself, and this bench a frail craft adrift on its open expanse. The glistening Spanish bayonets near the bench were moorings that receded when she finally

sought them, and the faint woeful trilling of a solitary cricket somewhere in the yard was an actuality that became, when she reached
for it, an illusion dissolving in the roll of waves. And the girls beside
her were no help in this extremity, for they too were adrift, Jane
close to her, Eleanor sitting a little away, both strangely subdued.
. . . She wondered what was going on inside this pair of pensive
young heads. What was it like to have most of life ahead and not
behind, most of time shining in the future instead of lying buried
in the past? Impossible to recall with any distinctness. Still, the general nature of Jane's thoughts could be surmised. It seemed a safe
guess that Jane was thinking of Jim, the center of her attention these
days. But there was simply no fathoming Eleanor's meditation, for
her fancies ranged too unpredictably wide and free. Of both girls
one thing only was sure: each was dreaming alone, as she herself was.
And in her own loneliness, her last resistance overwhelmed by the
immense white emptiness of the night, she turned home to Stephen
with an ache of longing. Tomorrow afternoon he had promised to
come out by boat with Eugenia and perhaps Joe to take them home
from the island, but she was ready for him right now. Tomorrow
seemed a long way off and she felt that already she had been away
from him for ages.

From somewhere in the vast aloofness of the night came an eerie
sound, illusory and intangible, till at last it materialized in a flying
wedge across the moon. For a moment the world was reduced to
calculable dimensions, but as the migrant flight of wings faded into
an eerie crying again the night swung back to vague immensity.
The event brought Eleanor and Jane briskly to life, but it made her
flinch and contract. She became aware with a shiver that the sea
breeze had turned into a cold wind from the west, and at the same
time winds from the past seemed to rush from the dark old house
behind her, striking to the marrow of her bones. She hated to give in,
but after a few moments of this hopeless disruption of the moonlight she had to suggest that it was time to be getting back to the
Robinsons'.

Back at the farmhouse, after the girls had gone to bed in Jim's
room, she stayed up to talk with Linda by the fire in the little sitting-
room. But for all her interest in Linda, her attention kept wandering
perversely away home to Stephen. Behind speech and hearing she
kept wishing she were there with him.

Before her talk with Linda was finished, she succeeded in putting him out of her mind long enough to give undivided attention to the subject of Jim. But later, when she was installed in Linda's bed, Linda being inflexible about sleeping on Jim's army cot in the sitting-room, her thoughts turned back to Stephen and she lay awake for a long time in the quiet darkness thinking of him. She wondered if he were missing her, too. By now Eugenia would have retired, after keeping him knitting company through the evening, and he would be sitting alone at the fireside in his easy-chair with his *News & Courier*. But he was not reading, she saw. His paper was resting on his knees, and he was smiling at her, still smiling over her reluctance to leave him for a single night. When she asked him if he was lonely, he nodded and got up with a sigh, and went to stand with his back to the fire. Then by some magic of mutual desire he seemed to move toward her, come toward her from the room and the house, crossing the river and the island, shedding years as he came. Till at last he stood before her as she had first known him, as she had first seen him one afternoon long ago in the yard of Seth's little store at Port Royal. It was the stifling hot and agonized day of Linda's birth, and he had arrived with Rusty on the laggard train from Charleston. Rusty was in the room with Martha and the newborn babe and she was on the stairway outside, and looking up at her from the yard was Rusty's cousin, Stephen Fenwick, not old and gray but dark and young. . . . Reluctantly she let the vision fade. And now he was back in his easy-chair, watching the reflections in the fire with a retrospective smile. He sat lost in reverie for such an extended time that finally she had to remind him how late it was. He refused to go to bed, but he closed his eyes, permitting her to take his head in her arms. Resting in his hard-won peace of spirit he looked like a tired little boy after a long day. She waited till she was sure he was sound asleep before she allowed herself to join him and share his dreaming.

Bright and early in the morning she was back with the girls at the house. She felt a certain hesitancy when she turned the key in the lock of the front door and crossed the threshold, and the hollow echoing emptiness of the cold bare hall was sharply disconcerting. But when the windows and blinds were opened and golden air and sunshine flowed in, driving out the stale clammy shadows, she breathed easier. And after the girls had explored all the rooms and every closet without surprising a single ghost, or even a mouse, they set to work to make a lark of their sweeping and cleaning ministrations: and their enthusiasm and enjoyment were contagious.

Some time later she was up in the attic with Jane, rummaging through boxes of old things stored away since the move to Marshlands, when she heard Eleanor call from the front yard. When the summons was repeated, Jane went down to see what her sister wanted. Presently both were calling. Through the cobwebbed weather-glazed dormer windows, which Stephen had taken the precaution to nail shut, she could see nothing; and when the calling persisted, she went down to the second-floor hall and out onto the verandah. After the dimness of the attic the dazzle of the Sound was blinding: she heard the girls call to her, "Boat coming!", but it was a moment before she could separate their forms, at the top of the landing steps, from the sparkling flame of the water.

"Must be Pappa and Aunt Gene!" Eleanor shouted gaily.

"And Uncle Joe," Jane chimed in.

And when she followed their pointing and looked to the west, there sure enough was a motorboat, heading toward the landing from the direction of the river and Beaufort. As she caught the *putt-putt* of its leisurely approach, a thought slashed obliquely across her consciousness: this was too early for Stephen and the others, for he had promised to come not till afternoon, late afternoon. But then in a flash she realized that he was appearing early for a surprise. And smiling with delight as she strained her eyes to catch sight of him in the boat, she decided it would be wise to withdraw from the verandah before he landed, so that she could do his surprise-party justice by being taken properly unawares somewhere in the house.

The boat, she soon recognized, was Captain Evans' *Lassie*, but before she could make out Stephen's form, strong young eyes at the landing steps identified another passenger. "That's Uncle Joe all right," Eleanor called, waving at the boat; "you can tell him a mile off." Yes, the figure standing at the bow was unmistakably Joe. She was about to leave the verandah then, without waiting to spot Stephen or see if Eugenia had come along too, when a sudden doubt checked and held her at the railing. And as the boat drew nearer, she could distinguish two passengers only, Joe at the bow and Captain Evans at the helm. Which simply meant, of course, that Stephen and Eugenia were concealed in the little cabin. When this failed to tally with Joe's conspicuousness, her mind swiftly rejected thought and turned defensively blank. Everything stopped functioning except her eyes, watching the boat. When at last it came alongside the landing, still without a sign of Stephen, all faculties beyond sight remained suspended.

But sight was acutely sharpened. With intense clarity she saw Jane come running toward the house. She saw Joe and Eleanor together at the top of the landing steps. Eleanor stopped and stood there by the bench irresolute, helpless as if caught by the flames of the Sound behind her, and Joe with his cane came plodding hurriedly on alone. She saw then what it was, but like one doomed in a dream she stood transfixed, unable to move or think, waiting for the blow to fall. Even when Joe stood below looking up at her, his flushed face and his voice magnified unmercifully, it took time for the piercing fragments to penetrate.

"Emily dear, Stephen——. Lucy—this morning—in the hall at the cellar stairs,—Lucy found him. I got here as soon as I could. . . ."

His message, broken, disjointed, seemed to repeat itself endlessly. And for a time she was able to keep denying that it was too late. For it could never be Stephen, not Stephen, not Stephen. . . . But then she could no longer see Joe's face. And then at last the bright sunlight turned brittle and shattered like glass: rushed back together again, steadied, and stood still, tingling and listening. Stood deathly still, listening and waiting, as her hands gripped the railing. She wanted to reach out to comfort Jane, and Joe, and Eleanor stricken by the bench at the landing steps. But her heart had shriveled to nothing, blood was ice in her veins, her lungs and throat were frozen.

VII

It was astounding how little his death altered the outward appearance and pace of the world. True, home was subdued and in mourning, faces were sorrowful, and there were the stark voids where he had been: his bedroom, his easy-chair by the living-room fire, and at the head of the dining-room table his place, which she now had to fill. Yet somehow the life of home went on its appointed way. The girls pursued their high-school course, Eugenia and Lucy seemed to find more to do than ever, Pearl continued to shine in the kitchen. And she herself kept busy in the house and the garden, "bearing up very well", as one of the solicitous neighbors said it was good to see. But inwardly the world was a wasteland, trackless, immeasurably desolate, and she was hopelessly old and weary, lost and alone. Every effort she made to escape this barren wilderness became a circle that brought her back to the starting-point of loneliness and despair. And in the end there was no will left to combat this appalling solitude and isolation.

Outwardly it was almost the Christmas holidays. The calendar said so, and the girls' intensified homework showed that school was on the strained verge of vacation, and Eugenia, sighing for Charleston shops, was making captious trips to Bay Street to search for presents. And in the garden, though coppery bits of autumn still clung to the crêpe-myrtles and though a few yellow leaves had yet to fall from the summer-house wistaria vine, the first camellia blossoms were opening, and that was a sure sign of Christmas time. But inwardly, in the secret sphere where time was actually measured, it was no season of the year. Hours and days were only a blur. Time was a stunned grayness, motionless and featureless like a lake under fog. . . . And yet, when she lay awake at night trying to return to solid ground, time was capable of assuming a fixity, a definiteness, a shape of the most tantalizing distinctness. So clearly she saw herself with him again, and at so many specific points in the past, all beckoning like lights in the darkness. If she could only reach any one of them, grope her way torturously back to him or strike out with frantic strength to rejoin him. But some power, some essential force of faith was lacking. Like a spent swimmer struggling vainly in nightmare waters to regain a far shore, she was always defeated, sinking again into the diffused blankness of time.

It was indeed a great mercy, as Eugenia maintained, that the end had come so swiftly: almost as if he had passed away in his sleep. no prolonged suffering, no lingering death, no knowing and waiting. But what consolation did this mercy offer for the silence that remained, that persisted unbreakable because it had not been broken at the end? Had it been a sparing dispensation that there had been no chance for last words with Rusty, or Miss Sophie, or Michael? If she had only learned long ago never to be lulled into forgetfulness of the mark of death on the forehead of every loved one!—for only that everlasting dread awareness could make the most of precious time against the hour of reckoning and bitterest regrets. And now she could no more reconcile herself to the loss of a last communion with Stephen, words that would somehow have redeemed all wasted time, than she could forgive herself for having been away from him the night of death. Even when she remembered Margaret's death,— the terrible last minutes together in the room at the Charleston hospital, after Dr. Ravenel and the nurse had left them alone,—even when she remembered that farewell, she still would have given anything to have had one last moment with Stephen. For the conviction was rooted that only a seed of final understanding planted then could be grown now to a force strong enough to break the tomb of death, this seal of silence, this enduring loneliness that not even the living presence of Eleanor and Jane could relieve.

It was Joe who worked hardest to help her. He alone seemed to realize the helpless depths of her loneliness. With Eleanor and Jane, who depended on her, it was necessary to keep up a brave front, and even Eugenia and Lucy were permitted to see nothing beyond grief; but with Joe she was unable to disguise her true state, her inner prostration and helplessness. She hated exposing herself to him, but it was unavoidable because of his prodigious solicitude, his straining to comfort her with distractions, which in his hands became probes that made her squirm into self-betrayal. Immediately after the funeral he had begun to practice his healing art, resuscitation by indirection, dedicating every afternoon to his campaign of diverting her; and soon, under the stress of trying to help him in his efforts to help her, her mask of sham courage had been torn away, exposing not grief but the fearful desolation that lay beneath grief.

Today he was making a supreme effort to rouse her by delivering a prolonged harangue on his favorite theme of Change and Decay. The late-December afternoon was warm enough for sitting out in the garden, and from his expansive place beside her on the seat of the summer-house he was blasting the frail still sunlight with denunciations of the new "river bugs" and all they stood for. The "river bugs" were the drab little gasoline tugs that now plied between Beaufort and Charleston, replacing the old white steamboats of pleasant memory: one of the bugs, carrying a cargo of freight and dusky passengers and belching black fumes from its exhaust, had passed the Point just as Joe was arriving for the afternoon, and that had served to launch him on his tirade. Snorting invective, driving his judgments home with jerks and thrusts of his cane, flustering his complexion from pink to purple, he was working himself into a frenzy of eloquence. And though she appreciated that he was outdoing himself for her benefit, in the hope of enlisting her interest, pro or con, yet she was unable to rouse herself to make the responses that would permit him to feel that he was accomplishing his purpose. She could only continue to listen; and she was doing even that very poorly, she was ashamed to find. . . . To her relief he finally ran out of breath and had to give up. Profoundly flushed and winded, he took off his square derby and mopped his distinguished brow, and with a rueful sigh joined her in silence.

He sat back at rest, airing his white-maned head, only long enough to recover his breath. Then he resumed his hat with a determined *bop* and started off on a fresh tack. But now his tone was altered. He spoke with restraint and deliberation, and he neglected his vehement cane and brought his pince-nez into play.

"Emily, there's something I'd like to discuss with you. I've always maintained that it was more blessed to wear out than rust out, but I've come to the conclusion that perhaps it's better to go slow than not to go at all. I mean to say, there's a limit and I feel that I've reached it."

He glanced at her over his pince-nez and, having assured himself that she was sufficiently attentive, went ponderously on. "I'm an old man, Emily. Certainly Beaufort's oldest inhabitant, and the parish's too, I daresay. Presently the *News & Courier* will be sending some young nincompoop to interview me about the old days, Confederate times and the gun-shoot at Bay Point. He won't want my opinions on the present state of the Union, but he'll get them nevertheless. The sear and yellow leaf will speak before it falls. . . . The sear and yellow leaf, Emily. Yes, I am an old man, and I can't expect to hang on much longer."

Roused by this unheard-of lugubriousness from Joe, who was always as confidently eternal as the great live-oak on the front lawn, she made an effort to rally her wits to contradict him. But before she could say anything, he contradicted himself by straightening up and sitting stoutly erect, with an air of ageless endurance, allowing his pince-nez to fall while he flashed at her a look of the most belligerent fortitude. And before she could pay tribute to this reassuring demonstration, he cleared his throat vigorously and strode sturdily on.

"Since—well, of late I've been thinking seriously of retiring from active practice. You can't know what such a decision means to a man who's been in harness all his life, but it's a step that must be taken at last. And now that Sally Broughton has secured a post at the Library I feel perfectly free to close the office. Her work as Librarian will keep her engaged without overtaxing her—only the afternoons and two evenings a week, I believe—and though it pays little enough in all conscience still it will cover her frugal living and permit her to preserve her savings intact. Of course I've offered her an honorarium, which she flatly refused. You know Sally. But at least I'll see to it that she gets an extra fee from time to time, for I'll still need her help on occasional mornings. I shall keep my shingle out at home, and no doubt certain special cases will arise that I shall feel bound to take."

"Well," she told him when he turned to her for approval, "I think you've worked everything out splendidly."

He nodded with a snort of satisfaction. "I'm glad you approve, my dear. Very glad. But now for your advice. . . . This morning a committee from the bank called at the office. It seems Ed Sands is resigning the presidency, and they want me to take his place. The Honorable Mr. Sands has decided that this is a dying country, and he's winding up his affairs here preparatory to transferring his peculiar talents to the great Northwest. Yes, it's hard to credit but it's true,—Beaufort is actually going to be rid of that cracker scoundrel. And with him out of the way I believe we can break up the whole cracker machine in this district."

He took time out here for a series of bellicose snorts, like a veteran war-horse getting the scent of battle, and then charged weightily on. "Yes, it's a magnificent stroke of good fortune and good riddance. But of course, as I hardly need say, the idea of succeeding Ed Sands in office is not exactly relishsome. Nor has it been made any less distasteful by the discovery that it was Ed Sands who proposed my name. My opponent has become my sponsor. Can you fathom that? Still, the presidency of the bank is in a sense a public office, a position of public trust, and hence a duty not lightly to be shirked. And if I find you approve, I shall accept."

"Why, Joe," she roused herself to respond, mustering a smile of appreciation for his reliance on her, "it sounds fine. But doesn't it rather clash with your good resolutions about retiring? Won't it be too much for you?"

Beaming floridly, he dismissed that objection with a flourishing shot of his cuffs. "I think not," he said, folding his arms serenely. "As a matter of fact, what they want—if I may say so—is simply a man of known probity and standing in the community. A figurehead to represent and personify the spirit of the bank. Naturally I'm honored, but I don't overestimate the importance of the post." And he added with a grave chuckle: "It's not unlike being the effigy on the prow of one of those old New England whaling ships I used to admire in Boston Harbor, in my Harvard days at the North. Still, I value the office because it seems a fit way to round out a lifetime of devotion to this place of my birth. . . . My life has come out very differently from what, in the buoyancy of youth, I confidently expected. I daresay I dreamed once of becoming a great legal light, a commanding figure on the bench, but circumstances have overruled me. However, I do not rate myself a vanquished figure, for I understand the working of things too well for that. I recognize I was born out of my time, too late, and have had to live in an era with which I am increasingly out of tune. But now I rest my case. And having your approval, I shall end my career by serving as president of the bank."

After she had given him further assurances of her approval, which he received with sundry nods and grumbles of satisfaction, he fell to polishing his pince-nez with a meditative handkerchief, lapsing by degrees into a massive abstracted silence. From which he was able to emerge only after a great clearing of his throat.

"My dear," he said finally, perching his glasses on the tip of his nose and turning to peer solemnly at her over them, "this bank business brings me to a matter I've been wanting to take up with you. That is, I hesitate to bring it up at this time, but Jack has written me from Atlanta. He's very anxious to help, Emily. He says he was unable to prevail upon you when he was here, but he seems to feel I might have some influence."

She shook her head.

He took off his glasses with a sigh and put them away. "I was afraid not," he frowned. "But you've got to let me help. Stephen——"

He stopped short, flustered with chagrin, as if he had broken an honor-bound resolution, violated a trust, in speaking the name. And hearing it spoken for the first time between them, she flinched in the shock of echoes flung back from the winter woods across the river, for it seemed the message of death uttered all over again. But then as the river and the garden returned to stillness, she felt a shudder of relief in the air, as if some ever-tightening cord had at last snapped free.

"No, Joe," she told him with sudden animation. "You know, and so does Jack, how much we appreciate your concern, but we just don't need help, from anyone. I know we haven't much, but it's enough with careful planning."

He greeted this with an expression of mixed approbation and pain.

"With all due respect for your ingenuity," he collected himself to protest, taking up his cane for vigorous gestures of emphasis, "you can't possibly see both girls through Smith College, or any Northern college, on what you have, your bank savings and a few Liberty Bonds. I mean to say, it's impossible. It simply can't be done. . . . Now if you would consider Charleston College, you might succeed. And I'm compelled to state that under the circumstances I strongly recommend such a compromise. At Charleston Eleanor and Jane will receive perfectly adequate training in whatever branches of the arts and sciences they elect to follow. And they'll be near home. . . . Have you stopped to consider that even though you're willing to send them away North, they'll never be willing to go when they realize the sacrifices involved?"

"But they won't know," she contradicted him. "They mustn't know, and you must help me in that. They're going North to college. It's Stephen's wish."

His name, coming at last from her own lips, acted like a mystic password: in an agony of release the wan sunlight of the garden sprang to radiant life. And having spoken his name, she longed to repeat it over and over, endlessly. In secret she called to him as she returned to Joe, her words stunned and slow at first, like prisoners released from darkness and chains, but then surer and surer, till at last they rushed confidently out.

"Can't you see, Joe? We're not going to fail now. We've planned it all out, and we can't fail now. You call the bank your final job,—well, this is ours, and we'll manage somehow. Even if we have to piece things out by taking in boarders, or by locating plantations for Dexter Giddings to sell to rich Yankees."

Through her blinding elation she saw Joe staring at her with injured amazement.

"Great Scott, Emily," he blustered, "you can't be serious. I admire your spirit and all that, but there's a limit."

"Don't worry," she reassured him with a smile of affection, "We'll save that as a last resort. But we're not quite ready to retire yet. We still have work to do. We haven't time to be old yet, not till the girls are well on their way."

And now she felt Stephen's presence so near that she could see his eyes and his smile, and touch his hand. And with him were Rusty, and Miss Sophie and Margaret, and Michael. Yes, and Jack. All her lost ones gathered together. All here with her in the clear bright sunlight.

VIII

Miss Sally Broughton maintained a remarkably even temper considering what she had had to put up with from fate, which had endowed her so generously for married life without granting her any fulfillment in that direction. She could sympathize with English girls of this post-war generation—for every three girls, she had read somewhere, there was only one man—but she could sympathize more deeply with the girls of her own generation: in the post-war days of her youth the situation had been ten times worse. And then there had been none of this emancipation-of-women business, from whose lusher details a whole crop of novels was sprouting, to the consternation of the ladies and gentlemen of the Library Board. None of this new freedom, which seemed to allow white women almost as much latitude and longitude as colored women had always enjoyed.

But Miss Sally was not given to repining. And she had plenty of company, suspended maidenhood being a by no means conspicuous predicament in Beaufort. There had never been enough eligible men, or indeed men of any sort, to go round; and of the few, most had always managed to escape to greener pastures. In Beaufort there were maidens of all ages, from the elderly Bramwell Girls down to crackerish young Viola Peters. The majority slipped into spinsterhood with a stoicism amazing to Sally, who though free from self-pity stood nevertheless in chronic rebellion against this unnatural state of affairs. Unable to fade or wither decisively, she remained, without any traces of belated winsomeness, incurably romantic.

Fate had not been entirely unkind to Sally Broughton. Her years of work at Turner Brothers' Hardware Emporium and then in Joseph Bramwell's law office had not only permitted her to support her invalid mother, and her brother till he was old enough to get a bank-clerk post in Savannah, but those years had also given her an outlet for her abundant energies as well as self-forgetfulness in a multitude of human contacts. She enjoyed people and respected them as individuals whether she liked them or not; and in return she was looked up to by everyone in town except a few extreme intransigents. Constitutionally sanguine she took Beaufort as she found it, from day to day and year in and year out, and made the best of it.

And now finally, in her position at the Library, she found herself more happily placed than ever. Here was a niche that she hoped she could occupy for the rest of her days. It had its drawbacks and vexations, of course, but by and large it was made to order for her. It was like being the public fount in the piazza of the little Italian hill town of the picture that hung between the windows behind her desk: the whole town, in all its variety, came to her to draw water and exchange gossip. A position more strategic and more dignified than Hattie Fowler's—the Widow Fowler with her eavesdropping earmuffs at the telephone exchange—it provided the amplest opportunities to live in other lives, and demonstrate that a woman could have a full and self-expressive existence without the intimate assistance of any man.

Leaving Joe Bramwell's office for this new post had at first turned her heart to stone. But then she had realized that his not seeing her all through the day except for a little while in the late afternoon, or on those occasional mornings when he needed her help, might be the very agent necessary to jar him into a real awareness of her existence. It was nerve-racking to wake, at this late hour, to the suspicion that in all those years of propinquity at the office she had only been defeating her own purpose, but she feared now that it was too true. So her stewardship of the Library became something more than a prized position. It was an unintentional, unpremeditated, and final maneuver of the utmost importance. Without cutting her off from Joe completely, it cut their contact down to such a sharp point that he could not fail to be pricked into appreciation of her company. . . . To date, however, the change had brought nothing resembling an awakening. He did seem to recognize that her position had shifted a little, but for the rest he took her as thoroughly for granted as ever.

In her earlier life Sally had received two proposals of marriage: one from Hal Turner, her former employer; the other from a stray Texan, a cattleman who had come all the way to Beaufort and Joe Bramwell's office to claim the property of a deceased brother. In neither case had Sally been left with any sense of regret, for Joe was the only man for her. He was ten years her senior, but as far back as she could remember she had never cared for anyone else. A terrible spell of years had passed since the day when her girlhood eyes had been smitten with the vision of Joseph Legerton Bramwell as an elegant young barrister of old Beaufort and Charleston, but the force of that vision had withstood all ravages of time. And even now, though the seasons of passion were forever spent, something still kept her from ever doubting—and this was the central consolation of her life—that at long last they would somehow come to share at least a fireside together.

Meanwhile she lived patiently alone in a little house tucked away in an alley not more than a stone's throw from Joe's Castle. One of the oldest houses in Beaufort, it had once been the home of Joe's legendary great-grandfather, the redoubtable pioneer Captain "Yemassee Jack" Bramwell. In the masonry foundation there were slits that Joe insisted had been used for musket fire against marauding Indians, though Sally's mother had spent her last wheelchair years contradicting him, insisting that she had always been told the slits were just ventilators to keep the cellar dry. In any case, Sally was most cozy in the cottage stronghold of Joe's ancestor. The yard was cramped, but there was room for a pair of white hydrangeas and beds of petunias and nasturtiums. And though there was no view of the river, there was one spot in the yard where she could stand and glimpse the Castle through the trees, and see the light in Joe's room at night. Spring and autumn, summer and winter.

When her mother had died and Sally had been faced with the strange business of living alone, she had seriously considered making conciliatory gestures to Eugenia Fenwick, who at that time was still living by herself in exile at Charleston. But on sober second thought she had decided that a companionate spinsterhood with Eugenia would be a business far stranger than solitary housekeeping. Of course if her brother had not gone away and married, she could be living with him, as naturally as Susan and Isabel with Joe,—but Sally didn't like to think of the Bramwell Girls, in that or any other connection.

They were the only human beings she really hated. She disliked several people in town, particularly Hattie Fowler of the telephone exchange, but her hate was reserved for Joe's sisters. It had taken her a long time to develop this emotion, for it had taken her a long time to realize that it was they who stood as prime obstacles between her and their brother. Now that so much of life was gone and the only sure allurements she could hold out to him were fireside companionship and household comfort, it was a vital misfortune that they were able to continue to fill all his requirements and meet his every need. Deprived of their ministrations he would turn instinctively, she felt, to her. But there was good reason to fear they might both survive him. They seemed in fact to be preserved like mummies against all further change.

Recently, to be sure, Isabel had been showing signs of definite mental wear-and-tear. During several of these spells of "nervousness", as Joe described them, she had had to be confined to her room. And on one bad occasion she had made a sudden sortie into the garden, pulled up by the roots every last one of Joe's prize chrysanthemums, and even succeeded in breaking down the old Rose-of-Sharon by the gate before Susan had been able to quiet her. These attacks of nervousness were becoming alarmingly frequent and increasingly spectacular; but far from weakening her vitality they seemed actually to renew it. And though they might lessen her value to Joe as a fireside companion and household comforter, they were binding him to her more inexorably than ever. Still, because of her growing affliction and a certain lingering charm of personality, it was impossible to feel quite so bitter about Isabel as about Susan. It was chiefly at Susan, her brother's everlastingly competent keeper, that the sharpest shafts of Sally's resentment were aimed.

But since there was nothing to be done about the situation, Sally continued to live patiently alone, waiting and hoping for a break in the impasse, ministering to Joe as best she could whenever she had him to herself for a few minutes, and presenting a smiling false front to his sisters, whom she knew she was not fooling for a second.

But it was not strictly true that Sally lived alone. There was Janet. And to live with Janet was certainly not to live alone.

Sally was aware that a cat was the very badge of spinsterhood, but she had no intention of allowing that to deprive her of Janet's company. She liked cats and she was particularly fond of Janet, who was far more tolerant, considerate, and cheerful than most people. They had many tastes in common and shared each other's antipathies. In fact the only marked point of difference between them was Janet's complete lack of virtue. But Sally was largely responsible for that: not one to take her own frustrations out on someone else, she found it impossible to deny Janet's fondness for moonlight strolling.

The present Janet, latest of a long and motley line of Janets, was without doubt the most promiscuous, color-blind, and prolific of the lot. A chaste and handsome gray-and-white, she had already produced three large litters of raffishly assorted offspring. Sally had strained to the limit the patience of her neighbors by presenting their children with nice pretty kittens that she hadn't the heart to drown. . . . Sally always pretended great indignation with the pagan Janet, each time it became apparent that Janet's size was due to something more permanent than a saucer of milk or a mouse or a mess of crickets and grasshoppers. Solemnly she detached from her house-slippers the strings that trailed bits of paper for Janet to frisk after, and regarded the miscreant with deep reproach.

"Janet! Janet! Just look at yourself. Now aren't you *too* ashamed?"

But Janet never was. Sitting in all her scandalous dignity she winked at Miss Sally and smiled complacently, secure in the knowledge that, though reproaches would continue up to the very hour of accouchement, her friend would not fail to provide a suitable layette behind the kitchen stove.

✔   ✔   ✔

Today, after lunch with Janet, Sally left early for her afternoon at the Library. The 1921 Spring catalogs, already overdue, would surely have arrived, and she wanted time to scan them before some member of the Book Committee appeared to carry them off. At least that was the excuse she offered Janet for her early departure: but as she closed the front door and waved good-bye (Janet's whiskered mew of protest came soundless from among the window plants), she had to admit to herself that she had not given Janet the real reason for her restlessness and haste. Joe Bramwell was back today from Charleston, after squiring his "nieces", his great-grandnieces

Eleanor and Jane Fenwick, to the St. Cecilia Ball. Of course, there was little hope of his arriving at the Library till his usual hour just before closing; but still, with so much to report, he might take it into his head to appear earlier, and on the strength of that frail possibility she was anxious to clear the stage for him.

And this combination of anxiety and anticipation, together with the February bleakness of the day, so quickened her pace that she was walking at top speed by the time she reached the post-office. There she stopped to pick up the Library mail, noting with satisfaction that some of the catalogs had at last arrived, and then with both arms ladened hurried on. Being like Joe a town personage, she was greeted by everyone she met, but today she was so preoccupied that she failed to acknowledge several greetings till too late, oversights she knew she would have to pay for in some form sooner or later. And, just as she had feared, there was a knot of youngsters already out of school and waiting for her at the Library steps. Why did today, of all days and after a week of spring-like weather, have to be so windy and raw that even the most outdoor and mercurial children were anxious to huddle in the warmth of her lair. She scolded them as she unlocked the door, but it was too cold to keep them out till official opening time.

After she had settled them in the children's alcove, she hung up her coat and hat on the rack behind her desk and furtively consulted the mirror she kept behind the *Readers Guide* on the reference shelf. Then she went down the steep cellar stairs to see if Old Clinch, once town lamplighter and now the Library's janitor and ward, had left the furnace right and had remembered to erase the latest obscene representations and scrawlings on the washroom wall. He had forgotten, of course. When she came back upstairs, flushed and a little short of breath, she studied the children's alcove speculatively while unwrapping and stamping the batch of new magazines. The washroom culprit, she decided as she placed the magazines on the periodical table, was probably one of the older boys who would be coming in later. Today she would keep a sharp watch on the cellar stairs, she resolved as she opened H. G. Wells' *Outline of History,* examined it skeptically, and set it aside for Joe's perusal. Then finally, after some necessary dusting to make up for Old Clinch's lick-and-promise, she settled down at her desk and glanced through the new catalogs, noting non-fiction items that might be of interest to Joe.

Facing her desk was the door, where presently the afternoon's quota of visitors would appear. And over the door hung the clock. But she refrained from giving it even a casual passing glance, for there was no hope of Joe for at least an hour yet.

When the hands of the clock were safely past four, Sally began to allow herself accidental glances at its familiar tick-tock face, as she dealt with incoming and outgoing books and their human escorts. When the hands reached four-thirty, she had to give the clock the satisfaction of seeing that she was definitely watching it. And by five she threw all caution to the winds and made no attempt to disguise the fact that she was also watching the window beyond the periodical table, the frame of street where Joe would appear.

It was getting dark in the Library, and outside the trees swayed dimly in the dreary February dusk; but Sally put off turning on the lights, for they would blot out what was left of her vision of the street. But when the clock said five-fifteen, she could no longer delay: she could hardly see what she was doing at her desk, and the children in the alcove were straining their eyes. Fortunately, at the moment she turned on the lights, the corner street lamp in the frame of Joe's window came on to counteract a little this inner glare.

By five-thirty, though there was still no sign of Joe, the stage was as good as cleared for him. The afternoon's expected people were disposed of; one or two stragglers might appear, but at this late hour they could be counted on not to tarry. And practically all the children were gone, drawn home by supper-time gnawings. One of the older boys, nice Bob Holden, was still poring over a stack of debate books, and one of the older girls, artful and precocious Miriam Tolivant was lingering on for obvious reasons; but Bob could be cleared out with a gentle hint at a moment's notice, and Miriam would quickly follow. That left only Hattie Fowler to worry about.

Hattie Fowler was the Library's steadiest customer. Every day, regular as clockwork, she consumed a book. Any work of fiction, good bad or indifferent, would do; she was interested in books as an additional source of gossip, for keeping track of Beaufort was not enough to satisfy her ravenous appetite. Age was not improving

Hattie Fowler: it seemed only to be sharpening her bad features, her horse face and prominent crooked teeth, her goiterish neck and violent eyes, and above all her long nose and vengeful tongue. And Joe hated the sight of her. They very seldom met to clash, however; five-thirty was her customary hour for stopping by to return one book and borrow another, on her way to the telephone exchange to relieve Louella Simpson at the switchboard for the night shift, and so normally she was safely off Miss Sally's little stage before Joe made his entrance at closing time. But today, when there was still a chance of Joe arriving earlier than usual, this would be the day that Hattie would pick to be late. It was as if she were deliberately delaying, lurking around the corner or in the shrubbery to time her arrival with Joe's.

But then, at twenty minutes to six and Joe not yet in sight, the door swung open and in bustled the tardy Hattie, well bundled up against the cold and carrying as usual her black knitting-bag. At that moment Miriam Tolivant was leaving, after giving Bob Holden a bare second's headstart, and Hattie stopped in her tracks to stare after the girl. When the door clicked closed, Hattie turned with a jerk of her head and came to the desk with eyebrows lifted and lips twisted.

"So that's the way the wind blows!" she flashed as she flopped her knitting-bag on the desk and turned down the ratty fur collar of her coat. "That Tolivant brat's after Sarah Holden's boy. Following in her man-crazy mother's footsteps. Somebody better open Sarah's eyes to what's going on around here."

Anxious as Sally was to dispose of Hattie Fowler as quickly as possible, it was impossible to ignore the implication that the Library was a place of assignation for the younger generation. "I don't think it's as serious as all that," she said coolly.

"Good grief, Sally Broughton," Hattie shot back, swelling her bosom and jerking her head, "you know as well as I do that every Tolivant female is a natural-born Jezebel. When a husband starts giving trouble in this town, you can be pretty sure there's a Tolivant at the bottom of it. I know Captain Fowler never so much as spoke to one of them up till the day I buried him, but I saw to that. Land, I'd like to see anything in pants make a fool out of me, upon my soul I would!"

Sally let that pass and held her peace till Hattie's head stopped jerking. Then she shifted her attention to the clock and with an air of simple discovery observed:

"You're quite late today, aren't you."

"It wouldn't surprise me if I was," Hattie nodded crossly. "Mabel Hitchcock dropped in just as I was leaving, and you know how she can talk. A body can't get a word in edgewise when she gets started. But then she has nothing better to do, having no children to worry about or no work to do like us. I feel real sorry for Mabel."

"Why feel sorry," Sally asked evenly but with an inward sigh of exasperation, "for people who don't feel sorry for themselves? Mabel appears to be satisfied with her life."

"*Appears* to be, perhaps," snapped Hattie. "But I happen to *know* different. If I had a mind to tell what I know."

The challenge was not taken up. And Hattie was visibly nettled: she liked to introduce a topic aggressively, but from that point on she preferred to be interviewed, to be questioned so that she could flash out answers and between deliveries sit back and look wise while preparing the next thrust. But heedless of Hattie's resentment Sally refused to rise to the Mabel Hitchcock bait. Instead, she actually held out her hand to compel Hattie to produce a book from the knitting-bag without further delay.

"You finished yesterday's book all right?" she asked to soften the impatience of her gesture.

A bright gleam came into Hattie's eyes, and she stopped dawdling and rummaged the book out of her congested knitting-bag in short order. "I did!" she exploded as she slapped the book down on the desk. "And as a member in good standing I want to know how this vile thing ever got into the Library! Where did it come from?"

Sally picked up *A Portrait of the Artist as a Young Man* and inspected it with a puzzled frown. "Oh," she finally realized, "this is one of the books given us by the brother of that artist woman. He brought them here the day she died, just before he went away. You remember the woman artist who died at the Sea Island Hotel at Christmas time."

"I remember," Hattie nodded grimly. "I remember she and her brother lived together in one room. *She* was an artist and *he* was supposed to be some kind of poet. And if I ever saw a guilty-looking pair of human beings, it was them."

It was not the first time Hattie Fowler had advanced this ugly

813

conjecture, but Sally couldn't help being shocked all over again.

"Now you know that's nonsense," she protested. "They lived in one room because they were poor, and he was taking care of her, nursing her."

"You can call it that if you like. But what I want to know is why didn't you tell me this book belonged to that pair? You know I wouldn't have touched it with gloves on!"

Sally, her cheeks on fire, hastened to explain. "Why, I had no idea there was anything wrong with it. What's it about?"

"I couldn't make heads or tails of the story," Hattie sniffed stiffly, "and I defy anybody else to. But I do know filth when I see it, even if I don't get the connection. Do you know what kind of language he uses in this book? Well, I'll give you just one word for a sample."

The word was so bad that Hattie had to lean over the desk to whisper it.

"What does it mean?" asked Sally in all innocence.

Hattie straightened up with a blink of fierce indignation, as if she had been slapped. "Now look here, Sally Broughton, don't try to put on airs with me!—we've known each other a little too long for that. What does it mean, my foot! You know as well as I do."

"I think I get the general idea," Sally conceded, to avoid prolonging the discussion.

"That's better," Hattie jerked.

"I'm sorry you got hold of the book," was all Sally could think of to add.

"Well, I'm not," said Hattie. "Suppose it had fallen into the hands of some child? I declare, it makes you wonder what we're coming to when they can print stuff like that in black and white. The garbage-can's the proper place for books like that."

"All right," Sally sighed wearily; "I'll see they're all disposed of."

But then Hattie abruptly changed her tune. "No, I don't say go that far," she compromised blandly. "You don't throw away a basket of eggs because one happens to be spoiled. Let's have a look at the others." And before Sally could intercept her, she stepped behind the desk and opened the cupboard under the shelves, where the rest of the offending gift books were lurking.

Fearing a Library scandal, Sally made an effort to take charge of the cupboard, but Hattie was not to be dislodged. She drew out a whole armful of the books, and held them up to the light one by one. After a sniffing-discarding process she was left clutching two survivors, Anatole France's *Thaïs* and Oscar Wilde's *Salomé,* and for a minute she was torn between them like a woman trying to focus her sixth sense at a bargain counter. But finally she rejected *Salomé* and retained *Thaïs.* "I'll try this one first," she announced, as she closed the cupboard.

Sally had no idea what *Thaïs* was about, but the illustrations were definitely alarming, and under the spur of apprehension she did her best to divest Hattie of the plum by tempting her with other fruit, from the current-fiction reserve shelf. But Hattie simply turned up her nose. No, she would just take *Thaïs* today. And report on it tomorrow.

"But," she bethought herself, "you better give me something good and clean to take the bad taste out of my mouth, in case. One of those Pollyanna books."

So in distress Sally watched *Thaïs* with a Pollyanna antidote disappear into the hungry maw of Hattie's knitting-bag. But there was at least one thing to be thankful for: now at last Hattie would have the decency to take herself off. She had her book and she couldn't very well procrastinate any longer, for the clock said six minutes to six and that left her barely time to get to the exchange and relieve Louella Simpson on the dot.

But Hattie hung on, like a nagging headache.

"Isn't Louella going to be worried about you?" Sally asked with an explicit glance at the clock, and then a side-glance at Joe's window.

"I suppose," said Hattie, not missing either glance, "you're anxious to hear how Joe Bramwell came out, carrying Eleanor and Jane Fenwick to Charleston. Seems to me it's a little soon for those girls to be traipsing to a party ball, with their grandfather hardly cold in his grave."

"I don't think so at all," Sally contradicted. "He died months ago. Besides, people should be allowed to decide such matters themselves."

"Some people," Hattie pursued, unperturbed, "can forget mighty quick and easy. Sorrow rolls off them like water off a duck's back. I'm still in weeds for Captain Fowler, but those Fenwicks took off mourning the day after the funeral, all except Eugenia. But what could you expect from Emily Fenwick? I was surprised she didn't

815

have him cremated heathen-style instead of giving him a decent Christian burial. She shows her face in church sometimes, but she's got no more religion than a Chinaman."

"You can't judge a person's religion," Sally retorted, "by church-going."

"Oh, is that so?" Hattie whinnied caustically. "Well, I'll thank you not to tell me how to judge a person's religion or anything else. You can stick up for her if you're a mind to, but not me. They say he put her through, and in more ways than one, but that's only her side of the story, and he was always a perfect gentleman to me, even back in the days when he used to drink like a fish. I never could understand why folks look up to her like she's some kind of tin saint. She never fooled me. She's always trying to butter me with that soft-soap of hers, but I always let her see she's not pulling any wool over my eyes. She sets herself up as leading lady of this town, but that don't cut no ice with me. And those girls. They hold their heads too high, Eleanor in particular. Beaufort ain't good enough for them. I hear they're going to some Yankee college up North. I suppose they'll try to catch men and live up there."

Hattie paused for breath, and for a moment she seemed on the verge of dropping into the chair by the desk. This, as Hattie well knew, was Joe's special Library chair, his place of honor respected by everyone; and while she didn't go so far as to actually occupy the sacred seat, the fact that she had even threatened to was enough to make Sally boiling mad. This was the last straw, and Sally stopped caring what she said.

"It's closing time now. And I'm not interested in the conversation anyway."

Hattie gave her a twisted smile. "Afraid I'll be on deck when your Joe appears?" she asked with a mild sting. But then she lashed out with pure venom: "When are you ever going to wake up?—he's about as much interested in you as he is in me! He's always been hipped on Emily Fenwick, and if you wasn't blind as a bat you'd have seen it long ago!"

When Sally could speak, she said quietly: "You better go now."

"I'll do nothing of the kind!" Hattie flung back at the top of her voice. "I'll leave when I'm good and ready, not a second sooner, and I'd like to see you put me out! It happens I want to see Joseph Bramwell myself. I got some questions to ask him about the bank. There's something funny going on, and I'm going to get to the bottom of it."

Sally straightened up in her chair to look Hattie right in the eye. "You better be careful what you say about the bank. That tongue of yours is going to get you in trouble yet. You can go to prison for spreading lies about a bank."

"Oh, I can, can I! Well, it won't be *me* that'll go to prison. I drew my money out of the bank three days ago, and nobody can stop me from telling it. And plenty of other folks is doing the same thing. And if you've got a grain of sense you'll get to Bay Street tomorrow morning and get your money out while the getting's still good. I figure Ed Sands is too slick an article to have quit and skipped town for nothing. If that bank ain't holler as a sucked egg it's certainly the next thing to it, and don't say I didn't warn you!"

And she added in a hoarse burst of confidence: "Ed Sands and I was always like that"—holding up crossed fingers—"but don't get any wrong impression. He and I was the same as raised together, and when Captain Fowler was taken and passed over, leaving me a poor widow, it was Ed that got me my position at the exchange. And last month when he was leaving town for good, he said, 'Hattie, I'm going to give you a parting word of advice that I wouldn't give nobody else,—keep it to yourself but just remember a sock is still the best place to put your pennies.' I didn't think nothing much of it at the time, but then here lately it come over me what he meant!"

Before Sally could collect herself for a scathing answer, the door swung open and in came Joe. A gust of raw wind swept the desk, and as Hattie turned to face the frowning hulk framed in the vestibule under the clock, Sally's heart stopped. For a moment she expected a frightful, historic clash; but as Joe advanced with solid dignity, like a veteran frigate, Hattie side-stepped and scuttled by him without firing a shot. In passing she saluted him with a jerk of her head, which he acknowledged with a grunt and snort. Then she flounced on out, closing the door behind her with a slam that jarred the windows.

It took a moment for the stunned echoes to subside.

As Joe confronted her at the desk, Sally tried to give him a nice unruffled smile, but she felt miserably shaken and upset.

"What's going on here?" he demanded with flushed gruffness. "What's the argument?"

"Oh nothing," said Sally lightly. "Just a little tiff."

"So little I could hear you out in the street. Tiffing about what?"

"Oh, just a piece of gossip Hattie's retailing."

"Gossip? What gossip? No matter,—the point is can't you women gossip without quarreling at the top of your lungs?"

The "you women" cut Sally, but she could resent nothing that came from Joe. She left her chair to relieve him of his overcoat and hat, while he grumbled as usual about not being able to stay more than a minute and with his usual cussedness hung onto his cane, which had to be pulled through the sleeve of the overcoat as usual. When she had hung his things up with her own on the rack in the corner, she stopped briefly at the *Readers Guide* on the reference shelf to give her hair a few pats in the hidden mirror: she felt as tousled as if her encounter with Hattie Fowler had been a hand-to-hand affair. When she came back to the desk she found Joe whisking the arms and seat of his special chair with flicks of his handkerchief,— as if she didn't always take special pains to see that it was free from even a speck of dust! But there was no trace of any reproach in her voice when she said to him, after he had ponderously settled himself:

"I thought you might come early today. You got back on the noon train?"

He nodded absently. "But I had to give Susan and Isabel a full account of the trip. And after dinner I stopped by, of course, to report to Emily. . . . Didn't I hear that Fowler woman blathering something about the bank?"

Sally's eyes were thrown into confusion. She succeeded finally in fixing them with rigid attention on her hands, which were locked tightly together on the desk. "Why yes," she had to admit. "Hattie's always gabbing about something."

"I'm well aware of that," Joe snorted, striking the floor with his cane. "But when it comes to the bank, she better guard her tongue. What did she say precisely?"

Sally's mouth was dry as a biscuit. "Why, she said she'd drawn her money out."

"So much the better," Joe rapped. "Is that all?"

"She said—plenty of other people would too."

Joe turned purple at that. Sally looked at him in alarm. He seemed so in danger of bursting a blood-vessel that it was a relief when he finally exploded:

"This has gone far enough! That woman's trying to start serious trouble, but I'll put a stop to it! I'll swear out a warrant for her arrest!"

Then he abruptly restrained his fury. "No, that would be bad policy. I'll find some other way to shut her up." And he asked with judicious composure: "What else did she have to say?" But when Sally hesitated, he leaned forward on his cane to blast out: "What else did she say!"

"She said something about Ed Sands," Sally told him wretchedly. "She said Ed Sands had given her a hint before he cleared out of town. About a sock being the best place for savings."

"So that's it! . . . Well, I'll now give you some inside facts, in strictest confidence. When I took office I found the bank in rotten shape—full of paper, frozen assets, bad real-estate loans contracted during the Ed Sands regime and the War boom. I might have stepped out then and there, but my resignation would have precipitated a crisis, and I felt it my duty to remain and do what I could to clean out the Augean stable."

He sat back in his chair, breathing hard. "Since the first of the year our Charleston parent bank has twice threatened to come down on us, but I've staved them off in both instances. And I can do it again if necessary. Given a little more time, a few months of grace, I'll have the whole mess straightened out. I'm working at cross-purposes with a group of skittish craven numskull directors, but I'll force them to coöperate if I have to take them by the scruffs of their necks and knock their cracker heads together! . . . But I haven't been figuring on outside interference. One squawking hen can stampede an entire barnyard. And if the bank were forced to close its doors today, the depositors wouldn't get ten cents on the dollar. No bank can stand the strain of fear and panic, and if our little bank is forced to the wall now, it will spell ruin for Beaufort and our people. That's the situation."

And he braced himself to add: "It seems to be my late mission in life to save what's left of my town from a final catastrophe. And you can rest assured I will. Starting tomorrow morning I'm taking a more active hand and a firmer stand at the bank. I'm laying down the law, and in no uncertain terms. And I'm going to silence that Fowler woman, if it's the last thing I ever do!"

"You better," Sally tensely approved. "She's dangerous, Joe. I'm afraid she's done some damage already. And you know how fast a thing can spread in Beaufort."

He shot a stringent glance at her. "Hasn't infected you, I hope."

"Hardly. Am I likely to worry about anything you're in charge of?"

"Very good," he nodded, appeased.

"I simply meant," Sally explained falteringly, "that unless she's called to order, she may really succeed in getting people stirred up. She's an expert at it, you know, and there are an awful pack of fools in this town."

"Are you insinuating," Joe swelled up to scoff indignantly, "that if things came to a serious pass people would allow themselves to be stampeded by that woman's squawkings when I stand for the bank? Are you suggesting that her tongue can undo me and what I stand for in this community? Is that what you mean to imply?"

"Of course not," Sally told him with a short distracted laugh. "But, Joe, Hattie's poison and dynamite rolled up in one package. You're too big to realize how much harm a mean small person's tongue can do. And she has her switchboard. I honestly think it might be a good idea to drop in on her at the exchange tonight."

Joe raised a silencing hand. "Now that will do. We won't bungle this matter with any hysterical feminine tactics. You leave Hattie to me,—I'll remove her sting in good time and with good judgment, I promise you that. I count on my name and my honor to counteract any poison that woman succeeds in injecting into the community, but as a precautionary measure I certainly intend to see her, sometime tomorrow. And we'll let the matter rest there. We'll say no more about it."

With her usual submissiveness where Joe was concerned Sally accepted this peremptory quietus meekly; and as Joe tapered off his indignation with huffings and puffings, she undertook to change the subject by producing the *Outline of History*. He received it absently, still grumbling to himself. Then, after staring at it for several moments, he fished his pince-nez out of his vest pocket and held them to his nose while he examined the bulky volume with an expression of profound distaste.

"Well," he finally decided, "it looks to me like a mess of condensed claptrap, but I'll run through it and make a few corrections before it goes into general circulation." And he put it down on the desk and resumed his cane with a morose frown.

After respecting his brooding silence for a minute or two Sally ventured to break in. Perking up in her chair she summoned her most receptive manner and inquired brightly: "Well, do tell me about your trip."

He was reluctant to be routed out of his scowling introspection, but once started he soon warmed to his theme, his scowl receding as his spirits expanded.

"Yes," he positively beamed at last in summing up his recital, "it was simply splendid. It was perfection, really, like a work of art. All Charleston was there in old Hibernian Hall, and I can't recall a finer St. Cecilia, a more brilliant gathering of the clans. Old faces missing, inevitably, but new faces to take their places and carry on the tradition,—the grand tradition that binds together its members, old and young, like a great family. . . . Many new faces, yes, but none to compare with my two young ladies, I can assure you. Eleanor was belle of the ball, without a doubt. Jane's wings are still untried, of course, but she'll catch up with her sister soon enough, and as it was she did very well indeed in her own set. Ah, but what pleased me even more than the beaux they collected was the way they made friends with my old friends. They show genuine respect and consideration for their elders, a quality all too rare among young people these days. And that virtue of deference, as I told Emily, is an index of prime importance, a sure sign of character as well as breeding. Yes, they passed all tests with flying colors, and introducing them to Charleston was an eminently pleasant honor. It was a proud day in my life."

He sighed reminiscently, and a faraway misty look came into his doughty old eyes. "It took me back to the days of my own youth, when I was squiring Susan and Isabel to their first ball. You were only a child then—a fat freckled tomboy, my dear!—but you must remember how lovely they were, and I myself thought their loveliness could be matched nowhere in the world, in any age or clime. But now, by George, I don't know. I won't go so disloyally far as to say these girls of Emily's are more attractive, but they do possess a certain natural sincerity and forthrightness that coupled with good taste and good manners makes a ravishing combination. Youth in itself is captivating, but when you have youth that seems to understand—among many other things—that you too were once young and would sell your soul to be again,—well, the total effect is irresistibly appealing. I mean to say, it can't be beat."

And he added with a self-indulgent chuckle: "I daresay I sound like a sentimental old fool, and I realize I'm expressing myself very badly, but it's something that calls for expression however inadequate. I used to think of my sisters as japonica blossoms, and I'm not ashamed to confess that I think of my nieces as all the flowers in the garden. Flesh-and-blood flowers, that's what they are to me,—yes, and they make me feel young and in love in some lost Eden of the world. Their company works like an elixir of life. They cast a spell over me, warming this old heart with their grace and charm, their shining eyes and smiles. Fair youth! It's the poetry of life, Sally. And to read it makes us sad, but it also restores the soul, makes us young and gallant again, revives our failing strength, our dreams, our faith."

Sally was wide-eyedly nonplussed by this unprecedented splurge of rhapsodizing from Joe. And while she was perfectly willing to admit that Eleanor and Jane were exceptional girls, they certainly did not make her feel young, and the only thing they revived in her was jealousy. Still, the fact that Joe was enjoying his rhapsody was enough for Sally; and she was on the point of asking him what the girls had worn, to encourage him to further enlarge on his fond theme, when the door of the Library swung open and a whirl of cold wind blew in.

It took Sally a bewildered moment to realize that the figure in the vestibule was not Old Clinch, come to bank the furnace and lock up. And even when she recognized that it was actually Hattie Fowler returned, it was still impossible to believe in her appearance, the picture she made. She was a sight scarcely human, a sight to strike terror to the heart, like some apparition of fiendish mythology, a hydra or a Gorgon-headed harpy.

Whether through histrionic instinct or sheer breathlessness the apparition let whole seconds pound away before it spoke. Then it struck out convulsively at Sally.

"I thought the pair of you might be interested to know *the bank's closed!*"

While Joe sat completely dumfounded, Sally managed to recover from consternation to say: "Why, of course, Hattie. It closed at three. What of it?"

"It's closed *for good!* It's *busted!* They've got a notice posted on the door! But I knew it was coming and I got *my* money out!"

Joe burst out of his speechlessness with a violent snort. "Confound it, woman!—what are you talking about?"

Turning from Sally to confront him, Hattie faltered for a goggling moment, twitching like all possessed. But having once succeeded in facing him, she struck with full force. "Don't you dare to curse me, you old—crook! Where were you when they were having their directors meeting after the close—*courting?* Don't suppose you knew they called an emergency meeting to close the bank, to keep from having a run!"

"Impossible!" Joe roared at her. "They can't act without me."

"Well, they did!" Hattie spat back. "And if you don't believe me, go see for yourself!"

And she added with quivering fury: "The beans is spilt, all right. And don't think you can try any cock-and-bull tricks to mend matters, like that Columbia bank outfit that called a mass meeting and got folks to raise good money to throw after bad! Your goose is cooked and you'll be lucky if you don't land in jail. Best thing you can do is get out of town, if you want to save that fine portly skin of yours!"

Joe's cane struck the floor. "Silence, woman!"

"Don't you dare to lay a hand on me!" Hattie sneered shrilly, her back against the door. "You can't bully me, you old windbag!"

Joe rose like a venerable lion goaded at last to ferocity.

"*Silence!*—blast you! Now get out of here! *Get out!*"

Hattie pulled the door wide open, and a rush of wind scattered the papers on Sally's desk like leaves. "Yes, I'll go!" she screeched in a spasm of triumph, "but not because I'm scared of you! I've finished with you two and now I've got other work to do! I'm going to see that everybody in town knows about the bank before they're through supper!"

And she bolted out into the bleak writhing street-lamp shadows, slamming the door with a terrific crash.

Joe sat down heavily and stared grimly aghast at the door, while Sally's senses reeled in the awful resounding silence. When the room steadied a little and the measured tick-tocking of the clock came back, she began mechanically to pick up the papers scattered on the floor.

823

"It can't be true," she choked out at dazed random. "It's all Hattie's doing, and she'll catch it when people come to their senses. And those cowardly skittish fools at the bank betrayed you. And Ed Sands,—he's probably across the border by now, in Canada or Mexico, but can't he be brought back and made to take the blame? He's responsible. But I believe the whole thing's a lie of Hattie's. We've got to find out. We can use the telephone across at the firehouse."

No answer came from Joe, and when she had put the papers on the desk she went to his side and placed a shaky hand on his sleeve. "Now don't you believe a word of this," she told him, trying to keep her voice from shaking too, "till we get to the bottom of it. Don't you want me to see what I can find out, while you stay here and rest a minute?"

Slumped in his chair, he turned his head and stared at her blankly, without recognition.

"It's no use," he said finally. "It's too late to do anything now. Except take my medicine. . . . If I could only take it alone."

Her eyes filled with tears as she watched him and waited.

"I'll put up my government bonds," he intoned flatly. "Susan and Isabel will just have to scrimp. Perhaps we can reopen the office."

"Of course," she quickly agreed. "And we'll all manage somehow. Oh, Joe dear, please don't worry."

He seemed not to hear her and went on in a mumbling voice as if talking to himself. "She'll never take a penny from Jack. But she'll see that Eleanor and Jane get their chance, if she has to take boarders."

His own words roused him at last.

"Where are my hat and coat?—I've got to see Emily."

Part Seven

I

THE SUAVE SHINING concrete of the highway came to an abrupt end, with a jounce of bags and tools in the rumble-seat. John Clark jammed on the brakes too late to avoid splashing the open roadster into a deep puddle left from the morning's rain.

Even on a perfect spring afternoon, he decided as he wiped his face, something could be said for not driving and daydreaming with the top down. When he leaned out to look past the edge of the splattered windshield, he found himself stalled in the rutted main street of a drab little settlement, where the double tracks of the Atlantic Coast Line to Florida crossed some decrepit local line. According to the map on the seat beside him this should be Yemassee. The guide-post ahead evaded his question and repudiated its surroundings by pointing out, through a rain-streaked film of ruddy dust, Augusta and Aiken to the right, Beaufort and Savannah to the left. But a sign on the dingy station across the tracks acknowledged that this was indeed Yemassee.

At hand was a combination store and filling-station sporting an orange pump, from which gas was being carefully measured into the battered tank of a tattered flivver loaded with darkies, while a parcel of white bench-warmers looked on. Behind the screen of his windshield John Clark peeled off his beret and chamois gloves and stuffed them into the pocket of his raglan. A pusillanimous retraction if I ever saw one, he thought; but after all the togs were Helen's idea, and why should the good people of Yemassee be entertained by his wife's conception of the latest things in continental male chic.

When the flivver had rattled away in a cloud of popping exhaust smoke, he drove over to the orange pump for gas and a clean windshield. The proprietor, in faded overalls and a greenish black hat and redolent of corn licker, turned out at close range to be a startling caricature of President Coolidge. And this Calvin of Yemassee looked as if he too had just chosen not to run, or even move. For a full minute he ruminated, surveying the car from radiator to taillight. Then he spat leisurely over the hood and drawled: "Hey, Jeff! . . . Dog that nigger, where's he at now?" The bench-warmers took up the nasal cry, and presently out the torn screen door of the store burst a black boy with a ragged grin.

While Jeff was applying himself to the windshield and Cal cautiously pumping gas, John Clark turned away from the frank stares of the bench-warmers. It was just as well, he thought with a twinge of lonely amusement, that Helen was not along. She would feel called upon to oblige this audience with some city-slicker business. . . . At the little station across the tracks several swank cars and station-wagons were parked in the sunshine; and on the cramped platform two distinct groups of expensive people were elaborately unaware of each other and their bucolic background, including the native peasantry, white and black.

The gentlemen on the platform were smartly dressed for Town, and the ladies for Country. The gentlemen were clearly sportsmen returning to New York from the chase on newly-acquired feudal domains. Captains of industry and finance returning to the wars, on the Sunday afternoon limited that would put them back in the front-line trenches in plenty of time Monday for a killing before the three-o'clock gong, Eastern Standard Time. Easter, this year of grace 1928, fell on April 8th, a week from this balmy Sunday of palms and fools: by Good Friday the captains would come trooping back, ladened with the fleeces of more lambs, to shoot duck and hound deer over the week-end. Well, a little late in the season for hunting, but there was always polo and the drags at Aiken and it must be about time for the Horse Show. . . . Five graceful years from now, say 1933, the Orange Blossom Special would be too slow for commuting and the sportsmen would be flying, shuttling back and forth by plane. By then Big Steel would have hit the ceiling, and Yemassee would be an Elizabethan village with an airport. This crossroads store of Cal's would be transformed into a half-timbered Dew Drop Inn. And they'd have Jeff in an orange beret and Cal in a zipper jerkin and puttees, dispensing Service with a Smile. That would be the millennium at last. Tiled rest-rooms for the humblest traveler, and a chicken in every pot. . . . And by then the best of the sportsmen, if they hadn't yet hoisted themselves on their own bloody petards, would be occupying suites of offices in the Ballard Building: the world's highest, widest, and handsomest, for a few minutes: Johnson, Blauvelt, & Clark, Architects.

Well, he told the sportsmen as he handed Cal a bill, you can have Yemassee and New York and the Ballard Building. And Johnson and Blauvelt. But you can't have Clark. At least, not for a few more days.

When Cal had counted change out of a greasy purse, he leaned against his orange pump and waited, without choosing to say a word about hurrying back, thereby shattering the tradition of hospitality that had prevailed as surely as cotton fields and stray cattle since the crossing of the Potomac. Feeling the need of some parting remark, John Clark said the first thing that came into his head as he glanced at the sallow hard-bitten face.

"Much malaria in these parts?"

Cal thrust his hands into his pockets, squinted, and spat accurately at the rear license-plate.

"New York, hey? Got many gangsters up your way?"

That brought a chuckle of applause from the bench-warmers, and Cal went on with a twang. "Mister, the malarium's so bad here even the skeeters take quinine. Interested in real-estate? Got a mighty pretty piece of land I can let go dirt cheap."

John Clark shook his head and stepped on the starter as he looked past Cal at the benchload of rock-ribbed Vermonters. "No thanks. I'm trying to get away from Republican territory."

"Well sir," Cal drawled back, without batting an eye at this obscure whimsy, "you sure come to the right place."

"You don't mean you're supporting Al Smith here?"

Cal spat at the license-plate again, but more loosely this time.

"Don't know what concern it is of your'n, mister, but don't mind tellin' you we ain't supportin' no Hoover, an' I reckon you won't catch us supportin' no wet Tammany Catholic. Ain't votin' neither way this trip,—reckon y'all got us hog-tied. Where you headin' for, mister?"

"Beaufort."

"Business or pleasure?"

"Escape."

That gave them pause. And while they were exchanging glances he leaned over to Jeff on the other side of the car and slipped him a quarter, with a private injunction: "Vote for East-Side Al, the People's Pal." Then straightening up to the wheel, he confronted Cal and his bench-warmers with a final amiable query.

"What about hurrying back?"

"Sure thing," Cal chewed moistly, pulling his hat so far down over his eyes that he had to tilt his head back to see. "Stop back long about mealtime. We eat Yankees round here, crust and all."

With a wry smile John Clark turned the car back to the road.

"Hey!" Cal called after him, pointing, "know you had a flat?"

When he braked the car and leaned out to see, Cal grinned: "April Fool, mister, an' no hard feelin's."

He drove on with the bench-warmers' jubilant guffaws in his ears.

Anyway, he smiled defensively, Helen would have liked it. And with her support, no coming off second best in any encounter, rural or urban.

It was bad to be alone. But he resented the necessity of turning back to her. As a drunkard, he thought, resents his bottle. Was it always going to be impossible to get along with her or without her?

The roadster rocked down the puddle-pocked street, swung to the left at the guide-post, and was back on concrete again. And then again the smooth flow and the healing beauty of April woods and fields. With a deep breath of relief he settled down to resume the enjoyment that Yemassee had interrupted.

Back in Central Park the poor caged trees were still shivering in the long cold stunting shadows of the towers, but here the glory of free trees in full panoply of spring. Southern spring, more tender and exquisite than any he had ever known. . . . At some places where the branches of giant live-oaks reached out over the road, there were patches of shade still wet from the morning showers; the tires made an agreeable swishing sound when they slashed across these slippery patches. And ahead at the end of each reach of the road, always receding like the horizon, were wet-looking patches where no shadows hung but where the sunshine smote the concrete with a black glisten, like the quivering heat mirage on a summer highway back North. It was mid-afternoon, but the light now seemed even more intense than when he had left Charleston at noon. There the spell had started: this enchantment of sapphire sky and renascent earth and soft vibrant air. Like some ancient charm, some magic release, and a recapture of eternal verities. It was like first love, innocent, pure, transcending self. The world was new again, as full of mystery and infinite possibilities as in childhood. The shining scented air. The rich soil of the fields. The delicate fresh green of the new leaves, jade mists floating against the dark sheen of the pines. And for contrast the drapings of gray moss; faded tattered pennants of past glory, ghostly rags of years and seasons long dead, cobwebs clinging to the branches of life like old memories.

None of the big billboards of the North to mar the landscape. Only an occasional little blemish, a small *Coca-Cola* or *Vick's* sign or a *Cardui* or *666* tacked on a tree or a fence-post, which could with only a slight effort be accepted as beauty-spots heightening the complexion of nature. And there was one sign that came in sections,— *The Bearded Lady—Tried a Jar—She's now—a Famous—Movie Star—BURMA SHAVE,*—which could be accepted as its own extenuation. But as he drove on even these minor jazz notes in the symphonic scenery became first disturbing, then annoying, and finally disruptive. Somehow they were breaking the spell of the country, making it flicker convulsively like a movie film off the track. They were reopening and deepening the Yemassee wedge, letting in New York and its bedlam of places and faces, spoiling this bright serene world that was both newer and older than his world with Helen. That jangled world of towers and subways, taxies and speakeasies, raw nerves, clenched teeth, short-circuits, till at last even his office and his drafting-board had become a tightrope stretched between blank walls over a roaring inferno of emptiness.

It was really Helen who should be moving into the penthouse of the Ballard Building, with her prize dogs,—schnauzers at the moment. Helen the fair, the brave, the face that launched a thousand straight-faced quips. One or two jumps ahead of almost everyone. The debonair problem child, burning with a hard gem-like and elegantly cock-eyed flame. Yes, it was Helen who should be perched like Columbia on the very crest of the wave, on top of the heap instead of merely on Murray Hill. But then, of course, she was too rare to be a living symbol of anything but herself and friends, that valiant little band of nimble spirits and career diplomats. To be a national or even metropolitan symbol, a perfect Columbia or Miss Manhattan, she would have to resemble Beatrice Lillie less and Miss Millicent Fannigan more. Miss Fannigan, the girl on the magazine cover, and presumptive mistress of the penthouse he had so passionately helped to conceive as a crown for the soaring tower. Ballard's latest-model tart, complete with pekingese, footman, and Duesenberg. Not that he had anything against Duesenbergs or footmen or pekingese, or glorified tarts, or Ballard for that matter: separately. But in combination and in possession of the penthouse, the pinnacle of a great dream of skill and labor: too much. If it didn't reduce all spires to a final absurdity, at least it raised a few doubts.

From the empty seat beside him came Helen's crisp poised voice. Whatever the occasion she always spoke with the same unobtrusive assurance with which she wore her clothes or smoked a cigarette; assurance that always reminded him of his own shortcomings, the general incompetence that ten years of New York had failed to correct. "You know," he distinctly heard her saying again, "I hate to bring it up but you used to be grand company, monkey. My! Before we were married, remember? And even after. Strangers commented on it, children followed us in the street, and neighbors rapped on the walls and complained to the management. But lately you've been going steadily grim on me, pet. I'm not bitter, but I seem to be getting a little stumped. I mean would you mind smiling or something? How about another honeymoon? We could try Harlem or Coney Island again. Have you ever heard the story about the Frenchman and the Englishman? Or would you just like to be Alone?"

The unfailing Lightness of Touch. Her armor and standard. The only virtue she claimed. And the only power, as her friends were constantly showing they understood, that had pulled her through one of the worst cases of shell-shock on record. . . . After all, she had lost her first love in the War; no-one could deny that. And her first husband, Barclay Mason the Illustrator, had gone into a tailspin of some sort. No doubt she had earned the right to feel that nothing could last, particularly the better things, so the only stand to take was that nothing mattered seriously.

"If you're really low," he recalled her saying, "by all means go off and have a stretch. A real stretch. I'm afraid I can't bear you grim, darling. You can be practically anything else, but not that. You haven't the flair for it, or the constitution. You're just not the type."

What type am I, he wondered. Well, among other things, the type that had been looking for the reassurance of a home-base and had somehow wound up as the nth stud of a pinwheel. But then she had never promised anything else, not directly. Only by inference. . . . A genuinely modern woman, with no use for any permanent illusion, unless it was the illusion that all illusions were transient and hence subtly invalid. And having no career beyond herself, she lived in picturesque circles, bent on "personal relations" which like the air she breathed had to be continually renewed for fear of staleness. Her spice-of-life variety: "Anything goes if it's amusing and you don't get your hair mussed." So all the windows and doors of marriage had to be always open to the fresh vagrant winds of change. Thus, by chance, things might be decoyed into lasting by assuming that they couldn't or wouldn't last. Portrait of my wife, the soul of honesty and witty wisdom, and a very great comfort in all but the most vital matters. . . . Perhaps there was no human cure for his particular brand of loneliness. Perhaps the only possible center was self; and the only *alter ego,* work. But when that combination began to crack up, what then?

Impertinently the figure of her divorced husband, Barclay Mason, rose up before the windshield in all his legendary trappings. There was a roman candle to match her pinwheel. Certainly the most spirited steed on her merry-go-round. Strange that she had ever dismounted. To sharpen her appreciation of him, perhaps, for now they were the best of friends again. As a matter of fact, as she had taken the trouble to explain, they had never really stopped being friends. No, that would have been quite childish. . . . And what, he asked her, do you still want with me?

He felt she was definitely smiling at that from the emptiness beside him. "After all, you're still you, more or less at odd moments. And you're a junior partner now, brains of the firm, and headed for the very top. I had the sense to pick you up when your stock was low, and now the market's going up, so why shouldn't I want to hang on to you? Besides, you'll always need a friend to save you from predatory females."

And then her final words on the subject came back to him. "Seriously, darling, you're going to break up or crumple if you don't get away from it all. You're denting too many fenders. You must take a vacation between blueprints and get a grip on yourself, and I know just the place for you."

Florida, it had developed, was out, for obvious reasons. Likewise Bermuda and Havana. Nassau in the Bahamas was still amusing, but too popular just now with drunks. And so on, till finally by a neat process of elimination: Beaufort, South Carolina, a restful little old place, well off the beaten track. "Madie Brokaw and I discovered it autumns ago, on the way back from Reno and ranching. There's quite an unusual inn there, run by a charming old lady. It's all been written up in the *Spur* and that sort of thing, so probably I better wire for a reservation for you." All kinds of people were becoming plantation conscious now, of course, but this place wouldn't be spoiled yet, and anyway the season was about over. He could coast down to Charleston, shedding persecution complexes and letting at least his nerves go native, and after a good stretch and some fishing at Beaufort he could loaf on through mammies and magnolias and mockingbirds to Savannah and New Orleans. By that time he should be ready to invite her to join him.

"We'll have a stack of sazeracs at Galatoire's and oysters Rockefeller at Antoine's, and then drive home upside-down through the Shenandoah Valley in a burst of apple blossoms,—and start all over again. There now, doesn't that help?"

He wondered how much it had helped so far, and pressed down the accelerator uneasily. But that was worse than useless: it was all blank ahead. Escape, if any, had to be internal, like digestion.

Well, anyway, he could elude the pursuing demons of short-circuit a little longer by doubling back to digest Charleston.

. . . He saw himself approaching it again by ferry, after the drive from Georgetown. A proud old city, floating Venice-like on the sunset waters, lights beginning to twinkle palely in its long low mass already half sunken in the rising tide of darkness, only a few points of accent surviving in charred silhouette against the flames of the west. To the north, grotesquely out of scale, loomed the unfinished arches of a new bridge spanning the Cooper River like a giant roller-coaster, and spelling imminent doom for the plodding old ferry. To the south, out in the middle of the harbor, brooded Fort Sumter.

"You'll land," Helen had warned, "at the height of the garden

834

season, and the place will be simply crawling with tourists. You really must see Middleton and Magnolia and some of the old plantation houses, but Charleston itself you'll find a bit too quaint." So, as a gesture of independence, he had set to work to find Charleston not too obviously quaint.

But that had presented grave difficulties. Fellow tourists, proclaiming the quaintness of the city, were everywhere. The hotels were swarming with them. Church Street was like a midway, congested with cars bearing the license-plates of every Northern state in the Union. Representatives of the better touring classes not only jampacked the sideshows—the labeled historic houses, the antique shops and artists' studios, the tearooms and taverns and bookstores— but they also had the initiative to go exploring on their own: seeking the "Catfish Row" of DuBose Heyward's *Porgy,* invading cobblestoned alleys for pearls of quaint dilapidation, and in some enterprising cases innocently finding themselves in the gardens of private houses. "So sorry, we thought this was open to the public"; and departing lingeringly, strewing tasteful appreciations, to make it perfectly plain that they too, in their own home towns, belonged to the cultivated and cloistered minority. With refined enthusiasm they penetrated every corner of the old quarter, tracking down the quaint with the thoroughness of an aniline dye.

In the end he gave up trying to distill peace from the lees of the past, and instead surrendered himself, with a kind of bitter relish, to the clash of contrasts that was living Charleston. Throughout the city discord was the dominant note. From minuet through polka, waltz, and two-step to jazz. Muted strings brooding over *Dixie,* with triumphant hot-trumpet overtones by the colored band of Jenkins Orphanage Home. *Weep No More* doing the Charleston.

In the lower city the fine Colonial houses and the stately residences of the Greek Revival were rudely elbowed by gingerbread monstrosities and upstart nonentities, and neatly parodied by the new development to the west of the obtrusive Fort Sumter Hotel: a conglomeration of "Colonial-style" homes, proudly owned in more than one case, no doubt, by the advanced descendants of Revolutionists and Signers. . . . In Broad Street, the Wall Street and divide of the city, musty old offices far outnumbered flashy new ones in the vicinity of the bluntly skyscraping bank; yet it was amply apparent that Charleston business men were, in their own fashion and well jogged by Coca-Colas, getting ahead in a plenty big enough way. Astonishing crowds, with lunatic fringes of stenographers and soda-jerkers, overflowed the staccato-ticking brokerage offices housed in antique buildings with ornamented cornices and slate roofs. . . . At the corner of Broad and Meeting, brightened by the baskets of flower women, traffic signals of the latest model turned from red to green for the fuming rush of cars that crossed under the clock and serene chimes of St. Michael's dreaming white spire. While within the old church's walled yard, barred from the living by gates of wrought-iron tracery, slumbered the great dead, exhausted from turning in their graves.

King Street, the narrow shopping artery of the city, presented a vivid cross-section of Charleston. Its thronging life and its stores and cafeterias and movie palaces (Clara Bow still silently "It" but *The Jazz Singer* crying out loud) were certainly indistinguishable from their Main Street mates anywhere. But when you raised your eyes above the ground-floor level of the street, you beheld an amazing range of upper stories. Colonial tops, tinted walls mellow with age, delicate cornices, old roofs with dormer windows and handsome tile-capped chimneys. Brick buildings of the golden age, soberly ornate, restrainedly sentimental, with pressed-iron balconies and grilles and molded window frames. And, in profusion, dingy façades of the gilded age and after: burlesque Gothic, hodge-podge Renaissance, cock-eyed Rococo.

In upper King Street, Jerusalem gone Harlem, the architectural diversity seemed even more striking, heightened perhaps by the dynamic blend of Jewish and Negro life that throbbed past the cheap stores. And then there were the backwashes of the city, where forgotten mansions served as tenements among gimcrack bungalows and plain shanties. But it was at Citadel Square, midtown, that impressions of the Queen City of the South came to a final focus. Here the Francis Marion Hotel dominated a shabby park where under the kindly eyes of a tall goateed patriarch policeman children played, men loafed, and brassy colored nursemaids gossiped, around two old public fountains and a bird-stained statue of Calhoun. And here, across the Square from the hotel, were a pair of prize bizarreries, either of which would serve as a neat epitome of Charleston quaintness.

It was hard, in fact, to choose between them. One was an old frame house with jalousied West Indian verandahs, its upper stories faded to ghostly gray, its basement living emphatically in the present with a blaring Radio Shoppe. The other was a filling-station, one of a chain of bright new "Georgian" filling-stations. What made this particular filling-station peculiarly interesting was its setting: it stood against the magnificent scarred shell of a real Georgian dwelling, whose classic gatehouse, an octagonal gem, had been tidily fitted into the service ensemble as a Ladies Rest Room.

Torn between these two symbols, the jalousied Radio Shoppe and the filling-station with background, he decided at last on the filling-station. Here, from one rank outsider's viewpoint at least, was the sum and substance of the matter, in a slightly obvious but convenient nutshell. And when he had finished a sketch while the car was being serviced,—the old house seemed to be serving as a rookery for as many families as there were rooms, and at the moment a ragged black boy on the front steps was obligingly hacking a portion of the hand-turned balustrade into kindlings,—he felt satisfied that he had captured something of the spirit of historic Charleston.

For Charleston was, without a doubt, the thing it claimed to be: America's most historic city. Here, in architectural forms dating from simple Colonial beginnings to the scrambled present, was the history of America, exposed like the history of the earth in geological strata. And if architecture expressed the soul of a nation, what could be said for this latest age?

He weighed the city's old hostelries, the Pink Tavern and the Planters Hotel and the Charleston House, against the many-storied Francis Marion and Fort Sumter; and St. Michael's Church against the Gloria, temple of cinema. Other contrasts were no less damning: always the scales tipped heavily to the past. And when he discounted the past's fragments, reminding himself that they were only the relics of an outworn creed, marks of the stagnation end of a long era in architecture and morals, still their weight remained. If buildings were outward and visible signs of inward and spiritual grace, there must have been eminent health and sanity in those faded days. Conversely, these days were eminently mad.

But the old city was dead. Most dead, perhaps, where it was most brightly restored. And, after all, the mess that had emerged from the decay of the earlier integrity was at least alive. This modern welter was a necessary transition between the past and the future; and out of it, someday and somehow, a cultural and spiritual unity would come again, a new age would be born,—an age, by the grace of God, a little finer and wiser than the old.

The New York Ballard Building and its fellows were portents of this great age to come. They were pioneer lances thrust toward the sky, significant in form, functional in character. . . . And what actually was their function? That was the rub. Crowded together, when they cried for space and light. Jostling and jostled Towers of Babel, when they dreamed of towering alone, each the heart of a gardened region, a generous and free community. Their function was to serve as vast warrens of promotion and advertising, hives of high-pressure salesmanship, topped off with penthouses for glorified parasites. Their function was to reduce the good term functional to a violent jest, a bigger and better futility.

When would we grow up, wake to the great future? How long must we hang suspended in a kind of crepuscular fetal sleep and epileptic dreaming, children of neither night nor day? How long must we remain lost, like Charleston, between two worlds: the old dead, the new powerless to be born? . . .

A sudden fork in the road jarred him out of this gloomy rut of reverie. To the right, Savannah; to the left, Beaufort. For a mutinous moment he considered skipping Beaufort. But that would be just another idle protest, and he swung the car to the left and sped on.

The Charleston reflections had successfully dislodged Helen; but when he picked up the map and folded it against the wheel to calculate the remaining distance to Beaufort, the sense of her presence snapped back like a rubber-band. Arrows and jottings in her firm hand demanded his attention.

"Note old dikes and floodgates here—abandoned ricefields."

"Amusing plantation house about here on highway—right."

"Worthwhile side trip—Sheldon—rather nice parish church ruins."

The abandoned ricefields and the amusing plantation house it was impossible not to note, but the worthwhile side trip to the rather nice ruins he snubbed with a pleasant feeling of insubordination.

He caught himself pulling out his cigarettes again, and crammed the package back into his pocket. To break a habit, he thought wryly, it is only necessary to make a fitting substitution. And for all the habits he wished broken what aggregate substitution could beat this healing sunshine, this radiant air, this Southern spring.

Such an aura of beauty invested this sea-island world. Yet it was an essentially melancholy country. But then the whole South seemed that, even where there were hills and no tidewater marshes, no cypress swamps, no cobwebs of moss. . . . He was passing now through a region of truck farms, broad rich acres of vegetables ripening for the markets of the North: a locality of bumper crops, surely, yet the people and their paintless homes betrayed the reign of chronic destitution. A state of affairs that had become thoroughly familiar since Virginia. The South, apparently, was made up of long stretches of rural poverty punctuated by towns of comparative plenty. And this was the "broad fundamental soundness" that was supporting the high towers of prosperity.

Pretty the way all fugitive trails led systematically back to the starting-point, like a labyrinth. Escape *via* Southern Charm was not going so well. Plenty of ground covered, but no progress: nerves still short-circuited, heart heavy as lead, head riddled by morbid moths.

But presently something clicked and flashed in his mind, as if his thoughts had reached a final wall and rebounded. The beauty of the country and the day sprang up around him like flame, enveloping him, taking possession of him within and without. In this benign crucible the worn fragments of his will were fused into wholeness and strength, and he felt himself lifted to a plane of transcendent well-being. It was like the heightened sensibility and appreciation of recovery from long illness. And in the spell of this potent magic a swift piercing snatch of song, a flash of cardinal wings across the windshield, was for an instant his own.

Or was it another mocking-bird, or a rubber duck, a Bronx birdie? . . . And as the spell snapped, he dropped back to the state of mind in which it seemed sufficient achievement to keep one's life going at all, achievement enough to keep muddling along—like the workaday world—on any basis, without benefit of wings or song. After all, he was lucky. He had his Career,—if he could ever get back into the swing of it. And Helen?—well, a pinwheel started out as a triangle and wound up as a sizzling circle, till finally there was nothing left but charred wood, which as a faithful retainer you might be allowed to have and hold forever. For the first time it was possible to feel sorry for Helen, and that was some comfort. It was also comforting to remind yourself that you didn't arrange things but that things arranged you, your role being to take it and like it. To make the best of things,—that was the whole battle. . . . To stop doing the splits and quit caring about the part of you that lagged behind, mourning the aborted dreams of youth. That was it. To throttle the still small voice that kept whispering success was failure, and let yourself go definitely modern Helen's way, not grimly but gracefully, with trimmings. To make the final compromise, negotiate the last lap to the tape she was patiently holding: accept the unfaith that was the faith of her world, and stop thinking of that world as a shambles of dreams,—that was ultimate wisdom.

And with a sigh he foresaw himself at some Western Union desk ahead, sending the inevitable wire inviting her to leave New York and meet him in New Orleans. For a stack of renewing sazeracs, a platter of oysters Rockefeller, and a pack of Camels. She would arrive with one or more of the prize schnauzers; and the Clark family would ride back to its apartment homestead in perfect safety and according to schedule, by way of the Shenandoah Valley in showers of apple blossoms, to make a fresh sporting start.

Definitely neurotic, he admitted. And extremely ungrateful.

II

Rows of palmettoes, flanking the highway like sentinels, gave the approach to Beaufort an air at once orderly and tropical. But this agreeable first impression was rudely shattered by a rash of signs. Arrows pointed to invisible real-estate developments: "Old Spanish Wells", "Beautiful Beaufort Shores", "River View Terrace". A banner, hanging across the road like a political streamer, bore the strange device, *See Mr. Blarker*. The side of a barn boasted that Beaufort had Everything, from Climate to Golf. A billboard in the middle of a sprouting cornfield threatened that "This Folksy Sunshine Garden City by the Sea" would eventually be "Your Dream Home—Why Not Now?". And thereafter a whole string of signs drummed in the injunction of the banner: *See Mr. Blarker, See Mr. Blarker, See Mr. Blarker.*

Evidently something had happened to restful little old Beaufort since Helen's visit. Beaufort, with the aid of Mr. Blarker, seemed to be going Florida. He began to look ahead with alarm.

At the edge of town, and opposite a brick-walled sanctuary labeled "Federal Cemetery No. 1", he stopped for directions at a Moorish filling-station backed by a squad of flimsy new cabins—"Kabin Kamps, $1 up". A clean-cut upstanding youth with a remarkable set of teeth came to the front.

"Looks like you're a long ways from home, sir," he observed with a friendly grin.

The sir and the long ways from home and the bright grin of youth produced a twinge of age in John Clark. When he apologized for not needing anything but directions to a place called Marshlands, the youth whipped a card out of his pocket and presented it with courteous enthusiasm. It said: "GEORGE WASHINGTON TAV-

ERN, Brand New, Minimum Rates, *See Mr. Blarker.*" And the youth, in language that could have been inspired only by Mr. Blarker himself, rattled off a list of the Tavern's virtues, winding up with a little persuasion of his own. "It sure is a fine place to stay, sir. They got Beautyrest beds and private baths just like they say, and country-style meals, and a radio playing in the lobby. Now the old Sea Island Hotel is kinda gone to seed, and Marshlands is kinda high-tone, but you're bound to like the George Washington Tavern, sir."

In the face of all this it was hard to be insistent about Marshlands.

"Well, you see, an old friend recommended the Marshlands place, so I'm afraid I'll have to try it for tonight at least. That is, if you don't think it's too high-tone."

The youth was crestfallen but quickly resilient. "Oh no, sir. It is high-tone like I say—you know, rich folks—but it's a mighty fine place to stay." And he supplied full directions, repeating them to make sure.

"Well, hurry back, sir."

John Clark nodded thanks to the friendly grin and turned the car back to the road, with a feeling of satisfaction at the restoration of the hurry-back tradition. And following directions, he pursued the concrete into town, passing first through a colored settlement of shanties and then blocks of assorted bungalows and old houses.

It was unmistakably Sunday afternoon in Beaufort. A bunch of boys were whooping it up on the village green, but this was highly exceptional; as a whole the little town was taking its day of rest seriously, despite the tonic spring air. A few car-owning families were out on the road, and a few young people were strolling along the path sidewalks, but the majority of the inhabitants were sitting on their porches, rocking and ruminating. Shining somnolence hung over the unpaved side streets, and over the precincts of the Post Office, the Court House, and the Public Library. And Bay Street, where he turned left according to directions, was deserted as the Street of Tombs.

At first glance, as he drove leisurely on (the tempo of the place was contagious), there was nothing to distinguish Bay Street from the main stem of any small town, his own home town for instance. Drab brick offices and stores, an *A & P,* a Busy Bee Lunch, a new bank and a defunct one, an untidy drugstore or two, and a Reliable garage. But on further inspection several items emerged to make Bay Street unusual. First there was the river, with its fishing craft and wharves, glimpsed at intervals between the waterfront buildings. Then there was Mr. Blarker's office, a startling Spanish villa of mottled stucco with Persian leanings and spear-supported awnings over windows and entrance. It was dormant today; evidently Beaufort sabbath was too holy even for Mr. Blarker, though it was hard to believe that he was not out somewhere doing a little quiet afterchurch promoting. But even in repose Mr. Blarker's villa was enough to make any main street, outside of Florida, extraordinary if not unique. And finally, opposite the villa in direct and astonishing contrast, stood an old house of purest Adam design. Paintless and faded, it somehow still retained the spirit and vitality of its prime. Noble, proud, undismayed even by the indignity of a barberpole fastened to its portico, it faced the *See Mr. Blarker* sign and the burlesque establishment across the way with an expression too aloof for contempt.

Near the end of Bay Street a new bridge reached across to a wooded island shore, and he stopped the car for a moment to take in the river scene. The tide was out; marsh flats exhaled a rich salt pungency. An old tire imbedded in the black mud at the foot of the bridge and the haunting cries of sea birds over the channel tended to give the scene a melancholy turn, but the lengthening sunlight touched the marshes and the green of the far shore with a golden felicity. In a cove across the river a cabin cruiser, a houseboat, and a cluster of lesser pleasure craft were moored among dingy workaday boats off a little shipyard. Down the river beyond curving bluffs lay shining open water, where several languid sailboats caught more sun than wind, their slack wings white against the deep blue of the horizon.

Driving on with a sense of remote reassurance, he was confronted at the end of the street by an architectural apparition. No need to read the sign to know that this was the George Washington Tavern and an offspring of Mr. Blarker's fertile brain. Less startlingly garish than Mr. Blarker's office villa, it was decidedly more appalling. It was made up of two distinct parts, joined by a sort of runway: the back part appeared to be an old house disguised with jaundiced stucco to match the front part, which seemed to be of cardboard construction. The feeling of the whole was probably Spanish, though the feature was a Normanish tower, poised like a silo on the brink of the river. To complete the picture an assortment of cars were parked at random on the treeless grounds, and on benches under bare trellis arbors several groups of people were sitting, apparently not yet recovered from the Tavern's country-style bounty. The total effect was not unlike the aftermath of a church picnic with an abandoned carnival concession for backdrop. But it did make a good conspicuous signpost for a left turn. And following the directions of the filling-station youth, he bore to the left and began to look for the next beacon, "a big old house like a castle".

The Castle was a pleasant surprise, particularly after the Tavern. By no means a big house, it still managed to give an impression of bigness; and it looked centuries old. A patina of countless seasons mellowed its walls, and its moldy Tudoresque battlements and chimneys seemed crumbling with age. Only a park was lacking to fill out the picture of an Elizabethan ancestral manor. As it was, the Castle sat unhappily cramped in a musty little garden, enclosed by a rotting brown board fence, which bore marks of an interminable struggle between chalk scrawls and a scrubbing-brush. But these discrepancies were compensated for by the venerable beards of moss that hung from the branches of a druid live-oak in the garden, and by the timeless marsh inlet whose dark mirror reflected one wing of the house. And the air of romantic age was further strengthened by the forbidding aspect of the upper-story windows, all shuttered, and by the heavy vine shroud that covered the entrance porch, hiding the front door. The place was definitely haunted. Its gloomy self-enfoldment, its weary withdrawal, its whole expression of sinister retirement and seclusion and surcease seemed so perfectly congenial to his own ingrown state of mind, seemed to offer such appropriate retreat for a man only one jump ahead of an old-fashioned breakdown, that he wondered what the hazards of approach would be, to see if the ghosts would take to the notion of a paying guest. But on second thought the Castle as an asylum fell flat. This was no place to be cornered by the bloodhounds.

Just beyond the Castle an arrow said Fenwick Street, and he swung to the right. After crossing a rumbling plank bridge,—the sound was a vague profundity, then abruptly and sharply an echo from the old covered bridge on the way to swimming, back in the country of boyhood,—the car settled down to a muffled tread. A small strange world, he thought homesickly. His old swimming-hole bridge thundering in Fenwick Street. . . .

Fenwick Street had evidently once been a fine neighborhood; its interesting old houses sat well back from the roadway and had plenty of elbow room. But now the street had a hopelessly rundown look; the houses were uniformly decrepit, the seedy lawns all ran together through broken picket fences and moth-eaten hedges, and the cobwebbed trees and straggly shrubs only accented the general forlornness. He looked ahead dubiously: Marshlands on the Point was going to be one of those charmingly shabby and inconvenient places.

The gates at the end of the road stood open graciously but inscrutably, and the flanking walls of greenery revealed nothing. So he was entirely unprepared for the little kingdom within. And then it seemed as if forlorn Fenwick Street had been carefully designed as a foil for this surprising place.

A short distance inside the gates the driveway forked, and he stopped to get his bearings and look around. From here he could see only a side of the house, but that was sufficient to satisfy him that it was a beauty. Not so fine in detail as the faded old house in Bay Street, but fine enough. The tabby foundation arches were banked with flowering shrubs, and standing out exquisitely against the whiteness of the house was a crimson swamp maple. A front lawn of fresh green, shaded by great live-oaks and magnolias, reached to a seawall where palmettoes stood watch over marsh and curving river. At his right was a side lawn with a path bordered by perky rows of narcissus and hyacinth, which wound through a mist of dogwood blossoms to a summer-house enfolded by azaleas and half buried under a mantle of wistaria and banksia rose. When he turned to look to the left, on a back lawn the blossom mist was repeated by flowering peaches, white and pink and red. And here gay daffodils were strewn at the feet of the trees, along the edges of the background planting, and at the base of a tall cedar that stood like a plume in the middle of this lawn. Except for the river vista the whole place was enclosed by solid walls of green, and it was as if all the most fragrant essences of spring were held willing captive here. The birds too were captivated by this dream-like little world: the slanting shafts of radiance quivered with their rejoicings.

845

As he was drinking in the heady enchantment of the place, he became aware of someone approaching the driveway from the direction of the summer-house. When he concentrated on the figure, he saw a very stout respectable-looking elderly woman lumbering across the lawn with a heavy rheumatic sway. She paused to wave a tiny handkerchief, and then resumed her plodding journey toward the car. Puzzled, he concluded this reception committee must be just an exuberant guest, for she hardly fitted Helen's description of the mistress of Marshlands. When she finally reached the driveway, she stopped quite out of breath and peered at him nearsightedly, looking a little puzzled herself.

"Oh, excuse me," she apologized, recovering slowly from confusion. Her benevolent smile was made tremulous by a set of treacherously unmanageable teeth. "I thought you were one of Mrs. Winship's young men."

The only answer he could find to make to that, as he stepped out of the car, was to offer an apology for disappointing her, by not being one of Mrs. Winship's young men.

"I have a little message I promised," the benevolent figure went on to explain, modestly disclosing a rolled pamphlet in her handkerchief hand. For a moment she seemed on the verge of giving him the little message anyway, but instead she inquired solicitously: "Are you one of Eleanor's friends from Charleston? Because she's gone to the island for the day with Miss Emily, to see Jane and the baby."

"Why no," he explained in turn, "you see, I'm just arriving for a visit, a short visit."

"Oh," the benevolent figure beamed, "you're just arriving. Isn't that nice. I'm Mrs. Albright,—I come here every winter. This is your first visit, isn't it?"

"Yes, it is," he bowed with a polite smile.

"I thought so. I didn't recall your face. You're not Mr. Clark, are you?"

"Why yes, I am."

"Well," Mrs. Albright nodded with sweet complacency, "I just thought you might be. They had a message from your wife to expect you. She said in the telegram that her name was Helen Mason when she was here several seasons ago, and I remember her well. Such a nice young woman. Too bad she couldn't come with you."

"Yes," he agreed, with a smile that was beginning to feel a little strained.

"I only wish," Mrs. Albright went placidly on to say, "my son and daughter and my grandchildren could be here with me. But of course Everet can't get away from his business—he's high up in Midwest Utilities and they're expanding all the time—and of course the children are in school, so I always have to come South alone. They think it's better for me out of Cleveland weather. But there are always so many nice people stopping here during the season that it's never lonely. . . . Well, I'm very pleased to meet you, but I didn't mean to detain you like this. Now I don't believe there's a soul in the house except Miss Eugenia, everybody seems to have gone out somewhere or other, but I'm sure Miss Eugenia will take good care of you."

After disengaging himself with thanks from Mrs. Albright's benevolent and myopic smile, he got back into the car with a private sigh and followed the right fork of the driveway round to the front of the house.

The spell of Marshlands had been slightly disrupted, but when he stopped at the entrance the spell was restored in full. He sat at the wheel for a minute admiring the proud face of the house. A handsome double porch, challenging the river, gave the front elevation dignity and distinction: tabby steps, flared at the bottom and flanked by a pair of camellia bushes bearing pink blooms among sleek leaves, led up to a fine fanlighted doorway. The heavy old door stood invitingly open; but on the mat crouched a watchdog, a veteran Irish setter, whose expression was far from inviting. I resent this intrusion, he seemed to be saying, and who are you anyway? But on further inspection it appeared that his expression was one of injury rather than hostility, as if he shared Mrs. Albright's plaintiveness because everybody had gone out somewhere or other without him. And when the stranger got out of the car and started up the steps, he rose to the occasion with a wide welcoming swing of his feathery tail and a smile of practiced hospitality.

When repeated taps of the brass knocker on the door failed to bring any response, John Clark decided to follow his host's lead into the hall. It was a spacious and pleasant area, flooded with late-afternoon sunlight from a palladian window at the landing of a generous flight of stairs, which divided there and reversed upward. At his right hand was a dining-room, set with tables of various sizes. A door to the left opened into a living-room. As he stood listening, uncertain what move to make next in this charming but strange establishment, his host went through a series of back-and-forth pacings that clearly indicated the living-room. And when he heeded the promptings and entered, his host disappeared, leaving him stranded.

He found himself in a white paneled room of excellent proportions. The furnishings were thoroughly assorted, from an Empire secretary and Sheraton side-tables through a Victorian horsehair sofa and an old-fashioned square piano to modern lamps and drapes and chintz-covered easy-chairs; but it was a thoroughly livable accumulation, and everything blended into a scheme of harmony and repose. A mantel of good design framed a simmering fire. In the over-mantel panel hung a picture, and here the whole room came to a focus.

He was drawn to the fireside by the picture, a painting of a verandahed old house by the sea. The scene was washed by shimmering sunlight, even the shadows were alive with this warm vibrant light, and the longer he studied the picture the more he liked it. He became so absorbed in its well-handled values and fine points of vision that he failed to respond at once to quick steps in the hall, and not till they stopped abruptly was he able to turn away from the picture. Then he saw that his host the setter had returned, bringing a tall thin pale woman, who stood poised on the threshold with a startled expression. And at first sight he had an illusion of having turned from one picture to another, for the figure framed in the doorway was a picture indeed: a portrait in lilac with throat-band to match and lace trimmings, sharp disdainful features contradicted by timid eyes, and a false-looking mass of raven hair brushed up into a high pompadour that emphasized tallness and was at least partly responsible for the startled look.

Trying not to look startled himself, he hastened to explain his presence.

"I'm sorry,—I knocked, but no-one answered, so I just walked in."

"It's quite all right," the portrait murmured in a demure tremolo, coming to life with a nod of stiff graciousness. "This is open house. Everyone comes and goes as they please."

She ventured into the room with a sort of angular poetry and stood with an easy-chair as buffer between them, eyes blinking rapidly, face working with nervous inquiry. Posed in the doorway she had managed to give an impression of middle-aged maidenliness, but at this closer range he saw that her face was old and etched with tiny lines.

"My name is Clark, John Clark. I've come to stay a day or two if I may."

"Oh yes, of course. I'm Miss Fenwick, Eugenia Fenwick. Rufus informed me of your arrival."

At the mention of his name, Rufus, with an air of duty well done, prepared to settle down on the hearth-rug. But Miss Eugenia Fenwick ordered him away, shooing him as if he were a cat. Casting a reproachful eye at her, and offering the guest a shamefaced grin, he retired with pensive stalking dignity, presumably to the doormat to await further developments.

"He's too spoiled for words," Miss Eugenia explained with a pallid sigh. "Everyone just spoils him to death."

"But he has such good manners."

"He used to have," corrected Miss Eugenia significantly, seeming to imply that everything had been better ordered in some former age of Marshlands. And the faintest suggestion of a smile, a smile of remotest coquetry, touched the thin lips for an instant. But then she quickly resumed her nervous blinking and her expression of startled inquiry. "We've been expecting you for several days, Mr. Clark. Your wife telegraphed."

"Yes,—well, you see," he apologized, longing for the impersonality of a hotel register, "I've gotten behind on my schedule. I overstayed in Charleston."

"It's just as well," said Miss Eugenia. "We've been full right up to yesterday." And she added with a sigh of long-suffering: "This has been our busiest season, and our last, I hope. . . . Mrs. Fenwick is at Land's End on the island, but I'll see if I can find the book, if you'll just have a seat."

She glided across the room to the desk by the piano and began an agitated search for "the book", murmuring harassed dear-me's and let-me-see's, while he turned back to the painting over the mantel, wondering if he should offer to help. "Oh, here it is right under my nose," he finally heard her discover, with a little exclamatory twitter that if it had been a snake it would have bitten her. "Now if you'll just write your name." But when she saw that he had been looking at the picture, she interrupted the formalities to glide over to the fireside.

"That's Land's End where they are today," she explained, blinking at the picture as if its highlights were too strong for her eyes. "My niece Jane painted it."

When he evinced interest, she went on in her constricted tremolo, with an overtone of pride properly tempered with modesty. "Both my nieces are young women of talent. Eleanor, my other niece, paints too and plays the piano very well indeed, but she hasn't much time for anything but her studies just now. She's finishing her course at the Charleston Medical School to become a—I never can remember the name for it but it means a child doctor."

Miss Eugenia remained startled-looking and continued her quick nervous blinking, but she was definitely unbending as she warmed to the theme of her nieces. "Jane's married now and has a husband and an infant son and a plantation to look after, but she keeps right on with her painting as if nothing had happened, and her music too. I declare I don't know how she does it. She's painted portraits of everyone in the family, and even the house servants and some of the island people."

John Clark nodded with patient attention.

"They tell me my portrait is the best she's done yet," Miss Eugenia told the picture over the mantel, "but I can't agree. She and Eleanor both use the new slapdash method and I don't feel it makes for a good likeness at all. I had on this very same dress but you'd never know it,—it came out mauve and magenta and watermelon pink, like a colored person. Jane says, I can't help it, Aunt Gene, that's the way I see it. Well, I tell her, they may have seen things too dark in my day, but at least the colors were true to life. I will say, though, the modeling of the hands came out very well."

Miss Eugenia's hands, which were long and finely tapered, attracted attention to themselves by flitting up to the mantelpiece, where with a tinkle of crystal prisms they straightened one of the girandoles that flanked the frame of the picture. But then she abruptly withdrew them with an abashed almost frightened expression, as if she had been guilty of indecent exposure.

"Many artists," she finished telling the picture in a frail chastened voice, "have admired my niece's work. Are you an artist, Mr. Clark?"

"No," he replied with a smiling shake of his head. And he was prepared to stand his ground on that simple negative. But when Miss Eugenia blinked at him expectantly, even suspiciously, he bowed to her curiosity and added: "I'm an architect."

"Oh indeed," she nodded with an ambiguous little cough; and for a moment she appeared at a loss how to proceed with an architect. But then she discovered that of course he must be interested in the subject of niece Jane's picture, the house itself, Land's End. "It's been in the family for generations. And this house is even older. My great-grandfather built them both." She seemed about to enlarge on this new theme, but checked herself, and, without giving him a chance to express interest in either house, turned back to formalities. "Now if you'll just sign the book,—I don't know much about these matters, but I believe it's the usual thing, first."

He followed her gliding lead to the desk, where she motioned him into a chair, opened a ledger before him with an entirely competent sweep of her elegant old hands, and with another telling sweep supplied him with a pen. While he signed, the hands hovered overhead with a blotter; and when he had finished his scrawl, they descended like swooping birds, blotted, and soared away, leaving John Clark nestling under a group of names bracketed by a common address: Montecito, Calif. Ida Wadhams Winship in bold calligraphy headed the list, followed by three nondescript male signatures. Could this, he wondered, be Mrs. Albright's Mrs. Winship and young men? And as he glanced up the page in putting the pen down, a name at the top caught his eye.

"Not *the* Eugene O'Neill?" he asked with polite incredulity as he got up, thinking of Helen and *Strange Interlude*.

"Yes indeed," nodded Miss Eugenia, stopping her blinking long enough to stare at him with an air of And-why-shouldn't-it-be? "Mr. O'Neill was here for several days last week. He's looking for a place to live on the sea islands. They say he writes the most dreadful plays, but he struck me as being a very mild sad gentleman. . . . Oh yes, we have many famous people. Henry Ford and his family were with us early in the year,—he's buying up whole counties down Savannah River way. And last month we had the President of the

Standard Oil Company of some Northern state or other. Well, I just couldn't begin to tell you all the famous people we've had stopping with us, particularly the past two seasons."

Some wayward thought or emotion compressed Miss Eugenia's thin white lips at this point, and her eyes closed for a moment. "Dear me," she murmured palely, "let me see what comes next." Then her eyes opened and began to blink faster than ever. Her fragile nerves seemed to be going all to pieces, and he quickly abandoned the idea of asking any embarrassing questions about rates. She looked the way he felt; and to keep from blinking back at her, he had to concentrate on steadying details of the room. "Where are we going to put you?" she was asking the world in general with perplexed flitterings of her hands. How about a nice snug strait jacket or a well-padded cell, he thought solemnly. But then, as if in answer to the baffling problem, another Marshlands figure appeared at the door. It was a little old colored woman with a face carved out of polished wood and a dress, apron, and cap immaculate and stiff-starched as a new doll's clothes. Her presence seemed to clear the air at once, and her soft resonant voice was like oil on troubled waters.

"You call me, Miss Gene?"

"Oh, why yes, Lucy," sighed Miss Eugenia in a tremolo of relief. "Where can we put Mr. Clark?"

It restored his balance, this contrast between Lucy's dark royal composure and Miss Eugenia's pale graces and incipient hysteria. He liked Lucy on sight, and was glad that the appraisal of her sagacious old eyes, respectful but penetrating, seemed not disapproving.

"In one de out room, I 'spec'," said Lucy, "fuh tonight anyhow, till some mo' de gues'-folk leabe. You be berry comfortable, suh."

She addressed him with a brief curtsy and smile, and he smiled back and wanted to bow, but refrained out of deference to Miss Eugenia's nerves.

"Has Able come back yet?" asked that startled lady, explaining in a blinking aside that the house servants were perfectly impossible to keep track of on Sunday.

"Yas'm," said Lucy. "He jes' now comin' in de yaa'd."

"Well, tell him to come get Mr. Clark's bags, and be quick about it."

And Miss Eugenia attempted to dispatch Lucy with flits of the

852

elegant harassed hands. But Lucy was not Rufus, to be lightly shooed. Imperturbably she waited till the hands had subsided, and then quietly asked: "Will de ge'man tek tea?"

"Oh yes," nodded Miss Eugenia, "won't you take some tea? Call Mrs. Albright, Lucy,—we won't wait for the others."

At the prospect of a dish of tea between Miss Eugenia and Mrs. Albright, for their good as well as his own he declined with hasty thanks.

"Well," Miss Eugenia sighed to Lucy, "better call Mrs. Albright anyway. And be sure to give us plenty of those little cakes she likes."

"She say she mus'n' tek no cek," said Lucy, "endurin' Lent."

"Never mind about that," replied Miss Eugenia in a sharpened tremolo. "You know she'll expect them, regardless. Now do hurry and send Able, and don't keep Mr. Clark waiting."

This time Lucy withdrew, as silently as she had come. And after a few more blinking moments with startled Miss Eugenia, he too was free to go. Able, Miss Eugenia said, would meet him out front at the car and guide him to his room: Sunday night supper was at seven.

Out on the porch he took a deep breath of the river garden and the golden sunlight. You would have here a very fine place for the nerves, he told Rufus as he patted the silky head, if you and Lucy and the house and garden were all there was to Marshlands. . . . As it is, he thought gloomily, tomorrow's sun will see the fugitive from justice on his weary way again.

From around a corner of the house appeared on the run a coal-black boy in a starched white coat, which he was buttoning as he came. This proved, indeed, to be Able. And riding on the running-board, grinning and gabbling in a dialect ten times thicker than Lucy's, he directed the way round to the back of the house. Here a wide flower-bordered court, with a green bay tree glistening in the slanting sunrays, separated a latticed kitchen yard from a stable garage and a long two-story brick building, where Able called a halt. Evidently once slave-quarters and now "out" quarters for guests, this mellow old building had a set of trim white doors on the ground floor and an outside stairway leading to the upper story. Able, gabbling his sea-islandese, opened one of the white doors and ushered the guest in.

It was a small room with a tight bath. A room no bigger than a cell, yet distinctly pleasant: a fireplace and an easy-chair, a comfortable-looking bed with a monk's-cloth spread, a maple side-chair, an old walnut bureau painted yellow, soft net curtaining at the windows, and on the rough plaster wall an Audubon print of a cardinal and his wife. After Able had brought in the suitcases, and the golf-bag that Helen had insisted on, he lighted the fire "fuh dribe-out de damp". After which he allowed himself to be detained for a minute of grinning talk. His talk was mostly an unintelligible jumble, but it had a grand swing. And when he finally bowed himself out, with a reminder that supper would "staa't se'm shaa'p", there was the crackling merriment of the fire and the agreeable snugness of the room.

It was good to be alone again, with a cheerful fire for company. So he felt at first, standing by it; but a few moments later when he looked at himself in the bathroom mirror, he felt cornered at last. Like a theatrical troupe completely sunk in the sticks, he thought as he turned back to the room to frown at his stranded luggage. A simile Helen would second with applause, for wasn't it her contention that his trouble was simply acute self-dramatics brought on by overwork, brain fag.

When he snapped open the larger suitcase he was greeted by *Time* and *The New Yorker*, both fresh as daisies from a Charleston newsstand. And the comforting bulge of a pajama-wrapped bottle of scotch, thus far neglected because of some strange lingering scruple about drinking alone. He glanced through *The New Yorker*, hoping for a slight touch of nostalgia, but all it had was a stale flat taste, like a morning-after living-room of glutted ashtrays and dead glasses. And when he opened *Time* at random, he landed on the Business & Finance page: "March madness," he read in snatches, "—shrill ecstacy on the Exchange—4,000,000 share sessions—the public has finally come in, tardily, clumsily, at the top as always. . . ." He turned back to the cover, where Harry Sinclair was facing the music with a jolly cigar-toothed jeer, over the caption "Long trials do not a prison make". The Spirit of Prosperity, he decided as he dropped *Time* on the bureau. Never mind, there was also the Spirit of St. Louis. America had wings as well as clay feet. And under the Great Engineer the music in the air would become sweller and sweller. Practically everybody that mattered said so. So it was high treason to harbor any misgivings and low heresy to entertain even lukewarm Democratic leanings, faint liberal wisps of the rebel ideals of youth.

As if election mattered, one way or the other.

What did matter?

Darling, he felt Helen say, isn't the holiday getting a bit thick? At this rate you'll have all your gears stripped. You won't even be presentable.

All right, he told her. Here in this pleasantly padded cell we'll go to the final mat, you and I. And he stretched out on the bed and locked his hands behind his head, determined to think things through.

But when he tried to switch back to New York as a preliminary to the showdown, some small but important part of him refused to move and remained moored in this room. . . . The breath of the garden and the sea stirred the filmy curtains at the window, and from beyond the footboard of the bed the dance of subsiding flames caressed Mr. Audubon's portrait of cardinal and wife. As John Clark's eyes closed with a sigh, he wondered if cardinals had triangle trouble. It was hard to believe. There might be problems on that brightest plane of life, but they would be problems directly met and so no trouble at all. And now the cardinal had left his static frame and was outside, saluting his mate and the world with a scarlet whistle of good cheer. From the garden came close and sharp the ecstacy of mocking-birds mixed with the scrappy brass of bluejays, so that the room was invested and its walls pierced by a multiple music of life. And lying at rest in this joyous turmoil of spring he lost all track of Helen.

Autumn in the city, he thought through fuzzy drowsiness, was not so bad, but spring there was a sorry affair. Spring in the city brought out all barrenness and made a man feel empty and lost: motherless, wifeless, and childless, homeless and friendless. But this Southern spring had a different swing: it was good, it was friendly, healing, fertile. You would have to go far back to remember such a spring. Back to the village and country of boyhood. To the spring that lay between winter's skating and summer's swimming.

He was glad he had had an old swimming-hole in his life. It was one thing that couldn't be lost. Its shapes and voices were there to be recalled at will. . . . Returning in spirit he could bask there alone in an element that was neither water nor earth nor air but the distilled essence of a long summer's day. A peace so still that a splash of water, the song of a meadow lark, the drunken flight of a bee were events of enormous significance in the deep sunshine. And here at last, in this releasing element, all weary confusions were dissolved away, leaving him floating naked and pure, newborn, weightless and free.

III

THE SOUND of a car roused him.

He was conscious then of having already fought off other arrivals. But this one was high-powered, strident and insistent. And when it stopped, with a rip of emergency brake after a final acceleration, a second car took up the refrain. And when this too died, a series of door clompings and a sharp exchange of voices completed his awakening.

Except for soft flashes from the fireplace it was dark in the room, but outside in the court it was still light, though the sun was gone. When he raised himself on an elbow to look out the window, he saw several cars besides his own. By the stable garage stood an old Ford sedan and a shiny new Lincoln, while near the house a Packard convertible was parked next to an elaborate foreign brougham, with G-B and R-F tags attached to its California license-plate to drive the foreign point home. And from this swank vehicle was emerging —with the group assistance of three young white men, a high-yellow chauffeur in cinnamon livery, and a cocky Filipino boy also in cinnamon—a woman.

She was a petite figure, dressed in a style of extreme, almost immature youthfulness; but even from this distance it was plain that she was far from young, mature enough in fact to be the mother of all the young men. As she alighted, with a sort of thwarted daintiness, she teetered precariously for a moment on stilted heels before she could get her balance for an effective stance. After she had given directions to her cinnamon retainers, with gestures as foreign as her car, she collected the three white men and started for the front of the house, by way of a rose and boxwood side garden. And as she minced with ticklish lightness along the brick walk, she paused to admire a bud here and a blossom there, singing exclamations to her trio of escorts. One, a tall and willowy young man, hovered over her appreciating everything. The other two brought up the rear at a stolid pace.

This, certainly, would be Mrs. Albright's Mrs. Winship and young men. More fellow guests to avoid, he thought crabbedly as he pulled out his watch. 3:33, it said, which was absurd on the face of it.

Southern charm seems to be working after all, he decided as he lay back with a yawn and a stretch. Judging from the sundown light outside it couldn't be much past six, so there was still plenty of time before supper at seven. The thing to do was to lie here in peaceful solitude till the last minute and avoid any unnecessary milling around with the guests. And for a few minutes he lay relaxed, enjoying the melodious commotion of wings settling down in the garden under the spell of evening's shadow wand. But presently he became aware of kitchen fragrances wafting into the room with the breath of the garden and the marshes, and hunger began to undermine unsociable caution. Perhaps he was miscalculating the time, perhaps as usual it was later than he thought. And on that basis he decided to get up and take a chance on the house.

When he went out into the court, he found the dusky air fresh and good, brisk but not chilly, just right for a spring evening. He was in the rose garden before he noticed over his shoulder the west's deep orange afterglow ascending through amber to cool jade, where a slender moon hung above the evening star. Here was starlight, first star bright, and a new moon thrown in for good measure: a wish would be doubly sure to come true tonight. And in remembrance of the lost credences of boyhood he pondered what wish to make on this diademed Venus. It would have something to do with being born again, he thought. But when he came out of the garden and stood in the front drive, looking at the dusk-bound river marshes, his wish was forgotten in a memory of city twilight, the remorseless night-blooming splendor of the canyons back North.

To repel the artificial sorcery of streets and towers he crossed the lawn to the seawall, to be close to the natural magic of the river. Veils of mist floated over the marshes like nebulous dreams, and the evening voices of waterfowl echoed the stillness of the dimming far shore. It was undeniably sad, this sea-island dusk, but it was a rich full sadness. A grand sadness. Not the tight jittery distress of the city; of being caged, shut in, lost in a jungle maze of walls and traffic; of being caught short in a panic no-man's-land between the day of business and the night of entertainment opiates. . . . In the city, he thought from the seawall as he watched the shadows stealing out from wooded points to encircle the river, dusk is a moment of fear. An exposure of all the blatant vanities of a labyrinth making less sense, having less purpose than a demented ant-hill. To Helen of course, and to plenty of other stout sports, this conception would be merely morbid, for New York was obviously the cream of the jest. Well, for him the cream had turned. Truth and reality were here in this sea-island country, while there in great Babylon of the hanging gardens all was confusion and vexation of the spirit. There dusk was a moment of unwelcome clarity before the dazzle of the towers came on in glittering tiers; while here dusk kindled the old stars of wonder and freedom, drawing a man out of his lonely little shell to become part of the world's whole greatness. Releasing him from his prison and at the same time restoring him to himself, giving him back the will to face the boundless mystery of existence, the eternity between light and darkness.

Darling, Helen asked without resentment, what if anything would that mean?

You wouldn't understand, he told her. I'm here now, alone and free, my own master. And the air he was breathing was not the poisonous reek of the city but the pure serenity of the isles of the sea. Here in this dusk was the feel of tomorrow's spring dawn already forming; and here was the womb of nature to which all city-trapped men longed to return, whether they knew it or not, to be born again. Yes, rebirth was here, and the nostalgia that troubled the city heart at dusk with glimpses of a new moon, an evening star, a frame of sunset splendor at the end of trammeled streets. . . . But as he watched this dark stream of river curving through the nightfall marshes toward the sea, he perceived that the tide had turned against him, that it was mocking him, flowing backward, northward, toward the city, toward Helen.

He turned his back on the river and started across the lawn toward the lights of the house.

When he opened the front door under the friendly fanlight and went into the hall, he saw there was plenty of company on tap. The living-room was loud with people. But now, confronted with human solace he found he had no stomach for it after all. He felt suddenly too gutless and drained for any mixing with fellow guests.

But it was too late to beat a retreat. Rufus waving a conspicuous tail was coming to greet him, and the living-room conversation was sagging with inquiring glances toward the hall. And Mrs. Albright, peering from a rocking-chair just inside the doorway, was giving him gentle nods of recognition. So he committed himself to the living-room as unobtrusively as possible and joined her, taking a firm stand by her rocker for an exchange of weather pleasantries.

When the weather was exhausted and Mrs. Albright showed signs of going introductory, he brought up the subject of Marshlands' spring garden to hold her attention. Then, feeling safely moored here, with the conversation of the room back in full swing, he relaxed a little and began to take casual note of his fellow guests. They were divided into two opposing camps of chatter: one near group by the piano and the desk, another and larger group over by the fireside. And he was vaguely wondering what Helen would make of this collection of sojourning Yankees when suddenly, with an agreeable shock, his eyes were arrested by one sharply particular figure in the fireside group.

She stood facing him with her back to the fire, and in the first flash of revelation she herself seemed an expression of fire, a straight slender flame burning upward to a crest of glowing gold. Even in a second moment of clearer vision, when he was able to note details, —the soft yellow undersweater she was wearing with a cardigan and skirt of soft green, and the perfect architecture of her legs, and that her hair was not golden blond but light brown,—she remained enveloped in an aura of flame like a girl in a dream. Come, come, he told himself rationally; but her eyes meeting his brought out the surprising lunacy, Haven't we met somewhere before? Lunatic yet unquestionably true, he felt, and she seemed to acknowledge its truth of instinctive recognition with a smile that made his head spin. She nodded and her lips moved, and he tried to read their message through Mrs. Albright's placidly insistent appreciation of the garden. But then he realized with a flush of chagrin that the smile, the nod, and the words were intended not for him but for the woman on the fireside sofa and for the young men of the group. And now even her eyes were denied him as she turned to speak to one of the young men.

But now the whole aspect of the room was changed. It was charged with an electric exhilaration. And the people looked different: they were warmed to interesting life by the flame of her. And now his one desire was to meet these fellow guests, have Mrs. Albright pass him on, touching off introductions that would carry him around to the fireside. But Mrs. Albright was a body not easily deflected; he had started the subject of Marshlands' spring garden and Mrs. Albright was finishing it, contentedly and at leisure. Her initial introducing tendencies having been discouraged, it was slow work getting her back on that track.

"Oh," she finally discovered "you haven't met any of these folks, have you." And she leaned to the left with a tactful cough to attract the attention of the piano-desk group of two men and a woman. "Oh, Mrs. Marks," she beamed in her sweet placid voice to the woman, "I just wanted to introduce Mr. Clark to you folks."

Mrs. Marks, a handsome woman impeccably correct, took him over with a gracious smile and presented him to her companions, her husband and a Right Reverend Mr. Macbeth. Both Mrs. and Mr. Marks were in riding attire, he in boots, she in jodhpurs, but they were too well-groomed and well-mannered to be anything but rankly amateur horsey: they smelled not of the stable and saddle but of Abercrombie & Fitch, and they had an air of being atmosphere in a society movie. And no-one would have suspected Mr. Macbeth of being Right Reverend; a bloated tweedy gentleman in knickers with a ready jocularity and without a trace of any clerical nonsense about him, he looked more like a conventioning banker than an anointed apostle of the Lord: he was plainly a man of the fashionable high-church world, at ease in all well-fed circles, and an expert fixer for rich camels worried about the eye of a needle. None of these three worthy people would have inspired much enthusiasm at any other time or place but here and now as means to a suddenly important end they were people to be treated with prompt respect.

After Mrs. Marks had established a basis of acquaintance with a few well-chosen questions and answers, Mr. Marks gave the conversation the inevitable financial slant. "How," he asked in a consequential tone, "did the market feel when you left? I try to keep in touch while touring, but you can't get the real feel of the ticker here in the South, with Radio jumping twenty points a day! Dangerous, don't you agree?"

Very dangerous, John Clark quickly agreed, hoping that would settle it and provide a lull and somehow a transition to the fireside group. But Mr. Marks was not satisfied with agreement: he wanted an argument, and when none was forthcoming he supplied it himself. The whole list should be sold short, he contended, and in the next breath he maintained that no man could afford to buck the trend. It was high time, he insisted, to get out from under all this pyramiding; and then he contradicted himself by citing the horrible example of a friend who had lost his nerve and gotten out of General Motors only to find he couldn't get in again. Whereupon the Right Reverend Mr. Macbeth stepped jovially in with word of an important parishioner of his, who from time to time favored him with confidential advice and had recently recommended that aviations were the best buys on the board, because of the impending rearmament race. For purely speculative purposes the friend liked the looks of Warner Brothers. When Mr. Marks denounced these recommendations, the Right Reverend beat an amiable retreat: after all, the market-place was not his province.

But golf was, decidedly. Dr. Macbeth, it seemed, was enjoying a sabbatical year of golf. And when he suggested a foursome for tomorrow, John Clark hastily accepted with the Markses, hoping to clear the way for an introduction to the fireside group without further delay. But the golf talk went blithely on.

He was beginning to feel definitely stymied, when, as if in response to his impatience, a member of the fireside group came to the rescue.

It was the tall willowy one of the young men, the three escorts of the elaborate little woman whose arrival in the courtyard had roused him from dreaming of the old swimming-hole. And after affably addressing Dr. Macbeth and the Markses, this providential stepping-stone to the fireside introduced himself with suave informality. Ainsworth Peck was the name, and he looked a complete New Yorker of the Madison Avenue decorator school. There was a slight touch of haberdashery swish in his smooth and easy manner but it was well under control, and under the circumstances it was a pleasure to have him take you by the arm and, with apologies to Mrs.

Marks for borrowing you for a moment, lead you over to the fireside.

But before being presented to the girl he was seeking, John Clark found himself facing the woman on the sofa.

"Lucky," crooned Ainsworth Peck, "this is Mr. Clark. Mr. Clark, Mrs. Winship."

He tried not to look startled at the sofa face and form. The form was bulging out of a tight mannish pin-striped *tailleur* softened by a very feminine cascade of chiffon at the throat. The face, under a rakish chapeau and a fringe of henna'd curls, looked like something from the French Court just before the Deluge: the ravished cheeks were daubed with rouge, the large nose was caked with powder, and the bouffant mouth heavily and crudely vermilioned. Traces of lipstick showed on vigorous teeth when the lips parted in greeting; and strong bright eyes, hooded and pouched, squinted almost shut with pleasure as Mrs. Winship leaned forward to extend a lax hand that seemed to expect to be bowed over in a French salute.

"Oh, Mr. Clark,—how nice," she purred in a voice a little too mellifluous and diffident to rhyme with the masterful eyes.

"Eleanor dear," she looked past him to nod dulcetly, "—Miss Fen-wick, Mr. Clark." And she relinquished him long enough to turn and meet the flame. Eleanor dear, he repeated to himself as he bowed formally to Miss Fenwick: and now he was able to see that her eyes were clearest blue, direct and frank, and that her smile was perfection. Eleanor, he thought with deep satisfaction; but then Ainsworth Peck crooned in facetiously, "And shake hands with. . . ." The names of the two other young men failed to register, their faces came as blanks, and he noticed only that they were no match for Ainsworth, being neither tall nor willowy, neither polished nor perfumed. And then, as he was turning back to Eleanor, Mrs. Winship reclaimed him.

"Won't you sit here, young man," she beckoned, patting the sofa with a peremptorily seductive hand. And when he was seated beside her, she fixed him with an expression of the most intense approval. "You're just the man I've been wanting to meet. Miss Eugenia tells us you're an architect. And Ainsworth says you're an important architect. Ainsworth, dear boy, is a perfect Who's Who,—he knows simply everyone important."

She flashed Ainsworth a glance of appreciation which he returned with a smile of languid self-deprecation. "Not quite that bad, Lucky. But I do happen to know that John Clark is the white-headed boy of our New York skyline."

"But how marvelous!" Mrs. Winship squinted with delight. "Isn't it marvelous the important people one meets quite by chance?" she asked, appealing to each of the group in turn: Eleanor, Ainsworth Peck, the two other young men, and finally the white-headed boy himself.

This seemed to call for more comeback than a mere laughing-off, internally wry.

"I'm afraid," he explained to Mrs. Winship's distended expectancy, "there's some mistake. I'm just a plain hack draftsman. Just a step-child of the setbacks, and petty observer of the zoning laws."

Which Mrs. Winship found charming, while Ainsworth applauded. But the other two young men remained abstracted and unimpressed; and Eleanor's eyes, though smiling, were calmly taking his measure. He offered her a silent apology and challenge: Sorry, but what would you do with the situation? And he added a mute appeal: I want to talk to you or just look at you and these people are in the way, can't you help?

"But what refreshing modesty," Mrs. Winship insisted. "And what a happy chance meeting for me. Eleanor, dear child, won't you entertain the boys while I improve the shining hour and tell Mr. Clark my problems."

And having thus segregated the sofa, with neatness and dispatch, Mrs. Winship proceeded without further preliminaries to make the most of the happy meeting.

Her problems, it developed, were highly architectural and she felt helpless before them. She had just acquired a superb old house on the Battery in Charleston, and she felt keenly the responsibility of owning such an heirloom; obviously it must be treated with utmost respect, it must of course be restored *literally*, but she was at a loss how to do it the justice it deserved while also doing justice to such elementary modern conveniences as plumbing and heating. This morning in the wee hours she had hit upon a scheme for installing a little elevator system running up through closets from floor to floor, and she had worked out a rough plan for partitioning off the bathrooms, but how to conceal hot-water pipes and furnace ducts

864

without tearing the walls and paneling apart? And on top of all this she was in the throes of buying a plantation, a sea-island shooting-box to go with the Charleston town house. She had found just the thing, she thought, in Holly Hill on the Combahee River near Beaufort; but it would require a new house, a large informal country place with guest cottages to match, and she confessed the idea of building terrified her: she wondered whether she had the stamina and courage for such an undertaking. So Holly Hill still belonged to its present owner Judge Bramwell, a kinsman of Eleanor's.

"You have very interesting problems," John Clark agreed with an appropriate frown, taking advantage of the opening to glance at Eleanor. But Mrs. Winship promptly recalled him to the sofa quarantine.

"I felt you'd understand," she smiled firmly. "But why do I bore you with my little troubles."

"Not at all," he assured her, trying to look strictly interested.

And as she went firmly on he became interested in spite of himself. Not in her troubles but in the woman herself. From certain lapses in delivery, particularly from a tendency of broad a's to go short and an inability of international accents to sustain themselves, he concluded that Mrs. Winship was not to her great-world manner born: there were traces of early silver-spooning, but her technique was of a much later stage and suggestive of indefatigable practice, probably with too many mirrors: her personality had been lifted at a fairly recent date and showed sagging scars behind the ears. But it didn't matter; she might be a bad actress, wobbling in and out of character, but she had an act that could hardly be ignored. And her voice was really magnificent, ranging from high flamboyant assurance to an appealing falter. In its artful modulations, and the accompanying shrugs, head tilts, and eyebrow play, the grotesqueness of henna'd curls was not only forgotten but actually translated into a kind of hideous charm. And even more remarkable than the voice and its accessories were the hands, which had an idiomatic life of their own. They gave an impression of being incased in tight gloves, and were further handicapped by arthritic bumps at their arched and lacquered tips, but they were amazingly vital and expressive, as fascinating to watch as an expert puppet-show.

"But meeting you," the voice was now narrowing down to a note of consummate simplicity, "gives me new courage. Frankly, young man, I take heart, feeling you will help me. I feel it has meaning for us both, this chance meeting."

"Why yes, of course,—anything I can do," he agreed mechanically, hypnotized by the compelling eyes. "You're really settling quite definitely in this neck of the woods, aren't you."

"Yes, isn't it," the bright eyes squinted with pleasure, and his words were repeated caressingly as if they were rare and special, "Yes, I'm really settling in this neck of the woods." But then the eyes opened wide, wavered, and fell, and the hands performed a pantomime of journey's end, the voice low and wayworn. "Yes, this is to be headquarters and home. Home at last. And what a long long search it's been."

Looking at the ravished face it was easy to believe that. And now the mobile mask was no longer a hangover from the French Court but the very countenance of the Wandering Jew. Even the eyes, fixed on him again, seemed to take on a deep dark cast and become the persecuted orbs of the pilgrim of the ages, the eternal home-seeker.

"I couldn't begin to tell you what a search it's been," she intoned wearily. She made an attempt at it, however, with hands galvanically excursive. "What divine discontent is it that drives us hither and yon like ships at sea, always seeking the golden clime? I've lived everywhere. Simply everywhere, in the States and abroad. Yet no place has held me. For a time I thought California was truly *simpatico,* a veritable Arcady, but even there one comes to feel rootless in the end. What is it, the pioneer crudeness of the country, the lack of tradition and finesse, a sense of living among the disinherited of the earth? Is it too many retired shopkeepers and farmers and—what does one call them—tincan tourists? Or is it simply too much sunshine?"

Knowing the Golden West only by hearsay he was unable to help her decide and could only share her puzzlement, while his inner attention tried to concentrate on Eleanor, busy entertaining the boys.

"In any case," Mrs. Winship shrugged sadly, "I weighed California and found even San Francisco wanting." And now her voice assumed a dramatic present. "One morning the emptiness of the climate jolts me like an earthquake and I flee, literally flee, leaving the servants to pack and close my Santa Barbara estate. I return to the East in despair and instruct my agents to throw the place on the market! And then," her voice faltered to a whisper, "I remember the South, my South, the place of my birth."

"Are you a Southerner?" he asked in genuine surprise, and added politely, "I thought you might be French."

The bright eyes flashed and squinted riantly and the voice purred with vivid intimacy: "Did you really? But how charmingly *naïf*. And yet you are not without reason. I have lived so much in Paris that even there I am mistaken for a native. But no, I am Southern. In fact I am planning a twofold tribute to my birthright. First, I wish to encourage struggling young Southern artists. And second, I want to bring birth-control to my Southland. Tell me, do you believe in birth-control?"

"Well," he stammered, "I'm afraid I haven't given it very careful thought."

"Ah, isn't that the way of youth," sighed Mrs. Winship indulgently. "But I have given it much thought, and with me it has become a passion. My plan is to start with the colored people at Holly Hill plantation—presuming of course that I do buy the place—and from there to branch out with tactful clinics in every direction. But before we can go into all this, young man, I fear you and I must become better acquainted. For you see I remain at heart as Victorian as my darling mother, and it is not easy for me to overcome the restrictions of a modesty that does not trouble you of the younger generation."

And with an air of plushest modesty she dismissed the subject and turned back to her return to the South, while Eleanor continued obligingly to entertain Ainsworth Peck and his two glum associates.

"Yes, Mr. Clark, we meet at the hour of my homecoming. Formerly I felt that there were but three rules for happiness: someone to love, something to do, and something to hope for. But of late I have come to realize that one other rule must be added to the formula: to live where one's childhood roots are. So you find me returning like a homing pigeon to take up my life where it began, among my own people. Actually, I was born in a little Texas town, and there someday"—a slight catch hampered her voice for the moment—"I shall rest beside my dear husband. But now I confess I prefer this coast country to the inland plains. And after all, Texas and Carolina, is it not all one, all South. Tell me, how do you like my country?"

"Why, who could resist it?"

Mrs. Winship seemed to take this as a subtly personal tribute. She squinted and sighed archly. "Who can resist it, that is it. Dear funny old South, so backward, so down-at-heel and shiftless, so appallingly provincial, and yet so proud, so steeped in tradition, so—gallant! Even its faults grow on one and become virtues, till in the end one finds oneself completely enamoured. Yes, your eyes show fatigue from the city but already they have a new light. And it is the same with me. Ah, but that you a Northerner should appreciate my South at once, love at first sight as it were, while I have taken so long to awake! . . . Of course I shall still travel a little, but now only for the joy of coming back to my Carolina Low Country. Yes, this is to be home at last. And the prodigal will make amends for long absence. I shall use all my resources to help the colored people and keep young talents from wasting themselves on the desert air. The South, I feel, trembles on the verge of a great renaissance, and I shall do everything in my power to encourage it." . . . Her voice veered abruptly to an almost plaintive humility. "But tell me, young man, do my plans make you feel I suffer from the delirium of grandeur?"

The sudden climaxing strangeness of the question made him suffer a slight internal delirium, but he managed to give her a solemn enough answer. "Why no, not at all,—quite the contrary."

"Yes," she nodded with an expression of the most childlike innocence and sincerity, "quite the contrary, that is just. Because I assure you, young man, I suffer from the inferiority complex. You will find me at bottom a very simple person, and in spite of my means a very lonely and helpless person, greatly in need of friendship and advice."

Fortunately at this strained point there was a welcome intrusion. Out of a clear but well-timed sky Rufus, the Irish setter, presented himself at the sofa, sat down, and extended an understanding paw. John Clark shook hands gratefully, relieving himself of accumulated amusement with a congested laugh. And the interruption gave him an excuse to turn back to Eleanor, who was appreciating the incident. You see, he told her, your dog approves of me. But her smile, though profoundly exhilarating, seemed thoroughly impersonal.

"But how charming!" Mrs. Winship purred in vivaciously. And

taking the center of the stage, she leaned forward till her lips were within an inch of Rufus's nose. In her little *pied-à-terre* at Washington, she assured him in baby patois, she had a Parisian poodle, Mademoiselle Mimi Froufrou, who was coming South soon. Mimi was chic, Mimi was very affectionate, Rufus would be mad about Mimi. But Rufus ignored Mrs. Winship's blandishments. He yawned in her face, in fact, and with a panting smile reoffered his paw to John Clark, who glanced at Eleanor for approval. And now it did seem that her smile was not quite so impersonal.

"You must come on our next picnic, boy," Mrs. Winship purred over Rufus, patting his silky red head to prove she harbored no resentment at his rude behavior. "Oh, we had such a thrilling picnic today!" she exclaimed to the fireside group as a whole. "The spring woods were simply heavenly, and the plantation darkies serenaded us with spirituals and other native airs. And we met the dearest old darky woman coming home from church carrying her shoes and smoking a pipe!—we crossed her palm with silver and she told all our fortunes. And Ainsworth took movies of everything. We must have another picnic tomorrow. And you mustn't fail us this time, Eleanor dear."

"I'm afraid I can't go tomorrow, thank you, Mrs. Winship," Eleanor answered, in a voice that warmed John Clark to the core.

"But what a pity," Mrs. Winship sighed, her lips twitching with some devious calculation. "But we won't reproach you, child. We know you must have much to do in your Easter holiday. And then your dear family has a prior claim on your time. Really I consider it impertinent of us to try to seduce you with our little frivolities. But you, young man," she veered, lightly touching John Clark's sleeve and then settling back into her original sofa pose, "we count on you to join us."

And firmly fixing him again, she sped on, hands volatile and incisive. "You must see the plantation at once, and help me decide what type of house to build. A pure Georgian house would be most suitable, of course. But don't you feel that even in the purest of Georgian houses one can afford to strike a French note in the boudoir suites? The reception rooms should have a feeling of classic restraint, but wouldn't it be a mistake not to let oneself go a little in the bedchambers?"

A decided mistake, he agreed with absent attention.

"I think," Mrs. Winship pressed on, indicating the fireplace with a fine flourish, "we should try to capture the spirit of that mantel. We should build the house around a copy of it. Isn't it a beauty?"

"Perfect," he nodded with enthusiasm.

"Such charming simplicity," pursued Mrs. Winship. "Such honesty and restraint. But perhaps too much restraint."

"A little too much restraint," he agreed.

When his attention failed to return to her from the mantel and Eleanor, Mrs. Winship became restive and a metallic note appeared in her melodious voice. "Oh, but you must see the mantel upstairs. It's really *exceptional.*" And leaning toward him she added in a sharp whisper, with a circular glance that took in all the fireside group but pointedly excluded the Marks-Macbeth group by the piano and Mrs. Albright in her rocker: "There's just time for a cocktail before supper,—give me one minute's headstart and then come up to my room, all of you."

And without waiting for anyone to accept or decline, Mrs. Winship took Ainsworth's alert hand, rose gallantly from the sofa, and accompanied by his hovering strides minced voluptuously out of the room.

Abruptly released by this sudden departure, John Clark found himself free to concentrate on Eleanor without interference. The problem now was to avoid studying her directly, openly, as she stood talking to the two young men that Mrs. Winship had thoughtfully left behind. And to keep from falling into a frank stare of pleasure he turned his attention to rubbing Rufus's sleek head, allowing himself only casual glances now and then in Eleanor's direction.

She was applying a friendly poultice to the defensive egos of the two young men, drawing them out of their sullen shells, and in the absence of their patroness they were responding like a pair of sleep-walkers surprised by the sun. One was a sad-eyed bird built like a wrestler and with a head bald as an eagle's, while the other was a sawed-off elf with a wild eye and wilder hair; both looked generally untidy. A fine pair of pets, he decided, jealous of the attention they were getting. Why didn't Mrs. Winship have the common decency to keep them on a leash. . . .

He was much obliged when the pair, after a few moments of unbending, decided that Mrs. Winship's headstart minute was up.

Allowing Eleanor to beg off, and ignoring him, they made a hurried exit for the hall and stairs.

When they were gone he joined her, standing beside her with his back to the fire. But though elated at having arrived at this close contact, he felt no nearer to her. In fact he felt farther away, for her words of polite interest in his Marshlands visit seemed to rebuke his urgent interest in her, requesting him to stay at an amicable distance. She was treating him just as she had treated the others, in the same friendly natural manner, as if there were no distinction between them and him, and he watched in vain for some trace of his own agitation in her voice or eyes. . . . What else could he expect, he wondered, presumption sobering. What did she know about him beyond what she could see, small recommendation certainly, and what she must have heard, that he was married. As for his feelings, if she was reading them between the strained lines of his talk, she must be rating him a little too susceptible. But despite this tightening sense of disqualification, he still was able to reassure himself with the odd notion that she must be sharing his awareness of an electric current or he wouldn't be feeling it so keenly.

A moment or two later Mr. and Mrs. Marks discovered it was time to change for supper and obligingly withdrew; and the Right Reverend Mr. Macbeth followed, dropping a few unctuous words in Mrs. Albright's ample lap in passing. And then a colored maid appeared at the door, announcing supper, and Mrs. Albright, parting company with her rocker, lumbered swayingly across the hall to the dining-room. But the fireside situation remained stubbornly unchanged. Now he was alone with her, but no better off. Worse off if anything, for now his end of the conversation was dropping into air-pockets: cross-tensions of exhilaration and anxiety were making him feel like a tongue-tied schoolboy, while she remained undisturbed as before. He was glad she didn't commit herself lightly, he told himself by way of encouragement, wishing in the same breath that she would slip for a split second into making a little less sense.

"Aren't you going up to see the mantel in Mrs. Winship's room?" she was asking him.

"Isn't it time for supper?" he countered with a lame smile, wondering if she was trying to ease him off her hands.

"That's just the first call. There's plenty of time for the mantel, unless you're too hungry."

"I'm starved. But I'll go if you will."

She nodded at a closed door to the left of the fireplace. "I'm waiting to see Uncle Joe. He's still closeted with Mother."

"Well," he told her obstinately, "I'm afraid I can't make it without support."

"All right, come along then," she surprised him by giving in, with a little laugh that made his blood race.

Following her out of the room was like walking on air. But in the hall on the way to the stairs he was brought down to earth by a jarring thought. Was she supporting him to avoid offending Mrs. Winship, who would blame her if he failed to appear? Or perhaps it was for the sake of Uncle Joe's plantation, for any stimulating architectural effect he might have on the pending deal. But she was incapable of such calculating, he quickly retracted, ashamed of his suspiciousness. No, she was just being courteous and obliging, accommodating one of the guests.

Being just an accommodated guest was no buoyant role, yet he was floating light-headed again in the pleasure of her company when they started up the stairs. But he was not in too ethereal a state to appreciate the deep grooves in the stair treads, worn by generations of her family and by her own steps since childhood. And the stair rail had a tingling feel that was almost like touching her hand, and through her the hands of the past, making him part of this friendly old house; giving him an acute awareness, a sense of recognition and belonging, as if he had always known this place of her birth and had climbed these stairs many times before.

At the landing the palladian window framed a picture that seemed more than familiar: bright crescent moon and evening star, above treetops and chimneys silhouetted darkly against the last afterglow in the west. And he wanted to stop here to tell her— what? Anything, before this moment alone with her was lost, before they were back again in the coils of Mrs. Winship. But the very pressure of necessity gagged him with its mounting briefness; and as they left the landing and went on up the stairs together, he ended by hastening the reintrusion of Mrs. Winship with a question he wanted to withdraw the instant he found himself asking it.

"Would Mrs. Winship," he whispered, "be an oil queen, or is it Listerine or Jell-o?"

"I think it's oil," came the whispered answer.

There was no rebuke in her voice, but facetious inquiry about guests of the house was scarcely the way to improve his standing with her. And he cursed himself and Mrs. Winship.

As they reached the upstairs hall, the oil queen stood poised teeteringly expectant in the doorway of a large discreetly-lighted bedroom, puffing a gallant cigarette. Somehow, possibly with the aid of a screen in the corner, she had managed to change from her tight tailored suit into an even tighter knitted sports dress of coral pink, which framed her royal squabbiness to perfection, while in the background hovered Ainsworth Peck noisily mixing martinis,—the two other young men, the bald wrestler and the shaggy elf, looking on with morose interest.

"But we had almost given you up!" sang Mrs. Winship, welcoming the arrivals into the room with hands flamboyantly gracious. "Eleanor dear, how specially sweet of you to come, since you don't take cocktails and must risk being bored. Sit here, dear, in this comfortable chair by the fire,—boys, pass Eleanor the cheesesticks and artichokes and do try to be entertaining. And now, young man, won't you come sit with me."

And mincing like a toe-dancer, Mrs. Winship led the way to a large pinewood lounge facing the fireplace with its back to the room's twin beds.

"One calls this an Aiken day-bed, I believe," she observed parenthetically as she approached it with a conciliatory sidle, committing her coral-pink back to its depths with cautious abandon. The Aiken day-bed was not designed to gracefully accommodate Mrs. Winship's particular build, but by wriggling and arranging her abbreviated skirt she was able to attain a position of some dignity and repose, one plump leg tucked girlishly under her, the other dangling overboard exposed from tight alligator pump to knee. "If we buy the plantation and build," she added with a little cough of relief in a wave of perfume, patting the space beside her invitingly and then signaling Ainsworth to speed the cocktails, "we must order several of these, one for the taproom and one for each of the guest cottages, don't you think."

He nodded agreeably, with a silent sigh for Eleanor; and after receiving a cocktail and napkin from Ainsworth he settled himself on the Aiken day-bed, as far as decently possible from Mrs. Winship's knee. Then he took in the room's oyster-white paneling, cornice, and mantel in a glance that brought him to Eleanor's chair, flanked by the elf and the wrestler, who had already emptied their glasses and were looking for more.

"This used to be the drawing-room and ballroom, didn't it, dear," Mrs. Winship purred stringently at Eleanor, commanding all attention. And giving the room an understanding appraisal she closed her eyes for a moment with a dramaturgical little sigh. "One feels the vibrations of the past so intensely here." But then her voice recovered its most vital pitch. "Ah, but now we have our brief hour on the stage. And haven't we a salon! A young lady student of medicine who is also a gifted pianist": this sweetly for Eleanor. "A poet and a painter": with a nod to the wrestler and the elf. "Ainsworth sings. And in you, my friend, we have the brilliant young exponent of architecture. While for me, I humbly pursue every art, not as a dilettante, I prefer to think, but as a lover, an amateur in the French sense. *Alors.* Shall we not drink a toast to our little circle?"

There was some confusion and delay while Ainsworth reprovingly refilled the glasses of the elf and the wrestler, and then Mrs. Winship touched John Clark's glass with her own. "Ah, what it must be to create a skyscraper! People take the miracles of the age so for granted, but for me I am in a constant state of wonder and admiration. Really, young man, I can't tell you how your skyscrapers affect me. Your marvelous shafts, they stir and thrill me with their gallant upthrust. A toast then to your handiwork, your—what can one say—your frozen music!" And fixing him with wide unblinking eyes Mrs. Winship trumped her own ace with a sudden *"Prosit!"*

Then she dropped her voice to a whisper that effectively insulated the Aiken day-bed. "I find," she confided, stressing hand and eyebrow articulations to make up for softness of tone, "I am losing interest in painting and poetry. Since acquiring the house in

874

Charleston I find myself turning to architecture. There is something so real, so substantial there. That is to say, one's head may be in the clouds but one's feet remain firmly on the ground, so to speak. Don't you agree?"

It was impossible to do anything else, with this resourceful obstacle preventing him from looking Eleanor's way or even listening for her voice, through the jabbering blockade of Ainsworth, the elf, and the wrestler, all three now encamped round her chair.

"Won't you smoke one of mine for a change?" Mrs. Winship insisted, producing a tortoise-shell cigarette-case with *Ida Wadhams Winship* in letters of gold, and then flourishing a lighter startlingly initialed *I. W. W.* . . . . "*Voilà,*" she squinted in delight when the lighter decided to work. And snuggling back, she asked archly: "Now really isn't this *gemütlich*—cozy? Where were we? But of course!—architecture."

But then this complex human predicament shot off at a new tangent of confidence. "Of course," she conveyed in a nimble undertone, between quick puffs of her cigarette, "Ainsworth will stay. He is not only a bachelor of all the decorative arts but also the only person who appreciates the burden of my affairs, the endless strain. And yet when it comes to deep understanding, even he fails me there. Poor undiscerning *Cheri,* he sees me as Proustian intellectual with a dash of Colette, whereas at heart I am a plain little *hausfrau*. Alas, fate has arranged for me *la vie vagabonde* when it is *la vie domestique* for which I have always yearned. To create an atmosphere of home. And can that not be a great art? Life itself—gracious living—is that not perhaps the greatest of the arts?"

She paused on that tilted note, and caught him glancing Eleanor's way. The bright eyes flashed metallic glint, but the next instant they were glazed with verve. "Do you mind if I call you by your first name, even though you are married. 'Mr. Clark' sounds so absurdly distant. And if you wish you may call me Lucky." And dropping her voice to its humblest register, she added apologetically: "One hesitates to rush friendship, isn't it, but time is so short, so—inexorable. Too desperately so for trivialities. You who are still young, you cannot feel that yet, the ticking of the clock, the awful pressure of time. . . . *Si jeunesse savoir,*" she chanted slowly, softly, "*si vieillesse pouvoir*. Ah, if youth only knew, if age but could."

She hung suspended on that sad strain, as if expecting contradiction. But under the awful pressure of time and her attention his endurance was crumpling, and his only response was an abstracted nod.

"But why," she then demanded of herself with a veering shrug, "why do we talk about me? Let us talk about you, my friend, you and your work. And the strange *à propos* of our meeting. . . . Fate, Deity, the Stars," she intoned confidentially with gestures, "who can say what power arranges our affairs? But the moment I saw you I knew at once we were in tune. *En rapport.* You see, I get at people through some fourth dimensional faculty, a sort of wireless telephony,—waves, vibrations. Something mental, possibly. I can't explain it, I can only feel it. It frightens me at times, but it never fails."

And she added in a hesitant murmur: "I feel that we come to each other in an hour of mutual extremity. I freely admit I need you. In Charleston I find no eager young architects to help me, only tired old mossbacks. So I humbly seek your support, your counsel and guidance. Money will not tempt you, I know,—though of course I would set no limit to the sums at your disposal,—so I must appeal to you on the simple grounds of friendship. And, frankly, I feel you need me too. New York has drained you. You need a complete change and rest from the hurly-burly of that life. Is it not so?"

"Oh, I feel better already," he managed to stammer.

"Do you really?" she smiled demurely; then frowned with concern. "But it is not enough that you escape for a week or a month. You must learn to relax. You must put yourself in my hands for a time, as I shall put myself in yours."

She paused expectantly, but before he could think of anything rational to say, she dashed on, vividly, almost with abandon, as if pursued by all the hounds of time. "These two struggling young men you find me helping at the moment, I'm tired of trying to wean them away from the primitive in art. This summer they can go to Mexico as they wish and dabble in the peon to their heart's content. Tell me, how much have you been abroad?"

"Not much," he confessed groggily. "We went to Sweden on our honeymoon."

That seemed to throw Mrs. Winship off for a moment, but

only for a moment. "Ah yes, Sweden," she sighed, "Venice of the North. What a novel place for a honeymoon. Dairy maids and modern architecture, what a delightful combination." And smiling without mirth, she darted on. "Ainsworth tells me your wife is such a charming person,—he met her at the Colony Club or Junior League theatricals or somewhere. I must get in touch with her at once. But perhaps she needs a holiday of her own. I know you modern young people. With you ties do not bind too tightly, and you understand far too well the value of variety."

With that Mrs. Winship's magnetic field suffered an abrupt eclipse; and as his attention shifted to Eleanor, he found it hard to even stay aware of his companion on the Aiken day-bed. He sensed only remotely her struggle to recover poise from realization that she had slightly overplayed her vibrations.

"But I shan't press you for an answer now," he heard her say in a tone reproachfully formal. *"Plus tard.* I fear hunger is making us a bit distrait. We are quite forgetting supper, isn't it. And the mantel!"

And joining his slant toward Eleanor, she called out melodiously: "Oh, won't you tell Mr. Clark about the mantel, dear? Isn't it charming!—so *ex*quisite, so *ar*istocratic—a veritable *mu*seum piece. Do step back out of the way, boys."

The boys, the elf and the wrestler, obligingly fell back, their empty glasses gravitating toward Ainsworth, leaving the mantel and Eleanor unobstructed. And her smile and clear cool voice, after his long confinement with Mrs. Winship's hectic nuances, came as a profound deliverance. All obstacles seemed swept away and for a moment he had an illusion that they were alone together in the room, unencumbered and free, and that she was talking for his sole benefit, privately, and telling much more than about the old white carved mantel.

"I'm afraid," she was saying, "I can't make much of a story of it. Uncle Joe Bramwell has a separate yarn for every scratch and scar, but the only one I can keep straight is about the empty space in the center. According to family history it once held a Wedgwood medallion of the seasons, four maidens depicting the moods of the year. When Beaufort was taken in the Civil War, they disappeared and haven't been seen since. That's all."

But Mrs. Winship was not content to let it rest there.

"But isn't that enough!" she exclaimed. "What could be more romantic? One condemns the vandal hand, of course, yet one can't help admiring the aesthetic instinct that chose such a prize, can one. And where is it now, this medallion? By now the vandal hand has surely withered away, but what has become of the hand's trophy, this symbol of the ageless seasons? May we not suppose that someday it will find its way home, brought back perhaps by a gallant grandson of the vandal, a young man of imagination and heart?"

"Why not," Eleanor smiled. "After all, a penitent vandal once took the trouble to return the pulpit Bible and registry to St. Helena's Church. And only last year a woman in Chicago offered to return some books her father had borrowed from the old Beaufort Library. There was a catch there, though. She wanted five hundred dollars for her pains."

"How contemptible," said Mrs. Winship. And then to John Clark: "Speaking of mantels, you must see the Adams mantel in the old Lafayette house on Bay Street. It's white marble, a perfect gem. We must have it copied for the plantation."

He nodded absently, now frankly preoccupied with Eleanor.

"Isn't she charming?" Mrs. Winship asked abruptly, touching his sleeve. And squinting at Eleanor sweetly she added with stinging graciousness: "Really, who would ever guess that such a lovely child was studying medicine, to be a doctor! And graduating this June, isn't it, dear? Oh, but do you know I quite forgot today is your birthday! Ainsworth, fill our glasses quickly. Do forgive me, my dear,—your twenty-first anniversary, I believe Miss Eugenia told us?"

"Twenty-fourth," Eleanor answered with good grace.

"Ah," sighed Mrs. Winship, poising her glass, "at your age one can afford to be so literal! And so confident. We drink to your career, my dear."

The toast was rousingly seconded by the elf and the wrestler, now completely out of their shells.

"I hope," Mrs. Winship pursued with ruthless sweetness, her gallant veneer peeling off in strips, "you won't permit your career to interfere with your happiness as a woman. But in your case I'm sure there's no cause for alarm,—even though you were willing

878

to permit it, there must be many young men desperate to prevent it. And I rather gather, from something Miss Eugenia let fall, that you are no longer fancy free. Candidly, my dear, isn't there one young man who meets with your particular favor?"

Eleanor was visibly flushed now, but her eyes continued to meet Mrs. Winship's squinted sweetness without resentment.

"Candidly," she smiled, "I think there is."

"What charming *naïveté*," purred Mrs. Winship. "You're not sure, my dear?"

"Not yet, thank you," Eleanor laughed lightly, getting up. "And now if you'll excuse me, I better not keep Emily waiting supper."

"But of course,—we must all go down," Mrs. Winship nodded, taking John Clark's arm to help her squirm off the Aiken day-bed. "I was going to urge you to have supper with us, my dear, but we've been selfish enough as it is. I know your dear grandmother wants every minute she can have with you." And speeding the parting guest with a conclusive squint, she turned with twitching lips to ask in an almost timid aside: "You will have supper with us, Mr. Clark?"

Since there was nothing else to do, he accepted with pleasure, as he regretfully watched Eleanor being escorted to the door by Ainsworth and the boys.

"How is your grandmother today, dear?" Mrs. Winship called mellifluously doorward, "—do give her my love." And to John Clark she loudly proclaimed, as Eleanor disappeared into the hall: "You haven't met Miss Emily yet, have you,—but you have a great treat in store. She reminds me so much of my own little mother."

Then as Eleanor's light steps came from the stairs, the tone slanted down to confidential candor, the eyes gleaming up sharply. "Isn't she an alluring child? Doesn't she make you wish you were ten years younger? But I'm forgetting how happily married you are! And in spite of her discreet disavowal, she seems most happily engaged. To a charming young Charleston man, a fellow medical student, I believe. I understand from Miss Eugenia they're to be married this summer right after graduation."

"He's a very lucky dog," John Clark observed absently.

"One hopes so, of course," Mrs. Winship murmured with a slight shrug and frown. "And yet as a woman I detect a certain coldness there, a more than virginal frigidity, an unyielding almost masculine quality, which I fear will make her a better doctor than wife. It seems so difficult for a woman to have a profession and remain truly feminine." And with a delicate catch in her voice, she added in a tone of softest yielding femininity: "But perhaps I'm mistaken in this case. Let us hope so. And now if you boys will start on down, I'll join you as soon as I powder my nose."

And showing her teeth with an arch play of eyebrows, she gave him a little sigh and minced away toward the screen in the corner, leaving him to join the boys with a profound sigh of his own.

On the way to the stairs Ainsworth applied his floorwalker arm-grip.

"You must find this all rather amusing," he assumed intimately. "Only Lucky would think of tackling a skyscraper expert to do a job of traditional house designing! But wouldn't it be swell if you decided to take her up. I'll be doing all the decorating, and it would be corking fun working with you. It would make a rather nice little thing for you, too, if you could sandwich it in between your regular commitments. The size of a commission means nothing to Lucky, of course, if it's something she's set her heart on. She's really a gorgeous person."

At the landing the old palladian west window revealed the slender scimitar moon, still guarding the star of Venus. But now Eleanor was gone, and John Clark could only wonder what he had done to deserve Mrs. Winship and Ainsworth Peck, and the strange twisted fate of this day.

"And of course," Ainsworth suavely continued as they went on downstairs, "I imagine the Fenwicks would greatly appreciate your interest in Lucky's house plans. Judge Bramwell, who hopes to sell his plantation to her, is related to Eleanor, you know."

"So I gather," John Clark nodded, glancing at Ainsworth's smooth face.

"You know," the smooth face added blandly, "it's really quite a coincidence, your arriving here just at this particular moment. You can be sort of a good fairy all around, if you know what I mean."

"I see what you mean," John Clark told him. "You have a re-markable insight into all the angles of the situation."

Ainsworth smiled modestly. "Rather amusing, the angles, don't you think? But I do hope you'll give the matter serious consideration."

"Very serious consideration," John Clark agreed.

✓   ✓   ✓

When supper was finally over and the party had adjourned to the living-room, Mrs. Winship immediately applied her energies to arranging a foursome for a little evening of bridge in her room, buttonholing the Right Reverend to invite him to play with Ainsworth, the wrestler, and the elf. It was clear that she was paving the way for a resumption of the *causerie intime,* and John Clark turned for help to Miss Eugenia Fenwick, who had made an unobtrusive gliding reappearance on the Marshlands scene. He would find the telephone, she informed him with her startled blink, in the back hall. So when Mrs. Winship closed in on him, her lips puckered in a smile of demure expectancy, he was ready with the excuse that he had several long-distance calls to make. And leaving her in the Right Reverend's jovial company, he escaped from the room.

In the back hall he found Mr. Marks fuming at an old-fashioned wall telephone, trying to get a New York connection. Not caring to return in defeat to the entanglements of the living-room, he lingered at a respectful distance from Mr. Marks and the refractory phone. At hand was a closed door flanked by a pair of bookcases, and as he absently perused the shelves in the dim hall light he decided Eleanor was in there. Between Mr. Marks's disjointed bickerings with central he tried to catch some sound of her voice.

"Of course I'm still here!" Mr. Marks was barking in final exasperation. "Yes, operator, I'm *holding* the line,—been holding it for the past hour."

Eventually it was all straightened out, and Marks, brow beaded with strain, passed him with a preoccupied nod and returned to the living-room, leaving the phone free.

He felt sure he heard Eleanor's voice with others in the room beyond the closed door. Would it do to knock and ask how to work the old coffee-grinder on the wall? He was staring at the phone, puzzling, when it responded with a sudden inspiration that made him jump guiltily. When it continued to jangle at him, three sharp alarms at a time and without bringing anyone to answer, he lifted the receiver.

"Charleston calling," a harsh-voiced central jabbed. "And if that's you listening in, Miss Bramwell, I'm ringing the Fenwicks, not you."

There was a moment's shocked silence on the line, and then a quick shrill voice protested: "You rang one long and two shorts plain as day."

"I rang," rasped central, *two shorts* and *one long* plain as the nose on your face, and I'll thank you to hang up, the line's in use."

"You're too insulting, Hattie Fowler," another quick voice shrilled in. "We'll see that Joe reports you in the morning!"

A deafening screech, followed by a derisive squawk and a gasp of outrage.

"Excuse it puh-lease," rasped central in best professional style. And when the outraged receiver clicked out: "Marshlands?—Charleston calling. Go ahead, Charleston, here's your party."

"Hello," John Clark repeated, deafly.

A gentlemanly voice, distinctly Charleston, asked: "May I speak to Miss Eleanor."

You may not, he felt like answering. And he resisted an impulse to tell this newest obstacle that Miss Eleanor was engaged. But then he realized that this was probably the man she was engaged to.

"Just a moment."

When he went to tap on the closed door, it was Lucy's dark polished face that answered his disconsolate summons. But as he was giving her the message, Eleanor appeared.

"Sorry if you were going to phone," she said as she came out into the hall. "I won't be a minute."

"No, no," he hastened to say.

The sight of her, after the long separation of supper, came now only to sharpen his loneliness. "Hello, Fred," he heard her say in a voice that sounded definitely engaged. And with the sense of being a completely fatuous interloper, he was about to retreat to the living-room in final defeat, when he heard a soft hail and turned to find Lucy in the hall inviting him back to the door.

"Mistuh Claa'k," she whispered over a tray she was carrying,

"Miss Em'ly wish to speak wid you, suh. Jes' step inside, if you please."

Grateful for this unexpected stay, he promptly complied and was ushered in with ceremony by Lucy, who closed the door behind him. Thus in the twinkling of an eye he found himself snatched from outer darkness and set down in the very citadel of the family.

It was a sort of bedroom study in which he found himself, an agreeable room of soft lamplight. An old four-poster stood in an alcove, while bookcases lined the walls, and there was a desk in the recess of a bay window, and a pair of easy-chairs by a cozy fireplace. Here a white-haired woman was sitting, waiting to greet him. But first he had to acknowledge the greeting of Rufus, who rose from the hearth rug with a wide wagging welcome.

"I see you two have already met," the woman nodded as Rufus conducted him to the fireside.

"Oh yes," he bowed, "we're getting to be old friends."

His hall gratitude for the sudden reprieve had turned, at the door, into fear that his disheveled state of mind would make him unpresentable to Eleanor's grandmother, unpresentable and uncomfortable. Instead, he felt immediately at ease with her, complications forgotten for the moment.

"Not very polite to ask you to come to me," she said in a voice of natural friendliness, "but I'm confined to my room this evening for bad behavior. It seems I've been too strenuous today. Won't you sit down?"

He took the easy-chair opposite hers with pleasure, thinking how good it was to be invited to sit with her instead of with Mrs. Winship.

But then as he settled down to comfortable talk, telling about his trip South and asking questions about Beaufort, he discovered that this was something better than good. He was enjoying, he began to realize, a positive privilege. For here certainly was age at its most fortunate best, charming, intelligent, and kind. In a world whose old people seemed to run to saddest extremes, here was one who had come through the battle in inspiring style. It had been a long hard fight, clearly enough,—the fine sensitive face was darkly lined and the form within the old-fashioned tight-waisted black dress appeared worn away to an irreducible slenderness,—but the eyes were undimmed, as bright blue and alert as Eleanor's, and the spirit that shone through seemed tempered to a final perfection.

It was easy now to see where Eleanor's charm came from. This was the source of light. And as he talked on with her, while Rufus stretched out drowsily on the hearth rug, he felt the force and warmth of this light with increasing conviction. He had met "radiant" people before, people whose flame of personality was immediately dazzling, and presently consuming, extinguishing. But this radiance felt benign and abiding: it burned steady and sure, a flame gentle and healing and illuminating rather than flashy and blinding. It seemed to come from deep sympathetic interest and understanding, a basic quality of unselfishness, a fine balance of heart and mind. Here, he decided, was someone who could be looked up to, a person whose friendship would be a treasure to have, if you could be worthy of it, if you could earn it.

And he found himself wanting to earn it. He wanted to be worthy of her esteem, for its own sake and not because of Eleanor. The problem of Eleanor, culminating in the hall conversation with Charleston, was losing its sting in the sudden importance of getting acquainted with "Miss Em'ly." But it was importance without strain, like liberation. It was like talking with Eleanor —an Eleanor known for a long while, all ice broken. Between these two, who were so much alike, the difference was only an element of time, and even this distinction soon faded. For Miss Em'ly was young too. Not in the desperate fashion of some unhappy old women, and not in the childish manner of others who gave an impression of youngness because they had never grown up, but in a style of her own, a youthfulness of spirit that belied the years, so that it was impossible to think of her as old: she seemed no age, or rather all ages blended together in an ultimate integrity and strength. And this strength was contagious, so that behind easy-going talk of Beaufort he found himself breaking free from the bonds that held him. In the light of her voice dark deep-seated bafflements and this day's added confusions seemed to dissolve. The feeling of disintegrating loneliness left him, and in its place was a feeling of homecoming, of peace and renewal in this house and this room.

He became so absorbed in the pleasure of talking with Miss

Em'ly that he lost all track of Eleanor, and he felt a sense of surprise and disruption when the door opened and she came in.

If she felt any surprise or disruption at finding him camped in the room, she failed to show it. She gave him a nod and smile, declining his chair, and with an apology for interrupting the conversation sat down on the fireside stool by her grandmother's chair.

"Fred Eustis wants to come down Wednesday," she explained in a quiet aside to Miss Em'ly and Rufus, "but I warned him we'd be up to our necks all vacation, cleaning up the Lafayette house. He seemed to think that's a strange way to spend Holy Week."

Before John Clark had time to digest that, the door opened again and Miss Eugenia Fenwick appeared, gliding in with her startled expression.

"Oh,—please don't get up," she blinked at him. "I just want to give Mrs. Fenwick a message. It's Mrs. Winship, Emmy. She wants basket lunches again tomorrow, for the whole party and one extra. Another picnic!"

"Well, I think we can arrange it with Lucy," said Miss Em'ly, calming the fluster.

He was afraid that at this point it was up to him to remember the telephone and retire to the hall. But before he could excuse himself, Miss Em'ly again came to the rescue like an intervening providence.

"Eleanor," she said, "won't you ask Mr. Clark to have some birthday cake while we discuss fried chicken?"

When Eleanor's smiling eyes interrogated him, he nodded with quick approval. And accompanied by Rufus he followed her to the bay-window desk, where the better half of a cake was waiting, its lemon icing glistening in a glow of lamplight.

"Hope you don't mind old-fashioned sponge cake," she said as she dismantled a row of candles and then broke off two pieces of the cake with a fork. "If you like something fancy you should be on hand for Aunt Eugenia's birthday,—Lucy always makes her a Lady Baltimore with all the trimmings. Only you can't eat that with your fingers. Of course, you can have this on a plate if you like."

"Not on your life, thanks," he told her, receiving his piece of cake with clumsy fingers. "Well, this takes me back about a hundred years. You don't happen to have any paper caps or snappers, or one of those curly whistles with a feather on the end?"

"Sorry. There isn't even any ice-cream to go with it. But there's a consolation prize, a lucky token, if Lucy didn't forget to put it in. It hasn't turned up yet, so maybe you'll get it."

"Sounds like a wedding cake."

"Oh, it isn't a ring. It's a thimble. If you get it, you get a wish. But it's quite a hard thimble, so you better go slow."

Following her example, he took a nibble of cake and munched it cautiously, while Rufus settled down on his haunches to watch the proceedings. Nothing whatever happened, and Rufus rocked with impatience, intently devouring first one piece of cake and then the other. When a second pair of nibbles still brought no results, Rufus groaned out loud. But the third wary bites broke the suspense. The gentleman guest seemed to have struck some obstacle, and presently he extracted and displayed what was undoubtedly a thimble.

"Without the loss of a tooth," he grinned, showing it to Eleanor and then to Rufus, who sniffed it indulgently.

"You get your wish," Eleanor smiled.

He shook his head. "I don't feel quite right about this."

"You can't use it?"

"Oh yes indeed," he told her soberly. "But after all, it's your birthday. You should have it."

"But I got my wish, thanks, when I blew out all the candles at one whack."

"Well then, how about Rufus? Couldn't he use a perfectly good wish?"

"A wish-bone, yes. But if you haven't one handy, a little cake would do very nicely. Wouldn't it, lamb pie?"

Rufus politely licked his chops. And when he was offered a fragment of cake, he received it delicately and instantly disposed of it, without batting an eye.

"How does this thimble business work?" John Clark asked. "Do you rub it like Aladdin's lamp?"

"I think it works best if you just put it on."

He fumbled around with the thimble, finally fitting it on his little finger. Then he closed his eyes for a moment of frowning concentration.

"All right," he announced. "Now may I tell what it was?"

"You're not supposed to."

"But I'm afraid I'll have to. I can't get it unless I do."

"Why?"

"Well, because I wished we could take a little stroll, all three of us, and have a look at Beaufort by night."

Through his own flush he saw that her smile was flushed now. The first encouraging sign, he decided with exhilaration. And for a moment her frank eyes looked confused, reflecting his own need, acknowledging and confirming his secret wishes. So it seemed for an instant, but she rallied too quickly for him to be sure.

"I'm afraid," she said with an even shake of her head, "we haven't any night life that would interest a New Yorker."

But now he was confident enough not to be discouraged by that. "But you see I'm not the genuine article. I never was anything but a poor imitation, and I'm not even that anymore. I've suffered a sea-island change into something that believes in magic again, so don't tell me yours doesn't work. Of course, I may have made too big a wish for this size thimble. But I still think Rufus would appreciate a little outing."

Rufus panted at the idea.

"You see? We're ganging up on you."

She studied him in silence for a disconcerting moment, but he managed to keep up an expectant smile.

"I see," she said finally. "Well, as a gang with a thimble you're too much for me. And as an architect how would you like to see our Lafayette house? The one with the marble mantel that Mrs. Winship mentioned."

"With you and Rufus?—fine!"

"We'll need some matches or something."

"We've got all kinds of matches," he told her exuberantly, as they started for the door to the hall.

On the way she stopped by her grandmother's chair at the fireside to explain.

"We're taking Rufus out for a little airing. And we're going to show Mr. Clark the Lafayette house, by match light."

"That's good," Miss Em'ly nodded without any sign of surprise.

But Miss Eugenia fluttered and blinked convulsively, looking more startled than ever.

His sense of exhilaration was heightened as they went down the hall to the front door, past the door of the living-room, where Mrs. Winship was still stuck with the jovial Right Reverend. But when he was safely outside with Eleanor and they were going down the steps together, exhilaration suddenly sobered at the realization that at last he actually had her to himself.

He was reluctant to speak, afraid that words would break the magic. The garden's afternoon song of rejoicing was reduced now to a faint trilling of crickets and the flowers were lost in darkness, yet their fragrance seemed enhanced, stronger than before, and in the mystery of shadows, this whispering stillness, the spell of things seemed to rise and spread. Venus and her crescent moon were set, yet now the whole sky was shining with stars. But this night of Southern spring could so easily be an illusion, a last wild flight from reality, an ultimate hallucination of cornered pride and loneliness. There seemed to be no question about his escape from New York to this country of the past, and it was easy to accept Marshlands up to the point of rest, his drowsiness in the little room with Mr. Audubon's cardinals; but from then on things had grown to have an unsubstantial air, as if he were still floating in old lost summers, dreaming of home and first love. From the moment he had seen her the spell had been taking shape, only sharpened by such all too fleshly figments as Mrs. Winship and the other guests, till now it had reached this critical stage. If it were true, this night of stars and this faint crunch of shell underfoot, there was no hurried need for words; if it were untrue, her youth and beauty moving beside him, he was in no rush to find out. She herself would have to put her spell to the test. And waiting in suspense he felt it was a good sign that she too seemed reluctant to speak, as they followed Rufus down the driveway.

So the silence went unbroken till they reached the gates and passed through to the street beyond. Then, as they took the dim sidewalk path, she was first to speak, but not to him.

"No chasing cats, young man," she cautioned Rufus as he started exploring the darkness of the lawns along the way.

But then she turned to say: "Beaufort night life seems to subdue you."

"It does indeed," he nodded with a grave breath of relief, finding

888

that words were not breaking the spell but giving it confident reality. "You see, I'd forgotten how nice and bright stars are."

"You don't have them in New York?"

"You can't be sure. Too many colored lights in the way."

"You certainly won't have that to contend with here. You're in darkest Africa."

"Dark? Seems to me it's more like coming up in Central Park from the subway, with the band playing and kids roller-skating on the Mall, on the finest day of the year. Ever come up like that, after a long ride?"

"Well, not exactly like that. I've come up once or twice at Carnegie Hall and Macy's."

"So you're an old hand at New York."

"Oh, I've been through the mill a little, on the way to college."

"And what do you make of it?"

"Well, after the first shock, very exciting. But isn't it a little rich for a steady diet?"

"That's about it. Too many calories and not enough vitamins."

"But I still think it's a nice place to visit once in a while."

"It's perfect, if you can work it that way. But just try staying on sometime and see what happens. See if it doesn't get to be like the game of electric bumping cars at an amusement park. Only it isn't for fun. Of course you don't notice that as long as your digestion holds up. When it doesn't, you suddenly find yourself in Beaufort, if you're lucky."

"But when your digestion mends, think how you'll appreciate getting back."

"You don't seem to take me very seriously as a reformed New Yorker. And yet I'd give an arm to change places with practically anybody in Beaufort."

"I wouldn't make that too loud. I think practically everybody here would be glad to take you up."

"You wouldn't."

"I'm afraid not. Beaufort and Charleston would be all I could ever hope to handle."

Mention of Charleston was a sudden letdown, an abrupt reminder of Fred Eustis, the boy who had the inside track. . . . Out of the frying-pan into this final fire, that was all the stars of this night spelled. From all angles a little late in the game of triangles to be finding the one and only girl.

"What is it you're going to be in your chosen field here?" he asked her with elaborate cheerfulness, promising himself to move on bright and early tomorrow morning, "—a child specialist, I think your aunt Miss Fenwick said."

"That or research. Pediatrics or bacteriology, that is the question. Which would you pick?"

"That's easy. Somehow I can't see you tucked away in a medical kitchen, tinkering with test-tubes and stewing up germs and things."

She laughed at that. And her laugh made tomorrow seem like a sentence of death.

She said: "I don't think you take the question very seriously."

"But you see I do. And my whole artistic instinct, such as it is, rebels at the picture of you cloistered in a laboratory. I suppose the regular hours would be pleasanter, though. Much pleasanter, certainly, for your future husband."

Angles of light from the house they were passing reached across the lawn to the path, but failed to reveal her eyes. They remained obscure, veiled in shadow, and only her smile was definite.

"I appreciate your looking at it that way," she nodded lightly. "But I don't think there's much danger of becoming cloistered. I'm afraid I'm not made of stern enough stuff for that." And she added soberly: "We've had two doctors in the family, and both wanted to do research work. But one never found time for it, and the other died before he could start. And now it looks as if that ambition would have to go on being frustrated, for another generation at least."

"I didn't realize it was an old family ambition. I just meant that I'd rather see somebody else filtering viruses and nursing spirochetes and things."

"Well, if I don't make the grade, maybe my nephew will be that somebody else. My sister has a little boy who's taken with microscopes. . . . Anyway, this summer before the hospital term starts I'm going to a camp in North Carolina to try a little practicing on the children. If they bear up under it, that will help decide the question."

"They'll never let you go into a laboratory, I can guarantee that.

. . . But I understood you were going to be married this June, right after graduation."

"That's interesting news. Mrs. Winship, by any chance?"

"Mrs. Winship by way of your aunt Miss Fenwick, I believe. She was very positive on the point. The lucky gentleman being from Charleston."

"Well, I'm awfully sorry to disappoint Aunt Gene, and particularly Mrs. Winship."

"Then you're not engaged?"

"Not that I know of."

"Not that it's any of my business, but is that official?"

"It really should be, don't you think?"

She turned her head to glance his way with a quiet little laugh. And now her amusement was a sudden reprieve, swift deliverance that turned tomorrow morning's doom into starry hope and all tomorrows into a present that was like a rush of wine in his veins, an uprush of joy in his heart that set him walking on air again as when he had first seen her.

And now he was aware of music in the air, music that he had only remotely sensed before, as a vague annoyance. It came mostly from a house across the street, but it was echoed from other houses in other streets. A very radio-conscious Beaufort seemed all intent on a single dance program. . . . It took a moment to get the drift, but then the melody came through unmistakable and clear. *Old Man River,*—minus Paul Robeson's voice and with a slight touch of static, but still rolling along. "He don't plant 'taters, he don't plant cotton, and them that plants 'em is soon forgotten." And he was deciding that for all its New York *Show Boat* connections, it was just right to be associated forever with this night, when abruptly it became a medley by swinging into *Make Believe.* That was enough to bring him back to earth. After all, the fact that she wasn't engaged proved nothing, except that the track was clear on her side of the fence. There was still the fence. And as the medley further lapsed into *Can't Help Loving That Man,* a favorite of Helen's, he felt a distinct pause. Even when the medley wound up with *Old Man River* again, it didn't sound quite the same.

Rather awkward point for a complete lull, he thought. But the only things he could find to say were of entirely too much consequence to be used for silence breakers; and she seemed to feel no urge to help. The street was narrowing down to a little bridge, bringing Rufus back into the fold from his lawn foraging, and she talked to him, congratulating him for his excellent judgment in digging up no cats.

The bridge, John Clark recognized, was the plank causeway he had crossed this afternoon on his way to Marshlands. Years ago, that seemed now, and the whole cast of the world was changed. But whether it was for better or for worse, impossible to say. Just as it was impossible to see whether the tide of the inlet was ebbing or flowing or just standing still. He felt there must be conflict below, troubled cross-currents of hope and anxiety, hesitation and unfathomable longing, as if the waters were unable to make up their mind under a surface of quiet suspense. But he could be sure only of the suspense: the rest was inscrutable as Eleanor's eyes in the darkness.

Ahead was a street-corner lamp, casting a pattern of palm fronds over the wing of a house. It was the mildewed Tudoresque place of this afternoon, the "castle" of the filling-station youth's directions to Marshlands; and if it had had a haunted look by day, now it was positively crawling with ghosts. The only sign of human survival was a thread of light that came from a crack in the shutters of a lower window. The rest was dank shadows, and a weird play of fireflies in the shrubbery of the garden; a melancholy chant of peepers; a scent of sweet decay from sprays of honeysuckle draping the board wall that enclosed the grounds and forced the sidewalk into the street.

For some obscure reason the board wall helped him make a resolve to be strong without the aid of silence. He would be simply a tourist from now on, and stop trying to wish himself—plus complications and consequences—on her accommodating good-nature, her natural friendliness.

"Here we have Beaufort's haunted house, I presume?" he asked his guide, as they reached the corner and turned to the left.

He caught the clear flash of her smile in the light, but her eyes remained shadowed.

"It looks as if it should be, doesn't it. But you'd be disappointed if you saw Uncle Joe Bramwell. He's really not much of a ghost."

"Sorry. I never would have guessed it was inhabited by any relative of yours. . . . And is your uncle the party who owns the plantation our friend Mrs. Winship has her eye on?"

"That's it."

She called to Rufus, who was sniffing the garden gate of the Castle. But before moving on he took time to display a fine contempt for ghosts.

Beyond the Castle the street curved narrowly. And as they followed the bend, Eleanor said with a reminiscent laugh:

"When Jane and I were in pigtails, we used to dash past that house for dear life. It was Uncle Joe's house and he was always a saint, but we were convinced that his sisters were witches. Lucy used them as a sort of switch to correct our deportment."

He liked the thought of her in pigtails. A proud independent soul, walking in the beauty that surrounds some children like an aura. Even in flight from witches, pigtails flying, even when deportment called for a little correction from Lucy's switch, she must have been a marvel of grace and dignity. She still had a definitely pigtail quality in her charm, and he was sure she would never lose it, not even in a clinic or laboratory.

But pigtails were all out of line with his tourist resolve, and he firmly dismissed them.

"What's it like inside the Castle?" he asked in a sightseeing tone. "Massive chests and armoires and suits of mail?"

"That's what I always imagined," she nodded. "But probably it's just horsehair and plush and tassels. I don't know, because I've never been inside. I've never been invited."

"Not very hospitable people, your relatives."

"Well, you see, Uncle Joe's sisters have never forgiven Emily for being a Yankee."

He wondered whether he liked the idea of her calling her grand-mother Emily, and decided it was entirely right. Sometimes she called her Mother, which was also right, and must mean her real mother was dead. And how about her father? But all that, like the present fact of Miss Em'ly being Yankee, was irrelevant. Everything concerning Eleanor, including her family and particularly Miss Em'ly, was too pertinent to be encouraged: he would stick to his sightseeing.

But setting his mind against his urgent desire for personal information only brought him back to her pigtails. And disentangling himself from them again left him discouragingly tied up in another knot of silence, which once again she cheerfully failed to help him out of.

But at the end of the curving street lay the waterfront and the beginning of Bay Street, and here another tourist landmark came into view. It was the George Washington Tavern, the stuccoed ensemble with the runway and the silo tower effect at the brink of the river, and he seized its red neon sign gratefully.

"Who's responsible for this tidy little item?" he asked with relief. "No relatives this time, I feel sure."

"No," she smiled at the sign. "This time it's a party by the name of Blarker."

"Not *See Mr. Blarker?*"

"The very same. And thereby hangs a tale, if you'd like to hear it."

"I can see it. And the horns too. Just who is this Old Nick in architect's clothing?"

"Well, nobody knows exactly. Some people seem to think he's Saint Nick. You see, he has a round face and little round belly that shakes when he laughs like a bowlful of jelly. And he arrived on the night before Christmas, a year ago."

"Did he appear in a miniature sleigh with eight tiny reindeer?"

"No, it wasn't quite that cunning. That style of approach wouldn't appeal to our Saint Nick. He sort of blew into town, in a large red limousine like a fire-engine, with the Florida hurricane still whistling in his whiskers."

"Distinctly the breezy type."

"Distinctly."

And as they turned their backs on the George Washington Tavern and started down deserted dim-lighted Bay Street, she went on to explain:

"When the Florida bubble burst, quite a lot of Mr. Blarkers landed around here. They're promoting skyscraper resorts in the Savannah swamps, and at Myrtle Beach, and even up in the mountains near Asheville. Of course our Mr. Blarker is one of the smaller fry, but he says he's big enough to stucco everything in Beaufort and put us right on the map."

"I see. He's going to fix Beaufort up like a Spanish omelet. Well, he seems to have made a pretty fair start, with the George Washington Tavern."

"Oh, that's just a sample. You should see some of his other jobs. He's particularly fond of stuccoing the old places. You may not believe it, but the rear section of the Tavern used to be one of the nicest houses in town."

"I'll have to take your word for it. But I wouldn't worry too much about Mr. Blarker's stucco. A few hard rains and I suspect you'll have your old places back again. If that's any comfort."

"It really is, coming from an architect."

They had reached a left turn-off from Bay Street that led out to the dim shape of a bridge, and he remembered having stopped here in the afternoon to look across the ebb-tide river at a wooded shore in golden sunlight, to the lonely tune of gulls. The shore was gone now and the gulls were still, and there was only a faint gleam of starlight to vouch for the river, and one bright particular star perched on the draw span to mark the arch of girders. He was about to speak, when the peremptory toot of a boat horn startled the night. A flashing finger of light came feeling along the waterfront from downstream, revealing wharves no longer balanced on stilts but resting at ease on the breast of high tide. The searching finger moved out to point at the draw of the bridge, which after a moment reluctantly responded, slowly swinging open. Then the finger withdrew, to become a stealthy mysterious approach, red and green snake-eyes advancing on the dark water.

Guided by Rufus, they walked out on the bridge a little way to watch the proceedings.

As the red and green eyes neared the bridge, the shape of a yacht grew discernible. And as it passed smoothly through the draw opening, cabin lights shone out with a muffled squawk of jazz.

"Palm Beach or Miami?" he wondered aloud. "And bound North for what frosty port, through this happy medium?"

Eleanor, leaning beside him on the bridge railing, said surprisingly: "Looks like the *Ibis,* bound home for Stamford."

"You must have good eyes," he said, peering hard at the stern of the yacht. But all he could see was a card-table with figures under a light on the after-deck.

"If you'd been watching yachts on this waterway all your life," she said, "you'd risk a shot in the dark too. They migrate through here like birds every autumn and spring, and you get to know the cut of them, even at night."

He liked the thought of her watching the migrations. It helped fill out the pigtail picture.

"You must have a good pair of binoculars and a long memory, and you must like yachts a lot, to get the names straight."

"I like everything that floats, from rowboats up. Someday I hope to have a boat of my own,—a yawl with snow-white sails, and Rufus for first mate, and a little colored boy for crew."

Rufus, head cocked with an air of nautical wisdom, watched through the side-rails of the bridge as the *Ibis's* wake washed against the seawall.

John Clark was thinking what a happy fate it would be to be crew on the yawl, when the horn of the *Ibis* tooted again, a snooty toot of thanks to the closing draw-bridge. And again the search-light flashed out, this time fingering the wooded far shore and the curve of the river at Marshlands point. A bell chimed primly, and the phantom shape picked up speed. Before the wash of wake had died along the seawall, the *Ibis* had rounded the bend and was gone, leaving the waterfront to settle back into stillness and repose.

He greeted this restoring of the night's enchantment with a sigh. In his youth he had never known anything like this waterfront of hers; but, perhaps because she had, he felt that it held the pro-foundest nostalgia of all, and the cure of all. The soft lapping of the tide, bright starlight, and the light of stray earthly stars winking over the dark waters, seemed now to compose the oldest music in the world, older and deeper than the spell of spring gardens, or the magic of crescent wishing moons, or even the lost swimming-hole and the fields and hills of boyhood. Sea-island night. . . . With an effort he reminded himself that he was just a transient here, a bird of passage like the *Ibis,* which no doubt had personal prob-lems too.

"To get back to Mr. Blarker," he said with deliberate matter-of-factness, "you would think he could find someplace else to reduce to a stucco shambles. Why pick on Beaufort?"

"That's the way Mother feels about it. But she's having a hard time convincing people Mr. Blarker's a public nuisance. He's a spellbinder from way back and he's got a lot of people hypnotized and all steamed up with civic pride. Even old friends of Emily's think she's trying to obstruct progress."

He looked at the tilt of her head, so miraculous against the stars. And the part he was trying to play, the role of detached tourist, became suddenly intolerable.

"You know, this is beginning to sound like a strictly grand row. I've always had a secret ambition to be an obstructionist. Any chance of signing up with the opposition?"

"But aren't you leaving tomorrow?"

"Not if there's a chance of getting in some obstructing,—between now and Easter. After that you go back to Charleston and medicine, don't you?"

"Yes, and Marshlands closes for the season. But you ought to be able to get in some worthwhile obstructing in a week. If Mrs. Winship doesn't get in your way."

She turned to him with her quiet laugh, without mockery. . . . She was the very spirit of this sea-island enchantment, and her laughter was life-giving faith, the breath of spring in a stir of soft wind and winking lights over the water. And he was overboard now, completely and finally, sink or swim and regardless of consequences.

"By the way," he said to the river darkness, in a voice whose calmness surprised him, "do you mind my telling you I've fallen in love?"

"Why no, if it's any relief," her voice answered promptly, in his own tone. "Mrs. Winship?"

"No, not Mrs. Winship. No, it's your grandmother. I hope you don't think it's too sudden."

"Well, it does seem a bit sudden. It must have been love at first sight."

"Well, it was. I admit I've only had about two words with her, and I don't know how to put it, but she makes me feel good. She makes life seem good again. It's a funny feeling, like coming home."

He could see her smile at that, but she was slow to reply. She was silent for so long a moment, in fact, that he had time to get anxious. Perhaps she found his admiration for her grandmother really a bit too sudden and easy, or a little too striving and presuming.

"She makes me feel good too, Emily does," she said finally, to his great relief. " . . . You really can help a lot, by just casting a professional eye on the Lafayette house. You see, we want to get it in shape as headquarters for the opposition."

"So that's where the Lafayette house comes in. It's much more than a marble mantel."

"It's the center of the fray. . . . See that hip roof with the two chimneys above all the flat roofs, there about a block down Bay Street?"

"Well, not exactly. I'm afraid your eyes are still better than mine. But I'll take your word it's there."

"Well, it really is,—right across the street from Mr. Blarker. He had his heart set on stuccoing it for his office, but Emily thwarted him. She got Sam Koenig, the owner, to give her an option on it. And now she's planning to deed it to the town, as a combination museum and community center and art club,—sort of a gentle and general reminder."

"And sort of a direct slap at Mr. Blarker?"

"A personal affront, if possible. And now are you ready for a closer inspection?"

"Well, I'm getting attached to this starlit river of yours. But if you think it will be here tomorrow night, I'm ready to get down to business."

"I think it will keep all right."

So they left the bridge and the wide river darkness and turned back to the sparse lights of Bay Street, to the very evident delight of Rufus, who seemed to have grown weary of tide smells.

Now, in the block ahead, the waterfront side of the street was no longer open to the river but cramped in with buildings, warehouses and stores blank-looking in the semi-gloom of Beaufort's lighting system. There was just enough light to reassure him of Eleanor's reality, the unquestionableness of her moving beside him down the deserted street. But though her presence was substantiated, it remained as mysterious as ever. It was as if he were lost with her in some forgotten corner of the world, wandering through some twilight zone of time, to meet a fate obscure as her eyes. But it was an obscurity he trusted implicitly, and a fate he welcomed with elation because it was in her hands.

"Where's everybody, in church?" he asked her.

"In church," she nodded, "or decently at home, and probably in bed by now."

"Even Mr. Blarker?"

"Mr. Blarker never misses church. And takes no chances. He goes to all three."

"Quite a feat, even for Mr. Blarker. How does he work it, with mirrors?"

"No, he just rotates."

"Oh. . . . Not that you miss people, but you would expect to meet an occasional straggler from curfew and church bells on a night like this."

"Not on Sunday night. Now on Saturday night, of course, the whole town turns out. The whole county, in fact. But other nights you're lucky to run into even the police force after dark. Still think you can stand a week of it?"

"Every week, indefinitely. . . . You know, I've been wondering if there'd be room for a Yankee architect in the South. In Charleston, for instance."

"Have you been wondering seriously?"

"Never more so."

"And what would become of New York?"

"New York would just have to totter along somehow. Oh, I could do a little commuting. Which reminds me there's a competition opening for a new auditorium to replace old Carnegie Hall. Fine problem in acoustic design there. But headquarters would be here. Think how much better work would go on this basis."

"It gets pretty hot and lazy here in summer."

"But there's the beach, and your North Carolina mountains."

"You really are quite a sudden person. You're so quick at working things out."

"No, the trouble is I'm too slow, particularly at geography. This thing has been brewing for years, but I've been too backward to know it. Ever since I left home and school I've been heading South, only I never realized it till now. Life would have been a lot sweeter if I had. But then there's the old catch, maybe I wouldn't be appreciating it so much. That's a lot of *I's,* but do you still think I'm quick?"

"You seem to be catching up quick."

"The real question is, am I getting South too late?"

"I don't think so. There should be room for a Yankee architect here."

"Mrs. Winship feels the South is trembling on the verge of a great renaissance. I'd certainly like to get in on that."

"But don't you think you better concentrate on this week, as a starter? What will you do about Mrs. Winship, for example?"

"I'm afraid it's a little late to do anything about Mrs. Winship. But I'll do her house plans, on the side, if she buys your uncle's plantation. How's that?"

"It's wonderful. But how will Mrs. Winship like being done on the side? Isn't it going to be a little complicated for you?"

"For some reason nothing seems complicated anymore. It must be the climate."

They had reached the spear-supported awning of Mr. Blarker's office, and here they stopped while Eleanor introduced him to the Lafayette house across the way. It was the noble old house whose direct opposition to Mr. Blarker he had noted with approval this afternoon. Now, in the gloomy light of Bay Street at night, it looked even older and more faded, but nobler too, larger and prouder, more challenging and more enduring. A discreet veil of shadow was drawn over the façade, concealing all ravages of time and change. Only a single blemish stood out undisguisably: from one chaste column of the portico, to which a double flight of steps led up, protruded a barber's pole.

"Very handsome headquarters for the opposition, all right," he said, as they started across the street. "But why is it called the Lafayette house? Was it one of the General's headquarters, or did he just stop here for a shave?"

"I was afraid of that," she said, with a shake of her head. "Something really should have been done about that pole before this, but we couldn't get the barber to vacate till yesterday. You'll agree it's the first thing that needs attention tomorrow morning."

"Why not now? We could wrap it up and leave it on Mr. Blarker's doorstep for a stick of peppermint candy,—after all, it's still April Fools' Day. But if that seems too droll, just overlook it. I'm feeling a little light-headed tonight."

And as they started up the steps of the house, Rufus climbing ahead, he said: "By the way, you don't suppose all this—the stars and everything—could be just an elaborate April Fool, do you?"

"Your staying over to help with the house isn't a joke, is it?"

"All right, no more questioning. It's just that I'm a little sensitive about the First of April. Something big always seems to happen. So far it's been bad, but I've always felt it would be good if All Fools' Day would only fall on a Sunday, particularly Palm Sunday. Did Lucy make a good superstitious Southerner of you?"

"Oh, very."

"Then you're impressed."

"I really am."

When they stood at the top of the steps, he asked her smile: "But why is it called the Lafayette house?"

"Because he spent a night here once, about a hundred years ago. Not as the dashing young hero of the Revolution, but as a tired old man, come to say farewell to the country he helped make. They gave him a royal welcome in Beaufort. He stood right here, with his hands on this railing, and thanked them with tears streaming down his cheeks. Or so I'm told."

He gave that some thought, hand on the railing.

"I wonder," he said after a moment, "what the old boy would make of his America now. Specially Mr. Blarker. I don't think he'd like Mr. Blarker."

Rufus was panting to get into the house, but he had to wait till Eleanor fished a key out from behind a blind. Then when the door was unlocked, he led the way in with cautious importance.

It was black dark inside and musty-smelling, and footsteps made a hollow sound.

When John Clark finally found a match, the tiny flare was blinding at first. Then it settled down to burn a brief hole in the blackness, revealing an empty hall, and at hand double doors open-ing into a large empty room.

"The mantel's in there," Eleanor said, as the match died out.

When he struck another to light the way, it saw them only over the threshold.

"At this rate," he said, "we ought to make it by midnight."

But then he remembered the lighter in his vest pocket. . . . He never expected to get used to this perforated brass cylinder, this old army lighter that had once belonged to Helen's first love, killed in action, and tonight it was a little too much. Typical of

Helen to have made him a present of it on their first April First together: it was an April Fool surprise because it always worked. And it always had, up to now.

"This clicking you hear," he explained to Eleanor, somewhere in the cavernous darkness, "is just an old April Fool lighter I've been carrying for a friend. It's never balked before. Must be the climate again."

"Maybe it's out of gas," she suggested. "Or just out of sorts."

"It's out of something," he said, working at it.

Voices had a strange magnified quality in the darkness, resonant and echoing. Even Rufus's sniffing around the edges of the room sounded exaggerated. And each scratch of the lighter was like the rasp of a file.

It made an occasional spark to encourage him to scrape on, but it refused to light. And in its refusal there was a sense of having lost her in the darkness, of being without her and alone again, clicking away at nothing.

"Still there?" he asked.

"Still here," her voice answered at his elbow.

Then suddenly, miraculously, the lighter took fire.

For an instant it was a dazzling blur: then sank down to a sad wavering little flame. Like a Christmas candle in the trenches, as Helen had once said in a moment of weakness. And now in this moment he felt a touch of pity for that moment, for all moments, for everyone lost in the darkness of time. In reaction to which the thought flashed: a pity that even this present couldn't be free from the past. First love was free from it: perhaps that was how it got its reputation for being the purest and best: later love was all mixed up, the later the worse mixed. . . . But then as the frail light spread, he met Eleanor's eyes smiling at him. Shining straight at him in the light, revealed at last. Not for effect as eyes had a way of doing, he saw, and not seeing themselves but seeing him, understanding and receiving him. It lasted only a bare moment, this meeting across the flame, but he felt it would last forever.

When her eyes turned away, it was impossible to see anything beyond her. But the whole incredibleness of this night and moment came to sober him with a quick caution. By doubting, by refusing to believe his eyes and heart, he might be able to hold his luck, keep it from getting scared away. And he hastened to look around the room with her, matter-of-factly, as if they were still just barely acquainted, she the obliging guide, he the accommodated tourist.

The room, he forced himself to observe, was not empty after all. There were living shadows, spirits of the darkness not dispelled by the lighter but only driven back into corners; and there was a barber's chair, seated by a window with a frayed shade, and explaining the room's faint aroma of bay rum. And then, directly facing them across the room, was the marble mantel. An elegant presence, soft white, graceful, proud.

He held the lighter high to peer at it.

"Well, it's a beauty sure enough. . . . A gem, as Mrs. Winship says."

He found he was whispering, as if the mantel, like the miracle of this night, might be scary too. And when he followed her across the worn floor, he stepped lightly, respectfully, practically tiptoeing.

On close inspection the top of the elegant mantel proved to be tattooed with cigarette burns.

"What do we do about that?" she asked him.

"Acid will take them off," he thought. "But don't you think we better leave them on till Mrs. Winship has that exact copy made?"

"That's right," she nodded gravely.

He put the lighter down on the tattooed top, and as he brought his hand back it touched hers with an electric shock.

"Think we can ever repair the damage?" she asked quickly, her hand calling his attention to the state of the walls and ceiling.

He looked around with a studied frown, trying to concentrate on the scarred cornices and moldings.

"It may take a little longer than a week," he decided. "Any good mechanics in Beaufort?"

"Two old colored men, the very best."

"Then it'll be easy. When do we start?"

"Right after breakfast, and a good night's rest. . . . I promise you the air will be better then. And you'll be able to see better."

From plain elation he was able to laugh at that.

"I'm sorry," he told her, "but I'm not sleepy, and I've never been able to see better in my life."

"Well, at least you can think better in the morning. I know I can."

Her eyes were smiling, but seemed to be asking him for time to think.

"Shall we start back now?"

"If you think we better," he nodded. "And if you know a nice long way back."

"Well, we can go round by St. Helena's Church. If we hurry we'll be in time for the closing hymn."

"Fine. I feel like a hymn, for some reason."

He picked up the lighter and turned back to the hall with her. Outside, he held it for her to see to lock the door and put the key away behind the blind. Then he blew it out and put it back in his pocket with a twinge of relief. . . . They were together under the stars again.

"I didn't know you locked doors in the South," he said as they started down the steps after Rufus.

"Oh, we didn't use to," her voice answered with a lightness that seemed like a sigh of relief.

"Back in the good old days, before Yankees and things?"

"That's it. But even now we still have an open-door policy, if you know where to look. You can usually find the key under the mat or somewhere handy."

As they reached the sidewalk and started on up Bay Street, following Rufus's knowing lead, she said: "You really like hymns?"

"Sure. I don't want to miss that last one. Maybe it will be *The Palms,* seeing it's Palm Sunday. *Hosanna—praise ye the Lord—blessed is He Who comes bringing to us—Salvation.* Isn't that something like it?"

"You're certainly warm, if not hot."

"I'm a little out of practice. . . . How about *Hark, Hark, My Soul.* That was always my favorite. And there's another grand one with a lot of *Halleluiahs.* Or is that more Easter?"

"A little more Easter. . . . You're a walking hymnal."

"I used to be. I was a confirmed Episcopalian once. At least I think I was."

"Strange sort of thing to be vague about, isn't it?"

"Well, I suppose it is. But it all seems such a long way back. . . . It's a nice thing to be getting back to hymns."

But underneath he was wondering how you told an old friend like Helen that you were being born again.

IV

Mrs. Albright decided she would walk to the Library by way of Bay Street. It was a roundabout way and meant that much more work for her lame knees, but then it was such a lovely lovely afternoon, and she had her letters to mail at the post-office and her messages to deliver.

And she had plenty of time on her hands before tea, she thought as she left the gates of Marshlands and started down Fenwick Street, treading with care because her knees were so treacherously crippled today. There would be nothing stirring at the house before tea-time; but then everybody would assemble again in the living-room and it would be like a play to watch. To be sure tea-time was not half as exciting as it had been at the height of the season, when the house had been packed with guests, stacks of mail on the hall table, telegrams arriving at all hours, and people long-distance telephoning to New York and Chicago and San Francisco and even Paris, France. But then there had been really too much going on, too much to keep track of. Now it was just right: no new people arriving and just enough left to keep straight. And plenty of spare cakes on the tea-tray, she thought with a myopic smile at the Rutherford lawn, where some dear little girls were having a tea-party for their dolls. Or were they skipping rope?—at this distance it was hard to be sure. Whichever it was, it seemed in a way only yesterday that she herself had been playing with dolls, and skipping rope too for that matter.

Yes, this was the very nicest time of the year. And it was true, as Everet had written, that people who were lucky enough to be South made a great mistake to leave or want to leave just when the weather was best. But still, as she had mustered the courage to write back to him, most people did like to be with their families at Easter, whatever the weather.

Easter. Here it was Wednesday and only three more days to Easter, another Easter. Imagine that, thought Mrs. Albright, solemnly. And because it was one of such a long procession of Resurrection Days, she hastened to avoid wondering what on earth had ever become of them all by wondering if the weather could possibly stay this perfect for Beaufort's little parade. She did hope that no Beaufort bonnet would be disappointed, and of course no Cleveland bonnet either. And for a blissful interval she saw herself back home with her family, riding to Easter service in the Buick with her son and her daughter and the children. But no, they were parading to church in crisp sparkling sunshine, that was it, and the children were laughing and coaxing and urging her along, using their pet hurrying names for her: Come on, Granny-dumpling, Granny-jumbo, Granny-jumdumps, hurry! Now children, now dears, Granny's hurrying, now don't pull Granny, dears, Granny might fall; but they were only pulling at her so they could reach her cheek to kiss. And her knees were doing fine now, why she was just rolling along. But when she tried to take a little surer grip of the children's hands, the sparkling sunshine turned to cold gray sleet, and before she knew it she was left behind, left alone, scarcely able to continue at all, her knees stiffening into their elephantine plod and sway in treacherous slush. Yes, alone, and the children's precious forms were skipping, skating, slipping and sliding away, their voices and their laughter fading, growing fainter and fainter. . . .

All is Unity, Mrs. Albright reminded herself in Beaufort sunshine, and Unity is God, and God is Good. But still her knees ached with every step, and still she felt vaguely sad inside. The calomel she had allowed herself yesterday didn't seem to have worked very well this time, and her after-lunch nap hadn't helped much either. Perhaps she shouldn't have taken the third shrimp croquette, but they were so good. . . . In her last letter to Everet she had come right out and asked him if it wasn't time for her to begin to think about packing for home, and she had even enclosed a clipping from the paper reporting that spring was early at the North this year. She had written him over a week ago, but she had had no answer yet. She did hope he wasn't offended,—Everet was so sensitive. She should never have sent the clipping: that was presumptuous and nagging. That deserved this silence. Of course, he was terribly busy and that might explain the delay. And of course there might be a message from him this afternoon, though the afternoon mail seldom brought anything.

Well, at least her Unity pamphlets had come in the morning mail, and that was some consolation. All is Unity, she thought, feeling in her handbag to make sure she had not forgotten and left them on the bureau. She wished now that she had ordered another dozen instead of just six.

Two of this latest batch were already gone: one to the nice young architect, Mr. Clark, who sat with her at lunch and was so interested in hearing about her grandchildren; the other to Lee, the nice little waitress, with a request that it be shared with Pearl the cook. She had considered offering one to Mrs. Winship, who in spite of all the money and young men did seem in sore need of Unity, but something in Mrs. Winship's eye had made her hesitate. To have presented Reverend Macbeth with a message of divine guidance and healing would have been impertinent; and as for the Markses, they had said politely that they were already "familiar" with Unity. So she still had four pamphlets to dispose of.

One of the remaining four was intended for Judge Bramwell's sisters, the Judge himself having proved unapproachable. She had never met the Misses Bramwell, in fact she had never really seen them, but from hints dropped by Miss Eugenia over a period of time she had gathered that Susan and Isabel Bramwell were no better than lost souls, that Bramwell Castle was a house divided against itself and indeed in need of Unity. Then another message was for Mr. Blarker, the real-estate man, who had so kindly insisted on taking her out in his car for a whole afternoon of seeing lots, though she had tried to tell him she was not even thinking of buying any land. And one was for the nice boy at the *A & P* store, for him and for the girl he was hoping to marry when he saved up enough money; and she thought of the nice boy at the Cleveland neighborhood *A & P* where she went marketing with her grandchildren, when she was allowed to be home for a few weeks between exiles. And, finally, one was for some unknown human destination by way of the Library. She would stick it firmly in the back of the book she was returning and trust to luck that it would escape the notice of Miss Sally Broughton, who had long ago been presented with her pamphlet. This last one was to be a special random offering, a shot in the dark, bread cast on the waters, a white messenger dove released to alight no telling where!

As Mrs. Albright plodded cheerfully along, looking down every other step or so to watch her footing, she remembered that this was the very way her own first Unity message had come. She had found it, a little white dove, nestling in a circulating-library book in St. Petersburg, where Everet had sent her for several winters after the War and before his big rise in Midwest Utilities. She had liked St. Pete, the easy-going crowds and the nice wide streets with plenty of benches, but Everet had decided it was not exclusive enough for his mother. Dear Everet: he had always been such a good thoughtful son, even as a boy; and she remembered all the Larkin products he had sold one summer for premiums to surprise her with a kitchen cabinet, denying himself a New-Departure coaster-brake bicycle. . . . How guilty she had felt at first when she had deserted her Methodist church to become part of Unity. *Showers of blessing, showers of blessing we need,—millions of mercies drop round us, but for our showers we plead.* The old hymns were hard to forget. And then there was the difficulty of holding the thought of mind over matter. Even now, this year when at last she had come to feel steeped enough in Unity to be worthy to pass the word on to others, even now she was often weak.

"You are nothing," she reminded her lumbering legs as they carried her down the afternoon street of soft spring sunshine. And to herself she added: My body is material but I am spirit, and all is Unity, all is health, all is peace.

The nonexistent aches in her knees did seem to be loosening up a little, and she was careful to let them know that she was stopping at the causeway bridge not on their account but simply for breath. She rested her hands on the railing with a sigh of relief and peered toward the shining river. The tide was ebbing, but there was still enough water left in the causeway inlet to reflect the wing of Bramwell Castle with its shuttered windows. On some of her afternoon walks she imagined she heard muffled screams or weird laughter in the Castle, but all was calm today. Only the remote cries of river gulls, and the voices of two barelegged boys crabbing along the edge of the marsh flats. . . . My grandsons, she thought. And as she looked down at the dark water ebbing reluctantly from under the causeway bridge, she saw herself mirrored alone, suspended over an abyss of blue. Her only company in this dizzy void was a lonely winter reed cast off by the new spring marshes, and as she clung to the railing this straw of realization pulled her down into sick emptiness. They all want to be rid of me, she saw: I'm an old nuisance to them and in the way and not wanted. And where were they planning to exile her next summer, for her "health"? It isn't fair, she told them; and as sickness sharpened into rebellion, she warned, Once I get home this time I won't budge, and you can't make me! But when she closed her eyes, with a peace peace be still, bitterness receded and sickness passed away. The moment of madness was gone and all was Unity again, Unity and resignation, resignation and remorse. I'm ashamed of you, she sighed at her material self. And then, remembering her messages, she brightened and trod stoutly on her way.

When she stopped at the garden gate of the Castle to deliver her first message, she was faced with an abrupt and serious problem. If she left the pamphlet plain-so at the gate, it would probably be found by old Judge Bramwell and never reach his sisters. Fortunately she was able to rummage an envelope and pencil out of her carry-all handbag, and enclosing the pamphlet she painfully addressed the envelope to *The Misses Bramwell—Personal* and stuck it in the gate. With surprise then she noticed that there was something strange about the look of the house: the entrance porch seemed to have lost its heavy vine shroud, exposing the front door. But that wasn't likely, her eyes must be playing another trick on her, and besides she couldn't tarry here peering like this. And she lumbered hurriedly away, feeling like a child in headlong flight after ringing a dangerous doorbell.

The giddy prankish goose-flesh feeling of having put over a neat one stayed with her the rest of the way to Bay Street. But there it sobered down to gentle anticipation of the next stop. Anticipation touched with regret, for she was sorry she was not offering a message to everybody she passed, each nice human face, white and colored.

There was nothing complicated about her *A & P* stop. When her boy came to meet her with his nice smile, she bought a box of fig newtons for a snack against night hunger and then pressed the promised message into his hand. "Read it just before bed," she beamed simply, "and sleep with it under your pillow." And touched by his pleased and grateful look, she toddled out of the store and plodded on to Mr. Blarker's office.

As she entered under the green spear-supported awning, passing from the warm sunshine of the street into the dampness of Mr. Blarker's headquarters, whose walls were plastered with visions of Beaufort fearfully and wonderfully developed, she was greeted by the cheery nasal brass of Mr. Blarker's stenographer, issuing from *True Romantic Confessions*. "Hi! Mis' Albright ma'm, how you feelin' this fine evenin'?" Mrs. Albright said she couldn't complain, and could she see Mr. Blarker. "Why the boss-man's out right now, ma'm, but he's just been tryin' to get you on the phone!—he's got just an *adorable* bargain lot to show you in the Casa Marina sub-division, and he says he can put you just the *cutest* little old hacienda house on it with a real tile patio for a price he says you'll just *never* be able to duplicate!—now if you'll just take a seat, sugar, I know he'll be right back, he just stepped out for a dope." Mrs. Albright was sorry but she'd just stepped in to leave a message she'd promised Mr. Blarker. Receiving the proffered pamphlet the pretty face fell, but rallied quickly: "Oh, all rightee, I'll tell him." "You'll be sure he gets it, won't you," said Mrs. Albright, "and you might like to glance over it yourself." "Uh-huh, yes ma'm," said the pretty face with a snap of chewing-gum.

Out in the nice sunshine again Mrs. Albright waited at the curb till all visible traffic, one automobile and a dray, was safely disposed of. Then with the way clear she crossed the street in an unwieldy panic, reaching the opposite curb with a puff of relief. All is Unity, she thought praisefully, and now only one final afternoon message remained to be delivered. . . . When she nodded to the Lafayette house in passing, she saw that a carpenter and a painter were at work in the open hall; and when she heard someone call her name from above, she peered up to see Eleanor with John Clark waving to her from a window. She waved back to them and paused to exchange a few words of greeting. Then, placidly reflecting their smiles, she plodded on to the corner, where she turned her back on Bay Street and the river and headed for the postoffice. There a letter from home was waiting for her, she felt sure, but as a sop to fate she pretended she didn't really expect anything.

The post-office steps, coming on top of her long missionary trek and her mail anticipation, took the last of her wind. And even after a pause before the Join-the-Navy poster and the Civil Service Examination lists on the bulletin-board, she arrived at the stamp window quite breathless. No, the nice plain face at the window reported, the only Marshlands mail this afternoon was a bunch of stuff for Mrs. Winship. "Well," said Mrs. Albright sweetly, not blaming the sympathetic face for the rebuff, "I just thought there might be something,—I'm expecting an important letter." And she turned her attention to the mail slot, where she tenderly deposited one at a time her missives to the family, a letter to Everet and picture postcards for the children: her disappointment taking the form of a regret that the range of Beaufort postcards was so limited that she had to repeat every other week, had to keep sending the same views over and over. Well, the nice plain face offered helpfully as she was leaving, maybe the letter she was looking for would be in the morning mail. "Oh yes," said Mrs. Albright gratefully, "I'm sure it will come by tomorrow."

But she didn't begin to recover from the post-office blow till she had descended the steps, with oblique caution. And for a minute thereafter, a minute of crushed respite on the sidewalk, the soft scented sunshine and the rejoicings of birds seemed cruelest mockery. But then she remembered the afternoon's final message still to be delivered, and somehow that thought insured a letter from home tomorrow, and with sense of Unity fully revived she started stoutly on toward the Library.

"Tomorrow," she repeated as she plodded on. And to her surprise she realized she was thinking out loud. Which reminded her of St. Petersburg winters and how, sitting on a sidewalk bench watching the crowd, she had often noticed people talking to themselves, young folks as well as old, lips moving audibly in smiling or grim self-communion. Yet not till this moment had she ever caught herself in the act, and she didn't know whether to laugh or sigh. Why, she was getting as bad as Judge Bramwell, she thought, remembering one particularly bad performance of his that she had witnessed from the garden summer-house only a day or two ago: he had come trudging through the gates of Marshlands and along the drive shaking his cane and mumbling and grumbling to himself at a great rate. But he had some excuse, poor old soul, for he was growing deaf as a post, he was hopelessly without Unity, and he was most likely worried about getting his plantation sold to Mrs. Winship. For herself she could find no excuse, having Unity, a letter from home tomorrow sure, and now a last message to deliver.

"Last but not least," she told the movie billboard in front of the Community Hall. It was John Gilbert coming next week in *The Big Parade,* which looked like a dreadful war picture, though with Marshlands about to be empty of guests and entertainment after Easter she might decide to take it in anyway. And with a prayer to Unity that next summer would somehow hold no lonely exile movies for her, she stopped by the billboard to arrange for the safe delivery of her last pamphlet, the special random message that would land no telling where. Getting out of her handbag *Mother India,* the Library book she was returning, she removed its neat wrapping-paper cover, the kind she always made for borrowed books, and for the children's schoolbooks whenever she had an opportunity between exiles; and firmly inserting the remaining pamphlet between pages near the back, she put it through several tests to see if it would fall out. Satisfied that it would not be easily dislodged, she then resumed her lumbering sway on toward the Library steps.

When she climbed the steps and pushed open the door, there were Miss Sally Broughton's tired nice brown eyes lifting from their desk work to greet her with a smile.

"Well, Mrs. Albright," said Miss Sally, "another fine day."

"Oh, isn't it lovely," beamed Mrs. Albright, a little short of breath from the steps and her secret excitement as she plodded over to the desk and put down *Mother India.*

Anxiously she watched, enlarging on the loveliness of the weather and how it just seemed too perfect to last till Easter, while Miss Sally's nimble old fingers searched a card out of the index file.

"How did you like it?" asked Miss Sally as she finally stamped *Mother India* and set it aside, without disturbing the hidden message.

"Well," Mrs. Albright sighed with relief, "I never did finish it. It goes into child marriage and all that, and as my son says we have enough mire to wade through in life without reading about it, and what's the good of it anyway."

Miss Sally nodded sympathetically. "I haven't read it myself," she apologized, folding her hands and frowning at the offensive volume, "but I'm sorry it leaves a bad taste. It's not your last book of this season, I hope. You're not leaving us yet?"

"Well," Mrs. Albright lied placidly, "my family begged me to be home for Easter, but it's so lovely here I just can't bear to leave. Of course I miss the children, but I'll have them all through summer vacation."

Miss Sally said she understood how that was, and now what would it be today? *Death Comes for the Archbishop* was in, and *An American Tragedy,* and *The Greene Murder Case.* . . . No, Mrs. Albright said she didn't think she wanted any detective stories. "My son reads all the mystery murders," she explained, "he says they rest his brain after business, but they just give me bad dreams. And I always say if you've read one you've read them all."

"Oh," she then remembered, "is *The Bridge of San Luis Rey* still out? My daughter writes me to be sure and not miss that. She says it's sad but just so human and sweetly written."

Miss Sally was sorry but *The Bridge* was still out. "But here's a little book I'm sure you'll enjoy. It's getting very popular."

"*Jalna,*" Mrs. Albright pronounced, peering at the title with placid doubt. "Well, is it pleasant? I mean does it come out right?"

Miss Sally was sure it was very pleasant and came out just right.

"Is there any sex in it?" Mrs. Albright asked in an anxious whisper.

Miss Sally was sure it was clean as a whistle.

So *Jalna* was finally settled on. And with the book tucked under her ample arm, Mrs. Albright took leave of Miss Sally and lumbered toward the door, wondering what needy soul would find the message hidden in *Mother India.*

All is Unity, she thought as her stout hand turned the knob, and tomorrow the letter from home will come without fail. And as she opened the door, her heart beaming in response to the song of a mocking-bird in the sweet spring air, she wondered if Lucy would remember this afternoon to have plenty of frosted cakes on the Marshlands tea-tray.

✓   ✓   ✓

Absently Sally watched Mrs. Albright's broad back go out. As the door clicked closed, Sally's eyes went up to the clock. 4:31, and at least an hour more before she could hope for Joe's arrival.

He would leave Marshlands after his regular visit with Emily Fenwick, and after performing for any Yankees gathered at tea-time; and then, as a sort of afterthought, he would condescend to stop by the Library. Would she ever get resigned to coming last with him, she wondered sadly as she went through Mrs. Albright's *Mother India*. She always went through every returned book after the person left, to smooth out dog-ears and remove markers: people used all kinds of odds-and-ends for markers and often forgot to remove them: matches and toothpicks, hairpins and letters, scraps of newspaper and even bits of toilet-paper. And sure enough out of *Mother India,* after much upside-down coaxing and shaking, skipped something. It slipped off the desk to the floor and when retrieved said *Unity,* which seemed vaguely familiar. But she couldn't recall the connection, and with a sigh for Joe she filed the little pamphlet away in the card index to save it for return to Mrs. Albright.

Joe was always late these days, and sometimes he failed her alto-gether, necessitating an evening call on his sisters at the Castle to find out what was wrong with him. Always late and sometimes never, yet already she was beginning to steal preliminary glances at his window, the frame of street where he would appear. And to-day her expectancy was particularly tense because today he would surely bring word that the plantation deal with Mrs. Winship was finally closed. But if she started watching for him this early she would be a perfect wreck by the time he came. She must control herself. Besides, these premature glances were producing a feeling of unreasonable animosity toward the new high-school principal. He was a nice enough young man, even if he did make her rustle up back numbers of magazines from the dust-bound stacks in the cellar, but today he happened to be sitting at the periodical table with his curly studious head directly between her and Joe's window.

But trying to control herself simply increased the strain, so she decided to just let herself go. And through the next stretch of the afternoon, as she kept glancing at the window from time to time and was always confronted by that wavy obstructive head, she de-veloped a mania to lop it clean off. Little by little, through her chats with members returning and borrowing books and through the clock-tocking intervals between, the mania grew from strength to strength.

By a quarter past five, when the afternoon's quota of visitors appeared completed and the only lingerers were the principal and two gigglish girls and a shabby stranger thumbing magazines in a corner, by then the head-lopping mania had become a really dangerous obsession. And had Mrs. Winship signed the deed papers today, or was the deal still hanging fire? It didn't seem to be Joe's price that was holding up the sale, but just the perversity of a rich woman. . . . Outwardly Sally remained her calm self, but within she was getting so tense that she was afraid she was going to scream or jump out of her skin. And at last for relief her nerves focussed on the pair of giggly girls, Natalie and Edna Lou, who were hanging around the shelves near the periodical table obviously to attract the young principal's attention. What a pleasure it would be to knock their silly tittering heads together. Instead she had to content herself with a quiet summons and a gentle reprimand.

"I can't understand," she chided them in a low moderate tone when they stood arraigned before her at the desk, "why you two girls want to be indoors on a fine afternoon like this, especially Easter vacation week."

Natalie, eyes wide with innocence, pertly explained: "Well, you see, Miss Sally, we have to prepare for a debate on Minimum Wage when school starts again."

"I wasn't aware," Sally replied with mild sarcasm, "that debate books had wings,—I didn't realize they'd flown from their place in the reference alcove to the shelves of the reading room. Now I'll have to ask you to confine your giggles to the children's side or else go home, one or the other."

Natalie and Edna Lou decided to stay where they belonged. And Sally, nerves relieved a little, resumed her desk work. But presently she became aware again of the girls' giggles and whispers, coming now from the reference alcove; and crossed with the tick-tock of the principal's block head, these alcove sounds were magnified into a discord that tightened her inner tension to the snapping-point again. . . . They were young, Natalie and Edna Lou, and she was old. She hated to think how many batches of Natalies and Edna Lous she had watched grow up in Beaufort, each batch crowding her a little closer to the wall. How she envied their flaunted youth and the ages of life they had ahead. If only she could start all over again in any one of these bright shapes of youth. And suddenly she felt cold as ice, which was senseless because the furnace was on enough to counteract the reading-room windows that the blockhead young principal had partly opened. Snatches of song from the late sunlight outside were wintry bleak, and the spring flowers on the desk seemed to be shivering and wilting under a breath of frost. . . . But then she remembered Hattie Fowler, and that thought stiffened and warmed her spine like a hot iron.

After the bank crash Sally Broughton had vowed never to speak to Hattie Fowler, never to even look at her again. In the cramped little circle of Beaufort life it had proved impossible to keep that vow to the letter, but for the six years since the crash Sally had succeeded in addressing Hattie only with the barest monosyllables and in looking at her only when absolutely necessary. Tactics that goaded Hattie to excesses of retaliation and spleen. So Sally could never afford to be taken off guard, caught in a moment of weakness; even when she was well braced, it was hard enough to withstand Hattie's onslaughts. Only by preparing in advance was she able to come through her daily passage with Hattie always unscathed, victorious by virtue of passive resistance and contemptuous control.

A glance at the clock now warned Sally that it was high time to prepare for today's ordeal. Five-thirty sharp was the signal for Hattie to appear like a demon cuckoo. And sure enough, right on the dot, in she marched.

It was easy to sense at once, without even looking at her, that she had several malicious bees in her ratty old bonnet. Nor did she lose any time bringing them out. As soon as she had returned her book and selected another for her night's ration at the telephone exchange, she got right down to business. Hattie's malevolent horse face seemed to be softening a speck with the years, but age was certainly not softening her tongue, and the shrill neighing force of her voice seemed sharper and stronger than ever; they had tried to retire Hattie from her post at the exchange, but that voice, so primed with scandal, was too well intrenched to be ousted and still ruled the party lines in triumph. Now, not from any deference to the Library's law of silence but to emphasize the import of her words, Hattie's voice was reduced to a sibilant whisper more penetrating than the average person's normal tone.

"I suppose you heard the news," she hissed across the desk.

Sally made no response, keeping her eyes on the index files that she had spread out like a shuffled deck of cards, as a precautionary counter-irritant.

"So you ain't interested," twitched Hattie. "My mistake. I thought anything that concerned Joe Bramwell concerned you."

Sally kept her eyes and fingers busy with the index cards, but she couldn't keep her ears from pricking up.

"I certainly hope," Hattie sighed, "he succeeds in selling his plantation to that rich Yankee woman. Then he can afford to put his sister Isabel away in the Columbia Asylum where she belongs, before she runs hog wild and murders somebody in their bed."

Sally couldn't help flashing a look of complete disdain at Hattie. And that was all the encouragement Hattie needed.

"You see," she disclosed in a casual hiss as she stuffed her book away in her black knitting-bag, "Sister Isabel had another *spell* this afternoon. The worst yet, from what I hear. She didn't do a thing this time but tear down the whole coral-vine off the front porch. They been training that old vine up the front of the Castle ever since Reconstruction times, maybe since Surrender, or at least as far back as I can remember. How long they been at it?—you'd know better than me, by a good ten years. Anyhow, there it lays at the foot of the steps, like a big old heap of seaweed throwed up by the tide. I just stopped by and saw it with my own eyes. And they tell me she pulled up Joe's mint bed by the roots before Susan and the butler got her back in the house. And before they got her quieted down, I hear she tore the better part of her clothes off and the butler's too, scratching and screaming fit to wake the dead."

Sally, quivering inside for Joe, tried to let her eyes betray no sign of shock but only profound contempt.

"Now to hear some folks talk," Hattie sneered at the ceiling, "you'd think Isabel was just a poor invalid. But it's going to be mighty hard pretending after this latest exhibition. Why she's crazy as a coot!"

Sally gnawed her tongue to keep from snapping back at her tormentor, and somehow she managed to keep her tingling fingers at work sorting the index cards.

"Well, I must say," Hattie sniffed in temporary defeat, "I thought you'd have spunk enough to stick up for Joe's sister, right or wrong. But I'm glad you've finally got the sense to admit she's cracked. . . . And where was your Joe Bramwell while all the rumpus was on? Having tea with his old friend Emily Fenwick as usual, I suppose."

Relieved to get off the delicate subject of Isabel, Sally allowed her eyes to return from their contempt of Hattie to the desk, where her fingers continued to sort the index cards into stacks, as if she were playing a quiet game of solitaire.

"Oh, by the way," Hattie wheezed staunchly, making a fresh start, "speaking of Emily Fenwick, hope you ain't voting on her side in the town meeting. If the Council gets instructions to accept that Lafayette house from her for a town museum or whatever it is, why it'll be the same as slapping Mr. Blarker right in the face. She's scheming to discourage him every way possible, trying to keep him from putting Beaufort on the map. Things is coming to a head at the meeting Saturday and we all got to get together and vote to throw the Lafayette house right back in her face. Voting'll be by ballot, so it won't take no nerve to do the right thing. And it's your big chance to get back at her, Sally Broughton."

Sally let that pass with a slight shrug.

"But of course," sniffed Hattie after a twitching moment, "you'll have to vote like Joe tells you. Some women was just born to play nigger for a man that don't scarcely know they're living. Why if he was to tell you to go jump in the river, you'd have it to do, even now. And if he said black was white, or the South won the War, you'd be ready to swear to it on a stack of Bibles. So I suppose it would just be wasting good breath to tell you his pet Eleanor ain't the tin angel he thinks she is."

Sally glanced significantly at the Library's *Silence* sign, and then past Hattie at the clock over the door.

"Did you know," Hattie gleamed, sharpening her hiss, "that the Yankee architect staying at Marshlands, John Clark, is married? Well, Eleanor knows it, I'll guarantee, but that don't stop her none. And her supposed to be engaged to one of them Charleston swells, there being nobody in Beaufort good enough for the likes of her! And did you know she was out with Clark all day yesterday? Supposed to be sailing and fishing, but Molly Ranger's husband on the pilot boat saw their boat pulled up on the beach at Old Fort and the pair of them off in the woods somewheres, looking at the ruins, I suppose. My foot. Day before yesterday they was out to Land's End, being chaperoned by Linda Robinson and Jane and Jim and the baby no doubt. And today they're together in the Lafayette house, flaunting theirselves in the face of the whole town."

Sally decided it was best to encourage Hattie to run her course as quickly as possible, so she stopped shuffling the index cards to show she was impressed.

"And that ain't the half of it," jerked Hattie. "Louella Simpson says there was a call put through yesterday afternoon to New York from the booth at the Sea Island Hotel. Says she recognized it was a female Yankee voice doing the calling, but she couldn't make out who it was till afterwards. And the call was for *Clark's wife.*" Hattie paused to let that sink in before she hissed on, in convulsive mimicry of a female Yankee voice: " 'Mrs. Clark,' she says, 'I hope my *namelessness* won't cause you to doubt my *sincerity*—I deem it only fair that you should know—your husband is *infatuated* with a young woman here.' I keep a scratch-pad on the switchboard for special occasions, and Louella swears she had the presence of mind to take the whole thing down just like she heard it. And you know what the wife said? 'Oh,' she says, 'how *amusing,* and how dreadfully *fair* of you—please accept my *sincere* thanks, and do congratulate the lucky party!' And then she laughed! Laughed right in her face. And you know who was doing the tattling at this end? But I don't suppose you'd be interested."

Eyebrows raised despisingly Sally resumed her solitaire, her pride smarting at being caught off guard by this old trick of suspense.

"Oh well," Hattie sniffed, "may as well tell you anyhow,—I know you're splitting to hear it. Well, it was that Winship creature. Yes, the same party your Joe Bramwell's trying to sell his plantation to. Beyond me why she should be sticking her nose in other people's affairs, if you ask me she should have her hands full minding her own business, with that menagerie of young men she's got. But it was her all right, because right after the call Louella says she looked out the window and saw her come traipsing out of the hotel to her car, with that tall skinny one with her. And that ain't all yet."

To speed Hattie Sally once again stopped her card sorting to show she was listening, though her eyes remained glued to the desk.

"Last night," Hattie twitched on, "long about eight, that flibber-tigibbet Charleston girl—the one that's always trying to put on airs copycatting them snippy Yankee operators—she come through with long-distance calling Mr. John Clark. Well. I knew right off who it was, before she even opened her mouth. *His wife.* And I wish you could have heard the voice on her!"

At this crucial point Hattie was interrupted by a display of impatience and protest from the young high-school principal at the periodical table in the reading room. But far from being chastened by his annoyance, Hattie simply glared back at him and swelled the volume and venom of her hiss as she continued her recital to Sally.

"I only wish I could take her off, the silly stuck-up way she talked and all. But at least I got most of it down on my pad and memorized word for word. First she asks him about Beaufort, and then she tells him about the big time she's having. *'Darling,'* she says, 'I can tell the South is simply making you over, and New York has never been such *fun,* so would you mind *terribly* if we postpone the *New Orleans reunion* or save it for another day?' 'Fine,' he says, 'because I'd like to drop back to Charleston after Easter—sorry now I skipped the gardens—then I'll be heading North *for a little talk.'* 'About life?' says she. 'That's about it,' says he. 'Sounds *too divine,'* she says, 'but remember one thing, darling, —going *native* is grand *tonic* providing you don't get in over your *head,* if you know what I mean. Don't look now,' she says, 'but a little bird tells me you're not being very *clandestine,* or don't you care. Couldn't you be a bit more *stylish,* darling. Mother knows best!' . . . Now how do you like that? Did you ever hear the likes of it?"

Sally refused to comment, but Hattie polished the subject off anyway.

"When they hung up I was just itching to step in and give her the real lowdown. And tell her she better not be so cocksure of him. A woman's a fool to let a man out of her sight and vice-verse. Now if it was me I'd never let on about no little bird. I'd kept it dark and hotfooted it down here and *trapped* the pair of them! . . . Eleanor goes back for her last term at medical school after Easter, and he's leaving for Charleston then too,—did you get that? And that's about all the rope they need to hang theirselves. It's nothing to me, I'm sure, but why don't Emily Fenwick put a stop to it, break it up? Why don't Joe do something about it? Maybe he will when you tell him what's going on. Only don't let on I told you, or I'll swear you're lying."

Sally still refused to comment. And Hattie, eyes bulging ferociously, stood twitching with frustration, and an obvious determination not to budge till she got a rise of some sort out of the desk's baffling composure. But at least her tenacity had the effect of dislodging other lingerers. With an expression of disgust the young principal gathered up his papers, removed his curly head from Sally's line of vision to Joe's window, and departed. And a moment later Natalie and Edna Lou followed him, leaving only the shabby stranger in the corner.

In departing the young principal had given Hattie a parting glare, which she had returned with interest. And now, when he and the two giggly girls were gone, she told the door: "You're riding for a fall, my fine friend." To which she added, addressing the desk: "He's been looking for trouble ever since he come here to teach, and I'm the one that can help him find it. I don't have enough on him yet, but I soon will have. Enough to get him a free ride out of town on a rail."

When Sally, showing no interest whatever in the young principal's affairs, quietly resumed her game of solitaire with the index cards, Hattie was reduced to extreme measures. After a moment of desperate twitching she suddenly, without warning, plumped herself down in the armchair by the desk, Joe's sacred seat.

It knocked the breath out of Sally. If Hattie had plumped down on her lap Sally would have been less shocked. All Beaufort knew the chair was Joe's throne and respected it as such, and not even Hattie had ever ventured—not even on the heels and strength of the bank crash—ever dared to profane it. By supreme self-control Sally refrained from exploding, but into her eyes she poured all the vials of her wrath and hate.

"If looks could kill," Hattie sneered with a taunting smirk, trying to appear comfortably seated. "Suppose you think this is Joe Bramwell's private chair. Well, this happens to be a Public Library, in case you don't know it."

Hands trembling, cheeks burning, Sally somehow still managed to hold her peace. But Hattie was quite satisfied now. "Well," she snapped with a cheerful toss of her head at the clock over the door, "I got to be going. I promised to relieve Louella on time. Poor fool, she thinks she's got a new beau on the hook." And with a twisted leer she prepared to vacate the forbidden chair. But first she leaned toward the desk for a parting shot. Her breath not having improved with age, Sally recoiled.

"Give *Judge* Bramwell my regards," the horse teeth clicked, "and tell him about his dear Eleanor. And tell him he better keep his dear sister Isabel under lock and key, before they put her away in the bughouse." And in a sardonic whisper she added: "And you better watch out for that man you got in the corner, Miss Sally,—ain't you afraid to be left alone with a specimen like that? If I bump into Joe outside I'll tell him to make haste."

Sally sat contemptuously rigid till the door opened and closed and Hattie Fowler was finally gone. Then she allowed herself to go limp in her chair, closing her eyes with a sigh of complete exhaustion.

Passive resistance had won another victory, but at what cost. Silent treatment, as dignified weapon of defense against Hattie's wild skirmishing raids and onslaughts, had a fearful kickback, particularly when Hattie was on a really offensive tear. A full year's growth lost in today's encounter, Sally decided, feeling like a very old rag. But then the thought of Joe came to revive her. And when she opened her eyes and discovered that the shabby stranger in the corner was looking at her, she quickly recovered an erect and businesslike posture.

When she had regained some measure of composure, and had put the index cards away, Sally got her dustcloth out of a lower drawer of the desk and proceeded to wipe Joe's violated chair, carefully rubbing off the Hattie desecration. After that she made a circuit of the children's alcove and the reading room to turn on all lights. Spring, which had arrived only yesterday, was already slanting toward summer, lengthening the days so that it was still light outside now at closing time; but inside gloomy shadows were creeping out from every corner. Not that she minded shadows in the least, Sally assured herself: she was turning on all lights simply to prepare a bright cheerful welcome for Joe. And when she closed the windows that the young high-school principal had opened, she paused at Joe's window to look up the street. But there was no sign of him yet.

Absently polishing the panes of Joe's window while studying the shabby stranger out of the corner of her eye, Sally reproached herself for being affected by Hattie's sly warning. Still it did feel a little creepy being alone with this unknown quantity in the late tocking hush of the clock. She had never had a tramp in the Library before, in fact she had never even seen one till recently; but since the Florida boom these Yankee products had become quite a frequent occurrence, particularly in autumn and spring when they passed through Beaufort like migrant birds. This one looked harmless enough, to be sure: he wore a disreputable army coat and his face bore a week's stubble, but somehow he didn't look in the least cutthroat. She hesitated to approach him, though, and when she finally worked up courage to move toward him it was like walking on needles and pins.

"I'm afraid," she told him tentatively, "it's closing time."

He looked up at her with the eyes of a whipped dog. "Yes ma'm," he nodded in a flat husky voice. And picking up a grimy cap he started for the door, hitching up his ragged trousers on the way.

When he was gone, Sally was left facing six o'clock with a twinge of regret and a vague sense of waste. After all, she realized as she tidied the magazines on the periodical table, he was some woman's wandering boy, and she could at least have offered him some supper in exchange for a little wood-chopping or something. But then she remembered how little there was in the house: nothing but scraps, and Janet's milk. And Joe would be violently disapproving. She had heard him on the subject of encouraging tramps, "aiding and abetting common vagrancy".

With a sigh she returned to her nook. And after a brief consultation with the mirror at the back of the *Readers Guide* shelf, she settled down to wait for Joe. She would wait, she told the clock, exactly ten minutes, and not one second longer.

It was exactly seventeen long minutes past six when she finally caught sight of him in the frame of his window. It was growing dark outside, but the street-corner light had come on to welcome the unmistakable pride of him, the authority of his cane, the wagging positiveness of his head. And if those characteristics were not

923

enough to distinguish him from all other men in Beaufort, or in the world for that matter, there was his hat, the broad-brimmed disreputably crumpled panama that he always exchanged for his old square derby on the first day of April, hot or cold, rain or shine. And there was his shawl. He never changed from his gray winter cutaway to pongee and baggy crash till after Memorial Day, but his overcoat was discarded early in the season and replaced by this shawl of Scotch plaiding. It was still a sore point with the Book Committee that in a weak moment three years ago they had allowed their honorary chairman to persuade them the Library needed a copy of *Tartans of the Scottish Clans;* Joe alone had made use of the manual before its retirement to dusty neglect, and a month after his perusal of the illustrated patterns he had blossomed out in a plaid shawl shrill as bagpipes, the tartan of the Clan Bramwell.

No-one but Joe could have carried off such a wild ancestral flourish. But as grand old man of Beaufort he could have donned a kilt without alarming people. Absolved long since of any blame for the bank crash, Joe was thoroughly accepted and indulged as the town's outstanding character. And how he fancied himself in the role of privileged eccentric, thought Sally tenderly, preparing with devoted heart for his entrance. It was meat and drink to him, she thought as she busied her hands on the desk, and the only career and honor left to him now.

She looked up with pleased surprise when the door opened and he came stomping in.

"Well!" she smiled, "I was afraid you weren't going to get here at all today."

Sally's voice was carefully distinct but not unduly raised. By diligent and expert adjustments she managed to keep pace with Joe's advancing deafness without any appearance of strain. But it was an increasingly nerve-racking process, for Joe scorned lip-reading as he scorned all earphone contraptions. He refused, in fact, to even admit his ailment. If he was a bit hard of hearing at times, it was because people had a way of mumbling their words nowadays, which was a blessing since it spared him much nonsense. That was all there was to it. And though he fiercely resented being shouted at he refused to keep his own voice down, pitching it higher and higher to confound the thundering silence that was closing in on him.

"A very busy afternoon," he grumbled loudly, thumping down on the desk the book he was returning. "Can't stay but a minute."

He allowed Sally to relieve him of his battered panama, retaining as usual his shawl and cane. His eyes looked bloodshot and tired, she thought as she hung his hat on the rack beside her own things, yet his face was strongly flushed and animated. He seemed more full of himself today than for ages, more like his high-tide self before the bank crash, his old stout full-bodied self. But perhaps an overdose of his standard remedy was responsible for that, she decided with a tolerant inward sigh, detecting an uncommonly rich aroma of bourbon in the air as she returned to her desk.

"Isabel had a bad day," he deigned to explain boomingly, using his handkerchief to slap-dust the seat of his chair, as if it wasn't perfectly spotless already and always.

"Oh, I'm sorry," Sally murmured, lapsing for a moment into her habitual Library tone as Hattie's desecration of the sacred chair clashed with Isabel's affliction and Joe's provoking handkerchief.

"What's that?" he demanded in a blare that startled the clock and every shelf and recess of the building.

"I say," said Sally, raising her voice, "I hope it's not serious."

"No, no," he rumbled petulantly, settling himself in the profaned chair. "Just a touch of nerves. She's all right now. . . . Strange," he frowned heavily, "that after each attack she seems better than ever."

But then he dismissed the subject with a ruffle of shawl and rattle of cane, his cavalier sword and cloak, and fishing his pince-nez out of a vest pocket he fell to polishing them with profound sanguinity. He was now waiting, Sally well knew, to be cross-examined about other events in his busy day. But to her surprise and shock she found her will set against his. Some perverse element, perhaps a demon caught from Hattie, was working in her heart: some obscurely mutinous tendency was stiffening her spine, inciting her to riot, or at least to stand her ground today and not cater to his ego, not play dependable water-boy to his everlasting pride.

"What's that?" he growled sharply, nipping mutiny in the bud.

It was impossible, of course, to tell him she had said nothing. "I asked," she capitulated meekly, her will collapsing, "if there were any developments in the Winship deal."

She expected him to have the pleasure of biting her head off with a snapped "No, not yet!" Instead he soberly put on his pince-nez and regarded her with affectionate tolerance. "The deal," he nodded quietly, "is closed. The papers were signed, sealed, and delivered to the party of the second part at Emily's this afternoon."

"Oh, Joe!" Sally gasped, forgetting how he hated any display of felicitation, "isn't that wonderful!"

He rejected her enthusiasm with a snort that toppled his glasses off his nose. "What's wonderful about it? It seems to have slipped your mind that Holly Hill has belonged to Bramwells since 1762. How many other Low Country grants remain in the hands of the original owners? Preserved through every vicissitude of fortune, from redskins and redcoats to Sherman and carpetbaggers, scalawags and black republicans, and finally this rising tide of white trash! And for what? To be sold at last like a faithful retainer or some cherished heirloom surrendered to the auction block through dire necessity. And you find it wonderful!"

"And remember," he added in a more temperate tone, before she could amend her congratulations with a word of sympathetic understanding, "I still have debts of honor to meet. But after everything's settled there'll be enough left over for a few government bonds, to provide comfortable security for Isabel and Susan. My mind's at ease on that score at least. And as I remarked to Emily, I find it possible to derive a certain grim consolation from the very irony of the transaction, the classic irony of the ransoms these Yankees will pay for relics of our plantation system, the civilization they themselves destroyed."

He allowed himself a grim dry chuckle and wagged his white-maned head over the classic irony of it all. Then resuming his pince-nez with solemn precision, he concluded generously: "I claim no credit for the sale. Emily engineered the whole thing, from start to finish. Though in justice some credit must go to her architect guest, John Clark. He's agreed to draw up plans for a mansion at Holly Hill, and that seems to have carried considerable weight with the flighty Winship woman. Fine young chap, Clark. We owe

926

him much. And he's been a boon to Eleanor, you know, in doing over the Lafayette house."

"Yes I know," said Sally, the demon influence of Hattie beginning to function again. "He's quite interested in Eleanor, isn't he. They seem to have become boon companions, from all I hear."

"Yes," Joe granted innocently, "they've become great friends. Well, he's a most likable chap, not at all Yankee. I took to him myself at once. I find him intelligent and well-informed, an excellent talker."

That, thought Sally, means he's an excellent listener.

"But isn't he married?" she found herself asking.

"Why yes, I believe so," Joe nodded, ruffling.

"Of course," Sally allowed, "that doesn't mean as much as it used to."

Joe's chronic ruddiness took on a purple cast from high stock to white mane. "And precisely what do you mean by that? Are you insinuating Clark isn't a man of honor?"

"That doesn't mean what it used to either," Sally flushed back.

Joe's mane bristled. "I resent that! Honor, like Justice, is a fixed quality, the same in every generation, and I believe I know an honorable man when I see one. I should be able to judge character by this time! I'll vouch for Clark. And I'll remind you that my niece is no child, but a responsible young woman."

"I'm afraid," Sally persisted with burning cheeks, "even that doesn't mean what it used to."

"Confound it!" Joe blasted, "what in perdition are you driving at? Do you insinuate that a respectable friendship can't exist between a lady and a gentleman because one of them happens to be married? Haven't I been a friend of Emily Fenwick's all the years of her married life? Has anyone ever dared to cast any reflection on our friendship?"

"I'm simply thinking about the welfare of your great-grand-niece," Sally retreated obliquely. "I'm simply wondering how this friendship is going to work out for her."

"Well, you don't need to!" Joe snorted with such violence that his glasses were dislodged again. "My niece is entirely competent to take care of her own affairs, thank you. I mean to say, I consider your attitude a piece of outrageous effrontery! And I'd like to know how you ever got started on it. It's not like you, and I won't have it. That's all."

Accepting the rebuke contritely, Sally ventured no further comment on the subject of Eleanor. Her only wonder now, as she tried to quiet the trembling of her hands on the desk, was how on earth she ever had got started, what ever could have possessed her to deliberately rouse Joe's wrath, when her everlasting purpose in life was to minister to him, soothe and smooth him. Well, nothing to do now but look abjectly chastened and wait for him to cool down.

He took his time about it. She had to endure a whole series of scathing snorts before his complexion returned to normal pink. Then he finished relieving his feelings by indignantly prodding the book on the desk with his cane.

"How was it?" she finally ventured to ask, brightly, though she was still trembling for having offended him.

"What I expected," he eventually growled at the well-prodded book. "More libel in the guise of history. Can no-one write accurately, fairly, or even sanely about the South? Must we forever be the victims of fools and slanderers? Persons who spell negro with a capital N, and call the War between the States the *Civil* War!"

Sally nodded encouragement, with a breath of relief that he was off on a favorite topic; and when he stopped his prodding and shifted the bone-shod tip of his cane to the floor for emphasizing taps, between appreciative nods she glanced through the obnoxious book. Plenty of underscoring and marginalia to be erased later, she noted. For a spell after the bank crash he had given up this slashing practice, a symptom of deflation that had worried her even more than his temporary loss of weight and his neglecting to apply a dusting handkerchief to the spotless seat of his chair; but now he was long since back at his old tricks. And today they seemed more violent than usual. Besides frequent recurrences of his customary "Incorrect!", she noted several cases of "Utter rot!", two "Ravings of a lunatic!", and one "Consummate asininity and gross prejudice!". And a less casual inspection would surely reveal plenty more jottings, all deeply engraved into the pages with a savage pencil. It would take endless eraser work to restore the book to order, yet she was glad to see that he was in such fine fettle.

"Facts," he was declaiming, "mean nothing to these latter-day scribes. The author of this so-called history of South Carolina hasn't the remotest understanding of his subject. To begin with, I would point out to this humbug"—the pince-nez came back into play with a judicial smack—"that our constitution was framed by Locke, after the pattern of Plato's model Republic. It was he who foresaw the perils of a too-numerous democracy."

Sally nodded attentively.

"Now Hamilton," Joe rumbled on, "saw the people simply as a great beast. An extreme view, perhaps, but containing a core of prophetic truth. For unless the rising tide of the masses can be stemmed, what remains of civilization must be engulfed, utterly wiped out. Keep down the rabble! That must become the watchword of these troublous times. . . . Remind me to make that point clear for once and for all in a letter to the *News & Courier,* hear."

Change-and-decay was Joe's pet hobby, and once astride he was capable of riding it for hours. So, while promising to remind him to write a letter to the paper, Sally stole a glance at the clock and decided to call a prompt halt. For if he was allowed to go on at length today it would make him late for supper, make it too late for him to escort her home on his way back to the Castle, make him scold her for letting him lose track of the time. Besides, it was bad for him to get worked up. And, incidentally, some busybody would be sure to report to the penny-pinching Board that Library lights were burning long after closing time.

"Well, what will it be today?" she asked hopefully, proposing as a starter *The Story of Philosophy.* "You haven't read this yet."

"Nor am I likely to," he glowered at it, "as long as my mental faculties remain unimpaired. The wisdom of the ages in capsule form! This is the third time you've tried to palm that monstrosity off on me, and I'll thank you not to try it again. When I need philosophic refreshment I turn to the proper authorities, the original sources, the classics."

Flustered, Sally turned in desperation to the fiction shelf. *Black April* caught her harassed eye, and in her extremity she dared to submit it. "Now really, Joe," she proposed with a courageous smile, "here's one book you shouldn't miss."

"Fiction?" he demanded, bristling.

"Well, I suppose it is, in a way. But it's by a Carolina woman, Julia Peterkin, and she's given a faithful picture of our colored people."

"Faithful poppycock!" Joe exploded. "Great Scott!—what next? What does any white person know about black people? I've lived among them all my life, eighty-odd years, and I claim to know nothing about them, nothing whatever. Sounds like Yankee business."

"There's really nothing offensive about it," Sally gently protested. "You see, no white characters appear in it at all. It's just about a group of gullah people living on an old river plantation, like Holly Hill. It's just the plain simple story of their daily life, their joys and sorrows."

"Is that all?" Joe inquired with purple restraint. "Proving, I suppose, that under their black skins they're just human beings like ourselves. Take it away! It makes my flesh crawl. You must be out of your mind, offering me such stuff. If you haven't anything decent, say so!"

Shriveled, Sally turned back in despair to the non-fiction shelf. The only remaining candidate, arrived at by panic elimination, was *Under The White Eagle*. He would almost certainly reject it with heat, but as a last resort she submitted it anyway.

"Is that the best you can do?" he snapped at her. "Another report on Russia! Has the book committee turned Bolshevik?"

"This one's about the White Russians," Sally explained weakly. "It tells what happened to the aristocrats. I thought you might be interested because it's so like what happened to us."

"Like what happened to us!" he rapped out with a sharp crack of his cane. "How can you make such a ridiculous statement? There's no parallel whatever. The Russian upheaval, like the French Revolution, was brought on by the gross folly and stupidity of the ruling class. They deserved their fate. While in our case it was an attack from the outside, undeserved, unprovoked, unutterably malicious and vicious. The South was a balanced democracy, patterned along supremely enlightened classic lines, and any minor imperfections that may have existed would all have been ironed out in the natural course of events, if the North had not overwhelmed us by sheer force of numbers and money. The Russian debacle has its tragic aspects, I grant you, but how can you speak of it in the same breath with the catastrophic downfall of our system?"

Shortness of breath choked him off for a moment, but then he vented his outrage in a full purple roar. *"Felix qui potuit rerum cognoscere causas!* The cost of the Confederate War, the monetary cost alone, far exceeded the value of all our slaves. But did the Abolitionists ever offer to relieve us of our property by purchase? —an offer we would have spurned of course. No indeed! And why? Because they wanted to break us! . . . Well, they succeeded. But in so doing they unwittingly sealed their own fate, though even now that fact is still unrecognized by most people, North and South. Nemesis is sometimes slow but always sure. It's only a matter of time. For when they broke our planter class, they broke the heart and backbone of the country. Since then this nation has been a monstrous thing, swelling to horrid proportions like some mindless creature of the primeval slime. In destroying us they loosed perdition, and some day their creature will turn and rend them. They that sow the wind shall reap the whirlwind. It's taking longer than I expected, but it will come."

Sally bowed to this familiar refrain with old acquiescence. And Joe, puffing for breath but somewhat appeased, lifted the tip of his cane to the desk to give *Under the White Eagle* a prod of contempt.

"However," he compromised with a grunt and grumble, "if it's all you have to offer, I may as well take it along. I daresay it needs a thorough going-over."

He moved in his chair and gathered his shawl in, as if about to rise; but instead he put down his cane, located his pince-nez at the end of their ribbon, breathed fragrantly on each lense, and set to polishing them with his big handkerchief, savagely at first, then more deliberately, and finally quite gently, meditatively.

"Last evening at Emily's," he cogitated, inspecting his glasses with reflective satisfaction, "I made that very point, that the soul of Democracy perished in the funeral pyre of the Confederacy. We had a general set-to, as a matter of fact, in Emily's room removed from the bridge-fiend guests. Jane and Jim were in from the island with the baby boy, and when I arrived after supper they were just leaving to get the rascal home to bed. Great nuisance their living at Land's End, I don't get to see half enough of my godson and namesake. You haven't seen him since the christening, have you. Well, he's a great little rascal, I can tell you,—a fine set of teeth now and learning to walk. Soon he'll be talking to his old godfather. And you know, I believe he does take after me in many respects. Jane, by the way, wants to paint a portrait of us together.

Ah, that youngster! I can frankly say that through him I feel my life is complete."

He sat bemused for a long moment over that felicity. Then rousing himself from reverie with a visible effort, he perched his glasses on the end of his nose to demand indignantly of Sally, as if she had interrupted his train of thought: "What did I start to say?—what was I talking about?"

"About a general set-to at Emily's," she prompted.

"Of course. That is, we discussed everything pro and con, from national politics and the election to world affairs in general. John Clark sided with Emily, Eleanor with me. But I always take her support with a grain of salt. Eleanor, for all her good sense, seems younger in some ways than Jane. . . . You know, I'm glad now that Jane married young. Everyone should settle down early, as our parents did. It makes for stability, steadiness, sanity. Naturally I would have picked someone besides Jim Robinson for her, but there's good blood there from somewhere, and I must admit he's making her a good husband and doing very well with his scientific farming."

Joe's eyes, staring over his glasses, looked befuddled for a moment; but this time he got back on the track without any prompting. "In any case, as I was saying," he reminded himself, "I had Eleanor's courtesy support, and together we laid down the law with a heavy hand. We drove Emily and Clark to cover all along the line."

He indulged in a reminiscent chuckle, but then sobered, frowning.

"However," he rumbled with a ponderous shake of head, "it was a hollow victory. It's no pleasure to establish what a sad state we're in. The New Freedom! . . . ."

And clearing his throat pregnantly, he leaned forward to rest an expansive arm on his cane. "Your modern world," he declaimed with forensic sageness, "is like the Roman Empire in its period of decline. Then and now the phenomena of degeneration are the same. Worship of money and bigness and show. Cosmopolitanism, with its flaunted decadence, its skepticism and sophistication, its smart intellectualism, too full of relatives for any positive faith. A falling birthrate among the better classes. A deplorable weakening of family ties. And, above all, the breeding of city mobs, those monsters of mischief and misrule, so easily swayed by bread and circuses, such perfect tools for the unscrupulous demagog. The Republic is dying and the stage is set for an age of Caesars. Yet people call this the age of Freedom and Progress and Prosperity!"

Shortness of breath and another spell of vagueness brought him to a halt, and for a moment he sat staring helplessly, his ruddy assurance faded to a pallor of indecision.

"What was I driving at?" he asked almost meekly, bowing his head to peer at Sally over his pince-nez.

"Progress," she prompted alertly. "But don't you think it's about time to leave? Susan and Isabel will blame me if you're late for supper, you know."

"Yes, yes,—one minute," he frowned in testy dismissal. "And what was I saying about progress?"

"That it's not what it's cracked up to be," Sally sighed, folding her hands on the desk.

"Precisely," he nodded. . . . "I venture to say no age has ever been poorer in inner life and light. Material riches but spiritual poverty. Ill fares the land, to hastening woes a prey, where wealth accumulates and men decay."

And he recited with a sonorous roll: "*Aetas parentum peior avis tulit nos nequiores, mox daturos progenium vitiosiorem.* 'Our grandsires' time bequeathed us one more ripe in crime—our sires did worse again beget—and we shall yield the basest yet!' A fitting motto for the next generation. . . . Horace, of course, was referring to the dissolution of family life as a major ill of his age. Some ass has advanced a malaria theory to account for the decline and fall of Rome, but I agree with Horace that the relaxing of family ties was the most important cause of disintegration. Reverence for home and parents insures the continuity of a culture. Without family solidarity the people perish."

Sally found she couldn't let that pass. "Family solidarity," she challenged with feeling, "can be mighty overdone. And family ties are often strangling."

"Strangling?" he stared at her in a fluster of surprise.

"You know as well as I do," she contended, "that most families are held together by habit and caution and hate of outsiders, not by affection. And even when it is a case of affection, it's not healthy."

"Exactly what do you mean by that?" he demanded.

"I mean that families that stick together get ingrown. Relatives should separate, before they get all tied up in knots. I think people would be better off if they didn't have any relatives."

"You're joking, of course," he told her indulgently. "That's the Russian ideal, I believe. But I hardly expected to hear such tommy-rot from you, even in jest. . . . As I was saying, a man must be a good member of a family before he can be a good member of society at large. The family, obviously, is the backbone of civilization. Hence family life, and all it stood for, was the nucleus, the very heart and core of the Old South."

He gave the floor a sound rapping with his cane. "I tell you, somehow we must find our way back! We've got to revive the old way of life, recapture the spirit of the past, return to first principles, as so clearly enunciated by our great scholar and gentleman, Gildersleeve. No-one has ever stated our case better than he. In his *Creed of the Old South,* published in *The Atlantic Monthly* of January 1892, he summed it all up. But he was writing no epitaph for the tomb of the Confederacy. He did set forth the virtues that made the Old South great, yes, but he was stressing the living truth that only those same virtues could make a great new South, or any future civilization worthy of the name. The Old South had an immortal soul, and to be saved we must embrace again the enduring elements of its grace, the everlasting tenets of its creed. Mark my words, a rebirth of that faith is our only salvation!"

He came to a snorting halt there, crimson and panting. And then for a moment he seemed overwhelmed again by pale vagueness. But he roused himself from befuddlement with a conclusive cane-rap, and clearing his throat with finality sat sanguinely wagging his head, awaiting her applause.

But for once in her life Sally failed to respond. This Gildersleeve harangue of his was the ultimate expression of his feelings on the subject dearest to his heart, and never before had she missed greeting it with proper respect and appreciation. Yet today something prevented her from giving it as much as a nod of agreement. She couldn't, in fact, even accord it a decent silence. She could only think, under demon promptings, how many times she had had to sit back and listen to it.

"Oh, I'm tired of hearing about the Old South," she found herself sitting forward to tell the clock. "It's nothing but a pack of illusions."

The clock stopped with a startled fugitive look, reflecting her own shock: then tocked up wildly. And she felt rather than saw Joe's dumfounded stare, and the mantling rage with which he finally yanked off his pince-nez.

"*Illusions?*" he recovered his voice to roar at her. "What in thunder do you mean by that? Are you insinuating you don't believe the old days were good?"

It was too late to turn back now, Sally saw. And there was a terrible exhilaration in plunging ahead.

"Not as good as you believe they were," she answered, in a low even tone calculated to double his infuriation. "Fond memory plays tricks on us. We remember the good and forget the bad."

"Bah!" he snorted in a purple fume. "Absolute stuff and nonsense! Great God!—after all, I was there, wasn't I? Do you mean to imply I can't correctly recall the circumstances of my own youth?"

"And so was I there, don't forget," Sally persisted with tense calmness.

"So much less excuse for you!" he stormed at her. "Confound it, what the devil's gotten into you? I don't expect most Southerners to properly evaluate the past, because they never belonged to it. But you did. You were a young girl then, to be sure, but old enough to realize and appreciate the antebellum world. You were part of it, and now you deny its validity, even its verity! The old way of life, our plantations, our people, white and black,—just an old man's fancy, an error of aging memory, is that it? Why, it's the only reality! This modern welter, this mess we live in, this is your pack of illusions!"

And after pausing for a panting glare, he spluttered at her: "What's the matter with you today? You're not yourself."

"Maybe that's the matter," she told the excited clock. "Maybe I'm being myself, for a change."

"You're being an ass, if you'll permit me to say so! And talking like one. And if you're deliberately trying to provoke me, you're doing a first-rate job, I can assure you!"

"Haven't I a right to my own opinions," she flashed at him, "without provoking you to call me an ass?"

935

"You don't have to shout!" he shouted at her. "I'm not deaf."

"I'm not shouting! Anyway, I have as much right to as you. You've been shouting at me for years."

"Now that's enough!" he rap-snorted in a wagging rage. "Confound it!—what's the meaning of this? I've known you since you were a child, but I'm damned if I've ever known you to act like this before. I mean to say, I'm not accustomed to bad temper and claptrap from you, and I'm not likely to start putting up with it now. I won't have it, is that clear?"

But now the demon current was tugging Sally loose from all moorings.

"*You* won't have it?" she fairly flung at him. "You mean *I* won't have it! I've been listening to you for a million years, and now you can sit back and listen to me for a change! For once in my life I'm going to tell you what I think. And I think these days are better than ours in a whole lot of ways. In our day we were all cooped up in a cage of rigid right and wrong. We were all slaves to a suffocating code. We couldn't breathe without transgressing. But now the air's improving. There's a fresh breeze blowing over the land. And how I envy these young people their emancipation!"

"Very poetic," Joe told her with apoplectic restraint. "You know, I believe Russia would suit you to perfection. They seem to be really advanced over there. The breezes, I hear, have swept that land clean of every tradition and standard. You should certainly look into this Russian business."

"I'm not afraid of Russia," said Sally with head held high. "I——"

"I *understand*," he boomed, cutting her short, "they're simply overrun with fresh air. No suffocation,—nothing but *freedom*. They've gone the whole hog and carried the modern trend to its logical conclusions, in one fell swoop. Too bad you can't be young again, my dear, and *Russian*."

"I wouldn't mind," she flung back at reckless random. "It would be a much better life, I know that much. You can jeer at Russia all you like, but I'm for it. It's the—the spearhead of the new age, and it's all to the good. You can have the past. Our age is dead and gone, and so are we just about. The only difference between you and me is that I'm ready to admit it while you're too blind and stubborn to see. And even if your old South was paradise itself, don't you realize you can't turn back the clock?"

936

The clock over the door threw up its hands at that, and for a lucid moment Sally quivered in agony under the fire of Joe's glare. But her own fire flashed back when he gave her desk a sharp crack with his cane.

"I hope to die," he lashed at her, "if I ever saw a clock that couldn't be turned back! And it's not too late even now. But if we don't turn back directly, if we commit ourselves any farther along this road to ruin,—well, I shudder to think what the world will have to go through before it finds its way back to redemption!" And he added with a magnificent toss of his mane: "If it's stubborn and blind to believe in what the Old South stood for, I gladly and proudly plead guilty to the charge on both counts. But do you honestly, from the bottom of your heart, mean what you've been saying? Come now, I'll give you another chance."

"Of course I mean it," Sally told her tightly clasped hands, feeling, in spite of her demon promptings, like Brutus and Peter and Judas all rolled into one. "I believe that when these young people recover from the first natural excesses of their freedom, they'll have a far better life than we ever knew. They won't miss the best things in life, for no reason. They won't waste their lives, as we have."

"Now what do you mean by *that?*" he demanded in a violent purple bluster. "I wasn't aware I'd wasted my life."

"Well, you've wasted mine."

And suddenly Sally was overwhelmed by the truth of that. It was all there, all the futility of her life, all the bitterness of the years. Now looking back it seemed to her that there had never been anything but bitterness, that she had never known any real happiness, or had ever been young and gay, or even middle-aged and hearty and content, content in her devotion to a lost cause. It seemed now that all the days of her life since girlhood had been wasted away, like blood falling drop by drop on heedless sands, like tears falling on ashes. Always she had been like this, dried-up and faded and old, a ghost of herself waiting for nothing at the end of a barren road: and at last the weary hopelessness of it all flowed over the rim of her will.

"It's all been wasted," she told him with quivering abandon. "You've just thrown everything away, that's all. All my life I've loved you, and what have you ever given me in return. The right to sit and listen to you talk, talk, talk! Year after year! All I was good for was to be your audience, to everlastingly sit and listen, and applaud at the right places!"

In an abrupt flash of reason she saw herself clearly for an instant, heard her words echoed with terrible distinctness by the walls of books. I deserve anything he says, she realized, aware of the clock washing its hands of her. Then she sat rigid in an appalling hush, feeling Joe's eyes, waiting to be blasted out of her chair. But when his voice came at last, it sounded startlingly far-off and small.

"It's hot in here," he said, sitting back in his chair with a brief little tap of his cane. "You must have the furnace going. And all the windows are closed. There's no air."

Something in his voice tended to bring her completely to her senses, but in her breast there was still a remnant of bitter grievance that had to be spent.

"Of course the furnace is going," she told him. "It's been on low all afternoon to keep the chill off. And naturally the windows are closed,—I locked up at six. I never know whether you're coming or not, and I didn't expect you to stay this long. Anyway, you wouldn't be hot if you'd take off that crazy plaid shawl."

And pushing her chair back from the desk she got up and started for the cellar door. "I'm going down to shut off the furnace, but please don't wait for me. You better hurry home to Susan and Isabel. I'll walk home alone."

Convulsive laughter choked her as she felt her way down the steep musty stairs. But as she groped for the light cord, laughter turned to racking sobs, so that she could hardly control her hand to shut the furnace damper. And then she stood aghast, shaking all over, hot tears of shame running down her shrunken cheeks.

It was all true, she tried to tell herself, and perfectly justified. But the next instant she was fiercely condemning herself. It was all false, what she had said, ridiculously false and horrid. And she must beg his forgiveness on bended knee. Take whatever punishment was coming to her and get back, quickly, to her life-time job. The privilege and honor of serving him, in her special capacity. . . . What more could she ask of life than that. And what did her pride matter. There was no room for that. What mattered was his pride. And she would never fail him again—never, never.

Joe dear, forgive me. . . .

She stood listening with throbbing heart for his tread on the floor above. But there was no sound of his leaving. He was waiting, then, to chasten and forgive her. And struggling to collect herself, she wiped her eyes and patted her hair, pulled out the light, and started up the stairs in thankful fear and trembling.

He was sitting just as she had left him, hunched in his chair, hands on cane, head bowed, pince-nez glistening at the end of their ribbon below the bottom button of his vest. Her eyes were too ashamed to look straight at him as she went to the desk, but at a glance his mood seemed to be one of profound hurt and humiliation rather than outrage or condemnation. And she was stabbed by an awareness that he had thrown off his shawl.

Yet for a moment it was impossible to say anything. She stood in anguish by the desk, cheeks on fire, teeth locked, mouth dry as dust.

"Joe," she finally managed to speak, stiffly, "I'm sorry for what I said. I don't know what made me fly off the handle like that."

He made no answer, and she tried again in a louder tone, finding it easier now that she had broken the silence. "I don't know what possessed me to talk like that. I didn't mean a word of it, of course. I must have been out of my mind, just as you said."

Still he refused to answer, or even to look up at her. And to keep her pride from stiffening, she turned to the coat-rack.

"You don't need to spare me," she told the little mirror at the back of the *Readers Guide* shelf as she put on her hat. "I know I deserve anything you say. But please say something."

But he continued to withhold judgment.

"Well, I don't know what more to say," she sighed shakily, bringing his hat to the desk, and then putting her hands to work retidying things. "Except I'm terribly sorry and disgusted with myself. I can't explain what came over me, but I didn't mean any of it. You know that."

But he still refused to make any response.

"Well," she told the clock with a miserable shrug, "if you won't even speak to me, I suppose we may as well leave. Maybe by tomorrow you won't hold it quite so much against me."

But he made no move to leave. He wouldn't even stir in his chair. He just sat hunched there, with his chin sunk in his chest, brooding.

She went round to his side of the desk then.

"Can't you forgive me this once, Joe? Please don't take it out on me by staying away tomorrow. I couldn't stand that."

She touched his arm in final appeal, and his cane fell to the floor with a shattering clatter.

The whole building seemed to shatter. Shelved walls rocked and swayed inward with a toppling avalanche of books. When she cried out, the only help was the face of the clock, hands paralyzed at the stroke of seven. And when she turned back to Joe, she was alone in a rending never-ending silence.

V

AT HER DESK, finishing a letter to Jack in far-off Atlanta, Emily thought how strangely quiet it was this afternoon of Easter. The house felt deserted, and it took an effort to recall why. For Joe's death had wiped out the bustle of guest departures. The Markses, the Right Reverend Macbeth, Mrs. Winship and party, they all seemed simply to have vanished, swallowed up in the wake of death. They were like the everyday sounds of town lost at noon, drowned out in that moment of shock and long obliteration when, as Lucy said, "de fiuh-house sireen holluh". . . .

They were really gone, the final batch of this season's guests. All but John Clark, with Eleanor at Land's End, and Mrs. Albright, who at last was going home to Cleveland and her grandchildren.

Of all extraneous events since Wednesday, only that last came back with any clarity: Western Union calling Mrs. Albright. Her poor knees plodding to answer the telephone summons, and then her beaming face, and her efforts to contain her joy out of respect for Judge Bramwell, who had always avoided her. And now from the room overhead came faint floor creakings: Mrs. Albright was packing again. For two solid days she had been packing, though she was not leaving till Tuesday, still two days off. . . . Long ago, in the same room but another world, there had been an even greater packer. For all trips, big or little, Miss Sophie had always been ready at least a week ahead. Miss Sophie, at whose side Joe was now lying in St. Helena's graveyard.

A moment ago he had been alive in this room, making his regular afternoon call. And now this letter to Jack, forcing her to acknowledge that he was gone forever. If she could only have waited a little longer for this open admission. But if she had put off writing, then

Jack might feel that she was offended with him for not coming to the funeral. . . . Fortunately, he would be expecting her to spare him any "details", any expression of feeling. All he would want was just what she had finally set down here: statements of fact about the burial service, the flowers, and the honors paid. And then there were these two *News & Courier* clippings to be enclosed. One, the death notice. *BRAMWELL, Suddenly on Wednesday at Beaufort, Joseph Legerton Bramwell, Survived by his sisters, Susan and Isabel Bramwell, Funeral services at St. Helena's Parish Church on Saturday at 3 o'clock.* The other, a memorial to "The Grand Old Man of Beaufort",—Assistant to Confederate Secretary of the Treasury Memminger, Friend of Wade Hampton, Judge of the Old School, Distinguished Mayor, Prominent Member of This and That, Honored Citizen of South Carolina and the Low Country. All so foreign to her own memories of him, back through the years. Joe, who had been so great a part of life.

The curtains at the window stirred softly, and the sunshine of the garden and the river seemed blurred and softened, its radiance subdued as if in mourning. And now the quiet that hung over the house was like a pall. Even the faint creak of Mrs. Albright's packing had ceased, and the only sound of life and home was a suppressed little clatter that came at intervals from the pantry, where Lucy was making her usual Sunday inspection of the dishes, in the after-dinner absence of the staff.

When she had sealed and addressed Jack's letter, and had propped it against the inkstand as a mailing reminder, she considered invading the pantry to remind Lucy of a solemn promise given, a promise to rest this afternoon instead of counting dishes. But she quickly thought better of that, for it would simply call Lucy's attention to the fact that someone else was not resting as promised. And Lucy would insist on her lying down, which would give a perfect opening to all the stirred-up memories waiting like darts in the deceptive air of this day.

From her desk at the bay window she could see a wide reach of the garden, from the boathouse landing to the walls of green at the west, from the seawall palmettoes to the flowering peach trees. But there was no escape out there. In all that home space, now at the flood-tide of glory, there was no rest or any peace. The flowers had a dark funereal look and their fragrance came fetid and stinging.

The wistaria and banksia-rose mantle of the summer-house and its encircling azaleas and dogwood, the hyacinths and jonquils bordering the paths and the driveway to the gates, the pink blossom mists around Michael's proud cedar,—in all this old spring magic of the garden there was not one blade of comfort, but only shadows of the past and sorrows resurrected, ghosts of other Easters long dead and gone.

As she sat staring numbly out the window, wishing she had gone with Eleanor and John Clark to Land's End and not stayed here to fight things out alone, there was a tap at the door. When she turned to answer the welcome summons, Eugenia appeared, looking refreshed and trimly collected in spite of her heavy mourning.

Yes, she admitted grudgingly as she came over to the desk, her headache was a little better.

"But I couldn't get a real rest. Mrs. Albright's been tramping around in her room the whole time. Thank goodness this is the last year, Emmy. You promised that, you know. As soon as Eleanor graduates, you said."

"I haven't forgotten, dear. You've been wonderful about everything, and now you're going to have a well-earned vacation."

"Oh, I'm not thinking about myself. You're the one that needs the vacation. This season has just about finished you. And the funeral coming on top of everything. Everybody leaning on you. Susan and Isabel letting you shoulder all the responsibility without a word. And Sally Broughton keeping you up most of last night, taking on like a colored person. Why she acted like she was the chief mourner. I thought that was the limit. But anybody can impose on you, sad to say."

Eugenia's strictures were interrupted by her discovery of Jack's letter on the desk.

"So that's what you've been doing instead of resting. Well, I think you make a great mistake writing him, so soon. You should have waited, at least. That would have shown him we're offended. He could have come to the funeral if he'd wanted to."

"But he explained that he just couldn't get away."

With a weary sigh Eugenia turned her back on the desk and moved to the bureau, where she shook her head sadly at the mirror.

"You're always finding excuses for people, Emmy. You know perfectly well Jack could have gotten here for the funeral if he'd tried.

943

Instead of telegraphing, and sending a hundred dollars for a lily exhibit. After all Joe did for him."

For a moment the mirror absorbed Eugenia's attention, but then she stood back for a final sorrowful comment.

"I helped raise Jack, goodness knows, but now if it was me I'd cut off my hand before I'd write him. He needn't ever trouble to come to my funeral, I'm sure. And I don't want any of his lilies, please remember that. There's nothing flattering about show-off flowers and tears from people who don't know you're living till you're dead."

And after giving herself a few finishing touches in the mirror she came back to the desk, to stare darkly out at the sunlight of the garden, her lace handkerchief fluttering up to soothe her nose.

When it was soothed, she tucked the handkerchief away with a last fragile sniffle and asked wanly: "Didn't I hear the phone ring after I went upstairs? Another Charleston call for Eleanor?"

"No, dear. It was Linda. She just wanted to talk about the baby."

"Well," Eugenia sighed, "I suppose it's a blessing they've finally got a phone at Land's End, but I can't see why Eleanor couldn't use it to tell them good-bye from here. For that matter why couldn't she have told them all good-bye after church, instead of traipsing off to the island this afternoon—with Mr. Clark. And you urged her to go. Anybody would think you were deliberately trying to throw them together. They'll be staying over for supper, I suppose."

"They'll be back early."

"I doubt that. They'll be back in time to pack, that's about all. It does look like we might have Eleanor to ourselves the last evening of her vacation, before he carries her off to Charleston tomorrow morning. He's monopolized her all week. The whole thing's beyond me, but I suppose I shouldn't be concerned if you aren't. And you certainly don't seem to be. You treat him like a long-lost son. Anybody would think he was a member of the family, instead of a disturbing influence. I haven't said a word up till now, and I have nothing personal against Mr. Clark, but really, Emmy, I can't understand——"

Eugenia interrupted herself with a pale gasp at the window.

A figure in black was coming through the gateway.

"Now who on earth could that be? . . . Why, it looks like—Susan. It *is* Susan. It's Susan Bramwell! It's Aunt Susie!"

And as the figure advanced resolutely up the drive, Eugenia fell back from the window in consternation.

"But it couldn't be," she whispered, dazed, hands a-flutter. "She'd never come here. She'd rather die than come near this house. She spoke to Eleanor and Jane at the funeral, but she'd never come here where you are. . . . She must want to see me! Goodness. Tell her I'm sick in bed. No!—tell her I won't see her. I'll tell Lucy. Let me get out of sight!"

In a panic Eugenia fled for the hall. But at the door she was overtaken by a wild surmise.

"Emmy, she's up to something! Don't let her trick you. I wouldn't put it beyond her to use Joe's passing as an excuse to get around you, for some purpose. But don't be taken in by her now, after all these years. You know how she's always hated you. She's always said the most dreadful things about you, and called you much worse names than carpetbagging Yankee. So if she does ask to see you, tell Lucy to tell her you're out. Whatever you do, don't see her, Emmy,—unless it's to give her the squelching of her life!"

The door closed with a quick click, and Emily was left alone with the incredible spectacle of Susan Bramwell marching up the driveway of home.

In amazement she watched the black-shrouded figure disappear round the corner of the house toward the front door. A minute later the knocker sounded with mettlesome sharpness. Then there was another minute of waiting before Lucy came to break the suspense.

"Miss Bram'l aksin' to see you, ma'm. In de livin'-room."

Only the bigness of Lucy's eyes betrayed her surprise. Her voice was perfectly normal, as if Susan Bramwell were just an old friend paying an afternoon call.

"Thank you, Lucy. I'll go right in."

Her own voice sounded quite normal and self-possessed, Emily thought. But at the fireside door to the living-room she hesitated, pausing to test her composure. An exchange of looks with Lucy was not reassuring. And when she opened the door it was with the feeling that her own eyes were big as saucers too.

In the middle of the living-room, rigid as a wooden soldier, stood Susan Bramwell.

Because of the heavy veil it was impossible to see the eyes or even

945

make out the features: only the dim outline of the face was discernible. Not till the unbelievable caller had been invited to the sofa was the veil lifted, revealing sensitive dark eyes set narrowly in a pointed shriveled face. An unknown face, for in all the years it had never been seen but from a distance or firmly averted. The Bramwell nose was recognizable, but there was no other resemblance to Joe or Sophie, or to the formidable conception that time and imagination had built up. Now at close range, face to face at last, this life-long enemy looked strangely small and slight, so different from what she had always seemed.

Sitting stiffly erect on the edge of the sofa, with a handkerchief clutched like a flag-of-truce in one black-gloved little hand, she spoke quickly in a tense shrill voice, as if delivering a belated speech, a speech that had had all expression but strain rehearsed out of it.

"I've come to thank you for all you did about the funeral. We were both so prostrated, Isabel and I, we were too stunned to know what was happening."

"Of course," Emily nodded gently.

"It was all so terribly sudden," the shrill voice sped tensely on. "We were hardly recovered enough to get to the church yesterday, to say nothing of tending to all the arrangements and the flowers and people. Sally Broughton was of absolutely no help to us in our bereavement. We would have been lost without your help."

For a moment the flag-of-truce handkerchief seemed about to fly up to comfort the hard-pressed eyes, but refrained. And Emily restrained a desire to extend a hand of sympathy and understanding. She wanted to show in a way clearer than words that she realized the sacrifice of pride this call was costing; but the caller must be allowed to set the pace, and in her quivering rigidity on the edge of the sofa Susan Bramwell showed no sign of weakening now but only a tightening tension.

"And now that I'm here," she hurried on to say, "I also want to tell you that Eleanor and Jane are to be our heirs. It was Joe's will, and now it's ours, Isabel's and mine. There wouldn't be anything but a mortgaged house if you hadn't helped him sell Holly Hill plantation. But we have many personal things to leave Eleanor and Jane."

After that Susan Bramwell's tenseness eased a little, and she permitted her handkerchief to go to the aid of her trembling lips. And now Emily felt it was safe to reach over and touch her hand. But

946

words must be spoken, too, and what words could be found to meet this occasion. The obvious things to say seemed so flat and inadequate, in the face of this astonishing surrender, that she rejected them all and ended by resorting to tea.

"I'm so glad to see you, and there's so much to say,—let me have Lucy bring us some tea."

"Oh no, please!" Susan Bramwell demurred, rigidly tense again on the edge of the sofa. "Forgive my haste, but I really must go. I must get back to Isabel. She's not well and I mustn't leave her for any length of time."

And getting quickly to her feet, almost jumping up, she seemed about to take abrupt leave when she was stopped by some afterthought.

"Oh," she remembered in a rush, taking an agitated stand by the sofa table, "there's a favor I'd like to ask, if it isn't too much trouble. The *News & Courier* has asked us for pictures of Joe for a special article they're printing in next Sunday's paper. They have his picture when he was Mayor, and we're loaning them the only other one we have, a daguerreotype taken when he was a young officer in the Beaufort Volunteer Artillery. Joe was always so shy about having his picture taken. But we seem to recall that he was in a group photograph of the Beaufort delegation to Washington, back in the 80's when they were fighting Charleston to get the Navy drydock here. Stephen was in it too, so we thought you might possibly have it. Do you remember it? Do you think you might still have it?"

"Why yes," Emily pondered, "I do remember it. And I'm sure I still have it. I think I know just where it is."

"Oh no, please don't trouble now! I just meant if you have time in the next day or two, and know just where to put your hand on it."

"But I can find it now easily, I'm sure, if you'll wait one minute."

And leaving Susan Bramwell murmuring perfunctory protests, Emily went back into her room.

There she stood for a moment unable to concentrate through the bewildering strangeness of what was happening. But then with an effort she recalled the picture, and remembered where it should be, in the silver-chest.

She remembered it was one of the few things she had preserved from the drastic cleaning-out of the attic the winter after Stephen's death. The ordeal of that time came back with painful vividness:

how she had planned to do it little by little, and then, finding that she was simply sorting things over, transferring them from one place to another, how finally with Lucy's support she had finished the whole task in one desperate day. It was a fearful accumulation of odds-and-ends he had left for her to dispose of at last, trunks and boxes to be emptied, the litter of years to be carried down to a funeral pyre behind the stable. Out of it all she had allowed herself to keep only a handful of things—among them the picture of the Beaufort delegation to Washington—to go into the silver-chest, place of final salvage.

Now when she went to the closet and opened the chest, lifting out the heavy-ladened top tray, it took several minutes to find the picture, for it had gravitated far down toward the bottom of things. And when she held it up to the light, she was shocked, for she had forgotten how faded and yellowed it was. One delegate at the left was in a state too ghostly for identification, and at the right Sam Koenig had lost an arm and old Mr. Rutherford a leg. But the delegates in the middle were intact and distinct, and fortunately Joe was there, with Stephen. Joe, pompously seated in his stoutest prime, glaring in profile at the elk's tooth on Mr Rutherford's watch-chain. And Stephen, standing so tall and handsomely straight, staring with fixed impatience off into space over Sam Koenig's bald head. The sight of him, his air of confidence in the first flush of success, the very suit he was wearing brought back the whole feel of the delayed honeymoon at White Sulphur Springs. He seemed to be secretly whispering to her: Take it easy, honey, it will all be over soon, and then we'll make up for lost time. . . .

Remembering her caller with a start, she hurried back to the living-room, where Susan Bramwell was standing in the same position by the sofa table, still murmuring protests.

"You really shouldn't have bothered to look for it now," she said, as her agitated little black-gloved hand received the yellowed picture. "But I'm too glad you found it. And could we possibly borrow it for a few days?"

"Of course. I'm sorry it's so faded."

"Yes," Susan Bramwell sighed, scrutinizing it closely and then holding it off at arm's-length. "But Joe looks all right. It's not a good likeness, of course,—no picture does him justice,—but at least it's distinct. And it's good of Stephen. It's very good of Stephen. . . .

I'll ask them to leave Joe and Stephen together and cut out the others. Then they'll have three pictures of Joe—this one and the other two—at three different periods in his life. That will give them quite a photographic record to print with their article."

And after a final moist squint at the picture Susan Bramwell tucked it away in the folds of her mourning, and brushing her eyes with her handkerchief she quickly tucked that away too, recovering full rigidity.

"When the *News & Courier* people telephoned from Charleston," she said with rapid stress, "we didn't know what to do, but finally we told them they could send a reporter to see us on Tuesday. They promised to take good care of any pictures we loaned them and to return them by the end of the week, so we'll have this one back to you by then without fail. And now I really must go, I must get back to Isabel."

At the front door her tenseness became acute. She seemed about to wrench out an abrupt leavetaking, but her lips faltered, straining mutely, and she postponed the attempt, allowing Emily to start down the steps with her. Then, half-way, she stopped to peer at the twin camellia bushes flanking the steps, their dark leaves glistening in the sun. A single flower still clung to one of them, a delicate pink rosette, a last perfect bloom that had not yet fallen from the weight of its perfection to the brown-petaled earth; and the sight of it seemed to ease her tenseness.

"Only one flower left," she observed quite calmly. "I suppose they were a mass of bloom earlier in the spring."

"Even up to last week, before it turned so warm," Emily nodded, grateful to them for relieving the strain.

Susan Bramwell nodded and sighed.

"Paul and Virginia, Sophie called them," she said reflectively. "I remember when she set them out, soon after she came here to live as the bride of Major Fenwick. Long before the War, that was, and I was a mere child, but I remember it well."

"Do you really remember when Miss Sophie planted them?" Emily asked by way of encouragement. "How big were they then?"

"Oh, there was little to them then," said Susan Bramwell, touching the shiny leaves. "But Sophie took great pains with them, coaxing and petting them. They were grown to tall handsome bushes at the time of Isabel's wedding, just before the—Union fleet came."

Sudden confusion seized her eyes, and for a moment her voice stumbled quaveringly. "You see, everything's so changed. The garden's too pretty . . . really lovely the way you have it . . . but it's hard to place things, after all these years. The house looks the same, but everything else is so changed. . . ." But then her eyes returned to the single surviving flower of the camellias and her voice steadied again. "They were nothing like this of course, Sophie's Paul and Virginia, but they were very fine even then, when last we saw them, that day of Isabel's wedding. She was married from this house, you know. We were still living on Holly Hill plantation—our present home was not finished then—so Isabel was married from here. It was autumn, but whenever I think of that day I always remember the japonicas as they were the spring before, all covered with blooms like this one."

Emily reached in among the leaves and broke the stem that held the last bloom of this spring, the flower that had been watched and intended for Joe's Easter buttonhole.

"Won't you take this to Isabel?"

"Oh, you shouldn't have!" Susan Bramwell protested, her troubled eyes brightening. "But I know how much Sister will appreciate it."

And as her hesitant black-gloved fingers took the waxen pink flower, a faint smile lightened the drawn face.

"Joe," she said in a voice of sadness touched with pride, "always called Isabel his japonica flower. I was the ugly duckling of his three sisters, Sophie was the domineering one, and Isabel was his favorite."

But then she seemed to feel she had said too much, and abruptly resumed her journey down the steps.

"Tea leaves," she said on the way, with stiff matter-of-factness, "make an excellent mulch for camellias, of course you know. My, how pretty your garden looks."

And at the foot of the steps she stood squinting at the summerhouse, where the blossom mists and the song of birds were most brightly gathered in the afternoon sunshine.

"I wish you'd let me show you the garden," Emily said.

"You're too kind," Susan Bramwell squinted tensely in the sun, "but I really must get back to Isabel. I've stayed much longer than I should have."

But still she seemed unable to say good-bye. And as her tenseness

950

threatened to become acute again, Emily said: "You'll come again soon, won't you?"

"And you'll come to see us," Susan Bramwell nodded.

Then, in a rush, she added: "I want you to know how much we admire your work in saving the Lafayette house from that Blarker creature. If that Northern vandal's allowed to have his way there'll be nothing left of Beaufort. If there's anything Isabel and I can do to help combat him, please don't fail to call on us. We Southerners must stand together."

And then, with a sudden handshake, she said good-bye, and lowering her veil turned quickly away.

Emily stood transfixed, watching her hurry with unsteady haste down the driveway. She stood watching till the slight proud figure passed through the gates and disappeared.

When she started slowly back up the steps, she found herself more touched and bewildered by the call than she had been while it was happening. Now it was all as strange and unbelievable as if it had been dreamed or imagined. But, half-way up the steps, Joe's last camellia was missing to prove that his sister had actually been here, that the call was no whim of fancy. And in the house Eugenia was waiting to further confirm its reality with reproachful eyes.

"Emmy," she said in her ghostliest tone of injury, "how could you! I begged you not to see her. I warned you she was up to something. And you even shook hands with her at the end! I didn't hear anything you said, but I couldn't help seeing that."

The reproaches continued down the hall and into the back room, where they reached a climax at the bay-window desk.

"If you were willing to forget your own pride, at least you might have considered mine. I still have a little, thank goodness. And I'd cut out my tongue before I'd receive her, or give her a civil word, or any satisfaction. . . . Well, aren't you going to tell me what happened?"

"A miracle," Emily told the garden.

"A miracle? A trick, you mean. She had something up her sleeve, I know that, or she never would have risked the snubbing of her life to come here. What was it? What did she want?"

"She wanted an old photograph of Joe."

"So that's the excuse she used to get into this house. And then what?"

"She just wanted to thank us for helping with the funeral arrangements."

"She needn't thank me. I hope she didn't get the impression we did it on her account, hers and Isabel's. Lucky for her she didn't ask to see me,—I'd have put her to rights in short order. What did she say about me? Did she mention my name?"

"No, not exactly. But I know she meant to include you in what she said."

"Oh no she didn't. She's not that big a fool. They know they could never get around me. Oh I've taken plenty of their browbeating and insults in the past, but you know yourself I haven't spoke to them since I came home from Charleston after Margaret passed away. I told them off then in a style they'll never forget, and I'm not likely to go back on it now, even at a time like this, just because you're willing to forgive them at a moment's notice, without considering me."

Emily turned away from the window to face the injured eyes.

"Sorry you feel that way about it, dear," she said with a spare smile. "But I had nothing to forgive. I never had anything against Joe's sisters. I only wish I could have known them long ago."

Eugenia threw up her hands at that, appealing to the room. "She never had anything against them! She only wishes she could have known them long ago! After all these years of hate, after all the names they've called her, all the lies they've told,—she has nothing to forgive! . . . Really, Emmy, that's too much. We always speak freely with each other, and I must say I don't see how a person can be as strong and as weak as you are. It's beyond me. . . . So that's what she came for, wasn't it?—to patch everything up with you sweet as you please, just like nothing had ever happened. She did come to bury the whole entire hatchet, now didn't she?"

"I suppose you could call it that," Emily nodded, turning back to the window.

"I knew it! Just what I was afraid of. Taking advantage of Joe's passing to bury the hatchet in his grave. And you let her. I'm surprised you all didn't kiss while you were at it. . . . How did she explain the sudden change of heart? How did she put it? What did she say?"

"Not very much. She just said, 'We Southerners must stand together'."

"Well. I declare. She said that to you? Sounds perfectly cracked. Must have been a dig. . . . Now listen to me, Emmy, it was all right to help with the funeral on Joe's account, and it was bad enough judgment to let them make up with you, but don't make the mistake of trusting them. Susie may have swallowed her pride in a moment of weakness, but it'll stick in her craw and be strangling her by nightfall. Give me credit for knowing a little something about human nature. And I certainly should know more than you about the ways of that old pair of guinea-hens. It can't last, this lovey-dovey reconciliation business. I can tell you that right now. It'll only make matters worse than before."

Eugenia paused for breath, and then went reproachfully on.

"I've learned one thing in my life. And that is that a transgressor never forgives. So you can expect them to go right on hating you, and all the more now, no matter how sweet they may be to your face. Mark my words. . . . What else did Susan say? She only popped in and out, but she must have had more to say for herself than you've told me so far."

"She said she and Isabel wanted Eleanor and Jane to be their heirs."

"Well! Now we're getting somewhere. So they're trying to bribe their way into our good graces. As if they had anyone else to leave their things to, unless they were to dig up some of the Savannah cousins. And what will they have to leave anyhow?—nothing but trash, and a house that's clammy as a morgue and infested with rats and roaches. . . . I see it all now. They want to get in with us because they're at the end of their rope and they've got no place else to turn. They're scared. All their lives they've been preparing a lonely bed for themselves and now they can't bear to lay in it."

A creaking tread on the stairs interrupted Eugenia's strictures.

"Mrs. Albright again," she sighed, pressing her fingers to her temples with an expression of long-suffering martyrdom. "And my headache's coming back. But it's the last day of the last season, so I suppose I oughtn't to mind entertaining her for the rest of the afternoon. No, Emmy, I'll do it. I *want* to do it. I always try to spare you, and anyhow it's my turn. Besides it's really no trouble, I'm so used to it by this time. I'll take her out in the garden and let her mirate on those grandchildren of hers, while you get a little rest before tea-time."

And with an air of patient self-sacrifce Eugenia started for the hall door, where she paused for a final thrust.

"After you've had a rest, Emmy, I do hope you won't be quite so vague about the call. Maybe you'll be able to tell me exactly what Susan said. You never were much good at repeating conversations, but in this case do try to recall every word, because I want to thrash the whole thing out with you later on and get to the bottom of it."

"I'll do my best," Emily nodded. "Because I'm hoping you'll go with me when I return the call. I think we should go to see Sally Broughton, too."

"Never," Eugenia tossed back. "I'll never speak to Sally as long as I live. Not even if you invite her to this house, not even if she comes crawling here on her hands and knees. As for Susan and Isabel, I'll show them there's one member of this family that don't forgive and forget so easy."

And she closed the door behind her with an emphatic click.

Her quick steps and fretted voice joined Mrs. Albright's slow heavy tread and placid monotone in the hall; and then as they went together to the front door, the room seemed to contract with a sigh.

Emily sat in her chair at the desk looking out the window, think-ing of Susan and Isabel Bramwell. She sat staring absently at the garden till Eugenia and Mrs. Albright appeared from the front drive-way and started across the side lawn toward the summer-house. Then in the tight silence of the room her thoughts came back to Joe.

She tried to turn away from pain by going to the silver-chest in the closet, to put back the things she had taken out in the search for the picture. But when she knelt before the old chest, everything her fingers touched quivered with a response of memory, and each memory set others in motion, till the whole past seemed trembling around her. It was like kneeling at a tomb among autumn leaves whispering in the wind. . . . Soon, she thought defensively, a bon-fire must be made of this yellowing litter: it must not be left for Eleanor and Jane to do. The enduring things, jewelry and trinkets, had already been divided; only these perishable scraps of the past, letters and papers, remained to be disposed of. And for a moment she felt she had the courage to do it now, this instant. But when she saw them reduced to cold ashes in the fireplace, courage left her. Soon, she thought, but not now. And she hastened to put back the top tray and close the lid of the chest, and then the closet door.

She stood staring at the fireplace, trying to conquer the empty silence of the room. Silence that said so convincingly that all time was past, and that life itself was only a longing to find the way back to death, a flame burning for the sleep of ashes, to rest forever from the pain of memory.

Her eyes fled to the brass fire-set and fastened there, as if that familiar shape of home could save her. Strange that in all the years of loss she had never really seen it before, how like a household god its center part stood, a steadfast cross supporting in tireless embrace the weak-kneed tongs and sagging hearthbroom, the old bent poker and battered shovel. But as she clung to this revelation of the commonplace, vanished hands returned to break her grip and make her face the room again.

But the room could no longer be endured. It was like a trap, walls pressing in to crush her with a sense of overpowering loneliness, a final denial of everything but loss. And when she thought of turning to Lucy, she saw that not even this oldest of friends could help her. No-one living could deliver her from this silence to which there was no longer any answer but surrender.

VI

WHILE SHE WAS WALKING she hardly remembered how she had left the house, or where she was going. Even when she reached the old wrought-iron side gate of St. Helena's graveyard, she failed to see clearly why she was here. She stood blinded for a moment, as if she had been walking through streets of deep shade and had come suddenly to a place of intense light.

It was the way the afternoon sun slanted through spring branches straight into her eyes, she realized. And as she opened the gate, the rays seemed so warm and benign, and the song of birds was so sweet in the air, that she felt she had somehow found her way to a place of peace, of respite and renewal. But then as she turned toward the Fenwick and Bramwell plots, she remembered her mission. And the last of her courage turned to cold despair as she faced Joe's grave.

She knew now that she had come here secretly hoping to break the spell of death, not to surrender but to turn defeat back into victory, somehow, once again: to prove by some desperate twist of will that the faith she had first won after Rusty's death, then lost and won again after Michael's death and Stephen's, was one thing that could never be taken from her. But now there was no will left to combat this sense of final defeat, the sheer weight of loss too great to be any longer borne. Her will lay dying beside those whom she had so proudly believed she could keep alive as long as she lived. . . . This new grave, which she had felt she could exorcise by some mystical power of confrontal, seemed now to make all the others new again, bringing back the freshness of death to all, all raw wounds again in the earth and in her heart, open and bleeding again and now never to be healed.

Her eyes flinched away from them, and now she sought only to accept their verdict and hurry from this place of death. But something in the sunlight held her, reminding her that there was no place left to turn to. And for a time she stood helpless, powerless to move, staring at the flowers on Joe's grave. . . . Pathetic symbols of resurrection and immortality, already wilting. What voice could refute their silent testimony. All she could summon to her aid was a prayer that her own turn would come next without fail, that she might be spared any further loss of loved ones, mortal as these flowers. But then even that ceased to matter, as if the future and all the lives of home had already gone to join the past, leaving a present in which there was nothing more to lose.

She was able finally to turn away, but only to the old mourning bench by the cedar tree, back against the wall.

Sitting here she could survey the extent of time's harvest. All the family dead lay here before her, under the new leaves and the hanging gray moss of the great sycamore whose web of roots spread everywhere. Under plain headstones with names and dates still clear, under brick-supported slabs of marble with lengthy epitaphs broken and blackened and almost erased, here they all lay, the recent living and the long dead, all contemporaries now, her own and those remote figures of legend, the unknown founders of the family, all bound together in this embrace of roots and earth.

Only Rusty was missing. His burial-place was of wind and wave, he was lost in the elements, and there was no marker with his name, no trace of his grave. Perhaps because of that it had always been so easy to feel him alive, in the wings and songs of his birds, in the island woods and fields, the marshes, quiet tidewaters at dawn and sunset, in the sun at noon, the sky at night, everywhere, always. But now even he seemed buried here with the others. At last, at this late hour of need, he too had come to fail her. He who had first taught her where to look for faith, cure of all ills, now he too was lost and nowhere to be found but here in this place where all meaning was extinct. . . .

When she had come into the churchyard there had been two figures in a far corner, a man and a woman, too far off across the maze of graves for her eyes to recognize. Now they were gone, and she was alone in the walled garden of death. Of all the music of the world only notes of ultimate mockery survived: the rapture of birds, the stirring of new leaves in the fragrant air, the whisper of palmetto fronds reaching over the wall behind her. Old conjury of spring that promised, today above all days, I am the Resurrection and the Life.

But presently even this bitter lingering mockery ceased to hurt. The sense of suffocation passed, and the world was reduced to ashes. The walls of the church and the yard, the grave stones, the cobwebs of moss trailing from the branches, all settled into a numbing haze around her, a nirvana of grayness in which she sat dully staring, feeling nothing but weariness and the heavy stillness of death.

From the depths of stillness a vague force welled up, a white cloud slowly and painfully taking shape in the gray void, a brightness rising from the ashes of the world. Formed and free at last, it rushed upward on wings of light. And in a flash it seemed to fill the whole sky with its singing, like some cosmic bird of revelation soaring through time and space, spreading faith and joy to the ends of eternity, dispelling every shadow of fear and doubt.

For an instant its reality was a dazzling conviction. But then as her senses cleared, the vision fled to the west and faded away in the late sunlight, to become the distant cry of a train. It was only the afternoon express, blowing for some remote crossing on its way from Savannah to Yemassee, both earthly enough stations far removed from the skies. But she had scarcely consigned it to this rational oblivion when it sounded again, to confound her reason with its mystery and suspense. . . . It never failed to reach her heart, this train call. Faint and far-away yet close as breathing, like music remembered from some moment long ago, it always brought a response of memory and longing from deep within, memory of old journeys, longing for journeys never made, for places and people never known, never to be known. But it held more than that today. Today it seemed to carry a heightened significance, overtones beyond the normal range of reverie and feeling. It seemed now to come not from inland, across pinelands and tide marshes, but from universes away and across immeasurable years. It was like the voice of infinity itself, spanning time and space, joining the separate syllables of the past and future with the present into one seamless word. And in this single word all meaning was locked, the whole secret of existence, truth eternal and absolute.

The train call was dying away, but its reflections and echoings persisted. The respite of stillness and dull weariness was broken, the trance of grayness gone, leaving her exposed again to the full impact of defeat. And now the hurt of this day, the sense of loss and futility and all the throbbings of memory, had reached a crisis of pain. In the quivering shafts of sunlight that pierced through spring branches to the graves at her feet, everything seemed fiercely intensified, charged with bitterest clarity, a culminating despair that seared the heart like flame.

So it was from final clear necessity that she drew courage to meet the challenge of the call. Here seemed to be a last summons, a last chance to read and answer the enigma, the cryptic message of the voice that summed up all meaning in one conclusive term. However miserably she failed, perhaps in the process of failing she might come to some final understanding of her own life, make some final pact with the enemy, the forces of darkness and doubt, silence and unfaith.

✦   ✦   ✦

A breath of wind from the west stirred through the trees, swaying the palm fronds and the branches of new leaves, seething them in sudden soft turmoil like a gust of spring rain. The slant crystal shafts of the sun were shattered for an instant into a confusion of myriad glancings. And then as the wind passed, the subsiding commotion of the leaves left a shimmering arabesque of light on her hands.

It all came back to self in the end. However you tried to escape your lonely prison, however you seemed to succeed at times in identifying your life with other lives and the life of the world, you were always thrown back on yourself at last. However taut you were able to stretch your tether, still the center stake held fast, making all your reachings circular, bringing you back to the beginning, home to your self, measure of all things. Space and time were curved, and there was a curvature of thought and feeling that bound you to return to yourself. In the end the ancient sunlight and the wind in the trees were no more than a shifting pattern of light and shadow on your hands, only an expression of you.

And yet was this you? Could these hands really be yours? For at this moment they seemed not to belong to you at all, or if they had once been part of you they were detached now and disowned. And even when, on second thought, you had to admit they were yours, they still felt as strange as they looked. Perhaps that was because they had been other hands, and still were somehow, underneath these brown veined covers. Once they had been as young and smooth as new doeskin: then for a long time they had been gloves for everyday work and wear, past any prettiness but good and serviceable: and now finally they were like a pair of crusty old garden mittens, fit only for the discard. They were like parched and withered autumn leaves, clinging to the branches of an old tree; but also, inside, they still had the durable quality of life's long summer, and even the soft vital texture of youth, the feel of spring leaves.

She remembered how in youth she had wondered of old people: could that poor thing ever have been young? In those years it had been impossible to believe in age, to see and feel oneself old, burdened down with the weight of times gone. It was an impossible state, a predicament too far-off and incredible to apply to oneself, as difficult to believe in as death itself. Now it was only too easy to believe, for death was now an imminent presence and age a state of being. And now it was possible to appreciate the essential indignity of age. Not that it was weighted down with years and memories and infirmities when you were least able to bear them, but that it was the least real phase of life, the least representative, the least you. You felt that this last stand was your poorest likeness, yourself caught off guard at a weakest moment. Age was an accumulation of all ages, and yet when your morale most needed bolstering you were forced to make your final appearance in these rags of decay, like a wretched old beggar, when still alive within you were a reasonably presentable and confident woman of maturity and a young woman dressed in robes of light, of eagerness and hope and trust.

It was strange to be really old. Old age had come so slowly, so gradually and without shock, so hidden in the press of years and hours, that you had failed to mark its approach till it was upon you. The final truth of *Snowbound,* first learned by light heart in girlhood, had at last come true. *How strange it seems with so much gone of life and love to still live on. . . .* How strange it seemed to be a contemporary now of Miss Sophie's, Stephen's mother, with whom he lay sleeping now in this womb of silence. How strange it was to be so much older than your own mother, whose grave back North you had once long ago planned to visit with Michael. But it was even stranger to feel that you were still younger than both mothers, Stephen's and yours, whose blood now was mingled in the veins of your children, the living and the dead and the unborn.

It was strange to have attained age without wisdom: to have surrendered the bright raiment of youth for this garment of sackcloth and ashes without winning any concessions from time, any final remission. To have exchanged youth's simple faith for this congested state of ungrace, whose only offering to youth was a prayer for its courage against a world of inscrutable contradictions. But it was strangest of all to find no peace in age, no release from the war, no relief from the pain of things. Age was supposed to carry its own anodyne, drugs of partial oblivion to blunt the sharpness of thought and feeling, sedatives to take the edge of care off life and induce a state of rest; an attitude of unworried reflection toward the world, which was the concern now of youth, belonged now to the young and strong; a pause before the end, a lull and calm not of indifference but of final proper perspective, of acquiescence, resignation. Perhaps when you got used to age this release would come, but it had not come yet.

And where was the gentle settling back into the folds of self that was also supposed to be a recompense of age? The lapsing into forgetfulness of recent years and the vivid remembering of long ago: the impairment of faculties that permitted the tired brain and heart to live backward, retrace steps, turn home to the beginning. . . . There were voices from the past that whispered in the stirring of leaves, and faces of childhood that appeared without summoning. But this was not new; it had always been true. Always there had been this returning to the lost world of home. In acceptance and love of the South there had always been this secret reservation, this loyalty to the old, this homesickness for the North. For the world whose center was Mother's room, the place of birth: the bed, the chair by the window, and the chestnut tree that was part of the room, a most important part. . . . Now in spring it was a glory again of fuzzy candle clusters, all lighted and glowing. Father complained of them because they "attracted insects", and when they fell they made the steps and the sidewalk unsightly and slippery; and Beebee—Bridget —complained because she was kept busy sweeping them into the gutter, as if she had nothing better to do. But everyone approved of the tree in summer. Then it made cool shade all day long, from the early clop-clop of the milk-cart—when you woke up but were not allowed to get up—till the last carriage at dark, after prayers and before sleep. Its summer shade was still there when you came back from the farm at Salem, just in time to gather a few of the big shiny reddish-brown nuts for a necklace, before the boys on the block got them all for their make-believe pipes and their show-off cracking game, with the nuts swinging at the end of a string. Then in autumn, after school started, the dark leaves turned yellow and began to drop, first one by one, and then in bunches when the wind shook them, littering the sidewalk with gold: more work for Beebee's broom. And then at last there were the bare branches of winter again, shivering outside the frosted panes of the window, looking so forlorn and cold that it was always a relief when the first exciting snow came whirling down to blanket them in furry white. . . . All through your life, at appointed moments, you had been drawn back to this deepest pool of memory. You were forever turning back to the beginning, returning to the world of the chestnut tree. Now in age no more than usual, and the colors there were no sharper now than they had always been.

No, so far there was neither of the promised reprieves in age, neither surcease nor any special homecoming. So far it was more like drowning than anything else. It was like sinking in the elements of Rusty's grave, a final sea of unrest, the whole of life and thought returning in a single long wave of engulfment. . . . It was no extraordinary life you had lived, and yet to have lived it and to remember it was strange as a dream. Life was truly like a dream, exceptional always, and age was a time of awakening to find that life was ended like a dream. All its wonders slipping from you, just when you felt you had learned at last to grasp their full wonder. . . .

The wind was stirring again in the branches, its gentle tempest rousing the birds to an ecstacy of life. But then for a moment the joyous turmoil seemed consternation and panic, and the soft breath of spring became a sudden autumnal jeopardy, agitation bleak and chill. For a haunted moment the sun seemed already set, its last golden radiance shivered into obscurity by a tide of dusk that rolled up from the earth and the graves. Loneness and dread gripped the heart as if they would never let go, and a voice of despair warned of the lateness of the hour, the hopelessness of trying to warm the dead with vain abstractions, the necessity of hurrying home to the living while there was still time.

But even as she moved to go, the spring branches with their tatters of moss swayed back to singing stillness. The last warm golden spell of the sun was restored around her. And now it was as if the voice of the wind had been only a sigh of closing day, while echoing in its wake was the sense of another voice that held her motionless. . . . From far away toward Charleston now, so faint and tenuous that listening could scarcely capture sound, it was the voice of the train again. Yet not so much again as still. For it was as if it had never stopped echoing from its earlier call, as if only her awareness of it had been interrupted for a time.

To Stephen a train whistle was a dismal sound, a wail, morbid and dreary. To Joe all machine noises—from the plain honk of an auto horn to the complicated roar of Jim's new tractor at Land's End, from the whine of an outboard motor or the spatting chug and crearing of a pineland sawmill to the great sky-boring drone of planes from the Parris Island airport—all were abominable, reconciling him to his growing deafness. Of old-timers to whom the sound of a train was as lifelong familiar as it was to her, only Rusty shared this mystical sense of its wonder, its profound meaning.

It was the voice of the world, this remote momentous cry, the voice of all voices, all in one. All the world's joy and pain were here, all gladness and sorrow, fortune and misfortune, her own and the good and evil of all men. Every color and shape of life, every form of living, every littleness and greatness found expression here: light and darkness, order and confusion, love and hate. Its immense and compressed reverberations reached every corner of space, expanding and contracting, echoing and re-echoing down all the corridors of distance, near and far. And all time was in its call: today and tomorrow, yesterday, and tomorrow, tomorrow and yesterday and today again, ever in conflict, ever in doubt, passing away and returning again, advancing and receding, ever changing and ever the same, echoing forever.

But it was more than an expression of countless diverse forces. It was summation, supreme integration: a meeting of opposites and a reconciliation of contrasts, a balancing of relatives in one absolute, infinite wisdom, eternal understanding. In its crucible of tone, so far away and small and yet so close and vast, all the little enigmas of life were melted into one whole great mystery again. In its rising and falling tide, flooding the world with a music at once major and minor, all dissonances were resolved, all chords blended, all voices joined, in one everlasting glory. It was like the mighty hosannas of Beethoven's Ode to Joy: like that and yet soaring above it, for this was music that transcended music. It was the echoing overtone that lived above great music, uniting sound and silence. life and death, all memory and all forgetting: tuning the past and future together in a diapason of omnipresent thought: gathering up all separate lives, the living and the dead and the unborn, in one great choral embrace.

It was the deathless voice of the world, this far-away call and echoing. And in its music, faint and tenuous as a dream, every note of fear and suffering was dissolved in pity and greatness, every negative phrase of life transmuted into a final affirmation. A peace that made of remorseless death only a return to earth, the mother of all to whom all returned at last like tired children at the end of day. A return that was neither defeat nor surrender, but only a going home to be one again with the earth and the sea and sky, the wind and the stars of night, where loved ones were.

So even as she turned to the gate, moving softly that the lingering echoes of the call might not be lost, it seemed to her that she was not turning away in flight. She was not deserting the dead, leaving them here alone, but taking them all home with her to the living.

And in this last secret echoing was the last word, the final meaning and answer. And she saw now that it was Rusty's answer, remembered from a sea-island day long ago in the dream of time. And it was more than faith in human continuity, or pride in being a member of the great tragic race, more even than courage to meet the lone hazards of chance and change.

Gratitude was the final response that life called for. Gratitude for the very briefness of living that made it so precious. For the hunger and thirst that made its fullness, the madness that gave it reason. Gratitude, above all else, for friends. For those loved ones living and gone, those companions known and unknown, who gave life its truest meaning, and made the havoc road to doom a journey of strangeness and wonder. Who made one believe at last with whole heart in all the dark splendor, all the terrible beauty of the world.

THE END

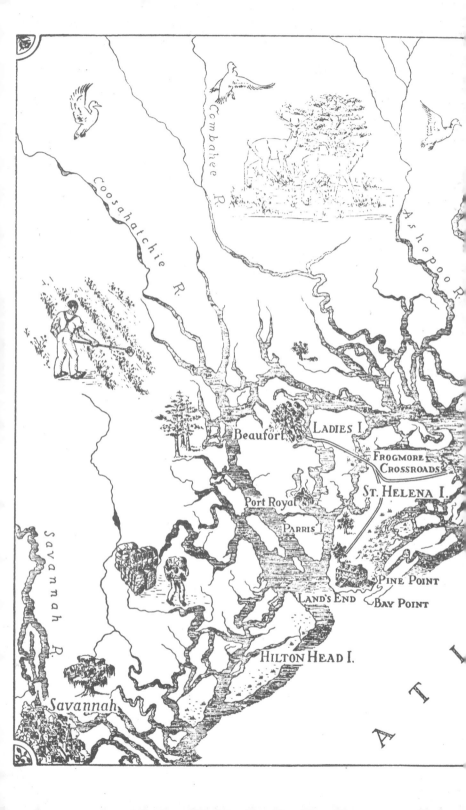